Morality and Moral Controversies

SIXTH EDITION

Morality and Moral Controversies

Readings in Moral, Social, and Political Philosophy

JOHN ARTHUR, Editor

Binghamton University—
State University of New York

Prentice
Hall

Upper Saddle River, New Jersey 07458

Library of Congress Cataloging-in-Publication Data

Morality and moral controversies: readings in moral, social, and political philosophy
John Arthur, editor.—6th ed.
   p. cm.
  Includes bibliographical references.
  ISBN 0-13-034155-X
  1. Ethics. 2. Social problems. I. Arthur, John, 1946–

BJ1025.M67 2002
170—dc21   2001036836

VP/Editorial Director: Charlyce Jones Owen
Acquisitions Editor: Ross Miller
Editorial Assistant: Carla Worner
Senior Managing Editor: Jan Stephan
Production Liaison: Fran Russello
Project Manager: Linda B. Pawelchak
Prepress and Manufacturing Buyer: Sherry Lewis
Cover Director: Jayne Conte
Cover Design: Kiwi Design
Cover Art: Casper David Friedrich, 1774–1840, German "White
   Cliffs at Ruegen." Oskar Reinhart Collection, Winterthur,
   Switzerland, A.K.G., Berlin/Superstock
Marketing Manager: Chris Ruel
Copy Editing: Laura Starret
Proofreading: Ann Sieger

This book was set in 10/11 Times Ten by Lithokraft II
and was printed and bound by Hamilton Printing Company.
The cover was printed by Phoenix Color Corp.

© 2002, 1999, 1996, 1993, 1986, 1981 by Pearson Education, Inc.
Upper Saddle River, New Jersey 07458

Printed in the United States of America
10 9 8 7 6 5 4 3 2

ISBN 0-13-034155-X

Pearson Education LTD., *London*
Pearson Education Australia PTY. Limited, *Sydney*
Pearson Education Singapore, Pte. Ltd.
Pearson Education North Asia Ltd., *Hong Kong*
Pearson Education Canada Ltd., *Toronto*
Pearson Educatión de Mexico, S.A. de C.V.
Pearson Education—Japan, *Tokyo*
Pearson Education Malaysia, Pte. Ltd.

Contents

PART I
MORAL THEORY

v

PART II
ISSUES OF LIFE AND DEATH

PART IV
PERSONAL RELATIONSHIPS

15

16

Marriage and the Family   603

Postscript to Instructors   654

Preface to the Sixth Edition

I continue to be pleased at the remarkable success of this book. Not only has it been widely used in ethics and moral problems courses, but it has also found its way into many classes in political and social philosophy. I have endeavored in this edition to increase the book's flexibility and coverage while maintaining the virtues of the previous one.

Much of the earlier edition remains intact, largely in response to reviewers and friends who report they and students have found the material works well and who therefore do not want it changed. I have revised slightly the basic organizational structure, dividing the book into four parts: Moral Theory, Issues of Life and Death, Political and Social Relationships, and Personal Relationships. Within this structure, the different sections have remained largely intact. I have included a total of eighteen new readings in this edition, each of which, I believe, further strengthens the book. Many of them bring the book up-to-date, discussing the implications of biotechnology and the information revolution on our ethical lives; others were suggested by reviewers, who wanted more coverage of capital punishment, for example, or on terrorism, relativism, and homosexuality.

The choice of these new articles reflects my fundamental editorial goals: (1) to ensure that the readings are philosophically sophisticated while at the same time they are accessible to typical undergraduate students; (2) to cover controversial positions on a wide array of topics, especially ones that students find interesting and that challenge received opinions; (3) to include articles that speak directly to one another, so that the issues are developed in a coherent fashion by authors who explicitly criticize the positions and arguments of those who have gone before; and (4) to increase the presence of different cultural, gender, and racial perspectives, along with better representation of women authors.

Part I, *Moral Theory,* includes expanded coverage of relativism and of the grounds of morality. The next part, *Issues of Life and Death,* now has an entire new section on "Violence, Terrorism, and War" that includes essays on gun control and terrorism. The readings on "Capital Punishment" include three new essays, essentially a debate between Jeffrey Reiman and Ernest van den Haag. The section on euthanasia has been expanded to "Euthanasia and Eugenics" and now includes an essay on the moral significance of biomedical technology. Part III, *Political and Social Relationships,* includes Marx and Engel's work along with a different selection from Walzer on hard work and desert. There are also new essays in the "Free Speech" section, on political correctness and on Internet censorship. The discussion of "Affirmative Action and Reparations" now includes a discussion of the claim that some form of reparations is due to African American descendants of victims of slavery and discrimination. Among the topics are the nature of reparations, the relevance of the fact that present-day whites had no role in slavery, the causes of economic inequalities, and the difficulties of determining how much is owed—and to whom. Part IV, *Personal Relationships,* includes new essays on the morality of homosexuality and the impact of the information age on personal relationships. The final section, on "Marriage and the Family," includes a debate on same-sex marriage and a critique of liberalism's no-fault approach to family that emphasizes individual freedom and the "unencumbered" self.

Each of the sections is independent of the others and can be included or omitted as desired. Thus, some readers might want to concentrate on social and political philosophy, ignoring issues of life and death entirely; others may want to concentrate on those questions, leaving topics such as justice and free speech aside. The entirety of Part I is also optional, although some of the later readings do assume at least an intuitive sense of the difference between utilitarian and deontological theories.

As before, each essay begins with a general introduction outlining what students can expect to find in the reading, and a series of review and discussion questions ends each essay. Longer, essay questions at the end of each section allow students to discuss two or more articles gathered around a single issue. These questions are designed to test students' understanding of the basic arguments presented in the book and to provoke discussion by suggesting possible lines of criticism and interesting comparisons with other essays or legal opinions.

In addition to these study aids included in the text, Prentice Hall has agreed to make available at no cost to students copies of my *Studying Philosophy: A Guide for the Perplexed.* In addition to material on how to read and discuss philosophy and how to write a good philosophy paper, the *Guide* also includes sections on basic grammar and punctuation rules, common spelling errors, tips for taking exams, guidelines and suggested forms for peer review of papers, and useful resources for studying philosophy.

Special thanks to reviewers and friends who have provided valuable suggestions and criticisms of this and earlier editions: Jim Abbott, Chesire Calhoun, Irwin Goldstein, Donald C. Hubin, Hugh LaFollette, Sarah Leffler, Elliot Leffler, Paul Menzel, Martin Perlmutter, Bill Shaw, Barbara Spencer, Amy Shapiro, Deni Elliott, David Haslett, Joseph Kupfer, Max Pensky, Joseph J. Tarala, and Richard L. Wilson. The reviewers for this edition were Larry D. McCargar, Massachusetts College of Art; Elizabeth Oljar, University of Detroit Mercy; Nancy A. Stanlick, University of Southern Florida; Richard Volkman, Southern Connecticut State University; and Harry van der Linden, Butler University.

John Arthur
Binghamton University

PART I

Moral Theory

1

Classical Theories of Morality

These selections include some of the most important works in moral theory ever produced by a philosopher. Each in its own way tries to provide a general, theoretical account of morality and moral argument. Topics include the ground or justification on which morality rests, the role of reason in morality, whether a single test for right and wrong exists, and what constitutes the ideal or best way of life. Selections range over great time and distance: from ancient Greece and Aristotle's *Nicomachean Ethics,* written more than two thousand years ago, to John Stuart Mill's classic work *Utilitarianism,* written in England during the nineteenth century.

Nicomachean Ethics

Aristotle

Aristotle (384–322 B.C.) was born in Stagira, a town near Macedonia. He went to Athens when he was seventeen years old and studied with Plato at the Academy for twenty years. When Plato died, Aristotle left Athens and traveled to Macedonia, where he tutored the young heir to the throne, who was later to become known as Alexander the Great. In 334 B.C., Aristotle returned to Athens and founded his own school, the Lyceum. When Alexander died in 323, there was strong anti-Macedonian feeling in Athens, and Aristotle left for Chalcis, where he died the next year at sixty-two. Aristotle studied and wrote about an astonishing range of subjects. No single person, it is often said, has ever founded and advanced so many fields of learning. Aristotle wrote separate treatises on physics, biology, logic, psychology, ethics, metaphysics, aesthetics, literary criticism, and political science. In the Middle Ages, he was known simply as "The Philosopher."

In this selection, taken from *Nicomachean Ethics,* Aristotle begins with a discussion of the study of ethics and of human nature and then turns to the nature of *eudaimonia*—that is, well-being or happiness. To understand happiness, it is necessary to understand the natural purpose or function of humans, which Aristotle describes as activity in accordance with reason. In that sense, happiness is also an excellent, specifically virtuous activity. Virtues, he argues, are those habits and traits that allow people to live well in communities, and true happiness is not, contrary to popular opinion, merely a pleasure. Nor is happiness to be found in economic wealth, although living a virtuous and happy life requires at least some wealth and certainly brings pleasure to the one who is able to achieve it. Turning finally to the nature of the virtues, Aristotle first distinguishes intellectual from moral virtue, arguing that whereas intellectual virtues can be taught, moral virtues must be acquired through habit and require a certain sort of community if they are to be realized. Using examples such as courage and liberality, he argues that moral virtues can best be understood as a mean between extremes.

BOOK I. HAPPINESS AND THE GOOD LIFE

Every art and every scientific inquiry, and similarly every action and purpose, may be said to aim at some good. Hence the good has been well defined as that at which all things aim. But it is clear that there is a difference in ends; for the ends are sometimes activities, and sometimes results beyond the mere activities. Where there are ends beyond the action, the results are naturally superior to the action.

As there are various actions, arts, and sciences, it follows that the ends are also various. Thus health is the end of the medical art, a ship of shipbuilding, victory of strategy, and wealth of economics. It often happens that a number of such arts or sciences combine for a single enterprise, as the art of making bridles and all such other arts as furnish the implements of horsemanship combine for horsemanship, and horsemanship and every military action for strategy; and in the same way, other arts or sciences combine for others. In all these cases, the ends of the master arts or sciences, whatever they may be, are more desirable than those of the subordinate arts or sciences, as it is for the sake of the former that the latter are pursued. It makes no difference to the argument whether the activities themselves are the ends of the action, or something beyond the activities, as in the above-mentioned sciences.

If it is true that in the sphere of action there is some end which we wish for its own sake, and for the sake of which we wish everything else, and if we do not desire everything for the sake of something else (for, if that is so, the process will go on ad infinitum, and our desire will be idle and futile), clearly this end will be good and the supreme good. Does it not follow then that the knowledge of this good is of great importance for the conduct of life? Like archers who have a mark at which to aim, shall we not have a better chance of attaining what we want? If this is so, we must endeavor to comprehend, at least in outline, what this good is, and what science or faculty makes it its object. . . .

From *Nicomachean Ethics*, trans. James E. C. Weldon (1892).

As every science and undertaking aims at some good, what is in our view the good at which political science [including moral and political theory] aims, and what is the highest of all practical goods? As to its name there is, I may say, a general agreement. The masses and the cultured classes agree in calling it happiness, and conceive that "to live well" or "to do well" is the same thing as "to be happy." But as to what happiness is they do not agree, nor do the masses give the same account of it as the philosophers. The former take it to be something visible and palpable, such as pleasure, wealth, or honor; different people, however, give different definitions of it, and often even the same man gives different definitions at different times. When he is ill, it is health, when he is poor, it is wealth; if he is conscious of his own ignorance, he envies people who use grand language above his own comprehension. Some philosophers, on the other hand, have held that, besides these various goods, there is an absolute good which is the cause of goodness in them all. [These were members of Plato's school of thought.] It would perhaps be a waste of time to examine all these opinions; it will be enough to examine such as are most popular or as seem to be more or less reasonable.

. . . Men's conception of the good or of happiness may be read in the lives they lead. Ordinary or vulgar people conceive it to be a pleasure, and accordingly choose a life of enjoyment. For there are, we may say, three conspicuous types of life, the sensual, the political, and, thirdly, the life of thought. Now the mass of men present an absolutely slavish appearance, choosing the life of brute beasts, but they have ground for so doing because so many persons in authority share the tastes of Sardanapalus. [A half legendary ruler of ancient Assyria, whose name to the Greeks stood for the extreme of Far Eastern luxury and extravagance.] Cultivated and energetic people, on the other hand, identify happiness with honor, as honor is the general end of political life. But this seems too superficial an idea for our present purpose; for honor depends more upon the people who pay it than upon the person to whom it is paid, and the good we feel is something which is proper to a man himself and cannot be easily taken away from him. Men too appear to seek honor in order to be assured of their own goodness. Accordingly, they seek it at the hands of the sage and of those who know them well, and they seek it on the ground of their virtue; clearly then, in their judgment at any rate, virtue is better than honor. Perhaps then we might look on virtue rather than honor as the end of political life. Yet even this idea appears not quite complete; for a man may possess virtue and yet be asleep or inactive throughout life, and not only so, but he may experience the greatest calamities and misfortunes. Yet no one would call such a life a life of happiness, unless he were maintaining a paradox. But we need not dwell further on this subject, since it is sufficiently discussed in popular philosophical treatises. The third life is the life of thought. . . .

The life of money making is a life of constraint; and wealth is obviously not the good of which we are in quest; for it is useful merely as a means to something else. It would be more reasonable to take the things mentioned before—sensual pleasure, honor, and virtue—as ends than wealth, since they are things desired on their own account. Yet these too are evidently not ends, although much argument has been employed to show that they are. . . .

But leaving this subject for the present, let us revert to the good of which we are in quest and consider what it may be. For it seems different in different activities or arts; it is one thing in medicine, another in strategy, and so on. What is the good in each of these instances? It is presumably that for the sake of which all else is done. In medicine this is health, in strategy victory, in architecture a house, and so on. In every activity and undertaking it is the end, since it is for the sake of the end that all people do whatever else they do. If then there is an end for all our activity, this will be the good to be accomplished; and if there are several such ends, it will be these.

Our argument has arrived by a different path at the same point as before; but we must endeavor to make it still plainer. Since there are more ends than one, and some of these ends—for example, wealth, flutes, and instruments generally—we desire as means to something else, it is evident that not all are final ends. But the highest good is clearly something final. Hence if there is only one final end, this will be the object of which we are in search; and if there are more than one, it will be the most final. We call that which is sought after for its own sake more final than that which is sought after as a means to something else; we call that which is never desired as a means to something else more final than things that are desired both for themselves and as means to something else. Therefore, we call absolutely final that which is always desired for itself and never as a means to something else. Now happiness more than anything else answers to this description. For happiness we always desire for its own sake and never as a means to something else, whereas honor, pleasure, intelligence, and every virtue we desire partly for their own sakes (for we should desire them independently of what might result from them), but partly also as means to happiness, because we suppose they will prove instruments of happiness. Happiness, on the other hand, nobody desires for the sake of these things, nor indeed as a means to anything else at all. . . .

Perhaps, however, it seems a commonplace to say that happiness is the supreme good; what is wanted is to define its nature a little more clearly. The best way of arriving at such a definition will probably be to ascertain the function of man. For, as with a flute player, a sculptor, or any artist, or in fact anybody who has a special function or activity, his goodness and excellence seem to lie in his function, so it would seem to be with man, if indeed he has a special function. Can it be said that, while a carpenter and a cobbler have special functions and activities, man, unlike them, is naturally functionless? Or, as the eye, the hand, the foot, and similarly each part of the body has a special function, so may man be regarded as having a special function apart from all these? What, then, can this function be? It is not life; for life is apparently something that man

shares with plants; and we are looking for something peculiar to him. We must exclude therefore the life of nutrition and growth. There is next what may be called the life of sensation. But this too, apparently, is shared by man with horses, cattle, and all other animals. There remains what I may call the active life of the rational part of man's being. Now this rational part is twofold; one part is rational in the sense of being obedient to reason, and the other in the sense of possessing and exercising reason and intelligence.

The function of man then is activity of soul in accordance with reason, or not apart from reason. Now, the function of a man of a certain kind, and of a man who is good of that kind—for example, of a harpist and a good harpist—are in our view the same in kind. This is true of all people of all kinds without exception, the superior excellence being only an addition to the function; for it is the function of a harpist to play the harp, and of a good harpist to play the harp well. This being so, if we define the function of man as a kind of life, and this life as an activity of the soul or a course of action in accordance with reason, and if the function of a good man is such activity of a good and noble kind, and if everything is well done when it is done in accordance with its proper excellence, it follows that the good of man is activity of soul in accordance with virtue, or, if there are more virtues than one, in accordance with the best and most complete virtue. But we must add the words "in a complete life." For as one swallow or one day does not make a spring, so one day or a short time does not make a man blessed or happy. . . .

Our account accords too with the view of those who hold that happiness is virtue or excellence of some sort; for activity in accordance with virtue is virtue. But there is plainly a considerable difference between calling the supreme good possession or use, a state of mind, or an activity. For a state of mind may exist without producing anything good—for example, if a person is asleep, or in any other way inert. Not so with an activity, since activity implies acting and acting well. As in the

Olympic games it is not the most beautiful and strongest who receive the crown but those who actually enter the combat, for from those come the victors, so it is those who act that win rightly what is noble and good in life.

Their life too is pleasant in itself. For pleasure is a state of mind, and whatever a man is fond of is pleasant to him, as a horse is to a lover of horses, a show to a lover of spectacles, and, similarly, just acts to a lover of justice, and virtuous acts in general to a lover of virtue. Now most men find a sense of discord in their pleasures, because their pleasures are not all naturally pleasant. But the lovers of nobleness take pleasure in what is naturally pleasant, and virtuous acts are naturally pleasant. Such acts then are pleasant both to these persons and in themselves. Nor does the life of such persons need more pleasure attached to it as a sort of charm; it possesses pleasure in itself. For, it may be added, a man who does not delight in noble acts is not good; as nobody would call a man just who did not enjoy just action, or liberal who did not enjoy liberal action, and so on. If this is so, it follows that acts of virtue are pleasant in themselves. They are also good and noble, and good and noble in the highest degree, for the judgment of the virtuous man on them is right, and his judgment is as we have described. Happiness then is the best and noblest and pleasantest thing in the world. . . .

Still it is clear, as we said, that happiness requires the addition of external goods; for it is impossible, or at least difficult, to do noble deeds with no outside means. For many things can be done only through the aid of friends or wealth or political power; and there are some things the lack of which spoils our felicity, such as good birth, wholesome children, and personal beauty. For a man who is extremely ugly in appearance or low born or solitary and childless can hardly be happy; perhaps still less so, if he has exceedingly bad children or friends, or has had good children or friends and lost them by death. As we said, then, happiness seems to need prosperity of this kind in addition to virtue. For this reason

some persons identify happiness with good fortune, though others do so with virtue. . . .

It is reasonable then not to call an ox or a horse or any other animal happy; for none of them is capable of sharing in this activity. For the same reason no child can be happy, since the youth of a child keeps him for the time being from such activity; if a child is ever called happy, the ground of felicitation is his promise, rather than his actual performance. For happiness demands, as we said, a complete virtue and a complete life. And there are all sorts of changes and chances in life, and the most prosperous of men may in his old age fall into extreme calamities, as Priam did in the heroic legends. [The disastrous fate of Priam, king of Troy, was part of the well-known Homeric tales.] And a person who has experienced such chances and died a miserable death, nobody calls happy. . . .

Now the events of chance are numerous and of different magnitudes. Small pieces of good fortune or the reverse do not turn the scale of life in any way, but great and numerous events make life happier if they turn out well, since they naturally give it beauty and the use of them may be noble and good. If, on the other hand, they turn out badly, they mar and mutilate happiness by causing pain and hindrances to many activities. Still, even in these circumstances, nobility shines out when a person bears with calmness the weight of accumulated misfortunes, not from insensibility but from dignity and greatness of spirit.

Then if activities determine the quality of life, as we said, no happy man can become miserable; for he will never do what is hateful and mean. For our idea of the truly good and wise man is that he bears all the chances of life with dignity and always does what is best in the circumstances, as a good general makes the best use of the forces at his command in war, or a good cobbler makes the best shoe with the leather given him, and so on through the whole series of the arts. If this is so, the happy man can never become miserable. I do not say that he will be fortunate if he meets such chances of life as Priam. Yet he will not be variable or constantly changing, for he will not be moved from his happiness easily or by ordinary misfortunes, but only by great and numerous ones; nor after them will he quickly regain his happiness. If he regains it at all, it will be only over a long and complete period of time and after great and notable achievement.

We may safely then define a happy man as one who is active in accord with perfect virtue and adequately furnished with external goods, not for some chance period of time but for his whole lifetime. . . .

Inasmuch as happiness is an activity of soul in accordance with complete or perfect virtue, it is necessary to consider virtue, as this will perhaps be the best way of studying happiness. . . .

BOOK II: VIRTUE AND THE MEAN

Virtue then is twofold, partly intellectual and partly moral, and intellectual virtue is originated and fostered mainly by teaching; it therefore demands experience and time. Moral virtue on the other hand is the outcome of habit. From this fact it is clear that moral virtue is not implanted in us by nature, for a law of nature cannot be altered by habituation. Thus a stone, that naturally tends to fall downwards, cannot be habituated or trained to rise upwards. It is neither by nature then nor in defiance of nature that virtues are implanted in us. Nature gives us the capacity of receiving them, and that capacity is perfected by habit.

Again, if we take the various natural powers which belong to us, we first possess the proper faculties and afterwards display the activities. It is obviously so with the senses. Not by seeing frequently or hearing frequently do we acquire the sense of seeing or hearing; on the contrary, because we have the senses we make use of them; we do not get them by making use of them. But the virtues we get by first practicing them, as we do in the arts. For it is by doing what we ought to do when we study the arts that we learn the arts themselves; we become builders by building

and harpists by playing the harp. Similarly, it is by doing just acts that we become just, by doing temperate acts that we become temperate, by doing brave acts that we become brave. The experience of states confirms this statement, for it is by training in good habits that lawmakers make the citizens good. This is the object all lawmakers have at heart; if they do not succeed in it, they fail of their purpose; and it makes the distinction between a good constitution and a bad one.

Again, the causes and means by which any virtue is produced and destroyed are the same. It is by our actions in dealing between man and man that we become either just or unjust. It is by our actions in the face of danger and by our training ourselves to fear or to courage that we become either cowardly or courageous. It is much the same with our appetites and angry passions. People become temperate and gentle, others licentious and passionate, by behaving in one or the other way in particular circumstances. In a word, moral states are the results of activities like the states themselves. It is our duty therefore to keep a certain character in our activities, since our moral states depend on the differences in our activities. So the difference between one and another training in habits in our childhood is not a light matter, but important, or rather, all-important.

Our present study is not, like other studies, purely theoretical in intention; for the object of our inquiry is not to know what virtue is but how to become good, and that is the sole benefit of it. We must, therefore, consider the right way of performing actions, for it is acts that determine the character of the resulting moral states.

That we should act in accordance with right reason is a common general principle, which may here be taken for granted. . . .

The first point to be observed is that in matters we are now considering deficiency and excess are both fatal. It is so, we see, in questions of health and strength. Too much or too little gymnastic exercise is fatal to strength. Similarly, too much or too little meat and drink is fatal to health, whereas a suitable amount produces, increases, and sustains it. . . .

It is the same with temperance, courage, and other moral virtues. A person who avoids and is afraid of everything and faces nothing becomes a coward; a person who is not afraid of anything but is ready to face everything becomes foolhardy. Similarly, he who enjoys every pleasure and abstains from none is licentious; he who refuses all pleasures, like a boor, is an insensible sort of person. For temperance and courage are destroyed by excess and deficiency but preserved by the mean. . . .

Every art then performs its function well, if it regards the mean and refers the works which it produces to the mean. This is the reason why it is usually said of successful works that it is impossible to take anything from them or to add anything to them, which implies that excess or deficiency is fatal to excellence but that the mean state ensures it. Good artists too, as we say, have an eye to the mean in their works. But virtue, like Nature herself, is more accurate and better than any art; virtue therefore will aim at the mean;—I speak of moral virtue, as it is moral virtue which is concerned with emotions and actions, and it is these which admit of excess and deficiency and the mean. Thus it is possible to go too far, or not to go far enough, in respect of fear, courage, desire, anger, pity, and pleasure and pain generally, and the excess and the deficiency are alike wrong; but to experience these emotions at the right times and on the right occasions and towards the right persons and for the right causes and in the right manner is the mean or the supreme good, which is characteristic of virtue. Similarly there may be excess, deficiency, or the mean, in regard to actions. But virtue is concerned with emotions and actions, and here excess is an error and deficiency a fault, whereas the mean is successful and laudable, and success and merit are both characteristics of virtue.

It appears then that virtue is a mean state, so far at least as it aims at the mean. . . .

On the other hand, there are many different ways of going wrong; for evil is in its nature infinite. [It] is easy to miss the mark but difficult to hit it. And so by reasoning excess and deficiency are characteristics of vice and the mean is a characteristic of virtue.

Virtue then is a state of deliberate moral purpose consisting in a mean that is relative to ourselves, the mean being determined by reason, or as a prudent man would determine it. . . .

But not every action or every emotion admits of a mean. There are some whose very name implies wickedness, as, for example, malice, shamelessness, and envy among the emotions, and adultery, theft, and murder among the actions. All these and others like them are marked as intrinsically wicked, not merely the excesses or deficiencies of them. It is never possible then to be right in them; they are always sinful. Right or wrong in such acts as adultery does not depend on our committing it with the right woman, at the right time, or in the right manner; on the contrary it is wrong to do it at all. It would be equally false to suppose that there can be a mean or excess of deficiency in unjust, cowardly, or licentious conduct. . . .

There are then three dispositions, two being vices, namely, excess and deficiency, and one virtue, which is the mean between them; and they are all in a sense morally opposed. Thus the brave man appears foolhardy compared with the coward, but cowardly compared with the foolhardy. Similarly, the temperate man appears licentious compared with the insensible man but insensible compared with the licentious; and the liberal man appears extravagant compared with the stingy man but stingy compared with the spendthrift. The result is that the extremes each denounce the mean as belonging to the other extreme; the coward calls the brave man foolhardy, and the foolhardy man calls him cowardly; and so on in other cases. . . .

That is why it is so hard to be good; for it is always hard to find the mean in anything; anybody can get angry—that is easy—and anybody can give or spend money, but to give it to the right person, to give the right amount of it, at the right time, for the right cause and in the right way, this is not what anybody can do, nor is it easy. That is why goodness is rare, praiseworthy, and noble. One who aims at the mean must begin by departing from the extreme, for of the two extremes one is more wrong than the other. . . . We must also note the weakness to which we are ourselves particularly prone, since different natures tend in different ways; and we may ascertain what our tendency is by observing our feelings of pleasure and pain. Then we must drag ourselves away towards the opposite extreme; for by pulling ourselves as far as possible from what is wrong we shall arrive at the mean.

In all cases we must especially be on our guard against the pleasant, or pleasure, for we are not impartial judges of pleasure. . . .

Undoubtedly this is a difficult task, especially in individual cases. It is not easy to determine the right matter, objects, occasion, and duration of anger. Sometimes we praise people who are deficient in anger, and call them gentle, and at other times we praise people who exhibit a fierce temper as high spirited. It is not however a man who deviates a little from goodness, but one who deviates a great deal, whether on the side of excess or of deficiency, that is blamed; for he is sure to call attention to himself. It is not easy to decide in theory how far and to what extent a man may go before he becomes blameworthy, but neither is it easy to define in theory anything else in the region of the senses; such things depend on circumstances, and our judgment of them depends on our perception.

REVIEW AND DISCUSSION QUESTIONS

1. What is the end or function of human beings, according to Aristotle?
2. How does Aristotle understand happiness? Why does he think it is the supreme good?
3. Why does Aristotle reject the pursuit of money or pleasure as the key to happiness?
4. Explain Aristotle's understanding of the nature of virtue and its connection with habit.
5. Explain the theory of the virtues as a mean between extremes. Give examples of the virtues.
6. Do you agree that happiness (or well-being) and virtue are connected? If not, what *is* the basis of happiness?

Leviathan

Thomas Hobbes

Thomas Hobbes was born in 1588 when the approach of the Spanish Armada was threatening Britain. "Fear and I were born twins," he would later say, emphasizing his conviction that the need for security was the foundation of society and the basis of political obligation. He lived during a critical and difficult period of English history, which included struggles over the traditional authority of the church and the emerging role of modern science. He also saw radical political change, including the absolutism of the Stuart monarchy, the English civil war, and the abolition and subsequent restoration of the monarchy. He died just before constitutional government won its final victory. Hobbes served as tutor for Charles II, who gave Hobbes a pension after being restored to the throne. After publishing early works expressing antiroyalist attitudes, Hobbes was sent into exile, condemned in the House of Commons, and, even after he died, his books were burned at Oxford. He was suspected of atheism, and, perhaps most important, he rejected the divine basis of political authority. God, he said, is beyond rational understanding; we can only know he exists as the first cause of the universe.

Hobbes lived until the age of ninety-one, enjoying a life of travel, study, polemical controversy, and literary and philosophical activity. He was personally temperate, lively, and a loyal friend; he played tennis until the age of seventy-five and attributed his lifelong good health to exercise and singing in bed. He wrote on a variety of subjects, but his most famous work by far is *Leviathan,* published in 1651.

Hobbes was heavily influenced by the new, Galilean scientific method and thought that physical laws could account for human behavior, just as they do all other phenomena. He sought to understand human beings (and politics) in accord with the new scientific methods.

Just before the selection reprinted here, Hobbes argued that the world, including human beings, is composed of material particles. Minds, he argued, are therefore no different from bodies; human "motion," such as walking, speaking, and other acts, is caused by our desires, appetites, and aversions. In this selection, Hobbes discusses how reason and the human condition induce people to leave a "state of nature" and agree to be ruled by a common power strong enough to enforce our contracts and ensure peace. Morality is, therefore, a form of convention, agreed to by all in order to avoid the war of all against all. Without an agreement, and the threat of harm imposed by the sovereign, there can be neither morality nor justice. Power and threats are the necessary bases of all obligations.

THE FIRST PART: OF MAN

Good. Evil. . . . Whatsoever is the object of any man's appetite or desire, that is it which he for his part calleth *good:* and the object of his hate and aversion, *evil;* and of his contempt, *vile* and *inconsiderable.* For these words of good, evil, and contemptible, are ever used with relation to the person that useth them: there being nothing simply and absolutely so. . . .

Deliberation. When in the mind of man, appetites, and aversions, hopes, and fears, concerning one and the same thing, arise alternately; and divers good and evil consequences of the doing, or omitting the thing propounded, come successively into our thoughts; so that sometimes we have an appetite to it; sometimes an aversion from it; sometimes hope to be able to do it; sometimes despair, or fear to attempt it; the whole sum of desires, aversions, hopes and fears continued till the thing be either done, or thought impossible, is that we call DELIBERATION. . . .

The Will. In *deliberation,* the last appetite, or aversion, immediately adhering to the action, or to the omission thereof, is that we call the WILL. . . .

Felicity. Continual success in obtaining those things which a man from time to time desireth, that is to say, continual prospering, is that men call FELICITY; I mean the felicity of this life. For there is no such thing as perpetual tranquility of mind, while we live here; because life itself is but motion, and can never be without desire, nor without fear, no more than without sense. . . .

Of the Natural Condition of Mankind as Concerning Their Felicity and Misery

Men by Nature Equal. Nature hath made men so equal, in the faculties of the body, and mind; as that though there be found one man sometimes manifestly stronger in body, or of quicker mind than another; yet when all is reckoned together, the difference between man, and man, is not so considerable, as that one man can thereupon claim to himself any benefit, to which another may not pretend, as well as he. For as to the strength of body, the weakest has strength enough to kill the strongest, either by secret machination, or by confederacy with others, that are in the same danger with himself.

From Thomas Hobbes, *Leviathan* (1651).

And as to the faculties of the mind, setting aside the arts grounded upon words, and especially that skill of proceeding upon general, and infallible rules, called science; which very few have, and but in few things; as being not a native faculty, born with us: nor attained, as prudence, while we look after somewhat else, I find yet a greater equality amongst men, than that of strength. For prudence, is but experience; which equal time, equally bestows on all men, in those things they equally apply themselves unto. That which may perhaps make such equality incredible, is but a vain conceit of one's own wisdom, which almost all men think they have in a greater degree, than the vulgar; that is, than all men but themselves, and a few others, whom by fame, or for concurring with themselves, they approve.

From Equality Proceeds Diffidence. From this equality of ability, ariseth equality of hope in the attaining of our ends. And therefore if any two men desire the same thing, which nevertheless they cannot both enjoy, they become enemies; and in the way to their end, which is principally their own conservation, and sometimes their delectation only, endeavor to destroy, or subdue one another. And from hence it comes to pass, that where an invader hath no more to fear, than another man's single power; if one plant, sow, build, or possess a convenient seat, others may probably be expected to come prepared with forces united, to dispossess, and deprive him, not only of the fruit of his labour, but also of his life, or liberty. And the invader again is in the like danger of another.

From Diffidence War. And from this diffidence of one another, there is no way for any man to secure himself, so reasonable, as anticipation; that is, by force, or wiles, to master the persons of all men he can, so long, till he see no other power great enough to endanger him: and this is no more than his own conservation requireth, and is generally allowed. Also because there be some, that taking pleasure in contemplating their own power in the acts of conquest, which they pursue farther than their security requires; if others, that otherwise would be glad to be at ease within modest bounds, should not by invasion increase their power, they would not be able, [for a] long time, by standing only on their defence, to subsist. And by consequence, such augmentation of dominion over men being necessary to a man's conservation, it ought to be allowed him.

Again, men have no pleasure, but on the contrary a great deal of grief, in keeping company, where there is no power able to overawe them all. For every man looketh that his companion should value him, at the same rate he sets upon himself: and upon all signs of contempt, or undervaluing, naturally endeavors, as far as he dares, (which amongst them that have no common power to keep them in quiet, is far enough to make them destroy each other), to extort a greater value from his contemners, by damage; and from others, by the example.

So that in the nature of man, we find three principal causes of quarrel. First, competition; secondly, diffidence; thirdly, glory.

The first, maketh men invade for gain; the second, for safety; and the third, for reputation. The first use violence, to make themselves masters of other men's persons, wives, children, and cattle; the second, to defend them; the third, for trifles, as a word, a smile, a different opinion, and any other sign of undervalue, either direct in their persons, or by reflection in their kindred, their friends, their nation, their profession, or their name.

Out of Civil States, There Is Always War of Every One Against Every One. Hereby it is manifest, that during the time men live without a common power to keep them all in awe, they are in that condition which is called war; and such a war, as is of every man, against every man. For WAR, consisteth not in battle only, or the act of fighting; but in a tract of time, wherein the will to contend by battle is sufficiently known: and therefore the notion of *time,* is to be considered in the nature of war; as it is in the nature of weather. For as the nature of foul weather, lieth not in a shower or two of rain; but in an inclination thereto of many days together: so the nature of war, consisteth not in actual fighting; but in the known disposition thereto, during all the time there is no assurance to the contrary. All other time is PEACE.

The Incommodities of Such a War. Whatsoever therefore is consequent to a time of war, where every man is enemy to every man; the same is consequent to the time, wherein men live without other security, than what their own strength, and their own invention shall furnish them withal. In such condition, there is no place for industry; because the fruit thereof is uncertain: and consequently no culture of the earth; no navigation, nor use of the commodities that may be imported by sea; no commodious building; no instruments of moving, and removing, such things as require much force; no knowledge of the face of the earth; no account of time; no arts; no letters; no society; and which is worst of all, continual fear, and danger of violent death; and the life of man, solitary, poor, nasty, brutish, and short.

It may seem strange to some man, that has not well weighed these things; that nature should thus dissociate, and render men apt to invade, and destroy one another: and he may therefore, not trusting to this inference, made from the passions, desire perhaps to have the same confirmed by experience. Let him therefore consider with himself, when taking a journey, he arms himself, and seeks to go well accompanied; when going to sleep, he locks his doors; when even in his house he locks his chests; and this when he knows there be laws, and public officers, armed, to revenge all injuries shall be done him; what opinion he has of his fellow-subjects, when he rides armed; of his fellow citizens, when he locks his doors; and of his children, and servants, when he locks his chests. Does he not there as much accuse mankind by his actions, as I do by my words? But neither of us accuse man's nature in it. The desires, and other passions of man, are in themselves no sin. No more are the actions, that proceed from those passions, till

they know a law that forbids them: which till laws be made they cannot know: nor can any law be made, till they have agreed upon the person that shall make it.

It may peradventure be thought, there was never such a time, nor condition of war as this; and I believe it was never generally so, over all the world: but there are many places, where they live so now. For the savage people in many places of America, except the government of small families, the concord whereof dependeth on natural lust, have no government at all; and live at this day in that brutish manner, as I said before. Howsoever, it may be perceived what manner of life there would be, where there were no common power to fear, by the manner of life, which men that have formerly lived under a peaceful government, use to degenerate into, in a civil war.

But though there had never been any time, wherein particular men were in a condition of war one against another; yet in all times, kings, and persons of sovereign authority, because of their independency, are in continual jealousies, and in the state and posture of gladiators; having their weapons pointing, and their eyes fixed on one another; that is, their forts, garrisons, and guns upon the frontiers of their kingdoms; and continual spies upon their neighbours; which is a posture of war. But because they uphold thereby, the industry of their subjects; there does not follow from it, that misery, which accompanies the liberty of particular men.

In Such a War Nothing Is Unjust. To this war of every man, against every man, this also is consequent; that nothing can be unjust. The notions of right and wrong, justice and injustice have there no place. Where there is no common power, there is no law: where no law, no injustice. Force, and fraud, are in war the two cardinal virtues. Justice, and injustice are none of the faculties neither of the body, nor mind. If they were, they might be in a man that were alone in the world, as well as his senses, and passions. They are qualities, that relate to men in society, not in solitude. It is consequent also to the same condition, that there be no propriety, no dominion, no *mine* and *thine* distinct; but only that to be every man's, that he can get: and for so long, as he can keep it. And thus much for the ill condition, which man by mere nature is actually placed in; though with a possibility to come out of it, consisting partly in the passions, partly in his reason.

The Passions That Incline Men to Peace.   The passions that incline men to peace, are fear of death; desire of such things as are necessary to commodious living; and a hope by their industry to obtain them. And reason suggesteth convenient articles of peace, upon which men may be drawn to agreement. These articles, are they, which otherwise are called the Laws of Nature: whereof I shall speak more particularly [below].

Of the First and Second Natural Laws, and of Contracts

Right of Nature What.   The RIGHT OF NATURE, which writers commonly call *jus naturale,* is the liberty each man hath, to use his own power, as he will himself, for the preservation of his own nature; that is to say, of his own life; and consequently, of doing any thing, which in his own judgment, and reason, he shall conceive to be the aptest means thereunto.

Liberty What.   By LIBERTY, is understood, according to the proper signification of the word, the absence of external impediments: which impediments, may oft take away part of a man's power to do what he would; but cannot hinder him from using the power left him, according as his judgment, and reason shall dictate to him.

A Law of Nature What. Difference of Right and Law.   A LAW OF NATURE, *lex naturalis,* is a precept or general rule, found out by reason, by which a man is forbidden to do that, which is destructive of his life, or taketh away the means of preserving the same; and to omit that, by which he thinketh it may be best preserved. . . .

Naturally Every Man Has Right to Every Thing. The Fundamental Law of Nature.   And because the condition of man, as hath been declared [above], is a condition of war of every one against every one; in which case every one is governed by his own reason; and there is nothing he can make use of, that may not be a help unto him, in preserving his life against his enemies; it followeth, that in such a condition, every man has a right to every thing; even to one another's body. And therefore, as long as this natural right of every man to every thing endureth, there can be no security to any man, how strong or wise soever he be, of living out the time, which nature ordinarily alloweth men to live. And consequently it is a precept, or general rule of reason, *that every man, ought to endeavor peace, as far as he has hope of obtaining it; and when he cannot obtain it, that he may seek, and use, all helps, and advantages of war. . . .*

The Second Law of Nature.   From this fundamental law of nature, by which men are commanded to endeavor peace, is derived this second law; *that a man be willing, when others are so too, as far-forth, as for peace, and defence of himself he shall think it necessary, to lay down this right to all things; and be contented with so much liberty against other men, as he would allow other men against himself.* For as long as every man holdeth this right, of doing any thing he liketh; so long are all men in the condition of war. But if other men will not lay down their right, as well as he; then there is no reason for anyone to divest himself of his: for that were to expose himself to prey, which no man is bound to, rather than to dispose himself to peace. . . .

Not All Rights Are Alienable.   Whensoever a man transferreth his right, or renounceth it; it is either in consideration of some right reciprocally transferred to himself; or for some other good he hopeth for thereby. For it is a voluntary act: and of the voluntary acts of every man, the object is some *good to himself.* And therefore there be some rights, which no man can be understood by any words, or other signs, to have abandoned, or transferred. As first a man cannot lay down the right of resisting them, that assault him by force, to take away his life; because he cannot be understood to aim thereby, at any good to himself. The same may be said of wounds, and chains, and imprisonment; because there is no benefit consequent to such patience; as there is to the patience of suffering another to be wounded, or imprisoned. . . .

Covenants of Mutual Trust, When Invalid. If a covenant be made, wherein neither of the parties perform presently, but trust one another; in the condition of mere nature, which is a condition of war of every man against every man, upon any reasonable suspicion, it is void; but if there be a common power set over them both, with right and force sufficient to compel performance, it is not void. For he that performeth first, has no assurance the other will perform after; because the bonds of words are too weak to bridle men's ambition, avarice, anger, and other passions, without the fear of some coercive power; which in the condition of mere nature, where all men are equal, and judges of the justness of their own fears, cannot possibly be supposed. And therefore he which performeth first does but betray himself to his enemy; contrary to the right, he can never abandon, of defending his life, and means of living. . . .

Covenants Extorted by Fear Are Valid. Covenants entered into by fear, in the condition of mere nature, are obligatory. For example, if I covenant to pay a ransom, or service for my life, to an enemy; I am bound by it: for it is a contract, wherein one receiveth the benefit of life; the other is to receive money, or service for it; and consequently, where no other law, as in the condition of mere nature, forbiddeth the performance, the covenant is valid. . . .

Of Other Laws of Nature

The Third Law of Nature, Justice. From that law of nature, by which we are obliged to transfer to another, such rights, as being retained, hinder the peace of mankind, there

followeth a third; which is this, *that men perform their covenants made:* without which, covenants are in vain, and but empty words; and the right of all men to all things remaining, we are still in the condition of war.

Justice and Injustice What. And in this law of nature, consisteth the fountain and original of JUSTICE. For where no covenant hath preceded, there hath no right been transferred, and every man has right to every thing; and consequently, no action can be unjust. But when a covenant is made, then to break it is unjust: and the definition of INJUSTICE, is no other than the not *performance of covenant.* And whatsoever is not unjust, is *just.*

Justice and Propriety Begin With the Constitution of Commonwealth. But because covenants of mutual trust, where there is a fear of not performance on either part, as hath been said in the former chapter, are invalid; though the original of justice be the making of covenants; yet injustice actually there can be none, till the cause of such fear be taken away; which while men are in the natural condition of war, cannot be done. Therefore before the names of just, and unjust can have place, there must be some coercive power, to compel men equally to the performance of their covenants, by the terror of some punishment, greater than the benefit they expect by the breach of their covenant; and to make good that propriety, which by mutual contract men acquire, in recompense of the universal right they abandon: and such power there is none before the erection of a commonwealth. . . .

Justice Not Contrary to Reason. The fool hath said in his heart, there is no such thing as justice; and sometimes also with his tongue: seriously alleging, that every man's conservation, and contentment, being committed to his own care, there could be no reason, why every man might not do what he thought conduced thereunto. He does not therein deny, that there are covenants; and that they are sometimes broken, sometimes kept; but he questioneth whether injustice, taking away the fear of God, may not sometimes stand

5. Explain how all of morality, not just politics, may be understood as an agreement for mutual advantage.

6. How does Hobbes respond to the "fool" who claims that justice is contrary to reason and that a rational person would act unjustly?

7. What is freedom, according to Hobbes? Do people have both freedom and free will? Explain.

8. Does Hobbes think morality applies in a state of war when there is no state or society? Explain.

9. Evaluate Hobbes's answer to question 8. Why do you agree or disagree?

The Fundamental Principles of the Metaphysic of Morals

Immanuel Kant

Immanuel Kant lived his entire life within a few miles of Koningsberg, in East Prussia, where he was born in 1724. Kant never married and was a man of remarkable organization and regularity of habits; it is even said that people would set their clocks based on his afternoon walks. Like Hobbes, he lived a long and very productive life, dying in 1804 at the age of eighty. Kant's writing has had and continues to have an immense impact on all areas of philosophy from epistemology and ethics to metaphysics and political theory.

Rejecting both Aristotle, who believed it necessary to study closely human psychology and the nature of human happiness in order to understand morality, and utilitarians who often believe sentiment and feeling to be at the root of morality, Kant argues that duty is based solely on reason. To be genuinely worthy, Kant argues, one must not just act *in accordance with* duty; one must also act for *duty's sake.* To do the right thing out of selfish motives (for fear of getting caught, for example) would not be to act for the sake of duty and, therefore, would not evidence the kind of value that actions done purely for the sake of duty do.

How then is one to know what duty requires? Kant argues that reason provides the foundation on which duty rests. An action is right, he claims, if it conforms to a moral rule that any agent must follow if he is to act rationally. That rule, which distinguishes right from wrong, is what Kant calls the *categorical* (that is, exceptionless) *imperative;* an imperative that Kant expresses as requiring that a person must never perform an act unless he or she can consistently will (or intend) that the maxim or principle that motivates the action could become a universal law. In this way, Kant argues, the categorical imperative comprises the heart of the distinction between right and wrong—a distinction that any rational being can comprehend and act on.

Kant also speaks of a second formulation of the categorical imperative that he believes is equivalent to the first. The second formulation states that one must act so as to treat people as ends in themselves, never merely as means. That second version, then, looks at actions from the perspective of the one acted upon rather than the agent. After discussing four examples of moral reasoning, Kant concludes with a description of what he terms the "kingdom of ends" as well as of human dignity and autonomy.

From *The Fundamental Principles of the Metaphysic of Morals,* (1785), trans. Thomas K. Abbott (1873).

THE GOOD WILL

Nothing can possibly be conceived in the world, or even out of it, which can be called good without qualification, except a *good will.* Intelligence, wit, judgment, and the other talents of the mind, however they may be named, or courage, resolution, perseverance, as qualities of temperament, are undoubtedly good and desirable in many respects; but these gifts of nature may also become extremely bad and mischievous if the will which is to make use of them, and which, therefore, constitutes what is called *character,* is not good. It is the same with the *gifts of fortune.* Power, riches, honor, even health, and the general well-being and contentment with one's condition which is called *happiness,* inspire pride, and often presumption, if there is not a good will to correct the influence of these on the mind, and with this also to rectify the whole principle of acting, and adapt it to its end. The sight of a being who is not adorned with a single feature of a pure and good will, enjoying unbroken prosperity, can never give pleasure to an impartial rational spectator. Thus a good will appears to constitute the indispensable condition even of being worthy of happiness.

There are even some qualities which are of service to this good will itself, and may facilitate its action, yet which have no intrinsic unconditional value, but always presuppose a good will, and this qualifies the esteem that we justly have for them, and does not permit us to regard them as absolutely good. Moderation in the affections and passions, self-control, and calm deliberation are not only good in many respects, but even seem to constitute part of the intrinsic worth of the person; but they are far from deserving to be called good without qualification, although they have been so unconditionally praised by the ancients. For without the principles of a good will, they may become extremely bad; and the coolness of a villain not only makes him far more dangerous, but also directly makes him more abominable in our eyes than he would have been without it.

A good will is good not because of what it performs or effects, not by its aptness for the attainment of some proposed end, but simply by virtue of the volition—that is, it is good in itself, and considered by itself is to be esteemed much higher than all that can be brought about by it in favor of any inclination, nay, even of the sum-total of all inclinations. Even if it should happen that, owing to special disfavor of fortune, or the niggardly provision of a stepmotherly nature, this will should wholly lack power to accomplish its purpose, if with its greatest efforts it should yet achieve nothing, and there should remain only the good will (not, to be sure, a mere wish, but the summoning of all means in our power), then, like a jewel, it would still shine by its own light, as a thing which has its whole value in itself. Its usefulness or fruitlessness can neither add to nor take away anything from this value. It would be, as it were, only the setting to enable us to handle it the more conveniently in common commerce, or to attract to it the attention of those who are not yet connoisseurs, but not to recommend it to true connoisseurs, or to determine its value. . . .

THE FIRST PROPOSITION OF MORALITY

We have then to develop the notion of a will which deserves to be highly esteemed for itself, and is good without a view to anything further. . . . [Consider] that it is always a matter of duty that a tradesman should not overcharge an inexperienced purchaser; and wherever there is much commerce the prudent tradesman does not overcharge, but keeps a fixed price of everyone, so that a child buys of him as well as any other. Men are thus honestly served, but this is not enough to make us believe that the tradesman acted from duty and from principles of honesty: his own advantage required it. Accordingly the action was done neither from duty nor from direct inclination, but merely with a selfish view. . . .

On the other hand, it is a duty to maintain one's life; and, in addition, everyone also has a direct inclination to do so. But on this account the often anxious care which most men take for it has no intrinsic worth, and their maxim has no moral import. They preserve their life *as duty requires,* no doubt, but not *because duty requires.* On the other hand, if adversity and hopeless sorrow have completely taken away the relish for life; if the unfortunate one, strong in mind, indignant at his fate rather than desponding or dejected, wishes for death, and yet preserves his life without loving it—not from inclination of fear, but from duty—then his maxim has a moral worth. . . .

To be beneficent when we can is a duty; and besides this, there are many minds so sympathetically constituted that, without any other motive of vanity or self-interest, they find a pleasure in spreading joy around them, and can take delight in the satisfaction of others so far as it is their own work. But I maintain that in such a case an action of this kind, however proper, however amiable it may be, has nevertheless no true moral worth, but is on a level with other inclinations, for example, the inclination to honor, which, if it is happily directed to that which is in fact of public utility and accordant with duty, and consequently honorable, deserves praise and encouragement, but not esteem. For the maxim[1] lacks the moral import, namely, that such actions be done *from duty,* not from inclination. Put the case that the mind of that philanthropist was clouded by sorrow of his own, extinguishing all sympathy with the lot of others, and that while he still has the power to benefit others in distress, he is not touched by their trouble because he is absorbed with his own; and now suppose that he tears himself out of this dead insensibility and performs the action without any inclination to it, but simply from duty, then . . . has his action its genuine moral worth. . . . It is just in this that the moral worth of the character is brought out which is incomparably the highest of all, namely, that he is beneficent, not from inclination, but from duty. . . .

It is in this manner, undoubtedly, that we are to understand those passages of Scripture in which we are commanded to love our neighbour, even our enemy. For love, as an affection, cannot be commanded, but beneficence for duty's sake may. This is *practical* love, and not *pathological*—a love that is seated in the will, and not in the propensities of feeling—in principles of action and not of tender sympathy; and it is this love alone which can be commanded.

THE SECOND AND THIRD PROPOSITIONS OF MORALITY

The second proposition is: That an action done from duty derives its moral worth, *not from the purpose* which is to be attained by it, but from the maxim by which it is determined, and therefore does not depend on the realization of the object of the action, but merely on the *principle of volition* by which the action has taken place, without regard to any object of desire. It is clear from what precedes that the purposes which we may have in view in our actions, or their effects regarded as ends and springs of the will, cannot give to actions any unconditional or moral worth. In what, then, can their worth lie if it is not to consist in the will and in reference to its expected effect? It cannot lie anywhere but in the *principle of the will* without regard to the ends which can be attained by the action. . . .

The third proposition, which is a consequence of the two preceding, I would express thus: *Duty is the necessity of acting from respect for the law.* I may have *inclination* for an object as the effect of my proposed action, but I cannot have respect for it just for this reason that it is an effect and not an energy of will. Similarly, I cannot have *respect* for inclination, whether my own or another's; I can at most, if my own, approve it; if another's, sometimes even love it, that is, look on it as favorable to my own interest. It is only what is connected with my will as a principle, by no means as an effect—what does not subserve my inclination, but overpowers it, or at least in case of choice excludes it from its calculation—in other words, simply the law of itself, which can be an object of respect, and hence a command. Now an action done from duty must wholly exclude the influence of inclination, and with it every object of the will, so that nothing remains which can determine the will except objectively the *law,* and subjectively *pure respect* for this practical law, and consequently the maxim[1] that I should follow this law even to the thwarting of all my inclinations.

Thus the moral worth of an action does not lie in the effect expected from it, nor in any principle of action which requires to borrow its motive from this expected effect. For all these effects—agreeableness of one's condition, and even the promotion of the happiness of others—could have been also brought about by other causes, so that for this there would have been no need of the will of a rational being; whereas it is in this alone that the supreme and unconditional good can be found. The pre-eminent good which we call moral can therefore consist in nothing else than *the conception of law* in itself, *which certainly is only possible in a rational being,* in so far as this conception, and not the expected effect, determines the will. This is a good which is already present in the person who acts accordingly, and we have not to wait for it to appear first in the result.

THE SUPREME PRINCIPLE OF MORALITY: THE CATEGORICAL IMPERATIVE

But what sort of law can that be the conception of which must determine the will, even without paying any regard to the effect expected from it, in order that this will may be called good absolutely and without qualification? As I have deprived the will of every impulse which could arise to it from obedience to any law, there remains nothing but the universal conformity of its actions to law in general, which alone is to serve the will as a principle, that is, I am never to act otherwise than so *that I could also will that my maxim should become a universal law.* Here, now, it is the simple conformity to law

in general, without assuming any particular law applicable to certain actions, that serves the will as its principle, and must so serve it if duty is not to be a vain delusion and a chimerical notion. The common reason of men in its practical judgments perfectly coincides with this, and always has in view the principle here suggested. Let the question be, for example: may I when in distress make a promise with the intention not to keep it? I readily distinguish here between the two significations which the question may have: whether it is prudent or whether it is right to make a false promise? The former may undoubtedly often be the case. I see clearly indeed that it is not enough to extricate myself from a present difficulty by means of this subterfuge, but it must be well considered whether there may not hereafter spring from this lie much greater inconvenience than that from which I now free myself, and as, with all my supposed *cunning,* the consequences cannot be so easily foreseen but that credit once lost may be much more injurious to me than any mischief which I seek to avoid at present, it should be considered whether it would not be more *prudent* to act herein according to a universal maxim, and to make it a habit to promise nothing except with the intention of keeping it. But it is soon clear to me that such a maxim will still only be based on the fear of consequences. Now it is a wholly different thing to be truthful from duty, and to be so from apprehension of injurious consequences. In the first case, the very notion of the action already implies a law for me; in the second case, I must first look about elsewhere to see what results may be combined with it which would affect myself. For to deviate from the principle of duty is beyond all doubt wicked; but to be unfaithful to my maxim of prudence may often be very advantageous to me, although to abide by it is certainly safer. The shortest way, however, and an unerring one, to discover the answer to this question whether a lying promise is consistent with duty, is to ask myself, Should I be content that my maxim (to extricate myself from difficulty by a false promise) should hold good as a universal law, for myself as well as for others; and should I be able to say to myself, "Every one may make a deceitful promise when he finds himself in a difficulty from which he cannot otherwise extricate himself"? Then I presently become aware that, while I can will the lie, I can by no means will that lying should be a universal law. For with such a law there would be no promises at all, since it would be in vain to allege my intention in regard to my future actions to those who would not believe this allegation, or if they over-hastily did so, would pay me back in my own coin. Hence my maxim, so soon as it should be made a universal law, would necessarily destroy itself.

I do not, therefore, need any far-reaching penetration to discern what I have to do in order that my will may be morally good. Inexperienced in the course of the world, incapable of being prepared for all its contingencies, I only ask myself: Canst thou also will that thy maxim should be a universal law? If not, then it must be rejected, and that not because of a disadvantage accruing from it to myself or even to others, but because it cannot enter as a principle into a possible universal legislation, and reason extorts from me immediate respect for such legislation. I do not indeed as yet *discern* on what this respect is based (this the philosopher may inquire), but at least I understand this—that it is an estimation of the worth which far outweighs all worth of what is recommended by inclination, and that the necessity of acting from pure respect for the practical law is what constitutes duty, to which every other motive must give place because it is the condition of a will being good *in itself,* and the worth of such a will is above everything.

Thus, then, without quitting the moral knowledge of common human reason, we have arrived at its principle. And although, no doubt, common men do not conceive it in such an abstract and universal form, yet they always have it really before their eyes and use it as the standard of their decision. Here it would be easy to show how, with this compass in hand, men are well able to distinguish, in every case that occurs, what is good, what bad, conformably to duty or inconsistent with it. . . .

IMPERATIVES: HYPOTHETICAL AND CATEGORICAL

Everything in nature works according to laws. Rational beings alone have the faculty of acting according *to the conception of laws,* that is according to principles, *i.e.,* have a *will.* Since the deduction of actions from principles requires *reason,* the will is nothing but practical reason. . . . The conception of an objective principle, in so far as it is obligatory for a will, is called a command (of reason), and the formula of the command is called an Imperative.

All imperatives are expressed by the word *ought* [or *shall*], and thereby indicate the relation of an objective law of reason to a will, which from its subjective constitution is not necessarily determined by it (an obligation). . . .

Now all *imperatives* command either *hypothetically* or *categorically.* The former represent the practical necessity of a possible action as means to something else that is willed (or at least which one might possibly will). The categorical imperative would be that which represented an action as necessary of itself without reference to another end, that is, as objectively necessary. . . .

If now the action is good only as a means to *something else,* then the imperative is *hypothetical;* if it is conceived as good *in itself* and consequently as being necessarily the principle of a will which of itself conforms to reason, then it is *categorical.* . . .

Accordingly the hypothetical imperative only says that the action is good for some purpose, *possible or actual.* In the first case it is a *problematical,* in the second an *assertorial* practical principle. The categorical imperative which declares an action to be objectively necessary in itself without reference to any purpose, that is, without any other end, is valid as an *apodictic* (practical) principle. . . .

FIRST FORMULATION
OF THE CATEGORICAL IMPERATIVE:
UNIVERSAL LAW

When I conceive a hypothetical imperative, in general I do not know beforehand what it will contain until I am given the condition. But when I conceive a categorical imperative, I know at once what it contains. For as the imperative contains besides the law only the necessity that the maxims[2] shall conform to this law, while the law contains no conditions restricting it, there remains nothing but the general statement that the maxim of the action should conform to a universal law, and it is this conformity alone that the imperative properly represents as necessary.

There is therefore but one categorical imperative, namely, this: *Act only on that maxim whereby thou canst at the same time will that it should become a universal law.*

Now if all imperatives of duty can be deduced from this one imperative as from their principle, then, although it should remain undecided whether what is called duty is not merely a vain notion, yet at least we shall be able to show what we understand by it and what this notion means. . . .

FOUR ILLUSTRATIONS

We will now enumerate a few duties, adopting the usual division of them into duties to ourselves and to others, and into perfect and imperfect duties.

1. A man reduced to despair by a series of misfortunes feels wearied of life, but is still so far in possession of his reason that he can ask himself whether it would not be contrary to his duty to himself to take his own life. Now he inquires whether the maxim of his action could become a universal law of nature. His maxim is: From self-love I adopt it as a principle to shorten my life when its longer duration is likely to bring more evil than satisfaction. It is asked then simply whether this principle founded on self-love can become a universal law of nature. Now we see at once that a system of nature of which it should be a law to destroy life by means of the very feeling whose special nature it is to impel to the improvement of life would contradict itself, and therefore could not exist as a system of nature; hence that maxim cannot possibly exist as a universal law of nature, and consequently would be wholly inconsistent with the supreme principle of all duty.

2. Another finds himself forced by necessity to borrow money. He knows that he will not be able to repay it, but sees also that nothing will be lent to him unless he promises stoutly to repay it in a definite time. He desires to make this promise, but he has still so much conscience as to ask himself: Is it not unlawful and inconsistent with duty to get out of a difficulty in this way? Suppose, however, that he resolves to do so, then the maxim of his action would be expressed thus: When I think myself in want of money, I will borrow money and promise to repay it, although I know that I never can do so. Now this principle of self-love or of one's own advantage may perhaps be consistent with my whole future welfare; but the question now is, Is it right? I change then the suggestion of self-love into a universal law, and state the question thus: How would it be if my maxim were a universal law? Then I see at once that it could never hold as a universal law of nature, but would necessarily contradict itself. For supposing it to be a universal law that everyone when he thinks himself in a difficulty should be able to promise whatever he pleases, with the purpose of not keeping his promise, the promise itself would become impossible, as well as the end that one might have in view in it, since no one would consider that anything was promised to him, but would ridicule all such statements as vain pretenses.

3. A third finds in himself a talent which with the help of some culture might make him a useful man in many respects. But he finds himself in comfortable circumstances and prefers to indulge in pleasure rather than to take pains in enlarging and improving his happy natural capacities. He asks, however, whether his maxim of neglect of his natural gifts, besides agreeing with his inclination to indulgence, agrees also with what is called duty. He sees then that a system of nature could indeed subsist with such a universal law, although men (like the South Sea islanders) should let their talents rest and resolve to devote their lives merely to idleness, amusement, and propagation of their species—in a word, to enjoyment; but he cannot possibly will that this should be a universal law of nature, or be implanted in us as such by a natural instinct. For, as a rational being, he necessarily wills that his faculties be developed, since they serve him, and have been given him, for all sorts of possible purposes.

4. A fourth, who is in prosperity, while he sees that others have to contend with great wretchedness and that he could help them, thinks: What concern is it of mine? Let everyone be as happy as Heaven pleases, or as he can make himself; I will take nothing from him nor even envy him, only I do not wish to contribute anything to his welfare or to his assistance in distress! Now no doubt, if such a mode of thinking were a universal law, the human race might very well subsist, and doubtless even better than in a state in which everyone talks of sympathy and good-will, or even takes care occasionally to put it into practice, but, on the other side, also cheats when he can, betrays the rights of men, or otherwise violates them. But although it is possible that a universal law of nature might exist in accordance with that maxim, it is impossible *to will* that such a principle should have the universal validity of a law of nature. For a will which resolved this would contradict itself, inasmuch as many cases might occur in which one would have need of the love and sympathy of others, and in which, by such a law of nature, sprung from his own will, he would deprive himself of all hope of the aid he desires.

These are a few of the many actual duties, or at least what we regard as such, which obviously fall into two classes on the one principle that we have laid down. We must be *able to will* that a maxim of our action should be a universal law. This is the canon of the moral

appreciation of the action generally. Some actions are of such a character that their maxim cannot without contradiction be even *conceived* as a universal law of nature, far from it being possible that we should *will* that it *should* be so. In others, this intrinsic impossibility is not found, but still it is impossible to *will* that their maxim should be raised to the universality of a law of nature, since such a will would contradict itself. . . .

SECOND FORMULATION OF THE CATEGORICAL IMPERATIVE: HUMANITY AS END IN ITSELF

The will is conceived as a faculty of determining oneself to action *in accordance with the conception of certain laws.* And such a faculty can be found only in rational beings. The ends which a rational being proposes to himself at pleasure as *effects* of his actions are all only relative, for it is only their relation to the particular desires of the subject that gives them their worth, which therefore cannot furnish principles universal and necessary for all rational beings and every volition, that is to say practical laws. Hence all these relative ends can give only hypothetical imperatives. Supposing, however, that there were something *whose existence* has *in itself* an absolute worth, something which, being *an end in itself,* could be a source of definite laws, then in this and this alone would lie the source of a possible categorical imperative, i.e. a practical law. . . .

Now I say: man and generally any rational being exists as an end in himself, *not merely as a means* to be arbitrarily used by this or that will, but in all his actions, whether they concern himself or other rational beings, must be always regarded at the same time as an end. All objects of the inclinations have only a conditional worth; for if the inclinations and the wants founded on them did not exist, then their object would be without value. Thus the worth of any object which is *to be acquired* by our action is always conditional. Beings whose existence depends not on our will but on nature's, have nevertheless, if they are nonrational beings, only a relative value as means, and are therefore called *things;* rational beings, on the contrary, are called *persons,* because their very nature points them out as ends in themselves, that is, as something which must not be used merely as means, and so far therefore restricts freedom of action (and is an object of respect). These, therefore, are not merely subjective ends whose existence has a worth *for us* as an effect of our action, but *objective ends,* that is, things whose existence is an end in itself—an end, moreover, for which no other can be substituted, which they should subserve *merely* as means, for otherwise nothing whatever would possess *absolute worth.* . . .

If then there is a supreme practical principle or, in respect of the human will, a categorical imperative, it must be one which, being drawn from the conception of that which is necessarily an end for everyone because it is *an end in itself,* constitutes an objective principle of will, and can therefore serve as a universal practical law. The foundation of this principle is: *rational nature exists as an end in itself.* Man necessarily conceives his own existence as being so: so far then this is a *subjective* principle of human actions. But every other rational being regards its existence similarly, just on the same rational principle that holds for me: so that it is at the same time an objective principle, from which as a supreme practical law all laws of the will must be capable of being deduced. Accordingly the practical imperative will be as follows: *So act as to treat humanity, whether in thine own person or in that of any other, in every case as an end withal, never as means only.* We will now inquire whether this can be practically carried out. . . .

THE KINGDOM OF ENDS

The conception of the will of every rational being as one which must consider itself as giving in all the maxims of its will universal laws, so as to judge itself and its actions from this point of view—this conception leads to another which depends on it and is very fruitful, namely that of a *kingdom of ends.*

By a *kingdom* I understand the union of different rational beings in a system by common laws. Now since it is by laws that ends are determined as regards their universal validity, hence, if we abstract from the personal differences of rational beings and likewise from all the content of their private ends, we shall be able to conceive all ends combined in a systematic whole (including both rational beings as ends in themselves, and also the special ends which each may propose to himself), that is to say, we can conceive a kingdom of ends, which on the preceding principles is possible.

For all rational beings come under the *law* that each of them must treat itself and all others *never merely as means,* but in every case *at the same time as ends in themselves.* Hence results a systematic union of rational beings by common objective laws, *i.e.,* a kingdom which may be called a kingdom of ends, since what these laws have in view is just the relation of these beings to one another as ends and means. It is certainly only an ideal.

A rational being belongs as a *member* to the kingdom of ends when although giving universal laws in it he is also himself subject to these laws. He belongs to it *as sovereign,* when while giving laws he is not subject to the will of any other.

A rational being must always regard himself as giving laws in a kingdom of ends which freedom of the will makes possible, whether it be as member or as sovereign. He cannot, however, maintain the latter position merely by the maxims of his will, but only in case he is a completely independent being without wants and with unrestricted power adequate to his will.

Morality consists then in the reference of all action to the legislation which alone can render a kingdom of ends possible. This legislation must be capable of existing in every rational being, and of emanating from his will, so that the principle of this will, is never to act on any maxim which could not without contradiction be also a universal law, and accordingly always so to act *that the will could at the same time regard itself as giving in its maxims universal laws.* If now the maxims of rational beings are not by their own nature coincident with this objective principle, then the necessity of acting on it is called practical obligation, *i.e., duty.* Duty does not apply to the sovereign in the kingdom of ends, but it does to every member of it and to all in the same degree.

The practical necessity of acting on this principle, i.e. duty, does not rest at all on feelings, impulses, or inclinations, but solely on the relation of rational beings to one another, a relation in which the will of a rational being must always be regarded as *legislative.* . . .

In the kingdom of ends everything has either Value or Dignity. Whatever has a value can be replaced by something else which is *equivalent;* whatever on the other hand is above all value, and therefore admits of no equivalent, has a dignity.

Whatever has reference to the general inclinations and wants of mankind has a *market value;* whatever without presupposing a want, corresponds to a certain taste, that is to a satisfaction in the mere purposeless play of our faculties, has a *fancy value;* but that which constitutes the condition under which alone anything can be an end in itself, this has not merely a relative worth, *i.e.,* value, but an intrinsic worth, that is, *dignity.*

Now morality is the condition under which alone a rational being can be an end in himself, since by this alone is it possible that he should be a legislating member in the kingdom of ends. Thus morality, and humanity as capable of it, is that which alone has dignity. Skill and diligence in labour have a market value; wit, lively imagination, and humour have a fancy value; on the other hand, fidelity to promises, benevolence from principle (not from instinct) have an intrinsic worth. Neither nature nor art contains anything which in default of these it could put in their place, for their worth consists not in the effects which spring from them, not in the use and advantage which they secure, but in the disposition of mind, that is the maxims of the will which are ready to manifest themselves in such actions, even though they should not have the desired effect. These actions also need no

recommendation from any subjective taste or sentiment, that they may be looked on with immediate favour and satisfaction: they need no immediate propensities or feeling for them; they exhibit the will that performs them as an object of an immediate respect, and nothing but reason is required to *impose* them on the will; not to *flatter* it into them, which in the case of duties would be a contradiction. This estimation therefore shows that the worth of such a disposition is dignity, and places it infinitely above all value, with which it cannot for a moment be brought into comparison or competition without as it were violating its sanctity.

What then is it which justifies virtue or the morally good disposition, in making such lofty claims? It is nothing less than the privilege it secures to the rational being of participating in the giving of universal laws, by which it qualifies him to be a member of a possible kingdom of ends, a privilege to which he was already destined by his own nature as being an end in himself, and on that account legislating in the kingdom of ends; free as regards all laws of physical nature, and obeying those only which he himself gives, and by which his maxims can belong to a system of universal law, to which at the same time he submits himself. For nothing has any worth except what the law assigns it. Now the legislation itself which assigns the worth of everything, must for that very reason possess dignity, that is an unconditional incomparable worth, and the word *respect* alone supplies a becoming expression for the esteem which a rational being must have for it. *Autonomy* then is the basis of the dignity of human and of every rational nature. . . .

THE AUTONOMY OF THE WILL

Autonomy of the will is the property that the will has of being a law to itself (independently of any property of the objects of volition). The principle of autonomy is this: Always choose in such a way that in the same volition the maxims of the choice are at the same time present as universal law.

If the will seeks the law that is to determine it anywhere but in the fitness of its maxims for its own legislation of universal laws, and if it thus goes outside of itself and seeks this law in the character of any of its objects, then heteronomy always results. The will in that case does not give itself the law, but the object does so because of its relation to the will. This relation, whether it rests on inclination or on representations of reason, admits only of hypothetical imperatives: I ought to do something because I will something else. On the other hand, the moral, and hence categorical, imperative says that I ought to act in this way or that way, even though I did not will something else. . . .

The Concept of Freedom Is the Key That Explains the Autonomy of the Will

The will is a kind of causality belonging to living beings in so far as they are rational, and *freedom* would be this property of such causality that it can be efficient, independently of foreign causes determining it; just as physical necessity is the property that the causality of all rational beings has of being determined to activity by the influence of foreign causes. . . .

What else then can freedom of the will be but autonomy, that is, the property of the will to be a law to itself? But the proposition: The will is in every action a law to itself, only expresses the principle to act on no other maxim than that which can also have as an object itself as a universal law. Now this is precisely the formula of the categorical imperative and is the principle of morality, so that a free will and a will subject to moral laws are one and the same. . . .

Freedom Must Be Presupposed as a Property of the Will of All Rational Beings

It is not enough to predicate freedom of our own will, from whatever reason, if we have not sufficient grounds for predicating the same of all rational beings. For as morality serves as a law for us only because we are rational beings, it must also hold for all rational beings. Now I say every being that cannot act except under the idea of freedom is just for that reason in a practical point of view really free, that is to say, all laws which are inseparably connected with freedom have the same force for him as if his will had been shown to be free in itself by a proof theoretically conclusive. (I adopt this method of assuming freedom merely as an idea which rational beings suppose in their actions, in order to avoid the necessity of proving it in theory. The form is sufficient for my purpose; for even though the speculative proof should not be made out, yet a being that cannot act except with the idea of freedom is bound by the same laws that would oblige a being who is actually free.) Now I affirm that we must attribute to every rational being which has a will that it has also the idea of freedom and acts entirely under this idea. For in such a being we conceive a reason that is practical, that is, has causality in reference to its objects. It must regard itself as the author of its principles independent of foreign influences. Consequently, as practical reason or as the will of a rational being it must regard itself as free, that is to say, the will of such a being cannot be a will of its own except under the idea of freedom. This idea must therefore in a practical point of view be ascribed to every rational being.

NOTES

1. A *maxim* is the subjective principle of volition. The objective principle (i.e., that which would also serve subjectively as a practical principle to all rational beings if reason had full power over the faculty of desire) is the practical law.
2. A maxim is a subjective principle of action, and must be distinguished from the objective principle, namely, practical law. The former contains the practical rule set by reason according to the conditions of the subject (often its ignorance or its inclinations), so that it is the principle on which the subject acts; but the law is the objective principle valid for every rational being, and is the principle which it *ought to act*—that is, an imperative.

REVIEW AND DISCUSSION QUESTIONS

1. What distinguishes acting from inclination and acting from duty? Which reflects genuine moral worth? Why?
2. How do hypothetical and categorical imperatives differ?
3. Describe the two versions Kant gives of the categorical imperative. Give an example of how the categorical imperative is applied.
4. What does Kant mean by a *maxim?*
5. Explain what Kant means by *autonomy.* Are persons autonomous?
6. Compare Kant's view of autonomy with Hobbes's view of freedom.
7. Explain how Kant would respond to those who emphasize the role of emotions and feelings in morality.

Utilitarianism

John Stuart Mill

John Stuart Mill (1806–1873) had an unusual childhood, by almost any standard. His father, James Mill, who was a friend of the economist David Ricardo and the legal theorist John Austin, was among the most devoted followers of Jeremy Bentham, the utilitarian philosopher. James developed a plan for the education of his son, John Stuart, that included a rigorous tutoring program and the isolation of the boy from other children. Young John was a brilliant student. By the age of three, he had begun learning Greek. At eight, he learned Latin and pursued mathematics and history. By the age of twelve, he was studying logic and political economy, and at fifteen, he studied law at University College, London, with John Austin.

At twenty-four, Mill began a lifelong friendship and intellectual collaboration with Harriet Taylor. Although they were close companions, Harriet Taylor remained married for two decades. When her husband John Taylor died, she and John Stuart Mill were married. The two then withdrew from "insipid society" and the gossip they had endured for years; they lived happily for seven years until her death. Mill served briefly as a member of Parliament and died in France (where he had bought a house near the cemetery in which Harriet was buried).

Mill's influence has been tremendous; he wrote important books on logic, philosophy of science, and economics, as well as on ethics and political philosophy. *The Subjection of Women* (see Section 14) remains a classic, as is *On Liberty,* his brilliant statement of the justification and limits of government (Section 10) and of freedom of speech (Section 11). In the following selections from *Utilitarianism,* Mill explains utilitarian moral theory, responds to critics, and explores the theory's philosophical basis.

GENERAL REMARKS

On the present occasion, I shall attempt to contribute something towards the understanding and appreciation of the Utilitarian or Happiness theory, and towards such proof as it is susceptible of. It is evident that this cannot be proof in the ordinary and popular meaning of the term. Questions of ultimate ends are not amenable to direct proof. We are not, however, to infer that its acceptance or rejection must depend on blind impulse, or

From John Stuart Mill, *Utilitarianism* (1861.).

arbitrary choice. Considerations may be presented capable of determining the intellect either to give or withhold its assent to the doctrine; and this is equivalent of proof.

WHAT UTILITARIANISM IS

The creed which accepts as the foundation of morals *utility* or the *greatest happiness principle* holds that actions are right in proportion as they tend to promote happiness, wrong as they tend to produce the reverse of happiness. By "happiness" is intended pleasure, and the absence of pain; by "unhappiness," pain, and the privation of pleasure. To give a clear view of the moral standard set up by the theory, much more requires to be said; in particular, what things it includes in the ideas of pain and pleasure, and to what extent this is left an open question. But these supplementary explanations do not affect the theory of life on which this theory of morality is grounded —namely, that pleasure, and freedom from pain, are the only things desirable as ends; and that all desirable things (which are as numerous in the utilitarian as in any other scheme) are desirable either for the pleasure inherent in themselves, or as means to the promotion of pleasure and the prevention of pain.

Now such a theory of life excites in many minds, and among them in some of the most estimable in feeling and purpose, inveterate dislike. To suppose that life has (as they express it) no higher end than pleasure—no better and nobler object of desire and pursuit—they designate as utterly mean and groveling; as a doctrine worthy only of swine. . . .

[But it] is quite compatible with the principle of utility to recognize the fact, that some *kinds* of pleasure are more desirable and more valuable than others. It would be absurd that while, in estimating all other things, quality is considered as well as quantity, the estimation of pleasures should be supposed to depend on quantity alone.

If I am asked what I mean by difference of quality in pleasures, or what makes one pleasure more valuable than another merely as a pleasure, except its being greater in amount, there is but one possible answer. Of two pleasures, if there be one to which all or almost all who have experience of both give a decided preference, irrespective of any feeling of moral obligation to prefer it, that is the more desirable pleasure. If one of the two is, by those who are competently acquainted with both, placed so far above the other that they prefer it, even though knowing it to be attended with a greater amount of discontent, and would not resign it for any quantity of the other pleasure which their nature is capable of, we are justified in ascribing to the preferred enjoyment a superiority in quality, so far outweighing quantity as to render it, in comparison, of small account.

Now it is an unquestionable fact that those who are equally acquainted with, and equally capable of appreciating and enjoying, both, do give a most marked preference to the manner of existence which employs their higher faculties. Few human creatures would consent to be changed into any of the lower animals, for a promise of the fullest allowance of a beast's pleasures; no intelligent human being would consent to be a fool; no instructed person would be an ignoramus; no person of feeling and conscience would be selfish and base, even though they should be persuaded that the fool, the dunce, or the rascal is better satisfied with his lot than they are with theirs. They would not resign what they possess more than he for the most complete satisfaction of all the desires which they have in common with him. If they ever fancy they would, it is only in cases of unhappiness so extreme, that to escape from it they would exchange their lot for almost any other, however undesirable in their own eyes. A being of higher faculties requires more to make him happy, is capable probably of more acute suffering, and certainly accessible to it at more points, than one of an inferior type; but in spite of these liabilities, he can never really wish to sink into what he feels to be a lower grade of existence. We may give what explanation we please of this unwillingness: we may attribute it to pride, a name which is given indiscriminately to some of the most and to some of the least estimable feelings of which mankind are capable; we may refer it to the love of liberty and personal independence, an appeal to which was with the Stoics one of the most effective means for the inculcation of it; to the love of power, or to the love of excitement, both of which do really enter into and contribute to it: but its most appropriate appellation is a sense of dignity, which all human beings possess in one form or other, and in some, though by no means in exact, proportion to their higher faculties, and which is so essential a part of the happiness of those in whom it is strong, that nothing which conflicts with it could be, otherwise than momentarily, an object of desire to them. . . .

From this verdict of the only competent judges I apprehend there can be no appeal. On a question which is the best worth having of two pleasures, or which of two modes of existence is the most grateful to the feelings, apart from its moral attributes and from its consequences, the judgment of those who are qualified by knowledge of both, or, if they differ, that of the majority among them, must be admitted as final. And there need be the less hesitation to accept this judgment respecting the quality of pleasures, since there is no other tribunal to be referred to even on the question of quantity. What means are there of determining which is the acutest of two pains, or the intensest of two pleasurable sensations, except the general suffrage of those who are familiar with both? Neither pains nor pleasures are homogeneous, and pain is always heterogeneous with pleasure. What is there to decide whether a particular pleasure is worth purchasing at the cost of a particular pain, except the feelings and judgment of the experienced? When, therefore, those feelings and judgment declare the pleasures derived from the higher faculties to be preferable in kind, apart from the question of intensity, to those of which the animal nature, disjoined from the higher faculties, is susceptible, they are entitled on this subject to the same regard. . . .

Though it is only in a very imperfect state of the world's arrangements that anyone can best serve the happiness of others by the absolute sacrifice of his own, yet so long as the world is in that imperfect state, I fully acknowledge that the readiness to make such a sacrifice is the highest virtue which can be found in man. I will add that in this condition of the world, paradoxical as the assertion may be, the conscious ability to do without happiness gives the best prospect of realizing such happiness as is attainable. For nothing except that consciousness can raise a person above the chances of life, by making him feel that, let fate and fortune do their worst, they have not power to subdue him. . . .

The utilitarian morality does recognize in human beings the power of sacrificing their own greatest good for the good of others. It only refuses to admit that the sacrifice is itself a good. A sacrifice which does not increase, or tend to increase, the sum total of happiness, it considers as wasted. . . .

The assailants of utilitarianism seldom have the justice to acknowledge, that the happiness which forms the utilitarian standard of what is right in conduct is not the agent's own happiness but that of all concerned. As between his own happiness and that of others, utilitarianism requires him to be as strictly impartial as a disinterested and benevolent spectator. In the golden rule of Jesus of Nazareth, we read the complete spirit of the ethics of utility. "To do as you would be done by," and "to love your neighbor as yourself," constitute the ideal perfection of utilitarian morality. As the means of making the nearest approach to this ideal, utility would enjoin, first, that laws and social arrangements should place the happiness or (as speaking practically, it may be called) the interest of every individual as nearly as possible in harmony with the interest of the whole; and, secondly, that education and opinion, which have so vast a power over human character, should so use that power as to establish in the mind of every individual an indissoluble association between his own happiness and the good of the whole, especially between his own happiness and the practice of such modes of conduct, negative and positive, as regard for the universal happiness prescribes; so that not only he may be unable to conceive the possibility of happiness to himself, consistent with the conduct opposed to the general good, but also that a direct impulse to promote the general good may be every individual one of the habitual motives of action, and the sentiments connected therewith may fill a large and prominent place in every human being's sentient existence. . . .

We not uncommonly hear the doctrine of utility inveighed against as a *godless* doctrine. If it be necessary to say anything at all against so mere an assumption, we may say that the question depends upon what idea we have formed of the moral character of the Deity. If it be a true belief that God desires, above all things, the happiness of his creatures, and that this was his purpose in their creation, utility is not only not a godless doctrine, but more profoundly religious than any other. If it be meant that utilitarianism does not recognize the revealed will of God as the supreme law of morals, I answer that a utilitarian who believes in the perfect goodness and wisdom of God necessarily believes that whatever God has thought fit to reveal on the subject of morals must fulfill the requirements of utility in a supreme degree. . . .

Again, defenders of utility often find themselves called upon to reply to such objections as this—that there is not time, previous to action, for calculating and weighing the effects of any line of conduct on the general happiness. This is exactly as if anyone were to say that it is impossible to guide our conduct by Christianity because there is not time, on every occasion on which anything has to be done, to read through the Old and New Testaments. The answer to the objection is that there has been ample time, namely, the whole past duration of the human species. During all that time mankind have been learning by experience the tendencies of actions; on which experience all the prudence as well as all the morality of life are dependent. The corollaries from the principle of utility, like

the precepts of every practical art, admit of indefinite improvement, and, in a progressive state of the human mind, their improvement is perpetually going on. But to consider the rules of morality as improvable is one thing; to pass over the intermediate generalization entirely and endeavor to test each individual action directly by the first principle is another. It is a strange notion that the acknowledgment of a first principle is inconsistent with the admission of secondary ones. To inform a traveler respecting the place of his ultimate destination is not to forbid the use of landmarks and direction-posts on the way. . . .

There exists no moral system under which there do not arise unequivocal cases of conflicting obligation. These are real difficulties, the knotty points both in the theory of ethics and in the conscientious guidance of personal conduct. They are overcome practically, with greater or with less success, according to the intellect and virtue of the individual; but it can hardly be pretended that anyone will be the less qualified for dealing with them, from possessing an ultimate standard to which conflicting rights and duties can be referred. If utility is the ultimate source of moral obligations, utility may be invoked to decide between them when their demands are incompatible. Though the application of the [utilitarian] standard may be difficult, it is better than none at all; while in other systems, the moral laws all claiming independent authority, there is no common umpire entitled to interfere between them; their claims to precedence one over another rest on little better than sophistry, and, unless determined, as they generally are, by the unacknowledged influence of consideration of utility, afford a free scope for the action of personal desires and partialities. We must remember that only in these cases of conflict between secondary principles is it requisite that first principles should be appealed to. There is no case of moral obligation in which some secondary principle is not involved; and if only one, there can seldom be any real doubt which one it is, in the mind of any person by whom the principle itself is recognized.

OF WHAT SORT OF PROOF THE PRINCIPLE OF UTILITY IS SUSCEPTIBLE

It has already been remarked that questions of ultimate ends do not admit of proof, in the ordinary acceptation of the term. To be incapable of proof by reasoning is common to all first principles; to the first premises of our knowledge, as well as to those of our conduct. But the former, being matters of fact, may be the subject of a direct appeal to the faculties which judge of fact—namely, our senses, and our internal consciousness. Can an appeal be made to the same faculties on questions of practical ends? Or by what other faculty is cognizance taken of them?

Questions about ends are, in other words, questions about what things are desirable. The utilitarian doctrine is, that happiness is desirable, and the only thing desirable, as an end; all other things being only desirable as means to that end. What ought to be required of this doctrine—what conditions is it requisite that the doctrine should fulfil—to make good its claim to be believed?

The only proof capable of being given that an object is visible, is that people actually see it. The only proof that a sound is audible, is that people hear it: and so of the other sources of our experience. In like manner, I apprehend, the sole evidence it is possible to produce that anything is desirable, is that people do actually desire it. If the end which the utilitarian doctrine proposes to itself were not, in theory and in practice, acknowledged to be an end, nothing could ever convince any person that it was so. No reason can be given why the general happiness is desirable, except that each person, so far as he believes it to be attainable, desires his own happiness. This, however, being a fact, we have not only all the proof which the case admits of, but all which it is possible to require, that happiness is a good: that each person's happiness is a good

to that person, and the general happiness, therefore, a good to the aggregate of all persons. Happiness has made out its title as one of the ends of conduct, and consequently one of the criteria of morality.

But it has not, by this alone, proved itself to be the sole criterion. To do that, it would seem, by the same rule, necessary to show, not only that people desire happiness, but that they never desire anything else. Now it is palpable that they do desire things which, in common language, are decidedly distinguished from happiness. They desire, for example, virtue, and the absence of vice, no less really than pleasure and the absence of pain. The desire of virtue is not as universal, but it is as authentic a fact, as the desire of happiness. And hence the opponents of the utilitarian standard deem that they have a right to infer that there are other ends of human action besides happiness, and that happiness is not the standard of approbation and disapprobation.

The ingredients of happiness are very various, and each of them is desirable in itself, and not merely when considered as swelling an aggregate. The principle of utility does not mean that any given pleasure, as music, for instance, or any given exemption from pain, as for example health, is to be looked upon as means to a collective something termed happiness, and to be desired on that account. They are desired and desirable in and for themselves; besides being a means, they are part of the end. Virtue, according to the utilitarian doctrine, is not naturally and originally part of the end, but is capable of becoming so; and in those who live disinterestedly it has become so, and is desired and cherished, not as a means to happiness, but as part of their happiness.

To illustrate this further, we may remember that virtue is not the only thing originally a means, and which if it were not a means to anything else would be and remain indifferent, but which by association with what it is a means to comes to be desired for itself, and that too with the utmost intensity. What, for example, shall we say of the love of money? There is nothing originally more desirable about money than about any heap of glittering pebbles. Its worth is solely that of the things which it will buy; the desires for other things than itself, which it is a means of gratifying. Yet the love of money is not only one of the strongest moving forces of human life, but money is, in many cases, desired in and for itself; the desire to possess it is often stronger than the desire to use it, and goes on increasing when all the desires which point to ends beyond it, to be compassed by it, are falling off. It may, then, be said truly that money is desired not for the sake of an end, but as part of the end. From being a means to happiness, it has come to be itself a principal ingredient of the individual's conception of happiness. The same may be said of the majority of the great objects of human life: power, for example, or fame, except that to each of these there is a certain amount of immediate pleasure annexed, which has at least the semblance of being naturally inherent in them—a thing which cannot be said of money. . . .

It results from the preceding considerations that there is in reality nothing desired except happiness. Whatever is desired otherwise than as a means to some end beyond itself, and ultimately to happiness, is desired as itself a part of happiness, and is not desired for itself until it has become so. . . .

We have now, then, an answer to the question, of what sort of proof the principle of utility is susceptible. If the opinion which I have now stated is psychologically true—if human nature is so constituted as to desire nothing which is not either a part of happiness or a means of happiness—we can have no other proof, and we require no other, that these are the only things desirable. If so, happiness is the sole end of human action, and the promotion of it the test by which to judge of all human conduct; from whence it necessarily follows that it must be the criterion of morality, since a part is included in the whole. . . .

ON THE CONNECTION BETWEEN JUSTICE AND UTILITY

In all ages of speculation, one of the strongest obstacles to the reception of the doctrine that Utility or Happiness is the criterion of right and wrong, has been drawn from the idea of Justice. . . .

To throw light upon this question, it is necessary to attempt to ascertain what is the distinguishing character of justice, or of injustice: . . .

In the first place it is mostly considered unjust to deprive anyone of his personal liberty, his property, or any other thing which belongs to him by law. Here, therefore, is one instance of the application of the terms just and unjust in a perfectly definite sense, namely, that it is just to respect, unjust to violate, the *legal rights* of any one. . . .

Secondly; the legal rights of which he is deprived, may be rights which *ought* not to have belonged to him; in other words, the law which confers on him these rights, may be a bad law. . . . When, however, a law is thought to be unjust, it seems to be regarded as being so in the same way in which a breach of law is unjust, namely, by infringing somebody's right; which, as it cannot in this case be a legal right . . . is called a moral right. We may say, therefore, that a second case of injustice consists in taking or withholding from any person that to which he has *a moral right.*

Thirdly, it is universally considered just that each person should obtain that (whether good or evil) which he *deserves;* and unjust that he should obtain a good, or be made to undergo an evil, which he does not deserve. . . . Speaking in a general way, a person is understood to deserve good if he does right, evil if he does wrong; and in a more particular sense, to deserve good from those to whom he does or has done good, and evil from those to whom he does or has done evil. . . .

Fourthly, it is confessedly unjust to *break faith* with any one: to violate an engagement, either express or implied, or disappoint expectations raised by our own conduct, at least if we have raised those expectations knowingly and voluntarily. . . .

Fifthly, it is, by universal admission, inconsistent with justice to be *partial*—to show favor or preference to one person over another in matters in which favor and preference do not apply. . . .

Among the many diverse applications of the term "justice" it is a matter of some difficulty to seize the mental link which holds them together. . . . In our survey of the various popular acceptations of justice, the term appeared generally to involve the idea of a personal right—a claim on the part of one or more individuals, like that which the law gives when it confers a proprietary or other legal right. Whether the injustice consists in depriving a person of a possession, or in breaking faith with him, or in treating him worse than he deserves, or worse than other people who have no greater claims—in each case the supposition implies two things: a wrong done, and some assignable person who is wronged. Injustice may also be done by treating a person better than others; but the wrong in this case is to his competitors, who are also assignable persons. It seems to me that this feature in the case—a right in some person, correlative to the moral obligation—constitutes the specific difference between justice and generosity or beneficence. Justice implies something which is not only right to do, and wrong not to do, but which some individual person can claim from us as his moral right. No one has a moral right to our generosity or beneficence because we are not morally bound to practice those virtues toward any given individual. . . .

[T]he idea of justice supposes two things; a rule of conduct, and a sentiment which sanctions the rule. The first must be supposed common to all mankind, and intended for their good. The other (the sentiment) is a desire that punishment may be suffered by those who infringe the rule. There is involved, in addition, the conception of some definite person who suffers by the infringement; whose rights (to use the expression appropriated to the case) are violated by it. And the sentiment of justice appears to me to be, the animal desire to repel or retaliate a hurt or damage to oneself, or to those with whom one sympathizes, widened so as to include all persons, by the human capacity of enlarged sympathy, and the human conception of intelligent self-interest. From the latter elements, the feeling derives its morality; from the former, its peculiar impressiveness, and energy of self-assertion.

I have, throughout, treated the idea of a *right* residing in the injured person, and violated by the injury, not as a separate element in the composition of the idea and sentiment, but as one of the forms in which the other two elements clothe themselves. These elements are, a hurt to some assignable person or persons on the one hand, and a demand for punishment on the other. An examination of our own minds, I think, will show, that these two things include all that we mean when we speak of violation of a right. When we call anything a person's right, we mean that he has a valid claim on society to protect him in the possession of it, either by the force of law, or by that of education and opinion. If he has what we consider a sufficient claim, on whatever account, to have something guaranteed to him by society, we say that he has a right to it. If we desire to prove that anything does not belong to him by right, we think this done as soon as it is admitted that society ought not to take measures for securing it to him, but should leave him to chance, or to his own exertions. Thus, a person is said to have a right to what he can earn in fair professional competition; because society ought not to allow any other person to hinder him from endeavouring to earn in that manner as much as he can. But he has not a right to three hundred a year, though he may happen to be earning it; because society is not called on to provide that he shall earn that sum. On the contrary, if he owns ten thousand pounds three per cent, stock, he *has* a right to three hundred a year; because society has come under an obligation to provide him with an income of that amount.

To have a right, then, is, I conceive, to have something which society ought to defend me in the possession of. If the objector goes on to ask, why it ought? I can give him no other reason than general utility. If that expression does not seem to convey a sufficient feeling of the strength of the obligation, nor to account for the peculiar energy of the feeling, it is because there goes to the composition of the sentiment, not a rational only but also an animal element—the thirst for retaliation; and this thirst derives its intensity, as well as its moral justification, from the extraordinarily important and impressive kind of utility which is concerned. The interest involved is that of security, to everyone's feelings the most vital of all interests. . . .

We are continually informed that utility is an uncertain standard, which every different person interprets differently, and that there is no safety but in the immutable, ineffaceable, and unmistakable dictates of justice, which carry their evidence in themselves. [But] not only have different nations and individuals different notions of justice, but in the mind of one and the same individual, justice is not some one rule, principle, or maxim but many which do not always coincide in their dictates, and, in choosing between which, he is guided either by some extraneous standard or by his own personal predilections.

For instance, there are some who say that it is unjust to punish anyone for the sake of example to others. Others maintain the extreme reverse, contending that to punish persons who have attained years of discretion for their own benefit, is despotism and injustice since, if the matter is solely their own good, no one has a right to control their own judgment of it; but that they may justly be punished to prevent evil to others. . . .

To escape these and other difficulties, a favorite contrivance has been the fiction of a contract whereby at some unknown period all members of society engaged to obey the laws and consented to be punished for any disobedience to them, thereby giving to their legislators the right, which it is assumed they would not otherwise have had, of punishing them, either for their own good or for that of the society. This happy thought was considered to get rid of the whole difficulty and to legitimate the infliction of punishment, in virtue of another received maxim of justice— that is not unjust which is done with the consent of the person who is supposed to be hurt by it. I need hardly remark that, even if consent were not a mere fiction, this maxim is not superior in authority to others which it is brought in to supersede. It is, on the contrary, an instructive specimen of the loose and irregular matter in which supposed principles of justice grow up. . . .

Again, . . . how many conflicting conceptions of justice come to light in discussing the proper apportionment of punishment to offenses. [One is] an eye for an eye, a tooth for a tooth. [Others think] it should be measured by the moral guilt of the culprit, [or] what amount of punishment is necessary to deter the offense. . . . Who shall decide between these appeals to conflicting principles of justice? Each, from his own point of view, is unanswerable; and any choice between them, on grounds of justice, must be perfectly arbitrary. Social utility alone can decide the preference. . . .

REVIEW AND DISCUSSION QUESTIONS

1. Some have argued that intensity and duration of a pain or pleasure matter, not its inherent nature. Mill rejects that. What does he mean in claiming that some pleasures are higher than others? What argument does Mill give for that conclusion?
2. Does Mill believe that people should think specifically in each case about what would maximize utility when deciding what to do, or should they rely on other standards or attitudes? Explain.
3. Discuss Mill's "proof" of the utility principle.

4. Explain how Mill accounts for the apparent fact that people value and desire virtue for its own sake.

5. Explain the issues that Mill thinks are questions of justice, indicating what features these have in common.

6. Contrast Mill's approach with the social contract theory. Why does Mill reject the social contract in favor of the utility principle?

7. Explain how Mill understands moral rights. Are they universally applicable, in all societies? Explain.

8. Philosopher Robert Nozick has raised an important question about value. Imagine, he suggests, that there existed an "experience machine" that would provide any experience you wanted. Such experiences would include great pleasures, wonderful accomplishments, important relationships, or anything else. The only catch, of course, is that it is all done via computers attached to the brain. The question, then, is whether there would be anything valuable to you that you would miss if your life took place entirely in the machine. How would Mill answer that question? What do you think the answer is?

Essay and Paper Topics for Section 1

1. Compare the different ways that Aristotle, Hobbes, and Mill understand human happiness or well-being. Which view seems closest to the truth? Explain.

2. It could be argued that Hobbes and Kant see morality in similar terms, since each imagines what people can reasonably agree to. Describe the two theories, indicating the extent to which you think they agree and disagree about the nature of morality.

3. Write an essay on the idea of impartiality and its role in moral theory, using three of the authors you have read in this section.

4. Discuss the following claim: Utilitarians such as Mill emphasize the role of sympathy in thinking about morality, while Kant emphasizes reason. In fact, however, we need both.

Contemporary Perspectives

Essays in this section represent a sampling of contemporary reflections on the moral theories presented in Section 1. The first essay, by W. D. Ross, discusses the nature of duty and the "'intuitions'" on which it rests. The next, by Onora O'Neill, offers a perspective on the dispute between utilitarians such as Mill, on one hand, and Kant, on the other, while at the same time giving her own interpretation and defense of Kant. Alasdair MacIntyre uses the question of whether patriotism is a virtue as a basis for inquiring into the strengths and limits of classical moral theories, while Virginia Held criticizes traditional theory from the feminist perspective. Though differing on other points, Held and MacIntyre agree in criticizing many of the classical theorists for their emphasis on the ideal of impartiality and for their aspiration to locate a universal basis of morality.

Intuitionism

W.D. Ross

In this selection, W.D. Ross offers an account of morality that is at once different from the moral theories already discussed (perhaps he may even be said to reject moral theory entirely), but which also, he argues, provides an accurate picture of both the nature of morality and of its ultimate justification. Central to Ross's account is the distinction between *prima facie* duties such as keeping promises and being truthful, on one hand, and our actual duty in a particular situation on the other. After identifying the different origins of *prima facie* duties, Ross then discusses the basis or grounding of moral knowledge. W.D. Ross (1877–1971) taught philosophy at Oxford University.

When a plain man fulfils a promise because he thinks he ought to do so, it seems clear that he does so with no thought of its total consequences, still less with any opinion that these are likely to be the best possible. He thinks in fact much more of the past than of the future. What makes him think it right to act in a certain way is the fact that he has promised to do so—that and, usually, nothing more. . . . It may be said that besides the duty of fulfilling promises I have and recognize a duty of relieving distress, and that when I think it right to do the latter at, the cost of not doing the former, it is not because I think I shall produce more good theory but because I think it the duty which is in the circumstances

From W.D. Ross, *The Right and the Good* (1930), published by Oxford University Press.

more of a duty. This account surely corresponds. . . closely with what we really think in such a situation. . . .

[Utilitarianism]. . . seems to simplify unduly our relations to our fellows. It says, in effect, that the only morally significant relation in which my neighbours stand to me is that of being possible beneficiaries by my action. They do stand in this relation to me, and this relation is morally significant. But they may also stand to me in the relation of promisee to promiser, of creditor to debtor, of wife to husband, of child to parent, of friend to friend, of fellow countryman to fellow countryman, and the like; and each of these relations is the foundation of a *prima facie* duty, which is more or less incumbent on me according to the circumstances of the case. When I am in a situation, as perhaps I always am, in which more than one of these *prima facie* duties is incumbent on me, what I have to do is to study the situation as fully as I can until I form the considered opinion (it is never more) that in the circumstances one of them is more incumbent than any other; then I am bound to think that to do this *prima facie* duty is my duty *sans phrase* in the situation.

I suggest "*prima facie* duty" or "conditional duty" as a brief way of referring to the characteristic (quite distinct from that of being a duty proper) which an act has, in virtue of being of a certain kind (e.g., the keeping of a promise), of being an act which would be a duty proper if it were not at the same time of another kind which is morally significant. Whether an act is a duty proper or actual duty depends on *all* the morally significant kinds it is an instance of. . . .

There is nothing arbitrary about these *prima facie* duties. Each rests or a definite circumstance which cannot seriously be held to be without moral significance. Of *prima facie* duties I suggest, without claiming completeness or finality for it, the following division.

(1) Some duties rest on previous acts of my own. These duties seem to include two kinds, (*a*) those resting on a promise or what may fairly be called an implicit promise, such as the implicit undertaking not to tell lies which

seems to be implied in the act of entering into conversation (at any rate by civilized men), or of writing books that purport to be history and not fiction. These may be called the duties of fidelity, (*b*) Those resting on a previous wrongful act. These may be called the duties of reparation. (2) Some rest on previous acts of other men, i.e. services done by them to me. These may be loosely described as the duties of gratitude. (3) Some rest on the fact or possibility of a distribution of pleasure or happiness (or of the means thereto) which is not in accordance with the merit of the persons concerned; in such cases there arises a duty to upset or prevent such a distribution. These are the duties of justice. (4) Some rest on the mere fact that them are other beings in the world whose condition we call make better in respect of virtue, or of intelligence, or of pleasure. These are the duties of beneficence. (5) Some rest on the fact that we can improve our own condition in respect of virtue or of intelligence. These are the duties of self-improvement. (6) I think that we should distinguish from (4) the duties that may be summed up under the title of "not injuring others." No doubt to injure others is incidentally to fail to do them good; but it seems to me clear that non-maleficence is apprehended as a duty of distinct from that of beneficence, and as a duty of a more stringent character. It will be noticed that this alone among the types of duty has been stated in a negative way. All attempt might no doubt be made to state this duty, like the others, in a positive way. It might be said that it is really the duty to prevent ourselves from acting either from an inclination to harm others or from an inclination to seek our own pleasure, in *doing* which we should incidentally harm them. But on reflection it seems clear that the primary duty here is the duty not to harm others, this being a duty whether or not we have an inclination that I if followed would lead to our harming them; and that when we have such an inclination the primary duty not to harm others gives rise to a consequential duty to resist the inclination. The recognition of this duty of non-maleficence is the first step of the way to the recognition of the duty of beneficence; and that accounts for the prominence of the commands "thou shalt not kill," "thou shalt not commit adultery," "thou shalt not steal," "thou shalt not bear false witness," in so early a code as the Decalogue. But even when we have come to recognize the duty of beneficence, it appears to me that the duty of non-maleficence is recognized as a distinct one, and as *prima facie* more binding. We should not in general consider it justifiable to kill one person in order to keep another alive or to steal from one in order to give alms to another. . . .

If the objection is made, that the catalogue of duties is an unsystematic one resting on no logical principle, it may be replied, first, that it makes no claim to being ultimate. It is a *prima facie* classification of the duties which reflection on our moral convictions seems actually to reveal. And if these convictions are, as I would claim that they are, of the nature of knowledge, and if I have not misstated them, the list will be a list of authentic conditional duties, correct as far as it goes though not necessarily complete. . . . . .

It may, again, be objected that our theory that there are these various and often conflicting types of *prima facie* duty leaves us with no principle upon which to discern what is our actual duty in particular circumstances. But . . . why should two sets of circumstances, or one set of circumstances, *not* possess different characteristics, any one of which makes a certain act our *prima facie* duty? When I ask what it is that makes me in certain cases sure that I have a *prima facie* duty to do so and so, I find that it lies in the fact that I have made a promise; when I ask the same question in another case, I find the answer lies in the fact that I have done a wrong. And if on reflection I find (as I think I do) that neither of these reasons is reducible to the other, I must not on any *a priori* ground assume that such a reduction is possible. . . .

In actual experience [*prima facie* duties] are compounded together in highly complex ways. Thus, for example, the duty of obeying the laws of one's country arises partly (as Socrates contends in the *Crito*) from the duty of gratitude for the benefits one has received from it; partly from the implicit promise to obey which seems to be involved in permanent residence in a country whose laws we know we are *expected* to obey, and still more clearly involved when we ourselves invoke the protection of its laws (this is the truth underlying the doctrine of the social contract); and partly (if we are fortunate in our country) from the fact that its laws are potent instruments for the general good.

Or again, the sense of a general obligation to bring about (so far as we can) a just apportionment of happiness to merit is often greatly reinforced by the fact that many of the existing injustices are due to a social and economic system which we have, not indeed created, but taken part in and assented to; the duty of justice is then reinforced by the duty of reparation.

It is necessary to say something by way of clearing up the relation between *prima facie* duties and the actual or absolute duty to do one particular act in particular circumstances. If, as almost all moralists except Kant are agreed, and as most plain men think, it is sometimes right to tell a lie or to break a promise, it must be maintained that there is a difference between *prima facie* duty and actual or absolute duty. When we think ourselves justified in breaking, and indeed morally obliged to break, a promise in order to relieve some one's distress, we do not for a moment cease to recognize a *prima facie* duty to keep our promise, and this leads us to feel, not indeed shame or repentance, but certainly compunction, for behaving as we do, we recognize, further, that it is our duty to make up somehow to the promisee for the breaking of the promise. We have to distinguish from the characteristic of being our duty that of tending to be our duty. Any act that we do contains various elements in virtue of which it falls under various categories. In virtue of being the breaking of a promise, for instance, it tends to be wrong; in virtue of being an instance of relieving distress it tends to be right. Tendency to be one's duty may be called a parti-resultant attribute, i.e. one which belongs to an act in virtue of some one component in its nature. *Being* one's duty is a toti-resultant attribute, one which belongs to an act in virtue of its whole nature and of nothing less than this. This distinction between parti-resultant and toti-resultant attributes is one which we shall meet in another context also. . . .

Something should be said of the relation between our apprehension of the *prima facie* rightness of certain types of act and our mental attitude towards particular acts. It is proper to use the word "apprehension" in the former case and not in the latter. That an act, *qua* fulfilling a promise, or *qua* effecting a just distribution of good, or *qua* returning services rendered, or *qua* promoting the good of others, or *qua* promoting the virtue or insight of the agent, is *prima facie* right, is self-evident; not in the sense that it is evident from the beginning of our lives, or as soon as we attend to the proposition for the first time, but in the sense that when we have reached sufficient mental maturity and have given sufficient attention to the proposition it is evident without any need of proof, or of evidence beyond itself. It is self-evident just as a mathematical axiom, or the validity of a form of inference, is evident. The moral order expressed in these propositions is just as much part of the fundamental nature of the universe (and, we may add, of any possible universe in which there were moral agents at all) as is the spatial or numerical structure expressed in the axioms of geometry or arithmetic. In our confidence that these propositions are true there is involved the same trust in our reason that is involved in our confidence in mathematics and we should have no justification for trusting it in the latter sphere and distrusting it in the former. In both cases we are dealing with propositions that cannot be proved, but that just as certainly need no proof. . . .

Our judgments about our actual duty in concrete situations have none of the certainty that attaches to our recognition of the general principles of duty. A statement is certain, i.e. is an expression of knowledge, only in one or other of two cases: when it is either self-evident, or a valid conclusion from self-evident premises. And our judgments about our particular duties have neither of these characters. (1) They are not self-evident. Where a possible act is seen to have two characteristics, in virtue of one of which it is *prima facie* right, and in virtue of the other *prima facie* wrong, we are (I think) well aware that we are not certain whether we ought or ought not to do it; that whether we do it or not, we are taking a moral risk. We come in the long run, after consideration, to think one duty more pressing than the other, but we do not feel certain that it is so. And though we do not always recognize that a possible act has two such characteristics, and though there *may* be cases in which it has not, we are never certain that any particular possible act has not, and therefore never certain that is right, nor certain that it is wrong. For, to go no further in the analysis, it is enough to point out that any particular act will in all probability in the course of time contribute to the bringing about of good or of evil for many human beings, and thus have a *prima facie* rightness or wrongness of which we know nothing. (2) Again, our judgments about our particular duties are not logical conclusions from self-evident premises. The only possible premises would be the general principles stating their *prima facie* rightness or wrongness *qua* having the different characteristics they do have; and even if we could (as we cannot) apprehend the extent to which an act will tend on the one hand, for example, to bring about advantages for our benefactors, and on the other hand to bring about disadvantages for fellow men who are not our benefactors, there is no principle by which we can draw the conclusion that it is on the whole right or on the whole wrong. In this respect the judgment as to the rightness of a particular act is just like the judgment as to the beauty of a . . . natural object or work of art. A poem is, for instance, in respect of certain qualities beautiful and in respect of certain others not beautiful, and our judgment as to the degree of beauty it possesses on the whole is never reached by logical reasoning from the apprehension of its particular beauties or particular defects. Both in this and in the moral case we have more or less probable opinions which are not logically justified conclusions from the general principles that are recognized as self-evident.

There is therefore much truth in the description of the right act as a fortunate act. If we cannot be certain that it is right, it is our good fortune if the act we do is the right act. This consideration does not, however, make the doing of our duty a mere matter of chance. There is a parallel here between the doing of duty and the doing of what will be to our personal advantage. We never *know* what act will in the long run be to our advantage. Yet it is certain that we are more likely in general to secure our advantage if we estimate to the best of our ability the probable tendencies of our actions in this respect, than if we act on caprice. And similarly we are more likely to do our duty if we reflect to the best of our ability on the *prima facie* rightness or wrongness of various possible acts in virtue of the characteristics we perceive them to have, than if we act without reflection. With this greater likelihood we must be content. . . .

In what has preceded, a good deal of use has been made of "what we really think" about moral questions. . . . It might be said that this is in principle wrong; that we should not be content to expound what our present moral consciousness tells us but should aim at a criticism of our existing moral consciousness in the light of theory. Now I do not doubt that the moral consciousness of men has in detail undergone a good deal of modification as regards the things we think right, at the hands of moral theory. But . . . we have to ask ourselves whether we really *can* get rid of our view that promise-keeping has a bindingness independent of productiveness of maximum good. In my own experience I find that I cannot, in spite of a very genuine attempt to do so, and I venture to think that most people will find the same, and that just because they cannot lose the sense of special obligation, they cannot accept as self-evident, or even as

true, the theory which would require them to do so. . . .

I would maintain, in fact, that what we are apt to describe as "what we think" about moral questions contains a considerable amount that we do not think but know, and that this forms the standard by reference to which the truth of any moral theory has to be tested, instead of having itself to be tested by reference to any theory. I hope that I have in what precedes indicated what in my view these elements of knowledge are that are involved in our ordinary moral consciousness.

It would be a mistake to found a natural science on "what we really think," i.e. on what reasonably thoughtful and well-educated people think about the subjects of the science before they have studied them scientifically. For such opinions are interpretations, and often misinterpretations, of sense-experience; and the man of science must appeal from these to sense-experience itself, which furnishes his real data. In ethics no such appeal is possible. We have no more direct way of access to the facts about rightness and goodness and about what things are right or good, than by thinking about them; the moral convictions of thoughtful and well-educated people are the data of ethics just as sense-perceptions are the data of a natural science. Just as some of the latter have to be rejected as illusory, so have some of the former; but as the latter are rejected only when they are in conflict with other more accurate sense-perceptions, the former are rejected only when they are in conflict with other convictions which stand better the test of reflection. The existing body of moral convictions of the best people is the cumulative product of the moral reflection of many generations, which has developed an extremely delicate power of appreciation of moral distinctions, and this the theorist cannot afford to treat with anything other than the greatest respect. The verdicts of the moral consciousness of the best people are the foundation on which he must build; though he must first compare them with one another and eliminate any contradictions they may contain.

REVIEW AND DISCUSSION QUESTIONS

1. What does Ross mean by prima facie duties and how does he distinguish them from actual duties?
2. Why does Ross reject utilitarianism?
3. How, according to Ross, do we know which are our prima facie duties? Does his answer to that question pay adequate attention, in your opinion, to the role which society plays in inculcating moral attitudes? To the diversity of moral attitudes among different peoples?

Kant and Utilitarianism Contrasted

Onora O'Neill

Onora O'Neill's description of the dispute between Kantian and utilitarian philosophers is useful not only because it provides a valuable review of Kant's ethical theory and how it differs from utilitarianism but also for its criticisms of utilitarianism. In this selection, she focuses in particular on the requirement that persons be treated as ends in themselves, and on the value of human life. Onora O'Neill teaches philosophy at Cambridge University.

Kant's moral theory has acquired the reputation of being forbiddingly difficult to understand and, once understood, excessively demanding in its requirements. I don't believe that this reputation has been wholly earned, and I am going to try to undermine it. . . . I shall try to reduce some of the difficulties. . . . [And then] I shall compare Kantian and utilitarian approaches and assess their strengths and weaknesses. The main method by which I propose to avoid some of the difficulties of Kant's moral theory is by explaining only one part of the theory. This does not seem to me to be an irresponsible approach in this case. One of the things that makes Kant's moral theory hard to understand is that he gives a number of different versions of the principle that he calls the Supreme Principle of Morality, and these different versions don't look at all like one another. They also don't look at all like the utilitarians' Greatest Happiness Principle. But the Kantian

principle is supposed to play a similar role in arguments about what to do.

Kant calls his Supreme Principle the *Categorical Imperative;* its various versions also have sonorous names. One is called the Formula of Universal Law; another is the Formula of the Kingdom of Ends. The one on which I shall concentrate is known as the *Formula of the End in Itself.* To understand why Kant thinks that these picturesquely named principles are equivalent to one another takes quite a lot of close and detailed analysis of Kant's philosophy. I shall avoid this and concentrate on showing the implications of this version of the Categorical Imperative.

THE FORMULA OF THE END IN ITSELF

Kant states the Formula of the End in Itself as follows:

"A Simplified Account of Kant's Ethics," by Onora O'Neill from *Matters of Life and Death,* ed. Toni Regan, 1986. McGraw-Hill Publishing Company. Reprinted by permission of The McGraw-Hill Companies.

Act in such a way that you always treat humanity, whether in your own person or in the person of any other, never simply as a means but always at the same time as an end.

To understand this we need to know what it is to treat a person as a means or as an end. According to Kant, each of our acts reflects one or more *maxims*. The maxim of the act is the principle on which one sees oneself as acting. A maxim expresses a person's policy, or if he or she has no settled policy, the principle underlying the particular intention or decision on which he or she acts. Thus, a person who decides "This year I'll give 10 percent of my income to famine relief" has as a maxim the principle of tithing his or her income for famine relief. In practice, the difference between intentions and maxims is of little importance, for given any intention, we can formulate the corresponding maxim by deleting references to particular times, places, and persons. In what follows I shall take the terms "maxim" and "intention" as equivalent. Whenever we act intentionally, we have at least one maxim and can, if we reflect, state what it is. (There is of course room for self-deception here—"I'm only keeping the wolf from the door" we may claim as we wolf down enough to keep ourselves overweight, or, more to the point, enough to feed someone else who hasn't enough food.)

When we want to work out whether an act we propose to do is right or wrong, according to Kant, we should look at our maxims and not at how much misery or happiness the act is likely to produce, and whether it does better at increasing happiness than other available acts. We just have to check that the act we have in mind will not use anyone as a mere means, and, if possible, that it will treat other persons as ends in themselves.

USING PERSONS AS MERE MEANS

To use someone as a *mere means* is to involve them in a scheme of action *to which they could not in principle consent*. Kant does not say that there is anything wrong about using someone as a means. Evidently we have to do so in any cooperative scheme of action. If I cash a check I use the teller as a means, without whom I could not lay my hands on the cash; the teller in turn uses me as a means to earn his or her living. But in this case, each party consents to her or his part in the transaction. Kant would say that though they use one another as means, they do not use one another as *mere* means. Each person assumes that the other has maxims of his or her own and is not just a thing or a prop to be manipulated.

But there are other situations where one person uses another in a way to which the other could not in principle consent. For example, one person may make a promise to another with every intention of breaking it. If the promise is accepted, then the person to whom it was given must be ignorant of what the promisor's intention (maxim) really is. If one knew that the promisor did not intend to do what he or she was promising, one would, after all, not accept or rely on the promise. It would be as though there had been no promise made. Successful false promising depends on deceiving the person to whom the promise is made about what one's real maxim is. And since the person who is deceived doesn't know that real maxim, he or she can't in principle consent to his or her part in the proposed scheme of action. The person who is deceived is, as it were, a prop or a tool—a mere means—in the false promisor's scheme. A person who promises falsely treats the acceptor of the promise as a prop or a thing and not as a person. In Kant's view, it is this that makes false promising wrong

One standard way of using others as mere means is by deceiving them. By getting someone involved in a business scheme or a criminal activity on false pretenses, or by giving a misleading account of what one is about, or by making a false promise or a fraudulent contract, one involves another in something to which he or she in principle cannot consent, since the scheme requires that he or she doesn't know what is going on. Another standard way of using others as mere means is by coercing them. If a rich or powerful person threatens a debtor with bankruptcy unless he or she joins in some scheme, then the creditor's intention is to coerce; and the debtor, if coerced, cannot consent to his or her part in the creditor's scheme. To make the example more specific: If a moneylender in an Indian village threatens not to renew a vital loan unless he is given the debtor's land, then he uses the debtor as a mere means. He coerces the debtor, who cannot truly consent to this "offer he can't refuse." (Of course the outward form of such transactions may look like ordinary commercial dealings, but we know very well that some offers and demands couched in that form are coercive.)

In Kant's view, acts that are done on maxims that require deception or coercion of others, and so cannot have the consent of those others (for consent precludes both deception and coercion), are wrong. When we act on such maxims, we treat others as mere means, as things rather than as ends in themselves. If we act on such maxims, our acts are not only wrong but unjust: such acts wrong the particular others who are deceived or coerced.

TREATING PERSONS AS ENDS IN THEMSELVES

Duties of justice are, in Kant's view (as in many others'), the most important of our duties. When we fail in these duties, we have used some other or others as mere means. But there are also cases where, though we do not use others as mere means, still we fail to use them as ends in themselves in the fullest possible way. To treat someone as an end in him or herself requires in the first place that one not use him or her as mere means, that one respects each as a rational person with his or her own maxims. But beyond that, one may also seek to foster others' plans and maxims by sharing some of their ends. To act beneficently is to seek others' happiness, therefore to intend to achieve some of the things that those others aim at with their maxims. If I want to make others happy, I will adopt

maxims that not merely do not manipulate them but that foster some of their plans and activities. Beneficent acts try to achieve what others want. However, we cannot seek everything that others want; their wants are too numerous and diverse, and, of course, sometimes incompatible. It follows that beneficence has to be selective.

There is then quite a sharp distinction between the requirements of justice and of beneficence in Kantian ethics. Justice requires that we act on *no* maxims that use others as mere means. Beneficence requires that we act on *some* maxims that foster others' ends, though it is a matter for judgment and discretion which of their ends we foster. Some maxims no doubt ought not to be fostered because it would be unjust to do so. Kantians are not committed to working interminably through a list of happiness-producing and misery-reducing acts; but there are some acts whose obligatoriness utilitarians may need to debate as they try to compare total outcomes of different choices, to which Kantians are stringently bound. Kantians will claim that they have done nothing wrong if none of their acts is unjust, and that their duty is complete if in addition their life plans have in the circumstances been reasonably beneficent.

In making sure that they meet all the demands of justice, Kantians do not try to compare all available acts and see which has the best effects. They consider only the proposals for action that occur to them and check that these proposals use no other as mere means. If they do not, the act is permissible; if omitting the act would use another as mere means, the act is obligatory. Kant's theory has less scope than utilitarianism. Kantians do not claim to discover whether acts whose maxims they don't know fully are just. They may be reluctant to judge others' acts or policies that cannot be regarded as the maxim of any person or institution. They cannot rank acts in order of merit. Yet, the theory offers more precision than utilitarianism when data are scarce. One can usually tell whether one's act would use others as mere means, even when its impact on human happiness is thoroughly obscure.

THE LIMITS OF KANTIAN ETHICS: INTENTIONS AND RESULTS

Kantian ethics differs from utilitarian ethics both in its scope and in the precision with which it guides action. Every action, whether of a person or of an agency, can be assessed by utilitarian methods, provided only that information is available about all the consequences of the act. The theory has unlimited scope, but, owing to lack of data, often lacks precision. Kantian ethics has a more restricted scope. Since it assesses actions by looking at the maxims of agents, it can only assess intentional acts. This means that it is most at home in assessing individuals' acts; but it can be extended to assess acts of agencies that (like corporations and governments and student unions) have decision-making procedures. It can do nothing to assess patterns of action that reflect no intention or policy, hence it cannot assess the acts of groups lacking decision-making procedures, such as the student movement, the women's movement, or the consumer movement.

It may seem a great limitation of Kantian ethics that it concentrates on intentions to the neglect of results. It might seem that all conscientious Kantians have to do is to make sure that they never intend to use others as mere means, and that they sometimes intend to foster others' ends. And, as we all know, good intentions sometimes lead to bad results and correspondingly, bad intentions sometimes do not harm, or even produce good. [Some philosophers have argued] that the good intentions of those who feed the starving lead to dreadful results in the long run. If some traditional arguments in favor of capitalism are right, the greed and selfishness of the profit motive have produced unparalleled prosperity for many.

But such discrepancies between intentions and results are the exception and not the rule. For we cannot just *claim* that our intentions are good and do what we will. Our intentions reflect what we expect the immediate results of our action to be. Nobody credits the "intentions" of a couple who practice neither celibacy nor contraception but still insist "we never mean to have (more) children." Conception is likely (and known to be likely) in such cases. Where people's expressed intentions ignore the normal and predictable results of what they do, we infer that (if they are not amazingly ignorant) their words do not express their true intentions. The Formula of the End in Itself applies to the intentions on which one acts—not to some prettified version that one may avow. Provided this intention—the agent's real intention—uses no other as mere means, he or she does nothing unjust. If some of his or her intentions foster others' ends, then he or she is sometimes beneficent. It is therefore possible for people to test their proposals by Kantian arguments even when they lack the comprehensive causal knowledge that utilitarianism requires. Conscientious Kantians can work out whether they will be doing wrong by some act even though it blurs the implications of the theory. If we peer through the blur, we see that the utilitarian view is that lives may indeed be sacrificed for the sake of a greater good even when the persons are not willing. There is nothing wrong with using another as a mere means provided that the end for which the person is so used is a happier result than could have been achieved any other way, taking into account the misery the means have caused. In utilitarian thought, persons are not ends in themselves. Their special moral status derives from their being means to the production of happiness. Human life has therefore a high though derivative value, and one life may be taken for the sake of greater happiness in other lives, or for ending of misery in that life. Nor is there any deep difference between ending a life for the sake of others' happiness by not helping (e.g., by triaging) and doing so by harming. Because the distinction between justice and beneficence is not sharply made within utilitarianism, it is not possible to say that triaging is a matter of not benefiting, while other interventions are a matter of injustice.

Utilitarian moral theory has then a rather paradoxical view of the value of human life. Living, conscious humans are (along with other sentient beings) necessary for the existence of everything utilitarians value. But it is not their being alive but the state of their consciousness that is of value. Hence, the best results may require certain lives to be lost—by whatever means—for the sake of the total happiness and absence of misery that can be produced.

KANT AND RESPECT FOR PERSONS

Kantians reach different conclusions about human life. Human life is valuable because humans (and conceivably other beings, e.g., angels or apes) are the bearers of rational life. Humans are able to choose and to plan. This capacity and its exercise are of such value that they ought not to be sacrificed for anything of lesser value. Therefore, no one rational or autonomous creature should be treated as mere means for the enjoyment or even the happiness of another. We may in Kant's view justifiably—even nobly—risk or sacrifice our lives for others. For in doing so we follow our own maxim and nobody uses us as mere means. But no others may use either our lives or our bodies for a scheme that they have either coerced or deceived us into joining. For in doing so they would fail to treat us as rational beings; they would use us as mere means and not as ends in ourselves.

It is conceivable that a society of Kantians, all of whom took pains to use no other as mere means, would end up with less happiness or with fewer persons alive than would some societies of complying utilitarians. For since the Kantians would be strictly bound only to justice, they might without wrongdoing be quite selective in their beneficence and fail to maximize either survival rates or happiness, or even to achieve as much of either as a strenuous group of utilitarians, who know that their foresight is limited and

that they may cause some harm or fail to cause some benefit. But they will not cause harms that they can foresee without this being reflected in their intentions.

UTILITARIANISM AND RESPECT FOR LIFE

From the differing implications that Kantian and utilitarian moral theories have for our actions towards those who do or may suffer famine, we can discover two sharply contrasting views of the value of human life. Utilitarians value happiness and the absence or reduction of misery. As a utilitarian one ought (if conscientious) to devote one's life to achieving the best possible balance of happiness over misery. If one's life plan remains in doubt, this will be because the means to this end are often unclear. But whenever the causal tendency of acts is clear, utilitarians will be able to discern the acts they should successively do in order to improve the world's balance of happiness over unhappiness.

This task is not one for the faint-hearted. First, it is dauntingly long, indeed interminable. Second, it may at times require the sacrifice of happiness, and even of lives, for the sake of a greater happiness. Such sacrfice may be morally required not only when the person whose happiness or even whose life is at stake volunteers to make the sacrifice. It may be necessary to sacrifice some lives for the sake of others. As our control over the means of ending and preserving human life has increased, analogous dilemmas have arisen in many areas for utilitarians. Should life be preserved at the cost of pain when modern medicine makes this possible? Should life be preserved without hope of consciousness? Should triage policies, because they may maximize the number of survivors, be used to determine who should be left to starve? Should population growth be fostered wherever it will increase the total of human happiness—or on some views so long as average happiness is not reduced? All these questions can be fitted into utilitarian frameworks and answered *if* we have the relevant information. And sometimes the answer will be that human happiness demands the sacrifice of lives, including the sacrifice of unwilling lives. Further, for most utilitarians, it makes no difference if the unwilling sacrifices involve acts of injustice to those whose lives are to be lost. It might, for example, prove necessary for maximal happiness that some persons have their allotted rations, or their hard-earned income, diverted for others' benefit. Or it might turn out that some generations must sacrifice comforts or liberties and even lives to rear "the fabric of felicity" for their successors. On the other hand, nobody will have been made an instrument of others' survival or happiness in the society of complying Kantians.

REVIEW AND DISCUSSION QUESTIONS

1. Which of the versions of Kant's categorical imperative does O'Neill discuss? Give examples of how people might fail to live up to that principle by treating people as mere means.

2. How, exactly, does O'Neill understand the requirement that we treat people as ends? How does promise keeping illustrate this?

3. O'Neill distinguishes sharply between duties of justice and of beneficence. What is that distinction, according to her?

4. Why do you think O'Neill says Kant offers more "precision" than utilitarians? Do you agree? Explain.

5. What specific, practical differences are there in the demands that utilitarians and Kantians make of people, according to O'Neill?

Is Patriotism a Virtue?

Alasdair MacIntyre

In this essay, Alasdair MacIntyre argues that classical "liberal" moral theories such as utilitarianism and Kantianism, which rest on familiar Enlightenment ideals of objectivity and impartiality, are deeply mistaken. Because such theories would have us judge actions from an impartial standpoint, it follows that patriotism, rather than being a virtue, would in fact be a moral vice since patriots are partial or biased in favor of their own nation. MacIntyre defends patriotism against this charge by questioning the adequacy of the liberal moral vision. Morality must finally rest, he claims, on the values found in the community in which people live rather than on the universal, cross-cultural norms of liberalism. The liberal vision should be replaced, he argues, by the patriot's willingness to exempt his or her nation's projects and practices from criticism. Such an exemption does not mean, however, that the patriot must support any particular policy or even government—but instead that he or she remains committed to the nation viewed as a historic project with a distinctive political and moral identity. Only through such a patriotic stance, he argues, can a satisfactory moral vision be supported, one that maintains the essentially historical connections that constitute a community's identity and provides people's lives with meaning. Alasdair MacIntyre is professor of philosophy at Duke University.

The Lindley Lecture, Department of Philosophy, University of Kansas (1984). © 1984 by the University of Kansas. Reprinted by permission.

46   Alasdair MacIntyre

I.

. . . It is quite clear that there are large dis-agreements about patriotism in our society. And although it would be a mistake to suppose that there are only two clear, simple and mutually opposed sets of beliefs about patriotism, it is at least plausible to suggest that the range of conflicting views can be placed on a spectrum with two poles. At one end is the view, taken for granted by almost everyone in the nineteenth century, a commonplace in the literary culture of the McGuffey readers, that "patriotism" names a virtue. At the other end is the contrasting view, expressed with sometimes shocking clarity in the nineteen sixties, that "patriotism" names a vice. It would be misleading for me to suggest that I am going to be able to offer good reasons for taking one of these views rather than the other. What I do hope to achieve is a clarification of the issues that divide them.

A necessary first step is to distinguish patriotism properly so-called from two other sets of attitudes that are all too easily assimilated to it. The first is that exhibited by those who are protagonists of their own nation's causes because and only because, so they assert, it is their nation which is the champion of some great moral ideal.

In the Great War of 1914–18 Max Weber claimed that Imperial Germany should be supported because its was the cause of *Kultur,* while Emile Durkheim claimed with equal vehemence that France should be supported because its was the cause of *civilization.* And here and now there are those American politicians who claim that the United States deserves our allegiance because it champions the goods of freedom against the evils of communism. What distinguishes their attitude from patriotism is twofold: first it is the ideal and not the nation which is the primary object of their regard; and secondly insofar as their regard for the ideal provides good reasons for allegiance to their country, it provides good reasons for anyone at all to uphold their country's cause, irrespective of their nationality or citizenship.

Patriotism by contrast is defined in terms of a kind of loyalty to a particular nation which only those possessing that particular nationality can exhibit. Only Frenchmen can be patriotic about France, while anyone can make the cause of *civilization* their own. But it would be all too easy in noticing this to fail to make a second equally important distinction. Patriotism is not to be confused with a mindless loyalty to one's own particular nation which has no regard at all for the characteristics of that particular nation. Patriotism does generally and characteristically involve a peculiar regard not just for one's own nation, but for the particular characteristics and merits and achievements of one's own nation. These latter are indeed valued as merits and achievements and their character as merits and achievements provides reasons supportive of the patriot's attitudes. But the patriot does not value in the same way precisely similar merits and achievements when they are the merits and achievements of some nation other than his or hers. For he or she—at least in the role of patriot—values them not just as merits and achievements, but as the merits and achievements of this particular nation. . . .

II.

The presupposition of the thesis [that patriotism is not a virtue] is an account of morality which has enjoyed high prestige in our culture. According to that account to judge from a moral standpoint is to judge impersonally. It is to judge as any rational person would judge, independently of his or her interests, affections and social position. And to act morally is to act in accordance with such impersonal judgments. Thus to think and to act morally involves a moral agent in abstracting him or herself from all social particularity and partiality. The potential conflict between morality so understood and patriotism is at once clear. For patriotism requires me to exhibit peculiar devotion to my nation and you to yours. It requires me to regard such contingent social facts as where I was born and what government ruled over that place at that time, who my parents were, who my great-great-grandparents were and so on, as deciding for me the question of what virtuous action is—at least insofar as it is the virtue of patriotism which is in question. Hence the moral standpoint and the patriotic standpoint are systematically incompatible.

Yet although this is so, it might be argued that the two standpoints need not be in conflict. For patriotism and all other such particular loyalties can be restricted in their scope so that their exercise is always within the confines imposed by morality. Patriotism need be regarded as nothing more than a perfectly proper devotion to one's own nation which must never be allowed to violate the constraints set by the impersonal moral standpoint. This is indeed the kind of patriotism professed by certain liberal moralists who are often indignant when it is suggested by their critics that they are not patriotic. To those critics however patriotism thus limited in its scope appears to be emasculated, and it does so because in some of the most important situations of actual social life either the patriotic standpoint comes into serious conflict with the standpoint of a genuinely impersonal morality or it amounts to no more than a set of practically empty slogans. What kinds of circumstances are these'? They are at least twofold.

The first kind arises from scarcity of essential resources, often historically from the scarcity of land suitable for cultivation and pasture, and perhaps in our own time from that of fossil fuels. What your community requires as the material prerequisites for your survival as a distinctive community and your growth into a distinctive nation may be exclusive use of the same or some of the same natural resources as my community requires for its survival and growth into a distinctive nation. When such a conflict arises, the standpoint of impersonal morality requires an allocation of goods such that each individual person counts for one and no more than one, while the patriotic standpoint requires that I strive to further the interests of my community

and you strive to further those of yours, and certainly where the survival of one community is at stake, and sometimes perhaps even when only large interests of one community are at stake, patriotism entails a willingness to go to war on one's community's behalf.

The second type of conflict-engendering circumstance arises from differences between communities about the right way for each to live. Not only competition for scarce natural resources, but incompatibilities arising from such conflict-engendering beliefs may lead to situations in which once again the liberal moral standpoint and the patriotic standpoint are radically at odds. The administration of the *pax Romana* from time to time required the Roman *imperium* to set its frontiers at the point at which they could be most easily secured. . . . But this required infringing upon the territory and the independence of barbarian border peoples. A variety of such peoples—Scottish Gaels, Iroquois Indians, Bedouin—have regarded raiding the territory of their traditional enemies living within the confines of such large empires as an essential constituent of the good life; whereas the settled urban or agricultural communities which provided the target for their depredations have regarded the subjugation of such peoples and their reeducation into peaceful pursuits as one of their central responsibilities. And on such issues once again the impersonal moral standpoint and that of patriotism cannot be reconciled.

For the impersonal moral standpoint, understood as the philosophical protagonists of modern liberalism have understood it, requires neutrality not only between rival and competing interests, but also between rival and competing sets of beliefs about the best way for human beings to live. Each individual is to be left free to pursue in his or her own way that way of life which he or she judges to be best; while morality by contrast consists of rules which, just because they are such that any rational person, independently of his or her interests or point of view on the best way for human beings to live, would assent to them, are equally binding on all persons. Hence in conflicts between nations or other communities over ways of life, the standpoint of morality will once again be that of an impersonal arbiter, adjudicating in ways that give equal weight to each individual person's needs, desires, beliefs about the good and the like, while the patriot is once again required to be partisan.

Notice that in speaking of the standpoint of liberal impersonal morality in the way in which I have done I have been describing a standpoint whose truth is both presupposed by the political actions and utterances of a great many people in our society and explicitly articulated and defended by most modern moral philosophers, and that it has at the level of moral philosophy a number of distinct versions—some with a Kantian flavour, some utilitarian, some contractarian. I do not mean to suggest that the disagreements between these positions are unimportant. Nonetheless the five central positions that I have ascribed to that standpoint appear in all these various philosophical guises: first, that morality is constituted by rules to which any rational person would under certain ideal conditions give assent; secondly, that those rules impose constraints upon and are neutral between rival and competing interests—morality itself is not the expression of any particular interest; thirdly, that those rules are also neutral between rival and competing sets of beliefs about what the best way for human beings to live is; fourthly, that the units which provide the subject-matter of morality as well as its agents are individual human beings and that in moral evaluations each individual is to count for one and nobody for more than one; and fifthly, that the standpoint of the moral agent constituted by allegiance to these rules is one and the same for all moral agents and as such is independent of all social particularity. What morality provides are standards by which all actual social structures may be brought to judgment from a standpoint independent of all of them. It is morality so understood allegiance to which is not only incompatible with treating patriotism as a virtue, but which requires that patriotism—at

least in any substantial version—be treated as a vice.

But is this the only possible way to understand morality? As a matter of history, the answer is clearly "No." This understanding of morality invaded post Renascence Western culture at a particular point in time as the moral counterpart to political liberalism and social individualism and its polemical stances reflect its history of emergence from the conflicts which those movements engendered and themselves presuppose alternatives against which those polemical stances were and are directed. Let me therefore turn to considering one of those alternative accounts of morality, whose peculiar interest lies in the place that it has to assign to patriotism.

III.

According to the liberal account of morality *where* and *from whom* I learn the principles of morality are and must be irrelevant both to the question of what the content of morality is and to that of the nature of my commitment to it, as irrelevant as *where* and *from whom* I learn the principles and precepts of mathematics are to the content of mathematics and the nature of my commitment to mathematical truths. By contrast on the alternative account of morality which I am going to sketch, the questions of *where* and *from whom* I learn my morality turn out to be crucial for both the content and the nature of moral commitment.

On this view it is an essential characteristic of the morality which each of us acquires that it is learned from, in and through the way of life of some particular community. Of course the moral rules elaborated in one particular historical community will often resemble and sometimes be identical with the rules to which allegiance is given in other particular communities, especially in communities with a shared history or which appeal to the same canonical texts. But there will characteristically be some distinctive features of the set of rules considered as a whole, and those distinctive features will often arise from the way in which members of that particular community responded to some earlier situation or series of situations in which particular features of difficult cases led to one or more rules being put in question and reformulated or understood in some new way. Moreover the form of the rules of morality as taught and apprehended will be intimately connected with specific institutional arrangements. The moralities of different societies may agree in having a precept enjoining that a child should honor his or her parents, but what it is so to honor and indeed what a father is and what a mother is will vary greatly between different social orders. So that what I learn as a guide to my actions and as a standard for evaluating them is never morality as such, but always the highly specific morality of some highly specific social order. . . .

[It] is not just that I first apprehend the rules of morality in some socially specific and particularised form. It is also and correlatively that the goods by reference to which and for the sake of which any set of rules must be justified are also going to be goods that are socially specific and particular. For central to those goods is the enjoyment of one particular kind of social life, lived out through a particular set of social relationships and thus what I enjoy is the good of *this* particular social life inhabited by me and I enjoy it as what it is. It may well be that it follows that I would enjoy and benefit equally from similar forms of social life in other communities; but this hypothetical truth in no way diminishes the importance of the contention that my goods are as a matter of fact found *here,* among *these* particular people, in *these* particular relationships. . . .

It follows that *I* find *my* justification for allegiance to these rules of morality in *my* particular community; deprived of the life of that community, *I* would have no reason to be moral. But this is not all. To obey the rules of morality is characteristically and generally a hard task for human beings. Indeed were it not so, our need for morality would not be what it is. It is because we are continually

liable to be blinded by immediate desire, to be distracted from our responsibilities, to lapse into backsliding and because even the best of us may at times encounter quite unusual temptations that it is important to morality that I can only be a moral agent because we are moral agents, that I need those around me to reinforce my moral strengths and assist in remedying my moral weaknesses. It is in general only within a community that individuals become capable of morality, are sustained in their morality and are constituted as moral agents by the way in which other people regard them and what is owed to and by them as well as by the way in which they regard themselves. . . .

Indeed the case for treating patriotism as a virtue is now clear. *If* first of all it is the case that I can only apprehend the rules of morality in the version in which they are incarnated in some specific community; and *if* secondly it is the case that the justification of morality must be in terms of particular goods enjoyed within the life of particular communities; and *if* thirdly it is the case that I am characteristically brought into being and maintained as a moral agent only through the particular kinds of moral sustenance afforded by my community, *then* it is clear that deprived of this community, I am unlikely to flourish as a moral agent. Hence my allegiance to the community and what it requires of me—even to the point of requiring me to die to sustain its life— could not meaningfully be contrasted with or counterposed to what morality required of me. Detached from my community, I will be apt to lose my hold upon all genuine standards of judgment. Loyalty to that community, to the hierarchy of particular kinship, particular local community and particular natural community, is on this view a prerequisite for morality. So patriotism and those loyalties cognate to it are not just virtues but central virtues. Everything however turns on the truth or falsity of the claims advanced in the three preceding if-clauses. . . . What we have here are two rival and incompatible moralities, each of which is viewed from within by its adherents as morality-as-such, each of which makes its exclusive claim to our allegiance. How are we to evaluate such claims?

One way to begin is. . . to focus attention on those accusations which the adherents of each bring against the rival position which the adherents of that rival position treat as of central importance to rebut. For this will afford at least one indication of the issues about the importance of which both sides agree and about the characterisation of which their very recognition of disagreement suggests that there must also be some shared beliefs. In what areas do such issues arise?

IV.

One such area is defined by a charge which it seems reasonable at least *prima facie* for the protagonists of patriotism to bring against liberal morality. The morality for which patriotism is a virtue offers a form of rational justification for moral rules and precepts whose structure is clear and rationally defensible. The rules of morality are justifiable if and only if they are productive of and partially constitutive of a form of shared social life whose goods are directly enjoyed by those inhabiting the particular communities whose social life is of that kind. Hence *qua* member of this or that particular community I can appreciate the justification for what morality requires of me from within the social roles that I live out in my community. By contrast, it may be argued, liberal morality requires of me to assume an abstract and artificial—perhaps even an impossible—stance, that of a rational being as such, responding to the requirements of morality not *qua* parent or farmer or quarterback, but *qua* rational agent who has abstracted him or herself from all social particularity, who has become not merely Adam Smith's impartial spectator, but a correspondingly impartial actor, and one who in his impartiality is doomed to rootlessness, to be a citizen of nowhere. How can I justify to myself performing this act of abstraction and detachment?

The liberal answer is clear: such abstraction and detachment is defensible, because it is a necessary condition of moral freedom, of emancipation from the bondage of the social, political and economic *status quo.* For unless I can stand back from every and any feature of that *status quo,* including the roles within it which I myself presently inhabit, I will be unable to view it critically and to decide for myself what stance it is rational and right for me to adopt towards it. This does not preclude that the outcome for such a critical evaluation may not be an endorsement of all or some of the existing social order; but even such an endorsement will only be free and rational if I have made it for myself in this way. . . . Thus liberal morality does after all appeal to an overriding good, the good of this particular kind of emancipating freedom. And in the name of this good it is able not only to respond to the question about how the rules of morality are to be justified, but also to frame a plausible and potentially damaging objection to the morality of patriotism.

It is of the essence of the morality of liberalism that no limitations are or can be set upon the criticism of the social *status quo.* No institution, no practice, no loyalty can be immune from being put in question and perhaps rejected. Conversely the morality of patriotism is one which precisely because it is framed in terms of the membership of some particular social community with some particular social, political and economic structure, must exempt at least some fundamental structures of that community's life from criticism. Because patriotism has to be a loyalty that is in some respects unconditional, so in just those respects rational criticism is ruled out. But if so the adherents of the morality of patriotism have condemned themselves to a fundamentally irrational attitude—since to refuse to examine some of one's fundamental beliefs and attitudes is to insist on accepting them, whether they are rationally justifiable or not, which is irrational—and have imprisoned themselves within that irrationality. What answer can the adherents of the morality of patriotism make to this kind of accusation? The reply must be threefold.

When the liberal moralist claims that the patriot is bound to treat his or her nation's projects and practices in some measure uncritically, the claim is not only that at any one time certain of these projects and practices will be being treated uncritically; it is that some at least must be permanently exempted from criticism. . . . What then is exempted? The answer is: the nation conceived *as a project,* a project somehow or other brought to birth in the past and carried on so that a morally distinctive community was brought into being which embodied a claim to political autonomy in its various organized and institutionalised expressions. . . . What the patriot is committed to is a particular way of linking a past which has conferred a distinctive moral and political identity upon him or her with a future for the project which is his or her nation which it is his or her responsibility to bring into being. Only this allegiance is unconditional and allegiance to particular governments or forms of government or particular leaders will be entirely conditional upon their being devoted to furthering that project rather than frustrating or destroying it. Hence there is nothing inconsistent in a patriot's being deeply opposed to his country's contemporary rulers, or plotting their overthrow as Adam von Trott did.

Yet although this may go part of the way towards answering the charge of the liberal moralist that the patriot must in certain areas be completely uncritical and therefore irrationalist, it certainly does not go all the way. For everything that I have said on behalf of the morality of patriotism is compatible with it being the case that on occasion patriotism might require me to support and work for the success of some enterprise of my nation as crucial to its overall project, crucial perhaps to its survival, when the success of that enterprise would not be in the best interests of mankind, evaluated from an impartial and an impersonal standpoint. The case of Adam von Trott is very much to the point.

Adam von Trott was a German patriot who was executed after the unsuccessful assassination attempt against Hitler's life in 1944. Trott deliberately chose to work inside Germany with the minuscule, but highly placed, conservative opposition to the Nazis with the aim of replacing Hitler from within, rather than to work for an overthrow of Nazi Germany which would result in the destruction of the Germany brought to birth in 1871. But to do this he had to appear to be identified with the cause of Nazi Germany and so strengthened not only his country's cause, as was his intention, but also as an unavoidable consequence the cause of the Nazis. This kind of example is a particularly telling one, because the claim that such and such a course of action is "to the best interests of mankind" is usually at best disputable, at worst cloudy rhetoric. But there are a very few causes in which so much was at stake—and that this is generally much clearer in retrospect than it was at the time does not alter that fact—that the phrase has clear application: the overthrow of Nazi Germany was one of them.

How ought the patriot then to respond? Perhaps in two ways. The first begins by reemphasising that from the fact that the particularist morality of the patriot is rooted in a particular community and inextricably bound up with the social life of that community, it does not follow that it cannot provide rational grounds for repudiating many features of that country's present organized social life. The conception of justice engendered by the notion of citizenship within a particular community may provide standards by which particular political institutions are found wanting. . . . Yes, the liberal critic of patriotism will respond, this indeed may happen; but it may not and it often will not. Patriotism turns out to be a permanent source of moral danger. And this claim, I take it, cannot in fact be successfully rebutted. . . .

That the rational protagonist of the morality of patriotism is compelled, if my argument is correct, to concede this does not mean that there is not more to be said in the debate.

And what needs to be said is that the liberal morality of impartiality and impersonality turns out also to be a morally dangerous phenomenon in an interestingly corresponding way. For suppose the bonds of patriotism to be dissolved: would liberal morality be able to provide anything adequately substantial in its place? What the morality of patriotism at its best provides is a clear account of and justification for the particular bonds and loyalties which form so much of the substance of the moral life. It does so by underlining the moral importance of the different members of a group acknowledging a shared history. Each one of us to some degree or other understands his or her life as an enacted narrative, and because of our relationships with others we have to understand ourselves as characters in the enacted narratives of other people's lives. Moreover the story of each of our lives is characteristically embedded in the story of one or more larger units. I understand the story of my life in such a way that it is part of the history of my family or of this farm or of this university or of this countryside; and I understand the story of the lives of other individuals around me as embedded in the same larger stories, so that I and they share a common stake in the outcome of that story and in what sort of story it both is and is to be: tragic, heroic, comic.

A central contention of the morality of patriotism is that I will obliterate and lose a central dimension of the moral life if I do not understand the enacted narrative of my own individual life as embedded in the history of my country. For if I do not so understand it I will not understand what I owe to others or what others owe to me, for what crimes of my nation I am bound to make reparation, for what benefits to my nation I am bound to feel gratitude. Understanding what is owed to and by me and understanding the history of the communities of which I am a part is on this view one and the same thing. . . .

In modern communities in which membership is understood only or primarily in terms of reciprocal self-interest, only two resources are generally available when destructive conflicts of interest threaten such reciprocity. One is the arbitrary imposition of some solution by force; the other is appeal to the neutral, impartial and impersonal standards of liberal morality. The importance of this resource is scarcely to be underrated; but how much of a resource is it? The problem is that some motivation has to be provided for allegiance to the standards of impartiality and impersonality which both has rational justification and can outweigh the considerations provided by interest. Since any large need for such allegiance arises precisely and only when and insofar as the possibility of appeals to reciprocity in interests has broken down, such reciprocity car no longer provide the relevant kind of motivation. And it is difficult to identify anything that can take its place. The appeal to moral agents *qua* rational beings to place their allegiance to impersonal rationality above that to their interests has just because it is an appeal to rationality, to furnish an adequate reason for so doing. And this is a point at which liberal accounts of morality are notoriously vulnerable. This vulnerability becomes a manifest practical liability at one key point in the social order.

Every political community except in the most exceptional conditions requires standing armed forces for its minimal security. Of the members of these armed forces it must require both that they be prepared to sacrifice their own lives for the sake of the community's security and that their willingness to do so be not contingent upon their own individual evaluation of the rightness or wrongness of their country's cause on some specific issue, measured by some standard that is neutral and impartial relative to the interests of their own community and the interests of other communities. And, that is to say, good soldiers may not be liberals and must indeed embody in their actions a good deal at least of the morality of patriotism. So the political survival of any polity in which liberal morality had secured large-scale allegiance would depend upon there still being enough young men and women who rejected that liberal morality. And in this sense liberal morality tends towards the dissolution of social bonds.

Hence the charge that the morality of patriotism can successfully bring against liberal morality is the mirror-image of that which liberal morality can successfully urge against the morality of patriotism. For while the liberal moralist was able to conclude that patriotism is a permanent source of moral danger because of the way it places our ties to our nation beyond rational criticism, the moralist who defends patriotism is able to conclude that liberal morality is a permanent source of moral danger because of the way it renders our social and moral ties too open to dissolution by rational criticism. And each party is in fact in the right against the other. . . .

REVIEW AND DISCUSSION QUESTIONS

1. Describe the two (mistaken) conceptions of patriotism that MacIntyre identifies.
2. Describe what it is that "liberal" moral theories have in common, giving examples from other readings.
3. Explain MacIntyre's argument that patriotism (however defined) must be a vice from the perspective of liberal moral theory.
4. MacIntyre outlines an alternative to liberal morality (which is often termed *communitarianism*). Explain the three facts that, he claims, lead naturally to this moral theory as opposed to liberalism.
5. How does MacIntyre think patriotism should be understood?
6. MacIntyre argues that communitarian morality has an advantage over liberalism when people are asked to join the military and fight. Explain his argument.
7. How do you think a nation could identify its "historical project"? Can it be done without in some way invoking universal moral standards?
8. Is MacIntyre right in thinking that true patriotism does not rest in the commitment to one's country based on the values it stands for (freedom, for example)?
9. Might MacIntyre's view lead to ethical relativism and thus the conclusion that, for example, the Nazis did not violate human rights? Explain.
10. Explain which of the philosophers in Section I comes closest to MacIntyre's position.
11. Select one of the moral philosophers in Section I you think exemplifies "liberalism," and write an essay explaining how you think that philosopher would respond to MacIntyre's criticisms.

Feminist Transformations of Moral Theory

Virginia Held

In this essay, Virginia Held discusses the history of ethics from the perspective of feminism. That history shows a distinctively male bias, she argues: its assumptions have reflected not human experience but men's experiences. In particular, Held criticizes the distinction often drawn between reason and emotion, the tendency to equate women with the emotions, the way that the public/private distinction has worked to privilege the male perspective, and the gender-biased view ethics presents of the person or self. Virginia Held is professor of philosophy at Hunter College and The Graduate School of the City University of New York.

The history of philosophy, including the history of ethics, has been constructed from male points of view, and has been built on assumptions and concepts that are by no means gender-neutral. Feminists characteristically begin with different concerns and give different emphases to the issues we consider than do nonfeminist approaches. And, as Lorraine Code expresses it, "starting points and focal points shape the impact of theoretical discussion."[1] Within philosophy, feminists often start with, and focus on, quite different issues than those found in standard philosophy and ethics, however "standard" is understood. Far from providing mere additional insights which can be incorporated into traditional theory, feminist explorations often require radical transformations of existing fields of inquiry and theory. From a feminist point of view, moral theory along with almost all theory will have to be transformed to take adequate account of the experience of women.

I shall in this paper [examine] how various fundamental aspects of the history of ethics have not been gender-neutral. And I shall discuss three issues where feminist rethinking is transforming moral concepts and theories.

Consider the ideals embodied in the phrase "the man of reason." As Genevieve Lloyd has told the story, what has been taken to characterize the man of reason may have changed from historical period to historical period, but in each, the character ideal of the man of reason has been constructed in conjunction with a rejection of whatever has been taken to be characteristic of the feminine. "Rationality," Lloyd writes, "has been conceived as transcendence of the 'feminine,' and the 'feminine' itself has been partly constituted by its occurrence within this structure."[2]

This has of course fundamentally affected the history of philosophy and of ethics. The split between reason and emotion is one of the most familiar of philosophical conceptions. And the advocacy of reason "controlling" unruly emotion, of rationality guiding responsible human action against the blindness of passion, has a long and highly influential history, almost as familiar to nonphilosophers as to philosophers. We should certainly now be alert to the ways in which reason has been associated with male endeavor, emotion with female weakness, and the ways in which this is of course not an accidental association. As Lloyd writes, "From the beginnings of philosophical thought, femaleness was symbolically associated with what Reason supposedly left behind—the dark powers of the earth goddesses, immersion in unknown forces associated with mysterious female powers. The early Greeks saw women's capacity to conceive as connecting them with the fertility of Nature. As Plato later expressed the thought, women 'imitate the earth.' "[3]

Reason, in asserting its claims and winning its status in human history, was thought to have to conquer the female forces of Unreason. Reason and clarity of thought were early associated with maleness, and as Lloyd notes, "what had to be shed in developing culturally prized rationality was, from the start, symbolically associated with femaleness."[4] In later Greek philosophical thought, the form/matter distinction was articulated, and with a similar hierarchical and gendered association. Maleness was aligned with active, determinate, and defining form; femaleness with mere passive, indeterminate, and inferior matter. Plato, in the *Timaeus,* compared the defining aspect of form with the father, and indefinite matter with the mother; Aristotle also compared the form/matter distinction with the male/female distinction. To quote Lloyd again, "This comparison . . . meant that the very nature of knowledge was implicitly associated with the extrusion of what was symbolically associated with the feminine."[5]

The associations between Reason, form, knowledge, and maleness, have persisted in various guises, and have permeated what has been thought to be moral knowledge as well

From *Philosophy and Phenomenological Research,* Fall 1990 (Supplement). Reprinted by permission.
This is the first part of a larger essay. Some footnotes omitted.

as what has been thought to be scientific knowledge, and what has been thought to be the practice of morality. The associations between the philosophical concepts and gender cannot be merely dropped, and the concepts retained regardless of gender, because gender has been built into them in such a way that without it, they will have to be different concepts. As feminists repeatedly show, if the concept of "human" were built on what we think about "woman" rather than what we think about "man," it would be a very different concept. Ethics, thus, has not been a search for universal, or truly human guidance, but a gender-biased enterprise.

Other distinctions and associations have supplemented and reinforced the identification of reason with maleness, and of the irrational with the female, on this and other grounds "man" has been associated with the human, "woman" with the natural. Prominent among distinctions reinforcing the latter view has been that between the public and the private, because of the way they have been interpreted. Again, these provide as familiar and entrenched a framework as do reason and emotion, and they have been as influential for nonphilosophers as for philosophers. It has been supposed that in the public realm, man transcends his animal nature and creates human history. As citizen, he creates government and law; as warrior, he protects society by his willingness to risk death; and as artist or philosopher, he overcomes his human mortality. Here, in the public realm, morality should guide human decision. In the household, in contrast, it has been supposed that women merely "reproduce" life as natural, biological matter. Within the household, the "natural" needs of man for food and shelter are served, and new instances of the biological creature that man is are brought into being. But what is distinctively human, and what transcends any given level of development to create human progress, are thought to occur elsewhere.

This contrast was made highly explicit in Aristotle's conceptions of polis and household; it has continued to affect the basic assumptions of a remarkably broad swath of thought ever since. In ancient Athens, women were confined to the household; the public sphere was literally a male domain. In more recent history, though women have been permitted to venture into public space, the associations of the public, historically male sphere with the distinctively human, and of the household, historically a female sphere, with the merely natural and repetitious, have persisted. These associations have deeply affected moral theory, which has often supposed the transcendent, public domain to be relevant to the foundations of morality in ways that the natural behavior of women in the household could not be. To take some recent and representative examples, David Heyd, in his discussion of supererogation, dismisses a mother's sacrifice for her child as an example of the supererogatory because it belongs, in his view, to "the sphere of natural relationships and instinctive feelings (which lie outside morality)"[6] J. O. Urmson had earlier taken a similar position. In his discussion of supererogation, Urmson said, "Let us be clear that we are not considering cases of natural affection, such as the sacrifice made by a mother for her child; such cases may be said with some justice not to fall under the concept of morality. . . ."[7] And in a recent article called "Distrusting Economics," Alan Ryan argues persuasively about the questionableness of economics and other branches of the social sciences built on the assumption that human beings are rational, self-interested calculators; he discusses various examples of non–self-interested behavior, such as of men in wartime, which show the assumption to be false, but nowhere in the article is there any mention of the activity of mothering, which would seem to be a fertile locus for doubts about the usual picture of rational man.[8] Although Ryan does not provide the kind of explicit reason offered by Heyd and Urmson for omitting the context of mothering from consideration as relevant to his discussion, it is difficult to understand the omission without a comparable assumption being implicit here, as it so often is elsewhere. Without feminist insistence on the relevance for morality of the experience in mothering, this context is largely ignored by moral theorists. And yet, from a gender-neutral point of view, how can this vast and fundamental domain of human experience possibly be imagined to lie "outside morality"?

The result of the public/private distinction, as usually formulated, has been to privilege the points of view of men in the public domains of state and law, and later in the marketplace, and to discount the experience of women. Mothering has been conceptualized as a primarily biological activity, even when performed by humans, and virtually no moral theory in the history of ethics has taken mothering, as experienced by women, seriously as a source of moral insight, until feminists in recent years have begun to. Women have been seen as emotional rather than as rational beings, and thus as incapable of full moral personhood. Women's behavior has been interpreted as either "natural" and driven by instinct, and thus as irrelevant to morality and to the construction of moral principles, or it has been interpreted as, at best, in need of instruction and supervision by males better able to know what morality requires and better able to live up to its demands.

The Hobbesian conception of reason is very different from the Platonic or Aristotelian conceptions before it, and from the conceptions of Rousseau or Kant or Hegel later; all have in common that they ignore and disparage the experience of reality of women. Consider Hobbes's account of man in the state of nature contracting with other men to establish society. These men hypothetically come into existence fully formed and independent of one another, and decide on entering or staying outside of civil society. As Christine Di Stefano writes, "What we find in Hobbes's account of human nature and political order is a vital concern with the survival of a self conceived in masculine terms. . . . This masculine dimension of Hobbes's atomistic egoism is powerfully underscored in his state of nature, which is effectively built on the foundation of denied maternity."[9] In *The Citizen,* where Hobbes gave his first systematic exposition of the state of nature, he asks us to "consider men as if but even now sprung out of the earth, and suddenly, like mushrooms, come to full maturity, without all kinds of engagement with each other."[10] As Di Stefano says, it is a most incredible and problematic feature of Hobbes's state of nature that the men in it "are not born of, much less nurtured by, women, or anyone else."[11] To abstract from the complex web of human reality an abstract man for rational perusal, Hobbes has, Di Stefano continues, "expunged human reproduction and early nurturance, two of the most basic and typically female-identified features of distinctively human life, from his account of basic human nature. Such a strategy ensures that he can present a thoroughly atomistic subject. . . ."[12] From the point of view of women's experience, such as subject or self is unbelievable and misleading, even as a theoretical construct. The Leviathan, Di Stefano writes, "is effectively comprised of a body politic of orphans who have reared themselves, whose desires are situated within and reflect nothing but independently generated movement. . . . These essential elements are natural human beings conceived along masculine lines."[13]

Rousseau, and Kant, and Hegel, paid homage to the emotional power, the aesthetic sensibility, and the familial concerns, respectively, of women. But since in their views morality must be based on rational principle, and women were incapable of full rationality, or a degree or kind of rationality comparable to that of men, women were deemed, in the view of these moralists, to be inherently wanting in morality. For Rousseau, women must be trained from childhood to submit to the will of men lest their sexual power lead both men and women to disaster. For Kant, women were thought incapable of achieving full moral personhood, and women lose all charm if they try to behave like men by engaging in rational pursuits. For Hegel, women's moral concern for their families could be admirable in its proper place, but is a threat to the more universal aims to which men, as members of the state, should aspire.

These images, of the feminine as what must be overcome if knowledge and morality are to be achieved, of female experience as naturally irrelevant to morality, and of women as inherently deficient moral creatures, are built into the history of ethics. Feminists examine these images, and see that they are not the incidental or merely idiosyncratic suppositions of a few philosophers whose views on many topics depart far from the ordinary anyway. Such views are the nearly uniform reflection in philosophical and ethical theory of patriarchal attitudes pervasive throughout human history. Or they are exaggerations even of ordinary male experience, which exaggerations then reinforce rather than temper other patriarchal conceptions and institutions. They distort the actual experience and aspirations of many men as well as of women. Annette Baier recently speculated about why it is that moral philosophy has so seriously overlooked the thrust between human beings that in her view is an utterly central aspect of moral life. She noted that "the great moral theorists in our tradition not only are all men, they are mostly men who had minimal adult dealings with (and so were then minimally influenced by) women."[14] They were for the most part "clerics, misogynists, and puritan bachelors," and thus it is not surprising that they focus their philosophical attention so single-mindedly on cool, distanced relations between more or less free and equal adult strangers. . . .[15] As feminists, we deplore the patriarchal attitudes that so much of philosophy and moral theory reflect. But we recognize that the problem is more serious even than changing those attitudes.

For moral theory as so far developed is incapable of correcting itself without an almost total transformation. It cannot simply absorb the gender that has been "left behind," even if both genders would want it to. To continue to build morality on rational principles opposed to the emotions and to include women among the rational will leave no one to reflect the promptings of the heart, which promptings can be moral rather than merely instinctive. To simply bring women into the public and male domain of the polis will leave no one to speak for the household. Its values have been hitherto unrecognized, but they are often moral values. Or to continue to seek contractual restraints on the pursuits of self-interest by atomistic individuals, and to have women join men in devotion to these pursuits, will leave no one involved in the nurturance of children and cultivation of social relations, which nurturance and cultivation can be of greatest moral import.

There are very good reasons for women not to want simply to be accorded entry as equals into the enterprise of morality as so far developed. In a recent survey of types of feminist moral theory, Kathryn Morgan notes that "many women who engage in philosophical reflection are acutely aware of the masculine nature of the profession and tradition, and feel their own moral concerns as women silenced or trivialized in virtually all the official settings that define the practice."[16] Women should clearly not agree, as the price of admission to the masculine realm of traditional morality, to abandon our own moral concerns as women. And so we are groping to shape new moral theory. Understandably, we do not yet have fully worked out feminist moral theories to offer. But we can suggest some directions our project of developing such theories is taking. As Kathryn Morgan points out, there is not likely to be a "star" feminist moral theorist on the order of a Rawls or Nozick: "There will be no individual singled out for two reasons. One reason is that vital moral and theoretical conversations are taking place on a large dialectical scale as the feminist community struggles to develop a feminist ethic. The second reason is that this community of feminist theoreticians is calling into question the very model of the individualized autonomous self presupposed by a star-centered male-dominated tradition. . . . We experience it as a common labour, a common task."[17]

The dialogues that are enabling feminist approaches to moral theory to develop are proceeding. As Alison Jaggar makes clear in her useful overview of them, there is no unitary view of ethics that can be identified as "feminist ethics." Feminist approaches to ethics share a commitment to "rethinking ethics with a view to correcting whatever forms of male bias it may contain."[18] While those who develop these approaches are "united by a shared project, they diverge widely in their views as to how this project is to be accomplished."[19]

Not all feminists, by any means, agree that there are distinctive feminist virtues or values. Some are especially skeptical of the attempt to give positive value to such traditional "feminine virtues" as a willingness to nurture, or an affinity with caring, or reluctance to seek independence. They see this approach as playing into the hands of those who would confine women to traditional roles. Other feminists are skeptical of all claims about women as such, emphasizing that women are divided by class and race and sexual orientation in ways that make any conclusion drawn from "women's experience" dubious. Still, it is possible, I think, to discern various important focal points evident in current feminist attempts to transform ethics into a theoretical and practical activity that could be acceptable from a feminist point of view. In the glimpse I have presented of bias in the history of ethics, I focused on what, from it feminist point of view, are three of its most questionable aspects: 1) the split between reason and emotion and the devaluation of emotion; 2) the public/private distinction and the relegation of the private to the natural; and 3) the concept of the self as constructed from a male point of view. . . .

NOTES

1. Lorraine Code, "Second Persons," in *Science, Morality and Feminist Theory,* ed. Marsha Hanen and Kai Nielsen (Calgary: University of Calgary Press, 1987), p. 360.
2. Genevieve Lloyd, *The Man of Reason: "Male" and "Female" in Western Philosophy* (Minneapolis: University of Minnesota Press, 1984), p. 104.
3. Ibid., p. 2.
4. Ibid., p. 3.
5. Ibid., p. 4.
6. David Heyd, *Supererogation: Its Status in Ethical Theory* (New York: Cambridge University Press, 1982), p. 134.
7. J.O. Urmson, "Saints and Heroes," in *Essays in Moral Philosophy,* ed. A. I. Melden (Seattle: University of Washington Press, 1958), p. 202. I am indebted to Marcia Baron for pointing out this and the previous example in her "Kantian ethics and Supererogation," *The Journal of Philosophy* 84 (May, 1987): 237–62.
8. Alan Ryan, "Distrusting Economics" *New York Review of Books* (May 18, 1989): 25–27. For a different treatment, see *Beyond Self-Interest,* ed. Jane Mansbridge (Chicago: University of Chicago Press, 1990).
9. Christine Di Stefano, "Masculinity as Ideology in Political Theory: Hobbesian Man Considered," *Women's Studies International Forum* (Special Issue: *Hypatia*), Vol. 6, No. 6 (1983): 633–44, p. 637.
10. Thomas Hobbes, *The Citizen: Philosophical Rudiments Concerning Government and Society,* ed. B. Gert (Garden City N.Y.: Doubleday, 1972 [1651]), p. 205.
11. Di Stefano, op. cit., p. 638.
12. Ibid.
13. Ibid., p. 639
14. Annette Baier, "Trust and Anti-Trust," *Ethics* 96 (1986): 231–60, pp. 247–48.
15. Ibid.
16. Kathryn Pauly Morgan, "Strangers in a Strange Land: Feminists Visit Relativists" in *Perspectives on Relativism,* ed. D. Odegaard and Carole Stewart (Toronto: Agathon Press, 1990).
17. Kathryn Morgan, "Women and Moral Madness," in *Science, Morality and Feminist Theory,* ed. Hanen and Nielsen, p. 223.
18. Alison M. Jaggar, "Feminist Ethics: Some Issues For The Nineties," *Journal of Social Philosophy,* 20 (Spring/Fall 1989), p. 91.
19. Ibid.

REVIEW AND DISCUSSION QUESTIONS

1. How does Held think the tendency in philosophy to distinguish reason from emotion has influenced the development of philosophical thought about ethics?
2. What is the "public/private" distinction, and why does Held think those who employ it privilege the male point of view?
3. In what way, according to Held, was Hobbes's view of human nature misleading from a female point of view? Was Kant any better? Explain.
4. Held thinks women have a different approach to philosophy than do men. Explain what she means. Do you agree?
5. Discuss critically the following claim: "Held unfairly criticizes traditional moral philosophy by attacking relatively unimportant, historically understandable features of the tradition without engaging the philosophical issues directly."

Essay and Paper Topics for Section 2

1. Discuss the utilitarian moral theory in light of O'Neill's or Ross's criticisms. In your essay, be sure to consider how the utilitarian philosopher might best respond to the criticisms and why you do or do not think that such a response is adequate.
2. Compare the essays written by MacIntyre and Held, paying special attention to similarities in their positions regarding patriotism and impartiality.
3. Is MacIntyre guilty of any of the charges Held makes against traditional philosophy, or does he successfully avoid them?

The Sources and Grounds of Morality

The essays in this section address a variety of related topics: the relationship between morality and religion, the grounding or justification of moral principles and judgments, the connections between morality and sentiments, and the possibility of criticizing another culture's moral practices. The first essay by John Arthur discusses arguments that morality is grounded in religion, thereby providing an objective basis for distinguishing right from wrong as well as giving people motives for doing what is right. Westermarck, however, argues that morality is at root based on feeling and social customs rather than either reason or religion, while David Hume famously defends the claim that morality is based on feelings and sentiments rather than reason and facts. Mary Midgley and William Shaw each consider moral relativism, while Thomas Nagel discusses the role of reflection and reason as well as feelings and desires. The final essay, by Joshua Cohen, discusses Martin Luther King Jr.'s suggestion that the universe is naturally hospitable to justice and right, and the related question of whether the "fact" of slavery's injustice contributed to its destruction.

Morality, Religion, and Conscience

John Arthur

What is morality? Does it depend in some way on religion, and if so how? This essay first describes, then assesses, three different ways in which it has sometimes been thought that morality requires religion as its basis. The article concludes with a brief discussion of John Dewey's suggestion that "morality is social" and what that might imply about moral reflection and about moral education. John Arthur is professor of philosophy and director of the Program in Philosophy, Politics, and Law at Binghamton University, State University of New York.

The question I discuss in this paper was famously captured by a character in Dostoyevsky's novel *The Brothers Karamazov:* "Without God" said Ivan, "everything is permitted." I want to argue that this is wrong: there is in fact no important sense in which morality depends on religion. Yet, I will also argue, there do remain important other respects in which the two *are* related. In the concluding section I extend the discussion of the origins of morality beyond religion by considering the nature of conscience, the ways morality is "social," and the implications of these ideas for moral education. First, however, I want to say something about the subjects: just what are we referring to when we speak of morality and of religion?

1. MORALITY AND RELIGION

A useful way to approach the first question— the nature of morality—is to ask what it would mean for a society to exist without a social moral code. How would such people think and behave? What would that society look like? First, it seems clear that such people would never feel guilt or resentment. For example, the notions that I ought to remember my parents' anniversary, that he has a moral responsibility to help care for his children after the divorce, that she has a right to equal pay for equal work, and that discrimination on the basis of race is unfair would be absent in such a society. Notions of duty, rights, and obligations would not be present, except perhaps in the legal sense; concepts of justice and fairness would also be foreign to these people. In short, people would have no tendency to evaluate or criticize the behavior of others, nor to feel remorse about their own behavior. Children would not be taught to be ashamed when they steal or hurt others, nor would they be allowed to complain when others treat them badly. (People might, however, feel regret at a decision that didn't turn out as they had hoped; but that would only be because their expectations were frustrated, not because they feel guilty.)

Such a society lacks a moral code. What, then, of religion? Is it possible that people lacking a morality would nonetheless have religious beliefs? It seems clear that it is possible. Suppose every day these same people file into their place of worship to pay homage to God (they may believe in many gods or in one all-powerful creator of heaven and earth). Often they can be heard praying to God for help in dealing with their problems and thanking Him for their good fortune. Frequently they give sacrifices to God, sometimes in the form of money spent to build beautiful temples and churches, other times by performing actions they believe God would approve such as helping those in need. These practices might also be institutionalized, in the sense that certain people are assigned important leadership roles. Specific texts might also be taken as authoritative, indicating the ways God has acted in history and His role in their lives or the lives of their ancestors.

To have a moral code, then, is to tend to evaluate (perhaps without even expressing it) the behavior of others and to feel guilt at certain actions when we perform them. Religion, on the other hand, involves beliefs in supernatural power(s) that created and perhaps also control nature, the tendency to worship and pray to those supernatural forces or beings, and the presence of organizational structures and authoritative texts. The practices of morality and religion are thus importantly different. One involves our attitudes toward various forms of behavior (lying and killing, for example), typically expressed using the notions of rules, rights, and obligations. The other, religion, typically involves prayer, worship, beliefs about the supernatural, institutional forms, and authoritative texts.

We come, then, to the central question: What is the connection, if any, between a society's moral code and its religious practices and beliefs? Many people have felt that morality is in some way dependent on religion or religious truths. But what sort of "dependence" might there be? In what follows I distinguish various ways in which one might claim that religion is necessary for morality, arguing against those who claim morality depends in some way on religion. I will also suggest, however, some other important ways in which the two are related, concluding with a brief discussion of conscience and moral education.

2. RELIGIOUS MOTIVATION AND GUIDANCE

One possible role which religion might play in morality relates to motives people have. Religion, it is often said, is necessary so that people will *do* right. Typically, the argument begins with the important point that doing what is right often has costs: refusing to shoplift or cheat can mean people go without some good or fail a test; returning a billfold means they don't get the contents. Religion is therefore said to be necessary in that it provides motivation to do the right thing. God rewards those who follow His commands by providing for them a place in heaven or by insuring that they prosper and are happy on earth. He also punishes those who violate the moral law. Others emphasize less self-interested ways in which religious motives may encourage people to act rightly. Since God is the creator of the universe and has ordained that His plan should be followed, they point out, it is important to live one's life in accord with this divinely ordained plan. Only by living a moral life, it is said, can people live in harmony with the larger, divinely created order.

The first claim, then, is that religion is necessary to provide moral motivation. The problem with that argument, however, is that religious motives are far from the only ones people have. For most of us, a decision to do the right thing (if that is our decision) is made for a variety of reasons: "What if I get caught? What if somebody sees me—what will he or she think? How will I feel afterwards? Will I regret it?" Or maybe the thought of cheating just doesn't arise. We were raised to be a decent person, and that's what we are—period. Behaving fairly and treating others

well is more important than whatever we might gain from stealing or cheating, let alone seriously harming another person. So it seems clear that many motives for doing the right thing have nothing whatsoever to do with religion. Most of us, in fact, do worry about getting caught, being blamed, and being looked down on by others. We also may do what is right just because it's right, or because we don't want to hurt others or embarrass family and friends. To say that we need religion to act morally is mistaken; indeed it seems to me that many of us, when it really gets down to it, don't give much of a thought to religion when making moral decisions. All those other reasons are the ones which we tend to consider, or else we just don't consider cheating and stealing at all. So far, then, there seems to be no reason to suppose that people can't be moral yet irreligious at the same time.

A second argument that is available for those who think religion is necessary to morality, however, focuses on moral guidance and knowledge rather than on people's motives. However much people may want to do the right thing, according to this view, we cannot ever know for certain what is right without the guidance of religious teaching. Human understanding is simply inadequate to this difficult and controversial task; morality involves immensely complex problems, and so we must consult religious revelation for help.

Again, however, this argument fails. First, consider how much we would need to know about religion and revelation in order for religion to provide moral guidance. Besides being sure that there is a God, we'd also have to think about which of the many religions is true. How can anybody be sure his or her religion is the right one? But even if we assume the Judeo-Christian God is the real one, we still need to find out just what it is He wants us to do, which means we must think about revelation.

Revelation comes in at least two forms, and not even all Christians agree on which is the best way to understand revelation. Some hold that revelation occurs when God tells us what he wants by providing us with His words:

The Ten Commandments are an example. Many even believe, as evangelist Billy Graham once said, that the entire Bible was written by God using thirty-nine secretaries. Others, however, doubt that the "word of God" refers literally to the words God has spoken, but believe instead that the Bible is an historical document, written by human beings, of the events or occasions in which God revealed Himself. It is an especially important document, of course, but nothing more than that. So on this second view revelation is not understood as *statements* made by God but rather as His *acts* such as leading His people from Egypt, testing Job, and sending His son as an example of the ideal life. The Bible is not itself revelation; it's the historical account of revelatory actions.

If we are to use revelation as a moral guide, then, we must first know what is to count as revelation—words given us by God, historical events, or both? But even supposing that we could somehow answer those questions, the problems of relying on revelation are still not over since we still must interpret that revelation. Some feel, for example, that the Bible justifies various forms of killing, including war and capital punishment, on the basis of such statements as "An eye for an eye." Others, emphasizing such sayings as "Judge not lest ye be judged" and "Thou shalt not kill," believe the Bible demands absolute pacifism. How are we to know which interpretation is correct? It is likely, of course, that the answer people give to such religious questions will be influenced in part at least by their own moral beliefs: if capital punishment is thought to be unjust, for example, then an interpreter will seek to read the Bible in a way that is consistent with that moral truth. That is not, however, a happy conclusion for those wishing to rest morality on revelation, for it means that their understanding of what God has revealed is itself dependent on their prior moral views. Rather than revelation serving as a guide for morality, morality is serving as a guide for how we interpret revelation.

So my general conclusion is that far from providing a short-cut to moral understanding, looking to revelation for guidance often creates more questions and problems. It seems wiser under the circumstances to address complex moral problems like abortion, capital punishment, and affirmative action directly, considering the pros and cons of each side, rather than to seek answers through the much more controversial and difficult route of revelation.

3. THE DIVINE COMMAND THEORY

It may seem, however, that we have still not really gotten to the heart of the matter. Even if religion is not necessary for moral motivation or guidance, it is often claimed, religion is necessary in another more fundamental sense. According to this view, religion is necessary for morality because without God there could be no right or wrong. God, in other words, provides the foundation or bedrock on which morality is grounded. This idea was expressed by Bishop R.C. Mortimer:

> God made us and all the world. Because of that He has an absolute claim on our obedience. . . . From [this] it follows that a thing is not right simply because we think it is. It is right because God commands it.[1]

What Bishop Mortimer has in mind can be seen by comparing moral rules with legal ones. Legal statutes, we know, are created by legislatures; if the state assembly of New York had not passed a law limiting the speed people can travel, then there would be no such legal obligation. Without the statutory enactments, such a law simply would not exist. Mortimer's view, *the divine command theory*, would mean that God has the same sort of relation to moral law as the legislature has to statutes it enacts: without God's commands there would be no moral rules, just as without a legislature there would be no statutes.

Defenders of the divine command theory often add to this a further claim, that only by assuming God sits at the foundation of morality can we explain the objective difference between right and wrong. This point was forcefully argued by F.C. Copleston in a 1948 British Broadcasting Corporation radio debate with Bertrand Russell.

Copleston: . . . The validity of such an interpretation of man's conduct depends on the recognition of God's existence, obviously. . . Let's take a look at the Commandant of the [Nazi] concentration camp at Belsen. That appears to you as undesirable and evil and to me too. To Adolph Hitler we suppose it appeared as something good and desirable. I suppose you'd have to admit that for Hitler it was good and for you it is evil.

Russell: No, I shouldn't go so far as that. I mean, I think people can make mistakes in that as they can in other things. If you have jaundice you see things yellow that are not yellow. You're making a mistake.

Copleston: Yes, one can make mistakes, but can you make a mistake if it's simply a question of reference to a feeling or emotion? Surely Hitler would be the only possible judge of what appealed to his emotions.

Russell: . . . You can say various things about that; among others, that if that sort of thing makes that sort of appeal to Hitler's emotions, then Hitler makes quite a different appeal to my emotions.

Copleston: Granted. But there's no objective criterion outside feeling then for condemning the conduct of the Commandant of Belsen, in your view. . . . The human being's idea of the content of the moral law depends certainly to a large extent on education and environment, and a man has to use his reason in assessing the validity of the actual moral ideas of his social group. But the possibility of criticizing the accepted moral code presupposes that there is an objective standard, that there is an ideal moral order, which imposes itself. . . . It implies the existence of a real foundation of God.[2]

Against those who, like Bertrand Russell, seek to ground morality in feelings and attitudes, Copleston argues that there must be a more solid foundation if we are to be able to claim truly that the Nazis were evil. God, according to Copleston, is able to provide the objective basis for the distinction, which we all know to exist, between right and wrong. Without divine commands at the root of human obligations, we would have no real reason for condemning the behavior of anybody, even Nazis. Morality, Copleston thinks, would then be nothing more than an expression of personal feeling.

To begin assessing the divine command theory, let's first consider this last point. Is it really true that only the commands of God can provide an objective basis for moral judgments? Certainly many philosophers have felt that morality rests on its own perfectly sound footing, be it reason, human nature, or natural sentiments. It seems wrong to conclude, automatically, that morality cannot rest on anything but religion. And it is also possible that morality doesn't have any foundation or basis at all, so that its claims should be ignored in favor of whatever serves our own self-interest.

In addition to these problems with Copleston's argument, the divine command theory faces other problems as well. First, we would need to say much more about the relationship between morality and divine commands. Certainly the expressions "is commanded by God" and "is morally required" do not *mean* the same thing. People and even whole societies can use moral concepts without understanding them to make any reference to God. And while it is true that God (or any other moral being for that matter) would tend to want others to do the right thing, this hardly shows that being right and being commanded by God are the same thing. Parents want their children to do the right thing, too, but that doesn't mean parents, or anybody else, can make a thing right just by commanding it!

I think that, in fact, theists should reject the divine command theory. One reason is what it implies. Suppose we were to grant (just for the sake of argument) that the divine command theory is correct, so that actions are right just because they are commanded by God. The same, of course, can be said about those deeds that we believe are wrong. If God hadn't commanded us not to do them, they would not be wrong.

But now notice this consequence of the divine command theory. Since God is all-powerful, and since right is determined solely by His commands, is it not possible that He might change the rules and make what we now think of as wrong into right? It would seem that according to the divine command theory the answer is "yes": it is theoretically possible that tomorrow God would decree that virtues such as kindness and courage have become vices while actions that show cruelty and cowardice will henceforth be the right actions. (Recall the analogy with a legislature and the power it has to change law.) So now rather than it being right for people to help each other out and prevent innocent people from suffering unnecessarily, it would be right (God having changed His mind) to create as much pain among innocent children as we possibly can! To adopt the divine command theory therefore commits its advocate to the seemingly absurd position that even the greatest atrocities might be not only acceptable but morally required if God were to command them.

Plato made a similar point in the dialogue *Euthyphro*. Socrates is asking Euthyphro what it is that makes the virtue of holiness a virtue, just as we have been asking what makes kindness and courage virtues. Euthyphro has suggested that holiness is just whatever all the gods love.

Socrates: Well, then, Euthyphro, what do we say about holiness? Is it not loved by all the gods, according to your definition?

Euthyphro: Yes.

Socrates: Because it is holy, or for some other reason?

Euthyphro: No, because it is holy.

Socrates: Then it is loved by the gods because it is holy: it is not holy because it is loved by them?

Euthyphro: It seems so.

Socrates: . . . Then holiness is not what is pleasing to the gods, and what is pleasing to the gods is not holy as you say, Euthyphro. They are different things.

Euthyphro: And why, Socrates?

Socrates: Because we are agreed that the gods love holiness because it is holy: and that it is not holy because they love it.[3]

This raises an interesting question: Why, having claimed at first that virtues are merely what is loved (or commanded) by the gods, would Euthyphro so quickly contradict this and agree that the gods love holiness *because* it's holy, rather than the reverse? One likely possibility is that Euthyphro believes that whenever the gods love something they do so with good reason, not without justification and arbitrarily. To deny this, and say that it is merely the gods' love that makes holiness a virtue, would mean that the gods have no basis for their attitudes, that they are arbitrary in what they love. Yet—and this is the crucial point—it's far from clear that a religious person would want to say that God is arbitrary in that way. If we say that it is simply God's loving something that makes it right, then what sense would it make to say God wants us to do right? All that could mean, it seems, is that God wants us to do what He wants us to do; He would have no reason for wanting it. Similarly "God is good" would mean little more than "God does what He pleases." The divine command theory therefore leads us to the results that God is morally arbitrary, and that His wishing us to do good or even God's being just mean nothing more than that God does what He does and wants whatever He wants. Religious people who reject that consequence would also, I am suggesting, have reason to reject the divine command theory itself, seeking a different understanding of morality.

This now raises another problem, however. If God approves kindness because it is a virtue and hates the Nazis because they were evil, then it seems that God discovers morality rather than inventing it. So haven't we then identified a limitation on God's power, since He now, being a good God, must love kindness and command us not to be cruel? Without the divine command theory, in other words, what is left of God's omnipotence?

But why, we may ask, is such a limitation on God unacceptable? It is not at all clear that God really can do anything at all. Can God, for example, destroy Himself? Or make a rock so heavy that He cannot lift it? Or create a universe which was never created by Him? Many have thought that God cannot do these things, but also that His inability to do them does not constitute a serious limitation on His power since these are things that cannot be done at all: to do them would violate the laws of logic. Christianity's most influential theologian, Thomas Aquinas, wrote in this regard that "whatever implies contradiction does not come within the scope of divine omnipotence, because it cannot have the aspect of possibility. Hence it is more appropriate to say that such things cannot be done than that God cannot do them."[4]

How, then, ought we to understand God's relationship to morality if we reject the divine command theory? Can religious people consistently maintain their faith in God the Creator and yet deny that what is right is right because He commands it? I think the answer to this is "yes." Making cruelty good is not like making a universe that wasn't made, of course. It's a moral limit on God rather than a logical one. But why suppose that God's limits are only logical?

One final point about this. Even if we agree that God loves justice or kindness because of their nature, not arbitrarily, there still remains a sense in which God could change morality even having rejected the divine command theory. That's because if we assume, plausibly I think, that morality depends in part on how we reason, what we desire and need, and the circumstances in which we find ourselves, then morality will still be under God's control since God could have constructed us or our environment very differently. Suppose, for instance, that he created us so that we couldn't be hurt by others or didn't care about freedom. Or perhaps our natural environment were created differently, so that all we have to do is ask and anything we want is given to us. If God had created either nature or us that way, then it seems

likely our morality might also be different in important ways from the one we now think correct. In that sense, then, morality depends on God whether or not one supports the divine command theory.

4. ON DEWEY'S THOUGHT THAT "MORALITY IS SOCIAL"

I have argued here that religion is not necessary in providing moral motivation or guidance, and against the divine command theory's claim that God is necessary for there to be morality at all. In this last section, I want first to look briefly at how religion and morality sometimes *do* influence each other. Then I will consider the development of moral conscience and the important ways in which morality might correctly be thought to be "social."

Nothing I have said so far means that morality and religion are independent of each other. But in what ways are they related, assuming I am correct in claiming morality does not *depend* on religion? First, of course, we should note the historical influence religions have had on the development of morality as well as on politics and law. Many of the important leaders of the abolitionist and civil rights movements were religious leaders, as are many current members of the pro-life movement. The relationship is not, however, one sided: morality has also influenced religion, as the current debate within the Catholic church over the role of women, abortion, and other social issues shows. In reality, then, it seems clear that the practices of morality and religion have historically each exerted an influence on the other.

But just as the two have shaped each other historically, so, too, do they interact at the personal level. I have already suggested how people's understanding of revelation, for instance, is often shaped by morality as they seek the best interpretations of revealed texts. Whether trying to understand a work of art, a legal statute, or a religious text, interpreters regularly seek to understand them in the best light—to make them as good as they can be, which requires that they bring moral judgment to the task of religious interpretation and understanding.

The relationship can go the other direction as well, however, as people's moral views are shaped by their religious training and beliefs. These relationships between morality and religion are often complex, hidden even from ourselves, but it does seem clear that our views on important moral issues, from sexual morality and war to welfare and capital punishment, are often influenced by our religious outlook. So not only are religious and moral practices and understandings historically linked, but for many religious people the relationship extends to the personal level—to their understanding of moral obligations as well as their sense of who they are and their vision of who they wish to be.

Morality, then, is influenced by religion (as is religion by morality), but morality's social character extends deeper even than that, I want to argue. First, of course, we possess a socially acquired language within which we think about our various choices and the alternatives we ought to follow, including whether a possible course of action is the right thing to do. Second, morality is social in that it governs relationships among people, defining our responsibilities to others and theirs to us. Morality provides the standards we rely on in gauging our interactions with family, lovers, friends, fellow citizens, and even strangers. Third, morality is social in the sense that we are, in fact, subject to criticism by others for our actions. We discuss with others what we should do, and often hear from them concerning whether our decisions were acceptable. Blame and praise are a central feature of morality.

While not disputing any of this, John Dewey has stressed another, less obvious aspect of morality's social character. Consider then the following comments regarding the origins of morality and conscience in an article he titled "Morality Is Social":

In language and imagination we rehearse the responses of others just as we dramatically enact other consequences. We foreknow how others will act, and the foreknowledge is the beginning of judgment passed on action. We know *with* them; there is conscience. An assembly is formed within our breast which discusses and appraises proposed and performed acts. The community without becomes a forum and tribunal within, a judgment-seat of charges, assessments and exculpations. Our thoughts of our own actions are saturated with the ideas that others entertain about them. . . . Explicit recognition of this fact is a prerequisite of improvement in moral education. . . . Reflection is morally indispensable.[5]

So Dewey's thought is that to consider matters from the moral point of view means we must think beyond ourselves, by which he means imagining how we as well as others might respond to various choices now being contemplated. To consider a decision from the *moral* perspective, says Dewey, requires that we envision an "assembly of others" that is "formed within our breast." That means, in turn, that morality and conscience cannot be sharply distinguished from our nature as social beings since conscience invariably brings with it, or constitutes, the perspective of the other. "Is this right?" and "What would this look like were I to have to defend it to others?" are not separable questions.[6]

It is important not to confuse Dewey's point here, however. He is *not* saying that what is right is finally to be determined by the reactions of actually existing other people, or even by the reaction of society as a whole. What is right or fair can never be finally decided by a vote, and indeed might not meet the approval of any specific others. But what then might Dewey mean in speaking of such an "assembly of others" as the basis of morality? The answer is that rather than actual people or groups, the assembly Dewey envisions is hypothetical or "ideal." The "community without" is thus transformed into a "forum and tribunal within, a judgment seat of charges, assessments and exculpations." So it is through the powers of our imagination that we can meet our moral responsibilities and exercise moral judgment, using these powers to determine what morality requires

68 John Arthur

by imagining the reaction of Dewey's "assembly of others."

Morality is therefore *inherently* social, in a variety of ways. It depends on socially learned language, is learned from interactions with others, and governs our interactions with others in society. But it also demands, as Dewey put it, that we know "with" others, envisioning for ourselves what their points of view would require along with our own. Conscience demands we occupy the positions of others.

Viewed in this light, God would play a role in a religious person's moral reflection and conscience since it is unlikely a religious person would wish to exclude God from the "forum and tribunal" that constitutes conscience. Rather, for the religious person conscience would almost certainly include the imagined reaction of God along with the reactions of others who might be affected by the action. Other people are also important, however, since it is often an open question just what God's reaction would be; revelation's meaning, as I have argued, is subject to interpretation. So it seems that for a religious person morality and God's will cannot be separated, though the connection between them is not the one envisioned by defenders of the divine command theory.

Which leads to my final point, about moral education. If Dewey is correct, then it seems clear there is an important sense in which morality not only can be taught but must be. Besides early moral training, moral thinking depends on our ability to imagine others' reactions and to imaginatively put ourselves into their shoes. "What would somebody (including, perhaps, God) think if this got out?" expresses more than a concern with being embarrassed or punished; it is also the voice of conscience and indeed of morality itself. But that would mean, thinking of education, that listening to others, reading about what others think and do, and reflecting within ourselves about our actions and whether we could defend them to others are part of the practice of morality itself. Morality cannot exist without the broader, social perspective introduced by others, and this social nature ties it, in that way, with education and with public discussion, both actual and imagined. "Private" moral reflection taking place independent of the social world would be no moral reflection at all. It follows that moral *education,* in the form of both studying others' moral ideas and subjecting our own to discussion and criticism, is not only possible, but essential.

NOTES

1. R.C. Mortimer, *Christian Ethics* (London: Hutchinson's University Library, 1950), pp. 7–8.
2. This debate was broadcast on the "Third Program" of the British Broadcasting Corporation in 1948.
3. Plato, *Euthyphro,* trans. H.N. Fowler (Cambridge, MA: Harvard University Press, 1947).
4. Thomas Aquinas, *Summa Theologica,* Part I, Q. 25, Art. 3.
5. John Dewey, "Morality Is Social" in *The Moral Writings of John Dewey,* rev. ed., ed. James Gouinlock (Amherst, N.Y.: Prometheus Books, 1994) pp. 182–84.
6. Obligations to animals raise an interesting problem for this conception of morality. Is it wrong to torture animals only because other *people* could be expected to disapprove? Or is it that the animal itself would disapprove? Or, perhaps, duties to animals rest on sympathy and compassion while human moral relations are more like Dewey describes, resting on morality's inherently social nature and on the dictates of conscience viewed as an assembly of others?

REVIEW AND DISCUSSION QUESTIONS

1. How does Arthur respond to those who argue that morality is necessary for moral motivation?

2. Arthur denies that morality is necessary for moral understanding or knowledge. Why does he think that?
3. How does the analogy with a legal system suggest that God may be necessary for there to be a right and wrong?
4. Why does Arthur reject the divine command theory?
5. In what ways are morality and religion connected, according to Arthur?
6. "Morality is social," said John Dewey. What did he mean by that?
7. What is the significance of Dewey's idea for moral education? What would Dewey probably have thought about a class in ethics?
8. In footnote 6, Arthur raises the problem of human's obligations to animals. How would you be inclined to answer the questions he asks there?

The Sources of Moral Ideas: Society, Custom, and Sympathy

Edward Westermarck

In this essay, Edward Westermarck begins by noting the importance of society and custom in teaching morality. Yet in many societies, it is also possible to take a critical stance toward traditional customs and practices, a stance that involves the intellect and reason. But despite this (limited) role of the intellect, Westermarck argues, it is the emotional constitution of people that shapes their sympathies and therefore their moral outlook. Reason therefore plays only a limited role in determining moral convictions.

Society is the school in which men learn to distinguish between right and wrong. The headmaster is Custom, and the lessons are the same for all. The first moral judgments were pronounced by public opinion; public indignation and public approval are the prototypes of the moral emotions. As regards questions of morality, there was, in early society, practically no difference of opinion; hence a character of universality, or objectivity, was from the very beginning attached to all moral judgments. And when, with advancing civilization, this unanimity was to some extent disturbed by individuals venturing to dissent from the opinions of the majority, the disagreement was largely due to facts which in no way affected the moral principle, but had reference only to its application.

Most people follow a very simple method in judging of an act. Particular modes of conduct have their traditional labels, many of which are learnt with language itself; and the moral judgment commonly consists simply in labelling the act according to certain obvious characteristics which it presents in common with others belonging to the same group. But a conscientious and intelligent judge proceeds in a different manner. He carefully examines all the details connected with the act, the external and internal conditions under which it was performed, its consequences, its motive; and, since the moral estimate in a large measure depends upon the regard paid to these circumstances, his judgment may differ greatly from that of the man in the street, even though the moral standard

From *The Origin and Development of the Moral Ideas* (1906).

which they apply be exactly the same. But to acquire a full insight into all the details which are apt to influence the moral value of an act is in many cases anything but easy, and this naturally increases the disagreement. There is thus in every advanced society a diversity of opinion regarding the moral value of certain modes of conduct which results from circumstances of a purely intellectual character—from the knowledge or ignorance of positive facts,—and involves no discord in principle.

Now it has been assumed by the advocates of various ethical theories that all the differences of moral ideas originate in this way, and that there is some ultimate standard which must be recognised as authoritative by everybody who understands it rightly. . . . [A]ll disagreement as to questions of morals is attributed to ignorance or misunderstanding.

The influence of intellectual considerations upon moral judgments is certainly immense. We shall find that the evolution of the moral consciousness to a large extent consists in its development from the unreflecting to the reflecting, from the unenlightened to the enlightened. All higher emotions are determined by cognitions, they arise from "the presentation of determinate objective conditions"; and moral enlightenment implies a true and comprehensive presentation of those objective conditions by which the moral emotions, according to their very nature, are determined. Morality may thus in a much higher degree than, for instance, beauty be a subject of instruction and of profitable discussion, in which persuasion is carried by the representation of existing data. But although in this way many differences may be accorded, there are points in which unanimity cannot be reached even by the most accurate presentation of facts or the subtlest process of reasoning.

Whilst certain phenomena will almost of necessity arouse similar moral emotions in every mind which perceives them clearly, there are others with which the case is different. The *emotional constitution of man* does not present the same uniformity as the human intellect. Certain cognitions inspire fear in nearly every breast; but there are brave men and cowards in the world, independently of the accuracy with which they realise impending danger. Some cases of suffering can hardly fail to awaken compassion in the most pitiless heart; but the sympathetic dispositions of men vary greatly, both in regard to the beings with whose sufferings they are ready to sympathise, and with reference to the intensity of the emotion. The same holds good for the moral emotions. The existing diversity of opinion as to the rights of different classes of men, and of the lower animals, which springs from emotional differences, may no doubt be modified by a clearer insight into certain facts, but no perfect agreement can be expected as long as the conditions under which the emotional dispositions are formed remain unchanged. Whilst an enlightened mind *must* recognise the complete or relative irresponsibility of an animal, a child, or a madman, and *must* be influenced in its moral judgment by the motives of an act—no intellectual enlightenment, no scrutiny of facts, can decide how far the interests of the lower animals should be regarded when conflicting with those of men, or how far a person is bound, or allowed, to promote the welfare of his nation, or his own welfare, at the cost of that of other nations or other individuals. Professor Sidgwick's well-known moral axiom, "I ought not to prefer my own lesser good to the greater good of another," would, if explained to a Fuegian or a Hottentot, be regarded by him, not as self-evident, but as simply absurd; nor can it claim general acceptance even among ourselves. Who is that "Another" to whose greater good I ought not prefer my own lesser good? A fellow-countryman, a savage, a criminal, a bird, a fish—all without distinction? It will, perhaps, be argued that on this, and on all other points of morals, there would be general agreement, if only the moral consciousness of men were sufficiently developed. But then, when speaking of a "sufficiently developed" moral consciousness (beyond insistence upon a full insight into the governing facts of each case), we practically mean nothing else than agreement with our own moral convictions. The expression is faulty and deceptive, because, if intended to mean anything more, it presupposes an objectivity of the moral judgments which they do not possess, and at the same time seems to be proving what it presupposes. We may speak of an intellect as sufficiently developed to grasp a certain truth, because truth is objective; but it is not proved to be objective by the fact that it is recognised as true by a "sufficiently developed" intellect. The objectivity of truth lies in the recognition of facts as true by all who understand them *fully*, whilst the appeal to a *sufficient* knowledge assumes their objectivity. To the verdict of a perfect intellect, that is, an intellect which knows everything existing, all would submit; but we can form no idea of a moral consciousness which could lay claim to a similar authority. . . .

The presumed objectivity of moral judgments thus being a chimera, there can be no moral truth in the sense in which this term is generally understood. The ultimate reason for this is, that the moral concepts are based upon emotions, and that the contents of an emotion fall entirely outside the category of truth.

REVIEW AND DISCUSSION QUESTIONS

1. What is the difference Westermarck sees between how people "commonly" think about moral issues and how a "conscientious and intelligent judge" approaches a moral question?
2. To what does Westermarck attribute moral disagreement, if not ignorance and misunderstanding?
3. Westermarck says that in general "higher emotions are determined by cognitions." Do you agree?
4. Is the answer Westermarck gives to question 3 consistent with his overall conclusion about the limited role of reason in morality?
5. Do you share Westermarck's conclusion that much of morality rests on people's emotional constitutions? What else might it rest on?

Morality Is Based on Sentiment

David Hume

David Hume (1711–1776) was a towering figure of the Scottish Enlightenment. He lived in Edinburgh, where he wrote on a wide array of subjects, including epistemology, history, religion, science, ethics, and politics. Hume attended Edinburgh University until he was about fifteen. By the age of twenty-eight, he had already published his massive, critical study of knowledge and morality titled *A Treatise of Human Nature*. Deeply disappointed by the book's reception, which, he wrote, "fell dead born from the press," Hume rewrote it as *An Enquiry Concerning Human Understanding* (1748) and *An Enquiry Concerning the Principles of Morals* (1751). He subsequently published *Political Discourses* (1752) and *History of England* (1754), which won him wide acclaim.

Hume was an amiable, moderate man whose company was widely sought. His philosophy, however, was radically critical. Taking his lead from modern science, especially Newton, Hume sought to use the tools of scientific observation and philosophical argument together to understand human knowledge, religion, morality, and politics. As an empiricist, Hume believed that things that can be present to the mind (which he termed "perceptions") are either impressions or ideas. Impressions occur whenever we feel an emotion or have an image of an external object; ideas are present whenever we reflect on impressions we have had. Ideas are therefore weaker than impressions, and all of our ideas are derived from sense impressions. Mathematics concerns itself merely with the relationships among our ideas.

Hume's key claim, then, is that reasoning can never motivate people, since it involves either the pure relations of ideas (mathematics) or the causes and effects of objects on other objects, including bodies. What does motivate us then must be our own feelings, which include our own pleasures and pains, of course, but also the sentiments we feel when thinking about the experiences of others. Values and morality are therefore sharply distinct from facts about the world or about mathematical ideas. Moral condemnation and approval arise from feelings alone, which are uniquely capable of motivating us to act. The selection concludes with a brief account of benevolence and its role in morality.

1. REASON SUBORDINATE TO EMOTION

Nothing is more usual in philosophy, and even in common life, than to talk of the combat of passion and reason, to give the preference to reason, and assert that men are only so far virtuous as they conform themselves to its dictates. Every rational creature, it is said, is obliged to regulate his actions by reason; and if any other motive or principle challenge the direction of his conduct, he ought to oppose it, till it be entirely subdued, or at least brought to a conformity with that superior principle. On this method of thinking the greatest part of moral philosophy, ancient and modern, seems to be founded. . . . I shall endeavor to prove *first,* that reason alone can never be a motive to any action of the will; and *secondly,* that it can never oppose passion in the direction of the will.

The understanding exerts itself after two different ways, as it judges from demonstration or probability; as it regards the abstract relations of our [mathematical] ideas, or those relations of objects, of which experience only gives us information. I believe it scarce will be asserted, and the first species of reasoning alone is ever the cause of any action. As its proper province is the world of ideas, and as the will always places us in that of realities, demonstration and volition seem, upon that account, to be totally removed from each other. Mathematics, indeed, are useful in all

mechanical operations, and arithmetic in almost every art and profession: but it is not of themselves they have any influence. Mechanics are the art of regulating the motions of bodies *to some designed end or purpose;* and the reason why we employ arithmetic in fixing the proportions of numbers, is only that we may discover the proportions of their influence and operation. A merchant is desirous of knowing the sum total of his accounts with any person: why? but that he may learn what sum will have the same *effects* in paying his debt, and going to market, as all the particular articles taken together. Abstract or demonstrative reasoning, therefore, never influences any of our actions, but only as it directs our judgment concerning causes and effects; which leads us to the second operation of the understanding.

It is obvious that when we have the prospect of pain or pleasure from any object, we feel a consequent emotion of aversion or propensity, and are carried to avoid or embrace what will give us this uneasiness or satisfaction. It is also obvious that this emotion rests not here, but making us cast our view on every side, comprehends whatever objects are connected with its original one by the relation of cause and effect. Here then reasoning takes place to discover this relation; and according as our reasoning varies, our actions receive a subsequent variation. But it is evident in this case, that the impulse arises not from reason,

From David Hume, *A Treatise of Human Nature* (1739–40) and *An Enquiry Concerning the Principles of Morals* (1751).

but is only directed by it. It is from the prospect of pain or pleasure that the aversion or propensity arises towards any object: and these emotions extend themselves to the causes and effects of that object, as they are pointed out to us by reason and experience. It can never in the least concern us to know that such objects are causes, and such others effects, if both the causes and effects be indifferent to us. Where the objects themselves do not affect us, their connection can never give them any influence; and it is plain, that as reason is nothing but the discovery of this connection, it cannot be by its means that the objects are able to affect us.

Since reason alone can never produce any action, or give rise to volition, I infer, that the same faculty is as incapable of preventing volition, or of disputing the preference with any passion or emotion. This consequence is necessary. . . .

A passion is an original existence, or, if you will, modification of existence, and contains not any representative quality, which renders it a copy of any other existence or modification. When I am angry, I am actually possessed with the passion, and in that emotion have no more a reference to any other object, than when I am thirsty, or sick, or more than five foot high. It is impossible, therefore, that this passion can be opposed by, or be contradictory to truth and reason; since this contradiction consists in the disagreement of ideas, considered as copies, with those objects, which they represent. . . .

It is certain, there are certain calm desires and tendencies, which, although they be real passions, produce little emotion in the mind, and are more known by their effects than by the immediate feeling or sensation. These desires are of two kinds; either certain instincts originally implanted in our natures, such as benevolence and resentment, the love of life, and kindness to children; or the general appetite to good, and aversion to evil, considered merely as such. When any of these passions are calm, and cause no disorder in the soul, they are very readily taken for the determinations for reason, and are supposed to proceed from the same faculty, with that,

which judges of truth and falsehood. Their nature and principles have been supposed the same, because their sensations are not evidently different.

Beside these calm passions, which often determine the will, there are certain violent emotions of the same kind, which have likewise a great influence on that faculty. When I receive any injury from another, I often feel a violent passion of resentment, which makes me desire his evil and punishment, independent of all considerations of pleasure and advantage to myself. When I am immediately threatened with any grievous ill, my fears, apprehensions, and aversions rise to a great height, and produce a sensible emotion.

The common error of metaphysicians has lain in ascribing the direction of the will entirely to one of these principles, and supposing the other to have no influence. Men often act knowingly against their interest: For which reason the view of the greatest possible good does not always influence them. Men often counteract a violent passion in prosecution of their interests and designs: It is not therefore the present uneasiness alone, which determines them. In general we may observe, that both these principles operate on the will; and where they are contrary, that either of them prevails, according to the *general* character or *present* disposition of the person. What we call strength of mind, implies the prevalence of the calm passions above the violent; although we may easily observe, there is no man so constantly possessed of this virtue, as never on any occasion to yield to the solicitations of passion and desire. . . .

According to this principle, which is so obvious and natural, it is only in two senses, that any affection can be called unreasonable. First, when a passion, such as hope or fear, grief or joy, despair or security, is founded on the supposition of the existence of objects, which really do not exist. Secondly, when in exerting any passion in action, we choose means insufficient for the designed end, and deceive ourselves in our judgment of causes and effects. Where a passion is neither founded on false suppositions, nor chooses means insufficient for the end, the understanding can neither justify nor condemn it. It is not contrary to reason to prefer the destruction of the whole world to the scratching of my finger. It is not contrary to reason for me to choose my total ruin to prevent the least uneasiness of an Indian or person wholly unknown to me. It is as little contrary to reason to prefer even my own acknowledged lesser good to my greater, and have a more ardent affection for the former than the latter. A trivial good may, from certain circumstances, produce a desire superior to what arises from the greatest and most valuable enjoyment; nor is there any thing more extraordinary in this, than in mechanics to see one pound weight raise up a hundred by the advantage of its situation. In short, a passion must be accompanied with some false judgment, in order to its being unreasonable; and even then it is not the passion, properly speaking, which is unreasonable, but the judgment.

The consequences are evident. Since a passion can never, in any sense, be called unreasonable, but when founded on a false supposition, or when it chooses means insufficient for the designed end, it is impossible, that reason and passion can ever oppose each other, or dispute for the government of the will and actions. The moment we perceive the falsehood of any supposition, or the insufficiency of any means, our passions yield to our reason without any opposition. I may desire any fruit as of an excellent relish; but whenever you convince me of my mistake, my longing ceases. I may will the performance of certain actions as means of obtaining any desired good; but as my willing of these actions is only secondary, and founded on the supposition, that they are causes of the proposed effect; as soon as I discover the falsehood of that supposition, they must become indifferent to me. . . .

2. MORAL DISTINCTIONS NOT DERIVED FROM REASON

It would be tedious to repeat all the arguments, by which I have proved, that reason is

perfectly inert, and can never either prevent or produce any action or affection. It will be easy to recollect what has been said upon that subject. I shall only recall on this occasion one of these arguments, which I shall endeavor to render still more conclusive, and more applicable to the present subject.

Reason is the discovery of truth or falsehood. Truth or falsehood consists in an agreement or disagreement either to the *real* relations of ideas, or to *real* existence and matter of fact. Whatever, therefore, is not susceptible of this agreement or disagreement, is incapable of being true or false, and can never be an object of our reason. Now it is evident our passions, volitions, and actions, are not susceptible of any such agreement or disagreement; being original facts and realities, complete in themselves, and implying no reference to other passions, volitions, and actions. It is impossible, therefore, they can be pronounced either true or false, and be either contrary or conformable to reason.

This argument is of double advantage to our present purpose. For it proves *directly,* that actions do not derive their merit from a conformity to reason, nor their blame from a contrariety to it; and it proves the same truth more *indirectly,* by showing us, that as reason can never immediately prevent or produce any action by contradicting or approving of it, it cannot be the source of moral good and evil, which are found to have that influence. Actions may be laudable or blameable; but they cannot be reasonable or unreasonable: laudable or blameable, therefore, are not the same with reasonable or unreasonable. The merit and demerit of actions frequently contradict, and sometimes control our natural propensities. But reason has no such influence. Moral distinctions, therefore, are not the offspring of reason. Reason is wholly inactive, and can never be the source of so active a principle as conscience, or a sense of morals. . . .

Take any action allowed to be vicious: wilful murder, for instance. Examine it in all lights, and see if you can find that matter of fact, or real existence, which you call *vice.* In whichever way you take it, you find only certain passions, motives, volitions and thoughts. There is no other matter of fact in the case. The vice entirely escapes you, as long as you consider the object. You never can find it, till you turn your reflection into your own breast, and find a sentiment of disapprobation, which arises in you, towards this action. Here is a matter of fact; but it is the object of feeling, not of reason. It lies in yourself, not in the object. So that when you pronounce any action or character to be vicious, you mean nothing, but that from the constitution of your nature you have a feeling or sentiment of blame from the contemplation of it. Vice and virtue, therefore, may be compared to sounds, colours, heat and cold, which, according to modern philosophy, are not qualities in objects, but perceptions in the mind: and this discovery in morals, like that other in physics, is to be regarded as a considerable advancement of the speculative sciences; though, like that too, it has little or no influence on practice. Nothing can be more real, or concern us more, than our own sentiments of pleasure and uneasiness; and if these be favourable to virtue, and unfavourable to vice, no more can be requisite to the regulation of our conduct and behaviour.

I cannot forbear adding to these reasonings an observation, which may, perhaps, be found of some importance. In every system of morality, which I have hitherto met with, I have always remarked, that the author proceeds for some time in the ordinary way of reasoning, and establishes the being of a God, or makes observations concerning human affairs; when of a sudden I am surprised to find, that instead of the usual copulations of propositions, *is,* and *is not,* I meet with no proposition that is not connected with an *ought,* or an *ought not.* This change is imperceptible; but is, however, of the last consequence. For as this *ought,* or *ought not,* expresses some new relation or affirmation, it is necessary that it should be observed and explained; and at the same time that a reason should be given, for what seems altogether inconceivable, how this new relation can be a

deduction from others, which are entirely different from it. But as authors do not commonly use this precaution, I shall presume to recommend it to the readers; and am persuaded, that this small attention would subvert all the vulgar systems of morality, and let us see, that the distinction of vice and virtue is not founded merely on the relations of objects, nor is perceived by reason.

3. WHY UTILITY PLEASES

. . . It has often been asserted, that, as every man has a strong connexion with society, and perceives the impossibility of his solitary subsistence, he becomes, on that account, favourable to all those habits or principles, which promote order in society, and insure to him the quiet possession of so inestimable a blessing. As much as we value our own happiness and welfare, as much must we applaud the practice of justice and humanity, by which alone the social confederacy can be maintained, and every man reap the fruits of mutual protection and assistance.

This deduction of morals from self-love, or a regard to private interest, is an obvious thought. . . . [Y]et is not this an affair to be decided by authority, and the voice of nature and experience seems plainly to oppose the selfish theory.

We frequently bestow praise on virtuous actions, performed in very distant ages and remote countries; where the utmost subtilty of imagination would not discover any appearance of self-interest, or find any connexion of our present happiness and security with events so widely separated from us.

A generous, a brave, a noble deed, performed by an adversary, commands our approbation; while in its consequences it may be acknowledged prejudicial to our particular interest. . . .

Usefulness is agreeable, and engages our approbation. This is a matter of fact, confirmed by daily observation. But, useful? For what? For somebody's interest, surely. Whose interest then? Not our own only: For our approbation frequently extends farther. It must, therefore, be the interest of those, who are served by the character of action approved of; and these we may conclude, however remote, are not totally indifferent to us. . . .

The human countenance, says Horace, borrows smiles or tears from the human countenance. Reduce a person to solitude, and he loses all enjoyment, except either of the sensual or speculative kind; and that because the movements of his heart are not forwarded by correspondent movements in his fellow-creatures. The signs of sorrow and mourning, though arbitrary, affect us with melancholy; but the natural symptoms, tears and cries and groans, never fail to infuse compassion and uneasiness. And if the effects of misery touch us in so lively a manner; can we be supposed altogether insensible or indifferent towards its causes; when a malicious or treacherous character and behaviour are presented to us? . . .

In general, it is certain, that, wherever we go, whatever we reflect on or converse about, everything still presents us with the view of human happiness or misery, and excites in our breast a sympathetic movement of pleasure or uneasiness. In our serious occupations, in our careless amusements, this principle still exerts its active energy. . . . We surely take into consideration the happiness and misery of others, in weighing the several motives of action, and incline to the former, where no private regards draw us to seek our own promotion or advantage by the injury of our fellow-creatures. And if the principles of humanity are capable, in many instances, of influencing our actions, they must, at all times, have *some* authority over our sentiments, and give us a general approbation of what is useful to society, and blame of what is dangerous or pernicious. The degrees of these sentiments may be the subject of controversy; but the reality of their existence, one should think, must be admitted in every theory or system. . . . Sympathy, we shall allow, is much fainter than our concern for ourselves, and sympathy with persons remote from us much fainter than that with persons near and contiguous; but for this very reason it is necessary for us, in

our calm judgments and discourse concerning the characters of men, to neglect all these differences, and render our sentiments more public and social. Besides, that we ourselves often change our situation in this particular, we every day meet with persons who are in a situation different from us, and who could never converse with us were we to remain constantly in that position and point of view, which is peculiar to ourselves. The intercourse of sentiments, therefore, in society and conversation, makes us form some general unalterable standard, by which we may approve or disapprove of characters and manners. . . .

It is sufficient for our present purpose, if it be allowed, what surely, without the greatest absurdity cannot be disputed, that there is some benevolence, however small, infused into our bosom; some spark of friendship for human kind; some particle of the dove kneaded into our frame, along with the elements of the wolf and serpent. Let these generous sentiments be supposed ever so weak; let them be insufficient to move even a hand or finger of our body, they must still direct the determinations of our mind, and where everything else is equal, produce a cool preference of what is useful and serviceable to mankind, above what is pernicious and dangerous. A *moral distinction,* therefore, immediately arises; a general sentiment of blame and approbation; a tendency, however faint, to the objects of the one, and a proportionable aversion to those of the other. . . .

Avarice, ambition, vanity, and all passions vulgarly, though improperly, comprised under the denomination of *self-love,* are here excluded from our theory concerning the origin of morals, not because they are too weak, but because they have not a proper direction for that purpose. The notion of morals implies some sentiment common to all mankind, which recommends the same object to general approbation, and makes every man, or most men, agree in the same opinion or decision concerning it. It also implies some sentiment, so universal and comprehensive as to extend to all mankind, and render the actions and conduct, even of the persons the most remote, an object of applause or censure, according as they agree or disagree with that rule of right which is established. . . .

When a man denominates another his *enemy,* his *rival,* his *antagonist,* his *adversary,* he is understood to speak the language of self-love, and to express sentiments, peculiar to himself, and arising from his particular circumstances and situation. But when he bestows on any man the epithets of *vicious* or *odious* or *depraved,* he then speaks another language and expresses sentiments, in which he expects all his audience to concur with him. He must here, therefore, depart from his private and particular situation, and must choose a point of view, common to him with others; he must move some universal principle of the human frame, and touch a string to which all mankind have an accord and symphony. If he mean, therefore, to express that this man possesses qualities, whose tendency is pernicious to society, he has chosen this common point of view, and has touched the principle of humanity, in which every man, in some degree, concurs. While the human heart is compounded of the same elements as at present, it will never be wholly indifferent to public good, nor entirely unaffected with the tendency of characters and manners. And though this affection of humanity may not generally be esteemed so strong as vanity or ambition, yet, being common to all men, it can alone be the foundation of morals, or of any general system of blame or praise.

REVIEW AND DISCUSSION QUESTIONS

1. Hume says it is common to think of reason and passion or sentiments in conflict. Why does he think passion cannot conflict with abstract relations of ideas?
2. Why does Hume think that the impulse to avoid a pain arises not from reason but from passion?
3. In what sense does Hume mean a passion can never be called "unreasonable"?
4. What is the difference between "calm desires and tendencies" and "violent" ones?
5. If neither moral judgment nor actions come from reason, where do they come from?
6. Explain what Hume means in saying that one can never derive an "ought" from an "is."
7. In what sense does Hume think morality rests not on self-love but on benevolence?

Trying Out One's New Sword

Mary Midgley

Moral isolationism, according to Mary Midgley, is the familiar position that respect and tolerance demand that members of one culture not criticize other cultures. Rejecting that position, she argues that it is little more than an internally inconsistent version of "immoralism." Nor, she claims, does it accurately describe the ways in which cultures are formed and changed. Using an ancient Samurai custom as an example, she suggests various ways in which cultures can, in fact, be criticized. Mary Midgley taught philosophy at the University of Newcastle-upon-Tyne for twenty years; now retired, she spends much of her time writing.

All of us are, more or less, in trouble today about trying to understand cultures strange to us. We hear constantly of alien customs. We see changes in our lifetime which would have astonished our parents. I want to discuss here one very short way of dealing with this difficulty, a drastic way which many people now theoretically favor. It consists in simply denying that we can ever understand any culture except our own well enough to make judgments about it. Those who recommend this hold that the world is sharply divided into separate societies, sealed units, each with its own system of thought. They feel that the respect and tolerance due from one system to another forbids us ever to take up a critical position to any other culture. Moral judgment, they suggest, is a kind of coinage valid only in its country of origin.

I shall call this position "moral isolationism." I shall suggest that it is certainly not forced upon us, and indeed that it makes no sense at all. People usually take it up because they think it is a respectful attitude to other cultures. In fact, however, it is not respectful. Nobody can respect what is entirely unintelligible to them. To respect someone, we have to know enough about him to make a *favorable* judgment, however general and tentative. And we do understand people in other cultures to this extent. Otherwise a great mass of our most valuable thinking would be paralysed.

To show this, I shall take a remote example, because we shall probably find it easier to think calmly about it than we should with a contemporary one, such as female circumcision in Africa or the Chinese Cultural Revolution. The principles involved will still be the same. My example is this. There is, it seems, a verb in classical Japanese which means "to try out one's new sword on a chance wayfarer." (The word is *tsujigiri*, literally "crossroads-cut.") A samurai sword had to be tried out because, if it was to work properly, it had to slice through someone at a single blow, from the shoulder to the opposite flank. Otherwise, the warrior bungled his stroke. This could injure his honour, offend his ancestors, and even let down his emperor.

So tests were needed, and wayfarers had to be expended. Any wayfarer would do—provided, of course, that he was not another Samurai. Scientists will recognize a familiar problem about the rights of experimental subjects.

Now when we hear of a custom like this, we may well reflect that we simply do not understand it; and therefore are not qualified to criticize it at all, because we are not members of that culture. But we are not members of any other culture either, except our own. So we extend the principle to cover all extraneous cultures, and we seem therefore to be moral isolationists. But this is, as we shall see, an impossible position. Let us ask what it would involve.

We must ask first: Does the isolating barrier work both ways? Are people in other cultures equally unable to criticize us? This question struck me sharply when I read a remark in *The Guardian* by an anthropologist about a South American Indian who had been taken into a Brazilian town for an operation, which saved his life. When he came back to his village, he made several highly critical remarks about the white Brazilians' way of life. They may very well have been justified. But the interesting point was that the anthropologist called these remarks "a damning indictment of Western civilization." Now the Indian had been in that town about two weeks. Was he in a position to deliver a damning indictment? Would we ourselves be qualified to deliver such an indictment on the Samurai, provided we could spend two weeks in ancient Japan? What do we really think about this?

My own impression is that we believe that outsiders can, in principle, deliver perfectly good indictments—only, it usually takes more than two weeks to make them damning. Understanding has degrees. It is not a slapdash yes-or-no matter. Intelligent outsiders can progress in it, and in some ways will be at an advantage over the locals. But if this is so, it must clearly apply to ourselves as much as anybody else.

Our next question is this: Does the isolating barrier between cultures block praise as well as blame? If I want to say that the Samurai culture has many virtues, or to praise the South American Indians, am I prevented from doing *that* by my outside status? Now, we certainly do need to praise other societies in this way. But it is hardly possible that we could praise them effectively if we could not, in principle, criticize them. Our praise would be worthless if it rested on definite grounds, if it did not flow from some understanding. Certainly we may need to praise things which we do not *fully* understand. We say "there's something very good here, but I can't quite make out what it is yet." This happens when we want to learn from strangers. And we can learn from strangers. But to do this we have to distinguish between those strangers who are worth learning from and those who are not. Can we then judge which is which?

This brings us to our third question: What is involved in judging? Now plainly there is no question here of sitting on a bench in a red robe and sentencing people. Judging simply means forming an opinion, and expressing it if it is called for. Is there anything wrong about this? Naturally, we ought to avoid forming—and expressing—*crude* opinions, like that of a simple-minded missionary, who might dismiss the whole Samurai culture as entirely bad, because non-Christian. But this is a different objection. The trouble with crude opinions is that they are crude, whoever forms them, not that they are formed by the wrong people. Anthropologists, after all, are outsiders quite as much as missionaries. Moral isolationism forbids us to form *any* opinions on these matters. Its ground for doing so is that we don't understand them. But there is much that we don't understand in our own culture too. This brings us to our last question: If we can't judge other cultures, can we really judge our own? Our efforts to do so will be much damaged if we are really deprived of our opinions about other societies, because these provide the range of comparison, the spectrum of alternatives against which we set what we want to understand. We would have to stop using the mirror which anthropology so helpfully holds up to us.

In short, moral isolationism would lay down a general ban on moral reasoning. Essentially, this is the programme of immoralism, and it carries a distressing logical difficulty. Immoralists like Nietzsche are actually just a rather specialized sect of moralists. They can no more afford to put moralizing out of business than smugglers can afford to abolish customs regulations. The power of moral judgment is, in fact, not a luxury, not a perverse indulgence of the self-righteous. It is a necessity. When we judge something to be bad or good, better or worse than something else, we are taking it as an example to aim at or avoid. Without opinions of this sort, we would have no framework of comparison for our own policy, no chance of profiting by other people's insights or mistakes. In this vacuum, we could form no judgments on our own actions.

Now it would be odd if *Homo sapiens* had really got himself into a position as bad as this—a position where his main evolutionary asset, his brain, was so little use to him. None of us is going to accept this skeptical diagnosis. We cannot do so, because our involvement in moral isolationism does not flow from apathy, but from a rather acute concern about human hypocrisy and other forms of wickedness. But we polarize that concern around a few selected moral truths. We are rightly angry with those who despise, oppress or steamroll other cultures. We think that doing these things is actually *wrong*. But this is itself a moral judgment. We could not condemn oppression and insolence if we thought that all our condemnations were just a trivial local quirk of our own culture. We could still less do it if we tried to stop judging altogether.

Real moral skepticism, in fact, could lead only to inaction, to our losing all interest in moral questions, most of all in those which concern other societies. When we discuss these things, it becomes instantly clear how far we are from doing this. Suppose, for instance, that I criticize the bisecting Samurai, that I say his behavior is brutal. What will usually happen next is that someone will protest, will say that I have no right to make criticisms like that of another culture. But it is most unlikely that he will use this move to end the discussion of the subject. Instead, he will justify the Samurai. He will try to fill in the background, to make me understand the custom, by explaining the exalted ideals of discipline and devotion which produced it. He will probably talk of the lower value which the ancient Japanese placed on individual life generally. He may well suggest that this is a healthier attitude than our own obsession with security. He may add, too, that the wayfarers did not seriously mind being bisected, that in principle they accepted the whole arrangement.

Now an objector who talks like this is implying that it *is* possible to understand alien customs. That is just what he is trying to make me do. And he implies, too, that if I do succeed in understanding them, I shall do something better than giving up judging them. He expects me to change my present judgment to a truer one—namely, one that is favourable. And the standards I must use to do this cannot just be Samurai standards. They have to be ones current in my own culture. Ideals like discipline and devotion will not move anybody unless he himself accepts them. As it happens, neither discipline nor devotion is very popular in the West at present. Anyone who appeals to them may well have to do some more arguing to make *them* acceptable, before he can use them to explain the Samurai. But if he does succeed here, he will have persuaded us, not just that there was something to be said for them in ancient Japan, but that there would be here as well.

Isolating barriers simply cannot arise here. If we accept something as a serious moral truth about one culture, we can't refuse to apply it—in however different an outward form—to other cultures as well, wherever circumstances admit it. If we refuse to do this, we just are not taking the other culture seriously. This becomes clear if we look at the last argument used by my objector—that of justification by consent of the victim. It is suggested that sudden bisection is quite in order, *provided* that it takes place between consenting adults. I cannot now discuss how

conclusive this justification is. What I am pointing out is simply that it can only work if we believe that *consent* can make such a transaction respectable—and this is a thoroughly modern and Western idea. It would probably never occur to a Samurai; if it did, it would surprise him very much. It is *our* standard. In applying it, too, we are likely to make another typically Western demand. We shall ask for good factual evidence that the wayfarers actually do have this rather surprising taste—that they are really willing to be bisected. In applying Western standards in this way, we are not being confused or irrelevant. We are asking the questions which arise *from where we stand,* questions which we can see the sense of. We do this because asking questions which you can't see the sense of is humbug. Certainly we can extend our questioning by imaginative effort. We can come to understand other societies better. By doing so, we may make their questions our own, or we may see that they are really forms of the questions which we are asking already. This is not impossible. It is just very hard work. The obstacles which often prevent it are simply those of ordinary ignorance, laziness and prejudice.

If there were really an isolating barrier, of course, our own culture could never have been formed. It is no sealed box, but a fertile jungle of different influences—Greek, Jewish, Roman, Norse, Celtic and so forth, into which further influences are still pouring—American, Indian, Japanese, Jamaican, you name it. The moral isolationist's picture of separate, unmixable cultures is quite unreal. People who talk about British history usually stress the value of this fertilizing mix, no doubt rightly. But this is not just an odd fact about Britain. Except for the very smallest and most remote, all cultures are formed out of many streams. All have the problem of digesting and assimilating things which, at the start, they do not understand. All have the choice of learning something from this challenge, or, alternatively, of refusing to learn, and fighting it mindlessly instead.

This universal predicament has been obscured by the fact that anthropologists used to concentrate largely on very small and remote cultures, which did not seem to have this problem. These tiny societies, which had often forgotten their own history, made neat, self-contained subjects for study. No doubt it was valuable to emphasize their remoteness, their extreme strangeness, their independence of our cultural tradition. This emphasis was, I think, the root of moral isolationism. But, as the tribal studies themselves showed, even there the anthropologists were able to interpret what they saw and make judgments—

often favourable—about the tribesmen. And the tribesmen, too, were quite equal to making judgments about the anthropologists—and about the tourists and Coca-Cola salesmen who followed them. Both sets of judgments, no doubt, were somewhat hasty, both have been refined in the light of further experience. A similar transaction between us and the Samurai might take even longer. But that is no reason at all for deeming it impossible. Morally as well as physically, there is only one world, and we all have to live in it.

REVIEW AND DISCUSSION QUESTIONS

1. What is moral isolationism?
2. Why does Midgley reject moral isolationism?
3. Explain what Midgley means in saying there is "only one world." Do you agree with her? Explain.
4. How might Westermarck respond to this essay? Would he defend the practice of trying out a new sword?
5 "Moral views cannot be proven true or false, therefore whatever you think is right is right for you." Describe carefully what somebody might mean by each part of that statement. In what sense, if any, do you agree with it? In what sense(s) do you disagree?

Relativism in Ethics

William H. Shaw

People sometimes describe themselves as "relativists" when it comes to morality, by which is meant either that there is no standard of right and wrong beyond what the individual may think, or no standard exists except what the cultural conventions and rules into which one is born require. In this essay, William H. Shaw discusses these claims, arguing that ethical relativism of either variety is unjustified. William H. Shaw teaches philosophy at San Jose State University.

The peoples and societies of the world are diverse; their institutions, fashions, ideas, manners, and mores vary tremendously. This is a simple truth. Sometimes an awareness of this diversity and of the degree to which our own beliefs and habits mirror those of the culture around us stimulates self-examination. In the realm of ethics, familiarity with strikingly different cultures has led many people to suppose that morality itself is relative to particular societies, that right and wrong vary from culture to culture.

This view is generally called "ethical relativism"; it is the normative theory that what is right is what the culture says is right. What is right in one place may be wrong in another, because the only criterion for distinguishing right from wrong—the only ethical standard for judging an action—is the moral system of the society in which the act occurs. Abortion, for example, is condemned as immoral in Catholic Spain, but practiced as a morally neutral form of birth control in Japan. According to the ethical relativist, then, abortion is wrong in Spain but morally permissible in Japan. The relativist is not saying merely that the Spanish believe abortion is abominable and the Japanese do not; that is acknowledged by everyone. Rather, the ethical relativist contends that abortion is immoral in Spain because the Spanish believe it to be immoral and morally permissible in Japan because the Japanese believe it to be so. There is no absolute ethical standard, independent of cultural context, no criterion of right and wrong by which to judge other than that of particular societies. In short, morality is relative to society.

A different sort of relativist might hold that morality is relative, not to the culture, but to the individual. The theory that what is right and wrong is determined by what a person thinks is right and wrong, however, is not very plausible. The main reason is that it collapses the distinction between thinking something is right and its actually being right. We have all done things we thought were right at the time, but later decided were wrong. Our normal view is that we were mistaken in our original thinking; we believed the action to have been right, but it was not. In the relativist view under consideration, one would have to say that the action in question was originally right, but later wrong as our thinking changed—surely a confused and confusing thing to say! Furthermore, if we accept this view, there would be no point in debating ethics with anyone, for whatever he thought right would automatically be right for him, and whatever we thought right would be right for us. Indeed, if right were determined solely by what we took to be right, then it would not be at all clear what we are doing when we try

to decide whether something is right or wrong in the first place—since we could never be mistaken! Certainly this is a muddled doctrine. Most likely its proponents have meant to emphasize that each person must determine for himself as best he can what actually is right or to argue that we ought not to blame people for acting according to their sincere moral judgments. These points are plausible, and with some qualifications, perhaps everyone would accept them, but they are not relativistic in the least.

The theory that morality is relative to society, however, is more plausible, and those who endorse this type of ethical relativism point to the diverseness of human values and the multiformity of moral codes to support their case. From our own cultural perspective, some seemingly "immoral" moralities have been adopted: polygamy, homosexuality, stealing, slavery, infanticide, and the eating of strangers have all been tolerated or even encouraged by the moral system of one society or another. In light of this, the ethical relativist feels that there can be no nonethnocentric standard by which to judge actions. We feel the individuals in some remote tribe are wrong to practice infanticide, while other cultures are scandalized that we eat animals. Different societies have different rules; what moral authority other than society, asks the relativist, can there be? Morality is just like fashion in clothes, beauty in persons, and legality in action—all of which are relative to, and determined by, the standards of a particular culture.

In some cases this seems to make sense. Imagine that Betty is raised in a society in which one is thought to have a special obligation to look after one's maternal aunts and uncles in their old age, and Sarah lives in a society in which no such obligation is supposed. Certainly we are inclined to say that Betty really does have an obligation that Sarah does not. Sarah's culture, on the other hand, may hold that if someone keeps a certain kind of promise to you, you owe him or her a favor, or that children are not required to tell the truth to adults. Again, it seems plausible that different sorts of obligations arise in Sarah's society; in her society, promisees really do owe their promisors and children are not wrong to lie, whereas this might not be so in other cultures.

Ethical relativism explains these cases by saying that right and wrong are determined solely by the standards of the society in question, but there are other, nonrelativistic ways of accounting for these examples. In Betty's society, people live with the expectation that their sister's offspring will look after them; for Betty to behave contrary to this institution and to thwart these expectations may produce bad consequences—so there is a reason to think she has this obligation other than the fact that her society thinks she has it. In Sarah's world, on the other hand, no adult expects children to tell the truth; far from deceiving people, children only amuse them with their tall tales. Thus, we are not required to be ethical relativists in order to explain why moral obligations may differ according to the social context. And there are other cases in which ethical relativism seems implausible. Suppose Betty's society thinks that it is wicked to engage in intercourse on Sundays. We do not believe it wrong of her to do so just because her society thinks such conduct is impermissible. Or suppose her culture thinks that it is morally reprehensible to wear the fur of rare animals. Here we may be inclined to concur, but if we think it is wrong of her to do this, we do not think it so because her society says so. In this example and the previous one, we look for some reason why her conduct should be considered immoral. The fact that her society thinks it so is not enough.

Ethical relativism undermines any moral criticism of the practices of other societies as long as their actions conform to their own standards. We cannot say that slavery in a slave society like that of the American South of the [nineteenth] century was immoral and unjust as long as that society held it to be morally permissible. Slavery was right for them, although it is wrong for us today. To condemn slave owners as immoral, says the relativist, is to attempt to extend the standards of our society illegitimately to another culture. But this is not the way we usually think. Not only do we wish to say that a society is mistaken if it thinks that slavery (or cannibalism, cruelty, racial bigotry) is morally permissible, but we also think we have justification for so saying and are not simply projecting ethnocentrically the standards of our own culture. Indeed, far from mirroring those standards in all our moral judgments, we sometimes criticize certain principles or practices accepted by our own society. None of this makes sense from the relativist's point of view. People can be censured for not living up to their society's moral code, but that is all; the moral code itself cannot be criticized. Whatever a society takes to be morally right really is right for it. Reformers who campaign against the "injustices" of their society are only encouraging people to be immoral—that is, to depart from the moral standards of their society—unless or until the majority of society agrees with the reformers. The minority can never be right in moral matters; to be right it must become the majority.

This raises some puzzles for the theory of ethical relativism. What proportion of a society must believe, say, that abortion is permissible for it to be morally acceptable in that society—90 percent? 75 percent? 51 percent? If the figure is set high (say 75 percent) and only 60 percent of the society condone abortion, then it would not be permissible; yet it would seem odd for the relativist to say that abortion was therefore wrong, given that a majority of the population believes otherwise. Without a sufficient majority either way, abortion would be neither morally permissible nor impermissible. On the other hand, if the figure is set lower, then there will be frequent moral flip-flops. Imagine that last year abortion was thought wrong by 51 percent of the populace, but this year only 49 percent are of that opinion; that means, according to the relativist, that it was wrong last year, but is now morally permissible—and things may change again. Surely, though, something is wrong with majority rule in matters of morality. In addition one might wonder what is to count, for the relativist, as a society. In a large and heterogeneous nation like the United States, are right and wrong determined by the whole country; or do smaller societies like Harlem, San Francisco, rural Iowa, or the Chicano community in Los Angeles set their own moral standards? But if these are cohesive enough to count as morality generating societies, what about such "societies" as outlaw bikers, the drug culture, or the underworld? And what, then, does the relativist say about conflicts between these group moralities or between them and the morality of the overall society? Since an individual may be in several overlapping "societies" at the same time, he may well be receiving conflicting moral instructions—all of which, it would seem, are correct according to the relativist.

These are all questions the relativist must answer if he is to make his theory coherent. To raise them is not to refute relativism, of course, since the relativist may be able to explain satisfactorily what he means by society," how its standards relate to those of other groups, and what is to count as moral approval by a given society. However the relativist attempts to refine his theory, he will still be maintaining that what is right is determined by what the particular society, culture, or group takes to be right and that this is the only standard by which an individual's actions can be judged. Not only does the relativist neglect to give us a reason for believing that a society's own views about morality are conclusive as to what is actually right and wrong, but also his theory does not square with our understanding of morality and the nature of ethical discourse. By contending that the moralities of different societies are all equally valid, the relativist holds that there can be no nonethnocentric ground for preferring one moral code to another, that one cannot speak of moral progress. Moralities may change, but they do not get better or worse. If words mean anything, however, it seems clear that a society that applauded the random torture of children would be immoral, even if it thought such a practice were right. It would simply be mistaken, and disastrously so. Since this is the

case, ethical relativism must be false as a theory of normative ethics. . . .

Reason-giving is essential to the nature of morality, at least as we understand it. Suppose that Smith and Jones both think that incest is immoral. Smith, when challenged, argues that it is unnatural, harmful to the family unit, and psychologically destructive to the individuals involved. Each of these reasons can be pursued in greater detail: For example, what is "unnatural," and is the unnatural always immoral? And we can raise other relevant issues with Smith about, say, consent, age, or individual rights. Jones, on the other hand, offers no reasons and does not assent to those Smith gives. When pressed, Jones merely says, "I don't need to give a reason; incest is simply wrong." At this point, one may doubt that Jones is making a moral judgment. He may well be troubled by the thought of incest; it may agitate him; he may be adamant in condemning it. But if he resists offering a justification for his opinion, we shall very likely refuse to recognize it as a moral position at all. Instead, we would suspect that he is only expressing a personal quirk or emotional reaction. The point I am making about our practice of morality—namely, that reason-giving and argumentation are essential to it—is attested to by the fact that prejudice frequently dresses itself in the language of reason. We recognize that the racist is only rationalizing his visceral bias when he attempts to justify segregation with spurious theories of racial differences, but his effort to so justify his prejudice at least acknowledges the fact that one must have reasons to back one's views if they are to count as a moral position in the first place—let alone be taken seriously. . . .

Not only are reasoning and argumentation basic to our practice of morality, but only certain sorts of reasons are countenanced by it. If Jones were to offer, as a justification of his judgment that incest is immoral, the reason that the idea is too gross for him to contemplate, or if a racist were to try to justify segregation by pointing to the skin color of the group he disdains, their "arguments" would simply be ruled out of bounds. By contrast, appeals to other sorts of considerations—for example, the rights of the persons involved, fairness, or the happiness produced—are perfectly appropriate and often suffice to establish at least the *prima facie* rightness or wrongness of the action. In other words, within moral discourse there are certain standard moves and relevant considerations—acknowledged by the vast majority of those who engage in it—just as there is an accepted framework of legal principles, policies, rules, and precedents on which a lawyer can and must draw in making his case. . . .

REVIEW AND DISCUSSION QUESTIONS

1. Why does Shaw reject the claim that morality is relative to the individual?
2. Why does he think it is more plausible to think morality is relative to society than to the individual?
3. Explain the major problems Shaw identifies with ethical relativism.
4. What is the role of reason-giving in morality, according to Shaw?
5. Does Shaw necessarily disagree with Hume, who claims that morality is based on sentiment and feeling? Or with Ross, who emphasized intuitions as the basis of morality? What do you think Shaw would say to each of those philosophers?

Ethics

Thomas Nagel

In this essay (taken from his book titled, interestingly, *The Last Word*), Thomas Nagel discusses a variety of issues that we have encountered in previous sections. He begins by looking at the differences between scientific and practical reasoning, the role played by empirical testing in each domain, and the claim that our moral views depend on the culture into which we happen to be born. He concludes with a brief discussion of whether moral issues can be dissolved by appeals to facts about history, culture, or even our own desires. Thomas Nagel is professor of philosophy at New York University.

Let me now turn to the question of whether moral reasoning is . . . fundamental and inescapable. Unlike logical or arithmetical reasoning, it often fails to produce certainty, justified or unjustified. It is easily subject to distortion by morally irrelevant factors, social and personal, as well as outright error. It resembles empirical reason in not being reducible to a series of self-evident steps.

I take it for granted that the objectivity of moral reasoning does not depend on its having an external reference. There is no moral analogue of the external world—a universe of moral facts that impinge on us causally. Even if such a supposition made sense, it would not support the objectivity of moral reasoning. Science, which this kind of reifying realism takes as its model, doesn't derive its objective validity from the fact that it starts from perception and other causal relations between us and the physical world. The real work comes after that, in the form of active scientific reasoning without which no amount of causal impact on us by the external world would generate a belief in Newton's or Maxwell's or Einstein's theories, or the chemical theory of elements and compounds, or molecular biology.

If we had rested content with the causal impact of the external world on us, we'd still be at the level of sense perception. We can regard our scientific beliefs as objectively true not because the external world causes us to have them but because we are able to arrive at those beliefs by methods that have a good claim to be reliable, by virtue of their success in selecting among rival hypotheses that survive the best criticisms and questions we can throw at them. Empirical confirmation plays a vital role in this process, but it cannot do so without theory.

Moral thought is concerned not with the description and explanation of what happens but with decisions and their justification. It is mainly because we have no comparably uncontroversial and well-developed methods for thinking about morality that a subjectivist position here is more credible than it is with regard to science. But just as there was no guarantee at the beginnings of cosmological and scientific speculation that we humans had the capacity to arrive at objective truth beyond the deliverances of sense-perception—that in pursuing it we were doing anything more than spinning collective fantasies—so there can be no decision in advance as to whether we are or are not talking about a real subject when we reflect and argue about morality. The answer must come from the results themselves. Only the effort to reason about morality can show us whether it is possible—whether, in thinking about what to do and how to live, we can find methods, reasons, and principles whose validity does not have to be subjectively or relativistically qualified.

Since moral reasoning is a species of practical reasoning, its conclusions are desires,

intentions, and actions, or feelings and convictions that can motivate desire, intention, and action. We want to know how to live, and why, and we want the answer in general terms, if possible. Hume famously believed that because a "passion" immune to rational assessment must underlie every motive, there can be no such thing as specifically practical reason, nor specifically moral reason either. That is false, because while "passions" are the source of some reasons, other passions or desires are themselves motivated and/or justified by reasons that do not depend on still more basic desires. And I would contend that either the question whether one should have a certain desire or the question whether, given that one has that desire, one should act on it, is always open to rational consideration.

The issue is whether the procedures of justification and criticism we employ in such reasoning, moral or merely practical, can be regarded finally as just something we do—a cultural or societal or even more broadly human collective practice, within which reasons come to an end. I believe that if we ask ourselves seriously how to respond to proposals for contextualization and relativistic detachment, they usually fail to convince. Although it is less clear than in some of the other areas we've discussed, attempts to get entirely outside of the object language of practical reasons, good and bad, right and wrong, and to see all such judgments as expressions of a contingent, nonobjective perspective will eventually collapse before the independent force of the first-order judgments themselves.

Suppose someone says, for example, "You only believe in equal opportunity because you are a product of Western liberal society. If you had been brought up in a caste society or one in which the possibilities for men and women were radically unequal, you wouldn't have the moral convictions you have or accept as persuasive the moral arguments you now accept." The second, hypothetical sentence is probably true, but what about the first—specifically the "only"? In general, the fact that I wouldn't believe something if I hadn't learned it proves nothing about the status of the belief or its grounds. It may be impossible to explain the learning without invoking the content of the belief itself, and the reasons for its truth; and it may be clear that what I have learned is such that even if I hadn't learned it, it would still be true. The reason the genetic fallacy is a fallacy is that the explanation of a belief can sometimes confirm it.

To have any content, a subjectivist position must say more than that my moral convictions are my moral convictions. That, after all, is something we can all agree on. A meaningful subjectivism must say that they are just my moral convictions—or those of my moral community. It must qualify ordinary moral judgments in some way, must give them a self-consciously first-person (singular or plural) reading. That is the only type of antiobjectivist view that is worth arguing against or that it is even possible to disagree with.

But I believe it is impossible to come to rest with the observation that a belief in equality of opportunity, and a wish to diminish inherited inequalities, are merely expressions of our cultural tradition. True or false, those beliefs are essentially objective in intent. Perhaps they are wrong, but that too would be a nonrelative judgment. Faced with the fact that such values have gained currency only recently and not universally, one still has to try to decide whether they are right—whether one ought to continue to hold them. That question is not displaced by the information of contingency: The question remains, at the level of moral content, whether I would have been in error if I had accepted as natural, and therefore justified, the inequalities of a caste society, or a fairly rigid class system, or the orthodox subordination of women. It can take in additional facts as material for reflection, but the question of the relevance of those facts is inevitably a moral question: Do these cultural and historical variations and their causes tend to show that I and others have less reason than we had supposed to favor equality of opportunity? Presentation of an array of historically and culturally conditioned attitudes, including my own, does not

disarm first-order moral judgment but simply gives it something more to work on—including information about influences on the formation of my convictions that may lead me to change them. But the relevance of such information is itself a matter for moral reasoning—about what are and are not good grounds for moral belief.

When one is faced with these real variations in practice and conviction, the requirement to put oneself in everyone's shoes when assessing social institutions—some version of universalizability—does not lose any of its persuasive force just because it is not universally recognized. It dominates the historical and anthropological data: Presented with the description of a traditional caste society, I have to ask myself whether its hereditary inequalities are justified, and there is no plausible alternative to considering the interests of all in trying to answer the question. If others feel differently, they must say why they find these cultural facts relevant—why they require some qualification to the objective moral claim. On both sides, it is a moral issue, and the only way to defend universalizability or equal opportunity against subjectivist qualification is by continuing the moral argument. It is a matter of understanding exactly what the subjectivist wants us to give up, and then asking whether the grounds for those judgments disappear in light of his observations.

In my opinion, someone who abandons or qualifies his basic methods of moral reasoning on historical or anthropological grounds alone is nearly as irrational as someone who abandons a mathematical belief on other than mathematical grounds. Even with all their uncertainties and liability to controversy and distortion, moral considerations occupy a position in the system of human thought that makes it illegitimate to subordinate them completely to anything else. Particular moral claims are constantly being discredited for all kinds of reasons, but moral considerations per se keep rising again to challenge in their own right any blanket attempt to displace, defuse, or subjectivize them.

This is an instance of the more general truth that the normative cannot be transcended by the descriptive. The question "What should I do?" like the question "What should I believe?" is always in order. It is always possible to think about the question in normative terms, and the process is not rendered pointless by any fact of a different kind—any desire or emotion or feeling, any habit or practice or convention, any contingent cultural or social background. Such things may in fact, guide our actions, but it is always possible to take their relation to action as an object of further normative reflection and ask, "How should I act, given that these things are true of me or of my situation?"

The type of thought that generates answers to this question is practical reason. But, further, it is always possible for the question to take a specifically moral form, since one of the successor questions to which it leads is, "What should anyone in my situation do?"—and consideration of that question leads in turn to questions about what everyone should do, not only in this situation but more generally.

Such universal questions don't always have to be raised, and there is good reason in general to develop a way of living that makes it usually unnecessary to raise them. But if they are raised, as they always can be, they require an answer of the appropriate kind—even though the answer may be that in a case like this one may do as one likes. They cannot be ruled out of order by pointing to something more fundamental—psychological, cultural, or biological—that brings the request for justification to an end. Only a justification can bring the request for justifications to an end. Normative questions in general are not undercut or rendered idle by anything, even though particular normative answers may be. (Even when some putative justification is exposed as a rationalization, that implies that something else could be said about the justifiability or nonjustifiability of what was done.)

REVIEW AND DISCUSSION QUESTIONS

1. What is the difference between scientific and practical reasoning? What makes scientific beliefs true, according to Nagel?
2. How does Nagel respond to those who say that we have our moral beliefs only because of our society and wouldn't have the ones we do if we'd been raised in a radically different society?
3. "Moral beliefs cannot be dissolved into cultural or factual ones." Discuss what this might mean, and why Nagel thinks it is true.

The Arc of the Moral Universe

Joshua Cohen

This essay by Joshua Cohen asks a question that involves the moral nature of the universe itself. Is it reasonable, Cohen asks, to fear or hate the world for its apparent indifference and even hostility toward justice? The answer, he argues, is "no." Cohen's particular focus is on slavery: why it was unjust, and whether the fact of its being unjust contributed to its destruction. He argues that the full explanation of slavery's demise goes beyond such historical facts as political and military power or the attitudes of people who opposed slavery. The institution's failure is also, says Cohen, explained by the fact that slavery *was* unjust.

Cohen begins by discussing the nature of slavery and the specific respects in which it was unjust. Assuming a broadly contractarian understanding of morality, he argues that slave laws and practices were unjust because they could not be the object of free and informed agreement among equals. Unlike other political and economic systems, slavery failed to recognize the *legitimate* interests of slaves in well-being, autonomy, and dignity. And because slavery could not be the object of agreement among people pursuing their legitimate interests, he argues, it was difficult for slavery to survive.

There are larger issues at stake here than the institution of slavery, however vile, which is why I have chosen to end the section with this essay. The most important, as Cohen puts it, is the "appropriate attitude toward the social world." The universe, he argues, is more friendly to justice than unjustice, so that Enlightenment views of the world and of morality were not so far wrong after all. The universe has a moral "arc" that bends toward justice, as Martin Luther King Jr. used to say. Joshua Cohen is professor of philosophy and Arthur and Ruth Sloan Professor of Political Science at the Massachusetts Institute of Technology.

I. ETHICAL EXPLANATION

William Williams was born into slavery in Salisbury, North Carolina. He escaped to Canada in 1849, where he was later interviewed by the American abolitionist Samuel Gridley Howe. It was two years into the American Civil War, and Williams said: "I think the North will whip the South, because I believe they are in the right."[1]

Williams's remark provides a striking example of an *ethical explanation*. Generally speaking, ethical explanations cite ethical norms—for example, norms of justice—in explaining why some specified social facts obtain, or, as in Williams's case, can be expected to obtain. The norms are offered in explanations of social facts, not only in appraisals of them: Williams expects the North to win because they are right. Similarly, the great abolitionist minister Theodore Parker predicted defeat for the "slave power" because it was wrong: Speaking to the New England Anti-Slavery Convention in 1858, he said of the slave power: "Its Nature of wickedness is its manifest Destiny of Ruin."[2]

Philosophers, historians, and social scientists often recoil from ethical explanations: How *could* the injustice of slavery contribute to explaining its demise? Or the justice of sexual subordination to explaining the instability of systems that subordinate women? Or the injustice of exclusion from the suffrage to explaining twentieth-century suffrage extension? Such explanations seem both too relaxed about distinctions between fact and value and too Panglossian: Does right really make might? Still, ethical explanations play an important role in certain common-sense schemes of social and historical understanding: they are elements of certain folk moralities, so to speak. Martin Luther King said that "the arc of the moral universe is long but it bends toward justice."[3] If there is an arc, King is right about its length. But is there one that bends toward justice? . . .

I think that some ethical explanations—for example, about slavery, sexual subordination, and suffrage extension—have force. That force derives from the general claim that the injustice of a social arrangement limits its viability. This general claim rests in turn on the role played by the notion of a voluntary system of social cooperation in plausible accounts of both justice and the long-term viability of social forms. Social arrangements better able to elicit voluntary cooperation have both moral and practical advantages over their more coercive counterparts.

This theme lies at the basis of Enlightenment theories of history: Adam Smith's account of the pressures that encourage the

From Joshua Cohen, "The Arc of the Moral Universe," *Philosophy and Public Affairs*, Vol. 26, No. 2 (1998), 91–134. © 1998 by Princeton University Press. Reprinted by permission of Princeton University Press.

emergence of a system of natural liberty, Hegel's account of the instabilities of social systems that enable only incomplete forms of human self-consciousness, and Marx's thesis that exploitative social relations ultimately give way because of the constraints they impose on the free development of human powers. . . .

[I will argue] that the injustice of slavery contributed to its demise. I will defend this claim by arguing for the following four:

> *Thesis One:* The basic structure of slavery as a system of power stands in sharp conflict with fundamental slave interests in material well-being, autonomy, and dignity.
>
> *Thesis Two:* Slavery is unjust because the relative powerlessness of slaves, reflected in the conflict between slavery and slave interests, implies that it could not be the object of a free, reasonable, and informed agreement.
>
> *Thesis Three:* The conflict between slavery and the interests of slaves is an important source of the limited viability of slavery.
>
> *Thesis Four:* Characterizing slavery as unjust conveys information relevant to explaining the demise of slavery that is not conveyed simply by noting that slavery conflicts with the interests of slaves.

. . . First, my focus here is on the role (if any) played by the injustice of slavery in explaining the ultimate demise of slavery. Slavery is unjust—as Lincoln said, "If slavery is not wrong, then nothing is wrong"[4]—and it has been abolished. But did its wrongness contribute to its demise? Historians continue to debate the role of moral convictions about the injustice of slavery—held, for example, by Quakers—in accounting for the abolition of slavery. I do not doubt the causal importance of these convictions, much less their sincerity. Indeed, I will eventually make them part of the story about *how* the injustice of slavery contributed to its demise. But my topic is different. I am not concerned principally with the causal importance of moral convictions in the decline of slavery but the importance of the *injustice itself* in accounting for that demise. In short, I am concerned with the consequences of slavery's injustice—whether

"Its Nature of wickedness is its manifest Destiny of Ruin"—and not simply the consequences of the fact that some people came to think of it as wrong. . . .

What is at stake is not the appropriate moral attitude toward slavery or philosophical outlook on morality, but the appropriate attitude toward the social world. How accommodating is the social world to injustice? Is it reasonable, from a moral point of view, to hate the world? . . .

II. SLAVERY

My argument that the injustice of slavery contributed to its demise depends on several background ideas about slavery and slave interests. Briefly summarized, I propose that slavery is a distinctive distribution of de facto *power,* that this distribution was reproduced through both force and "consent," and that patterns in the use of force and strategies for inducing consent provide a basis for attributing to slaves basic interests in material well-being, autonomy, and dignity. . . .

Power

Slavery is best understood, I suggest, in terms of the notion of *de facto power,* rather than, for example, in terms of familiar cultural or legal representations of slaves—as extensions of the will of masters, or as property. To be specific: a slave is, in the first instance, someone largely lacking the power to dispose of his/her physical and mental powers, including both the capacity to produce and control of the body generally (extending to sexuality and reproduction); the power to dispose of the means of production; the power to select a place a residence; the power to associate with others and establish stable bonds; the power to decide on the manner in which one's children will be raised; and the (political) power to fix the rules governing the affairs of the states in which one resides. . . .

But slaves were not entirely powerless— mere extensions and instruments of another's will. To be sure, their power was highly confined, dangerous to exercise, and nearly always insufficient to overturn slavery itself. But slaves did not, as a general matter, lack all forms of power, and sometimes asserted it to improve their conditions and shape the terms of order within the framework of slavery. As an ex-slave and blacksmith named J. W. Lindsay put it in an 1863 interview with the Freedman's Inquiry Commission, "Of course, they treated me pretty well, for the reason that I would not allow them to treat me in any other way. If they attempted to use any barbarity, I would walk off before their faces."[5] Though Lindsay's remark is almost certainly an exaggeration, and certainly not a plausible generalization, it captures a truth put more subtly by Harriet Jacobs, who said, "My master had power and law on his side; I had a determined will. There is might in each."[6]

The power of slaves was most clearly in evidence in the range of activities commonly grouped together as "slave resistance."

First, a variety of forms of resistance could be pursued individually and were not threatening to slavery, including: "taking" from masters (what slaves called "taking" the masters called "stealing"), lying, feigning illness, slowing down the pace of work, damaging tools and animals, self-mutilation, suicide, infanticide, abortion, arson, murdering the master, and running away. . . .

A second form of resistance—less frequent, but also more collective and threatening—was the widespread phenomenon of "maroon" communities. Established by runaway slaves, some maroon communities were quite small. . . . Others were large-scale and long-standing. . . .

Finally, most dramatically, there are slave revolts. . . .

These examples underscore the limits of the extension-of-will and ownership conceptions of slavery: To appreciate the power of slaves we must distinguish real from legal disabilities, and from the public interpretation of those disabilities. Slaves of course suffered from legal disabilities, which both codified and contributed to their lack of power. But

their general lack of legally codified or publicly acknowledged rights also exaggerated their real situation. Thus slaves were commonly able to do what the law denied them the right to do.

For example, slave "marriages" were not recognized at law, but more or less stable unions were part of the practice of virtually all slave societies. And while slaves had no legal right to control the pace of their work, they had, as a general matter, some power—highly qualified, limited, and always dangerous to exercise—to help to shape it through various forms of resistance and threats of resistance. While, then, the actual terms of association among slaves themselves and between slaves and masters reflected the need to find a stable accommodation between agents with vastly different powers, the legal and moral representation of those relations denied that need, emphasizing instead the unilateral dictation of terms and conditions by masters, and the absence of a capacity for independent action on the part of slaves.

Force and Consent

Premising this conception of slavery as distinctive form of power, we come now to the question: How was this form reproduced? . . .

Limited in their power, slaves drew limited benefits from social cooperation, and, since they did not have to sell their labor to gain their subsistence, such benefits as they did get were importantly independent from their activity. So masters faced problems in motivating slaves to work. Force was one solution (we will come to the others). As Adam Smith put it, "A person who can acquire no property, can have no other interest but to eat as much, and to labor as little as possible. Whatever work he does beyond what is sufficient to purchase his own maintenance, can be squeezed out of him by violence only, and not by any interest of his own."[7] Smith's contention about "violence only" is overstated, in ways that will become clear when I discuss the use of positive incentives. But it does capture an important problem for masters, and provides a good characterization of the basis of the productive use of force.

Appreciating the scope and limits of the productive use of force requires attention to the costs (to masters) of using force as distinct from other incentives. It might require a staff of overseers, or some other diversion of resources from more productive uses, and might damage the human beings one is seeking to "motivate." . . .

The maintenance of slavery could not, then, proceed through force alone. Masters wanted to elicit greater effort, slaves typically faced impossible odds if they sought their own emancipation, and the result was superficially more consensual forms of servitude. Abstracting from endless varieties of compromise and accommodation, varying across time and place, we can distinguish two broad ways to make servitude (superficially) more voluntary: First, masters deployed positive incentives . . . including material reward, authority, autonomy, family security, and manumission. The importance of the strategic use of incentives is a common theme in ancient and modern treatises on slave management. Genovese quotes an overseer making the strategic case for permitting slaves to pursue private cultivation: "Every means are used to encourage them, and impress on their minds the advantage of holding property, and the disgrace attached to idleness. Surely, if industrious for themselves, they will be so for their masters, and no Negro, with a well-stocked poultry house, a small crop advancing, a canoe partly finished, or a few tubs unsold, all of which he calculates soon to enjoy, will ever run away. In ten years I have lost by absconding, forty-seven days, out of nearly six hundred Negroes."[8] . . .

A majority of slave systems relied as well on practices of manumission through which slaves were individually emancipated by their masters, though rates of manumission varied greatly across different slave systems. The practice might take the form of self-purchase, with the slave using his or her *peculium* to pay for freedom (the Cuban

coartacion and Islamic *murgu* both involved gradual self-purchase). Other standard processes included the freeing of concubines, the emancipation of the children of concubines, and the manumission of slaves as displays of piety in Islamic societies. . . .

Alongside force and positive incentives, cultural representations of slavery as reasonable—religious and ethical representations justifying slavery—also figure in explaining compliance.

Rousseau's *Social Contract* emphasizes what has come to be a commonplace of modern social theory: that the "strongest is never strong enough to be master all the time, unless he transforms force into right and obedience into duty."[9] The thought is that existing power is made more powerful by public ideas that represent it as a necessity, make a virtue of such necessity, and thereby suggest that the terms of order are an object of common consent and that subjects willingly comply. . . . But three qualifications are equally important.

First, slaves typically did not simply embrace the dominant religious and ethical interpretations of their nature and their condition. . . .

American Afro-Baptism, for example, rejected doctrines of original sin and predestination, and emphasized Old Testament themes of earthly deliverance, comparing the situation and prospects of slaves with the deliverance of the Jews from bondage in Egypt. Thus, the Freedman's Hymn: "Shout the glad tidings o'er Egypt's Dark Sea; Jehovah has triumphed, his people are free." Similarly, the religious views characteristic of East African coastal slaves blended hinterland beliefs and practices with a distinctive form of Islam, which rejected the dominant conception of sharp divisions within God's creation in favor of an emphasis on the importance of love for the Prophet and the possibility of attaining religious purity through that love.

Second, even when slave understandings served as a basis for an accommodation to slavery, the fact that they were not fully accommodations turned them into potential sources of "internal normative criticism" and resistance. By "internal normative criticism" (sometimes called "restorationist" or "traditionalist" criticism) I mean the criticism of practices by appeal to understandings, norms, and values that are, at some level of generality, widely shared. . . .

Finally, no sharp and useful distinction can be drawn between the use of internal norms to criticize practices and more radical forms of criticism that reject those norms in favor of other norms. And the views of some slaves—how many we will never know—seem most plausibly characterized as continuing internal normative criticism to the point where it passes into external criticism. . . .

But if we are to understand better the critical uses of norms, the development of alternative interpretations of norms, the uses slaves made of their power, and the importance and prevalence of positive incentives, we need an account of the interests of slaves.

Interests

Slaves had interests in material well-being, autonomy, and dignity. Perhaps that goes without saying. But the enterprise of attributing interests to people seems to some arbitrary, and attributions of these interests to slaves may strike others as anachronistic, romantic, ideologically blinded, or simply ignorant. These interests, however, play two roles in my argument: the case for both the injustice of slavery and its limited viability turns on the claim that slavery conflicts with the legitimate interests of slaves in material well-being, autonomy, and dignity. So I need to say enough about them to explain why that later appeal to them is plausible.

As a general matter, then, a course of action or state of affairs is in a person's interest just in case that course or state is the best way to realize an end that he or she would affirm on reflection given full information and full imaginative powers. . . . Given this, I will sketch some evidence that slaves cared

substantially about material well-being, autonomy, and dignity.

First, then, the phenomena of resistance and revolt support the view that at least some slaves cared greatly about autonomy—enough to accept significant risks, e.g., the risks taken by the 6,000 crucified slaves who lined the road from Capua to Rome after the defeat of the rebellion led by Spartacus (100,000 slaves were killed in this revolt). This willingness to accept risks for autonomy is clearest in the case of individual runaways, maroons, and rebels. . . .

Second, the provision of material incentives and manumission, and the various other paraphernalia of voluntary servitude, indicate that slaves wanted material improvement and autonomy, and that masters, aware of those wants, sought to elicit more cooperative behavior by promising to reward such behavior by satisfying those wants. . . .

Third, evidence for the desire for autonomy is provided by American slave narratives, and the interviews conducted by both the Freedman's Inquiry Commission and the WPA. They provide substantial testimony on the aspiration to autonomy; indeed the slave narratives are organized around that aspiration. And they commonly return to the theme suggested by the phenomenon of manumission: that the desire for autonomy is not simply in service of material improvement. . . .

Fourth, the central role of force in establishing and sustaining slave systems also argues for the presence of interests in material well-being and autonomy. The fact that slave "recruitment" typically involved force indicates that slavery was rarely chosen by slaves—and then only under difficult circumstances—and that observing the conditions of others who had been enslaved did not encourage self-enslavement. . . .

Coming now to dignity: the central feature of dignity for our purposes is its social aspect—that it involves a desire for public recognition of one's worth. . . .

Several considerations support the attribution to slaves of an interest in conditions that support and are appropriate to a sense of dignity. First, when we consider the few oral and written records left by slaves, from the fables collected by Phaédrus to American slave narratives, what we find is repeated assertions of their sense of self-worth, and the ways that their conditions violate that sense.[10]

Second, as I already indicated, the normative understandings of slavery held by slaves press the worth of the slaves into focus. . . . A particularly striking statement of this is provided by an ex-slave named Benjamin Miller. In a Freedman's Inquiry Commission interview, Miller says: "I was in bondage in Missouri, too. I can't say that my treatment was bad. In one respect I say it was not bad, but in another I consider it was as bad as could be. I was a slave. That covers it all. I had not the rights of a man.[11]

Taking these remarks about the different interests together, I will hereafter use the term "fundamental interests" as shorthand for the three interests I have just discussed.

III. INJUSTICE AND THE LIMITS OF SLAVERY

Slavery, I have proposed, is best understood as a particular form of power; that form was reproduced through force, strategic incentives, and moral-religious norms; and slave interests in material improvement, autonomy, and dignity are revealed in the practices that reproduce slavery. With these claims as background, I come to the main argument about the injustice of slavery and its viability, which I will pursue by taking up, in turn, the four theses stated earlier.

Slavery and Slave Interests

Thesis One: The basic structure of slavery as a system of power stands in sharp conflict with fundamental slave interests in material well-being, autonomy, and dignity.

Consider, first, the interest in material well-being. The intuitive argument for this

aspect of Thesis One is that being a slave is materially undesirable because slaves are relatively powerless. Limited power means limited capacity to protect basic material interests in nourishment and health. So it seems plausible that it is materially better not to be a slave, even if one is a serf or poor peasant. Given the breadth and depth of the limits that define the condition of slave, one can expect to have more power if one is not a slave and to be able to turn that power to material advantage. . . .

Autonomy is a matter of being able to set and pursue one's aspirations. To be in the relatively powerless position of slave is on the whole to lack just such power, or to have it as a result of conditions that are more fortuitous in the lives of slaves than they are even in the lives of other socially subordinate groups. This is clear not just in the arena of work, but (particularly for women slaves) with respect to sexuality as well.

The case of dignity seems equally clear. A characteristic feature of slave systems is that both the organization of power and the symbolic understandings of that organization—especially the pervasive symbolism of social death—deny that slave interests command public respect. Thus the organization of power largely deprived slaves of the powers required for advancing their interests; and the symbolic expression of that organization represented slaves as extensions of the wills of their masters or as their property, as having no legitimate social place, and as legitimately denied the powers required for protecting and advancing their interests. . . .

Injustice

Thesis Two: Slavery is unjust because the relative powerlessness of slaves, reflected in the conflict between slavery and slave interests, implies that it could not be the object of a free, reasonable, and informed agreement.

In stating this second thesis, I introduce a particular account of justice, based on an idealized notion of consensus—a free, reasonable, and informed agreement.[12] I will not defend this account of justice here, nor does the argument depend on its details. What does matter are the intuitive ideas that the ideal consensus view articulates: that a just arrangement gives due consideration to the interests of all its members, and that we give due consideration when we treat people as equals, taking their good fully into account in our social arrangements. The ideal consensus view articulates this requirement of treating people as equals by asking what arrangements people themselves would agree to, if they looked for arrangements acceptable to all, understood as equals. By a *free* agreement, then, I mean an agreement reached under conditions in which there are no bargaining advantages. An agreement is *reasonable* only if it is reached on the basis of interests that can be advanced consistent with the aim of arriving at a free agreement. I will hereafter call such interests "legitimate interests." An *informed* agreement is one in which the parties correctly understand the consequences of the agreement.

According to this ideal consensus view of justice, then, slavery is unjust because it could not be the object of a free and reasonable agreement. Why not? What features of slavery preclude it from being the object of such an agreement? Given the relative powerlessness that defines the condition of slavery, the force essential to sustaining it, and the public interpretation of slaves that is encouraged by that distribution of power, it is reasonable for slaves to have very low expectations about the satisfaction of their fundamental interests, lower even than in alternative systems of direct social subordination. Given this low expectation, slaves could only "consent" to their condition if the relations of power between masters and slaves determined the rational course of their conduct. But such power is excluded by the requirement of a free agreement.

This rejection is reasonable because the fundamental slave interests that lie at its foundation are legitimate. Advancing them was consistent with acknowledging that everyone has the fundamental interests, and that the structure of the social order ought to accommodate those interests. . . . The rejection of slavery would have been reasonable, then, because the elimination of slavery would have improved the conditions of slaves with respect to their fundamental interests; but that improvement need not have imposed on any group a burden at all comparable to that borne by slaves under slavery.

Consider, by contrast, the interest in having slaves—which I suppose at least some masters to have had. This was not a morally legitimate interest, since it could not be advanced as a basis for an agreement consistent with the aim of reaching a free agreement on terms of cooperation. Slavery was in the sharpest conflict with the fundamental interests of slaves. Given that slaves had these interests, masters could only propose slavery if they were not aiming to find mutually acceptable terms of social order, but instead seeking to advance their particular interests. And masters could not reasonably expect slaves to agree to terms that conflict with their interests simply because such an agreement would be advantageous to masters—not as part of a free agreement.

This rejection of slavery would have been an *informed* rejection in that it turns on the general features of slavery that I sketched earlier: that slaves are relatively powerless; because they are relatively powerless their legitimate interests in material well-being and autonomy are at best marginally and insecurely protected; such protection as they in fact receive results either from the whims of masters or from a precarious and shifting balance of power between masters and slaves; and since their interests are typically not recognized as significant either in the organization of power or in the dominant conceptions of slaves and their social standing, slavery is an insult to their dignity. This argument does not turn on identifying slavery with its most murderous forms or slaves as utterly powerless. . . .

Limited Viability

> *Thesis Three:* The conflict between slavery and the interests of slaves is an important source of the limited viability of slavery.

Slavery is unjust, then, because it conflicts with certain interests of slaves—interests that are identified as morally legitimate by the ideal consensus view (and no doubt by other views). Does this injustice-making conflict help to account for the demise of slavery? And where, if at all, does the injustice itself enter in? As a first step to answering these questions, I defend the third thesis by sketching two sources of the limited viability of slavery—two lines of argument that figure as important strands in plausible accounts of abolition.

The first source emphasizes the *recognition of injustice.* The idea is that slavery is undermined in part because it was unjust, because that injustice was recognized, and that recognition motivated opposition. Here the injustice of slavery plays an explanatory role, roughly, by virtue of its being cognized and then serving to motivate moral opposition.

Let's separate the contention that recognition of injustice is relevant to explaining the demise of slavery into three components: some consequential opposition to slavery was motivated by moral conviction; the content of those moral convictions can plausibly by represented by the ideal consensus conception of justice that I have presented here; and those moral convictions are themselves explained in part by the injustice of slavery. Without this third point, it would not be the injustice itself that helps to explain the demise, but only the belief that slavery is wrong. I will consider the first two points here, and return later to the third.

First, then, it seems clear that moral opposition motivated at least some eighteenth- and nineteenth-century abolitionist opponents of slavery who fought against the slave trade and for the abolition of slavery, who objected to slavery on grounds of principle, whose interests are not sufficient to explain their opposition—Quakers being only the most familiar case—and whose opposition was important to abolition. Fogel, who emphasizes the economic success and viability of American slavery, puts the case especially strongly: "[Slavery's] death was an act of 'econocide,' a political execution of an immoral system at its peak of economic success, incited by men ablaze with moral fervor."[13] Moral conviction also provides an explanation of some of the motivations of slaves, particularly those who were animated by external moral criticisms of slavery.

Concerning the second point: Slaves, I have suggested, were motivated to oppose slavery in part by indignation and outrage, and not only by their interests. But this does not suffice to show that they were motivated by a recognition of the injustice of slavery as I have characterized the notion of injustice here. Sometimes—in the case of internal moral criticism—their indignation could be explained by the fact that masters had violated traditional norms and customary understandings. But . . . not all slave opposition can be explained in those terms. Among the forms of opposition that cannot be are the views advanced in the course of the Haitian Revolution, in slave petitions in the United States, in Jamaica's 1831 Christmas rebellion, and in the views that animated the participation of ex-slaves in the fight against the Confederacy. In all these cases, opposition was shaped in part by the notions of due consideration and treating people as equals that provide the intuitive foundation of the ideal consensus conception.

More generally, the conception of slavery—and not merely their own individual enslavement or the violations by masters of customary expectations—as unjust helps explain the late eighteenth century shift that Genovese has described from restorationist rebellions to revolutionary opposition to slavery. Furthermore, this opposition (particularly the revolution in Ste. Dominque) was consequential, and contributed to the end of slavery by, among other things, helping to limit the expansion of slavery and contributing strength to movements to end the slave trade.

The case for the first two aspects of the recognition-of-injustice view seems plausible. Still, we have not yet arrived fully at the recognition of injustice; for that we must also vindicate the claim that there is an explanatory connection between the injustice of slavery and moral beliefs about it. I will discuss this issue later on, and respond in particular to the objection that all that matters here are beliefs about injustice, and that talk about "recognition" is misplaced.

The second view is what I call the *conflicting interests* account. This view locates viability problems in slavery directly in the conflict between slavery and the fundamental slave interests, without the mediation of moral beliefs. The contention is that these conflicts are a key source of pressure to move from slave to nonslave systems, because they are a source of conflict within slave systems and of disadvantages that slave systems face when they compete economically and conflict militarily with nonslave systems.

To bring out the content of this view, I want to note that it helps to explain the force and limits of classical economic arguments about the limits of slavery. Those arguments emphasize the costliness of slave labor, deriving from high enforcement costs, constrained productivity, and difficulties of securing a biologically reproductive slave population. Adam Smith, for example, thought that slave labor was the most costly, and was imposed because of false pride and a desire to dominate, not for sound economic reasons. The conflicting interests view argues that these liabilities of slavery result principally from difficulties in inducing the willing cooperation of slaves, and that those problems of motivation in turn reflect the underlying conflict of interests.

If that explanation is right then we should expect problems deriving from the conflicting interests to have noneconomic manifestations as well—for example, relative military weakness, overt slave resistance, and a loss of political confidence by owners.

Consider the military issue. Wars present two problems for slave systems. First, in a wide range of systems, slaves were either not trusted to fight, or otherwise excluded from fighting. With a segment of the population thus excluded, military potential is diminished. . . .

In general, then, the conflicting-interests view contends that the demise of slavery results in part from the *practical advantages* in competition and conflict available to systems less sharply in conflict with the interests of their members than slavery is—advantages expressed through mechanisms akin to natural selection.

A problem for the conflicting interests theory is that it may appear to explain "too much." Although conflicts between slavery and slave interests may have been fundamental and persistent, slavery was not in permanent crisis. But the conflicting interests account does not imply that it would be. That account is not intended to provide a comprehensive explanation of the evolution and demise of slavery, but rather to characterize one important, destabilizing determinant of that evolution. . . .

Justice and Viability

> *Thesis Four:* Characterizing slavery as unjust conveys information relevant to explaining the demise of slavery that is not conveyed simply by noting that slavery conflicts with the interests of slaves.

Suppose, then, that the conflict between slave interests and slavery limits the viability of slavery. What, then, does injustice have to do with limited viability? Why would the same limits not exist even if slave interests were not legitimate? What force is added to the explanation by noting that slave interests are morally weighty?

I suggest two ways that our understanding of the limits of slavery is aided by noting that moral weight. The first is provided by considerations about the recognition of injustice. Recall where we left the discussion of that recognition: I indicated that moral convictions motivated some consequential opposition to slavery, and that the content of those convictions could reasonably be characterized by the ideal consensus conception of justice.

Still, the injustice of slavery is not perhaps evident in this argument: How does the injustice itself shape the moral motivations of opponents? It be might be said that simple beliefs on the part of abolitionists and slaves that slavery is unjust suffice to motivate opposition, quite apart from the actual injustice of slavery.

The objection seems to me not to have much force since it is natural to want an explanation of the moral beliefs as well. And part of the explanation for the moral belief is that slaves have interests in material well-being, autonomy, and dignity, and are recognized as having them; that slavery sharply conflicts with those interests, and is recognized as so conflicting; and that those interests are legitimate, and recognized as such. And why is this sequence of points not naturally captured by saying that people believe slavery to be unjust in part because it is unjust? To see why this rendering is appropriate, consider the force of the "because" in "because it is unjust." We can interpret it as follows: Suppose people reason morally about the rightness or wrongness of slavery, and pursue that reasoning in light of an understanding of certain facts about slave interests and the conflict between slavery and those interests. Because the reasoning is moral, it is guided by the thought that the interests of slaves need to be given due consideration, as they are, for example, in the requirement of free agreement. Pursuing that reasoning, they will be driven to the conclusion that slavery is wrong: they do not see how slavery could result from a free agreement. (It is not that difficult to see how this might go: after all, we do something like this now when we ask whether slavery is wrong.)

What is essential is to acknowledge that slaves have legitimate interests. And the key to that acknowledgment is to see that slaves have the properties—for example, the interests and the capacity for deliberate action—that others have (masters, or other members of the free population) in virtue of which people are prepared to attribute legitimate interests to those others. But this recognition is available to anyone who reflects on the practices that help to sustain slavery, in particular on the practice of providing the incentives that I mentioned earlier. For those incentives are in effect the homage paid by a scheme of domination to fundamental human aspirations; to provide them is in effect to acknowledge that slaves have the relevant interests and capacities. . . .

To say, then, that the wrongness of slavery explains the moral belief is to note the following: that moral reasoning mandates the conclusion that slavery is unjust; and that the moral belief is produced in part by that kind of reasoning. And once the injustice is recognized, it is reasonable to expect that that recognition plays some role in motivation, that it contributes to the antagonism of slaves to slavery, that it adds nonslave opponents to the slave opponents, and that, once slavery is abolished, it helps to explain why there are not strong movements to bring it back.

The moral weight also figures implicitly in the conflicting interests view. To see how, keep in mind that an explanation of the demise of slavery is not simply an account of opposition to slavery, or of shifts away from slavery—an account of the evolution of institutional variation—but also an account of the eventual retention of nonslave arrangements, of the absence of "wandering" from slave to nonslave and then back. The competitive disadvantages of slave systems are important to understanding this retention. The conflict of slavery with legitimate slave interests, and the fact that masters' interests in preserving slavery are not legitimate, plausibly helps to "tip the balance" in favor of stable departures from slavery.

To see how, consider a remark from a nineteen-year-old black soldier and ex-slave, who, after the Battle of Nashville, used his furlough to pay a visit to his former mistress. She asked him: "You remember when you were sick and I had to bring you to the house and nurse you." When he replied that he did remember, she responded: "And now you are fighting me." To which the soldier said: "No'm, I ain't fighting you. I'm fighting to get free."[14] To appreciate the bearing of this remark on the issue here, recall that the rejection of slavery was reasonable and slave interests legitimate because the fundamental interests of slaves could be advanced consistent with the aim of reaching a free agreement. The fundamental interests that provide the basis for a reasonable rejection of slavery are shared by masters, and slavery imposes great hardship on slaves while alternatives to slavery do not impose a hardship on any other group comparable to the hardship imposed on slaves by slavery. Alternatives to slavery accommodate the interests of subordinate groups better than slavery does. Moreover, they provide substantial protections of the fundamental interests at the superordinate positions. By contrast, the slaveowner interest in maintaining slavery was not shared by slaves. Because slaves and masters shared the fundamental interests, slaves could reject slavery consistent with extending to masters the same standing that they desired for themselves. But masters could not have advanced their interest in maintaining slavery except by failing to extend to slaves the same recognition masters desired for themselves. These facts about common and conflicting interests are the basis for the moral condemnation of slavery.

Suppose slave interests were not legitimate. Slaves might still have resisted just as much. But the economic and military disadvantages of slavery, the abolition of slavery, and the apparent stability of that abolition, would be more surprising. Suppose in particular that the fundamental interests were not capable of mutual satisfaction. Then we would expect dissatisfaction with abolition leading to struggles for its reimposition. We would also not expect any particular practical advantage to be conferred by the absence of slavery if those other systems conflicted with the interests of some of their members as sharply as slavery does with some of its members. For if the conflicts were as sharp, then they would have the same difficulties as slavery in eliciting cooperation. Of course, other systems of social subordination are also unjust. But slavery is on the extreme end of powerlessness; alternatives to it permit greater space

for material improvement, increased scope for autonomy, and do not rest on an enslaving denial of dignity. So the sources of conflict and instability in the alternatives to slavery do not tend to produce returns to slavery. And the fact that those replacements are improvements with respect to justice makes the stability of the shift away from slavery less surprising.

Thus the fact that there is not wandering back and forth between slavery and abolition reflects the fact that the fundamental slave interests were shared and so could serve as the basis of an agreement. Stating that slavery is unjust and that slave interests are legitimate interests conveys all these relevant facts about the conflict between slavery and the interests of slaves. It represents a second, distinct reason for citing the injustice in an explanation of the end of slavery. We cite the injustice itself, first, then, to indicate that moral reasoning mandates a certain conclusion, that people arrived at the conclusion because they reasoned, and were motivated to act. And we cite it, second, to convey information about the features of the system and of the alternatives to it in virtue of which the moral reasoning condemns it as unjust, and to claim that those very features are a source of instability. . . .

In sum, then, we have no reason to correct William Williams or Theodore Parker. Ethical explanations have some force, given certain plausible background beliefs about the connections between the satisfaction of fundamental interests and the justice of social forms, the tendency of people to act on their interests, and the relationship between the satisfaction of those interests and the viability of social arrangements (especially when those arrangements operate under conditions of competition and conflict). . . .

IV. SCAFFOLD AND THRONE

Appeals to the injustice of slavery can play a role in explaining the demise of slavery. But that role is limited, no greater than the advantages conferred by moral improvements. Those limits in turn underscore the length of the arc of the moral universe. King often coupled his reference to that arc with a stanza from James Russell Lowell:

Truth forever on the scaffold,
Wrong forever on the throne;
Yet that scaffold sways the future,
And behind the dim unknown

Standeth God within the shadow
Keeping watch above His own.

Many of us do not share Lowell's faith—or King's—in a God who keeps watch above His own. But even if we do not, we can find some support for the hopefulness of Lowell, King, and William Williams in the human aspirations and powers that shape the arc of our part of the moral universe.

NOTES

1. Cited in John W. Blassingame, ed., *Slave Testimony* (Baton Rouge: Louisiana State University Press, 1977), p. 437.
2. Theodore Parker, *The Relation of Slavery to a Republican Form of Government* (Boston: William Kent and Company, 1858), p. 20. Strictly speaking, Williams and Parker make ethical predictions: they predict a change in a world, and base the predictions on norms of rightness. No doubt they would have embraced the claim that the North won because it was in the right.
3. The phrase "arc of the moral universe" or variants on it occur throughout King's writing and speeches. See Martin Luther King, Jr., *A Testament of Hope: The Essential Writings of Martin Luther King, Jr.,* ed. James Washington (San Francisco: Harper and Row, 1986), pp. 141, 207, 230, 277, 438.
4. Quoted in David M. Potter, *The Impending Crisis: 1848–1861,* completed and edited by Don E. Fehrenbacher (New York: Harper and Row, 1976), p. 342. The passage comes from Lincoln's letter to Albert G. Hodges (April 4, 1864).
5. Blassingame, *Slave Testimony*. p. 397.
6. Cited in Elizabeth Fox-Genovese, *Within the Plantation Household: Black and White Women of the Old South* (Chapel Hill: University of North Carolina Press, 1988), p. 290.
7. Adam Smith, *Wealth of Nations*. New York: Random House, p. 365.
8. Genovese, *Roll, Jordan, Roll*. New York: Panthean, 1974, p. 539.
9. Jean-Jacques Rousseau, *Social Contract,* ed. Roger D. Masters, trans. Judith R. Masters (New York: St. Martin's Press, 1978), p. 48.
10. "There is," according to Patterson, "absolutely no evidence from the long and dismal annals of slavery to suggest that any group of slaves ever internalized the conception of degradation held by their masters." Patterson, *Slavery and Social Death*. Cambridge, MA: Harvard University Press, p. 97.
11. Blassingame, *Slave Testimony,* p. 439.
12. I draw, as will be evident, on Rawls, *Theory of Justice;* T. M. Scanlon, "Contractualism and Utilitarianism," in Amartya Sen and Bernard Williams, eds., *Utilitarianism and Beyond* (Cambridge: Cambridge University Press, 1982).
13. Fogel, *Without Consent on Contract*. New York: Norton, 1989, p. 410.
14. Cited in Litwack, *Been in the Storm So Long*. New York: Vintage, p. 97.

REVIEW AND DISCUSSION QUESTIONS

1. Describe the three legitimate interests slaves had that slavery largely ignored. What does Cohen mean in saying these interests are "legitimate"? How does he argue slaves had those interests?
2. In what sense was slavery unjust?
3. Why was the conflict of interests slavery created a source of weakness and limited viability for the system?
4. Describe the two ways that Cohen says slavery's injustice (in Cohen's sense) is relevant to understanding its destruction.

5. Explain how Cohen's argument might be applied to another type of injustice, for instance, religious oppression or oppression of women. Is the argument as strong in those cases? Why or why not?

6. Cohen thinks his argument makes a difference for how people should view the universe, even if they are not religious. Why do you think he says that? Is he right? Explain.

Essay and Paper Topics for Section 3

1. Using the various authors you have read in this section, write a brief essay on the nature of morality and its relationship with custom, with reason or intellect, and with feelings.

2. Describe whether you think morality is objective or subjective, being careful to define what you mean by those terms.

3. Write an essay comparing the views of Cohen and Nagel with those of Kant.

4. How might Hume defend his claim that morality depends on sentiment against one of the authors in this section who takes the opposite position?

PART II

Issues of Life and Death

4

Violence, Terrorism, and War

We begin our discussion of life and death by looking at questions of violence in different contexts: terrorism, gun control, and war. The articles represent different perspectives and look at a range of issues, including whether gun control reduces crime, how best to deal with terrorism, whether morality is relevant to war at all, the justification or lack of it of going to war, and the legitimacy of killing innocents in wartime.

Do Guns Mean Crime?

The Economist

The second amendment to the U.S. Constitution states that "A well regulated militia, being necessary to the security of a free State, the right of the people to keep and bear Arms, shall not be infringed." The U.S. Supreme Court has held, however, that this does not prevent states from limiting or even banning certain types of guns, for instance machine guns. Whether the right to bear arms applies to individuals or merely to state militias is also an oft-debated question. But most agree that one central issue in the debate is whether banning guns reduces crime. In this short essay, taken from *The Economist* magazine, the author reviews recent evidence and then discusses an interesting new study that uses magazine sales as a proxy for gun ownership and asks whether increased gun ownership reduces or increases crime.

The second amendment of the American constitution concerns the "right of the people to keep and bear Arms," and the intent of that language is the subject of a perpetual debate, one that will be sharpened by the incoming [George W. Bush] administration's gun-leaning instincts. Economists are not usually in the business of making value judgments. But some recent research about the effects on crime of gun ownership ought to play a part in informing society's decisions.

From a hypothetical perspective, gun ownership could promote crime by facilitating violence; or it could deter it, by implicitly threatening retribution. Empirically, the question has been hard to resolve. Economists seeking to map the relationship between American gun ownership and crime face a formidable obstacle: data on gun ownership exists only at the national level.

It is not for economists, however, to be put off by a paucity of data. Some academics have spent years squirrelling around for proxies for gun ownership in given geographical areas. Until recently, the most notorious of their studies used the passage of legislation that allowed private citizens to carry concealed firearms as a proxy indicator of gun ownership. The findings[1] of John Lott of Yale University and David Mustard of the University of Georgia (both at the time at the University of Chicago) suggested that such laws, and the increases in gun ownership that presumably accompanied them, diminished violent crime.

While the National Rifle Association feasted upon these results, other academics voiced scepticism about their statistical rigour. Just a year later, a paper[2] using the same data and more advanced econometric methods showed that concealed-weapon legislation had made only a small contribution to falling murder rates, and may even have boosted robberies. This second paper was feasted upon less than the first.

The search for a more reliable proxy continued, and has now led to a forthcoming paper[3] by Mark Duggan of the University of Chicago. Mr. Duggan obtained state- and county-level sales data from one of America's largest gun magazines, betting that sales would be strongly correlated with gun ownership. This particular magazine concentrates on handguns, the type most commonly used in crime. Although Mr. Duggan does not assume that subscribers are likely to be criminals, he does point out that the majority of guns used in crimes are obtained through burglaries or secondhand sales. Still, even before considering the link to crime, how do you prove that a correlation exists with magazine sales, when gun ownership is itself such an unknown quantity?

BURDEN OF PROOF

Mr. Duggan attacked this problem from several directions. First, he showed that the counties with high gun-magazine sales had similar demographics to those associated with the profile of typical gun-owners in national-level surveys. Next, he found a strong relationship between the level of magazine sales and the number of gun shows in states. To assume that gun shows and gun ownership are highly correlated is no great leap of logic. But then again, the logical link between gun ownership and the sales of gun magazines can hardly be called tenuous. Mr. Duggan also used government health statistics to demonstrate that states with higher magazine sales suffered higher rates of gun-related death.

Armed with a high-powered proxy, Mr. Duggan set his sights on crime. With data stretching from 1980 to 1998, he calculated that a 10% increase in an average state's rate of gun ownership, proxied by magazine sales, was associated with a 2% rise in its homicide rate. However, these concurrent changes could support either of two hypotheses: that crime rises when individuals own more guns, or that individuals purchase more guns to defend themselves against rising crime. To sort out this confusion, Mr. Duggan checked the direction of the relationship over time; increases in gun ownership led to increases in crime in the *following* year, but the reverse did not hold. The same pattern was found at the county level.

As a further check, Mr. Duggan divided his pool into homicides that involved guns and those that did not. Changes in magazine sales were not associated with changes in non-gun homicides—a reassuring point in favour of the proxy. Mr. Duggan also examined other forms of crime. Perhaps most striking for those who believe in the deterrent effect of gun-ownership, burglary (theft with forcible entry) and larceny (theft without forcible entry or threat of harm) rose significantly following growth in gun ownership, by roughly half as much as homicides. On the other hand, rates of robbery (theft with threat of harm), assault, rape and car theft remained largely unchanged, a finding which, at least for violent crimes, contradicts Messrs. Lott's and Mustard's paper.

The author also took on the Lott-Mustard results explicitly. Mr. Duggan reasoned that for guns to deter crime, the passage of concealed-weapons laws must either lead to more gun ownership or to more frequent carrying of previously owned weapons. But the passage of such legislation did not lead to significant changes in gun ownership. And those counties where gun ownership was highest (where an increase in gun carrying could occur) did not see any significant changes in crime when their states passed concealed-weapons laws.

Perhaps those in favour of concealed-weapons laws will argue that it is merely the increased fear that your victim might be armed that would be enough to deter criminals; and that concealed-weapons laws might create such fears regardless of whether actual gun ownership, or gun carrying, increased. Still, the central tenet of Mr. Duggan's findings stands: on balance, the evidence suggests that guns foster crime, not the other way around.

NOTES

1. "Crime, Deterrence, and Right-to-Carry Concealed Handguns." By John Lott and David Mustard. *Journal of Legal Studies,* January 1997.
2. "Lives Saved or Lives Lost? The Effects of Concealed-Handgun Laws on Crime." By Hashem Dezhbakhsh and Paul H. Rubin. *American Economic Review,* May 1998.
3. "More Guns, More Crime." By Mark Duggan. Forthcoming in the *Journal of Political Economy,* 2001.

REVIEW AND DISCUSSION QUESTIONS

1. How does Duggan try to address the problem of determining the level of gun ownership? Why does he think that this is a good "proxy"?
2. What is the conclusion of the Duggan study? On what basis does the author reach that conclusion?
3. How do you think a defender of the claim that guns do not lead to greater crime might respond to this study?
4. Are you persuaded that banning guns, by law, will increase crime, decrease crime, or have no effect? Explain your reasoning.

Terrorism

R.G. Frey and Christopher W. Morris

Beginning with the observation that violence is often not rejected absolutely in all circumstances, Frey and Morris go on to consider the nature of violence and whether terrorism is justified from either a consequentialist or from a natural law and Kantian moral perspective. R.G. Frey and Christopher Morris are professors of philosophy at Bowling Green State University in Ohio.

Unless one is a pacifist, one is likely to find it relatively easy to think of scenarios in which the use of force and violence against others is justified. Killing other people in self-defense, for example, seems widely condoned, but so, too, does defending our citizens abroad against attack from violent regimes. Violence in these cases appears reactive, employed to defeat aggression against or violence toward vital interests. Where violence comes to be seen as much more problematic, if not simply prohibited, is in its direct use for social/political ends. It then degenerates into terrorism, many people seem to think, and terrorism, they hold, is quite wrong. But what exactly is terrorism? And why is it wrong?

Most of us today believe terrorism to be a serious problem, one that raises difficult and challenging questions. The urgency of the problem, especially to North Americans and Western Europeans, may appear to be that terrorism is an issue that we confront from outside—that, as it were. it is an issue for us, not because violence for political ends is something approved of in our societies, but because we are the objects of such violence. The difficulty of the questions raised by contemporary terrorism has to do, we may suppose, with the complexity of issues having to do with the use of violence generally for political ends.

The first question, that of the proper characterization of terrorism, is difficult, in part because it is hard to separate from the second, evaluative question, that of the wrongness of terrorism. We may think of terrorism as a type of violence, that is, a kind of force that inflicts damage or harm on people and property. Terrorism thus broadly understood raises the same issues raised generally by the use of violence by individuals or groups. If we think of violence as being a kind of force, then the more general issues concern the evaluation of the use of force, coercion, and the like: When may we restrict people's options so that they have little or no choice but to do what we wish them to do? Violence may be used as one would use force, in order to obtain some end. But violence inflicts harm or damage and consequently adds a new element to the nonviolent use of force. When, then, if ever, may we inflict harm or damage on someone in the pursuit of some end? This question and the sets of issues it raises are familiar topics of moral and political philosophy.

Without preempting the varying characterizations of terrorism . . . we can think of it more narrowly; that is, we can think of it as a particular use of violence, typically for social/political ends, with several frequently conjoined characteristics. On this view, terrorism, as one would expect from the use of the term, usually involves creating terror or fear, even, perhaps, a sense of panic in a population. This common feature of terrorism is related to another characteristic, namely, the seemingly random or arbitrary use of violence. This in turn is related to a third feature, the targeting of the innocent or of "noncombatants." This

From *Violence, Terrorism, and Justice,* ed. R.G. Frey amd Christopher W. Morris (New York: Cambridge University Press, 1991). 1–11. Reprinted with permission of Cambridge University Press.

last, of course, is a more controversial feature than the others, since many terrorists attempt to justify their acts by arguing that their victims are not (wholly) innocent.

Thus characterized, terrorism raises specific questions that are at the center of contemporary philosophical debate. When, if ever, may one intentionally harm the innocent? Is the justification of terrorist violence to be based entirely on consequences, beneficial or other? Or are terrorist acts among those that are wrong independently of their consequences? What means may one use in combating people who use violence without justification? Other questions, perhaps less familiar, also arise. What does it mean for people to be innocent, that is, not responsible for the acts, say, of their governments? May there not be some justification in terrorists' targeting some victims but not others? May terrorist acts be attributed to groups or to states? What sense, if any, does it make to think of a social system as terrorist?

Additionally, there are a variety of issues that specifically pertain to terrorists and their practices. What is the moral standing generally of terrorists? That is, what, if any, duties do we have to them? How do their acts, and intentions, affect their standing? How does that standing affect our possible responses to them? May we, for instance, execute terrorists or inflict forms of punishment that would, in the words of the American Constitution, otherwise be "cruel and unusual"? What obligations might we, or officials of state, have in our dealings with terrorists? Is bargaining, of the sort practiced by virtually all Western governments, a justified response to terrorism? How, if at all, should our responses to terrorists be altered in the event that we admit or come to admit, to some degree, the justice of their cause?

Considered broadly, as a type of violence, or, even more generally, as a type of force, terrorism is difficult to condemn out of hand. Force is a common feature of political life. We secure compliance with law by the use and threat of force. For many, this may be the sole reason for compliance. Force is used, for instance, to ensure that people pay their taxes, and force, even violence, is commonplace in the control of crime. In many instances, there is not much controversy about the general justification of the use of force. The matter, say, of military conscription, though endorsed by many, is more controversial. In international contexts, however, the uses of force, and of violence, raise issues about which there is less agreement. Examples will come readily to mind.

More narrowly understood, involving some or all of the three elements mentioned earlier (the creation of terror, the seemingly random use of violence, and the targeting of the innocent or of noncombatants), the justification of terrorism is more problematic, as a brief glance at several competing moral theories will reveal.

Act-consequentialists, those who would have us evaluate actions solely in terms of their consequences, would presumably condone some terrorist acts. Were some such act to achieve a desirable goal, with minimal costs, the consequentialist might approve. Care, however, must be taken in characterizing the terrorists' goals and means. For contemporary consequentialists invariably are universalists; the welfare or ends of all people (and, on some accounts, all sentient beings) are to be included. Thus, terrorists cannot avail themselves of such theories to justify furthering the ends of some small group at the cost of greater damage to the interests of others. Merely to argue that the ends justify the means, without regard to the nature of the former, does not avail to one the resources of consequentialist moral theory.

Two factors will be further emphasized. First, consequentialist moral theory will focus upon effectiveness and efficiency, upon whether terrorist acts are an effective, efficient means to achieving desirable goals. The question naturally arises, then, whether there is an alternative means available, with equal or better likelihood of success in achieving the goal at a reduced cost. If resort to terrorism is a tactic, is there another tactic, just as likely to achieve the goal, at a cost more easy for us to bear? It is here, of course, that alternatives such as passive resistance and nonviolent civil disobedience will arise and need to be considered. It is here also that account must be taken of the obvious fact that terrorist acts seem often to harden the resistance of those the terrorists oppose. Indeed, the alleged justice of the terrorists' cause can easily slip into the background, as the killing and maiming come to preoccupy and outrage the target population. Second, consequentialist moral theory will focus upon the goal to be achieved: Is the goal that a specific use of terrorism is in aid of desirable enough for us to want to see it realized in society, at the terrible costs it exacts? It is no accident that terrorists usually portray their cause as concerned with the rectification and elimination of injustice; for this goal seems to be one the achievement of which we might just agree was desirable enough for us to tolerate significant cost. And it is here, of course, that doubts plague us, because we are often unsure where justice with respect to some issue falls. In the battle over Ireland, and the demand of the Irish Republican Army for justice, is there nothing to be said on the English side? Is the entire matter black and white? Here, too, a kind of proportionality rule may intrude itself. Is the reunification of Ireland worth all the suffering and loss the IRA inflicts? Is this a goal worth, not only members of the IRAs dying for, but also their making other people die for? For consequentialists, it typically will not be enough that members of the IRA think so; those affected by the acts of the IRA cannot be ignored.

Finally, consequentialist moral theory will stress how unsure we sometimes are about what counts as doing justice. On the one hand, we sometimes are genuinely unsure about what counts as rectifying an injustice. For instance, is allowing the Catholics of Northern Ireland greater and greater control over their lives part of the rectification process? For the fact remains that there are many more Protestants than Catholics in the North, so that democratic votes may well not materially change the condition of the latter, whatever their degree of participation in the process. On the other hand, we sometimes are genuinely unsure whether we can rectify or eliminate one injustice without

perpetrating another. In the Arab–Israeli conflict, for example, can we remove one side's grievances without thereby causing additional grievances on the other side? Is there any way of rectifying an injustice in that conflict without producing another?

Thus, while consequentialist moral theory can produce a justification of terrorist acts, it typically will do so here, as in other areas, only under conditions that terrorists in the flesh will find it difficult to satisfy.

It is the seeming randomness of the violence emphasized by terrorism, understood in the narrower sense, that leads many moral theorists to question its legitimacy. Many moral traditions, especially nonconsequentialist ones, impose strict limits on the harm that may be done to the innocent. Indeed, some theories, such as those associated with natural law and Kantian traditions, will impose an indefeasible prohibition on the intentional killing of the innocent, which "may not be overridden, whatever the consequences." Sometimes this prohibition is formulated in terms of the rights of the innocent not to be killed (e.g., the right to life), other times in terms merely of our duties not to take their lives. Either way the prohibition is often understood to be indefeasible.

If intentionally killing the innocent is indefeasibly wrong, that is, if it may never be done whatever the consequences, than many, if not most, contemporary terrorists stand condemned. Killing individuals who happen to find themselves in a targeted store, café, or train station may not be done, according to these traditions. Contemporary terrorists, who intend to bring about the deaths of innocent people by their acts, commit one of the most serious acts of injustice, unless, of course, they can show that these people are not innocent. Much turns on their attempts, therefore, to attack the innocence claim.

Just as natural law and Kantian moral theories constrain our behavior and limit the means we may use in the pursuit of political ends, so they constrain our responses to terrorists. We may not, for instance, intentionally kill innocent people (e.g., bystanders, hostages) while combating those who attack us. Our hands may thus be tied in responding to terrorism. Many commentators have argued that a morally motivated reluctance to use the non-discriminating means of terrorists makes us especially vulnerable to them.

Some natural law or Kantian thinkers invoke the notions of natural or human rights to understand moral standing, where these are rights which we possess simply by virtue of our natures or of our humanity. Now if our nature or our humanity is interpreted, as it commonly is in these traditions, as something we retain throughout our lives, at least to the extent that we retain those attributes and capacities that are characteristic of humans, then even those who violate the strictest prohibitions of justice will retain their moral standing. According to this view, a killer acts wrongly without thereby ceasing to be the sort of being that possesses moral standing. Terrorists, then, retain their moral standing, and consequently, there are limits to what we may do to them, by way either of resistance or of punishment. Conversely, though there is reason to think consequentialists, including those who reject theories of rights to understand moral standing, would not deny terrorists such standing, what may be done to terrorists may not be so easily constrained. For harming those who harm the innocent seems less likely to provoke outrage and opposition and so negative consequences . . .

Whether we follow these theories in understanding the prohibition on the intentional killing of the innocent to be indefeasible or not, this principle figures importantly in most moral traditions. Care, however, must be taken in its interpretation and application. Even if we understand terrorism narrowly as involving attacks on the innocent, it may not be clear here as elsewhere exactly who is innocent. As made clear in the just war and abortion literature, the term "innocent" is ambiguous. The usual sense is to designate some individual who is not guilty of moral or legal wrongdoing, a sense usually called the moral or juridical sense of the term. By contrast, in discussing what are often called "innocent threats"—for instance, an approaching infant who unwittingly is boobytrapped with explosives, a fetus whose continued growth threatens the life of the woman—it is common to distinguish a "technical" or "causal" sense of "innocence." People lack innocence in this second sense insofar as they threaten, whatever their culpability.

Determining which sense of "innocence" is relevant (and this is not to prejudge the issue of still further, different senses) is controversial. In discussions of the ethics of war, it is often thought that "noncombatants" are not legitimate targets, because of their innocence. Noncombatants, however, may share some of the responsibility for the injustice of a war or the injustice of the means used to prosecute the war, or they may threaten the adversary in certain ways. In the first case, they would not be fully innocent in the moral or juridical sense; in the second, they would lack, to some degree, causal innocence.

This distinction is relevant to the moral evaluation of terrorist acts aimed at noncombatants. Sometimes attempts are made at justification by pointing to the victims' lack of innocence, in the first sense. Perhaps this is what Emile Henry meant when he famously said, in 1894, after exploding a bomb in a Paris café, "There are no innocents." Presumably in such cases, where the relevant notion of innocence is that of nonculpability, terrorists would strike only at members of certain national or political groups. Other times it might be argued that the victims in some way (for instance, by their financial, electoral, or tacit support for a repressive regime) posed a threat. In these cases, terrorists would view themselves as justified in striking at anyone who, say, was present in a certain location. The distinction may also be of importance in discussions of the permissibility of various means that might be used in response to terrorist acts. If the relevant sense of innocence is causal, then certain means, those endangering the lives of victims, might be permissible.

Of course it is hard to understand how the victims of the Japanese Red Army attack at

Israel's Lod airport in 1972 or of a bomb in a Paris department store in 1986 could be thought to lack innocence in either sense. In the first case, the victims were travelers (e.g., Puerto Rican Christians); in the second case, the store in question was frequented by indigent immigrants and, at that time of year, by mothers and children shopping for school supplies. It is this feature of some contemporary terrorism that has led many commentators to distinguish it from earlier forms and from other political uses of violence.

The analogies here with another issue that has preoccupied moral theorists recently, that of the ethics of nuclear deterrence and conflict, are significant. The United States, of course, dropped atomic weapons on two Japanese cities at the end of the last world war. For several decades now, American policy has been to threaten the Soviet Union with a variety of kinds of nuclear strikes in the event that the latter attacked the United States or its Western allies with nuclear or, in the case of an invasion of Western Europe, merely with conventional weapons. These acts or practices involve killing or threatening to kill noncombatants in order to achieve certain ends: unconditional surrender in the case of Japan, deterrence of aggression in that of the Soviet Union. The possible analogies with terrorism have not gone unnoticed. Furthermore, just as some defenders of the atomic strikes against the Japanese have argued, those we attack, or threaten to attack, with nuclear weapons are themselves sufficiently similar to terrorists to justify our response.

A still different perspective on these issues may be obtained by turning from the usual consequentialist and natural law or Kantian theories to forms of contractarianism in ethics. Although this tradition has affinities with natural law and Kantian theories, especially with regard to the demands of justice or the content of moral principles, there are differences that are especially noteworthy in connection with the issues that are raised by terrorist violence.

According to this tradition, justice may be thought of as a set of principles and dispositions that bind people insofar as those to whom they are obligated reciprocate. In the absence of constraint by others, one has little or no duty to refrain from acting toward them in ways that normally would be unjust. Justice may be thus thought, to borrow a phrase from John Rawls, to be a sort of "cooperative venture for mutual advantage." According to this view, justice is not binding in the absence of certain conditions, one of which would be others' cooperative behavior and dispositions.

Adherents to this tradition might argue that we would be in a "state of nature," that is, a situation where few if any constraints of justice would bind us, with regard to terrorists who attack those who are innocent (in the relevant sense). . . . Unlike the earlier views, then, this view holds that terrorists who, by act or by intent, forswear the rules of justice may thereby lose the protection of those rules, and so a major part of their moral standing.

Similarly, partisans of terrorism might argue that it is the acts of their victims or of their governments that make impossible cooperative relations of fair dealing between themselves and those they attack. The acts, or intentions, of the latter remove them from the protection of the rules of justice.

In either case, the acts of terrorists and our response to them take place in a world beyond, or prior to, justice. Students of international affairs and diplomacy will recognize here certain of the implications of a family of skeptical positions called "realism."

Consequentialists, it should be noted, are likely to find this exclusive focus on the virtue of justice to be misguided, and they are likely to be less enamored of certain distinctions involving kinds of innocence or types of violence that are incorporated into contractarianism. In general, they will argue, as noted earlier, that terrorism can be justified by its consequences, where these must include the effects not merely on the terrorists but also on their victims (and others). As terrorist acts appear often not to produce sufficient benefits to outweigh the considerable costs they inevitably exact, there will most likely be a moral presumption, albeit defensible, against them. But wrongful terrorism will be condemned, not because of the existence of mutually advantageous conventions of justice, but because of the overall harm or suffering caused. Consequentialists, then, will doubtless stand out against natural law or Kantian ones.

The foregoing, then, is a sketch of different ways terrorism may be understood and of different types of moral theories in which its justification may be addressed. There is serious controversy on both counts, and this fact alone, whatever other differences may exist, makes the works of philosophers and political and social scientists on terrorism contentious even among themselves.

REVIEW AND DISCUSSION QUESTIONS

1. What are the three features of violence, according to the authors?
2. Why might some consequentialists condone terrorism?
3. How would a consequentialist be likely to view the means terrorists use? The goals of terrorists?
4. What problems and questions do the authors believe would be raised by Kantian and natural law theories?
5. Who are "noncombatants" and what is their relevance in thinking about terrorist violence, according to the authors?

On the Morality of War

Richard A. Wasserstrom

When is war justified, if at all? And what are the moral limits on how wars should be fought? Some say war *itself* is simply beyond the bounds of morality; if not everything is fair in love, at least it is in war. In this essay, Richard A. Wasserstrom discusses both the question of applying morality to war and the various issues that arise as one begins to think about the justification of war as well as the rules governing how wars should be fought. He also weighs the issues surrounding killing innocents. Richard A. Wasserstrom is professor of philosophy at the University of California at Santa Cruz.

1. WAR AND MORAL NIHILISM

Before we examine the moral criteria for assessing war, we must examine the claim that it is not possible to assess war in moral terms. . . . For want of a better name for this general view, I shall call it moral nihilism in respect to war. If it is correct, there is, of course, no point in going further.

. . . During the controversy over the rightness of the Vietnam War there have been any number of persons, including a large number in

From Richard A. Wasserstrom, "On the Morality of War: A Preliminary Inquiry," *Stanford Law Review,* 21, no. 6 (June 1969), pp. 1627–1656. ©1969 by the Board of Trustees of Leland Stanford Junior University. Reprinted by permission of the *Stanford Law Review* and the author. Some footnotes omitted.

the university, who have claimed that in matters of war (but not in other matters) morality has no place. The war in Vietnam may, they readily concede, be stupid, unwise, or against the best interests of the United States, but it is neither immoral nor unjust—not because it is moral or right, but because these descriptions are *in this context* either naive or meaningless or inapplicable.

Nor is this view limited to the Vietnam War. Consider, for example, the following passage from a speech given only a few years ago by Dean Acheson:

> [T]hose involved in the Cuban crisis of October, 1962, will remember the irrelevance of the supposed moral considerations brought out in the discussions. Judgment centered about the appraisal of dangers and risks, and weighing of the need for decisive and effective action against considerations of prudence; the need to do enough, against the consequences of doing too much. Moral talk did not bear on the problem. Nor did it bear upon the decision of those called upon to advise the President in 1949 whether and with what degree or urgency to press the attempt to produce a thermonuclear weapon. A respected colleague advised me that it would be better that our nation and people should perish rather than be party to a course so evil as producing that weapon. I told him that on the Day of Judgment his view might be confirmed and that he was free to go forth and preach the necessity for salvation. It was not, however, a view which I would entertain as a public servant.[1]

. . . Whatever may be the correct exegesis of this text, I want to treat it as illustrative of the position that morality has no place in the assessment of war. There are several things worth considering in respect to such a view. In the first place, the claim that in matters of war morality has no place is ambiguous. To put it somewhat loosely, the claim may be descriptive, or it may be analytic, or it may be prescriptive. Thus, it would be descriptive if it were merely the factual claim that matters relating to war uniformly turn out to be decided on grounds of national interest or expediency rather than by appeal to what is moral. This claim I will not consider further; it is an empirical one better answered by students of American (and foreign) diplomatic relations.

It would be a prescriptive claim were it taken to assert that matters relating to war ought always be decided by appeal to (say) national interest rather than an appeal to the moral point of view. For reasons which have yet to be elucidated, on this view the moral criteria are capable of being employed but it is undesirable to do so. I shall say something more about this view in a moment.

The analytic point is not that morality ought not be used, but rather that it cannot. On this view the statement "The United States is behaving immorally in the way it is waging war in Vietnam" (or, "in waging war in Vietnam") is not wrong but meaningless.

What are we to make of the analytic view? As I have indicated, it could, of course, be advanced simply as an instance of a more sweeping position concerning the general meaninglessness of the moral point of view. What I find particularly interesting, though, is the degree to which this thesis is advanced as a special view about war and not as a part of a more general claim that all morality is meaningless.

I think that there are at least [three] reasons why this special view may be held. First, the accusation that one's own country is involved in an immoral war is personally very threatening. For one thing, if the accusation is well-founded it may be thought to imply that certain types of socially cooperative behavior are forbidden to the citizen and that other kinds of socially deviant behavior are obligatory upon him. Yet, in a time of war it is following just this sort of dictate that will be treated more harshly by the actor's own government. Hence the morally responsible citizen is put in a most troublesome moral dilemma. If his country is engaged in an immoral war then he may have a duty to oppose and resist; yet opposition and resistance will typically carry extraordinarily severe penalties.

The pressure is, I suspect, simply too great for many of us. We are unwilling to pay the fantastically high personal price that goes with the moral point of view, and we are equally unwilling to plead guilty to this most serious charge of immorality. So we solve the problem by denying the possibility that war can be immoral. The relief is immediate; the moral "heat" is off. If war cannot be immoral, then one's country cannot be engaged in an immoral war, but only a stupid or unwise one. And whatever one's obligation to keep one's country from behaving stupidly or improvidently, they are vastly less stringent and troublesome than obligations imposed by the specter of complicity in an immoral war. We may, however, pay a price for such relief since we obliterate the moral distinctions between the Axis and the Allies in World War II at the same time as the distinctions between the conduct of the United States in 1941–45 and the conduct of the United States in 1967–68 in Vietnam.

Second, I think the view that moral judgments are meaningless sometimes seems plausible because of the differences between personal behavior and the behavior of states. There are not laws governing the behavior of states in the same way in which there are positive laws governing the behavior of citizens. International law is a troublesome notion just because it is both like and unlike our concept of positive law.

Now, how does skepticism about the law-like quality of international law lead to the claim that it is impossible for war to be either moral or immoral? It is far from obvious. Perhaps it is because there is at least one sense of justice that is intimately bound up with the notion of rule-violation; namely, that which relates justice to the following of rules and to the condemnation and punishment of those who break rules. In the absence of positive laws governing the behavior of states, it may be inferred (although I think mistakenly) that it is impossible for states to behave either justly or unjustly. But even if justice can be said to be analyzable solely in terms of following rules, morality certainly cannot. Hence the absence of international laws cannot serve to make the moral appraisal of war impossible.

. . . More plausible, is the view that says there can be no moral assessment of war just because there is, by definition, no morality in war. If war is an activity in which anything goes, moral judgments on war are just not possible.

To this there are two responses. To begin with, it is not, as our definitional discussion indicates, a necessary feature of war that it be an activity in which everything is morally permissible. There is a difference between the view that war is unique because killing and violence are morally permissible in contexts and circumstances where they otherwise would not be and the view that war is unique because everything is morally permissible.

A less absolutist argument for the absurdity of discussing the morality of war might be that at least today the prevailing (although not necessary) conception of war is one that as a practical matter rules out no behavior on moral grounds. After all, if flame throwers are deemed perfectly permissible, if the bombing of cities is applauded and not condemned, and if thermonuclear weapons are part of the arsenal of each of the major powers, then the remaining moral prohibitions on the conduct of war are sufficiently insignificant to be ignored.

The answer to this kind of an argument requires, I believe, that we distinguish the question of what is moral in war from that of the morality of war or of war generally. . . . Paradoxically, the more convincing the argument from war's conduct, the stronger is the moral argument *against* engaging in war at all. For the more it can be shown that engaging in war will inevitably lead to despicable behavior to which no moral predicates are deemed applicable, the more this also constitutes an argument against bringing such a state of affairs into being.

There is still another way to take the claim that in matters of war morality has no place. That is what I have called the prescriptive view: that national interest ought to determine policies in respect to war, not morality. This is surely one way to interpret the remarks of Dean Acheson reproduced earlier. It is also, perhaps, involved in President Truman's defense of the dropping of the atomic bomb on Hiroshima. What he said was this:·

> Having found the bomb, we have to use it. We have used it against those who attacked us without warning at Pearl Harbor, against those who have starved and beaten and executed American prisoners of war, against those who have abandoned all pretense of obeying international laws of warfare. We have used it in order to shorten the agony of war, in order to save the lives of thousands and thousands of young Americans.[2]

Although this passage has many interesting features, I am concerned only with President Truman's insistence that the dropping of the bomb was justified because it saved the lives "of thousands and thousands of young Americans."

Conceivably, this is merely an elliptical way of saying that on balance fewer lives were lost through the dropping of the bomb and the accelerated cessation of hostilities than through any alternative course of conduct. Suppose, though, that this were not the argument. Suppose, instead, that the justification were regarded as adequate provided only that it was reasonably clear that fewer *American* lives would be lost than through any alternative course of conduct. Thus, to quantify the example, we can imagine someone maintaining that Hiroshima was justified because 20,000 fewer Americans died in the Pacific theater than would have died if the bomb had not been dropped. And this is justified even though 30,000 more Japanese died than would have been killed had the war been fought to an end with conventional means. Thus, even though 10,000 more people died than would otherwise have been the case, the bombing was justified because of the greater number of American lives saved.

On this interpretation the argument depends upon valuing the lives of Americans higher than the lives of persons from other countries. As such, is there anything to be said for the argument? Its strongest statement, and the only one that I shall consider, might go like this: Truman was the President of the United States and as such had an obligation always to choose that course of conduct that appeared to offer the greatest chance of maximizing the interests of the United States. As President, he was obligated to prefer the lives of American soldiers over those from any other country, and he was obligated to prefer them just because they were Americans and he was their President.

Some might prove such a point by drawing an analogy to the situation of a lawyer, or a parent, or a corporation executive. A lawyer has a duty to present his client's case in the fashion most calculated to ensure his client's victory; and he has this obligation irrespective of the objective merits of his client's case. Similarly, we are neither surprised nor dismayed when a parent prefers the interests of his child over those of other children. A parent *qua* parent is certainly not behaving immorally when he acts so as to secure satisfactions for his child, again irrespective of the objective merits of the child's needs or wants. And, *mutatis mutandis,* a corporate executive has a duty to maximize profits for his company. Thus, as public servants, Dean Acheson and Harry Truman had no moral choice but to pursue those policies that appeared to them to be in the best interest of the United States. And to a lesser degree, all persons *qua* citizens of the United States have a similar, if slightly more attenuated, obligation. Therefore, morality has no real place in war.

The analogy, however, must not stop halfway. It is certainly both correct and important to observe that public officials, like parents, lawyers, and corporate executives, do have special moral obligations that are imposed by virtue of the position or role they fill. A lawyer does have a duty to prefer his client's interests in a way that would be improper were the person anyone other than a client. And the same sort of duty, I think, holds for a parent, an executive, a President, and a citizen in their respective roles. The point becomes distorted, however, when it is supposed that such an obligation always, under all circumstances, overrides any and all other obligations that the person might have. The case of the lawyer is instructive. While he has an obligation to attend to his client's interests in very special ways, there are many other things that it is impermissible for the lawyer to do in furtherance of his client's interests—irrespective, this time, of how significantly they might advance that interest.

The case for the President, or for public servants generally, is similar. While the President may indeed have an obligation to prefer and pursue the national interests, this obligation could only be justifiable—could only be a moral obligation—if it were enmeshed in a comparable range of limiting and competing obligations. If we concede that the President has certain obligations to prefer the national interest that no one else has, we must be equally sensitive to the fact that the President also has some of the same obligations to other persons that all other men have—if for no other reason than that all persons have the right to be treated or not treated in certain ways. So, whatever special obligations the President may have cannot by themselves support the view that in war morality ought have no place. . . .

But the major problem with the national-interest argument is its assumption that the national interest not only is something immutable and knowable but also that it limits national interest to narrowly national concerns. It is parochial to suppose that the American national interest really rules out solicitude for other states in order to encourage international stability.

Finally, national interest as a goal must itself be justified. The United States' position of international importance may have imposed on it a duty of more than national concern. The fact that such a statement has become hackneyed by constant use to justify American interference abroad should not blind us to the fact that it may be viable as an argument for a less aggressive international responsibility.

2. ASSESSING THE MORALITY OF WARS

If we turn now to confront more directly the question of the morality of wars, it is evident that there is a variety of different perspectives from which, or criteria in terms of which, particular wars may be assessed. First, to the extent to which the model of war as a game continues to have a place, wars can be evaluated in terms of the degree to which the laws of war—the rules for initiating and conducting war—are adhered to by the opposing countries. Second, the rightness or wrongness of wars is often thought to depend very much upon the cause for which a war is fought. And third, there is the independent justification for a war that is founded upon an appeal of some kind to a principle of self-defense.

In discussing the degree to which the laws of war are followed or disregarded there are two points that should be stressed. First, a skepticism as to the meaningfulness of any morality *within* war is extremely common. The gnomic statement is Sherman's: "War is hell." The fuller argument depends upon a rejection of the notion of war as a game. It goes something like this. War is the antithesis of law or rules. It is violence, killing and all of the horror they imply. Even if moral distinctions can be made in respect to such things as the initiation and purposes of a war, it is absurd to suppose that moral distinctions can be drawn once a war has begun. All killing is bad, all destruction equally wanton.

Now, there does seem to me to be a fairly simple argument of sorts that can be made in response. Given the awfulness of war, it nonetheless appears plausible to discriminate among degrees of awfulness. A war in which a large number of innocent persons are killed is, all other things being equal, worse than one in which only a few die. A war in which few combatants are killed is, *ceteris paribus,* less immoral than one in which many are killed.

And more to the point, perhaps, any unnecessary harm to others is surely unjustifiable. To some degree, at least, the "laws of war" can be construed as attempts to formalize these general notions and to define instances of unnecessary harm to others.

The second criterion, the notion of the cause that can be invoked to justify a war may involve two quite different inquiries. On the one hand, we may intend the sense in which cause refers to the *consequences* of waging war, to the forward-looking criteria of assessment. Thus, when a war is justified as a means by which to make the world safe for democracy, or on the grounds that a failure to fight now will lead to a loss of confidence on the part of one's allies, or as necessary to avoid fighting a larger, more destructive war later, when these sorts of appeals are made, the justification is primarily consequential or forward-looking in character. Here the distinction between morality and prudence—never a very easy one to maintain in international relations—is always on the verge of collapse. On the other hand, a war may be evaluated through recourse to what may be termed backward-looking criteria. Just as in the case of punishment or blame where what happened in the past is relevant to the justice of punishing or blaming someone, so in the case of war, what has already happened is, on this view, relevant to the justice or rightness of the war that is subsequently waged. The two backward-looking criteria that are most frequently invoked in respect to war are the question of whether the war involved a violation of some prior promise, typically expressed in the form of a treaty or concord.

Two sorts of assertions are often made concerning the role of the treaty in justifying resort to war. First, if a country has entered into a treaty not to go to war and if it violates that treaty, it is to be condemned for, in effect, having broken its promise. And second, if a country has entered into a treaty in which it has agreed to go to war under certain circumstances and if those circumstances come to pass, then the country is at least justified in

going to war—although it is not in fact obligated to do so.

Once again . . . it is clear that treaties can be relevant but not decisive factors. This is so just because it is sometimes right to break our promises and sometimes wrong to keep them. The fact that a treaty is violated at best tends to make a war unjust or immoral in some degree, but it does not necessarily render the war unjustified.

The other backward-looking question, that of aggression, is often resolved by concluding that under no circumstances is the initiation of a war of aggression justified. This is a view that Americans and America have often embraced. Such a view was expounded at Nuremberg by Mr. Justice Jackson when he said:

[T]he wrong for which their [the German] fallen leaders are on trial is not that they lost the war, but that they started it. And we must not allow ourselves to be drawn into a trial of the causes of war, for our position is that no grievances or policies will justify resort to aggressive war. . . . Our position is that whatever grievances a nation may have, however objectionable it finds that *status quo,* aggressive warfare is an illegal means for settling those grievances or for altering those conditions.[3]

A position such as this is typically thought to imply two things: (1) the initiation of war is never justifiable; (2) the warlike response to aggressive war is justifiable. Both views are troublesome.

To begin with, it is hard to see how the two propositions go together very comfortably. Conceivably, there are powerful arguments against the waging of aggressive war. Almost surely, though, the more persuasive of these will depend, at least in part, on the character of war itself—on such things as the supreme importance of human life, or the inevitable injustices committed in every war. If so, then the justifiability of meeting war with war will to that degree be called into question.

To take the first proposition alone, absent general arguments about the unjustifiability of all war, it is hard to see how aggressive war can be ruled out in a wholly a priori fashion. Even if we assume that no problems are presented in determining what is and is not aggression, it is doubtful that the quality of aggression could always be morally decisive in condemning the war. Would a war undertaken to free innocent persons from concentration camps or from slavery always be unjustifiable just because *it was aggressive?* Surely this is to rest too much upon only one of a number of relevant considerations.

From a backward-looking point of view, the claim that a warring response to aggressive war is always justified is even more perplexing. . . .

In order to understand the force of the doctrine of self-defense when invoked in respect to war, and to assess its degree of legitimate applicability, it is necessary that we look briefly at self-defense as it functions as a doctrine of municipal criminal law. . . .

[W]hat is important is that we keep in mind two of the respects in which the law qualifies resort to the claim of self-defense. On one hand, the doctrine cannot be invoked successfully if the intended victim could have avoided the encounter through a reasonable escape or retreat unless the attack takes place on one's own property. And on the other hand, the doctrine requires that no more force be employed than is reasonably necessary to prevent the infliction of comparable harm.

Now how does all of this apply to self-defense as a justification for engaging in war? In the first place, to the extent to which the basic doctrine serves as an excuse, the applicability to war seems doubtful. While it may make sense to regard self-defense of one's person as a natural, instinctive response to an attack, it is only a very anthropomorphic view of countries that would lead us to elaborate a comparable explanation here.

In the second place, it is not even clear that self-defense can function very persuasively as a justification. For it to do so it might be necessary, for example, to be able to make out a case that countries die in the same way in which persons do, or that a country can be harmed in the same way in which a person can be. Of

course, persons in the country can be and killed by war, and I shall return t point in a moment, but we can also imagin attack in which none of the inhabitants of t country will be killed or even physically harmed unless they fight back. But the country, as a separate political entity, might nonetheless disappear. Would we say that this should be regarded as the equivalent of human death? That it is less harmful? More harmful? These are issues to which those who readily invoke the doctrine of self-defense seldom address themselves.

Even if we were to decide, however, that there is no question but that a country is justified in relying upon a doctrine of self-defense that is essentially similar to that which obtains in the criminal law, it would be essential to observe the constraints that follow. Given even the unprovoked aggressive waging of war by one country against another, the doctrine of self-defense could not be invoked by the country so attacked to justify waging unlimited defensive war or insisting upon unconditional surrender. Each or both of these responses might be justifiable, but not simply because a country was wrongly attacked. It would, instead, have to be made out that something analogous to retreat was neither possible nor appropriate, and, even more, that no more force was used than was reasonably necessary to terminate the attack.

There is, to be sure, an answer to this. The restrictions that the criminal law puts upon self-defense are defensible, it could be maintained, chiefly because we have a municipal police force, municipal laws, and courts. If we use no more than reasonable force to repel attacks, we can at least be confident that the attacker will be apprehended and punished and, further, that we live in a society in which this sort of aggressive behavior is deterred by a variety of means. It is the absence of such a context that renders restrictions on an international doctrine of self-defense inappropriate.

I do not think this answer is convincing. It is relevant to the question of what sorts of

...perative on the behavior ...untries, but it is not persua-...nvocation of *self*-defense as a ...or war. To use more force than is ...y necessary to defend oneself is, in ...o do more than defend oneself. If such ...self-defensive behavior is to be justified, ...must appeal to some different principle or set of principles.

There are, therefore, clearly cases in which a principle of self-defense does appear to justify engaging in a war: at a minimum, those cases in which one's country is attacked in such a way that the inhabitants are threatened with deadly force and in which no more force than is reasonably necessary is employed to terminate the attack.

3. WAR AND INNOCENTS

The strongest argument against war is that which rests upon the connection between the morality of war and the death of innocent persons. The specter of thermonuclear warfare makes examination of this point essential; yet the problem was both a genuine and an urgent one in the preatomic days of air warfare, particularly during the Second World War.

The argument based upon the death of innocent persons goes something like this: Even in war innocent people have a right to life and limb that should be respected. It is no less wrong and no more justifiable to kill innocent persons in war than at any other time. Therefore, if innocent persons are killed in a war, that war is to be condemned.

The argument can quite readily be converted into an attack upon all modern war. Imagine a thoroughly unprovoked attack upon another country—an attack committed, moreover, from the worst of motives and for the most despicable of ends. Assume too, for the moment, that under such circumstances there is nothing immoral about fighting back and even killing those who are attacking. Nonetheless, if in fighting back innocent persons will be killed, the defenders will be acting immorally. However, given any war fought today, innocent persons will inevitably be killed. Therefore, any war fought today will be immoral.

There are a variety of matters that require clarification before the strength of this argument can be adequately assessed. In particular, there are four questions that must be examined: (1) What is meant by "innocence" in this context? (2) Is it plausible to suppose that there are any innocents? (3) Under what circumstances is the death of innocent persons immoral? (4) What is the nature of the connection between the immorality of the killing of innocent persons and the immorality of the war in which this killing occurs?

It is anything but clear what precisely is meant by "innocence" or "the innocent" in an argument such as this. One possibility would be that all noncombatants are innocent. But then, of course, we would have to decide what was meant by "noncombatants." Here we might be tempted to claim that noncombatants are all of those persons who are not in the army—not actually doing the fighting; the combatants are those who are. There are, however, serious problems with this position. For it appears that persons can be noncombatants in this sense and yet indistinguishable in any apparently relevant sense from persons in the army. Thus, civilians may be manufacturing munitions, devising new weapons, writing propaganda, or doing any number of other things that make them indistinguishable from many combatants vis-à-vis their relationship to the war effort.

A second possibility would be to focus upon an individual's causal connection with the attempt to win the war rather than on his status as soldier or civilian. In this view only some noncombatants would be innocent and virtually no combatants would be. If the causal connection is what is relevant, meaningful distinctions might be made among civilians. One might distinguish between those whose activities or vocations help the war effort only indirectly, if at all, and those whose activities are more plausibly described as directly beneficial. Thus the distinctions would be between a typical grocer or a tailor on the one hand, and a worker in an armaments plant on the other. Similarly, children, the aged, and the infirm would normally not be in a position to play a role causally connected in this way with the waging of war.

There are, of course, other kinds of possible causal connections. In particular, someone might urge that attention should also be devoted to the existence of a causal connection between the individual's civic behavior and the war effort. Thus, for example, a person's voting behavior, or the degree of his political opposition to the government, or his financial contributions to the war effort might all be deemed to be equally relevant to his status as an innocent.

Still a fourth possibility, closely related to those already discussed, would be that interpretation of innocence concerned with culpability rather than causality per se. On this view a person would properly be regarded an innocent if he could not fairly be held responsible for the war's initiation or conduct. Clearly, the notion of culpability is linked in important ways with that of causal connection, but they are by no means identical. So it is quite conceivable, for example, that under some principles of culpability many combatants might not be culpable and some noncombatants might be extremely culpable, particularly if culpability were to be defined largely in terms of state of mind and enthusiasm for the war. Thus, an aged or infirm person who cannot do very much to help the war effort but is an ardent proponent of its aims and objectives might be more culpable (and less innocent in this sense) than a conscriptee who is firing a machine gun only because the penalty for disobeying the command to do so is death.

But we need not propose an airtight definition of "innocence" in order to answer the question of whether, in any war, there will be a substantial number of innocent persons involved. For irrespective of which sense or senses of innocence are ultimately deemed most instructive or important, it does seem clear that there will be a number of persons in any country (children are probably the clearest example) who will meet any test of inn that is proposed.

The third question enumerated earlie Under what circumstances is the death innocent persons immoral? One possible view is that which asserts simply that it is unimportant which circumstances bring about the death of innocent persons. As long as we know that innocent persons will be killed as a result of war, we know all we need to know to condemn any such war.

Another, and perhaps more plausible, view is that which regards the death of innocent persons as increasingly unjustifiable if it was negligently, recklessly, knowingly, or intentionally brought about. Thus, if a country engages in acts of war with the intention of bringing about the death of children, perhaps to weaken the will of the enemy, it would be more immoral than if it were to engage in acts of war aimed at killing combatants but which through error also kill children.

A different sort of problem arises if someone asks how we are to differentiate the deaths of children in war from, for example, the deaths of children that accompany the use of highways or airplanes in times of peace. Someone might, that is, argue that we permit children to ride in cars on highways and to fly in airplanes even though we know that there will be accidents and that as a result of these accidents innocent children will die. And since we know this to be the case, the situation appears to be indistinguishable from that of engaging in acts of war where it is known that the death of children will be a direct, although not intended, consequence.

I think that there are three sorts of responses that can be made to an objection of this sort. In the first place, in a quite straightforward sense the highway does not, typically, cause the death of the innocent passenger; the careless driver or the defective tire does. But it is the intentional bombing of the heavily populated city that does cause the death of the children who live in the city.

In the second place, it is one thing to act where one knows that certain more or less identifiable persons will be killed (say, bombing

one knows that those chil-
the vicinity of the camp will
), and quite another thing to
onduct in which all one can say is
be predicted with a high degree of
ence that over a given period of time a
ain number of persons (including chil-
ren) will be killed. . . .

In the third place, there is certainly a difference in the two cases in respect to the possibility of deriving benefits from the conduct. That is to say, when a highway is used, one is participating in a system or set of arrangements in which benefits are derived from that use (even though risks, and hence costs, are also involved). It is not easy to see how a similar sort of analysis can as plausibly be proposed in connection with typical acts of war.

The final and most important issue that is raised by the argument concerning the killing of the innocent in time of war is that of the connection between the immorality of the killing of innocent persons and the immorality of the war in which this killing occurs. Writers in the area often fail to discuss the connection.

Miss Anscombe puts the point this way: "[I]t is murderous to attack [the innocent] or make them a target for an attack which [the attacker] judges will help him toward victory. For murder is the deliberate killing of the innocent, whether for its own sake or as a means to some further end.". . .

It is likely that Miss Anscombe means to assert an absolutist view here—that there are no circumstances under which the intentional killing of innocent persons, even in time of war, can be justified. It is always immoral to do so. At least their arguments are phrased in absolutist terms. If this is the view that they intend to defend, it is, I think, a hard one to accept. This is so just because it ultimately depends upon too complete a rejection of the relevance of consequences to the moral character of action. It also requires too rigid a dichotomy between acts and omissions. It seems to misunderstand the character of our moral life to claim that, no matter what the consequences, the intentional killing of an innocent person could never be justifiable—even, for example, if a failure to do so would bring about the death of many more innocent persons. . . .

My own view is that as a theoretical matter an absolutist position is even less convincing here. Given the number of criteria that are relevant to the moral assessment of any war and given the great number of persons involved in and the extended duration of most wars, it would be false to the complexity of the issues to suppose that so immediately simple a solution were possible.

But having said all of this, the *practical,* as opposed to the theoretical, thrust of the argument is virtually unabated. If wars were conducted, or were likely to be conducted, so as to produce only the occasional intentional killing of the innocent, that would be one thing. We could then say with some confidence that on this ground at least wars can hardly be condemned out of hand. Unfortunately, though, mankind no longer lives in such a world and, as a result, the argument from the death of the innocent has become increasingly more convincing. The intentional, or at least knowing, killing of the innocent on a large scale became a practically necessary feature of war with the advent of air warfare. And the genuinely indiscriminate killing of very great numbers of innocent persons is the dominant legacy of the birth of thermonuclear weapons. At this stage the argument from the death of the innocent moves appreciably closer to becoming a decisive objection to war. For even if we reject, as I have argued we should, both absolutist interpretations of the argument, the core of truth that remains is the insistence that in war, no less than elsewhere, the knowing killing of the innocent is an evil that throws up the heaviest of justificatory burdens. My own view is that in any major war that can or will be fought today, none of those considerations that can sometimes justify engaging in war will in fact come close to meeting this burden. But even if I am wrong, the argument from the death of the innocent does, I believe, make it clear both where the burden is and how unlikely it is today to suppose that it can be honestly discharged.

NOTES

1. D. Acheson, "Ethics in International Relations Today," in *The Vietnam Reader,* ed. M. Raskin and B. Fall (1965), p. 13.
2. Address to the Nation by President Harry S.
Truman, Aug. 9, 1945, quoted in R. Tucker, *The War* (1960), pp. 21–22, n. 14.
3. Quoted in R. Tucker, supra note 2, p. 12.

REVIEW AND DISCUSSION QUESTIONS

1. Describe and evaluate the argument that warfare is amoral.
2. What considerations does Wasserstrom think could justify war? Describe the limitations of each.
3. "War is wrong because it inevitably means the deaths of innocents." How does Wasserstrom assess this argument?
4. Under what circumstances would it be right to say that a war is unjust?

Essay and Paper Topics for Section 4

1. Many features of our lives might be thought to encourage violence, including sports, video games, movies. Discuss whether you think these practices do or do not encourage violence, along with whether or not there is reason to ban them.
2. "Terrorism is never justified." Critically assess that claim. Under what circumstances, if any, would you think terrorism is justified? How would you answer the person who offers what you think is the best argument against your conclusion?
3. Using the approach the authors used in discussing terrorism, write an essay in which you discuss how the different approaches to moral philosophy would assess wars.

tal Punishment

...e next topic on our consideration of issues of life and death is one about which there is growing controversy: capital punishment. The first selection is taken from the U.S. Supreme Court's opinion in which it held that executions are not unconstitutional violations of the Eighth Amendment's ban on cruel and unusual punishment. That case is followed by two articles, one by Martin Perlmutter and the other by Ernest van den Haag. Perlmutter discusses the justification of executions from a utilitarian and retributivist perspective, while van den Haag replies to the arguments of capital punishment's critics. Next is an essay in which Jeffrey Reiman argues that the death penalty, like torture, is simply beyond the pale of what civilized societies do to their own. The last reading is a brief response to Reiman by van den Haag.

The Death Penalty

Gregg v. Georgia

The Eighth Amendment to the U.S. Constitution says in part that no "cruel and unusual punishment" shall be inflicted. But what, precisely, does that mean? Some examples are clear enough, for instance drawing and quartering, burning at the stake, and other extreme forms of mutilation or torture. But what about executions? The Supreme Court has consistently held that the meaning of "cruel and unusual" is not fixed, but instead it must be adjusted as society evolves. In this case, the question before the Court is whether executions for murder are unconstitutional. In an earlier case, *Furman* v. *Georgia* (1972), the Court overturned a death sentence in part because the specific procedures used made imposition of the penalty "arbitrary." A minority of the justices had also argued in *Furman* that executions per se were unconstitutional. In this opinion, the Court again considers both questions: the constitutionality of executions and the constitutionality of the procedures by which it is determined who shall die. In doing so, it also considers the important philosophical issues surrounding punishment and its justification.

Mr. Justice Stewart, with Justices Powell and Stevens Concurring: We address initially the basic contention that the punishment of death for the crime of murder is, under all circumstances, "cruel and unusual" in violation of the Eighth and Fourteenth Amendments of the Constitution. [Later in] this opinion, we will consider the sentence of death imposed under the Georgia statutes at issue in this case. . . .

Gregg v. *Georgia* 428 U.S. 153 (1976).

The substantive limits imposed by the Eighth Amendment on what can be made criminal and punished were discussed in *Robinson* v. *California* (1962). The Court found unconstitutional a state statute that made the status of being addicted to a narcotic drug a criminal offense. It held, in effect, that it is "cruel and unusual" to impose any punishment at all for the mere status of addiction. The cruelty in the abstract of the actual sentence imposed was irrelevant: "Even one day in prison would be a cruel and unusual punishment for the 'crime' of having a common cold." *Id.,* at 667. Most recently, in *Furman* v. *Georgia*, . . . three Justices in separate concurring opinions found the Eighth Amendment applicable to procedures employed to select convicted defendants for the sentence of death.

It is clear from the foregoing precedents that the Eighth Amendment has not been regarded as a static concept. As Mr. Chief Justice Warren said, in an oft-quoted phrase, "[t]he Amendment must draw its meaning from the evolving standards of decency that mark the progress of a maturing society." Thus, an assessment of contemporary values concerning the infliction of a challenged sanction is relevant to the application of the Eighth Amendment. As we develop below more fully, . . . this assessment does not call for a subjective judgment. It requires, rather, that we look to objective indicia that reflect the public attitude toward a given sanction.

But our cases also make clear that public perceptions of standards of decency with respect to criminal sanctions are not conclusive. A penalty also must accord with "the dignity of man," which is the "basic concept underlying the Eighth Amendment." *Trop* v. *Dulles.* This means, at least, that the punishment not be "excessive." When a form of punishment in the abstract (in this case, whether capital punishment may ever be imposed as a sanction for murder) rather than in the particular (the propriety of death as a penalty to be applied to a specific defendant for a specific crime) is under consideration, the inquiry into "excessiveness" has two aspects. First, the punishment must not involve the unnecessary

and wanton infliction of pain. . . . Secon punishment must not be grossly out of portion to the severity of the crime. . . .

The imposition of the death penalty for th crime of murder has a long history of acceptance both in the United States and in England. The common-law rule imposed as mandatory death sentence on all convicted murderers. . . . And the penalty continued to be used into the 20th century by most American States, although the breadth of the common-law rule was diminished, initially by narrowing the class of murders to be punished by death and subsequently by widespread adoption of laws expressly granting juries the discretion to recommend mercy. . . .

It is apparent from the text of the Constitution itself that the existence of capital punishment was accepted by the Framers. At the time the Eighth Amendment was ratified, capital punishment was a common sanction in every State. Indeed, the First Congress of the United States enacted legislation providing death as the penalty for specified crimes. . . .

The most marked indication of society's endorsement of the death penalty for murder is the legislative response to *Furman.* The legislatures of at least 35 States have enacted new statutes that provide for the death penalty for at least some crimes that result in the death of another person. And the Congress of the United States, in 1974, enacted a statute providing the death penalty for aircraft piracy that results in death. These recently adopted statutes have attempted to address the concerns expressed by the Court in *Furman* primarily (i) by specifying the factors to be weighed and the procedures to be followed in deciding when to impose a capital sentence, or (ii) by making the death penalty mandatory for specified crimes. . . .

[H]owever, the Eighth Amendment demands more than that a challenged punishment be acceptable to contemporary society. The Court also must ask whether it comports with the basic concept of human dignity at the core of the Amendment. . . . Although we cannot "invalidate a category of penalties because we deem less severe penalties adequate to serve ogy," *Furman* v. *Georgia*, . . . , J., dissenting), the sanction not be so totally without peno- . . . ification that it results in the gratu- . . . liction of suffering. . . .

. . . e death penalty is said to serve two princi- . . . social purposes: retribution and deterrence of capital crimes by prospective offenders.[1]

In part, capital punishment is an expression of society's moral outrage at particularly offensive conduct. This function may be unappealing to many, but it is essential in an ordered society that asks its citizens to rely on legal processes rather than self-help to vindicate their wrongs.

> "The instinct for retribution is part of the nature of man, and channeling that instinct in the administration of criminal justice serves an important purpose in promoting the stability of a society governed by law. When people begin to believe that organized society is unwilling or unable to impose upon criminal offenders the punishment they 'deserve,' then there are sown the seeds of anarchy—of self-help, vigilante justice, and lynch law." *Furman* v. *Georgia*, . . . at 308 (Stewart, J., concurring).

"Retribution is no longer the dominant objective of the criminal law," *Williams* v. *New York*, (1949), but neither is it a forbidden objective nor one inconsistent with our respect for the dignity of men. . . . Indeed, the decision that capital punishment may be the appropriate sanction in extreme cases is an expression of the community's belief that certain crimes are themselves so grievous an affront to humanity that the only adequate response may be the penalty of death.

Statistical attempts to evaluate the worth of the death penalty as a deterrent to crimes by potential offenders have occasioned a great deal of debate. The results simply have been inconclusive. . . .

Although some of the studies suggest that the death penalty may not function as a significantly greater deterrent than lesser penalties, there is no convincing empirical evidence either supporting or refuting this view. We

may nevertheless assume safely that there are murderers, such as those who act in passion, for whom the threat of death has little or no deterrent effect. But for many others, the death penalty undoubtedly is a significant deterrent. There are carefully contemplated murders, such as murders for hire, where the possible penalty of death may well enter into the cold calculus that precedes the decision to act.[2] And there are some categories of murder, such as murder by a life prisoner, where other sanctions may not be adequate.

The value of capital punishment as a deterrent of crime is a complex factual issue the resolution of which properly rests with the legislatures, which can evaluate the results of statistical studies in terms of their own local conditions and with a flexibility of approach that is not available to the courts. . . . Indeed, many of the post-*Furman* statutes reflect just such a responsible effort to define those crimes and those criminals for which capital punishment is most probably an effective deterrent.

In sum, we cannot say that the judgment of the Georgia Legislature that capital punishment may be necessary in some cases is clearly wrong. Considerations of federalism, as well as respect for the ability of a legislature to evaluate, in terms of its particular State, the moral consensus concerning the death penalty and its social utility as a sanction, require us to conclude, in the absence of more convincing evidence, that the infliction of death as a punishment for murder is not without justification and thus is not unconstitutionally severe.

Finally, we must consider whether the punishment of death is disproportionate in relation to the crime for which it is imposed. There is no question that death as a punishment is unique in its severity and irrevocability. . . .

When a defendant's life is at stake, the Court has been particularly sensitive to ensure that every safeguard is observed. . . . But we are concerned here only with the imposition of capital punishment for the crime of murder, and when a life has been taken deliberately by the offender, we cannot say that the punishment is invariably disproportionate to the crime. It is an extreme sanction, suitable to the most extreme of crimes.

We hold that the death penalty is not a form of punishment that may never be imposed, regardless of the circumstances of the offense, regardless of the character of the offender, and regardless of the procedure followed in reaching the decision to impose it.

We now consider whether Georgia may impose the death penalty on the petitioner in this case. . . . Because of the uniqueness of the death penalty, *Furman* held that it could not be imposed under sentencing procedures that created a substantial risk that it would be inflicted in an arbitrary and capricious manner. Mr. Justice White concluded that "the death penalty is exacted with great infrequency even for the most atrocious crimes and there is no meaningful basis for distinguishing the few cases in which it is imposed from the many cases in which it is not." *Id.*, at 313 (concurring). Indeed, the death sentences examined by the Court in *Furman* were "cruel and unusual in the same way that being struck by lightning is cruel and unusual. For, of all the people convicted of [capital crimes], many just as reprehensible as these, the petitioners [in *Furman* were] among a capriciously selected random handful upon whom the sentence of death has in fact been imposed. . . . [T]he Eighth and Fourteenth Amendments cannot tolerate the infliction of a sentence of death under legal systems that permit this unique penalty to be so wantonly and so freakishly imposed." *Id.*, at 309–310 (Stewart, J., concurring). . . .

In summary, the concerns expressed in *Furman* that the penalty of death not be imposed in an arbitrary or capricious manner can be met by a carefully drafted statute that ensures that the sentencing authority is given adequate information and guidance. As a general proposition these concerns are best met by a system that provides for a bifurcated proceeding at which the sentencing authority is apprised of the information relevant to the imposition of sentence and provided with standards to guide its use of the information. . . .

The basic concern of *Furman* centered on those defendants who were being condemned to death capriciously and arbitrarily. Under the procedures before the Court in that case, sentencing authorities were not directed to give attention to the nature or circumstances of the crime committed or to the character or record of the defendant. Left unguided, juries imposed the death sentence in a way that could only be called freakish. The new Georgia sentencing procedures, by contrast, focus the jury's attention on the particularized nature of the crime and the particularized characteristics of the individual defendant. While the jury is permitted to consider any aggravating or mitigating circumstances, it must find and identify at least one statutory aggravating factor before it may impose a penalty of death. In this way the jury's discretion is channeled. No longer can a jury wantonly and freakishly impose the death sentence; it is always circumscribed by the legislative guidelines. In addition, the review function of the Supreme Court of Georgia affords additional assurance that the concerns that prompted our decision in *Furman* are not present to any significant degree in the Georgia procedure applied here.

For the reasons expressed in this opinion, we hold that the statutory system under which Gregg was sentenced to death does not violate the Constitution. Accordingly, the judgment of the Georgia Supreme Court is affirmed.

It is so ordered.

Mr. Justice Brennan, Dissenting: The Cruel and Unusual Punishments Clause "must draw its meaning from the evolving standards of decency that mark the progress of a maturing society."[3] . . .

In *Furman* v. *Georgia,* . . . I read "evolving standards of decency" as requiring focus upon the essence of the death penalty itself and not primarily or solely upon the procedures under which the determination to inflict the penalty upon a particular person was made. I there said:

"From the beginning of our Nation, the punishment of death has stirred acute public controversy. Although pragmatic arguments for and against the punishment have been frequently advanced, this longstanding and heated controversy cannot be explained solely as the result of differences over the practical wisdom of a particular government policy. At bottom, the battle has been waged on moral grounds. The country has debated whether a society for which the dignity of the individual is the supreme value can, without a fundamental inconsistency, follow the practice of deliberately putting some of its members to death. In the United States, as in other nations of the western world, 'the struggle about this punishment has been one between ancient and deeply rooted beliefs in retribution, atonement or vengeance on the one hand, and, on the other, beliefs in the personal value and dignity of the common man that were born of the democratic movement of the eighteenth century, as well as beliefs in the scientific approach to an understanding of the motive forces of human conduct, which are the result of the growth of the sciences of behavior during the nineteenth and twentieth centuries.' It is this essentially moral conflict that forms the backdrop for the past changes in and the present operation of our system of imposing death as a punishment for crime." *Id.,* at 296.[4]

That continues to be my view. For the Clause forbidding cruel and unusual punishments under our constitutional system of government embodies in unique degree moral principles restraining the punishments that our civilized society may impose on those persons who transgress its laws. Thus, I too say: "For myself, I do not hesitate to assert the proposition that the only way the law has progressed from the days of the rack, the screw and the wheel is the development of moral concepts, or, as stated by the Supreme Court the application of 'evolving standards of decency.' . . ."[5]

This Court inescapably has the duty, as the ultimate arbiter of the meaning of our Constitution, to say whether, when individuals condemned to death stand before our Bar, "moral concepts" require us to hold that the law has progressed to the point where we should declare that the punishment of death, like punishments on the rack, the screw, and the wheel, is no longer morally tolerable in our civilized society. . . . I emphasize only that foremost among the "moral concepts" recognized in our cases and inherent in the Clause is the primary moral principle that the State, even as it punishes, must treat its citizens in a manner consistent with their intrinsic worth as human beings—a punishment must not be so severe as to be degrading to human dignity. A judicial determination whether the punishment of death comports with human dignity is therefore not only permitted but compelled by the Clause. . . .

The fatal constitutional infirmity in the punishment of death is that it treats "members of the human race as nonhumans, as objects to be toyed with and discarded. [It is] thus inconsistent with the fundamental premise of the Clause that even the vilest criminal remains a human being possessed of common human dignity." *Id.,* at 273. As such it is a penalty that "subjects the individual to a fate forbidden by the principle of civilized treatment guaranteed by the [Clause]." I therefore would hold, on that ground alone, that death is today a cruel and unusual punishment prohibited by the Clause. "Justice of this kind is obviously no less shocking than the crime itself, and the new 'official' murder, far from offering redress for the offense committed against society, adds instead a second defilement to the first."[6]

Mr. Justice Marshall, Dissenting: In *Furman* I concluded that the death penalty is constitutionally invalid for two reasons. First, the death penalty is excessive. . . . And second, the American people, fully informed as to the purposes of the death penalty and its liabilities, would in my view reject it as morally unacceptable. . . .

Since the decision in *Furman,* the legislatures of 35 States have enacted new statutes authorizing the imposition of the death sentence for certain crimes, and Congress has enacted a law providing the death penalty for air piracy resulting in death. . . . I would be less than candid if I did not acknowledge that these developments have a significant bearing on a realistic assessment of the moral acceptability of the death penalty to the American people. But if the constitutionality of the death penalty turns, as I have urged, on the opinion of an *informed* citizenry, then even the enactment of new death statutes cannot be viewed as conclusive. In *Furman,* I observed that the American people are largely unaware of the information critical to a judgment on the morality of the death penalty, and concluded that if they were better informed they would consider it shocking, unjust, and unacceptable. . . . A recent study, conducted after the enactment of the post-*Furman* statutes, has confirmed that the American people know little about the death penalty, and that the opinions of an informed public would differ significantly from those of a public unaware of the consequences and effects of the death penalty.[7]

Even assuming, however, that the post-*Furman* enactment of statutes authorizing the death penalty renders the prediction of the views of an informed citizenry an uncertain basis for a constitutional decision, the enactment of those statutes has no bearing whatsoever on the conclusion that the death penalty is unconstitutional because it is excessive. An excessive penalty is invalid under the Cruel and Unusual Punishments Clause "even though popular sentiment may favor" it. . . . The inquiry here, then, is simply whether the death penalty is necessary to accomplish the legitimate legislative purposes in punishment, or whether a less severe penalty—life imprisonment—would do as well. . . .

The two purposes that sustain the death penalty as nonexcessive in the Court's view are general deterrence and retribution. In *Furman,* I canvassed the relevant data on the deterrent effect of capital punishment. . . . The state of knowledge at that point, after literally centuries of debate, was summarized as follows by a United Nations Committee:

"It is generally agreed between the retentionists and abolitionists, whatever their opinions about the validity of comparative studies of deterrence, that the data which now exist show no correlation between the existence of capital punishment and lower rates of capital crime."[8]

The available evidence, I concluded in *Furman,* was convincing that "capital punishment is not necessary as a deterrent to crime in our society." *Id.,* at 353. . . .

The other principal purpose said to be served by the death penalty is retribution. . . . It is this notion that I find to be the most disturbing aspect of today's unfortunate decisions.

The concept of retribution is a multifaceted one, and any discussion of its role in the criminal law must be undertaken with caution. On one level, it can be said that the notion of retribution or reprobation is the basis of our insistence that only those who have broken the law be punished, and in this sense the notion is quite obviously central to a just system of criminal sanctions. But our recognition that retribution plays a crucial role in determining who may be punished by no means requires approval of retribution as a general justification for punishment.[9] It is the question whether retribution can provide a moral justification for punishment—in particular, capital punishment—that we must consider.

My Brothers Stewart, Powell, and Stevens offer the following explanation of the retributive justification for capital punishment:

"The instinct for retribution is part of the nature of man, and channeling that instinct in the administration of criminal justice serves an important purpose in promoting the stability of a society governed by law. When people begin to believe that organized society is unwilling or unable to impose upon criminal offenders the punishment they 'deserve,' then there are sown the seeds of anarchy—of self-help, vigilante justice, and lynch law."

This statement is wholly inadequate to justify the death penalty. As my Brother Brennan stated in *Furman,* "[t]here is no evidence whatever that utilization of imprisonment rather than death encourages private blood feuds and other disorders." . . . at 303 (concurring opinion). It simply defies belief to suggest that the death penalty is necessary to prevent the American people from taking the law into their own hands.

In a related vein, it may be suggested that the expression of moral outrage through the imposition of the death penalty serves to reinforce basic moral values—that it marks some crimes as particularly offensive and therefore to be avoided. The argument is akin to a deterrence argument, but differs in that it contemplates the individual's shrinking from antisocial conduct, not because he fears punishment, but because he has been told in the strongest possible way that the conduct is wrong. This contention, like the previous one, provides no support for the death penalty. It is inconceivable that any individual concerned about conforming his conduct to what society says is "right" would fail to realize that murder is "wrong" if the penalty were simply life imprisonment.

The foregoing contentions—that society's expression of moral outrage through the imposition of the death penalty preempts the citizenry from taking the law into its own hands and reinforces moral values—are not retributive in the purest sense. They are essentially utilitarian in that they portray the death penalty as valuable because of its beneficial results. These justifications for the death penalty are inadequate because the penalty is, quite clearly I think, not necessary to the accomplishment of those results.

There remains for consideration, however, what might be termed the purely retributive justification for the death penalty—that the death penalty is appropriate, not because of its beneficial effect on society, but because the taking of the murderer's life is itself morally good. Some of the language of the opinion of my Brothers Stewart, Powell, and Stevens . . . appears positively to embrace this notion of retribution for its own sake as a justification for capital punishment. They state:

"[T]he decision that capital punishment may be the appropriate sanction in extreme cases is an expression of the community's belief that certain crimes are themselves so grievous an affront to humanity that the only adequate response may be the penalty of death."

They then quote with approval from Lord Justice Denning's remarks before the British Royal Commission on Capital Punishment:

"The truth is that some crimes are so outrageous that society insists on adequate punishment, because the wrong-doer deserves it, irrespective of whether it is a deterrent or not."

Of course, it may be that these statements are intended as no more than observations as to the popular demands that it is thought must be responded to in order to prevent anarchy. But the implication of the statements appears to me to be quite different—namely, that society's judgment that the murderer "deserves" death must be respected not simply because the preservation of order requires it, but because it is appropriate that society make the judgment and carry it out. It is this latter notion, in particular, that I consider to be fundamentally at odds with the Eighth Amendment. . . . The mere fact that the community demands the murderer's life in return for the evil he has done cannot sustain the death penalty, for as Justices Stewart, Powell, and Stevens remind us, "the Eighth Amendment demands more than that a challenged punishment be acceptable to contemporary society." To be sustained under the Eighth Amendment, the death penalty must "comport with the basic concept of human dignity at the core of the Amendment," *ibid.;* the objective in imposing it must be "[consistent] with our respect for the dignity of [other] men." Under these standards, the taking of life "because the wrongdoer deserves it" surely must fall, for such a punishment has as its very basis the total denial of the wrongdoer's dignity and worth.

The death penalty, unnecessary to promote the goal of deterrence or to further any legitimate notion of retribution, is an excessive penalty forbidden by the Eighth and Fourteenth Amendments. I respectfully dissent from the Court's judgment upholding the sentences of death imposed upon the petitioners in these cases.

NOTES

1. Another purpose that has been discussed is the incapacitation of dangerous criminals and the consequent prevention of crimes that they may otherwise commit in the future.
2. Other types of calculated murders, apparently occurring with increasing frequency, include the use of bombs or other means of indiscriminate killings, the extortion murder of hostages or kidnap victims, and the execution-style killing of witnesses to a crime.
3. *Trop* v. *Dulles,* 356 U.S. 86, 101 (1958) (plurality opinion of Warren, C. J.).
4. Quoting T. Sellin, *The Death Penalty,* A Report for the Model Penal Code Project of the American Law Institute 15 (1959).
5. *Novak* v. *Beto,* 453 F. 2d 661, 672 (CA5 1971) (Tuttle, J., concurring in part and dissenting in part).
6. A. Camus, *Reflections on the Guillotine* 5–6 (Fridtjof-Karla Pub. 1960).
7. Sarat and Vidmar, "Public Opinion, The Death Penalty, and the Eighth Amendment: Testing the Marshall Hypothesis," 1976 *Wis. L. Rev.* 171.
8. United Nations, Department of Economic and Social Affairs, *Capital Punishment*, pt. II, ¶ 159, p. 123 (1968).
9. See, *e.g.,* H. Hart, *Punishment and Responsibility* 8–10, 71–83 (1968); H. Packer, *Limits of the Criminal Sanction* 38–39, 66 (1968).

REVIEW AND DISCUSSION QUESTIONS

1. How would you define *punishment?* How is it different from taxation?
2. The Supreme Court states that the Eighth Amendment means that punishment cannot be "excessive." What two reasons do the justices who defend executions give to prove that capital punishment is not excessive?
3. How do the two dissenters respond to the argument that executions are not excessive punishment?
4. Besides not being excessive, the death penalty must also be compatible with society's "evolving standards of decency." Why does Justice Stewart think it is not incompatible?
5. Why do the dissenters think executions are not compatible with evolving standards of decency? How does Justice Marshall respond to Justice Stewart's point about what state legislatures had done after the *Furman* decision?
6. Consider the following argument: the death penalty must deter, no matter what statistics say, because almost everybody would prefer life in prison to execution. Do you agree with that argument?

Desert and Capital Punishment

Martin Perlmutter

Martin Perlmutter argues that the utilitarian approach to punishment, emphasizing the usefulness of deterrence, protection, and rehabilitation, is inadequate, primarily because it views punishment as "forward looking." Rather, he claims, the proper focus of punishment is on the past; people are punished for past wrongdoing. If the wrongdoing is serious enough, he argues, then capital punishment is appropriate and the wrongdoer deserves death. Perlmutter concludes by arguing that, in a sense, the criminal has a right to be punished—that to fail to do so treats him or her as less than a person. Martin Perlmutter is professor of philosophy at the University of Charleston, South Carolina.

"Shall we receive good at the hand of God and shall we not receive evil?" In all this Job did not sin with his lips.

Job 2:10

Punishment is a form of harm or deprivation; in punishing somebody, we are making that person worse off than he was before. And since it seems that we have a *prima facie* obligation not to make others worse off, the practice of punishment needs a justification in virtue of which that *prima facie* obligation is overridden. Why are we entitled to harm persons when we punish them?

There are two general answers to this question. The first looks to the future and to the overall consequences of inflicting the harm; it maintains that one is entitled to make a person worse off if the consequences of doing so outweigh the harm done. Inflicting harm is justified when the harm done is part of a larger chain in which that harm results in yet greater good. The good produced by the harm might be the rehabilitation of the offender, the protection of others from the offender, or the deterrence of other future offenders. This answer is utilitarian; it looks to future goods, which outweigh the present harm, as the justification of the present harm. The second looks to the past and to the past deeds of the offender; it maintains that one is entitled to make a person worse off if that person's past deeds are such that he deserves to be punished. Just as it is fitting to reward someone who does well with some goods, whether those be a trophy, a better job, or a salary increase, so it is appropriate to deprive someone who does poorly of those same goods. Of course, it would be nice if good consequences proceeded from the punishment, just as it would be nice if good consequences proceeded from giving the trophy to the winner rather than to the loser, but good consequences, like rehabilitation, protection, or deterrence, are not in any way integral to punishment. This answer is the retributive view of punishment; it looks to past deeds in virtue of which the harm is deserved as justification of the harm.[1]

In this paper I will argue that punishment focuses on the past; it is thus a retributive concept. Just as the concepts "praise," "blame," and, more importantly, "desert" have a backward focus, so too "punishment" looks to the past. The justification of punishment is another matter. I will argue that the practice of punishment is justified, because the individual who did the wrong also "chose" the punishment; in punishing the wrongdoer, we are honoring that individual's choice. The justification of punishment is to be found in the broader notion of desert, another backward-looking concept. I will also argue that capital punishment is defensible; there are some crimes that are so serious, so offensive to the moral community, that their perpetrators deserve death for committing them. As Justice Stewart points out in *Gregg* v. *Georgia*, "the decision that capital punishment may be the appropriate sanction in extreme cases is an expression of the community's belief that certain crimes are themselves so grievous an affront to humanity that the only adequate response may be the penalty of death." Finally, as a postscript, I will make some general remarks about treating somebody as a person. In doing so, I will try to make sense of the seemingly absurd Hegelian view that "in punishment the offender is honored as a rational being, since the punishment is looked on as his right."

1. THE CONCEPT OF PUNISHMENT

Before we ask questions about the justification of punishment, we should be clear about what punishment is. Otherwise, we would not know whether or not it is punishment that we are justifying. So, for example, justifying the reform or rehabilitation of an offender might not be a difficult task, but it would be a justification of punishment only if punishment were essentially a reformative or rehabilitative notion.

There are two features of punishment that are essential to it. First, punishment is inflicting harm; nothing can count as punishment unless it is a deprivation or causes pain or suffering to the person on whom it is inflicted. This is not quite right since a person might prefer his punishment to the alternatives available to him; on occasion, a drunkard might prefer a warm cell with a mattress to the cold outside, and a child might rather be banished to his room than continue to play with his friends. The intention in punishing, however, is to do harm; in punishing somebody, we intend to make the person worse off than he would be without the punishment.[2] So, punishment must involve pain or other consequences normally considered unpleasant.

Not every case of making a person worse off, however, is an instance of punishment. Confining a person who has an infectious disease, hitting somebody just for the fun of it, and taxing the wealthy might well be instances of harming persons, but they are not cases of punishment, even if they were deprivations that we were justified in imposing. For a deprivation to be a punishment, it has to be associated with past wrongdoing. A heavily taxed wealthy person would be overstating his case if he complained that he was being punished for being wealthy, for there is no presumption of any past wrongdoing in his case.

Second, then, a person may be punished if and only if there is some presumption of past wrongdoing. Again, this is a conceptual requirement; it is part of the meaning of "punishment." Imposing harm is not punishment unless the imposition of the harm is connected with a supposed past wrongdoing.

This connection between wrongdoing and the imposition of harm is so strong that some have maintained a conceptual link between them. It has been claimed that the very concept of wrongdoing must contain a reference to punishment; that is, an act is an instance of wrongdoing if and only if the agent is subject to punishment for performing it. In legal contexts, a natural home for the discussion of punishment, such a view has had some currency. An act is a legal offense just in case there is a sanction that attaches to performing it; a rule of law requires that a person perform or forbear from performing some act and promises harm in case of noncompliance. As a more general thesis, however, it is false; wrongdoing or offense cannot have liability to punishment

in its explication, for there are many offenses that do not subject the offender to any penalty. Punishment, however, does require reference to both harm and wrongdoing.

The imposition of harm and past wrongdoing are closely related. The harm imposed is in virtue of the past wrongdoing; the person deserves to suffer because he committed an offense. It is appropriate that the person suffer harm or deprivation because of the person's past deeds; had the person not done wrong, he would not have deserved the suffering. This is central to punishment.

The connection can be seen in the nature of rules, whether they be the regulations of baseball, the laws of society, or the rules of bridge. Rules are constitutive of baseball, society, and bridge. The rules define the practice, they distribute the benefits and the burdens, and they determine acceptable behavior within the practice. In violating a rule, the person is competing unfairly; that is an improper way of gaining an advantage. Throwing a spitball, stealing a car, or surreptitiously signaling the ace of spades are all unacceptable ways of getting ahead. Persons who attempt to benefit by violating a rule are subject to a penalty for so doing because they are benefiting from the practice, but are participating unfairly in it. Typically, there are procedures for determining whether the rule has been violated, what the penalty should be, and who should administer the penalty.

The legitimate domain of punishment is restricted to special relationships. A state can legitimately punish its citizens; it is within a parent's province to punish his or her child; and a teacher has the authority to punish his or her students.

So too the tournament director at bridge, the umpire, and the baseball commissioner. Not everyone, however, is entitled to punish, even in response to past wrongdoing. As a general rule, a citizen cannot punish the state, a child cannot punish a parent, and a student cannot punish a teacher.

Although blame is similar to punishment in many ways—in blaming a person, we are causing that person a limited sort of harm in virtue of a past wrongdoing—blame is more general than punishment in this way.[3] The legitimate domain of blame is not restricted to special relationships. While it may be morally unacceptable to blame somebody, though he is blameworthy, that unacceptability is in virtue of considerations of the future. On occasion, the bad consequences of expressing the blame make such expressions unacceptable even to someone who is blameworthy. It might be unacceptable to blame somebody for past deeds if that person is on his deathbed; it might be silly for you to blame somebody if doing so would upset you a great deal; and there might be no point to blaming somebody who would enjoy the loss of your esteem. In each of these cases, it might be morally unacceptable or imprudent to blame him, even though he is blameworthy. But it is not a question of authority; blame, unlike punishment, is not restricted to special relationships. Each of these three cases would be a paradigmatic instance of blaming, just as a morally unacceptable case of telling the truth would be a paradigmatic instance of truth-telling.

2. A UTILITARIAN CRITIQUE OF PUNISHMENT

A utilitarian might focus on the analogy of punishment to blame to argue that though punishment has a backward focus, the moral acceptability of inflicting the harm must derive from the future consequences of the harm inflicted. If it is morally unacceptable to express blame to a person on his deathbed, though the person is blameworthy, then blameworthiness is not sufficient for the moral acceptability of blaming. And it is forward-looking considerations that make expressing the blame morally unacceptable; that is, since nothing good will be accomplished by expressing the blame and somebody will be worse off for it, the blame should not be expressed. Similarly, in punishment, past wrongdoing is not sufficient for the moral acceptability of inflicting the harm. Even if inflicting harm requires past wrongdoing for it to be punishment, it requires

good consequences for it to be morally acceptable. As a result, in the utilitarian view, it is the consequences of inflicting harm that determine whether or not it is morally acceptable to inflict the harm, though it is backward-looking considerations that determine whether or not it is punishment. Just as taxing the wealthy might be a morally acceptable way of harming the wealthy only if the consequences justify it, so too fining a traffic offender is morally acceptable only if the consequences justify it. Of course, taxing the wealthy is not based on past wrongdoing, so it is not punishment, whereas fining the traffic offender is punishment. But whether or not inflicting harm is punishment is only a detail and does not speak to the moral acceptability of inflicting it.

This utilitarian view is general and not restricted to punishment. According to it, one should always do what has the best consequences. What has already happened is relevant only insofar as the future is concerned. The fact that a person has committed an offense might be a reason for inflicting harm on the person, but only in virtue of the future benefits of the harm. Thus, a past offense might serve as evidence for future offenses and future offenses are to be avoided, so it might be best to protect his future victims by imprisoning him. Or, it might be best to discourage future offenders by inflicting harm on this offender for this offense. But unless there is a justification in the future, it would be morally unacceptable to inflict the harm. For if there were no such future benefits, then, all things considered, in punishing one is increasing the amount of suffering in the world and that is morally unacceptable.

This utilitarian challenge might require abandoning the practice of punishment. If punishment involves intending to make a person worse off because of past wrongdoing, then the only utilitarian defense of punishment could be deterrence. For reform of the offender or protection of society from the offender's future offenses does not involve intentionally making the offender worse off any more than curing a person of an infectious disease involves that intention. Were we able to cure a person of a disease without inconveniencing the victim, one would surely do so. Similarly, if reform were the aim of punishment, punishment would not necessarily involve making the offender worse off, even temporarily. The same holds true for societal protection as an aim of punishment; it too does not necessarily involve making a person worse off. Deterrence fares a little better, but even it does not require actually inflicting the harm as opposed to merely appearing to others to inflict the harm. Punishment necessarily involves harm or deprivation, whereas reform, deprivation, and even deterrence do not.

An example might help. Suppose my son lies to me and suppose also that I am persuaded that I have no evidence that sending him to his room will do any more good than not sending him to his room. I might still think that he deserves to be punished for what he did and send him to his room, thereby inflicting harm on him for what he did. A utilitarian would claim that I should not have done it, for no good will result from my harming my son in this way. If he is right, it is not because he has a different theory of punishment which yields a different result in this case. Rather, it is because punishment is not justified; it is because, in his view, I am not entitled to inflict harm unless a greater good will result. The utilitarian is giving a critique of punishment, not an alternative theory of punishment.

Even if the utilitarian does not provide an alternative theory of punishment, he might be right in his critique of punishment. My punishing my son for lying might be morally unacceptable, because reform, protection, or deterrence is not gained by it. It might be morally unacceptable to do anything whose foreseeable consequences involve more harm than good. And if it is, then the practice of punishment ought to be abandoned.

3. A CRITIQUE OF UTILITARIANISM

The utilitarian contention ignores the fact that many of our moral concepts are backward-looking. Most often, we are morally required to do things because of what happened in the past. It is that which makes social contract theories appealing; we are obligated to behave in accordance with an implicit contract, something which we already tacitly agreed to do. More simply, though, we are required to keep a promise because we made it, we are required to award the prize to the winner because he won the race, and we are required to repay a debt because we borrowed the money. Frequently, it is the past and not the future which determines the moral acceptability of an action. Of course, keeping a promise has consequences for the practice of promise-keeping and the fact that a promise was made also has consequences since the promise created expectations. But what makes it right to keep a promise is the past fact that a promise was made. So, the well-known example of a secret promise to a dying man to deliver a hoard of money, which he entrusts to me, to his already rich son is relevant. It is the promise, and not the consequences, which makes it right to give his son the money.

The utilitarian is correct in recognizing that, on occasion, we are morally required to look to the future and that the future sometimes affects what it is morally acceptable to do, even in the case of backward-looking concepts. Thus, though a promise was made, perhaps to meet somebody for lunch, it would be morally unacceptable to do so if it would result in somebody's death, because of the need to rush somebody to the hospital. But in cases such as this, it is not *merely* minimizing harm or maximizing benefit that is operative. Rather, a rational person would not expect the promise to be kept to him in a case such as this. The commitment involved in promises does not create an obligation in such a case.

So, even though the utilitarian contention about maximizing benefits and minimizing harm has some plausibility, it does not conform to our everyday moral intuitions about what is morally acceptable. Of course, a utilitarian might urge that it is unreasonable to take the past as seriously as we do. But until we become persuaded by such urgings, and it is not clear that we should become persuaded by them, we should continue to take our everyday moral notions seriously and reject the utilitarian contention. Promises should be kept because they were made, debts should be re-paid because they were incurred, and awards should be given because they are deserved. Moral notions such as these show that the past plays a much larger role in justifying behavior than a utilitarian acknowledges.

The notion of desert is central to punishment. What a person deserves is most often determined by what he has done. Does a person ever deserve to have harm inflicted on him for what he has done? The answer seems straightforward. On occasion, when a person knowingly and intentionally does wrong, he should be punished for what he did. In much the same way as a person occasionally deserves to be blamed, deserves the loss of another's esteem, a person occasionally deserves to have harm inflicted upon him.

Even a view which emphasizes deterrence as the rationale for inflicting the harm requires such a notion of desert. Otherwise, harming an innocent person to deter others would be morally acceptable. A plausible deterrence view must insist that in doing wrong a person made it acceptable to have harm inflicted upon himself, thereby deterring others. That is, he deserves the harm; the punishment is morally acceptable because of the past misdeed. So, even a theory which emphasizes deterrence requires a retributive underpinning.

4. CAPITAL PUNISHMENT

The view that the severity of the punishment should be determined by the severity of the crime is a natural extension of the retributive view that punishment is a person's due in virtue of the wrong that the person committed. That is, the crime should not only legitimate that the person be punished, but it should also determine the extent of the punishment. Simply put, the more serious the crime, the more severe the penalty.

Lex talionis, literally the law of retaliation, is the custom of inflicting a similar injury on the person who injures another. The person who causes another to lose an eye must himself lose an eye; the person who murders another must himself be put to death. That was a common practice of punishment in earlier societies and is included in the Biblical corpus of laws (Exodus 21:23–25, for example). Most often, *lex talionis* is inapplicable, since most wrongs do not have analogous injuries applicable to the offender. But the view that the severity of the offense should determine the severity of the punishment remains a plausible view, one which many of us intuitively accept. The U.S. Supreme Court used this principle as a negative test when it upheld the death penalty in *Gregg* v. *Georgia:* "The punishment must not be grossly out of proportion to the severity of the crime."

Of course, one cannot grade wrongs with mathematical precision and there is no scientific procedure for ranking punishments. But some wrongs are worse than others. Missing an appointment altogether is worse than being five minutes late; robbing a bank is worse than not feeding a parking meter; marking the deck of cards is worse than neglecting to inform one's opponents of a bridge convention; and intentionally losing a baseball game is worse than questioning an umpire's third-strike call. More generally, a third offense is worse than a first offense, a premeditated act is worse than an impulsive or negligent one; and an altogether self-interested criminal act is worse than a criminal act designed to benefit another. Punishments are more easily ranked. A thousand dollar fine is worse than a hundred dollar fine; ten years in prison is worse than one year in prison; and solitary confinement is worse than imprisonment in a minimum security detention facility.

Are there any limits on the appropriate punishments? Is life imprisonment, capital punishment, bodily mutilation, or castration beyond the pale of acceptable punishment? Two issues need to be separated. First, the appropriateness of the punishment for the particular crime. Life imprisonment would be too severe a penalty for a parking violation, even though life imprisonment might be appropriate for other offenses. Second, the appropriateness of the punishment for any crime.[4] Some harms are unacceptable because they are not the sorts of thing that persons are ever entitled to do, even as a punishment. Maiming, bodily mutilation, and torture seem to be disqualified for this reason.

Clearly, there are cultural factors which are relevant as response to these questions. How serious the crime and what punishments are compatible with conceptions of human dignity vary from culture to culture. And there are objective criteria which can be used to determine both issues. Sexual relations between consenting adults is generally allowed in our culture, but is a serious wrong in others. In our cultural setting, bodily mutilation is a form of humiliation that is unacceptable; it is not compatible with our fundamental standards of human dignity and decency. Nobody should be allowed to mutilate another, even as a response to a serious crime (such as mutilating another). Imprisonment, even for a long term, is different, since our society clearly thinks that imprisonment is an appropriate response to wrongdoing. Depriving a person of his liberty is an acceptable response to wrongdoing; bodily mutilation is not.

A person might reasonably prefer an unacceptable punishment to an acceptable one. Having one's hand cut off or being castrated seems less severe as a punishment than life imprisonment; a person might well prefer a life without a hand or a life without some sexual pleasures to a life without liberty, even though our society allows the latter as a punishment and disallows the former. The issue is not a matter of preference or severity; the punishment has to accord with human dignity. In our society, bodily integrity and privacy are important values that preclude maiming, bodily mutilation, or castration.

What about capital punishment? Again, we need to separate two questions. First, is death too severe a penalty to impose for any offense? Are there any crimes that are so serious that death is an appropriate penalty for them? Second, is capital punishment compatible with our views of human dignity and decency?

In our society, murder is a crime for which death is a fitting punishment. Not only does murder result in the death of another, it undermines the very fabric of a moral community. A murderer should be altogether and completely cut off from the moral community which he sought to undermine. The murderer caused death and deserves death in response. Life imprisonment is not adequate because it makes the criminal a dependent of the community, a ward of the community he sought to undermine. The murderer's only claim is that he be treated in a way that is compatible with society's standards of human dignity.

Others might want to restrict capital punishment to other crimes—to mass murder, to the killing of a police officer, or to political assassination. There is no scientific way to determine what crimes are so egregious that capital punishment is appropriate for them and I need not argue for the appropriateness of capital punishment for any particular crime. But I do want to insist that if our standards of decency allow death as an acceptable punishment, then there are some crimes that warrant it as a punishment.

But does our view of human dignity allow for capital punishment? The legislature of most every state has enacted new statutes authorizing the death penalty for certain crimes, the Congress has made air piracy punishable by death, and the Supreme Court has ruled that the death penalty is not cruel and unusual punishment. Surveys indicate that the vast majority of Americans support the death penalty for some crimes, and seemingly rational persons occasionally choose death when their life prospects are sufficiently grim. So, there is excellent evidence that capital punishment is not humiliating in an unacceptable way and that capital punishment is compatible with standards of human dignity.

5. PUNISHMENT AND DESERT

We are now in a position to understand the Hegelian view that "in punishment the offender is honored as a rational being, since the punishment is looked on as his right." If the offender deserves to be punished in virtue of his past wrongdoing, then if we do not punish him, we should have some reason for not treating him as he deserves. If we are in no way excusing what he did but merely exempting him from the harm, then we are not dealing with him as he deserves. In choosing to do wrong and in realizing the consequences of what he did, he brought the punishment upon himself. In punishing him, we are respecting his choice. The punishment is his due in much the same way as the prize is the due of the winner. If we refused the winner the prize merely because we did not want him to benefit, then we would be acting illegitimately by not giving him his desert. So too with punishment. In punishment we are honoring the integrity of the agent by giving him his due.

The right to be punished is a strange sort of right. Rights are generally associated with what is in one's interest, so we must say that it is in the offender's interest to be punished. Pain or suffering is undesirable, however, so people will ordinarily not claim their right to be punished. Nevertheless, persons do have an interest in being treated as persons, as genuine members of the moral community. Such treatment requires that one's choices are honored and that one is dealt with in a manner appropriate to those choices. The right to be punished, then, is derivative on the right to be treated as a person. Just as persons deserve to be rewarded, so too persons deserve to be punished. Both rewarding and punishing are instances of respecting persons.

On occasion, it is more appropriate to use a therapy model than the model of honoring the integrity of human beings. Wrongdoing is occasionally pathological and should be dealt with much as one deals with other pathological conditions. If the agent is himself a victim, then it is appropriate to treat him as a victim in the way that a therapy model does. If kleptomania is a disease, then the person should be treated for it, not punished for it. So, one might treat the person for this illness much as one would treat a person for a cancer. In treating a person in this way, however, one is treating him as a victim, not as an agent; one is not respecting his choices; and one is not honoring him as a human being.

Most often, the therapy model is inappropriate. When it is inappropriate, the person as a moral agent has a right to be punished, not treated. It is demeaning to have our choices treated as if they were something over which we have no control. It is in our interest to be treated as a person, as an autonomous moral agent; we ordinarily do want our choices to be respected as emanating from us, rather than to be dealt with as symptoms of an ailment over which we have no control.

A deathbed scenario is sometimes used to criticize this retributive view. Should we punish a person on his deathbed for a past wrongdoing? The retributive view suggests that we should, that in doing so we are honoring his choices as a human being, and that he deserves the punishment in virtue of the wrong that he did. A utilitarian disagrees. He thinks that such treatment is inhumane, that respecting him as a human being requires that we forgo the punishment.

The correct answer depends on how the person on his deathbed is viewed. If the only interest, or the overwhelming interest, that we associate with a dying person is a peaceful death, then we should not punish him. A dying person would require special treatment in virtue of that dominant interest. If he wants a promise to be made, even an unreasonable promise, it might be best to make it, later to break it. If he is blameworthy, it might be unacceptable to blame him. It might even be acceptable to lie to him about his prospects for survival. But insofar as we are entitled to do all these things, we are compromising his status as a full-fledged member of the moral community. If the pressing interest to die comfortably and untroubled overrides his generally more important interest to be treated as a person, then our ordinary moral discourse fails. It is not, however, because we respect him as a person that we are willing to do these things. Rather, it is because his situation is so dire that it demands that his immediate needs be met. Issues of desert are overwhelmed by issues of immediate need.

Most often, however, it is desert that determines the moral acceptability of behavior. Occasionally, what one deserves is for harm to be inflicted. On those occasions, one deserves to be punished; it is one's right as a person.

NOTES

1. These two general answers do get a bit more complex. For the utilitarian might go on to maintain that inflicting harm can only be punishment if it is in virtue of a past deed that the harm is inflicted. Taking from the wealthy to feed starving children might be a morally acceptable way of harming the wealthy, but it is a conceptual mistake to view it as a punishment. Inflicting harm to prevent yet greater harm or to produce beneficial consequences might be morally acceptable, but it is not punishment unless it is backward-looking enough so that it is inflicted in virtue of some past misdeed. And the retributivist might not want to be saddled with punishing a person when no possible earthly benefit will derive from it. It seems severe to inflict harm on another in those cases when absolutely nothing will be gained from it, except perhaps a balancing of the moral scales. So, punishment may become a bit backward-looking for the utilitarian and a bit forward-looking for the retributivist.

   Thus, both views, when modified, seem to agree that both backward-looking and forward-looking considerations are relevant for determining the moral acceptability of punishment. Yet, the focus of the two views is different. For the retributivist thinks that it is the past wrongdoing which makes inflicting harm morally acceptable, whereas the utilitarian maintains that inflicting harm can be made morally acceptable only by considering the future consequences of the harm. Thus, the retributivist is not committed to the view that inflicting the harm is morally acceptable only if doing so produces better consequences than not inflicting it, for he believes that the justification lies in the past.

2. Again, this will not do. A judge might realize that the drunken defendant prefers the warm cell, yet punish him by sentencing him to a night in jail. Presumably, a night in jail is normally considered less pleasant than not spending a night in jail, even if it is not so in every case. In legal contexts, the penalty is determined by what is normally considered harmful or unpleasant.

3. There are two features associated with blame that need to be distinguished. First, there is blameworthiness. Blameworthiness is wholly backward-looking, focusing exclusively on the agent and his past deeds. Blameworthiness is analogous to responsibility, another backward-looking concept. Second, there is expressing the blame, typically to the blameworthy person. On occasion, it is morally unacceptable to express the blame, though blame is appropriate. The deathbed case might be such a case. Clearly, the fact that a man is dying does not affect his blameworthiness, for it has nothing whatever to do with his being accountable for his past misdeeds.

4. In his provocative essay, "Why I Am Not a Christian," Bertrand Russell criticizes Christ's teaching of hell. He says, "I do not myself feel that any person who is really profoundly humane can believe in everlasting punishment." For Russell, eternal damnation is always an inappropriate punishment, never deserved by any misdeed. He thinks it altogether too severe.

REVIEW AND DISCUSSION QUESTIONS

1. Explain why Perlmutter thinks utilitarians miss the point of punishment.

2. Why does Perlmutter think that to punish someone is to honor that person, while failing to punish may show disrespect?

3. Retributivists take the view that the *degree* of punishment should match the degree of moral blameworthiness of the act. How would such a view of punishment treat attempted crimes as compared with successful ones? Is that a reasonable approach?

4. How might a retributivist be expected to view punishment of drunk drivers? Drivers who kill when drunk? Drivers who kill after falling asleep?

5. Are there ever cases in which we should punish people who are not morally blameworthy? Explain.

6. Do utilitarians ignore the fact that some moral concepts are "backward looking," as Perlmutter says? How might Mill respond to that claim? Is his response adequate?

The Ultimate Punishment

Ernest van den Haag

Ernest van den Haag is among capital punishment's best known and most enthusiastic supporters. In this essay, he reviews the case on behalf of executions, beginning with the topic of its "maldistribution" among those who deserve it. He then discusses the concern that it is applied incorrectly to those who are innocent, whether it deters crime, its cost to society and to the executed, and whether it "brutalizes" society. He concludes with a brief discussion of capital punishment's supposed excessiveness and with Justice Brennan's claim that it "degrades" and is inconsistent with "human dignity." Ernest van den Haag was professor of jurisprudence and public policy at Fordham University.

The death penalty is our harshest punishment.* It is irrevocable: it ends the existence of those punished, instead of temporarily imprisoning them. Further, although not intended to cause physical pain, execution is the only corporal punishment still applied to adults.[1] These singular characteristics contribute to the perennial, impassioned controversy about capital punishment.

1. DISTRIBUTION

Consideration of the justice, morality, or usefulness of capital punishment is often conflated with objections to its alleged discriminatory or capricious distribution among the guilty. Wrongly so. If capital punishment is immoral *in se,* no distribution among the guilty could make it moral. If capital punishment is moral, no distribution would make it immoral. Improper distribution cannot affect the quality of what is distributed, be it punishments or rewards. Discriminatory or capricious distribution thus could not justify abolition of the death penalty. Further, maldistribution inheres

no more in capital punishment than in any other punishment.

Maldistribution between the guilty and the innocent is, by definition, unjust. But the injustice does not lie in the nature of the punishment. Because of the finality of the death penalty, the most grievous maldistribution occurs when it is imposed upon the innocent. However, the frequent allegations of discrimination and capriciousness refer to maldistribution among the guilty and not to the punishment of the innocent.

Maldistribution of any punishment among those who deserve it is irrelevant to its justice or morality. Even if poor or black convicts guilty of capital offenses suffer capital punishment, and other convicts equally guilty of the same crimes do not, a more equal distribution, however desirable, would merely be more equal. It would not be more just to the convicts under sentence of death.

Punishments are imposed on persons, not on racial or economic groups. Guilt is personal. The only relevant question is: does the person to be executed deserve the punishment? Whether or not others who deserved the same punishment, whatever their economic or racial group, have avoided execution is irrelevant. If they have, the guilt of the executed convicts would not be diminished, nor would their punishment be less deserved.

---

*Some writers . . . have thought that life imprisonment is more severe. . . . However, the overwhelming majority of both abolitionists and of convicts under death sentence prefer life imprisonment to execution.

To put the issue starkly, if the death penalty were imposed on guilty blacks, but not on guilty whites, or, if it were imposed by a lottery among the guilty, this irrationally discriminatory or capricious distribution would neither make the penalty unjust, nor cause anyone to be unjustly punished, despite the undue impunity bestowed on others.*

Equality, in short, seems morally less important than justice. And justice is independent of distributional inequalities. The ideal of equal justice demands that justice be equally distributed, not that it be replaced by equality. Justice requires that as many of the guilty as possible be punished, regardless of whether others have avoided punishment. To let these others escape the deserved punishment does not do justice to them, or to society. But it is not unjust to those who could not escape.

These moral considerations are not meant to deny that irrational discrimination, or capriciousness, would be inconsistent with constitutional requirements. But I am satisfied that the Supreme Court has in fact provided for adherence to the constitutional requirement of equality as much as is possible. Some inequality is indeed unavoidable as a practical matter in any system.† But, *ultra posse nemo obligatur.* (Nobody is bound beyond ability.)

Recent data reveal little direct racial discrimination in the sentencing of those arrested and convicted of murder.[2] The abrogation of the death penalty for rape has eliminated a major source of racial discrimination. Concededly, some discrimination based on the race of murder victims may exist; yet, this discrimination affects criminal victimizers in an unexpected way. Murderers of whites are thought more likely to be executed than murderers of blacks. Black victims, then, are less fully vindicated than white ones. However, because most black murderers kill blacks, black murderers are spared the death penalty more often than are white murderers. They fare better than most white murderers.* The motivation behind unequal distribution of the death penalty may well have been to discriminate against blacks, but the result has favored them. Maldistribution is thus a straw man for empirical as well as analytical reasons.

II. MISCARRIAGES OF JUSTICE

In a recent survey Professors Hugo Adam Bedau and Michael Radelet found that 7000 persons were executed in the United States between 1900 and 1985 and that 25 were innocent of capital crimes.[3] Among the innocents they list Sacco and Vanzetti as well as Ethel and Julius Rosenberg. Although their data may be questionable, I do not doubt that, over a long enough period, miscarriages of justice will occur even in capital cases.

Despite precautions, nearly all human activities, such as trucking, lighting, or construction, cost the lives of some innocent bystanders. We do not give up these activities, because the advantages, moral or material, outweigh the unintended losses. Analogously, for those who think the death penalty just, miscarriages of justice are offset by the moral benefits and the usefulness of doing justice. For those who

___

*Justice Douglas, concurring in *Furman* v. *Georgia,* 408 U.S. 238 (1972), wrote that "a law which. . . . reaches that [discriminatory] result in practice has no more sanctity than a law which in terms provides the same." *Id.* at 256 (Douglas, J., concurring). Indeed, a law legislating this result "in terms" would be inconsistent with the "equal protection of tile laws" provided by the fourteenth amendment, as would the discriminatory result reached in practice. But that result could be changed by changing the distributional practice. Thus, Justice Douglas notwithstanding, a discriminatory result does not make the death penalty unconstitutional, unless the penalty ineluctably must produce that result to an unconstitutional degree.

†The ideal of equality, unlike the ideal of retributive justice (which can be approximated separately in each instance), is clearly unattainable unless all guilty persons are apprehended, and thereafter tried, convicted and sentenced by the same court, at the same time. Unequal justice is the best we can do; it is still better than the injustice, equal or unequal, which occurs if, for the sake of equality, we deliberately allow some who could be punished to escape.

___

* It barely need be said that any discrimination *against* (for example, black murderers of whites) must also be discrimination *for* (for example, black murderers of blacks).

think the death penalty unjust even when it does not miscarry, miscarriages can hardly be decisive.

III. DETERRENCE

Despite much recent work, there has been no conclusive statistical demonstration that the death penalty is a better deterrent than are alternative punishments.[4] However, deterrence is less than decisive for either side. Most abolitionists acknowledge that they would continue to favor abolition even if the death penalty were shown to deter more murders than alternatives could deter.* Abolitionists appear to value the life of a convicted murderer or, at least, his nonexecution, more highly than they value the lives of the innocent victims who might be spared by deterring prospective murderers.

Deterrence is not altogether decisive for me either. I would favor retention of the death penalty as retribution even if it were shown that the threat of execution could not deter prospective murderers not already deterred by the threat of imprisonment.[†] Still, I believe the death penalty, because of its finality, is more feared than imprisonment, and deters some prospective murderers not deterred by the threat of imprisonment. Sparing the lives of even a few prospective victims by deterring their murderers is more important than preserving the lives of convicted murderers because of the possibility, or even the

probability, that executing them would not deter others. Whereas the lives of the victims who might be saved are valuable, that of the murderer has only negative value, because of his crime. Surely the criminal law is meant to protect the lives of potential victims in preference to those of actual murderers.

Murder rates are determined by many factors; neither the severity nor the probability of the threatened sanction is always decisive. However, for the long run, I share the view of Sir James Fitzjames Stephen: "Some men, probably, abstain from murder because they fear that if they committed murder they would be hanged. Hundreds of thousands abstain from it because they regard it with horror. One great reason why they regard it with horror is that murderers are hanged."[5] Penal sanctions are useful in the long run for the formation of the internal restraints so necessary to control crime. The severity and finality of the death penalty is appropriate to the seriousness and the finality of murder.*

IV. INCIDENTAL ISSUES: COST, RELATIVE SUFFERING, BRUTALIZATION

Many nondecisive issues are associated with capital punishment. Some believe that the monetary cost of appealing a capital sentence is excessive.[6] Yet most comparisons of the cost of life imprisonment with the cost of execution, apart from their dubious relevance, are flawed at least by the implied assumption that life prisoners will generate no judicial costs during their imprisonment. At any rate, the actual monetary costs are trumped by the importance of doing justice.

---

*For most abolitionists, the discrimination argument, *see supra,* is similarly nondecisive: they would favor abolition even if there could be no racial discrimination.

†If executions were shown to increase the murder rate in the long run, I would favor abolition. Sparing the innocent victims who would be spared, *ex hypothesi,* by the nonexecution of murderers would be more important to me than the execution, however just, of murderers. But although there is a lively discussion of the subject, no serious evidence exists to support the hypothesis that executions produce a higher murder rate. *Cf.* Phillips, *The Deterrent Effect of Capital Punishment: New Evidence on an Old Controversy* 86 *Am. J. Soc.* 139 (1980) (arguing that murder rates drop immediately after executions of criminals).

---

* *Weems* v. *United States,* 217 U.S. 349 (1910), suggests that penalties be proportionate to the seriousness of the crime—a common theme of the criminal law. Murder, therefore, demands more than life imprisonment, if, as I believe, it is a more serious crime than other crimes punished by life imprisonment. In modern times, our sensibility requires that the range of punishments be narrower than the range of crimes—but not so narrow as to exclude the death penalty.

Others insist that a person sentenced to death suffers more than his victim suffered, and that this (excess) suffering is undue according to the *lex talionis* (rule of retaliation).[7] We cannot know whether the murderer on death row suffers more than his victim suffered; however, unlike the murderer, the victim deserved none of the suffering inflicted. Further, the limitations of the *lex talionis* were meant to restrain private vengeance, not the social retribution that has taken its place. Punishment—regardless of the motivation—is not intended to revenge, offset, or compensate for the victim's suffering, or to be measured by it. Punishment is to vindicate the law and the social order undermined by the crime. This is why a kidnapper's penal confinement is not limited to the period for which he imprisoned his victim; nor is a burglar's confinement meant merely to offset the suffering or the harm he caused his victim; nor is it meant only to offset the advantage he gained.*

Another argument . . . is that, by killing a murderer, we encourage, endorse, or legitimize unlawful killing. Yet, although all punishments are meant to be unpleasant, it is seldom argued that they), legitimize the unlawful imposition of identical unpleasantness. Imprisonment is not thought to legitimize kidnapping; neither are fines thought to legitimize robbery. The difference between murder and execution, or between kidnapping and imprisonment, is that the first is unlawful and undeserved, the second a lawful and deserved punishment for an unlawful act. The physical similarities of the punishment to the crime are irrelevant. The relevant difference is not physical, but social.†

V. JUSTICE, EXCESS, DEGRADATION

We threaten punishments in order to deter crime. We impose them not only to make the threats credible but also as retribution (justice) for the crimes that were not deterred. Threats and punishments are necessary to deter and deterrence is a sufficient practical justification for them. Retribution is an independent moral justification.[8] Although penalties can be unwise, repulsive, or inappropriate, and those punished can be pitiable, in a sense the infliction of legal punishment on a guilty person cannot be unjust. By committing the crime, the criminal volunteered to assume the risk of receiving a legal punishment that he could have avoided by not committing the crime. The punishment he suffers is the punishment he voluntarily risked suffering and, therefore, it is no more unjust to him than any other event for which one knowingly volunteers to assume the risk. Thus, the death penalty cannot be unjust to the guilty criminal.*

There remain, however, two moral objections. The penalty may be regarded as always excessive as retribution and always morally

---

*Thus restitution (a civil liability) cannot satisfy the punitive purpose of penal sanctions, whether the purpose be retributive or deterrent.

†Some abolitionists challenge: if the death penalty is just and serves as a deterrent, why not televise executions? The answer is simple. The death even of a murderer, however well-deserved, should not serve as public entertainment. It so served in earlier centuries. But in this respect our sensibility has changed for the better, I believe. Further, television unavoidably would trivialize executions, wedged in, as they would be, between game shows, situation comedies, and the like. Finally, because

televised executions would focus on the physical aspects of the punishment, rather than the nature of the crime and the suffering of the victim, a televised execution would present the murderer as the victim of the state. Far from communicating the moral significance of the execution, television would shift the focus to the pitiable fear of the murderer. We no longer place in cages those sentenced to imprisonment to expose them to public view. Why should we so expose those sentenced to execution?

* An explicit threat of punitive action is necessary to the justification of any legal punishment: *nulla poena sine lege* (no punishment without [preexisting] law). To be sufficiently justified, the threat must in turn have a rational and legitimate purpose. "Your money or your life" does not qualify; nor does the threat of an unjust law; nor, finally, does a threat that is altogether disproportionate to the importance of its purpose. In short, preannouncement legitimizes the threatened punishment only if the threat is warranted. But this leaves a very wide range of justified threats. Furthermore, the punished person is aware of the penalty for his actions and thus volunteers to take the risk even of an unjust punishment. His victim, however, did not volunteer to risk anything. The question whether any self-inflicted injury—such as a legal punishment—ever can be unjust to a person who knowingly risked it is a matter that requires more analysis than is possible here.

degrading. To regard the death penalty as always excessive, one must believe that no crime—no matter how heinous—could possibly justify capital punishment. Such a belief can be neither corroborated nor refuted; it is an article of faith.

Alternatively, or concurrently, one may believe that everybody, the murderer no less than the victim, has an imprescriptible (natural?) right to life. The law therefore should not deprive anyone of life. I share Jeremy Bentham's view that any such "natural and imprescriptible rights" are "nonsense upon stilts."[†]

Justice Brennan has insisted that the death penalty is "uncivilized," "inhuman," inconsistent with "human dignity" and with "the sanctity of life,"[9] that it "treats members of the human race as nonhumans, as objects to be toyed with and discarded,"[10] that it is "uniquely degrading to human dignity"[11] and "by its very nature, [involves] a denial of the executed person's humanity."[12] Justice Brennan does not say why he thinks execution "uncivilized." Hitherto most civilizations have had the death penalty, although it has been discarded in Western Europe, where it is currently unfashionable probably because of its abuse by totalitarian regimes.

By "degrading," Justice Brennan seems to mean that execution degrades the executed convicts. Yet philosophers, such as Immanuel Kant and G. W. F. Hegel, have insisted that,

when deserved, execution, far from degrading the executed convict, affirms his humanity by affirming his rationality and his responsibility for his actions. They thought that execution, when deserved, is required for the sake of the convict's dignity. (Does not life imprisonment violate human dignity more than execution, by keeping alive a prisoner deprived of all autonomy?)

Common sense indicates that it cannot be death—our common fate—that is inhuman. Therefore, Justice Brennan must mean that death degrades when it comes not as a natural or accidental event, but as a deliberate social imposition. The murderer learns through his punishment that his fellow men have found him unworthy of living; that because he has murdered, he is being expelled from the community of the living. This degradation is self-inflicted. By murdering, the murderer has so dehumanized himself that he cannot remain among the living. The social recognition of his self-degradation is the punitive essence of execution. To believe, as Justice Brennan appears to, that the degradation is inflicted by the execution reverses the direction of causality.

Execution of those who have committed heinous murders may deter only one murder per year. If it does, it seems quite warranted. It is also the only fitting retribution for murder I can think of.

NOTES

1. For a discussion of the sources of opposition to corporal punishment, see E. van den Haag, *Punishing Criminals* 196–206 (1975).
2. *See* Bureau of Justice Statistics, U.S. Dept. of Justice, Bulletin No. NCJ-98, 399, *Capital Punishment 1984*, at 9 (1985); Johnson, *The Executioner's Bias, Nat'l Rev.*, Nov. 15, 1985, at 44.

3. Bedau & Radelet, *Miscarriages of Justice in Potentially Capital Cases* (1st draft, Oct. 1985) (on file at Harvard Law School Library).
4. For a sample of conflicting views on the subject, see Baldus & Cole, *A Comparison of the Work of Thorsten Sellin and Isaac Ehrlich on the Deterrent Effect of Capital Punishment*, 85 *Yale L. J.* 170 (1975); Bowers & Pierce, *Deterrence or Brutalization: What Is the Effect of Executions?*, 26 *Crime & Delinq.* 453 (1980); Bowers & Pierce, *The Illusion of Deterrence in Isaac Ehrlich's Research on Capital Punishment*, 85 *Yale L. J.* 187 (1975); Ehrlich, *Fear of Deterrence: A Critical Evaluation of the "Report of the Panel on Research on Deterrent and Incapacitative Effects,"* 6 *J. Legal Stud.* 293 (1977); Ehrlich, *The Deterrent Effect of Capital Punishment: A Question of Life and*

†*The Works of Jeremy Bentham* 105 (J. Bowring ed. 1972). However, I would be more polite about prescriptible natural rights, which Bentham described as "simple nonsense." *Id.* (It does not matter whether natural rights are called "moral" or "human" rights as they currently are by most writers.)

Death, 65 *Am. Econ. Rev.* 397, 415–16 (1975); Ehrlich & Gibbons, *On the Measurement of the Deterrent Effect of Capital Punishment and the Theory of Deterrence*, 6 *J. Legal Stud.* 35 (1977).

5. H. Gross, *A Theory of Criminal Justice* 489 (1979) (attributing this passage to Sir James Fitzjames Stephen).

6. *Cf.* Kaplan, *Administering Capital Punishment*, 36 *U. Fla. L. Rev.* 177, 178, 190–91 (1984) (noting the high cost of appealing a capital sentence).

7. For an example of this view, see A. Camus, *Reflections on the Guillotine* 24–30 (1959). On the limitations allegedly imposed by the *lex talionis,* see Reiman, *Justice, Civilization, and the Death Penalty: Answering van den Haag*, 14 *Phil. & Pub. Aff.* 115, 119–34 (1985).

8. *See* van den Haag, *Punishment as a Device for Controlling the Crime Rate*, 33 *Rutgers L. Rev.* 706, 719 (1981) (explaining why the desire for retribution, although independent, would have to be satisfied even if deterrent were the only purpose of punishment).

9. *The Death Penalty in America* 256–63 (H. Bedau ed., 3d ed. 1982) quoting *Furman* v. *Georgia*, 408 U.S. 238, 286, 305 (1972) (Brennan, J., concurring).

10. *Id.* at 272–73; see also *Gregg* v. *Georgia*, 428 U.S. 153, 230 (1976) (Brennan, J., dissenting).

11. *Furman* v. *Georgia*, 408 U.S. 238, 291 (1972) (Brennan, J., concurring).

12. *Id.* at 290.

REVIEW AND DISCUSSION QUESTIONS

1. How does van den Haag respond to those who would reject capital punishment because it falls disproportionately on minorities and the poor? Because it sometimes leads to executions of innocents?

2. Why does van den Haag believe capital punishment deters criminals?

3. How does the author respond to Justice Brennan's claim that executions violate "human dignity"?

Justice, Civilization, and the Death Penalty

Jeffrey H. Reiman

It is often assumed that if the death penalty is deserved then it follows that it should be administered. Jeffrey Reiman disputes this claim, arguing instead that like torture, capital punishment should not be administered because of how horrible it is. He then goes on to assess the central claims made by Ernest van den Haag in defense of capital punishment. Jeffrey Reiman is William Fraser McDowell Professor of Philosophy at The American University.

CIVILIZATION, PAIN, AND JUSTICE

. . . [F]rom the fact that something is justly deserved, it does not automatically follow that it should be done, since there may be other moral reasons for not doing it such that, all told, the weight of moral reasons swings the balance against proceeding. The same argument that I have given for the justice of the death penalty for murderers proves the justice of beating assaulters, raping rapists, and torturing torturers. Nonetheless, I believe, and suspect that most would agree, that it would not be right for us to beat assaulters, rape rapists, or torture torturers, *even though it were their just deserts*—and even if this were the only way to make them suffer as much as they had made their victims suffer. Calling for the abolition of the death penalty, though it be just, then, amounts to urging that as a society we place execution in the same category of sanction as beating, raping, and torturing, and treat it as something it would not be right for us to do to offenders, *even if it were their just deserts. . . .*

Progress in civilization is characterized by a lower tolerance for one's own pain and that suffered by others. And this is appropriate, since, via growth in knowledge, civilization brings increased power to prevent or reduce pain and, via growth in the ability to communicate and interact with more and more people, civilization extends the circle of people with whom we empathize.[1] If civilization is characterized by lower tolerance for our own pain and that of others, then publicly refusing to do horrible things to our fellows both signals the level of our civilization *and, by our example, continues the work of civilizing.* And this gesture is all the more powerful if we refuse to do horrible things to those who deserve them. I contend then that the more things we are able to include in this category, the more civilized we are and the more civili*zing.* Thus we gain from including torture in this category, and if execution is especially horrible, we gain still more by including it. . . .

What can be said of reducing the horrible things that we do to our fellows even when deserved? First of all, given our vulnerability to pain, it seems clearly a gain. Is it however an unmitigated gain? That is, would such a reduction ever amount to a loss? It seems to me that there are two conditions under which it would be a loss, namely, if the reduction made our lives more dangerous, or if not doing what is justly deserved were a loss in itself. Let us leave aside the former, since, as I have already suggested and as I will soon indicate in greater detail, I accept that if some horrible punishment is necessary to deter equally or more horrible acts, then we may have to impose the punishment. Thus my claim is that reduction in the horrible things we do to our fellows is an

advance in civilization *as long as our lives are not thereby made more dangerous,* and that it is only then that we are called upon to extend that reduction as part of the work of civilization. Assuming then, for the moment, that we suffer no increased danger by refraining from doing horrible things to our fellows when they justly deserve them, does such refraining to do what is justly deserved amount to a loss?

It seems to me that the answer to this must be that refraining to do what is justly deserved is only a loss where it amounts to doing an injustice. But such refraining to do what is just is not doing what is unjust, unless what we do instead falls below the bottom end of the range of just punishments. Otherwise, it would be unjust to refrain from torturing torturers, raping rapists, or beating assaulters. In short, I take it that if there is no injustice in refraining from torturing torturers, then there is no injustice in refraining to do horrible things to our fellows generally, when they deserve them, as long as what we do instead is compatible with believing that they do deserve them. And thus that if such refraining does not make our lives more dangerous, then it is no loss, and given our vulnerability to pain, it is a gain. Consequently, reduction in the horrible things we do to our fellows, when not necessary to our protection, is an advance in civilization that we are called upon to continue once we consciously take upon ourselves the work of civilization.

To complete the argument, however, I must show that execution is horrible enough to warrant its inclusion alongside torture. Against this it will be said that execution is not especially horrible since it only hastens a fate that is inevitable for us. I think that this view overlooks important differences in the manner in which people reach their inevitable ends. I contend that execution is especially horrible, and it is so in a way similar to (though not identical with) the way in which torture is especially horrible. I believe we view torture as especially awful because of two of its features, which also characterize execution: intense pain and the spectacle of one human being completely subject to the power of another. This latter is separate from the issue of pain since it is something that offends us about unpainful things, such as slavery (even voluntarily entered) and prostitution (even voluntarily chosen as an occupation).[2] Execution shares this separate feature, since killing a bound and defenseless human being enacts the total subjugation of that person to his fellows. I think, incidentally, that this accounts for the general uneasiness with which execution by lethal injection has been greeted. Rather than humanizing the event, it seems only to have purchased a possible reduction in physical pain at the price of increasing the spectacle of subjugation—with no net gain in the attractiveness of the death penalty. Indeed, its net effect may have been the reverse.

In addition to the spectacle of subjugation, execution, even by physically painless means, is also characterized by a special and intense psychological pain that distinguishes it from the loss of life that awaits us all. Interesting in this regard is the fact that although we are not terribly squeamish about the loss of life itself, allowing it in war, self-defense, as a necessary cost of progress, and so on, we are, as the extraordinary hesitance of our courts testifies, quite reluctant to execute. I think this is because execution involves the most psychologically painful features of deaths. We normally regard death from human causes as worse than death from natural causes, since a humanly caused shortening of life lacks the consolation of unavoidability And we normally regard death whose coming is foreseen by its victim as worse than sudden death, because a foreseen death adds to the loss of life the terrible consciousness of that impending loss. As a humanly caused death whose advent is foreseen by its victim, an execution combines the worst of both.

Thus far, by analogy with torture, I have argued that execution should be avoided because of how horrible it is to the one executed. But there are reasons of another sort that follow from the analogy with torture. Torture is to be avoided not only because of what it says about *what* we are willing to do to our fellows, but also because of what it says about *us* who are willing to do it. To torture

someone is an awful spectacle not only because of the intensity of pain imposed, but because of what is required to be able to impose such pain on one's fellows. The tortured body cringes, using its full exertion to escape the pain imposed upon it—it literally begs for relief with its muscles as it does with its cries. To torture someone is to demonstrate a capacity to resist this begging, and that in turn demonstrates a kind of hardheartedness that a society ought not parade.

And this is true not only of torture, but of all severe corporal punishment. Indeed, I think this constitutes part of the answer to the puzzling question of why we refrain from punishments like whipping, even when the alternative (some months in jail versus some lashes) seems more costly to the offender. Imprisonment is painful to be sure, but it is a reflective pain, one that comes with comparing what is to what might have been, and that can be temporarily ignored by thinking about other things. But physical pain has an urgency that holds body and mind in a fierce grip. Of physical pain, as Orwell's Winston Smith recognized, "you could only wish one thing: that it should stop."[3] Refraining from torture in particular and corporal punishment in general, we both refuse to put a fellow human being in this grip *and* refuse to show our ability to resist this wish. The death penalty is the last corporal punishment used officially in the modern world. And it is corporal not only because administered via the body, but because the pain of foreseen, humanly administered death strikes us with the urgency that characterizes intense physical pain, causing grown men to cry, faint, and lose control of their bodily functions. There is something to be gained by refusing to endorse the hardness of heart necessary to impose such a fate.

By placing execution alongside torture in the category of things we will not do to our fellow human beings even when they deserve them, we broadcast the message that totally subjugating a person to the power of others *and* confronting him with the advent of his own humanly administered demise is too horrible to be done by civilized human beings to their fellows even when they have earned it: too horrible to do, and too horrible to be capable of doing. And I contend that broadcasting this message loud and clear would in the long run contribute to the general detestation of murder and be, to the extent to which it worked itself into the hearts and minds of the populace, a deterrent. In short, refusing to execute murderers though they deserve it both reflects and continues the taming of the human species that we call civilization. Thus, I take it that the abolition of the death penalty, though it is just punishment for murder, is part of the civilizing mission of modern states.

CIVILIZATION, SAFETY, AND DETERRENCE

Earlier I said that judging a practice too horrible to do even to those who deserve it does not exclude the possibility that it could be justified if necessary to avoid even worse consequences. Thus, were the death penalty clearly proven a better deterrent to the murder of innocent people than life in prison, we might have to admit that we had not yet reached a level of civilization at which we could protect ourselves without imposing this horrible fate on murderers, and thus we might have to grant the necessity of instituting the death penalty.[4] But this is far from proven. The available research by no means clearly indicates that the death penalty reduces the incidence of homicide more than life imprisonment does. Even the econometric studies of Isaac Ehrlich, which purport to show that each execution saves seven or eight potential murder victims, have not changed this fact, as is testified to by the controversy and objections from equally respected statisticians that Ehrlich's work has provoked.[5]

Conceding that it has not been proven that the death penalty deters more murders than life imprisonment, van den Haag has argued that neither has it been proven that the death penalty does *not* deter more murders, and thus we must follow common sense which teaches that the higher the cost of something, the fewer people will choose it, and therefore at

least some potential murderers who would not be deterred by life imprisonment will be deterred by the death penalty. . . . Those of us who recognize how common-sensical it was, and still is, to believe that the sun moves around the earth, will be less willing than Professor van den Haag to follow common sense here, especially when it comes to doing something awful to our fellows. Moreover, there are good reasons for doubting common sense on this matter. Here are four:

1. From the fact that one penalty is more feared than another, it does not follow that the more feared penalty will deter more than the less feared, unless we know that the less feared penalty is not fearful enough to deter everyone who can be deterred—and this is just what we don't know with regard to the death penalty. Though I fear the death penalty more than life in prison, I can't think of any act that the death penalty would deter me from that an equal likelihood of spending my life in prison wouldn't deter me from as well. Since it seems to me that whoever would be deterred by a given likelihood of death would be deterred by an *equal* likelihood of life behind bars, I suspect that the common-sense argument only seems plausible because we evaluate it unconsciously assuming that potential criminals will face larger likelihoods of death sentences than of life sentences. If the likelihoods were equal, it seems to me that where life imprisonment was improbable enough to make it too distant a possibility to worry much about, a similar low probability of death would have the same effect. After all, we are undeterred by small likelihoods of death every time we walk the streets. And if life imprisonment were sufficiently probable to pose a real deterrent threat, it would pose as much of a deterrent threat as death. And this is just what most of the research we have on the comparative deterrent impact of execution versus life imprisonment suggests.

2. In light of the fact that roughly 500 to 700 suspected felons are killed by the police in the line of duty every year, and the fact that the number of privately owned guns in America is substantially larger than the number of households in America, it must be granted that anyone contemplating committing a crime *already* faces a substantial risk of ending up dead as a result. It's hard to see why anyone *who is not already deterred by this* would be deterred by the addition of the more distant risk of death after apprehension, conviction, and appeal. Indeed, this suggests that people consider risks in a much crueler way than van den Haag's appeal to common sense suggests—which should be evident to anyone who contemplates how few people use seatbelts (14% of drivers, on some estimates), when it is widely known that wearing them can spell the difference between life (outside prison) and death.

3. Van den Haag has maintained that deterrence doesn't work only by means of cost-benefit calculations made by potential criminals. It works also by the lesson about the wrongfulness of murder that is slowly learned in a society that subjects murderers to the ultimate punishment . . . . But if I am correct in claiming that the refusal to execute even those who deserve it has a civilizing effect, then the refusal to execute also teaches a lesson about the wrongfulness of murder. My claim here is admittedly speculative, but no more so than van den Haag's to the contrary. And my view has the added virtue of accounting for the failure of research to show an increased deterrent effect from executions *without having to deny the plausibility of van den Haag's common-sense argument that at least some additional potential murderers will be deterred by the prospect of the death penalty*. If there is a deterrent effect from *not executing*, then it is understandable that while executions will deter some murderers, this effect will be balanced out by the weakening of the deterrent effect of not executing, such that no net reduction in murders will result. And this, by the way, also disposes of van den Haag's argument that, in the absence of knowledge one way or the other on the deterrent effect of executions, we should execute murderers rather than risk the lives of innocent people whose murders might have been deterred if we had. If there is a deterrent effect of not executing, it follows

that we risk innocent lives either way. And if this is so, it seems that the only reasonable course of action is to refrain from imposing what we know is a horrible fate.

4. Those who still think that van den Haag's common-sense argument for executing murderers is valid will find that the argument proves more than they bargained for. Van den Haag maintains that, in the absence of conclusive evidence on the relative deterrent impact of the death penalty versus life imprisonment, we must follow common sense and assume that if one punishment is more fearful than another, it will deter some potential criminals not deterred by the less fearful punishment. Since people sentenced to death will almost universally try to get their sentences changed to life in prison, it follows that death is more fearful than life imprisonment, and thus that it will deter some additional murderers. Consequently, we should institute the death penalty to save the lives these additional murderers would have taken. But, since people sentenced to be tortured to death would surely try to get their sentences changed to simple execution, the same argument proves that death-by-torture will deter still more potential murderers. Consequently, we should institute death-by-torture to save the lives these additional murderers would have taken. Anyone who accepts van den Haag's argument is then confronted with a dilemma: Until we have conclusive evidence that capital punishment is a greater deterrent to murder than life imprisonment, we must grant *either* that we should not follow common sense and not impose the death penalty; *or* we should follow common sense and torture murderers to death. In short, either we must abolish the electric chair or reinstitute the rack. Surely, this is the *reductio ad absurdum* of van den Haag's common-sense argument.

CONCLUSION: HISTORY, FORCE, AND JUSTICE

I believe that, taken together, these arguments prove that we should abolish the death penalty though it is a just punishment for murder. Let me close with an argument of a different sort. When you see the lash fall upon the backs of Roman slaves, or the hideous tortures meted out in the period of the absolute monarchs, you see more than mere cruelty at work. Surely you suspect that there is something about the injustice of imperial slavery and royal tyranny that requires the use of extreme force to keep these institutions in place. That is, for reasons undoubtedly related to those that support the second part of Durkheim's first law of penal evolution, we take the amount of force a society uses against its own people as an inverse measure of its justness. And though no more than a rough measure, it is a revealing one nonetheless, because when a society is limited in the degree of force it can use against its subjects, it is likely to have to be a juster society since it will have to gain its subjects' cooperation by offering them fairer terms than it

would have to, if it could use more force. From this we cannot simply conclude that reducing the force used by our society will automatically make our society more just—but I think we can conclude that it will have this tendency, since it will require us to find means other than force for encouraging compliance with our institutions, and this is likely to require us to make those institutions as fair to all as possible. Thus I hope that America will pose itself the challenge of winning its citizens' cooperation by justice rather than force, and that when future historians look back on the twentieth century, they will find us with countries like France and England and Sweden that have abolished the death penalty, rather than with those like South Africa and the Soviet Union and Iran that have retained it—with all that this suggests about the countries involved.

NOTES

1. Van den Haag writes that our ancestors "were not as repulsed by physical pain as we are. The change has to do not with our greater smartness or moral superiority but with a new outlook pioneered by the French and American revolutions [namely, that assertion of human equality and with it 'universal identification'], and by such mundane things as the invention of anesthetics, which make pain much less of an everyday experience" ([Ernest van den Haag and John P. Conrad, *The Death Penalty: A Debate* (New York: Plenum Press, 1983)], p. 215; cf. van den Haag's *Punishing Criminals* [New York: Basic Books, 1975], pp. 196-206).
2. I am not here endorsing this view of voluntarily entered slavery or prostitution. I mean only to suggest that it is *the belief* that these relations involve the extreme subjugation of one person to the power of another that is at the basis of their offensiveness. What I am saying is quite compatible with finding that this belief is false with respect to voluntarily entered slavery or prostitution.
3. George Orwell, *1984* (New York: New American Library, 1983; originally published in 1949), p. 197.
4. I say "might" here to avoid the sticky question of just how effective a deterrent the death penalty would have to be to justify overcoming our scruples about executing. It is here that the other considerations often urged against capital punishment—discrimination, irrevocability, the possibility of mistake, and so

on—would play a role. Omitting such qualifications, however, my position might crudely be stated as follows: *Just desert limits what a civilized society may do to deter crime, and deterrence limits what a civilized society may do to give criminals their just deserts.*
5. Isaac Ehrlich, "The Deterrent Effect of Capital Punishment: A Question of Life or Death," *American Economic Review* 65 (June 1975): 397–417. For reactions to Ehrlich's work, see Alfred Blumstein, Jacqueline Cohen, and Daniel Nagin, eds., *Deterrence and Incapacitation: Estimating the Effects of Criminal Sanctions on Crime Rates* (Washington, D.C. National Academy of Sciences, 1978), esp. pp. 59–63 and 336–60; Brian E. Forst, "The Deterrent Effect on Capital Punishment: A Cross-State Analysis," *Minnesota Law Review* 61 (May 1977): 743–67, Deryck Beyleveld, "Ehrlich's Analysis of Deterrence," *British Journal of Criminology* 22 (April 1982): 101–23, and Isaac Ehrlich, "On Positive Methodology, Ethics and Polemics in Deterrence Research," *British Journal of Criminology* 22 (April 1982): 124–39. Much of the criticism of Ehrlich's work focuses on the fact that he found a deterrence impact of executions in the period from 1933–1969, which includes the period 1963–1969, a time when hardly any executions were carried out and crime rates rose for reasons that are arguably independent of the existence or nonexistence of capital punishment. When the 1963–1969 period is excluded, no significant

deterrent effect shows. Prior to Ehrlich's work, research on the comparative deterrent impact of the death penalty versus life imprisonment indicated no increase in the incidence of homicide in states that abolished the death penalty and no greater incidence of homicide in states without the death penalty compared to similar states with the death penalty. See Thorsten Sellin, *The Death Penalty* (Philadelphia: American Law Institute, 1959).

REVIEW AND DISCUSSION QUESTIONS

1. How does Reiman understand social progress?
2. Explain why Reiman thinks that the failure to abolish capital punishment signifies a low level of civilization. What analogy does he make to substantiate his claim?
3. Describe each of Reiman's responses to van den Haag's argument that capital punishment deters.

Refuting Reiman

Ernest van den Haag

In the previous essay, Jeffrey Reiman argued that van den Haag is wrong in supposing that capital punishment deters and that it is therefore justified. In this response, van den Haag provides his response to Reiman's criticisms.

Reiman believes the death penalty is deserved by some murderers, but should never be imposed. Moral scruples should preclude it. If the punishment deserved . . . is morally repugnant, we may impose less, provided the suffering imposed *in lieu* of what is deserved is proportional to the suffering inflicted on the crime victim. However, suffering exceeding that of his victim can never be deserved by the offender; to impose it would be "unjust for the same reasons that make punishment of the innocent unjust."[1] . . .

I share some of Reiman's scruples: although he deserves it, I do not want to see the torturer tortured. Other scruples strike me as unjustified.

POVERTY AND CULPABILITY

Reiman believes "that the vast majority of murders in America are a predictable response to the frustrations and disabilities of impoverished social circumstances" which could be, but are not remedied because "others in America benefit," wherefore we have "no right to exact the full cost . . . from our murderers until we have done everything possible to rectify the conditions that produce their crimes." Murder here seems to become the punishment for the sins of the wealthy. According to Reiman, "the vast majority" of current murderers are not fully culpable, since part of the blame for their

Ernest van den Haag, "Refuting Reiman and Nathanson," *Philosophy and Public Affairs* 14 (Spring 1985). Copyright © 1985 by Princeton University Press. Reprinted by permission of Princeton University Press.

crimes must be placed on those who fail to "rectify the conditions that produce their crimes."

I grant that certain social conditions predictably produce crime more readily than others. Does it follow that those who commit crimes in criminogenic conditions are less responsible, or blameworthy, than they would be if they did not live in these conditions? Certainly not. Predictability does not reduce responsibility. Reiman remains responsible for his predictable argument. Culpability is reduced only when the criminal's ability to control his actions, or to realize that they are wrong, is abnormally impaired. If not, the social conditions in which the criminal lives have no bearing on his responsibility for his acts. Conditions, such as poverty, just or unjust, may increase the temptation to commit crimes. But poverty is neither a necessary nor a sufficient condition for crime, and thus certainly not a coercive one. If there is no compulsion, temptation is no excuse. The law is meant to restrain, and to hold responsible, those tempted to break it. It need not restrain those not tempted, and it cannot restrain those who are unable to control their actions.

Reiman's claim, that even "though criminals can control their actions, when crimes are predictable responses to unjust circumstances, then those who benefit from and do not remedy those conditions bear some responsibility for the crimes and thus the criminals cannot be held *wholly* responsible for them. . . ." seems quite unjustified. Those responsible for unjust conditions must be blamed for them,[2] but not for crimes that are "predictable responses to unjust circumstances," if the respondents could have avoided these crimes, as most people living in unjust conditions do.

If crimes are political, that is, address not otherwise remediable "unjust circumstances," they may be held to be morally, if not legally, excusable, on some occasions. But the criminal's moral, let alone legal, responsibility for a crime which he committed for personal gain and could have avoided, is not diminished merely because he lives in unjust circumstances, and his crime was a predictable response to them. Suppose the predictable response to unjust wealth were drunken driving, or rape. Would his wealth excuse the driver or the rapist? Why should poverty, if wealth would not?

Crime is produced by many circumstances, "just" and "unjust." The most just society may have no less crime than the least just (unless "just" is defined circularly as the absence of crime). Tracing crime to causal circumstances is useful and may help us to control it. Suggesting that they *eo ipso* are excuses confuses causality with nonresponsibility. . . . Excuses require specific circumstances that diminish the actor's control over his actions. . . .

CIVILIZATION

Reiman thinks that the death penalty is not civilized, because it involves the total subjugation of one person to others, as does slavery, or prostitution.[3]

Whereas slavery usually is not voluntary, the murderer runs the risk of execution voluntarily: he could avoid it by not murdering. I find nothing uncivilized in imposing the risk of subjugation and death on those who decide to murder.

Nota bene: Persons who act with diminished capacity, during moments of passion, are usually convicted of manslaughter rather than murder. Even if convicted of murder, they are not sentenced to death; only if the court believes the murderer did have a choice, and intended to murder, can he receive the death sentence.

Reiman refers to research finding a brutalization effect, such that executions lead to more homicides. The data are unpersuasive. Some researchers find an increase, some a decrease, of homicides immediately after an execution.[4] Either effect seem[s] ephemeral, involving bunching, rather than changes in the annual homicide rate.

To argue more generally, as Reiman also does, that capital punishment is inconsistent with the advancement of civilization, is to rely on arbitrary definitions of "advancement" and "civilization" for a circular argument. If civilization actually had "advanced" in the direction Reiman, quoting Durkheim, thinks it has, why is that a reason for not preferring "advancement" in some other, perhaps opposite, direction? I cannot find the *moral* (normative) argument in Reiman's description.

DETERRENCE

The death penalty should be retained if abolition would endanger us, Reiman believes. But he does not believe that abolition would. He may be right. However, some of his arguments seem doubtful.

He thinks that whatever marginal deterrent effect capital punishment has, if it has any, is not needed, since life imprisonment provides all the deterrence needed. How can it be ascertained that punishment x deters "everyone who can be deterred" so that punishment x-plus would not deter additional persons? I can see no way to determine this, short of experiments we are unlikely to undertake. Reiman may fear life imprisonment as much, or more, than death. Couldn't someone else fear death more and be insufficiently deterred by life imprisonment?

I cannot prove conclusively that the death penalty deters more than life imprisonment, or that the added deterrence is needed. Reiman cannot prove conclusively that the added deterrence is not needed, or produced. I value the life of innocents more than the life of murderers. Indeed, I value the life of murderers negatively. Wherefore I prefer over- to underprotection. I grant this is a preference.

SELF-DEFENSE

Reiman also believes that murderers who are not deterred by the risk they run because their victims may defend themselves with guns will not be deterred by the risk of execution. This seems unrealistic. Murderers rarely run much risk from self-defense since they usually ambush unsuspecting victims.

TORTURE

On my reasoning, Reiman contends, torture should be used, since it may deter more than execution; or else, even if more deterrent than alternatives, the death penalty should be abolished as torture was: "either we must abolish the electric chair or reinstitute the rack," is his colorful phrase. But there is a difference. I do not oppose torture as undeserved or nondeterrent (although I doubt that the threat of the rack, or of anything adds deterrence to the threat of execution), but simply as repulsive. Death is not; nor is the death penalty. Perhaps repulsiveness is not enough to exclude the rack. If Reiman should convince me that the threat of the rack adds a great deal of deterrence to the threat of execution he might persuade me to overcome my revulsion and to favor the rack as well. It certainly can be deserved. . . .

MODES OF EXECUTION

As Reiman stresses, the spectacle of execution is not pretty. Nor is surgery. Wherefore both should be attended only by the necessary personnel. I do not find Reiman's aesthetic or moral scruples sufficient to preclude execution or surgery. However, I share his view that lethal injections are particularly unpleasant, not so much because of the subjugation which disturbs him, but because of the veterinary air. (We put animals "to sleep" when sick or inconvenient.) In contrast, shooting strikes me as dignified; it is painless too and probably the best way of doing what is necessary.

LIFE IMPRISONMENT

Reiman proposes life imprisonment without parole instead of execution. Although less feared, and therefore likely to be less deterrent, actual lifelong imprisonment strikes me as more cruel than execution even if perceived as less harsh. Its comparative cruelty was stressed already by Cesare Bonesana, Marchese di Beccaria, and by many others since.

Life imprisonment also becomes unde-served over time. A person who committed a murder when twenty years old and is executed within five years—far too long and cruel a delay in my opinion—is, when executed, still the person who committed the murder for which he is punished. His identity changes lit-tle in five years. However, a person who com-mitted a murder when he was twenty years old and is kept in prison when sixty years old, is no longer the same person who committed the crime for which he is still being punished. The sexagenarian is unlikely to have much in com-mon with the twenty-year-old for whose act he is being punished; his legal identity no longer reflects reality. Personality and actual identity are not that continuous. In effect, we punish an innocent sexagenarian who does not deserve punishment, instead of a guilty twenty-year-old who did. This spectacle should offend our moral sensibilities more than the deserved execution of the twenty-year-old. Those who deserve the death penalty should be executed while they deserve it, not kept in prison when they no longer deserve any punishment.

NOTES

1. See Jeffrey H. Reiman, "Justice, Civilization, and the Death Penalty: Answering van den Haag," *Philosophy & Public Affairs* 14, no. 2: 128. Unless otherwise noted, all my quotations are taken from Reiman's article.
2. Who are they? They are not necessarily the benefici-aries, as Reiman appears to believe. I benefit from rent control, which I think unjust to my landlord, but I'm not responsible for it. I may benefit from low prices for services or goods, without being responsi-ble for them, or for predictable criminal responses to them. Criminals benefit from the unjust exclusionary rules of our courts. Are they to blame for these rules?
3. Prostitution does not involve total subjugation and is voluntary. In an ambiguous footnote Reiman asserts that it is the perception of prostitution as subjugation that makes it offensive. But this perception, derived from pulp novels more than from reality, is not what makes the voluntary act offensive. Rather, it is the sale of sex as a fungible service, divorced from affec-tion and depersonalized that is offensive. Anyway, when something is offensive because misperceived it is not the thing that is offensive.
4. David P. Philips, "The Deterrent Effect of Capital Punishment: New Evidence on an Old Controversy," *The American Journal of Sociology* (July 1980). For further discussion see loc. cit., July 1982. See also Lester, *Executions as a Deterrent to Homicides* 44 *Psychological Rep.* 562 (1979).

REVIEW AND DISCUSSION QUESTIONS

1. Why does van den Haag think that poverty does not excuse people from execution?
2. Reiman argued that capital punishment is not civilized. Describe his argument, and then indicate how van den Haag responds to him in this essay.
3. Why does van den Haag reject life in prison?

Essay and Paper Topics for Section 5

1. Suppose we do not know whether capital punishment deters criminals. Is it bet-ter, all things considered, if we assume that it does deter, and we are wrong, or if we assume it does not deter and we are wrong? Explain your answer.
2. On balance, do you think capital punishment is justified or that it should be abolished? What argument poses the strongest challenge to your conclusion? How do you respond to it?

3. Compare the moral issues raised by killing in war and capital punishment. Might a person take the view that capital punishment is unjustified, whereas killing in war is acceptable? Or should people who oppose capital punishment also be pacifists?

4. If van den Haag is right about life in prison, then is he also right about capital punishment's deterrence value? Explain.

5. Using the general moral theory from Part I that you found most reasonable, write an essay in which you discuss how that theory would evaluate the position of two philosophers you have read on the subject of capital punishment.

6

Animals
and the Natural Environment

We assume human lives are valuable and worth protecting; but what about other forms of life? Are species themselves important, for example? Or what about other natural entities such as forests, rivers, and oceans? Or are ecosystems in general valuable? Essays in this section consider when and why nonhuman life is worthy of moral consideration, and whether that value depends ultimately on satisfying human wants or needs. This leads to further problems and questions, for instance, whether nonhuman life is not only valuable but of equal value to humans, and to conflicts between defenders of animal rights and those who see hunting as a natural activity of human as well as nonhuman animals.

All Animals Are Equal

Peter Singer

In this influential essay, taken from his book *Animal Liberation,* Peter Singer argues that equality applies to animals as well as humans and that our ordinary attitudes toward nonhuman animals betray a bias toward our species that is rather like the attitudes of a racist or sexist. Both our eating habits and our use of animals in experiments are, he argues, morally wrong. Peter Singer is professor of bioethics at Princeton University.

"Animal Liberation" may sound more like a parody of other liberation movements than a serious objective. The idea of "The Rights of Animals" actually was once used to parody the case for women's rights. When Mary Wollstonecraft, a forerunner of today's feminists, published her *Vindication of the Rights of Women* in 1792, her views were widely regarded as absurd, and before long an anonymous publication appeared entitled *A Vindication of the Rights of Brutes.* The author of this satirical work (now known to have been Thomas Taylor, a distinguished Cambridge philosopher) tried to refute Mary Wollstonecraft's arguments by showing that they could be carried one stage further. If the argument for equality was sound when applied to women, why should it not be applied to dogs, cats, and horses? The reasoning seemed to hold for these "brutes" too; yet to hold that brutes had rights was manifestly absurd; therefore the reasoning by which this

From Peter Singer, *Animal Liberation* (New York: Avon Books, 1977). Reprinted by permission. Section titles added.

conclusion had been reached must be unsound, and if unsound when applied to brutes, it must also be unsound when applied to women, since the very same arguments had been used in each case.

1. SEXUAL AND RACIAL EQUALITY

In order to explain the basis of the case for the equality of animals, it will be helpful to start with an examination of the case for the equality of women. . . . The extension of the basic principle of equality from one group to another does not imply that we must treat both groups in exactly the same way, or grant exactly the same rights to both groups. Whether we should do so will depend on the nature of the members of the two groups. The basic principle of equality does not require equal or identical *treatment;* it requires equal *consideration.* Equal consideration for different beings may lead to different treatment and different rights. . . .

When we say that all human beings, whatever their race, creed, or sex, are equal, what is it that we are asserting? Those who wish to defend hierarchical, inegalitarian societies have often pointed out that by whatever test we choose it simply is not true that all humans are equal. Like it or not we must face the fact that humans come in different shapes and sizes; they come with different moral capacities, different intellectual abilities, different amounts of benevolent feeling and sensitivity to the needs of others, different abilities to communicate effectively, and different capacities to experience pleasure and pain. In short, if the demand for equality were based on the actual equality of all human beings, we would have to stop demanding equality.

Still, one might cling to the view that the demand for equality among human beings is based on the actual equality of different races and sexes. Although, it may be said, humans differ as individuals there are no such differences between races and sexes *as such.* From the mere fact that a person is black or a woman we cannot infer anything about that person's intellectual or moral capacities. This, it may be said, is why racism and sexism are wrong. The white racist claims that whites are superior to blacks, but this is false. . . . The opponent of sexism would say the same: a person's sex is no guide to his or her abilities, and this is why it is unjustifiable to discriminate on the basis of sex.

The existence of individual variations that cut across the lines of race or sex, however, provides us with no defense at all against a more sophisticated opponent of equality, one who proposes that, say, the interests of all those with IQ scores below 100 be given less consideration than the interests of those with ratings over 100. . . .

There is a second important reason why we ought not to base our opposition to racism and sexism on any kind of actual equality, even the limited kind that asserts that variations in capacities and abilities are spread evenly between the different races and sexes: we can have no absolute guarantee that these capacities and abilities really are distributed evenly, without regard to race or sex, among human beings. So far as actual abilities are concerned there do seem to be certain measurable differences between both races and sexes. These differences do not, of course, appear in each case, but only when averages are taken. More important still, we do not yet know how much of these differences is really due to different genetic endowments of the different races and sexes, and how much is due to poor schools, poor housing, and other factors that are the result of past and continuing discrimination. Perhaps all the important differences will eventually prove to be environmental rather than genetic. Anyone opposed to racism and sexism will certainly hope that this will be so, for it will make the task of ending discrimination a lot easier; nevertheless it would be dangerous to rest the case against racism and sexism on the belief that all significant differences are environmental in origin. The opponent of, say, racism who takes this line will be unable to avoid conceding that *if* differences in ability do after all prove to have some genetic connection with race, racism would in some way be defensible.

Fortunately there is no need to pin the case for equality to one particular outcome of a scientific investigation. The appropriate response to those who claim to have found evidence of genetically based differences in ability between the races or sexes is not to stick to the belief that the genetic explanation must be wrong, whatever evidence to the contrary may turn up: instead we should make it quite clear that the claim to equality does not depend on intelligence, moral capacity, physical strength, or similar matters of fact. Equality is a moral idea, not an assertion of fact. There is no logically compelling reason for assuming that a factual difference in ability between two people justifies any difference in the amount of consideration we give to their needs and interests. *The principle of equality of human beings is not a description of an alleged actual equality among humans: it is a prescription of how we should treat humans.*

Jeremy Bentham, the founder of the reforming utilitarian school of moral philosophy, incorporated the essential basis of moral equality into his system of ethics by means of the formula: "Each to count for one and none for more than one." In other words, the interests of every being affected by an action are to be taken into account and given the same weight as the like interests of any other being. A later utilitarian, Henry Sidgwick, put the point in this way: "The good of any one individual is of no more importance, from the point of view (if I may say so) of the Universe, than the good of any other."

It is an implication of this principle of equality that our concern for others and our readiness to consider their interests ought not to depend on what they are like or on what abilities they may possess. Precisely what this concern or consideration requires us to do may vary according to the characteristics of those affected by what we do: concern for the well-being of a child growing up in America would require that we teach him to read; concern for the well-being of a pig may require no more than that we leave him alone with other pigs in a place where there is adequate food and room to run freely. But the basic element—the taking into account of the interests of the being, whatever those interests may be—must, according to the principle of equality, be extended to all beings, black or white, masculine or feminine, human or non-human.

Thomas Jefferson, who was responsible for writing the principle of the equality of men into the American Declaration of Independence, saw this point. It led him to oppose slavery even though he was unable to free himself fully from his slaveholding background. He wrote in a letter to the author of a book that emphasized the notable intellectual achievements of Negroes in order to refute the then common view that they had limited intellectual capacities:

> Be assured that no person living wishes more sincerely than I do, to see a complete refutation of the doubts I have myself entertained and expressed on the grade of understanding allotted to them by nature, and to find that they are on a par with ourselves but whatever be their degree of talent it is no measure of their rights. Because Sir Isaac Newton was superior to others in understanding, he was not therefore lord of the property or person of others.[1]

Similarly when in the 1850s the call for women's rights was raised in the United States a remarkable black feminist named Sojourner Truth made the same point in more robust terms at a feminist convention:

> . . . they talk about this thing in the head; what do they call it? ["Intellect," whispered someone near by.] That's it. What's that got to do with women's rights or Negroes' rights? If my cup won't hold but a pint and yours holds a quart, wouldn't you be mean not to let me have my little half-measure full?[2]

It is on this basis that the case against racism and the case against sexism must both ultimately rest; and it is in accordance with this principle that the attitude that we may call "speciesism," by analogy with racism, must also be condemned.

2. SPECIESISM AND THE EQUALITY OF ANIMALS

Speciesism—the word is not an attractive one, but I can think of no better term—is a prejudice or attitude of bias toward the interests of members of one's own species and against those of members of other species. It should be obvious that the fundamental objections to racism and sexism made by Thomas Jefferson and Sojourner Truth apply equally to speciesism. If possessing a higher degree of intelligence does not entitle one human to use another for his own ends, how can it entitle humans to exploit nonhumans for the same purpose?[3]

Many philosophers and other writers have proposed the principle of equal consideration of interests, in some form or other, as a basic moral principle; but not many of them have recognized that this principle applies to members of other species as well as to our own. Jeremy Bentham was one of the few who did realize this. In a forward-looking passage written at a time when black slaves had been freed by the French but in the British dominions were still being treated in the way we now treat animals, Bentham wrote:

> The day *may* come when the rest of the animal creation may acquire those rights which never could have been withholden from them but by the hand of tyranny. The French have already discovered that the blackness of the skin is no reason why a human being should be abandoned without redress to the caprice of a tormentor. It may one day come to be recognized that the number of the legs, the villosity of the skin, or the termination of the *os sacrum* are reasons equally insufficient for abandoning a sensitive being to the same fate. What else is it that should trace the insuperable line? Is it the faculty of reason, or perhaps the faculty of discourse? But a full-grown horse or dog is beyond comparison a more rational, as well as a more conversable animal, than an infant of a day or a week or even a month, old. But suppose they were otherwise, what would it avail? The question is not, Can they *reason?* nor Can they *talk?* but, *Can they suffer?*[4]

In this passage Bentham points to the capacity for suffering as the vital characteristic that gives a being the right to equal consideration. The capacity for suffering—or more strictly, for suffering and/or enjoyment or happiness—is not just another characteristic like the capacity for language or higher mathematics. Bentham is not saying that those who try to mark "the insuperable line" that determines whether the interests of a being should be considered happen to have chosen the wrong characteristic. By saying that we must consider the interests of all beings with the capacity for suffering or enjoyment Bentham does not arbitrarily exclude from consideration any interests at all—as those who draw the line with reference to the possession of reason or language do. The capacity for suffering and enjoyment is *a prerequisite for having interests at all,* a condition that must be satisfied before we can speak of interests in a meaningful way. It would be nonsense to say that it was not in the interests of a stone to be kicked along the road by a schoolboy. A stone does not have interests because it cannot suffer. Nothing that we can do to it could possibly make any difference to its welfare. A mouse, on the other hand, does have an interest in not being kicked along the road, because it will suffer if it is.

If a being suffers there can be no moral justification for refusing to take that suffering into consideration. No matter what the nature of the being, the principle of equality requires that its suffering be counted equally with the like suffering—in so far as rough comparisons can be made—of any other being. If a being is not capable of suffering, or of experiencing enjoyment or happiness, there is nothing to be taken into account. So the limit of sentience (using the term as a convenient if not strictly accurate shorthand for the capacity to suffer and/or experience enjoyment) is the only defensible boundary of concern for the interests of others. To mark this boundary by some other characteristic like intelligence or rationality would be to mark it in an arbitrary manner. Why not choose some other characteristic, like skin color?

The racist violates the principle of equality by giving greater weight to the interests of members of his own race when there is a clash between their interests and the interests of those of another race. The sexist violates the principle of equality by favoring the interests of his own sex. Similarly the speciesist allows the interests of his own species to override the greater interests of members of other species. The pattern is identical in each case.

Most human beings are speciesists. Ordinary human beings—not a few exceptionally cruel or heartless humans, but the overwhelming majority of humans—take an active part in, acquiesce in, and allow their taxes to pay for practices that require the sacrifice of the most important interests of members of other species in order to promote the most trivial interests of our own species. . . .

3. SPECIESISM IN PRACTICE

For the great majority of human beings, especially in urban, industrialized societies, the most direct form of contact with members of other species is at mealtimes: We eat them. In doing so we treat them purely as means to our ends. We regard their life and well-being as subordinate to our taste for a particular kind of dish. I say "taste" deliberately—this is purely a matter of pleasing our palate. There can be no defense of eating flesh in terms of satisfying nutritional needs, since it has been established beyond doubt that we could satisfy our need for protein and other essential nutrients far more efficiently with a diet that replaced animal flesh by soy beans, or products derived from soy beans, and other high protein vegetable products.[5]

It is not merely the act of killing that indicates what we are ready to do to other species in order to gratify our tastes. The suffering we inflict on the animals while they are alive is perhaps an even clearer indication of our speciesism than the fact that we are prepared to kill them.[6] In order to have meat on the table at a price that people can afford, our society tolerates methods of meat production that confine sentient animals in cramped, unsuitable conditions for the entire duration of their lives. Animals are treated like machines that convert fodder into flesh, and any innovation that results in a higher "conversion ratio" is liable to be adopted. As one authority on the subject has said, "cruelty is acknowledged only when profitability ceases."[7] So hens are crowded four or five to a cage with a floor area of twenty inches by eighteen inches, or around the size of a single page of the *New York Times*. The cages have wire floors, since this reduces cleaning costs, though wire is unsuitable for the hens' feet; the floors slope, since this makes the eggs roll down for easy collection, although this makes it difficult for the hens to rest comfortably. In these conditions all the birds' natural instincts are thwarted: They cannot stretch their wings fully, walk freely, dust-bathe, scratch the ground, or build a nest. Although they have never known other conditions, observers have noticed that the birds vainly try to perform these actions. Frustrated at their inability to do so, they often develop what farmers call "vices," and peck each other to death. To prevent this, the beaks of young birds are often cut off.

This kind of treatment is not limited to poultry. Pigs are now also being reared in cages inside sheds. These animals are comparable to dogs in intelligence, and need a varied, stimulating environment if they are not to suffer from stress and boredom. Anyone who kept a dog in the way in which pigs are frequently kept would be liable to prosecution, in England at least, but because our interest in exploiting pigs is greater than our interest in exploiting dogs, we object to cruelty to dogs while consuming the produce of cruelty to pigs. Of the other animals, the condition of veal calves is perhaps worst of all, since these animals are so closely confined that they cannot even turn around or get up and lie down freely. In this way they do not develop unpalatable muscle. They are also made anaemic and kept short of roughage, to keep their flesh pale, since white veal fetches a higher price; as a result they develop a craving for iron and roughage, and have been observed to gnaw wood off the sides of their stalls, and lick greedily at any rusty hinge that is within reach.

Since, as I have said, none of these practices cater to anything more than our pleasures of taste, our practice of rearing and killing other animals in order to eat them is a clear instance of the sacrifice of the most important interests of other beings in order to satisfy trivial interests of our own. To avoid speciesism we must stop this practice, and each of us has a moral obligation to cease supporting the practice. Our custom is all the support that the meat industry needs. The decision to cease giving it that support may be difficult, but it is no more difficult than it would have been for a white Southerner to go against the traditions of his society and free his slaves; if we do not change our dietary habits, how can we censure those slaveholders who would not change their own way of living?

The same form of discrimination may be observed in the widespread practice of experimenting on other species in order to see if certain substances are safe for human beings, or to test some psychological theory about the effect of severe punishment on learning, or to try out various new compounds just in case something turns up. People sometimes think that all this experimentation is for vital medical purposes, and so will reduce suffering overall. This comfortable belief is very wide of the mark. Drug companies test new shampoos and cosmetics that they are intending to put on the market by dropping them into the eyes of rabbits, held open by metal clips, in order to observe what damage results. Food additives, like artificial colorings and preservatives, are tested by what is known as the "LD50"—a test designed to find the level of consumption at which 50 percent of a group of animals will die. In the process, nearly all of the animals are made very sick before some finally die, and others pull through. If the substance is relatively harmless, as it often is, huge doses have to be forcefed to the animals, until in some cases sheer volume or concentration of the substance causes death.

Much of this pointless cruelty goes on in the universities. In many areas of science, nonhuman animals are regarded as an item of laboratory equipment, to be used and expended as desired. In psychology laboratories experimenters devise endless variations and repetitions of experiments that were of little value in the first place. To quote just one example, from the experimenter's own account in a psychology journal: At the University of Pennsylvania, Perrin S. Cohen hung six dogs in hammocks with electrodes taped to their hind feet. Electric shock of varying intensity was then administered through the electrodes. If the dog learned to press its head against a panel on the left, the shock was turned off, but otherwise it remained on indefinitely. Three of the dogs, however, were required to wait periods varying from 2 to 7 seconds while being shocked before making the response that turned off the current. If they failed to wait, they received further shocks. Each dog was given from 26 to 46 "sessions" in the hammock, each session consisting of 80 "trials" or shocks, administered at intervals of one minute. The experimenter reported that the dogs, who were unable to move in the hammock, barked or bobbed their heads when the current was applied. The reported findings of the experiment were that there was a delay in the dogs' responses that increased proportionately to the time the dogs were required to endure the shock, but a gradual increase in the intensity of the shock had no systematic effect in the timing of the response. The experiment was funded by the National Institutes of Health, and the United States Public Health Service.[8]

In this example, and countless cases like it, the possible benefits to mankind are either nonexistent or fantastically remote, while the certain losses to members of other species are very real. This is, again, a clear indication of speciesism. . . .

4. THE VALUE OF LIVES: HUMANS AND NONHUMANS

If I give a horse a hard slap across its rump with my open hand, the horse may start, but it presumably feels little pain. Its skin is thick enough to protect it against a mere slap. If I slap a baby in the same way, however, the baby will cry and presumably does feel pain, for its skin is more sensitive. So it is worse to slap a baby than a horse, if both slaps are administered with equal force. But there must be some kind of blow—I don't know exactly what it would be, but perhaps a blow with a heavy stick—that would cause the horse as much pain as we cause a baby by slapping it with our hand. That is what I mean by "the same amount of pain," and if we consider it wrong to inflict that much pain on a baby for no good reason then we must, unless we are speciesists, consider it equally wrong to inflict the same amount of pain on a horse for no good reason.

There are other differences between humans and animals that cause other complications. Normal adult human beings have mental capacities which will, in certain circumstances, lead them to suffer more than animals would in the same circumstances. If, for instance, we decided to perform extremely painful or lethal scientific experiments on normal adult humans, kidnapped at random from public parks for this purpose, every adult who entered a park would become fearful that he would be kidnapped. The resultant terror would be a form of suffering additional to the pain of the experiment. The same experiments performed on nonhuman animals would cause less suffering since the animals would not have the anticipatory dread of being kidnapped and experimented upon. This does not mean, of course, that it would be right to perform the experiment on animals, but only that there is a reason, which is not speciesist, for preferring to use animals rather than normal adult humans, if the experiment is to be done at all. It should be noted, however, that this same argument gives us a reason for preferring to use human infants—orphans perhaps—or retarded humans for experiments, rather than adults, since infants and retarded humans would also have no idea of what was going to happen to them. So far as this argument is concerned nonhuman animals and infants and retarded humans are in the same category; and if we use this argument to justify experiments on nonhuman animals we have to ask ourselves whether we are also

prepared to allow experiments on human infants and retarded adults; and if we make a distinction between animals and these humans, on what basis can we do it, other than a barefaced—and morally indefensible—preference for members of our own species?

There are many areas in which the superior mental powers of normal adult humans make a difference: anticipation, more detailed memory, greater knowledge of what is happening, and so on. Yet these differences do not all point to greater suffering on the part of the normal human being. Sometimes an animal may suffer more because of his more limited understanding. If, for instance, we are taking prisoners in wartime we can explain to them that while they must submit to capture, search, and confinement they will not otherwise be harmed and will be set free at the conclusion of hostilities. If we capture a wild animal, however, we cannot explain that we are not threatening its life. A wild animal cannot distinguish an attempt to overpower and confine from an attempt to kill; the one causes as much terror as the other.

It may be objected that comparisons of the sufferings of different species are impossible to make, and that for this reason when the interests of animals and humans clash the principle of equality gives no guidance. It is probably true that comparisons of suffering between members of different species cannot be made precisely, but precision is not essential. Even if we were to prevent the infliction of suffering on animals only when it is quite certain that the interests of humans will not be affected to anything like the extent that animals are affected, we would be forced to make radical changes in our treatment of animals that would involve our diet, the farming methods we use, experimental procedures in many fields of science, our approach to wildlife and to hunting, trapping and the wearing of furs, and areas of entertainment like circuses, rodeos, and zoos. As a result, a vast amount of suffering would be avoided.

So far I have said a lot about the infliction of suffering on animals, but nothing about killing them. This omission has been deliberate. The application of the principle of equality to the infliction of suffering is, in theory at least, fairly straightforward. Pain and suffering are bad and should be prevented or minimized, irrespective of the race, sex, or species of the being that suffers. How bad a pain is depends on how intense it is and how long it lasts, but pains of the same intensity and duration are equally bad, whether felt by humans or animals.

The wrongness of killing a being is more complicated. I have kept, and shall continue to keep, the question of killing in the background because in the present state of human tyranny over other species the more simple, straightforward principle of equal consideration of pain or pleasure is a sufficient basis for identifying and protesting against all the major abuses of animals that humans practice. Nevertheless, it is necessary to say something about killing.

Just as most humans are speciesists in their readiness to cause pain to animals when they would not cause a similar pain to humans for the same reason, so most humans are speciesists in their readiness to kill other animals when they would not kill humans. We need to proceed more cautiously here, however, because people hold widely differing views about when it is legitimate to kill humans, as the continuing debates over abortion and euthanasia attest. Nor have moral philosophers been able to agree on exactly what it is that makes it wrong to kill humans, and under what circumstances killing a human being may be justifiable.

Let us consider first the view that it is always wrong to take an innocent human life. We may call this the "sanctity of life" view. People who take this view oppose abortion and euthanasia. They do not usually, however, oppose the killing of nonhumans—so perhaps it would be more accurate to describe this view as the "sanctity of *human* life" view.

The belief that human life, and only human life, is sacrosanct is a form of speciesism. To see this, consider the following example.

Assuming that, as sometimes happens, an infant has been born with massive and irreparable brain damage. The damage is so severe that the infant can never be any more than a "human vegetable," unable to talk, recognize other people, act independently of others, or develop a sense of self-awareness. The parents of the infant, realizing that they cannot hope for any improvement in their child's condition and being in any case unwilling to spend, or ask the state to spend, the thousands of dollars that would be needed annually for proper care of the infant, ask the doctor to kill the infant painlessly.

Should the doctor do what the parents ask? Legally, he should not, and in this respect the law reflects the sanctity of life view. The life of every human being is sacred. Yet people who would say this about the infant do not object to the killing of nonhuman animals. How can they justify their different judgments? Adult chimpanzees, dogs, pigs, and many other species far surpass the brain-damaged infant in their ability to relate to others, act independently, be self-aware, and any other capacity that could reasonably be said to give value to life. With the most intensive care possible, there are retarded infants who can never achieve the intelligence level of a dog. Nor can we appeal to the concern of the infant's parents, since they themselves, in this imaginary example (and in some actual cases), do not want the infant kept alive.

The only thing that distinguishes the infant from the animal, in the eyes of those who claim it has a "right to life," is that it is, biologically, a member of the species *Homo sapiens*, whereas chimpanzees, dogs, and pigs are not. But to use *this* difference as the basis for granting a right to life to the infant and not to the other animals is, of course, pure speciesism.[9] It is exactly the kind of arbitrary difference that the most crude and overt kind of racist uses in attempting to justify racial discrimination.

This does not mean that to avoid speciesism we must hold that it is as wrong to kill a dog as it is to kill a normal human being. The only position that is irredeemably speciesist is the one that tries to make the boundary of the right to life run exactly parallel to the boundary of our own species. Those who hold the sanctity of life view do this because while distinguishing sharply between humans and other animals they allow no distinctions to be made within our own species, objecting to the killing of the severely retarded and the hopelessly senile as strongly as they object to the killing of normal adults.

To avoid speciesism we must allow that beings which are similar in all relevant respects have a similar right to life—and mere membership in our own biological species cannot be a morally relevant criterion for this right. Within these limits we could still hold that, for instance, it is worse to kill a normal adult human, with a capacity for self-awareness, and the ability to plan for the future and have meaningful relations with others, than it is to kill a mouse, which presumably does not share all of these characteristics; or we might appeal to the close family and other personal ties which humans have but mice do not have to the same degree; or we might think that it is the consequences for other humans, who will be put in fear of their own lives, that makes the crucial difference; or we might think it is some combination of these factors, or other factors altogether.

Whatever criteria we choose, however, we will have to admit that they do not follow precisely the boundary of our own species. We may legitimately hold that there are some features of certain beings which make their lives more valuable than those of other beings; but there will surely be some nonhuman animals whose lives, by any standards, are more valuable than the lives of some humans. A chimpanzee, dog, or pig, for instance, will have a higher degree of self-awareness and a greater capacity for meaningful relations with others than a severely retarded infant or someone in a state of advanced senility. So if we base the right to life on these characteristics we must grant these animals a right to life as good as, or better than, such retarded or senile humans.

Now this argument cuts both ways. It could be taken as showing that chimpanzees, dogs, and pigs, along with some other species, have a right to life and we commit a grave moral offense whenever we kill them, even when they are old and suffering and our intention is to put them out of their misery. Alternatively

one could take the argument as showing that the severely retarded and hopelessly senile have no right to life and may be killed for quite trivial reasons, as we now kill animals.

Since my focus here is on ethical questions concerning animals and not on the morality of euthanasia I shall not attempt to settle this issue finally. I think it is reasonably clear, though, that while both of the positions just described avoid speciesism, neither is entirely satisfactory. What we need is some middle position which would avoid speciesism but would not make the lives of the retarded and senile as cheap as the lives of pigs and dogs now are, nor make the lives of pigs and dogs so sacrosanct that we think it wrong to put them out of hopeless misery. What we must do is bring nonhuman animals within our sphere of moral concern and cease to treat their lives as expendable for whatever trivial purposes we may have. At the same time, once we realize that the fact that a being is a member of our own species is not in itself enough to make it always wrong to kill that being, we may come to reconsider our policy of preserving human lives at all costs, even when there is no prospect of a meaningful life or of existence without terrible pain.

I conclude, then, that a rejection of speciesism does not imply that all lives are of equal worth. While self-awareness, intelligence, the capacity for meaningful relations with others, and so on are not relevant to the question of inflicting pain—since pain is pain, whatever other capacities, beyond the capacity to feel pain, the being may have—these capacities may be relevant to the question of taking life. It is not arbitrary to hold that the life of a self-aware being, capable of abstract thought, of planning for the future, of complex acts of communication, and so on, is more valuable than the life of a being without these capacities. To see the difference between the issues of inflicting pain and taking life, consider how we would choose within our own species. If we had to choose to save the life of a normal human or a mentally defective human, we would probably choose to save the life of the normal human; but if we had to choose between preventing pain in the normal human or the mental defective—imagine that both have received painful but superficial injuries, and we only have enough painkiller for one of them—it is not nearly so clear how we ought to choose. The same is true when we consider other species. The evil of pain is, in itself, unaffected by the other characteristics of the being that feels the pain; the value of life is affected by these other characteristics.

Normally this will mean that if we have to choose between the life of a human being and the life of another animal we should choose to save the life of the human, but there may be special cases in which the reverse holds true, because the human being in question does not have the capacities of a normal human being. . . .

5. A DISTINCTIVE HUMAN DIGNITY?

[The] idea of a distinctive human dignity and worth has a long history. Contemporary philosophers have cast off its original metaphysical and religious shackles, and freely invoke the idea of human dignity without feeling any need to justify the idea at all. Why should we not attribute "intrinsic dignity" or "intrinsic worth" to ourselves? Why should we not say that we are the only things in the universe that have intrinsic value? . . .

The truth is that the appeal to the intrinsic dignity of human beings appears to solve the egalitarian philosopher's problems only as long as it goes unchallenged. Once we ask why it should be that all humans—including infants, mental defectives, criminal psychopaths, Hitler, Stalin, and the rest—have some kind of dignity or worth that no elephant, pig, or chimpanzee can ever achieve, we see that this question is as difficult to answer as our original request for some relevant fact that justifies the inequality of humans and other animals. In fact, these two questions are really one: talk of intrinsic dignity or moral worth does not help, because any satisfactory defense of the claim that all and only humans have intrinsic dignity would need to refer to some relevant capacities or characteristics that only human beings have, in virtue of which they have this unique dignity or worth. To introduce ideas of dignity and worth as a substitute for other reasons for distinguishing humans and animals is not good enough. Fine phrases are the last resource of those who have run out of arguments. . . .

NOTES

1. Letter to Henri Gregoire, February 25, 1809.
2. Reminiscences by Francis D. Gage, from Susan B. Anthony, *The History of Woman Suffrage,* vol. 1; the passage is to be found in the extract in Leslie Tanner, ed., *Voices from Women's Liberation* (New York: Signet, 1970).
3. I owe the term *speciesism* to Richard Ryder.
4. *Introduction to the Principles of Morals and Legislation,* chapter 17.
5. In order to produce 1 lb. of protein in the form of beef or veal, we must feed 21 lbs. of protein to the animal. Other forms of livestock are slightly less inefficient, but the average ratio in the U.S. is still 1:8. It has been estimated that the amount of protein lost to humans in this way is equivalent to 90 percent of the annual world protein deficit. For a brief account, see Frances Moore Lappe, *Diet for a Small Planet* (New York: Friends of the Earth/Ballantine, 1971), pp. 4–11.
6. Although one might think that killing a being is obviously the ultimate wrong one can do to it, I think that the infliction of suffering is a clearer indication of speciesism because it might be argued that at least part of what is wrong with killing a human is that most humans are conscious of their existence over time, and have desires and purposes that extend into the future. Of course, if one took this view one would have to hold that killing a human infant or mental defective is not in itself wrong, and is less serious than killing certain higher mammals that probably do have a sense of their own existence over time.
7. Ruth Harrison, *Animal Machines* (London: Stuart, 1964). This book provides an eye-opening account of intensive farming methods for those unfamiliar with the subject.
8. *Journal of the Experimental Analysis of Behavior,* 13, no. 1 (1970). Any recent volume of this journal, or of other journals in the field, such as the *Journal of Comparative and Physiological Psychology,* will contain reports of equally cruel and trivial experiments.

9. I am here putting aside religious views, for example, the doctrine that all and only humans have immortal souls, or are made in the image of God. Historically these views have been very important, and no doubt are partly responsible for the idea that human life has a special sanctity. Logically, however, these religious views are unsatisfactory, since a reasoned explanation of why it should be that all humans and no nonhumans have immortal souls is not offered. This belief too, therefore, comes under suspicion as a form of speciesism. In any case, defenders of the "sanctity of life" view are generally reluctant to base their position on purely religious doctrines, since these doctrines are no longer as widely accepted as they once were.

REVIEW AND DISCUSSION QUESTIONS

1. What reasons does Singer give for rejecting the idea that human equality rests on factual similarities?
2. What does Singer think human equality does mean? What are the implications of that for our treatment of animals?
3. Describe the practices that most clearly demonstrate our speciesism.
4. What facts about humans might you point to in defending the notion that a living human has rights that other animals lack?
5. Suppose a meat eater argued that although factory farms do involve some suffering, the animals are still better off for having lived. How would that claim, if true, affect Singer's argument for vegetarianism?
6. Singer disputes the claim that humans have a special "dignity." How would Kant respond to that? Whose position do you think is more reasonable? Explain.
7. Describe what you think would be the implications of Singer's position for euthanasia and abortion.

Speciesism and the Idea of Equality

Bonnie Steinbock

Bonnie Steinbock rejects Peter Singer's attack on "speciesism," defending instead the view that membership in the human species is in itself morally important. Human beings, she claims, have important characteristics that warrant treating us differently from nonhuman animals even though, she admits, animal suffering is also morally important. Bonnie Steinbock is professor of philosophy at Albany University, State University of New York.

Most of us believe that we are entitled to treat members of other species in ways which would be considered wrong if inflicted on members of our own species. We kill them for food, keep them confined, use them in painful experiments. The moral philosopher has to ask what relevant difference justifies this difference in treatment. A look at this question will lead us to re-examine the distinctions which we have assumed make a moral difference.

It has been suggested by Peter Singer[1] that our current attitudes are "speciesist," a word intended to make one think of "racist" or "sexist." The idea is that membership in a species is

From Bonnie Steinbock, "Speciesism and the Idea of Equality," *Philosophy* 53, no. 204 (April 1978) © 1978 University Press. Reprinted with the permission of Cambridge University Press.

in itself not relevant to moral treatment, and that much of our behaviour and attitudes toward nonhuman animals is based simply on this irrelevant fact.

There is, however, an important difference between racism or sexism and "speciesism." We do not subject animals to different moral treatment simply because they have fur and feathers, but because they are in fact different from human beings in ways that could be morally relevant. It is false that women are incapable of being benefited by education, and therefore that claim cannot serve to justify preventing them from attending school. But this is not false of cows and dogs, even chimpanzees. Intelligence is thought to be a morally relevant capacity because of its relation to the capacity for moral responsibility.

What is Singer's response? He agrees that nonhuman animals lack certain capacities that human animals possess, and that this may justify different *treatment*. But it does not justify giving less consideration to their needs and interests. According to Singer, the moral mistake which the racist or sexist makes is not essentially the factual error of thinking that blacks or women are inferior to white men. For even if there were no factual error, even if it were true that blacks and women are less intelligent and responsible than whites and men, this would not justify giving less consideration to their needs and interests. It is important to note that the term "speciesism" is in one way like, and in another way unlike, the terms "racism" and "sexism." What the term "speciesism" has in common with these terms is the reference to focusing on a characteristic which is, in itself, irrelevant to moral treatment. And it is worth reminding us of this. But Singer's real aim is to bring us to a new understanding of the idea of equality. The question is, on what do claims to equality rest? The demand for *human* equality is a demand that the interests of all human beings be considered equally, unless there is a moral justification for not doing so. But why should the interests of all human beings be considered equally? In order to answer this question, we have to give some sense to the phrase, "All

men (human beings) are created equal." Human beings are manifestly *not* equal, differing greatly in intelligence, virtue and capacities. In virtue of what can the claim to equality be made?

It is Singer's contention that claims to equality do not rest on factual equality. Not only do human beings differ in their capacities, but it might even turn out that intelligence, the capacity for virtue, etc., are not distributed evenly among the races and sexes:

> The appropriate response to those who claim to have found evidence of genetically based differences in ability between the races or sexes is not to stick to the belief that the genetic explanation must be wrong, whatever evidence to the contrary may turn up; instead we should make it quite clear that the claim to equality does not depend on intelligence, moral capacity, physical strength, or similar matters of fact. Equality is a moral ideal, not a simple assertion of fact. There is no logically compelling reason for assuming that a factual difference in ability between two people justifies any difference in the amount of consideration we give to satisfying their needs and interests. The principle of equality of human beings is not a description of an alleged actual equality among humans: it is a prescription of how we should treat humans.[2]

In so far as the subject is human equality, Singer's view is supported by other philosophers. Bernard Williams, for example, is concerned to show that demands for equality cannot rest on factual equality among people, for no such equality exists.[3] The only respect in which all men are equal, according to Williams, is that they are all equally men. This seems to be a platitude, but Williams denies that it is trivial. Membership in the species *Homo sapiens* in itself has no special moral significance, but rather the fact that all men are human serves as a *reminder* that being human involves the possession of characteristics that are morally relevant. But on what characteristics does Williams focus? Aside from the desire for self-respect (which I will discuss later), Williams is not concerned with uniquely human capacities. Rather, he focuses on the capacity to feel pain and the capacity to feel affection. It is in virtue of these capacities, it seems, that the idea of equality is to be justified.

Apparently Richard Wasserstrom has the same idea as he sets out the racist's "logical and moral mistakes" in "Rights, Human Rights and Racial Discrimination."[4] The racist fails to acknowledge that the black person is as capable of suffering as the white person. According to Wasserstrom, the reason why a person is said to have a right not to be made to suffer acute physical pain is that we all do in fact value freedom from such pain. Therefore, if anyone has a right to be free from suffering acute physical pain, everyone has this right, for there is no possible basis of discrimination. Wasserstrom says, "For, if all persons do have equal capacities of these sorts and if the existence of these capacities is the reason for ascribing these rights to anyone, then all persons ought to have the right to claim equality of treatment in respect to the possession and exercise of these rights."[5] The basis of equality, for Wasserstrom as for Williams, lies not in some uniquely human capacity, but rather in the fact that all human beings are alike in their capacity to suffer. Writers on equality have focused on this capacity, I think, because it functions as some sort of lowest common denominator, so that whatever the other capacities of a human being, he is entitled to equal consideration because, like everyone else, he is capable of suffering.

If the capacity to suffer is the reason for ascribing a right to freedom from acute pain, or a right to well being, then it certainly looks as though these rights must be extended to animals as well. This is the conclusion Singer arrives at. The demand for human equality rests on the equal capacity of all human beings to suffer and to enjoy well being. But if this is the basis of the demand for equality, then this demand must include all beings which have an equal capacity to suffer and enjoy well being. That is why Singer places at the basis of the demand for equality, not intelligence or reason, but sentience. And equality will mean, not equality of treatment, but "equal consideration of interests." The equal consideration of interests will often mean quite different treatment, depending on the nature of the entity being considered. (It would be as absurd to talk of a dog's right to vote, Singer says, as to talk of a man's right to have an abortion.)

It might be thought that the issue of equality depends on a discussion of rights. According to this line of thought, animals do not merit equal consideration of interests because, unlike human beings, they do not, or cannot, have rights. But I am not going to discuss rights, important as the issue is. The fact that an entity does not have rights does not necessarily imply that its interests are going to count for less than the interests of entities which are right-bearers. According to the view of rights held by H. L. A. Hart and S. I. Benn, infants do not have rights, nor do the mentally defective, nor do the insane, in so far as they all lack certain minimal conceptual capabilities for having rights.[6] Yet it certainly does not seem that either Hart or Benn would agree that therefore their interests are to be counted for less, or that it is morally permissible to treat them in ways in which it would not be permissible to treat right-bearers. It seems to mean only that we must give different sorts of reasons for our obligations to take into consideration the interests of those who do not have rights.

We have reasons concerning the treatment of other people which are clearly independent of the notion of rights. We would say that it is wrong to punch someone because doing that infringes his rights. But we could also say that it is wrong because doing that hurts him, and that is, ordinarily, enough of a reason not to do it. Now this particular reason extends not only to human beings, but to all sentient creatures. One has a *prima facie* reason not to pull the cat's tail (whether or not the cat has rights) because it hurts the cat. And this is the only thing, normally, which is relevant in this case. The fact that the cat is not a "rational being," that it is not capable of moral responsibility, that it cannot make free choices or shape its life—all of these differences from us have nothing to do with the justifiability of pulling its tail. Does this show that rationality and the rest of it are irrelevant to moral treatment?

I hope to show that this is not the case. But first I want to point out that the issue is not one of cruelty to animals. We all agree that cruelty is wrong, whether perpetrated on a moral or nonmoral, rational or nonrational agent. Cruelty is defined as the infliction of unnecessary pain or suffering. What is to count as necessary or unnecessary is determined, in part, by the nature of the end pursued. Torturing an animal is cruel, because although the pain is logically necessary for the action to be torture, the end (deriving enjoyment from seeing the animal suffer) is monstrous. Allowing animals to suffer from neglect or for the sake of large profits may also be thought to be unnecessary and therefore cruel. But there may be some ends, which are very good (such as the advancement of medical knowledge), which can be accomplished by subjecting animals to pain in experiments. Although most people would agree that the pain inflicted on animals used in medical research ought to be kept to a minimum, they would consider pain that cannot be eliminated "necessary" and therefore not cruel. It would probably not be so regarded if the subjects were nonvoluntary human beings. Necessity, then, is defined in terms of human benefit, but this is just what is being called into question. The topic of cruelty to animals, while important from a practical viewpoint, because much of our present treatment of animals involves the infliction of suffering for no good reason, is not very interesting philosophically. What is philosophically interesting is whether we are justified in having different standards of necessity for human suffering and for animal suffering.

Singer says, quite rightly I think, "If a being suffers, there can be no moral justification for refusing to take that suffering into consideration."[7] But he thinks that the principle of equality requires that, no matter what the nature of the being, its suffering be counted equally with the like suffering of any other being. In other words sentience does not simply provide us with reasons for acting; it is the only relevant consideration for equal consideration of interests. It is this view that I wish to challenge.

I want to challenge it partly because it has such counter-intuitive results. It means, for

example, that feeding starving children before feeding starving dogs is just like a Catholic charity's feeding hungry Catholics before feeding hungry non-Catholics. It is simply a matter of taking care of one's own, something which is usually morally permissible. But whereas we would admire the Catholic agency which did not discriminate, but fed all children, first come, first served, we would feel quite differently about someone who had this policy for dogs and children. Nor is this, it seems to me, simply a matter of a sentimental preference for our own species. I might feel much more love for my dog than for a strange child—and yet I might feel morally obliged to feed the child before I fed my dog. If I gave in to the feelings of love and fed my dog and let the child go hungry, I would probably feel guilty. This is not to say that we can simply rely on such feelings. Huck Finn felt guilty at helping Jim escape, which he viewed as stealing from a woman who had never done him any harm. But while the existence of such feelings does not settle the morality of an issue, it is not clear to me that they can be explained away. In any event, their existence can serve as a motivation for trying to find a rational justification for considering human interests above nonhuman ones.

However, it does seem to me that this requires a justification. Until now, common sense (and academic philosophy) have seen no such need. Benn says, "No one claims equal consideration for all mammals—human beings count, mice do not, though it would not be easy to say why not. . . . Although we hesitate to inflict unnecessary pain on sentient creatures, such as mice or dogs, we are quite sure that we do not need to show good reasons for putting human interests before theirs."[8]

I think we do have to justify counting our interests more heavily than those of animals. But how? Singer is right, I think, to point out that it will not do to refer vaguely to the greater value of human life, to human worth and dignity:

Faced with a situation in which they see a need for some basis for the moral gulf that is commonly thought to separate humans and animals, but can find no concrete difference that will do this without undermining the equality of humans, philosophers tend to waffle. They resort to high-sounding phrases like "the intrinsic dignity of the human individual." They talk of "the intrinsic worth of all men" as if men had some worth that other beings do not have or they say that human beings, and only human beings, are "ends in themselves," while "everything other than a person can only have value for a person." . . . Why should we not attribute "intrinsic dignity" or "intrinsic worth" to ourselves? Why should we not say that we are the only things in the universe that have intrinsic value? Our fellow human beings are unlikely to reject the accolades we so generously bestow upon them and those to whom we deny the honour are unable to object.[9]

Singer is right to be skeptical of terms like "intrinsic dignity" and "intrinsic worth." These phrases are no substitute for a moral argument. But they may point to one. In trying to understand what is meant by these phrases, we may find a difference or differences between human beings and nonhuman animals that will justify different treatment while not undermining claims for human equality. While we are not compelled to discriminate among people because of different capacities, if we can find a significant difference in capacities between human and nonhuman animals, this could serve to justify regarding human interests as primary. It is not arbitrary or smug, I think, to maintain that human beings have a different moral status from members of other species because of certain capacities which are characteristic of being human. We may not all be equal in these capacities, but all human beings possess them to some measure, and nonhuman animals do not. For example, human beings are normally held to be responsible for what they do. In recognizing that someone is responsible for his or her actions, you accord that person a respect which is reserved for those possessed of moral autonomy, or capable of achieving such autonomy. Secondly, human beings can be expected to reciprocate in a way that nonhuman animals cannot. Nonhuman animals cannot be motivated by altruistic or moral reasons; they cannot treat you fairly or unfairly. This does not

rule out the possibility of an animal being motivated by sympathy or pity. It does rule out altruistic motivation in the sense of motivation due to the recognition that the needs and interests of others provide one with certain reasons for acting.[10] Human beings are capable of altruistic motivation in this sense. We are sometimes motivated simply by the recognition that someone else is in pain, and that pain is a bad thing, no matter who suffers it. It is this sort of reason that I claim cannot motivate an animal or any entity not possessed of fairly abstract concepts. (If some nonhuman animals do possess the requisite concepts—perhaps chimpanzees who have learned a language—they might well be capable of altruistic motivation.) This means that our moral dealings with animals are necessarily much more limited than our dealings with other human beings. If rats invade our houses, carrying disease and biting our children, we cannot reason with them, hoping to persuade them of the injustice they do us. We can only attempt to get rid of them. And it is this that makes it reasonable for us to accord them a separate and not equal moral status, even though their capacity to suffer provides us with some reason to kill them painlessly, if this can be done without too much sacrifice of human interests. Thirdly, as Williams points out, there is the "desire for self-respect": "a certain human desire to be identified with what one is doing, to be able to realize purposes of one's own, and not to be the instrument of another's will unless one has willingly accepted such a role."[11] Some animals may have some form of this desire, and to the extent that they do, we ought to consider their interest in freedom and self-determination. (Such considerations might affect our attitudes toward zoos and circuses.) But the desire for self-respect *per se* requires the intellectual capacities of human beings, and this desire provides us with special reasons not to treat human beings in certain ways. It is an affront to the dignity of a human being to be a slave (even if a well-treated one); this cannot be true for a horse or a cow. To point this out is of course only to say that the justification for the treatment of an entity will depend on the sort of entity in question. In our treatment of other entities, we must consider the desire for autonomy, dignity and respect, but only where such a desire exists. Recognition of different desires and interests will often require different treatment, a point Singer himself makes.

But is the issue simply one of different desires and interests justifying and requiring different treatment? I would like to make a stronger claim, namely, that certain capacities, which seem to be unique to human beings, entitle their possessors to a privileged position in the moral community. Both rats and human beings dislike pain, and so we have a *prima facie* reason not to inflict pain on either. But if we can free human beings from crippling diseases, pain and death through experimentation which involves making animals suffer, and if this is the only way to achieve such results, then I think that such experimentation is justified because human lives are more valuable than animal lives. And this is because of certain capacities and abilities that normal human beings have which animals apparently do not, and which human beings cannot exercise if they are devastated by pain or disease.

My point is not that the lack of the sorts of capacities I have been discussing gives us a justification for treating animals just as we like, but rather that it is these differences between human beings and nonhuman animals which provide a rational basis for different moral treatment and consideration. Singer focuses on sentience alone as the basis of equality, but we can justify the belief that human beings have a moral worth that nonhuman animals do not, in virtue of specific capacities, and without resorting to "high-sounding phrases."

Singer thinks that intelligence, the capacity for moral responsibility, for virtue, etc., are irrelevant to equality, because we would not accept a hierarchy based on intelligence any more than one based on race. We do not think that those with greater capacities ought to have their interests weighed more heavily than those with lesser capacities, and this, he thinks, shows that differences in such capacities are irrelevant to equality. But it does not show this at all. Kevin Donaghy argues (rightly, I think) that what entitles us human beings to a privileged

position in the moral community is a certain minimal level of intelligence, which is a prerequisite for morally relevant capacities.[12] The fact that we would reject a hierarchical society based on degree of intelligence does not show that a minimal level of intelligence cannot be used as a cut-off point, justifying giving greater consideration to the interests of those entities which meet this standard.

Interestingly enough, Singer concedes the rationality of valuing the lives of normal human beings over the lives of nonhuman animals.[13] We are not required to value equally the life of a normal human being and the life of an animal, he thinks, but only their suffering. But I doubt that the value of an entity's life can be separated from the value of its suffering in this way. If we value the lives of human beings more than the lives of animals, this is because we value certain capacities that human beings have and animals do not. But freedom from suffering is, in general, a minimal condition for exercising these capacities, for living a fully human life. So, valuing human life more involves regarding human interests as counting for more. That is why we regard human suffering as more deplorable than comparable animal suffering.

But there is one point of Singer's which I have not yet met. Some human beings (if only a very few) are less intelligent than some nonhuman animals. Some have less capacity for moral choice and responsibility. What status in the moral community are these members of our species to occupy? Are their interests to be considered equally with ours? Is experimenting on them permissible where such experiments are painful or injurious, but somehow necessary for human well being? If it is certain of our capacities which entitle us to a privileged position, it looks as if those lacking those capacities are not entitled to a privileged position. To think it is justifiable to experiment on an adult chimpanzee but not on a severely mentally incapacitated human being seems to be focusing on membership in a species where that has no moral relevance. (It is being "speciesist" in a perfectly reasonable use of the word.) How are we to meet this challenge?. . .

I doubt that anyone will be able to come up with a concrete and morally relevant difference that would justify, say, using a chimpanzee in an experiment rather than a human being with less capacity for reasoning, moral responsibility, etc. Should we then experiment on the severely retarded? Utilitarian considerations aside (the difficulty of comparing intelligence between species, for example), we feel a special obligation to care for the handicapped members of our own species, who cannot survive in this world without such care. Nonhuman animals manage very well, despite their "lower intelligence" and lesser capacities; most of them do not require special care from us. This does not, of course, justify experimenting on them. However, to subject to experimentation those people who depend on us seems even worse than subjecting members of other species to it. In addition, when we consider the severely retarded, we think, "That could be me." It makes sense to think that one might have been born retarded, but not to think that one might have been born a monkey. And so, although one can imagine one's self in the monkey's place, one feels a closer identification with the severely retarded human being. Here we are getting away from such things as "morally relevant differences" and are talking about something much more difficult to articulate, namely, the role of feeling and sentiment in moral thinking. We

would be horrified by the use of the retarded in medical research. But what are we to make of this horror? Has it moral significance or is it "mere" sentiment, of no more importance than the sentiment of whites against blacks? It is terribly difficult to know how to evaluate such feelings.[14] I am not going to say more about this, because I think that the treatment of severely incapacitated human beings does not pose an insurmountable objection to the privileged status principle. I am willing to admit that my horror at the thought of experiments being performed on severely mentally incapacitated human beings in cases in which I would find it justifiable and preferable to perform the same experiments on nonhuman animals (capable of similar suffering) may not be a moral emotion. But it is certainly not wrong of us to extend special care to members of our own species, motivated by feelings of sympathy, protectiveness, etc. If this is speciesism, it is stripped of its tone of moral condemnation. It is not racist to provide special care to members of your own race; it is racist to fall below your moral obligation to a person because of his or her race. I have been arguing that we are morally obliged to consider the interests of all sentient creatures, but not to consider those interests equally with human interests. Nevertheless, even this recognition will mean some radical changes in our attitude toward and treatment of other species.[15]

NOTES

1. Peter Singer, *Animal Liberation* (New York: Avon Books, 1977).
2. Singer, p. 5.
3. Bernard Williams, "The Idea of Equality," *Philosophy, Politics and Society* (Second Series), ed. Laslett and Runciman (Blackwell, 1962), pp. 110–13, reprinted in *Moral Concepts,* ed. Feinberg (Oxford, 1970), pp. 153–71.
4. Richard Wasserstrom, "Rights, Human Rights, and Racial Discrimination," *Journal of Philosophy* 61, no. 20 (1964), reprinted in *Human Rights,* ed. A. I. Melden (Wadsworth, 1970), pp. 96–110.
5. Ibid., p. 106.
6. H.L.A. Hart, "Are There Any Natural Rights?" *Philosophical Review* 64 (1955), and S. I. Benn,
"Abortion, Infanticide, and Respect for Persons," in *The Problem of Abortion,* ed. Feinberg (Wadsworth, 1973), pp. 92–104.
7. Singer, p. 9.
8. Benn, "Equality, Moral and Social," *The Encyclopedia of Philosophy* 3, no. 40.
9. Singer, pp. 266–7.
10. This conception of altruistic motivation comes from Thomas Nagel's *The Possibility of Altruism* (Oxford, 1970).
11. Williams, p. 157.
12. Kevin Donaghy, "Singer on Speciesism," *Philosophic Exchange* (Summer 1974).
13. Singer, p. 22.
14. We run into the same problem when discussing

abortion. Of what significance are our feelings toward the unborn when discussing its status? Is it relevant or irrelevant that it looks like a human being?

15. I would like to acknowledge the help of, and offer thanks to, Professor Richard Arneson of the University of California, San Diego; Professor Sidney Gendin of Eastern Michigan University; and Professor Peter Singer of Monash University, all of whom read and commented on earlier drafts of this paper.

REVIEW AND DISCUSSION QUESTIONS

1. Describe how Peter Singer understands equality and the relevance of that understanding to how we should treat animals.
2. How does Steinbock distinguish racism and sexism from speciesism?
3. Why does Steinbock reject Singer's understanding of equality?
4. Why does Steinbock think it is acceptable to treat a human being's interests more seriously than those of nonhuman animals?
5. How might Singer respond to Steinbock's claim that it may be correct to give mentally defective humans greater moral concern than nonhuman animals? Is that response adequate? Explain.

People or Penguins

William F. Baxter

What sorts of beings have moral standing and deserve moral consideration? How is that standing to be determined? In this essay, William F. Baxter opens the discussion by arguing that the key question that always needs to be addressed is: what are our goals? Instead of seeking simply to protect natural life, he argues, we must constantly be aware of other, competing values and make choices accordingly. Baxter thus defends what he terms a "cost-benefit" approach to nature and the environment—a view that, he argues, is sound from the perspective of nature as well as human beings. It is also, he claims, the only approach that is realistic. The soundest policy is to take account of only the needs and interests of people, not penguins or pine trees. Nature itself has no independent moral standing and will receive sufficient protection through a wise, human-centered ethic. The question always to be asked is therefore what is the optimal amount of pollution, not how pollution can be eliminated. William F. Baxter is William Benjamin Scott and Luna M. Scott Professor of Law at Stanford University.

I start with the modest proposition that, in dealing with pollution, or indeed with any problem, it is helpful to know what one is attempting to accomplish. Agreement on how and whether to pursue a particular objective, such as pollution control, is not possible unless some more general objective has been identified and stated with reasonable precision. We talk loosely of having clean air and clean water, of preserving our wilderness areas, and so forth. But none of these is a sufficiently general objective: each is more accurately viewed as a means rather than as an end.

With regard to clean air, for example, one

may ask, "how clean?" and "what does clean mean?" It is even reasonable to ask, "why have clean air?" Each of these questions is an implicit demand that a more general community goal be stated—a goal sufficiently general in its scope and enjoying sufficiently general assent among the community of actors that such "why" questions no longer seem admissible with respect to that goal.

If, for example, one states as a goal the proposition that "every person should be free to do whatever he wishes in contexts where his actions do not interfere with the interests of other human beings," the speaker is unlikely to be met with a response of "why"? The goal may be criticized as uncertain in its implications or difficult to implement, but it is so basic a tenet of our civilization—it reflects a cultural value so broadly shared, at least in the abstract—that the question "why" is seen as impertinent or imponderable or both.

I do not mean to suggest that everyone would agree with the "spheres of freedom" objective just stated. Still less do I mean to suggest that a society could subscribe to four or five such general objectives that would be adequate in their coverage to serve as testing criteria by which all other disagreements might be measured. One difficulty in the attempt to construct such a list is that each new goal added will conflict, in certain applications, with each prior goal listed; and thus each goal serves as a limited qualification on prior goals.

Without any expectation of obtaining unanimous consent to them, let me set forth four goals that I generally use as ultimate testing criteria in attempting to frame solutions to problems of human organization. My position regarding pollution stems from these four criteria. If the criteria appeal to you and any part of what appears hereafter does not, our disagreement will have a helpful focus: Which of us is correct, analytically, in supposing that his position on pollution would better serve these general goals? If the criteria do not seem acceptable to you, then it is to be expected that our more particular judgments will differ, and the task will then be yours to identify the basic set of criteria upon which your particular judgments rest.

My criteria are as follows:

1. The spheres of freedom criterion stated above.

2. Waste is a bad thing. The dominant feature of human existence is scarcity—our available resources, our aggregate labors, and our skill in employing both have always been, and will continue for some time to be, inadequate to yield to every man all the tangible and intangible satisfactions he would like to have. Hence, none of those resources, or labors, or skills, should be wasted—that is, employed so as to yield less than they might yield in human satisfactions.

3. Every human being should be regarded as an end rather than as a means to be used for the betterment of another. Each should be afforded dignity and regarded as having an absolute claim to an evenhanded application of such rules as the community may adopt for its governance.

4. Both the incentive and the opportunity to improve his share of satisfactions should be preserved to every individual. Preservation of incentive is dictated by the "no-waste" criterion and enjoins against the continuous, totally egalitarian redistribution of satisfactions, or wealth; but subject to that constraint, everyone should receive, by continuous redistribution if necessary, some minimal share of aggregate wealth so as to avoid a level of privation from which the opportunity to improve his situation becomes illusory.

The relationship of these highly general goals to the more specific environmental issues at hand may not be readily apparent, and I am not yet ready to demonstrate their pervasive implications. But let me give one indication of their implications. Recently scientists have informed us that use of DDT in food production is causing damage to the penguin population. For the present purposes let us accept that assertion as an indisputable scientific fact. The scientific fact is often asserted as if the correct implication—that we must stop agricultural use of DDT—followed from the mere statement of the fact of penguin damage. But plainly it does not follow if my criteria are employed.

My criteria are oriented to people, not penguins. Damage to penguins, or sugar pines, or geological marvels is, without more, simply irrelevant. One must go further, by my criteria, and say: Penguins are important because people enjoy seeing them walk about rocks; and furthermore, the well-being of people would be less impaired by halting use of DDT than by giving up penguins. In short, my observations about environmental problems will be people-oriented, as are my criteria. I have no interest in preserving penguins for their own sake.

It may be said by way of objection to this position, that it is very selfish of people to act as if each person represented one unit of importance and nothing else was of any importance. It is undeniably selfish. Nevertheless I think it is the only tenable starting place for analysis for several reasons. First, no other position corresponds to the way most people really think and act—i.e., corresponds to reality.

Second, this attitude does not portend any massive destruction of nonhuman flora and fauna, for people depend on them in many obvious ways, and they will be preserved because and to the degree that humans do depend on them.

Third, what is good for humans is, in many respects, good for penguins and pine trees—clean air for example. So that humans are, in these respects, surrogates for plant and animal life.

Fourth, I do not know how we could administer any other system. Our decisions are either private or collective. Insofar as Mr. Jones is free to act privately, he may give such preferences as he wishes to other forms of life: he may feed birds in winter and do with less himself, and he may even decline to resist an advancing polar bear on the ground that the bear's appetite is more important than those portions of himself that the bear may choose to eat. In short my basic premise does not rule out private altruism to competing life-forms. It does rule out, however, Mr. Jones' inclination to feed Mr. Smith to the bear, however hungry the bear, however despicable Mr. Smith.

Insofar as we act collectively on the other hand, only humans can be afforded an opportunity to participate in the collective decisions. Penguins cannot vote now and are unlikely subjects for the franchise—pine trees more unlikely still. Again each individual is free to cast his vote so as to benefit sugar pines if that is his inclination. But many of the more extreme assertions that one hears from some conservationists amount to tacit assertions that they are specially appointed representatives of sugar pines, and hence that their preferences should be weighted more heavily than the preferences of other humans who do not enjoy equal rapport with "nature." The simplistic assertion that agricultural use of DDT must stop at once because it is harmful to penguins is of that type.

Fifth, if polar bears or pine trees or penguins, like men, are to be regarded as ends rather than means, if they are to count in our calculus of social organization, someone must tell me how much each one counts, and someone must tell me how these life-forms are to be permitted to express their preferences, for I do not know either answer. If the answer is that certain people are to hold their proxies, then I want to know how those proxy-holders are to be selected: self-appointment does not seem workable to me.

Sixth, and by way of summary of all the foregoing, let me point out that the set of environmental issues under discussion—although they raise very complex technical questions of how to achieve any objective—ultimately raise a normative question: what ought we to do. Questions of ought are unique to the human mind and world—they are meaningless as applied to a nonhuman situation.

I reject the proposition that we ought to respect the "balance of nature" or to "preserve the environment" unless the reason for doing so, express or implied, is the benefit of man.

I reject the idea that there is a "right" or "morally correct" state of nature to which we should return. The word "nature" has no normative connotation. Was it "right" or "wrong" for the earth's crust to heave in contortion and create mountains and seas? Was it "right" for the first amphibian to crawl up out of the primordial ooze? Was it "wrong" for plants to reproduce themselves and alter the atmospheric composition in favor of oxygen? For animals to alter the atmosphere in favor of carbon dioxide both by breathing oxygen and eating plants? No answers can be given to these questions because they are meaningless questions.

All this may seem obvious to the point of being tedious, but much of the present controversy over environment and pollution rests on tacit normative assumptions about just such nonnormative phenomena: that it is "wrong" to impair penguins with DDT, but not to slaughter cattle for prime rib roasts; that it is wrong to kill stands of sugar pines with industrial fumes, but not to cut sugar pines and build housing for the poor. Every man is entitled to his own preferred definition of Walden Pond, but there is no definition that has any moral superiority over another, except by reference to the selfish needs of the human race.

From the fact that there is no normative definition of the natural state, it follows that there is no normative definition of clean air or pure water—hence no definition of polluted air—or of pollution—except by reference to the needs of man. The "right" composition of the atmosphere is one which has some dust in it and some lead in it and some hydrogen sulfide in it—just those amounts that attend a sensibly organized society thoughtfully and knowledgeably pursuing the greatest possible satisfaction for its human members.

The first and most fundamental step toward solution of our environmental problems is a clear recognition that our objective is not pure air or water but rather some optimal state of pollution. That step immediately suggests the question: How do we define and attain the level of pollution that will yield the maximum possible amount of human satisfaction?

Low levels of pollution contribute to human satisfaction but so do food and shelter and education and music. To attain ever lower levels of pollution, we must pay the cost of having less of these other things. I contrast that view of the cost of pollution control with the more popular statement that pollution control will "cost" very large numbers of dollars. The popular statement is true in some senses, false in others; sorting out the true and false senses is of some importance. The first step in that sorting process is to achieve a clear understanding of the difference between dollars and resources. Resources are the wealth of our nation; dollars are merely claim checks upon those resources. Resources are of vital importance; dollars are comparatively trivial.

Four categories of resources are sufficient for our purposes: At any given time a nation, or a planet if you prefer, has a stock of labor, of technological skill, of capital goods, and of natural resources (such as mineral deposits, timber, water, land, etc.). These resources can be used in various combinations to yield goods and services of all kinds—in some limited quantity. The quantity will be larger if they are combined efficiently, smaller if combined inefficiently. But in either event the resource stock is limited, the goods and services that they can be made to yield are limited; even the most efficient use of them will yield less than our population, in the aggregate, would like to have.

If one considers building a new dam, it is appropriate to say that it will be costly in the sense that it will require x hours of labor, y tons of steel and concrete, and z amount of capital goods. If these resources are devoted to the dam, then they cannot be used to build hospitals, fishing rods, schools, or electric can openers. That is the meaningful sense in which the dam is costly.

Quite apart from the very important question of how wisely we can combine our resources to produce goods and services, is the very different question of how they get distributed—who gets how many goods? Dollars constitute the claim checks which are distributed among people and which control their share of national output. Dollars are nearly valueless pieces of paper except to the extent that they do represent claim checks to some fraction of the output of goods and services. Viewed as claim checks, all the dollars outstanding during any period of time are worth, in the aggregate, the goods and services that are available to be claimed with them during that period—neither more nor less.

It is far easier to increase the supply of dollars than to increase the production of goods and services—printing dollars is easy. But printing more dollars doesn't help because each dollar then simply becomes a claim to fewer goods, i.e., becomes worth less.

The point is this: many people fall into error upon hearing the statement that the decision to build a dam, or to clean up a river, will cost $X million. It is regrettably easy to say: "It's only money. This is a wealthy country, and we have lots of money." But you cannot build a dam or clean a river with $X million—unless you also have a match, you can't even make a fire. One builds a dam or cleans a river by diverting labor and steel and trucks and factories from making one kind of goods to making another. The cost in dollars is merely a shorthand way of describing the extent of the diversion necessary. If we build a dam for $X million, then we must recognize that we will have $X million less housing and food and medical care and electric can openers as a result.

Similarly, the costs of controlling pollution are best expressed in terms of the other goods we will have to give up to do the job. This is not to say the job should not be done. Badly as we need more housing, more medical care, and more can openers, and more symphony orchestras, we could do with somewhat less of them, in my judgment at least, in exchange for somewhat cleaner air and rivers. But that is the nature of the trade-off, and analysis of the problem is advanced if that unpleasant reality is kept in mind. Once the trade-off relationship is clearly perceived, it is possible to state in a very general way what the optimal level of pollution is. I would state it as follows:

People enjoy watching penguins. They enjoy relatively clean air and smog-free vistas. Their health is improved by relatively clean water and air. Each of these benefits is a type of good or service. As a society we would be well advised to give up one washing machine if the resources that would have gone into that washing machine can yield greater human satisfaction when diverted into pollution control. We should give up one hospital if the resources thereby freed would yield more human satisfaction when devoted to elimination of noise in our cities. And so on, trade-off by trade-off, we should divert our productive capacities from the production of existing goods and services to the production of a cleaner, quieter, more pastoral nation up to—and no further than—the point at which we value more highly the next washing machine or hospital that we would have to do without than we value the next unit of environmental improvement that the diverted resources would create.

Now this proposition seems to me unassailable but so general and abstract as to be unhelpful—at least unadministerable in the form stated. It assumes we can measure in some way the incremental units of human satisfaction yielded by very different types of goods. The proposition must remain a pious abstraction until I can explain how this measurement process can occur. But I insist that the proposition stated describes the result for which we should be striving—and again, that it is always useful to know what your target is even if your weapons are too crude to score a bull's eye.

REVIEW AND DISCUSSION QUESTIONS

1. What are the basic tests or criteria Baxter uses to assess human decisions and organizations?
2. What are the reasons Baxter gives for thinking that his is the best approach to environmental issues?

3. Why does he speak of the optimal amount of pollution instead of its elimination?
4. How, specifically, would Peter Singer respond to this essay? How would Baxter respond to Singer?
5. Would Steinbock be likely to agree or disagree with Baxter? Explain.
6. Compare Baxter's view of nature with the view of people who criticize homosexuality as "unnatural."

The Land Ethic

J. Baird Callicott

J. Baird Callicott first distinguishes three philosophical positions: *ethical humanists,* who defend the special status of humans; *humane moralists* (like Peter Singer), who reject the notion of a special status for human beings in favor of "animal liberation"; and defenders of the *"land ethic"* (as represented by Aldo Leopold in his book *A Sand County Almanac*), who focus on the good of the "biotic community" as a whole. Each position offers its own account of what is valuable, but it is the land ethic, Callicott argues, that is the most creative, interesting, and practical of the alternatives. This environmentalist position also offers a different perspective on such questions as hunting and meat eating, as well as on the value of nonanimal life. J. Baird Callicott is professor of philosophy at the University of Wisconsin, Stevens Point.

ENVIRONMENTAL ETHICS AND ANIMAL LIBERATION

Partly because it is so new to Western philosophy (or at least heretofore only scarcely represented) *environmental ethics* has no precisely fixed conventional definition in glossaries of philosophical terminology. Aldo Leopold, however, is universally recognized as the father or founding genius of recent environmental ethics. His "land ethic" has become a modern classic and may be treated as the standard example, the paradigm case, as it were, of what an environmental ethic is. *Environmental ethics* then can be defined ostensively by using Leopold's land ethic as the exemplary type. I do not mean to suggest that all environmental ethics should necessarily conform to Leopold's paradigm, but the extent to which an ethical system resembles Leopold's land ethic might be used, for want of

anything better, as a criterion to measure the extent to which it is or is not of the environmental sort.

It is Leopold's opinion, and certainly an overall review of the prevailing traditions of Western ethics, both popular and philosophical, generally confirms it, that traditional Western systems of ethics have not accorded moral standing to nonhuman beings.[1] Animals and plants, soils and waters, which Leopold includes in his community of ethical beneficiaries, have traditionally enjoyed no moral standing, no rights, no respect, in sharp contrast to human persons whose rights and interests ideally must be fairly and equally considered if our actions are to be considered "ethical" or "moral." One fundamental and novel feature of the Leopold land ethic, therefore, is the extension of direct ethical considerability from people to nonhuman natural entities.

From J. Baird Callicott, "Animal Liberation: A Triangular Affair," *Environmental Ethics* 2, no. 4 (Winter 1980), pp. 311–38. Reprinted by permission.

At first glance, the recent ethical movement usually labeled "animal liberation" or "animal rights" seems to be squarely and centrally a kind of environmental ethics. The more uncompromising among the animal liberationists have demanded equal moral consideration on behalf of cows, pigs, chickens, and other apparently enslaved and oppressed nonhuman animals. The theoreticians of this new hyperegalitarianism have coined such terms as *speciesism* (on analogy with *racism* and *sexism*) and *human chauvinism* (on analogy with male chauvinism), and have made animal liberation seem, perhaps not improperly, the next and most daring development of political liberalism. Aldo Leopold also draws upon metaphors of political liberalism when he tells us that his land ethic "changes the role of *Homo sapiens* from conqueror of the land community to plain member and citizen of it."[2] For animal liberationists it is as if the ideological battles for equal rights and equal consideration for women and for racial minorities have been all but won, and the next and greatest challenge is to purchase equality, first theoretically and then practically, for all (actually only some) animals, regardless of species. This more rhetorically implied than fully articulated historical progression of moral rights from fewer to greater numbers of "persons" (allowing that animals may also be persons) as advocated by animal liberationists, also parallels Leopold's scenario in "The Land Ethic" of the historical extension of "ethical criteria" to more and more "fields of conduct" and to larger and larger groups of people during the past three thousand or so years.[3] As Leopold develops it, the land ethic is a cultural "evolutionary possibility," the next "step in a sequence."[4] For Leopold, however, the next step is much more sweeping, much more inclusive than the animal liberationists envision, since it "enlarges the boundaries of the [moral] community to include soils, waters, [and] plants . . . " as well as animals.[5] Thus, the animal liberation movement *could* be construed as partitioning Leopold's perhaps undigestible and totally inclusive environmental ethic into a series of more assimilable stages: today animal rights, tomorrow equal rights for

plants, and after that full moral standing for rocks, soil, and other earthy compounds, and perhaps sometime in the still more remote future, liberty and equality for water and other elementary bodies.

Put just this way, however, there is something jarring about such a graduated progression in the exfoliation of a more inclusive environmental ethic, something that seems absurd. A more or less reasonable case might be made for rights for some animals, but when we come to plants, soils, and waters, the frontier between plausibility and absurdity appears to have been crossed. Yet, there is no doubt that Leopold sincerely proposes that *land* (in his inclusive sense) be ethically regarded. The beech and chestnut, for example, have in his view as much "biotic right" to life as the wolf and the deer, and the effects of human actions on mountains and streams for Leopold is an ethical concern as genuine and serious as the comfort and longevity of brood hens.[6] In fact, Leopold to all appearances never considered the treatment of brood hens on a factory farm or steers in a feed lot to be a pressing moral issue. He seems much more concerned about the integrity of the farm wood lot and the effects of clear-cutting steep slopes on neighboring streams.

Animal liberationists put their ethic into practice (and display their devotion to it) by becoming vegetarians, and the moral complexities of vegetarianism have been thoroughly debated in the recent literature as an adjunct issue to animal rights. (No one however has yet expressed, as among Butler's Erewhonians, qualms about eating plants, though such sentiments might be expected to be latently present, if the rights of plants are next to be defended.) Aldo Leopold, by contrast, did not even condemn hunting animals, let alone eating them, nor did he personally abandon hunting, for which he had had an enthusiasm since boyhood, upon becoming convinced that his ethical responsibilities extended beyond the human sphere. There are several interpretations for this behavioral peculiarity. One is that Leopold did not see that his land ethic actually ought to prohibit hunting, cruelly killing, and eating animals. A corollary of this interpretation is that Leopold was so unperspicacious as deservedly to be thought stupid—a conclusion hardly comporting with the intellectual subtlety he usually evinces in most other respects. If not stupid, then perhaps Leopold was hypocritical. But if a hypocrite, we should expect him to conceal his proclivity for blood sports and flesh eating and to treat them as shameful vices to be indulged secretively. As it is, bound together between the same covers with "The Land Ethic" are his unabashed reminiscences of killing and consuming *game*. This term (like *stock*) when used of animals, moreover, appears to be morally equivalent to referring to a sexually appealing young woman as a "piece" or to a strong, young black man as a "buck"—if animal rights, that is, are to be considered as on a par with women's rights and the rights of formerly enslaved races. A third interpretation of Leopold's approbation of regulated and disciplined sport hunting (and *a fortiori* meat eating) is that it is a form of human/animal behavior not inconsistent with the land ethic as he conceived it. A corollary of this interpretation is that Leopold's land ethic and the environmental ethic of the animal liberation movement rest upon very different theoretical foundations, and that they are thus two very different forms of environmental ethics.

The urgent concern of animal liberationists for the suffering of *domestic* animals, toward which Leopold manifests an attitude which can only be described as indifference, and the urgent concern of Leopold, on the other hand, for the disappearance of species of plants as well as animals and for soil erosion and stream pollution, appear to be symptoms not only of very different ethical perspectives, but profoundly different cosmic visions as well. The neat similarities, noted at the beginning of this discussion, between the environmental ethic of the animal liberation movement and the classical Leopoldian land ethic appear in light of these observations to be rather superficial and to conceal substrata of thought and value which are not at all similar. The theoretical foundations of the animal liberation movement and those of the Leopoldian land ethic

may even turn out not to be companionable, complementary, or mutually consistent. The animal liberationists may thus find themselves not only engaged in controversy with the many conservative philosophers upholding *apartheid* between man and "beast," but also faced with an unexpected dissent from another, very different, system of environmental ethics. Animal liberation and animal rights may well prove to be a triangular rather than, as it has so far been represented in the philosophical community, a polar controversy.

ETHICAL HUMANISM AND HUMANE MORALISM

The orthodox response of "ethical humanism" (as this philosophical perspective may be styled) to the suggestion that nonhuman animals should be accorded moral standing is that such animals are not worthy of this high perquisite. Only human beings are rational, or capable of having interests, or possess *self-awareness*, or have linguistic abilities, or can represent the future, it is variously argued. These essential attributes taken singly or in various combinations make people somehow exclusively deserving of moral consideration. The so-called "lower animals," it is insisted, lack the crucial qualification for ethical considerability and so may be treated (albeit humanely, according to some, so as not to brutalize man) as things or means, not as persons or as ends.

The theoreticians of the animal liberation movement ("humane moralists" as they may be called) typically reply as follows. Not all human beings qualify as worthy of moral regard, according to the various criteria specified. Therefore, by parity of reasoning, human persons who do not so qualify as moral patients may be treated, as animals often are, as mere things or means (e.g., used in vivisection experiments, disposed of if their existence is inconvenient, eaten, hunted, etc., etc.). But the ethical humanists would be morally outraged if irrational and inarticulate infants, for example, were used in painful or lethal medical experiments, or if severely retarded people were hunted for pleasure. Thus, the double-dealing, the hypocrisy, of ethical humanism appears to be exposed. Ethical humanism, though claiming to discriminate between worthy and unworthy ethical patients on the basis of objective criteria impartially applied, turns out after all, it seems, to be *speciesism,* a philosophically indefensible prejudice (analogous to racial prejudice) against animals. . . .

The humane moralists, for their part, insist upon *sentience* (*sensibility* would have been a more precise word choice) as the only relevant capacity a being need possess to enjoy full moral standing. If animals, they argue, are conscious entities who, though deprived of reason, speech, forethought or even *self*-awareness (however that may be judged), are capable of suffering, then their suffering should be as much a matter of ethical concern as that of our fellow human beings, or strictly speaking, as our very own. . . . As a *moral* agent, I should not consider my pleasure and pain to be of greater consequence in determining a course of action than that of other persons. Thus, by the same token, if animals suffer pain—and among philosophers only strict Cartesians would deny that they do—then we are morally obliged to consider their suffering as much an evil to be minimized by conscientious moral agents as human suffering. Certainly actions of ours which contribute to the suffering of animals, such as hunting them, butchering and eating them, experimenting on them, etc., are on these assumptions morally reprehensible. Hence, a person who regards himself or herself as not aiming in life to live most selfishly, conveniently, or profitably, but rightly and in accord with practical principle, if convinced by these arguments, should, among other things, cease to eat the flesh of animals, to hunt them, to wear fur and leather clothing and bone ornaments and other articles made from the bodies of animals, to eat eggs and drink milk, if the animal producers of these commodities are retained under inhumane circumstances, and to patronize zoos (as sources of psychological if not physical torment of animals). On the other hand, since certain very simple animals are almost certainly insensible to pleasure and pain, they may and indeed should be treated as morally inconsequential. Nor is there any *moral* reason why trees should be respected or rivers or mountains or anything which is, though living or tributary to life processes, unconscious. The humane moralists, like the moral humanists, draw a firm distinction between those beings worthy of moral consideration and those not. They simply insist upon a different but quite definite cut-off point on the spectrum of natural entities, and accompany their criterion with arguments to show that it is more ethically defensible (granting certain assumptions) and more consistently applicable than that of the moral humanists.

THE FIRST PRINCIPLE
OF THE LAND ETHIC

The fundamental principle of humane moralism, as we see, is Benthamic. [*Jeremy Bentham famously defended the view known as hedonism, that the only states of affairs that are good in themselves, and not as means to something else, are experiences of pleasure. Money, for instance, while valued is not good except as a means to pleasure.—Ed.*] Good is equivalent to pleasure and, more pertinently, evil is equivalent to pain. The presently booming controversy between moral humanists and humane moralists appears, when all the learned dust has settled, to be essentially internecine; at least, the lines of battle are drawn along familiar watersheds of the conceptual terrain.* A classical ethical theory, Bentham's, has been refitted and pressed into

---

*John Rodman, "The Liberation of Nature" (p. 95), comments: "Why do our 'new ethics' seem so old? Because the attempt to produce a 'new ethics' by the process of 'extension' perpetuates the basic assumptions of the conventional modern paradigm, however much it fiddles with the boundaries." When the assumptions remain conventional, the boundaries are, in my view, scaler, but triangular when both positions are considered in opposition to the land ethic. The scaler relation is especially clear when two other positions, not specifically discussed in the text, the reverence-for-life ethic and pan-moralism, are considered.

service to meet relatively new and unprecedented ethically relevant situations—the problems raised especially by factory farming and
ever more exotic and frequently ill-conceived
scientific research employing animal subjects.
Then, those with . . . Kantian ethical affiliation
have heard the bugle and have risen to arms. . . .
The familiar historical positions have simply
been retrenched, applied, and exercised.

But what about the third (and certainly
minority) party to the animal liberation
debate? What sort of reasonable and coherent moral theory would at once urge that animals (and plants and soils and waters) be
included in the same class with people as
beings to whom ethical consideration is owed
and yet not object to some of them being
slaughtered (whether painlessly or not) and
eaten, others hunted, trapped, and in various
other ways seemingly cruelly used? Aldo
Leopold provides a concise statement of what
might be called the categorical imperative or
principal precept of the land ethic: "A thing is
right when it tends to preserve the integrity,
stability, and beauty of the biotic community.
It is wrong when it tends otherwise."[7] What is
especially noteworthy, and that to which
attention should be directed in this proposition, is the idea that the good of the biotic
community is the ultimate measure of the
moral value, the rightness or wrongness,
of actions. Thus, to hunt and kill a white-
tailed deer in certain districts may not only be

ethically permissible, it might actually be a
moral requirement, necessary to protect the
local environment, taken as a whole, from the
disintegrating effects of a cervid population
explosion. On the other hand, rare and
endangered animals like the lynx should
be especially nurtured and preserved. The
lynx, cougar, and other wild feline predators,
from the neo-Benthamite perspective (if consistently and evenhandedly applied) should
be regarded as merciless, wanton, and incorrigible murderers of their fellow creatures, who
not only kill, it should be added, but cruelly
toy with their victims, thus increasing the
measure of pain in the world. From the perspective of the land ethic, predators generally
should be nurtured and preserved as critically
important members of the biotic communities
to which they are native. Certain plants, similarly, may be overwhelmingly important to
the stability, integrity, and beauty of biotic
communities, while some animals, such as
domestic sheep (allowed perhaps by egalitarian and humane herdspersons to graze freely
and to reproduce themselves without being
harvested for lamb and mutton) could be a
pestilential threat to the natural floral community of a given locale. Thus, the land ethic
is logically coherent in demanding at once
that moral consideration be given to plants as
well as to animals and yet in permitting animals to be killed, trees felled, and so on. In
every case the effect upon ecological systems

The reverence-for-life ethic (as I am calling it in deference to Albert Schweitzer) seems to be the next step on the scale after the humane ethic. William Frankena considers it so in "Ethics and the Environment," *Ethics and Problems of the 21st Century,* pp. 3–20. W. Murry Hunt ("Are Mere Things Morally Considerable," *Environmental Ethics* 2 [1980]: 59–65) has gone a step past Schweitzer, and made the bold suggestion that *everything* should be accorded moral stand-ing, pan-moralism. Hunt's discussion shows clearly that there is a similar logic ("slippery slope" logic) involved in taking each downward step, and thus a certain commonal-ity of underlying assumptions among all the ethical types to which the land ethic stands in opposition. Hunt is not unaware that his suggestion may be interpreted as a *reduc-tio ad absurdum* of the whole matter, but insists that that is not his intent. The land ethic is not part of this linear series of steps and hence may be represented as a point off the

scale. The principal difference . . . is that the land ethic is collective or "holistic" while the others are distributive or "atomistic." Another relevant difference is that moral humanism, humane moralism, reverence-for-life ethics, and the limiting case, pan-moralism, either openly or implicitly espouse a pecking-order model of nature. The land ethic, founded upon an ecological model of nature emphasizing the contributing roles played by various species in the econ-omy of nature, abandons the "higher"/"lower" ontological and axiological schema, in favor of a functional system of value. The land ethic, in other words, is inclined to establish value distinctions not on the basis of higher and lower orders of being, but on the basis of the importance of organ-isms, minerals, and so on to the biotic community. Some bacteria, for example, may be of greater value to the health or economy of nature than dogs, and thus command more respect.

is the decisive factor in the determination of the ethical quality of actions.

THE LAND ETHIC AND THE ECOLOGICAL POINT OF VIEW

. . . Since ecology focuses upon the relationships between and among things, it inclines its students toward a more holistic vision of the world. Before the rather recent emergence of ecology as a science the landscape appeared to be, one might say, a collection of objects, some of them alive, some conscious, but all the same, an aggregate, a plurality of separate individuals. With this "atomistic" representation of things it is no wonder that moral issues might be understood as competing and mutually contradictory clashes of the "rights" of separate individuals, each separately pursuing its "interests." Ecology has made it possible to apprehend the same landscape as an articulate unity (without the least hint of mysticism or ineffability). Ordinary organic bodies have articulated and discernible parts (limbs, various organs, myriad cells); yet, because of the character of the network of relations among those parts, they form in a perfectly familiar sense a second-order whole. Ecology makes it possible to see land, similarly, as a unified system of integrally related parts, as, so to speak, a third-order organic whole.

Another analogy that has helped ecologists to convey the particular holism which their science brings to reflective attention is that land is integrated as a human community is integrated. The various parts of the "biotic community" (individual animals and plants) depend upon one another *economically* so that the system as such acquires distinct characteristics of its own. Just as it is possible to characterize and define collectively peasant societies, agrarian communities, industrial complexes, capitalist, communist, and socialist economic systems, and so on, ecology characterizes and defines various biomes as desert, savanna, wetland, tundra, wood land, etc., communities, each with its particular "professions," "roles," or "niches."

Now we may think that among the duties we as moral agents have toward ourselves is the duty of self-preservation, which may be interpreted as a duty to maintain our own organic integrity. It is not uncommon in historical moral theory, further, to find that in addition to those peculiar responsibilities we have in relation both to ourselves and to other persons severally, we also have a duty to behave in ways that do not harm the fabric of society *per se*. The land ethic, in similar fashion, calls our attention to the recently discovered integrity—in other words, the unity—of the biota and posits duties binding upon moral agents in relation to that whole. . . . Hence, the representation of the natural environment as, in Leopold's terms, "one humming community" (or, less consistently in his discussion, a third-order organic being) brings into play, whether rationally or not, those stirrings of conscience which we feel in relation to delicately complex, functioning social and organic systems.

The neo-Benthamite humane moralists have, to be sure, digested one of the metaphysical implications of modern biology. They insist that human beings must be understood continuously with the rest of organic nature. People are (and are only) animals, and much of the rhetorical energy of the animal liberation movement is spent in fighting a rear guard action for this aspect of Darwinism against those philosophers who still cling to the dream of a special metaphysical status for people in the order of "creation." To this extent the animal liberation movement is biologically enlightened. . . . [B]ut the biological information of the animal liberation movement seems to extend no further than this—the continuity of human with other animal life forms. The more recent ecological perspective especially seems to be ignored by humane moralists. The holistic outlook of ecology and the associated value premium conferred upon the biotic community, its beauty, integrity, and stability may simply not have penetrated the thinking of the animal liberationists, or it could be that to include it would involve an intolerable contradiction with the Benthamite foundations of their ethical theory. Bentham's view of the "interests of the community" was bluntly reductive. With his characteristic bluster, Bentham wrote, "The community is a fictitious *body* composed of the individual persons who are considered as constituting as it were its *members.* The interest of the community then is, what?—the sum of the interests of the several members who compose it."[8] Bentham's very simile—the community is like a body composed of members—gives the lie to his reduction of its interests to the sum of its parts taken severally. The interests of a person are not those of his or her cells summed up and averaged out. Our organic health and well-being, for example, require vigorous exercise and metabolic stimulation which cause stress and often pain to various parts of the body and a more rapid turnover in the life cycle of our individual cells. For the sake of the person taken as whole, some parts may be, as it were, unfairly sacrificed. On the level of social organization, the interests of society may not always coincide with the sum of the interests of its parts. Discipline, sacrifice, and individual restraint are often necessary in the social sphere to maintain social integrity as within the bodily organism. A society, indeed, is particularly vulnerable to disintegration when its members become preoccupied totally with their own particular interest, and ignore those distinct and independent interests of the community as a whole. One example, unfortunately, our own society, is altogether too close at hand to be examined with strict academic detachment. The United States seems to pursue uncritically a social policy of reductive utilitarianism, aimed at promoting the happiness of all its members severally. Each special interest accordingly clamors more loudly to be satisfied while the community as a whole becomes noticeably more and more infirm economically, environmentally, and politically. . . .

ETHICAL HOLISM

Before we take up this question, however, some points of interest remain to be considered on the matter of a holistic versus a reductive environmental ethic. To pit the one against the other as I have done without further qualification would be mistaken. A society is constituted by its members, an organic body by its cells, and the ecosystem by the plants, animals, minerals, fluids, and gases which compose it. One cannot affect a system as a whole without affecting at least some of its components. An environmental ethic which takes as its *summum bonum* the integrity, stability, and beauty of the biotic community is not conferring moral standing on something else besides plants, animals, soils, and waters. Rather, the former, the good of the community as a whole, serves as a standard for the assessment of the relative value and relative ordering of its constitutive parts and therefore provides a means of adjudicating the often mutually contradictory demands of the parts considered separately for equal consideration. If diversity does indeed contribute to stability (a classical "law" of ecology), then specimens of rare and endangered species, for example, have a *prima facie* claim to preferential consideration from the perspective of the land ethic. Animals of those species, which, like the honey bee, function in ways critically important to the economy of nature, moreover, would be granted a greater claim to moral attention than psychologically more complex and sensitive ones, say, rabbits and moles, which seem to be plentiful, globally distributed, reproductively efficient, and only routinely integrated into the natural economy. Animals and plants, mountains, rivers, seas, the atmosphere are the *immediate* practical beneficiaries of the land ethic. The well-being of the biotic community, the biosphere as a whole, cannot be logically separated from their survival and welfare.

Some suspicion may arise at this point that the land ethic is ultimately grounded in human interests, not in those of nonhuman natural entities. . . . It is my view that there can be no value apart from an evaluator, that all value is as it were in the eye of the beholder. The value that is attributed to the ecosystem, therefore, is humanly dependent or (allowing that other living things may take a certain delight in the well-being of the whole of things, or that the gods may) at least dependent upon some variety of morally and aesthetically sensitive consciousness. Granting this, however, there is a further, very crucial distinction to be drawn. It is possible that while things may only have value because we (or someone) values them, they may nonetheless be valued for themselves as well as for the contribution they might make to the realization of our (or someone's) interests. Children are valued for themselves by most parents. Money, on the other hand, has only an instrumental or indirect value. Which sort of value has the health of the biotic community and its members severally for Leopold and the land ethic? It is especially difficult to separate these two general sorts of value, the one of moral significance, the other merely selfish, when something that may be valued in both ways at once is the subject of consideration. Are pets, for example, well-treated, like children, for the sake of themselves, or, like mechanical appliances, because of the sort of services they provide their owners? Is a healthy biotic community something we value because we are so utterly and (to the biologically well-informed) so obviously dependent upon it not only for our happiness but for our very survival, or may we also perceive it disinterestedly as having an independent worth? Leopold insists upon a noninstrumental value for the biotic community and mutatis mutandis for its constituents. According to Leopold, collective enlightened self-interest on the part of human beings does not go far enough; the land ethic in his opinion (and no doubt this reflects his own moral intuitions) requires "love, respect, and admiration for land, and a high regard for its value." The land ethic, in Leopold's view, creates "obligations over and above self-interest." And "obligations have no meaning without conscience, and the problem we face is the extension of the social conscience from people to land."[9] If, in other words, any genuine ethic is possible, if it is possible to value *people* for the sake of themselves, then it is equally possible to value land in the same way. . . .

The biospheric perspective does not exempt *Homo sapiens* from moral evaluation in relation to the well-being of the community of nature taken as a whole. The preciousness of individual deer, as of any other specimen, is inversely proportional to the population of the species. Environmentalists, however reluctantly and painfully, do not omit to apply the same logic to their own kind. As omnivores, the population of human beings should, perhaps, be roughly twice that of bears, allowing for differences of size. A global population of more than four billion persons and showing no signs of an orderly decline presents an alarming prospect to humanists, but it is at present a global disaster (the more *per capita* prosperity, indeed, the more disastrous it appears) for the biotic community. . . . Edward Abbey in his enormously popular *Desert Solitaire* bluntly states that he would sooner shoot a man than a snake.[10] Abbey may not be simply depraved; this is perhaps only his way of dramatically making the point that the human population has become so disproportionate from the biological point of view that if one had to choose between a specimen of *Homo sapiens* and a specimen of a rare even if unattractive species, the choice would be moot. . . .

REAPPRAISING DOMESTICITY

Among the last philosophical remarks penned by Aldo Leopold before his untimely death in 1948 is the following: "Perhaps such a shift of values [as implied by the attempt to weld together the concepts of ethics and ecology] can be achieved by reappraising things unnatural, tame, and confined in terms of things natural, wild, and free."[11] John Muir, in a similar spirit of reappraisal, had noted earlier the difference between the wild mountain sheep of the Sierra and the ubiquitous domestic variety. The latter, which Muir described as "hooved locusts," were only, in his estimation, "half alive" in comparison with their natural and autonomous counterparts.[12] One of the more distressing aspects of the animal liberation movement is the failure of almost all its exponents to draw a sharp distinction between the very different plights (and rights) of wild and domestic animals. But this distinction lies at the very center of the land ethic. Domestic animals are creations of man. They are living artifacts, but artifacts nevertheless, and they constitute yet another mode of extension of the works of man into the ecosystem. From the perspective of the land ethic a herd of cattle, sheep, or pigs is as much or more a ruinous blight on the landscape as a fleet of four-wheel drive off-road vehicles. There is thus something profoundly incoherent (and insensitive as well) in the complaint of some animal liberationists that the "natural behavior" of chickens and bobby calves is cruelly frustrated on factory farms. It would make almost as much sense to speak of the natural behavior of tables and chairs.

Here a serious disanalogy (which no one to my knowledge has yet pointed out) becomes clearly evident between the liberation of blacks from slavery (and more recently, from civil inequality) and the liberation of animals from a similar sort of subordination and servitude. Black slaves remained, as it were, metaphysically autonomous: they were by nature if not by convention free beings quite capable of living on their own. They could not be enslaved for more than a historical interlude, for the strength of the force of their freedom was too great. They could, in other words, be retained only by a continuous counterforce, and only temporarily. This is equally true of caged wild animals. African cheetahs in American and European zoos are captive, not indentured, beings. But this is not true of cows, pigs, sheep, and chickens. They have been bred to docility, tractability, stupidity, and dependency. It is literally meaningless to suggest that they be liberated. It is, to speak in hyperbole, a logical impossibility.

Certainly it is a practical impossibility. Imagine what would happen if the people of the world became morally persuaded that domestic animals were to be regarded as oppressed and enslaved persons and accordingly set free. In one scenario we might imagine that like former American black slaves they would receive the equivalent of forty acres and a mule and be turned out to survive on their own. Feral cattle and sheep would hang around

farm outbuildings waiting forlornly to be sheltered and fed, or would graze aimlessly through their abandoned and deteriorating pastures. Most would starve or freeze as soon as winter settled in. Reproduction which had been assisted over many countless generations by their former owners might be altogether impossible in the feral state for some varieties, and the care of infants would be an art not so much lost as never acquired. And so in a very short time, after much suffering and agony, these species would become abruptly extinct. Or, in another scenario beginning with the same simple emancipation from human association, survivors of the first massive die-off of untended livestock might begin to recover some of their remote wild ancestral genetic traits and become smaller, leaner, heartier, and smarter versions of their former selves. An actual contemporary example is afforded by the feral mustangs ranging over parts of the American West. In time such animals as these would become (just as the mustangs are now) competitors both with their former human masters and (with perhaps more tragic consequences) indigenous wildlife for food and living space.

Foreseeing these and other untoward consequences of immediate and unplanned liberation of livestock, a human population grown morally more perfect than at present might decide that they had a duty, accumulated over thousands of years, to continue to house and feed as before their former animal slaves (whom they had rendered genetically unfit to care for themselves), but not to butcher them or make other ill use of them, including frustrating their "natural" behavior, their right to copulate freely, reproduce, and enjoy the delights of being parents. People, no longer having meat to eat, would require more vegetables, cereals, and other plant foods, but the institutionalized animal incompetents would still consume all the hay and grains (and more since they would no longer be slaughtered) than they did formerly. This would require clearing more land and bringing it into agricultural production with further loss of wildlife habitat and ecological destruction. Another possible scenario might be a decision on the part of people not literally to liberate domestic animals but simply to cease to breed and raise them. When the last livestock have been killed and eaten (or permitted to die "natural" deaths), people would become vegetarians and domestic livestock species would thus be rendered deliberately extinct (just as they had been deliberately created). But there is surely some irony in an outcome in which the beneficiaries of a humane extension of conscience are destroyed in the process of being saved.

The land ethic, it should be emphasized, as Leopold has sketched it, provides for the *rights* of nonhuman natural beings to a share in the life processes of the biotic community. The conceptual foundation of such rights, however, is less conventional than natural, based upon, as one might say, evolutionary and ecological entitlement. Wild animals and native plants have a particular place in nature, according to the land ethic, which domestic animals (because they are products of human art and represent an extended presence of human beings in the natural world) do not have. The land ethic, in sum, is as much opposed, though on different grounds, to commercial traffic in wildlife, zoos, the slaughter of whales and other marine mammals, etc., as is the humane ethic. Concern for animal (and plant) rights and well-being is as fundamental to the land ethic as to the humane ethic, but the difference between naturally evolved and humanly bred species is an essential consideration for the one, though not for the other.

The "shift of values" which results from our "reappraising things unnatural, tame, and confined in terms of things natural, wild, and free" is especially dramatic when we reflect upon the definitions of *good* and *evil* espoused by Bentham and Mill and uncritically accepted by their contemporary followers. Pain and pleasure seem to have nothing at all to do with good and evil if our appraisal is taken from the vantage point of ecological biology. Pain in particular is primarily information. In animals, it informs the central nervous system of stress, irritation, or trauma in outlying regions of the organism. A certain level of pain under optimal organic circumstances is indeed desirable

as an indicator of exertion—of the degree of exertion needed to maintain fitness, to stay "in shape," and of a level of exertion beyond which it would be dangerous to go. An arctic wolf in pursuit of a caribou may experience pain in her feet or chest because of the rigors of the chase. There is nothing bad or wrong in that. Or, consider a case of injury. Suppose that a person in the course of a wilderness excursion sprains an ankle. Pain informs him or her of the injury and by its intensity the amount of further stress the ankle may endure in the course of getting to safety. Would it be better if pain were not experienced upon injury or, taking advantage of recent technology, anaesthetized? Pleasure appears to be, for the most part (unfortunately it is not always so) a reward accompanying those activities which contribute to organic maintenance, such as the pleasures associated with eating, drinking, grooming, and so on, or those which contribute to social solidarity like the pleasures of dancing, conversation, teasing, etc., or those which contribute to the continuation of the species, such as the pleasures of sexual activity and of being parents. The doctrine that life is the happier the freer it is from pain and that the happiest life conceivable is one in which there is continuous pleasure uninterrupted by pain is biologically preposterous. A living mammal which experienced no pain would be one which had a lethal dysfunction of the nervous system. The idea that pain is evil and ought to be minimized or eliminated is as primitive a notion as that of a tyrant who puts to death messengers bearing bad news on the supposition that thus his well-being and security is improved.

More seriously still, the value commitments of the humane movement seem at bottom to betray a world-denying or rather a life-loathing philosophy. The natural world as actually constituted is one in which one being lives at the expense of others. Each organism, in Darwin's metaphor, struggles to maintain its own organic integrity. The more complex animals seem to experience (judging from our own case, and reasoning from analogy) appropriate and adaptive psychological accompaniments to organic existence. There is a palpable passion for self-preservation. There are desire, pleasure in the satisfaction of desires, acute agony attending injury, frustration, and chronic dread of death. But these experiences are the psychological substance of living. To live is to be anxious about life, to feel pain and pleasure in a fitting mixture, and sooner or later to die. That is the way the system works. If nature as a whole is good, then pain and death are also good. Environmental ethics in general require people to play fair in the natural system. The neo-Benthamites have in a sense taken the uncourageous approach. People have attempted to exempt themselves from the life/death reciprocities of natural processes and from ecological limitations in the name of a prophylactic ethic of maximizing rewards (pleasure) and minimizing unwelcome information (pain). To be fair, the humane moralists seem to suggest that we should attempt to project the same values into the nonhuman animal world and to widen the charmed circle—no matter that it would be biologically unrealistic to do so or biologically ruinous if, per impossible, such an environmental ethic were implemented.

There is another approach. Rather than imposing our alienation from nature and natural processes and cycles of life on other animals, we human beings could reaffirm our participation in nature by accepting life as it is given without a sugar coating. Instead of imposing artificial legalities, rights, and so on on nature, we might take the opposite course and accept and affirm natural biological laws, principles, and limitations in the human personal and social spheres. Such appears to have been the posture toward life of tribal peoples in the past. The chase was relished with its dangers, rigors, and hardships as well as its rewards: animal flesh was respectfully consumed; a tolerance for pain was cultivated; virtue and magnanimity were prized; lithic, floral, and faunal spirits were worshipped; population was routinely optimized by sexual continency, abortion, infanticide, and stylized warfare; and other life forms, although certainly appropriated, were respected as fellow players in a magnificent and awesome, if not

altogether idyllic, drama of life. It is impossible today to return to the symbiotic relationship of Stone Age man to the natural environment, but the ethos of this by far the longest era of human existence could be abstracted and integrated with a future human culture seeking a viable and mutually beneficial relationship with nature. Personal, social, and environmental *health* would, accordingly, receive a premium value rather than comfort, self-indulgent pleasure, and anaesthetic insulation from pain. Sickness would be regarded as a worse evil than death. The pursuit of health or wellness at the personal, social, and environmental levels would require self-discipline in the form of simple diet, vigorous exercise, conservation, and social responsibility.

Leopold's prescription for the realization and implementation of the land ethic—the reappraisal of things unnatural, tame, and confined in terms of things natural, wild, and free—does not stop, in other words, with a reappraisal of nonhuman domestic animals in terms of their wild (or willed) counterparts; the human ones should be similarly reappraised. This means, among other things, the reappraisal of the comparatively recent values and concerns of "civilized" *Homo sapiens* in terms of those of our "savage" ancestors. Civilization has insulated and alienated us from the rigors and challenges of the natural environment. The hidden agenda of the humane ethic is the imposition of the anti-natural prophylactic ethos of comfort and soft pleasure on an even wider scale. The land ethic, on the other hand, requires a shrinkage, if at all possible, of the domestic sphere; it rejoices in a recrudescence of wilderness and a renaissance of tribal cultural experience.

The converse of those goods and evils, axiomatic to the humane ethic, may be illustrated and focused by the consideration of a single issue raised by the humane morality: a vegetarian diet. Savage people seem to have had, if the attitudes and values of surviving tribal cultures are representative, something like an intuitive grasp of ecological relationships and certainly a morally charged appreciation of eating. There is nothing more intimate than eating, more symbolic of the connectedness of life, and more mysterious. What we eat and how we eat is by no means an insignificant ethical concern.

From the ecological point of view, for human beings universally to become vegetarians is tantamount to a shift of trophic niche from omnivore with carnivorous preferences to herbivore. . . . The human population would probably, as past trends overwhelmingly suggest, expand in accordance with the potential thus afforded. The net result would be fewer nonhuman beings and more human beings, who, of course, have requirements of life far more elaborate than even those of domestic animals, requirements which would tax other "natural resources" (trees for shelter, minerals mined at the expense of topsoil and its vegetation, etc.) more than under present circumstances. A vegetarian human population is therefore *probably* ecologically catastrophic.

Meat eating as implied by the foregoing remarks may be more *ecologically* responsible than a wholly vegetable diet. Meat, however, purchased at the supermarket, externally packaged and internally laced with petrochemicals, fattened in feed lots, slaughtered impersonally, and, in general, mechanically processed from artificial insemination to microwave roaster, is an affront not only to physical metabolism and bodily health but to conscience as well. From the perspective of the land ethic, the immoral aspect of the factory farm has to do far less with the suffering and killing of nonhuman animals than with the monstrous transformation of living things from an organic to a mechanical mode of being. . . .

Ethical vegetarianism to all appearances insists upon the human consumption of plants (in a paradoxical moral gesture toward those animals whose very existence is dependent upon human carnivorousness), even when the tomatoes are grown hydroponically, the lettuce generously coated with chlorinated hydrocarbons, the potatoes pumped up with chemical fertilizers, and the cereals stored with the help of chemical preservatives. The land ethic takes as much exception to the transmogrification of plants by mechanicochemical means as to that of animals. The important thing, I would think, is not to eat vegetables as opposed to animal flesh, but to resist factory farming in all its manifestations, including especially its liberal application of pesticides, herbicides, and chemical fertilizers to maximize the production of *vegetable* crops.

The land ethic, with its ecological perspective, helps us to recognize and affirm the organic integrity of self and the untenability of a firm distinction between self and environment. On the ethical question of what to eat, it answers, not vegetables instead of animals, but organically as opposed to mechanicochemically produced food. Purists like Leopold prefer, in his expression, to get their "meat from God," i.e., to hunt and consume wildlife and to gather wild plant foods, and thus to live within the parameters of the aboriginal human ecological niche. Second best is eating from one's own orchard, garden, henhouse, pigpen, and barnyard. Third best is buying or bartering organic foods from one's neighbors and friends.

CONCLUSION

Philosophical controversy concerning animal liberation/rights has been most frequently represented as a polar dispute between traditional moral humanists and seemingly *avant garde* humane moralists. Further, animal liberation has been assumed to be closely allied with environmental ethics, possibly because in Leopold's classical formulation moral standing and indeed rights (of some unspecified sort) are accorded nonhuman beings, among them animals. The purpose of this discussion has been to distinguish sharply environmental ethics from the animal liberation/rights movement both in theory and practical application and to suggest, thereupon, that there is an underrepresented, but very important, point of view respecting the problem of the moral status of nonhuman animals. The debate over animal liberation, in short, should be conceived as triangular, not polar, with land ethics or environmental ethics, the third and, in my judgment, the most creative, interesting, and practicable alternative. Indeed, from this third point of view moral humanism and humane moralism appear to have much more in common with one another than either have with environmental or land ethics. On reflection one might even be led to suspect that the noisy debate between these parties has served to drown out the much deeper challenge to "business-as-usual" ethical philosophy represented by Leopold and his exponents, and to keep ethical philosophy firmly anchored to familiar modern paradigms.

Moral humanism and humane moralism, to restate succinctly the most salient conclusions of this essay, are *atomistic* or distributive in their theory of moral value, while environmental ethics (again, at least, as set out in Leopold's outline) is *holistic* or collective. Modern ethical theory, in other words, has consistently located moral value in individuals and set out certain metaphysical reasons for including some individuals and excluding others . . . while environmental ethics locates ultimate value in the "biotic community" and assigns differential moral value to the constitutive individuals relatively to that standard. This is perhaps the most fundamental theoretical difference between environmental ethics and the ethics of animal liberation.

Allied to this difference are many others. One of the more conspicuous is that in environmental ethics, plants are included within the parameters of the ethical theory as well as animals. Indeed, inanimate entities such as oceans and lakes, mountains, forests, and wetlands are assigned a greater value than individual animals and in a way quite different from systems which accord them moral considerability through a further multiplication of competing individual loci of value and holders of rights. . . .

Environmental ethics sets a very low priority on domestic animals as they very frequently contribute to the erosion of the integrity, stability, and beauty of the biotic communities into which they have been insinuated. On the other hand, animal liberation, if pursued at the practical as well as rhetorical level, would have ruinous consequences on plants, soils, and waters, consequences which could not be directly reckoned according to humane moral theory. As this last remark suggests, the animal liberation/animal rights movement is in the final analysis utterly unpracticable. An imagined society in which all animals capable of sensibility received equal consideration or held rights to equal consideration would be so ludicrous that it might be more appropriately and effectively treated in satire than in philosophical discussion. The land ethic, by contrast, even though its ethical purview is very much wider, is nevertheless eminently practicable, since, by reference to a single good, competing individual claims may be adjudicated and relative values and priorities assigned to the myriad components of the biotic community. This is not to suggest that the implementation of environmental ethics as social policy would be easy. Implementation of the land ethic would require discipline, sacrifice, retrenchment, and massive economic reform, tantamount to a virtual revolution in prevailing attitudes and life styles. Nevertheless, it provides a unified and coherent practical principle and thus a decision procedure at the practical level which a distributive or atomistic ethic may achieve only artificially and so imprecisely as to be practically indeterminate.

NOTES

1. Aldo Leopold, *A Sand County Almanac* (New York: Oxford University Press, 1949), pp. 202–3.
2. Ibid., p. 204.
3. Ibid., pp. 201–3.
4. Ibid., p. 203.
5. Ibid., p. 204.
6. Ibid., p. 221 (trees); pp. 129–33 (mountains); p. 209 (streams).
7. Ibid., pp. 224–25.
8. *An Introduction to the Principles of Morals and Legislation* (Oxford: Oxford University Press, 1823), chap. 1, sec. 4.

9. Leopold, *Sand County Almanac*, pp. 223 and 209.
10. Edward Abbey, *Desert Solitaire* (New York: Ballantine Books, 1968), p. 20.
11. Leopold, *Sand County Almanac*, p. ix.
12. See John Muir, "The Wild Sheep of California," *Overland Monthly* 12 (1874), p. 359.

REVIEW AND DISCUSSION QUESTIONS

1. How does Callicott think environmental ethics differs from animal liberation (humane moralism)?
2. What is the first principle of the land ethic?
3. What does Callicott mean by saying that animal liberationists like Bentham are "bluntly reductive"?
4. How does the environmental ethic differ from moral humanism?
5. Describe the reasons that seem to lead Callicott to conclude that the environmental ethic is superior to the others.
6. What practical implications do Callicott and you see from the adoption of the land ethic, as opposed to animal liberation?

Essay and Paper Topics for Section 6

1. How might Peter Singer most reasonably respond to Callicott's argument? Is that response adequate?
2. Which of Callicott's three positions is closest to Steinbock's? How might she respond to Callicott's essay?
3. Discuss the following claim: "Callicott argues that 'wild' animals have a 'place in nature' that domestic ones do not. But if humans are part of nature, then there is no reason to suppose our dependents are less valuable or less a part of nature than the dependents of nonhuman animals."
4. Using the general moral theory from Part I that you found most reasonable, write an essay in which you discuss how that theory would evaluate the position of two philosophers you have read on the subject of our obligations to animals and to nature.

Abortion

Essays in this section represent a broad range of views on one of the most controversial moral and legal issues in the United States: abortion. Three themes run through these readings. The first, and most often discussed, is the moral status of the fetus. Is it, as some have suggested, no more valuable than any other piece of human tissue, like a tonsil? Or is it, as others passionately believe, the moral equivalent of a newborn baby and therefore entitled to the same moral and legal respect we give each other? Or is its value somewhere between these two and, if so, where? The second question involves women's rights and the question of political domination. Can a pregnant woman legitimately get an abortion, based on her right to control her body, even if there is another person inside her? A third set of questions involves fathers: are their choices and desires of no consequence in the abortion decision? Or might the father legitimately demand that the mother not get an abortion? We begin the discussions with the U.S. Supreme Court's most far-reaching decision on this issue, in which it argued that governments are strictly limited in the ways they may restrict abortions.

The Constitutional Right to Abortion

Roe v. *Wade*

Few constitutional cases have created more controversy, both moral and legal, than abortion. *Roe* v. *Wade* is the famous Supreme Court decision that guarantees women the right to get an abortion. The case began in August 1969 when Norma McCorvey discovered she was pregnant. Too poor to travel from Texas to California, the nearest state where abortions were legal, she sought help. A friend introduced her to two recent law school graduates, Sarah Weddington and Linda Coffee, and the three decided to challenge the constitutionality of Texas's law forbidding abortion.

Norma McCorvey never got her abortion, nor did she see her baby girl again after leaving the hospital. Hoping to remain anonymous, she became Jane Roe for purposes of the lawsuit she was bringing against Henry Wade, District Attorney for Dallas County, Texas. Four years later, the Supreme Court took the controversial step of extending the right to privacy to include the right to get an abortion. Justice Blackmun wrote the majority opinion in this famous case; Justice White wrote a dissenting opinion. Justice Blackmun continued for years after this

Roe v. *Wade* 410 U.S. 113 (1973). Some citations and footnotes omitted.

decision to get hate mail and threats; once, a pro-life advocate fired a bullet into his house.

Justice Blackmun Delivered the Opinion of the Court: Three reasons have been advanced to explain historically the enactment of criminal abortion laws in the nineteenth century and to justify their continued existence.

It has been argued occasionally that these laws were the product of a Victorian social concern to discourage illicit sexual conduct. Texas, however, does not advance this justification in the present case. . . .

A second reason is concerned with abortion as a medical procedure. When most criminal abortion laws were first enacted, the procedure was a hazardous one for the woman. . . .

Modern medical techniques have altered this situation. Appellants and various *amici* refer to medical data indicating that abortion in early pregnancy, that is, prior to the end of first trimester, although not without its risk, is now relatively safe. . . . The State has a legitimate interest in seeing to it that abortion, like any other medical procedure, is performed under circumstances that insure maximum safety for the patient. This interest obviously extends at least to the performing physician and his staff, to the facilities involved, to the availability of aftercare, and to adequate provision for any complication or emergency that might arise. The prevalence of high mortality rates at illegal "abortion mills" strengthens, rather than weakens, the State's interest in regulating the conditions under which abortions are performed. Moreover, the risk to the woman increases as her pregnancy continues. Thus the State retains a definite interest in protecting the woman's own health and safety when an abortion is proposed at a late stage of pregnancy.

The third reason is the State's interest—some phrase it in terms of duty—in protecting prenatal life. Some of the argument for this justification rests on the theory that a new human life is present from the moment of conception. The State's interest and general obligation to protect life then extends, it is argued, to prenatal life. Only when the life of the pregnant mother herself is at stake, balanced

against the life she carries within her, should the interest of the embryo or fetus not prevail. Logically, of course, a legitimate state interest in this area need not stand or fall on acceptance of the belief that life begins at conception or at some other point prior to live birth. In assessing the State's interest, recognition may be given to the less rigid claim that as long as at least *potential* life is involved, the State may assert interests beyond the protection of the pregnant woman alone.

Parties challenging state abortion laws have sharply disputed in some courts the contention that a purpose of these laws, when enacted, was to protect prenatal life. . . . There is some scholarly support for this view of original purpose. The few state courts called upon to interpret their laws in the nineteenth and early twentieth centuries did focus on the State's interest in protecting the woman's health rather than in preserving the embryo and fetus. . . .

The Constitution does not explicitly mention any right of privacy. In a line of decisions, however, . . . the Court has recognized that a right of personal privacy, or a guarantee of certain areas or zones of privacy, does exist under the Constitution. . . .

This right of privacy, whether it be founded in the Fourteenth Amendment's concept of personal liberty and restrictions upon state action, as we feel it is, or, as the District Court determined, in the Ninth Amendment's reservation of rights to the people, is broad enough to encompass a woman's decision whether or not to terminate her pregnancy. The detriment that the State would impose upon the pregnant woman by denying this choice altogether is apparent. Specific and direct harm medically diagnosable even in early pregnancy may be involved. Maternity, or additional offspring, may force upon the woman a distressful life and future. Psychological harm may be imminent. Mental and physical health may be taxed by child care. There is also the distress, for all concerned, associated with the unwanted child, and there is the problem of bringing a child into a family already unable, psychologically and otherwise, to care for it. In other cases, as in this one, the additional difficulties and continuing stigma of unwed motherhood may be involved. All these are factors the woman and her responsible physician necessarily will consider in consultation.

On the basis of elements such as these, appellants and some *amici* argue that the woman's right is absolute and that she is entitled to terminate her pregnancy at whatever time, in whatever way, and for whatever reason she alone chooses. With this we do not agree. Appellant's arguments that Texas either has no valid interest at all in regulating the abortion decision, or no interest strong enough to support any limitation upon the woman's sole determination, is unpersuasive. The Court's decisions recognizing a right of privacy also acknowledge that some state regulation in areas protected by that right is appropriate. As noted above, a state may properly assert important interests in safeguarding health, in maintaining medical standards, and in protecting potential life. At some point in pregnancy, these respective interests become sufficiently compelling to sustain regulation of the factors that govern the abortion decision. The privacy right involved, therefore, cannot be said to be absolute. In fact, it is not clear to us that the claim asserted by some *amici* that one has an unlimited right to do with one's body as one pleases bears a close relationship to the right of privacy previously articulated in the Court's decisions. . . .

Where certain "fundamental rights" are involved, the Court has held that regulation limiting these rights may be justified only by a "compelling state interest," . . . and that legislative enactments must be narrowly drawn to express only the legitimate state interests at stake. . . .

A. The appellee and certain *amici* argue that the fetus is a "person" within the language and meaning of the Fourteenth Amendment. In support of this they outline at length and in detail the well-known facts of fetal development. If this suggestion of personhood is established, the appellant's case, of course, collapses, for the fetus' right to life is then guaranteed specifically by the Amendment.

The appellant conceded as much on reargument. On the other hand, the appellee conceded on reargument that no case should be cited that holds that a fetus is a person within the meaning of the Fourteenth Amendment.

The Constitution does not define "person" in so many words. . . . But in nearly all these instances, the use of the word is such that it has application only postnatally. None indicates with any assurance that it has any possible pre-natal application.[1]

All this, together with our observation, *supra,* that throughout the major portion of the nineteenth century prevailing legal abortion practices were far freer than they are today, persuades us that the word "person," as used in the Fourteenth Amendment, does not include the unborn. . . .

This conclusion, however, does not of itself fully answer the contentions raised by Texas, and we pass on to other considerations.

B. The pregnant woman cannot be isolated in her privacy. She carries an embryo and, later, a fetus, if one accepts the medical definitions of the developing young in the human uterus. . . .

Texas urges that, apart from the Fourteenth Amendment, life begins at conception and is present throughout pregnancy, and that, therefore, the State has a compelling interest in protecting that life from and after conception. We need not resolve the difficult question of when life begins. When those trained in the respective disciplines of medicine, philosophy, and theology are unable to arrive at any consensus, the judiciary, at this point in the development of man's knowledge, is not in a position to speculate as to the answer.

It should be sufficient to note briefly the wide divergence of thinking on this most sensitive and difficult question. There has always been strong support for the view that life does not begin until live birth. This was the belief of the Stoics. It appears to be the predominant, though not the unanimous, attitude of the Jewish faith. It may be taken to represent also the position of a large segment of the Protestant community, insofar as that can be ascertained; organized groups that have taken a formal position on the abortion issue have generally regarded abortion as a matter for the conscience of the individual and her family. As we have noted, the common law found greater significance in quickening. Physicians and their scientific colleagues have regarded that event with less interest and have tended to focus either upon conception or upon live birth or upon the interim point at which the fetus becomes "viable," that is, potentially able to live outside the mother's womb, albeit with artificial aid. Viability is usually placed at about seven months (28 weeks) but may occur earlier, even at 24 weeks. The Aristotelian theory of "mediate animation," that held sway throughout the Middle Ages and the Renaissance in Europe, continued to be official Roman Catholic dogma until the nineteenth century, despite opposition to this "ensoulment" theory from those in the Church who would recognize the existence of life from the moment of conception. The latter is now, of course, the official belief of the Catholic Church. As one of the briefs *amicus* discloses, this is a view strongly held by many non-Catholics as well, and by many physicians. Substantial problems for precise definition of this view are posed, however, by new embryological data that purport to indicate that conception is a "process" over time, rather than an event, and by new medical techniques such as menstrual extraction, the "morning-after" pill, implantation of embryos, artificial insemination, and even artificial wombs.

In areas other than criminal abortion the law has been reluctant to endorse any theory that life, as we recognize it, begins before live birth or to accord legal rights to the unborn except in narrowly defined situations and except when the rights are contingent upon live birth. For example, the traditional rule of tort law had denied recovery for prenatal injuries even though the child was born alive. That rule has been changed in almost every jurisdiction. In most States recovery is said to be permitted only if the fetus was viable, or at least quick, when the injuries were sustained, though few courts have squarely so held. . . . [U]nborn children have been recognized as acquiring rights or interests by way of inheritance or other devolution of property, and have been represented by guardians. . . .

In view of all this, we do not agree that, by adopting one theory of life, Texas may override the rights of the pregnant woman that are at stake. We repeat, however, that the State does have an important and legitimate interest in preserving and protecting the health of the pregnant woman, whether she be a resident of the State or a non-resident who seeks medical consultation and treatment there, and that it has still another important and legitimate interest in protecting the potentiality of human life. These interests are separate and distinct. Each grows in substantiality as the woman approaches term and, at a point during pregnancy, each becomes "compelling."

With respect to the State's important and legitimate interest in the health of the mother, the "compelling" point, in the light of present medical knowledge, is at approximately the end of the first trimester. This is so because of the now established medical fact, referred to above, that until the end of the first trimester mortality in abortion is less than mortality in normal childbirth. It follows that, from and after this point, a State may regulate the abortion procedure to the extent that the regulation reasonably relates to the preservation and protection of maternal health. Examples of permissible state regulation in this area are requirements as to the qualifications of the person who is to perform the abortion; as to the licensure of that person; as to the facility in which the procedure is to be performed, that is, whether it must be a hospital or may be a clinic or some other place of less-than-hospital status; as to the licensing of the facility; and the like.

This means, on the other hand, that, for the period of pregnancy prior to this "compelling" point, the attending physician, in consultation with his patient, is free to determine, without regulation by the State, that in his medical judgment the patient's pregnancy should be terminated. If that decision is reached, the judgment may be effectuated by an abortion free of interference by the State.

With respect to the State's important and legitimate interest in potential life, the "compelling" point is at viability. This is so because the fetus then presumably has the capability of meaningful life outside the mother's womb. State regulation protective of fetal life after viability thus has both logical and biological justifications. If the State is interested in protecting fetal life after viability, it may go so far as to proscribe abortion during that period except when it is necessary to preserve the life or health of the mother.

Measured against these standards, Art. 1196 of the Texas Penal Code, in restricting legal abortions to those "procured or attempted by medical advice for the purpose of saving the life of the mother," sweeps too broadly. The statute makes no distinction between abortions performed early in pregnancy and those performed later, and it limits to a single reason, "saving" the mother's life, the legal justification for the procedure. The statute, therefore, cannot survive the constitutional attack made upon it here.

Mr. Justice White, . . . Dissenting: At the heart of the controversy in these cases are those recurring pregnancies that pose no danger whatsoever to the life or health of the mother but are nevertheless unwanted for any one or more of a variety of reasons—convenience, family planning, economics, dislike of children, the embarrassment of illegitimacy, etc. The common claim before us is that for any one of such reasons, or for no reason at all, and without asserting or claiming any threat to life or health, any woman is entitled to an abortion at her request if she is able to find a medical advisor willing to undertake the procedure.

The Court for the most part sustains this position: During the period prior to the time the fetus becomes viable, the Constitution of the United States values the convenience, whim or caprice of the putative mother more than the life or potential life of the fetus; the Constitution, therefore, guarantees the right to an abortion as against any state law or policy seeking to protect the fetus from an abortion not prompted by more compelling reasons of the mother.

With all due respect, I dissent. I find nothing in the language or history of the Constitution to support the Court's judgment. The Court simply fashions and announces a new constitutional right for pregnant mothers and, with scarcely any reason or authority for its action, invests that right with sufficient substance to override most existing state abortion statutes. The upshot is that the people and the legislatures of the 50 States are constitutionally disentitled to weigh the relative importance of the continued existence and development of the fetus on the one hand against a spectrum of possible impacts on the mother on the other hand. As an exercise of raw judicial power, the Court perhaps has authority to do what it does today; but in my view its judgment is an improvident and extravagant exercise of the power of judicial review which the Constitution extends to this Court.

The Court apparently values the convenience of the pregnant mother more than the continued existence and development of the life or potential life which she carries. Whether or not I might agree with that marshalling of values, I can in no event join the Court's judgment because I find no constitutional warrant for imposing such an order of priorities on the people and legislatures of the States. In a sensitive area such as this, involving as it does issues over which reasonable men may easily and heatedly differ, I cannot accept the Court's exercise of its clear power of choice by interposing a constitutional barrier to state efforts to protect human life and by investing mothers and doctors with the constitutionally protected right to exterminate it. This issue, for the most part, should be left with the people and to the political processes the people have devised to govern their affairs.

It is my view, therefore, that the Texas statute is not constitutionally infirm because it denies abortions to those who seek to serve only their convenience rather than to protect their life or health. . . .

NOTE

1. When Texas urges that a fetus is entitled to Fourteenth Amendment protection as a person, it faces a dilemma. Neither in Texas nor in any other State are all abortions prohibited. Despite broad proscription, an exception always exists. The exception contained in Art. 1196, for an abortion procured or attempted by medical advice for the purpose of saving the life of the mother, is typical. But if the fetus is a person who is not to be deprived of life without due process of law, and if the mother's condition is the sole determinant, does not the Texas exception appear to be out of line with the Amendment's command?

   There are other inconsistencies between Fourteenth Amendment status and the typical abortion statute. It has already been pointed out that in Texas the woman is not a principal or an accomplice with respect to an abortion upon her. If the fetus is a person, why is the woman not a principal or an accomplice? Further, the penalty for criminal abortion specified by Art. 1195 is significantly less than the maximum penalty for murder prescribed by Art. 1257 of the Texas Penal Code. If the fetus is a person, may the penalties be different?

REVIEW AND DISCUSSION QUESTIONS

1. According to Justice Blackmun, what have been the state's reasons for preventing abortion?
2. Why does the Court reject the view that a fetus is a "person" within the meaning of the Constitution?
3. Explain the "trimester" approach taken by Justice Blackmun in this case.
4. On what basis does Justice White dissent?
5. Does Blackmun's majority opinion successfully avoid the issue of the moral status of a fetus, as he suggests? Explain.

A Defense of Abortion

Judith Jarvis Thomson

It has seemed to many people that abortion obviously involves taking the life of an innocent human being. At conception, it is claimed, life is started, and it is undeniably human since it has a human genetic code. Indeed, each of us could trace our own development to such a point. Nor can it be doubted that the organism living inside the mother is alive, just like every other cell in the body. Only this one, it is argued, is different, because if left alone it will likely develop to the point of birth and childhood. Finally, the argument concludes, there is nothing else that occurs after conception that could possibly justify saying that before it occurred the human organism could be killed but not afterward. Birth, for example, amounts to no more than a change of location and the start of respiration and digestion, and neither location nor being on one's own respirative and digestive systems is necessary to be a living person, as we know from visiting any hospital. Viability, similarly, means nothing more than that the fetus is developed enough to survive on its own systems—a fact that we know from seeing others who depend on such systems is not the test for a being's status as a living human being. So only conception (the argument concludes) provides a morally significant point in

Thomson, Judith Jarvis, "A Defense of Abortion," *Philosophy and Public Affairs,* 1, no. 1 (1971), 47–66. © 1971 by Princeton University Press. Reprinted by permission of Princeton University Press. Section titles added.

the continuous development of a person. And since abortion involves killing such a person, it is impermissible. This article, one of the best known in recent philosophical writing, is an attempt to answer this argument while leaving intact the claim that the fetus is a person. Employing an ingenious set of analogies, including one about a kidnapped violinist, Thomson argues that even assuming the fetus is a living person, a mother's right to her body allows her to get an abortion in all but the most extreme circumstances. Judith Jarvis Thomson is professor of philosophy at Massachusetts Institute of Technology.

Most opposition to abortion relies on the premise that the fetus is a human being, a person, from the moment of conception. The premise is argued for, but, as I think, not well. Take, for example, the most common argument. We are asked to notice that the development of a human being from conception through birth into childhood is continuous; then it is said that to draw a line, to choose a point in this development and say "before this point the thing is not a person, after this point it is a person" is to make an arbitrary choice, a choice for which in the nature of things no good reason can be given. It is concluded that the fetus is, or anyway that we had better say it is, a person from the moment of conception. But this conclusion does not follow. Similar things might be said about the development of an acorn into an oak tree, and it does not follow that acorns are oak trees, or that we had better say they are. Arguments of this form are sometimes called "slippery slope arguments"—the phrase is perhaps self-explanatory—and it is dismaying that opponents of abortion rely on them so heavily and uncritically.

I am inclined to agree, however, that the prospects for "drawing a line" in the development of the fetus look dim. I am inclined to think also that we shall probably have to agree that the fetus has already become a human person well before birth. Indeed, it comes as a surprise when one first learns how early in its life it begins to acquire human characteristics. By the tenth week, for example, it already has a face, arms and legs, fingers and toes; it has internal organs, and brain activity is detectable. On the other hand, I think that the premise is false, that the fetus is not a person from the moment of conception. A newly fertilized ovum, a newly implanted clump of cells, is no more a person than an acorn is an oak tree. But I shall not discuss any of this. For it seems to me to be of great interest to ask what happens if, for the sake of argument, we allow the premise. How, precisely, are we supposed to get from there to the conclusion that abortion is morally impermissible? Opponents of abortion commonly spend most of their time establishing that the fetus is a person, and hardly any time explaining the step from there to the impermissibility of abortion. Perhaps they think the step too simple and obvious to require much comment. Or perhaps instead they are simply being economical in argument. Many of those who defend abortion rely on the premise that the fetus is not a person, but only a bit of tissue that will become a person at birth; and why pay out more arguments than you have to? Whatever the explanation, I suggest that the step they take is neither easy nor obvious, that it calls for closer examination than it is commonly given, and that when we do give it this closer examination we shall feel inclined to reject it.

I propose, then, that we grant that the fetus is a person from the moment of conception. How does the argument go from here? Something like this, I take it. Every person has a right to life. So the fetus has a right to life. No doubt the mother has a right to decide what shall happen in and to her body; everyone would grant that. But surely a person's right to life is stronger and more stringent than the mother's right to decide what happens in and to her body, and so outweighs it. So the fetus may not be killed; an abortion may not be performed.

It sounds plausible. But now let me ask you to imagine this. You wake up in the morning and find yourself back to back in bed with an unconscious violinist. A famous unconscious violinist. He has been found to have a fatal kidney ailment, and the Society of Music Lovers has canvassed all the available medical records and found that you alone have the right blood type to help. They have therefore kidnapped you, and last night the violinist's circulatory system was plugged into yours, so that your kidneys can be used to extract poisons from his blood as well as your own. The director of the hospital now tells you, "Look, we're sorry the Society of Music Lovers did this to you—we would never have permitted it if we had known. But still, they did it, and the violinist now is plugged into you. To unplug you would be to kill him. But never mind, it's only for nine months. By then he will have recovered from his ailment, and can safely be unplugged from you." Is it morally incumbent on you to accede to this situation? No doubt it would be very nice of you if you did, a great kindness. But do you have to accede to it? What if it were not nine months, but nine years? Or longer still? What if the director of the hospital says, "Tough luck, I agree, but you've now got to stay in bed, with the violinist plugged into you, for the rest of your life. Because remember this. All persons have a right to life, and violinists are persons. Granted you have a right to decide what happens in and to your body, but a person's right to life outweighs your right to decide what happens in and to your body. So you cannot ever be unplugged from him." I imagine you would regard this as outrageous, which suggests that something really is wrong with that plausible-sounding argument I mentioned a moment ago.

In this case, of course, you were kidnapped; you didn't volunteer for the operation that plugged the violinist into your kidneys. Can those who oppose abortion on the ground I mentioned make an exception for a pregnancy due to rape? Certainly. They can say that persons have a right to life only if they didn't come into existence because of rape; or they can say that all persons have a right to life, but that some have less of a right to life than others, in particular, that

those who come into existence because of rape have less. But these statements have a rather unpleasant sound. Surely the question of whether you have a right to life at all, or how much of it you have, shouldn't turn on the question of whether or not you are the product of a rape. And in fact the people who oppose abortion on the ground I mentioned do not make this distinction, and hence do not make an exception in case of rape.

Nor do they make an exception for a case in which the mother has to spend the nine months of her pregnancy in bed. They would agree that would be a great pity, and hard on the mother; but all the same, all persons have a right to life, the fetus is a person, and so on. I suspect, in fact, that they would not make an exception for a case in which, miraculously enough, the pregnancy went on for nine years, or even the rest of the mother's life.

Some won't even make an exception for a case in which continuation of the pregnancy is likely to shorten the mother's life; they regard abortion as impermissible even to save the mother's life. Such cases are nowadays very rare, and many opponents of abortion do not accept this extreme view. All the same, it is a good place to begin: a number of points of interest come out in respect to it.

1. THE EXTREME ANTI-ABORTION VIEW

Let us call the view that abortion is impermissible even to save the mother's life "the extreme view." I want to suggest first that it does not issue from the argument I mentioned earlier without the addition of some fairly powerful premises. Suppose a woman has become pregnant, and now learns that she has a cardiac condition such that she will die if she carries the baby to term. What may be done for her? The fetus, being a person, has a right to life, but as the mother is a person too, so has she a right to life. Presumably they have an equal right to life. How is it supposed to come out that an abortion may not be performed? If mother and child have an equal right to life, shouldn't we perhaps flip a coin?

Or should we add to the mother's right to life her right to decide what happens in and to her body, which everybody seems to be ready to grant—the sum of her rights now outweighing the fetus' right to life?

The most familiar argument here is the following. We are told that performing the abortion would be directly killing the child, whereas doing nothing would not be killing the mother, but only letting her die. Moreover, in killing the child, one would be killing an innocent person, for the child has committed no crime, and is not aiming at his mother's death. . . . If directly killing an innocent person is murder, and thus is impermissible, then the mother's directly killing the innocent person inside her is murder, and thus is impermissible. But it cannot seriously be thought to be murder if the mother performs an abortion on herself to save her life. It cannot seriously be said that she must refrain, that she *must* sit passively by and wait for her death. Let us look again at the case of you and the violinist. There you are, in bed with the violinist, and the director of the hospital says to you, "It's all most distressing, and I deeply sympathize, but you see this is putting an additional strain on your kidneys, and you'll be dead within the month. But you *have* to stay where you are all the same. Because unplugging you would be directly killing an innocent violinist, and that's murder, and that's impermissible." If anything in the world is true, it is that you do not commit murder, you do not do what is impermissible, if you reach around to your back and unplug yourself from that violinist to save your life.

The main focus of attention in writings on abortion has been on what a third party may or may not do in answer to a request from a woman for an abortion. This is in a way understandable. Things being as they are, there isn't much a woman can safely do to abort herself. So the question asked is what a third party may do, and what the mother may do, if it is mentioned at all, is deduced, almost as an afterthought, from what it is concluded that third parties may do. But it seems to me that to treat the matter in this way is to refuse to grant to the mother that very status of person which is so firmly insisted on for the fetus. For we cannot simply read off what a person may do from what a third party may do. Suppose you find yourself trapped in a tiny house with a growing child. I mean a very tiny house, and a rapidly growing child—you are already up against the wall of the house and in a few minutes you'll be crushed to death. The child on the other hand won't be crushed to death; if nothing is done to stop him from growing he'll be hurt, but in the end he'll simply burst open the house and walk out a free man. Now I could well understand it if a bystander were to say, "There's nothing we can do for you. We cannot choose between your life and his, we cannot be the ones to decide who is to live, we cannot intervene." But it cannot be concluded that you too can do nothing, that you cannot attack it to save your life. However innocent the child may be, you do not have to wait passively while it crushes you to death. Perhaps a pregnant woman is vaguely felt to have the status of [a] house, to which we don't allow the right of self-defense. But if the woman houses the child, it should be remembered that she is a person who houses it.

I should perhaps stop to say explicitly that I am not claiming that people have a right to do anything whatever to save their lives. I think, rather, that there are drastic limits to the right of self-defense. If someone threatens you with death unless you torture someone else to death, I think you have not the right, even to save your life, to do so. But the case under consideration here is very different. In our case there are only two people involved, one whose life is threatened, and one who threatens it. Both are innocent: the one who is threatened is not threatened because of any fault, the one who threatens does not threaten because of any fault. For this reason we may feel that we bystanders cannot intervene. But the person threatened can.

In sum, a woman surely can defend her life against the threat to it posed by the unborn child, even if doing so involves its death. And this shows that the extreme view of abortion is false, and so we need not canvass any other possible ways of arriving at it from the argument I mentioned at the outset.

The extreme view could of course be weakened to say that while abortion is permissible to save the mother's life, it may not be performed by a third party, but only by the mother herself. But this cannot be right either. For what we have to keep in mind is that the mother and the unborn child are not like two tenants in a small house which has, by an unfortunate mistake, been rented to both: the mother owns the house. The fact that she does adds to the offensiveness of deducing that the mother can do nothing from the supposition that third parties can do nothing. But it does more than this: it casts a bright light on the supposition that third parties can do nothing. Certainly it lets us see that a third party who says "I cannot choose between you" is fooling himself if he thinks this is impartiality. If Jones has found and fastened on a certain coat, which he needs to keep from freezing, but which Smith also needs to keep him from freezing, then it is not impartiality that says "I cannot choose between you" when Smith owns the coat. Women have said again and again, "This body is my body!" and they have reason to feel angry, reason to feel that it has been like shouting into the wind. Smith, after all, is hardly likely to bless us if we say to him, "Of course it's your coat, anybody would grant that it is. But no one may choose between you and Jones who is to have it."

We should really ask what it is that says "no one may choose" in the face of the fact that the body that houses the child is the mother's body. It may be simply a failure to appreciate this fact. But it may be something more interesting, namely the sense that one has a right to refuse to lay hands on people, even where it would be just and fair to do so, even where justice seems to require that somebody do so. Thus justice might call for somebody to get Smith's coat back from Jones, and yet you have a right to refuse to be the one to lay hands on Jones, a right to refuse to do physical violence to him. This, I think, must be granted. But then what should be said

is not "no one may choose," but only "I cannot choose," and indeed not even this, but "I will not act," leaving it open that somebody else can or should, and in particular that anyone in a position of authority, with the job of securing people's rights, both can and should. So this is no difficulty. I have not been arguing that any given third party must accede to the mother's request that he perform an abortion to save her life, but only that he may. . . .

2. THE RIGHT TO LIFE

Where the mother's life is not at stake, the argument I mentioned at the outset seems to have a much stronger pull. "Everyone has a right to life, so the unborn person has a right to life." And isn't the child's right to life weightier than anything other than the mother's own right to life, which she might put forward as ground for an abortion?

This argument treats the right to life as if it were unproblematic. It is not, and this seems to me to be precisely the source of the mistake.

For we should now, at long last, ask what it comes to, to have a right to life. In some views having a right to life includes having a right to be given at least the bare minimum one needs for continued life. But suppose that what in fact is the bare minimum a man needs for continued life is something he has no right at all to be given? If I am sick unto death, and the only thing that will save my life is the touch of Henry Fonda's cool hand on my fevered brow, then all the same, I have no right to be given the touch of Henry Fonda's cool hand on my fevered brow. It would be frightfully nice of him to fly in from the West Coast to provide it. It would be less nice, though no doubt well meaning, if my friends flew out to the West Coast and carried Henry Fonda back with them. But I have no right at all against anybody that he should do this for me. Or again, to return to the story I told earlier, the fact that for continued life that violinist needs the continued use of your kidneys does not establish that he has a right to be given the continued use of your kidneys. He certainly has no right against you that you should give him continued use of your kidneys. For nobody has any right to use your kidneys unless you give him such a right; and nobody has the right against you that you shall give him this right—if you do allow him to go on using your kidneys, this is a kindness on your part, and not something he can claim from you as his due. Nor has he any right against anybody else that *they* should give him continued use of your kidneys. Certainly he had no right against the Society of Music Lovers that they should plug him into you in the first place. And if you now start to unplug yourself, having learned that you will otherwise have to spend nine years in bed with him, there is nobody in the world who must try to prevent you, in order to see to it that he is given something he has a right to be given.

Some people are rather stricter about the right to life. In their view, it does not include the right to be given anything, but amounts to, and only to, the right not to be killed by anybody. But here a related difficulty arises. If everybody is to refrain from killing that violinist, then everybody must refrain from doing a great many different sorts of things. Everybody must refrain from slitting his throat, everybody must refrain from shooting him—and everybody must refrain from unplugging you from him. But does he have a right against everybody that they shall refrain from unplugging you from him? To refrain from doing this is to allow him to continue to use your kidneys. It could be argued that he has a right against us that we should allow him to continue to use your kidneys. That is, while he had no right against us that we should give him the use of your kidneys, it might be argued that he anyway has a right against us that we shall not now intervene and deprive him of the use of your kidneys. I shall come back to third-party interventions later. But certainly the violinist has no right against you that you shall allow him to continue to use your kidneys. As I said, if you do allow him to use them, it is a kindness on your part, and not something you owe him. . . .

3. THE RIGHT TO USE THE MOTHER'S BODY

There is another way to bring out the difficulty. In the most ordinary sort of case, to deprive someone of what he has a right to is to treat him unjustly. Suppose a boy and his small brother are jointly given a box of chocolates for Christmas. If the older boy takes the box and refuses to give his brother any of the chocolates, he is unjust to him, for the brother has been given a right to half of them. But suppose that, having learned that otherwise it means nine years in bed with that violinist, you unplug yourself from him. You surely are not being unjust to him for you gave him no right to use your kidneys, and no one else can have given him any such right. But we have to notice that in unplugging yourself, you are killing him; and violinists, like everybody else, have a right to life, and thus in the view we were considering just now, the right not to be killed. So here you do what he supposedly has a right you shall not do, but you do not act unjustly to him in doing it.

The emendation which may be made at this point is this: the right to life consists not in the right not to be killed, but rather in the right not to be killed unjustly. This runs a risk of circularity, but never mind; it would enable us to square the fact that the violinist has a right to life with the fact that you do not act unjustly toward him in unplugging yourself, thereby killing him. For if you do not kill him unjustly, you do not violate his right to life, and so it is no wonder you do him no injustice.

But if this emendation is accepted, the gap in the argument against abortion stares us plainly in the face: it is by no means enough to show that the fetus is a person, and to remind us that all persons have a right to life—we need to be shown also that killing the fetus violates its right to life, i.e., that abortion is unjust killing. And is it?

I suppose we may take it as a datum that in a case of pregnancy due to rape the mother has not given the unborn person a right to the use of her body for food and shelter. Indeed, in what pregnancy could it be supposed that the mother has given the unborn person such a right? It is not as if there were unborn persons drifting about the world, to whom a woman who wants a child says, "I invite you in."

But it might be argued that there are other ways one can have acquired a right to the use of another person's body than by having been invited to use it by that person. Suppose a woman voluntarily indulges in intercourse, knowing of the chance it will issue in pregnancy, and then she does become pregnant; is she not in part responsible for the presence, in fact the very existence, of the unborn person inside her? No doubt she did not invite it in. But doesn't her partial responsibility for its being there itself give it a right to the use of her body? If so, then her aborting it would be more like the boy's taking away the chocolates, and less like your unplugging yourself from the violinist—doing so would be depriving it of what it does have a right to, and thus would be doing it an injustice.

And then, too, it might be asked whether or not she can kill it even to save her own life: If she voluntarily called it into existence, how can she now kill it, even in self-defense?

The first thing to be said about this is that it is something new. Opponents of abortion have been so concerned to make out the independence of the fetus, in order to establish that it has a right to life, just as its mother does, that they have tended to overlook the possible support they might gain from making out that the fetus is *dependent* on the mother, in order to establish that she has a special kind of responsibility for it, a responsibility that gives it rights against her which are not possessed by any independent person—such as an ailing violinist who is a stranger to her.

On the other hand, this argument would give the unborn person a right to its mother's body only if her pregnancy resulted from a voluntary act, undertaken in full knowledge of the chance a pregnancy might result from it. It would leave out entirely the unborn person whose existence is due to rape. Pending the availability of some further argument, then, we would be left with the conclusion that unborn persons whose existence is due to rape have no right to the use

of their mothers' bodies, and thus that aborting them is not depriving them of anything they have a right to and hence is not unjust killing.

And we should also notice that it is not at all plain that this argument really does go even as far as it purports to. For there are cases and cases, and the details make a difference. If the room is stuffy, and I therefore open a window to air it, and a burglar climbs in, it would be absurd to say, "Ah, now he can stay, she's given him a right to the use of her house—for she is partially responsible for his presence there, having voluntarily done what enabled him to get in, in full knowledge that there are such things as burglars, and that burglars burgle." It would be still more absurd to say this if I had had bars installed outside my windows, precisely to prevent burglars from getting in, and a burglar got in only because of a defect in the bars. It remains equally absurd if we imagine it is not a burglar who climbs in, but an innocent person who blunders or falls in. Again, suppose it were like this: people-seeds drift about in the air like pollen, and if you open your windows, one may drift in and take root in your carpets or upholstery. You don't want children, so you fix up your windows with fine mesh screens, the very best you can buy. As can happen, however, and on very, very rare occasions does happen, one of the screens is defective; and a seed drifts in and takes root. Does the person-plant who now develops have a right to the use of your house? Surely not—despite the fact that you voluntarily opened your windows, you knowingly kept carpets and upholstered furniture, and you knew that screens were sometimes defective. Someone may argue that you are responsible for its rooting, that it does have a right to your house, because after all you could have lived out your life with bare floors and furniture, or with sealed windows and doors. But this won't do—for by the same token anyone can avoid a pregnancy due to rape by having a hysterectomy, or anyway by never leaving home without a (reliable!) army.

It seems to me that the argument we are looking at can establish at most that there are some cases in which the unborn person has a right to the use of its mother's body, and therefore some cases in which abortion is unjust killing. There is room for much discussion and argument as to precisely which, if any. But I think we should sidestep this issue and leave it open, for at any rate the argument certainly does not establish that all abortion is unjust killing.

4. RIGHTS AND THEIR LIMITS

There is room for yet another argument here, however. We surely must all grant that there may be cases in which it would be morally indecent to detach a person from your body at the cost of his life. Suppose you learn that what the violinist needs is not nine years of your life, but only one hour: all you need do to save his life is to spend one hour in that bed with him. Suppose also that letting him use your kidneys for that one hour would not affect your health in the slightest. Admittedly you were kidnapped. Admittedly you did not give anyone permission to plug him into you. Nevertheless it seems to me plain you *ought* to allow him to use your kidneys for that hour—it would be indecent to refuse.

Again, suppose pregnancy lasted only an hour, and constituted no threat to life or health. And suppose that a woman becomes pregnant as a result of rape. Admittedly she did not voluntarily do anything to bring about the existence of a child. Admittedly she did nothing at all which would give the unborn person a right to the use of her body. All the same it might well be said, as in the newly emended violinist story, that she *ought* to allow it to remain for that hour—that it would be indecent for her to refuse. . . .

Suppose that the box of chocolates I mentioned earlier was given only to the older boy. There he sits, stolidly eating his way through the box, his small brother watching enviously. Here we are likely to say "You ought not to be so mean. You ought to give your brother some of those chocolates." My own view is that it just does not follow from the truth of this that the brother has any right to any of the chocolates. If the boy refuses to give his brother any, he is greedy, stingy, callous—but not unjust. . . . Take the case of Henry Fonda again. I said earlier that I had no right to the touch of his cool hand on my fevered brow, even though I needed it to save my life. I said it would be frightfully nice of him to fly in from the West Coast to provide me with it, but that I had no right against him that he should do so. But suppose he isn't on the West Coast. Suppose he has only to walk across the room, place a hand briefly on my brow—and lo, my life is saved. Then surely he *ought* to do it, it would be indecent to refuse. . . .

So my own view is that even though you ought to let the violinist use your kidneys for the one hour he needs, we should not conclude that he has a right to do so—we would say that if you refuse, you are, like the boy who owns all the chocolates and will give none away, self-centered and callous, indecent in fact, but not unjust. And similarly, that even supposing a case in which a woman pregnant due to rape ought to allow the unborn person to use her body for the hour he needs, we should not conclude that he has a right to do so; we should conclude that she is self-centered, callous, indecent, but not unjust, if she refuses. The complaints are no less grave; they are just different. . . . And so it is for the mother and unborn child. Except in such cases as the unborn person has a right to demand it—and we are leaving open the possibility that there may be such cases—nobody is morally *required* to make large sacrifices, of health, of all other interests and concerns, of all other duties and commitments, for nine years, or even for nine months, in order to keep a person alive.

5. THE GOOD SAMARITAN AND THE RESPONSIBILITIES OF PARENTS

We have in fact to distinguish between two kinds of Samaritan: the Good Samaritan and what we might call the Minimally Decent Samaritan. . . . The Good Samaritan went out of his way, at some cost to himself, to help one in need of it. . . . These things are a matter of degree, of course, but there is a difference, and it comes out perhaps most clearly in the story of Kitty Genovese, who, as you will remember, was murdered while thirty-eight people watched or listened, and did nothing at all to help her. A Good Samaritan would have rushed out to give direct assistance against the murderer. Or perhaps we had better allow that it would have been a Splendid Samaritan who did this, on the ground that it would have involved a risk of death for himself. But the thirty-eight not only did not do this, they did not even trouble to pick up a phone to call the police. Minimally Decent Samaritanism would call for doing at least that, and their not having done it was monstrous. . . . It seems plain that it was not morally required of any of the thirty-eight that he rush out to give direct assistance at the risk of his own life, and that it is not morally required of anyone that he give long stretches of his life—nine years or nine months—to sustain the life of a person who has no special right (we were leaving open the possibility of this) to demand it. . . .

What we should ask is not whether anybody should be compelled by law to be a Good Samaritan, but whether we must accede to a situation in which somebody is being compelled—by nature, perhaps—to be a Good Samaritan. . . . There you are, you were kidnapped, and nine years in bed with that violinist lie ahead of you. You have your own life to lead. You are sorry, but you simply cannot see giving up so much of your life to the sustaining of his. You cannot extricate yourself, and ask us to do so. I should have thought that—in light of his having no right to the use of your body—it was obvious that we do not have to accede to your being forced to give up so much. We can do what you ask. There is no injustice to the violinist in our doing so. . . .

It may be said that what is important is not merely the fact that the fetus is a person, but that it is a person for whom the woman has a special kind of responsibility issuing from the fact that she is its mother. . . . Surely we do not have any such "special responsibility" for a person unless we have assumed it, explicitly or implicitly. If a set of parents do not try to prevent pregnancy, do not obtain an abortion, but rather take it home with them, then they have assumed responsibility for it, and have given it rights, and they cannot *now* withdraw support from it at the cost of its life because they now find it difficult to go on providing for it. But if they have taken all reasonable precautions against having a child, they do not simply by virtue of their biological relationship to the child who comes into existence have a special responsibility for it. . . .

I have argued that you are not morally required to spend nine months in bed, sustaining the life of that violinist; but to say this is by no means to say that if, when you unplug yourself, there is a miracle and he survives, you then have a right to turn around and slit his throat. You may detach yourself even if this costs him his life; you have no right to be guaranteed his death, by some other means, if unplugging yourself does not kill him. There are some people who will feel dissatisfied by this feature of my argument. A woman may be utterly devastated by the thought of a child, a bit of herself, put out for adoption and never seen or heard of again. . . . All the same, I agree that the desire for the child's death is not one which anybody may gratify, should it turn out to be possible to detach a child alive.

At this place, however, it should be remembered that we have only been pretending throughout that the fetus is a human being from the moment of conception. A very early abortion is surely not the killing of a person, and so is not dealt with by anything I have said.

REVIEW AND DISCUSSION QUESTIONS

1. How does Thomson understand the right to life? Why shouldn't the fetus's having such a right prevent the mother from getting an abortion?
2. Suppose the violinist needed your kidneys for only five minutes. Does Thomson think you should allow him to use them? Why?

3. "Abortions almost always occur in cases in which the mother voluntarily had sex, so the violinist analogy doesn't apply." How does Thomson respond to this claim? Is her response adequate?

4. Suppose you found a baby in your mountain cabin just after the winter snows arrived. Should you now let it share your cabin (to which, let's assume, you have a right) for nine months if the only alternative is to put it outside to die? Is this situation a good analogy to abortion?

5. Is it important that it is her own child the mother kills, whereas the violinist is a stranger? Explain how Thomson understands this issue. Do you agree?

On the Moral and Legal Status of Abortion

Mary Anne Warren

In this essay, Mary Anne Warren begins by discussing Judith Jarvis Thomson's defense of abortion. Finding that defense inadequate, Warren concludes that the status of the fetus is of central importance in assessing abortion. Warren's approach rests on a fundamental distinction that, if she is correct, would undermine the traditional pro-life position that life begins at conception and that no other event after conception can carry the moral weight needed to say that before then killing is justified beyond those rare cases when both the mother and baby will die. It is crucial, according to Warren, to distinguish between a biological human being, on one hand, and a member of the "moral community" whose members enjoy full and equal moral rights, on the other. Merely being a member of the species *Homo sapiens* is not, she argues, sufficient to qualify as a moral person. Warren then goes on to discuss the circumstances in which a being should be regarded as having full moral rights; what, she asks, are the criteria for "personhood"? In the last sections of her paper, Warren explores some of the consequences of her theory. Even very late abortions do not take the life of a person, she contends, nor is it relevant that a (merely) potential person is killed in abortions since its rights cannot outweigh the rights of already existing women. Mary Anne Warren is professor of philosophy at San Francisco State University.

We will be concerned with both the moral status of abortion, which for our purposes we may define as the act which a woman performs in voluntarily terminating, or allowing another person to terminate, her pregnancy, and the legal status which is appropriate for this act. I will argue that, while it is not possible to produce a satisfactory defense of a woman's right to obtain an abortion without showing that a fetus is not a human being, in the morally relevant sense of that term, we ought not to conclude that the difficulties involved in determining whether or not a fetus is human make it impossible to produce any satisfactory solution to the problem of the moral status of abortion. For it is possible to show that, on the basis of intuitions which we may expect even the opponents of abortion to share, a fetus is not a person, and hence not the sort of entity to which it is proper to ascribe full moral rights.

Of course, while some philosophers would deny the possibility of any such proof,[1] others will deny that there is any need for it, since the moral permissibility of abortion appears to them to be too obvious to require proof. But

From *The Monist*, 1973. © 1973 *The Monist*, La Salle, IL 61301. Reprinted by permission.

the inadequacy of this attitude should be evident from the fact that both the friends and the foes of abortion consider their position to be morally self-evident. Because proabortionists have never adequately come to grips with the conceptual issues surrounding abortion, most if not all, of the arguments which they advance in opposition to laws restricting access to abortion fail to refute or even weaken the traditional antiabortion argument, i.e., that a fetus is a human being, and therefore abortion is murder.

These arguments are typically of one of two sorts. Either they point to the terrible side effects of the restrictive laws, e.g., the deaths due to illegal abortions, and the fact that it is poor women who suffer the most as a result of these laws, or else they state that to deny a woman access to abortion is to deprive her of her right to control her own body. Unfortunately, however, the fact that restricting access to abortion has tragic side effects does not, in itself, show that the restrictions are unjustified, since murder is wrong regardless of the consequences of prohibiting it; and the appeal to the right to control one's body, which is generally construed as a property right, is at best a rather feeble argument for the permissibility of abortion. Mere ownership does not give me the right to kill innocent people whom I find on my property, and indeed I am apt to be held responsible if such people injure themselves while on my property. It is equally unclear that I have any moral right to expel an innocent person from my property when I know that doing so will result in his death.

Furthermore, it is probably inappropriate to describe a woman's body as her property, since it seems natural to hold that a person is something distinct from her property, but not from her body. Even those who would object to the identification of a person with his body, or with the conjunction of his body and his mind, must admit that it would be very odd to describe, say, breaking a leg, as damaging one's property, and much more appropriate to describe it as injuring *oneself.* Thus it is probably a mistake to argue that the right to

obtain an abortion is in any way derived from the right to own and regulate property.

But however we wish to construe the right to abortion, we cannot hope to convince those who consider abortion a form of murder of the existence of any such right unless we are able to produce a clear and convincing refutation of the traditional antiabortion argument, and this has not, to my knowledge, been done. With respect to the two most vital issues which that argument involves, i.e., the humanity of the fetus and its implication for the moral status of abortion, confusion has prevailed on both sides of the dispute.

Thus, both proabortionists and antiabortionists have tended to abstract the question of whether abortion is wrong to that of whether it is wrong to destroy a fetus, just as though the rights of another person were not necessarily involved. This mistaken abstraction has led to the almost universal assumption that if a fetus is a human being, with a right to life, then it follows immediately that abortion is wrong (except perhaps when necessary to save the woman's life), and that it ought to be prohibited. It has also been generally assumed that unless the question about the status of the fetus is answered, the moral status of abortion cannot possibly be determined. . . .

The question which we must answer in order to produce a satisfactory solution to the problem of the moral status of abortion is this: How are we to define the moral community, the set of beings with full and equal moral rights, such that we can decide whether a human fetus is a member of this community or not? What sort of entity, exactly, has the inalienable rights to life, liberty, and the pursuit of happiness? Jefferson attributed these rights to all *men,* and it may or may not be fair to suggest that he intended to attribute them *only* to men. Perhaps he ought to have attributed them to all human beings. If so, then we arrive, first, at the problem of defining what makes a being human, and, second, at the equally vital question . . . namely, What reason is there for identifying the moral community with the set of all human beings, in whatever way we have chosen to define that term?

ON THE DEFINITION OF "HUMAN"

One reason why this vital second question is so frequently overlooked in the debate over the moral status of abortion is that the term "human" has two distinct, but not often distinguished, senses. This fact results in a slide of meaning, which serves to conceal the fallaciousness of the traditional argument that since (1) it is wrong to kill innocent human beings, and (2) fetuses are innocent human beings, then (3) it is wrong to kill fetuses. For if "human" is used in the same sense in both (1) and (2) then, whichever of the two senses is meant, one of these premises is question-begging. And if it is used in two different senses then of course the conclusion doesn't follow.

Thus, (1) is a self-evident moral truth,[2] and avoids begging the question about abortion, only if "human being" is used to mean something like "a full-fledged member of the moral community." (It may or may not also be meant to refer exclusively to members of the species *Homo sapiens.*) We may call this the *moral* sense of "human." It is not to be confused with what we will call the *genetic* sense, i.e., the sense in which *any* member of the species is a human being, and no member of any other species could be. If (1) is acceptable only if the moral sense is intended, (2) is non-question-begging only if what is intended is the genetic sense.

In "Deciding Who is Human," Noonan argues for the classification of fetuses with human beings by pointing to the presence of the full genetic code, and the potential capacity for rational thought.[3] It is clear that what he needs to show, for his version of the traditional argument to be valid, is that fetuses are human in the moral sense, the sense in which it is analytically true that all human beings have full moral rights. But, in the absence of any argument showing that whatever is genetically human is also morally human, and he gives none, nothing more than genetic humanity can be demonstrated by the presence of the human genetic code. And, as we will see, the *potential* capacity for rational thought can at most show that an entity has the potential for *becoming* human in the moral sense.

DEFINING THE MORAL COMMUNITY

Can it be established that genetic humanity is sufficient for moral humanity? I think that there are very good reasons for not defining the moral community in this way. I would like to suggest an alternative way of defining the moral community, which I will argue for only to the extent of explaining why it is, or should be, self-evident. The suggestion is simply that the moral community consists of all and only *people,* rather than all and only human beings;[4] and probably the best way of demonstrating its self-evidence is by considering the concept of personhood, to see what sorts of entity are and are not persons, and what the decision that a being is or is not a person implies about its moral rights.

What characteristics entitle an entity to be considered a person? This is obviously not the place to attempt a complete analysis of the concept of personhood, but we do not need such a fully adequate analysis just to determine whether and why a fetus is or isn't a person. All we need is a rough and approximate list of the most basic criteria of personhood, and some idea of which, or how many, of these an entity must satisfy in order to properly be considered a person.

In searching for such criteria, it is useful to look beyond the set of people with whom we are acquainted, and ask how we would decide whether a totally alien being was a person or not. (For we have no right to assume that genetic humanity is necessary for personhood.) Imagine a space traveler who lands on an unknown planet and encounters a race of beings utterly unlike any he has ever seen or heard of. If he wants to be sure of behaving morally toward these beings, he has to somehow decide whether they are people, and hence have full moral rights, or whether they are the sort of thing which he need not feel guilty about treating as, for example, a source of food.

How should he go about making this decision? If he has some anthropological background, he might look for such things as religion, art, and the manufacturing of tools, weapons, or shelters, since these factors have been used to distinguish our human from our prehuman ancestors, in what seems to be closer to the moral than the genetic sense of "human." And no doubt he would be right to consider the presence of such factors as good evidence that the alien beings were people, and morally human. It would, however, be overly anthropocentric of him to take the absence of these things as adequate evidence that they were not, since we can imagine people who have progressed beyond, or evolved without ever developing, these cultural characteristics.

I suggest that the traits which are most central to the concept of personhood, or humanity in the moral sense, are, very roughly, the following:

1. consciousness (of objects and events external and/or internal to the being), and in particular the capacity to feel pain;
2. reasoning (the *developed* capacity to solve new and relatively complex problems);
3. self-motivated activity (activity which is relatively independent of either genetic or direct external control);
4. the capacity to communicate, by whatever means, messages of an indefinite variety of types, that is, not just with an indefinite number of possible contents, but on indefinitely many possible topics;
5. the presence of self-concepts, and self-awareness, either individual, or racial, or both.

Admittedly, there are apt to be a great many problems involved in formulating precise definitions of these criteria, let alone in developing universally valid behavioral criteria for deciding when they apply. But I will assume that both we and our explorer know approximately what (1)–(5) mean, and that he is also able to determine whether or not they apply. How, then, should he use his findings to decide whether or not the alien beings are people? We needn't suppose that an entity must have *all* of these attributes to be properly considered a person; (1) and (2) alone may well be sufficient for personhood, and quite probably (1)–(3) are sufficient. Neither do we need to insist that any one of these

criteria is *necessary* for personhood, although once again (1) and (2) look like fairly good candidates for necessary conditions, as does (3), if "activity" is construed so as to include the activity of reasoning.

All we need to claim, to demonstrate that a fetus is not a person, is that any being which satisfies *none* of (1)–(5) is certainly not a person. I consider this claim to be so obvious that I think anyone who denied it, and claimed that a being which satisfied none of (1)–(5) was a person all the same, would thereby demonstrate that he had no notion at all of what a person is—perhaps because he had confused the concept of a person with that of genetic humanity. If the opponents of abortion were to deny the appropriateness of these five criteria, I do not know what further arguments would convince them. We would probably have to admit that our conceptual schemes were indeed irreconcilably different, and that our dispute could not be settled objectively.

I do not expect this to happen, however, since I think that the concept of a person is one which is very nearly universal (to people), and that it is common to both proabortionists and antiabortionists, even though neither group has fully realized the relevance of this concept to the resolution of their dispute. Furthermore, I think that on reflection even the antiabortionists ought to agree not only that (1)–(5) are central to the concept of personhood, but also that it is a part of this concept that all and only people have full moral rights. The concept of a person is in part a moral concept; once we have admitted that x is a person we have recognized, even if we have not agreed to respect, x's right to be treated as a member of the moral community. It is true that the claim that x is a *human being* is more commonly voiced as part of an appeal to treat x decently than is the claim that x is a person, but this is either because "human being" is here used in the sense which implies personhood, or because the genetic and moral senses of "human" have been confused.

Now if (1)–(5) are indeed the primary criteria of personhood, then it is clear that genetic humanity is neither necessary nor sufficient for establishing that an entity is a person. Some human beings are not people, and there may well be people who are not human beings. A man or woman whose consciousness has been permanently obliterated but who remains alive is a human being which is no longer a person; defective human beings, with no appreciable mental capacity, are not and presumably never will be people; and a fetus is a human being which is not yet a person, and which therefore cannot coherently be said to have full moral rights. Citizens of the next century should be prepared to recognize highly advanced, self-aware robots or computers, should such be developed, and intelligent inhabitants of other worlds, should such be found, as people in the fullest sense, and to respect their moral rights. But to ascribe full moral rights to an entity which is not a person is as absurd as to ascribe moral obligations and responsibilities to such an entity.

FETAL DEVELOPMENT AND THE RIGHT TO LIFE

Two problems arise in the application of these suggestions for the definition of the moral community to the determination of the precise moral status of a human fetus. Given that the paradigm example of a person is a normal adult human being, then (1) How like this paradigm, in particular how far advanced since conception, does a human being need to be before it begins to have a right to life by virtue, not of being fully a person as of yet, but of being *like* a person? and (2) To what extent, if any, does the fact that a fetus has the *potential* for becoming a person endow it with some of the same rights? Each of these questions requires some comment.

In answering the first question, we need not attempt a detailed consideration of the moral rights of organisms which are not developed enough, aware enough, intelligent enough, etc., to be considered people, but which resemble people in some respects. It does seem reasonable to suggest that the more like a person, in the relevant respects, a being is,

the stronger is the case for regarding it as having a right to life, and indeed the stronger its right to life is. Thus we ought to take seriously the suggestion that, insofar as "the human individual develops biologically in a continuous fashion . . . the rights of a human person might develop in the same way."[3] But we must keep in mind that the attributes which are relevant in determining whether or not an entity is enough like a person to be regarded as having some of the same moral rights are no different from those which are relevant to determining whether or not it is fully a person—i.e., are no different from (1)–(5)—and that being genetically human, or having recognizably human facial and other physical features, or detectable brain activity, or the capacity to survive outside the uterus, are simply not among these relevant attributes.

Thus it is clear that even though a seven- or eight-month fetus has features which make it apt to arouse in us almost the same powerful protective instinct as is commonly aroused by a small infant, nevertheless it is not significantly more personlike than is a very small embryo. It is *somewhat* more personlike; it can apparently feel and respond to pain, and it may even have a rudimentary form of consciousness, insofar as its brain is quite active. Nevertheless, it seems safe to say that it is not fully conscious, in the way that an infant of a few months is, and that it cannot reason, or communicate messages of indefinitely many sorts, does not engage in self-motivated activity, and has no self-awareness. Thus, in the *relevant* respects, a fetus, even a fully developed one, is considerably less personlike than is the average mature mammal, indeed the average fish. And I think that a rational person must conclude that if the right to life of a fetus is to be based upon its resemblance to a person, then it cannot be said to have any more right to life than, let us say, a newborn guppy (which also seems to be capable of feeling pain), and that a right of that magnitude could never override a woman's right to obtain an abortion, at any stage of her pregnancy.

There may, of course, be other arguments in favor of placing legal limits upon the stage of pregnancy in which an abortion may be performed. Given the relative safety of the new techniques of artificially inducing labor during the third trimester, the danger to the woman's life or health is no longer such an argument. Neither is the fact that people tend to respond to the thought of abortion in the later stages of pregnancy with emotional repulsion, since mere emotional responses cannot take the place of moral reasoning in determining what ought to be permitted. Nor, finally, is the frequently heard argument that legalizing abortion, especially late in the pregnancy, may erode the level of respect for human life, leading, perhaps, to an increase in unjustified euthanasia and other crimes. For this threat, if it is a threat, can be better met by educating people to the kinds of moral distinctions which we are making here than by limiting access to abortion (which limitation may, in its disregard for the rights of women, be just as damaging to the level of respect for human rights).

Thus, since the fact that even a fully developed fetus is not personlike enough to have any significant right to life on the basis of its personlikeness shows that no legal restrictions upon the stage of pregnancy in which an abortion may be performed can be justified on the grounds that we should protect the rights of the older fetus and since there is no other apparent justification for such restrictions, we may conclude that they are entirely unjustified. Whether or not it would be *indecent* (whatever that means) for a woman in her seventh month to obtain an abortion just to avoid having to postpone a trip to Europe, it would not, in itself, be *immoral,* and therefore it ought to be permitted.

POTENTIAL PERSONHOOD
AND THE RIGHT TO LIFE

We have seen that a fetus does not resemble a person in any way which can support the claim that it has even some of the same rights. But what about its *potential*, the fact that if nurtured and allowed to develop naturally it will very probably become a person? Doesn't that alone give it at least some right to life? It is hard to deny that the fact that an entity is a potential person is a strong prima facie reason for not destroying it; but we need not conclude from this that a potential person has a right to life, by virtue of that potential. It may be that our feeling that it is better, other things being equal, not to destroy a potential person is better explained by the fact that potential people are still (felt to be) an invaluable resource, not to be lightly squandered. Surely, if every speck of dust were a potential person, we would be much less apt to conclude that every potential person has a right to become actual.

Still, we do not need to insist that a potential person has no right to life whatever. There may be something immoral, and not just imprudent, about wantonly destroying potential people, when doing so isn't necessary to protect anyone's rights. But even if a potential person does have some prima facie right to life, such a right could not possibly outweigh the right of a woman to obtain an abortion, since the rights of any actual person invariably outweigh those of any potential person, whenever the two conflict. Since this may not be immediately obvious in the case of a human fetus, let us look at another case.

Suppose that our space explorer falls into the hands of an alien culture, whose scientists decide to create a few hundred thousand or more human beings, by breaking his body into its component cells, and using these to create fully developed human beings, with, of course, his genetic code. We may imagine that each of these newly created men will have all of the original man's abilities, skills, knowledge, and so on, and also have an individual self-concept, in short that each of them will be a bona fide (though hardly unique) person. Imagine that the whole project will take only seconds, and that its chances of success are extremely high, and that our explorer knows all of this, and also knows that these people will be treated fairly. I maintain that in such a situation he would have every right to escape if he could, and thus to deprive all of these potential people of their potential lives; for his right to life outweighs all of theirs together, in spite of the fact that they are all genetically human, all innocent, and all have a very high probability of becoming people very soon, if only he refrains from acting.

Indeed, I think he would have a right to escape even if it were not his life which the alien scientists planned to take, but only a year of his freedom, or, indeed, only a day. Nor would he be obligated to stay if he had gotten captured (thus bringing all these people-potentials into existence) because of his own carelessness, or even if he had done so deliberately, knowing the consequences. Regardless of how he got captured, he is not morally obligated to remain in captivity for *any* period of time for the sake of permitting any number of potential people to come into actuality, so great is the margin by which one actual person's right to liberty outweighs whatever right to life even a hundred thousand potential people have. And it seems reasonable to conclude that the rights of a woman will outweigh by a similar margin whatever right to life a fetus may have by virtue of its potential personhood.

Thus, neither a fetus's resemblance to a person, nor its potential for becoming a person provides any basis whatever for the claim that it has any significant right to life. Consequently, a woman's right to protect her health, happiness, freedom, and even her life,[6] by terminating an unwanted pregnancy, will always override whatever right to life it may be appropriate to ascribe to a fetus, even a fully developed one. And thus, in the absence of any overwhelming social need for every possible child, the laws which restrict the right to obtain an abortion, or limit the period of pregnancy during which an abortion may be performed, are a wholly unjustified violation of a woman's most basic moral and constitutional rights.

NOTES

1. For example, Roger Wertheimer, who in "Understanding the Abortion Argument" (*Philosophy and Public Affairs*, 1, no. 1 [Fall 1971], 67–95), argues that the problem of the moral status of abortion is insoluble, in that the dispute over the status of the fetus is not a question of fact at all, but only a question of how one responds to the facts.
2. Of course, the principle that it is (always) wrong to kill innocent human beings is in need of many other modifications, e.g., that it may be permissible to do so to save a greater number of other innocent human beings, but we may safely ignore these complications here.
3. John Noonan, "Deciding Who Is Human," *Natural Law Forum,* 13 (1968), p. 135.
4. From here on, we will use "human" to mean genetically human, since the moral sense seems closely connected to, and perhaps derived from, the assumption that genetic humanity is sufficient for membership in the moral community.
5. Thomas L. Hayes, "A Biological View," *Commonweal*, 85 (March 17, 1967), 677–78, quoted by Daniel Callahan in *Abortion, Law, Choice, and Morality* (London: Macmillan, 1970).
6. That is, insofar as the death rate, for the woman, is higher for childbirth than for early abortion.

REVIEW AND DISCUSSION QUESTIONS

1. How does Warren answer those who defend the right to an abortion based on the "terrible side effects" of antiabortion laws?
2. How does Warren respond to those who defend abortion on the ground that the woman "owns" her body?
3. Explain the biological or genetic sense of the term *human,* indicating how Warren thinks that sense differs from the "moral" sense of the term.
4. On what basis does Warren think a human fetus is not a moral person?
5. How does Warren respond to those who argue that even if a fetus isn't a person, it is still a potential one and for that reason should not be killed?

6. Do you agree that, in theory at least, it is possible for there to be a "person" who is not a biological human? Explain, indicating the significance of that position for abortion.

7. When, in the course of your development, would Warren say you became a moral "person"?

8. In response to those who point out her view might justify infanticide, Warren has responded that it does not because (a) other people, besides the mother, would like to raise the infant themselves and (b) others also value infants and would prefer they not be killed. Are those responses adequate, in your opinion? Explain.

9. "One virtue of Warren's approach is that it solves not only the abortion problem but also helps resolve cases in which a human being has become a 'human vegetable' and therefore should not be kept alive." Explain that comment, indicating whether or not you agree.

Abortion and the Concept of a Person

Jane English

The writer of the preceding essay, like most people generally, assumes that the abortion controversy depends in large measure on the concept of a person: if a fetus is a person, it is almost always wrong to get an abortion; if it is not a person, then abortion is almost always acceptable. Jane English doubts that this approach, thinking about the nature of a person, is the right one. The concept of a person includes a family of characteristics, she argues, and it cannot provide an answer to the legitimacy of abortion. English then discusses the senses in which it may, or may not, be true that the woman is entitled to get an abortion out of self-defense and concludes with some thoughts about morality in general, including the importance of our psychology in our attitudes toward babies, other persons, and animals. Jane English was professor of philosophy at the University of North Carolina.

The abortion debate rages on. Yet the two most popular positions seem to be clearly mistaken. Conservatives maintain that a human life begins at conception and that therefore abortion must be wrong because it is murder. But not all killings of humans are murders. Most notably, self-defense may justify even the killing of an innocent person.

Liberals, on the other hand, are just as mistaken in their argument that since a fetus does not become a person until birth, a woman may do whatever she pleases in and to her own body. First, you cannot do as you please with your own body if it affects other people adversely.[1] Second, if a fetus is not a person, that does not imply that you can do to it anything you wish. Animals, for example, are not persons, yet to kill or torture them for no reason at all is wrong.

At the center of the storm has been the issue of just when it is between ovulation and adulthood that a person appears on the scene. Conservatives draw the line at conception, liberals at birth. In this paper I first examine our concept of a person and conclude that no single criterion can capture the concept of a person and no sharp line can be drawn. Next I argue that if a fetus is a person, abortion is still justifiable in many cases; and if a fetus is not a person, killing it is still wrong in many cases. To a large extent, these two solutions are in agreement. I conclude that our concept

Jane English, "Abortion and the Concept of a Person," *Canadian Journal of Philosophy* 5 (October 1974): 233–243. Reprinted with permission of the *Canadian Journal of Philosophy,* and the Jane English Memorial Fund at the University of North Carolina.

of a person cannot and need not bear the weight that the abortion controversy has thrust upon it.

I

The several factions in the abortion argument have drawn battle lines around various proposed criteria for determining what is and what is not a person. For example, Mary Anne Warren[2] lists five features (capacities for reasoning, self-awareness, complex communications, etc.) as her criteria for personhood and argues for the permissibility of abortion because a fetus falls outside this concept. Baruch Brody[3] uses brain waves. Michael Tooley[4] picks having-a-concept-of-self as his criterion and concludes that infanticide and abortion are justifiable, while the killing of adult animals is not. On the other side, Paul Ramsey[5] claims a certain gene structure is the defining characteristic. John Noonan[6] prefers conceived-of-humans and presents counterexamples to various other candidate criteria. For instance, he argues against viability as the criterion because the newborn and infirm would then be non-persons, since they cannot live without the aid of others. He rejects any criterion that calls upon the sorts of sentiments a being can evoke in adults on the grounds that this would allow us to exclude other races as non-persons if we could just view them sufficiently unsentimentally

These approaches are typical: foes of abortion propose sufficient conditions for personhood which fetuses satisfy, while friends of abortion counter with necessary conditions for personhood which fetuses lack. But these both presuppose that the concept of a person can be captured in a straightjacket of necessary and/or sufficient conditions.[7] Rather, "person" is a cluster of features, of which rationality, having a self-concept and being conceived of humans are only a part.

What is typical of persons? Within our concept of a person we include, first, certain biological factors: descended from humans, having a certain genetic make-up, having a head, hands, arms, eyes, capable of locomotion, breathing, eating, sleeping. There are psychological factors: sentience, perception, having a concept of self and of one's own interests -and desires, and the ability to use tools, the ability to use language or symbol systems, the ability to joke, to be angry, to doubt. There are rationality factors: the ability to reason and draw conclusions, the ability to generalize and to learn from past experience, the ability to sacrifice present interests for greater gains in the future. There are social factors: the ability to work in groups and respond to peer pressures, the ability to recognize and consider as valuable the interests of others, seeing oneself as among "other minds," the ability to sympathize, encourage, love, the ability to evoke from others the responses of sympathy, encouragement, love, the ability to work with others for mutual advantage. Then there are legal factors: being subject to the law and protected by it, having the ability to sue and enter contracts, being counted in the census, having a name and citizenship, the ability to own property, inherit, and so forth.

Now the point is not that this list is incomplete, or that you can find counterinstances to each of its points. People typically exhibit rationality, for instance, but someone who was irrational would not thereby fail to qualify as a person. On the other hand, something could exhibit the majority of these features and still fail to be a person, as an advanced robot might. There is no single core of necessary and sufficient features which we can draw upon with the assurance that they constitute what really makes a person; there are only features that are more or less typical.

This is not to say that no necessary or sufficient conditions can be given. Being alive is a necessary condition for being a person, and being a U.S. Senator is sufficient. But rather than falling inside a sufficient condition or outside a necessary one, a fetus lies in the penumbra region where our concept of a person is not so simple. For this reason I think a conclusive answer to the question whether a fetus is a person is unattainable.

Here we might note a family of simple fallacies that proceed by stating a necessary condition for personhood and showing that a fetus has that characteristic. This is a form of the fallacy of affirming the consequent. For example, some have mistakenly reasoned from the premise that a fetus is human (after all, it is a human fetus rather than, say, a canine fetus), to the conclusion that it is a human. Adding an equivocation on "being," we get the fallacious argument that since a fetus is something both living and human, it is a human being.

Nonetheless, it does seem clear that a fetus has very few of the above family of characteristics, whereas a newborn baby exhibits a much larger proportion of them—and a two-year-old has even more. Note that one traditional antiabortion argument has centered on pointing out the many ways in which a fetus resembles a baby. They emphasize its development ("It already has ten fingers . . .") without mentioning its dissimilarities to adults (it still has gills and a tail). They also try to evoke the sort of sympathy on our part that we only feel toward other persons ("Never to laugh . . . or feel the sunshine?"). This all seems to be a relevant way to argue, since its purpose is to persuade us that a fetus satisfies so many of the important features on the list that it ought to be treated as a person. Also note that a fetus near the time of birth satisfies many more of these factors than a fetus in the early months of development. This could provide reason for making distinctions among the different stages of pregnancy, as the U.S. Supreme Court has done.[8]

Historically, the time at which a person had been said to come into existence has varied widely. Muslims date personhood from fourteen days after conception. Some medievals followed Aristotle in placing ensoulment at forty days after conception for a male fetus and eighty days for a female fetus.[9] In European common law since the seventeenth century, abortion was considered the killing of a person only after quickening, the time when a pregnant woman first feels the fetus move on its own. Nor is this variety of opinions surprising.

Biologically, a human being develops gradually. We shouldn't expect there to be any specific time or sharp dividing point when a person appears on the scene.

For these reasons I believe our concept of a person is not sharp or decisive enough to bear the weight of a solution to the abortion controversy. To use it to solve that problem is to clarify *obscurum per obscurius*.

II

Next let us consider what follows if a fetus is a person after all. Judith Jarvis Thomson's landmark article, "A Defense of Abortion,"[10] correctly points out that some additional argumentation is needed at this point in the conservative argument to bridge the gap between the premise that a fetus is an innocent person and the conclusion that killing it is always wrong. To arrive at this conclusion, we would need the additional premise that killing an innocent person is always wrong. But killing an innocent person is sometimes permissible, most notably in self-defense. Some examples may help draw out our intuitions or ordinary judgments about self-defense.

Suppose a mad scientist, for instance, hypnotized innocent people to jump out of the bushes and attack innocent passers-by with knives. If you are so attacked, we agree you have a right to kill the attacker in self-defense, if killing him is the only way to protect your life or to save yourself from serious injury. It does not seem to matter here that the attacker is not malicious but himself an innocent pawn, for your killing of him is not done in a spirit of retribution but only in self-defense.

How severe an injury may you inflict in self-defense? In part this depends upon the severity of the injury to be avoided: you may not shoot someone merely to avoid having your clothes torn. This might lead one to the mistaken conclusion that the defense may only equal the threatened injury in severity; that to avoid death you may kill, but to avoid a black eye you may only inflict a black eye or the equivalent. Rather, our laws and customs seem to say that you may create an injury somewhat, but not enormously, greater than the injury to be avoided. To fend off an attack whose outcome would be as serious as rape, a severe beating or the loss of a finger, you may shoot; to avoid having your clothes torn, you may blacken an eye.

Aside from this, the injury you may inflict should only be the minimum necessary to deter or incapacitate the attacker. Even if you know he intends to kill you, you are not justified in shooting him if you could equally well save yourself by the simple expedient of running away. Self-defense is for the purpose of avoiding harms rather than equalizing harms.

Some cases of pregnancy present a parallel situation. Though the fetus is itself innocent, it may pose a threat to the pregnant woman's well-being, life prospects or health, mental or physical. If the pregnancy presents a slight threat to her interests, it seems self-defense cannot justify abortion. But if the threat is on a par with a serious beating or the loss of a finger, she may kill the fetus that poses such a threat, even if it is an innocent person. If a lesser harm to the fetus could have the same defensive effect, killing it would not be justified. It is unfortunate that the only way to free the woman from the pregnancy entails the death of the fetus (except in very late stages of pregnancy). Thus a self-defense model supports Thomson's point that the woman has a right only to be freed from the fetus, not a right to demand its death.[11]

The self-defense model is most helpful when we take the pregnant woman's point of view. In the pre-Thomson literature, abortion is often framed as a question for a third party: do you, a doctor, have a right to choose between the life of the woman and that of the fetus? Some have claimed that if you were a passer-by who witnessed a struggle between the innocent hypnotized attacker and his equally innocent hypnotized victim, you would have no reason to kill either in defense of the other. They have concluded that the self-defense model implies that a woman may attempt to abort herself, but that a doctor should not assist her. I think the position of the third party is somewhat more complex. We do feel some inclination to intervene on behalf of the victim rather than the attacker, other things equal. But if both parties are innocent, other factors come into consideration. You would rush to the aid of your husband whether he was attacker or attackee. If a hypnotized famous violinist were attacking a skid row bum, we would try to save the individual who is of more value to society. These considerations would tend to support abortion in some cases.

But suppose you are a frail senior citizen who wishes to avoid being knifed by one of these innocent hypnotics, so you have hired a bodyguard to accompany you. If you are attacked, it is clear we believe that the bodyguard, acting as your agent, has a right to kill the attacker to save you from a serious beating. Your rights of self-defense are transferred to your agent. I suggest that we should similarly view the doctor as the pregnant woman's agent in carrying out a defense she is physically incapable of accomplishing herself.

Thanks to modern technology, the cases are rare in which a pregnancy poses as clear a threat to a woman's bodily health as an attacker brandishing a switchblade. How does self-defense fare when more subtle, complex, and long-range harms are involved?

To consider a somewhat fanciful example, suppose you are a highly trained surgeon when you are kidnapped by the hypnotic attacker. He says he does not intend to harm you but to take you back to the mad scientist who, it turns out, plans to hypnotize you to have a permanent mental block against all your knowledge of medicine. This would automatically destroy your career which would in turn have a serious adverse impact on your family, your personal relationships and your happiness. It seems to me that if the only way you can avoid this outcome is to shoot the innocent attacker, you are justified in so doing. You are defending yourself from a drastic injury to your life prospects. I think it is no exaggeration to claim that 'unwanted pregnancies (most obviously among teenagers) often have such adverse life-long-consequences as the surgeon's loss of livelihood.

Several parallels arise between various views on abortion and the self-defense model. Let's suppose further that these hypnotized attackers only operate at night, so that it is well known that they can be avoided completely by the considerable inconvenience of never leaving your house after dark. One view is that since you could stay home at night, therefore if you go out and are selected by one of these hypnotized people, you have no right to defend yourself. This parallels the view that abstinence is the only acceptable way to avoid pregnancy. Others might hold that you ought to take along some defense such as Mace which will deter the hypnotized person without killing him, but that if this defense fails, you are obliged to submit to the resulting injury, no matter how severe it is. This parallels the view that contraception is all right but abortion is always wrong, even in cases of contraceptive failure.

A third view is that you may kill the hypnotized person only if he will actually kill you, but not if he will only injure you. This is like the position that abortion is permissible only if it is required to save a woman's life. Finally we have the view that it is all right to kill the attacker, even if only to avoid a very slight inconvenience to yourself and even if you knowingly walked down the very street where all these incidents have been taking place without taking along any Mace or protective escort. If we assume that a fetus is a person, this is the analogue of the view that abortion is always justifiable, "on demand."

The self-defense model allows us to see an important difference that exists between abortion and infanticide, even if a fetus is a person from conception. Many have argued that the only way to justify abortion without justifying infanticide would be to find some characteristic of personhood that is acquired at birth. Michael Tooley, for one, claims infanticide is justifiable because the really significant characteristics of a person are acquired some time after birth. But all such approaches look to characteristics of the developing human and ignore the relation between the fetus and the woman. What if, after birth, the

presence of an infant or the need to support it posed a grave threat to the woman's sanity or life prospects? She could escape this threat by the simple expedient of running away. So a solution that does not entail the death of the infant is available. Before birth, such solutions are not available because of the biological dependence of the fetus on the woman. Birth is the crucial point not because of any characteristics the fetus gains, but because after birth the woman can defend herself by a means less drastic than killing the infant. Hence self-defense can be used to justify abortion without necessarily thereby justifying infanticide.

III

On the other hand, supposing a fetus is not after all a person, would abortion always be morally permissible? Some opponents of abortion seem worried that if a fetus is not a full-fledged person, then we are justified in treating it in any way at all. However, this does not follow. Non-persons do get some consideration in our moral code, though of course they do not have the same rights as persons have (and in general they do not have moral responsibilities), and though their interests may be overridden by the interests of persons. Still, we cannot just treat them in any way at all.

Treatment of animals is a case in point. It is wrong to torture dogs for fun or to kill wild birds for no reason at all. It is wrong Period, even though dogs and birds do not have the same rights persons do. However, few people think it is wrong to use dogs as experimental animals, causing them considerable suffering in some cases, provided that the resulting research will probably bring discoveries of great benefit to people. And most of us think it is all right to kill birds for food or to protect our crops. People's rights are different from the consideration we give to animals, then, for it is wrong to experiment on people, even if others might later benefit a great deal as a result of their suffering. You might volunteer to be a subject, but this would be supererogatory; you certainly, have a right to refuse to be a medical guinea pig.

But how do we decide what you may or may not do to non-persons? This is a difficult problem, one for which I believe no adequate account exists. You do not want to say, for instance, that torturing dogs is all right whenever the sum of its effects on people is good—when it doesn't warp the sensibilities of the torturer so much that he mistreats people. If that were the case, it would be all right to torture dogs if you did it in private, or if the torturer lived on a desert island or died soon afterward, so that his actions had no effect on people. This is an inadequate account, because whatever moral consideration animals get, it has to be indefeasible, too. It will have to be a general proscription of certain actions, not merely a weighing of the impact on people on a case-by-case basis.

Rather, we need to distinguish two levels on which consequences of actions can be taken into account in moral reasoning. The traditional objections to Utilitarianism focus on the fact that it operates solely on the first level, taking all the consequences into account in particular cases only. Thus Utilitarianism is open to "desert island" and "lifeboat" counterexamples because these cases are rigged to make the consequences of actions severely limited.

Rawls's theory could be described as a teleological sort of theory, but with teleology operating on a higher level.[12] In choosing the principles to regulate society from the original position, his hypothetical choosers make their decision on the basis of the total consequences of various systems. Furthermore, they are constrained to choose a general set of rules which people can readily learn and apply. An ethical theory must operate by generating a set of sympathies and attitudes toward others which reinforce the functioning of that set of moral principles. Our prohibition against killing people operates by means of certain moral sentiments including sympathy, compassion, and guilt. But if these attitudes are to form a coherent set, they carry us further: we tend to perform supererogatory actions, and we tend to feel similar compassion toward person-like non-persons.

It is crucial that psychological facts play a role here. Our psychological constitution makes it the case that for our ethical theory to work, it must prohibit certain treatment of non-persons which are significantly person-like. If our moral rules allowed people to treat some person-like non-persons in ways we do not want people to be treated, this would undermine the system of sympathies and attitudes that makes the ethical system work. For this reason, we would choose in the original position to make mistreatment of some sorts of animals wrong in general (not just wrong in the cases with public impact), even though animals are not themselves parties in the original position. Thus it makes sense that it is those animals whose appearance and behavior are most like those of people that get the most consideration in our moral scheme.

It is because of "coherence of attitudes," I think, that the similarity of a fetus to a baby is very significant. A fetus one week before birth is so much like a newborn baby in our psychological space that we cannot allow any cavalier treatment of the former while expecting full sympathy and nurturative support for the latter. Thus, I think that anti-abortion forces are indeed giving their strongest arguments when they point to the similarities between a fetus and a baby, and when they try to evoke our emotional attachment to and sympathy for the fetus. An early horror story from New York about nurses who were expected to alternate between caring for six-week premature infants and disposing of viable 24-week aborted fetuses is just that—a horror story. These beings are so much alike that no one can be asked to draw a distinction and treat them so very differently.

Remember, however, that in the early weeks after conception, a fetus is very much unlike a person. It is hard to develop these feelings for a set of genes which doesn't yet have a head, hands, beating heart, response to touch or the ability to move by itself. Thus it seems to me that the alleged "slippery slope" between conception and birth is not so very slippery. In the early stages of pregnancy, abortion can hardly be compared to murder for psychological reasons, but in the latest stages it is psychologically akin to murder.

Another source of similarity is the bodily continuity between fetus and adult. Bodies play a surprisingly central role in our attitudes toward persons. One has only to think of the philosophical literature on how far physical identity suffices for personal identity or Wittgenstein's remark that the best picture of the human soul is the human body. Even after death, when all agree the body is no longer a person, we still observe elaborate customs of respect for the human body; like people who torture dogs, necrophiliacs are not to be trusted with people.[13] So it is appropriate that we show respect to a fetus as the body continuous with the body of a person. This is a degree of resemblance to persons that animals cannot rival.

Michael Tooley also utilizes a parallel with animals. He claims that it is always permissible to drown newborn kittens and draws conclusions about infanticide.[14] But it is only permissible to drown kittens when their survival would cause some hardship. Perhaps it would be a burden to feed and house six more cats or to find other homes for them. The alternative of letting them starve produces even more suffering than the drowning. Since the kittens get their rights secondhand, so to speak, *via* the need for coherence in our attitudes, their interests are often overridden by the interests of full-fledged persons. But if their survival would be no inconvenience to people at all, then it is wrong to drown them, *contra* Tooley.

Tooley's conclusions about abortion are wrong for the same reason. Even if a fetus is not a person, abortion is not always permissible, because of the resemblance of a fetus to a person. I agree with Thomson that it would be wrong for a woman who is seven months pregnant to have an abortion just to avoid having to postpone a trip to Europe. In the early months of pregnancy when the fetus hardly resembles a baby at all, then, abortion is permissible whenever it is in the interests of the pregnant woman or her family. The reasons would only need to outweigh the pain and inconvenience of the abortion itself. In the middle months, when the fetus comes to resemble a person, abortion would be justifiable only when the continuation of the pregnancy or the birth of the child would cause harms—physical, psychological, economic or social—to the woman. In the late months of pregnancy, even on our current assumption that a fetus is not a person, abortion seems to be wrong except to save a woman from significant injury or death.

The Supreme Court has recognized similar gradations in the alleged slippery slope stretching between conception and birth. To this point, the present paper has been a discussion of the moral status of abortion only, not its legal status. In view of the great physical, financial and sometimes psychological costs of abortion, perhaps the legal arrangement most compatible with the proposed moral solution would be the absence of restrictions, that is, so-called abortion "on demand."

So I conclude, first, that application of our concept of a person will not suffice to settle the abortion issue. After all, the biological development of a human being is gradual. Second, whether a fetus is a person or not, abortion is justifiable early in pregnancy to avoid modest harms and seldom justifiable late in pregnancy except to avoid significant injury or death.

NOTES

1. We also have paternalistic laws which keep us from harming our own bodies even when no one else is affected. Ironically, anti-abortion laws were originally designed to protect pregnant women from a dangerous but tempting procedure.

2. Mary Anne Warren, "On the Moral and Legal Status of Abortion," *Monist* 5 (1973), p. 55.
3. Baruch Brody, "Fetal Humanity and the Theory of Essentialism," in Robert Baker and Frederick Elliston (eds.), *Philosophy and Sex* (Buffalo, N.Y., 1975).

4. Michael Tooley, "Abortion and Infanticide," *Philosophy and Public Affairs* 1 (1971).
5. Paul Ramsey, "The Morality of Abortion," in James Rachels, ed., *Moral Problems* (New York, 1971).
6. John Noonan, "Abortion and the Catholic Church: A Summary History," *Natural Law Forum* 12 (1967):125–131.
7. Wittgenstein has argued against the possibility of so capturing the concept of a game, *Philosophical Investigations* (New York, 1958), §66–71.
8. Not because the fetus is partly a person and so has some of the rights of persons but rather because of the rights of personlike non-persons. . . .
9. Aristotle himself was concerned, however, with the different question of when the soul takes form. For historical data, see Jimmye Kimmey, "How the Abortion Laws Happened," *Ms.* 1 (April, 1973):48ff and John Noonan, *loc. cit.*
10. J. J. Thomson, "A Defense of Abortion," *Philosophy and Public Affairs* 1 (1971).
11. Ibid.
12. John Rawls, *A Theory of Justice* (Cambridge, Mass., 1971), §3–4.
13. On the other hand, if they can be trusted with people, then our moral customs are mistaken. It all depends on the facts of psychology.
14. Tooley, *op. cit.*

REVIEW AND DISCUSSION QUESTIONS

1. What is the "typical" approach to the abortion question, according to English?

2. In what ways does English think a fetus resembles a person? In what ways does it not?

3. What conclusion does English reach about the attempt to solve the abortion question by asking if the fetus is a person?

4. Explain English's reasoning about self-defense and its relevance to the abortion controversy.

5. Suppose you were Judith Jarvis Thomson. Write an essay explaining whether and in what ways you either agree or disagree with the English essay.

6. Compare Michael Tooley's position on the nature of a person with other articles in this section. What problems do you see with Tooley's position? How might he respond?

7. What does English mean by "coherence of attitudes"? What is the importance of such coherence in attitudes for how we treat fetuses, according to English?

An Argument That Abortion Is Wrong

Dan Marquis

After a brief critical discussion of Thomson's defense of abortion, Dan Marquis develops an approach to the abortion question that first looks at the broader question of why it is wrong to kill, say, the readers of this book. The reason why standard murder is wrong, he claims, is that it deprives the victim of a future, just as abortion deprives another human being of a future. After giving four reasons why we should accept the "future like our own" theory, he concludes by responding to three objections to the position he has presented. Dan Marquis is professor of philosophy at the University of Kansas.

From *Ethics In Practice,* ed. Hugh Lafollette (Blackwell Publishers, 1997). © Blackwell Publishers Ltd. 1997 and *The Journal of Philosophy,* 84, 4 (April 1989): 183–202. Reprinted by permission.

The purpose of this essay is to set out an argument for the claim that abortion, except perhaps in rare instances, is seriously wrong.[1] One reason for these exceptions is to eliminate from consideration cases whose ethical analysis should be controversial and detailed for clear-headed opponents of abortion. Such cases include abortion after rape and abortion during the first fourteen days after conception when there is an argument that the fetus is not definitely an individual. Another reason for making these exceptions is to allow for those cases in which the permissibility of abortion is compatible with the argument of this essay. Such cases include abortion when continuation of a pregnancy endangers a woman's life and abortion when the fetus is anencephalic. When I speak of the wrongness of abortion in this essay, a reader should presume the above qualifications. I mean by an abortion an action intended to bring about the death of a fetus for the sake of the woman who carries it. (Thus, as is standard on the literature on this subject, I eliminate spontaneous abortions from consideration.) I mean by a fetus a developing human being from the time of conception to the time of birth. (Thus, as is standard, I call embryos and zygotes fetuses.)

The argument of this essay will establish that abortion is wrong for the same reason as killing a reader of this essay. I shall just assume, rather than establish, that killing you is seriously wrong. I shall make no attempt to offer a complete ethics of killing. Finally, I shall make no attempt to resolve some very fundamental and difficult general philosophical issues into which this analysis of the ethics of abortion might lead.

WHY THE DEBATE OVER ABORTION SEEMS INTRACTABLE

Symmetries that emerge from the analysis of the major arguments on either side of the abortion debate may explain why the abortion debate seems intractable. Consider the following standard anti-abortion argument: Fetuses are both human and alive. Humans have the right to life. Therefore, fetuses have the right to life. Of course, women have the right to control their own bodies, but the right to life overrides the right of a woman to control her own body. Therefore, abortion is wrong. . . .

Thomson's View. Judith Thomson (1971) has argued that even if one grants (for the sake of argument only) that fetuses have the right to life, this argument fails. Thomson invites you to imagine that you have been connected while sleeping, bloodstream to bloodstream, to a famous violinist. The violinist, who suffers from a rare blood disease, will die if disconnected. Thomson argues that you surely have the right to disconnect yourself. She appeals to our intuition that having to lie in bed with a violinist for an indefinite period is too much for morality to demand. She supports this claim by noting that the body being used is your body, not the violinist's body. She distinguishes the right to life, which the violinist clearly has, from the right to use someone else's body when necessary to preserve one's life, which it is not at all obvious the violinist has. Because the case of pregnancy is like the case of the violinist, one is no more morally obligated to remain attached to a fetus than to remain attached to the violinist.

It is widely conceded that one can generate from Thomson's vivid case the conclusion that abortion is morally permissible when a pregnancy is due to rape (Warren, 1973, p. 49 and Steinbock, 1992, p. 79). But this is hardly a general right to abortion. Do Thomson's more general theses generate a more general right to an abortion? Thomson draws our attention to the fact that in a pregnancy, although a fetus uses a woman's body as a life support system, a pregnant woman does not use a fetus's body as a life support system. However, an opponent of abortion might draw our attention to the fact that in an abortion the life that is lost is the fetus's, not the woman's. This symmetry seems to leave us with a stand-off.

Thomson points out that a fetus's right to life does not entail its right to use someone else's body to preserve its life. However, an opponent of abortion might point out that woman's right to use her own body does not entail her right to end someone else's life in order to do what she wants with her body. In reply, one might argue that a pregnant woman's right to control her own body doesn't come to much if it is wrong for her to take any action that ends the life of the fetus within her. However, an opponent of abortion can argue that the fetus's right to life doesn't come to much if a pregnant woman can end it when she chooses. The consequence of all of these symmetries seems to be a stand-off. But if we have the stand-off, then one might argue that we are left with a conflict of rights: a fetal right to life versus the right of a woman to control her own body. One might then argue that the right to life seems to be a stronger right than the right to control one's own body in the case of abortion because the loss of one's life is a greater loss than the loss of the right to control one's own body in one respect for nine months. Therefore, the right to life overrides the right to control one's own body and abortion is wrong. Considerations like these have suggested to both opponents of abortion and supporters of choice that a Thomsonian strategy for defending a general right to abortion will not succeed. In fairness, one must note that Thomson did not intend her strategy to generate a general moral permissibility of abortion.

Do Fetuses Have the Right to Life? The above considerations suggest that whether abortion is morally permissible boils down to the question of whether fetuses have the right to life. An argument that fetuses either have or lack the right to life must be based upon some general criterion for having or lacking the right to life. Opponents of abortion, on the one hand, look around for the broadest possible plausible criterion, so that fetuses will fall under it. This explains why classic arguments against abortion appeal to the criterion of being human. This criterion appears plausible: The claim that all humans, whatever their race, gender, religion or *age* have the right to life seems evident enough. In addition, because the fetuses we are concerned with don't, after all, belong to another species, they are clearly human. Thus, the syllogism that generates the conclusion that fetuses have the right to life is apparently sound.

On the other hand, those who believe abortion is morally permissible wish to find a narrow, but plausible, criterion for possession of the right to life so that fetuses will fall outside of it. This explains, in part, why the standard pro choice arguments in the philosophical literature appeal to the criterion of being a person [*Warren, 1973 (reprinted earlier)—Ed.*]. This criterion appears plausible: The claim that only persons have the right to life seems evident enough. Furthermore, because fetuses are neither rational nor possess the capacity to communicate in complex ways nor possess a concept of self that continues through time, no fetus is a person. Thus, the syllogism needed to generate the conclusion that no fetus possesses the right to life is apparently sound. Given that no fetus possesses the right to life, a woman's right to control her own body easily generates the general right to abortion. The existence of two apparently defensible syllogisms which support contrary conclusions helps to explain why partisans on both sides of the abortion dispute often regard their opponents as either morally depraved or mentally deficient.

Which syllogism should we reject? The anti-abortion syllogism is usually attacked by attacking its major premise: the claim that whatever is biologically human has the right to life. This premise is subject to scope problems because the class of the biologically human includes too much: human cancer cell cultures are biologically human, but they do not have the right to life. Moreover, this premise also is subject to moral relevance problems: the connection between the biological and the moral is merely assumed. It is hard to think of a good *argument* for such a connection. If one wishes to consider the category of human a moral category, as some people find it plausible to do in other contexts, then one is left with no way of showing that the fetus is fully human without begging the question. Thus, the classic anti-abortion argument appears subject to fatal difficulties.

These difficulties with the classic anti-abortion argument are well known and thought by many to be conclusive. The symmetrical difficulties with the classic pro choice syllogism are not as well recognized. The pro choice syllogism can be attacked by attacking its major premise: Only persons have the right to life. This premise is subject to scope problems because the class of persons includes too little: infants, the severely retarded, and some of the mentally ill seem to fall outside the class of persons as the supporter of choice understands the concept. The premise is also subject to moral relevance problems: Being a person is understood by the pro choicer as having certain psychological attributes. If the pro choicer questions the connection between the biological and the moral, the opponent of abortion can question the connection between the psychological and the moral. If one wishes to consider person a moral category, as is often done, then one is left with no way of showing that the fetus is not a person without begging the question. . . .

The argument of this section has attempted to establish, albeit briefly, that the classic anti-abortion argument and the pro choice argument favored by most philosophers both face problems that are mirror images of one another. A stand-off results. The abortion debate requires a different strategy.

THE "FUTURE LIKE OURS" ACCOUNT OF THE WRONGNESS OF KILLING

Why do the standard arguments in the abortion debate fail to resolve the issue? The general principles to which partisans in the debate appeal are either truisms most persons would affirm in the absence of much reflection or very general moral theories. All are subject to major problems. A different approach is needed.

Opponents of abortion claim that abortion is wrong because abortion involves killing someone like us, a human being who just happens to be very young. Supporters of choice claim that ending the life of a fetus is not in the same moral category as ending the life of an adult human being. Surely this controversy cannot be resolved in the absence of an account of what it is about killing us that makes

killing us wrong. On the one hand, if we know what property we possess that makes killing us wrong, then we can ask whether fetuses have the same property. On the other hand, suppose that we do not know what it is about us that makes killing us wrong. If this is so, we do not understand even easy cases in which killing is wrong. Surely, we will not understand the ethics of killing fetuses, for if we do not understand easy cases, then we will not understand hard cases. Both pro choicer and anti-abortionist agree that it is obvious that it is wrong to kill us. Thus, a discussion of what it is about us that makes killing us, not only wrong, but seriously wrong seems to be the right place to begin a discussion of the abortion issue.

Who is primarily wronged by a killing? The wrong of killing is not primarily explained in terms of the loss to the family and friends of the victim. Perhaps the victim is a hermit. Perhaps one's friends find it easy to make new friends. The wrong of killing is not primarily explained in terms of the brutalization of the killer. The great wrong to the victim explains the brutalization, not the other way around. The wrongness of killing us is understood in terms of what killing does to us. Killing us imposes on us the misfortune of premature death. That misfortune underlies the wrongness.

Premature death is a misfortune because when one is dead, one has been deprived of life. This misfortune can be more precisely specified. Premature death cannot deprive me of my past life. That part of my life is already gone. If I die tomorrow or if I live thirty more years my past life would be no different. It has occurred on either alternative. Rather than my past, my death deprives me of my future, of the life that I would have lived if I live out my natural life span.

The loss of a future biological life does not explain the misfortune of death. Compare two scenarios: In the former I now fall into a coma from which I do not recover until my death in thirty years. In the latter I die now. The latter scenario does not seem to describe a greater misfortune than the former.

The loss of our future conscious life is what underlies the misfortune of premature death.

Not any future conscious life qualifies, however. Suppose that I am terminally ill with cancer. Suppose also that pain and suffering would dominate my future conscious life. If so, then death would not be a misfortune for me.

Thus, the misfortune of premature death consists of the loss to us of the future goods of consciousness. What are these goods? Much can be said about this issue, but a simple answer will do for the purposes of this essay. The goods of life are whatever we get out of life. The goods of life are those items toward which we take a pro attitude. They are completed projects of which we are proud, the pursuit of our goals, aesthetic enjoyments, friendships, intellectual pursuits, and physical pleasures of various sorts. The goods of life are what make life worth living. In general, what makes life worth living for one person will not be the same as what makes life worth living for another. Nevertheless, the list of goods in each of our lives will overlap. The lists are usually different in different stages of our lives.

What makes the goods of my future good for me? One possible, but wrong, answer is my desire for those goods now. This answer does not account for those aspects of my future life that I now believe I will later value, but about which I am wrong. Neither does it account for those aspects of my future that I will come to value, but which I don't value now. What is valuable to the young may not be valuable to the middle aged. What is valuable to the middle aged may not be valuable to the old. Some of life's values for the elderly are best appreciated by the elderly. Thus it is wrong to say that the value of my future to me is just what I value now. What makes my future valuable to me are those aspects of my future that I will (or would) value when I will (or would) experience them whether I value them now or not.

It follows that a person can believe that she will have a valuable future and be wrong. Furthermore, a person can believe that he will not have a valuable future and also be wrong. This is confirmed by our attitude toward many of the suicidal. We attempt to save the lives of the suicidal and to convince them that they have made an error in judgment. This does not

mean that the future of an individual obtains value from the value that others confer on it. It means that, in some cases, others can make a clearer judgment of the value of a person's future *to that person* than the person herself. This often happens when one's judgment concerning the value of one's own future is clouded by personal tragedy.

Thus, what is sufficient to make killing us wrong, in general, is that it causes premature death. Premature death is a misfortune. Premature death is a misfortune, in general, because it deprives an individual of a future of value. An individual's future will be valuable to that individual if that individual will come, or would come, to value it. We know that killing us is wrong. What makes killing us wrong, in general, is that it deprives us of a future of value. Thus, killing someone is wrong, in general, when it deprives her of a future like ours. I shall call this "a FLO."

ARGUMENTS IN FAVOR OF THE FLO THEORY

At least four arguments support this FLO account of the wrongness of killing.

The Considered Judgment Argument. The FLO account of the wrongness of killing is correct because it fits with our considered judgment concerning the nature of the misfortune of death. The analysis of the previous section is an exposition of the nature of this considered judgment. This judgment can be confirmed. If one were to ask individuals with AIDS or with incurable cancer about the nature of their misfortune, I believe that they would say or imply that their impending loss of a FLO makes their premature death a misfortune. If they would not, then the FLO account would plainly be wrong.

The Worst of Crimes Argument. The FLO account of the wrongness of killing is correct because it explains why we believe that killing is one of the worst of crimes. My being killed deprives me of more than my being robbed or beaten or harmed in some other way because my being killed deprives me of all of the value of my future, not merely part of it. This explains why we make the penalty for murder greater than the penalty for other crimes.

As a corollary the FLO account of the wrongness of killing also explains why killing an adult human being is justified only in the most extreme circumstances, only in circumstances in which the loss of life to an individual is outweighed by a worse outcome if that life is not taken. Thus, we are willing to justify killing in self-defense, killing in order to save one's own life, because one's loss if one does not kill in that situation is so very great. We justify killing in a just war for similar reasons. We believe that capital punishment would be justified if, by having such an institution, fewer premature deaths would occur. The FLO account of the wrongness of killing does not entail that killing is always wrong. Nevertheless, the FLO account both explains why killing is one of the worst of crimes and, as a corollary, why the exceptions to the wrongness of killing are so very rare. A correct theory of the wrongness of killing should have these features.

The Appeal to Cases Argument. The FLO account of the wrongness of killing is correct because it yields the correct answers in many life and death cases that arise in medicine and have interested philosophers.

Consider medicine first. Most people believe that it is not wrong deliberately to end the life of a person who is permanently unconscious. Thus we believe that it is not wrong to remove a feeding tube or a ventilator from a permanently comatose patient knowing that such a removal will cause death. The FLO account of the wrongness of killing explains why this is so. A patient who is permanently unconscious cannot have a future that she would come to value, whatever her values. Therefore, according to the FLO theory of the wrongness of killing, death could not, *ceteris paribus,* be a misfortune to her. Therefore, removing the feeding tube or ventilator does not wrong her.

By contrast, almost all people believe that it is wrong, *ceteris paribus,* to withdraw medical treatment from patients who are temporarily unconscious. The FLO account of the wrongness of killing also explains why this is so. Furthermore, these two unconsciousness cases explain why the FLO account of the wrongness of killing does not include present consciousness as a necessary condition for the wrongness of killing.

Consider now the issue of the morality of legalizing active euthanasia. Proponents of active euthanasia argue that if a patient faces a future of intractable pain and wants to die, then, *ceteris paribus,* it would not be wrong for a physician to give him medicine that she knows would result in his death. This view is so universally accepted that even the strongest *opponents* of active euthanasia hold it. The official Vatican view is that it is permissible for a physician to administer to a patient morphine sufficient (although no more than sufficient) to control his pain even if she foresees that the morphine will result in his death. Notice how nicely the FLO account of the wrongness of killing explains this unanimity of opinion. A patient known to be in severe intractable pain is presumed to have a future without positive value. Accordingly, death would not be a misfortune for him and an action that would (foreseeably) end his life would not be wrong.

Contrast this with the standard emergency medical treatment of the suicidal. Even though the suicidal have indicated that they want to die, medical personnel will act to save their lives. This supports the view that it is not the mere *desire* to enjoy a FLO which is crucial to our understanding of the wrongness of killing. *Having* a FLO is what is crucial to the account, although one would, of course, want to make an exception in the case of fully autonomous people who refuse life saving medical treatment. Opponents of abortion can, of course, be willing to make an exception for fully autonomous fetuses who refuse life supports.

The FLO theory of the wrongness of killing also deals correctly with issues that have concerned philosophers. It implies that it would be wrong to kill (peaceful) persons from outer space who come to visit our planet even though they are biologically utterly unlike us. Presumably, if they are persons, then they would have futures that are sufficiently like ours so that it would be wrong to kill them. The FLO account of the wrongness of killing shares this feature with the personhood views of the supporters of choice. Classical opponents of abortion who locate the wrongness of abortion somehow in the biological humanity of a fetus cannot explain this.

The FLO account does not entail that there is another species of animals whose members ought not be killed. Neither does it entail that it is permissible to kill any non-human animal. On the one hand, a supporter of animals' rights might argue that since some non-human animals have a future of value, it is wrong to kill them also, or at least it is wrong to kill them without a far better reason than we usually have for killing non-human animals. On the other hand, one might argue that the futures of non-human animals are not sufficiently like ours for the FLO account to entail that it is wrong to kill them. Since the FLO account does not specify which properties a future of another individual must possess so that killing that individual is wrong, the FLO account is indeterminate with respect to this issue. The fact that the FLO account of the wrongness of killing does not give a determinate answer to this question is not a flaw in the theory. A sound ethical account should yield the right answers in the obvious cases; it should not be required to resolve every disputed question.

A major respect in which the FLO account is superior to accounts that appeal to the concept of person is the explanation the FLO account provides of the wrongness of killing infants. There was a class of infants who had futures that include a class of events that are identical to the futures of the readers of this essay. Thus, reader, the FLO account explains why it was as wrong to kill you when you were an infant as it is to kill you now. This account can be generalized to almost all infants. Notice that the wrongness of killing infants can be explained in the absence of an account of what makes a future of an individual sufficiently valuable so that it is wrong to kill that individual. The absence of such an account explains why the

FLO account is indeterminate with respect to the wrongness of killing nonhuman animals.

If the FLO account is the correct theory of the wrongness of killing, then because abortion involves killing fetuses and fetuses have FLO's for exactly the same reasons that infants have FLO's, abortion is presumptively seriously immoral. This inference lays the necessary groundwork for a fourth argument in favor of the FLO account that shows that abortion is wrong.

The Analogy with Animals Argument. Why do we believe it is wrong to cause animal suffering? We believe that, in our own case and in the case of other adults and children, suffering is a misfortune. It would be as morally arbitrary to refuse to acknowledge that animal suffering is wrong as it would be to refuse to acknowledge that the suffering of persons of another race is wrong. It is, on reflection, suffering that is a misfortune, not the suffering of white males or the suffering of humans. Therefore, infliction of suffering is presumptively wrong no matter on whom it is inflicted and whether it is inflicted on persons or nonpersons. Arbitrary restrictions on the wrongness of suffering count as racism or speciesism. Not only is this argument convincing on its own, but it is the only way of justifying the wrongness of animal cruelty. Cruelty toward animals is clearly wrong. [*This famous argument is due to Singer, 1979 (reprinted earlier).—Ed.*]

The FLO account of the wrongness of abortion is analogous. We believe that, in our own case and the cases of other adults and children, the loss of a future of value is a misfortune. It would be as morally arbitrary to refuse to acknowledge that the loss of a future of value to a fetus is wrong as to refuse to acknowledge that the loss of a future of value to Jews (to take a relevant 20th Century example) is wrong. It is, on reflection, the loss of a future of value that is a misfortune; not the loss of a future of value to adults or loss of a future of value to non-Jews. To deprive someone of a future of value is wrong no matter on whom the deprivation is inflicted and no matter whether the deprivation is inflicted on persons or nonpersons. Arbitrary restrictions on the wrongness of this deprivation count as racism, genocide or ageism. Therefore, abortion is wrong. This argument that abortion is wrong should be convincing because it has the same form as the argument for the claim that causing pain and suffering to non-human animals is wrong. Since the latter argument is convincing, the former argument should be also. Thus, an analogy with animals supports the thesis that abortion is wrong.

REPLIES TO OBJECTIONS

The four arguments in the previous section establish that abortion is, except in rare cases, seriously immoral. Not surprisingly, there are objections to this view. There are replies to the [three] most important objections to the FLO argument for the immorality of abortion.

The Potentiality Objection. The FLO account of the wrongness of abortion is a potentiality argument. To claim that a fetus *has* a FLO is to claim that a fetus now has the potential to be in a state of a certain kind in the future. It is not to claim that all ordinary fetuses *will* have FLO's. Fetuses who are aborted, of course, will not. To say that a standard fetus has a FLO is to say that a standard fetus either will have or would have a life it will or would value. To say that a standard fetus would have a life it would value is to say that it will have a life it will value if it does not die prematurely. The truth of this conditional is based upon the nature of fetuses (including the fact that they naturally age) and this nature concerns their potential.

Some appeals to potentiality in the abortion debate rest on unsound inferences. For example, one may try to generate an argument against abortion by arguing that because persons have the right to life, potential persons also have the right to life. Such an argument is plainly invalid as it stands. The premise one needs to add to make it valid would have to be something like: 'If X's have the right to Y, then potential X's have the right to Y. This premise is plainly false. Potential presidents don't have

the rights of the presidency; potential voters don't have the right to vote.

In the FLO argument potentiality is not used in order to bridge the gap between adults and fetuses as is done in the argument in the above paragraph. The FLO theory of the wrongness of killing adults is based upon the adult's potentiality to have a future of value. Potentiality is in the argument from the very beginning. Thus, the plainly false premise is not required. Accordingly, the use of potentiality in the FLO theory is not a sign of an illegitimate inference.

The Argument from Interests. A second objection to the FLO account of the immorality of abortion involves arguing that even though fetuses have FLO's, nonsentient fetuses do not meet the minimum conditions for having any moral standing at all because they lack interests. Steinbock (1992, p. 5) has presented this argument clearly:

> Beings that have moral status must be capable of caring about what is done to them. They must be capable of being made, if only in a rudimentary sense, happy or miserable, comfortable or distressed. Whatever reasons we may have for preserving or protecting nonsentient beings, these reasons do not refer to their own interests. For without conscious awareness, beings cannot have interests. Without interests, they cannot have a welfare of their own, Without a welfare of their own, nothing can be done for their sake. Hence, they lack moral standing or status.

Medical researchers have argued that fetuses do not become sentient until after 22 weeks of gestation (Steinbock, 1992, p. 50). If they are correct, and if Steinbock's argument is sound, then we have both an objection to the FLO account of the wrongness of abortion and a basis for a view on abortion minimally acceptable to most supporters of choice.

Steinbock's conclusion conflicts with our settled moral beliefs. Temporarily unconscious human beings are nonsentient, yet no one believes that they lack either interests or moral standing. Accordingly, neither conscious awareness nor the capacity for conscious awareness is a necessary condition for having interests.

The counter example of the temporarily unconscious human being shows that there is something internally wrong with Steinbock's argument. The difficulty stems from an ambiguity. One cannot *take* an interest in something without being capable of caring about what is done to it. However, something can be *in* someone's interest without that individual being capable of caring about it, or about anything. Thus, life support can be *in* the interests of a temporarily unconscious patient even though the temporarily unconscious patient is incapable of *taking* an interest in that life support. If this can be so for the temporarily unconscious patient, then it is hard to see why it cannot be so for the temporarily unconscious (that is, nonsentient) fetus who requires placental life support. Thus the objection based on interests fails. . . .

The Contraception Objection.

The strongest objection to the FLO argument for the immorality of abortion is based on the claim that, because contraception results in one less FLO, the FLO argument entails that contraception, indeed, abstention from sex when conception is possible, is immoral. Because neither contraception nor abstention from sex when conception is possible is immoral, the FLO account is flawed.

There is a cogent reply to this objection.

If the argument of the early part of this essay is correct, then the central issue concerning the morality of abortion is the problem of whether fetuses are individuals who are members of the class of individuals whom it is seriously presumptively wrong to kill. The properties of being human and alive, of being a person, and of having a FLO are criteria that participants in the abortion debate have offered to mark off the relevant class of individuals. The central claim of this essay is that having a FLO marks off the relevant class of individuals. A defender of the FLO view could, therefore, reply that since, at the time of contraception, there is no individual to have a FLO, the FLO account does not entail that contraception is wrong. The wrong of killing is primarily a wrong to the individual who is

killed; at the time of contraception there is no individual to be wronged.

However, someone who presses the contraception objection might have an answer to this reply. She might say that the sperm and egg are the individuals deprived of a FLO at the time of contraception. Thus, there are individuals whom contraception deprives of a FLO and if depriving an individual of a FLO is what makes killing wrong, then the FLO theory entails that contraception is wrong.

There is also a reply to this move. In the case of abortion, an objectively determinate individual is the subject of harm caused by the loss of a FLO. This individual is a fetus. In the case of contraception, there are far more candidates. (See Norcross, 1990.) Let us consider some possible candidates in order of the increasing number of individuals harmed: (1) The single harmed individual might be the combination of the particular sperm and the particular egg that would have united to form a zygote if contraception had not been used. (2) The two harmed individuals might be the particular sperm itself, and, in addition, the ovum itself that would have physically combined to form the zygote. (This is modeled on the double homicide of two persons who would otherwise in a short time fuse. (1) is modeled on harm to a single entity some of whose parts are not physically contiguous, such as a university.) (3) The many harmed individuals might be the millions of *combinations* of sperm and released ovum whose (small) chances of having a FLO were reduced by the successful contraception. (4) The even larger class of harmed individuals (larger by one) might be the class consisting of all of the individual sperm in an ejaculate and, in addition, the individual ovum released at the time of the successful contraception. (1) through (4) are all candidates for being the subject(s) of harm in the case of successful contraception or abstinence from sex. Which should be chosen? Should we hold a lottery? There seems to be no non-arbitrarily determinate subject of harm in the case of successful contraception. But if there is no such subject of harm, then no determinate thing was harmed. If no determinate thing was harmed, then (in the case of contraception) no wrong has been done. Thus, the FLO account of the wrongness of abortion does not entail that contraception is wrong.

CONCLUSION

This essay contains an argument for the view that, except in unusual circumstances, abortion is seriously wrong. Deprivation of a FLO explains why killing adults and children is wrong. Abortion deprives fetuses of FLO's. Therefore, abortion is wrong. This argument is based on an account of the wrongness of killing

that is a result of our considered judgment on the nature of the misfortune of premature death. It accounts for why we regard killing as one of the worst of crimes. It is superior to alternative accounts of the wrongness of killing that are intended to provide insight into the ethics of abortion. This account of the wrongness of killing is supported by the way it handles cases in which our moral judgments are settled. This account has an analogue in the most plausible account of the wrongness of causing animals to suffer. This account makes no appeal to religion. Therefore, the FLO account shows that abortion, except in rare instances, is seriously wrong.

NOTE

1. This essay is an updated version of a view that first appeared in the *Journal of Philosophy* (1989). This essay incorporates attempts to deal with the objections of McInerney (1990), Norcross (1990), Shirley (1995), Steinbock (1992), and Paske (1994) to the original version of the view.

BIBLIOGRAPHY

Marquis, D.B.: "Why abortion is immoral," *Journal of Philosophy*, 86 (1989) 183–202.

McInerney, P.: "Does a fetus already have a future-like ours?," *Journal of Philosophy*, 87 (1990) 264–268.

Norcross, A.: "Killing, abortion, and contraception: a reply to Marquis," *Journal of Philosophy*, 87 (1990) 268–277.

Paske, G.: "Abortion and the neo-natal right to life: a critique of Marquis's futurist argument," *The Abortion Controversy: A Reader*, ed. L.P. Pojman and F.J. Beckwith (Boston: Jones and Bartlett, 1994) 343–353.

Sacred Congregation for the Propagation of the Faith: *Declaration on Euthanasia* (Vatican City, 1980).

Shirley, E.S.: "Marquis' argument against abortion: a critique," *Southwest Philosophy Review*, 11 (1995) 79–89.

Singer, P.: "Not for humans only: the place of nonhumans in environmental issues," *Ethics and Problems of the 21st Century*, ed. K.E. Goodpaster and K.M. Sayre (South Bend: Notre Dame University Press, 1979).

Steinbock, B.: *Life Before Birth: The Moral and Legal Status of Embryos and Fetuses* (New York: Oxford University Press, 1992).

Warren, M.A.: "On the moral and legal status of abortion," *Monist*, 57 (1973) 43–61.

REVIEW AND DISCUSSION QUESTIONS

1. Why does Marquis reject Thomson's defense of abortion?
2. Describe the "future like ours" account of why killing a human being is wrong.
3. What are the four reasons Marquis gives in support of the FLO theory?
4. Explain why Marquis does not believe his theory rests on a mistaken premise about the value of potential persons.
5. Warren claims that without consciousness, beings cannot have interests. How does Marquis respond to that claim?
6. Who is right on the interests question, in your view? Explain.
7. How does Marquis answer those who claim that his FLO position leads to the absurd conclusion that contraception and even abstention from sex are wrong and, therefore, that FLO must be rejected?

Fathers and Fetuses

George W. Harris

In his essay, George Harris looks at an issue that has, he points out, been largely ignored in discussions about abortion: the interests and desires of the father. Is it wrong, he asks, for a woman to get an abortion on the ground that it wrongs the father? Using five very different cases as illustrations, Harris argues that the central moral issue involves how to respect the autonomy of the father, and in that light he considers how abortion decisions affect the father's legitimate interests. George W. Harris is professor of philosophy at the College of William and Mary.

Conspicuously absent from most discussions of the abortion issue are considerations of third-party interests, especially those of the father. A survey of the literature reveals an implicit assumption by most writers that the issue is to be viewed as a two-party conflict—the rights of the fetus versus the rights of the mother—and that an adequate analysis of the balance of these rights is sufficient to determine the conditions under which abortion is morally permissible. I shall argue, however, that in some cases it would be morally impermissible for a woman to have an abortion because it would be a wrongful harm to the father and a violation of his autonomy. Moreover, I shall argue for this on principles that I believe require a strong stand on women's rights.

I

The issue I wish to discuss then is whether or not it would ever be morally wrong for a woman to have an abortion on the grounds that it would be a wrong done to the father. I leave aside the issue of the rights of the fetus since I do not consider here whether abortion under the circumstances raised might be wrong on other grounds.

Consider then the following cases which are arranged to elucidate the moral considerations involved in the analysis. The extreme cases 1 and 5 are included not so much for

their intrinsic importance but because of the light they shed on the analysis of cases 2, 3, and 4. Now, to the cases.

Case 1. Karen, a healthy twenty-five-year-old woman, becomes pregnant as the result of being raped by a man with severe psychological problems. After therapy and significant improvement in his mental health, the man recognizes what he has done and is willing to accept liability for the harms he has caused and even punishment should the victim deem it necessary. His only plea is that Karen carry the fetus to term and then give it to him if she does not care to raise the child herself. Unable, however, to dissociate the fetus from the trauma of the rape, Karen decides to abort.

Case 2. Jane and Jack, two attractive, healthy individuals, meet at a party given by mutual friends. During the weeks and months that follow, a casual but pleasant sexual relationship develops between them. As a result, Jane becomes pregnant. But after learning of the pregnancy, Jack reveals that he is a moderately serious Catholic and from a combined sense of guilt, responsibility, and parental instinct proposes that they be married. Jane, on the other hand, being neither Catholic nor desirous of a husband, decides to abort. Respecting her religious differences and her right to marry whomever she pleases, Jack offers to pay all of Jane's medical expenses, to take complete responsibility for the child after it is born, and to pay her a large sum of money to carry the fetus to term. Jane nonetheless decides to proceed with the abortion.

Case 3. Susan and Charles, both in perfect health, are in the fifth year of their marriage. Aside from his love for Susan, the prospect of raising a family is the most important thing in Charles's life—more important than career, possessions, sports, or any of the other things thought to be of the utmost importance to men. Susan, on the other hand, is secretly ambivalent about having children due to her indecisiveness between having a career and having a family. But because of her love for Charles and the fear of causing him what she believes might be unnecessary anxiety, she allows him to believe that her reluctance is only with when rather than with whether to have children. And despite reasonable efforts at birth control, Susan becomes pregnant just at a point at which her career takes a significant turn for the better. In the situation, it is a career rather than children that she wants, and she decides to have an abortion. Distraught, Charles tries to dissuade her by offering to forgo his own career and to take on the role traditionally reserved for mothers. But to no avail.

Case 4. Michelle and Steve, like Susan and Charles, are also in the fifth year of their marriage. And Steve, like Charles, is equally and similarly desirous of a family. Michelle, however, knows all along that she does not want children but avoids discussing the issue with Steve, allowing him to think that the beginning of their family is just a matter of time. She believes that eventually she can disabuse him of the values of family life in favor of a simple life together. But due to the unpleasantness of broaching the subject, Michelle procrastinates and accidentally becomes pregnant. And despite Steve's expectations, his pleas, and his offer to take on the major responsibilities of raising the child, Michelle decides to abort.

Case 5. Anne is a man hater. Resentment brought on in part by traditional male chauvinistic attitudes toward women has led her to stereotype all men as little more than barbarians. Mark is a reasonably decent man, who, like Charles and Steve, desires very much to be a parent. After meeting Mark, Anne devises a plan to vicariously vent her rage through Mark on the entire male sex. Carefully playing the role of a conventionally attractive woman with traditional life plans, she sets out to seduce Mark. Soon he falls in love with her and, thinking that he has met the ideal mate, proposes marriage. She accepts and after the wedding convinces Mark that if they are to have a happy married life and a healthy environment in which to raise children he must give up his lucrative realty business and the house he inherited from his parents. Valuing his life with Anne and the prospects of a family more than his career, he sells the business at a considerable loss and takes a less lucrative job. He also sells his home and buys another, again at a considerable financial loss. Finally, Anne becomes pregnant. Initially, she plays the adorable expectant mother, intentionally heightening Mark's expectations. But later she has an abortion. Relishing Mark's horror, she further reveals her scheme and explains that his pain and loss are merely the just deserts of any man for the things that men have done to women.

In all these cases, the issue is this: if we assume that all the men could be acceptable parents and that the pregnancies are physically normal, would any of the abortions by the woman in these cases constitute a moral wrong done to any of the men? In the following sections, I shall argue that only in the third, fourth, and fifth cases is a wrongful harm done to the father and that only in the fourth and fifth cases would it be morally impermissible for the woman to proceed with the abortion. By a "wrongful harm," I shall mean a harm that could reasonably have been avoided. I shall argue that in the cases where abortion is claimed to be morally impermissible it is so on the grounds that it violates the father's autonomy; that is, it invades the man's morally legitimate interest in self-determination. The Kantian notion of treating persons as ends— as autonomous agents in pursuit of morally legitimate interests—underlies my argument. Its role will become clearer as the argument proceeds.

II

Much of the analysis presented here turns on the issue of when it is morally significant to say that the fetus is the father's as well as the mother's. One of the things that a woman can do without violating her interest in the autonomous control of her own body is to have a baby. I do not mean that she can do this alone but that, with the cooperation of a man, she can become pregnant as a matter of unencumbered choice. And though things are a bit more difficult for a man, one of the things he can do with his body, in cooperation with a woman, is to bring new life into the world. The interest in autonomy and the interest in procreation are therefore quite compatible and are common to both women and men. The significance of this, I believe, is that when a man and a woman autonomously decide to become parents together, a harm done to the fetus by a third party without the consent of both parents is a prima facie wrong done both to the man and to the woman because it is an interference with his autonomy as well as with hers. Moreover, a harm done to the fetus is a harm done to the man as well as to the woman because the fetus is both the object and the result of his pursuing a morally legitimate interest, that is, the interest in procreation. To harm the fetus, then, is to invade the morally legitimate interest in procreation of both the father and the mother and thereby to interfere with the man's as well as the woman's autonomy. Further exploration of these observations, I believe, is crucial to the analysis of the cases already presented.

In the first case, Karen's abortion, whatever its moral standing relative to the fetus, is not a wrong done to the man who raped her. This is true despite the fact that the man was not in control of his behavior and therefore was not responsible for his actions. The biological connection between the fetus and the father in this case is not sufficient to establish that the fetus is a morally legitimate object of interest for the man. The reason is obvious. Although procreation is a morally legitimate interest that men can have, the pursuit of this interest is restricted by the equipment that men respect the autonomy of women in this regard. And since the fetus was forced upon Karen by the man, she is not required to view the fetus as a legitimate object of interest for him. The fetus then is his only in a biological sense. Any harm done to the fetus is therefore neither a violation of his autonomy nor a harm done to him by Karen. It is important to note, however, that she could decide to keep it without violating her own or anyone else's autonomy. And this makes the fetus hers in a way that it is not the man's.

Similarly, in the second case, the fetus is Jane's in a way that it is not Jack's. The reasons, however, are slightly different than in the first case. Although Jane and Jack here each autonomously decide to pursue the interests in sex, neither has decided to pursue an interest in procreation. The fact that Jack has neglected to reveal his beliefs about abortion vitiates any claim he has that a harm done to the fetus is a violation of his autonomous pursuit of procreation. Rather, he has left it to Jane to assume that his only interest is in the pleasure of sex with her, and it is only this interest that she has a moral obligation to honor in terms of his autonomy. Had she promised him love and a family in order to have sex with him, she would have violated his autonomy both in regard to his interest in sex with love and his interest in procreation. Neither of these has occurred here. But though Jane is free from considerations of Jack's autonomy in deciding whether to abort or to keep the fetus, she could decide to keep it without violating her own sense of autonomy. It is this fact that makes the fetus hers in a way that it is not Jack's. Yet by parity of reasoning, Jack is equally free from any responsibility to Jane in terms of the fetus should she decide to keep it. For, like Jane he has not given his consent to the use of his body for the pursuit of her interest in procreation. He could, however, autonomously decide to take on the responsibility for the fetus. But she could not lay claim to a violation of her autonomy if he did not so choose. Had he promised her love and a family in order to have sex with her, he would have violated her autonomy in regard to her interest in sex with love and her interest in procreation. But since he has done neither of these, she has no valid claim that the fetus is a moral liability for him.[1] Thus the pursuit of casual sex can be quite compatible with the principle of autonomy; it is nonetheless morally perilous for both men and women.

In the third case, Charles is the victim of a wrongful harm and his autonomy has been violated. Due to the fact that both men and women have a morally legitimate interest in procreation, couples have an obligation to each other to be forthright and informative about their desires and reservations about family planning. Such forthrightness is necessary if each is to pursue morally legitimate interests without violating the autonomy of the other. Susan, in this case, has clearly been negligent in this responsibility to Charles. She has allowed him to believe that his sex life with her is more than casual and includes more than an expression of his love for her; it is, in part, a legitimate pursuit of his interest in procreation.

Moreover, he has not violated her autonomy as the rapist did with Karen in the first case. Consequently, the fetus is a morally legitimate object of interest for him, and to harm it is to harm Charles—a harm that could reasonably have been avoided by Susan had she told him about her reservations and informed him that should a pregnancy occur she might very well decide in favor of abortion. And it is no excuse that she had not led Charles to believe that she would carry through with any pregnancy, for she has led him to believe that she would carry through with some pregnancy and has now made a decision that thwarts any such expectation. As a result of Susan's negligence, then, the abortion causes a wrongful harm to Charles and is a violation of his autonomy because the fetus is his as well as hers.

But does it follow from this that the abortion is morally impermissible for Susan? The abortion would be morally impermissible if and only if she has a moral obligation to carry the fetus to term. And the issue we are considering here is whether she has such an obligation to Charles. By withholding important information relevant to her own interest in procreation, she has violated his autonomy in regard to two of his legitimate interests—his interest in procreation and his interest in respecting her autonomy in regard to procreation. Therefore, since the fetus is the result of his pursuing a morally legitimate interest in a morally legitimate way with due respect for her autonomy, the fetus is his as well as hers and she has a prima facie obligation to him not to harm it. What considerations then could possibly absolve her of her obligation to Charles?

The answer cannot be found in ranking the interest in a career over an interest in procreation; I cannot see that a career is a more legitimate means of self-determination than procreation or vice versa. Rather, I believe that the answer can be found in Susan's general interest in the control of her own body when compared with the nature of her negligence. To undertake a pregnancy is a serious investment of a woman's bodily and psychological resources—an undertaking that is not similarly possible for a man. The fetus then is a threat to the mother's autonomy in a way that it is not to the father's. And though Susan is responsible for being forthright about such matters, it is certainly understandable for a woman, as it is for a man, to be undecided about how to rank an interest in a career versus an interest in a possible family. Moreover, it is understandable, though far from mature or laudable, for a person to find it difficult to talk with his or her spouse about such matters when the spouse has strong desires for a family. To say that Susan has an obligation to carry his fetus to term in this case and to sacrifice the control of her own body is, it seems to me, to overestimate the fault of her negligence by not allowing for understandable weaknesses in regard to the responsibilities of autonomy. But we must be careful not to underestimate it. She has caused Charles a serious harm, and she has violated his autonomy. For that, she is guilty.

The fourth case is much like the third except the violation of Steve's autonomy and the consequent wrongful harm are done with deceit rather than negligence. The burden to overcome the prima facie obligation not to harm the fetus is therefore stronger for Michelle than it was for Susan because Michelle could have been expected more reasonably to have avoided the harm. Again it is understandable, though neither mature nor laudable, for a person who is deeply in love with someone with significantly different life plans, perhaps as a result of self-deception, to think that the other person can be brought around to seeing things the other way. But it is not excusable. Surely, given the importance the interest in procreation plays in the lives of some people, a normal adult can be expected on the grounds of the other person's autonomy to be honest in such situations. If so, then in the absence of countervening moral considerations it would be a wrong to Steve for Michelle to have the abortion.

The fifth case involves malicious deceit with the intent to cause harm. Only a crazed ideologue could think that the harm caused Mark is not wrongful. And only someone who thinks that men have no legitimate moral interest in procreation could think that Anne's plan does not involve a violation of his autonomy. The fetus is clearly a morally legitimate object of interest for him and therefore his as well as hers. To harm the fetus then is a prima facie harm done to Mark. And given the extent of his sacrifices, the intensity of his expectations, and the depravity of Anne's intentions, it is difficult to see how the general interest in the autonomous control of one's own body could ever be morally significant enough to allow a woman like Anne to culminate the harm she has planned by having the abortion unless the fetus seriously threatened her most fundamental welfare. To think that the general interest in the autonomous control of one's body allows a woman this kind of freedom is to sanctify female autonomy and to trivialize male autonomy—the mirror image of the chauvinism Anne claims to despise. Assuming then that Anne is physically healthy and the pregnancy is not a threat to her fundamental welfare, for her to abort is morally wrong. She has an obligation to Mark to carry through with the pregnancy. . . .

IV

Someone might argue, however, that the wrongs in these cases can be accounted for on moral grounds that are independent of special considerations of the father or the fetus. The negligence of Susan, the deceit of Michelle, the malice of Anne, all—it might be argued—are wrongs independent of abortion, and there is nothing special about abortion amid these wrongs.

Certainly negligence, deceit, and malice are wrongs independent of abortion, but it does not follow from this that there is nothing special about the wrongs here. Susan, Michelle, and Anne would, respectively, be guilty of negligence, deceit, and malice even had Charles, Steve, and Mark turned out unknowingly to be sterile. But the fact that the men were not sterile and the fact that the women did become pregnant make possible an additional wrong that is special to the abortion issue and that involves fathers and fetuses. The nonmalicious deceit of Michelle illustrates this well. Had Steve been unknowingly sterile, Michelle would have wronged him by lying to him, but she would not have wrongfully harmed him. In fact, the particular harm Anne planned to inflict upon Mark would have been impossible had he been sterile. And had he been knowingly sterile, Anne could not have violated his autonomy by invading an interest that was impossible for him to pursue. Nonetheless, she would have wronged him in other ways. The fact that these other wrongs can affect a man's legitimate interest in procreation gives them special significance here. It might also be objected that one disquieting implication of the argument is that abortion would be said to constitute a "wrongful harm" to anyone and anything that has a "morally legitimate interest" in it. So, for example, in an underpopulated country like Norway or Australia, society might have a morally legitimate interest in childbearing, and every woman opting for an abortion might be said to do a "wrongful harm to society." Or grandparents might have a "morally legitimate" interest in grandchildren being born; and a woman aborting would be said to have done a "wrongful harm" to the would-be grandparents.[2]

Certainly these results are unacceptable, but I do not believe that they are consistent with the concept of autonomy I have in mind here. We might distinguish between interests that are prima facie morally legitimate and those that are morally legitimate simpliciter or legitimate after all moral considerations are in. An interest that is prima facie morally legitimate is one that in itself is a morally permissible interest to have. The interest in sex and the interest in procreation are two such interests, as are the interest in grandparents having grandchildren and the interest of a country in having a larger population. But one way in which prima facie morally legitimate interests can fail to be morally legitimate simpliciter is for a person who has these interests to pursue them in ways that are morally illegitimate.

Assume that the rapist has an interest in sex (which is doubtful, at least that it is his primary interest). This interest fails to be morally legitimate simpliciter when the pursuit of it invades the morally legitimate interest his victim has in her choice of sexual partners. And it is the primacy of the importance of individual choice and its moral legitimacy that is at the heart of the concept of autonomy employed here. Thus a prima facie morally legitimate interest can fail to be morally legitimate simpliciter if it is pursued in a way that does not respect the autonomy of others to pursue their morally legitimate interests. So like the rapist who has an interest in sex, there is nothing wrong with what the country wants in wanting a larger population or in what potential grandparents want in wanting grandchildren. These interests become morally illegitimate, however, when the autonomy of the women involved is violated by the rapist, the country, or the grandparents in the pursuit of their interests. And it

is the importance of autonomy to my argument that prevents the disquieting implication.

A final objection might be that too much of the argument turns on the extremity and implausibility of case [5]. There is an ambiguity, however, in the charge of "implausibility." On the one hand, it might mean that the case is far-fetched in that cases like it are not at all likely to occur. Or on the other hand, it might mean that the analysis of the case is either unconvincing or that it sheds no light on the other cases. The first construal of the charge renders it irrelevant. We hope that there are and will be no such cases. But this is beside the point. If the analysis of the case can be defended against the charge of implausibility of the second kind, the case serves to shed light on moral issues in other contexts. This is what Judith Jarvis Thomson's violinist example [is] designed to do.[3] And no one thinks that these examples are implausible on the grounds that they are unlikely to occur. Those who think these examples are implausible think so on the grounds that they are misleading or otherwise uninformative in terms of analysis. The objection then turns on the second construal of the charge.

That the analysis is unconvincing might be argued either by claiming that Anne has not wronged Mark or that the wrong is independent of the abortion issue. Since I do not believe that anyone would upon reflection seriously claim the former and since I have already addressed the latter claim, the second charge must turn on the claim that the case fails to illuminate the issues in other contexts. But I believe that it does illuminate the issues of other cases. Most important, it establishes that a serious wrong that a woman can do to a man is to harm him by killing his fetus, and it shows how this might involve other wrongs that are done with intentional malice. Once these two points are established, the issue naturally arises as to whether the wrong of harming a man by killing his fetus might be done in other ways involving other wrongs that are not accompanied by malicious intent. I have argued that abortion constitutes a wrongful harm in cases involving neglect and nonmalicious deceit.

Viewed from this perspective, cases 3 and 4 are illuminated by case 5. And viewed from this perspective, we can see that there are other ways—ways that are more likely to occur—in which we can wrong others by failing to take their autonomy and their interest seriously than just in cases where we intentionally and maliciously set out to do so. The latter cases are easy to recognize; the former are not always. Being alive to this is important, and that is why cases 3 and 4 and perhaps other more subtle ones are most important in the analysis.

I have spoken about the rights of autonomy. It is time now to say something about its responsibilities. On any plausible view of the importance of autonomy, anyone who claims to have a right that others respect his or her autonomy must recognize the obligation to take seriously the autonomy of others. Men and women in their relations with each other as members of the opposite sex have not always done this. Let me briefly mention two ways in which men and women have failed in this responsibility.

The first has to do with equality. If the interest in procreation and the interest in, say, a career are equally legitimate, then a man cannot consistently require a woman with whom he is involved to take seriously his interest in a family if he does not take seriously her interest in a career. It is notoriously true that many men are chauvinistic in this regard. But by the same token, a woman cannot consistently require a man with whom she is involved to take seriously her interest in a career if she does not take seriously his interest in a family. This does not mean that she must have children with him, but it does mean that in working out her relationship with him she must grant that men have as legitimate an interest in being parents as do women. I am not sure that many women—nor for that matter that many men—are emotionally prepared to admit this. Although we are making some progress in thinking that women have an equal right to a career as men and that men have equal obligations in child rearing as women, we are still hesitant to think that a man could be an equal to a woman in parenthood.

The second way in which men and women have failed to take each other's autonomy seriously involves forthrightness. Men, it is said with some justification, are unwilling to talk about their feelings. This often puts an unfair burden on the woman with whom a man is involved to understand what his interests are, and without adequate information regarding his interests, the woman is poorly positioned to respect his autonomy in regard to those interests. Thus one aspect of the responsibility to be forthright involves letting the other person know what your interests are so that your autonomy can be respected. This was Jack's failure in case 2.

Another aspect of the responsibility to be forthright has to do with allowing the other person to make an informed choice. Certainly, it is an interference with another person's autonomy to purposefully provide them with or knowingly allow them to believe erroneous information relevant to their choices. This is what Susan, Michelle, and Anne have done in the cases considered. Such motivation to be less than forthright is not always selfish, but it is almost always a failure to take autonomy seriously.

V

To summarize: In order for a man to lay claim to the fetus being his in a sense that the mother is obligated to respect, the fetus must be the result of his pursuing the legitimate interest in procreation in a morally legitimate way. In cases 1 and 2, the men—in different ways—have not satisfied the requirement of acting in a way that is consistent with the responsibilities of autonomy. It would therefore not be a wrong done to these men for Karen and Jane to have their abortions. However, when a man has satisfied the requirements of autonomy in regard to the interest in procreation both in regard to himself and to his sexual partner, the woman has a prima facie obligation to him not to harm the fetus. And unless there is some countervening moral consideration to override this prima facie obligation, the abortion of the fetus is morally impermissible. I have argued that the latter is true in cases 4 and 5.

NOTES

1. These observations do not contradict the practice of the courts in holding liable for support men who have simply become uninterested in their wives and children. What is being maintained is that the fact that a man is the biological father of a child is not sufficient either to give him rights to the child or to put him under an obligation to it or to the mother.

2. I owe this objection to Robert Goodin. The grandparents case was also mentioned to me by James F. Hill.
3. See Judith Jarvis Thomson, "A Defense of Abortion," *Philosophy and Public Affairs* I (1971), 46–66 [reprinted above].

REVIEW AND DISCUSSION QUESTIONS

1. Is Harris right in thinking that in case 1, the woman has no responsibility to respect the man's autonomy? Explain.
2. Why in case 2 does Harris think that Jack's autonomy is not violated by an abortion and that the fetus is Jane's?
3. Discuss case 3, indicating why the fetus belongs to both and whether there are reasons showing that nonetheless Susan may get an abortion.
4. Why in case 4 is it wrong for Michelle to have an abortion?
5. Why is Anne obligated not to get an abortion, according to Harris?
6. Harris thinks that we should respect others' autonomy if we want them to respect ours, and that this includes respecting their legitimate interests in being parents. Discuss this claim, indicating whether you agree and why.

Essay and Paper Topics for Section 7

1. Discuss Thomson's defense of abortion in light of the criticisms of it given by Warren and Marquis. How might Thomson respond to those criticisms? Do you think her responses would be adequate?
2. Compare the positions of Warren, English, and Marquis on the moral status or importance of the fetus. Which of the three seems the most reasonable to you? Explain why, indicating what problems you see with the others and the strength of the position you think most reasonable.
3. Discuss whether anti-abortion laws have political and social consequences for women and their role in society. What do you believe the consequences are? Are the consequences an important argument that should be considered in thinking about abortion rights? Explain.
4. Laws have traditionally included the "maternal presumption," which means that the law assumes mothers, rather than fathers, should be given custody of children after a divorce. Does that presumption make sense, in light of the ideal of gender equality? How do you think Harris would respond to the maternal presumption? Might a feminist disagree? Explain.
5. Using the general moral theory you found most reasonable from earlier sections, write an essay in which you discuss how that theory would evaluate the arguments of two philosophers you have read on the subject of abortion.

Euthanasia and Eugenics

Essays in Section 8 focus first on euthanasia—that is, the killing of human beings who are either terminally ill, suffering tremendously, or severely retarded. Authors take varying positions, some rejecting virtually all forms of euthanasia and others arguing that it should be allowed much more often than current law generally permits. Another issue running through many of the readings is the debate about the merits of distinguishing, legally and morally, between actively killing and passively allowing a person to die. A third, and related, topic is the value of human life: Are some lives worth more than others? Are some lives not worth living? The section then turns to increasingly troubling questions involving eugenics. Genetic engineering and cloning often evoke strong, negative reactions; the question, however, is whether such reactions are justified and if so on what grounds. The section begins, however, with one of the U.S. Supreme Court's most important cases on the subject of euthanasia.

Removing Life-Support Systems

Cruzan v. Director, Missouri Department of Health

In this case, the U.S. Supreme Court reviews a Missouri court's decision not to allow the parents of Nancy Cruzan, who was in a "persistent vegetative state" as a result of an auto accident, to remove feeding and hydration tubes that kept her alive. The Missouri court had required that there be "clear and convincing" proof that such a decision expresses Nancy Cruzan's desires and held that no such proof had been presented. In what follows, a majority of the U.S. Supreme Court agreed with the Missouri court, holding that the U.S. Constitution does not require Missouri to allow the parents to remove the tubes from their daughter, nor does it prevent a state from imposing such a heavy burden of proof on those who may wish not to be kept on life-support systems. Two justices, however, wrote strong dissents.

Chief Justice Rehnquist Delivered the Opinion of the Court: "Petitioner Nancy Beth Cruzan was rendered incompetent as a result of severe injuries sustained during an automobile accident. Co-petitioners Lester and Joyce Cruzan, Nancy's parents and co-guardians, sought a

court order directing the withdrawal of their daughter's artificial feeding and hydration equipment after it became apparent that she had virtually no chance of recovering her cognitive faculties. The Supreme Court of Missouri held that because there was no clear and

Cruzan v. *Director, Missouri Department of Health* 496 U.S. (1990).

convincing evidence of Nancy's desire to have life-sustaining treatment withdrawn under such circumstances, her parents lacked authority to effectuate such a request. We granted certiorari, and now affirm. . . .

After it had become apparent that Nancy Cruzan had virtually no chance of regaining her mental faculties her parents asked hospital employees to terminate the artificial nutrition and hydration procedures. All agree that such a removal would cause her death. The employees refused to honor the request without court approval. The parents then sought and received authorization from the state trial court for termination. The court found that a person in Nancy's condition had a fundamental right under the State and Federal Constitutions to refuse or direct the withdrawal of "death prolonging procedures." The court also found that Nancy's "expressed thoughts at age twenty-five in somewhat serious conversation with a housemate friend that if sick or injured she would not wish to continue her life unless she could live at least halfway normally suggests that given her present condition she would not wish to continue on with her nutrition and hydration." . . .

We granted certiorari to consider the question of whether Cruzan has a right under the United States Constitution which would require the hospital to withdraw life-sustaining treatment from her under these circumstances.

At common law, even the touching of one person by another without consent and without legal justification was a battery. [This] notion of bodily integrity has been embodied in the requirement that informed consent is generally required for medical treatment. Justice Cardozo, while on the Court of Appeals of New York, aptly described this doctrine: "Every human being of adult years and sound mind has a right to determine what shall be done with his own body; and a surgeon who performs an operation without his patient's consent commits an assault, for which he is liable in damages." *Schloendorff* v. *Society of New York Hospital* (1914). The informed consent doctrine has become firmly entrenched in American tort law.

The logical corollary of the doctrine of informed consent is that the patient generally possesses the right not to consent, that is, to refuse treatment. . . .

The Fourteenth Amendment provides that no State shall "deprive any person of life, liberty, or property, without due process of law." . . . For purposes of this case, we assume that the United States Constitution would grant a competent person a constitutionally protected right to refuse life-saving hydration and nutrition.

The difficulty with petitioners' claim is that in a sense it begs the question: an incompetent person is not able to make an informed and voluntary choice to exercise a hypothetical right to refuse treatment or any other right. Such a "right" must be exercised for her, if at all, by some sort of surrogate. Here, Missouri has in effect recognized that under certain circumstances a surrogate may act for the patient in electing to have hydration and nutrition withdrawn in such a way as to cause death, but it has established a procedural safeguard to assure that the action of the surrogate conforms as best it may to the wishes expressed by the patient while competent. Missouri requires that evidence of the incompetent's wishes as to the withdrawal of treatment be proved by clear and convincing evidence. The question, then, is whether the United States Constitution forbids the establishment of this procedural requirement by the State. We hold that it does not.

Whether or not Missouri's clear and convincing evidence requirement comports with the United States Constitution depends in part on what interests the State may properly seek to protect in this situation. Missouri relies on its interest in the protection and preservation of human life, and there can be no gainsaying this interest. As a general matter, the States—indeed, all civilized nations—demonstrate their commitment to life by treating homicide as serious crime. Moreover, the majority of States in this country have laws imposing criminal penalties on one who assists another to commit suicide. We do not think a State is required to remain neutral in the face of an

informed and voluntary decision by a physi-
cally-able adult to starve to death.

But in the context presented here, a State
has more particular interests at stake. The
choice between life and death is a deeply personal decision of obvious and overwhelming
finality. We believe Missouri may legitimately
seek to safeguard the personal element of this
choice through the imposition of heightened
evidentiary requirements. . . . Finally, we think
a State may properly decline to make judgments about the "quality" of life that a particular individual may enjoy, and simply assert an
unqualified interest in the preservation of
human life to be weighed against the constitutionally protected interests of the individual.

In our view, Missouri has permissibly
sought to advance these interests through the
adoption of a "clear and convincing" standard
of proof to govern such proceedings. . . .

[N]ot only does the standard of proof
reflect the importance of a particular adjudication, it also serves as "a societal judgment
about how the risk of error should be distributed between litigants." *Santosky*. The more
stringent the burden of proof a party must
bear, the more that party bears the risk of an
erroneous decision. We believe that Missouri
may permissibly place an increased risk of an
erroneous decision on those seeking to terminate an incompetent individual's life-sustaining
treatment. An erroneous decision not to terminate results in a maintenance of the status
quo; the possibility of subsequent developments such as advancements in medical science,
the discovery of new evidence regarding the
patient's intent, changes in the law, or simply
the unexpected death of the patient despite
the administration of life-sustaining treatment, at least create the potential that a wrong
decision will eventually be corrected or its
impact mitigated. An erroneous decision to
withdraw life-sustaining treatment, however,
is not susceptible of correction. . . .

In sum, we conclude that a State may apply
a clear and convincing evidence standard in
proceedings where a guardian seeks to discontinue nutrition and hydration of a person diagnosed to be in a persistent vegetative state. . . .

No doubt is engendered by anything in this
record but that Nancy Cruzan's mother and
father are loving and caring parents. If the
State were required by the United States
Constitution to repose a right of "substituted
judgment" with anyone, the Cruzans would
surely qualify. But we do not think the Due
Process Clause requires the State to repose
judgment on these matters with anyone but
the patient herself. Close family members
may have a strong feeling—a feeling not at all
ignoble or unworthy, but not entirely disinterested, either—that they do not wish to witness
the continuation of the life of a loved one
which they regard as hopeless, meaningless,
and even degrading. But there is no automatic
assurance that the view of close family members will necessarily be the same as the
patient's would have been had she been confronted with the prospect of her situation
while competent. All of the reasons previously
discussed for allowing Missouri to require
clear and convincing evidence of the patient's
wishes lead us to conclude that the State may
choose to defer only to those wishes, rather
than confide the decision to close family
members.

***Justice Brennan, with Whom Justice Marshall
and Justice Blackmun Join, Dissenting:*** A
grown woman at the time of [her] accident,
Nancy Cruzan had previously expressed her
wish to forgo continuing medical care under
circumstances such as these. Her family and
her friends are convinced that this is what she
would want. A guardian *ad litem* appointed by
the trial court is also convinced that this is
what Nancy would want. . . .

Because I believe that Nancy Cruzan has a
fundamental right to be free of unwanted artificial nutrition and hydration, which right is
not outweighed by any interests of the State,
and because I find that the improperly biased
procedural obstacles imposed by the Missouri
Supreme Court impermissibly burden that
right, I respectfully dissent. Nancy Cruzan is
entitled to choose to die with dignity. . . .

[Although] the right to be free of unwanted
medical intervention, like other constitutionally

protected interests, may not be absolute, no State interest could outweigh the rights of an individual in Nancy Cruzan's position....

The only state interest asserted here is a general interest in the preservation of life. But the State has no legitimate general interest in someone's life, completely abstracted from the interest of the person living that life, that could outweigh the person's choice to avoid medical treatment.... Thus, the State's general interest in life must accede to Nancy Cruzan's particularized and intense interest in self-determination in her choice of medical treatment. There is simply nothing legitimately within the State's purview to be gained by superseding her decision.

Moreover, there may be considerable danger that Missouri's rule of decision would impair rather than serve any interest the State does have in sustaining life. Current medical practice recommends use of heroic measures if there is a scintilla of a chance that the patient will recover, on the assumption that the measures will be discontinued should the patient improve. When the President's Commission [for the Study of Ethical Problems in Medicine and Biomedical and Behavioral Research] in 1982 approved the withdrawal of life support equipment from irreversibly vegetative patients, it explained that "[a]n even more troubling wrong occurs when a treatment that might save life or improve health is not started because the health care personnel are afraid that they will find it very difficult to stop the treatment if, as is fairly likely, it proves to be of little benefit and greatly burdens the patient."...

This is not to say that the State has no legitimate interests to assert here. As the majority recognizes, Missouri has a parens patriae interest in providing Nancy Cruzan, now incompetent, with as accurate as possible a determination of how she would exercise her rights under these circumstances. Second, if and when it is determined that Nancy Cruzan would want to continue treatment, the State may legitimately assert an interest in providing that treatment. But until Nancy's wishes have been determined, the only state interest

that may be asserted is an interest in safeguarding the accuracy of that determination.

Accuracy, therefore, must be our touchstone. Missouri may constitutionally impose only those procedural requirements that serve to enhance the accuracy of a determination of Nancy Cruzan's wishes or are at least consistent with an accurate determination. The Missouri "safeguard" that the Court upholds today does not meet that standard. The determination needed in this context is whether the incompetent person would choose to live in a persistent vegetative state on life-support or to avoid this medical treatment. Missouri's rule of decision imposes a markedly asymmetrical evidentiary burden. Only evidence of specific statements of treatment choice made by the patient when competent is admissible to support a finding that the patient, now in a persistent vegetative state, would wish to avoid further medical treatment. Moreover, this evidence must be clear and convincing. No proof is required to support a finding that the incompetent person would wish to continue treatment....

To be sure, courts have long erected clear and convincing evidence standards to place the greater risk of erroneous decisions on those bringing disfavored claims. In such cases, however, the choice to discourage certain claims was a legitimate, constitutional policy choice. In contrast, Missouri has no such power to disfavor a choice by Nancy Cruzan to avoid medical treatment, because Missouri has no legitimate interest in providing Nancy with treatment until it is established that this represents her choice. Just as a State may not override Nancy's choice directly, it may not do so indirectly through the imposition of a procedural rule....

Even more than its heightened evidentiary standard, the Missouri court's categorical exclusion of relevant evidence dispenses with any semblance of accurate fact finding. The court adverted to no evidence supporting its decision, but held that no clear and convincing, inherently reliable evidence had been presented to show that Nancy would want to avoid further treatment. In doing so, the court failed to consider statements Nancy had made to family members and a close friend. The court also failed to consider testimony from Nancy's mother and sister that they were certain that Nancy would want to discontinue artificial nutrition and hydration, even after the court found that Nancy's family was loving and without malignant motive. The court also failed to consider the conclusions of the guardian ad litem, appointed by the trial court, that there was clear and convincing evidence that Nancy would want to discontinue medical treatment and that this was in her best interests. . . .

[The] Missouri court's disdain for Nancy's statements in serious conversations not long before her accident, for the opinions of Nancy's family and friends as to her values, beliefs and certain choice, and even for the opinion of an outside objective fact finder appointed by the State evinces a disdain for Nancy Cruzan's own right to choose. The rules by which an incompetent person's wishes are determined must represent every effort to determine those wishes. The rule that the Missouri court adopted and that this Court upholds, however, skews the result away from a determination that as accurately as possible reflects the individual's own preferences and beliefs. It is a rule that transforms human beings into passive subjects of medical technology. . . .

As many as 10,000 patients are being maintained in persistent vegetative states in the United States, and the number is expected to increase significantly in the near future. Medical technology, developed over the past 20 or so years, is often capable of resuscitating people after they have stopped breathing or their hearts have stopped beating. Some of those people are brought fully back to life. Two decades ago, those who were not and could not swallow and digest food, died. Intravenous solutions could not provide sufficient calories to maintain people for more than a short time. Today, various forms of artificial feeding have been developed that are able to keep people metabolically alive for years, even decades. In addition, in this century, chronic or degenerative ailments have replaced communicable diseases as the primary causes of death. [A] fifth of all adults surviving to age 80 will suffer a progressive dementing disorder prior to death. . . .

[Missouri] and this Court have displaced Nancy's own assessment of the processes associated with dying. They have discarded evidence of her will, ignored her values, and deprived her of the right to a decision as closely approximating her own choice as humanly possible. They have done so disingenuously in her name, and openly in Missouri's own. That Missouri and this Court may truly be motivated only by concern for incompetent patients makes no matter. As one of our most prominent jurists warned us decades ago: "Experience should teach us to be most on our guard to protect liberty when the government's purposes are beneficent. . . . The greatest dangers to liberty lurk in insidious encroachment by men of zeal, well meaning but without understanding." *Olmstead* v. *United States* (1928) (Brandeis, J., dissenting).

I respectfully dissent.

Justice Stevens, Dissenting: Our Constitution is born of the proposition that all legitimate governments must secure the equal right of every person to "Life, Liberty, and the pursuit of Happiness." In the ordinary case we quite naturally assume that these three ends are compatible, mutually enhancing, and perhaps even coincident. . . .

[I]n my view, the Constitution requires the State to care for Nancy Cruzan's life in a way that gives appropriate respect to her own best interests. . . .

Nancy Cruzan's death, when it comes, cannot be an historic act of heroism; it will inevitably be the consequence of her tragic accident. But Nancy Cruzan's interest in life, no less than that of any other person, includes an interest in how she will be thought of after her death by those whose opinions mattered to her. There can be no doubt that her life made her dear to her family, and to others. How she dies will affect how that life is remembered. The trial court's order authorizing

Nancy's parents to cease their daughter's treatment would have permitted the family that cares for Nancy to bring to a close her tragedy and her death. Missouri's objection to that order subordinates Nancy's body, her family, and the lasting significance of her life to the State's own interests. . . .

Missouri asserts that its policy is related to a state interest in the protection of life. In my view, however, it is an effort to define life, rather than to protect it, that is the heart of Missouri's policy. Missouri insists, without regard to Nancy Cruzan's own interests, upon equating her life with the biological persistence of her bodily functions. Nancy Cruzan, it must be remembered, is not now simply incompetent. She is in a persistent vegetative state, and has been so for seven years. The trial court found, and no party contested, that Nancy has no possibility of recovery and no consciousness.

It seems to me that the Court errs insofar as it characterizes this case as involving "judgments about the 'quality' of life that a particular individual may enjoy." Nancy Cruzan is obviously "alive" in a physiological sense. But for patients like Nancy Cruzan, who have no consciousness and no chance of recovery, there is a serious question as to whether the mere persistence of their bodies is "life" as that word is commonly understood, or as it is used in both the Constitution and the Declaration of Independence. The State's unflagging determination to perpetuate Nancy Cruzan's physical existence is comprehensible only as an effort to define life's meaning, not as an attempt to preserve its sanctity.

This much should be clear from the oddity of Missouri's definition alone. Life, particularly human life, is not commonly thought of as a merely physiological condition or function. Its sanctity is often thought to derive from the impossibility of any such reduction. When people speak of life, they often mean to describe the experiences that comprise a person's history, as when it is said that somebody "led a good life." They may also mean to refer to the practical manifestation of the human spirit, a meaning captured by the familiar

observation that somebody "added life" to an assembly. If there is a shared thread among the various opinions on this subject, it may be that life is an activity which is at once the matrix for and an integration of a person's interest. In any event, absent some theological abstraction, the idea of life is not conceived separately from the idea of a living person. Yet, it is by precisely such a separation that Missouri asserts an interest in Nancy Cruzan's life in opposition to Nancy Cruzan's own interests. The resulting definition is uncommon indeed.

[My] disagreement with the Court is thus unrelated to its endorsement of the clear and convincing standard of proof for cases of this kind. Indeed, I agree that the controlling facts must be established with unmistakable clarity. The critical question, however, is not how to improve the controlling facts but rather what proven facts should be controlling. In my view, the constitutional answer is clear: the best interests of the individual, especially when buttressed by the interests of all related third parties, must prevail over any general state policy that simply ignores those interests. Indeed, the only apparent secular basis for the State's interest in life is the policy's persuasive impact upon people other than Nancy and her family. [The] failure of Missouri's policy to heed the interests of a dying individual with respect to matters so private is ample evidence of the policy's illegitimacy.

Only because Missouri has arrogated to itself the power to define life, and only because the Court permits this usurpation, are Nancy Cruzan's life and liberty put into disquieting conflict. If Nancy Cruzan's life were defined by reference to her own interests, so that her life expired when her biological existence ceased serving any of her own interests, then her constitutionally protected interest in freedom from unwanted treatment would not come into conflict with her constitutionally protected interest in life. Conversely, if there were any evidence that Nancy Cruzan herself defined life to encompass every form of biological persistence by a human being, so that the continuation of treatment would serve Nancy's own liberty, then once again there would be no conflict between life and liberty. The opposition of life and liberty in this case are thus not the result of Nancy Cruzan's tragic accident, but are instead the artificial consequence of Missouri's effort, and this Court's willingness, to abstract Nancy Cruzan's life from Nancy Cruzan's person.

Both this Court's majority and the state court's majority express great deference to the policy choice made by the state legislature. . . . [The] Court's deference seems ultimately to derive from the premise that chronically incompetent persons have no constitutionally cognizable interests at all, and so are not persons within the meaning of the Constitution. Deference of this sort is patently unconstitutional. It is also dangerous in ways that may not be immediately apparent. Today the State of Missouri has announced its intent to spend several hundred thousand dollars in preserving the life of Nancy Beth Cruzan in order to vindicate its general policy favoring the preservation of human life. Tomorrow, another State equally eager to champion an interest in the "quality of life" might favor a policy designed to ensure quick and comfortable deaths by denying treatment to categories of marginally hopeless cases. If the State in fact has an interest in defining life, and if the State's policy with respect to the termination of life-sustaining treatment commands deference from the judiciary, it is unclear how any resulting conflict between the best interests of the individual and the general policy of the State would be resolved. I believe the Constitution requires that the individual's vital interest in

liberty should prevail over the general policy in that case, just as in this.

That a contrary result is readily imaginable under the majority's theory makes manifest that this Court cannot defer to any State policy that drives a theoretical wedge between a person's life, on the one hand, and that person's liberty or happiness, on the other. The consequence of such a theory is to deny the personhood of those whose lives are defined by the State's interests rather than their own. This consequence may be acceptable in theology or in speculative philosophy, but it is radically inconsistent with the foundation of all legitimate government. Our Constitution presupposes a respect for the personhood of every individual, and nowhere is strict adherence to that principle more essential than in the Judicial Branch.

[The] Cruzan family's continuing concern provides a concrete reminder that Nancy Cruzan's interests did not disappear with her vitality or her consciousness. However commendable may be the State's interest in human life, it cannot pursue that interest by appropriating Nancy Cruzan's life as a symbol for its own purposes. Lives do not exist in abstraction from persons, and to pretend otherwise is not to honor but to desecrate the State's responsibility for protecting life. A State that seeks to demonstrate its commitment to life may do so by aiding those who are actively struggling for life and health. In this endeavor, unfortunately, no State can lack for opportunities: there can be no need to make an example of tragic cases like that of Nancy Cruzan.

I respectfully dissent.

REVIEW AND DISCUSSION QUESTIONS

1. Explain how the majority opinion, written by Justice Rehnquist, places this case in the context of other common-law decisions.
2. What "interests" does Justice Rehnquist think the state has in this case?
3. How does Justice Rehnquist defend the "standard of proof" required by Missouri law before a patient can be removed from life-support systems?
4. Summarize the grounds on which Justice Brennan dissents.
5. Justice Stevens wrote a separate dissent. Describe the similarities and differences between his analysis and the dissent by Justice Brennan.
6. If you were on the Court, how would you have ruled in this case? Explain.

Comparing Human Lives:
The Archbishop and the Chambermaid

William Godwin

In this selection from his book on political justice, William Godwin confronts the question of whether all human lives are of equal value, and argues that in fact human lives have very different worth. His book, including this passage, aroused heated discussion. In it, he argued that morality rests on impartial sympathy for others, and that only in small societies can we hope to live in a world without prejudice and thus be able to bring about the greatest happiness for all. William Godwin (1756–1836) was an English philosopher and novelist.

In a loose and general view I and my neighbour are both of us men, and of consequence entitled to equal attention. But in reality it is probable that one of us is a being of more worth and importance than the other. A man is of more worth than a beast, because, being possessed of higher faculties, he is capable of a more refined and genuine happiness. In the same manner the illustrious archbishop of Cambrai [Fenelon] was of more worth than his chambermaid, and there are few of us that would hesitate to pronounce, if his palace were in flames and the life of only one of them could be preserved, which of the two ought to be preferred. But there is another ground of preference beside the private consideration of one of them being farther removed from the state of a mere animal. We are not connected with one or two percipient beings, but with a society, a nation, and in some sense with the whole family of mankind. Of consequence that life ought to be preferred which will be most conducive to the general good. In saving the life of Fenelon, suppose at the moment when he was conceiving the project of his immortal *Telemachus,* I should be promoting the benefit of thousands who have been cured by the perusal of it of some error, vice and consequent unhappiness. Nay, my benefit would extend farther than this, for every individual thus cured has become a better member of society and has contributed in his turn to the happiness, the information and improvement of others. Supposing I had been myself the chambermaid, I ought to have chosen to die rather than that Fenelon should have died. The life of Fenelon was really preferable to that of the chambermaid. But understanding is the faculty that perceives the truth of this and similar propositions; and justice is the principle that regulates my conduct accordingly. It would have been just in the chambermaid to have preferred the archbishop to herself. To have done otherwise would have been a breach of justice.

Supposing the chambermaid had been my wife, my mother or my benefactor. This would not alter the truth of the proposition. The life of Fenelon would still be more valuable than that of the chambermaid; and justice—pure, unadulterated justice—would still have preferred that which was most valuable. Justice would have taught me to save the life of Fenelon at the expense of the other. What magic is there in the pronoun "my" to overturn the decisions of everlasting truth? My wife or my mother may be a fool or a prostitute, malicious, lying or dishonest. If they be, of what consequence is it that they are mine?

"But my mother endured for me the pains of child bearing, and nourished me in the helplessness of infancy." When she first subjected herself to the necessity of these cares, she was probably influenced by no particular motives of benevolence to her future offspring. Every voluntary benefit however entitles the bestower to

From William Godwin, *An Enquiry Concerning Political Justice* (1793).

some kindness and retribution. But why so? Because a voluntary benefit is an evidence of benevolent intention; that is, of virtue. It is the disposition of the mind, not the external action, that entitles to respect. But the merit of this disposition is equal whether the benefit was conferred upon me or upon another. I and another man cannot both be right in preferring our own individual benefactor, for no man can be at the same time both better and worse than his neighbour. My benefactor ought to be esteemed, not because he bestowed a benefit upon me, but because he bestowed it upon a human being. His desert will be in exact proportion to the degree in which that human being was worthy of the distinction conferred. Thus every view of the subject brings us back to the consideration of my neighbour's moral worth and his importance to the general weal as the only standard to determine the treatment to which he is entitled. Gratitude therefore, a principle which has so often been the theme of the moralist and the poet, is no part either of justice or virtue.

REVIEW AND DISCUSSION QUESTIONS

1. Why are human lives worth more than those of the "beasts"? What do you think Godwin means by "higher faculties"?

2. On what grounds does Godwin think the archbishop's life is worth more than his maid's?

3. Suppose Godwin viewed the archbishop in a way that is similar to how you revere, say, Martin Luther King, Jr. Or imagine somebody else who you respect tremendously: a great scientist, for instance, or perhaps a teacher or an artist. Do you think that person's life was worth no more than anybody else's? If you disagree with Godwin, explain the sense in which you think the two lives *are* worth the same. Is what you think about that incompatible with Godwin's position? Explain.

4. Godwin hated prejudice and thought it the source of much that is wrong in the world. He also stressed the importance of impartiality. Can you believe those ideals without agreeing with him about the value of human lives? Explain.

An Alternative to the Ethic of Euthanasia

Arthur J. Dyck

In this selection, Arthur J. Dyck raises an array of objections to euthanasia, arguing that it is inherently wrong for people to kill themselves and that euthanasia is a dangerous social policy. Responding to those who defend euthanasia on grounds of compassion and autonomy, Dyck proposes another approach, which he terms "benemortasia" or good death.

The arguments for euthanasia focus upon two humane and significant concerns: compassion for those who are painfully and terminally ill; and concern for the human dignity associated with freedom of choice. Compassion and freedom are values that sustain and enhance the common good. The question here, however, is how these values affect our behavior toward the dying.

The argument for compassion usually occurs

From Arthur J. Dyck, "An Alternative to the Ethic of Euthanasia," in *To Live and to Let Die*, ed. R. H. Williams (New York: Springer-Verlag, 1973), pp. 98–112. Reprinted by permission of the publisher.

in the form of attacking the inhumanity of keeping dying people alive when they are in great pain or when they have lost almost all of their usual functions, particularly when they have lost the ability or will to communicate with others. . . . The argument for compassion is supplemented by an argument for greater freedom for a patient to choose how and when he or she will die. For one thing, the patient should not be subjected to medical treatment to which that patient does not consent. Those who argue for voluntary euthanasia extend this notion by arguing that the choice to withhold techniques that would prolong life is a choice to shorten life. Hence, if one can choose to shorten one's life, why cannot one ask a physician by a simple and direct act of intervention to put an end to one's life? Here it is often argued that physicians already curtail life by means of pain-killing drugs, which in the doses administered, will hasten death. Why should not the law recognize and sanction a simple and direct hastening of death, should the patient wish it?

How do the proponents of euthanasia view the general prohibition against killing? First of all, they maintain that we are dealing here with people who will surely die regardless of the intervention of medicine. They advocate the termination of suffering and the lawful foreshortening of the dying process. Secondly, although the patient is committing suicide, and the physician is an accomplice in such a suicide, both acts are morally justifiable to cut short the suffering of one who is dying.

It is important to be very clear about the precise moral reasoning by which advocates of voluntary euthanasia justify suicide and assisting a suicide. They make no moral distinction between those instances when a patient or a physician chooses to have life shortened by failing to accept or use life-prolonging techniques and those instances when a patient or a physician shortens life by employing a death-dealing chemical or instrument. They make no moral distinction between a drug given to kill pain, which also shortens life, and a substance given precisely to shorten life and for no other reason. Presumably these distinctions are not

honored, because regardless of the stratagem employed—regardless of whether one is permitting to die or killing directly—the result is the same, the patient's life is shortened. Hence, it is maintained that, if you can justify one kind of act that shortens the life of the dying, you can justify any act that shortens the life of the dying when this act is seen to be willed by the one who is dying. Moral reasoning of this sort is strictly utilitarian; it focuses solely on the consequences of acts, not on their intent. . . .

Because of this loss of a merely descriptive term for a happy death, it is necessary to invent a term for a happy or good death— namely, benemortasia. The familiar derivatives for this new term are *bene* (good) and *mors* (death). . . . An ethic of benemortasia does not stand in opposition to the values of compassion and human freedom. It differs, however, from the ethic of euthanasia in its understanding of how these values are best realized. In particular, certain constraints upon human freedom are recognized and emphasized as enabling human beings to increase compassion and freedom rather than diminish them. . . .

Our ethic of benemortasia acknowledges the freedom of patients who are incurably ill to refuse interventions that prolong dying and the freedom of physicians to honor such wishes. However, these actions are not acts of suicide and assisting in suicide. In our ethic of benemortasia, suicide and assisting in suicide are unjustifiable acts of killing. Unlike the ethic of those who would legalize voluntary euthanasia, our ethic makes a moral distinction between acts that permit death and acts that cause death. . . . From the point of view of the dying person, when could his or her decisions be called a deliberate act to end life, the act we usually designate as suicide? Only, it seems to me, when the dying person commits an act that has the immediate intent of ending life and has no other purpose. That act may be to use, or ask the physician to use, a chemical or an instrument that has no other immediate effect than to end the dying person's life. If, for the sake of relieving pain, a dying person chooses drugs administered in potent doses, the intent of this act is not to shorten life, even though it has that effect. It is a choice as to how to live while dying. Similarly, if a patient chooses to forego medical interventions that would have the effect of prolonging his or her life without in any way promising release from death, this also is a choice as to what is the most meaningful way to spend the remainder of life, however short that may be. The choice to use drugs to relieve pain and the choice not to use medical measures that cannot promise a cure for one's dying are no different in principle from the choices we make throughout our lives as to how much we will rest, how hard we will work, how little and how much medical intervention we will seek or tolerate, and the like. For society or physicians to map out life styles for individuals with respect to such decisions is surely beyond anything that we find in Stoic, Jewish, or Christian ethics. Such intervention in the liberty of individuals is far beyond what is required in any society whose rules are intended to constrain people against harming others.

But human freedom should not be extended to include the taking of one's own life. Causing one's own death cannot generally be justified, even when one is dying. To see why this is so, we have to consider how causing one's death does violence to one's self and harms others.

The person who causes his or her own death repudiates the meaningfulness and worth of his or her own life. To decide to initiate an act that has as its primary purpose to end one's life is to decide that that life has no worth to anyone, especially to oneself. It is an act that ends all choices regarding what one's life and whatever is left of it is to symbolize.

Suicide is the ultimately effective way of shutting out all other people from one's life. Psychologists have observed how hostility for others can be expressed through taking one's own life. People who might want access to the dying one to make restitution, offer reparation, bestow last kindnesses, or clarify misunderstandings are cut off by such an act. Every kind of potentially and actually meaningful contact and relation among persons is

irrevocably severed except by means of memories and whatever life beyond death may offer. Certainly for those who are left behind by death, there can remain many years of suffering occasioned by that death. The sequence of dying an inevitable death can be much better accepted than the decision on the part of a dying one that he or she has no worth to anyone. An act that presupposes that final declaration leaves tragic overtones for anyone who participated in even the smallest way in that person's dying.

But the problem is even greater. If in principle a person can take his or her own life whenever he or she no longer finds it meaningful, there is nothing in principle that prevents anyone from taking his or her life, no matter what the circumstances. For if the decision hinges on whether one regards his or her own life as meaningful, anyone can regard his or her own life as meaningless even under circumstances that would appear to be most fortunate and opportune for an abundant life.

What about those who would commit suicide or request euthanasia in order to cease being a "burden" on those who are providing care for them? If it is a choice to accept death by refusing non-curative care that prolongs dying, the freedom to embrace death or give one's life in this way is honored by our ethic of benemortasia. What is rejected is the freedom to cause death whether by suicide or by assisting in one.

How a person dies has a definite meaning for those to whom that person is related. In the first year of bereavement, the rate of death among bereaved relatives of those who die in hospitals is twice that of bereaved relatives of those who die at home; sudden deaths away from hospital and home increase the death rate of the bereaved even more.

The courage to be, as expressed in Christian and Jewish thought, is more than the overcoming of the fear of death, although it includes that Stoic dimension. It is the courage to accept one's own life as having worth no matter what life may bring, including the threat of death, because that life remains meaningful and is regarded as worthy by God, regardless of what that life may be like. . . . The courage to be as a part recognizes that one is not merely one's own, that one's life is a gift bestowed and protected by the human community and by the ultimate forces that make up the cycle of birth and death. In the cycle of birth and death, there may be suffering, as there is joy, but suffering does not render a life meaningless or worthless. Suffering people need the support of others; suffering people should not be encouraged to commit suicide by their community, or that community ceases to be a community.

This consideration brings us to a further difficulty with voluntary euthanasia and its legalization. Not only does euthanasia involve suicide, but also, if legalized, it sanctions assistance in suicide by physicians. Legislation like the Voluntary Euthanasia Act of 1969 makes it a duty of the medical profession to take someone else's life for him. Here the principle not to kill is even further eroded and violated by giving the physician the power and the encouragement to decide that someone else's life is no longer worth living. The whole notion that a physician can engage in euthanasia implies acceptance of the principle that another person's life is no longer meaningful enough to sustain, a principle that does not afford protection for the lives of any of the most defenseless, voiceless, or otherwise dependent members of a community. Everyone in a community is potentially a victim of such a principle, particularly among members of racial minorities, the very young, and the very old.

Those who would argue that these consequences of a policy of voluntary euthanasia cannot be predicted fail to see two things: that we have already had an opportunity to observe what happens when the principle that sanctions euthanasia is accepted by a society; and that regardless of what the consequences may be of such acts, the acts themselves are wrong in principle.

With respect to the first point, Leo Alexander's (1949) very careful analysis of medical practices and attitudes of German physicians before and during the reign of Nazism in Germany should serve as a definite warning against the consequences of making euthanasia a public policy. He notes that the outlook of German physicians that led to their cooperation in what became a policy of mass murders,

> started with the acceptance of that attitude, basic in the euthanasia movement, that there is such a thing as life not worthy to be lived. This attitude in its early stages concerned itself merely with the severely and chronically sick. Gradually the sphere of those to be included in this category was enlarged to include the socially unproductive, the racially unwanted, and finally all non-Germans. But it is important to realize that the infinitely small wedged-in lever from which this entire trend of mind received its impetus was the attitude toward the nonrehabilitable sick.

Those who reject out of hand any comparison of what happened in Nazi Germany with what we can expect here in the United States should consider current examples of medical practice in this nation. The treatment of mongoloids is a case in point. Now that the notion is gaining acceptance that a fetus diagnosed in the womb as mongoloid can, at the discretion of a couple or the pregnant woman, be justifiably aborted, instances of infanticide in hospitals are being reported. At Johns Hopkins Hospital, for example, an allegedly mongoloid infant whose parents would not permit an operation that is generally successful in securing normal physical health and development, was ordered to have "nothing by mouth," condemning that infant to a death that took 15 days. . . .

Someone may argue that the mongoloid was permitted to die, not killed. But this is faulty reasoning. In the case of an infant whose future life and happiness could be reasonably assured through surgery, we are not dealing with someone who is dying and with intervention that has no curative effect. The fact that some physicians refer to this as a case of permitting to die is an ominous portent of the dangers inherent in accepting the principle that a physician or another party can decide for a patient that his or her life is not worth living. Equally ominous is the assumption that this principle, once accepted, can easily be limited to cases of patients for whom no curative intervention is known to exist. . . .

The hesitation to commit suicide and the ambivalence of the dying about their worth should give one pause before one signs a declaration that empowers a physician to decide that at some point one can no longer be trusted as competent to judge whether or not one wants to die. Physicians are also frail humans, and mistaken diagnoses, research interests, and sometimes errors of judgment that stem from a desire for organs, are part of the practice of medicine.

Comatose patients pose special problems for an ethic of benemortasia as they do for the advocates of voluntary euthanasia. Where patients are judged to be irreversibly comatose and where sustained efforts have been made to restore such persons to consciousness, no clear case can be made for permitting to die, even though it seems merciful to do so. It seems that the best we can do is to develop some rough social and medical consensus about a reasonable length of time for keeping "alive" a person's organ systems after "brain death" has been decided. Because of the pressures to do research and to transplant organs, it may also be necessary to employ special patient advocates who are not physicians and nurses. These patient advocates, trained in medical ethics, would function as ombudsmen.

In summary, even if the practice of euthanasia were to be confined to those who voluntarily request an end to their lives, no physician could in good conscience participate in such an act. To decide directly to cause the death of a patient is to abandon a cardinal principle of medical practice—namely, to do no harm to one's patient. The relief of suffering, which is surely a time-honored role for the physician, does not extend to an act that presupposes that the life of a patient who is suffering is not worthy to be lived. As we have argued, not even the patient who is dying can justifiably and unilaterally universalize the principle by which a dying life would be declared to be worthless.

REVIEW AND DISCUSSION QUESTIONS

1. Describe the practical difficulties and dangers that Dyck envisions with policies allowing euthanasia. Are there other problems associated with euthanasia policies that would have to be dealt with? Do you think that Dyck is right to believe these problems are severe enough to reject euthanasia?
2. Explain Dyck's argument that euthanasia is wrong because it involves suicide. What does he think is wrong with suicide?
3. Most people feel better about euthanasia if there is informed consent from the person to be killed or allowed to die. What problems are there in being sure that the consent is truly voluntary? Truly informed?
4. Does suicide "repudiate the meaningfulness and worth of life"? Why or why not?
5. Do you agree that the distinction between causing and permitting death is important? Explain.
6. How would Dyck view the *Cruzan* opinion? Was it a euthanasia case? Was her life "meaningful" in Dyck's terms?
7. Is self-sacrifice (falling on a grenade to save a comrade, for example) suicide in Dyck's view? If not, then why is taking a pain-killing drug that leads to death also not suicide, assuming it is equally clear in both cases that the person will die?

Active and Passive Euthanasia

James Rachels

In this essay, James Rachels does not defend euthanasia directly; instead, he argues that if we are going to use euthanasia, then we should use active rather than passive means to kill. Not only is it more humane, but the widely respected distinction between killing and letting die, he argues, makes no moral difference. Reliance on the distinction also encourages people to make medical decisions on irrelevant grounds, according to Rachels. James Rachels is University Professor of Philosophy at the University of Alabama, Birmingham.

The distinction between active and passive euthanasia is thought to be crucial for medical ethics. The idea is that it is permissible, at least in some cases, to withhold treatment and allow a patient to die, but it is never permissible to take any direct action designed to kill the patient. This doctrine seems to be accepted by most doctors, and is endorsed in a statement adopted by the House of Delegates of the American Medical Association on December 4, 1973:

> The intentional termination of the life of one human being by another—mercy killing—is contrary to that for which the medical profession stands and is contrary to the policy of the American Medical Association.
>
> The cessation of the employment of extraordinary means to prolong the life of the body when there is irrefutable evidence that biological death is imminent is the decision of the patient and/or his immediate family. The advice and judgment of the physician should be freely available to the patient and/or his immediate family.

However, a strong case can be made against this doctrine. In what follows I will set out some of the relevant arguments, and urge doctors to reconsider their views on this matter.

To begin with a familiar type of situation, a patient who is dying of incurable cancer of the throat is in terrible pain, which can no longer be satisfactorily alleviated. He is certain to die within a few days, even if present treatment is continued, but he does not want to go on living for those days since the pain is unbearable. So he asks the doctor for an end to it, and his family joins in the request.

Suppose the doctor agrees to withhold treatment, as the conventional doctrine says he may. The justification for his doing so is that the patient is in terrible agony, and since he is going to die anyway, it would be wrong to prolong his suffering needlessly. But now notice this. If one simply withholds treatment, it may take the patient longer to die, and so he may suffer more than he would if more direct action were taken and a lethal injection given. This fact provides strong reason for thinking that, once the initial decision not to prolong his agony has been made, active euthanasia is actually preferable to passive euthanasia, rather than the reverse. To say otherwise is to endorse the option that leads to more suffering rather than less, and is contrary to the humanitarian impulse that prompts the decision not to prolong his life in the first place.

Part of my point is that the process of being "allowed to die" can be relatively slow and painful, whereas being given a lethal injection is relatively quick and painless. Let me give a different sort of example. In the United States about one in 600 babies is born with Down's syndrome. Most of these babies are otherwise healthy—that is, with only the usual pediatric care, they will proceed to an otherwise normal infancy. Some, however, are born with congenital defects such as intestinal obstructions that require operations if they are to live.

Reprinted with permission from *The New England Journal of Medicine,* 292, no. 2 (Jan. 9, 1975), pp. 78–80.

Sometimes, the parents and the doctor will decide not to operate, and let the infant die. Anthony Shaw describes what happens then.

> ... When surgery is denied [the doctor] must try to keep the infant from suffering while natural forces sap the baby's life away. As a surgeon whose natural inclination is to use the scalpel to fight off death, standing by and watching a salvageable baby die is the most emotionally exhausting experience I know. It is easy at a conference, in a theoretical discussion, to decide that such infants should be allowed to die. It is altogether different to stand by in the nursery and watch as dehydration and infection wither a tiny being over hours and days. This is a terrible ordeal for me and the hospital staff—much more so than for the parents who never set foot in the nursery.[1]

I can understand why some people are opposed to all euthanasia, and insist that such infants must be allowed to live. I think I can also understand why other people favor destroying these babies quickly and painlessly. But why should anyone favor letting "dehydration and infection wither a tiny being over hours and days"? The doctrine that says that a baby may be allowed to dehydrate and wither, but may not be given an injection that would end its life without suffering, seems so patently cruel as to require no further refutation. The strong language is not intended to offend, but only to put the point in the clearest possible way.

My second argument is that the conventional doctrine leads to decisions concerning life and death made on irrelevant grounds.

Consider again the case of the infants with Down's syndrome who need operations for congenital defects unrelated to the syndrome to live. Sometimes, there is no operation, and the baby dies, but when there is no such defect, the baby lives on. Now, an operation such as that to remove an intestinal obstruction is not prohibitively difficult. The reason why such operations are not performed in these cases is, clearly, that the child has Down's syndrome and the parents and doctor judge that because of that fact it is better for the child to die.

But notice that this situation is absurd, no matter what view one takes of the lives and potentials of such babies. If the life of such an infant is worth preserving, what does it matter if it needs a simple operation? Or, if one thinks it better that such a baby should not live on, what difference does it make that it happens to have an unobstructed intestinal tract? In either case, the matter of life and death is being decided on irrelevant grounds. It is the Down's syndrome, and not the intestines, that is the issue. The matter should be decided, if at all, on that basis, and not be allowed to depend on the essentially irrelevant question of whether the intestinal tract is blocked.

What makes this situation possible, of course, is the idea that when there is an intestinal blockage, one can "let the baby die," but when there is no such defect there is nothing that can be done, for one must not "kill" it. The fact that this idea leads to such results as deciding life or death on irrelevant grounds is another good reason why the doctrine should be rejected.

One reason why so many people think that there is an important moral difference between active and passive euthanasia is that they think killing someone is morally worse than letting someone die. But is it? Is killing, in itself, worse than letting die? To investigate this issue, two cases may be considered that are exactly alike except that one involves killing whereas the other involves letting someone die. Then, it can be asked whether this difference makes any difference to the moral assessments. It is important that the cases be exactly alike, except for this one difference, since otherwise one cannot be confident that it is this difference, and not some other that accounts for any variation in the assessments of the two cases. So, let us consider this pair of cases:

In the first, Smith stands to gain a large inheritance if anything should happen to his six-year-old cousin. One evening while the child is taking his bath, Smith sneaks into the bathroom and drowns the child, and then arranges things so that it will look like an accident.

In the second, Jones also stands to gain if anything should happen to his six-year-old cousin. Like Smith, Jones sneaks in planning to drown the child in his bath. However, just as he enters the bathroom Jones sees the child slip and hit his head, and fall face down in the water. Jones is delighted; he stands by, ready to push the child's head back under if it is necessary, but it is not necessary. With only a little thrashing about, the child drowns all by himself, "accidentally," as Jones watches and does nothing.

Now Smith killed the child, whereas Jones "merely" let the child die. That is the only difference between them. Did either man behave better, from a moral point of view? If the difference between killing and letting die were in itself a morally important matter, one should say that Jones's behavior was less reprehensible than Smith's. But does one really want to say that? I think not. In the first place, both men acted from the same motive, personal gain, and both had exactly the same end in view when they acted. It may be inferred from Smith's conduct that he is a bad man, although that judgment may be withdrawn or modified if certain further facts are learned about him— for example, that he is mentally deranged. But would not the very same thing be inferred about Jones from his conduct? And would not the same further considerations also be relevant to any modification of this judgment? Moreover, suppose Jones pleaded, in his own defense, "After all, I didn't do anything except just stand there and watch the child drown. I didn't kill him; I only let him die." Again, if letting die were in itself less bad than killing, this defense should have at least some weight. But it does not. Such a "defense" can only be regarded as a grotesque perversion of moral reasoning. Morally speaking, it is no defense at all.

Now it may be pointed out, quite properly, that the cases of euthanasia with which doctors are concerned are not like this at all. They do not involve personal gain or the destruction of normal healthy children. Doctors are concerned only with cases in which the patient's life is of no further use to him, or in which the patient's life has become or will soon become a terrible burden. However, the point is the same in these cases: the bare difference between

killing and letting die does not, in itself, make a moral difference. If a doctor lets a patient die, for humane reasons, he is in the same moral position as if he had given the patient a lethal injection for humane reasons. If his decision was wrong—if, for example, the patient's illness was in fact curable—the decision would be equally regrettable no matter which method was used to carry it out. And if the doctor's decision was the right one, the method used is not in itself important.

The AMA policy statement isolates the crucial issue very well; the crucial issue is "the intentional termination of the life of one human being by another." But after identifying this issue, and forbidding "mercy killing," the statement goes on to deny that the cessation of treatment is the intentional termination of a life. This is where the mistake comes in, for what is the cessation of treatment, in these circumstances, if it is not "the intentional termination of the life of one human being by another"? Of course it is exactly that, and if it were not, there would be no point to it.

Many people will find this judgment hard to accept. One reason, I think, is that it is very easy to conflate the question of whether killing is, in itself, worse than letting die, with the very different question of whether most actual cases of killing are more reprehensible than most actual cases of letting die. Most actual cases of killing are clearly terrible (think, for example, of all the murders reported in the newspapers), and one hears of such cases every day. On the other hand, one hardly ever hears of a case of letting die, except for the actions of doctors who are motivated by humanitarian reasons. So one learns to think of killing in a much worse light than of letting die. But this does not mean that there is something about killing that makes it in itself worse than letting die, for it is not the bare difference between killing and letting die that makes the difference in these cases. Rather, the other factors—the murderer's motive of personal gain, for example, contrasted with the doctor's humanitarian motivation—account for different reactions to the different cases.

I have argued that killing is not in itself any worse than letting die; if my contention is right, it follows that active euthanasia is not any worse than passive euthanasia. What arguments can be given on the other side? The most common, I believe, is the following:

"The important difference between active and passive euthanasia is that, in passive euthanasia, the doctor does not do anything to bring about the patient's death. The doctor does nothing, and the patient dies of whatever ills already afflict him. In active euthanasia, however, the doctor does something to bring about the patient's death; he kills him. The doctor who gives the patient with cancer a lethal injection has himself caused his patient's death; whereas if he merely ceases treatment, the cancer is the cause of the death."

A number of points need to be made here. The first is that it is not exactly correct to say that in passive euthanasia the doctor does nothing, for he does do one thing that is very important: he lets the patient die. "Letting someone die" is certainly different, in some respects, from other types of action—mainly in that it is a kind of action that one may perform by way of not performing certain other actions. For example, one may let a patient die by way of not giving medication, just as one may insult someone by way of not shaking his hand. But for any purpose of moral assessment, it is a type of action nonetheless. The decision to let a patient die is subject to moral appraisal in the same way that a decision to kill him would be subject to moral appraisal: it may be assessed as wise or unwise, compassionate or sadistic, right or wrong. If a doctor deliberately let a patient die who was suffering from a routinely curable illness, the doctor would certainly be to blame for what he had done, just as he would be to blame if he had needlessly killed the patient. Charges against him would then be appropriate. If so, it would be no defense at all for him to insist that he didn't "do anything." He would have done something very serious indeed, for he let his patient die.

Fixing the cause of death may be very important from a legal point of view, for it may determine whether criminal charges are brought against the doctor. But I do not think that this notion can be used to show a moral difference between active and passive euthanasia. The reason why it is considered bad to be the cause of someone's death is that death is regarded as a great evil—and so it is. However, if it has been decided that euthanasia—even passive euthanasia—is desirable in a given case, it has also been decided that in this instance death is no greater an evil than the patient's continued existence. And if this is true, the usual reason for not wanting to be the cause of someone's death simply does not apply.

Finally, doctors may think that all of this is only of academic interest—the sort of thing that philosophers may worry about but that has no practical bearing on their own work. After all, doctors must be concerned about the legal consequences of what they do, and active euthanasia is clearly forbidden by the law. But even so, doctors should also be concerned with the fact that the law is forcing upon them a moral doctrine that may well be indefensible, and has a considerable effect on their practices. Of course, most doctors are not now in the position of being coerced in this matter, for they do not regard themselves as merely going along with what the law requires. Rather, in statements such as the AMA policy statement that I have quoted, they are endorsing this doctrine as a central point of medical ethics. In that statement, active euthanasia is condemned not merely as illegal but as "contrary to that for which the medical profession stands," whereas passive euthanasia is approved. However, the preceding considerations suggest that there is really no moral difference between the two, considered in themselves (there may be important moral differences in some cases in their consequences, but, as I pointed out, these differences may make active euthanasia, and not passive euthanasia, the morally preferable option). So, whereas doctors may have to discriminate between active and passive euthanasia to satisfy the law, they should not do any more than that. In particular, they should not give the distinction any added authority and weight by writing it into official statements of medical ethics.

NOTE

1. A. Shaw, "Doctor, Do We Have a Choice?" *The New York Times Magazine,* Jan. 30, 1972, p. 54.

REVIEW AND DISCUSSION QUESTIONS

1. How does Rachels explain the generally held belief that it is worse to kill than allow to die?
2. Describe the relevance of the Smith and Jones cases to Rachels's thesis.
3. What difference is there between the drowning-child case and euthanasia? Does that difference weaken Rachels's argument?
4. Are there arguments you think important that weaken Rachels's position that a doctor who lets a person die is in the same moral position as one who gives a lethal injection?

Defective Newborns and the Morality of Termination

Richard B. Brandt

Whether done passively or actively, the decision to administer euthanasia to severely defective newborns is among the most difficult of all to make. Here Richard Brandt argues that each of four relevant considerations leads to the conclusion that in some cases, at least, euthanasia is the best thing to do. Richard B. Brandt was professor of philosophy of the University of Michigan.

One of the ethical issues uppermost in the minds of practicing physicians at the present time is what they should do, or recommend to be done, when a seriously defective infant is born. . . .

Historically, many writers, including Pope Pius XI in *Casti Connubii* (1930), have affirmed an absolute prohibition against killing anyone who is neither guilty of a capital crime, nor an unjust assailant threatening one's life (killing in self-defense), except in case of "extreme necessity." This view leaves some questions open. It certainly implies that a defective newborn may not be given a lethal injection. But it is far from clear that it requires complicated and expensive surgery and other treatment, over a period of years, in order to save a life. I wish merely to point out this ambiguity. Historically, I believe this tradition of absolute prohibition of "killing" derives from the Biblical injunction, "Thou shalt not kill," which itself seems to involve the same ambiguity. Does "not killing" mean saving a life by use of extraordinary means? However that may be, the Biblical injunction requires interpretation. Does it forbid suicide, killing of animals or even plants? If we ask ourselves, for instance, whether it is morally wrong for a terminally ill patient in great pain to terminate his own life, I think we feel that the

From Richard B. Brandt, "Defective Newborns and the Morality of Termination," in *Infanticide and the Value of Life,* ed. Marvin Kohl (Buffalo: Prometheus Books, 1978). Reprinted by permission.

Biblical injunction needs qualification, or at least reflection! And once we see that interpretation of the scope of a proposed moral principle must be undertaken, we see that its force for the problem of interest to us must be reconsidered. My belief is that virtually all of us would think that there are circumstances in which it is morally not wrong for a person to terminate his own life. And I suggest that the Biblical injunction does not settle the question whether it is morally right or wrong, in the case of some defective newborns, not to perform surgery to prolong their lives, or even to terminate them painlessly.

I want now to consider four lines of thinking, which I believe bear on a reasonable answer to our problem. They all rest on what I take to be rather widespread moral convictions, which I imagine all of you will share.

1. THE PROSPECTIVE QUALITY OF LIFE OF DEFECTIVE NEWBORNS

Suppose that killing a defective newborn, or allowing it to die, would not be an *injury,* but would rather be doing the infant a favor. In that case we should feel intuitively less opposed to termination of newborns, and presumably rational persons would be more inclined to support a moral code permitting such an action. In that case we would feel rather as we do about frustrating a suicide attempt in order that the person be elaborately tortured to death at a later stage. André Malraux, in *Man's Fate,* describes an incident of the capture of a group of revolutionary soldiers by Chiang Kai-shek's army. There was no trial. One by one they were being taken to a nearby steam locomotive, with the firebox roaring, and they were executed by being thrust, headfirst, into the firebox. One of the captives had a few cyanide pills. He gave all but one of these to his friends, who accepted and used them gratefully. He kept one for himself. Then he spied a young boy, also one who was to be killed, shaking in terror. He gave his last pill to the young boy, electing to be killed in the firebox himself. I believe everybody would think he had done the young boy a favor, and

that he performed a heroic act. Doubtless this is an extreme case, but we do sometimes do a person a favor by giving a person the means to shorten his own life. Are we doing something like this if we do not treat, or even painlessly terminate the life of, a severely defective newborn? A British physician, John Lorber, has claimed, on the basis of experience with over 1,000 *spina bifida* babies treated at Sheffield, England, that, in the words of Dr. Robert Reid's recent article in a Report of the Hastings Center, it is "possible to say with accuracy on the first day of life whether that baby would have an existence compatible with health, dignity and all other factors which contribute to a reasonable quality of life."

It may be said that we have no way of knowing what the conscious experiences of defective children are like, and that we have no competence in any case to decide when or what kind of life is bad or not worth living. Further, it may be said that predictions about a defective newborn's prospects for the future are precarious, in view of possible further advances of medicine. It does seem, however, that here as everywhere the rational person will follow the evidence about the present or future facts. But there is a serious question for philosophers, how to decide whether a life is bad or not worth living.

In the case of *some* defective newborns, it seems clear that their prospective life is bad. Suppose, as sometimes happens, a child is hydrocephalic with an extremely low I.Q., is blind and deaf, has no control over its body, and can only lie on its back all day and have all its needs taken care of by others, and even cries out with pain when it is touched or lifted. Infants born with *spina bifida*—and these number over 2 per 1,000 births—are normally not so badly off, but sometimes they are so.

But what criterion are we using if we say that such a life is bad? One criterion might be called a "happiness" criterion. If a person likes a moment of experience while he is having it, his life is so far good; if a person dislikes a moment of experience while he is having it, his life is so far bad. Based on such reactions, we might construct a "happiness curve" for a person, going up above the indifference axis when a moment of experience is liked—and how far above depending on how strongly it is liked—and dipping down below the line when a moment is disliked. Then this criterion would say that a life is worth living if there is a net balance of positive area. . . .

Is the prospective life of the seriously defective newborn, like the one described above, bad or good according to this criterion? One thing seems clear: that it is less good than is the prospective life of a normal infant. But is it bad?

We have to do some extrapolating from what we know. For instance, such a child will presumably suffer from severe sensory deprivation; he is simply not getting interesting stimuli. On the basis of laboratory data, it is plausible to think the child's experience is at best boring or uncomfortable. Insofar as the child's experience is painful, of course, its moments are on the negative side. One must suppose that such a child hardly suffers from disappointment, since it will not learn to expect anything exciting, beyond being fed and fondled, and these events will be regularly forthcoming. One might expect such a child to suffer from isolation and loneliness, but insofar as this is true the object of dislike probably should be classified as just sensory deprivation; dislike of loneliness seems to depend on the deprivation of past pleasure of human company. There are also some positive enjoyments: of eating, drinking, elimination, and so on. But the brief enjoyments can hardly balance the long stretches of boredom, discomfort, or even pain. I speculate that on the whole the lives of such children are bad, on the happiness criterion.

Naturally we cannot generalize about the cases of *all* "defective" newborns: there are all sorts of defects, and the cases I have described are about the worst. A child with moderately severe *spina bifida* may, if he survives the numerous operations, I suppose, adjust to the frustrations of immobility; he may become accustomed to the embarrassments of no bladder or bowel control; he may have some intellectual enjoyments like playing chess; he will

suffer from observing what others have but he cannot, such as sexual satisfactions, in addition to the pain of repeated surgery. How does it all balance out? Surely not as very good, but perhaps above the indifference level.

It may fairly be said, I think, that the lives of some defective newborns are destined to be bad on the whole, and it would be a favor to them if their lives were terminated. Contrariwise, the prospective lives of many defective newborns are modestly pleasant, and it would be some injury to them to be terminated, albeit the lives they will live are ones some of us would prefer not to live at all.

2. CONSENT

Let us now leave the question whether termination of a defective newborn would be doing him a favor, and ask whether he might possibly be construed to *consent* to nontreatment or termination. The suggestion that the newborn might be so construed may seem absurd at the outset, but I wish to pursue the point. The reason I wish to pursue it is that intuitively we would all, I think, be *more* favorably inclined to conclude that it is right to let the defective die if we could think he did not object; and I think also that, in case he could be construed to consent, rational persons would be more ready to support a moral code permitting termination. Notice that we think that if an ill person has signified what we think a rational and deliberated desire to die, we are morally better justified in withdrawing life-supporting measures than we otherwise would be.

The newborn, however, is incapable of expressing his preference (giving consent) at all, much less expressing a rational deliberated preference. There could in theory be court-appointed guardians or proxies, presumably disinterested parties, authorized to give such consent on his behalf; but even so this would not be his consent.

Nevertheless, there is a fact about the mental life of the newborn (defective or not) such that, when we understand it, it seems to us clear that he would not *object*—even rationally or after deliberation if that were possible—to his life being terminated, or to his parents substituting another child in his place. This suggestion may seem absurd, but let us see. The explanation runs along the lines of an argument I once used to support the morality of abortion. I quote the paragraph in which this argument was introduced:[1]

> Suppose I were seriously ill, and were told that, for a sizable fee, an operation to save "my life" could be performed, of the following sort: my brain would be removed to another body which could provide a normal life, but the unfortunate result of the operation would be that my memory and learned abilities would be wholly erased, and that the forming of memory brain traces must begin again from scratch, as in a newborn baby. Now, how large a fee would I be willing to pay for this operation, when the alternative is my peaceful demise? My own answer would be: None at all. I would take no interest in the continued existence of "myself" in that sense, and I would rather add the sizable fee to the inheritance of my children. I cannot see the point of forfeiting my children's inheritance in order to start off a person who is brand new except that he happens to enjoy the benefit of having my present brain, without the memory traces. It appears that some continuity of memory is a necessary condition for personal identity *in an important sense*.

My argument was that the position of a fetus, at the end of the first trimester, is essentially the same as that of the person contemplating this operation: he will consider that the baby born after six months will not be *he* in any *important* and *motivating* sense (there will be no continuity of memory, and indeed maybe nothing to have been remembered), and the later existence of this baby, in a sense bodily continuous with his present body, would be a matter of indifference to him. So, I argued, nothing is being done to the fetus that he would object to having done if he understood the situation.

What do I think is necessary in order for the continuation of my body with its conscious experiences to be worthwhile? One thing is that it be able to remember the events I can now remember; another is that it takes some interest in the projects I am now planning and remembers them as my projects; another is that it recognizes my friends and has warm feelings for them, and so on. Reflection on these states of a future continuation of my body with its experiences is what makes the idea motivating. Now such motivating reflection for a newborn is impossible: he has no memories that he wants recalled later; he has no plans to execute; he has no warm feelings for other persons. He has simply not had the length of life necessary for these to come about. Not only that: the conception of these things *cannot* be motivating because the prospect of some future state of affairs being motivating requires roughly a past experience in which similar states of affairs were satisfying, and he has not lived long enough for the requisite conditioning to have taken place. (The most one could say is that the image of warm milk in the child's mouth is attractive; he might answer affirmatively if it could be put to him whether he would be aversive to the idea of no more warm milk.) So we can say, not merely that the newborn does not *want the continuation of himself as a subject of experiences* (he has not the conceptual framework for this); he does not want *anything* which his own survival would promote. It is like the case of the operation: there is nothing I want which the survival of my brain with no memory would promote. Give the newborn as much *conceptual* framework as you like; the wants are not there, which could give significance to him of the continuance of his life.

The newborn, then, is bound to be *indifferent* to the idea of a continuation of the steam of his experiences, even if he has the idea of that clearly. It seems we can know this about him.

The fact that the newborn would be indifferent, however, is still not enough for it to be the case that the newborn, defective or not, gives *consent* to, or expresses a preference for, the termination of his life. *Consent* is a performance, normally linguistic, but always requiring some conventional *sign*. A newborn who has not yet learned how to signalize consent, cannot give consent. And it may be thought that this difference makes all the difference.

In order to see what difference it does make in this case, we should ask what makes adult consent morally important. Why is it that we think euthanasia can be practiced on an adult only if he gives his consent, at least his implied consent (e.g., by previous statements)? There seem to be two reasons. The first is that a person is likely to be concerned with his own welfare, and to take steps to secure his own welfare, more than are others, even his good friends. Giving an individual control over his own life, and not permitting others to take control except when he consents, is normally to help secure his welfare. An individual may, of course, behave stupidly or shortsightedly, but we think that on the whole a person's welfare is best secured if decisions about it are in his hands; and it is *best for society in the normal case* if persons' own lives are well-served. There is a second reason. That is the feeling of security a person can have if he knows that major decisions about himself are in his own hands. When they are not, a person can easily, and in some cases very reasonably, suppose that other persons may well be able to do something to him which he would very much like them not to do. He does not have to worry about that if he knows they cannot do it without his consent.

Are things different with the newborn? At least he, like the fetus, is not yet able to suffer from insecurity; he cannot worry about what others may do to him. So the second reason for requiring consent cannot have any importance in his case. His situation is thus very unlike that of the senile adult; for an adult can worry about what others may do to him if they judge him senile. And this worry can well cast a shadow over a lot of life. But how about the first reason? Here matters are more complex. In the case of children, we think their own lives are better cared for if certain decisions are in the hands of *others:* the child may not want to visit the dentist, but the parents know that his best interests are served by going, and they make him go. The same for compulsory

school attendance. And the same for the newborn. It seems that the newborn's interests may be as well served if other persons of goodwill, who know what his future is going to be like, make the decision for him.

But there is another point. This is that society in certain cases has a strong interest in what happens to a person, and in some of these cases we do not think that the individual's own consent is decisive. We do not think an individual must consent before he is inducted into the armed forces in a just war; nor do we think that we must have a criminal's consent before he is punished for a crime; nor do we think we need an aggressor's consent before we use force to repel his aggression. If there is only one kidney machine, and after careful reflection we think that Mr. A has a much better claim to its use than does Mr. B, must we get Mr. B's consent before we are justified in allocating its use to Mr. A? Now, we must ask whether the position of the seriously defective newborn, a full-scale treatment of which may consume the time of many people and cost millions of dollars, is perhaps somewhat similar.

Everything considered, then, it seems that explicit or even implied consent does not have the moral weight in the case of the newborn that it has in the case of the normal adult.

On the one hand, then, the newborn will not care whether his life is terminated, even if he understood his situation perfectly; and, on the other hand, it seems that there are various reasons casting doubt on whether explicit *consent* has in any case the moral weight in his case that it has for adults. So, while it seems true that we would feel better about permitting termination of defective newborns if only they could give rational and deliberated consent and gave it, nevertheless when we bear the foregoing points in mind, the absence of consent does not seem morally crucial in their case. We can understand why rational persons deciding which moral code to support for their society might not make the giving of consent a necessary condition of feeling free to terminate an infant's life when such action was morally indicated by the other features of the situation.

3. REPLACEMENT IN ORDER
TO GET A BETTER LIFE

I now wish to call your attention to some convictions which most of us share, which seem to
bear on our problem. Suppose a woman wants
a child, but is told that if she conceives a child
now it will be defective, whereas if she waits
three months she will produce a normal child.
Obviously we think it would be outrageous
morally for the mother not to delay. Of course,
if she delays, she will not have the *same* child
as the one she would have had if she had not
delayed; but we do not think we need worry
about any rights of the child she might have
had, in view of the fact that the later-conceived
child will have a better life.

Suppose, however, a woman conceives but
discovers three months later, after amniocentesis, that the fetus will develop into a defective child, but that in all probability she can
have a normal child later if she has an abortion
and tries again. Now this time there is still the
same reason for having the abortion that there
was formerly for the delay: that she will produce another child with a better life. Ought
she then to have the abortion? If the child's
life is bad, he could well complain that he had
been injured by being brought to term, and in
fact some court suits along this line have actually been filed. Would the child about to be
aborted in favor of the later normal child, be
inclined to complain, if he could grasp the situation? Not if the argument stated earlier is
correct. I have not really stated that the
mother in this case should have an abortion; I
have only asked a rhetorical question, and that
is not an argument. I do believe, however, that
the vast majority of persons would think she
should, and it is for this reason that amniocentesis is becoming so widespread, when there
are reasons to expect congenital defects.

But now suppose the woman cannot discover until after she gives birth, that her child
is seriously defective. She learns then that,
were she to conceive again, it is highly probable that she would have a normal child. Are
things really different, in the first few days?
One might think that a benevolent person
would want, in each of these cases, the substitution of a normal child for the defective one,
of the better life for the worse one.

4. THE PSYCHOLOGICAL
AND MATERIAL COSTS
AND THEIR RELEVANCE

It is agreed that the burden of care for a seriously defective infant, say one born with *spina
bifida,* is huge. The cost of surgery alone for
an infant with *spina bifida* has been estimated
to be around $275,000. In many places this
cost must be borne by the family of the child,
and there is in addition the cost of care in an
institution if the child's condition does not
permit care at home—and a very modest estimate of the monthly cost at present is $1,100.
To meet even the surgical costs, not to mention monthly payments for continuing care,
the lives of members of the family may have to
be lived at a spartan level, for many years.
The siblings of the defective may have to be
deprived of a college education, and so on.

The psychological effects of the situation,
and probably the more so if care is provided at
home, are far-reaching. Just what are these
costs? Doubtless they vary from case to case.
One knows of cases in which the suicide of a
sibling seems very clearly to have been caused
by the presence of the defective infant in the
home. The life of the parents may come to
revolve in a small circle around the child. The
family may feel unable to have a social life
because it is uncomfortable to have guests to a
meal given the unpredictable behavior of the
defective family member. If the child is in
the home, either the parents must remain at
home or they must put up with the continuing
presence of a caretaker. One can go on and on
in spelling out just what life in such a family
may be like, in the case of a severely defective
infant. In one way or another the continued
existence of the child is apt to reduce dramatically the quality of life of the family as a whole.

It can be and has been argued that such
costs, while real, are irrelevant to the moral
problem of what should be done. (Professor

Philippa Foot so argues in a recent article on "Euthanasia," in *Philosophy and Public Affairs* [6, 1977, 85–112.) She says: "So it is not for their sake but to avoid trouble to others that they are allowed to die. When brought out into the open this seems unacceptable; at least we do not easily accept the principle that adults who need special care should be counted too burdensome to be kept alive." I would think that "to avoid trouble to others" is hardly the terminology to describe the havoc that is apt to be produced. I agree that adults should not be allowed to die, or actively terminated, without their consent, except possibly when they cannot give consent but are in pain; but the reasons which justify different behavior in the two situations have already been discussed. It seems obvious, however, that rational persons, when deciding which moral code to support, would take these human costs into account. As indeed they should: for the parents and siblings are also human beings with lives to live, and any sacrifices a given law or moral system might call on them to make must be taken into account in deciding between laws and moral codes. Everyone will feel sympathy for a helpless newborn; but everyone should also think equally vividly, of all the others who will suffer and just how they will suffer—and, of course, as indicated above, of just what kind of life the defective newborn will have in any case. There is a choice here between allowing a newborn to die (possibly a favor to it, and in any case not a serious loss), and imposing a very heavy burden on the family for many years to come.

Philosophers who think the cost to others is irrelevant to what should be done should reflect that we do not accept the general principle that lives should be saved at no matter what cost. For instance, ships are deliberately built with only a certain margin of safety; they could be built so that they would hardly sink in any storm, but to do so would be economically unfeasible. We do not think we should require a standard of safety for automobiles that goes beyond a certain point of expense and inconvenience; we are prepared to risk a few extra deaths. And how about the lives we

are willing to lose in war, in order to assure a certain kind of economic order, or democracy or free speech? Surely there is a point at which the loss of a life (or rather the abbreviation of a life) and the cost to others become comparable. Is it obvious that the continuation of a marginal kind of life for a child takes moral precedence over providing a college education for one or more of his siblings? Some comparisons will be hard to make, but continuing even a marginally *pleasant* life hardly has *absolute* priority. . . .

5. DRAWING LINES

There are two final questions which must be answered in any complete account of what is the morally right thing to do about defective newborns.

The first is: If a decision to terminate is made, how soon must it be made and the conclusion effectuated? Obviously it could not be postponed to the age of five, or of three, or even a year and a half. At those ages, all the reasons for insisting on consent are already cogent. And at those ages, the child will already care what happens to him. But ten days is tolerable. Doubtless advances in medicine will permit detection of serious prospective defects early in pregnancy, and this issue of how many days will not arise.

Second, the argument from the quality of the prospective life of the defective newborn requires that we decide which defects are so serious that the kind of life the defective child can have gives it no serious claim as compared with the social costs. Obviously this issue must be thought through and some guidelines established. Some guidelines have been proposed, and used, for instance by Dr. Lorber in Sheffield. Roughly his guidelines are, to cite Dr. Reid's paper, "First, the site of the *spina bifida*: if this is on the lower half of the back then the baby will be severely paralysed and incontinent and probably have severe hydrocephalus. Second, paralysis: if a baby is paralysed at birth, it will never recover its muscle power. Third, gross distortion of the spine as a result of, for example, kyphosis: those affected are among the most handicapped children and the consequences tend to worsen with time. Fourth, gross hydrocephalus: a simple tape measure round the baby's head can establish the extent of the problem. Fifth, other gross congenital malformations: along with *spina bifida,* conditions such as congenital heart disease and mongolism can occur together." Dr. Lorber's proposal was that a child with any of these characteristics should not be recommended for treatment.

Criteria of this sort can be thought through and established by the medical profession,

rather in the way in which the American Law Institute has drawn up recommendations for the reform of the penal codes of the various states. This task of framing criteria is certainly not one for philosophers. As I see it, it is a task to be undertaken by thoughtful medical specialists with wide experience, who at the same time are familiar with the morally relevant considerations, such as those I have been discussing. We might criticize specific proposals, but it would seem that the framing of some is a step in the right direction, which it is to be hoped the medical profession will undertake.

NOTE

1. "The morality of abortion," in an earlier form in *The Monist* 56 (1972), 504–526, and in revised form in *Abortion: Pro and Con,* ed. R. L. Perkins (Cambridge, MA: Schenkman, 1974).

REVIEW AND DISCUSSION QUESTIONS

1. How would Brandt decide when a life is not worth living?
2. Why does Brandt argue that an infant (even a healthy one) would be indifferent to being killed?
3. Brandt argues that the reasons to seek consent generally do not apply to infants. Why?
4. Are there other reasons, besides the ones Brandt mentions, that make getting consent important?
5. Why does Brandt think that active euthanasia is better than passive euthanasia?

Playing God: Genes, Clones, and Luck

Ronald Dworkin

Prospects of genetic engineering and especially cloning often provoke strong reactions in people, and many times they are strongly negative. Part of that reaction may be historical, as people recall the eugenic policies of the Nazi era. But is such a reaction rational? In this essay, Ronald Dworkin weighs a variety of arguments that might be advanced to regulate or ban the use of biomedical technology to create people with specific characteristics. Sometimes the objections are grounded in concern about the dangers of the technology itself; sometimes in worries about whether it will be limited to only the wealthy; and sometimes the concern rests on the desire to maintain biodiversity within the human population. Dworkin discusses each of these arguments, arguing that none of them has substantial weight. Rather than these concerns, he argues, the hostility to genetic engineering is grounded in the fact that if we were to use it we would be "playing God." He concludes with a discussion of the meaning, and the merits, of that claim. Ronald Dworkin is professor of philosophy at New York University and London University.

A. WHY NOT

The most arresting of the possibilities geneticists are now exploring would give scientists and doctors the power to choose which human beings there will be. People gained that power long ago, in a broad and clumsy way, when they came to understood that allowing certain people rather than others to mate would have consequences for the kind of children they produced. Eugenics, which was supported by George Bernard Shaw and Oliver Wendell Holmes as well as Adolf Hitler, was modeled on that simple insight. But genetic science now holds out the possibility, at least as comprehensible fantasy, of creating particular human beings who have been designed, one by one, according to a detailed blueprint, or of changing existing human beings, either as fetuses or later, to create people with chosen genetic properties.

Even the fantasy of this, when the technology was first described, was greeted with shock and indignation, and that shock crystallized when scientists in Scotland cloned an adult sheep, and other scientists and publicists speculated that the technique could be used to clone human beings. Committees hurriedly appointed by governments and international bodies all immediately denounced the very idea. President Clinton ruled that federal funds could not be used to finance research into human cloning, and the United States Senate considered forbidding, through preposterously over-broad and panicky legislation, any and all such research. The possibility of comprehensive genetic engineering—altering a zygote's genetic composition to produce a battery of desired physical, mental, and emotional propensities—has also aroused great fear and

revulsion, and any success in engineering mammals, comparable to the creation of the sheep Dolly, would undoubtedly provoke a similar official response. (In this discussion I shall often use the word "engineering" to include both comprehensive genetic alteration and human cloning, the latter being treated as a special case of the former. Of course engineering and cloning are very different techniques, but many of the social and moral issues they raise are the same.)

The rhetoric of the European Parliament is not untypical of the reaction that prospects of genetic engineering have produced. In its "resolution on the cloning of the human embryo," that body declared its "firm conviction that the cloning of human beings, whether on an experimental basis, in the context of fertility treatments, preimplantation diagnosis, for tissue transplantation, or for any other purpose whatsoever, is unethical, morally repugnant, contrary to respect for the person, and a grave violation of fundamental human rights which can not under any circumstances be justified or accepted." How might we justify, or even explain, this blunderbuss reaction? We might explore three grounds of objection that are frequently mentioned. First, genetic research is said to pose great danger, and extreme caution is therefore urged. If human cloning or other comprehensive genetic engineering is possible at all, research into it or attempts at it might result in an unacceptable number of miscarriages or in the birth of an unacceptable number of deformed children, for example. Second, some people resist research into genetic engineering on grounds of social justice. Cloning, if available, is bound to be hideously expensive for a long time, and hence would be available only to rich people who would want,

From Ronald Dworkin, *Sovereign Virtue* (Cambridge: Harvard University Press, 2000). Reprinted by permission of the author.

out of vanity, to clone themselves, increasing the unfair advantages of wealth. (Opponents horrified by the prospect of cloning have cited the specter of thousands of Rupert Murdochs or Donald Trumps.) Third, much of the hostile reaction has been generated by a detached and reasonably familiar aesthetic value. Engineering, if available, might well be used to perpetuate now desired traits of height, intelligence, color and personality, and the world would be robbed of the variety that seems essential to novelty, originality and fascination. We must discuss each of these supposed justifications for a ban on research and development, but in my own view they do not separately or together explain the dogmatic strength of the reaction I described.

Security. It is unclear how far the Dolly precedent should be relied on in predicting the likely results of experimentation into human cloning. On the one hand, technical skill will presumably improve; on the other, human cloning may prove exponentially more difficult than cloning sheep. Several hundred attempts were necessary to produce one sheep, but, as I understand it, the rest were lost through early miscarriage, and no deformed but viable sheep was produced. Nor is there much reason to think that either cloning or engineering would produce germ-line damage threatening generations of deformity, or deformity that would not appear for generations. In any case, however, these dangers are not enough, on their own, to justify forbidding the further research that could refine our appreciation of them, and perhaps our ability to forestall or reduce whichever threats are in fact genuine. True, the sudden appearance of Dr. Seed, in the headlines and on the screen, promising to clone anyone for a high price, was enough to terrify anyone. But regulation can rein him in, along with the thousands of other cloning cowboys who would be bound to appear, without closing down research altogether. If we are assessing the risks of damage that experimentation or testing might produce, moreover, we must also take into account the hope that advancing and

refining the techniques of genetic engineering will vastly decrease the number of defects and deformities with which people are now born or into which they inexorably grow. The balance of risk might well be thought to tilt in favor of experimentation.

Justice. We can easily imagine genetic engineering's becoming a perquisite of the rich, and therefore as exacerbating the already savage injustice of both prosperous and impoverished societies. But these techniques have uses beyond vanity, and these uses may justify research and trials, even if we decide that vanity is an inappropriate and forbidden motive. We noticed, earlier, the important medical gains that have already been achieved through selective engineering, and more comprehensive engineering can confidently be expected to expand these enormously. Cloning may prove to have particularly dramatic medical benefits. Parents of a desperately sick child might want another child, whom they would love as much as any other, but whose blood or marrow might save the life of the sick child from which it was cloned. Cloning individual human stem cells to produce a particular organ for transplant, rather than an entire organism, might have even more evident benefits. A reengineered and then heavily cloned cell, taken from a cancer patient, might prove to be a cure for that cancer when the clones were reintroduced. We must also count benefits beyond the narrowly medical. Childless couples, for example, or single women or single men might wish to procreate through cloning, which they might think better than the alternatives available. Or they may have no alternative at all.

Perhaps we could regulate engineering to screen out all but approved motives. If this is possible, does justice demand it, even if we assume that there are no other objections to it? I do not believe so. We should not . . . seek to improve equality by leveling down, and, as in the case of more orthodox genetic medicine, techniques available for a time only to the very rich often produce discoveries of much more general value for everyone. The remedy for injustice is redistribution, not denial of benefits to some with no corresponding gain to others.

Aesthetics. We already have clones—genetically identical multiple births (which have increased as a result of infertility treatment) produce clones—and the history of genetically identical children shows that identical genes do not produce identical phenotypes. We may have underestimated nature in years past, but nurture remains important too, and the reaction to the prospect of engineering has underestimated its importance in turn. Nevertheless, people do fear that if we replace the genetic "lottery" with engineered reproduction, the welcome diversity of human types will be progressively replaced with uniformity dictated by vogue. To some degree, of course, greater uniformity is unambiguously desirable: there is no value, aesthetic or otherwise, in the fact that some people are doomed to a disfigured and short life. But it is widely believed better that, within limits, people look different and act differently in ways that might well be the consequence of different alleles. This thought appeals to a derivative value [*"Derivative" values are based on people's interests. "Detached" values are not derived from people's interests but are inherent in things. Nature and works of art are often cited as examples of things with detached value—Ed.*]: that it is better for everyone to live in a world of differences. But it might also be seen as appealing to a detached value: many people think that diversity is a value in itself, so that it would remain valuable even if, for some reason, people came to prefer uniformity.

What is not plain, however, is how far engineering, even if it were freely and inexpensively available, would actually threaten desirable diversity. Presumably all parents, if given a choice, would wish their children to have the level of intelligence and other skills that we now regard as normal, or even that we now believe superior. But we cannot regard that as undesirable: it is, after all, the object of education, ordinary as well as remedial, to improve intelligence and skill levels across the board. Do we have good reason to fear that if parents had the choice they would often prefer cloning one of them—or cloning a third person—to sexual reproduction that produces a child bearing the genes of both? Or that they would choose cloning for reasons other than to exclude damaging alleles, or because they were incapable of sexual reproduction? That seems unlikely. Do we have reason to fear (as many people do fear) that parents will engineer a reproductive zygote in order to make it a male rather than a female child, for example? It is true that in certain communities—in northern India, for example—male children are apparently preferred to female ones. But that preference seems so sensitive to economic circumstances, as well as to shifting cultural prejudices, that it offers no reason for thinking that the world will suddenly be swamped with a generation dominated by males. Selective abortion for sex has been available, as a result of amniocentesis and liberal abortion laws, for some time now, and no such general trend seems to have been established. In any case, we would not be justified in stopping experimentation on the basis of such thin speculation.

The fear, however, goes beyond a fear of sexual asymmetry: it is a fear that one phenotype—say, blond, conventionally good-looking, nonaggressive, tall, musically talented, and witty—will come to dominate a culture in which that phenotype is particularly valued. We should pause to notice the scientific assumptions embedded in that fear: it supposes not only that comprehensive genetic design is possible, but that the various properties of the preferred phenotype can be assembled in the same person through that design, as if each property were the product of a single allele whose possession made the property at least very highly likely, and that could be specified, and would have that consequence, independently of the specification of or phenotypic expression of other alleles. Each of those assumptions seems improbable, and their combination highly so. It seems much more likely that even parents with state of the art engineering at their disposal would have fewer combinations to choose from, and more risks to run about the impact of nurture and experience, and that they would make these choices differently in response to the very differences among them that we now celebrate. The later impact of differing personal choices by their offspring themselves, perhaps in search of individuality, would enlarge on those differences.

The basic motivational assumptions behind the fear seem equally as dubious as the scientific assumptions, moreover. Most people delight in the mysteries of reproduction—that value is, after all, at the root of the very objection we are considering—and many, and perhaps the great bulk, of people would forgo engineering, beyond trying to eliminate obvious defects and handicaps, as distasteful. If all this is right, the aesthetic objection is overblown or, at best, premature. We would need much more information, of a kind that could be produced only through research and experimentation, before we could even judge the assumptions on which the objection is founded, and it would therefore seem irrational to rely on that objection to prevent that research.

B. PLAYING GOD

The arguments and objections we have so far been canvassing do not provide what T. S. Eliot called an "objective correlative" for the immediate and largely sustained revulsion that I described. People feel some deeper, less articulate ground for that revulsion, even if they have not or perhaps cannot fully articulate that ground, but can express it only in heated and logically inappropriate language, like the bizarre reference to "fundamental human rights" in the European Parliament resolution I quoted earlier. We will not adequately appreciate the real power of the political and social resistance to further research into genetic engineering, or the genuine moral and ethical issues that such research presents, until we have better understood that deeper ground, and we might begin with another familiar piece of rhetoric. It is wrong, people say, particularly after more familiar objections have been found wanting, to play God.

This objection appeals to what I called a detached rather than a derivative value. Playing God is thought wrong in itself, quite apart from any bad consequences it will or may have for any identifiable human being. Nevertheless it is deeply unclear what the injunction really means—unclear what playing God is, and what, exactly, is wrong with it. It can't mean that it is always wrong for human beings to attempt to resist natural catastrophes, or to improve upon the hand that nature has dealt them. People do that—always have done that—all the time. What is the difference, after all, between inventing penicillin and using engineered and cloned genes to cure even more terrifying diseases than penicillin cures? What is the difference between setting your child strenuous exercises to reduce his weight or increase his strength and altering his genes, while an embryo, with the same end in view?

These are not rhetorical questions. We must try to answer them, but we must begin at some distance from them, in the overall structure of our moral and ethical experience. For that structure depends, crucially, on a fundamental distinction between what we are responsible for doing or deciding, individually or collectively, and what is given to us, as a background against which we act or decide, but which we are powerless to change. For the Greeks, this was a distinction between themselves and their fate or destiny, which was in the hands or the laps of the gods. For people, even today, who are religious in a conventional way, it is a distinction between how God designed the world, including our natural condition in it, and the scope of the free will he also created. More sophisticated people use the language of science to the same effect: for them the fundamental distinction falls between what nature, including evolution, has created, by way of particles and energy and genes, and what we do in that world and with those genes. For everyone, the distinction, however they describe it, draws a line between who and what we are, for which either a divine will or no one but a blind process is responsible, and what we do with that inheritance, for which we are indeed, separately or together, responsible.

That crucial boundary between chance and choice is the spine of our ethics and our morality, and any serious shift in that boundary is seriously dislocating. Our sense of a life well lived, for example, is fundamentally shaped by supposed givens about the upper limits of human life span. If people could suddenly be expected to live ten times as long as we now do, we would have to recreate the whole range of our opinions about what an attractive kind of life would be, and also our opinions about what activities that carry some risk of accidental death for others, like driving, are morally permissible. History already offers, in our own time, less dramatic but nevertheless profound examples of how scientific change radically dislocates values. People's settled convictions about the responsibilities of leaders to protect their own soldiers in war, at any cost, changed when scientists split the atom and vastly increased the carnage that those convictions could justify. People's settled convictions about euthanasia and suicide changed when deathbed medicine dramatically increased a doctor's power to extend life beyond the point at which that life had any meaning for the patient. In each case a period of moral stability was replaced by moral insecurity, and it is revealing that in both episodes people reached for the expression "playing God," in one case to accuse the scientists who had dramatically increased our powers over nature by cracking what had been thought fundamental in God's design, and in the other to criticize dying patients for taking upon themselves a decision that the past limits of medicine had made it easy to treat as God's alone.

My hypothesis is that genetic science has suddenly made us aware of the possibility of a similar though far greater pending moral dislocation. We dread the prospect of people designing other people because that possibility in itself shifts—much more dramatically than in these other examples—the chance/choice boundary that structures our values as a whole, and such a shift threatens, not to offend any of our present values, derivative or detached, but, on the contrary, to make a great part of these suddenly obsolete. Our

physical being—the brain and body that furnishes each person's material substrate—has long been the absolute paradigm of what is both devastatingly important to us and, in its initial condition, beyond our power to alter and therefore beyond the scope of our responsibility, either individual or collective. The popularity of the term "genetic lottery" itself shows the centrality of our conviction that what we most basically *are* is a matter of chance not choice. I do not mean that genetic continuity provides the key to the technical philosophical problem of personal identity, though some philosophers have indeed thought this. I mean to make a psychological point: people think that the very essence of the distinction between what God or nature provides, and what they are responsible for making of or with that provision, is to be defined physically, in terms of what is in "the genes" or, in a metaphor reflecting an older science, "the blood."

If we were to take seriously the possibility we are now exploring—that scientists really have gained the capacity to create a human being having any phenotype that they or their prospective parents choose—then we could chart the destruction of settled moral and ethical attitudes starting at almost any point. We use the chance/choice distinction not simply in our assignments of responsibility for situations or events, for example, but in our assessments of pride, including pride in what nature has given us. It is a striking phenomenon, now, that people take pride in physical attributes or skills they did not choose or create, like physical appearance or strength, but not when these can be seen to be the results of the efforts of others in which they played no part. A woman who puts herself in the hands of a cosmetic surgeon may rejoice in the result but can take no pride in it; certainly not the pride she would have taken if she had been born into the same beauty. What would happen to pride in our physical attributes, or even what we made of them, if these were the inexorable results not of a nature in whose pride we are allowed, as it were, to share, but of the decision of our parents and their hired geneticists?

But the most dramatic use of the fundamental chance/choice distinction is in the assignment of personal and collective responsibility, and it is here that the danger of moral insecurity seems greatest. We now accept the condition in which we were born as a parameter of our responsibility—we must make the best of it that we can—but not as itself a potential arena of blame, except in those special cases, themselves of relatively recent discovery, in which someone's behavior altered his embryonic development, through smoking, for example, or drugs. Otherwise, though we may curse fate for how we are . . . we may blame no one else. The same distinction holds, at least for most people, and for many reflective moral philosophers, for social responsibility as well. We feel a greater responsibility to compensate victims of industrial accidents and of racial prejudice, as in both cases victims, though in different ways, of society generally, than we feel to compensate those born with genetic defects or those injured by lightning or in those other ways that lawyers and insurance companies call "acts of God." How would all this change if everyone was as he is through the decisions of others, including the decision of some parents not to intervene but to let nature take its course?

Change it must. But how and why? Once again, these questions are not rhetorical. I do not know the answers, and can hardly guess at them. But that is the point. The terror many of us feel at the thought of genetic engineering is not a fear of what is wrong; it is rather a fear of losing our grip on what is wrong. We are not entitled—it would be a serious confusion—to think that even the most dramatic shifts in the chance/choice boundary somehow challenge morality itself; that there will one day be no more wrong or right. But we are entitled to worry that our settled convictions will, in large numbers, be undermined, that we will be in a kind of moral free-fall, that we will have to think again against a new background and with uncertain results. Playing God is playing with fire.

Suppose that this hypothesis, at least as it might be corrected and improved, makes sense, and accounts for the powerful surd in people's emotional reaction to genetic engineering that is not accounted for by the more discrete grounds we first examined. Have we then discovered not only an explanation but a justification for the objection, a reading of "don't play God" that shows why, at least in this instance, we shouldn't? I think not. We would have discovered a challenge that we must take up rather than a reason for turning back. For our hypothesis implicates no *value* —derivative or detached—at all. It reveals only reasons why our contemporary values, of both kinds, may be wrong or at least ill considered. If we are to be morally and ethically responsible, there can be no turning back once we find, as we have found, that some of the most basic presuppositions of these values are mistaken. Playing God is indeed playing with fire. But that is what we mortals have done since Prometheus, the patron saint of dangerous discovery. We play with fire and take the consequences, because the alternative is cowardice in the face of the unknown.

REVIEW AND DISCUSSION QUESTIONS

1. Why does Dworkin think we should not ban research and development in genetic engineering on the ground that it is too risky?

2. Explain why justice is not a good reason to reject genetic engineering, according to Dworkin.

3. What is the difference between "derivative" and "detached" values?

4. How does Dworkin answer those who claim that genetic engineering would result in loss of aesthetic value?

5. What, exactly, is the concern that Dworkin has in mind with the idea of "playing God"? How is it related to the boundary between chance and choice?

6. What decisions does Dworkin think we face, in light of scientific progress in genetic engineering?

7. Has Dworkin adequately answered those who claim we should forbid the use of cloning and other products of genetic engineering because we would be "playing God"? Explain your answer.

Essay and Paper Topics for Section 8

1. Compare the positions of Godwin, Dyck, and Brandt on euthanasia and the value of life.

2. Suppose, after deciding not to have the brain transplant described in Brandt's essay, that you find out that the body in which your brain is now located will be tortured. Would you still take no interest in the transfer?

3. How would Dyck respond to Brandt's essay? Which position do you find more reasonable? Explain.

4. Compare and contrast the positions of the authors in this section with those of the Supreme Court Justices who wrote the *Cruzan* decision.

5. Using Godwin's essay and Jane English's essay "What Do Grown Children Owe Their Parents?" (reprinted in Section 16) as a starting place, write an essay in which you discuss how medical resources should be distributed.

6. Are medical advances making contraception and abortion accessible to most people examples of what Dworkin terms "playing God"? What lessons, if any, might be drawn from those or other technological advances about the question Dworkin asks, but does not answer, about the attitudes we should take in the future toward cloning?

7. Using the general moral theory from Part I that you found most reasonable, write an essay in which you discuss the position of two philosophers you have read on the subject of euthanasia or cloning in the light of that theory.

PART III

Political and Social Relationships

9

Justice and Economic Distribution

How should economic wealth be distributed? Is private property justified? Is capitalism justified? Do people deserve what they earn from hard work? Behind these are other, more general questions about the nature and legitimacy of political authority and the ideal of justice itself. These and other questions are at the center of this section. Readings begin with John Locke's famous defense of individual rights, property, and the right of revolution—a position that many see as the foundation of the Declaration of Independence. It is followed by David Hume's account of economic justice and property, and then by Karl Marx and Friedrich Engel's famous critique of capitalism and private property and defense of communism as both inevitable and better than what has gone before. The next reading is from what many regard as the most important work in political philosophy of the twentieth century, in which John Rawls seeks to revive social contract theory in the service of a liberal, egalitarian vision of government and social justice. That is followed by essays by two other philosophers who look at the issue from radically opposed perspectives: a libertarian opponent of all redistribution schemes and a utilitarian who claims morality demands that the wealthy give substantial aid to the poor. Questions about whether people deserve the fruits of their labor, and what that desert might encompass, are the subjects of the last two readings.

The Second Treatise of Government

John Locke

Born in 1632, John Locke was an important figure in both British and American politics; indeed, there are few, if any, philosophers who were more influential in the development of American political institutions and beliefs than John Locke. Locke's father was a politically influential lawyer who supported Oliver Cromwell and the British Parliament against King Charles I. John Locke was sent to Oxford at fifteen, where he became friendly with noted chemist Robert Boyle as well as other scientists, all of whom exerted an important influence on young John. After graduation, Locke served as a tutor in Greek. Then, after serving a period as a diplomat, he returned to Oxford to study medicine. Locke was active throughout his life in political and public affairs. At one point he was forced into exile by the king, but he returned to England after the Glorious Revolution in 1688. He died in 1704 at the age of seventy-two. Locke's influence is evident, among other places, in the U.S. Declaration of Independence. In his *First Treatise of Government,* Locke attacks the divine right of kings; in the *Second Treatise,* from which the following selection is taken, he addresses the legitimate role of government together with the limits on governmental power. Locke begins by imagining persons in a state of nature in which each is independently pursuing his or her own interests. In that situation, he argues, people possess natural moral rights to life, property, and liberty, rights that are not to be transgressed by others. Given the realities of such a state of nature, it is in the interests of people to move toward cooperation and trade and to establish common institutions to provide protection of life and property. Governmental action is severely limited, however, by people's natural rights—a topic to which he devotes considerable attention. Locke also considers the related and important question of how a previously unowned resource may justly become the property of one person.

OF THE STATE OF NATURE

To understand political power aright, and derive it from its original, we must consider what state all men are naturally in, and that is a state of perfect freedom to order their actions and dispose of their possessions and persons as they think fit, within the bounds of the law of nature, without asking leave, or depending upon the will of any other man.

A state also of equality, wherein all the power and jurisdiction is reciprocal, no one having more than another; there being nothing more evident than that creatures of the same species and rank, promiscuously born to all the same advantages of nature, and the use of the same faculties, should also be equal one amongst another without subordination or subjection, unless the Lord and Master of them all should by any manifest declaration of His will set one above another, and confer on him by an evident and clear appointment an undoubted right to domination and sovereignty.

From *The Second Treatise of Government: An Essay Concerning the Origin, Extent and End of Civil Government* (1690).

But though this be a state of liberty, yet it is not a state of license; though man in that state have an uncontrollable liberty to dispose of his person or possessions, yet he has not liberty to destroy himself, or so much as any creature in his possession, but where some nobler use than its bare preservation calls for it. The state of nature has a law of nature to govern it, which obliges everyone; and reason, which is that law, teaches all mankind who will but consult it, that, being all equal and independent, no one ought to harm another in his life, health, liberty, or possessions. For men being all the workmanship of one omnipotent and infinitely wise Maker—all the servants of one sovereign Master, sent into the world by His order, and about His business—they are His property, whose workmanship they are, made to last during His, not one another's pleasure; and being furnished with like faculties, sharing all in one community of nature, there cannot be supposed any such subordination among us, that may authorize us to destroy one another, as if we were made for one another's uses, as the inferior ranks of creatures are for ours. Everyone, as he is bound to preserve himself, and not to quit his station willfully, so, by the like reason, when his own preservation comes not in competition, ought he, as much as he can, to preserve the rest of mankind, and not, unless it be to do justice on an offender, take away or impair the life, or what tends to the preservation of the life, the liberty, health, limb, or goods of another.

And that all men may be restrained from invading others' rights, and from doing hurt to one another, and the law of nature be observed, which willeth the peace and preservation of all mankind, the execution of the law of nature is in that state put into every man's hand, whereby everyone has a right to punish the transgressors of that law to such a degree as may hinder its violation. For the law of nature would, as all other laws that concern men in this world, be in vain if there were nobody that, in the state of nature, had a power to execute that law, and thereby preserve the innocent and restrain offenders. And if anyone in the state of nature may punish another for any evil he has done, everyone may do so. For in that state of perfect equality, where naturally there is no superiority or jurisdiction of one over another, what any may do in prosecution of that law, everyone must needs have a right to do.

And thus in the state of nature one man comes by a power over another; but yet no absolute or arbitrary power, to use a criminal, when he has got him in his hands, according to the passionate heats or boundless extravagance of his own will; but only to retribute to him so far as calm reason and conscience dictate what is proportionate to his transgression, which is so much as may serve for reparation and restraint. For these two are the only reasons why one man may lawfully do harm to another, which is that we call punishment. In transgressing the law of nature, the offender declares himself to live by another rule than that of common reason and equity, which is that measure God has set to the actions of men, for their mutual security; and so he becomes dangerous to mankind, the tie which is to secure them from injury and violence being slighted and broken by him. Which, being a trespass against the whole species, and the peace and safety of it, provided for by the law of nature, every man upon this score, by the right he hath to preserve mankind in general, may restrain, or, where it is necessary, destroy things noxious to them, and so may bring such evil on anyone who hath transgressed that law, as may make him repent the doing of it, and thereby deter him, and by his example others, from doing the like mischief. And in this case, and upon this ground, every man hath a right to punish the offender, and be executioner of the law of nature. . . .

Besides the crime which consists in violating the law, and varying from the right rule of reason, whereby a man so far becomes degenerate, and declares himself to quit the principles of human nature, and to be a noxious creature, there is commonly injury done, and some person or other, some other man receives damage by his transgression, in which case he who hath received any damage, has, besides the right of punishment common to him with other men, a particular right to seek reparation from him that has done it. And any other person who finds it just, may also join with him that is injured, and assist him in recovering from the offender so much as may make satisfaction for the harm he has suffered.

. . . The magistrate, who by being magistrate hath the common right of punishing put into his hands, can often, where the public good demands not the execution of the law, remit the punishment of criminal offenses by his own authority, but yet cannot remit the satisfaction due to any private man for the damage he has received. That he who has suffered the damage has a right to demand in his own name, and he alone can remit. The damnified person has this power of appropriating to himself the goods or service of the offender, by right of self-preservation, as every man has a power to punish the crime, to prevent its being committed again, by the right he has of preserving all mankind, and doing all reasonable things he can in order to that end. And thus it is that every man in the state of nature has a power to kill a murderer, both to deter others from doing the like injury, which no reparation can compensate, by the example of the punishment that attends it from everybody, and also to secure men from the attempts of a criminal who having renounced reason, the common rule and measure God hath given to mankind, hath by the unjust violence and slaughter he hath committed upon one, declared war against all mankind, and therefore may be destroyed as a lion or a tiger, one of those wild savage beasts with whom men can have no society nor security. . . .

To this strange doctrine—viz., that in the state of nature everyone has the executive power of the law of nature—I doubt not but it will be objected that it is unreasonable for men to be judges in their own cases, that self-love will make men partial to themselves and their friends. And on the other side, that ill-nature, passion, and revenge will carry them too far in punishing others; and hence nothing but confusion and disorder will follow; and that

therefore God hath certainly appointed government to restrain the partiality and violence of men. I easily grant that civil government is the proper remedy for the inconveniences of the state of nature, which must certainly be great where men may be judges in their own case, since 'tis easy to be imagined that he who was so unjust as to do his brother an injury, will scarce be so just as to condemn himself for it. But I shall desire those who make this objection, to remember that absolute monarchs are but men, and if government is to be the remedy of those evils which necessarily follow from men's being judges in their own cases, and the state of nature is therefore not to be endured, I desire to know what kind of government that is, and how much better it is than the state of nature, where one man commanding a multitude, has the liberty to be judge in his own case, and may do to all his subjects whatever he pleases, without the least question or control of those who execute his pleasure; and in whatsoever he doth, whether led by reason, mistake, or passion, must be submitted to, which men in the state of nature are not bound to do one to another? And if he that judges, judges amiss in his own or any other case, he is answerable for it to the rest of mankind.

'Tis often asked as a mighty objection, Where are, or ever were there, any men in such a state of nature? To which it may suffice as an answer at present: that since all princes and rulers of independent governments all through the world are in a state of nature, 'tis plain the world never was, nor ever will be, without numbers of men in that state. I have named all governors of independent communities, whether they are or are not in league with others. For 'tis not every compact that puts an end to the state of nature between men, but only this one of agreeing together mutually to enter into one community, and make one body politic; other promises and compacts men may make one with another, and yet still be in the state of nature. The promises and bargains for truck, etc., between the two men in Soldania, in or between a Swiss and an Indian, in the woods of America, are binding to them, though they are perfectly in a state of nature in reference to one another. For truth and keeping of faith belong to men as men, and not as members of society. . . .

OF PROPERTY

Whether we consider natural reason, which tells us that men being once born have a right to their preservation, and consequently to meat and drink and such other things as nature affords for their subsistence; or revelation, which gives us an account of those grants God made of the world to Adam, and to Noah and his sons, 'tis very clear that God, as King David says, Psalm cxv. 16, "has given the earth to the children of men," given it to mankind in common. But this being supposed, it seems to some a very great difficulty how anyone should ever come to have a property in anything. I will not content myself to answer that if it be difficult to make out property upon a supposition that God gave the world to Adam and his posterity in common, it is impossible that any man but one universal monarch should have any property upon a supposition that God gave the world to Adam and his heirs in succession, exclusive of all the rest of his posterity. But I shall endeavor to show how men might come to have a property in several parts of that which God gave to mankind in common, and that without any express compact of all the commoners.

God, who hath given the world to men in common, hath also given them reason to make use of it to the best advantage of life and convenience. The earth and all that is therein is given to men for the support and comfort of their being. And though all the fruits it naturally produces, and beasts it feeds, belong to mankind in common, as they are produced by the spontaneous hand of nature; and nobody has originally a private dominion exclusive of the rest of mankind in any of them as they are thus in their natural state; yet being given for the use of men, there must of necessity be a means to appropriate them some way or other before they can be of any use or at all beneficial to any particular

man. The fruit or venison which nourishes the wild Indian, who knows no enclosure, and is still a tenant in common, must be his, and so his, i.e., a part of him, that another can no longer have any right to it, before it can do any good for the support of his life.

Though the earth and all inferior creatures be common to all men, yet every man has a property in his own person; this nobody has any right to but himself. The labor of his body and the work of his hands we may say are properly his. Whatsoever, then, he removes out of the state that nature hath provided and left it in, he hath mixed his labor with, and joined to it something that is his own, and thereby makes it his property. It being by him removed from the common state nature placed it in, it hath by this labor something annexed to it that excludes the common right of other men. For this labor being the unquestionable property of the laborer, no man but he can have a right to what that is once joined to, at least where there is enough, and as good left in common for others.

He that is nourished by the acorns he picked up under an oak, or the apples he gathered from the trees in the wood, has certainly appropriated them to himself. Nobody can deny but the nourishment is his. I ask, then, When did they begin to be his—when he digested, or when he ate, or when he boiled, or when he brought them home, or when he picked them up? And 'tis plain if the first gathering made them not his, nothing else could. That labor put a distinction between them and common; that added something to them more than nature, the common mother of all, had done, and so they became his private right. And will anyone say he had no right to those acorns or apples he thus appropriated, because he had not the consent of all mankind to make them his? Was it a robbery thus to assume to himself what belonged to all in common? If such a consent as that was necessary, man had starved, notwithstanding the plenty God had given him. We see in commons which remain so by compact that 'tis the taking any part of what is common and removing it out of the state nature leaves it in, which begins the property; without which the common is of no use. And the taking of this or that part does not depend on the express consent of all the commoners. Thus the grass my horse has bit, the turfs my servant has cut, and the ore I have dug in any place where I have a right to them in common with others, become my property without the assignation or consent of anybody. The labor that was mine removing them out of that common state they were in, hath fixed my property in them. . . .

It will perhaps be objected to this, that if gathering the acorns, or other fruits of the earth, etc., makes a right to them, then anyone may engross as much as he will. To which I answer, Not so. The same law of nature that does by this means give us property, does also bound that property too. "God has given us all things richly" (1 Tim. vi. 17), is the voice of reason confirmed by inspiration. But how far has He given it to us? To enjoy. As much as anyone can make use of to any advantage of life before it spoils, so much he may by his labor fix a property in; whatever is beyond this, is more than his share, and belongs to others. Nothing was made by God for man to spoil or destroy. And thus considering the plenty of natural provisions there was a long time in the world, and the few spenders, and to how small a part of that provision the industry of one man could extend itself, and engross it to the prejudice of others—especially keeping within the bounds, set by reason, of what might serve for his use—there could be then little room for quarrels or contentions about property so established. . . .

OF THE BEGINNING AND ENDS OF POLITICAL SOCIETIES

Men being, as has been said, by nature all free, equal, and independent, no one can be put out of this estate, and subjected to the political power of another, without his own consent, which is done by agreeing with other men to join and unite into a community for their comfortable, safe, and peaceable living one amongst another, in a secure enjoyment of their properties, and a greater security against any that are not of it. This any number of men may do, because it injures not the freedom of the rest; they are left as they were in the liberty of the state of nature. When any number of men have so consented to make one community or government, they are thereby presently incorporated, and make one body politic, wherein the majority have a right to act and conclude the rest.

For when any number of men have, by the consent of every individual, made a community, they have thereby made that community one body, with a power to act as one body, which is only by the will and determination of the majority. For that which acts any community being only the consent of the individuals of it, and it being one body must move one way, it is necessary the body should move that way whither the greater force carries it, which is the consent of the majority; or else it is impossible it should act or continue one body, one community, which the consent of every individual that united into it agreed that it should; and so everyone is bound by that consent to be concluded by the majority. And therefore we see that in assemblies empowered to act by positive laws, where no number is set by that positive law which empowers them, the act of the majority passes for the act of the whole, and of course determines, as having by the law of nature and reason the power of the whole.

And thus every man, by consenting with others to make one body politic under one government, puts himself under an obligation to every one of that society, to submit to the determination of the majority, and to be concluded by it; or else this original compact, whereby he with others incorporates into one society, would signify nothing, and be no compact, if he be left free and under no other ties than he was in before in the state of nature. For what appearance would there be of any compact? What new engagement if he were no farther tied by any decrees of the society, than he himself thought fit, and did actually consent to? This would be still as great a liberty as he himself had before his compact, or anyone else in the state of nature hath, who may submit himself and consent to any acts of it if he thinks fit. . . .

Universal consent is next to impossible ever to be had. . . . [So] where the majority cannot conclude the rest, there they cannot act as one body, and consequently will be immediately dissolved again.

Whosoever therefore out of a state of nature unite into a community must be understood to give up all the power necessary to the ends for which they unite into society, to the majority of the community, unless they expressly agreed in any number greater than the majority. And this is done by barely agreeing to unite into one political society, which is all the compact that is, or needs be, between the individuals that enter into or make up a commonwealth. . . .

Every man being, as has been shown, naturally free, and nothing being able to put him into subjection to any earthly power but only his own consent, it is to be considered what shall be understood to be sufficient declaration of a man's consent to make him subject to the laws of any government. There is a common distinction of an express and a tacit consent, which will concern our present case. Nobody doubts but an express consent of any man entering into any society makes him a perfect member of that society, a subject of that government. The difficulty is, what ought to be looked upon as a tacit consent, and how far it binds i.e., how far anyone shall be looked on to have consented, and thereby submitted to any government, where he has made no expressions of it at all. And to this I say that every man that hath any possession or enjoyment of any part of the dominions of any government doth thereby give his tacit consent, and is as far forth obliged to obedience to the laws of that government during such enjoyment as anyone under it; whether this his possession be of land to him and his heirs for ever, or a lodging only for a week; or whether it be barely traveling freely on the highway; and in effect it reaches as far as the very being of anyone within the territories of that government.

To understand this the better, it is fit to consider that every man when he at first incorporates himself into any commonwealth, he, by his uniting himself thereunto, annexed also, and submits to the community those possessions which he has or shall acquire that do not already belong to any other government; for it would be a direct contradiction for anyone to enter into society with others for the securing and regulating of property, and yet to suppose his land, whose property is to be regulated by the laws of the society, should be exempt from the jurisdiction of that government to which he himself, and the property of the land, is a subject. . . .

But since the government has a direct jurisdiction only over the land, and reaches the possessor of it (before he has actually incorporated himself in the society), only as he dwells upon, and enjoys that: the obligation anyone is under, by virtue of such enjoyment, to submit to the government, begins and ends with the enjoyment; so that whenever the owner, who has given nothing but such a tacit consent to the government, will by donation, sale, or otherwise, quit the said possession, he is at liberty to go and incorporate himself into any other commonwealth, or to agree with others to begin a new one . . . in any part of the world they can find free and unpossessed. . . .

The reason why men enter into society is the preservation of their property; and the end why they choose and authorize a legislative is that there may be laws made, and rules set, as guards and fences to the properties of all the members of the society to limit the power and moderate the dominion of every part and member of the society. For since it can never be supposed to be the will of the society that the legislative should have a power to destroy that which everyone designs secure by entering into society, and for which the people submitted themselves to legislators of their own making, whenever the legislators endeavor to take away and destroy the property of the people, or to reduce them to slavery under arbitrary power, they put themselves into a state of war with the people, who are thereupon absolved from any further obedience, and are left to the common refuge which God hath provided for all men against force and violence. Whensoever, therefore, the legislative shall transgress this fundamental rule of society, and either by ambition, fear, folly, or corruption, endeavor to grasp themselves or put into the hands of any other an absolute power over the lives, liberties, and estates of the people, by this breach of trust they forfeit the power the people had put into their hands, for quite contrary ends, and it devolves to the people, who have a right to resume their original liberty, and by the establishment of the new legislative (such as they shall think fit) provide for their own safety and security, which is the end for which they are in society.

REVIEW AND DISCUSSION QUESTIONS

1. Describe the "state of nature" as Locke envisions it. In what sense(s) is every person an equal there?
2. How does Locke view nature and humankind's relationship to it?
3. Why are people motivated to leave the state of nature?
4. What justifies or makes legitimate a government? When may citizens revolt, according to Locke?
5. What justifies somebody's taking an unowned resource for his or her own use? What provisos or limitations does Locke place on the acquisition of unowned resources?

Of Justice

David Hume

In this essay, which is from his *An Enquiry Concerning the Principles of Morals* (another selection of which was reprinted in Section 3), David Hume discusses why economic justice is necessary given the scarcity of resources, the reasons why property should be protected, and the importance of utility in deciding these issues.

That Justice is so useful to society, and consequently that *part* of its merit, at least, must arise from that consideration, it would be a superfluous undertaking to prove. That public utility is the *sole* origin of justice, and that reflections on the beneficial consequences of this virtue are the *sole* foundation of its merit; this proposition, being more curious and important, will better deserve our examination and enquiry.

Let us suppose that nature has bestowed on the human race such profuse *abundance* of all *external* conveniences, that, without any uncertainty in the event, without any care or industry on our part, every individual finds himself fully provided with whatever his most voracious appetites can want, or luxurious imagination wish or desire. His natural beauty, we shall suppose, surpasses all acquired ornaments: the perpetual clemency of the seasons renders useless all clothes or covering; the raw herbage affords him the most delicious fare; the clear fountain, the richest beverage. No laborious occupation required: no tillage:

From David Hume, *An Enquiry Concerning the Principles of Morals* (1751).

no navigation. Music, poetry, and contemplation form his sole business: conversation, mirth, and friendship his sole amusement.

It seems evident that, in such a happy state, every other social virtue would flourish, and receive tenfold increase; but the cautious, jealous virtue of justice would never once have been dreamed of. For what purpose make a partition of goods, where every one has already more than enough? Why give rise to property, where there cannot possibly be any injury? Why call this object mine, when upon the seizing of it by another, I need but stretch out my hand to possess myself to what is equally valuable? Justice, in that case, being totally useless, would be an idle ceremonial, and could never possibly have place in the catalogue of virtues.

We see, even in the present necessitous condition of mankind, that, wherever any benefit is bestowed by nature in an unlimited abundance, we leave it always in common among the whole human race, and make no subdivisions of right and property. Water and air, though the most necessary of all objects, are not challenged as the property of individuals; nor can any man commit injustice by the most lavish use and enjoyment of these blessings. In fertile extensive countries, with few inhabitants, land is regarded on the same footing.

Again; suppose, that, though the necessities of human race continue the same as at present, yet the mind is so enlarged, and so replete with friendship and generosity, that every man has the utmost tenderness for every man, and feels no more concern for his own interest than for that of his fellows; it seems evident, that the use of justice would, in this case, be suspended by such an extensive benevolence, nor would the divisions and barriers of property and obligation have ever been thought of. Why should I bind another, by a deed or promise, to do me any good office, when I know that he is already prompted, by the strongest inclination, to seek my happiness, and would, of himself, perform the desired service; except the hurt, he thereby receives, be greater than the benefit accruing to me? . . .

To make this truth more evident, let us reverse the foregoing suppositions; and carrying everything to the opposite extreme, consider what would be the effect of these new situations. Suppose a society to fall into such want of all common necessaries, that the utmost frugality and industry cannot preserve the greater number from perishing, and the whole from extreme misery; it will readily, I believe, be admitted, that the strict laws of justice are suspended, in such a pressing emergence, and give place to the stronger motives of necessity and self-preservation. Is it any crime, after a shipwreck, to seize whatever means or instrument of safety one can lay hold of, without regard to former limitations of property? Or if a city besieged were perishing with hunger; can we imagine, that men will see any means of preservation before them, and lose their lives, from a scrupulous regard to what, in other situations, would be the rules of equity and justice? The use and tendency of that virtue is to procure happiness and security, by preserving order in society: but where the society is ready to perish from extreme necessity, no greater evil can be dreaded from violence and injustice; and every man may now provide for himself by all the means, which prudence can dictate, or humanity permit. . . .

The common situation of society is a medium amidst all these extremes. We are naturally partial to ourselves, and to our friends; but are capable of learning the advantage resulting from a more equitable conduct. Few enjoyments are given us from the open and liberal hand of nature; but by art, labor, and industry, we can extract them in great abundance. Hence the ideas of property become necessary in all civil society: Hence justice derives its usefulness to the public: And hence alone arises its merit and moral obligation. . . .

If we examine the *particular* laws, by which justice is directed, and property determined; we shall still be presented with the same conclusion. The good of mankind is the only object of all these laws and regulations. Not only is it requisite, for the peace and interest of society, that men's possessions should be separated; but the rules, which we follow, in making the separation, are such as can best be contrived to serve farther the interests of society. . . . Render possessions ever so equal, men's different degrees of art, care, and industry will immediately break that equality. Or if you check these virtues, you reduce society to the most extreme indigence; and instead of preventing want and beggary in a few, render it unavoidable to the whole community. . . .

Who sees not, for instance, that whatever is produced or improved by man's art or industry ought, for ever, to be secured to him, in order to give encouragement to such *useful* habits and accomplishments? That the property ought to also descend to children and relations, for the same *useful* purpose? That it may be alienated by consent, in order to beget that commerce and intercourse, which is so *beneficial* to human society? And that all contracts and promises ought carefully to be fulfilled, in order to secure mutual trust and confidence, by which the general *interest* of mankind is so much promoted? . . .

Examine the writers on the laws of nature; and you will always find, that, whatever principles they set out with, they are sure to terminate here at last, and to assign, as the ultimate reason for every rule which they establish, the convenience and necessities of mankind.

What is man's property? Anything which it is lawful for him, and for him alone, to use. *But what rule have we by which we can distinguish these objects?* Here we must have recourse to statutes, customs, precedents, analogies, and a hundred other circumstances; some of which are constant and inflexible, some variable and arbitrary. But the ultimate point, in which they all professedly terminate, is the interest and happiness of human society. . . .

All birds of the same species in every age and country, built their nests alike: in this we see the force of instinct. Men, in different times and places, frame their houses differently: here we perceive the influence of reason and custom. A like inference may be drawn from comparing the instinct of generation and the institution of property.

How great soever the variety of municipal laws, it must be confessed, that their chief outlines pretty regularly concur; because the purposes, to which they tend, are everywhere exactly similar. In like manner, all houses have a roof and walls, windows and chimneys; though diversified in their shape, figure, and materials. The purposes of the latter, directed to the conveniences of human life, discover not more plainly their origin from reason and reflection, than do those of the former, which points all to a like end. . . .

The convenience, or rather necessity, which leads to justice is so universal, and everywhere points so much to the same rules, that the habit takes place in all societies; and it is not without some scrutiny, that we are able to ascertain its true origin. The matter, however, is not so obscure, but that even in common life we have every moment recourse to the principle of public utility, and ask, *What must become of the world, if such practices prevail? How could society subsist under such disorders?* Were the distinction or separation of possessions entirely useless, can any one conceive, that it ever should have obtained in society?

Thus we seem, upon the whole, to have attained a knowledge of the force of that principle here insisted on, and can determine what degree of esteem or moral approbation may result from reflections on public interest and utility. The necessity of justice to the support of society is the sole foundation of that virtue.

REVIEW AND DISCUSSION QUESTIONS

1. Hume imagines possible worlds in which available resources are different from our own world, and in which human beings are different. What are those worlds?
2. What is the point Hume makes about property, by describing our actual world and how it might have been different?

3. Explain how Hume thinks property rights should be determined in society. What justifies private property, according to Hume?

The Communist Manifesto

Karl Marx and Fredrich Engels

Karl Marx was born into a middle-class family in Trier, Germany in 1818. After receiving a doctorate in philosophy and marrying his childhood sweetheart, he moved to Paris. In September of 1844, Marx met Engels, the son of a prosperous manufacturer. A lifelong friendship and intellectual collaboration began.

In 1848, they wrote *The Communist Manifesto* for a small workers' organization to which they belonged, the Communist League. *The Communist Manifesto* was a polemical political pamphlet, written when Marx and Engels were relatively young. But because it expresses in succinct form their understanding of history and their vision of politics, they allowed it to be republished many times and to be translated into many different languages during their lives—even though they went on to elaborate the ideas it contains with greater sophistication in their later work.

Marx and Engels were active in Germany during the upheavals of 1848, but when the revolutionary movement collapsed, they settled in England, Engels in Manchester working at the family firm, and Marx in London studying at the British Museum and writing *Capital,* his masterpiece. Marx died in 1883, but Engels lived for another twelve years, doing scholarly research, editing his friend's unfinished work, and popularizing their political views.

The Communist Manifesto portrays history as the history of struggle between classes—in the modern era, between the capitalist or bourgeois class and the class of workers or proletarians. Although Marx and Engels credit the bourgeoisie with having broken the bonds of feudalism and with having developed modern industry to extraordinary heights of productivity, they believed that capitalism was plagued by internal contradictions, which would provoke the working class to overthrow it and replace it by a socialist or communist system that would better serve human needs. In *The Communist Manifesto,* Marx and Engels lay down a challenge to any philosophical theory of justice and community that ignores the importance of socioeconomic development and class divisions in understanding human society.

I. BOURGEOIS AND PROLETARIANS[1]

The history of all hitherto existing society[2] is the history of class struggles.

Free man and slave, patrician and plebian, lord and serf, guild master and journeyman, in a word, oppressor and oppressed, stood in constant opposition to one another, carried on an uninterrupted, now hidden, now open fight, a fight that each time ended either in a revolutionary reconstitution of society at large or in the common ruin of the contending classes.

In the earlier epochs of history we find almost everywhere a complicated arrangement of society into various orders, a manifold gradation of social rank. In ancient Rome we have patricians, knights, plebians, slaves; in the Middle Ages, feudal lords, vassals, guild masters, journeymen, apprentices, serfs; in almost all of these classes, again, subordinate gradations.

From Karl Marx and Friedrich Engels, *Manifesto of the Communist Party* (New York: International Publishers, 1932).

The modern bourgeois society that has sprouted from the ruins of feudal society has not done away with class antagonisms. It has but established new classes, new conditions of oppression, new forms of struggle in place of the old ones.

Our epoch, the epoch of the bourgeoisie, possesses, however, this distinctive feature: it has simplified the class antagonisms. Society as a whole is more and more splitting up into two great hostile camps, into two great classes directly facing each, other: bourgeoisie and proletariat.

From the serfs of the Middle Ages sprang the chartered burghers of the earliest towns. From these burgesses the first elements of the bourgeoisie were developed.

The discovery of America, the rounding of the Cape opened up fresh ground for the rising bourgeoisie. The East Indian and Chinese markets, the colonization of America, trade with the colonies, the increase in the means of exchange and in commodities generally, gave to commerce, to navigation, to industry an impulse never before known, and thereby, to the revolutionary element in the tottering feudal society, a rapid development.

The feudal system of industry, under which industrial production was monopolized by closed guilds, now no longer sufficed for the growing wants of the new markets. The manufacturing system took its place. The guild-masters were pushed on one side by the manufacturing middle class; division of labor between the different corporate guilds vanished in the face of division of labor in each single workshop.

Meantime the markets kept ever growing, the demand ever rising. Even manufacturers no longer sufficed. Thereupon steam and machinery revolutionized industrial production. The place of manufacture was taken by the giant, modern industry, the place of the industrial middle class by industrial millionaires, the leaders of whole industrial armies, the modern bourgeois.

Modern industry has established the world market, for which the discovery of America paved the way. This market has given an immense development to commerce, to navigation, to communication by land. This development has, in its turn, reacted on the extension of industry; and in proportion as industry, commerce, navigation, railways extended, in the same proportion the bourgeoisie developed, increased its capital, and pushed into the background every class handed down from the Middle Ages.

We see, therefore, how the modern bourgeoisie is itself the product of a long course of development, of a series of revolutions in the modes of production and of exchange.

Each step in the development of the bourgeoisie was accompanied by a corresponding political advance of that class. An oppressed class under the sway of the feudal nobility, an armed and self-governing association in the medieval commune; here independent urban republic (as in Italy and Germany), there taxable "third estate" of the monarchy (as in France), afterwards, in the period of manufacture proper, serving either the semi-feudal or the absolute monarchy as a counterpoise against the nobility, and, in fact, cornerstone of the great monarchies in general, the bourgeoisie has at last, since the establishment of modern industry and of the world market, conquered for itself, in the modern representative state, exclusive political sway. The executive of the modern state is but a committee for managing the common affairs of the whole bourgeoisie.

The bourgeoisie, historically, has played a most revolutionary part.

The bourgeoisie, wherever it has got the upper hand, has put an end to all feudal, patriarchal, idyllic relations. It has pitilessly torn asunder the motley feudal ties that bound man to his "natural superiors," and has left remaining no other nexus between man and man than naked self-interest, than callous "cash payment." It has drowned the most heavenly ecstasies of religious fervor, of chivalrous enthusiasm, of Philistine sentimentalism in the icy water of egotistical calculation. It has resolved personal worth into exchange value and, in place of the numberless indefeasible chartered freedoms, has set up that single, unconscionable freedom—free trade. In one word, for exploitation, veiled by religious and political illusions, it has substituted naked, shameless, direct, brutal exploitation.

The bourgeoisie has stripped of its halo every occupation hitherto honored and looked up to with reverent awe. It has converted the physician, the lawyer, the priest, the poet, the man of science into its paid wage laborers.

The bourgeoisie has torn away from the family its sentimental veil, and has reduced the family relation to a mere money relation.

The bourgeoisie has disclosed how it came to pass that the brutal display of vigor in the Middle Ages, which reactionists so much admire, found its fitting complement in the most slothful indolence. It has been the first to show what man's activity can bring about. It has accomplished wonders far surpassing Egyptian pyramids, Roman aqueducts, and Gothic cathedrals; it has conducted expeditions that put in the shade all former exoduses of nations and crusades.

The bourgeoisie cannot exist without constantly revolutionizing the instruments of production, and thereby the relations of production, and with them the whole relations of society. Conservation of the old of production in unaltered form was, on the contrary, the first condition of existence for all earlier industrial classes. Constant revolutionizing of production, uninterrupted disturbance of all social conditions, everlasting uncertainty and agitation distinguish the bourgeois epoch from all earlier ones. All fixed, fast-frozen relations, with their train of ancient and venerable prejudices and opinions, are swept away, all new-formed ones become antiquated before they can ossify. All that is solid melts into air, all that is holy is profaned, and man is at last compelled to face with sober senses his real conditions of life and his relations with his kind.

The need of a constantly expanding market for its products chases the bourgeoisie over the whole surface of the globe. It must nestle everywhere, settle everywhere, establish connections everywhere.

The bourgeoisie has through its exploitation of the world market given a cosmopolitan character to production and consumption in every country. To the great chagrin of reactionists, it has drawn from under the feet of industry the national ground on which it stood. All old-established national industries have been destroyed or are daily being destroyed. They are dislodged by new industries, whose introduction becomes a life and death question for all civilized nations by industries that no longer work up indigenous raw material, but raw material drawn from the remotest zones; industries whose products are consumed not only at home, but in every quarter of the globe. In place of the old wants, satisfied by the productions of the country, we find new wants, requiring for their satisfaction the products of distant lands and climes. In place of the old local and national seclusion and self-sufficiency we have intercourse in every direction, universal interdependence of nations. And as in material, so also in intellectual production. The intellectual creations of individual nations become common property. National one-sidedness and narrow-mindedness become more and more impossible, and from the numerous national and local literatures there arises a world literature.

The bourgeoisie, by the rapid improvement of all instruments of production, by the immensely facilitated means of communication, draws all, even the most barbarian, nations into civilization. The cheap prices of its commodities are the heavy artillery with which it batters down all Chinese walls, with which it forces the barbarians' intensely obstinate hatred of foreigners to capitulate. It compels all nations, on pain of extinction, to adopt the bourgeois mode of production; it compels them to introduce what it calls civilization into their midst, i.e., to become bourgeois themselves. In one word, it creates a world after its own image.

The bourgeoisie has subjected the country to the rule of the towns. It has created enormous cities, has greatly increased the urban population as compared with the rural, and has thus rescued a considerable part of the population from the idiocy of rural life. Just as it has made the country dependent on the towns, so it has made barbarian and semi-barbarian countries dependent on the civilized ones, nations of peasants on nations of bourgeois, the East on the West.

The bourgeoisie keeps more and more doing away with the scattered state of the population, of the means of production, and of property. It has agglomerated population, centralized means of production, and has concentrated property in a few hands. The necessary consequence of this was political centralization. Independent, or but loosely connected provinces, with separate interests, laws, governments and systems of taxation, became lumped together into one nation, with one government, one code of laws, one national class interest, one frontier, and one customs tariff.

The bourgeoisie, during its rule of scarce one hundred years, has created more massive and more colossal productive forces than have all preceding generations together. Subjection of nature's forces to man, machinery, application of chemistry to industry and agriculture, steam navigation, railways, electric telegraphs, clearing of whole continents for cultivation, canalization of rivers, whole populations conjured out of the ground—what earlier century had even a presentiment that such productive forces slumbered in the lap of social labor?

We see then: the means of production and of exchange, on whose foundation the bourgeoisie built itself up, were generated in feudal society. At a certain stage in the development of these means of production and of exchange, the conditions under which feudal society produced and exchanged, the feudal organization of agriculture and manufacturing industry, in one word, the feudal relations of property, became no longer compatible with the already developed productive forces; they became so many fetters. They had to be burst asunder; they were burst asunder.

Into their place stepped free competition, accompanied by a social and political

constitution adapted to it, and by the economic and political sway of the bourgeois class.

A similar movement is going on before our own eyes. Modern bourgeois society with its relations of production, of exchange, and of property, a society that has conjured up such gigantic means of production and of exchange, is like the sorcerer who is no longer able to control the powers of the nether world whom he has called up by his spells. For many a decade past, the history of industry and commerce is but the history of the revolt of modern productive forces against modern conditions of production, against the property relations that are the conditions for the existence of the bourgeoisie and of its rule. It is enough to mention the commercial crises that by their periodic return put on its trial, each time more threateningly, the existence of the entire bourgeois society. In these crises a great part not only of the existing products but also of the previously created productive forces are periodically destroyed. . . .

The weapons with which the bourgeoisie felled feudalism to the ground are now turned against the bourgeoisie itself.

But not only has the bourgeoisie forged the weapons that bring death to itself; it has also called into existence the men who are to wield those weapons—the modern working class—the proletarians.

In proportion as the bourgeoisie, i.e., capital, is developed, in the same proportion is the proletariat, the modern working class, developed—a class of laborers, who live only so long as they find work, and who find work only so long as their labor increases capital. These laborers, who must sell themselves piecemeal, are a commodity, like every other article of commerce, and are consequently exposed to all the vicissitudes of competition, to all the fluctuations of the market.

Owing to the extensive use of machinery and to division of labor, the work of the proletarians has lost all individual character and, consequently, all charm for the workman. He becomes an appendage of the machine, and it is only the simplest, most monotonous, and most easily acquired knack that is required of him. Hence the cost of production of a workman is restricted, almost entirely, to the means of subsistence that he requires for his maintenance and for the propagation of his race. But the price of a commodity, and therefore also of labor, is equal to its cost of production. In proportion, therefore, as the repulsiveness of the work increases, the wage decreases. Nay, more, in proportion as the use of machinery and division of labor increases, in the same proportion the burden of toil also increases, whether by prolongation of the working hours, by increase of the work exacted in a given time, or by increased speed of the machinery, etc.

Modern industry has converted the little workshop of the patriarchal master into the great factory of the industrial capitalist. Masses of laborers, crowded into the factory, are organized like soldiers. As privates of the industrial army they are placed under a command of a perfect hierarchy of officers and sergeants. Not only are they slaves of the bourgeois class, and of the bourgeois state; they are daily and hourly enslaved by the machine, by the overlooker, and, above all, by the individual bourgeois manufacturer himself. The more openly this despotism proclaims gain to be its end and aim, the more petty, the more hateful, and the more embittering it is.

The less the skill and exertion of strength implied in manual labor, in other words, the more modern industry becomes developed, the more is the labor of men superseded by that of women. Differences of age and sex have no longer any distinctive social validity for the working class. All are instruments of labor, more or less expensive to use, according their age and sex. . . .

Now and then the workers are victorious, but only for a time. The real fruit of their battles lies not in the immediate result, but in the ever expanding union of the workers. This union is helped on by the improved means of communication that are created by modern industry and that place the workers of different localities in contact with one another. It was just this contact that was needed to centralize the numerous local struggles, all of the same character, into one national struggle between classes. But every class struggle is a political struggle. . . .

All previous historical movements were movements of minorities, or in the interest of minorities. The proletarian movement is the self-conscious, independent movement of the immense majority, in the interests of the immense majority. . . .

Hitherto every form of society has been based, as we have already seen, on the antagonism of oppression and oppressed classes. But in order to oppress a class certain conditions must be assured to it under which it can, at least, continue its slavish existence. The serf, in the period of serfdom, raised himself to membership in the commune, just as the petty bourgeois, under the yoke of feudal absolutism, managed to develop into a bourgeois. The modern laborer, on the contrary, instead of rising with the progress of industry, sinks deeper and deeper below the conditions of existence of his own class. He becomes a pauper, and pauperism develops more rapidly than population and wealth. And here it becomes evident that the bourgeoisie is unfit any longer to be the ruling class in society, and to impose its conditions of existence upon society as an overriding law. It is unfit to rule because it is incompetent to assure an existence to its slave within his slavery, because it cannot help letting him sink into such a state that it has to feed him instead of being fed by him. Society can no longer live under this bourgeoisie: in other words, its existence is no longer compatible with society.

The essential condition for the existence, and for the sway of the bourgeois class, is the formation and augmentation of capital; the condition for capital is wage labor. Wage labor rests exclusively on competition between the laborers. The advance of industry, whose involuntary promoter is the bourgeoisie, replaces the isolation of the laborers, due to competition, by their revolutionary combination, due to association. The development of modern industry, therefore, cuts from under its feet the very foundation on which the bourgeoisie produces and appropriates products. What the bourgeoisie, therefore, produces, above all, is its own gravediggers, Its fall and the victory of the proletariat are equally inevitable.

II. PROLETARIANS AND COMMUNISTS

In what relation do the communists stand to the proletarians as a whole?

The communists do not form a separate party opposed to other working-class parties.

They have no interests separate and apart from those of the proletariat as a whole. . . .

The immediate aim of the communists is the same as that of all the other proletarian parties. . . . formation of the proletariat into a class, overthrow of the bourgeois supremacy, conquest of political power by the proletariat.

The theoretical conclusions of the communists are in no way based on ideas or principles that have been invented, or discovered, by this or that would-be universal reformer.

They merely express, in general terms, actual relations springing from an existing class struggle, from a historical movement going on under our very eyes. The abolition of existing property relations is not at all a distinctive feature of communism.

All property relations in the past have continually been subject to historical change consequent upon the change in historical conditions.

The French Revolution, for example, abolished feudal property in favor of bourgeois property.

The distinguishing feature of communism is not the abolition of property generally, but the abolition of bourgeois property. But modern bourgeois private property is the final and most complete expression of the system of producing and appropriating products that is based on class antagonisms, on the exploitation of the many by the few.

In this sense the theory of the community may be summed up in the single sentence: Abolition of private property.

We communists have been reproached with the desire of abolishing the right of personally acquiring property as the fruit of man's own labor, which property is alleged to be the groundwork of all personal freedom, activity, and independence.

Hard-won, self-acquired, self-earned property! Do you mean the property of the petty artisan and of the small peasant, a form of property that preceded the bourgeois form? There is no need to abolish that; the development of industry has to a great extent already destroyed it, and is still destroying it daily.

Or do you mean modern bourgeois private property?

But does wage labor create any property for the laborer? Not a bit. It creates capital, i.e., that kind of property which exploits wage labor, and which cannot increase except upon condition of begetting a new supply of wage labor for fresh exploitation. Property, in its present form, is based on the antagonism of capital and wage labor. Let us examine both sides of this antagonism.

To be a capitalist is to have not only a purely personal but a social *status* in production. Capital is a collective product, and only by the united action of many members, nay, in the last resort only by the united action of all members of society, can it be set in motion.

Capital is, therefore, not a personal, it is a social power.

When, therefore, capital is converted into common property, into the property of all members of society, personal property is not thereby transformed into social property. It is only the social character of the property that is changed. It loses its class character.

Let us now take wage labor.

The average price of wage labor is the minimim wage, i.e., that quantum of the means of subsistence which is absolutely requisite to keep the laborer in bare existence as a laborer. What, therefore, the wage laborer appropriates by means of his labor merely suffices to prolong and reproduce a bare existence. We by no means intend to abolish this personal appropriation of the products of labor, an appropriation that is made for the maintenance and reproduction of human life, and that leaves no surplus wherewith to command the labor of others. All that we want to do away with is the miserable character of this appropriation, under which the laborer lives merely to increase capital, and is allowed to live only in so far as the interest of the ruling class requires it.

In bourgeois society, living labor is but means to increase accumulated labor. In communist society accumulated labor is but a means to widen, to enrich, to promote the existence of the laborer.

In bourgeois society, therefore, the past dominates the present; in communist society the present dominates the past. In bourgeois society capital is independent and has individuality, while the living person is dependent and has no individuality.

And the abolition of this state of things is called by the bourgeois, abolition of individuality and freedom! And rightly so. The abolition of bourgeois individuality, bourgeois independence, and bourgeois freedom is undoubtedly aimed at.

By freedom is meant, under the present bourgeois conditions of production, free trade, free selling and buying.

But if selling and buying disappear, free selling and buying disappear also. This talk about free selling and buying, and all the other "brave words" of our bourgeoisie about free in general, have a meaning, if any, only in contrast with restricted selling and buying, with the fettered traders of the Middle Ages, but have no meaning when opposed to the communistic abolition of buying and selling, of the bourgeois conditions of production, and of the bourgeoisie itself.

You are horrified at our intending to do away with private property. But in your existing society private property is already done away with for nine tenths of the population; its existence for the few is solely due to its non-existence in the hands of those nine tenths. You reproach us, therefore, with intending to do away with a form of property the necessary condition for whose existence is the non-existence of any property for the immense majority of society.

In one word, you reproach us with intending to do away with your property. Precisely so; that is just what we intend.

From the moment when labor can no longer be converted into capital, money, or rent, into a social power capable of being monopolized, i.e., from the moment when individual property can no longer be transformed into bourgeois property, into capital, from that moment, you say, individuality vanishes.

You must, therefore, confess that by "individual" you mean no other person than the bourgeois, than the middle-class owner of property. This person must, indeed, be swept out of the way and made impossible.

Communism deprives no man of the power to appropriate the products of society; all that it does is to deprive him of the power to subjugate the labor of others by means of such appropriation.

It has been objected that upon the abolition of private property all work will cease and universal laziness will overtake us.

According to this, bourgeois society ought long ago have gone to the dogs through sheer idleness, for those of its members who. work acquire nothing and those who acquire anything do not work. The whole of this objection is but another expression of the tautology that there can no longer be any wage labor when there is no longer any capital. . . .

But don't wrangle with us so long as you apply, to our intended abolition of bourgeois property, the standard of your bourgeois notions of freedom, culture, law, etc. Your very ideas are but the outgrowth of the conditions of your bourgeois production and bourgeois property, just as your juris-prudence is but the will of your class made into a law for all, a will whose essential character and direction are determined by the economic conditions of existence of your class.

The selfish misconception that induces you to transform into eternal laws of nature and of reason the social forms springing from your present mode of production and form of property—historical relations that rise and disappear in the progress of production—this misconception you share with every ruling class that has preceded you. What you see clearly in the case of ancient property, what you admit in the case of feudal property, you are of course forbidden to admit in the case of your own bourgeois form of property.

Abolition of the family! Even the most radical flare up at this infamous proposal of the communists.

On what foundation is the present family, the bourgeois family based? On capital, on private gain. In its completely developed form this family exists only among the bourgeoisie. But this state of things finds its complement in the practical absence of the family among the proletarians, and in public prostitution.

The bourgeois family will vanish as a matter of course when its complement vanishes, and both will vanish with the vanishing of capital.

Do you charge us with wanting to stop the exploitation of children by their parents? To this crime we plead guilty.

But you will say, we destroy the most hallowed of relations when we replace home education by social.

And your education! Is not that also social, and determined by the social conditions under which you educate, by the intervention, direct or indirect, of society, by means of schools, etc.? The communists have not invented the intervention of society in education; they do but seek to alter the character of that intervention, and to rescue education from the influence of the ruling class.

The bourgeois claptrap about the family and education, about the hallowed co-relation of parent and child, becomes all the more disgusting, the more, by the action of modern industry, all family ties among the proletarians are torn asunder and their children transformed into simple articles of commerce and instruments of labor. . . .

The communists are further reproached with desiring to abolish countries and nationality.

The workingmen have no country. We cannot take from them what they have not got. Since the proletariat must first of all acquire political supremacy, must rise to be the leading class of the nation, must constitute itself *the* nation, it is, so far, itself national, though not in the bourgeois sense of the word. . . .

Does it require deep intuition to comprehend that man's ideas, views, and conceptions, in one word, man's consciousness, change with every change in the conditions of his material existence, in his social relations, and in his social life?

What else does the history of ideas prove than that intellectual production changes its character in proportion as material production is changed? The ruling ideas of each age have been the ideas of its ruling class.

When people speak of ideas that revolutionize society they do not express the fact that within the old society the elements of a new one have been created, and that the dissolution of the old ideas keeps even pace with the dissolution of the old conditions of existence. . . .

But let us have done with the bourgeois objections to communism.

We have seen above that the first step in the revolution by the working class is to raise the proletariat to the position of ruling class, to win the battle of democracy.

The proletariat will use its political supremacy to wrest, by degrees, all capital from the bourgeoisie, to centralize all instruments of production in the hands of the state, i.e., of the proletariat organized as the ruling class, and to increase the total of productive forces as rapidly as possible.

Of course, in the beginning this cannot be effected except by means of despotic inroads on the rights of property and on the conditions of bourgeois production; by means of measures, therefore, which appear economically insufficient and untenable, but which, in the course of the movement, outstrip themselves, necessitate further inroads upon the old social order, and are unavoidable as a means of entirely revolutionizing the mode of production.

These measures will of course be different in different countries.

Nevertheless, in the most advanced countries the following will be pretty generally applicable:

1. Abolition of property in land and application of all rents of land to public purposes.
2. A heavy progressive or graduated income tax.
3. Abolition of all right of inheritance.
4. Confiscation of the property of all emigrants and rebels.
5. Centralization of credit in the hands of the state, by means of a national bank with state capital and an exclusive monopoly.
6. Centralization of the means of communication and transport in the hands of the state.
7. Extension of factories and instruments of production owned by the state; the bringing into cultivation of wastelands, and the improvement of the soil generally in accordance with a common plan.
8. Equal liability of all to labor. Establishment of industrial armies, especially for agriculture.
9. Combination of agriculture with manufacturing industries; gradual abolition of the distinction between town and country, by a more equable distribution of the population over the country.
10. Free education for all children in public schools. Abolition of children's factory labor in its present form. Combination of education with industrial production, etc.

When, in the course of development, class distinctions have disappeared and all production has been concentrated in the hands of a vast association of the whole nation, the public power will lose its political character. Political power, properly so called, is merely the organized power of one class for oppressing another. If the proletariat during its contest with the bourgeoisie is compelled, by the force of circumstances, to organize itself as a class, if, by means of a revolution, it makes itself the ruling class and, as such, sweeps away by force the old conditions of production, then it will, along with these conditions, have swept away the conditions for the existence of class antagonisms and of classes generally, and will thereby have abolished its own supremacy as a class.

In place of the old bourgeois society, with its classes and class antagonisms, we shall have an association in which the free development of each is the condition for the free development of all.

NOTES

1. By bourgeoisie is meant the class of modern capitalists, owners of the means of social production and employers of wage-labor. By proletariat, the class of modern wage-laborers who, having no means of production of their own, are reduced to selling their labor-power in order to live (Note by Engels in English edition of 1888).
2. That is, all *written* history. In 1847, the pre-history of society, the social organization existing previous to recorded history, was all but unknown. Since then ... village communities were found to be, or to have been the primitive form of society everywhere from India to Ireland. ... With the dissolution of these primeval communities society begins to be differentiated into separate and finally antagonistic classes. ... (Note by Engels in the English edition of 1888).

REVIEW AND DISCUSSION QUESTIONS

1. How do Marx and Engels characterize the bourgeoisie? The proletariat?
2. Marx famously argued that the level of technological advancement (forces of production) determine the economic and social structure of the society. He also speaks in terms of 'inherent "contradictions" existing within a given socioeconomic system. Explain what he means.

3. What advantages do Marx and Engels see in the system of capitalism, as opposed to feudalism?
4. What do Marx and Engles mean by "exploitation"?
5. Where do philosophical ideas about rights, justice, and entitlements originate, according to Marx and Engels?
6. Describe their vision of a communist society. What will happen to class antagonisms? To the family? To private ownership of the means of production, (factories, land, etc.)?

A Theory of Justice

John Rawls

Political philosophy has experienced a renaissance in recent years, in large part because of the work of John Rawls. His book, *A Theory of Justice,* now in its second edition, has been translated into Japanese, Chinese, and Korean, as well as every major European language. In it, Rawls revives the social contract tradition. The focus of social justice is what he terms society's *basic structure,* by which he means its constitution, laws, and its economic system, not the justice or injustice of individual acts. Rawls' social contract is hypothetical rather than historical: correct principles of justice are ones that *would be* chosen in a fair position of equality. That, in turn, requires us to imagine ourselves in an "original position" behind a "veil of ignorance" that prevents us from relying on such morally irrelevant factors as race, gender, social class, or even our particular talents. By forcing ourselves to choose under fair circumstances, he argues, justice is assured. Situated in such a position, he then argues, people would choose to construct their government according to principles that (1) respect basic liberties and (2) allow social and economic inequalities only if they benefit everybody, in particular society's least advantaged, and assure that everyone is given genuine (fair) equality of opportunity to seek various positions. John Rawls is emeritus professor of philosophy at Harvard University.

THE MAIN IDEA OF THE THEORY OF JUSTICE

My aim is to present a conception of justice which generalizes and carries to a higher level of abstraction the familiar theory of the social contract as found, say, in Locke, Rousseau, and Kant. In order to do this we are not to think of the original contract as one to enter a particular society or to set up a particular form of government. Rather, the guiding idea is that the principles of justice for the basic structure of society are the object of the original agreement. They are the principles that free and rational persons concerned to further their own interests would accept in an initial position of equality as defining the fundamental terms of their association. These principles are to regulate all further agreements; they specify the kinds of social cooperation that can be entered into and the forms of government that can be established. This way of regarding the principles of justice I shall call justice as fairness.

Thus we are to imagine that those who engage in social cooperation choose together, in one joint act, the principles which are to assign basic rights and duties and to determine the division of social benefits. Men are to decide in advance how they are to regulate their claims against one another and what is to be the foundation charter of their society. Just as each person must decide by rational reflection what constitutes his good, that is, the system of ends which it is rational for him to pursue, so a group of persons must decide once and for all what is to count among them as just and unjust. The choice which rational men would make in this hypothetical situation of equal liberty, assuming for the present that this choice problem has a solution, determines the principles of justice.

In justice as fairness the original position of equality corresponds to the state of nature in the traditional theory of the social contract. This original position is not, of course, thought of as an actual historical state of affairs, much less as a primitive condition of culture. It is understood as a purely hypothetical situation characterized so as to lead to a certain conception of justice. Among the essential features of this situation is that no one knows his place in society, his class position or social status, nor does any one know his fortune in the distribution of natural assets and abilities, his intelligence, strength, and the like. I shall even assume that the parties do not know their conceptions of the good or their special psychological propensities. The principles of justice are chosen behind a veil of ignorance. This ensures that no one is advantaged or disadvantaged in the choice of principles by the outcome of natural chance or the contingency of social circumstances. Since all are similarly situated and no one is able to design principles to favor his particular condition, the principles of justice are the result of a fair agreement or bargain. For given the circumstances of the original position, the symmetry of everyone's relations to each other, this initial situation is fair between individuals as moral persons, that is, as rational beings with their own ends and capable, I shall

assume, of a sense of justice. The original position is, one might say, the appropriate initial status quo, and thus the fundamental agreements reached in it are fair. This explains the propriety of the name "justice as fairness": it conveys the idea that the principles of justice are agreed to in an initial situation that is fair. The name does not mean that the concepts of justice and fairness are the same, any more than the phrase "poetry as metaphor" means that the concepts of poetry and metaphor are the same.

Justice as fairness begins, as I have said, with one of the most general of all choices which persons might make together, namely, with the choice of the first principles of a conception of justice which is to regulate all subsequent criticism and reform of institutions. Then, having chosen a conception of justice, we can suppose that they are to choose a constitution and a legislature to enact laws, and so on, all in accordance with the principles of justice initially agreed upon. Our social situation is just if it is such that by this sequence of hypothetical agreements we would have contracted into the general system of rules which defines it. Moreover, assuming that the original position does determine a set of principles (that is, that a particular conception of justice would be chosen), it will then be true that whenever social institutions satisfy these principles those engaged in them can say to one another that they are cooperating on terms to which they would agree if they were free and equal persons whose relations with respect to one another were fair. They could all view their arrangements as meeting the stipulations which they would acknowledge in an initial situation that embodies widely accepted and reasonable constraints on the choice of principles. The general recognition of this fact would provide the basis for a public acceptance of the corresponding principles of justice. No society can, of course, be a scheme of cooperation which men enter voluntarily in a literal sense; each person finds himself placed at birth in some particular position in some particular society, and the nature of this position materially affects his life prospects. Yet a society satisfying the principles of justice as fairness comes as close as a society can to being a voluntary scheme, for it meets the principles which free and equal persons would assent to under circumstances that are fair. In this sense its members are autonomous and the obligations they recognize self-imposed.

One feature of justice as fairness is to think of the parties in the initial situation as rational and mutually disinterested. This does not mean that the parties are egoists, that is, individuals with only certain kinds of interests, say in wealth, prestige, and domination. But they are conceived as not taking an interest in one another's interests. They are to presume that even their spiritual aims may be opposed, in the way that the aims of those of different religions may be opposed. Moreover, the concept of rationality must be interpreted as far as possible in the narrow sense, standard in economic theory, of taking the most effective means to given ends. . . . [O]ne must try to avoid introducing into it any controversial ethical elements. The initial situation must be characterized by stipulations that are widely accepted.

In working out the conception of justice as fairness one main task clearly is to determine which principles of justice would be chosen in the original position. To do this we must describe this situation in some detail and formulate with care the problem of choice which it presents. . . . It may be observed, however, that once the principles of justice are thought of as arising from an original agreement in a situation of equality, it is an open question whether the principle of utility would be acknowledged. Offhand it hardly seems likely that persons who view themselves as equals, entitled to press their claims upon one another, would agree to a principle which may require lesser life prospects for some simply for the sake of a greater sum of advantages enjoyed by others. Since each desires to protect his interests, his capacity to advance his conception of the good, no one has a reason to acquiesce in an enduring loss for himself in order to bring about a greater net balance of satisfaction. In the absence of strong and

lasting benevolent impulses, a rational man would not accept a basic structure merely because it maximized the algebraic sum of advantages irrespective of its permanent effects on his own basic rights and interests. Thus it seems that the principle of utility is incompatible with the conception of social cooperation among equals for mutual advantage. It appears to be inconsistent with the idea of reciprocity implicit in the notion of a well-ordered society. Or, at any rate, so I shall argue.

I shall maintain instead that the persons in the initial situation would choose two rather different principles: the first requires equality in the assignment of basic rights and duties, while the second holds that social and economic inequalities, for example inequalities of wealth and authority, are just only if they result in compensating benefits for everyone, and in particular for the least advantaged members of society. These principles rule out justifying institutions on the grounds that the hardships of some are offset by a greater good in the aggregate. It may be expedient but it is not just that some should have less in order that others may prosper. But there is no injustice in the greater benefits earned by a few provided that the situation of persons not so fortunate is thereby improved. The intuitive idea is that since everyone's well-being depends upon a scheme of cooperation without which no one could have a satisfactory life, the division of advantages should be such as to draw forth the willing cooperation of everyone taking part in it, including those less well situated. Yet this can be expected only if reasonable terms are proposed. The two principles mentioned seem to be a fair agreement on the basis of which those better endowed, or more fortunate in their social position, neither of which we can be said to deserve, could expect the willing cooperation of others when some workable scheme is a necessary condition of the welfare of all. Once we decide to look for a conception of justice that nullifies the accidents of natural endowment and the contingencies of social circumstance as counters in quest for political and economic advantage, we are led to these principles. They express the result of leaving aside those aspects of the social world that seem arbitrary from a moral point of view. . . .

THE ORIGINAL POSITION AND JUSTIFICATION

I have said that the original position is the appropriate initial status quo which ensures that the fundamental agreements reached in it are fair. This fact yields the name "justice as fairness." It is clear, then, that I want to say that one conception of justice is more reasonable than another, or justifiable with respect to it, if rational persons in the initial situation would choose its principles over those of the other for the role of justice. Conceptions of justice are to be ranked by their acceptability to persons so circumstanced. Understood in this way the question of justification is settled by working out a problem of deliberation: we have to ascertain which principles it would be rational to adopt given the contractual situation. This connects the theory of justice with the theory of rational choice.

If this view of the problem of justification is to succeed, we must, of course, describe in some detail the nature of this choice problem. A problem of rational decision has a definite answer only if we know the beliefs and interests of the parties, their relations with respect to one another, the alternatives between which they are to choose, the procedure whereby they make up their minds, and so on. . . . The concept of the original position, as I shall refer to it, is that of the most philosophically favored interpretation of this initial choice situation for purposes of a theory of justice.

But how are we to decide on the most favored interpretation? . . . To justify a particular description of the initial situation one shows that it incorporates these commonly held presumptions. One argues from widely accepted but weak premises to more specific conclusions. Each of the presumptions should by itself be natural and plausible; some of

them may seem innocuous or even trivial. The aim of the contract approach is to establish that taken together they impose significant bounds on acceptable principles of justice. . . .

One should not be misled, then, by the somewhat unusual conditions which characterize the original position. The idea here is simply to make vivid to ourselves the restrictions that it seems reasonable to impose on arguments for principles of justice, and therefore on these principles themselves. Thus it seems reasonable and generally acceptable that no one should be advantaged or disadvantaged by natural fortune or social circumstances in the choice of principles.

[Rawls thus argues in a later section that it is reasonable in the original position to exclude knowledge of "natural talents" such as intelligence as well as inherited wealth and social class, race, and gender, because all of these are "morally arbitrary." Social class and natural talents are not "deserved," and one's "character" also "depends in large part on fortunate family and social circumstances."—Ed.]

It also seems widely agreed that it should be impossible to tailor principles to the circumstances of one's own case. We should ensure further that particular inclinations and aspirations, and persons' conceptions of their good do not affect the principles adopted. The aim is to rule out those principles that it would be rational to propose for acceptance, however little the chance of success, only if one knew certain things that are irrelevant from the standpoint of justice. For example, if a man knew that he was wealthy, he might find it rational to advance the principle that various taxes for welfare measures be counted unjust; if he knew that he was poor, he would most likely propose the contrary principle. To represent the desired restrictions one imagines a situation in which everyone is deprived of this sort of information. One excludes the knowledge of those contingencies which sets men at odds and allows them to be guided by their prejudices. In this manner the veil of ignorance is arrived at in a natural way. This concept should cause no difficulty if we keep in mind the constraints on arguments that it is meant to express. At any time we can enter the original position, so to speak, simply by following a certain procedure, namely, by arguing for principles of justice in accordance with these restrictions.

It seems reasonable to suppose that the parties in the original position are equal. That is, all have the same rights in the procedure for choosing principles; each can make proposals, submit reasons for their acceptance, and so on. Obviously the purpose of these conditions is to represent equality between human beings as moral persons, as creatures having a conception of their good and capable of a sense of justice. The basis of equality is taken to be similarity in these two respects. Systems of ends are not ranked in value; and each man is presumed to have the requisite ability to understand and to act upon whatever principles are adopted. Together with the veil of ignorance, these conditions define the principles of justice as those which rational persons concerned to advance their interests would consent to as equals when none are known to be advantaged or disadvantaged by social and natural contingencies.

There is, however, another side to justifying a particular description of the original position. This is to see if the principles which would be chosen match our considered convictions of justice or extend them in an acceptable way. We can note whether applying these principles would lead us to make the same judgments about the basic structure of society which we now make intuitively and in which we have the greatest confidence; or whether, in cases where our present judgments are in doubt and given with hesitation, these principles offer a resolution which we can affirm on reflection. There are questions which we feel sure must be answered in a certain way. For example, we are confident that religious intolerance and racial discrimination are unjust. We think that we have examined these things with care and have reached what we believe is an impartial judgment not likely to be distorted by an excessive attention to our own interests. These convictions are provisional fixed points which we presume any conception of justice must fit. But we have much less assurance as to what is the correct distribution of wealth and authority. Here we may be looking for a way to remove our doubts. We can check an interpretation of the initial situation, then, by the capacity of its principles to accommodate our firmest convictions and to provide guidance where guidance is needed.

In searching for the most favored description of this situation we work from both ends. . . . By going back and forth, sometimes altering the conditions of the contractual circumstances, at others withdrawing our judgments and conforming them to principle, I assume that eventually we shall find a description of the initial situation that both expresses reasonable conditions and yields principles which match our considered judgments duly pruned and adjusted. This state of affairs I refer to as reflective equilibrium. It is an equilibrium because at last our principles and judgments coincide: and it is reflective since we know to what principles our judgments conform and the premises of their derivation. At the moment everything is in order. But this equilibrium is not necessarily stable. It is liable to be upset by further examination of the conditions which should be imposed on the contractual situation and by particular cases which may lead us to revise our judgments. Yet for the time being we have done what we can to render coherent and to justify our convictions of social justice. We have reached a conception of the original position. . . .

In arriving at the favored interpretation of the initial situation there is no point at which an appeal is made to self-evidence. . . . A conception of justice cannot be deduced from self-evident premises or conditions on principles; instead, its justification is a matter of the mutual support of many considerations, of everything fitting together into one coherent view.

A final comment. We shall want to say that certain principles of justice are justified because they would be agreed to in an initial situation of equality. I have emphasized that this original position is purely hypothetical. It is natural to ask why, if this agreement is never actually entered into, we should take any interest in these principles, moral or otherwise. The answer is that the conditions embodied in the description of the original position are ones that we do in fact accept. Or if we do not, then perhaps we can be persuaded to do so by philosophical reflection. Each aspect of the contractual situation can be given supporting grounds. Thus what we shall do is to collect together into one conception a number of conditions on principles that we are ready upon due consideration to recognize as reasonable. These constraints express what we are prepared to regard as limits on fair terms of social cooperation. One way to look at the idea of the original position, therefore, is to see it as an expository device which sums up the meaning of these conditions and helps us to extract their consequences. On the other hand, this conception is also an intuitive notion that suggests its own elaboration, so that led on by it we are drawn to define more clearly the standpoint from which we can best interpret moral relationships. We need a conception that enables us to envision our objective from afar: the intuitive notion of the original position is to do this for us. . . .

TWO PRINCIPLES OF JUSTICE

I shall now state in a provisional form the two principles of justice that I believe would be chosen in the original position. . . . The first statement of the two principles reads as follows.

First: each person is to have an equal right to the most extensive scheme of equal basic liberties compatible with a similar scheme of liberties for others.

Second: social and economic inequalities are to be arranged so that they are both (a) reasonably expected to be to everyone's advantage, and (b) attached to positions and offices open to all. . . .

These principles primarily apply, as I have said, to the basic structure of society and govern the assignment of rights and duties and regulate the distribution of social and economic advantages. Their formulation presupposes that, for the purposes of a theory of justice, the social structure may be viewed as having two more or less distinct parts, the first principle applying to the one, the second principle to the other. Thus we distinguish between the aspects of the social system that define and secure the equal basic liberties and the aspects that specify and establish social and economic inequalities. Now it is essential to observe that the basic liberties are given by a list of such liberties. Important among these are political liberty (the right to vote and to hold public office) and freedom of speech and assembly; liberty of conscience and freedom of thought; freedom of the person, which includes freedom from psychological oppression and physical assault and dismemberment (integrity of the person); the right to hold personal property and freedom from arbitrary arrest and seizure as defined by the concept of the rule of law. These liberties are to be equal by the first principle.

The second principle applies, in the first approximation, to the distribution of income and wealth and to the design of organizations that make use of differences in authority and responsibility. While the distribution of wealth and income need not be equal, it must be to everyone's advantage, and at the same time, positions of authority and responsibility must be accessible to all. One applies the second principle by holding positions open, and then, subject to this constraint, arranges social and economic inequalities so that everyone benefits.

These principles are to be arranged in a serial order with the first principle prior to the second. This ordering means that infringements of the basic equal liberties protected by the first principle cannot be justified, or compensated for, by greater social and economic advantages. These liberties have a central range of application within which they can be limited and compromised only when they conflict with other basic liberties. Since they may be limited when they clash with one another, none of these liberties is absolute; but however they are adjusted to form one system, this system is to be the same for all. It is difficult, and perhaps impossible, to give a complete specification of these liberties independently from the particular circumstances —social, economic, and technological—of a given society. The hypothesis is that the general form of such a list could be devised with sufficient exactness to sustain this conception of justice. Of course, liberties not on the list, for example, the right to own certain kinds of property (e.g., means of production) and freedom of contract as understood by the doctrine of laissez-faire are not basic; and so they are not protected by the priority of the first principle. Finally, in regard to the second principle, the distribution of wealth and income, and positions of authority and responsibility, are to be consistent with both the basic liberties and equality of opportunity.

The two principles are rather specific in their content, and their acceptance rests on certain assumptions that I must eventually try to explain and justify. For the present, it should be observed that these principles are a special case of a more general conception of justice that can be expressed as follows.

> All social values—liberty and opportunity, income and wealth, and the social bases of self respect—are to be distributed equally unless an unequal distribution of any, or all, of these values is to everyone's advantage.

Injustice, then, is simply inequalities that are not to the benefit of all. Of course, this conception is extremely vague and requires interpretation.

As a first step, suppose that the basic structure of society distributes certain primary goods, that is, things that every rational man is presumed to want. These goods normally have a use whatever a person's rational plan of life. For simplicity, assume that the chief primary goods at the disposition of society are rights, liberties, and opportunities, and

income and wealth. . . . These are the social primary goods. Other primary goods such as health and vigor, intelligence and imagination, are natural goods; although their possession is influenced by the basic structure, they are not so directly under its control. Imagine, then, a hypothetical initial arrangement in which all the social primary goods are equally distributed: everyone has similar rights and duties, and income and wealth are evenly shared. This state of affairs provides a benchmark for judging improvements. If certain inequalities of wealth and differences in authority would make everyone better off than in this hypothetical starting situation, then they accord with the general conception.

Now it is possible, at least theoretically, that by giving up some of their fundamental liberties men are sufficiently compensated by the resulting social and economic gains. . . . We need not suppose anything so drastic as consenting to a condition of slavery. Imagine instead that people seem willing to forego certain political rights when the economic returns are significant. It is this kind of exchange which the two principles rule out; being arranged in serial order they do not permit exchanges between basic liberties and economic and social gains except under extenuating circumstances.

For the most part, I shall leave aside the general conception of justice and examine instead the two principles in serial order. The advantage of this procedure is that from the first the matter of priorities is recognized and an effort made to find principles to deal with it. One is led to attend throughout to the conditions under which the absolute weight of liberty with respect to social and economic advantages, as defined by the lexical order of the two principles, would be reasonable. Offhand, this ranking appears extreme and too special a case to be of much interest; but there is more justification for it than would appear at first sight. Or at any rate, so I shall maintain. [*Rawls argues it is rational after a certain level of economic development has been achieved by the society.—Ed.*] Furthermore, the distinction between fundamental rights and liberties and economic and social benefits marks a difference among primary social goods that suggests an important division in the social system. . . .

Now the second principle insists that each person benefit from permissible inequalities in the basic structure. This means that it must be reasonable for each relevant representative man defined by this structure, when he views it as a going concern, to prefer his prospects with the inequality to his prospects without it. One is not allowed to justify differences in income or in positions of authority and responsibility on the ground that the disadvantages of those in one position are outweighed by the greater advantages of those in another. Much less can infringements of liberty be counterbalanced in this way. It is obvious, however, that there are indefinitely many, ways in which all may be advantaged when the initial arrangement of equality is taken as a benchmark. How then are we to choose among these possibilities? The principles must be specified so that they yield a determinate conclusion. I now turn to this problem.

THE REASONING LEADING TO THE TWO PRINCIPLES OF JUSTICE

I [now] take up the choice between the two principles of justice and the principle of average utility. Determining the rational preference between these two options is perhaps the central problem in developing the conception of justice as fairness as a viable alternative to the utilitarian tradition. . . .

Now consider the point of view of anyone in the original position. There is no way for him to win special advantages for himself. Nor, on the other hand, are there grounds for his acquiescing in special disadvantages. Since it is not reasonable for him to expect more than an equal share in the division of social primary goods, and since it is not rational for him to agree to less, the sensible thing is to acknowledge as the first step a principle of justice requiring an equal distribution. Indeed,

this principle is so obvious given the symmetry of the parties that it would occur to everyone immediately. Thus the parties start with a principle requiring equal basic liberties for all, as well as fair equality of opportunity and equal division of income and wealth.

But even holding firm to the priority of the basic liberties and fair equality of opportunity [*By fair equality of opportunity Rawls means that two equally talented children would have the same chance to reach their goals, regardless of socioeconomic background.—Ed.*] there is no reason why this initial acknowledgment should be final. Society should take into account economic efficiency and the requirements of organization and technology. If there are inequalities in income and wealth, and differences in authority and degrees of responsibility, that work to make everyone better off in comparison with the benchmark of equality, why not permit them? One might think that ideally individuals should want to serve one another. But since the parties are assumed to be mutually disinterested, their acceptance of these economic and institutional inequalities is only the recognition of the relations of opposition in which men stand in the circumstances of justice. They have no grounds for complaining of one another's motives. Thus the parties would agree to these differences only if they would be dejected by the bare knowledge or perception that others are better situated; but I suppose that they decide as if they are not moved by envy. Thus the basic structure should allow these inequalities so long as these improve everyone's situation, including that of the least advantaged, provided that they are consistent with equal liberty and fair opportunity. Because the parties start from an equal division of all social primary goods, those who benefit least have, so to speak, a veto. Thus we arrive at the difference principle. Taking equality as the basis of comparison, those who have gained more must do so on terms that are justifiable to those who have gained the least.

By some such reasoning, then, the parties might arrive at the two principles of justice in serial order. I shall not try to justify this ordering here, but the following remarks may convey the intuitive idea. I assume that the parties view themselves as free persons who have fundamental aims and interests in the name of which they think it legitimate for them to make claims on one another concerning the design of the basic structure of society. The religious interest is a familiar historical example; the interest in the integrity of the person is another. In the original position the parties do not know what particular forms these interests take; but they do assume that they have such interests and that the basic liberties necessary for their protection are guaranteed by the first principle. Since they must secure these interests, they rank the first principle prior to the second. The case for the two principles can be strengthened by spelling out in more detail the notion of a free person. Very roughly the parties regard themselves as having a highest-order interest in how all their other interests, including even their fundamental ones, are shaped and regulated by social institutions. They do not think of themselves as inevitably bound to, or as identical with, the pursuit of any particular complex of fundamental interests that they may have at any given time, although they want the right to advance such interests (provided they are admissible). Rather, free persons conceive of themselves as beings who can revise and alter their final ends and who give first priority to preserving their liberty in these matters. Hence, they not only have final ends that they are in principle free to pursue or to reject, but their original allegiance and continued devotion to these ends are to be formed and affirmed under conditions that are free. Since the two principles secure a social form that maintains these conditions, they would be agreed to rather than the principle of utility. Only by this agreement can the parties be sure that their highest-order interest as free persons is guaranteed.

The priority of liberty means that whenever the basic liberties can be effectively established, a lesser or an unequal liberty cannot be exchanged for an improvement in economic well-being. It is only when social circumstances do not allow the effective establishment of these basic rights that one can concede their limitation; and even then these restrictions can be granted only to the extent that they are necessary to prepare the way for the time when they are no longer justified. The denial of the equal liberties can be defended only when it is essential to change the conditions of civilization so that in due course these liberties can be enjoyed. Thus in adopting the serial order of the two principles, the parties are assuming that the conditions of their society, whatever they are, admit the effective realization of the equal liberties. Or that if they do not, circumstances are nevertheless sufficiently favorable so that the priority of the first principle points out the most urgent changes and identifies the preferred path to the social state in which all the basic liberties can be fully instituted. The complete realization of the two principles in serial order is the long-run tendency of this ordering, at least under reasonably fortunate conditions.

It seems from these remarks that the two principles are at least a plausible conception of justice. The question, though, is how one is to argue for them more systematically. Now there are several things to do.

One can work out their consequences for institutions and note their implications for fundamental social policy. In this way they are tested by a comparison with our considered judgments of justice. . . .

But one can also try to find arguments in their favor that are decisive from the standpoint of the original position. In order to see how this might be done, it is useful as a heuristic device to think of the two principles as the maximin solution to the problem of social justice. There is a relation between the two principles and the maximin rule for choice under uncertainty. This is evident from the fact that the two principles are those a person would choose for the design of a society in which his enemy is to assign him his place. The maximin rule tells us to rank alternatives by their worst possible outcomes: we are to adopt the alternative the worst outcome of which is superior to the worst outcomes of the others.* The persons in the original position do not, of course, assume that their initial place in society is decided by a malevolent opponent. . . . They should not reason from false premises. The veil of ignorance does not violate this idea, since an absence of information is not misinformation. But that the two principles of justice would be chosen if the parties were forced to protect themselves against such a contingency explains the sense in which this conception is the maximin solution. And this analogy suggests that if the original position has been described so that it is rational for the parties to adopt the conservative attitude expressed by this rule, a conclusive argument can indeed be constructed for these principles. Clearly the maximin rule is not, in general, a suitable guide for choices under uncertainty. But it holds only in situations marked by certain special features. My aim, then, is to show that a good case can be made for the two principles based on the fact that position has these features to a very high degree.

Now there appear to be three chief features of situations that give plausibility to this unusual rule. First, since the rule takes no account of the likelihoods of the possible circumstances, there must be some reason for sharply discounting estimates of these probabilities. . . .

The second feature that suggests the maximum rule is the following: the person choosing has a conception of the good such that he cares very little, if anything, for what he might gain above the minimim stipend that he can, in fact, be sure of by following the maximin rule. It is not worthwhile for him to take a chance for the sake of a further advantage, especially when it may turn out that he loses much that is important to him. This last provision brings in the third feature, namely, that the rejected alternatives have outcomes that one can hardly accept. The situation involves grave risks. Of course these features work most effectively in combination. The paradigm situation for following the maximin rule is when all three features are realized to the highest degree.

Let us review briefly the nature of the original position with these three special features in mind. To begin with, the veil of ignorance excludes all knowledge of likelihoods. The parties have no basis for determining the probable nature of their society, or their place in it. Thus they have no basis for probability calculations. They must also take into account the fact that their choice of principles should seem reasonable to others, in particular their descendants, whose rights will be deeply affected by it. These considerations are strengthened by the fact that the parties know

---

*Consider the gain-and-loss table below. It represents the gains and losses for a situation which is not a game of strategy. There is no one playing against the person making the decision; instead he is faced with several possible circumstances which may or may not obtain. Which circumstances happen to exist does not depend upon what the person choosing decides or whether he announces his moves in advance. The numbers in the table are monetary values (in hundreds of dollars) in comparison with some initial situation. The gain (g) depends upon the individual's decision (d) and the circumstances (c). Thus $g = f(d, c)$. Assuming that there are three possible decisions and three possible circumstances, we might have this gain-and-loss table.

The maximin rule requires that we make the third decision. For in this case the worst that can happen is that

one gains five hundred dollars, which is better than the worst for the other actions. If we adopt one of these we may lose either eight or seven hundred dollars. Thus, the choice of d_3 maximizes $f(d,c)$ for that value of c, which for a given d, minimizes f. The term "maximin" means the *maximum minimorum;* and the rule directs our attention to the worst that can happen under any proposed course of action, and to decide in the light of that.

Decisions	Circumstances		
	c_1	c_2	c_3
d_1	−7	8	12
d_2	−8	7	14
d_3	5	6	8

very little about the possible states of society. Not only are they unable to conjecture the likelihoods of the various possible circumstances, they cannot say much about what the possible circumstances are, much less enumerate them and foresee the outcome of each alternative available. Those deciding are much more in the dark than illustrations by numerical tables suggest. It is for this reason that I have spoken only of a relation to the maximin rule.

Several kinds of arguments for the two principles of justice illustrate the second feature. Thus, if we can maintain that these principles provide a workable theory of social justice, and that they are compatible with reasonable demands of efficiency, then this conception guarantees a satisfactory minimim. There may be, on reflection, little reason for trying to do better. . . . The minimum assured by the two principles in lexical order is not one that the parties wish to jeopardize for the sake of greater economic and social advantages.

Finally, the third feature holds if we can assume that other conceptions of justice may lead to institutions that the parties would find intolerable. For example, it has sometimes been held that under some conditions the utility principle (in either form) justifies, if not slavery or serfdom, at any rate serious infractions of liberty for the sake of greater social benefits. We need not consider here the truth of this claim. For the moment, this contention is only to illustrate the way in which conceptions of justice may allow for outcomes which the parties may not be able to accept. And having the ready alternative of the two principles of justice which secure a satisfactory minimum, it seems unwise, if not irrational, for them to take a chance that these conditions are not realized.

So much, then, for a brief sketch of the features of situations in which the maximin rule is a useful maxim and of the way in which the arguments for the two principles of justice can be subsumed under them. Thus. . . . these principles would be selected by the rule. The original position exhibits these special features to a sufficiently high degree in view of the fundamental character of the choice of a conception of justice.

REVIEW AND DISCUSSION QUESTIONS

1. What does Rawls mean by the "basic structure" of society?
2. Describe the original position: Behind the veil of ignorance, what do people know, and what do they not know?
3. What are "social primary goods"? What role do they play in Rawls's theory?
4. In what sense are the social contractors equal? How does Rawls's theory express the idea that all persons are "created equal"?
5. What is the "maximin rule" and what three reasons does Rawls give for thinking it would be rational for people to follow it in the original position?
6. Explain why Rawls thinks people would choose his two principles instead of utilitarianism.
7. Why does Rawls term his theory "justice as fairness"? What reasons does Rawls give for using this hypothetical thought experiment of a veil of ignorance?
8. It is sometimes said that Rawls unreasonably assumes people can "forget" their social class, natural talents, and conception of the good when, in fact, they cannot do so. How would Rawls respond to that objection?
9. Describe other circumstances in which we expect people to ignore what they know in making a decision.
10. Does Rawls assume people are in fact only concerned with their own well-being? Explain.

The Entitlement Theory

Robert Nozick

Like John Locke, Robert Nozick begins with a strong commitment to prepolitical individual rights—rights that may not be transgressed by others, either as individuals or collectively as the state. Commonly called *negative rights,* they constitute "side constraints" on the actions of others, ensuring a person's freedom from interference in the pursuit of his or her own life. These rights are negative because they require only that others refrain from acting in certain ways; in particular, that they refrain from interfering with us. Beyond this, no one is obliged to do anything positive for us; we have no right, for example, to expect others to provide us with satisfying work or with any material goods we might need. Each individual is to be seen as autonomous and responsible and should be left to fashion his or her own life free from the interference of others—as long as this is compatible with the right of others to do the same. Only the acknowledgment of this almost absolute right to be free from coercion, argues Nozick, fully respects the distinctiveness of persons, each with a unique life to lead. This framework of individual rights and corresponding duties constitutes the basis of what power the government may legitimately have. In Nozick's view, the only morally legitimate state is the so-called night-watchman state, one whose functions are restricted to protecting the negative rights of citizens, that is, to protecting them against force, theft, fraud, and so on. In the selection that follows, Nozick is especially concerned with rejecting the claim that a larger state is necessary in order to achieve a just economic distribution.

In contrast to theories he calls *end-state* and *patterned,* Nozick proposes the *entitlement theory of justice.* According to this theory, a distribution is just if it arises from a prior just distribution by just means. For example, as Locke also argued, unowned resources may be acquired originally by one's taking something from nature, subject to certain provisos. And, once legitimately owned, there are a number of ways of legitimately transferring justly acquired objects—gifts and voluntary exchange are among them, theft and blackmail are not. There is, however, no pattern to which a just distribution should conform. In the absence of force and fraud, people may do what they wish with their holdings. They have a right to acquire and dispose of their property as they see fit, and individuals are entitled to their personal talents and characteristics and to whatever property they can obtain with them, as long as the negative rights of others are not violated in the process. Taxation for purposes of redistribution, he then argues, is on a par with forced labor.

In the final section, "The Tale of the Slave," Nozick creates an imaginary series of events meant to illustrate and extend his argument that taking property is tantamount to slavery. Robert Nozick teaches philosophy at Harvard University.

The term "distributive justice" is not a neutral one. Hearing the term "distribution," most people presume that some thing or mechanism uses some principle or criterion to give out a supply of things. Into this process of distributing shares some error may have crept.

So it is an open question, at least, whether *re*distribution should take place; whether we should do again what has already been done once, though poorly. However, we are not in the position of children who have been given portions of pie by someone who now makes last minute adjustments to rectify careless cutting. There is no *central* distribution, no person or group entitled to control all the resources, jointly deciding how they are to be doled out. What each person gets, he gets from others who give to him in exchange for something, or as a gift. In a free society, diverse persons control different resources, and new holdings arise out of the voluntary exchanges and actions of persons. There is no more a distributing or distribution of shares than there is a distributing of mates in a society in which persons choose whom they shall marry. The total result is the product of many individual decisions which the different individuals involved are entitled to make. . . . We shall speak of people's holdings; a principle of justice in holdings describes (part of) what justice tells us (requires) about holdings.

THE ENTITLEMENT THEORY

The subject of justice in holdings consists of three major topics. The first is the *original acquisition of holdings,* the appropriation of unheld things. This includes the issues of how unheld things may come to be held, the process, or processes, by which unheld things may come to be held, the things that may come to be held by these processes, the extent of what comes to be held by a particular process, and so on. We shall refer to the complicated truth about this topic, which we shall not formulate here, as the principle of justice in acquisition. The second topic concerns the *transfer of holdings* from one person to another. By what processes may a person transfer holdings to another? How may a person acquire a holding from another who holds it? Under this topic come general descriptions of voluntary exchange, and gift and (on the other hand) fraud, as well as reference to particular conventional details fixed upon in a given society. The complicated truth about this subject (with placeholders for conventional details) we shall call the principle of justice in transfer. (And we shall suppose it

also includes principles governing how a person may divest himself of a holding, passing it into an unheld state.)

If the world were wholly just, the following inductive definition would exhaustively cover the subject of justice in holdings.

1. A person who acquires a holding in accordance with the principle of justice in acquisition is entitled to that holding.
2. A person who acquires a holding in accordance with the principle of justice in transfer, from someone else entitled to the holding, is entitled to the holding.
3. No one is entitled to a holding except by (repeated) applications of 1 and 2.

The complete principle of distributive justice would say simply that a distribution is just if everyone is entitled to the holdings they possess under the distribution.

A distribution is just if it arises from another just distribution by legitimate means. The legitimate means of moving from one distribution to another are specified by the principle of justice in transfer. The legitimate first "moves" are specified by the principle of justice in acquisition. Whatever arises from a just situation by just steps is itself just. The means of change specified by the principle of justice in transfer preserve justice. . . .

Not all actual situations are generated in accordance with the two principles of justice in holdings: the principle of justice in acquisition and the principle of justice in transfer. Some people steal from others, or defraud them, or enslave them, seizing their product and preventing them from living as they choose, or forcibly exclude others from competing in exchanges. None of these are permissible modes of transition from one situation to another. And some persons acquire holdings by means not sanctioned by the principle of justice in acquisition. The existence of past injustice (previous violations of the first two principles of justice in holdings) raises the third major topic under justice in holdings: the *rectification of injustice in holdings.* If past injustice has shaped present holdings in various ways, some identifiable and some not, what now, if anything, ought to be done to rectify these injustices? What obligations do the performers of injustice have toward those whose position is worse than it would have been had the injustice not been done? Or, than it would have been had compensation been paid promptly? How, if at all, do things change if the beneficiaries and those made worse off are not the direct parties in the act of injustice, but, for example, their descendants? Is an injustice done to someone whose holding was itself based upon an unrectified injustice? How far back must one go in wiping clean the historical slate of injustices? What may victims of injustice permissibly do in order to rectify the injustices being done to them, including the many injustices done by persons acting through their government? I do not know of a thorough or theoretically sophisticated treatment of such issues. Idealizing greatly, let us suppose theoretical investigation will produce a principle of rectification. This principle uses historical information about previous situations and injustices done in them (as defined by the first two principles of justice and rights against interference), and information about the actual course of events that flowed from these injustices, until the present, and it yields a description (or descriptions) of holdings in the society. The principle of rectification presumably will make use of its best estimate of subjunctive information about what would have occurred (or a probability distribution over what might have occurred, using the expected value) if the injustice had not taken place. If the actual description of holdings turns out not to be one of the descriptions yielded by the principle, then one of the descriptions yielded must be realized.

The general outlines of the theory of justice in holdings are that the holdings of a person are just if he is entitled to them by the principles of justice in acquisition and transfer, or by the principle of rectification of injustice (as specified by the first two principles). If

each person's holdings are just, then the total set (distribution) of holdings is just. . . .

HISTORICAL PRINCIPLES AND END-RESULT PRINCIPLES

The general outlines of the entitlement theory illuminate the nature and defects of other conceptions of distributive justice. The entitlement theory of justice in distribution is *historical;* whether a distribution is just depends upon how it came about. In contrast, *current time-slice principles* of justice hold that the justice of a distribution is determined by how things are distributed (who has what) as judged by some *structural* principle(s) of just distribution. A utilitarian who judges between any two distributions by seeing which has the greater sum of utility and, if the sums tie, applies some fixed equality criterion to choose the more equal distribution, would hold a current time-slice principle of justice. . . .

Most persons do not accept current time-slice principles as constituting the whole story about distributive shares. They think it relevant in assessing the justice of a situation to consider not only the distribution it embodies, but also how that distribution came about. If some persons are in prison for murder or war crimes, we do not say that to assess the justice of the distribution in the society we must look only at what this person has, and that person has, and that person has. . . . at the current time. We think it relevant to ask whether someone did something so that he *deserved* to be punished, deserved to have a lower share. Most will agree to the relevance of further information with regard to punishments and penalties. Consider also desired things. One traditional socialist view is that workers are entitled to the product and full fruits of their labor; they have earned it; a distribution is unjust if it does not give the workers what they are entitled to. Such entitlements are based upon some past history. No socialist holding this view would find it comforting to be told that because the actual distribution A happens to coincide structurally with the one he desires D, A therefore is no less just than D; it differs only in that the "parasitic" owners of capital receive under A what the workers are entitled to under D, and the workers receive under A what the owners are entitled to under D, namely very little. This socialist rightly, in my view, holds onto the notions of earning, producing, entitlement, desert, and so forth, and he rejects current time-slice principles that look only to the structure of the resulting set of holdings. (The set of holdings resulting from what? Isn't it implausible that how holdings are produced and come to exist has no effect at all on who should hold what?) His mistake lies in his view of what entitlements arise out of what sorts of productive processes.

We construe the position we discuss too narrowly by speaking of *current* time-slice principles. Nothing is changed if structural principles operate upon a time sequence of current time-slice profiles and, for example, give someone more now to counterbalance the less he has had earlier. . . . Henceforth, we shall refer to such unhistorical principles of distributive justice, including the current time-slice principles, as *end-result principles* or *end-state principles.*

In contrast to end-result principles of justice, *historical principles* of justice hold that past circumstances or actions of people can create differential entitlements or differential deserts to things. . . .

PATTERNING

The entitlement principles of justice in holdings that we have sketched are historical principles of justice. To better understand their precise character, we shall distinguish them from another subclass of the historical principles. Consider, as an example, the principle of distribution according to moral merit. This principle requires that total distributive shares vary directly with moral merit; no person should have a greater share than anyone

whose moral merit is greater. (If moral merit could be not merely ordered but measured on an interval or ratio scale, stronger principles could be formulated.) Or consider the principle that results by substituting "usefulness to society" for "moral merit" in the previous principle. . . . The principle of distribution in accordance with moral merit is a patterned historical principle, which specifies a patterned distribution. "Distribute according to I.Q." is a patterned principle that . . . is not historical, however, in that it does not look to any past actions creating differential entitlements to evaluate a distribution; it requires only distributional matrices whose columns are labeled by I.Q. scores. The distribution in a society, however, may be composed of such simple patterned distributions, without itself being simply patterned. Different sectors may operate different patterns, or some combination of patterns may operate in different proportions across a society. A distribution composed in this manner, from a small number of patterned distributions, we also shall term "patterned." And we extend the use of "pattern" to include the overall designs put forth by combinations of end-state principles.

Almost every suggested principle of distributive justice is patterned: to each according to his moral merit, or needs, or marginal product, or how hard he tries, or the weighted sum of the foregoing, and so on. The principle of entitlement we have sketched is *not* patterned. There is no one natural dimension or weighted sum or combination of a small number of natural dimensions that yields the distributions generated in accordance with the principle of entitlement. The set of holdings that results when some persons receive their marginal products, others win at gambling, others receive a share of their mate's income, others receive gifts from foundations, others receive interest on loans, others receive gifts from admirers, others receive returns on investment, others make for themselves much of what they have, others find things, and so on, will not be patterned . . .

HOW LIBERTY UPSETS PATTERNS

It is not clear how those holding alternative conceptions of distributive justice can reject the entitlement conception of justice in holdings. For suppose a distribution favored by one of these nonentitlement conceptions is realized. Let us suppose it is your favorite one and let us call this distribution D_1; perhaps everyone has an equal share, perhaps shares vary in accordance with some dimension you treasure. Now suppose that Wilt Chamberlain is greatly in demand by basketball teams, being a great gate attraction. (Also suppose contracts run only for a year, with players being free agents.) He signs the following sort of contract with a team: in each home game, twenty-five cents from the price of each ticket of admission goes to him. (We ignore the question of whether he is "gouging" the owners, letting them look out for themselves.) The season starts, and people cheerfully attend his team's games; they buy their tickets, each time dropping a separate twenty-five cents of their admission price into a special box with Chamberlain's name on it. They are excited about seeing him play; it is worth the total admission price to them. Let us suppose that in one season one million persons attend his home games, and Wilt Chamberlain winds up with $250,000, a much larger sum than the average income and larger even than anyone else has. Is he entitled to this income? Is this new distribution D_2, unjust? If so, why? There is *no* question about whether each of the people was entitled to the control over the resources they held in D_1; because that was the distribution (your favorite) that (for the purposes of argument) we assumed was acceptable. Each of these persons chose to give twenty-five cents of their money to Chamberlain. They could have spent it on going to the movies, or on candy bars, or on copies of *Dissent* magazine, or of *Monthly Review*. But they all, at least one million of them, converged on giving it to Wilt Chamberlain in exchange for watching him play basketball. If D_1 was a just distribution, and people voluntarily moved from it to D_2, transferring parts of their shares they were given under D_1 (what was it for if not to do something with?), isn't D_2 also just? If the people were entitled to dispose of the resources to which they were entitled (under D_1), didn't this include their being entitled to give it to, or exchange it with, Wilt Chamberlain? Can anyone else complain on grounds of justice? Each other person already has his legitimate share under D_1. Under D_1, there is nothing that anyone has that anyone else has a claim of justice against. After someone transfers something to Wilt Chamberlain, third parties *still* have their legitimate shares; *their* shares are not changed. By what process could such a transfer among two persons give rise to a legitimate claim of distributive justice on a portion of what was transferred, by a third party who had no claim of justice on any holding of the others *before* the transfer? . . .

The general point illustrated by the Wilt Chamberlain example. . . . is that no end-state principle or distributional-patterned principle of justice can be continuously realized without continuous interference with people's lives. Any favored pattern would be transformed into one unfavored by the principle, by people choosing to act in various ways; for example, by people exchanging goods and services with other people, or giving things to other people, things the transferrers are entitled to under the favored distributional pattern. To maintain a pattern one must either continually interfere to stop people from transferring resources as they wish to, or continually (or periodically) interfere to take from some persons resources that others for some reason chose to transfer to them. . . .

REDISTRIBUTION AND PROPERTY RIGHTS

Apparently, patterned principles allow people to choose to spend upon themselves, but not upon others, those resources they are entitled to (or rather, receive) under some favored distributional pattern D_1. For if each of several persons chooses to expend some of his D_1 resources upon one other person, then that other person will receive more than his D_1 share, distributing the favored distributional pattern. Maintaining a distributional pattern is individualism with a vengeance! Patterned distributional principles do not give people what entitlement principles do, only better distributed. For they do not give the right to choose what to do with what one has; they do not give the right to choose to pursue an end involving (intrinsically, or as a means) the enhancement of another's position. To such views, families are disturbing; for within a family occur transfers that upset the favored distributional pattern. Either families themselves become units to which distribution takes place, the column occupiers (on what rationale?), or loving behavior is forbidden. We should note in passing the ambivalent position of radicals toward the family. Its loving relationships are seen as a model to be emulated and extended across the whole society, at the same time that it is denounced as a suffocating institution to be broken and condemned as a focus of parochial concerns that interfere with achieving radical goals. Need we say that it is not appropriate to enforce across the wider society the relationships of love and care appropriate within a family, relationships which are voluntarily undertaken?* Incidentally, love is an interesting instance of another relationship that is historical, in that (like justice) it depends upon what actually occurred. An adult may come to love another because of the other's characteristics; but it is the other person, and not the characteristics, that is loved. The love is not transferable to someone else with the same characteristics, even to one who "scores" higher for these characteristics. And the love endures through changes of the characteristics that give rise to it. One loves the particular person one actually encountered. Why love is historical, attaching to persons in this way and not to characteristics, is an interesting and puzzling question.

Proponents of patterned principles of distributive justice focus upon criteria for determining who is to receive holdings; they consider the reasons for which someone should have something, and also the total picture of holdings. Whether or not it is better to give than to receive, proponents of patterned principles ignore giving altogether. In considering the distribution of goods, income, and so forth, their theories are theories of recipient justice; they completely ignore any right a person might have to give something to someone. Even in exchanges where each party is simultaneously giver and recipient, patterned principles of justice focus only upon the recipient role and its supposed rights. Thus discussions tend to focus on whether people (should) have a right to inherit, rather than on whether people (should) have a right to bequeath or on whether persons who have a right to hold also have a right to choose that others hold in their place. I lack a good explanation of why the usual theories of distributive justice are so recipient oriented; ignoring givers and transferrers and their rights is of a piece with ignoring producers and their entitlements. But why is it *all* ignored?

Patterned principles of distributive justice necessitate *re*distributive activities. The likelihood is small that any actual freely-arrived-at set of holdings fits a given pattern; and the likelihood is nil that it will continue to fit the pattern as people exchange and give. From the point of view of an entitlement theory, redistribution is a serious matter indeed,

*One indication of the stringency of Rawls' difference principle is its inappropriateness as a governing principle even within a family of individuals who love one another. Should a family devote its resources to maximizing the position of its least well off and least talented child, holding back the other children or using resources of their education and development only if they will follow a policy through their lifetimes of maximizing the position of their least fortunate sibling? Surely not. How then can this even be considered as the appropriate policy for enforcement in the wider society? (I discuss below what I think would be Rawls' reply: that some principles apply at the macro level which do not apply to micro-situations.)

involving, as it does, the violation of people's rights. (An exception is those takings that fall under the principle of the rectification of injustices.) From other points of view, also, it is serious.

Taxation of earnings from labor is on a par with forced labor.* Some persons find this claim obviously true: taking the earnings of n hours labor is like taking n hours from the person; it is like forcing the person to work n hours for another's purpose. Others find the claim absurd. But even these, *if* they object to forced labor, would oppose forcing unemployed hippies to work for the benefit of the needy. And they would also object to forcing each person to work five extra hours each week for the benefit of the needy. But a system that takes five hours' wages in taxes does not seem to them like one that forces someone to work five hours, since it offers the person forced a wider range of choice in activities than does taxation in kind with the particular labor specified. (But we can imagine a gradation of systems of forced labor, from one that specifies a particular activity, to one that gives a choice among two activities, to . . . ; and so on up.) Furthermore, people envisage a system with something like a proportional tax on everything above the amount necessary for basic needs. Some think this does not force someone to work extra hours, since there is no fixed number of extra hours he is forced to work, and since he can avoid the tax entirely by earning only enough to cover his basic needs. This is a very uncharacteristic view of forcing for those who *also* think people are forced to do something *whenever* the alternatives they face are considerably worse. However, *neither* view is correct. The fact that others intentionally intervene, in violation of

a side constraint against aggression, to threaten force to limit the alternatives, in this case to paying taxes or (presumably the worse alternative) bare subsistence, makes the taxation system one of forced labor and distinguishes it from other cases of limited choices which are not forcings.

The man who chooses to work longer to gain an income more than sufficient for his basic needs prefers some extra goods or services to the leisure and activities he could perform during the possible nonworking hours: whereas the man who chooses not to work the extra time prefers the leisure activities to the extra goods or services he could acquire by working more. Given this, if it would be illegitimate for a tax system to seize some of a man's leisure (forced labor) for the purpose of serving the needy, how can it be legitimate for a tax system to seize some of a man's goods for that purpose? Why should we treat the man whose happiness requires certain material goods or services differently from the man whose preferences and desires make such goods unnecessary for his happiness? Why should the man who prefers seeing a movie (and who has to earn money for a ticket) be open to the required call to aid the needy, while the person who prefers looking at a sunset (and hence need earn no extra money) is not? Indeed, isn't it surprising that redistributionists choose to ignore the man whose pleasures are so easily attainable without extra labor, while adding yet another burden to the poor unfortunate who must work for his pleasures? If anything, one would have expected the reverse. Why is the person with the nonmaterial or nonconsumption desire allowed to proceed unimpeded to his most favored feasible alternative, whereas the man whose pleasures or desires involve material things and who must work for extra money (thereby serving whomever considers his activities valuable enough to pay him) is constrained in what he can realize? Perhaps there is no difference in principle. And perhaps some think the answer concerns merely administrative convenience. (These questions

---

*I am unsure as to whether the arguments I present below show that such taxation merely is forced labor; so that "is on a par with" means "is one kind of." Or alternatively, whether the arguments emphasize the great similarities between such taxation and forced earnings, to show it is plausible and illuminating to view such taxation in the light of forced labor.

and issues will not disturb those who think that forced labor to serve the needy or to realize some favored end-state pattern is acceptable.) In a fuller discussion we would have (and want) to extend our argument to include interest, entrepreneurial profits, and so on. Those who doubt that this extension can be carried through, and who draw the line here at taxation of income from labor, will have to state rather complicated patterned *historical* principles of distributive justice, since end-state principles would not distinguish *sources* of income in any way. It is enough for now to get away from end-state principles and to make clear how various patterned principles are dependent upon particular views about the sources or the illegitimacy or the lesser legitimacy of profits, interest, and so on; which particular views may well be mistaken.

What sort of right over others does a legally institutionalized end-state pattern give one? The central core of the notion of a property right in *X*, relative to which other parts of the notion are to be explained, is the right to determine what shall be done with *X;* the right to choose which of the constrained set of options concerning *X* shall be realized or attempted. The constraints are set by other principles or laws operating in the society; in our theory, by the Lockean rights people possess (under the minimal state). My property rights in my knife allow me to leave it where I will, but not in your chest. I may choose which of the acceptable options involving the knife is to be realized. This notion of property helps us to understand why earlier theorists spoke of people as having property in themselves and their labor. They viewed each person as having a right to decide what would become of himself and what he would do, and as having a right to reap the benefits of what he did. . . .

When end-result principles of distributive justice are built into the legal structure of a society, they (as do most patterned principles) give each citizen an enforceable claim to some portion of the total social product; that is, to some portion of the sum total of the individually and jointly made products. This total product is produced by individuals laboring, using means of production others have saved to bring into existence, by people organizing production or creating means to produce new things or things in a new way. It is on this batch of individual activities that patterned distributional principles give each individual an enforceable claim. Each person has a claim to the activities and the products of other persons, independently of whether the other persons enter into particular relationships that give rise to these claims, and independently of whether they voluntarily take these claims upon themselves, in charity or in exchange for something.

Whether it is done through taxation on wages or on wages over a certain amount, or through seizure of profits, or through there being a big *social pot* so that it's not clear what's coming from where and what's going where, patterned principles of distributive justice involve appropriating the actions of other persons. Seizing the results of someone's labor is equivalent to seizing hours from him and directing him to carry on various activities. If people force you to do certain work, or unrewarded work, for a certain period of time, they decide what you are to do and what purposes your work is to serve apart from your decisions. This process whereby they take this decision from you makes them a *part-owner* of you; it gives them a property right in you. Just as having such partial control and power of decision, by right, over an animal or inanimate object would be to have a property right in it.

End-state and most patterned principles of distributive justice institute (partial) ownership by others of people and their actions and labor. These principles involve a shift from the classical liberals' notion of self-ownership to a notion of (partial) property rights in *other* people. . . .

May a person emigrate from a nation that has institutionalized some end-state or patterned distributional principle? . . . Consider a nation having a compulsory scheme of minimal social provision to aid the neediest (or one organized so as to maximize the position of the worst-off group); no one may opt out of participating in it. (None may say, "Don't compel me to contribute to others and don't provide for me via this compulsory mechanism if I am in need.") Everyone above a certain level is forced to contribute to aid the needy. But if emigration from the country were allowed, anyone could choose to move to another country that did not have compulsory social provision but otherwise was (as much as possible) identical. In such a case, the person's *only* motive for leaving would be to avoid participating in the compulsory scheme of social provision. And if he does leave, the needy in his initial country will receive no (compelled) help from him. What rationale yields the result that the person be permitted to emigrate, yet forbidden to stay and opt out of the compulsory scheme of social provision? If providing for the needy is of overriding importance, this does militate against allowing internal opting out; but it also speaks against allowing external emigration. (Would it also support, to some extent, the kidnaping of persons living in a place without compulsory social provision, who could be forced to make a contribution to the needy in your community?) . . .

THE TALE OF THE SLAVE

Consider the following sequence of cases, which we shall call *The Tale of the Slave,* and imagine it is you.

1. There is a slave completely at the mercy of his brutal master's whims. He often is cruelly beaten, called out in the middle of the night, and so on.
2. The master is kindlier and beats the slave only for stated infractions of his rules (not fulfilling the work quota, and so on). He gives the slave some free time.
3. The master has a group of slaves, and he decides how things are to be allocated among them on nice grounds, taking into account their needs, merit, and so on.
4. The master allows his slaves four days on their own and requires them to work only three

days a week on his land. The rest of the time is their own.
5. The master allows his slaves to go off and work in the city (or anywhere they wish) for wages. He requires only that they send back to him three-sevenths of their wages. He also retains the power to recall them to the plantation if some emergency threatens his land; and to raise or lower the three-sevenths amount required to be turned over to him. He further retains the right to restrict the slaves from participating in certain dangerous activities that threaten his financial return, for example, mountain climbing, cigarette smoking.
6. The master allows all of his 10,000 slaves, except you, to vote, and the joint decision is made by all of them. There is open discussion, and so forth, among them, and they have the power to determine to what uses to put whatever percentage of your (and their) earnings they decide to take; what activities may legitimately be forbidden to you, and so on.

Let us pause in this sequence of cases to take stock. If the master contracts this transfer of power so that he cannot withdraw it, you have a change of master. You now have 10,000 masters instead of just one; rather you have one 10,000-headed master. Perhaps the 10,000 even will be kindlier than the benevolent master in case 2. Still, they are your master. However, still more can be done. A kindly single master (as in case 2) might allow his slave(s) to speak up and try to persuade him to make a certain decision. The 10,000-headed master can do this too.

7. Though still not having the vote, you are at liberty (and are given the right) to enter into the discussions of the 10,000 to try to persuade them to adopt various policies and to treat you and themselves in a certain way. They then go off to vote to decide upon policies covering the vast range of their powers.
8. In appreciation of your useful contributions to discussion, the 10,000 allow you to vote if they are deadlocked; they commit themselves to this procedure. After the discussion you mark your vote on a slip of paper, and they go off and vote. In the eventuality that they divide evenly on some issue, 5,000 for and 5,000 against, they look at your ballot and count it.

This has never yet happened; they have never yet had the occasion to open your ballot. (A single master also might commit himself to letting his slave decide any issue concerning about which he, the master, was absolutely indifferent.)

9. They throw your vote in with theirs. If they are exactly tied your vote carries the issue.

Otherwise it makes no difference to the electoral outcome.

The question is: which transition from case 1 to case 9 made it no longer the tale of a slave?

REVIEW AND DISCUSSION QUESTIONS

1. Why does Nozick think that the notion of "distributive justice" is misleading?
2. What are the three topics that, he thinks, constitute the subject of justice in holdings?
3. Distinguish historical from end-result principles.
4. What is a patterned principle?
5. Using the Wilt Chamberlain example, explain Nozick's argument that no patterned principle is compatible with freedom.
6. In what way does Nozick think taxation is comparable to forced labor?
7. What does Nozick mean by "self-ownership" and how is it relevant to entitlements?
8. Explain *The Tale of the Slave,* indicating the point Nozick is making with the parable.
9. How would you answer the question at the end of Nozick's essay?

Rich and Poor

Peter Singer

Death resulting from starvation, disease, and preventable violence is widely reported throughout the world. How much do those of us who are well-off owe those in need? Rejecting the Lockean vision of a state of nature and natural rights, Peter Singer argues that such a libertarian view of property is mistaken and that we all have a duty to provide far more aid than we now give. He then considers several objections to his position—that people should "take care of their own," that the right to property contradicts his position, and that we are relieved of the obligation to assist because helping now would only increase overpopulation and make the problem worse. Peter Singer is professor of bio-ethics at Princeton University.

SOME FACTS

Consider these facts: by the most cautious estimates, 400 million people lack the calories, protein, vitamins, and minerals needed for a normally healthy life. Millions are constantly hungry; others suffer from deficiency diseases and from infections they would be able to resist on a better diet. Children are worst affected. According to one estimate, 15 million children under five die every year from the combined effects of malnutrition and

From Peter Singer, *Practical Ethics.* New York: Cambridge University Press, 1979. © 1979. Reprinted with the permission of Cambridge University Press.

infection. In some areas, half the children born can be expected to die before their fifth birthday. . . .

Death and disease apart, absolute poverty remains a miserable condition of life, with inadequate food, shelter, clothing, sanitation, health services and education. According to World Bank estimates which define absolute poverty in terms of income levels insufficient to provide adequate nutrition, something like 800 million people—almost 40 percent of the people of developing countries—live in absolute poverty. Absolute poverty is probably the principal cause of human misery today. . . .

The problem is not that the world cannot produce enough to feed and shelter its people. People in the poor countries consume, on average, 400 lbs. of grain a year, while North Americans average more than 2,000 lbs. The difference is caused by the fact that in the rich countries we feed most of our grain to animals, converting it into meat, milk and eggs. Because this is an inefficient process, wasting up to 95 percent of the food value of the animal feed, people in rich countries are responsible for the consumption of far more food than those in poor countries who eat few animal products. If we stopped feeding animals on grains, soybeans and fishmeal the amount of food saved would—if distributed to those who need it—be more than enough to end hunger throughout the world.

These facts about animal food do not mean that we can easily solve the world food problem by cutting down on animal products, but they show that the problem is essentially one of distribution rather than production. The world does produce enough food. Moreover the poorer nations themselves could produce far more if they made more use of improved agricultural techniques. . . .

At this stage I am making no ethical judgments about absolute affluence, merely pointing out that it exists. Its defining characteristic is a significant amount of income above the level necessary to provide for the basic human needs of oneself and one's dependents. By this standard Western Europe, North America, Japan, Australia, New Zealand and the oil-rich Middle Eastern states are all absolutely affluent, and so are many, if not all, of their citizens. The [former] USSR and Eastern Europe might also be included on this list. To quote [former Secretary of Defense] Robert McNamara . . . :

> The average citizen of a developed country enjoys wealth beyond the wildest dreams of the one billion people in countries with per capita incomes under $200.

These, therefore, are the countries—and individuals—who have wealth which they could, without threatening their own basic welfare, transfer to the absolutely poor.

At present, very little is being transferred. Members of the Organization of Petroleum Exporting Countries lead the way, giving an average of 2.1 percent of their Gross National Product. Apart from them, only Sweden, The Netherlands and Norway have reached the modest UN target of 0.7 percent of GNP. Britain gives 0.38 percent of its GNP in official development assistance and a small additional amount in unofficial aid from voluntary organizations. The total comes to less than £1 per month per person, and compares with 5.5 percent of GNP spent on alcohol, and 3 percent on tobacco. Other, even wealthier nations, give still less: Germany gives 0.27 percent, the United States 0.22 percent and Japan 0.21 percent. . . .

THE MORAL EQUIVALENT OF MURDER?

If these are the facts, we cannot avoid concluding that by not giving more than we do, people in rich countries are allowing those in poor countries to suffer from absolute poverty, with consequent malnutrition, ill health and death. . . . If, then, allowing someone to die is not intrinsically different from killing someone, it would seem that we are all murderers.

Is this verdict too harsh? . . . (It might be said that the plight of the hungry is not my doing, and so I cannot be held responsible for it.) On the one hand we feel ourselves to be under a greater obligation to help those whose misfortunes we have caused. (It is for this reason that advocates of overseas aid often argue that Western nations have created the poverty of Third World nations, through forms of economic exploitation which go back to the colonial system.) On the other hand any consequentialist would insist that we are responsible for all the consequences of our actions, and if a consequence of my spending money on a luxury item is that someone dies, I am responsible for that death. It is true that the person would have died even if I had never existed, but what is the relevance of that? The fact is that I do exist, and the consequentialist will say that our responsibilities derive from the world as it is, not as it might have been.

One way of making sense of the non-consequentialist view of responsibility is by basing it on a theory of rights of the kind proposed by John Locke or, more recently, Robert Nozick. If everyone has a right to life, and this right is a right *against* others who might threaten my life, but not a right *to* assistance from others when my life is in danger, then we can understand the feeling that we are responsible for acting to kill but not for omitting to save. The former violates the rights of others, the latter does not.

Should we accept such a theory of rights? If we build up our theory of rights by imagining, as Locke and Nozick do, individuals living independently from each other in a "state of nature," it may seem natural to adopt a conception of rights in which as long as each leaves the other alone, no rights are violated. I might, on this view, quite properly have maintained my independent existence if I had wished to do so. So if I do not make you any worse off than you would have been if I had had nothing at all to do with you, how can I have violated your rights? But why start from such an unhistorical, abstract and ultimately inexplicable idea as an independent individual? We now know that our ancestors were social beings long before they were human

beings, and could not have developed the abilities and capacities of human beings if they had not been social beings first. In any case we are not, now, isolated individuals. If we consider people living together in a community, it is less easy to assume that rights must be restricted to rights against interference. We might, instead, adopt the view that taking rights to life seriously is incompatible with standing by and watching people die when one could easily save them. . . .

THE ARGUMENT FOR AN OBLIGATION TO ASSIST

The path from the library at my university to the Humanities lecture theatre passes a shallow ornamental pond. Suppose that on my way to give a lecture I notice that a small child has fallen in and is in danger of drowning. Would anyone deny that I ought to wade in and pull the child out? This will mean getting my clothes muddy, and either canceling my lecture or delaying it until I can find something dry to change into; but compared with the avoidable death of a child this is insignificant.

A plausible principle that would support the judgment that I ought to pull the child out is this: if it is in our power to prevent something very bad happening, without thereby sacrificing anything of comparable moral significance, we ought to do it. This principle seems uncontroversial. It will obviously win the assent of consequentialists; but non-consequentialists should accept it too, because the injunction to prevent what is bad applies only when nothing comparably significant is at stake. Thus the principle cannot lead to the kinds of actions of which non-consequentialists strongly disapprove—serious violations of individual rights, injustice, broken promises, and so on. If a non-consequentialist regards any of these as comparable in moral significance to the bad thing that is to be prevented, he will automatically regard the principle as not applying in those cases in which the bad thing can only be prevented by violating rights, doing injustice, breaking promises, or whatever else is at stake. Most non-consequentialists hold that we ought to prevent what is bad and promote what is good. Their dispute with consequentialists lies in their insistence that this is not the sole ultimate ethical principle: that it is an ethical principle is not denied by any plausible ethical theory.

Nevertheless the uncontroversial appearance of the principle that we ought to prevent what is bad when we can do so without sacrificing anything of comparable moral significance is deceptive. If it were taken seriously and acted upon, our lives and our world would be fundamentally changed. For the principle applies, not just to rare situations in which one can save a child from a pond, but to the everyday situation in which we can assist those living in absolute poverty. In saying this I assume that absolute poverty, with its hunger and malnutrition, lack of shelter, illiteracy, disease, high infant mortality and low life expectancy, is a bad thing. And I assume that it is within the power of the affluent to reduce absolute poverty, without sacrificing anything of comparable moral significance. If these two assumptions and the principle we have been discussing are correct, we have an obligation to help those in absolute poverty which is no less strong than our obligation to rescue a drowning child from a pond. Not to help would be wrong, whether or not it is intrinsically equivalent to killing. Helping is not, as conventionally thought, a charitable act which it is praiseworthy to do, but not wrong to omit; it is something that everyone ought to do. . . .

Our affluence means that we have income we can dispose of without giving up the basic necessities of life, and we can use this income to reduce absolute poverty. Just how much we will think ourselves obliged to give up will depend on what we consider to be of comparable moral significance to the poverty we could prevent: colour television, stylish clothes, expensive dinners, a sophisticated stereo system, overseas holidays, a (second?) car, a larger house, private schools for our children. . . .

OBJECTIONS TO THE ARGUMENT

Taking Care of Our Own

Anyone who has worked to increase overseas aid will have come across the argument that we should look after those near us, our families and then the poor in our own country, before we think about poverty in distant places.

No doubt we do instinctively prefer to help those who are close to us. Few could stand by and watch a child drown; many can ignore a famine in Africa. But the question is not what we usually do, but what we ought to do, and it is difficult to see any sound moral justification for the view that distance, or community membership, makes a crucial difference to our obligations.

Consider, for instance, racial affinities. Should whites help poor whites before helping poor blacks? Most of us would reject such a suggestion out of hand, and our discussion of equal consideration of interests *[see "All Animals Are Equal," reprinted earlier.—Ed.]* has shown why we should reject it: people's need for food has nothing to do with their race, and if blacks need food more than whites, it would be a violation of the principle of equal consideration to give preference to whites.

The same point applies to citizenship or nationhood. Every affluent nation has some relatively poor citizens, but absolute poverty is limited largely to the poor nations. Those living on the streets of Calcutta, or in a drought-stricken region of the Sahel, are experiencing poverty unknown in the West. Under these circumstances it would be wrong to decide that only those fortunate enough to be citizens of our own community will share our abundance.

We feel obligations of kinship more strongly than those of citizenship. Which parents could give away their last bowl of rice if their own children were starving? To do so would seem unnatural, contrary to our nature as biologically evolved beings—although whether it would be wrong is another question altogether. In any case, we are not faced with that situation, but with one in which our own children are well-fed, well-clothed, well-educated, and would now like new bikes, a stereo set, or their own car. In these circumstances any special obligations we might have to our children have been fulfilled, and the needs of strangers make a stronger claim upon us.

The element of truth in the view that we should first take care of our own, lies in the advantage of a recognized system of responsibilities. When families and local communities look after their own poorer members, ties of affection and personal relationships achieve ends that would otherwise require a large, impersonal bureaucracy. Hence it would be absurd to propose that from now on we all regard ourselves as equally responsible for the welfare of everyone in the world; but the argument for an obligation to assist does not propose that. It applies only when some are in absolute poverty, and others can help without sacrificing anything of comparable moral significance. To allow one's own kin to sink into absolute poverty would be to sacrifice something of comparable significance; and before that point had been reached, the breakdown of the system of family and community responsibility would be a factor to weigh the balance in favour of a small degree of preference for family and community. This small degree of preference is, however, decisively outweighed by existing discrepancies in wealth and property.

Property Rights

Do people have a right to private property, a right which contradicts the view that they are under an obligation to give some of their wealth away to those in absolute poverty? According to some theories of rights (for instance, Robert Nozick's) provided one has acquired one's property without the use of

unjust means like force and fraud, one may be entitled to enormous wealth while others starve. This individualistic conception of rights is in contrast to other views, like the early Christian doctrine to be found in the works of Thomas Aquinas, which holds that since property exists for the satisfaction of human needs, "whatever a man has in superabundance is owed, of natural right, to the poor for their sustenance." A socialist would also, of course, see wealth as belonging to the community rather than the individual, while utilitarians, whether socialist or not, would be prepared to override property rights to prevent great evils. . . .

The argument for an obligation to assist can survive, with only minor modifications, even if we accept the individualistic theory of property rights. In any case, however, I do not think we should accept such a theory. It leaves too much to chance to be an acceptable ethical view. For instance, those whose forefathers happened to inhabit some sandy wastes around the Persian Gulf are now fabulously wealthy, because oil lay under those sands; while those whose forefathers settled on better land south of the Sahara live in absolute poverty, because of drought and bad harvests. Can this distribution be acceptable from an impartial point of view? If we imagine ourselves about to begin life as a citizen of either Kuwait or Chad—but we do not know which—would we accept the principle that citizens of Kuwait are under no obligation to assist people living in Chad?

Population and the Ethics of Triage

Perhaps the most serious objection to the argument that we have an obligation to assist is that since the major cause of absolute poverty is overpopulation, helping those now in poverty will only ensure that yet more people are born to live in poverty in the future.

In its most extreme form, this objection is taken to show that we should adopt a policy of "triage". The term comes from medical policies adopted in wartime. With too few doctors to cope with all the casualties, the wounded were divided into three categories:

those who would probably survive without medical assistance, those who might survive if they received assistance, but otherwise probably would not, and those who even with medical assistance probably would not survive. Only those in the middle category were given medical assistance. The idea, of course, was to use limited medical resources as effectively as possible. For those in the first category, medical treatment was not strictly necessary; for those in the third category, it was likely to be useless. It has been suggested that we should apply the same policies to countries, according to their prospects of becoming self-sustaining. We would not aid countries which even without our help will soon be able to feed their populations. We would not aid countries which, even with our help, will not be able to limit their population to a level they can feed. We would aid those countries where our help might make the difference between success and failure in bringing food and population into balance.

Advocates of this theory are understandably reluctant to give a complete list of the countries they would place into the "hopeless" category; but Bangladesh is often cited as an example. Adopting the policy of triage would, then, mean cutting off assistance to Bangladesh and allowing famine, disease and natural disasters to reduce the population of that country (now around 80 million) to the level at which it can provide adequately for all.

In support of this view Garrett Hardin has offered a metaphor: we in the rich nations are like the occupants of a crowded lifeboat adrift in a sea full of drowning people. If we try to save the drowning by bringing them aboard our boat will be overloaded and we shall all drown. Since it is better that some survive than none, we should leave the others to drown. In the world today, according to Hardin, "lifeboat ethics" apply. The rich should leave the poor to starve, for otherwise the poor will drag the rich down with them.

Against this view, some writers have argued that overpopulation is a myth. The world produces ample food to feed its population, and could, according to some estimates, feed ten

times as many. People are hungry because of inequitable land distribution, the manipulation of Third World economies by the developing nations, wastage of food in the West, and so on. . . . [I]t is true, as we have already seen, that the world now produces enough to feed its inhabitants—the amount lost to animals itself being enough to meet existing grain shortages. Nevertheless population growth cannot be ignored. . . . [But] the consequences of triage on this scale are so horrible that we are inclined to reject it without further argument. How could we sit by our television sets, watching millions starve while we do nothing? Would not that (far more than the proposals for legalizing euthanasia) be the end of all notions of human equality and respect for human life? Don't people have a right to our assistance, irrespective of the consequences?

Anyone whose initial reaction to triage was not one of repugnance would be an unpleasant sort of person. Yet initial reactions based on strong feelings are not always reliable guides. Advocates of triage are rightly concerned with the long-term consequences of our actions. They say that helping the poor and starving now merely ensures more poor and starving in the future. When our capacity to help is finally unable to cope—as one day it must be—the suffering will be greater than it would be if we stopped helping now. If this is correct, there is nothing we can do to prevent absolute starvation and poverty, in the long run, and so we have no obligation to assist. Nor does it seem reasonable to hold that under these circumstances people have a right to our assistance. If we do accept such a right, irrespective of the consequences, we are saying that, in Hardin's metaphor, we would continue to haul the drowning into our lifeboat until the boat sank and we all drowned.

If triage is to be rejected it must be tackled on its own ground, within the framework of consequentialist ethics. Here it is vulnerable. Any consequentialist ethics must take probability of outcome into account. A course of action that will certainly produce some benefit is to be preferred to an alternative course that may lead to a slightly larger benefit, but is equally likely to result in no benefit at all. Only if the greater magnitude of the uncertain benefit outweighs its uncertainty should we choose it. Better one certain unit of benefit than a 10 percent chance of 5 units; but better a 50 percent chance of 3 units than a single certain unit. The same principle applies when we are trying to avoid evils.

The policy of triage involves a certain, very great evil: population control by famine and disease. Tens of millions would die slowly. Hundreds of millions would continue to live in absolute poverty, at the very margin of existence. Against this prospect, advocates of the policy place a possible evil which is greater still: the same process of famine and disease, taking place in, say, fifty years time, when the world's population may be three times its present level, and the number who will die from famine, or struggle on in absolute poverty, will be that much greater. The question is: how probable is this forecast that continued assistance now will lead to greater disasters in the future?

Forecasts of population growth are notoriously fallible, and theories about the factors which affect it remain speculative. One theory, at least as plausible as any other, is that countries pass through a "demographic transition" as their standard of living rises. When people are very poor and have no access to modern medicine their fertility is high, but population is kept in check by high death rates. The introduction of sanitation, modern medical techniques and other improvements reduces the death rate, but initially has little effect on the birth rate. Then population grows rapidly. Most poor countries are now in this phase. If standards of living continue to rise, however, couples begin to realize that to have the same number of children surviving to maturity as in the past, they do not

need to give birth to as many children as their parents did. The need for children to provide economic support in old age diminishes. Improved education and the emancipation and employment of women also reduce the birthrate, and so population growth begins to level off. Most rich nations have reached this stage, and their populations are growing only very slowly.

If this theory is right, there is an alternative to the disasters accepted as inevitable by supporters of triage. We can assist the poor countries to raise the living standards of the poorest members of their population. We can encourage the governments of these countries to enact land reform measures, improve education, and liberate women from a purely child-bearing role. We can also help other countries to make contraception and sterilization widely available. There is a fair chance that these measures will hasten the onset of the demographic transition and bring population growth down to a manageable level. Success cannot be guaranteed; but the evidence that improved economic security and education reduce population growth is strong enough to make triage ethically unacceptable. We cannot allow millions to die from starvation and disease when there is a reasonable probability that population can be brought under control without such horrors.

Population growth is therefore not a reason against giving overseas aid, although it should make us think about the kind of aid to give. Instead of food handouts, it may be better to give aid that hastens the demographic transition. This may mean agricultural assistance for the rural poor, or assistance with education, or the provision of contraceptive services. Whatever kind of aid proves most effective in specific circumstances, the obligation to assist is not reduced. . . .

REVIEW AND DISCUSSION QUESTIONS

1. Describe the analogy Singer uses to develop his argument. What principle does he say establishes the duty to prevent absolute poverty?
2. Singer rejects the Lockean view of property rights for two reasons. Explain each.

3. Describe triage and its relevance to Singer's position. On what grounds does Singer reject the triage argument?

4. Would Singer's principle demand that you give your second kidney to save another's life? Your savings? Explain why or why not.

What People Deserve

James Rachels

Often, it is claimed, people should be rewarded by society with economic or other goods because they deserve them. But what, exactly, is "desert"? In this essay, James Rachels begins with a discussion of justice, arguing that desert is part, but only a part, of treating people justly. While Nozick and others are correct in thinking that justice demands respecting people's rights, including the right to hire and fire as one wishes, desert is also an important component of justice. To deserve something, he says, requires that we reward or punish people in virtue of their past actions. People ought to be treated according to their deserts, he further claims, because this increases their control over their lives and shows them respect. James Rachels is professor of philosophy at the University of Alabama at Birmingham.

1. THE RELATION BETWEEN JUSTICE AND DESERT

The fact that people are, or are not, treated as they deserve to be treated is one kind of reason why an action or social policy may be just or unjust. I say "one kind of reason" because there are also other sorts of reasons relevant to supporting claims of justice. Besides requiring that people be treated as they deserve, justice may also require that people's rights be respected, which is different. . . .

The term "distributive justice" is commonly used by philosophers, but as Nozick points out, it can be misleading. It suggests that there is a central supply of things which some authority has to dole out; but for most goods, there is no such supply and no such authority. Goods are produced by diverse individuals and groups who then have rights with respect to them, and the "distribution" of holdings at any particular time will depend, at least in part, on the voluntary exchanges and agreements those people have made. Jobs, for example, do not come from some great stockpile, to be handed out by a master "distributor" who may or may not follow principles of "justice." Jobs are created by the independent decisions of countless business people, who are entitled, within some limits of course, to operate their own businesses according to their own judgments. In a free society those people get to choose with whom they will make what sorts of agreements, and this means, among other things, that they get to choose who is hired from among the various job applicants.

These observations suggest an argument in defense of reverse discrimination: if private business people have a right to hire whomever they please, don't they have a right to hire blacks and women in preference to others? In her paper on "Preferential Hiring"

"What People Deserve," from John Arthur and William H. Shaw, *Justice and Economic Distribution* (Englewood Cliffs, NJ: Prentice Hall, 1978). Preprinted by permission.

Judith Jarvis Thomson[1] advances an argument based on exactly this idea. The argument begins with this principle:

> No perfect stranger has a right to be given a benefit which is yours to dispose of; no perfect stranger even has a right to be given an equal chance at getting a benefit which is yours to dispose of.[2]

Since many jobs are benefits which private employers have a right to dispose of, those employers violate no one's rights in hiring whomever they wish. If they choose to hire blacks, or women, rather than other applicants, they have a perfect right to do so. Therefore, she concludes, "there is no problem about preferential hiring," at least in the case of private business.

Thomson's principle is plausible. If something is *yours,* then no one else has a right to it—at least, no perfect stranger who walks in off the street wanting it. Suppose you have a book which you don't need and decide to give away as a gift. Smith and Jones both want it, and you decide to give it to Smith. Is Jones entitled to complain? Apparently not, since he had no claim on it in the first place. If it was your book, you were entitled to give it to whomever you chose; you violated no right of Jones in giving it to Smith. Why shouldn't the same be true of jobs? If you start a business, on your own, why shouldn't you be free to hire whomever you please to work with you? You violate no one's rights in hiring whomever you please, since no one had a right to be hired by you in the first place.

This is an important and powerful argument because it calls attention to a fact that is often overlooked, that people do not naturally have claims of right to jobs and other benefits which are privately produced. However, the argument also depends on another assumption which is false, namely, the assumption that people are treated unjustly only if their rights are violated. In fact, a person may be treated unjustly even though no right of his is violated, because he is not treated as he deserves to be treated. Suppose

one applicant for a job has worked very hard to qualify himself for it; he has gone to night-school, at great personal sacrifice, to learn the business, and so on. Another applicant could have done all that, but chose not to; instead, he has frittered away his time and done nothing to prepare himself. In addition, the first applicant has worked hard at every previous job he has held, making a good record for himself, whereas the second is a notorious loafer—and it's his own fault; he has no good excuse. Now it may be true that neither applicant has a right to the job, in the sense that the employer has the right to give the job to whomever he pleases. However, the first man is clearly more deserving, and if the employer is concerned to treat job applicants fairly he will not hire the second man over the first.

Now let me return to Nozick.[3] In Part II of *Anarchy, State and Utopia* he defends capitalism, not merely as efficient or workable, but as the only moral economic system, because it is the only such system which respects individual rights. Under capitalism people's holdings are determined by the voluntary exchanges (of services and work as well as goods) they make with others. Their right to liberty requires that they be allowed to make such exchanges, providing that they violate no one else's rights in doing so. Having acquired their holdings by such exchanges, they have a right to them; so it violates their rights for the government (or anyone else) to seize their property and give it to others. It is impermissible, therefore, for governments to tax some citizens in order to provide benefits for others.

The obvious objection is that such an arrangement could produce a disastrously unfair distribution of goods. Some lucky entrepreneurs could become enormously rich, while other equally deserving people are poor, and orphans starve. In reply Nozick contends that even if unmodified capitalism did lead to such a distribution, that would not necessarily be unjust. The justice of a distribution, he says, can be determined only by considering the historical process which led to it. We cannot tell whether a distribution is just simply by checking whether it conforms to some nonhistorical pattern, for example the pattern of everyone having equal shares, or everyone having what he or she needs. To show this Nozick gives a now-famous argument starring the basketball player Wilt Chamberlain. First, he says, suppose the goods in a society are distributed according to some pattern which you think just. Call this distribution D_1. Since you regard D_1 as a just distribution, you will agree that under it each person has a right to the holdings in his or her possession. Now suppose a million of these people each decide to give Wilt Chamberlain twenty-five cents to watch him play basketball. Chamberlain becomes rich, and the original pattern is upset. But if the original distribution was just, mustn't we admit that the new distribution (D_2) is also just? . . .

> Each of these persons *chose* to give twenty-five cents of their money to Chamberlain. They could have spent it on going to the movies, or on candy bars, or on copies of *Dissent* magazine, or of *Monthly Review.* But they all, at least one million of them, converged on giving it to Wilt Chamberlain in exchange for watching him play basketball. If D_1 was a just distribution, and people voluntarily moved from it to D_2, transferring parts of their shares they were given under D_1 (what was it for if not to do something with?), isn't D_2 also just? . . . Can anyone else complain on grounds of justice? . . . After someone transfers something to Wilt Chamberlain, third parties *still* have their legitimate shares; *their* shares are not changed.[4]

The main argument here seems to depend on the principle that *If* D_1 *is a just distribution, and* D_2 *arises from* D_1 *by a process in which no one's rights are violated, then* D_2 *is also just.* Now Nozick is surely right that the historical process which produces a situation is one of the things that must be taken into account in deciding whether it is just. But that need not be the only relevant consideration. The historical process *and* other considerations, such as desert, must be weighed together to determine what is just. Therefore, it would not follow that a distribution is just *simply* because it is the result of a certain process, even a

process in which no one's rights are violated. So this argument cannot answer adequately the complaint against unmodified capitalism.

To make the point less abstract, consider the justice of inherited wealth. A common complaint about inherited wealth is that some people gain fortunes which they have done nothing to deserve, while others, of equal merit, have nothing. This seems unjust on the face of it. Nozick points out that if the testators legitimately own their property—if it is *theirs*—then they have a right to give it to others as a gift. (The holdings of third parties will not be changed, etc.) Bequests are gifts; therefore property owners have a right to pass on their property to their heirs. This is fair enough, but at most it shows only that there is more than one consideration to be taken into account here. That some people have more than others, without deserving it, counts against the justice of the distribution. That they came by their holdings in a certain way may count in favor of the justice of the same distribution. It should come as no surprise that in deciding questions of justice competing claims must often be weighed against one another, for that is the way it usually is in ethics.

2. DESERT AND PAST ACTIONS

Deserts may be positive or negative, that is, a person may deserve to be treated well or badly; and they may be general or specific, that is, a person may deserve to be treated in a generally good or bad way, or he may deserve some specific kind of good or bad treatment. An example may make the latter distinction clear. Suppose a woman has always been kind and generous with others. As a general way of dealing with her, she deserves that others be kind and generous in return. Here we need not specify any *particular* act of kindness to say what she deserves, although of course treating her kindly will involve some particular act or other. What she deserves is that people treat her decently in *whatever* situation might arise. By way of contrast, think of someone who has worked hard to earn promotion in his job. He may deserve, *specifically,* to be promoted.

I wish to argue that the basis of all desert is a person's own past actions. In the case of negative desert, this is generally conceded. In order for a person to deserve punishment, for example, he must have done something to deserve it. Moreover, he must have done it "voluntarily," in Aristotle's sense, without any excuse such as ignorance, mistake, or coercion. In allowing these excuses and others like them, the law attempts to restrict punishment to cases in which it is deserved.

But not every negative desert involves punishment, strictly speaking. They may involve more informal responses to other people's misconduct. Suppose Adams and Brown work at the same factory. One morning Adams' car breaks down and he calls Brown to ask for a ride to work. Brown refuses, not for any good reason, but simply because he won't be bothered. Later, Brown finds himself in the same fix: his car won't start, and he can't get to work; so he calls Adams to ask for a lift. Now if Adams is a kind and forgiving person, he may grant Brown's request. And perhaps we all ought to be kind and forgiving. However, if Adams does choose to help Brown, he will be treating Brown better than Brown deserves. Brown deserves to be left in the lurch. Here I am not arguing that we ought to treat people as they deserve—although I do think there are reasons for so treating people, which I will mention presently—here I am only describing what the concept of desert involves. What Brown *deserves,* as opposed to what kindness or any other value might decree, is to be treated as well, or as *badly,* as he himself chooses to treat others.

If I am right, then the familiar lament "What did I do to deserve this?," asked by a victim of misfortune, is more than a mournful cliché. If there is no satisfactory answer, then in fact one does *not* deserve the misfortune. And since there is always a presumption against treating people badly, if a person does not deserve bad treatment it is likely to be wrong to treat him in that way. On the other side, in the case of positive deserts, we may notice a corresponding connection between the concept of desert and the idea of *earning* one's way, which also supports my thesis.

To elaborate an example I used earlier, think of an employer who has to decide which of two employees to give a promotion. One has worked very hard for the company for several years. He has always been willing to do more than his share of work; he has put in a lot of overtime when no one else would; and so on. The other has always done the least he could get by with, never taking on any extra work or otherwise exerting himself beyond the necessary minimim. Clearly, if the choice is between these two candidates, it is the first who deserves the promotion. It is important to notice that this conclusion does not depend on any estimate of how the two candidates are likely to perform in the future. Even if the second candidate were to reform, so that he would work just as hard (and well) in the new position as the first candidate, the first is still more deserving. What one deserves depends on what one has done, not on what one will do.

Of course there may be any number of reasons for not giving the promotion to the most deserving candidate: perhaps it is a family business, and the second candidate is the boss's son, and he will be advanced simply because of who he is. But that does not make him the most deserving candidate; it only means that the promotion is to be awarded on grounds other than desert. Again, the boss might decide to give the position to the second candidate because he is extraordinarily smart and talented, and the boss thinks for that reason he will do a better job (he has promised to work harder in the future). This is again to award the job on grounds other than desert, for no one deserves anything *simply* in virtue of superior intelligence and natural abilities. As Rawls emphasizes, a person no more deserves to be intelligent or talented than he deserves to be the boss's son—or, than he deserves to be born white in a society prejudiced against non-whites. These things are all matters of chance, at least as far as the lucky individual himself is concerned.

Three questions naturally arise concerning this view. First, aren't there bases of desert *other than* a person's past actions, and if not, why not? Second, if a person may not deserve things in virtue of being naturally talented or intelligent or fortunate in some other way, how can he deserve things by working for them? After all, isn't it merely a matter of luck that one person grows up to be industrious—perhaps as the result of a rigorous upbringing by his parents—while another person is not encouraged, and ends up lazy for reasons beyond his control? And finally, even if I am right about the basis of desert, what reason is there actually to treat people according to their deserts? Why should desert matter? I will take up these questions in order. The answers, as we shall see, are interrelated.

(a) . . . Does the most skillful player deserve to win an athletic competition? It seems a natural enough thing to say. But suppose the less skilled player has worked very hard, for weeks, to prepare himself for the match. He has practiced nine hours a day, left off drinking, and kept to a strict regimen. Meanwhile, his opponent, who is a "natural athlete," has partied, stayed drunk, and done nothing in the way of training. *But he is still the most skilled,* and as a result can probably beat the other guy anyway. Does he *deserve* to win the game, simply because he is better endowed by nature? Does he *deserve* the acclaim and benefits which go with winning? Of course, skills are themselves usually the product of past efforts. People must work to sharpen and develop their natural abilities; therefore, when we think of the most skillful as the most deserving, it may be because we think of them as having worked hardest. (Ted Williams practiced hitting more than anyone else on the Red Sox.) But sometimes that assumption is not true.

Do the prettiest and most handsome deserve to win beauty contests? Again, it seems a natural enough thing to say. There is no doubt that the *correct* decision for the judges of such a competition to make is to award the prize to the best-looking. But this may have little to do with the contestants' deserts. Suppose a judge were to base his decision on desert; we might imagine him reasoning like this: "Miss Montana isn't the prettiest, but after all, she'd done her best with what nature provided. She's studied the use of make-up, had her teeth and nose fixed, and spent hours practicing walking down runways in high-heeled shoes. That smile didn't just happen; she had to learn it by spending hours before a mirror. Miss Alabama, on the other hand, is prettier, but she just entered the contest on a lark—walked in, put on a bathing suit, and here she is. Her make-up isn't even very good." If all this seems ridiculous, it is because the point of such contests is not to separate the more deserving from the less (and maybe because beauty contests are themselves a little ridiculous, too). The criterion is beauty, not desert, and the two have little to do with one another. The same goes for athletic games: the purpose is to see who is the best player, or at least who is able to defeat all the others, and not to discover who is the most deserving competitor.

There is a reason why past actions are the only bases of desert. A fair amount of our dealings with other people involves holding them responsible, formally or informally, for one thing or another. It is unfair to hold people responsible for things over which they have no control. People have no control over their native endowments—over how smart, or athletic, or beautiful they naturally are—and so we may not hold them responsible for those things. They are, however, in control of (at least some of) their own actions, and so they may rightly be held responsible for the situations they create, or allow to exist, by their voluntary behavior. But those are the only things for which they may rightly be held responsible. The concept of desert serves to signify the ways of treating people that are appropriate responses to them, given that they are responsible for those actions or states of affairs. That is the role played by desert in our moral vocabulary. And, as ordinary-language philosophers used to like to say, if there weren't such a term, we'd have to invent one. Thus the explanation of why past actions are the only bases of desert connects with the fact that if people were never responsible for their own conduct—if hard determinism were true—no one would ever deserve anything, good or bad.

(b) According to the view I am defending, we may deserve things by working for them, but not simply by being naturally intelligent or talented or lucky in some other way. Now it may be thought that this view is inconsistent, because whether someone is willing to work is just another matter of luck, in much the same way that intelligence and talent are matters of luck. Rawls takes this position when he says:

> Perhaps some will think that the person with greater natural endowments deserves those assets and the superior character that made their development possible. Because he is more worthy in this sense, he deserves the greater advantages that he could achieve with them. This view, however, is surely incorrect. It seems to be one of the fixed points of our considered judgments that no one deserves his place in the distribution of native endowments, any more than one deserves one's initial starting place in society. The assertion that a man deserves the superior character that enables him to make the effort to cultivate his abilities is equally problematic; for his character depends in large part upon fortunate family and social circumstances for which he can claim no credit. The notion of desert seems not to apply to these cases.[5]

So if a person does not deserve anything on account of his intelligence or natural abilities, how can he deserve anything on account of his industriousness? Isn't willingness to work just another matter of luck?

The first thing to notice here is that people do not deserve things on account of their willingness to work, but only on account of their actually having worked. The candidate for promotion does not deserve it because he has been willing to work hard in his old job, or because he is willing to work hard in the new job. Rather he deserves the promotion because he actually *has* worked hard. Therefore it is no objection to the view I am defending to say that willingness to work is a character trait that one does not merit. For, on this view, the basis of desert is not a character trait of any kind, not even industriousness. The basis of desert is a person's past actions.

Now it may be that some people have been so psychologically devastated by a combination of poor native endowment and unfortunate family and social circumstances that they no longer have the capacity for making anything of their lives. If one of these people has a job, for example, and doesn't work very hard at it, it's no use blaming him because, as we would say, he just hasn't got it in him to do any better. On the other hand, there are those in whom the capacity for effort has not been extinguished. Among these, some choose to work hard, and others, who *could* so choose, do not. It is true of everyone in this latter class that he is *able,* as Rawls puts it, "to strive conscientiously." The explanation of why some strive, while others don't, has to do with their own choices. When I say that those who work hard are more deserving of success, promotions, etc., than those who don't, I have in mind comparisons made among people in this latter class, in whom the capacity for effort has not been extinguished.[6]

There is an important formal difference between industriousness, considered as a lucky asset, and other lucky assets such as intelligence. For only by exercising this asset—i.e., by working—can one utilize his other assets, and achieve anything with them. Intelligence alone produces nothing; intelligence plus work can produce something. And the same relation holds between industriousness and every other natural talent or asset. Thus "willingness to work," if it is a lucky asset, is a sort of superasset which enables one's other assets to be utilized. Working is simply the way one uses whatever else one has. This point may help to explain why the concept of desert is tied to work in a way in which it is not tied to intelligence or talents. And at the same time it may also provide a rationale for the following distinction: if a person displays intelligence and talent in his work, and earns a certain benefit by it, then he deserves the benefit not because of the intelligence or talent shown, but only on account of the work done.

(c) Finally, we must ask why people ought to be treated according to their deserts. Why should desert matter? In one way, it is an odd question. The reason why the conscientious employee ought to be promoted is precisely that he has earned the promotion by working for it. That is a full and sufficient justification for promoting him, which does not require supplementation of any sort. If we want to know why he should be treated in that way, that is the answer. It is not easy to see what else, by way of justification, is required.

Nevertheless, something more may be said. Treating people as they deserve is one way of treating them as autonomous beings, responsible for their own conduct. A person who is punished for his misdeeds is *held responsible* for them in a concrete way. He is not treated as a mindless automaton, whose defective performance must be "corrected," or whose good performance promoted, but as a responsible agent whose actions merit approval or

resentment. The recognition of deserts is bound up with this way of regarding people. Moreover, treating people as they deserve *increases* their control over their own lives and fortunes, for it allows people to determine, through their own actions, how others will respond to them. It can be argued on grounds of kindness that people should not always be treated as they deserve, when they deserve ill. But this should not be taken to imply that deserts count for nothing. They can count for something, and still be overridden in some cases. To deny categorically that desert matters would not only excuse the malefactors; it would leave all of us impotent to earn the good treatment and other benefits which others have to bestow, and thus would deprive us of the ability to control our own destinies as social beings.

[Rachels discusses the implications for what he has been saying here in a section titled "Reverse Discrimination," which appears in the section 14.—Ed.]

NOTES

1. Judith Jarvis Thomson, "Preferential Hiring," *Philosophy and Public Affairs,* 2, no. 4 (Summer 1973), pp. 364–384.
2. Ibid., p. 369.
3. The following is from my review of *Anarchy, State and Utopia* in *Philosophia,* 7 (1977).
4. Robert Nozick, *Anarchy, State and Utopia* (New York: Basic Books, 1974), p. 161.
5. John Rawls, *A Theory of Justice* (Cambridge, MA: Harvard University Press, 1971), pp. 103–104.
6. What I am resisting—and what I think Rawls' view leads us towards—is a kind of determinism that would make all moral evaluation of persons meaningless. On this tendency in Rawls, see Nozick, pp. 213–214.

REVIEW AND DISCUSSION QUESTIONS

1. What are the two parts of justice, according to Rachels?
2. Describe the Wilt Chamberlain example and how it might be relevant to the distribution of income.
3. How does Rachels understand desert?
4. What is the moral and philosophical grounding of desert, according to Rachels? Why does he think people should be given what they deserve?
5. Explain the significance of Rachels's position on the importance of desert for welfare, indicating the sorts of welfare policies you think he would support.

Markets and Hard Work

Michael Walzer

Sometimes it seems that everything is for sale in a capitalist state, or at least almost everything. Michael Walzer begins by describing the range of "blocked exchanges," that is, the many different types of goods that are not for sale. Turning to the market sphere, where goods and labor are for sale, he discusses the oft-heard claim that the market rewards those who deserve it for their hard, dangerous, or unpleasant work. Walzer disputes this claim, by describing a group of garbage collectors who formed a company that linked hard and unpleasant work with other activities such as self-government and economic reward. He concludes with some suggestions about how the United States might transform hard work in ways that benefit the workers and the community as a whole. Michael Walzer is professor of politics at Harvard University.

MONEY AND COMMODITIES

Blocked Exchanges

Let me try to suggest the full set of blocked [market] exchanges in the United States today. I will rely in part on the first chapter of Arthur Okun's *Equality and Efficiency,* where Okun draws a line between the sphere of money and what he calls "the domain of rights."[1] Rights of course, are proof against sale and purchase, and Okun revealingly recasts the Bill of Rights as a series of blocked exchanges. But it's not only rights that stand outside the cash nexus. Whenever we ban the use of money, we do indeed establish a right—namely, that this particular good be distributed in some other way. But we must argue about the meaning of the good before we can say anything more about its rightful distributions. . . . Blocked exchanges set limits on the dominance of wealth.

1. Human beings cannot be bought and sold. The sale of slaves, even of oneself as a slave, is ruled out. This is an example of what Okun calls "prohibitions on exchanges born of desperation."[2] There are many such prohibitions; but the others merely regulate the labor market, and I will list them separately. This one establishes what is and is not marketable: not persons or the liberty of persons, but only their labor power and the things they make. (Animals are marketable because we conceive them to be without personality, even though liberty is undoubtedly a value for some of them.) Personal liberty is not, however, proof against conscription or imprisonment; it is proof only against sale and purchase.

2. Political power and influence cannot be bought and sold. Citizens cannot sell their votes or officials their decisions. Bribery is an illegal transaction. It hasn't always been so; in many cultures gifts from clients and suitors are a normal part of the remuneration of office holders. But here the gift relationship will only work—that is, fit into a set of more or less coherent meanings—when "office" hasn't fully emerged as an autonomous good, and when the line between public and private is hazy and indistinct. It won't work in a republic, which draws the line sharply: Athens, for example, had an extraordinary set of rules designed to repress bribery; the more offices the citizens shared, the more elaborate the rules became.

3. Criminal justice is not for sale. It is not only that judges and juries cannot be bribed, but that the services of defense attorneys are a matter of communal provision—a necessary form of welfare given the adversary system.

4. Freedom of speech, press, religion, assembly: none of these require money payments; none of them are available at auction; they are simply guaranteed to every citizen. It's often said that the exercise of these freedoms costs money, but that's not strictly speaking the case: talk and worship are cheap; so is the meeting of citizens; so is publication in many of its forms. Quick access to large audiences is expensive, but that is another matter, not of freedom itself but of influence and power.

5. Marriage and procreation rights are not for sale. Citizens are limited to one spouse and cannot purchase a license for polygamy. And if limits are ever set on the number of children we can have, I assume that these won't take the form [of] licenses to give birth that can be traded on the market.

6. The right to leave the political community is not for sale. The modern state has, to be sure, an investment in every citizen, and it might legitimately require that some part of that investment be repaid, in work or money, before permitting emigration. The Soviet Union has adopted a policy of this sort, chiefly as a mechanism to bar emigration altogether. Used differently, it seems fair enough, even if it then has differential effects on successful and unsuccessful citizens. But the citizens can claim, in their turn, that they never sought the health care and education that they received (as children, say) and owe nothing in return. That claim underestimates the benefits of citizenship, but nicely captures its consensual character. And so it is best to let them go, once they have fulfilled those obligations-in-kind (military service) that are fulfilled in any case by young men and women who aren't yet fully consenting citizens. No one can buy his way out of these.

7. And so, again, exemptions from military service, from jury duty, and from any other form of communally imposed work cannot be sold by the government or bought by citizens—for reasons I have already given.

8. Political offices cannot be bought; to buy them would be a kind of simony, for the political community is like a church in this sense, that its services matter a great deal to its members and wealth is no adequate sign of a capacity to deliver those services. Nor can professional standing be bought, insofar as this is regulated by the community, for doctors and lawyers are our secular priests; we need to be sure about their qualifications.

9. Basic welfare services like police protection or primary and secondary schooling are purchasable only at the margins. A minimim is guaranteed to every citizen and doesn't have to be paid for by individuals. If policemen dun shopkeepers for protection money, they are acting like gangsters, not like policemen. But shopkeepers can hire security guards and nightwatchmen for the sake of a higher level of protection than the political community is willing to pay for. Similarly, parents can hire private tutors for their children or send them to private schools. The market in services is subject to restraint only if it distorts the character, or lowers the value, of communal provision. (I should also note that some goods are partially provided, hence partially insulated from market control. The mechanism here is not the blocked but the subsidized exchange—as in the case of college and University education, many cultural activities, travel generally, and so on.)

10. Desperate exchanges, "trades of last resort," are barred, though the meaning of desperation is always open to dispute. The eight-hour day, minimim wage laws, health and safety regulations: all these set a floor, establish basic standards, below which workers cannot bid against one another for employment. Jobs can be auctioned off, but only within these limits. This is a restraint of market liberty for the sake of some communal conception of personal liberty, a reassertion, at lower levels of loss; of the ban on slavery.

11. Prizes and honors of many sorts, public and private, are not available for purchase. The Congressional Medal of Honor cannot be bought, nor can the Pulitzer Prize or the Most Valuable Player Award, or even the trophy given by a local Chamber of Commerce to the "businessman of the year." Celebrity is certainly for sale, though the price can be high, but a good name is not. Prestige, esteem, and status stand somewhere between these two. Money is implicated in their distribution; but even in our own society, it is only sometimes determinative.

12. Divine grace cannot be bought—and not only because God doesn't need the money. His servants and deputies often do need it. Still, the sale of indulgences is commonly thought to require reform, if not Reformation.

13. Love and friendship cannot be bought, not on our common understanding of what these two mean. Of course, one can buy all sorts of things—clothing, automobiles, gourmet foods, and so on—that make one a better candidate for love and friendship or more self-confident in the pursuit of lovers and friends. Advertisers commonly play on these possibilities, and they are real enough.

. . . But the direct purchase is blocked, not in the law but more deeply, in our shared morality and sensibility. Men and women marry for money, but this is not a "marriage of true minds." Sex is for sale, but the sale does not make for "a meaningful relationship." People who believe that sexual intercourse is morally tied to love and marriage are likely to favor a ban on prostitution—just as, in other cultures, people believed that intercourse was a sacred ritual would have deplored the behavior of priestesses who tried to make a little money on the side. Sex can be sold only when it is understood in terms of pleasure and not exclusively in terms of married love or religious worship.

14. Finally, a long series of criminal sales are ruled out. Murder, Inc., cannot sell its services; blackmail is illegal; heroin cannot be sold, nor can stolen goods, or goods fraudulently described, or adulterated milk, or information thought vital to the security of the state. And arguments go on about unsafe cars, guns, inflammable shirts, drugs with uncertain side effects, and so on. All these are useful illustrations of the fact that the sphere of money and commodities is subject to continuous redefinition.

I think that this is an exhaustive list, though it is possible that I have omitted some crucial category. In any case, the list is long enough to suggest that if money answereth all things, it does so, as it were, behind the backs of many of the things and in spite of their social meanings. The market where exchanges of these sorts are free is a black market, and the men and women who frequent it are likely to do so sneakily and then to lie about what they are doing.

What Money Can Buy

What is the proper sphere of money? What social goods are rightly marketable? The obvious answer is also the right one; it points us to a range of goods that have probably always been marketable, whatever else has or has not been: all those objects, commodities, products, services, beyond what is communally provided, that individual men and women find useful or pleasing, the common stock of bazaars, emporiums, and trading post. . . .

The market produces and reproduces inequalities; people end up with more or less, with different numbers and different kinds of possessions. There is no way to ensure that everyone is possessed of whatever set of things marks the "average American," for any such effort will simply raise the average. Here is a sad version of the pursuit of happiness: communal provision endlessly chasing consumer demand. Perhaps there is some point beyond which the fetishism of commodities will lose its grip. Perhaps, more modestly, there is some lower point at which individuals are safe against any radical loss of status. That last possibility suggests the value of partial redistributions in the sphere of money, even if the result is something well short of simple equality. But it also suggests that we must look outside that sphere and strengthen autonomous distributions elsewhere. There are, after all, activities more central to the meaning of membership than owning and using commodities.

Our purpose is to tame "the inexorable dynamic of a money economy," to make money harmless—or at least to make sure that the harms experienced in the sphere of money are not mortal, not to life and not to social standing [as equal citizens] either. But the market remains a competitive sphere, where risk is common, where the readiness to take risks is often a virtue, and where people win and lose. An exciting place: for even when money buys only what it should buy, it is still a very good thing to have. It answereth some things that nothing else can answer. And once we have blocked every wrongful exchange and controlled the sheer weight of money itself, we have no reason to worry about the answers the market provides. Individual men and women still have reason to worry, and so they will try to minimize their risks, or to share them or spread them out, or to buy themselves insurance. In the regime of complex equality, certain sorts of risks will regularly be shared, because the power to impose risks on others, to make authoritative decisions in factories and corporations, is not a marketable good. This is only one more example of a blocked exchange; I will take it up in detail later. Given the right blocks, there is no such thing as a maldistribution of consumer goods. It just doesn't matter, from the standpoint of complex equality, that you have a yacht and I don't. . . .

The Marketplace

There is a stronger argument about the sphere of money, the common argument of the defenders of capitalism: that market outcomes matter a great deal because the market, if it is free, gives to each person exactly what he deserves. The market rewards us all in accordance with the contributions we make to one another's well-being. The goods and services we provide are valued by potential consumers in such-and-such a way, and these values are aggregated by the market, which determines the price we receive. And that price is our desert, for it expresses the only worth our goods and services can have, the worth they actually have for other people. But this is to misunderstand the meaning of desert. Unless there are standards of worth independent of what people want (and are willing to buy) at this or that moment in time, there can be no deservingness at all. We would never know what a person deserved until we saw what he had gotten. And that can't be right.

Imagine a novelist who writes what he hopes will be a best seller. He studies his potential audience, designs his book to meet the current fashion. Perhaps he had to violate the canons of his art in order to do that, and perhaps he is a novelist for whom the violation was painful. He has stooped to conquer. Does he now deserve the fruits of his conquest? Does he deserve a conquest that bears fruit? His novel appears, let's say, during a depression when no one has money for books, and very few copies are sold; his reward is small. Has he gotten less than he deserves? (His fellow writers smile at his disappointment; perhaps that's what he deserves.) Years later, in better times, the book is reissued and does well. Has its author become more deserving? Surely desert can't hang on the state of the economy. There is too much luck involved here; talk of desert makes little sense. We would do better to say simply that the writer is entitled to his royalties, large or small. . . .

HARD WORK

Equality and Hardness

It is not a question here of demanding or strenuous work. In that sense of the word, we can work hard in almost any office and at almost any job. I can work hard writing this book, and sometimes do. A task or a cause that seems to us worth the hard work it entails is clearly a good thing. For all our natural laziness, we go looking for it. But *hard* has another sense—as in "hard winter" and "hard heart"—where it means harsh, unpleasant, cruel, difficult to endure. . . .

This kind of work is a negative good, and it commonly carries other negative goods in its train: poverty, insecurity, ill health, physical danger, dishonor and degradation. And yet it is socially necessary work, it needs to be done, and that means that someone must be found to do it.

The conventional solution to this problem has the form of a simple equation: the negative good is matched by the negative status of the people into whose hands it is thrust. Hard work is distributed to degraded people. Citizens are set free; the work is imposed on slaves, resident aliens, "guest workers"—outsiders all. Alternatively, the insiders do the work are turned into "inside" aliens, like the Indian untouchables or the American blacks after emancipation. In many societies, women have been the most important group of "inside" aliens, doing the work that men disdained and freeing the men not only for more rewarding economic activities but also for citizenship and politics. Indeed, the household work that women traditionally have done—cooking, cleaning, caring for the sick and the old—makes up a substantial part of the hard work of the economy today, for which aliens are recruited (and women prominently among them).

The idea in all these cases is a cruel one: negative people for a negative good. The work should be done by men and women whose qualities it is presumed to fit. Because of their race or sex, or presumed intelligence, or social status, they deserve to do it, or they don't deserve not to do it, or they somehow qualify for it. It's not the work of citizens, free men, white men, and so on. But what sort of desert, what sort of qualification is this? It would be hard to say what the hard workers of this or any other society have done to

deserve the danger and degradation their work commonly entails; or how they, and they alone, have qualified for it. What secrets have we learned about their moral character? When convicts do hard labor, we can at least argue that they deserve their punishment. But even they are not state slaves; their degradation is (most often) limited and temporary, and it is by no means clear that the most oppressive sorts of work should be assigned to them. And if not to them, surely to no one else. Indeed, if convicts are driven to hard labor, then ordinary men and women should probably be protected from it, so as to make it clear that they are not convicts and have never been found guilty by a jury of their peers. And if even convicts shouldn't be forced to endure the oppression (imprisonment being oppression enough), then it is *a fortiori* true that no one else should endure it.

Nor can it be imposed on outsiders. . . . [T]he people who do this sort of work are so closely tied into the everyday life of the political community that they can't rightly be denied membership. Hard work is a naturalization process, and it brings membership to those who endure the hardship. At the same time, there is something attractive about a community whose members resist hard work (and whose new members are naturalized into the resistance). They have a certain sense of themselves and their careers that rules out the acceptance of oppression; they refuse to be degraded and have the strength to sustain the refusal. Neither the sense of self nor the personal strength are all that common in human history. They represent a significant achievement of modern democracy, closely connected to economic growth, certainly, but also to the success or the partial success of complex equality in the sphere of welfare. . . .

Dangerous Work

Soldiering is a special kind of hard work. In many societies, in fact, it is not conceived to be hard work at all. It is the normal occupation of young men, their social function, into which they are not so much drafted as ritually initiated, and where they find the rewards of camaraderie, excitement, and glory. It would be as odd, in these cases, to talk about conscripts as to talk about volunteers; neither category is relevant. . . .

Even when its true character is understood, however, soldiering is not a radically degraded activity. Rank-and-file soldiers are often recruited from the lowest classes, or from outcasts or foreigners, and they are often regarded with contempt by ordinary citizens. But the perceived value of their work is subject to sudden inflation, and there is always the chance that they will one day appear as the saviors of the country they defend. Soldiering is socially necessary, at least sometimes; and when it is, the necessity is visible and dramatic. At those times, soldiering is also dangerous, and it is dangerous in a way that makes a special mark on our imaginations. The danger is not natural but human; the soldier inhabits a world where other people—his enemies and ours, too—are trying to kill him. And he must try to kill them. He runs the risk of killing and being killed. For these reasons, I think, this is the first form of hard work that citizens are required, or require each other, to share. Conscription has other purposes too—above all, to produce the vast numbers of troops needed for modern warfare. But its moral purpose is to universalize or randomize the risks of war over a given generation of young men.

When the risks are of a different sort, however, the same purpose seems less pressing. Consider the case of coal mining. "The rate of accidents among miners is so high," wrote George Orwell in *The Road to Wigan Pier* ". . . that casualties are taken for granted as they would be in a minor war."[3] It isn't easy, however, to imagine this sort of work being shared. Mining may not be highly skilled work, but it is certainly very difficult, and it's best done by men who have done it for a long time. It requires something more than "basic training." "At a pitch," wrote Orwell, "I could be a tolerable road-sweeper, or . . . a tenth-rate farm hand. But by no conceivable amount of effort or training could I become a coal-miner; the work would kill me in a few weeks."[4] Nor does it make much sense to break in upon the solidarity of the miners. Work in the pits breeds a strong bond, a tight community that is not welcoming to transients. That community is the great strength of the miners. A deep sense of place and clan and generations of class struggle have made for staying power. . . .

Dirty Work

In principle, there is no such thing as intrinsically degrading work; degradation is a cultural phenomenon. It is probably true in practice, however, that a set of activities having to do with dirt, waste, and garbage has been the object of disdain and avoidance in just about every human society. The precise list will vary from one time and place to another, but the set is more or less common. In India, for example, it includes the butchering of cows and the tanning of cowhide—jobs that have a rather different standing in Western cultures. . . . . .

So long as there is a reserve army, a class of degraded men and women driven by their poverty and their impoverished sense of their own value, the market will never be effective. Under such conditions, the hardest work is also the lowest paid, even though nobody wants to do it. But given a certain level of communal provision and a certain level of self-valuation, the work won't be done unless it is very well paid indeed (or unless the working conditions are very good). The citizens will find that if they want to hire their fellows as scavengers and sweepers, the rates will be high—much higher, in fact, than for more prestigious or pleasant work. This is a direct consequence of the fact that they are hiring *fellow* citizens. It is sometimes claimed that under conditions of genuine fellowship, no one would agree to be a scavenger or a sweeper. In that case, the work would have to be shared. But the claim is probably false. "We are so accustomed," as Shaw has written, "to see dirty work done by dirty and poorly paid people that we have come to think that it is disgraceful to do it, and that unless a dirty and disgraced class existed, it would not be done at all."[5] If sufficient money or leisure were offered, Shaw rightly insisted, people would come forward.

His own preference was for rewards that take the form of leisure or "liberty"—which will always be, he argued, the strongest incentive and the best compensation for work that carries with it little intrinsic satisfaction:

> In a picture gallery you will find a nicely dressed lady sitting at a table with nothing to do but to tell anyone who asks what is the price of any particular picture, and take an order for it if one is given. She has many pleasant chats with journalists and artists; and if she is bored she can read a novel. . . . But the gallery has to be scrubbed and dusted each day; and its windows have to be kept clean. It is clear that the lady's job is a much softer one than the charwoman's. To balance them you must either let them take their turns at the desk and at the scrubbing on alternate days or weeks; or else, as a first-class scrubber and duster and cleaner might make a very bad business lady, and a very attractive business lady might make a very bad scrubber, you must let the charwoman go home and have the rest of the day to herself earlier than the lady at the desk.[6]

The contrast between the "first-rate" charwoman and the "very attractive" business lady nicely combines the prejudices of class and sex. If we set aside those prejudices, the periodic exchange of work is less difficult to imagine. The lady, after all, will have to share in the scrubbing, dusting, and cleaning at home (unless she has, as Shaw probably expected her to have, a charwoman there, too). And what is the charwoman to do with her leisure? Perhaps she will paint pictures or read books about art. But then, though the exchange is easy, it may well be resisted by the charwoman herself. One of the attractions of Shaw's proposal is that it establishes hard work as an opportunity for people who want to protect their time. So they will clean or scrub or collect garbage for the sake of their leisure, and avoid if they can any more engaging, competitive, or time-consuming employment.

Under the right conditions, the market provides a kind of sanctuary from the pressures of the market. The price of the sanctuary is so many hours a day of hard work—for some people, at least, a price worth paying.

The major alternative to Shaw's proposal is the reorganization of the work so as to change, not its physical requirements (for I'm assuming that they are not changeable), but its moral character. The history of garbage collecting in the city of San Francisco offers a nice example of this sort of transformation, which I want to dwell on briefly. . . .

The San Francisco Scavengers. For the past sixty years, roughly half of the garbage of the city of San Francisco has been collected and disposed of by the Sunset Scavenger Company, a cooperative owned by its workers, the men who drive the trucks and carry the cans. In 1978 the sociologist Stewart Perry published a study of Sunset, a fine piece of urban ethnography and a valuable speculation on "dirty work and the pride of ownership"—it is my sole source in the paragraphs that follow. The cooperative is democratically run, its officers elected from the ranks and paid no more than the other workers. Forced by the Internal Revenue Service in the 1930s to adopt bylaws in which they are referred to as "stockholders," the members nevertheless insisted that they were, and would remain, faithful to the program of the original organizers "who intended to form and carry on a cooperative . . . where every member was a worker and actually engaged in the common work and where every member did his share of the work and expected every other member to work and do his utmost to increase the collective earnings."[7] Indeed, earnings have increased (more than those of manual workers generally); the company has grown; its elected officers have shown considerable entrepreneurial talent. Perry believes that the cooperative provides better-than-average service to the citizens of San Francisco and, what is more important here, better-than-average working conditions to its own members. That doesn't mean that the work is physically easier; rather, cooperation has made it more pleasant—has even made it a source of pride.

In one sense, the work is in fact easier: the accident rate among Sunset members is significantly lower than the industry average. Garbage collecting is a dangerous activity. In the United States today, no other occupation has a higher risk of injury (though miners are subject to more serious injury). The explanation of these statistics is not clear. Garbage collecting is strenuous work, but no more so than many other jobs that turn out to have better safety records. Perry suggests that there may be a connection between safety and self-valuation. "The 'hidden injuries' of the status system may be linked to the apparent injuries that public health and safety experts can document."[8] The first "accident" of garbage collecting is the internalization of disrespect, and then other accidents follow. Men who don't value themselves don't take proper care of themselves. If this view is right, the better record of Sunset may be connected to the shared decision making and the sense of ownership.

Membership in the Sunset Scavenger Company is distributed by a vote of the current members and then by the purchase of shares (it has generally not been difficult to borrow the necessary money, and the shares have steadily increased in value). The founders of the company were Italian-Americans, and so are the bulk of the members today; about half of them are related to other members; a fair number of sons have followed their fathers into the business. The success of the cooperative may owe something to the easiness of the members with one another. In any case, and whatever one wants to say about the work, they have made membership into a good thing. They don't distribute the good they have created, however, in accordance with "fair equality of opportunity." In New York City, because of a powerful union, garbage collecting is also a widely desired job, and there the job has been turned into an office. Candidates must qualify for the work by taking a civil service exam.[9] It would be interesting to know something about the self-valuation of the men who pass the exam and are hired as public employees. They probably earn more than the members of the Sunset cooperative, but they don't have the same security; they don't own their jobs. And they don't share risks and opportunities; they don't manage their own company. The New Yorkers call themselves "sanitationmen"; the San Franciscans, "scavengers": who has the greater pride? If the advantage lies, as I think it does, with the members of Sunset, then it is closely connected to the character of Sunset: a company of companions, who choose their own fellows. There is no way to qualify for the work except to appeal to the current members of the company. No doubt the members look for men who can do the necessary work and do it well, but they also look, presumably, for good companions.

But I don't want to underestimate the value of unionization, for this can be another form of self-management and another way of making the market work. There can't be any doubt that unions have been effective in winning better wages and working conditions for their members; sometimes they have even succeeded in breaking the link between income differentials and the status hierarchy (the New York garbage collectors are a prime example). Perhaps the general rule should be that wherever work can't be unionized or run cooperatively, it should be shared by the citizens—not symbolically and partially, but generally. Indeed, when union or cooperative work is available to everyone (when there is no reserve army), other work just won't get done unless people do it for themselves. This is clearly the case with domestic cooking and cleaning, an area where jobs are increasingly filled by new immigrants, not by citizens. "Mighty few young black women are doin' domestic work [today]," Studs Terkel was told by a very old black woman, a servant all her life. "And I'm glad. That's why I want my kids to go to school. This one lady told me, 'All you people are gettin' like that.' I said, 'I'm glad.' There's no more gettin' on their knees"[10] This is the sort of work that is largely dependent on its (degraded) moral character. Change the character, and the work may well become un-doable, not only from the perspective of the worker but from that of the employer, too. "When domestic servants are treated as human beings," wrote Shaw, "it is not worthwhile to keep them. . . ."[11]

What is most attractive in the experience of the Sunset company (as of the Israeli kibbutz) is the way in which hard work is connected to other activities—in this case, the meetings of the "stockholders," the debates over policy, the election of officers and new members. The company has also expanded into land-fill and salvage operations, providing new and diversified employment (including managerial jobs) for some of the members; though all of them, whatever they do now, have spent years riding the trucks and carrying the cans. Throughout most of the economy, the division of labor has developed very differently, continually separating out rather than integrating the hardest sorts of work. This is especially true in the area of the human services, in the care we provide for the sick and the old. Much of that work is still done in the home, where it is connected with a range of other jobs, and its difficulties are relieved by the relationships it sustains. Increasingly, however, it is institutional work; and within the great caretaking institutions—hospitals, mental asylums, old-age homes—the hardest work, the dirty work, the most intimate service and supervision, is relegated to the most subordinate employees. Doctors and nurses, defending their place in the social hierarchy, shift it onto the shoulders of aides, orderlies, and attendants—who do for strangers, day in and day out, what we can only just conceive of doing in emergencies for the people we love.

Perhaps the aides, orderlies, and attendants win the gratitude of their patients or of the families of their patients. That's not a reward I would want to underestimate, but gratitude is most often and most visibly the reward of doctors and nurses, the healers rather than merely the caretakers of the sick. The resentment of the caretakers is well known. W. H. Auden was clearly thinking of the patients, not the hospital staff, when he wrote:

> . . . the hospitals alone remind us of the equality of man.[12]

Orderlies and attendants have to cope for long hours with conditions that their institutional superiors see only intermittently, and that the general public doesn't see at all and doesn't want to see. Often they took after men and women whom the rest of the world has given up on (and when the world gives up, it turns away). Underpaid and overworked, at the bottom of the status system, they are nevertheless the last comforters of humanity—though I suspect that unless they have a calling for the work, they give as little comfort as they get. And sometimes they are guilty of those petty cruelties that make their jobs a little easier, and that their superiors, they firmly believe, would be as quick to commit in their place.

"There is a whole series of problems here," Everett Hughes has written, "which cannot be solved by some miracle of changing the social selection of those who enter the job."[13] In fact, if caretaking were shared—if young men and women from different social backgrounds took their turns as orderlies and attendants— the internal life of hospitals, asylums, and old-age homes would certainly be changed for the better. Perhaps this sort of thing is best organized locally rather than nationally, so as to establish a connection between caretaking and neighborliness; it might even be possible, with a little invention, to reduce somewhat the rigid impersonality of institutional settings. But such efforts will be supplementary at best. Most of the work will have to be done by people who have chosen it as a career, and the choice will not be easy to motivate in a society of equal citizens. Already, we must recruit foreigners to do a great deal of the hard and dirty work of our caretaking institutions. If we wish to avoid that sort of recruitment (and the oppression it commonly entails), we must, again, transform the work. "I have a notion," says Hughes, "that . . . 'dirty work' can be more easily endured when it is part of a good role, a role that is full of rewards to one's self. A nurse might do some things with better grace than a person who is not allowed to call herself a nurse, but is dubbed 'subprofessional' or 'non-professional.'"[14] That is exactly right. National service might be effective because, for a time at least, the role of neighbor or citizen would cover the necessary work. But over a longer period, the work can be covered only by an enhanced sense of institutional or professional place. . . .

We can share (and partially transform) hard work through some sort of national service; we can reward it with money or leisure; we can make it more rewarding by connecting it to other sorts of activity—political, managerial, and professional in character. We can conscript, rotate, cooperate, and compensate; we can reorganize the work and rectify its names. We can do all these things, but we will not have abolished hard work; nor will we have abolished the class of hard workers. The first kind of abolitionism is, as I have already argued, impossible; the second would merely double hardness with coercion. The measures that I have proposed are at best partial and incomplete. They have an end appropriate to a negative good: a distribution of hard work that doesn't corrupt the distributive spheres with which it overlaps, carrying poverty into the sphere of money, degradation into the sphere of honor, weakness and resignation into the sphere of power. To rule out negative dominance: that is the purpose of collective bargaining, cooperative management, professional conflict, the rectification of names—the politics of hard work. The outcomes of this politics are indeterminate, certain to be different in different times and places, conditioned by previously established hierarchies and social understandings. But they will also be conditioned by the solidarity, the skillfulness, and the energy of the workers themselves.

NOTES

1. Arthur Okun, *Equality and Efficiency: The Big Tradeoff* (Washington, D.C., 1975), pp. 6ff.
2. Ibid., p. 20.
3. George Orwell, *The Road to Wigan Pier* (New York, 1958), p. 44.
4. Ibid., pp. 32–33.
5. George Bernard Shaw, *The Intelligent Woman's Guide to Socialism, Capitalism, Sovietism, and Fascism* (Hammondsworth, England, 1937).
6. Ibid., p. 109.
7. Stewart E. Perry, *San Francisco Scavengers* (Berkeley, 1978).
8. Ibid., p. 8.
9. Ibid., pp. 188–91.
10. Studs Terkel *Working* (New York, 1975), p. 168.
11. Bernard Shaw, "Maxims for Revolutionists," *Man and Superman*, in *Seven Plays* (New York, 1951), p. 736.
12. W.H. Auden, "In Time of War" (XXV), in *The English Auden: Poems, Essays, and Dramatic Writings 1927–1939*, ed. Edward Mendelson (New York, 1978), p. 261.
13. Everett Hughes, *The Sociological Eye* (Chicago, 1971), p. 345.
14. Ibid., p. 314.

REVIEW AND DISCUSSION QUESTIONS

1. What are the different sorts of "blocked exchanges" that Walzer describes?
2. What is the proper sphere of the market?
3. How does Walzer distinguish hard, dangerous, and dirty work?
4. What is the Sunset Scavenger Company? How does it work?
5. What reforms does Walzer propose in how our society understands and distributes work?

Essay and Paper Topics for Section 9

1. Compare the three differing conceptions of the social contract presented by Hobbes, Locke, and Rawls.

2. Using the idea of the basic structure, explain how Rawls might respond to Nozick's Chamberlain example. Would Rawlsian contractors accept Nozick's entitlement principle? Explain.

3. Compare Rawls's view of equality with that of Peter Singer.

4. Compare the views of Locke and Singer on the relationship between humans and the natural environment. Can social contract theory provide an adequate account of human obligations to animals and to nature? Explain.

5. Compare the essays by Walzer and Rachels. Would Walzer accept Rachels's claim that economic income should be distributed according to desert? Explain.

6. Compare Nozick's approach to economic justice and property rights with that of Marx and Engels, focusing on the ideas of exploitation and self-ownership.

10

Civil Disobedience and the Rule of Law

Law surrounds us from before we are born until long after we are dead. It limits what we may do to others, and what they may do to us. It decides if we are to be born, whether we attend school, what our jobs are like, who we marry, and how we die. It also punishes us when we violate the law, even though we may sometimes believe the law to be unjust. Essays in this section address a range of interrelated problems about legal obligation and the ideal of the rule of law, including the basis of legal obligation, the justification of rights against government, whether civil disobedience is justified, the nature and importance of the rule of law, how officials should handle persons who break laws they believe are unjust, and the nature of law itself. The section begins with probably the most famous, and certainly one of the earliest, discussions of the basis of legal obligation.

Crito

Plato

Plato was born into an aristocratic family in Athens around 427 B.C. Socrates (470–399 B.C.) was a friend of Plato's family from the time Plato was a schoolboy. Although a young Athenian of Plato's class would normally have pursued a political career, Plato chose philosophy instead. He achieved great fame as Socrates' most talented student and one of the world's greatest philosophers. In 387 B.C., Plato founded the Academy, a school of higher education and research (which existed for more than 900 years), and he was its head until his death in 347 B.C. at the age of eighty. Plato wrote some twenty-five dialogues, including "Crito" and the book-length *Republic.*

"Crito" begins after Socrates has been condemned to death for corrupting the youth of Athens through his teaching. Friends try to convince Socrates to allow them to save his life by breaking him out of jail, but Socrates will agree only if he can be convinced that violating the law would be just. "Crito" thus sets the stage for centuries of debate over the nature and extent of legal obligation. (Socrates, in fact, refused to disobey and was executed.)

From *The Dialogues of Plato,* 3rd ed., trans. Benjamin Jowett (London: Oxford University Press, 1892).

SCENE: THE PRISON OF SOCRATES

Socrates: Dear Crito, . . . I am and always have been one of those natures who must be guided by reason, whatever the reason may be which upon reflection appears to me to be the best; and now that this fortune has come upon me, I can not put away the reasons which I have before given: the principles which I have hitherto honored and revered I still honor, and unless we can find other and better principles on the instant, I am certain not to agree with you; no, not even if the power of the multitude could inflict many more imprisonments, confiscations, deaths, frightening us like children with hobgoblin terrors. But what will be the fairest way of considering the question? Shall I return to your old argument about the opinions of men some of which are to be regarded, and others, as we were saying, are not to be regarded? Now were we right in maintaining this before I was condemned? And has the argument which was once good now proved to be talk for the sake of talking;—in fact an amusement only, and altogether vanity? That is what I want to consider with your help, Crito:— whether, under my present circumstances, the argument appears to be in any way different or not; and is to be allowed by me or disallowed. That argument, which, as I believe, is maintained by many who assume to be authorities, was to the effect, as I was saying, that the opinions of some men are to be regarded, and of other men not to be regarded. Now you, Crito, are a disinterested person who is not going to die tomorrow—at least, there is no human probability of this, and you are therefore not liable to be deceived by the circumstances in which you are placed. Tell me then, whether I am right in saying that some opinions, and the opinions of some men only, are to be valued, and other opinions and the opinions of other men, are not to be valued. I ask you whether I was right in maintaining this?

Crito: Certainly.

Socrates: Very good; and is not this true, Crito, of other things which we need not separately enumerate? In the matter of just and unjust, fair and foul, good and evil, which are the subjects of our present consultation, ought we to follow the opinion of the many and to fear them; or the opinion of the one man who has understanding, and whom we ought to fear and reverence more than all the rest of the world: and whom deserting we shall destroy and injure that principle in us which may be assumed to be improved by justice and deteriorated by injustice;—is there not such a principle?

Crito: Certainly there is, Socrates.

Socrates: Take a parallel instance:—if, acting under the advice of men who have no understanding, we destroy that which is improvable by health and deteriorated by disease—when that has been destroyed, I say, would life be worth having? And that is—the body?

Crito: Yes.

Socrates: Could we live, having an evil and corrupted body?

Crito: Certainly not.

Socrates: And will life be worth having, if that higher part of man be depraved, which is improved by justice and deteriorated by injustice? Do we suppose that principle, whatever it may be in man, which has to do with justice and injustice, to be inferior to the body?

Crito: Certainly not.

Socrates: More honored, then?

Crito: Far more honored.

Socrates: Then, my friend, we must not regard what the many say of us; but what he, the one man who has understanding of just and unjust, will say, and what the truth will say. And therefore you begin in error when you suggest that we should regard the opinion of the many about just and unjust, good and evil, honorable and dishonorable.—Well, some one will say, "but the many can kill us."

Crito: Yes, Socrates; that will clearly be the answer.

Socrates: That is true: but still I find with surprise that the old argument is, as I conceive, unshaken as ever. And I should like to know whether I may say the same of another proposition—that not life, but a good life, is to be chiefly valued?

Crito: Yes, that also remains.

Socrates: And a good life is equivalent to a just and honorable one—that holds also?

Crito: Yes, that holds.

Socrates: From these premises I proceed to argue the question whether I ought not to try and escape without the consent of the Athenians: and if I am clearly right in escaping, then I will make the attempt; but if not, I will abstain. The other considerations which you mention, of money and loss of character and the duty of educating children, are, as I fear, only the doctrines of the multitude, who would be as ready to call people to life, if they were able, as they are to put them to death—and with as little reason. But now, since the argument has thus far prevailed, the only question which remains to be considered is, whether we shall do rightly either in escaping or in suffering others to aid in our escape and paying them in money and thanks, or whether we shall not do rightly; and if the latter, then death or any other calamity which may ensue on my remaining here must not be allowed to enter into the calculation.

Crito: I think that you are right, Socrates; how then shall we proceed?

Socrates: Let us consider the matter together, and do you either refute me if you can, and I will be convinced; or else cease, my dear friend, from repeating to me that I ought to escape against the wishes of the Athenians: for I am extremely desirous to be persuaded by you, but not against my own better judgment. And now please to consider my first position, and do your best to answer me.

Crito: I will do my best.

Socrates: Are we to say that we are never intentionally to do wrong, or that in one way we ought and in another way we ought not to do wrong, or is doing wrong always evil and dishonorable, as I was just now saying, and as has been already acknowledged by us? Are all our former admissions which were made within a few days to be thrown away? And have we, at our age, been earnestly discoursing with one another all our life long only to discover that we are no better than children? Or are we to rest assured, in spite of the opinion of the many, and in spite of consequences whether better or worse, of the truth of what was then said, that injustice is always an evil and dishonor to him who acts unjustly? Shall we affirm that?

Crito: Yes.

Socrates: Then we must do no wrong?

Crito: Certainly not.

Socrates: Nor when injured injure in return, as the many imagine; for we must injure no one at all?

Crito: Clearly not.

Socrates: Again, Crito, may we do evil?

Crito: Surely not, Socrates.

Socrates: And what of doing evil in return for evil, which is the morality of the many—is that just or not?

Crito: Not just.

Socrates: For doing evil to another is the same as injuring him?

Crito: Very true.

Socrates: Then we ought not to retaliate or render evil for evil to any one, whatever evil we may have suffered from him. But I would have you consider, Crito, whether you really mean what you are saying. For this opinion has never been held, and never will be held, by any considerable number of persons; and those who are agreed and those who are not agreed upon this point have no common ground, and can only despise one another when they see how widely they differ. Tell me, then, whether you agree with and assent to my first principle, that neither injury nor retaliation nor warding off evil by evil is ever right. And shall that be the premise of our argument? Or do you decline and dissent from this? For this has been of old and is still my opinion; but, if you are of another opinion, let me hear what you have to say. If, however, you remain of the same mind as formerly, I will proceed to the next step.

Crito: You may proceed, for I have not changed my mind.

Socrates: Then I will proceed to the next step, which may be put in the form of a question:—Ought a man to do what he admits to be right, or ought he to betray the right?

Crito: He ought to do what he thinks right.

Socrates: But if this is true, what is the application? In leaving the prison against the will of the Athenians, do I wrong any? Or rather do I not wrong those whom I ought least to wrong? Do I not desert the principles which were acknowledged by us to be just? What do you say?

Crito: I can not tell, Socrates, for I do not know.

Socrates: Then consider the matter in this way:—Imagine that I am about to play truant (you may call the proceeding by any name which you like), and the laws and the government come and interrogate me: "Tell us, Socrates," they say; "what are you about? Are you going by an act of yours to overturn us— the laws and the whole state, as far as in you lies? Do you imagine that a state can subsist and not be overthrown, in which the decisions of law have no power, but are set aside and overthrown by individuals?" What will be our answer, Crito, to these and the like words? Any one, and especially a clever rhetorician, will have a good deal to urge about the evil of setting aside the law which requires a sentence to be carried out; and we might reply, "Yes; but the state has injured us and given an unjust sentence." Suppose I say that?

Crito: Very good, Socrates.

Socrates: "And was that our agreement with you?" the law would say; "or were you to abide by the sentence of the state?" And if I were to express astonishment at their saying this, the law would probably add: "Answer, Socrates, instead of opening your eyes: you are in the habit of asking and answering questions. Tell us what complaint you have to make against us which justifies you in attempting to destroy us and the state? In the first place did we not bring you into existence? Your father married your mother by our aid and begat you. Say whether you have any objection to urge against those of us who regulate marriage?" None, I should reply. "Or against those of us who regulate the system of nurture and education of children in which you were trained? Were not the laws, who have the charge of this, right in commanding your father to train you in music

and gymnastic?" Right, I should reply, "Well then, since you were brought into the world and nurtured and educated by us, can you deny in the first place that you are our child and slave, as your fathers were before you? And if this is true you are not on equal terms with us; nor can you think that you have a right to do to us what we are doing to you. Would you have any right to strike or revile or do any other evil to a father or to your master, if you had one, when you have been struck or reviled by him, or received some other evil at his hands?—you would not say this? And because we think right to destroy you, do you think that you have any right to destroy us in return, and your country as far as in you lies? And will you, O professor of true virtue, say that you are justified in this? Has a philosopher like you failed to discover that our country is more to be valued and higher and holier far than mother or father or any ancestor, and more to be regarded in the eyes of the gods and of men of understanding? Also to be soothed, and gently and reverently entreated when angry, even more than a father, and if not persuaded, obeyed? And when we are punished by her, whether with imprisonment or stripes, the punishment is to be endured in silence; and if she lead us to wounds or death in battle, thither we follow as is right; neither may any one yield or retreat or leave his rank, but whether in battle or in a court of law, or in any other place, he must do what his city and his country order him; or he must change their view of what is just: and if he may do no violence to his father or mother, much less may he do violence to his country." What answer shall we make to this, Crito? Do the laws speak truly, or do they not?

Crito: I think that they do.

Socrates: Then the laws will say: "Consider, Socrates, if this is true, that in your present attempt you are going to do us wrong. For, after having brought you into the world, and nurtured and educated you, and given you and every other citizen a share in every good that we had to give, we further proclaim and give the right to every Athenian, that if he does not like us when he has come of age and has seen the ways of the city, and made our acquaintance, he may go where he pleases and take his goods with him; and none of us laws will forbid him or interfere with him. Any of you who does not like us and the city, and who wants to go to a colony or to any other city, may go where he likes, and take his goods with him. But he who has experience of the manner in which we order justice and administer the state, and still remains, has entered into an implied contract that he will do as we command him. And he who disobeys us is, as we maintain, thrice wrong; first, because in disobeying us he is disobeying his parents; secondly, because we are the authors of his education; thirdly, because he has made an agreement with us that he will duly obey our commands; and he neither obeys them nor convinces us that our commands are wrong; and we do not rudely impose them, but give them the alternative of obeying or convincing us;—that is what we offer, and he does neither. These are the sort of accusations to which, as we were saying, you, Socrates, will be exposed if you accomplish your intentions; you, above all other Athenians." Suppose I ask, why is this? they will justly retort upon me that I above all other men have acknowledged the agreement. "There is clear proof," they will say, "Socrates, that we and the city were not displeasing to you. Of all Athenians you have been the most constant resident in the city, which, as you never leave, you may be supposed to love. For you never went out of the city either to see the games, except once when you went to the Isthmus, or to any other place unless you were on military service; nor did you travel as other men do. Nor had you any curiosity to know other states or their laws: your affections did not go beyond us and our state; we were your special favorites, and you acquiesced in our government of you; and this is the state in which you begat your children, which is a proof of your satisfaction. Moreover, you might, if you had liked, have fixed the penalty at banishment in the course of the trial—the state which refuses to let you go now would have let you go then. But you

pretended that you preferred death to exile, and that you were not grieved at death. And now you have forgotten these fine sentiments, and pay no respect to us the laws, of whom you are the destroyer; and are doing what only a miserable slave would do, running away and turning your back upon the compacts and agreements which you made as a citizen. And first of all answer this very question: Are we right in saying that you agreed to be governed according to us in deed, and not in word only? Is that true or not?" How shall we answer that, Crito? Must we not agree?

Crito: There is no help, Socrates.

Socrates: Then will they not say: "You, Socrates, are breaking the covenants and agreements which you made with us at your leisure, not in any haste or under any compulsion or deception, but having had seventy years to think of them, during which time you were at liberty to leave the city, if we were not to your mind, or if our covenants appeared to you to be unfair. You had your choice, and might have gone either to Lacedaemon or Crete, which you often praise for their good government, or to some other Hellenic or foreign state. Whereas you, above all other Athenians, seemed to be so fond of the state, or, in other words, of us her laws (for who would like a state that has no laws), that you never stirred out of her; the halt, the blind, the maimed were not more stationary in her than you were. And now you run away and forsake your agreements. Not so, Socrates, if you will take our advice; do not make yourself ridiculous by escaping out of the city.

"Listen, then, Socrates, to us who have brought you up. Think not of life and children first, and of justice afterwards, but of justice first, that you may be justified before the princes of the world below. For neither will you nor any that belong to you be happier or holier or juster in this life, or happier in another, if you do as Crito bids. Now you depart in innocence, a sufferer and not a doer of evil; a victim, not of the laws, but of men. But if you go forth, returning evil for evil, and injury for injury, breaking the covenants and agreements which you have made with us, and wronging those whom you ought least to wrong, that is to say, yourself, your friends, your country, and us, we shall be angry with you while you live, and our brethren, and laws in the world below, will receive you as an enemy; for they will know that you have done your best to destroy us. Listen, then, to us and not to Crito."

This is the voice which I seem to hear murmuring in my ears, like the sound of the flute in the ears of the mystic; that voice, I say, is humming in my ears, and prevents me from hearing any other. And I know that anything more which you may say will be vain. Yet speak, if you have anything to say.

Crito: I have nothing to say, Socrates.

Socrates: Then let me follow the intimations of the will of God.

REVIEW AND DISCUSSION QUESTIONS

1. Elaborate on Socrates' notion that the law is like a parent and so deserves obedience from its citizens.
2. Sometimes we can lead others to expect us to behave in a certain way even though we never overtly promise to do so. Give an example of such behavior, and then discuss whether Socrates has done anything that can fairly be interpreted as leading others to expect him to obey the law.
3. At his trial, Socrates made an argument in his own defense. Is that relevant to the present issue?
4. Obviously, Socrates has benefited from living in Athens, and has gladly accepted these benefits. Does that constitute an "implied contract" to obey?
5. What is gratitude? Does Socrates think part of his obligation to remain and serve his sentence is based on gratitude? Explain.

Taking Rights Seriously

Ronald Dworkin

Rights are central to many of our political and moral discussions: we often find ourselves disagreeing about the limits of free speech and religion, as well as the rights of the unborn, the environment, minorities, the terminally ill, the victims of crimes, and animals, to mention only a few examples. The legitimate role of governments, we also often say, is in part defined by rights. But what does it mean to say that an individual has a right, as opposed to something being the right thing for that person to do? And what must government do if it is to respect the rights of its citizens? Ronald Dworkin discusses these questions in detail, arguing that rights are like trump cards citizens hold against their government, sometimes justifying their claim to break the law. Rights can be exercised even when it is not in the collective public interest for citizens to do so; rights thus rest on a model that places the dignity of the individual at center stage. Dworkin concludes this essay with a discussion of whether it is wise for government to take rights seriously, given the social costs of doing so. Ronald Dworkin teaches philosophy and law at London University and at New York University.

From Ronald Dworkin, *Taking Rights Seriously* (Cambridge: Harvard University Press, 1977), pp. 184–205. Reprinted by permission of the author.

1. THE RIGHTS OF CITIZENS

The language of rights now dominates political debate in the United States. Does the Government respect the moral and political rights of its citizens? Or does the Government's foreign policy, or its race policy, fly in the face of these rights? Do the minorities whose rights have been violated have the right to violate the law in return? Or does the silent majority itself have rights, including the right that those who break the law be punished? It is not surprising that these questions are now prominent. The concept of rights, and particularly the concept of rights against the Government, has its most natural use when a political society is divided, and appeals to co-operation or a common goal are pointless.

The debate does not include the issue of whether citizens have *some* moral rights against their Government. It seems accepted on all sides that they do. Conventional lawyers and politicians take it as a point of pride that our legal system recognizes, for example, individual rights of free speech, equality, and due process. They base their claim that our law deserves respect, at least in part, on that fact, for they would not claim that totalitarian systems deserve the same loyalty.

I shall not be concerned, in this essay, to defend the thesis that citizens have moral rights against their governments; I want instead to explore the implications of that thesis for those, including the present United States Government, who profess to accept it.

It is much in dispute, of course, what *particular* rights citizens have. Does the acknowledged right to free speech, for example, include the right to participate in nuisance demonstrations? In practice the Government will have the last word on what an individual's rights are, because its police will do what its officials and courts say. But that does not mean that the Government's view is necessarily the correct view; anyone who thinks it does must believe that men and women have only such moral rights as Government chooses to grant, which means that they have no moral rights at all.

All this is sometimes obscured in the United States by the constitutional system. The American Constitution provides a set of individual *legal* rights in the First Amendment, and in the due process, equal protection, and similar clauses. Under present legal practice the Supreme Court has the power to declare an act of Congress or of a state legislature void if the Court finds that the act offends these provisions. This practice has led some commentators to suppose that individual moral rights are fully protected by this system, but that is hardly so, nor could it be so.

The Constitution fuses legal and moral issues, by making the validity of a law depend on the answer to complex moral problems, like the problem of whether a particular statute respects the inherent equality of all men. This fusion has important consequences for the debates about civil disobedience; I have described these elsewhere[1] and I shall refer to them later. But it leaves open two prominent questions. It does not tell us whether the Constitution, even properly interpreted, recognizes all the moral rights that citizens have, and it does not tell us whether, as many suppose, citizens would have a duty to obey the law even if it did invade their moral rights.

Even if the Constitution were perfect, of course, and the majority left it alone, it would not follow that the Supreme Court could guarantee the individual rights of citizens. A Supreme Court decision is still a legal decision, and it must take into account precedent and institutional considerations like relations between the Court and Congress, as well as morality. And no judicial decision is necessarily the right decision. Judges stand for different positions on controversial issues of law and morals and, as the fights over Nixon's Supreme Court nominations showed, a President is entitled to appoint judges of his own persuasion, provided that they are honest and capable.

So, though the Constitutional system adds something to the protection of moral rights against the Government, it falls far short of guaranteeing these rights, or even establishing what they are.

2. RIGHTS AND THE RIGHT TO BREAK THE LAW

In most cases when we say that someone has a "right" to do something, we imply that it would be wrong to interfere with his doing it, or at least that some special grounds are needed for justifying any interference. I use this strong sense of right when I say that you have the right to spend your money gambling, if you wish, though you ought to spend it in a more worthwhile way. I mean it would be wrong for anyone to interfere with you even though you propose to spend your money in a way that I think is wrong.

There is a clear difference between saying that someone has a right to do something in this sense and saying that it is the "right" thing for him to do, or that he does no "wrong" in doing it. Someone may have the right to do something that is the wrong thing for him to do, as might be the case with gambling. Conversely, something may be the right thing for him to do and yet he may have no right to do it, in the sense that it would not be wrong for someone to interfere with his trying. If our army captures an enemy soldier, we might say that the right thing for him to do is to try to escape, but it would not follow that it is wrong for us to try to stop him. We might admire him for trying to escape, and perhaps even think less of him if he did not. But there is no suggestion here that it is wrong of us to stand in his way; on the contrary, if we think our cause is just, we think it right for us to do all we can to stop him. . . .

These distinctions enable us to see an ambiguity in the orthodox question: Does a man ever have a right to break the law? Does that question mean to ask whether he ever has a right to break the law in the strong sense, so that the Government would do wrong to stop him, by arresting and prosecuting him? Or does it mean to ask whether he

ever does the right thing to break the law, so that we should all respect him even though the Government should jail him?

Conservatives and liberals do agree that sometimes a man does not do the wrong thing to break a law, when his conscience so requires. They disagree, when they do, over the different issue of what the State's response should be. Both parties do think that sometimes the State should prosecute. But this is not inconsistent with the proposition that the man prosecuted did the right thing in breaking the law. . . .

I said that in the United States citizens are supposed to have certain fundamental rights against their Government, certain moral rights made into legal rights by the Constitution. If this idea is significant, and worth bragging about, then these rights must be rights in the strong sense I just described. The claim that citizens have a right to free speech must imply that it would be wrong for the Government to stop them from speaking, even when the Government believes that what they will say will cause more harm than good. The claim cannot mean, on the prisoner-of-war analogy, only that citizens do no wrong in speaking their minds, though the Government reserves the right to prevent them from doing so.

This is a crucial point, and I want to labour it. Of course a responsible government must be ready to justify anything it does, particularly when it limits the liberty of its citizens. But normally it is a sufficient justification, even for an act that limits liberty, that the act is calculated to increase what the philosophers call general utility—that it is calculated to produce more over-all benefit than harm. So, though the New York City Government needs a justification for forbidding motorists to drive up Lexington Avenue, it is sufficient justification if the proper officials believe, on sound evidence, that the gain to the many will outweigh the inconvenience to the few. When individual citizens are said to have rights against the Government, however, like the right of free speech, that must mean that this sort of justification is not enough. Otherwise the claim would not argue that individuals have special protection against the law when their rights are in play, and that is just the point of the claim.

Not all legal rights, or even Constitutional rights, represent moral rights against the Government. I now have the legal right to drive either way on Fifty-seventh Street, but the Government would do no wrong to make that street one-way if it thought it in the general interest to do so. I have a Constitutional right to vote for a congressman every two years, but the national and state governments would do no wrong if, following the amendment procedure, they made a congressman's term four years instead of two, again on the basis of a judgment that this would be for the general good.

But those Constitutional rights that we call fundamental, like the right of free speech, are supposed to represent rights against the Government in the strong sense; that is the point of the boast that our legal system respects the fundamental rights of the citizen. If citizens have a moral right of free speech, then governments would do wrong to repeal the First Amendment that guarantees it, even if they were persuaded that the majority would be better off if speech were curtailed.

I must not overstate the point. Someone who claims that citizens have a right against the Government need not go so far as to say that the State is *never* justified in overriding that right. He might say, for example, that although citizens have a right to free speech, the Government may override that right when necessary to protect the rights of others, or to prevent a catastrophe, or even to obtain a clear and major public benefit (though if he acknowledged this last as a possible justification he would be treating the right in question as not among the most important or fundamental). What he cannot do is to say that the Government is justified in overriding a right on the minimal grounds that would be sufficient if no such right existed. He cannot say that the Government is entitled to act on no more than a judgment that its act is likely to produce, overall, a benefit to the community.

That admission would make his claim of a right pointless, and would show him to be using some sense of "right" other than the strong sense necessary to give his claim the political importance it is normally taken to have. . . .

I said that any society that claims to recognize rights at all must abandon the notion of a general duty to obey the law that holds in all cases. This is important, because it shows that there are no short cuts to meeting a citizen's claim to right. If a citizen argues that he has a moral right not to serve in the Army, or to protest in a way he finds effective, then an official who wants to answer him, and not simply bludgeon him into obedience, must respond to the particular point he makes, and cannot point to the draft law or a Supreme Court decision as having even special, let alone decisive, weight. Sometimes an official who considers the citizen's moral arguments in good faith will be persuaded that the citizen's claim is plausible, or even right. It does not follow, however, that he will always be persuaded or that he always should be.

I must emphasize that all these propositions concern the strong sense of right, and they therefore leave open important questions about the right thing to do. If a man believes he has the right to break the law, he must then ask whether he does the right thing to exercise that right. He must remember that reasonable men can differ about whether he has a right against the Government, and therefore the right to break the law, that he thinks he has; and therefore that reasonable men can oppose him in good faith. He must take into account the various consequences his acts will have, whether they involve violence, and such other considerations as the context makes relevant; he must not go beyond the rights he can in good faith claim, to acts that violate the rights of others. . . .

3. CONTROVERSIAL RIGHTS

The argument so far has been hypothetical: if a man has a particular moral right against the Government, that right survives contrary legislation or adjudication. But this does not tell us what rights he has, and it is notorious that reasonable men disagree about that. There is wide agreement on certain clear-cut cases; almost everyone who believes in rights at all would admit, for example, that a man has a moral right to speak his mind in a nonprovocative way on matters of political concern, and that this is an important right that the State must go to great pains to protect. But there is great controversy as to the limits of such paradigm rights, and the so-called "anti-riot" law involved in the famous Chicago Seven trial is a case in point.

The defendants were accused of conspiring to cross state lines with the intention of causing a riot. This charge is vague—perhaps unconstitutionally vague—but the law apparently defines as criminal emotional speeches which argue that violence is justified in order to secure political equality. Does the right of free speech protect this sort of speech? That, of course, is a legal issue, because it invokes the free-speech clause of the First Amendment of the Constitution. But it is also a moral issue, because, as I said, we must treat the First Amendment as an attempt to protect a moral right. It is part of the job of governing to "define" moral rights through statutes and judicial decisions, that is, to declare officially the extent that moral rights will be taken to have in law. Congress faced this task in voting on the anti-riot bill, and the Supreme Court has faced it in countless cases. How should the different departments of government go about defining moral rights?

They should begin with a sense that whatever they decide might be wrong. History and their descendants may judge that they acted unjustly when they thought they were right. If they take their duty seriously, they must try to limit their mistakes, and they must therefore try to discover where the dangers of mistake lie.

They might choose one of two very different models for this purpose. The first model recommends striking a balance between the rights of the individual and the demands of society at large. If the Government *infringes*

on a moral right (for example, by defining the right of free speech more narrowly than justice requires), then it has done the individual a wrong. On the other hand, if the Government *inflates* a right (by defining it more broadly than justice requires) then it cheats society of some general benefit, like safe streets, that there is no reason it should not have. So a mistake on one side is as serious as a mistake on the other. The course of government is to steer to the middle, to balance the general good and personal rights, giving to each its due. . . .

The first model, described in this way, has great plausibility, and most laymen and lawyers, I think, would respond to it warmly. The metaphor of balancing the public interest against personal claims is established in our political and judicial rhetoric, and this metaphor gives the model both familiarity and appeal. Nevertheless, the first model is a false one, certainly in the case of rights generally regarded as important, and the metaphor is the heart of its error.

The institution of rights against the Government is not a gift of God, or an ancient ritual, or a national sport. It is a complex and troublesome practice that makes the Government's job of securing the general benefit more difficult and more expensive, and it would be frivolous and wrongful practice unless it served some point. Anyone who professes to take rights seriously, and who praises our Government for respecting them, must have some sense of what that point is. He must accept, at the minimum, one or both of two important ideas. The first is the vague but powerful idea of human dignity. This idea, associated with Kant, but defended by philosophers of different schools, supposes that there are ways of treating a man that are inconsistent with recognizing him as a full member of the human community, and holds that such treatment is profoundly unjust.

The second is the more familiar idea of political equality. This supposes that the weaker members of a political community are entitled to the same concern and respect of their government as the more powerful members have secured for themselves, so that if some men have freedom of decision whatever the effect on the general good, then all men must have the same freedom. I do not want to defend or elaborate these ideas here, but only to insist that anyone who claims that citizens have rights must accept ideas very close to these.[2]

It makes sense to say that a man has a fundamental right against the Government, in the strong sense, like free speech, if that right is necessary to protect his dignity, or his standing as equally entitled to concern and respect, or some other personal value of like consequence. It does not make sense otherwise.

So if rights make sense at all, then the invasion of a relatively important right must be a very serious matter. It means treating a man as less than a man, or as less worthy of concern than other men. The institution of rights rests on the conviction that this is a grave injustice, and that it is worth paying the incremental cost in social policy or efficiency that is necessary to prevent it. But then it must be wrong to say that inflating rights is as serious as invading them. If the Government errs on the side of the individual, then it simply pays a little more in social efficiency than it has to pay; it pays a little more, that is, of the same coin that it has already decided must be spent. But if it errs against the individual it inflicts an insult upon him that, on its own reckoning, it is worth a great deal of that coin to avoid.

So the first model is indefensible. It rests, in fact, on a mistake I discussed earlier, namely the confusion of society's rights with the rights of members of society. "Balancing" is appropriate when the Government must choose between competing claims of right— between the Southerner's claim to freedom of association, for example, and the black man's claim to an equal education. The Government can do nothing but estimate the merits of the competing claims, and act on its estimate. The first model assumes that the "right" of the majority is a competing right that must be balanced in this way; but that, as I argued before, is a confusion that threatens to destroy the concept of individual rights. It

is worth noticing that the community rejects the first model in that area where the stakes for the individual are highest, the criminal process. We say that it is better that a great many guilty men go free than that one innocent man be punished, and that homily rests on the choice of the second model for government.

The second model treats abridging a right as much more serious than inflating one, and its recommendations follow from that judgment. It stipulates that once a right is recognized in clear-cut cases, then the Government should act to cut off that right only when some compelling reason is presented, some reason that is consistent with the suppositions on which the original right must be based. It cannot be an argument for curtailing a right, once granted, simply that society would pay a further price for extending it. There must be something special about that further cost, or there must be some other feature of the case, that makes it sensible to say that although great social cost is warranted to protect the original right, this particular cost is not necessary. Otherwise, the Government's failure to extend the right will show that its recognition of the right in the original case is a sham, a promise that it intends to keep only until that becomes inconvenient.

How can we show that a particular cost is not worth paying without taking back the initial recognition of a right? I can think of only three sorts of grounds that can consistently be used to limit the definition of a particular right. First, the Government might show that the values protected by the original right are not really at stake in the marginal case, or are at stake only in some attenuated form. Second, it might show that if the right is defined to include the marginal case, then some competing right, in the strong sense I described earlier, would be abridged. Third, it might show that if the right were so defined, then the cost to society would not be simply incremental, but would be of a degree far beyond the cost paid to grant the original right, a degree great enough to justify whatever assault on dignity or equality might be involved. . . .

But what of the individual rights of those who will be destroyed by a riot, of the passer-by who will be killed by a sniper's bullet or the shop-keeper who will be ruined by looting? To put the issue in this way, as a question of competing rights, suggests a principle that would undercut the effect of uncertainty. Shall we say that some rights to protection are so important that the Government is justified in doing all it can to maintain them? Shall we therefore say that the Government may abridge the rights of others to act when their acts might simply increase the risk, by however slight or speculative a margin, that some person's right to life or property will be violated?

Some such principle is relied on by those who oppose the Supreme Court's recent liberal rulings on police procedure. These rulings increase the chance that a guilty man will go free, and therefore marginally increase the risk that any particular member of the community will be murdered, raped, or robbed. Some critics believe that the Court's decision must therefore be wrong.

But no society that purports to recognize a variety of rights, on the ground that a man's dignity or equality may be invaded in a variety of ways, can accept such a principle. If forcing a man to testify against himself, or forbidding him to speak, does the damage that the rights against self-incrimination and the right of free speech assume, then it would be contemptuous for the State to tell a man that he must suffer this damage against the possibility that other men's risk of loss may be marginally reduced. If rights make sense, then the degrees of their importance cannot be so different that some count not at all when others are mentioned.

Of course the Government may discriminate and may stop a man from exercising his right to speak when there is a clear and substantial risk that his speech will do great damage to the person or property of others, and no other means of preventing this are at hand, as in the case of the man shouting "Fire!" in a theater. But we must reject the suggested principle that the Government can simply ignore rights to speak when life and property are in question. So long as the impact of speech on these other rights remains speculative and marginal, it must look elsewhere for levers to pull.

4. WHY TAKE RIGHTS SERIOUSLY?

I said at the beginning of this essay that I wanted to show what a government must do that professes to recognize individual rights. It must dispense with the claim that citizens never have a right to break its laws, and it must not define citizens' rights so that these are cut off for supposed reasons of the general good. Any Government's harsh treatment of civil disobedience, or campaign against vocal protest, may therefore be thought to count against its sincerity.

One might well ask, however, whether it is wise to take rights all that seriously after all. . . .

[Former Vice President] Spiro Agnew supposed that rights are divisive, and that national unity and a new respect for law may be developed by taking them more skeptically. But he [was] wrong. America will continue to be divided by its social and foreign policy, and if the economy grows weaker again the divisions will become more bitter. If we want our laws and our legal institutions to provide the ground rules within which these issues will be contested, then these ground rules must not be the conqueror's law that the dominant class imposes on the weaker, as Marx supposed the law of a capitalist society must be. The bulk of the law—that part which defines and implements social, economic, and foreign policy—cannot be neutral. It must state, in its greatest part, the majority's view of the common good. The institution of rights is therefore crucial, because it represents the majority's promise to the minorities that their dignity and equality will be respected. When the divisions among the groups are most violent, then this gesture, if law is to work, must be most sincere.

The institution requires an act of faith on the part of the minorities, because the scope of their rights will be controversial whenever they are important, and because the officers of the majority will act on their own notions of what these rights really are. Of course these officials will disagree with many of the claims that a minority makes. That makes it all the more important that they take their decisions gravely. They must show that they understand what rights are, and they must not cheat on the full implications of the doctrine. The Government will not re-establish respect for law without giving the law some claim to respect. It cannot do that if it neglects the one feature that distinguishes law from ordered brutality.

NOTES

1. See "On Not Prosecuting Civil Disobedience" [reprinted in this section].
2. He need not consider these ideas to be axiomatic. He may, that is, have reasons for insisting that dignity or equality are important values, and these reasons may be utilitarian. He may believe, for example, that the general good will be advanced, in the long run, only if we treat indignity or inequality as very great injustices, and never allow our opinions about the general good to justify them. I do not know of any good arguments for or against this sort of "institutional" utilitarianism, but it is consistent with my point, because it argues that we must treat violations of dignity and equality as special moral crimes, beyond the reach of ordinary utilitarian justification.

REVIEW AND DISCUSSION QUESTIONS

1. What does Dworkin mean by "right" in the "strong" sense? In what ways does the U.S. Constitution protect citizens' rights in that sense?
2. Describe the two models that might be used to understand the rights of citizens. Which model does Dworkin find most appealing, and why?
3. Why is the "equal dignity" view of rights more concerned to avoid abridging a basic right than to avoid inflating a right?
4. Has Dworkin responded adequately to the arguments Plato offers in defense of the claim that citizens must obey the law? What do you imagine Plato would say in response to Dworkin's arguments?
5. Consider carefully what Dworkin says in note 2, and compare it with Mill's position. Could Mill agree with Dworkin?

Civil Disobedience and the Social Contract

John Rawls

Ours is a multicultural, diverse society that includes many incompatible visions of the good life, of religion, and of the meaning and purposes of human existence. We also have a tradition of respecting individual rights, as well as a commitment to majority rule. Given that diversity and those commitments, it seems inevitable that there will be conflicts over the nature and extent of rights as well as about the limits on governmental power. Such conflicts can lead to disobedience, and thus to philosophical questions about the basis of legal obligation, the justification of civil disobedience, and, ultimately, the nature of social justice itself.

Few twentieth-century philosophers have had as much influence on our thinking about these issues as John Rawls. His seminal work, *A Theory of Justice* (a selection of which is reprinted in section 9), offers a new and important work in the social contract tradition. Rawls argues that principles governing a constitution and laws enacted under it should be chosen behind a "veil of ignorance" in which people ignore their social class, race, and religion, as well as any other facts that are morally arbitrary and that, if known, would allow the laws to be tailored so as to advantage one group over another. He calls the theory "justice as fairness" because the veil of ignorance (corresponding to the traditional social contract) assures that the chosen principles are fair. Forced to choose a constitution and laws behind such a veil of ignorance, Rawls argues that people would secure for themselves basic rights, assure equality of opportunity, and allow economic inequality only if everybody benefits from it, including the least advantaged.

In the following essay, John Rawls discusses the related questions of legal obligation and civil disobedience, both within the context of social contract theory. Legal obligation, he argues, is based on the duty of fair play. Even assuming the constitution is just, there is no assurance laws enacted in accordance with its procedures will also be just. Nonetheless, Rawls argues, citizens may have an obligation to obey that is based on their having benefited from the (generally) just regime. He concludes with a discussion of the role of civil disobedience in a constitutional democracy, including the circumstances in which it would be justified. John Rawls is emeritus professor of philosophy at Harvard University.

INTRODUCTION

I should like to discuss briefly, and in an informal way, the grounds of civil disobedience in a constitutional democracy. Thus, I shall limit my remarks to the conditions under which we may, by civil disobedience, properly oppose legally established democratic authority; I am not concerned with the situation under other kinds of government nor, except incidentally, with other forms of resistance. My thought is that in a reasonably just (though of course not perfectly just) democratic regime, civil disobedience, when it is justified, is normally to be understood as a political action which addresses the sense of justice of the majority in order to urge reconsideration of the measures protested and to warn that in the firm opinion of the dissenters the conditions of social cooperation are not being honored. This characterization of civil disobedience is intended to apply to dissent on fundamental questions of internal policy, a limitation which I shall follow to simplify our question.

THE SOCIAL CONTRACT DOCTRINE

It is obvious that the justification of civil disobedience depends upon the theory of political obligation in general, and so we may appropriately begin with a few comments on this question. The two chief virtues of social institutions are justice and efficiency, where by the efficiency of institutions I understand their effectiveness for certain social conditions and ends the fulfillment of which is to everyone's advantage. We should comply with and do our part in just and efficient social arrangements for at least two reasons: first of all, we have a natural duty not to oppose the establishment of just and efficient institutions (when they do not yet exist) and to uphold and comply with them (when they do exist); and second, assuming that we have knowingly accepted the benefits of these institutions and plan to continue to do so, and that we have encouraged and expect others to do their part, we also have an obligation to do our share when, as the arrangement requires,

From *Civil Disobedience*, ed. Hugo Bedau (Pegasus, 1969), and *Law and Philosophy*, ed. Sidney Hook (New York: New York University Press, 1968). Reprinted by permission of the author.

it comes our turn. Thus, we often have both a natural duty as well as an obligation to support just and efficient institutions, the obligation arising from our voluntary acts while the duty does not.

Now all this is perhaps obvious enough, but it does not take us very far. Any more particular conclusions depend upon the conception of justice which is the basis of a theory of political obligation. I believe that the appropriate conception, at least for an account of political obligation in a constitutional democracy, is that of the social contract theory from which so much of our political thought derives. If we are careful to interpret it in a suitably general way, I hold that this doctrine provides a satisfactory basis for political theory, indeed even for ethical theory itself, but this is beyond our present concern.[1] The interpretation I suggest is the following: that the principles to which social arrangements must conform, and in particular the principles of justice, are those which free and rational men would agree to in an original position of equal liberty; and similarly, the principles which govern men's relations to institutions and define their natural duties and obligations are the principles to which they would consent when so situated. It should be noted straightway that in this interpretation of the contract theory the principles of justice are understood as the outcome of a hypothetical agreement. They are principles which would be agreed to if the situation of the original position were to arise. There is no mention of an actual agreement nor need such an agreement ever be made. Social arrangements are just or unjust according to whether they accord with the principles for assigning and securing fundamental rights and liberties which would be chosen in the original position. This position is, to be sure, the analytic analogue of the traditional notion of the state of nature, but it must not be mistaken for a historical occasion. Rather it is a hypothetical situation which embodies the basic ideas of the contract doctrine; the description of this situation enables us to work out which principles would be adopted. I must now say something about these matters.

The contract doctrine has always supposed that the persons in the original position have equal powers and rights, that is, that they are symmetrically situated with respect to any arrangements for reaching agreement, and that coalitions and the like are excluded. But it is an essential element (which has not been sufficiently observed although it is implicit in Kant's version of the theory) that there are very strong restrictions on what the contracting parties are presumed to know. In particular, I interpret the theory to hold that the parties do not know their position in society, past, present, or future; nor do they know which institutions exist. Again, they do not know their own place in the distribution of natural talents and abilities, whether they are intelligent or strong, man or woman, and so on. Finally, they do not know their own particular interests and preferences or the system of ends which they wish to advance: they do not know their conception of the good. In all these respects the parties are confronted with a veil of ignorance which prevents any one from being able to take advantage of his good fortune or particular interests or from being disadvantaged by them. What the parties do know (or assume) is that Hume's circumstances of justice obtain: namely, that the bounty of nature is not so generous as to render cooperative schemes superfluous nor so harsh as to make them impossible. Moreover, they assume that the extent of their altruism is limited and that, in general, they do not take an interest in one another's interests. Thus, given the special features of the original position, each man tries to do the best he can for himself by insisting on principles calculated to protect and advance his system of ends whatever it turns out to be.

I believe that as a consequence of the peculiar nature of the original position there would be an agreement on the following two principles for assigning rights and duties and for regulating distributive shares as these are determined by the fundamental institutions of society: first, each person is to have an equal right to the most extensive liberty compatible with a like liberty for all; second, social and economic inequalities (as defined by the institutional structure or fostered by it) are to be arranged so that they are both to everyone's advantage and attached to positions and offices open to all. In view of the content of these two principles and their application to the main institutions of society, and therefore to the social system as a whole, we may regard them as the two principles of justice. Basic social arrangements are just insofar as they conform to these principles, and we can, if we like, discuss questions of justice directly by reference to them. But a deeper understanding of the justification of civil disobedience requires, I think, an account of the derivation of these principles provided by the doctrine of the social contract. Part of our task is to show why this is so.

THE GROUNDS OF COMPLIANCE WITH AN UNJUST LAW

If we assume that in the original position men would agree both to the principle of doing their part when they have accepted and plan to continue to accept the benefits of just institutions (the principle of fairness), and also to the principle of not preventing the establishment of just institutions and of upholding and complying with them when they do exist, then the contract doctrine easily accounts for our having to conform to just institutions. But how does it account for the fact that we are normally required to comply with unjust laws as well? The injustice of a law is not a sufficient ground for not complying with it any more than the legal validity of legislation is always sufficient to require obedience to it. Sometimes one hears these extremes asserted, but I think that we need not take them seriously.

An answer to our question can be given by elaborating the social contract theory in the following way. I interpret it to hold that one is to envisage a series of agreements as follows:

first, men are to agree upon the principles of justice in the original position. Then they are to move to a constitutional convention in which they choose a constitution that satisfies the principles of justice already chosen. Finally they assume the role of a legislative body and guided by the principles of justice enact laws subject to the constraints and procedures of the just constitution. The decisions reached in any stage are binding in all subsequent stages. Now whereas in the original position the contracting parties have no knowledge of their society or of their own position in it, in both a constitutional convention and a legislature they do know certain general facts about their institutions, for example, the statistics regarding employment and output required for fiscal and economic policy. But no one knows particular facts about his own social class or his place in the distribution of natural assets. On each occasion the contracting parties have the knowledge required to make their agreement rational from the appropriate point of view, but not so much as to make them prejudiced. They are unable to tailor principles and legislation to take advantage of their social or natural position; a veil of ignorance prevents their knowing what this position is. With this series of agreements in mind, we can characterize just laws and policies as those which would be enacted were this whole process correctly carried out.

In choosing a constitution the aim is to find among the just constitutions the one which is most likely, given the general facts about the society in question, to lead to just and effective legislation. The principles of justice provide a criterion for the laws desired; the problem is to find a set of political procedures that will give this outcome. I shall assume that, at least under the normal conditions of a modern state, the best constitution is some form of democratic regime affirming equal political liberty and using some sort of majority (or other plurality) rule. Thus it follows that on the contract theory a constitutional democracy of some sort is required by the principles of justice. At the same time it is essential to observe that the constitutional process is always a case of what we may call imperfect procedural justice: that is, there is no feasible political procedure which guarantees that the enacted legislation is just even though we have (let us suppose) a standard for just legislation. In simple cases, such as games of fair division, there are procedures which always lead to the right outcome (assume that equal shares is fair and let the man who cuts the cake take the last piece). These situations are those of perfect procedural justice. In other cases it does not matter what the outcome is as long as the fair procedure is followed: fairness of the process is transferred to the result (fair gambling is an instance of this). These situations are those of pure procedural justice. The constitutional process, like a criminal trial, resembles neither of these; the result matters and we have a standard for it. The difficulty is that we cannot frame a procedure which guarantees that only just and effective legislation is enacted. Thus even under a just constitution unjust laws may be passed and unjust policies enforced. Some form of the majority principle is necessary but the majority may be mistaken, more or less willfully in what it legislates. . . .

LEGAL OBLIGATION AND THE DUTY OF FAIR PLAY

. . . There is, then, the question as to how it can be morally justifiable to acknowledge a constitutional procedure for making legislative enactments when it is certain (for all practical purposes) that laws will be passed that by one's own principles are unjust. It would be impossible for a person to undertake to change his mind whenever he found himself in the minority; it is not impossible, but entirely reasonable, for him to undertake to abide by the enactments made, whatever they are, provided that they are within certain limits. But what more exactly are the conditions of this undertaking?

First of all, it means, as previously suggested, that the constitutional procedure is misinterpreted as a procedure for making legal rules. It is a process of social decision that does not produce a statement to be believed (that B is the best policy) but a rule to be followed. Such a procedure, say involving some form of majority rule, is necessary because it is certain that there will be disagreement on what is the best policy. . . . If one thinks of the constitution as a fundamental part of the scheme of social cooperation, then one can say that if the constitution is just, and if one has accepted the benefits of its working and intends to continue doing so, and if the rule enacted is within certain limits, then one has an obligation, based on the principle of fair play, to obey it when it comes one's turn. In accepting the benefits of a just constitution one becomes bound to it, and in particular one becomes bound to one of its fundamental rules: given a majority vote in behalf of a statute, it is to be enacted and properly implemented.

The principle of fair play may be defined as follows. Suppose there is a mutually beneficial and just scheme of social cooperation, and that the advantages it yields can only be obtained if everyone, or nearly everyone, cooperates. Suppose further that cooperation requires a certain sacrifice from each person, or at least involves a certain restriction of his liberty. Suppose finally that the benefits produced by cooperation are, up to a certain point, free: that is, the scheme of cooperation is unstable in the sense that if any one person knows that all (or nearly all) of the others will continue to do their part, he will still be able to share a gain from the scheme even if he does not do his part. Under these conditions a person who has accepted the benefits of the scheme is bound by a duty of fair play to do his part and not to take advantage of the free benefit by not cooperating. The reason one must abstain from this attempt is that the existence of the benefit is the result of everyone's effort, and prior to some understanding as to how it is to be shared, if it can be shared at all, it belongs in fairness to no one.

Now I want to hold that the obligation to obey the law, as enacted by a constitutional procedure, even when the law seems unjust to us, is a case of the duty of fair play as defined. It is, moreover, an obligation in the more limited sense in that it depends upon our having accepted and our intention to continue accepting the benefits of a just scheme of cooperation that the constitution defines. In this sense it depends on our own voluntary acts. . . .

THE PLACE OF CIVIL DISOBEDIENCE IN A CONSTITUTIONAL DEMOCRACY

We are now in a position to say a few things about civil disobedience. I shall understand it to be a public, nonviolent, and conscientious act contrary to law usually done with the intent to bring about a change in the policies or laws of the government.[2] Civil disobedience is a political act in the sense that it is an act justified by moral principles which define a conception of civil society and the public good. It rests, then, on political conviction as opposed to a search for self or group interest; and in the case of a constitutional democracy, we may assume that this conviction involves the conception of justice (say that expressed by the contract doctrine) which underlies the constitution itself. That is, in a viable democratic regime there is a common conception of justice by reference to which its citizens regulate their political affairs and interpret the constitution. Civil disobedience is a public act which the dissenter believes to be justified by this conception of justice and for this reason it may be understood as addressing the sense of justice of the majority in order to urge reconsideration of the measures protested and to warn that, in the sincere opinion of the dissenters, the conditions of social cooperation are not being honored. For the principles of justice express precisely such conditions, and their persistent and deliberate violation in regard to basic liberties over any extended period of time cuts the ties of community and invites either submission or forceful resistance. By engaging in civil disobedience a minority leads the majority to consider whether it wants to have its acts taken in this way, or whether, in view of the common sense of justice, it wishes to acknowledge the claims of the minority.

Civil disobedience is also civil in another sense. Not only is it the outcome of a sincere conviction based on principles which regulate civil life, but it is public and nonviolent, that is, it is done in a situation where arrest and punishment are expected and accepted without resistance. In this way it manifests a respect for legal procedures. Civil disobedience expresses disobedience to law within the limits of fidelity to law, and this feature of it helps to establish in the eyes of the majority that it is indeed conscientious and sincere, that it really is meant to address their sense of justice.[3] Being completely open about one's acts and being willing to accept the legal consequences of one's conduct is a bond given to make good one's sincerity, for that one's deeds are conscientious is not easy to demonstrate to another or even before oneself. No doubt it is possible to imagine a legal system in which conscientious belief that the law is unjust is accepted as a defense for noncompliance, and men of great honesty who are confident in one another might make such a system work. But as things are such a scheme would be unstable; we must pay a price in order to establish that we believe our actions have a moral basis in the convictions of the community.

The nonviolent nature of civil disobedience refers to the fact that it is intended to address the sense of justice of the majority and as such it is a form of speech, an expression of conviction. To engage in violent acts likely to injure and to hurt is incompatible with civil disobedience as a mode of address. Indeed, an interference with the basic rights of others tends to obscure the civilly disobedient quality of one's act. Civil disobedience is nonviolent in the further sense that the legal penalty for one's action is accepted and that resistance is not (at least for the moment) contemplated. Nonviolence in this sense is to be distinguished from nonviolence as a religious or pacifist principle. While those engaging in civil disobedience have often held some such principle, there is no necessary connection between it and civil disobedience. For on the interpretation suggested, civil disobedience in a democratic society is best understood as an appeal to the principles of justice, the fundamental conditions of willing social cooperation among free men, which in the view of the community as a whole are expressed in the constitution and guide its interpretation. Being an appeal to the moral basis of public life, civil disobedience is a political and not primarily a religious act. It addresses itself to the common principles of justice which men can require one another to follow and not to the aspirations of love which they cannot. Moreover by taking part in civilly disobedient acts one does not foreswear indefinitely the idea of forceful resistance; for if the appeal against injustice is repeatedly denied, then the majority has declared its intention to invite submission or resistance and the latter may conceivably be justified even in a democratic regime. We are not required to acquiesce in the crushing of fundamental liberties by democratic majorities which have shown themselves blind to the principles of justice upon which justification of the constitution depends.

THE JUSTIFICATION
OF CIVIL DISOBEDIENCE

So far we have said nothing about the justification of civil disobedience, that is, the conditions under which civil disobedience may be engaged in consistent with the principles of justice that support a democratic regime. Our task is to see how the characterization of civil disobedience as addressed to the sense of justice of the majority (or to the citizens as a body) determines when such action is justified.

First of all, we may suppose that the normal political appeals to the majority have already been made in good faith and have been rejected, and that the standard means of redress have been tried. Thus, for example, existing political parties are indifferent to the claims of the minority and attempts to repeal the laws protested have been met with further repression since legal institutions are in the control of the majority. While civil disobedience should be recognized, I think, as a form of political action within the limits of fidelity to the rule of law, at the same time it is a rather desperate act just within these limits, and therefore it should, in general, be undertaken as a last resort when standard democratic processes have failed. In this sense it is not a normal political action. When it is justified there has been a serious breakdown; not only is there grave injustice in the law but a refusal more or less deliberate to correct it.

Second, since civil disobedience is a political act addressed to the sense of justice of the majority, it should usually be limited to substantial and clear violations of justice and preferably to those which, if rectified, will establish a basis for doing away with remaining injustices. For this reason there is a presumption in favor of restricting civil disobedience to violations of the first principle of justice, the principle of equal liberty, and to barriers which contravene the second principle, the principle of open offices which protects equality of opportunity. It is not, of course, always easy to tell whether these principles are satisfied. But if we think of them as guaranteeing the fundamental equal political and civil liberties (including freedom of conscience and liberty of thought) and equality of opportunity, then it is often relatively clear whether their principles are being honored. After all, the equal liberties are defined by the visible structure of social institutions; they are to be incorporated into the recognized practice, if not the letter, of social arrangements. When minorities are denied the right to vote or to hold certain political offices, when certain religious groups are repressed and others denied equality of opportunity in the economy, this is often obvious and there is no doubt that justice is not being given. However, the first part of the second principle which requires that inequalities be to everyone's advantage is a much more imprecise and controversial matter. Not only is there a problem of assigning it a determinate and precise sense, but even if we do so and agree on what it should be, there is often a wide variety of reasonable opinion as to whether the principle is satisfied. The reason for this is that the principle applies primarily to fundamental economic and social policies. The choice of these depends upon theoretical and speculative beliefs as well as upon a wealth of concrete information, and all of this mixed with judgment and plain hunch, not to mention in actual cases prejudice and self-interest. Thus unless the laws of taxation are clearly designed to attack a basic equal liberty, they should not be protested by civil disobedience; the appeal to justice is not sufficiently clear and its resolution is best left to the political process. But violations of the equal liberties that define the common status of citizenship are another matter. The deliberate denial of these more or less over any extended period of time in the face of normal political protest is, in general, an appropriate object of civil disobedience. We may think of the social system as divided roughly into two parts, one which incorporates the fundamental equal liberties (including equality of opportunity) and another which embodies social and economic policies properly aimed at promoting the advantage of everyone. As a rule civil disobedience is best limited to the former where the appeal to justice is not only more definite and precise, but where, if it is effective, it tends to correct the injustices in the latter.

Third, civil disobedience should be restricted to those cases where the dissenter is willing to affirm that everyone else similarly subjected to the same degree of injustice has the right to protest in a similar way. That is, we must be prepared to authorize others to dissent in similar situations and in the same way, and to accept the consequences of their doing so. Thus, we may hold, for example, that the widespread disposition to disobey civilly clear violations of fundamental liberties more or less deliberate over an extended period of time would raise the degree of justice throughout society and would insure men's self-esteem as well as their respect for one another. Indeed, I believe this to be true, though certainly it is partly a matter of conjecture. As the contract doctrine emphasizes,

since the principles of justice are principles which we would agree to in an original position of equality when we do not know our social position and the like, the refusal to grant justice is either the denial of the other as an equal (as one in regard to whom we are prepared to constrain our actions by principles which we would consent to) or the manifestation of a willingness to take advantage of natural contingencies and social fortune at his expense. In either case, injustice invites submission or resistance; but submission arouses the contempt of the oppressor and confirms him in his intention. If straightway, after a decent period of time to make reasonable political appeals in the normal way, men were in general to dissent by civil disobedience from infractions of the fundamental equal liberties, these liberties would, I believe, be more rather than less secure. Legitimate civil disobedience properly exercised is a stabilizing device in a constitutional regime, tending to make it more firmly just. . . .

The final condition, of a different nature, is the following. We have been considering when one has a right to engage in civil disobedience, and our conclusion is that one has the right should three conditions hold: when one is subject to injustice more or less deliberate over an extended period of time in the face of normal political protests; where the injustice is a clear violation of the liberties of equal citizenship; and provided that the general disposition to protest similarly in similar cases would have acceptable consequences. These conditions are not, I think, exhaustive but they seem to cover the more obvious points; yet even when they are satisfied and one has the right to engage in civil disobedience, there is still the different question of whether one should exercise this right, that is, whether by doing so one is likely to further one's ends. Having established one's right to protest one is then free to consider these tactical questions. We may be acting within our rights but still foolishly if our action only serves to provoke the harsh retaliation of the majority; and it is likely to do so if the majority lacks a sense of justice or if the action is poorly timed or not well designed to make the appeal to the sense of justice effective. It is easy to think of instances of this sort, and in each case these practical questions have to be faced. From the standpoint of the theory of political obligation we can only say that the exercise of the right should be rational and reasonably designed to advance the protester's aims, and that weighing tactical questions presupposes that one has already established one's right, since tactical advantages in themselves do not support it.

CONCLUSION: SEVERAL OBJECTIONS CONSIDERED

In a reasonably affluent democratic society justice becomes the first virtue of institutions. Social arrangements irrespective of their efficiency must be reformed if they are significantly unjust. No increase in efficiency in the form of greater advantages for many justifies the loss of liberty of a few. That we believe this is shown by the fact that in a democracy the fundamental liberties of citizenship are not understood as the outcome of political bargaining nor are they subject to the calculus of social interests. Rather these liberties are fixed points which serve to limit political transactions and which determine the scope of calculations of social advantage. It is this fundamental place of the equal liberties which makes their systematic violation over any extended period of time a proper object of civil disobedience. For to deny men these rights is to infringe the conditions of social cooperation among free and rational persons, a fact which is evident to the citizens of a constitutional regime since it follows from the principles of justice which underlie their institutions. The justification of civil disobedience rests on the priority of justice and the equal liberties which it guarantees.

It is natural to object to this view of civil disobedience that it relies too heavily upon the existence of a sense of justice. Some may hold that the feeling for justice is not a vital political force, and that what moves men are

various other interests, the desire for wealth, power, prestige, and so on. Now this is a large question the answer to which is highly conjectural and each tends to have his own opinion. But there are two remarks which may clarify what I have said: first, I have assumed that there is in a constitutional regime a common sense of justice the principles of which are recognized to support the constitution and to guide its interpretation. In any given situation particular men may be tempted to violate these principles, but the collective force in their behalf is usually effective since they are seen as the necessary terms of cooperation among free men; and presumably the citizens of a democracy (or sufficiently many of them) want to see justice done. Where these assumptions fail, the justifying conditions for civil disobedience (the first three) are not affected, but the rationality of engaging in it certainly is. In this case, unless the costs of repressing civil dissent injures the economic self-interest (or whatever) of the majority, protest may simply make the position of the minority worse. No doubt as a tactical matter civil disobedience is more effective when its appeal coincides with other interests, but a constitutional regime is not viable in the long run without an attachment to the principles of justice of the sort which we have assumed.

Then, further, there may be a misapprehension about the manner in which a sense of justice manifests itself. There is a tendency to think that it is shown by professions of the relevant principles together with actions of an altruistic nature requiring a considerable degree of self-sacrifice. But these conditions are obviously too strong, for the majority's sense of justice may show itself simply in its being unable to undertake the measures required to suppress the minority and to punish as the law requires the various acts of civil disobedience. The sense of justice undermines the will to uphold unjust institutions, and so a majority despite its superior power may give way. It is unprepared to force the minority to be subject to injustice. Thus, although the majority's action is reluctant and grudging, the role of the sense of justice is nevertheless essential, for without it the majority would have been willing to enforce the law and to defend its position. Once we see the sense of justice as working in this negative way to make established injustices indefensible, then it is recognized as a central element of democratic politics.

Finally, it may be objected against this account that it does not settle the question of who is to say when the situation is such as to justify civil disobedience. And because it does not answer this question, it invites anarchy by encouraging every man to decide the matter for himself. Now the reply to this is that each man must indeed settle this question for himself, although he may, of course, decide wrongly. This is true on any theory of political duty and obligation, at least on any theory compatible with the principles of a democratic constitution. The citizen is responsible for what he does. If we usually think that we should comply with the law, this is because our political principles normally lead to this conclusion. There is a presumption in favor of compliance in the absence of good reasons to the contrary. But because each man is responsible and must decide for himself as best he can whether the circumstances justify civil disobedience, it does not follow that he may decide as he pleases. It is not by looking to our personal interests or to political allegiances narrowly construed, that we should make up our mind. The citizen must decide on the basis of the principles of justice that underlie and guide the interpretation of the constitution and in the light of his sincere conviction as to how these principles should be applied in the circumstances. If he concludes that conditions obtain which justify civil disobedience and conducts himself accordingly, he has acted conscientiously and perhaps mistakenly, but not in any case at his convenience.

In a democratic society each man must act as he thinks the principles of political right require him to. We are to follow our understanding of these principles, and we cannot do otherwise. There can be no morally binding legal interpretation of these principles, not even by a supreme court or legislature. Nor is there any infallible procedure for determining what or who is right. In our system the Supreme Court, Congress, and the President often put forward rival interpretations of the Constitution. Although the Court has the final say in settling any particular case, it is not immune from powerful political influence that may change its reading of the law of the land. The Court presents its point of view by reason and argument; its conception of the Constitution must, if it is to endure, persuade men of its soundness. The final court of appeal is not the Court, or Congress, or the President, but the electorate as a whole. The civilly disobedient appeal in effect to this body. There is no danger of anarchy as long as there is a sufficient working agreement in men's conceptions of political justice and what it requires. That men can achieve such an understanding when the essential political liberties are maintained is the assumption implicit in democratic institutions. There is no way to avoid entirely the risk of divisive strife. But if legitimate civil disobedience seems to threaten civil peace, the responsibility falls not so much on those who protest as upon those whose abuse of authority and power justifies such opposition.

NOTES

1. By the social contract theory, I have in mind the doctrine found in Locke, Rousseau, and Kant.
2. Here I follow H. A. Bedau's definition of civil disobedience. See his "On Civil Disobedience," *Journal of Philosophy* (October 1961).
3. For a fuller discussion on this point, to which I am indebted, see Charles Fried, "Moral Causation," *Harvard Law Review* (1964).

REVIEW AND DISCUSSION QUESTIONS

1. Describe what Rawls means by justice as "fairness."
2. Why does Rawls think that the basic principles used to select a constitution and laws governing citizens' rights and opportunities should be chosen behind a "veil of ignorance"?
3. "Even a just constitution can lead to unjust laws." Explain this statement, using the analogy of a criminal trial.
4. Rawls thinks that the obligation to obey the law (assuming a just constitution) rests on the duty of fair play. Explain what he means.
5. How does Rawls define civil disobedience? What role does civil disobedience play in a constitutional democracy?
6. Under what circumstances does Rawls think civil disobedience is justified?
7. How does Rawls respond to those who suggest his view is naive because it is based on the view that civil disobedience is an appeal to a majority's "sense of justice?"
8. Compare Rawls's conception of civil disobedience with conscientious refusal, on religious grounds, to kill in war.

On Not Prosecuting Civil Disobedience

Ronald Dworkin

Besides legal obligation, civil disobedience raises further philosophical questions about the nature of law itself and whether those who engage in civil disobedience should be prosecuted. Ronald Dworkin begins with a familiar argument, that since society could not function if everybody were allowed to pick and choose the laws that he or she wishes to obey, *fairness* demands uniform prosecution of all acts of civil disobedience. But in order to assess the argument, Dworkin maintains, we must first ask ourselves what we expect fellow citizens to do when they sincerely believe a law is unjust or immoral. In the American constitutional system, according to Dworkin, law and morality are not easily separated, which means that the validity of law is itself often an issue in civil disobedience cases and therefore that officials should think of civil disobedients differently from ordinary criminals. Ronald Dworkin teaches philosophy and law at London University and New York University.

How should the government deal with those who disobey the draft laws out of conscience? Many people think the answer is obvious: the government must prosecute the dissenters, and if they are convicted it must punish them. Some people reach this conclusion easily, because they hold the mindless view that conscientious disobedience is the same as lawlessness. They think that the dissenters are anarchists who must be punished before their corruption spreads. Many lawyers and intellectuals come to the same conclusion, however, on what looks like a more sophisticated argument. They recognize that disobedience to law may be *morally* justified, but they insist that it cannot be *legally* justified, and they think that it follows from this truism that the law must be enforced. Erwin Griswold,

From Ronald Dworkin, *Taking Rights Seriously* (Cambridge: Harvard University Press, 1977), pp. 206–222. Reprinted by permission of the author.

the Solicitor General of the United States, and the former dean of the Harvard Law School, appears to have adopted this view in a recent statement. "[It] is of the essence of law," he said, "that it is equally applied to all, that it binds all alike, irrespective of personal motive. For this reason, one who contemplates civil disobedience out of moral conviction should not be surprised and must not be bitter if a criminal conviction ensues. And he must accept the fact that organized society cannot endure on any other basis." . . .

But the argument that, because the government believes a man has committed a crime, it must prosecute him is much weaker than it seems. Society "cannot endure" if it tolerates all disobedience; it does not follow, however, nor is there evidence, that it will collapse if it tolerates some. In the United States prosecutors have discretion whether to enforce criminal laws in particular cases. A prosecutor may properly decide not to press charges if the lawbreaker is young, or inexperienced, or the sole support of the family, or is repentant, or turns state's evidence, or if the law is unpopular or unworkable or generally disobeyed, or if the courts are clogged with more important cases, or for dozens of other reasons. This discretion is not license—we expect prosecutors to have good reasons for exercising it—but there are, at least *prima facie,* some good reasons for not prosecuting those who disobey the draft laws out of conscience. One is the obvious reason that they act out of better motives than those who break the law out of greed or a desire to subvert government. Another is the practical reason that our society suffers a loss if it punishes a group that includes—as a group of draft dissenters does—some of its most thoughtful and loyal citizens. Jailing such men solidifies their alienation from society, and alienates many like them who are deterred by the threat.

Those who think that conscientious draft offenders . . . should always be punished must show that these are not good reasons for exercising discretion, or they must find contrary reasons that outweigh them. What arguments might they produce? . . . Dean Griswold and

those who agree with him seem to rely on a fundamental moral argument that it would be unfair, not merely impractical, to let the dissenters go unpunished. They think it would be unfair, I gather, because society could not function if everyone disobeyed laws he disapproved of or found disadvantageous. If the government tolerates those few who will not "play the game," it allows them to secure the benefits of everyone else's deference to law, without shouldering the burdens, such as the burden of the draft.

This argument is a serious one. It cannot be answered simply by saying that the dissenters would allow everyone else the privilege of disobeying a law he believed immoral. In fact, few draft dissenters would accept a changed society in which sincere segregationists were free to break civil rights laws they hated. The majority want no such change, in any event, because they think that society would be worse off for it; until they are shown this is wrong, they will expect their officials to punish anyone who assumes a privilege which they, for the general benefit, do not assume.

There is, however, a flaw in the argument. The reasoning contains a hidden assumption that makes it almost entirely irrelevant to the draft cases, and indeed to any serious case of civil disobedience in the United States. The argument assumes that the dissenters know that they are breaking a valid law, and that the privilege they assert is the privilege to do that. Of course, almost everyone who discusses civil disobedience recognizes that in America a law may be invalid because it is unconstitutional. . . .

Doubtful law is by no means special or exotic in cases of civil disobedience. On the contrary. In the United States, at least, almost any law which a significant number of people would be tempted to disobey on moral grounds would be doubtful—if not clearly invalid—on constitutional grounds as well. The constitution makes our conventional political morality relevant to the question of validity; any statute that appears to compromise that morality raises constitutional questions, and if the compromise is serious, the constitutional doubts are serious also.

[Dworkin illustrates this by pointing out that moral objections to the Vietnam War—for example, that the United States was using immoral weapons, that Congress had never officially declared war, and that it had been made a crime to "counsel" draft resistance— have parallels in law, for example international treaties we signed banning certain weapons, Congress's exclusive power to declare war, and First Amendment protections of free speech. These moral/legal arguments thus provide the basis for thinking that, in fact, the laws in question are invalid.—Ed.]

. . . We cannot conclude from these arguments that the draft (or any part of it) was unconstitutional. . . . But the arguments of unconstitutionality were at least plausible and a reasonable and competent lawyer might think that they present a stronger case, on balance, than the counterarguments. . . .

Therefore we cannot assume, in judging what should have been done with the draft dissenters, that they were asserting a privilege to disobey valid laws. We cannot decide that fairness demanded their punishment until we try to answer further questions: What should a citizen do when the law is unclear, and when he thinks it allows what others think it does not? I do not mean to ask, of course, what it is *legally* proper for him to do, or what his *legal* rights are—that would be begging the question, because it depends upon whether he is right or they are right. I mean to ask what his proper course is as a citizen, what, in other words, we would consider to be "playing the game." That is a crucial question, because it cannot be unfair not to punish him if he is acting as, given his opinions, we think he should.[1]

There is no obvious answer on which most citizens would readily agree, and that is itself significant. If we examine our legal institutions and practices, however, we shall discover some relevant underlying principles and policies. I shall set out three possible answers to the question, and then try to show which

of these best fits our practices and expectations. The three possibilities I want to consider are these:

1. If the law is doubtful, and it is therefore unclear whether it permits someone to do what he wants, he should assume the worst, and act on the assumption that it does not. He should obey the executive authorities who command him, even though he thinks they are wrong, while using the political process, if he can, to change the law.

2. If the law is doubtful, he may follow his own judgment, that is, he may do what he wants if he believes that the case that the law permits this is stronger than the case that it does not. But he may follow his own judgment only until an authoritative institution, like a court, decides the other way in a case involving him or someone else. Once an institutional decision has been reached, he must abide by that decision, even though he thinks that it was wrong. (There are, in theory, many subdivisions of this second possibility. We may say that the individual's choice is foreclosed by the contrary decision of any court, including the lowest court in the system if the case is not appealed. Or we may require a decision of some particular court or institution. I shall discuss this second possibility in its most liberal form, namely that the individual may properly follow his own judgment until a contrary decision of the highest court competent to pass on the issue, which, in the case of the draft, was the United States Supreme Court.)

3. If the law is doubtful, he may follow his own judgment, even after a contrary decision by the highest competent court. Of course, he must take the contrary decision of any court into account in making his judgment of what the law requires. Otherwise the judgment would not be an honest or reasonable one, because the doctrine of precedent, which is an established part of our legal system, has the effect of allowing the decision of the courts to change the law. Suppose, for example, that a taxpayer believes that he is not required to pay tax on certain forms of income. If the Supreme Court decides to the contrary, he should, taking into account the practice of according great weight to the decisions of the Supreme Court on tax matters, decide that the Court's decision has itself tipped the balance, and that the law now requires him to pay the tax.

Someone might think that this qualification erases the difference between the third and the second models, but it does not. The doctrine of precedent gives different weights to the decisions of different courts, and greatest weight to the decisions of the Supreme Court, but it does not make the decisions of any court conclusive. Sometimes, even after a contrary Supreme Court decision, an individual may still reasonably believe that the law is on his side; such cases are rare, but they are most likely to occur in disputes over constitutional law when civil disobedience is involved. The Court has shown itself more likely to overrule its past decisions if these have limited important personal or political rights, and it is just these decisions that a dissenter might want to challenge.

We cannot assume, in other words, that the Constitution is always what the Supreme Court says it is. Oliver Wendell Holmes, for example, did not follow such a rule in his famous dissent in the *Gitlow* case. A few years before, in *Abrams,* he had lost his battle to persuade the court that the First Amendment protected an anarchist who had been urging general strikes against the government. A similar issue was presented in *Gitlow,* and Holmes once again dissented. "It is true," he said, "that in my opinion this criterion was departed from [in *Abrams*] but the convictions that I expressed in that case are too deep for it to be possible for me as yet to believe that it . . . settled the law." Holmes voted for acquitting Gitlow, on the ground that what Gitlow had done was no crime, even though the Supreme Court had recently held that it was.

Here then are three possible models for the behavior of dissenters who disagree with the executive authorities when the law is doubtful.

Which of them best fits our legal and social practices?

I think it plain that we do not follow the first of these models, that is, that we do not expect citizens to assume the worst. If no court has decided the issue, and a man thinks, on balance, that the law is on his side, most of our lawyers and critics think it perfectly proper for him to follow his own judgment. Even when many disapprove of what he does—such as peddling pornography—they do not think he must desist just because the legality of his conduct is subject to doubt.

It is worth pausing a moment to consider what society would lose if it did follow the first model or, to put the matter the other way, what society gains when people follow their own judgment in cases like this. When the law is uncertain, in the sense that lawyers can reasonably disagree on what a court ought to decide, the reason usually is that different legal principles and policies have collided, and it is unclear how best to accommodate these conflicting principles and policies.

Our practice, in which different parties are encouraged to pursue their own understanding, provides a means of testing relevant hypotheses. If the question is whether a particular rule would have certain undesirable consequences, or whether these consequences would have limited or broad ramifications, then, before the issue is decided, it is useful to know what does in fact take place when some people proceed on that rule. (Much anti-trust and business regulation law has developed through this kind of testing.) If the question is whether and to what degree a particular solution would offend principles of justice or fair play deeply respected by the community, it is useful, again, to experiment by testing the community's response. The extent of community indifference to anti-contraception laws, for example, would never have become established had not some organizations deliberately flouted those laws.

If the first model were followed, we would lose the advantages of these tests. The law would suffer, particularly if this model were applied to constitutional issues. When the validity of a criminal statute is in doubt, the statute will almost always strike some people as being unfair or unjust, because it will infringe some principle of liberty or justice or fairness which they take to be built into the Constitution. If our practice were that whenever a law is doubtful on these grounds, one must act as if it were valid, then the chief vehicle we have for challenging the law on moral grounds would be lost, and over time the law we obeyed would certainly become less fair and just, and the liberty of our citizens would certainly be diminished. . . .

We must also reject the second model, that if the law is unclear a citizen may properly follow his own judgment until the highest court has ruled that he is wrong. This fails to take into account the fact that any court, including the Supreme Court, may overrule itself. In 1940 the Court decided that a West Virginia law requiring students to salute the Flag was constitutional. In 1943 it reversed itself, and decided that such a statute was unconstitutional after all. What was the duty as citizens, of those people who in 1941 and 1942 objected to saluting the Flag on grounds of conscience, and thought that the Court's 1940 decision was wrong? We can hardly say that their duty was to follow the first decision. They believed that saluting the Flag was unconscionable, and they believed, reasonably, that no valid law required them to do so. The Supreme Court later decided that in this they were right. The Court did not simply hold that after the second decision failing to salute would not be a crime; it held (as in a case like this it almost always would) that it was no crime after the first decision either.

Some will say that the flag-salute dissenters should have obeyed the Court's first decision, while they worked in the legislatures to have the law repealed, and tried in the courts to find some way to challenge the law again without actually violating it. That would be, perhaps, a plausible recommendation if conscience were not involved, because

it would then be arguable that the gain in orderly procedure was worth the personal sacrifice of patience. But conscience was involved, and if the dissenters had obeyed the law while biding their time, they would have suffered the irreparable injury of having done what their conscience forbade them to do. It is one thing to say that an individual must sometimes violate his conscience when he knows that the law commands him to do it. It is quite another to say that he must violate his conscience even when he reasonably believes that the law does not require it, because it would inconvenience his fellow citizens if he took the most direct, and perhaps the only, method of attempting to show that he is right and they are wrong.

Since a court may overrule itself, the same reasons we listed for rejecting the first model count against the second as well. If we did not have the pressure of dissent, we would not have a dramatic statement of the degree to which a court decision against the dissenter is felt to be wrong, a demonstration that is surely pertinent to the question of whether it was right. We would increase the chance of being governed by rules that offend the principles we claim to serve. . . .

Thus the third model, or something close to it, seems to be the fairest statement of a man's social duty in our community. A citizen's allegiance is to the law, not to any particular person's view of what the law is, and he does not behave unfairly so long as he proceeds on his own considered and reasonable view of what the law requires. Let me repeat (because it is crucial) that this is not the same as saying that an individual may disregard what the courts have said. The doctrine of precedent lies near the core of our legal system, and no one can make a reasonable effort to follow the law unless he grants the courts the general power to alter it by their decisions. But if the issue is one touching fundamental personal or political rights, and it is arguable that the Supreme Court has made a mistake, a man is within his social rights in refusing to accept that decision as conclusive. . . .

I have been talking about the case of a man who believes that the law is not what other people think, or what the courts have held. This description may fit some of those who disobey the draft laws out of conscience, but it does not fit most of them. Most of the dissenters are not lawyers or political philosophers; they believe that the laws on the books are immoral, and inconsistent with their country's legal ideals, but they have not considered the question of whether they may be invalid as well. Of what relevance to their situation, then, is the proposition that one may properly follow one's own view of the law?

To answer this, I shall have to return to the point I made earlier. The Constitution, through the due process clause [government cannot deprive citizens of "life, liberty, or property without due process of law"], the equal protection clause [states cannot deny citizens the "equal protection of the laws"], the First Amendment [government cannot "abridge freedom of speech" or make a law "respecting the establishment of religion, or prohibiting the free exercise thereof"], and the other provisions I mentioned, injects an extraordinary amount of our political morality into the issue of whether a law is valid. The statement that most draft dissenters are unaware that the law is invalid therefore needs qualification. They hold beliefs that, if true, strongly support the view that the law is on their side; the fact that they have not reached that further conclusion can be traced, in at least most cases, to their lack of legal sophistication. If we believe that when the law is doubtful people who follow their own judgment of the law may be acting properly, it would seem wrong not to extend that view to those dissenters whose judgments come to the same thing. No part of the case that I made for the third model would entitle us to distinguish them from their more knowledgeable colleagues.

We can draw several tentative conclusions from the argument so far: When the law is uncertain, in the sense that a plausible case can be made on both sides, then a citizen who follows his own judgment is not behaving unfairly. Our practices permit and encourage him to follow his own judgment in such cases. For that reason, our government has a special responsibility to try to protect him, and soften his predicament, whenever it can do so without great damage to other policies. It does not follow that the government can guarantee him immunity—it cannot adopt the rule that it will prosecute no one who acts out of conscience, or convict no one who reasonably disagrees with the courts. That would paralyze the government's ability to carry out its policies; it would, moreover, throw away the most important benefit of following the third model. If the state never prosecuted, then the courts could not act on the experience and the arguments the dissent has generated. But it does follow that when the practical reasons for prosecuting are relatively weak in a particular case, or can be met in other ways, the path of fairness lies in tolerance. The popular view that the law is the law and must always be enforced refuses to distinguish the man who acts on his own judgment of a doubtful law, and thus behaves as our practices provide, from the common criminal. I know of no reason, short of moral blindness, for not drawing a distinction in principle between the two cases.

I anticipate a philosophical objection to these conclusions: that I am treating law as a "brooding omnipresence in the sky." I have spoken of people making judgments about what the law requires, even in cases in which the law is unclear and undemonstrable. I have spoken of cases in which a man might think that the law requires one thing, even though the Supreme Court has said that it requires another, and even when it was not likely that the Supreme Court would soon change its mind. I will therefore be charged with the view that there is always a "right answer" to a legal problem to be found in natural law or locked up in some transcendental strongbox.

The strongbox theory of law is, of course, nonsense. When I say that people hold views on the law when the law is doubtful, and that these views are not merely predictions of what the courts will hold, I intend no such metaphysics. I mean only to summarize as accurately as I can many of the practices that are part of our legal process.

Lawyers and judges make statements of legal right and duty, even when they know these are not demonstrable, and support them with arguments even when they know that these arguments will not appeal to everyone. They make these arguments to one another, in the professional journals, in the classrooms, and in the courts. They respond to these arguments, when others make them, by judging them good or bad or mediocre. In so doing they assume that some arguments for a given doubtful position are better than others. They also assume that the case on one side of a doubtful proposition may be stronger than the case on the other, which is what I take a claim of law in a doubtful case to mean. . . .

Our legal system pursues these goals (the development and testing of the law through experimentation by citizens and through the adversary process) by inviting citizens to decide the strengths and weaknesses of legal arguments for themselves, or through their own counsel, and to act on these judgments, although that permission is qualified by the limited threat that they may suffer if the courts do not agree. Success in this strategy depends on whether there is sufficient agreement within the community on what counts as a good or bad argument, so that, although different people will reach different judgments, these differences will be neither so profound nor so frequent as to make the system

unworkable, or dangerous for those who act by their own lights. I believe there is sufficient agreement on the criteria of the argument to avoid these traps, although one of the main tasks of legal philosophy is to exhibit and clarify these criteria. In any event, the practices I have described have not yet been shown to be misguided; they therefore must count in determining whether it is just and fair to be lenient to those who break what others think is the law.

I have said that the government has a special responsibility to those who act on a reasonable judgment that a law is invalid. It should make accommodation for them as far as possible, when this is consistent with other policies. It may be difficult to decide what the government ought to do, in the name of that responsibility, in particular cases. The decision will be a matter of balance, and flat rules will not help. . . .

Some lawyers will be shocked by my general conclusion that we have a responsibility toward those who disobey the draft laws out of conscience, and that we may be required not to prosecute them, but rather to change our laws or adjust our sentencing procedures to accommodate them. The simple Draconian propositions, that crime must be punished, and that he who misjudges the law must take the consequences, have an extraordinary hold on the professional as well as the popular imagination. But the rule of law is more complex and more intelligent than that and it is important that it survive.

NOTE

1. I do not mean to imply that the government should always punish a man who deliberately breaks a law he knows is valid. There may be reasons of fairness or practicality, like those I listed in the third paragraph, for not prosecuting such men. But cases like the draft cases present special arguments for tolerance; I want to concentrate on these arguments and therefore have isolated these cases.

REVIEW AND DISCUSSION QUESTIONS

1. Describe how Dworkin understands the relationship between morality and law. Why is it often difficult to know whether a law is valid?
2. What service does he think civil disobedients provide in our system?

3. Dworkin argues that it is not unfair to refuse to prosecute civil disobedients. His argument relies on a discussion of three courses of action open to citizens who object to law, and what we as a society reasonably expect of our fellow citizens. Explain his argument.

4. What does Dworkin mean in rejecting the "strongbox" view of law? If law and morality are connected, as he suggests, how is the law to be tested and legal arguments assessed?

5. In light of one or two of the cases you have read, is Dworkin's description of the connections between law and morality an accurate one?

The Problem of the Grudge Informer

Lon L. Fuller

Earlier essays in this section have focused on various questions associated with the nature of legal obligation and the justification of civil disobedience. But parallel questions emerged as well, about whether to punish those who apparently violate the law and even about the nature of law itself. Using an issue that is facing societies today as they undergo rapid political change, Lon Fuller uses an ingenious narrative to explore whether to prosecute people who took advantage of a previous, deeply unjust regime to work out personal grudges by informing on their personal enemies to the police. What policy should a newly elected, democratic government take toward those who benefited from a corrupt and antidemocratic regime in the past? Answering this, Fuller suggests, exposes fascinating questions about the ideal of the rule of law and the nature of law itself. Lon Fuller was professor of law at Harvard Law School.

By a narrow margin you have been elected Minister of Justice of your country, a nation of some twenty million inhabitants. At the outset of your term of office you are confronted by a serious problem that will be described below. But first the background of this problem must be presented.

For many decades your country enjoyed a peaceful, constitutional and democratic government. However, some time ago it came upon bad times. Normal relations were disrupted by a deepening economic depression and by an increasing antagonism among various factional groups, formed along economic, political, and religious lines. The proverbial man on horseback appeared in the form of the Headman of a political party or society that called itself the Purple Shirts.

In a national election attended by much disorder the Headman was elected President of the Republic and his party obtained a majority of the seats in the General Assembly. The success of the party at the polls was partly brought about by a campaign of reckless promises and ingenious falsifications, and partly by the physical intimidation of night-riding Purple Shirts who frightened many people away from the polls who would have voted against the party.

When the Purple Shirts arrived in power they took no steps to repeal the ancient Constitution or any of its provisions. They also left intact the Civil and Criminal Codes and the Code of Procedure. No official action was taken to dismiss any government official or to remove any judge from the bench. Elections continued to be held at intervals and ballots were counted with apparent honesty. Nevertheless, the country lived under a reign of terror.

Judges who rendered decisions contrary to the wishes of the party were beaten and murdered. The accepted meaning of the Criminal Code was perverted to place political opponents in jail. Secret statutes were passed, the contents of which were known only to the upper levels of the party hierarchy. Retroactive statutes were enacted which made acts criminal that were legally innocent when committed. No attention was paid by the government to the restraints of the Constitution, of antecedent laws, or even of its own laws. All opposing political parties were disbanded. Thousands of political opponents were put to death, either methodically in prisons or in sporadic night forays of terror. A general amnesty was declared in favor of persons under sentence for acts "committed in defending the fatherland against subversion." Under this amnesty a general liberation of all prisoners who were members of the Purple Shirt party was effected. No one not a member of the party was released under the amnesty.

The Purple Shirts as a matter of deliberate policy preserved an element of flexibility in their operations by acting at times through the party "in the streets," and by acting at other times through the apparatus of the state which they controlled. Choice between the two methods of proceeding was purely a matter of expediency. For example, when the inner circle of the party decided to ruin all the former Socialist-Republicans (whose party put up a last-ditch resistance to the new regime), a dispute arose as to the best way of confiscating their property. One faction, perhaps still influenced by prerevolutionary conceptions, wanted to accomplish this by a statute declaring their goods forfeited for criminal acts. Another wanted to do it by compelling the owners to deed their property over at the point of a bayonet. This group argued against the proposed statute on the ground that it would attract unfavorable comment abroad. The Headman decided in favor of direct action through the party to be followed by a secret statute ratifying the party's action and confirming the titles obtained by threats of physical violence.

The Purple Shirts have now been overthrown and a democratic and constitutional government restored. Some difficult problems have, however, been left behind by the deposed regime. These you and your associates in the new government must find some way of solving. One of these problems is that of the "grudge informer."

During the Purple Shirt regime a great many people worked off grudges by reporting their enemies to the party or to the government authorities. The activities reported were such things as the private expression of views critical of the government, listening to foreign radio broadcasts, associating with known wreckers and hooligans, hoarding more than the permitted amount of dried eggs, failing to report a loss of identification papers within five days, etc. As things then stood with the administration of justice, any of these acts, if proved, could lead to a sentence of death. In some cases this sentence was authorized by "emergency" statutes; in others it was imposed without statutory warrant, though by judges duly appointed to their offices.

After the overthrow of the Purple Shirts, a strong public demand grew up that these grudge informers be punished. The interim government, which preceded that with which you are associated, temporized on this matter. Meanwhile it has become a burning issue and a decision concerning it can no longer be postponed. Accordingly, your first act as Minister of Justice has been to address yourself to it. You have asked your five Deputies to give thought to the matter and to bring their recommendations to conference. At the conference the five Deputies speak in turn as follows:

First Deputy: "It is perfectly clear to me that we can do nothing about these so-called grudge informers. The acts they reported were unlawful according to the rules of the government then in actual control of the nation's affairs. The sentences imposed on their victims were rendered in accordance with principles of law then obtaining. These principles differed from those familiar to us in ways that we consider detestable. Nevertheless they were then the law of the land. One of the principal differences between that law and our own lies in the much wider discretion it accorded to the judge in criminal matters. This rule and its consequences are as much entitled to respect by us as the reform which the Purple Shirts introduced into the law of wills, whereby only two witnesses were required instead of three. It is immaterial that the rule granting the judge a more or less uncontrolled discretion in criminal cases was never formally enacted but was a matter of tacit acceptance. Exactly the same thing can be said of the opposite rule which we accept that restricts the judge's discretion narrowly. The difference between ourselves and the Purple Shirts is not that theirs was an unlawful government—a contradiction in terms— but lies rather in the field of ideology. No one has a greater abhorrence than I for Purple Shirtism. Yet the fundamental difference between our philosophy and theirs is that we permit and tolerate differences in viewpoint, while they attempted to impose their monolithic code on everyone. Our whole system of government assumes that law is a flexible thing, capable of expressing and effectuating many different aims. The cardinal point of our creed is that when an objective has been duly incorporated into a law or judicial decree it must be provisionally accepted even by those that hate it, who must await their chance at the polls, or in another litigation, to secure a legal recognition for their own aims. The Purple Shirts, on the other hand, simply disregarded laws that incorporated objectives of which they did not approve, not even considering it worth the effort involved to repeal them. If we now seek to unscramble the acts of the Purple Shirt regime, declaring this judgment invalid, that statute void, this sentence excessive, we shall be doing exactly the thing we most condemn in them. I recognize that it will take courage to carry through with the program I recommend and we shall have to resist strong pressures of public opinion. We shall also have to be prepared to prevent the people from taking the law into their own hands. In the long run, however, I believe the course I recommend is the only one that will insure the triumph of the conceptions of law and government in which we believe."

Second Deputy: "Curiously, I arrive at the same conclusion as my colleague, by an exactly opposite route. To me it seems absurd to call the Purple Shirt regime a lawful government. A legal system does not exist simply because policemen continue to patrol the streets and wear uniforms or because a constitution and code are left on the shelf unrepealed. A legal system presupposes laws that are known, or can be known, by those subject to them. It presupposes some uniformity of action and that like cases will be given like treatment. It presupposes the absence of some lawless power, like the Purple Shirt Party, standing above the government and able at any time to interfere with the administration of justice whenever it does not function according to the whims of that power. All of these presuppositions enter into the very conception of an order of law and have nothing to do with political and economic ideologies. In my opinion law in any ordinary sense of the word ceased to exist when the Purple Shirts came to power. During their regime we had, in effect, an interregnum in the rule of law. Instead of a government of laws we had a war of all against all conducted behind barred doors, in dark alleyways, in palace intrigues, and prison yard conspiracies. The acts of these so-called grudge informers were just one phase of that war. For us to condemn these acts as criminal would involve as much incongruity as if we were to attempt to apply juristic conceptions to the struggle for existence that goes on in the jungle or beneath the surface of the sea. We must put this whole dark, lawless chapter of our history behind us like a bad dream. If we stir among its hatreds, we shall bring upon ourselves something of its evil spirit and risk infection from its miasmas. I therefore say with my colleague, let bygones be bygones. Let us do nothing about the so-called grudge informers. What they did do was neither lawful nor contrary to law, for they lived, not under a regime of law, but under one of anarchy and terror."

Third Deputy: "I have a profound suspicion of any kind of reasoning that proceeds by an 'either-or' alternative. I do not think we need to assume either, on the one hand, that in some manner the whole of the Purple Shirt regime was outside the realm of law, or, on the other, that all of its doings are entitled to full credence as the act of a lawful government. My two colleagues have unwittingly delivered powerful arguments against these extreme assumptions by demonstrating that both of them lead to the same absurd conclusion, a conclusion that is ethically and politically impossible. If one reflects about the matter without emotion it becomes clear that we did not have during the Purple Shirt regime a 'war of all against all.' Under the surface much of what we call normal human life went on—marriages were contracted, goods were sold, wills were drafted and executed. This life was attended by the usual dislocations—automobile accidents, bankruptcies, unwitnessed wills, defamatory misprints in the newspapers. Much of this normal life and most of these equally normal dislocations of it were unaffected by the Purple Shirt ideology. The legal questions that arose in this area were handled by the courts much as they had been formerly and much as they are being handled today. It would invite an intolerable chaos if we were to declare everything that happened under the Purple Shirts to be without legal basis. On the other hand, we certainly cannot say that the murders committed in the streets by members of the party acting under orders

from the Headman were lawful simply because the party had achieved control of the government and its chief had become President of the Republic. If we must condemn the criminal acts of the party and its members, it would seem absurd to uphold every act which happened to be canalized through the apparatus of a government that had become, in effect, the alter ego of the Purple Shirt party. We must therefore, in this situation, as in most human affairs, discriminate. Where the Purple Shirt philosophy intruded itself and perverted the administration of justice from its normal aims and uses, there we must interfere. Among these perversions of justice I would count, for example, the case of a man who was in love with another man's wife and brought about the death of the husband by informing against him for a wholly trivial offense, that is, for not reporting a loss of his identification papers within five days. This informer was a murderer under the Criminal Code which was in effect at the time of his act and which the Purple Shirts had not repealed. He encompassed the death of one who stood in the way of his illicit passions and utilized the courts for the realization of his murderous intent. He knew that the courts were themselves the pliant instruments of whatever policy the Purple Shirts might for the moment consider expedient. There are other cases that are equally clear. I admit that there are also some that are less clear. We shall be embarrassed, for example, by the cases of mere busybodies who reported to the authorities everything that looked suspect. Some of these persons acted not from desire to get rid of those they accused, but with a desire to curry favor with the party, to divert suspicions (perhaps ill-founded) raised against themselves, or through sheer officiousness. I don't know how these cases should be handled, and make no recommendation with regard to them. But the fact that these troublesome cases exist should not deter us from acting at once in the cases that are clear, of which there are far too many to permit us to disregard them."

Fourth Deputy: "Like my colleague I too distrust 'either-or' reasoning, but I think we need to reflect more than he has about where we are headed. This proposal to pick and choose among the acts of the deposed regime is thoroughly objectionable. It is, in fact, Purple Shirtism itself, pure and simple. We like this law, so let us enforce it. We like this judgment, let it stand. This law we don't like, therefore it never was a law at all. This governmental act we disapprove, let it be deemed a nullity. If we proceed this way, we take toward the laws and acts of the Purple Shirt government precisely the unprincipled attitude they took toward the laws and acts of the government they supplanted. We shall have chaos, with every judge and every prosecuting attorney a law unto himself. Instead of ending the abuses of the Purple Shirt regime, my colleague's proposal would perpetuate them. There is only one way of dealing with this problem that is compatible with our philosophy of law and government and that is to deal with it by duly enacted law, I mean, by a special statute directed toward it. Let us study this whole problem of the grudge informer, get all the relevant facts, and draft a comprehensive law dealing with it. We shall not then be twisting old laws to purposes for which they were never intended. We shall furthermore provide penalties appropriate to the offense and not treat every informer as a murderer simply because the one he informed against was ultimately executed. I admit that we shall encounter some difficult problems of draftsmanship. Among other things, we shall have to assign a definite legal meaning to 'grudge' and that will not be easy. We should not be deterred by these difficulties, however, from adopting the only course that will lead us out of a condition of lawless, personal rule."

Fifth Deputy: "I find a considerable irony in the last proposal. It speaks of putting a definite end to the abuses of the Purple Shirtism, yet it proposes to do this by resorting to one of the most hated devices of the Purple Shirt regime, the ex post facto criminal statute. My colleague dreads the confusion that will result if we attempt without a statute to undo and redress 'wrong' acts of the departed order, while we uphold and enforce its 'right' acts. Yet he seems not to realize that his proposed statute is a wholly specious cure for this uncertainty. It is easy to make a plausible argument for an undrafted statute; we all agree it would be nice to have things down in black and white on paper. But just what would this statute provide? One of my colleagues speaks of someone who had failed for five days to report a loss of his identification papers. My colleague implies that the judicial sentence imposed for that offense, namely death, was so utterly disproportionate as to be clearly wrong. But we must remember that at that time the underground movement against the Purple Shirts was mounting in intensity and that the Purple Shirts were being harassed constantly by people with false identification papers. From their point of view they had a real problem, and the only objection we can make to their solution of it (other than the fact that we didn't want them to solve it) was that they acted with somewhat more rigor than the occasion seemed to demand. How will my colleague deal with this case in his statute, and with all of its cousins and second cousins? Will he deny the existence of any need for law and order under the Purple Shirt regime? I will not go further into the difficulties involved in drafting this proposed statute, since they are evident enough to anyone who reflects. I shall instead turn to my own solution. It has been said on very respectable authority that the main purpose of the criminal law is to give an outlet to the human instinct for revenge. There are times, and I believe this is one of them, when we should allow that instinct to express itself directly without the intervention of forms of law. This matter of the grudge informers is already in process of straightening itself out. One reads almost every day that a former lackey of the Purple Shirt regime has met his just reward in some unguarded spot. The people are quietly handling this thing in their own way and if we leave them alone, and instruct our public prosecutors to do the same, there will soon be no problem left for us to solve. There will be some disorders, of course, and a few innocent heads will be broken. But our government and our legal system will not be involved in the affair and we shall not find ourselves hopelessly bogged down in an attempt to unscramble all the deeds and misdeeds of the Purple Shirts."

As Minister of Justice which of these recommendations would you adopt?

REVIEW AND DISCUSSION QUESTIONS

1. Describe the problem faced by the Minister of Justice; then outline each of the five alternatives that the various deputies defend.
2. Fuller's dialogue raises two issues. The first is whether or not a state may legitimately punish someone whose acts were wrong but not illegal. How would you respond to that issue?
3. The second issue deals with the validity of laws during the reign of the Purple Shirts. In light of the deputies' arguments, is the law of the Purple Shirts valid? Were laws from the previous constitutional regime still valid? How does that question bear on the choice among the five deputies' positions?
4. How would you answer the question raised at the end of the article? Explain why you reject the advice of each deputy whose position you think is mistaken.

Essay and Paper Topics for Section 10

1. Write an essay in which you discuss whether or not you believe there is at least a general, if not absolute, moral obligation to obey the law, using any of the authors you have read in this section.
2. "The law's the law; judges should apply it and pay no attention to whether it's just." Discuss this claim, using any of the essays in this section you think relevant.
3. Using the essay by Lon Fuller, discuss the idea of the rule of law and the way(s) in which it is important for society to be ruled by law. If law does not guarantee justice or other values, then can it really be important? Explain.

Liberty and Freedom

We all tend to assume freedom is valuable and respecting it important. Why is this the case? Philosophers have offered different answers to this question, but the classic defense of individual liberty comes from John Stuart Mill, who famously claims that people have a right to act however they wish as long as they do not harm others. Following Mill's classic essay *On Liberty* are four readings on legal paternalism. Under what circumstances, they ask, may government interfere with freedom in the name of keeping people from doing harm to themselves? The issue is focused on two topics: refusal of medical treatment and use of potentially harmful drugs. In the last essay, Janet Radcliffe Richards begins with Mill's conception of freedom and goes on to discuss the familiar idea that society and social conditioning limit women's freedom.

On Liberty

John Stuart Mill

None of Mill's works has had a greater impact than *On Liberty;* its ideas are often discussed by academics, politicians, and the general public, even by people who have never heard of him. According to letters and other material from Mill's life, *On Liberty* should be thought of as a joint work authored by Mill himself and his longtime friend Harriet Taylor. Mill even said in a letter that there was not a sentence in the book that the two did not go over together many times. (Harriet Taylor also had a major role in other works, including *The Subjection of Women,* reprinted in Section 13.) For a brief description of John Stuart Mill's life, see the introduction to his essay in Section 1.

In *On Liberty,* Mill examines a fundamental question of political philosophy: what are the limits of society's power over the individual? Mill's answer is that society may interfere with an individual's speech or actions only on the grounds of self-protection. Accordingly, Mill first discusses the history of the fight of the individual against tyrannical government. He then explores the importance of individuality to a person's overall well-being, and, finally, he considers his famous "harm principle," which provides that government is justified in interfering with a citizen's liberty only if there is the threat of harm to others.

INTRODUCTORY

The subject of this essay is . . . civil, or social liberty: the nature and limits of power which can be legitimately exercised by society over the individual. . . . The struggle between liberty and authority is the most conspicuous feature in the portions of history with which we are earliest familiar, particularly in that of Greece, Rome, and England. But in old times this contest was between subjects, or some classes of subjects, and the government. By liberty, was meant protection against the tyranny of the political rulers. The rulers were conceived (except in some of the popular governments of Greece) as in a necessarily antagonistic position to the people whom they ruled. . . .

A time, however, came, in the progress of human affairs, when men ceased to think it a necessity of nature that their governors should be an independent power, opposed in interest to themselves. It appeared to them much better that the various magistrates of the State should be their tenants or delegates, revocable at their pleasure. In that way alone, it seemed, could they have complete security that the powers of government would never be abused to their disadvantage. By degrees this new demand for elective and temporary rulers became the prominent object of the exertions of the popular party, wherever any such party existed; and superseded, to a considerable extent, the previous efforts to limit the power of rulers. . . .

But in political and philosophical theories, as well as in persons, success discloses faults and infirmities which failure might have concealed from observation. . . . It was now perceived that such phrases as "self- government," and "the power of the people over themselves," do not express the true state of the case. The "people" who exercise the power are not always the same people with those over whom it is exercised; and the "self-government" spoken of is not the government of each by himself, but of each by all the rest. The will of the people, moreover, practically means the will of the most numerous or the most active *part* of the people—the majority, or those who succeed in making themselves accepted as the majority; the people, consequently, may desire to oppress a part of their number, and precautions are as much needed against this as against any other abuse of power. The limitation, therefore, of

the power of government over individuals loses none of its importance when the holders of power are regularly accountable to the community, that is, to the strongest party therein. . . .

The object of this essay is to assert one very simple principle, as entitled to govern absolutely the dealings of society with the individual in the way of compulsion and control, whether the means used be physical force in the form of legal penalties or the moral coercion of public opinion. That principle is, that the sole end for which mankind are warranted, individually or collectively, in interfering with the liberty of action of any of their number, is self-protection. That the only purpose for which power can be rightfully exercised over any member of a civilized community, against his will, is to prevent harm to others. His own good, either physical or moral, is not a sufficient warrant. He cannot rightfully be compelled to do or forbear because it will be better for him to do so, because it will make him happier, because, in the opinions of others, to do so would be wise or even right. These are good reasons for remonstrating with him, or reasoning with him, or persuading him, or entreating him, but not for compelling him or visiting him with any evil in case he do otherwise. To justify that, the conduct from which it is desired to deter him must be calculated to produce evil to someone else. The only part of the conduct of anyone, for which he is amenable to society, is that which concerns others. In the part which merely concerns himself, his independence is, of right, absolute. Over himself, over his own body and mind, the individual is sovereign.

It is, perhaps, hardly necessary to say that this doctrine is meant to apply only to human beings in the maturity of their faculties. We are not speaking of children, or of young persons below the age which the law may fix as that of manhood or womanhood. Those who are still in a state to require being taken care

From John Stuart Mill, *On Liberty* (1859).

of by others, must be protected against their own actions as well as against external injury. For the same reason, we may leave out of consideration those backward states of society in which the race itself may be considered as in its nonage. The early difficulties in the way of spontaneous progress are so great, and there is seldom any choice of means for overcoming them; and a ruler full of the spirit of improvement is warranted in the use of any expedients that will attain an end, perhaps otherwise unattainable. Despotism is a legitimate mode of government in dealing with barbarians, provided the end be their improvement, and the means justified by actually effecting that end. Liberty, as a principle, has no application to any state of things anterior to the time when mankind have become capable of being improved by free and equal discussion. Until then, there is nothing for them but implicit obedience to an Akbar or a Charlemagne, if they are so fortunate as to find one. But as soon as mankind have attained the capacity of being guided to their own improvement by conviction or persuasion (a period long since reached in all nations with whom we need here concern ourselves), compulsion, either in the direct form or in that of pains and penalties for noncompliance, is no longer admissible as a means to their own good, and justifiable only for the security of others.

It is proper to state that I forego any advantage which could be derived to my argument from the idea of abstract right, as a thing independent of utility. I regard utility as the ultimate appeal on all ethical questions; but it must be utility in the largest sense, grounded on the permanent interests of a man as a progressive being. These interests, I contend, authorized the subjection of individual spontaneity to external control, only in respect to those actions of each which concern the interest of other people. If anyone does an act hurtful to others, there is a *prima facie* case for punishing him, by law, or, where legal penalties are not safely applicable, by general disapprobation. There are also many positive acts for the benefit of others, which he may

rightfully be compelled to perform: such as to give evidence in a court of justice; to bear his fair share in the common defense, or in any other joint work necessary to the interest of the society of which he enjoys the protection; and to perform certain acts of individual beneficence, such as saving a fellow-creature's life, or interposing to protect the defenseless against ill-usage, things which whenever it is obviously a man's duty to do, he may rightfully be made responsible to society for not doing. A person may cause evil to others not only by his actions but by his inaction, and in either case he is justly accountable to them for the injury. The latter case, it is true, requires a much more cautious exercise of compulsion than the former. . . .

This, then is the appropriate region of human liberty. It comprises, *first,* the inward domain of consciousness; demanding liberty of conscience in the most comprehensive sense; liberty of thought and feeling; absolute freedom of opinion and sentiment on all subjects, practical or speculative, scientific, moral or theological. . . .

Secondly, the principle requires liberty of tastes and pursuits; of framing the plan of our life to suit our own character; of doing as we like, subject to such consequences as may follow: without impediment from our fellow-creatures, so long as what we do does not harm them, even though they should think our conduct foolish, perverse, or wrong.

Thirdly, from this liberty of each individual, follows the liberty, within the same limits, of combinations among individuals; freedom to unite, for any purpose not involving harm to others: the persons combining being supposed to be of full age, and not forced or deceived.

No society in which these liberties are not, on the whole, respected, is free, whatever may be its form of government; and none is completely free in which they do not exist absolute and unqualified. The only freedom which deserves the name, is that of pursuing our own good in our own way, as long as we do not attempt to deprive others of theirs, or impede their efforts to obtain it. Each is the proper guardian of his own health, whether bodily, or mental and spiritual. . . . *[Mill now discusses liberty of thought and discussion, an essay which is reprinted in the next section.—Ed.]*

OF INDIVIDUALITY, AS ONE OF THE ELEMENTS OF WELL-BEING

No one pretends that actions should be as free as opinions. On the contrary, even opinions lose their immunity when the circumstances in which they are expressed are such as to constitute their expression a positive instigation to some mischievous act. An opinion that corn-dealers are starvers of the poor, or that private property is robbery, ought to be unmolested when simply circulated through the press, but may justly incur punishment when delivered orally to an excited mob assembled before the house of a corn-dealer, or when handed about among the same mob in the form of a placard. . . . It is desirable, in short, that in things which do not primarily concern others, individuality should assert itself. Where not the person's own character, but the traditions or customs of other people are the rule of conduct, there is wanting one of the principal ingredients of human happiness, and quite the chief ingredient of individual and social progress. . . .

Few persons, out of Germany, even comprehend the meaning of the doctrine which Wilhelm von Humboldt, so eminent both as a savant and as a politician, made the text of a treatise—that "the end of man, or that which is prescribed by the eternal or immutable dictates of reason, and not suggested by vague and transient desires, is the highest and most harmonious development of his powers to a complete and consistent whole," that, therefore, the object "towards which every human being must ceaselessly direct his efforts, and on which especially those who design to influence their fellow-men must ever keep their eyes, is the individuality of power and development"; that for this there are two requisites, "freedom, and variety of situations"; and that from the union of these arise "individual vigor and manifold diversity," which combine themselves in "originality." . . .

He who lets the world, or his own portion of it, choose his plan of life for him, has no need of any other faculty than the ape-like one of imitation. He who chooses his plan for himself, employs all his faculties. He must use observation to see, reasoning and judgments to foresee, activity to gather materials for decision, discrimination to decide, and when he has decided, firmness and self-control to hold to his deliberate decision. And these qualities he requires and exercises exactly in proportion as the part of his conduct which he determines according to his own judgment and feelings is a large one. It is possible that he might be guided in some good path, and kept out of harm's way, without any of these things. But what will be his comparative worth as a human being? It really is of importance, not only what men do, but also what manner of men they are that do it. Among the works of man which human life is rightly employed in perfecting and beautifying, the first in importance surely is man himself. . . . Human nature is not a machine to be built after a model, and set to do exactly the work prescribed for it, but a tree, which requires to grow and develop itself on all sides, according to the tendency of the inward forces which make it a living thing. . . .

But society has now fairly got the better of individuality. . . . In our times, from the highest class of society down to the lowest, everyone lives as under the eye of a hostile and dreaded censorship. Not only in what concerns others, but in what concerns only themselves, the individual or the family do not ask themselves—what do I prefer? or, what would suit my character and disposition? or, what would allow the best and highest in me to have fair play, and enable it to grow and thrive? They ask themselves, what is suitable to my position? what is usually done by persons of my station and pecuniary circumstances? or (worse still) what is usually done by persons of a station and circumstances superior to mine? I do not mean that they choose what is customary in preference to what suits their own inclination. It does not occur to them to have any inclination, except for what is customary. Thus the mind itself is bowed to the yoke: even in what people do for pleasure, conformity is the first thing thought of; they like crowds; they exercise choice only among things commonly done: peculiarity of taste, eccentricity of conduct, are shunned equally with crimes: until by dint of not following their own nature they have no nature to follow: their human capacities are withered and starved: they become incapable of any strong wishes or native pleasures, and are generally without either opinions or feelings of home growth, or properly their own. Now is this, or is it not, the desirable condition of human nature?. . .

OF THE LIMITS TO THE AUTHORITY OF SOCIETY OVER THE INDIVIDUAL

Though society is not founded on a contract, and though no good purpose is answered by inventing a contract in order to deduce social obligations from it, everyone who receives the protection of society owes a return for the benefit, and the fact of living in society renders it indispensable that each should be bound to observe a certain line of conduct towards the rest. This conduct consists, *first,* in not injuring the interests of one another; or rather certain interests, which either by express legal provision or by tacit understanding, ought to be considered as rights; and *secondly,* in each person's bearing his share (to be fixed on some equitable principle) of the labors and sacrifices incurred for defending the society or its members from injury and molestation. These conditions society is justified in enforcing, at all costs to those who endeavor to withhold fulfillment. Nor is this all that society may do. The acts of an individual may be hurtful to others, or wanting in due consideration for their welfare, without going to the length of violating any of their constituted rights. The offender may then be justly punished by opinion,

though not by law. As soon as any part of a person's conduct affects prejudicially the interests of others, society has jurisdiction over it, and the question whether the general welfare will or will not be promoted by interfering with it, becomes open to discussion. But there is no room for entertaining any such question when a person's conduct affects the interests of no persons besides himself, or need not affect them unless they like (all the persons concerned being of full age, and the ordinary amount of understanding). In all such cases, there should be perfect freedom, legal and social, to do the action and stand the consequences.

It would be a great misunderstanding of this doctrine to suppose that it is one of selfish indifference, which pretends that human beings have no business with each other's conduct in life, and that they should not concern themselves about the well-doing or well-being of one another, unless their own interest is involved. Instead of any diminution, there is need of a great increase of disinterested exertion to promote the good of others. But disinterested benevolence can find other instruments to persuade people to their good than whips and scourges, either of the literal or the metaphorical sort. I am the last person to undervalue the self-regarding virtues: they are only second in importance, if even second, to the social. It is equally the business of education to cultivate both. But even education works by conviction and persuasion as well as by compulsion, and it is by the former only that, when the period of education is passed, the self-regarding virtues should be inculcated. Human beings owe to each other help to distinguish the better from the worse, and encouragement to choose the former and avoid the latter. They should be forever stimulating each other to increased exercise of their higher faculties, and increased direction of their feelings and aims towards wise instead of foolish, elevating instead of degrading, objects and contemplations. But neither one person, nor any number of persons, is warranted in saying to another human creature of ripe years, that he shall not do with his life for his own benefit what he chooses to do with it. He is the person most interested in his own well-being: the interest which any other person, except in cases of strong personal attachment, can have in it, is trifling, compared with that which he himself has; the interest which society has in him individually (except as to conduct to others) is fractional, and altogether indirect; while with respect to his own feelings and circumstances, the most ordinary man or woman has means of knowledge immeasurably surpassing those that can be possessed by anyone else. The interference of society to overrule his judgment and purposes in what only regards himself must be grounded on general presumptions; which may be altogether wrong, and even if right, are as likely as not to be misapplied to individual cases, by persons no better acquainted with the circumstances of such cases than those are who look at them merely from without. In this department, therefore, of human affairs, individuality has its proper field of action. In the conduct of human beings towards one another it is necessary that general rules should for the most part be observed, in order that people may know what they have to expect; but in each person's own concerns his individual spontaneity is entitled to free exercise. Considerations to aid his judgment, exhortations to strengthen his will, may be offered to him, even obtruded on him, by others: but he himself is the final judge. All errors which he is likely to commit against advice and warning are far outweighed by the evil of allowing others to constrain him to what they deem his good. . . .

Though doing no wrong to anyone, a person may so act as to compel us to judge him, and feel to him, as a fool, or as a being of an inferior order; and since this judgment and feeling are a fact which he would prefer to avoid, it is doing him a service to warn him of it beforehand, as of any other disagreeable consequence to which he exposes himself. . . . We have a right, also, in various ways, to act upon our unfavorable opinion of anyone, not to the oppression of his individuality, but in the exercise of ours. We are not bound,

for example, to seek his society; we have a right to avoid it (though not to parade the avoidance), for we have a right to choose the society most acceptable to us. We have a right, and it may be our duty, to caution others against him, if we think his example or conversation likely to have a pernicious effect on those with whom he associates. We may give others a preference over him in optional good offices, except those which tend to his improvement. In these various modes a person may suffer very severe penalties at the hands of others for faults which directly concern only himself; but he suffers these penalties only in so far as they are the natural and, as it were, the spontaneous consequences of the faults themselves, not because they are purposely inflicted on him for the sake of punishment. . . .

What I contend for is, that the inconveniences which are strictly inseparable from the unfavorable judgment of others, are the only ones to which a person should ever be subjected for that portion of his conduct and character which concerns his own good, but which does not affect the interest of others in their relations with him. Acts injurious to others require a totally different treatment. Encroachment on their rights; infliction on them of any loss or damage not justified by his own rights; falsehood or duplicity in dealing with them; unfair or ungenerous use of advantages over them; even selfish abstinence from defending them against injury—these are fit objects of moral reprobation, and, in grave cases, of moral retribution and punishment. And not only these acts, but the dispositions which lead to them, are properly immoral, and fit subjects of disapprobation which may rise to abhorrence. . . .

The distinction here pointed out between the part of a person's life which concerns only himself, and that which concerns others, many persons will refuse to admit. How (it may be asked)—can any part of the conduct of a member of society be a matter of indifference to the other members? No person is an entirely isolated being; it is impossible for a person to do anything seriously or permanently hurtful to himself, without mischief reaching at least to his near connections, and often far beyond them. If he injures his property, he does harm to those who directly or indirectly derived support from it, and usu-ally diminishes, by a greater or less amount, the general resources of the community. If he deteriorates his bodily or mental faculties, he not only brings evil upon all who depended on him for any portion of their happiness, but disqualifies himself for rendering the services which he owes to his fellow-creatures generally; perhaps becomes a burden on their affection or benevolence; and if such conduct were very frequent, hardly an offense that is committed would detract more from the general sum of good. Finally, if by his vices or follies a person does not direct harm to others, he is nevertheless (it may be said) injurious by his example; and ought to be compelled to control himself, for the sake of those whom the sight or knowledge of his conduct might corrupt or mislead.

And even (it will be added) if the consequences of misconduct could be confined to the vicious or thoughtless individual, ought society to abandon to their own guidance those who are manifestly unfit for it? If protection against themselves is confessedly due to children and persons under age, is not society equally bound to afford it to persons of mature years who are equally incapable of self-government? If gambling, or drunkenness, or incontinence, or idleness, or uncleanliness, are as injurious to happiness, and as great a hindrance to improvement, as many or most of the acts prohibited by law, why (it may be asked) should not law, so far as is consistent with practicability and social convenience, endeavor to repress these also? And as a supplement to the unavoidable imperfections of law, ought not opinion at least to organize a powerful police against these vices, and visit rigidly with social penalties those who are known to practice them? There is no question here (it may be said) about restricting individuality, or impeding the trial of new and original experiments in living. The only things it is sought to prevent are things which have been tried and condemned

from the beginning of the world until now; things which experience has shown not to be useful or suitable to any person's individuality. There must be some length of time and amount of experience after which a moral or prudential truth may be regarded as estalished: and it is merely desired to prevent generation after generation from falling over the same precipice which has been fatal to their predecessors.

I fully admit that the mischief which a person does to himself may seriously affect, both through their sympathies and their interests, those nearly connected with him and, in a minor degree, society at large. When, by conduct of this sort, a person is led to violate a distinct and assignable obligation to any other person or persons, the case is taken out of the self-regarding class and becomes amenable to moral disapprobation in the proper sense of the term. If, for example, a man, through intemperance or extravagance, becomes unable to pay his debts, or, having undertaken the moral responsibility of a family, becomes from the same cause incapable of supporting or educating them, he is deservedly reprobated, and might be justly punished; but it is for the breach of duty to his family or creditors, not for the extravagance. If the resources which ought to have been devoted to them, had been diverted from them for the most prudent investment, the moral culpability would have been the same. George Barnwell murdered his uncle to get money for his mistress, but if he had done it to set himself up in business he would equally have been hanged. Again, in the frequent case of a man who causes grief to his family by addiction to bad habits, he deserves reproach for his unkindness or ingratitude; but so he may for cultivating habits not in themselves vicious, if they are painful to those with whom he passes his life, or who from personal ties are dependent on him for their comfort. Whoever fails in the consideration generally due to the interests and feelings of others, not being compelled by some more imperative duty, or justified by allowable self-preference, is a subject of moral disapprobation for that failure, but not for the cause of it, nor for the errors, merely personal to himself, which may have remotely led to it. In like manner, when a person disables himself, by conduct purely self-regarding, from the performance of some definite duty incumbent on him to the public, he is guilty of a social offense. No person ought to be punished simply for being drunk; but a soldier or policeman should be punished for being drunk on duty. Whenever, in short, there is a definite damage, or a definite risk of damage, either to an individual or to the public, the case is taken out of the province of liberty and placed in that of morality or law.

But with regard to the merely contingent or, as it may be called, constructive injury which a person causes to society by conduct which neither violates any specific duty to the public, nor occasions perceptible hurt to any assignable individual except himself, the inconvenience is one which society can afford to bear, for the sake of the greater good of human freedom. If grown persons are to be punished for not taking proper care of themselves, I would rather it were for their own sake than under pretense of preventing them from impairing their capacity or rendering to society benefits which society does not pretend it has a right to exact. But I cannot consent to argue the point as if society had no means of bringing its weaker members up to its ordinary standard of rational conduct, except waiting till they do something irrational, and then punishing them, legally or morally, for it. Society has had absolute power over them during all the early portion of their existence; it has had the whole period of childhood and nonage in which to try whether it could make them capable of rational conduct in life. The existing generation is master both of the training and the entire circumstances of the generation to come; it cannot indeed make them perfectly wise and good, because it is itself so lamentably deficient in goodness and wisdom; and its best efforts are not always, in individual cases, its most successful ones; but it is perfectly well able to make the rising generation, as a whole, as good as, and

a little better than, itself. If society lets any considerable number of its members grow up mere children, incapable of being acted on by rational consideration of distant motives, society has itself to blame for the consequences. Armed not only with all the powers of education, but with the ascendancy which the authority of a received opinion always exercises over the minds who are least fitted to judge for themselves, and aided by the *natural* penalties which cannot be prevented from falling on those who incur the distaste or the contempt of those who know them—let not society pretend that it needs, besides all this, the power to issue commands and enforce obedience in the personal concerns of individuals in which, on all principles of justice and policy, the decision ought to rest with those who are to abide the consequences. Nor is there anything which tends more to discredit and frustrate the better means of influencing conduct than a resort to the worse. If there be among those whom it is attempted to coerce into prudence or temperance any of the material of which vigorous and independent characters are made, they will infallibly rebel against the yoke. No such person will ever feel that others have a right to control him in his concerns, such as they have to prevent him from injuring them in theirs; and it easily comes to be considered a mark of spirit and courage to fly in the face of such usurped authority and do with ostentation the exact opposite of what it enjoins, as in the fashion of grossness which succeeded, in the time of Charles II, to the fanatical moral intolerance of the Puritans. With respect to what is said of the necessity of protecting society from the bad example set to others by the vicious or the self-indulgent, it is true that bad example may have a pernicious effect, especially the example of doing wrong to others with impunity to the wrongdoer. But we are now speaking of conduct which, while it does no wrong to others, is supposed to do great harm to the agent himself; and I do not see how those who believe this can think otherwise than that the example, on the whole, must be more salutary than hurtful, since, if it displays the misconduct, it displays also the painful or degrading consequences which, if the conduct is justly censured, must be supposed to be in all or most cases attendant on it.

But the strongest of all the arguments against the interference of the public with purely personal conduct is that, when it does interfere, the odds are that it interferes wrongly and in the wrong place. On questions of social morality, of duty to others, the opinion of the public, that is, of an overruling majority, though often wrong, is likely to be still oftener right, because on such questions they are only required to judge of their own interests, of the manner in which some mode of conduct, if allowed to be practiced, would affect themselves. But the opinion of a similar majority, imposed as a law on the minority, on questions of self-regarding conduct is quite as likely to be wrong as right, for in these cases public opinion means, at the best, some people's opinion of what is good or bad for other people, while very often it does not even mean that—the public, with the most perfect indifference, passing over the pleasure or convenience of those whose conduct they censure and considering only their own preference. There are many who consider as an injury to themselves any conduct which they have a distaste for, and resent it as an outrage to their feelings; as a religious bigot, when charged with disregarding the religious feelings of others, has been known to retort that they disregard his feelings by persisting in their abominable worship or creed. But there is no parity between the feeling of a person for his own opinion and the feeling of another who is offended at his holding it, no more than between the desire of a thief to take a purse and the desire of the right owner to keep it. And a person's taste is as much his own peculiar concern as his opinion or his purse. It is easy for anyone to imagine an ideal public which leaves the freedom and choice of individuals in all uncertain matters undisturbed and only requires them to abstain from modes of conduct which universal experience has condemned. But where has there

been seen a public which set any such limit to its censorship? Or when does the public trouble itself about universal experience? In its interferences with personal conduct it is seldom thinking of anything but the enormity of acting or feeling differently from itself. . . .

APPLICATIONS

. . . It is a proper office of public authority to guard against accidents. If either a public officer or anyone else saw a person attempting to cross a bridge which had been ascertained to be unsafe, and there were no time to warn him of his danger, they might seize him and turn him back, without any real infringement of his liberty; for liberty consists in doing what one desires, and he does not desire to fall into the river. Nevertheless, when there is not a certainty, but only a danger of mischief, no one but the person himself can judge of the sufficiency of the motive which may prompt him to incur the risk; in this case, therefore (unless he is a child, or delirious, or in some state of excitement or absorption incompatible with the full use of the reflecting faculty), he ought, I conceive, to be only warned of the danger; not forcibly prevented from exposing himself to it. . . .

[However] in this and most other civilized countries an engagement by which a person should sell himself, or allow himself to be sold, as a slave, would be null and void; neither enforced by law nor by opinion. The ground for thus limiting his power of voluntarily disposing of his own lot in life, is apparent, and is very clearly seen in this extreme case. The reason for not interfering unless for the sake of others, with a person's voluntary acts, is consideration for his liberty. His voluntary choice is evidence that what he so chooses is desirable, or at least endurable, to him, and his good is on the whole best provided for by allowing him to take his own means of pursuing it. But by selling himself for a slave, he abdicates his liberty; he foregoes any future use of it beyond that single act.

He therefore defeats, in his own case, the very purpose which is the justification of allowing him to dispose of himself. He is no longer free; but is thenceforth in a position which has no longer the presumption in its favor, that would be afforded by his voluntarily remaining in it. The principle of freedom cannot require that he should be free not to be free. It is not freedom to be allowed to alienate his freedom. . . .

REVIEW AND DISCUSSION QUESTIONS

1. Mill argues that the good life involves more than mere contentment. Of what else, specifically, does true well-being consist?
2. What "faculties" does Mill believe people living truly worthwhile and valuable lives will employ?
3. Mill admits that many acts may affect others, but he insists that unless they also harm others, government may not intervene. How does Mill define *harm?*
4. Describe how Mill thinks society may try to influence people whose actions are harmless to others, yet either immoral or not in their true interest.
5. What reasons does Mill give to support his claim that harming others is necessary to justify punishment?
6. Sometimes, Mill says, society is wise not to interfere even though an act is harmful to another. Give an example of such an act; then explain why Mill thinks society should nevertheless not interfere.
7. What does Mill say may be done if somebody is about to walk off a bridge? May society prevent suicide? Explain.
8. Why may a person not sell himself or herself into slavery, according to Mill? Is this position consistent with the rest of his essay? Explain.

Requiring Medical Treatment

JFK Memorial Hospital v. *Heston*

Legal paternalism is the position that legal coercion may be used to protect individuals from self-inflicted harm; it therefore implies that sometimes the state knows the interests of individual citizens better than they themselves do. The following case, argued before the New Jersey Supreme Court, concerns a young woman who for religious reasons refused a blood transfusion deemed medically necessary to save her life.

The Opinion of the Court Was Delivered by Weintraub, C. J.: Delores Heston, age 22 and unmarried, was severely injured in an automobile accident. She was taken to the plaintiff's hospital where it was determined that she would expire unless operated upon for a ruptured spleen and that if operated upon she would expire unless whole blood was administered. Miss Heston and her parents are Jehovah's Witnesses and a tenet of their faith forbids blood transfusions. Miss Heston insists she expressed her refusal to accept blood, but the evidence indicates she was in shock on admittance to the hospital and in the judgment of the attending physicians and nurses was then or soon became disoriented and incoherent. Her mother remained adamant in her opposition to a transfusion, and signed a release of liability for the hospital and medical personnel. Miss Heston did not execute a release; presumably she could not. Her father could not be located.

Death being imminent, plaintiff on notice to the mother made application at 1:30 A.M. to a judge of the Superior Court for the appointment of a guardian for Miss Heston with directions to consent to transfusions as needed to save her life. At the hearing, the mother and her friends thought a certain doctor would pursue surgery without a transfusion, but the doctor, in response to the judge's telephone call, declined the case. The court appointed a guardian with authority to consent to blood transfusions "for the preservation of the life of Delores Heston." Surgery was performed at 4:00 A.M. the same morning. Blood was administered. Miss Heston survived.

Defendants then moved to vacate the order. Affidavits were submitted by both sides. The trial court declined to vacate the order. This appeal followed. We certified it before argument in the Appellate Division.

The controversy is moot. Miss Heston is well and no longer in plaintiff's hospital. The prospect of her return at some future day in like circumstances is too remote to warrant a declaratory judgment as between the parties. Nonetheless, the public interest warrants a resolution of the cause, and for that reason we accept the issue. . . .

In *Perricone,* we sustained an order for compulsory blood transfusion for an infant despite the objection of the parents who were Jehovah's Witnesses. In *Raleigh Fitkin-Paul Morgan Memorial Hospital* v. *Anderson, N.J.* (1964), it appeared that both the mother, a Jehovah's Witness, and the child she was bearing would die if blood were not transfused should she hemorrhage. We held that a blood

transfusion could be ordered if necessary to save the lives of the mother and the unborn child. We said:

> We have no difficulty in so deciding with respect to the infant child. The more difficult question is whether an adult may be compelled to submit to such medical procedures when necessary to save his life. Here we think it is unnecessary to decide that question in broad terms because the welfare of the child and the mother are so intertwined and inseparable that it would be impracticable to attempt to distinguish between them with respect to the sundry factual patterns which may develop. The blood transfusions (including transfusions made necessary by the delivery) may be administered if necessary to save her life or the life of her child, as the physician in charge at the time may determine.

The case at hand presents the question we thus reserved in *Raleigh Fitkin-Paul Morgan Memorial Hospital.*

It seems correct to say there is no constitutional right to choose to die. Attempted suicide was a crime at common law and was held to be a crime under N.J.S.A. 2A:85–1. It is now denounced as a disorderly persons offense. N.J.S.A. 2A:170–25.6. Ordinarily nothing would be gained by a prosecution, and hence the offense is rarely charged. Nonetheless the Constitution does not deny the State an interest in the subject. It is commonplace for the police and other citizens, often at great risk to themselves, to use force or stratagem to defeat efforts at suicide, and it could hardly be said that thus to save someone from himself violated a right of his under the Constitution subjecting the rescuer to civil or penal consequences.

Nor is constitutional right established by adding that one's religious faith ordains his death. Religious beliefs are absolute, but conduct in pursuance of religious beliefs is not wholly immune from governmental restraint. *Mountain Lakes Bd. of Educ.* v. *Maas, N.J.* (1960) (vaccination of children); *Bunn* v. *North Carolina* (1949) (the use of snakes in a religious ritual); *Baer* v. *City of Bend, Or.* (1956) (fluoridation of drinking water). Of immediate interest is *Reynolds* v. *United States* (1878), in which it was held that Congress could punish polygamy in a territory notwithstanding that polygamy was permitted or demanded by religious tenet, and in which the Court said:

> Laws are made for the government of actions, and while they cannot interfere with mere religious belief and opinions, they may with practices. Suppose one believed that human sacrifices were a necessary part of religious worship, would it be seriously contended that the civil government under which he lived could not interfere to prevent a sacrifice? Or if a wife religiously believed it was her duty to burn herself upon the funeral pile of her dead husband, would it be beyond the power of the civil government to prevent her carrying her belief into practice?

Complicating the subject of suicide is the difficulty of knowing whether a decision to die is firmly held. Psychiatrists may find that beneath it all a person bent on self-destruction is hoping to be rescued, and most who are rescued do not repeat the attempt, at least not at once. Then, too, there is the question whether in any event the person was and continues to be competent (a difficult concept in this area) to choose to die. And of course there is no opportunity for a trial of these questions in advance of intervention by the State or a citizen.

Appellant suggests there is a difference between passively submitting to death and actively seeking it. The distinction may be merely verbal, as it would be if an adult sought death by starvation instead of a drug. If the State may interrupt one mode of self-destruction, it may with equal authority interfere with the other. It is arguably different when an individual, overtaken by illness, decides to let it run a fatal course. But unless the medical option itself is laden with the risk of death or of serious infirmity, the State's interest in sustaining life in such circumstances is hardly distinguishable from its interest in the case of suicide.

Here we are not dealing with deadly options. The risk of death or permanent injury because of a transfusion is not a serious factor. Indeed, Miss Heston did not resist a transfusion on that basis. Nor did she wish to die. She wanted to live, but her faith demanded that she refuse blood even at the price of her life. The question is not whether the State could punish her for refusing a transfusion. It may be granted that it would serve no State interest to deal criminally with one who resisted a transfusion on the basis of religious faith. The question is whether the State may authorize force to prevent death or may tolerate the use of force by others to that end. Indeed, the issue is not solely between the State and Miss Heston, for the controversy is also between Miss Heston and a hospital and staff who did not seek her out and upon whom the dictates of her faith will fall as a burden.

Hospitals exist to aid the sick and the injured. The medical and nursing professions are consecrated to preserving life. That is their professional creed. To them, a failure to use a simple, established procedure in the circumstances of this case would be malpractice, however the law may characterize that failure because of the patient's private convictions. A surgeon should not be asked to operate under the strain of knowing that a transfusion may not be administered even though medically required to save this patient. The hospital and its staff should not be required to decide whether the patient is or continues to be competent to make a judgment upon the subject, or whether the release tendered by the patient or a member of his family will protect them from civil responsibility. The hospital could hardly avoid the problem by compelling the removal of a dying patient, and Miss Heston's family made no effort to take her elsewhere.

When the hospital and staff are thus involuntary hosts and their interests are pitted against the belief of the patient, we think it reasonable to resolve the problem by permitting the hospital and its staff to pursue their functions according to their professional standards. The solution sides with life, the conservation of which is, we think, a matter of State interest. A prior application to a court is appropriate if time permits it, although in the nature of the emergency the only question that can be explored satisfactorily is whether death will probably ensue if medical procedures are not followed. If a court finds, as the trial court did, that death will likely follow unless a transfusion is administered, the hospital and the physician should be permitted to follow that medical procedure.

For the reasons already given, we find that the interest of the hospital and its staff, as well as the State's interest in life, warranted the transfusion of blood under the circumstances of this case. The judgment is accordingly affirmed.

REVIEW AND DISCUSSION QUESTIONS

1. On what ground does the court reach its opinion that Delores Heston should be forced to accept the transfusion?
2. How would Mill respond to this case? Explain.
3. If the woman's reasons were not based on established religious doctrine, do you think the courts would have had so much difficulty with these decisions? Would you? Explain.
4. In Michigan, a court considered the question whether a law requiring motorcycle helmets was constitutional. Using the essays that you have read in this section, explain whether or not you think such a law is philosophically justified. (The Michigan court in fact held that the law was unconstitutional and invalidated it, saying that it could not find a strong enough relationship between the law and public health, safety, or welfare.)

The Ethics of Addiction: An Argument in Favor of Letting Americans Take Any Drug They Want

Thomas Szasz

Relying explicitly on John Stuart Mill's discussion of liberty, Thomas Szasz discusses the legalization of drugs. After reviewing the historical effects of prohibition, he argues that such policies lead to socially harmful consequences and also fail to respect the legitimate control citizens may exercise over their own lives. A decent regard for individual liberty demands that government respect its citizens' right to "life, liberty, and the pursuit of highs." Thomas Szasz is a psychiatrist and the author of many books.

To avoid clichés about "drug abuse," let us analyze its official definition. According to the World Health Organization, "Drug addiction is a state of periodic or chronic intoxication detrimental to the individual and to society, produced by the repeated consumption of a drug (natural or synthetic). Its characteristics include: (1) an overpowering desire or need (compulsion) to continue taking the drug and to obtain it by any means, (2) a tendency to increase the dosage, and (3) a psychic (psychological) and sometimes physical dependence on the effects of the drug."

Since this definition hinges on the harm

done to both the individual and society, it is clearly an ethical one. Moreover, by not specifying what is "detrimental," it consigns the problem of addiction to psychiatrists who define the patient's "dangerousness to himself and others."

Next, we come to the effort to obtain the addictive substance "by any means." This suggests that the substance must be prohibited, or is very expensive, and is hence difficult for the ordinary person to obtain (rather than that the person who wants it has an inordinate craving for it). If there were an abundant and inexpensive supply of what the "addict" wants, there would be no reason for him to go to "any means" to obtain it. Thus by the WHO's definition, one can be addicted only to a substance that is illegal or otherwise difficult to obtain. This surely removes the problem of addiction from the realm of medicine and psychiatry, and puts it squarely into that of morals and law.

In short, drug addiction or drug abuse cannot be defined without specifying the proper and improper uses of certain pharmacologically active agents. The regular administration of morphine by a physician to a patient dying of cancer is the paradigm of the proper use of a narcotic; whereas even its occasional self-administration by a physically healthy person for the purpose of "pharmacological pleasure" is the paradigm of drug abuse.

I submit that these judgments have nothing whatever to do with medicine, pharmacology, or psychiatry. They are moral judgments. Indeed, our present views on addiction are astonishingly similar to some of our former views on sex. Until recently, masturbation— or self-abuse, as it was called—was professionally declared, and popularly accepted, as both the cause and the symptom of a variety of illnesses. Even today, homosexuality— called a "sexual perversion"—is regarded as a disease by medical and psychiatric experts as well as by "well-informed" laymen.

To be sure, it is now virtually impossible to cite a contemporary medical authority to support the concept of self-abuse. Medical opinion holds that whether a person masturbates or not is medically irrelevant: and that engaging in the practice or refraining from it is a matter of personal morals or life-style. On the other hand, it is virtually impossible to cite a contemporary medical authority to oppose the concept of drug abuse. Medical opinion holds that drug abuse is a major medical, psychiatric, and public health problem; that drug addiction is a disease similar to diabetes, requiring prolonged (or lifelong) and careful, medically supervised treatment; and that taking or not taking drugs is primarily, if not solely, a matter of medical responsibility.

Thus the man on the street can only believe what he hears from all sides—that drug addiction is a disease, "like any other," which has now reached "epidemic proportions," and whose "medical" containment justifies the limitless expenditure of tax monies and the corresponding aggrandizement and enrichment of noble medical warriors against this "plague."

PROPAGANDA TO JUSTIFY PROHIBITION

Like any social policy, our drug laws may be examined from two entirely different points of view: technical and moral. Our present inclination is either to ignore the moral perspective or to mistake the technical for the moral.

Since most of the propagandists against drug abuse seek to justify certain repressive policies because of the alleged dangerousness of various drugs, they often falsify the facts about the true pharmacological properties of the drugs they seek to prohibit. They do so for two reasons: first, because many substances in daily use are just as harmful as the substances they want to prohibit: second, because they realize that dangerousness alone is never a sufficiently persuasive argument to justify the prohibition of any drug, substance, or artifact. Accordingly, the more they ignore the moral dimensions of the problem, the more they must escalate their fraudulent claims about the dangers of drugs.

To be sure, some drugs are more dangerous than others. It is easier to kill oneself with heroin than with aspirin. But it is also easier to kill oneself by jumping off a high building than a low one. In the case of drugs, we regard their potentiality for self-injury as justification for their prohibition; in the case of buildings, we do not.

Furthermore, we systematically blur and confuse the two quite different ways in which narcotics may cause death: by a deliberate act of suicide or by accidental overdosage.

Every individual is capable of injuring or killing himself. This potentiality is a fundamental expression of human freedom. Self-destructive behavior may be regarded as sinful and penalized by means of informal sanctions. But it should not be regarded as a crime or (mental) disease, justifying or warranting the use of the police powers of the state for its control.

Therefore, it is absurd to deprive an adult of a drug (or of anything else) because he might use it to kill himself. To do so is to treat everyone the way institutional psychiatrists treat the so-called suicidal mental patient: they not only imprison such a person but take everything away from him—shoelaces, belts, razor blades, eating utensils, and so forth—until the "patient" lies naked on a mattress in a padded cell—lest he kill himself. The result is degrading tyrannization.

Death by accidental overdose is an altogether different matter. But can anyone doubt that this danger now looms so large precisely because the sale of narcotics and many other drugs is illegal? Those who buy illicit drugs cannot be sure what drug they are getting or how much of it. Free trade in drugs, with governmental action limited to safeguarding the purity of the product and the veracity of the labeling, should reduce the risk of accidental overdose with "dangerous drugs" to the same levels that prevail, and that we find acceptable, with respect to other chemical agents and physical artifacts that abound in our complex technological society.

This essay is not intended as an exposition on the pharmacological properties of narcotics and other mind-affecting drugs. However, I want to make it clear that in my view, *regardless* of their danger, all drugs should be "legalized" (a misleading term I employ reluctantly as a concession to common usage). Although I recognize that some drugs—notably heroin, the amphetamines, and LSD, among those now in vogue—may have undesirable or dangerous consequences, I favor free trade in drugs for the same reason the Founding Fathers favored free trade in ideas. In an open society, it is none of the government's business what idea a man puts into his mind; likewise, it should be none of the government's business what drug he puts into his body.

WITHDRAWAL PAINS FROM TRADITION

It is a fundamental characteristic of human beings that they get used to things: one becomes habituated, or "addicted," not only to narcotics, but to cigarettes, cocktails before dinner, orange juice for breakfast, comic strips, and so forth. It is similarly a fundamental characteristic of living organisms that they acquire increasing tolerance to various chemical agents and physical stimuli: the first cigarette may cause nothing but nausea and headache; a year later, smoking three packs a day may be pure joy. Both alcohol and opiates are "addictive" in the sense that the more regularly they are used, the more the user craves them and the greater his tolerance for them becomes. Yet none of this involves any mysterious process of "getting hooked." It is simply an aspect of the universal biological propensity for *learning*, which is especially well developed in man. The opiate habit, like the cigarette habit or food habit, can be broken—and without any medical assistance—provided the person wants to break it. Often he doesn't. And why, indeed, should he, if he has nothing better to do with his life? Or, as happens to be the case with morphine, if he can live an essentially normal life while under its influence?

Actually, opium is much less toxic than alcohol. Just as it is possible to be an "alcoholic" and work and be productive, so it is (or, rather, it used to be) possible to be an opium addict and work and be productive. According to a definitive study published by the American Medical Association in 1929, ". . . morphine addiction is not characterized by physical deterioration or impairment of physical fitness. . . . There is no evidence of change in the circulatory, hepatic, renal, or endocrine functions. When it is considered that these subjects had been addicted for at least five years, some of them for as long as twenty years, these negative observations are highly significant." In a 1928 study, Lawrence Kolb, an Assistant Surgeon General of the United States Public Health Service, found that of 119 persons addicted to opiates through medical practice, "90 had good industrial records and only 29 had poor ones. . . . Judged by the output of labor and their own statements, none of the normal persons had [his] efficiency reduced by opium. Twenty-two of them worked regularly while taking opium for twenty-five years or more; one of them, a woman aged 81 and still alert mentally, had taken 3 grains of morphine daily for 65 years. [The usual therapeutic dose is one-quarter grain, three to four grains being fatal for the nonaddict.] She gave birth to and raised six children, and managed her household affairs with more than average efficiency. A widow, aged 66, had taken 17 grains of morphine daily for most of 37 years. She is alert mentally, does physical labor every day, and makes her own living."

I am not citing this evidence to recommend the opium habit. The point is that we must, in plain honesty, distinguish between pharmacological effects and personal inclinations. Some people take drugs to help them function and conform to social expectations; others take them for the very opposite reason, to ritualize their refusal to function and conform to social expectations. Much of the "drug abuse" we now witness—perhaps nearly all of it—is of the second type. But instead of acknowledging that "addicts" are unfit or unwilling to work and be "normal," we prefer to believe that they act as they do because certain drugs—especially heroin, LSD, and the

amphetamines—make them "sick." If only we could get them "well," so runs this comforting view, they would become "productive" and "useful" citizens. To believe this is like believing that if an illiterate cigarette smoker would only stop smoking, he would become an Einstein. With a falsehood like this, one can go far. No wonder that politicians and psychiatrists love it.

The concept of free trade in drugs runs counter to our cherished notion that everyone must work and idleness is acceptable only under special conditions. . . . [Drug users] are, in principle at least, capable of working and supporting themselves. But they refuse: they "drop out"; and in doing so, they challenge the most basic values of our society.

The fear that free trade in narcotics would result in vast masses of our population spending their days and nights smoking opium or mainlining heroin, rather than working and taking care of their responsibilities, is a bugaboo that does not deserve to be taken seriously. Habits of work and idleness are deep-seated cultural patterns. Free trade in abortions has not made an industrious people like the Japanese give up work for fornication. Nor would free trade in drugs convert such a people from hustlers to hippies. Indeed, I think the opposite might be the case: it is questionable whether, or for how long, a responsible people can tolerate being treated as totally irresponsible with respect to drugs and drug-taking. In other words, how long can we live with the inconsistency of being expected to be responsible for operating cars and computers, but not for operating our own bodies?

Although my argument about drug-taking is moral and political, and does not depend upon showing that free trade in drugs would also have fiscal advantages over our present policies, let me indicate briefly some of its economic implications.

The war on addiction is not only astronomically expensive; it is also counterproductive. On April 1, 1967, New York State's narcotics addiction control program, hailed as "the most massive ever tried in the nation," went into effect. "The program, which may cost up to $400 million in three years," reported the *New York Times,* "was hailed by Governor Rockefeller as 'the start of an unending war.'" Three years later, it was conservatively estimated that the number of addicts in the state had tripled or quadrupled. New York State Senator John Hughes reports that the cost of caring for each addict during this time was $12,000 per year (as against $4,000 per year for patients in state mental hospitals). It's been a great time, though, for some of the ex-addicts. In New York City's Addiction Services Agency, one ex-addict started at $6,500 a year in 1967, and was making $16,000 seven months later. Another started at $6,500 and soon rose to $18,100. The salaries of the medical bureaucrats in charge of these programs are similarly attractive. In short, the detection and rehabilitation of addicts is good business. We now know that the spread of witchcraft in the late Middle Ages was due more to the work of witchmongers than to the lure of witchcraft. Is it not possible that the spread of addiction in our day is due more to the work of addictmongers than to the lure of narcotics?

Let us see how far some of the monies spent on the war on addiction could go in supporting people who prefer to drop out of society and drug themselves. Their "habit" itself would cost next to nothing: free trade would bring the price of narcotics down to a negligible amount. During the 1969–70 fiscal year, the New York State Narcotics Addiction Control Commission had a budget of nearly $50 million, excluding capital construction. Using these figures as a tentative base for calculation, here is what we come to: $100 million will support 30,000 drug addicts at $3,300 per year. Since the population of New York State is roughly one-tenth that of the nation, if we multiply its operating budget for addiction control by ten, we arrive at a figure of $500 million, enough to support 150,000 addicts.

I am not advocating that we spend our hard-earned money in this way. I am only trying to show that free trade in narcotics would be more economical for those of us who work, even if we had to support legions of addicts, than is our present program of trying to "cure" them. Moreover, I have not even made use, in my economic estimates, of the incalculable sums we would save by reducing crimes now engendered by the illegal traffic in drugs.

THE RIGHT OF SELF-MEDICATION

Clearly, the argument that marijuana—or heroin, methadone, or morphine—is prohibited because it is addictive or dangerous cannot be supported by facts. For one thing, there are many drugs, from insulin to penicillin, that are neither addictive nor dangerous but are nevertheless also prohibited; they can be obtained only through a physician's prescription. For another, there are many things, from dynamite to guns, that are much more dangerous than narcotics (especially to others) but are not prohibited. As everyone knows, it is still possible in the United States to walk into a store and walk out with a shotgun. We enjoy this right not because we believe that guns are safe but because we believe even more strongly that civil liberties are precious. At the same time, it is not possible in the United States to walk into a store and walk out with a bottle of barbiturates, codeine, or other drugs.

I believe that just as we regard freedom of speech and religion as fundamental rights, so we should also regard freedom of self-medication as a fundamental right. Like most rights, the right of self-medication should apply only to adults; and it should not be an unqualified right. Since these are important qualifications, it is necessary to specify their precise range.

John Stuart Mill said (approximately) that a person's right to swing his arm ends where his neighbor's nose begins. And Oliver Wendell Holmes said that no one has a right to shout "Fire!" in a crowded theater. Similarly, the limiting condition with respect to self-medication should be the inflicting of actual (as against symbolic) harm on others.

Our present practices with respect to alcohol embody and reflect this individualistic ethic. We have the right to buy, possess, and consume alcoholic beverages. Regardless of how offensive drunkenness might be to a person, he cannot interfere with another person's "right" to become inebriated so long as that person drinks in the privacy of his own home or at some other appropriate location, and so long as he conducts himself in an otherwise law-abiding manner. In short, we have a right to be intoxicated—in private. Public intoxication is considered an offense to others and is therefore a violation of the criminal law. It makes sense that what is a "right" in one place may become, by virtue of its disruptive or disturbing effect on others, an offense somewhere else.

The right to self-medication should be hedged in by similar limits. Public intoxication, not only with alcohol but with any drug, should be an offense punishable by the criminal law. Furthermore, acts that may injure others—such as driving a car—should, when carried out in a drug-intoxicated state, be punished especially strictly and severely. The right to self-medication must thus entail unqualified responsibility for the effects of one's drug-intoxicated behavior on others. For unless we are willing to hold ourselves responsible for our own behavior, and hold others responsible for theirs, the liberty to use drugs (or to engage in other acts) degenerates into a license to hurt others.

Such, then, would be the situation of adults, if we regarded the freedom to take drugs as a fundamental right similar to the freedom to read and worship. What would be the situation of children? Since many people who are now said to be drug addicts or drug abusers are minors, it is especially important that we think clearly about this aspect of the problem.

I do not believe, and I do not advocate, that children should have a right to ingest, inject, or otherwise use any drug or substance they want. Children do not have the right to drive, drink, vote, marry, or make binding contracts. They acquire these rights at various ages, coming into their full possession at maturity, usually between the ages of eighteen and twenty-one. The right to self-medication should similarly be withheld until maturity.

In short, I suggest that "dangerous" drugs be treated, more or less, as alcohol is treated now. Neither the use of narcotics, nor their possession, should be prohibited, but only their sale to minors. Of course, this would result in the ready availability of all kinds of drugs among minors—though perhaps their availability would be no greater than it is now, but would only be more visible and hence more easily subject to proper controls. This arrangement would place responsibility for the use of all drugs by children where it belongs: on parents and their children. This is where the major responsibility rests for the use of alcohol. It is a tragic symptom of our refusal to take personal liberty and responsibility seriously that there appears to be no public desire to assume a similar stance toward other "dangerous" drugs.

Consider what would happen should a child bring a bottle of gin to school and get drunk there. Would the school authorities blame the local liquor stores as pushers? Or would they blame the parents and the child himself? There is liquor in practically every home in America and yet children rarely bring liquor to school. Whereas marijuana, Dexedrine, and heroin—substances children usually do not find at home and whose very possession is a criminal offense—frequently find their way into the school.

Our attitude toward sexual activity provides another model for our attitude toward drugs. Although we generally discourage children below a certain age from engaging in sexual activities with others, we do not prohibit such activities by law. What we do prohibit by law is the sexual seduction of children by adults. The "pharmacological seduction" of children by adults should be similarly punishable. In other words, adults who give or sell drugs to children should be regarded as offenders. Such a specific and limited prohibition—as against the kinds of generalized prohibitions that we had under the Volstead Act or have now with respect to countless drugs—

would be relatively easy to enforce. More-over, it would probably be rarely violated, for there would be little psychological interest and no economic profit in doing so.

THE TRUE FAITH: SCIENTIFIC MEDICINE

What I am suggesting is that while addiction is ostensibly a medical and pharmacological problem, actually it is a moral and political problem. We ought to know that there is no necessary connection between facts and val-ues, between what is and what ought to be. Thus, objectively quite harmful acts, objects, or persons may be accepted and tolerated—by minimizing their dangerousness. Conver-sely, objectively quite harmless acts, objects, or persons may be prohibited and perse-cuted—by exaggerating their dangerousness. It is always necessary to distinguish—and especially so when dealing with social pol-icy—between description and prescription, fact and rhetoric, truth and falsehood.

In our society, there are two principal methods of legitimizing policy: social tradi-tion and scientific judgment. More than any-thing else, time is the supreme ethical arbiter. Whatever a social practice might be, if people engage in it, generation after generation, that practice becomes acceptable.

Many opponents of illegal drugs admit that nicotine may be more harmful to health than marijuana; nevertheless, they urge that smok-ing cigarettes should be legal but smoking marijuana should not be, because the former habit is socially accepted while the latter is not. This is a perfectly reasonable argument. But let us understand it for what it is—a plea for legitimizing old and accepted practices, and for illegitimizing novel and unaccepted ones. It is a justification that rests on prece-dent, not evidence.

The other method of legitimizing policy, ever more important in the modern world, is through the authority of science. In matters of health, a vast and increasingly elastic cate-gory, physicians play important roles as legit-imizers and illegitimizers. This, in short, is why we regard being medicated by a doctor as drug use, and self-medication (especially with certain classes of drugs) as drug abuse.

This, too, is a perfectly reasonable arrange-ment. But we must understand that it is a plea for legitimizing what doctors do, because they do it with "good therapeutic" intent; and for illegitimizing what laymen do, because they do it with bad self-abusive ("masturbatory" or mind-altering) intent. This justification rests on the principles of professionalism, not of pharmacology. Hence we applaud the system-atic medical use of methadone and call it "treatment for heroin addiction," but decry the occasional nonmedical use of marijuana and call it "dangerous drug abuse."

Our present concept of drug abuse articu-lates and symbolizes a fundamental policy of scientific medicine—namely, that a layman should not medicate his own body but should place its medical care under the supervision of a duly accredited physician. Before the Refor-mation, the practice of True Christianity rested on a similar policy—namely, that a layman should not himself commune with God but should place his spiritual care under the super-vision of a duly accredited priest. The self-interests of the church and of medicine in such policies are obvious enough. What might be less obvious is the interest of the laity: by delegating responsibility for the spiritual and medical welfare of the people to a class of authoritatively accredited specialists, these policies—and the practices they ensure—relieve individuals from assuming the burdens of responsibility for themselves. As I see it, our present problems with drug use and drug abuse are just one of the consequences of our pervasive ambivalence about personal auton-omy and responsibility.

I propose a medical reformation analo-gous to the Protestant Reformation: specifi-cally, a "protest" against the systematic mystification of man's relationship to his body and his professionalized separation from it. The immediate aim of this reform would be to remove the physician as intermediary between man and his body and to give the layman direct access to the language and contents of the pharmacopoeia. If man had unencumbered access to his own body and the means of chemically altering it, it would spell the end of medicine, at least as we now know it. This is why, with faith in scientific medicine so strong, there is little interest in this kind of medical reform. Physicians fear the loss of their privileges; laymen, the loss of their protections.

Finally, since luckily we still do not live in the utopian perfection of "one world," our technical approach to the "drug problem" has led, and will undoubtedly continue to lead, to some curious attempts to combat it.

Here is one such attempt: the American government is now pressuring Turkey to restrict its farmers from growing poppies (the source of morphine and heroin). If turnabout is fair play, perhaps we should expect the Turkish government to pressure the United States to restrict its farmers from growing corn and wheat. Or should we assume that Muslims have enough self-control to leave alcohol alone, but Christians need all the controls that politicians, policemen, and physicians can bring to bear on them to enable them to leave opiates alone?

LIFE, LIBERTY, AND THE PURSUIT OF HIGHS

Sooner or later we shall have to confront the basic moral dilemma underlying this problem: does a person have the right to take a drug, any drug—not because he needs it to cure an illness, but because he wants to take it?

The Declaration of Independence speaks of our inalienable right to "life, liberty, and the pursuit of happiness." How are we to interpret this? By asserting that we ought to be free to pursue happiness by playing golf or watching television, but not by drinking alcohol, or smoking marijuana, or ingesting pep pills?

The Constitution and the Bill of Rights are silent on the subject of drugs. This would seem to imply that the adult citizen has, or

ought to have, the right to medicate his own body as he sees fit. Were this not the case, why should there have been a need for a Constitutional Amendment to outlaw drinking? But if ingesting alcohol was, and is now again, a Constitutional right, is ingesting opium, or heroin, or barbiturates, or anything else, not also such a right? If it is, then the Harrison Narcotic Act is not only a bad law but is unconstitutional as well, because it prescribes in a legislative act what ought to be promulgated in a Constitutional Amendment.

The questions remain: as American citizens, should we have the right to take narcotics or other drugs? If we take drugs and conduct ourselves as responsible and law-abiding citizens, should we have a right to remain unmolested by the government? Lastly, if we take drugs and break the law, should we have a right to be treated as persons accused of crime, rather than as patients accused of mental illness?

These are fundamental questions that are conspicuous by their absence from all contemporary discussions of problems of drug addiction and drug abuse. The result is that instead of debating the use of drugs in moral and political terms, we define our task as the ostensibly narrow technical problem of protecting people from poisoning themselves with substances for whose use they cannot possibly assume responsibility. This, I think, best explains the frightening national consensus against personal responsibility for taking drugs and for one's conduct while under their influence. In 1965, for example, when President Johnson sought a bill imposing tight federal controls over pep pills and goof balls, the bill cleared the House by a unanimous vote, 402 to 0.

The failure of such measures to curb the "drug menace" has only served to inflame our legislators' enthusiasm for them. In October 1970 the Senate passed, again by a unanimous vote (54 to 0), "a major narcotics crackdown bill."

To me, unanimity on an issue as basic and complex as this means a complete evasion of the actual problem and an attempt to master it by attacking and overpowering a scape-goat—"dangerous drugs" and "drug abusers." There is an ominous resemblance between the unanimity with which all "reasonable" men—and especially politicians, physicians, and priests—formerly supported the protective measures of society against witches and Jews, and that with which they now support them against drug addicts and drug abusers.

After all is said and done, the issue comes down to whether we accept or reject the ethical principle John Stuart Mill so clearly enunciated: "The only purpose [he wrote in *On Liberty*] for which power can be rightfully exercised over any member of a civilized community, against his will, is to prevent harm to others. His own good, either physical or moral, is not a sufficient warrant. He cannot rightfully be compelled to do or forbear because it will make him happier, because in the opinions of others, to do so would be wise, or even right. . . . In the part [of his conduct] which merely concerns himself, his independence is, of right, absolute. Over himself, over his own body and mind, the individual is sovereign."

By recognizing the problem of drug abuse for what it is—a moral and political question rather than a medical or therapeutic one—we can choose to maximize the sphere of action of the state at the expense of the individual, or of the individual at the expense of the state. In other words, we could commit ourselves to the view that the state, the representative of many, is more important than the individual; that it therefore has the right, indeed the duty, to regulate the life of the individual in the best interests of the group. Or we could commit ourselves to the view that individual dignity and liberty are the supreme values of life, and that the foremost duty of the state is to protect and promote these values.

In short, we must choose between the ethic of collectivism and individualism, and pay the price of either—or of both.

REVIEW AND DISCUSSION QUESTIONS

1. Describe the "myths" that Szasz says surround drug addiction.
2. What, specifically, does Szasz propose should be done about drug laws? What motivates him to make that proposal?
3. Is this proposal one that Mill would accept? Why?
4. How does Szasz understand addiction? Do you agree with Szasz's analysis? Explain.
5. This article was written more than twenty years ago. What lessons can be learned from the events since then? Would Szasz be likely to feel vindicated or refuted by recent history? Explain.

The Ethics of Smoking

Robert E. Goodin

Unlike the previous author, who doubted whether alcohol and other drugs cause people to lose control, Robert Goodin claims that tobacco's addictive nature means people do not voluntarily choose to smoke and therefore do not freely accept its risks. Beyond these "Kantean style" questions about consent, he argues, lie other, more utilitarian issues about the social costs of smoking. Goodin describes those costs and then responds to two familiar arguments that defenders of smoking have offered in an attempt to show that smoking is not, in fact, economically costly. He concludes with a discussion of three proposals: mandatory warnings, bans, and "medicalization"—that is, making tobacco a prescription drug. Robert E. Goodin is professorial fellow in philosophy at the Australian National University.

1. DO SMOKERS VOLUNTARILY ACCEPT THE RISKS?

Given what we know of the health risks from smoking, we may well be tempted to "ban cigarette manufacturers from continuing to manufacture their product on the grounds that we are preventing them from causing illness to others in the same way that we prevent other manufacturers from releasing pollutants into the atmosphere, thereby causing danger to members of the community." That would be to move too quickly. As Dworkin (1972/1983, p. 22) continues, "The difference is . . . that in the former but not the latter case the harm is of such a nature that it could be avoided by those individuals affected, if they so chose. The incurring of the harm requires the active cooperation of the victim. It would be a mistake in theory and hypocritical in practice to assert that our interference in such cases is just like our interference in standard cases of protecting others from harm." Courts have been as sensitive to this distinction as moral philosophers, appealing to the venerable legal maxim, *volenti non fit injuria,* to hold that through their voluntary assumption of the risk smokers have waived any claims against cigarette manufacturers. In perhaps one of the most dramatic cases (given the well-established synergism between smoking and asbestos inhalation) the Fifth Circuit refused to enjoin cigarette manufacturers as codefendants in a suit against Johns-Manville, saying that "the danger is to the smoker who willingly courts it."[1]

Certainly there is, morally speaking, a world of difference between the harms that others inflict upon you and the harms that you inflict upon yourself. The question is simply whether, in the case of smoking, the active cooperation of the smoker really is such as to constitute voluntary acceptance of the consequent risks of illness and death. This question is decomposable into two further ones. The first concerns the question of whether smokers knew the risks. The second concerns the question of whether, even if smoking in full knowledge of the risks, they could be said to have "accepted" the risks in a sense that was fully voluntary.

The first is essentially a question of "informed consent." People can be held to have consented only if they knew to what they were supposedly consenting. In the personalized context of medical encounters, this means that each and every person being treated is told, in terms he or she understands, by the attending physician what the risks of the treatment might be (Gorovitz 1982, chap. 3). For largely anonymous transactions in the market, such personalized standards are inappropriate. Instead, we are forced to infer consent from what people know or should have known (in the standard legal construct, what a "reasonable" person should have been expected to know) about the product. And in the anonymous world of the market, printed warnings necessarily take the place of face-to-face admonitions.

Cigarette manufacturers, in defending against product liability suits, have claimed on both these grounds that smokers should be construed as having consented to the risks that they have run. They claim, first, that any "reasonable" person should have known, and the "ordinary consumer" did indeed know, that smoking was an "inherently dangerous" activity. Their interrogatories constantly seek to establish that plaintiffs had, in their youth, consorted with people calling cigarettes "coffin nails," and so on. Manufacturers claim,

From Robert E. Goodin, "The Ethics of Smoking," *Ethics,* 99, no. 3. © 1989 University of Chicago Press. Reprinted by permission. Some notes and references omitted.

second, that printing of government-mandated health warnings on cigarette packets from 1966 onward has constituted further, explicit warning to users.

Now, of course, there are some risks (e.g., Buerger's disease, a circulatory condition induced, often in quite young people, by smoking that can result in amputation of limbs) of which smokers were never warned, by grandmother or government health warnings either. Indeed, the warnings of both folk wisdom and cigarette packets in the 1960s and 1970s at least were desperately nonspecific; and there is a more general question whether an all-purpose warning that "X may be hazardous to your health," without specifying just how likely X is to cause just what sorts of harms, is adequate warning to secure people's informed consent at all.

Furthermore, cigarette manufacturers take back through their advertising what is given by way of warnings.[2] The problem is not so much one of literally deceptive advertising—though there is evidence of that, too (U.S. FTC 1981, 1984, 1985)—as it is one of the widespread use of deceptively healthy imagery (U.S. FTC 1981, pp. 428a, 491a). The printed warnings may say "smoking kills," but the advertising images are the very picture of robust good health. Cowboys, sports, and the great outdoors figure centrally in the ads. The U.S. Federal Trade Commission has continually warned Congress that "current practices and methods of cigarette advertising" have the effect of "reducing anxieties about the health risks posed by cigarette smoking" (U.S. FTC 1984, p. 5), "negat[ing] the effect of health warnings because they imply that smoking is a habit which is compatible with performing various outdoor activities and having a strong healthy body" (U.S. FTC 1985, p. 5).[3] The point is not that advertising bypasses consumers' capacity to reason and somehow renders them unfree to choose intelligently whether or not to consume the product. The point is, rather, that tobacco companies in effect are giving out—and, more important, consumers are receiving—conflicting information. The implicit health claims of the advertising imagery conflict with the explicit health warnings and thus undercut any *volenti* or informed-consent defense companies might try to mount on the basis of those warnings

Despite tobacco companies' best efforts, however, nearly everyone—smokers included—knows, in broad outline, the health risks that smoking entails. In a 1978 Gallup poll, only 24 percent of heavy smokers claimed they were unaware of or did not believe the evidence that smoking is hazardous. How that recalcitrant residual should be handled is a hard question. Having smoked thousands of packets containing increasingly stern warnings, and having been exposed to hundreds of column inches of newspaper reporting and several hours of broadcasting about smoking's hazards, they are presumably incorrigible in their false beliefs in this regard. Providing them with still more information is likely to prove pointless.

Ordinarily it is not the business of public policy to prevent people from relying on false inferences from full information which would harm only themselves. Sometimes, however, it is. One such case comes when the false beliefs would lead to decisions that are "far-reaching, potentially dangerous, and irreversible"—as, for example, with people who believe that when they jump out of a tenth-story window they will float upward (Dworkin 1972/1983, p. 31).

We are particularly inclined toward intervention when false beliefs with such disastrous results are traceable to familiar, well-understood forms of cognitive defect. One is "wishful thinking": smokers believing the practice is safe because they smoke rather than smoking because they believe it to be safe (Pears 1984). There is substantial evidence that smokers believe, groundlessly, that they are less vulnerable to smoking-related diseases; there is also evidence that they came to acquire those beliefs, and to "forget" what they previously knew about the dangers of smoking, after they took up the habit (Leventhal, Glynn, and Fleming 1987). Another cognitive defect is the "anchoring" fallacy (Kahneman, Slovic, and Tversky 1982): people smoke many times without any (immediately perceptible) bad effects; and . . . extrapolating from their own experience, they therefore quite reasonably but quite wrongly conclude that smoking is safe for them. Yet another phenomenon, sometimes regarded as a cognitive defect, is "time-discounting": since young smokers will not suffer the full effects of smoking-related diseases for some years to come, they may puff away happily now with little regard for the consequences, if they attach relatively little importance to future pains relative to present pleasures in their utility functions (Fuchs 1982). All of these cognitive defects point to relatively weak forms of irrationality. In and of themselves, they would not be enough to justify interference with people's liberty, perhaps. But when they lead people to make decisions that are far-reaching, potentially dangerous, and irreversible, perhaps intervention would be justified.

Interfering with people's choices in such cases is paternalistic, admittedly. But there are many different layers of paternalism. What is involved here is a relatively weak form of paternalism, working within the individual's own theory of the good and merely imposing upon him better means of achieving his own ends.[4] It is one thing to stop people who want to commit suicide from doing so, but quite another to stop people who want to live from acting in a way that they falsely believe to be safe. Smokers who deny the health risks fall into that latter, easier category.

The larger and harder question is how to deal with the great majority of smokers who, knowing the risks, continue smoking anyway. Of course, it might be said that they do not really know the risks. Although most acknowledge that smoking is "unhealthy," in some vague sense, few know exactly what chances they run of exactly what diseases. In one poll, 49 percent of smokers did not know that smoking causes most cases of lung cancer, 63 percent that it causes most cases of bronchitis, and 85 percent that it causes most cases of emphysema. Overestimating badly the risks of

dying in other more dramatic ways (car crashes, etc.), people badly underestimate the relative risks of dying in the more mundane ways associated with smoking—thus allowing them to rationalize further their smoking behavior as being "not all that dangerous," compared to other things that they are also doing.[5] Besides all that, there is the distinction between "knowing intellectually" some statistic and "feeling in your guts" its full implications. Consent counts—morally, as well as legally—only if it is truly informed consent, only if people know what it is to which they are consenting. That, in turn, requires not only that we can state the probabilities but also that we "appreciate them in an emotionally genuine manner" (Dworkin 1972/1983, p. 30). There is reason to believe that smokers do not.

It may still be argued that, as long as people had the facts, they can and should be held responsible if they chose not to act upon them when they could have done so. It may be folly for utilitarian policymakers to rely upon people's such imperfect responses to facts for purposes of constructing social welfare functions, and framing public policies around them. But there is the separate matter of who ought to be blamed when some self-inflicted harm befalls people. There, arguably, responsibility ought to be on people's own shoulders (Knowles 1977; Wikler 1987). Arguably, we ought to stick to that judgment, even if people were "pressured" into smoking by the bullying of aggressive advertising or peer pressure.

What crucially transforms the "voluntary acceptance" argument is evidence of the addictive nature of cigarette smoking. Of course, saying that smoking is addictive is not to say that no one can ever give it up. Many have done so. By the same token, though, more than 70 percent of American servicemen addicted to heroin in Vietnam gave it up when returning to the United States; yet we still rightly regard heroin as an addictive drug. The test of addictiveness is not impossibility but rather difficulty of withdrawal. . . .

To establish a substance as addictive, we require evidence of "physical need" for the substance among its users. That evidence is necessary to prove smoking is an addiction rather than just a "habit" (U.S. DHEW 1964, chaps. 13–14), a psychological dependence, or a matter of mere sociological pressure (Daniels 1985, p. 159)—none of which would undercut, in a way that addictiveness does, claims that the risks of smoking are voluntarily incurred. That physical link has now been established, though. Particular receptors for the active ingredients of tobacco smoke have been discovered in the brain; the physiological sites and mechanisms by which nicotine acts on the brain have now been well mapped, and its tendency to generate compulsive, repetitive behavior in consequence has been well established. Such evidence—summarized in the surgeon general's 1988 report—has been one of the crucial factors leading the World Health Organization and the American Psychiatric Association to classify "nicotine dependence" as an addiction.

None of that evidence proves that it would be literally impossible for smokers to resist the impulse to smoke. Through extraordinary acts of will, they might. Nor does any of that evidence prove that it is literally impossible for them to break their dependence altogether. Many have. Recall, however, that the issue is not one of impossibility but rather of how hard people should have to try before their will is said to be sufficiently impaired that their agreement does not count as genuine consent.

The evidence suggests that nicotine addicts have to try very hard indeed. This is the second crucial fact to establish in proving a substance addictive.[6] Central among the WHO/APA criteria for diagnosing nicotine dependence is the requirement of evidence of "continuous use of tobacco for at least one month with . . . unsuccessful attempts to stop or significantly reduce the amount of tobacco use on a permanent basis." A vast majority of smokers do indeed find themselves in this position. The surgeon general reports that 90 percent of regular smokers have tried to quit. Another 1975 survey found that 84 percent of smokers had attempted to stop, but that only

36 percent of them had succeeded in maintaining their changed behavior for a whole year.[7]

Such evidence of smokers trying and failing to stop is rightly regarded as central to the issue of addiction, philosophically as well as diagnostically. Some describe free will in terms of "second-order volitions"—desires about desires—controlling "first-order" ones (Frankfurt 1971). Others talk of one's "evaluational structure" controlling one's "motivational structure," so one strives to obtain something if and only if one thinks it of value (Watson 1975, 1977). Addiction—the absence of free will—is thus a matter of first-order volitions winning out over second-order ones, and surface desires prevailing over the agent's own deeper values. In the case of smoking, trying to stop can be seen as a manifestation of one's second-order volitions or one's deeper values, and failing to stop as evidence of the triumph of first-order surface desires over them. The same criteria the WHO/APA use to diagnose nicotine dependence also establish the impairment of the smoker's free will, philosophically.

Various policy implications follow from evidence of addictiveness. One might be that over-the-counter sales of cigarettes should be banned. If the product is truly addictive, then we have no more reason to respect a person's voluntary choice (however well informed) to abandon his future volition to an addiction than we have for respecting a person's voluntary choice (however well informed) to sell himself into slavery (Mill 1859/1975, pp. 126–27). I am unsure how far to press this argument. After all, we do permit people to bind their future selves (through contracts, e.g.). But if it is the size of the stakes or the difficulty of breaking out of the bonds that makes the crucial difference, then acquiring a lethal and hard-to-break addiction is much more like a slavery contract than it is like an ordinary commercial commitment.

In any case, addictiveness thus defined makes it far easier to justify interventions that on their face appear paternalistic. In some sense, they would then be not paternalistic at all. Where people "wish to stop smoking, but do not have the requisite willpower . . . we are not imposing a good on someone who rejects it. We are simply using coercion to enable people to carry out their own goals" (Dworkin 1972/1983, p. 32). It is, of course, genuinely difficult to decide which is the "authentic" self: with whom should we side, when the person who asks us to help him "enforce rules on himself" repudiates the rules at the time they need to be enforced? But at least we have more of a warrant for interference in such cases than if we were never asked for assistance at all. Much of the assistance we render in such situations will necessarily be of a very personal nature and outside the scope of public policy. There is nonetheless a substantial role for public policy in these realms. Banning or restricting smoking in public places (especially the workplace) can contribute crucially to an individual's own efforts at smoking cessation, for example.

The force of the addiction findings . . . is to undercut the claim that there is any continuing consent to the risks involved in smoking. There might have been consent in the very first instance—in smoking your first cigarette. But once you were hooked, you lost the capacity to consent in any meaningful sense on a continuing basis. As Hume (1760) says, to consent implies the possibility of doing otherwise; and addiction substantially deprives you of the capacity to do other than continue smoking. So once you have become addicted to nicotine, your subsequent smoking cannot be taken as indicating your consent to the risks.

If there is to be consent at all, then, it can only be consent in the very first instance, that is, when you first began to smoke. That, in turn, seriously undercuts the extent to which cigarette manufacturers can rely upon *volenti* or informed-consent defenses in product liability litigation and its moral analogues. Many of those now dying from tobacco-induced diseases started smoking well before warnings began appearing on packets in 1966; their consent to the risks of smoking could only have been based on "common knowledge" and "folk wisdom."

That is a short-term problem, though, since that cohort of smokers will eventually die off. The more serious, continuing problem is this. A vast majority of smokers began smoking in their early to middle teens. Evidence suggests that "of those teenagers who smoke more than a single cigarette only 15 percent avoid becoming regular dependent smokers"; and a great majority, perhaps up to 95 percent, of regular adult smokers are thought to have been addicted before they were twenty-one years of age. Being below the age of consent, they were incapable of consenting in the first instance;[8] and being addicted by the time they reached the age of consent they were incapable of consenting later, either.

2. DO THE BENEFITS OUTWEIGH THE COSTS?

In addition to Kantian-style questions about informed consent, there are utilitarian-style questions of overall social welfare to be considered in this connection. Presumably it is in these latter terms that public health measures are ordinarily justified. We do not leave it to the discretion of consumers, however well informed, whether or not to drink grossly polluted water, ingest grossly contaminated foods, or inject grossly dangerous drugs. We simply prohibit such things, on grounds of public health, by appeal to utilitarian calculations of one sort or another.

To some extent, the same considerations that lead us to believe such measures are justified on grounds of social utility might also give us grounds for presuming people's (at least hypothetical) consent to them, also. To some extent, we can appeal to externality arguments to justify the measures: contagious diseases and costly cures affect the community as a whole. But to some extent, the justification of public health measures must be baldly paternalistic, turning on the benefits accruing to the person himself from avoiding diseases that he might otherwise cavalierly court.

All those considerations are in play in the case of smoking. Paternalistic elements have been canvassed above. There are contagion effects, too: being among smokers exerts strong social pressure upon people to start smoking and makes it difficult for people to stop; and these contagion effects are particularly pronounced among young people, whose smoking behavior is strongly affected by that of parents and peers. As regards externalities, smoking is believed to cause at least half of residential fires, harming family and neighbors as well as the smokers themselves; treating smoking-induced illnesses is costly, and even in the United States some 40 percent of those costs are borne by the public; premature deaths cost the economy productive members and entail pain and suffering for family and friends; and so on.

Dealing just in those nonquantified terms of human costs, smoking must surely stand indicted. The U.S. surgeon general says it is the "chief, single, avoidable cause of death in our society and the most important public health problem of our time." Cigarettes kill 25 percent of their users, even when used as their manufacturers intended they be used. Suppose a toaster or lawnmower had a similar record. It would be whipped off the market forthwith. On utilitarian grounds, there would seem to be no reason why cigarettes should be treated any differently.

For those preferring hard, solid numbers, economists (focusing principally upon medical costs and lost productivity) calculate that smoking costs the American economy on net $52–$62 billion per year. By that reckoning, too, there is clearly a case to answer against smoking, on grounds of social utility.

There are, in fact, rejoinders available on two levels. One is a micro-level argument couched in terms of benefits to smokers themselves from the practice. The other is a macro-level argument, querying the real costs to society from the practice.

The first style of argument . . . is that cost-benefit calculations should take into account whatever subjective pleasures smokers derive from the practice. In the boldest statement of

this very standard microeconomic proposition, Buchanan (1970) argues that, if fully informed people would be willing to buy the product in preference to all others on the market, then we would be making them worse off (in preference—which for him equates to welfare—terms) by banning that product from the market. . . .

The . . . way around the microeconomic argument . . . starts from the observation that cigarette sales are substantially price inelastic [i.e., sales do not go up and down much as prices fluctuate—Ed.]. Estimates of just how inelastic vary. But much evidence suggests that even rather large increases in the price of the product (induced, e.g., by increased excise taxes) result in only slight decreases in sales to adult consumers. We might infer either of two conclusions from that fact. One would be that there is an enormous "consumer's surplus" (subjective benefit, net of subjective cost) that smokers enjoy, which even large taxes would not extinguish. Price inelasticity would then be taken as evidence that there are substantial subjective gains to consumers from smoking, which ought to be set off against the calculated social costs in any utilitarian decision procedure. Which would predominate we cannot say in advance. But other things being equal, utilitarians ought be more inclined to allow smoking the more satisfaction consumers derive from it.

Alternatively, we might infer from price inelasticity that people are indeed addicted to the product. Present users will pay any price for cigarettes for the same reason they will pay any price for heroin: they cannot help themselves. Most of them would rather not, according to surveys. Most wish they were not hooked but backslide every time they try to get unhooked.

There is, admittedly, a bit of a problem in determining what should count as a "benefit" to addicts. In one sense, they benefit from having their habits serviced—certainly they would suffer in some obvious sense otherwise. So in a way, the implication of the addiction interpretation would be much the same as that of the consumer surplus interpretation, that is, present users benefit, as indicated by their willingness to pay, from smoking. In another way, however, they would benefit—even in terms of subjective preferences—if they were to stop. In the same terms, others would benefit if they were never to start.

Addictive substances are not ordinary economic goods. Ordinarily, cultivating new tastes (acquiring a taste for fine foods, e.g.) is thought to make you better off—able to derive more pleasure—than before. With addictions, however, you are worse off, even in your own eyes, than before; whatever momentary pleasures you derive from servicing the addiction, you would prefer to stop but find that you cannot. Thus, we should do whatever we can to prevent new addicts, who would be subjectively worse off once addicted than they were before. As regards existing addicts, there may be a utilitarian case for continuing to service their habits, though even they would be subjectively better off in the long run if they could be helped to break the habit.

Whereas the first rejoinder to the utilitarian argument for curbing smoking alleges an underestimate of consumer benefits from smoking, a second rejoinder alleges an overestimate of net social costs. The less interesting versions of this argument point to the tobacco industry's contribution to the aggregate economy—but a contribution of $3.3 billion to the Gross National Product, set off against the $52–$62 billion cost estimates described above, leave the industry's account well in the red.

A more interesting version of this argument alleges that the above procedures overstate true social costs. As regards the narrow question of health care costs, everyone dies of something sooner or later. For an accurate assessment of the medical costs of smoking-related diseases, then, we must deduct the costs that would have been incurred had the people killed by smoking died of something else later (Wikler 1978/1983, p. 46). In terms of hospital bed days and overall medical expenditure, over the course of their lives as a whole, there is some evidence to suggest that

there may be no significant difference between smokers and nonsmokers.

Similarly, perhaps we need not worry too much about externalities, in the sense of the unfair imposition of burdens on others. Smokers could be refused treatment in public hospital beds and made to pay their own way. They could be required to carry complete insurance against smoking-related diseases; and to avoid unfairness to coinsureds, we could further require that risks to smokers be pooled only with those of other smokers (Wikler 1978/1983, p. 49), as is increasingly done by insurance companies for purely commercial reasons, anyway. Alternatively, and perhaps more practically, "users of cigarettes and alcohol . . . could be made to pay an excise tax, the proceeds of which would cover the costs of treatment for lung cancer and other resulting illnesses" (Wikler 1978/1983, p. 49).

In those narrow terms, at least, smokers already more than pay their own way. In the United Kingdom, the cigarette tax accounts for over 8 percent of total government revenue. It has been estimated that in Ontario it takes only 8 percent of tobacco tax revenues to pay for all public health care expenditure on smoking-related disease. Even in the United States, if we count only the share of health care costs borne by the federal government, that is almost exactly counterbalanced by the federal excise tax on cigarettes—although there, as in those other cases as well, matters would look very different if we were to count total costs to the economy and society (e.g., lost productivity) as well as just medical costs borne by the government.

In other ways, too, smokers save us money by dying early. Just think: "Smoking tends to cause few problems during a person's productive years and then to kill the individual before the need to provide years of social security and pension payments. From this perspective, the truly burdensome individual may be the unreasonably fit senior citizen who lives on for thirty years after retirement, contributing to the bankruptcy of the social security system, and using up savings that would have reverted to the public purse via inheritance taxes, had an immoderate life-style brought an early death" (Wikler 1978/ 1983, p. 46).

In the eyes of many, this will appear to be a reductio ad absurdum. What it seems to suggest is nothing less than a thinly veiled form of not-altogether-voluntary euthanasia. Many suppose it is unjust, if not necessarily uneconomic, to encourage people to die off promptly upon their ceasing to be productive members of the work force (cf. Battin 1987).

What this is a reductio [i.e., reduction to absurdity] of, however, is not the utilitarian calculus but, rather, an economic calculus that serves as such a poor proxy for it. Most people who are already retired would wish to enjoy a long and happy retirement; most people still in the work force would wish the same for themselves and, indeed, for their elders. Those preferences, too, must be factored into any proper calculus of social utility. Once they are, early deaths induced by smoking are almost certain to turn out to be costs rather than benefits in the broader social scale of values.

3. POLICY OPTIONS

Publicity

Mandatory health warnings on cigarette packages and advertisements, and public health campaigns more generally, are [a] popular government response to smoking. Some thirty-eight countries now require such warnings. Among the more important reasons for the popularity of this strategy is that health warnings and public information campaigns are seen as the least paternalistic forms of government intervention. Mill (1859/1975, p. 118) himself holds that "labelling [a] drug with some word expressive of its dangerous character, may be enforced without violation of liberty," since presumably "the buyer cannot wish not to know that the thing he possesses has poisonous qualities." In this judgment, Mill has been followed by a host of more recent commentators.

No doubt publicizing health risks reduces smoking. Publication of the two great official reports—by the Royal College of Physicians in 1962 and the surgeon general in 1964—produced long-term drops in cigarette consumption by between 7 percent and 14 percent. The antismoking television advertisements, allowed under the Fairness Doctrine in the United States until the 1970 legislation banning television advertising of cigarettes altogether, seemed to have an effect almost twice as strong.

There are reasons to believe that health campaigns cannot work in isolation from other policy initiatives, though. Specifically, allowing cigarette advertising undercuts health messages by inducing newspapers and magazines to engage in self-censorship of health reports that might offend their tobacco sponsors. Thus, a publicity campaign might not really succeed unless coupled with something stronger: an advertising ban. Otherwise the message simply might not get carried effectively.

Bans

There are, in fact, various regulatory options under this general heading. Most modestly, we might ban cigarette advertising, either in particular settings (e.g., on television) or in general. More dramatically, we might ban sales of cigarettes, either to a certain group (e.g., children) or in general. Most dramatically, we might ban use of tobacco, either in particular settings (e.g., where there is a particular fire hazard, as in elevators, theaters, and subways, or where there are synergistic effects with other substances in the immediate vicinity, such as asbestos) or in general.

These are separable policy options, any one of which can be pursued independently of any other. From 1975, Norway has banned advertising but not sale of cigarettes. Similarly, we can ban sale without banning consumption. (Most states allow you to eat game birds and fish you shoot or catch yourself but not to sell them.) Though there is no modern experience of a general ban on sale or use of tobacco, advertising bans are reasonably common: fifteen countries have total bans, and another twelve have strong partial bans.

Advertising bans can be particularly helpful in reducing cigarette consumption among adolescents, with whom we should be especially concerned on grounds of "informed consent." There is good evidence that cigarette advertising in general, and sport sponsorship in particular, appeals to children. Conversely, banning advertising of cigarettes in Norway in 1975 led to a sharp decline in the percentage of teenagers who subsequently became daily smokers.

Against bans on the use or sale of tobacco, the Prohibition analogy is standardly urged. Already we have evidence of substantial "bootlegging" (or "buttlegging") of cigarettes between states with low cigarette taxes and those with high ones. Any more serious ban on sale or use of tobacco would no doubt lead to even more illicit activity of this sort. Even accepting such slippage, however, this strategy is still bound to reduce smoking substantially. Whether more would be lost in terms of respect for the law than would be gained in terms of public health remains an open question.

Medicalization

If smoking tobacco is addictive, then perhaps a medical rather than legal or economic response is indicated. The idea here would be to make tobacco a prescription drug, available to registered users only.[9] The model would be methadone maintenance programs for heroin addicts, perhaps. The aim in making tobacco a prescription drug would be to respond humanely to the needs of present addicts, while discouraging new users. Again, it would be impossible to stop all new users—they can always smoke the cigarettes of registered users illicitly, unless we require registered users to smoke only in the clinics. But again, such a policy would have a strong tendency in the desired direction.

REFERENCES

Battin, Margaret P., "Age Rationing and the Just Distribution of Health Care: Is There a Duty to Die?" *Ethics* 97 (1987): 317–40.

Buchanan, James M., "In Defense of Caveat Emptor," *University of Chicago Law Review* 38(1970): 64–73.

Daniels, Norman, *Just Health Care.* Princeton, N.J.: Princeton University Press, 1985.

Dworkin, Gerald, "Paternalism," *Monist* 56, no. 1(1972): 64–84. Reprinted in Sartorius, ed., 1983, pp. 19–34.

Feinberg, Joel, "Legal Paternalism," *Canadian Journal of Philosophy* 1(1971):106–24. Reprinted in Sartorius, ed., 1983, pp. 3–18.

Frankfurt, Harry G., "Freedom of the Will and the Concept of a Person," *Journal of Philosophy* 68(1971): 5–20.

Fuchs, Victor R., "Time Preference and Health: An Exploratory Study," in *Economic Aspects of Health,* ed. Victor R. Fuchs, pp. 93–120. Chicago: University of Chicago Press.

Gorovitz, Samuel, *Doctors' Dilemmas.* New York: Oxford University Press, 1982.

Hume, David, "Of the Original Contract," in *Essays, Literary, Moral and Political.* London: A. Millar, 1760.

Kahneman, D., P. Slovic, and A. Tversky, eds., *Judgment under Uncertainty.* Cambridge: Cambridge University Press, 1982.

Knowles, John H., "The Responsibility of the Individual," *Daedalus* 106, no. 1(1977): 57–80.

Leventhal, Howard, Kathleen Glynn, and Raymond Fleming, "Is the Smoking Decision an 'Informed Choice'?" *Journal of the American Medical Association* 257(1987): 3373–76.

Lichtenstein, S., P. Slovic, B. Fischhoff, M. Layman, and B. Combs, "Judged Frequency of Lethal Events," *Journal of Experimental Psychology* (Human Learning and Memory) 4(1978): 551–78.

Mill, John Stuart, *On Liberty. In Three Essays,* ed. Richard Wollheim, pp. 1–141. Oxford: Oxford University Press, 1975 (1859).

Pears, David, *Motivated Irrationality.* Oxford: Clarendon, 1984.

Sartorius, Rolf, ed., *Paternalism.* Minneapolis: University of Minnesota Press, 1983.

Slovic, P., B. Fischhoff, and S. Lichtenstein, "Fact vs. Fears: Understanding Perceived Risks," in Kahneman, Slovic, and Tversky, eds., 1982, pp. 463–89.

United States Department of Health, Education and Welfare (U.S. DHEW), *Smoking and Health.* Report of the Advisory Committee to the Surgeon General of the Public Health Service. Washington, DC: Government Printing Office, 1964.

United States Federal Trade Commission (U.S. FTC), *Staff Report on the Cigarette Advertising Investigation,* Matthew L. Meyers, chairman. Public version. Washington, DC: FTC, 1981.

U.S. FTC, *A Report to the Congress Pursuant to the Federal Cigarette Labelling and Advertising Act.* Washington, DC: Government Printing Office, 1984.

U.S. FTC, *A Report to the Congress Pursuant to the Federal Cigarette Labelling and Advertising Act.* Washington, DC: Government Printing Office, 1985.

Watson, Gary, "Free Agency," *Journal of Philosophy* 72(1975): 205–20.

Watson, Gary, "Skepticism about Weakness of Will," *Philosophical Review* 86(1977): 316–39,

Wikler, Daniel, "Persuasion and Coercion for Health: Ethical Issues in Government Efforts to Change Life-styles," *Health and Society* (now *Milbank Quarterly*) 56 (1978): 303–38. Reprinted in Sartorius, ed., 1983, pp. 35–59.

Wikler, Daniel, "Personal Responsibility for Illness," in *Health Care Ethics,* ed. D. van de Veer and T. Regan, pp. 326–58. Philadelphia: Temple University Press, 1987.

NOTES

1. *Johns-Manville Sales Corp.* v. *International Association of Machinists, Machinists Local 1609,* 621 F.2d 756 at 759 (5th Cir. 1980).

2. Warnings that "smoking may be dangerous," when conjoined with pictures of people enjoying dangerous sports (white-water rafting, etc.), perversely serve to make smoking more attractive; warnings that "smoking may complicate pregnancy," when conjoined with sexually provocative photos in a magazine devoted to casual sex without procreation, again perversely undercut the health warnings.

3. Literally, of course, it is—at least broadly speaking and in the short run. But in the medium to long term, participation even in purely recreational sport (not to mention serious sport, where peak performance is required) is impaired by the consequences of smoking. Insofar as young smokers are encouraged in the belief that they can always quit, should smoking become a problem later, that is a false belief (as shown by the addiction evidence, discussed below); and advertisements carrying any such implications once again would count as clearly deceptive advertising.

4. One of a person's ends—continued life—at least. Perhaps the person has other ends ("relaxation," or whatever) that are well served by smoking, and insofar as "people taking risks actually value the direct consequences associated with them . . . it is more difficult to intrude paternalistically" (Daniels 1985, pp. 158, 163). But assuming that smoking is not the only means to the other ends—not the only way to relax, etc.—the intrusion is only minimally difficult to justify.

5. Logically, it would be perfectly possible for people both to underestimate the extent of the risk and simultaneously to overreact to it. People might suppose the chances of snakebite are slight but live in mortal fear of it nonetheless. Psychologically, however, the reverse seems to happen. People's subjective probability estimates of an event's likelihood increase the more they dread it and the more "psychologically available" the event therefore is to them (Kahneman, Slovic, and Tversky 1982). Smoking-related diseases, in contrast, tend to be "quiet killers" of which people have little direct or indirect experience, which tend to be underreported in newspapers and which act on people one at a time rather than catastrophically killing many people at once (Lichtenstein et al. 1983, p. 567). Smoking-related diseases being psychologically less available to people in these ways, they underestimate their frequency dramatically—by a factor of eight, in the case of lung cancer, according to one study (Slovic, Fischhoff, and Lichtenstein 1982, p. 469).

6. There are other physical needs that we would have trouble renouncing—such as our need for food—that we would be loath to call "addictions." Be that as it may, we would also be loath, for precisely those reasons, to say that we "eat of our own free will" (we would have no hesitation that someone who makes a credible threat of preventing us from eating has "coerced" us, etc.). Since involuntariness and impairment of free will are what is really at issue here, those thus do seem to be the aspects of addictiveness that matter in the present context.

7. The graphs mapping the relapse rate after a given period of time are almost identical for nicotine and for heroin, although it might be wrong to make too much of that fact. (Perhaps heroin addicts find both that it is harder to give up and that they have more reason to do so: then relapse rates would appear the same, even though heroin is more addictive in the sense of being harder to give up.) Pointing to the addiction evidence, U.S. federal courts have decided that "smoking can be an involuntary act for some persons" and that social security disability benefits may not therefore be routinely withheld from victims of smoking-related diseases on the grounds that they are suffering from voluntarily self-inflicted injuries (*Gordon* v. *Schweiker,* 725 F.2d 231, 236 [1984]).

8. Strictly speaking, ability to consent is not predicated—legally or morally—upon attaining some arbitrary age but, rather, upon having attained the capacity to make reasoned choices in the matter at hand. The level of understanding manifested by teenagers about smoking clearly suggests that their decision to start smoking cannot be deemed an informed choice, however (Leventhal, Glynn, and Fleming 1987).

9. Ironically, nicotine-containing chewing gum is a controlled prescription drug in the United States, United Kingdom, Sweden, and Canada, whereas wet snuff (whose risks are, if anything, greater) is freely available over the counter to adult purchasers. Czechoslovakia now requires consumers of twenty or more cigarettes per day to register with the medical service that monitors respiratory diseases, perhaps as a first step in this "medicalization" direction (*Daily Express*, London, February 17, 1986).

REVIEW AND DISCUSSION QUESTIONS

1. What role do ads play in encouraging smoking, according to Goodin?
2. Describe the three "cognitive defects" that Goodin thinks are relevant in assessing smoking.
3. In what "weak" sense does Goodin agree that interfering with smoking is paternalistic?
4. Describe how Goodin responds to those who say people voluntarily accept the risks of smoking.
5. What are the costs of smoking, according to Goodin?
6. How does Goodin respond to those who claim the benefits of smoking are often underestimated?
7. How does Goodin respond to those who claim that the costs of smoking are often overestimated?
8. What response does Goodin give to each of the three policy options?

Addiction and Drug Policy

Daniel Shapiro

Much of the debate surrounding drug legalization revolves around the nature of drug addiction and the extent to which it is possible for addicts to quit. In this essay, Daniel Shapiro attacks what he terms the "standard view" that heroin and cocaine are inherently addictive. Instead, he claims, we should see drug use not in terms of pharmacology and addictive potency but rather in terms of how the experience is interpreted, focusing specifically on the "setting" and the "set" of drug use. He concludes by looking at cigarette smoking and how its pharmacological effects, social setting, and personal set interact. Daniel Shapiro is professor of philosophy at West Virginia University.

Most people think that illegal drugs, such as cocaine and heroin, are highly addictive. Usually, their addictiveness is explained by pharmacology: their chemical composition and its effects on the brain are such that, after a while, it's hard to stop using them. This view of drug addiction—I call it the standard view—underlies most opposition to legalizing cocaine and heroin. James Q. Wilson's (1990) arguments are typical: legalization increases access, and increased access to addictive drugs increases addiction. The standard view also underlies the increasingly popular opinion, given a philosophical defense by Robert Goodin (1989), that cigarette smokers are addicts in the grip of a powerful drug.

However, the standard view is false: pharmacology, I shall argue, does not by itself do much to explain drug addiction. I will offer a different explanation of drug addiction, and discuss its implications for the debate about drug legalization.

PROBLEMS WITH THE STANDARD VIEW

We label someone as a drug addict because of his behavior. A drug addict uses drugs repeatedly, compulsively, wants to stop or cut back on his use but finds it's difficult to do so; at its worst, drug addiction dominates or crowds out other activities and concerns. The standard view attempts to explain this compulsive behavior by the drug's effects on the brain. Repeated use of an addictive drug induces cravings, and the user comes to need a substantial amount to get the effect she wants, i.e., develops tolerance. If the user tries to stop, she then suffers very disagreeable effects, called withdrawal symptoms. (For more detail on the standard view, see American Psychiatric Association 1994: 176–81.)

Cravings, tolerance, and withdrawal symptoms: do these explain drug addiction? A craving or strong desire to do something doesn't *make* one do something: one can act on a desire, *or* ignore it *or* attempt to extinguish it. Tolerance explains why the user increases her intake to get the effect she wants, but that doesn't explain why she would find it difficult to *stop wanting* this effect. Thus the key idea in the standard view is really withdrawal symptoms, because that is needed to explain the difficulty in extinguishing the desire to take the drug or to stop wanting the effects the drug produces.

However, for this explanation to work, these symptoms have to be really bad, for if they aren't, why not just put up with them as a small price to pay for getting free of the drug? However, withdrawal symptoms aren't *that* bad. Heroin is considered terribly addictive, yet pharmacologists describe its withdrawal symptoms as like having a bad flu for about a week: typical withdrawal symptoms include fever, diarrhea, sneezing, muscle cramps, and vomiting (Kaplan 1983: 15, 19, 35). While a bad flu is quite unpleasant, it's not so bad that one has little choice but to take heroin rather than experience it. Indeed, most withdrawal symptoms for any drug cease within a few weeks, yet most heavy users who relapse do so after that period and few drug addicts report withdrawal symptoms as the reason for their relapse (Peele 1985: 19–20, 67, Schacter 1982: 436–44, Waldorf 1991: 241).

Thus cravings, tolerance, and withdrawal symptoms cannot explain addiction. An additional problem for the standard view is that most drug users, whether they use legal or illegal drugs, do not become addicts, and few addicts remain so permanently. (Cigarette smokers are a partial exception, which I discuss later.) Surveys of drug users by the National Institute on Drug Abuse (1990) indicate that less than 5% of powder cocaine users use it daily, and the figures are probably only somewhat higher for crack cocaine (Erickson 1994: 167–74, 231–32) and heroin (Husak 1992: 125, Trebach 1982: 3–4). (Notice, incidentally, that a daily user need not be an addict; someone who drinks daily is not thereby an alcoholic.) These surveys have been confirmed by longitudinal studies—studies of a set of users over time—which indicate that moderate and/or controlled use of these drugs is the norm, not the exception, and that even heavy users do not inevitably march to addiction, let alone remain permanent addicts (Waldorf 1991, Erickson 1994, Zinberg 1984: 111–34, 152–71). The standard view has to explain the preeminence of controlled use by arguing that drug laws reduce access to illegal drugs. However I argue below that even with easy access to drugs most people use them responsibly, and so something other than the law and pharmacology must explain patterns of drug use.

AN ALTERNATIVE VIEW

I will defend a view of addiction summed up by Norman Zinberg's book, *Drug, Set, and Setting* (1984). "Drug" means pharmacology, "set" means the individual's mindset, his personality, values, and expectations, and "setting" means the cultural or social surroundings of drug use. This should sound like common sense. Humans are interpretative animals and so what results from drug use depends not just on the experience or effects produced by the drug but *also* on the interpretation of that experience or effects. And how one interprets or understands the experience depends on one's individuality and the cultural or social setting.

I begin with setting. Hospital patients that get continuous and massive doses of narcotics rarely get addicted or crave the drugs after release from the hospital (Peele 1985: 17, Falk 1996: 9). The quantity and duration of their drug use pales in significance compared with the setting of their drug consumption: subsequent ill effects from the drug are rarely interpreted in terms of addiction. A study of Vietnam veterans, the largest study of untreated heroin users ever conducted, provides more dramatic evidence of the role of setting. Three quarters of Vietnam vets who used heroin in Vietnam became addicted, but after coming home, only half of heroin users in Vietnam continued to use and of those only 12% were addicts (Robins 1980). Wilson also mentions this study, and says that the change was because heroin is illegal in the US (1990: 22), and while this undoubtedly played a role, so did the difference in social setting: Vietnam, with its absence of work and family, as well as loneliness and fear of death, helped to promote acceptance of heavy drug use.

Along the same lines, consider the effects of alcohol in different cultures. In Finland, for example, violence and alcohol are linked, for sometimes heavy drinkers end up in fights; in Greece, Italy, and other Mediterranean countries, however, where drinking is moderate and controlled, there is no violence-alcohol link (Peele 1985: 25). Why the differences? Humans are social or cultural animals, not just products of their biochemistry, and this means, in part, that social norms or rules play a significant role in influencing behavior. In cultures where potentially intoxicating drugs such as alcohol are viewed as supplements or accompaniments to life, moderate and controlled use will be the norm—hence even though Mediterranean cultures typically consume large amounts of alcohol, there is little alcoholism—while in cultures where alcohol is also viewed as a way of escaping one's problems, alcoholism will be more prevalent, which may explain the problem in Finland and some other Scandinavian cultures. In addition to cultural influences, most people learn to use alcohol responsibly by observing their parents. They see their parents drink at a ballgame or to celebrate special occasions, or with food at a meal, but rarely on an empty stomach; they learn it's wrong to be drunk at work, to drink and drive; they learn that uncontrolled behavior with alcohol is generally frowned upon; they absorb certain norms and values such as "know your limit," "don't drink alone," "don't drink in the morning" and so forth. They learn about rituals which reinforce moderation, such as the phrase "let's have *a* drink." These informal rules and rituals teach most people how to use alcohol responsibly (Zinberg 1987: 258–62).

While social controls are harder to develop with illicit drugs—accurate information is pretty scarce, and parents feel uncomfortable teaching their children about controlled use—even here sanctions and rituals promoting moderate use exist. For example, in a study of an 11-year follow-up of an informal network of middle-class cocaine users largely connected through ties of friendship, and most of whom were moderate users, the authors concluded that:

> Rather than cocaine overpowering user concerns with family, health, and career, we found that the high value most of our users placed upon family, health, and career achievement . . . mitigated against abuse and addiction. Such group norms and the informal social controls that seemed to stem from them (e.g., expressions of concern, warning about risks, the use of pejorative names like "coke hog," refusal to share with abusers) mediated the force of pharmacological, physiological, and psychological factors which can lead to addiction. (Murphy 1989: 435)

Even many heavy cocaine users are able to prevent their use from becoming out of control (or out of control for significant periods of time) by regulating the time and circumstances of use (not during work, never too late at night, limit use on weekdays) using with friends rather than alone, employing fixed rules (paying bills before spending money on cocaine), etc. (Waldorf 1991).

Unsurprisingly, these studies of controlled cocaine use generally focus on middle-class users: their income and the psychological support of friends and family put them at less of a risk of ruining their lives by drug use than those with little income or hope (Peele 1991: 159–60).

I now examine the effects of set on drug use, that is the effect of expectations, personality, and values. Expectations are important because drug use occurs in a pattern of ongoing activity, and one's interpretation of the drug's effects depends upon expectations of how those effects will fit into or alter those activities. Expectations explain the well-known placebo effect: if people consume something they mistakenly believe will stop or alleviate their pain it often does. Along the same lines, in experiments with American college-age men, aggression and sexual arousal increased when these men were told they were drinking liquor, even though they were drinking zero percent proof, while when drinking liquor and told they are not, they

acted normally (Peele 1985: 17). The role of expectations also explains why many users of heroin, cocaine, and other psychoactive drugs do not like or even recognize the effects when they first take it, and have to be taught to or learn how to appreciate the effects (Peele 1985: 13–14, Waldorf, 1991: 264, Zinberg 1984: 117). The importance of expectations means that those users who view the drug as overpowering them will tend to find their lives dominated by the drug, while those who view it as an enhancement or a complement to certain experiences or activities will tend not to let drugs dominate or overpower their other interests (Peele 1991: 156–8, 169–70).

As for the individual's personality and values, the predictions of common sense are pretty much accurate. Psychologically healthy people are likely to engage in controlled, moderate drug use, or if they find themselves progressing to uncontrolled use, they tend to cut back. On the other hand, drug addicts of all kinds tend to have more psychological problems before they started using illicit drugs (Peele 1991: 153–54, 157, Zinberg 1984: 74–76). People who are motivated to control their own lives will tend to make drug use an accompaniment or an ingredient in their lives, not the dominant factor. Those who place a high value on responsibility, work, family, productivity, etc., will tend to fit drug use into their lives, rather than letting it run their lives (Waldorf 1991: 267, Peele 1991: 160–66). That's why drug use of all kinds, licit or illicit, tends to taper off with age: keeping a job, raising a family, and so forth leave limited time or motivation for uncontrolled or near continuous drug use (Peele 1985: 15). And it's why it's not uncommon for addicts to explain their addiction by saying that they drifted into the addict's life; with little to compete with their drug use, or lacking motivation to substitute other activities or interests, drug use comes to dominate their lives (DeGrandpre 1996: 44–46). Those with richer lives, or who are motivated on an individual and/or cultural level to get richer lives, are less likely to succumb to addiction.

To summarize: even with easy access to intoxicating drugs, most drug users don't become addicts, or if they do, don't remain addicts for that long, because most people have and are motivated to find better things to do with their lives. These better things result from their individual personality and values and their social or cultural setting.

CIGARETTE SMOKING AND THE ROLE OF PHARMACOLOGY

I've discussed how set and setting influence drug use, but where does pharmacology fit in? Its role is revealed by examining why it is much harder to stop smoking cigarettes—only half of smokers that try to stop smoking succeed in quitting—than to stop using other substances. (For more detail in what follows, see Shapiro 1994, and the references cited therein.)

Smokers smoke to relax, to concentrate, to handle anxiety, stress and difficult interpersonal situations, as a way of taking a break during the day, as a social lubricant, as a means of oral gratification—and this is a partial list. Since smoking is a means to or part of so many activities, situations, and moods, stopping smoking is a major life change and major life changes do not come easily. Part of the reason smoking is so integrated into people's lives is pharmacological. Nicotine's effects on the brain are mild and subtle: it doesn't disrupt your life. While addicts or heavy users of other drugs such as cocaine, heroin, or alcohol *also* use their drugs as a means to or part of a variety of activities, situations, and moods, most users of these drugs are not life-long addicts or heavy users, because these drugs are not so mild, and heavy use has a stronger tendency over time to disrupt people's lives.

The pharmacology of smoking, however, cannot be separated from its social setting. Smoking doesn't disrupt people's lives in part because it is legal. Even with increasing regulations, smokers still can smoke in a variety of

situations (driving, walking on public streets, etc.) where one cannot use illegal drugs except in a furtive and secretive manner. Furthermore, the mild effects of nicotine are due to its mild potency—smokers can carefully control their nicotine intake, getting small doses throughout the day—and its mild potency is due partly to smoking being legal. Legal drugs tend to have milder potencies than illegal ones for two reasons. First, illegal markets create incentives for stronger potencies, as sellers will favor concentrated forms of a drug that can be easily concealed and give a big bang for the buck. Second, in legal markets different potencies of the same drug openly compete, and over time the weaker ones come to be preferred—consider the popularity of low tar/nicotine cigarettes and wine and beer over hard liquor.

Thus pharmacology and setting interact: smoking is well-integrated into people's lives because the nicotine in cigarettes has mild pharmacological effects and because smoking is legal, and nicotine has those mild effects in part because smoking is legal. Pharmacology also interacts with what I've been calling set. The harms of smoking are slow to occur, are cumulative, and largely affect one's health, not one's ability to perform normal activities (at least prior to getting seriously ill.) Furthermore, to eliminate these harms requires complete smoking cessation; cutting back rarely suffices (even light smokers increase their chances of getting lung cancer, emphysema, and heart disease). Thus, quitting smoking requires strong motivation, since its bad effects are not immediate, and it does not disrupt one's life. Add to this what I noted earlier, that stopping smoking means changing one's life, and it's unsurprising that many find it difficult to stop.

If my explanation of the relative difficulty of quitting smoking is correct, then the standard view of an addictive drug is quite suspect. That view suggests that knowledge of a drug's pharmacology provides a basis for making reasonable predictions about a drug's addictiveness. However, understanding nicotine's effects upon the brain does not tell us that it's hard to stop smoking; we only know that once we add information about set and setting. Generalizing from the case of smoking, all we can say is:

The milder the effects upon the brain, the easier for adults to purchase, the more easily integrated into one's life, and the more the bad effects are cumulative, slow-acting and only reversible upon complete cessation, the more addictive the drug.

Besides, however, being a mouthful, this understanding of drug addiction requires introducing the *interaction* of set and setting with pharmacology to explain the addictiveness potential of various drugs. It is simpler and less misleading to say that people tend to *addict themselves* to various substances (and activities), this tendency varying with various cultural and individual influences.

CONCLUSION

My argument undercuts the worry that legalizing cocaine and heroin will produce an explosion of addiction because people will have access to inherently and powerfully addictive drugs. The standard view that cocaine and heroin are *inherently* addictive is false, because no drug is inherently addictive. The desire of most people to lead responsible and productive lives, in a social setting that rewards such desires, is what controls and limits most drug use. Ironically, if cocaine and heroin in a legal market would be as disruptive as many drug prohibitionists fear, then that is an excellent reason why addiction would not explode under legalization—drug use that tends to thrive is drug use that is woven into, rather than disrupts, responsible people's lives.

REFERENCES

American Psychiatric Association. (1994). *Diagnostic and Statistical Manual of Mental Disorders* (4th ed.), Washington, D.C.: Author.

DeGrandpre, R., and White E. (1996). "Drugs: In Care of the Self," *Common Knowledge,* 3: 27–48.

Erickson, P., Edward, E., Smart, R., and Murray, G. (1994). *The Steel Drug: Crack and Cocaine in Perspective* (2nd ed.). New York: MacMillan.

Falk, J. (1996). "Environmental Factors in the Instigation and Maintenance of Drug Abuse," in (eds.) W. Bickel and R. DeGrandpre, *Drug Policy and Human Nature.* New York: Plenum Press.

Goodin, R. (1989). "The Ethics of Smoking," *Ethics,* 99: 574–624.

Husak, D. (1992). *Drugs and Rights.* New York: Cambridge University Press.

Kaplan, J. (1983). *The Hardest Drug: Heroin and Public Policy.* Chicago: University of Chicago Press.

Murphy, S., Reinarman, C., and Waldorf, D. (1989). "An 11 Year Follow-Up of a Network of Cocaine Users," *British Journal of Addiction,* 84: 427–36.

National Institute of Drug Abuse. (1990). *National Household Survey on Drug Abuse.* Washington, DC: Department of Health and Human Services.

Peele, S. (1985). *The Meaning of Addiction: Compulsive Experience and Its Interpretation.* Lexington, MA: D.C. Heath and Company.

Peele, S. (1991). *The Diseasing of America: Addiction Treatment Out of Control.* Boston: Houghton Mifflin.

Robins, L., Helzer, J., Hesselbrock, M., and Wish, E. (1980). "Vietnam Veterans Three Years After Vietnam: How Our Study Changed Our View of Heroin," in (eds.) L. Brill and C. Winick, *The Yearbook of Substance Use and Abuse* (Vol. 2). New York: Human Sciences Press.

Schacter, S. (1982). "Recidivism and Self-Cure of Smoking and Obesity," *American Psychologist,* 37: 436–44.

Shapiro, D. (1994). "Smoking Tobacco: Irrationality, Addiction and Paternalism," *Public Affairs Quarterly,* 8: 187–203.

Trebach, A. (1982). *The Heroin Solution.* New Haven, CT: Yale University Press.

Waldorf, D., Reinarman, C., and Murphy, S. (1991). *Cocaine Changes: The Experience of Using and Quitting.* Philadelphia: Temple University Press.

Wilson, J. (1990). "Against the Legalization of Drugs," *Commentary,* 89: 21–28.

Zinberg, N. (1984). *Drug, Set, and Setting.* New Haven, CT: Yale University Press.

Zinberg, N. (1987). "The Use and Misuse of Intoxicants," in (ed.) R. Hamowy, *Dealing with Drugs.* Lexington, MA: D.C. Heath and Company.

REVIEW AND DISCUSSION QUESTIONS

1. What does Shapiro mean by the "standard view" of addiction?
2. Describe the objections Shapiro raises against the standard view of addiction.
3. The alternative view of addiction relies on two notions: "set" and "setting." Explain this alternative understanding of addiction.
4. Describe Shapiro's understanding of the role of tobacco's pharmacological effects in smoking.
5. What are the policy implications of Shapiro's conclusions?

Freedom, Conditioning, and the Real Woman

Janet Radcliffe Richards

In this selection from her book *The Skeptical Feminist,* Janet Radcliffe Richards argues that we are free to the extent others' desires do not keep us from realizing our own, and that freedom is valuable as an end in itself. Some feminists, however, seem to doubt this. Contending that women have been conditioned by male society, they believe that a truly liberated woman is not one who is free to choose without restraints but, rather, a woman who makes certain choices. In response, Radcliffe Richards argues that the fact that women are as they are because of social influences does not show that their choices are not their own. She explores carefully the relation between freedom and conditioning and discusses the ways in which conditioning ought to be properly attacked. Janet Radcliffe Richards is lecturer in philosophy at the Open University in England.

A DEFENCE OF LIBERTY

Here, then, is [my account] of freedom as a possession: you are free to the extent that other people's desires do not come between you and your own. Another, apparently rival, account will appear later in the chapter, but for now we shall concentrate on this one. If this is freedom, what is its value?

One obvious and common defence of freedom is that it is a means to happiness. People who approve of freedom say that it leads to happiness because we are made unhappy if we know that other people control what we do, or because we know better than anyone else what we want and will be made happiest by being left to decide for ourselves, or because

freedom leads to strength and self reliance which in turn lead to happiness. Other people are doubtful about these arguments, and say that, on the contrary, too much freedom makes people unhappy. People do not really know what is best for them, it is argued, so they may be happier if other people make the decisions. Midge Decter, for instance, in her arguments against Women's Liberation, says that what is making women dissatisfied is not a lack of freedom but a surfeit of it.[1]

All these arguments are of course important, but here they are beside the point. Here the issue is not whether freedom is an effective means to some *other* end like happiness, but whether it is good *as an end in itself.* Can we argue that freedom is good irrespective of

From Janet Radcliffe Richards, *The Skeptical Feminist* (Harmondsworth, England: Penguin, 1982). Reprinted by permission.

whether it leads to happiness or anything else we value? And if so, how valuable is it in comparison with these other things?

In some sense there can be very little argument on subjects like this one, because with questions of ultimate values there does not seem to be any common ground for discussion between people who disagree. If people really, in the last analysis, value different things, there is nothing more to be said. However it is possible to do something not unlike arguing. It does seem possible to make it clear by illustration that a great many people, whether they realize it or not, do in fact value freedom as an end in itself, and that many value it even more than happiness. . . .

Suppose, for instance, you were an outstandingly gifted but miserably neurotic artist or musician, and someone offered you a drug which would make you happy, but would result in your losing all your ability. There are already drugs along these lines, but we are to think of one so entirely effective that once having taken it the patient would not even regret having lost the desire or ability to compose or paint. Suppose also that you had complete faith in its efficacy, and in the intentions of the person who offered it. Would you take it? Some people would no doubt be very happy to, but there must be many who in such a situation would rather remain unhappy than achieve happiness at the cost of losing a skill they valued far more than any prospect of happiness.

Suppose, again, you lived in a country with a political regime you disliked intensely, with no way of escaping and not much hope of making things more to your liking. Suppose also that the government had a programme of "re-education" which you believed would be completely effective and which would make you entirely happy with the political situation afterwards. Would you be willing to undergo this programme? Many people would certainly not. They would rather remain unhappy than be so radically changed. Or suppose that you were very dissatisfied with your life as it was. Would you welcome the opportunity (to take a classic example) to become a satisfied pig? Again, probably not.

Of course these thought experiments are all rather artificial. They presuppose impossibilities, and anyway are not specific enough: whether we should be willing to become satisfied pigs would probably depend a good deal on the degree of our unhappiness as human beings. Nevertheless, the arguments are useful because they do suggest that to many people there are things which are more important than happiness.

So far, of course, this does not prove that anyone prefers *freedom* to happiness because the discussion has only been about which of two things we should take if we were in a position to choose, and as long as there is a question of choice some freedom is built into the example. All this shows is that there are occasions where people would choose to cling to what might be called their identities, rather than lose them for the sake of happiness. No doubt they would like happiness as well, but given the necessity of choice, happiness might well be abandoned first. However, it is possible to look at the question of freedom by considering similar cases which involve other people.

Why is it, for instance, that so many people object to Soviet dissidents' being put in psychiatric hospitals? Of course there are several reasons. We may not think the "treatment" will work, and we may not like the system the patients' minds are being changed to fit. However, even supposing we did approve of the political system, and supposing we did believe that after treatment the dissidents would fit happily into Russian society and regard their former activities and attitudes as absurd, would we then approve of the practice? Probably not. We might be happy for people to be offered such treatment if they wanted it, but still think that they should be allowed to choose for themselves whether they would rather be altered and made happy, or remain unhappy but still themselves. And if we think that it is more important to give people this choice than to force happiness on them, it means we are in favour of freedom, and regard it as more important than happiness.

There are many other examples of this sort of attitude. For instance, most of us would be shocked by this advertisement described by Sheila Rowbotham:[2] "There was a picture of a young mother with a pram in front of a big block of flats and the heading 'She can't change her environment but you can change her mood with Serenid-D.'" There are all kinds of reasons for being upset about putting people on happiness drugs, including being afraid of side effects and long-term consequences. Nevertheless, part of the objection is to the idea of making women happy *without fulfilling their desires*. If we were concerned only with happiness for people we should not worry about putting them on effective happiness drugs. If happiness is all that matters there is nothing intrinsically wrong with brainwashing, or forcible medication, or giving people sedatives and tranquilizers instead of coping with their emotional problems. Most of us do care about allowing people to determine the course of their own lives, rather than having other people make them happy in ways they do not want. Since there can hardly be a feminist in existence who would regard it as an acceptable solution to women's problems that someone should invent some kind of medication or special process of re-education which would make women happy in their present lot, but had to be administered against their wills, we must think that most feminists value freedom more than happiness for women. The firm feminist rejection of male paternalism comes not only through the recognition that men's apparent concern for women's well-being is by some curious coincidence remarkably well adapted to the interests of men. Even if men's dominance were wholly good for women, we should still reject its being forced on them. As Kant said, "paternalism is the worst despotism imaginable." And as Mill said, "the only purpose for which power can be rightfully exercised over any member of a civilized community, against his will, is to prevent harm to others. His own good, either physical or moral, is not a sufficient warrant."[3]

There is probably no way of arguing with any feminist who disagrees with all this, as doubtless some must. However, the principle of freedom will be taken as fundamental to feminism throughout this book, and where it produces statements with which feminists disagree, at least it will be obvious where the disagreement stems from. Freedom is being taken as a fundamental good in its own right, and a thing of which we should, therefore, all have as much as possible. How much each individual should have when the claims of other people are taken into consideration is a question of distributive justice. . . .

INNER FREEDOM

Two main propositions have been argued for in the previous two sections. One is that we are free to the extent that we can do as we like (which means that we are not properly described as free or not-free, only as more or less free). The other is that freedom, understood in this way, is good in itself. We should all have as much of it as possible, and if our freedom is to be curtailed it is to be for the sake only of other people, not ourselves.

However, we now have to look at the question of whether feminists do indeed think that freedom is a good thing, and want it for women. If freedom is the ability to fulfill one's desires, and if feminists do want it for women, they should surely be trying to make the world as much as possible as women would like it to be. However, it is a most conspicuous fact about some feminists that they seem to include among their aims things which not only men find objectionable, but which women do too. There are all kinds of things which women seem to want and have no wish to change, and yet which many feminists apparently want to abolish. Traditional marriage and division of labour seem to be happily chosen by many women; many enjoy making themselves attractive to men, and giving men certain kinds of service in return for being protected by them. Many would rather look after a home and family than do anything else. And many, with the appearance of total freedom, choose to enter beauty competitions (which are watched as willingly by millions more women), or to become striptease artists, "hostesses" of various sorts, and prostitutes.

Of course, you can argue here that some of these apparently free choices are not very free at all, because choosing the best of a bad lot does not give women what they really want. They probably would not choose to become housewives or prostitutes if better things were readily available to them. There is much truth in that, no doubt, but it does not provide the slightest reason for taking away the best there is and leaving these women with something which must, in their eyes, be still worse. The true liberator can always be recognized by her wanting to increase the options open to the people who are to be liberated, and there is never any justification for taking a choice away from a group you want to liberate unless it is demonstrable beyond all reasonable doubt that removing it will bring other, more important, options into existence. To give women freedom we must give them more choice, and then if they really do not want the things they are choosing now, like homes and families, those things will just die out without our having to push them.

Of course there are many feminists who do want to increase the options open to women. Consider, for instance, the programme for the picketing of a Miss America Pageant, which stated "There will be . . . Lobbying Visits to the contestants urging our sisters to reject the Pageant Farce and join us . . . we do not plan heavy disruptive tactics. . . ."[4] That was genuinely liberating. The women entering the competition might not have thought of other routes to success, or they might not have realized that there were groups of people where different things were valued. However that is, or at least seems (it is not always easy to know how literally things are to be taken) a very different matter from the demonstrations at the Miss World competition in London where feminist protestors would apparently have liked to disrupt the whole proceedings. To prevent women from doing what they have chosen to do is not to be concerned with their freedom. Nevertheless, that does seem to be the aim of some feminists.

But that is not the end of the matter. This kind of feminist need not accept yet the accusation that she is not really offering women freedom. In general, when the liberators of women or anyone else take the view that they know better than the beneficiaries of their efforts what should be done for them, they will argue that these people are *conditioned,* and therefore not in a state of mind to be able to choose freely no matter how many alternatives are open to them. *That* is why the liberators sometimes have to make choices on their behalf.

This kind of view certainly has intuitive plausibility about it. However, it does present many problems, and in particular the immediate one of seeming to call for (at least) a modification of the account of freedom so far given. It has been argued so far that an individual's freedom is a function mainly of how many choices there are available. If we are to accept, however, that it may sometimes be acceptable to restrict such choices in the name of freedom, on the grounds that the person to be liberated is conditioned and therefore unable to choose, a new element seems to have entered into the idea of liberty. It seems that to be free it is not enough to have a wide range of options open. As well as, or perhaps even instead of, having such options, the free individual must be in a certain state of mind. Freedom must be at least in part an internal thing.

There certainly is no doubt that some such view is widespread in feminism. Perhaps the most striking indication of it is the use of the word "liberated" when applied to women. To the outsider as well as to the feminist a liberated woman is not one who is free to choose among a great many options, but one who makes *certain kinds of choices;* she is not a woman with a tolerant and helpful husband who encourages her to achieve all her ambitions, but one who would not stand any nonsense from her husband if he tried any.

Now there is indeed a long philosophical tradition of saying that true freedom does not consist in being in an environment which permits you to do as you please, but consists (at least partly, depending on the theory) in being in a particular state of mind. Theories like these still do keep to the basic idea of freedom as the satisfaction of desire, but it is differently interpreted and analyzed. There are innumerable variants on the theme, but we need consider only two, and without too much detail.

The first and more extreme, is the idea that freedom is contained entirely within the mind of the free person, with outside circumstances irrelevant. According to this view you are truly free when your desires have been so adjusted that you desire nothing you cannot get. According to the Stoic idea, for instance, if the slave reaches total tranquility of mind while the master is in the grips of unrealized desire, the slave is the freer of the two. And in Christianity, the reason for saying that perfect freedom is to be found in the service of God is that once the Christian has achieved a state of mind in which nothing is desired but to do the will of God, that desire need never be unfulfilled: the will of God can be done in any circumstances whatever. This extreme idea of freedom is not much found in feminism, although there are traces of it. The woman who determines that she will no longer care about things which previously obsessed her, like the approval of men, may be looking for freedom in this way. If she ceases to care about what men think she can act to please herself rather than men, and so lessen the extent of her unfulfilled desire.

The second, more moderate, view of internal freedom is one more commonly found in feminism. This idea is that being in the right state of mind is not enough on its own to make you free: to be free you also need the kind of freedom we have been discussing . . . which involves being able to do as you like. However, that is not enough on its own, and a necessary condition of your choosing freely is that you should be in the right state of mind before deciding among the options which are open to you. There are all kinds of variants on this idea, but common to them all is something like the view that each individual has a *true self* which should be doing the choosing,

but that its activities are obstructed by various contaminants which have got into the person in some way, and which prevent real choice as effectively as obstructions in the environment do. Plato, for instance, thought that there were parts of the soul, and that the lower parts were always trying to pull the highest part from its chosen path. A common idea in religion is that the uncontaminated soul would choose what was good, but that evil powers may take possession of it and force evil choices. More recently, there is the psychoanalytic idea that you cannot be truly free without getting rid of the neuroses which come between yourself and your real desires. Of course, an idea along these lines is very common in feminism. The domination of men has been so complete that the male has entered women's souls, making them choose on behalf of men and against their own interests. That they think themselves free is beside the point: all that shows is how well the work of conditioning has been done.

Now it is quite clear that however difficult all this may be to work out in detail, there is something in it. It is also true that (risky as it may sound) it is *sometimes* reasonable to override people's immediate wishes in the cause of their greater freedom, even when the earlier definition of freedom is taken and we say that people are free to the extent that they can do as they like. For instance, if a friend wanted to achieve something which was very important to her, and we knew beyond any doubt that she was setting about it the wrong way but could not persuade her to change, we might override her immediate wishes because we wanted her to get something which we knew she wanted more. Or again, since freedom is not simply a matter of how many immediate choices there are, but also of *scope* of choice, we might override some trivial choice to make sure that there was a greater range of choices later on. This is always being done in the case of children. Parents are not (necessarily) working against their children's freedom if, for instance, they do not let the children decide which schools they should go to. If a school is so much better than another that it will allow the children far more important choices later on in life, it is in the interests of the children's freedom that they should not be allowed to choose now.

Nevertheless, it is obvious that if we are going to take this sort of line, we have to take *great care*. If women's wishes are to be ignored in the name of their freedom, on the grounds that they are conditioned, it is essential to know exactly what is meant by conditioning, why it is supposed to impair freedom, to what extent it is legitimate to ignore what people want if they are conditioned, and how to distinguish women who are conditioned from the ones who are not. If we do not take care, we run the risk of planning a scheme in which the only freedom women get is the freedom to do what their liberators want them to do.

That is a tempting line anyway. As an early feminist Margaret Rhondda said, "the passion to decide to look after your fellowmen, to do good to them in your way, is far more common than the desire to put into everyone's hand the power to look after themselves."[5] The danger becomes intensified a thousand times when you can do this but still be able to convince yourself that you are offering freedom because the whole issue has been obscured under more or less indiscriminate accusations of conditioning. If the idea of conditioning is to be used to enhance freedom, and not as a general device by which a liberation movement can do as it likes in the name of freedom, it must be pinned down more precisely.

CONDITIONING AND THE REAL WOMAN

There is one point which must be made quite clear before going any further. The conditioning which was referred to in the previous section is supposed to be a sort of thing which is *actually a constraint* on a woman; something which comes between herself and her true desires. Now the word "conditioning" is one which is extremely commonly used in feminism, in all kinds of circumstances, and what must on no account be presumed is that whenever the word is used the so-called conditioned

desires, attitudes and responses are things which actually do prevent the real woman from fulfilling her real desires.

In feminist contexts the usual ground for making an accusation of conditioning is to point to the social root of the habit of mind in question (which is, of course, always one which is disapproved of). Women want to make themselves beautiful only because society has made them want to; they think that their mission in life is to be mothers because everyone has been drumming it into them since the age of two; they lack ambition because they have been brought up from birth to think that the female is the natural servant of the male and on no account to compete with him. This may all be true. However, to establish that a woman is conditioned in *that* sense of the word is nothing like enough to show that she is conditioned in the very different sense of having something in her personality which gets between herself and the fulfillment of her real desires, and therefore that these environmentally produced characteristics limit her freedom.

The reason why conditioning in the sense of "coming from a (disapproved of) social influence" cannot be the same as conditioning in the sense of "getting in the way of the true woman's desires" is obvious from the discussion of the nature of woman. . . . You cannot distinguish between the woman as she now is and what is supposed to be the "true" woman by pointing to the way society has shaped her. It is absolutely inevitable that the adult woman should be as she is partly as a result of social influence, and it is a thing we cannot possibly object to unless we are to suggest that people should be sent to grow up among wolves (and anyway there are social pressures even among wolves). We cannot say of social pressures *in general* that they turn the woman into something which is not her true self; on the contrary, they cannot be anything other than a contribution to what she actually is.

Of course we may not *like* the way women are at present, and if we do not we can argue that their upbringing ought to be changed. Very obviously, for instance, feminists are bound to disapprove of any upbringing which is so much at odds with women's intrinsic natures that they are bound to be unhappy. They can also reasonably object to women's being brought up to depend on men in the achievement of what they want, because that is unreliable and their success in life should be more firmly based. They can disapprove of women's being encouraged to see their main aim in life as relationships with men, and all their ambitions directed towards pleasing men in one way or another, because it is undignified and they want women to be dignified. They can say that women ought not to be brought up to confine their interests and activities to domestic matters and concentrate their energies on trivia, because they would prefer them to be well-educated, ambitious and serious-minded. Since there is no neutral way to bring children up (they must be surrounded by influences of one kind or another) we have a good deal of choice about how adults eventually turn out. We certainly could make women other than they are now, and it is not surprising that feminists would like to see a good many changes.

On the other hand, none of this provides any reason at all for saying that women as they are now, with the desires they have now, are not *free*. We may think it a good thing that women should be brought up to be happy, dignified, independent, serious and useful, but, once again, everything is what it is. Happiness is happiness, dignity is dignity, independence is independence: none of these things is freedom. Even though there may be some difficulty about finding a definitive account of freedom there are limits to what we can reasonably decide to adopt, and it really would be travesty of the language (as well as potentially treacherous) to say that people were not free just because we did not like the way they were, or that in making them into something we liked better we should be giving them freedom. We may argue with perfect justice that women are as they are because of social influences, but that is not enough to show that the choices they are making are not their own real choices. And if by "conditioned" we want to mean "not in a state to make free choices" we

must mean something more than "influenced by social pressures we disapprove of."

Of course we can still, if we want to, say that "conditioned" does just refer to socially induced characteristics in women, rather than aspects of a woman's character which somehow do get in the way of her real desires. However, this is dangerous. The word has now such deeply entrenched connotations of interference with freedom that if we take a definition which does not include those connotations we open the floodgates to mistakes and double dealing. I shall therefore take it that "conditioning" is properly used only when it does refer to a real restriction on freedom. The problem is, now that we have decided that a woman brought up one way is no less her real self than a woman brought up any other way, to work out what form conditioning might take.

FREEDOM AND CONDITIONING

Since we are trying to distinguish the social pressures which condition a woman from the ones which simply form her character, one obvious starting point is the fact that from the point of view of each individual there is a great difference between different kinds of social pressure. Whereas some are congenial and easily conformed to, others are not: some social pressures push people towards doing things for which they have an intrinsic dislike.

Nevertheless, people often go along even with these, because doing so is less unpleasant than suffering the social consequences of resistance. So a woman who has no natural interest in beauty may make herself as beautiful as she can; or one who is not interested in children may do her best to absorb herself in the concerns of a family; or a woman by nature apt to explore jungles may become a secretary, because that is the feminine thing to do and that way she will get social approval. None of this shows conditioning. The environment is constricting, but nevertheless a woman who makes the best choice among the limited set available to her is behaving perfectly rationally and choosing in her own interest, and as long as she is doing that the only restrictions on her freedom are external, not internal.

However, what happens to these women who go along with uncongenial social pressures when liberators appear on the scene, and suggest to them that the world would be a better place if women did not spend so much time on their appearance, or that children are not necessarily the ideal object of every woman's devotion? Or what happens if they find themselves in a situation where the uncongenial social pressures are beginning to lessen, and following their natural inclinations would bring down less social censure?

If they thoroughly understand the situation in which they have grown up there may be no difficulty. They may instantly join in the campaign to change the things which are alien to their natures, or at least take advantage of any changes which come about. But this may well not happen. Usually when children are subjected to pressures in growing up they do not think separately about what they would like to do and what adult pressures and encouragements compel them to do; they just get into habits of doing what produces the least unacceptable consequences. The result is that when the situation changes, or when there is some prospect of its changing, they may not rush to embrace the new but cling to the habits they have grown up with. Probably they do not understand that their present preferences came about by the forcible suppression of their natural (that is, inherent) inclinations, but even if they do they may well have difficulty in ridding themselves of the habits they have gathered. These habits may then come between the adults and their real desires.

A simple analogy can be drawn from an entirely different context. When you learn to drive you rapidly pick up the skills of braking and steering, and your responses to various situations become so automatic that you can usually do the right thing without thinking. But you may well learn these habits without knowing much about how braking and steering work, and the result is that the first time you skid you react in the way you always have

reacted when the car moves too fast in the wrong direction, by braking as hard as possible and hauling the steering wheel round. The consequences are exactly the opposite of what you want. In order to avoid the situation in future you have to do two things. The first is to understand the theory, so that you know under what conditions the usual methods will and will not work, and the second is to free yourself of your habitual actions.

As a motorist you have very definite desires (to move in particular directions), but you yourself may interfere with their fulfillment through ignorance, or bad habits, or both. Much the same may happen with women. Their failure to understand the situation they are in, and the persistence of deeply entrenched habits, may get in the way of what they want to do. And where this happens we can say that a woman's state of mind is obstructing her desires, *without having to resort to dubious theories about hidden desires in the core of her imaginary real self.*

Failure to understand the nature of the world and the structure of possibilities within it acts against women in all kinds of ways. For instance, many women (if not all) are by nature as inclined as men to seek fame and fortune, but the traditional restricted upbringing of a woman means that in most cases there is only a limited number of forms in which she is capable of casting this ambition: she may think as a matter of course that success for a woman must take the form of being pursued by men, envied by women and renowned for beauty. But if that is the only way in which she can imagine making an impact on the world she is likely to have condemned herself to failure before even setting out. Few women succeed in being renowned for beauty, and anyway beauty does not last. Or she may have more specific ambitions, and look for political power, but may automatically presume that political success for a woman must take the form of being the wife of a politician, and in that case her potential for success is restricted from the start by the casting of her ambitions in a form which sets a low upper limit on possible success. If women squeeze their desires into a conventionally feminine mould they are likely to be doomed to failure from the first. But even if they succeed in it, [they] may still fail because of habits of mind which interfere: perhaps she cannot avoid feeling that she ought to take care with her dress, or feeling guilty if she lets her husband do his fair share of the housework, however clearly she may understand the unreasonableness of such feelings. Her ingrained habits of mind prevent the fulfillment of her strongest desires.

This analysis seems to provide a very good account of what it is to be conditioned, and there is no difficulty at all about seeing it as an internal lack of freedom: something about the woman which prevents her from doing as she really wants. One aspect of conditioning is *ignorance,* probably the greatest curtailer of freedom there is, because if someone does not know or fully grasp that the world contains certain possibilities, as far as that person is concerned they might just as well not exist. The other aspect is the inability to change unwelcome aspects of oneself, which is as much a restriction on the fulfillment of desire as the inability to change anything in the outside world. If you want to be more beautiful, or run faster, or be stronger, or be able to charm people, but cannot do whatever it is, you are as curtailed in your desires as you would be through not having money, or influence, or a car, or tools for a trade.

The upshot of all this is that feminists are indeed right in thinking that lack of freedom can be internal: a woman may be in a state where her own mind prevents her from achieving what she really wants (a matter which must not be confused with her mind preventing what she would have wanted if she had been someone else). However, although the comparisons drawn in the last paragraph between internal and external restrictions on freedom do show that freedom can be limited by aspects of the mind, what they also show at the same time is that there is no intrinsic difference between external and internal lack of freedom; they are essentially the same sort of thing. Internal lack of freedom does not consist in being in a special state of mind or

having a particular set of desires, only in having within oneself (rather than in surrounding circumstances) the things which prevent fulfillment of desire. This means that, in fact, there is no problem about reconciling the concept of internal freedom with the first account of freedom given in this chapter. The only acceptable interpretation of "internal freedom" (the only account of it which does not involve calling something quite different by the name of freedom, or presuming that the real woman is something uninfluenced by society) is one which makes it essentially a matter of being unimpeded in one's desires by one's own ignorance and habits. This is important. Once it is clear people will be less likely to be confused by the vague way in which "conditioned" is often used, or lured into thinking that if women have socially induced desires which the liberators disapprove of, they are necessarily not free.

THE ATTACK ON CONDITIONING

When women are really conditioned, their preconceptions and immediate desires do get in the way of what, in some perfectly obvious way, they really want. If they are conditioned, therefore, it does seem that other people may be justified in overriding their immediate desires in order to produce not what the liberators think they should want, but what they actually do want.

However, there is an obvious danger in taking this attitude, because the only case in which it would be reasonable to override a woman's wishes in the name of her freedom would be where it was absolutely certain that she was conditioned, and equally certain what she really wanted and how it could be brought about. And the simple fact of the matter is that it is virtually impossible even to approach certainty in cases like this, let alone reach it. It is very hard to tell when, and to what extent, people are conditioned.

The main reason why this must be so is probably obvious from what has gone before. The point is that it is quite impossible to tell conditioned women from unconditioned ones[6] by their preferences. The pressures on women to be beautiful and maternal and domestic and deferential to men have no doubt left in many women habits of mind which will prevent their ever achieving what they really want to achieve, but we are not entitled to presume that the pressures which produced these mental blocks in some women did the same for all. For the women to whom these pressures were congenial, as they must have been for some, the desires produced became their own most basic desires, and not obstacles to the fulfillment of others. If a woman is interested mainly in dress or nursery design it is no doubt true to say that it can be attributed to her background to some extent: if she had been brought up differently she would have had different interests. However, these may be genuinely hers, and ideally suited to her nature. The "conditioned" responses may be genuinely her own. It is therefore impossible to tell whether or not a woman is conditioned just by knowing about her likes and dislikes, or about her formative influences.

What that means is that the only attack which can be safely mounted against conditioning must be directed to its source. It is too dangerous to try to "free" women who are regarded as conditioned by forcing them to do what the prevailing feminist ideology presumes they must want, because with that method there is always the danger of ignoring women's real wishes. They may not be conditioned at all. The only thing to do is start from the beginning and try, even at this late stage, to remove the cause of the trouble, and give conditioned women a chance to become unconditioned in a way which runs no risk of damaging those who are not, because it still leaves women to make their own choices.

There are two stages to this process, corresponding to the two aspects of conditioning. The first is to increase understanding of how the present state of things came about and how it works, so that women who have been doing what does not suit them can understand

why, and at the same time what alternatives are possible. The second is to make help available to women who decide as a result of this that they do want to change their habits.

There are all kinds of ways in which advances could be made on these two fronts. The key to the first is *diversity*. Women must be exposed to kinds of new influences and information (in addition to the old, of course, not instead of them) to make them fully aware of the possibilities the world contains. Some people, no doubt, will try to turn the freedom argument against this procedure by saying that if people have new alternatives thrust before them they are *forced to choose,* and that in itself is an infringement of liberty because people ought to have the freedom not to choose if that is what they would prefer. However, that argument cannot possibly work. This is because it is true as a matter of *logic* that people cannot be the ultimate determiners of their own degree of freedom. Whatever anyone chooses to do, that choice comes from among alternatives which already exist, and those alternatives were not themselves chosen. Since, therefore, the ultimate degree of freedom is always out of the hands of the individual we are right to insist that the choice given should always be as great as possible. We cannot, in the name of liberty for women, force them to do anything against their wills or bring about states of society they do not like, but we are bound to give them more knowledge of possibilities.

The second part of the attack on conditioning is to reinforce this for women who do decide that they would like to change their lives by giving them every help in overcoming unwelcome habits of mind: help ranging from the support of other women who understand the position to full-scale psychotherapy. As long as this was directed to bringing about what women themselves wanted, and not to persuading them into something they did not want, it would be genuinely liberating.

Still, however energetically we pursued such a programme, we should have to be hopelessly optimistic to think that we should actually eliminate all existing conditioning as a result of it, and perhaps this seems to justify the wish of some feminists to make a firm attack on the symptoms of conditioning, rather than going in this gentle way for its cause. However much we may want freedom for women, they could argue, even the freedom to stay conditioned, can we allow them this freedom if the price of it is to trap other women in the same bonds? Can we allow a conditioned mother to bring up her daughter in the same way? Surely for the sake of the daughters we ought to be willing to run the risk of attacking directly what we believe to be the mothers' conditioned desires, even though we may run some risk of going against their real wishes? Surely we should work directly against bad influences, and deliberately get rid of (for instance), beauty competitions, sexist literature in schools, and anything else we think objectionable, whatever the conditioned mothers may think of the matter?

However, even though conditioned mothers will certainly tend to bring up conditioned daughters, and although we certainly cannot allow that, this conclusion is not the proper one to draw. The way to prevent the daughters from becoming conditioned is not to keep them out of the range of influence of the things which are believed to have conditioned their mothers, because it was not *being in the range of those influences* which did the harm, but *being out of the range of others*. If we bring the daughters up on a diet of so-called non-sexist literature (much of what is around at present is actually *female* sexist) to think that there

should be no sex roles, that does not free them from conditioning: it only brings them up with a different sort. If to get feminist approval a little girl is forced to sneer at the idea of beauty competitions, she is as much coerced as her mother was by parents who expected her to look pleased when she was given dolls and pretty party frocks. Once again, whether or not a girl is conditioned cannot be judged by which slogans she grows up chanting, because in theory she could be conditioned into chanting any.

The solution to the problem, as always with questions of freedom, is once again diversity. We can perhaps summarize the conditioned mothers and those of daughters who are to be rescued from conditioning by proposing a solution to the widely debated problem of how free a parent should be to determine a child's education. We can put it this way. Within practicable limits, the parent should be allowed to say that the child *must* learn certain things, and have lessons from people of particular political, moral or religious views. On the other hand, no parent should have the right to *prevent* the child's learning anything (going to scripture classes in the wrong religion or having sex education) or being exposed to other people's views. The education authorities should have a positive duty to diversify influences, since in that way the parent's wishes are respected but the child's freedom is not impaired. That should be what feminists want. As Germaine Greer said of a similar problem, "censorship is the weapon of the opposition, not ours."[7]

NOTES

1. Midge Decter, *The New Chastity,* p. 51.
2. Sheila Rowbotham, *Woman's Consciousness, Man's World,* pp. 75–6.
3. John Stuart Mill, "On Liberty," in *The Essential Works of John Stuart Mill,* ed. Lerner, p. 263.
4. "No More Miss America!" in *Sisterhood is Powerful,* ed. Morgan, p. 584.
5. Margaret Rhondda, quoted in Firestone, *The Dialectic of Sex,* p. 20.
6. More accurately, of course, *more* or *less* conditioned, and in certain ways rather than just in general. Throughout arguments of this sort it must not be forgotten that freedom is a matter of degree.
7. Germaine Greer, *The Female Eunuch,* p. 309.

REVIEW AND DISCUSSION QUESTIONS

1. How does Radcliffe Richards define freedom? What is the alternative, "inner" way of understanding freedom that she discusses?
2. In what ways does Radcliffe Richards agree with those who advocate "inner" freedom? What does she mean by the term?
3. How does Radcliffe Richards distinguish pressures that "condition"—that is, restrict freedom—from those that merely play a part in the general formation of a person?
4. Why is Radcliffe Richards skeptical of those who argue that women who dress for men or participate in beauty pageants are not truly free? What solutions does Radcliffe Richards think will help assure women are not, in fact, choosing in accord with conditioning rather than choosing freely?
5. Explain how censorship can damage women's freedom, according to Radcliffe Richards. How can education help women?
6. How would Radcliffe Richards respond to Catharine MacKinnon, who argues that women's choices are "structured" and that marriage, prostitution, and sexual harassment are "indistinguishable"? Explain.

Essay and Paper Topics for Section 11

1. Compare Mill's discussion of individuality in this selection with his description of the "higher" pleasures in utilitarianism, and with Aristotle's discussion of happiness in *Nicomachean Ethics*.
2. Compare Shapiro's understanding of addiction with that of Szasz and Goodin.
3. Discuss, in light of the material in this section, whether or not you think drugs should be legalized.
4. Compare Radcliffe Richards's essay with Mill's *On Liberty*, and with Held's discussion of feminist moral theory in Section 2.

12

Free Speech

Freedom of speech is regarded as among the most important rights; yet all rights have limits, and speech is no exception. Nobody thinks the right to speak freely extends to publishing military secrets or burning down buildings in a protest. Two forms of speech, in particular, have created controversy: hate speech and pornography. These debates have recently moved into a new area, as the Internet has expanded access to information beyond what seemed impossible only a few years ago. This section begins with a chapter from Mill's *On Liberty,* a work that is widely regarded as one of the most important and articulate defenses of free expression ever written. It is followed by a 1989 U.S. Supreme Court case asking whether burning the U.S. flag is protected by the Constitution, another legal decision involving the right of Nazis to march in a town that included many survivors of Nazi concentration camps, and two selections on limiting hate speech on campus and political correctness. The discussion of pornography begins with two articles taking opposing views on the legitimacy of censoring pornography, followed by a major legal decision on the subject. The section concludes with two opposing perspectives on whether, and how, censorship should be extended to the Internet in order to protect children.

Of the Liberty of Thought and Discussion

John Stuart Mill

In the following selection, taken from his classic work *On Liberty,* John Stuart Mill provides what may be the best known and most widely quoted defense of freedom of conscience and speech ever written. Arguing that along with other liberties, protecting freedom of conscience and speech is of vital social importance, Mill vigorously upholds freedom of opinion, regardless of whether the belief is true or false. Indeed, he argues, it is especially important that false and evil opinions be freely expressed. For a brief description of John Stuart Mill's life, see the introduction to *Utilitarianism* (section 1). Other selections from *On Liberty* are reprinted in section 11.

The time, it is to be hoped, is gone by, when any defense would be necessary of the "liberty of the press" as one of the securities against corrupt or tyrannical government. No argument, we may suppose, can now be needed against permitting a legislature or an executive, not identified in interest with the people, to prescribe opinions to them, and determine what doctrines or what arguments they shall be allowed to hear. . . . Let us suppose . . . that government is entirely at one with the people, and never thinks of exerting any power of coercion unless in agreement with what it conceives to be their voice. But I deny the right of the people to exercise such coercion, either by themselves or by their government. The power itself is illegitimate. The best government has no more title to it than the worst. It is as noxious, or more noxious, when exerted in accordance with public opinion than when in opposition to it. If all mankind minus one were of one opinion, mankind would be no more justified in silencing that one person than he, if he had the power, would be justified in silencing mankind. Were an opinion a personal possession of no value except to the owner, if to be obstructed in the enjoyment of it were simply a private injury, it would make some difference whether the injury was inflicted only on a few persons or on many. But the peculiar evil of silencing the expression of an opinion is that it is robbing the human race, posterity as well as the existing generation—those who dissent from the opinion, still more than those who hold it. If the opinion is right, they are deprived of the opportunity of exchanging error for truth; if wrong, they lose, what is almost as great a benefit, the clearer perception and livelier impression of truth produced by its collision with error.

It is necessary to consider separately these two hypotheses, each of which has a distinct branch of the argument corresponding to it. We can never be sure that the opinion we are endeavoring to stifle is a false opinion; and if we were sure, stifling it would be an evil still.

First, the opinion which it is attempted to suppress by authority may possibly be true. Those who desire to suppress it, of course, deny its truth; but they are not infallible. They have no authority to decide the question for all mankind and exclude every other person from the means of judging. To refuse a hearing to an opinion because they are sure that it is false to assume that *their* certainty is the same thing as *absolute* certainty. All silencing of discussion is an assumption of infallibility. Its condemnation may be allowed to rest on this common argument, not the worse for being common.

Unfortunately for the good sense of mankind, the fact of their fallibility is far from carrying the weight in their practical judgment which is always allowed to it in theory; for while everyone well knows himself to be fallible, few think it necessary to take any precautions against their own fallibility, or admit the supposition that any opinion of which they feel very certain may be one of the examples of the error to which they acknowledge themselves to be liable. . . .

The objection likely to be made to this argument would probably take some such form as the following. There is no greater assumption of infallibility in forbidding the propagation of error than in any other thing which is done by public authority on its own judgment and responsibility. . . . It is the duty of governments, and of individuals, to form the truest opinions they can; to form them carefully, and never impose them upon others unless they are quite sure of being right. But when they are sure (such reasoners may say), it is not conscientiousness but cowardice to shrink from acting on their opinions and allow doctrines which they honestly think dangerous to the welfare of mankind, either in this life or in another, to be scattered abroad without restraint, because other people, in less enlightened times, have persecuted opinions now believed to be true. . . . There is no such thing as absolute certainty, but there is assurance sufficient for the purposes of human life. We may, and must, assume our opinion to be true for the guidance of our own conduct; and it is assuming no more when we forbid bad men to pervert society by the propagation of opinions which we regard as false and pernicious.

I answer, that it is assuming very much

From John Stuart Mill, *On Liberty* (1859).

more. There is the greatest difference between presuming an opinion to be true because, with every opportunity for contesting it, it has not been refuted, and assuming its truth for the purpose of not permitting its refutation. Complete liberty of contradicting and disproving our opinion is the very condition which justifies us in assuming its truth for purposes of action; and on no other terms can a being with human faculties have any rational assurance of being right. . . .

Let us now pass to the second division of the argument, and dismissing the supposition that any of the received opinions may be false, let us assume them to be true and examine into the worth of the manner in which they are likely to be held when their truth is not freely and openly canvassed. However unwillingly a person who has a strong opinion may admit the possibility that his opinion may be false, he ought to be moved by the consideration that, however true it may be, if it is not fully, frequently, and fearlessly discussed, it will be held as a dead dogma, not a living truth. . . .

If the cultivation of the understanding consists in one thing more than in another, it is surely in learning the grounds of one's own opinions. Whatever people believe, on subjects on which it is of the first importance to believe rightly, they ought to be able to defend against at least the common objections. . . . The greatest orator, save one, of antiquity, has left it on record that he always studied his adversary's case with as great, if not still greater, intensity than even his own. What Cicero practiced as the means of forensic success requires to be imitated by all who study any subject in order to arrive at the truth. He who knows only his own side of the case knows little of that. His reasons may be good, and no one may have been able to refute them. But if he is equally unable to refute the reasons on the opposite side, if he does not so much as know what they are, he has no ground for preferring either opinion. The rational position for him would be suspension of judgment, and unless he contents himself with that, he is either led by authority or adopts, like the generality of the world, the side to which he feels most inclination. Nor is it enough that he should hear the arguments of adversaries from his own teachers, presented as they state them, and accompanied by what they offer as refutations. That is not the way to do justice to the arguments or bring them into real contact with his own mind. He must be able to hear them from persons who actually believe them, who defend them in earnest and do their very utmost for them. He must know them in their most plausible and persuasive form; he must feel the whole force of the difficulty which the true view of the subject has to encounter and dispose of, else he will never really possess himself of the portion of truth which meets and removes that difficulty. . . .

The fact . . . is that not only the grounds of the opinion are forgotten in the absence of discussion, but too often the meaning of the opinion itself. The words which convey it cease to suggest ideas, or suggest only a small portion of those they were originally employed to communicate. Instead of a vivid conception and a living belief, there remain only a few phrases retained by rote; or, if any part, the shell and husk only of the meanings is retained, the finer essence being lost. The great chapter in human history which this fact occupies and fills cannot be too earnestly studied and meditated on. . . .

We have hitherto considered only two possibilities: that the received opinion may be false, and some other opinion, consequently, true; or that, the received opinion being true, a conflict with the opposite error is essential to a clear apprehension and deep feeling of its truth. But there is a commoner case than either of these: when the conflicting doctrines, instead of being one true and the other false, share the truth between them, and the nonconforming opinion is needed to supply the remainder of the truth of which the received doctrine embodies only a part. Popular opinions, on subjects not palpable to sense, are often true, but seldom or never the whole truth. They are a part of the truth, sometimes a greater, sometimes a smaller part, but exaggerated, distorted, and disjointed from the truths by which they ought to be accompanied and limited. Heretical opinions, on the other hand, are generally some of these suppressed and neglected truths, bursting the bonds which kept them down, and either seeking reconciliation with the truth contained in the common opinion, or fronting it as enemies, and setting themselves up, with similar exclusiveness, as the whole truth. The latter case is hitherto the most frequent, as, in the human mind, one-sidedness has always been the rule, and many-sidedness the exception. . . . Such being the partial character of prevailing opinions, even when resting on a true foundation, every opinion which embodies somewhat of the portion of truth which the common opinion omits ought to be considered precious, with whatever amount of error and confusion that truth may be blended. . . .

We have now recognized the necessity to the mental well-being of mankind (on which all their other well-being depends) of freedom of opinion, and freedom of the expression of opinion, on four distinct grounds, which we will now briefly recapitulate:

First, if any opinion is compelled to silence, that opinion may, for aught we can certainly know, be true. To deny this is to assume our own infallibility.

Secondly, although the silenced opinion be an error, it may, and very commonly does, contain a portion of truth; and since the general or prevailing opinion on any subject is rarely or never the whole truth, it is only by the collision of adverse opinions that the remainder of the truth has any chance of being supplied.

Thirdly, even if the received opinion be not only true, but the whole truth; unless it is suffered to be, and actually is, vigorously and earnestly contested, it will, by most of those who receive it, be held in the manner of a prejudice, with little comprehension or feeling of its rational grounds. And not only this, but fourthly, the meaning of the doctrine itself will be in danger of being lost or enfeebled, and deprived of its vital effect on the character and conduct: the dogma becoming a mere formal profession, inefficacious for good, but cumbering the ground and preventing the growth of any real and heartfelt conviction from reason or personal experience.

REVIEW AND DISCUSSION QUESTIONS

1. What values or purposes does Mill think are served by freedom of speech?
2. Why does Mill think that false speech should be tolerated or even encouraged?
3. Explain why Mill thinks those who would censor speech are assuming, falsely, that they are "infallible."
4. How does Mill respond to those who say that "offensive" speech may be banned?
5. Describe how Mill's discussion of free speech fits into his larger discussion of liberty and individuality in *On Liberty*.
6. Suppose somebody defends censorship of Nazi propaganda based on the claim that unless their ideas are suppressed Nazis might eventually gain power, as occurred in post–World War I Germany. How would Mill respond to such an argument? Is that response sound?

Flag Burning as Constitutionally Protected

Texas v. *Johnson*

After burning the U.S. flag as an act of political protest, Gregory Lee Johnson was convicted of desecrating a flag in violation of Texas law. The state of Texas, after losing in lower courts, appealed to the U.S. Supreme Court, which had to decide whether Johnson's conviction was consistent with the First Amendment's protection of freedom of speech. By a narrow five-to-four vote, the Court again held that the Texas law was unconstitutional. Delivering the opinion of the Court, Justice Brennan argues that the state cannot "prescribe what shall be orthodox" by punishing symbolic actions like flag burning. The way to preserve the flag's special role in our national life, he argues, is not to punish those who feel differently about this symbol but to persuade them that they are wrong. In their separate dissents, Justice Rehnquist and Justice Stevens reject the idea that the flag is just another symbol, toward which it would be unconstitutional to require minimal respect.

Justice Brennan: As in *Spence* [v. *Washington*, a 1974 case on expressive conduct], "[w]e are confronted with a case of prosecution for the expression of an idea through activity," and "[a]ccordingly, we must examine with particular care the interests advanced by [petitioner] to support its prosecution.". . . . Johnson was not, we add, prosecuted for the expression of just any idea; he was prosecuted for his expression of dissatisfaction with the policies of this country, expression situated at the core of our First Amendment values.

Moreover, Johnson was prosecuted because he knew that his politically charged expression would cause "serious offense." If he had burned the flag as a means of disposing of it because it was dirty or torn, he would not have been convicted of flag desecration under this Texas law: federal law designates burning as the preferred means of disposing of a flag "when it is in such condition that it is no longer a fitting emblem for display." . . .

If we are to hold that a state may forbid flag-burning wherever it is likely to endanger the flag's symbolic role, but allow it wherever burning a flag promotes that role—as where, for example, a person ceremoniously burns a

dirty flag—we would be saying that when it comes to impairing the flag's physical integrity, the flag itself may be used as a symbol—as a substitute for the written or spoken word or a "short cut from mind to mind"—only in one direction. We would be permitting a state to "prescribe what shall be orthodox" by saying that one may burn the flag to convey one's attitude toward it and its referents only if one does not endanger the flag's representation of nationhood and national unity.

We never before have held that the government may ensure that a symbol be used to express only one view of that symbol or its referents. . . .

We are fortified in today's conclusion by our conviction that forbidding criminal punishment for conduct such as Johnson's will not endanger the special role played by our flag or the feelings it inspires. To paraphrase Justice [Oliver Wendell] Holmes, we submit that nobody can suppose that this one gesture of an unknown man will change our nation's attitude towards its flag. . . . Indeed, Texas's argument that the burning of an American flag "is an act having a high likelihood to cause a breach of peace," . . . . and its statute's

Texas v. *Johnson.* 57 L.W. 4770 (1989).

implicit assumption that physical mistreatment of the flag will lead to "serious offense," tend to confirm that the flag's special role is not in danger; if it were, no one would riot or take offense because a flag had been burned.

We are tempted to say, in fact, that the flag's deservedly cherished place in our community will be strengthened, not weakened, by our holding today. Our decision is a reaffirmation of the principles of freedom and inclusiveness that the flag best reflects, and of the conviction that our toleration of criticism such as Johnson's is a sign and source of our strength. Indeed, one of the proudest images of our flag, the one immortalized in our own national anthem, is of the bombardment it survived at Fort McHenry. It is the nation's resilience, not its rigidity, that Texas sees reflected in the flag—and it is that resilience that we reassert today.

The way to preserve the flag's special role is not to punish those who feel differently about these matters. It is to persuade them that they are wrong. "To courageous, self-reliant men, with confidence in the power of free and fearless reasoning applied through the processes of popular government, no danger flowing from speech can be deemed clear and present, unless the incidence of the evil apprehended is so imminent that it may befall before there is opportunity for full discussion. If there be time to expose through discussion the falsehood and fallacies, to avert the evil by the processes of education, the remedy to be applied is more speech, not enforced silence." . . . And, precisely because it is our flag that is involved, one's response to the flag-burner may exploit the uniquely persuasive power of the flag itself. We can imagine no more appropriate response to burning a flag than waving one's own, no better way to counter a flag-burner's message than by saluting the flag that burns, no surer means of preserving the dignity even of the flag that burned than by—as one witness here did—according its remains a respectful burial. We do not consecrate the flag by punishing its desecration, for in doing so we dilute the freedom that this cherished emblem represents.

Johnson was convicted for engaging in expressive conduct. The state's interest in preventing breaches of the peace does not support his conviction because Johnson's conduct did not threaten to disturb the peace. Nor does the state's interest in preserving the flag as a symbol of nationhood and national unity justify his criminal conviction for engaging in political expression. The judgment of the Texas Court of Criminal Appeals is therefore affirmed.

Justice Rehnquist, Dissenting: In holding this Texas statute unconstitutional, the court ignores Justice Holmes's familiar aphorism that "a page of history is worth a volume of logic." . . . For more than 200 years, the American flag has occupied a unique position as the symbol of our nation, a uniqueness that justifies a governmental prohibition against flag burning in the way respondent Johnson did here. . . .

In the First and Second World Wars, thousands of our countrymen died on foreign soil fighting for the American cause. At Iwo Jima in the Second World War, United States Marines fought hand-to-hand against thousands of Japanese. By the time the Marines reached the top of Mount Suribachi, they raised a piece of pipe upright and from one end fluttered a flag. That ascent had cost nearly 6,000 American lives. . . .

During the Korean War, the successful amphibious landing of American troops at Inchon was marked by the raising of an American flag within an hour of the event. . . .

The government is simply recognizing as a fact the profound regard for the American flag created by that history when it enacts statutes prohibiting the disrespectful public burning of the flag.

The court concludes its opinion with a regrettably patronizing civics lecture, presumably addressed to members of both houses of Congress, the members of the 48 state legislatures that enacted prohibitions against flag burning and the troops fighting under that flag in Vietnam who objected to its being burned: "The way to preserve the flag's special role is not to punish those who feel differently about these matters. It is to persuade them that they are wrong." . . .

The court's role as the final expositor of the Constitution is well established, but its role as a platonic guardian admonishing those responsible to public opinion as if they were truant school children has no similar place in our system of government. The cry of "no taxation without representation" animated those who revolted against the English crown to found our nation—the idea that those who submitted to government should have some say as to what kind of laws would be passed. Surely one of the high purposes of a democratic society is to legislate against conduct that is regarded as evil and profoundly offensive to the majority of people—whether it be murder, embezzlement, pollution or flag burning.

Our Constitution wisely places limits on powers of legislative majorities to act, but the declaration of such limits by this court "is, at all times, a question of much delicacy, which ought seldom, if ever, to be decided in the affirmative, in a doubtful case." . . . Uncritical extension of constitutional protection to the burning of the flag risks the frustration of the very purpose for which organized governments are instituted. The court decides that the American flag is just another symbol, about which not only must opinions pro and con be tolerated, but for which the most minimal public respect may not be enjoined. The government may conscript men into the armed forces where they must fight and perhaps die for the flag, but the government may not prohibit the public burning of the banner under which they fight. I would uphold the Texas statute as applied in this case.

Justice Stevens, Dissenting: As the court analyzes this case, it presents the question whether the state of Texas, or indeed the federal government, has the power to prohibit the public desecration of the American flag. The question is unique. In my judgment, rules that apply to a host of other symbols, such as state flags, armbands or various privately promoted emblems of political or commercial

identity, are not necessarily controlling. Even if flag burning could be considered just another species of symbolic speech under the logical application of the rules that the court has developed in its interpretation of the First Amendment in other contexts, this case has an intangible dimension that makes those rules inapplicable.

A country's flag is a symbol of more than "nationhood and national unity." . . . It also signifies the ideas that characterize the society that has chosen that emblem as well as the special history that has animated the growth and power of those ideas. The fleurs-de-lis and the tricolor both symbolized "nationhood and national unity," but they had vastly different meanings. The message conveyed by some flags—the swastika, for example—may survive long after it has outlived its usefulness as a symbol of regimented unity in a particular nation.

So it is with the American flag. It is more than a proud symbol of the courage, the determination and the gifts of nature that transformed 13 fledgling colonies into a world power. It is a symbol of freedom, of equal opportunity, of religious tolerance and of goodwill for other peoples who share our aspirations. The symbol carries its message to dissidents both at home and abroad who may have no interest at all in our national unity or survival.

The value of the flag as a symbol cannot be measured. Even so, I have no doubt that the interest in preserving that value for the future is both significant and legitimate. Conceivably that value will be enhanced by the court's conclusion that our national commitment to free expression is so strong that even the United States as ultimate guarantor of that freedom is without power to prohibit the desecration of its unique symbol. But I am unpersuaded. . . .

The case has nothing to do with "disagreeable ideas." . . . [I]t involves disagreeable conduct that, in my opinion, diminishes the value of an important national asset.

The court is therefore quite wrong in blandly asserting that respondent "was prosecuted for his expression of dissatisfaction with the policies of this country, expression situated at the core of our First Amendment values." . . . Respondent was prosecuted because of the method he chose to express his dissatisfaction with those policies. Had he chosen to spray paint—or perhaps convey with a motion picture projector—his message of dissatisfaction on the facade of the Lincoln Memorial, there would be no question about the power of the government to prohibit his means of expression. The prohibition would be supported by the legitimate interest in preserving the quality of an important national asset. Though the asset at stake in this case is intangible, given its unique value, the same interest supports a prohibition on the desecration of the American flag.

The ideas of liberty and equality have been an irresistible force in motivating leaders like Patrick Henry, Susan B. Anthony and Abraham Lincoln, schoolteachers like Nathan Hale and Booker T. Washington, the Philippine Scouts who fought at Bataan, and the soldiers who scaled the bluff at Omaha Beach. If those ideas are worth fighting for—and our history demonstrates that they are—it cannot be true that the flag that uniquely symbolizes their power is not itself worthy of protection from unnecessary desecration.

I respectfully dissent.

REVIEW AND DISCUSSION QUESTIONS

1. What does Texas argue is the danger in allowing flag burning?
2. What is the "fixed star" in our constitutional system that Justice Brennan argues is at the heart of this issue?
3. Why, according to Justice Brennan, might allowing such political protests actually *increase* people's sense of patriotism?
4. Why does Justice Rehnquist think government is justified in prohibiting flag burning?
5. On what basis does Justice Stevens dissent?
6. How might it be argued that preventing flag burning is *not* tantamount to establishing political orthodoxy?

Nazi Marches

Village of Skokie v. *National Socialist Party*

Skokie, Illinois, was the home of more than forty thousand Jews and five to seven thousand survivors of Nazi concentration camps. When the National Socialist Party (the American Nazi Party) tried to march in Skokie, the village won an injunction preventing various forms of conduct. An appeals court modified that injunction but allowed the ban on displaying the swastika to stand. Here the Supreme Court of Illinois considers an appeal by the Nazi leader, Frank Collin, of the lower court's ban. (The U.S. Supreme Court later refused to reconsider this decision of the Illinois Supreme Court.)

Per Curiam: [D]efendant Frank Collin, who testified that he was "party leader," stated that on or about March 20, 1977, he sent officials of the plaintiff village a letter stating that the party members and supporters would hold a peaceable, public assembly in the village on May 1, 1977, to protest the Skokie Park District's requirement that the party procure

$350,000 of insurance prior to the party's use of the Skokie public parks for public assemblies. The demonstration was to begin at 3 P.M., last 20 to 30 minutes, and consist of 30 to 50 demonstrators marching in single file, back and forth, in front of the village hall. The marchers were to wear uniforms which include a swastika emblem or armband. They were to carry a party banner containing a swastika emblem and signs containing such statements as "White Free Speech," "Free Speech for the White Man," and "Free Speech for White America." The demonstrators would not distribute handbills, make any derogatory statements directed to any ethnic or religious group, or obstruct traffic. They would cooperate with any reasonable police instructions or requests.

At the hearing on plaintiff's motion for an "emergency injunction" a resident of Skokie testified that he was a survivor of the Nazi holocaust. He further testified that the Jewish community in and around Skokie feels the purpose of the march in the "heart of the Jewish population" is to remind the two million survivors "that we are not through with you" and to show "that the Nazi threat is not over, it can happen again." Another resident of Skokie testified that as the result of defendants' announced intention to march in Skokie, 15 to 18 Jewish organizations, within the village and surrounding area, were called and a counterdemonstration of an estimated 12,000 to 15,000 people was scheduled for the same day. There was opinion evidence that defendants' planned demonstration in Skokie would result in violence. . . .

In defining the constitutional rights of the parties who come before this court, we are, of course, bound by the pronouncements of the United States Supreme Court in its interpretation of the United States Constitution. The decisions of that court, particularly *Cohen* v. *California* . . . in our opinion compel us to permit the demonstration as proposed, including display of the swastika.

"It is firmly settled that under our Constitution the public expression of ideas may not be prohibited merely because the ideas are themselves offensive to some of their hearers" . . . and it is entirely clear that the wearing of distinctive clothing can be symbolic expression of a thought or philosophy. The symbolic expression of thought falls within the free speech clause of the first amendment . . . and the plaintiff village has the heavy burden of justifying the imposition of a prior restraint upon defendants' right to freedom of speech. . . . The village of Skokie seeks to meet this burden by application of the "fighting words" doctrine first enunciated in *Chaplinsky* v. *New Hampshire* (1942). . . . That doctrine was designed to permit punishment of extremely hostile personal communication likely to cause immediate physical response, "no words being 'forbidden except such as have a direct tendency to cause acts of violence by the persons to whom, individually, the remark is addressed.'" . . . In *Cohen* the Supreme Court restated the description of fighting words as "those personally abusive epithets which, when addressed to the ordinary citizen, are, as a matter of common knowledge, inherently likely to provoke violent reaction." . . . Plaintiff urges, and the appellate court has held, that the exhibition of the Nazi symbol, the swastika, addresses to ordinary citizens a message which is tantamount of fighting words. Plaintiff further asks this court to extend *Chaplinsky,* which upheld a statute punishing the use of such words, and hold that the fighting-words doctrine permits a prior restraint on defendants' symbolic speech. In our judgment we are precluded from doing so.

In *Cohen,* defendant's conviction stemmed from wearing a jacket bearing the words "Fuck the Draft" in a Los Angeles County courthouse corridor. The Supreme Court for reasons we believe applicable here refused to find that the jacket inscription constituted fighting words. That court stated:

Village of Skokie v. *National Socialist Party.* 373 N.E. 2d 21 (Ill. 1978).

"The constitutional right of free expression is powerful medicine in a society as diverse and populous as ours. It is designed and intended to remove governmental restraints from the arena of public discussion, putting the decision as to what views shall be voiced largely into the hands of each of us, in the hope that use of such freedom will ultimately produce a more capable citizenry and more perfect polity and in the belief that no other approach would comport with the premise of individual dignity and choice upon which our political system rests. . . .

To many, the immediate consequence of this freedom may often appear to be only verbal tumult, discord, and even offensive utterance. These are, however, within established limits, in truth necessary side effects of the broader enduring values which the process of open debate permits us to achieve. That the air may at times seem filled with verbal cacophony is, in this sense not a sign of weakness but of strength. We cannot lose sight of the fact that, in what otherwise might seem a trifling and annoying instance of individual distasteful abuse of a privilege, these fundamental societal values are truly implicated. . . . '[S]o long as the means are peaceful, the communication need not meet standards of acceptability,' . . .

Against this perception of the constitutional policies involved, we discern certain more particularized considerations that peculiarly call for reversal of this conviction. First, the principle contended for by the State seems inherently boundless. How is one to distinguish this from any other offensive word [emblem]? Surely the State has no right to cleanse public debate to the point where it is grammatically palatable to the most squeamish among us. Yet no readily ascertainable general principle exists for stopping short of that result were we to affirm the judgment below. For, while the particular four-letter word [emblem] being litigated here is perhaps more distasteful than most others of its genre, it is nevertheless often true that one man's vulgarity is another's lyric. Indeed, we think it is largely because governmental officials cannot make principled distinctions in this area that the Constitution leaves matters of taste and style so largely to the individual. . . .

Finally, and in the same vein, we cannot indulge the facile assumption that one can forbid particular words without also running a substantial risk of suppressing ideas in the process. Indeed, governments might soon seize upon the censorship of particular words [emblems] as a convenient guise for banning the expression of unpopular views. We have been able, as noted above, to discern little social benefit that might result from running the risk of opening the door to such grave results." . . .

The display of the swastika, as offensive to the principles of a free nation as the memories it recalls may be, is symbolic political speech intended to convey to the public the beliefs of those who display it. It does not, in our opinion, fall within the definition of "fighting words," and that doctrine cannot be used here to overcome the heavy presumption against the constitutional validity of a prior restraint.

Nor can we find that the swastika, while not representing fighting words, is nevertheless so offensive and peace threatening to the public that its display can be enjoined. We do not doubt that the sight of this symbol is abhorrent to the Jewish citizens of Skokie, and that the survivors of the Nazi persecutions, tormented by their recollections, may have strong feelings regarding its display. Yet it is entirely clear that this factor does not justify enjoining defendants' speech. The *Cohen* court spoke to this subject.

"Finally, in arguments before this Court much has been made of the claim that Cohen's distasteful mode of expression was thrust upon unwilling or unsuspecting viewers, and that the State might therefore legitimately act as it did in order to protect the sensitive from otherwise unavoidable exposure to appellant's crude form of protest. Of course, the mere presumed presence of unwitting listeners or viewers does not serve automatically to justify curtailing all speech capable of giving offense. . . . While this Court has recognized that government may properly act in many situations to prohibit intrusion into the privacy of the home of unwelcome views and ideas which cannot be totally banned from the public dialogue we have at the same time consistently stressed that 'we are often "captives" outside the sanctuary of the home and subject to objectionable speech.' The ability of government, consonant with the Constitution, to shut off discourse solely to protect others from hearing it is, in other words, dependent upon a showing that substantial privacy interests are being invaded in an essentially intolerable manner. Any broader view of this authority would effectively empower a majority to silence dissidents simply as a matter of personal predilections."

Rockwell v. *Morris* . . . also involved an American Nazi leader, George Lincoln Rockwell, who challenged a bar to his use of a New York City park to hold a public demonstration where anti-Semitic speeches would be made. Although approximately $2\frac{1}{2}$ million Jewish New Yorkers were hostile to Rockwell's message, the court ordered that a permit to speak be granted, stating:

"A community need not wait to be subverted by street riots and storm troopers; but, also, it cannot, by its policemen or commissioners, suppress a speaker, in prior restraint, on the basis of news reports, hysteria, or inference that what he did yesterday, he will do today. Thus, too, if the speaker incites others to immediate unlawful action he may be punished—in a proper case, stopped when disorder actually impends; but this is not to be confused with unlawful action from others who seek unlawfully to suppress or punish the speaker.

So, the unpopularity of views, their shocking quality, their obnoxiousness, and even their alarming impact is not enough. Otherwise, the preacher of any strange doctrine could be stopped; the anti-racist himself could be suppressed, if he undertakes to speak in 'restricted' areas; and one who asks that public schools be open indiscriminately to all ethnic groups could be lawfully suppressed, if only he choose to speak where persuasion is needed most." . . .

In summary, as we read the controlling Supreme Court opinions, use of the swastika is a symbolic form of free speech entitled to first amendment protections. Its display on uniforms or banners by those engaged in peaceful demonstrations cannot be totally precluded solely because that display may provoke a violent reaction by those who view it. Particularly is this true where, as here, there has been advance notice by the demonstrators of their plans so that they have become, as the complaint alleges, "common knowledge" and those to whom sight of the swastika banner or uniforms would be offense are forewarned and need not view them. A speaker who gives prior notice of his message has not compelled a confrontation with those who voluntarily listen.

As to those who happen to be in a position to be involuntarily confronted with the swastika, the following observations from *Erznoznik* v. *City of Jacksonville* . . . are appropriate:

"The plain, if at all times disquieting, truth is that in our pluralistic society, constantly proliferating new and ingenious forms of expression, 'we are inescapably captive audiences for many purposes.' . . . Much that we encounter offends our esthetic, if not our political and moral, sensibilities. Nevertheless, the Constitution does not permit government to decide which types of otherwise protected speech are sufficiently offensive to require protection for the unwilling listener or viewer. Rather, absent the narrow circumstances described above [home intrusion or captive audience], the burden normally falls upon the viewer to 'avoid further bombardment of [his] sensibilities simply by averting [his] eyes.'"

REVIEW AND DISCUSSION QUESTIONS

1. Describe the factual background and legal issues in this case.
2. The court relied on an earlier U.S. Supreme Court case, *Cohen* v. *California,* in deciding this one. What happened in *Cohen?* Why does the court think it is relevant to *Skokie?*
3. What do you think the intention of the Nazis was in deciding to march in Skokie, if not to win political converts to their cause? Should the court have considered their purposes?
4. How does the court distinguish this case from *Chaplinsky* and the "fighting words" exception?
5. It is sometimes said that had the court ruled otherwise it would be put on a slippery slope of trying to balance the offensiveness of speech against the First Amendment rights of the speaker, with the result that important political acts like civil rights marches would have been jeopardized. Do you agree? Explain.

Prohibiting Racist Speech on Campus: A Debate

Charles Lawrence and Gerald Gunther

The following is a debate between two law professors, offered in response to Stanford University's speech code. (In 1990, Stanford revised the code, along the lines described in the questions after the reading.) Charles Lawrence is professor of law at Georgetown University, and Gerald Gunther is professor of law at Stanford University.

By Charles Lawrence

I have spent the better part of my life as a dissenter. As a high-school student, I was threatened with suspension for my refusal to participate in a civil-defense drill, and I have been a conspicuous consumer of my First Amendment liberties ever since. There are very strong reasons for protecting even speech that is racist. Perhaps the most important is that such protection reinforces our society's commitment to tolerance as a value. By protecting bad speech from government regulation, we will be forced to combat it as a community.

I have, however, a deeply felt apprehension about the resurgence of racial violence and the corresponding increase in the incidence of verbal and symbolic assault and harassment to which blacks and other traditionally excluded groups are subjected. I am troubled by the way the debate has been framed in response to the recent surge of racist incidents on college and university campuses and in response to some universities' attempts to regulate harassing speech. The problem has been framed as one in which the liberty of free speech is in conflict with the elimination of racism. I believe this has placed the bigot on the moral high ground and fanned the rising flames of racism.

Above all, I am troubled that we have not listened to the real victims—that we have shown so little understanding of their injury, and that we have abandoned those whose race, gender, or sexual orientation continues to make them second-class citizens. It seems to me a very sad irony that the first instinct of civil libertarians has been to challenge even the smallest, most narrowly framed efforts by universities to provide black and other minority students with the protection the Constitution, in my opinion, guarantees them.

The landmark case of *Brown* v. *Board of Education* is not a case that we normally think of as a case about speech. But *Brown* can be broadly read as articulating the principle of equal citizenship. *Brown* held that segregated schools were inherently unequal because of the message that segregation conveyed: that black children were an untouchable caste, unfit to go to school with white children. If we understand the necessity of eliminating the system of signs and symbols that signal the inferiority of blacks, then we should hesitate before proclaiming that all racist speech that stops short of physical violence must be defended.

University officials who have formulated policies to respond to incidents of racial harassment have been characterized in the press as "thought police," even though such policies generally do nothing more than impose sanctions against intentional face-to-face insults. Racist speech takes the form of face-to-face insults, catcalls, or other assaultive speech aimed at an individual or small

From Charles Lawrence and Gerald Gunther, "Good Speech, Bad Speech—Yes," and "Good Speech, Bad Speech—No," *Stanford Lawyer*, 24 (1990), pp. 6, 8, 40, and 7, 9, 41. Reprinted with permission.

group of persons and falls directly within the "fighting words" exception to the First Amendment protection. The Supreme Court has held in *Chaplinsky* v. *New Hampshire* that words which "by their very utterance inflict injury or tend to incite an immediate breach of the peace" are not protected by the First Amendment.

If the purpose of the First Amendment is to foster the greatest amount of speech, racial insults disserve that purpose. Assaultive racist speech functions as a preemptive strike. The invective is experienced as a blow, not as a proffered idea. And once the blow is struck, a dialogue is unlikely to follow. Racial insults are particularly undeserving of First Amendment protection, because the perpetrator's intention is not to discover truth or initiate dialogue but to injure the victim. In most situations, members of minority groups realize that they are likely to lose if they fight back, and are forced to remain silent and submissive.

Courts have held that offensive speech may not be regulated in public forums (such as streets, where the listener may avoid the speech by moving on). But the regulation of otherwise protected speech has been permitted when the speech invades the privacy of the unwilling listener's home, or when the unwilling listener cannot avoid the speech. Racist posters, fliers, and graffiti in dormitories, bathrooms, and other common living spaces would seem to fall within the reasoning of these cases. Minority students should not be required to remain in their rooms in order to avoid racial insult. Minimally, they should find a safe haven in their dorms and in all other common rooms that are a part of their daily routine.

I would also argue that the university's responsibility for ensuring that these students receive an equal educational opportunity provides a compelling justification for regulations that ensure them safe passage in all common areas. A minority student should not have to risk becoming the target of racially assaulting speech every time he or she chooses to walk across campus. Regulating vilifying speech that cannot be anticipated or avoided need not

preclude announced speeches and rallies—situations that would give minority-group members and their allies the opportunity to organize counterdemonstrations or avoid the speech altogether.

The most commonly advanced argument against the regulation of racist speech proceeds something like this: We recognize that minority groups suffer pain and injury as the result of racist speech, but we must allow this hate mongering for the benefit of society as a whole. Freedom of speech is the lifeblood of our democratic system. It is especially important for minorities, because often it is their only vehicle for rallying support for the redress of their grievances. It will be impossible to formulate a prohibition so precise that it will prevent the racist speech you want to suppress, without catching in the same net all kinds of speech that it would be unconscionable for a democratic society to suppress.

Such arguments seek to strike a balance between our concern, on the one hand, for the continued free flow of ideas and the democratic process dependent on that flow, and, on the other, our desire to further the cause of equality. There can, however, be no meaningful discussion of how we should reconcile our commitment to equality with our commitment to free speech, until it is acknowledged that racist speech inflicts real harm, and that this harm is far from trivial.

To engage in a debate about the First Amendment and racist speech without a full understanding of the nature and extent of that harm is to risk making the First Amendment an instrument of domination rather than a vehicle of liberation. We have not all known the experience of victimization by racist, misogynist, and homophobic speech, nor do we equally share the burden of the harm it inflicts. We are often quick to say that we have heard the cry of the victims when we have not.

The *Brown* case is again instructive, because it speaks directly to the psychic injury inflicted by racist speech by noting that the symbolic message of segregation affected "the hearts and minds" of Negro children "in a way unlikely ever to be undone." Racial epithets and harassment often cause deep emotional scarring and feelings of anxiety and fear that pervade every aspect of a victim's life.

Brown also recognized that black children did not have an equal opportunity to learn and participate in the school community when they bore the additional burden of being subjected to the humiliation and psychic assault contained in the message of segregation. University students bear an analogous burden when they are forced to live and work in an environment where at any moment they may be subjected to denigrating verbal harassment and assault. The same injury was addressed by the Supreme Court when it held that, under Title VII of the Civil Rights Act of 1964, sexual harassment which creates a hostile or abusive work environment violates the ban on sex discrimination in employment.

Carefully drafted university regulations could bar the use of words as assault weapons while at the same time leaving unregulated even the most heinous of ideas provided those ideas are presented at times and places and in manners that provide an opportunity for reasoned rebuttal or escape from immediate insult. The history of the development of the right to free speech has been one of carefully evaluating the importance of free expression and its effects on other important societal interests. We have drawn the line between protected and unprotected speech before without dire results. (Courts have, for example, exempted from the protection of the First Amendment obscene speech and speech that disseminates official secrets, defames or libels another person, or is used to form a conspiracy or monopoly.)

Blacks and other people of color are skeptical about the argument that even the most injurious speech must remain unregulated because, in an unregulated marketplace of ideas, the best ones will rise to the top and gain acceptance. Experience tells quite the opposite. People of color have seen too many demagogues elected by appealing to America's racism, and too many sympathetic politicians shy away from issues that might brand them as being too closely allied with disparaged groups.

Whenever we decide that racist speech must be tolerated because of the importance of maintaining societal tolerance for all unpopular speech, we are asking blacks and other subordinated groups to bear the burden for the good of all. We must be careful that the ease with which we strike the balance against the regulation of racist speech is in no way influenced by the fact that the cost will be borne by others. We must be certain that those who will pay that price are fairly represented in our deliberations and that they are heard.

At the core of the argument that we should resist all government regulation of speech is the ideal that the best cure for bad speech is good—that ideas that affirm equality and the worth of all individuals will ultimately prevail. This is an empty ideal unless those of us who would fight racism are vigilant and unequivocal in that fight. We must look for ways to offer assistance and support to students whose speech and political participation are chilled in a climate of racial harassment.

Civil rights lawyers might consider suing on behalf of blacks whose right to an equal education is denied by a university's failure to ensure a non-discriminatory educational climate or conditions of employment. We must embark upon the development of a First Amendment jurisprudence grounded in the reality of our history and our contemporary experience. We must think hard about how best to launch legal attacks against the most indefensible forms of hate speech. Good lawyers can create exceptions and narrow interpretations that limit the harm of hate speech without opening the floodgates of censorship.

Everyone concerned with these issues must find ways to engage actively in actions that resist and counter the racist ideas that we would have the First Amendment protect. If we fail in this, the victims of hate speech must rightly assume that we are on the bigots' side.

By Gerald Gunther

I am deeply troubled by current efforts—however well-intentioned—to place new limits on freedom of expression at this and other campuses. Such limits are not only incompatible with the mission and meaning of a university; they also send exactly the wrong message from academia to society as a whole. University campuses should exhibit greater, not less, freedom of expression than prevails in society at large.

Proponents of new limits argue that historic First Amendment rights must be balanced against "Stanford's commitment to the diversity of ideas and persons." Clearly, there is ample room and need for vigorous University action to combat racial and other discrimination. But curbing freedom of speech is the wrong way to do so. The proper answer to bad speech is usually more and better speech—not new laws, litigation, and repression.

Lest it be thought that I am insensitive to the pain imposed by expressions of racial or religious hatred, let me say that I have suffered that pain and empathize with others under similar verbal assault. My deep belief in the principles of the First Amendment arises in part from my own experiences.

I received my elementary education in a public school in a very small town in Nazi Germany. There I was subjected to vehement anti-Semitic remarks from my teacher, classmates and others—"Judensau" (Jew pig) was far from the harshest. I can assure you that they hurt. More generally, I lived in a country where ideological orthodoxy reigned and where the opportunity for dissent was severely limited.

The lesson I have drawn from my childhood in Nazi Germany and my happier adult life in this country is the need to walk the sometimes difficult path of denouncing the bigots' hateful ideas with all my power, yet at the same time challenging any community's attempt to suppress hateful ideas by force of law.

Obviously, given my own experience, I do not quarrel with the claim that words can do harm. But I firmly deny that a showing of harm suffices to deny First Amendment protection, and I insist on the elementary First Amendment principle that our Constitution usually protects even offensive, harmful expression.

That is why—at the risk of being thought callous or doctrinaire—I feel compelled to speak out against the attempt by some members of the Stanford community to enlarge the area of forbidden speech under the Fundamental Standard. Such proposals, in my view, seriously undervalue the First Amendment and far too readily endanger its precious content. Limitations on free expression beyond those established by law should be eschewed in an institution committed to diversity and the First Amendment.

In explaining my position, I will avoid extensive legal arguments. Instead, I want to speak from the heart, on the basis of my own background and of my understanding of First Amendment principles—principles supported by an even larger number of scholars and Supreme Court justices, especially since the days of the Warren Court.

Among the core principles is that any official effort to suppress expression must be viewed with the greatest skepticism and suspicion. Only in very narrow, urgent circumstances should government or similar institutions be permitted to inhibit speech. True, there are certain categories of speech that may be prohibited; but the number and scope of these categories has steadily shrunk over the last fifty years. Face-to-face insults are one such category; incitement to immediate illegal action is another. But opinions expressed in debates and arguments about a wide range of political and social issues should not be suppressed simply because of disagreement with those views, with the content of the expression.

Similarly, speech should not and cannot be banned simply because it is "offensive" to substantial parts or a majority of a community. The refusal to suppress offensive speech is one of the most difficult obligations the free speech principle imposes upon all of us; yet it is also one of the First Amendment's greatest glories—indeed it is a central test of a community's commitment to free speech.

The Supreme Court's 1989 decision to allow flag-burning as a form of political protest, in *Texas* v. *Johnson,* warrants careful pondering by all those who continue to advocate campus restraints on "racist speech." As Justice Brennan's majority opinion in Johnson reminded, "If there is a bedrock principle underlying the First Amendment, it is that the Government may not prohibit the expression of an idea simply because society finds the idea itself offensive or disagreeable." In refusing to place flag-burning outside the First Amendment, moreover, the *Johnson* majority insisted (in words especially apt for the "racist speech" debate): "The First Amendment does not guarantee that other concepts virtually sacred to our Nation as a whole—*such as the principle that discrimination on the basis of race is odious and destructive*—will go unquestioned in the marketplace of ideas. We decline, therefore, to create for the flag an exception to the joust of principles protected by the First Amendment." (Italics added.)

Campus proponents of restricting offensive speech are currently relying for justification on the Supreme Court's allegedly repeated reiteration that "fighting words" constitute an exception to the First Amendment. Such an exception has indeed been recognized in a number of lower court cases. However, there has only been one case in the history of the Supreme Court in which a majority of the Justices has ever found a statement to be a punishable resort to "fighting words." That was *Chaplinsky* v. *New Hampshire,* a nearly fifty-year-old case involving words which would very likely not be found punishable today.

More significant is what has happened in the nearly half-century since: Despite repeated appeals to the Supreme Court to recognize the applicability of the "fighting words" exception by affirming challenged convictions, the Court has in every instance refused. One must wonder about the strength of an exception that, while theoretically recognized, has for so long not been found apt in practice. (Moreover, the proposed Stanford rules are not limited to face-to-face insults to an addressee, and thus go well beyond the traditional, albeit fragile, "fighting words" exception.)

The phenomenon of racist and other offensive speech that Stanford now faces is not a new one in the history of the First Amendment. In recent decades, for example, well-meaning but in my view misguided majorities have sought to suppress not only racist speech but also antiwar and antidraft speech, civil rights demonstrators, the Nazis and the Ku Klux Klan, and left-wing groups.

Typically, it is people on the extremes of the political spectrum (including those who advocate overthrow of our constitutional system and those who would not protect their opponents' right to dissent were they the majority) who feel the brunt of repression and have found protection in the First Amendment; typically, it is well-meaning people in the majority who believe that their "community standards," their sensibilities, their sense of outrage, justify restraints.

Those in power in a community recurrently seek to repress speech they find abhorrent; and their efforts are understandable human impulses. Yet freedom of expression—and especially the protection of dissident speech, the most important function of the First Amendment—is an anti-majoritarian principle. Is it too much to hope that, especially on a university campus, a majority can be persuaded of the value of freedom of expression and of the resultant need to curb our impulses to repress dissident views?

The principles to which I appeal are not new. They have been expressed, for example, by the most distinguished Supreme Court justices ever since the beginning of the Court's confrontations with First Amendment issues nearly seventy years ago. These principles are reflected in the words of so imperfect a First Amendment defender as Justice Oliver Wendell Holmes: "If there is any principle of the Constitution that more imperatively calls for attachment than any other it is the principle of free thought—not free thought for those who agree with us but freedom for the thought that we hate."

This is the principle most elaborately and eloquently addressed by Justice Louis D. Brandeis, who reminded us that the First Amendment rests on a belief "in the power of reason as applied through public discussion" and therefore bars "silence coerced by law—the argument of force in its worst form."

This theme, first articulated in dissents, has repeatedly been voiced in majority opinions in more recent decades. It underlies Justice Douglas's remark in striking down a conviction under a law banning speech that "stirs the public to anger": "A function of free speech [is] to invite dispute. . . . Speech is often provocative and challenging. That is why freedom of speech [is ordinarily] protected against censorship or punishment."

It also underlies Justice William J. Brennan's comment about our "profound national commitment to the principle that debate on public issues should be uninhibited, robust and wide-open, and that it may well include vehement, caustic and sometimes unpleasantly sharp attacks"—a comment he followed with a reminder that constitutional protection "does not turn upon the truth, popularity or social utility of the ideas and beliefs which are offered."

These principles underlie as well the repeated insistence by Justice John Marshall Harlan, again in majority opinions, that the mere "inutility or immorality" of a message cannot justify its repression, and that the state may not punish because of "the underlying content of the message." Moreover, Justice Harlan, in one of the finest First Amendment opinions on the books, noted, in words that Stanford would ignore at its peril at this time:

> The constitutional right of free expression is powerful medicine in a society as diverse and populous as ours. . . . To many, the immediate consequence of this freedom may often appear to be only verbal tumult, discord and even offensive utterance. These are, however, within established limits, in truth necessary side effects of the broader enduring values which the process of open debate permits us to achieve. That the air may at times seem filled with verbal cacophony is, in this sense, not a sign of weakness but of strength.

In this same passage, Justice Harlan warned that a power to ban speech merely because it is offensive is an "inherently boundless" notion, and added that "we think it is largely because governmental officials cannot make principled distinctions in this area that the Constitution leaves matters of taste and style so largely to the individual." (The Justice made these comments while overturning the conviction of an antiwar protestor for "offensive conduct." The defendant had worn, in a courthouse corridor, a jacket bearing the words "Fuck the Draft." It bears noting, in light of the ongoing campus debate, that Justice Harlan's majority opinion also warned that "we cannot indulge in the facile assumption that one can forbid particular words without also running the substantial risk of suppressing ideas in the process.")

I restate these principles and repeat these words for reasons going far beyond the fact that they are familiar to me as a First Amendment scholar. I believe—in my heart as well as my mind—that these principles and ideals are not only established but right. I hope that the entire Stanford community will seriously reflect upon the risks to free expression, lest we weaken hard-won liberties at Stanford and, by example, in this nation.

REVIEW AND DISCUSSION QUESTIONS

1. Explain why Lawrence supports the code. What values does he argue are at stake?
2. Why does Gunther oppose the code? How does he address the concerns raised by Lawrence?
3. How might Lawrence respond to Gunther, if he were given the opportunity?

4. Stanford's new policy is directed at either verbal or symbolic harassment that must be "intended to stigmatize an individual or small number of individuals." Harassment is defined as behavior "commonly understood to convey direct and visceral hatred or contempt for human beings on the basis of their sex, race, color, handicap, religion, sexual orientation, or national or ethnic origin." Would this definition answer the objections raised by Gunther?

5. Discuss how Lawrence would view a racist attack by a member of a minority against a white male or against a woman.

Political Correctness, Speech Codes, and Diversity

Alan M. Dershowitz

In this essay, Alan Dershowitz raises questions about political correctness and its relationship to the demand for greater diversity on campus. Dershowitz is concerned that others who share his generally leftist ideology are increasingly inclined to use the law against their opponents. Alan M. Dershowitz is professor of law at Harvard Law School.

There is now a debate among the pundits over whether the "political correctness" movement on college and university campuses constitutes a real threat to intellectual freedom or merely provides conservatives with a highly publicized opportunity to bash the left for the kind of intolerance of which the right has often been accused.

My own sense, as a civil libertarian whose views lean to the left, is that the "P.C." movement is dangerous and that it is also being exploited by hypocritical right wingers.

In addition to being intellectually stifling, the P.C. movement is often internally inconsistent. Among its most basic tenets are (1) the demand for "greater diversity" among students and faculty members; and (2) the need for "speech codes," so that racist, sexist and homophobic ideas, attitudes and language do not "offend" sensitive students.

Is it really possible that the bright and well-intentioned students (and faculty) who are pressing the "politically correct" agenda do not realize how inherently self-contradictory these two basic tenets really are? Can they be blind to the obvious reality that true diversity of viewpoints is incompatible with speech codes that limit certain diverse expressions and attitudes?

I wonder if most of those who are pressing for diversity really want it. What many on the extreme left seem to want is simply more of their own: more students and faculty who think like they do, vote like they do and speak like they do. The last thing they want is a truly diverse campus community with views that are broadly reflective of the multiplicity of attitudes in the big, bad world outside of the ivory towers.

How many politically correct students are demanding—in the name of diversity—an increase in the number of Evangelical Christians, National Rifle Association members, and Right to Life advocates? Where is

Alan M. Dershowitz, "Political Correctness, Speech Codes, and Diversity," *Harvard Law Record*, September 20, 1991. Reprinted by permission.

the call for more anti-communist refugees from the Soviet Union, Afro-Americans who oppose race-specific quotas, and women who are antifeminist?

Let's be honest: the demand for diversity is at least in part a cover for a political power grab by the left. Most of those who are recruited to provide politically correct diversity—Afro-Americans, women, gays—are thought to be supporters of the left. And historically, the left—like the right—has not been a bastion of diversity.

Now the left—certainly the extreme left that has been pushing hardest for political correctness—is behind the demands for speech codes. And if they were to get their way these codes would not be limited to racist, sexist, or homophobic epithets. They would apply as well to politically incorrect ideas that are deemed offensive by those who would enforce the codes. Such ideas would include criticism of affirmative action programs, opposition to rape-shield laws, advocacy of the criminalization of homosexuality and defense of pornography.

I have heard students argue that the expression of such ideas—both in and out of class, both by students and professors—contributes to an atmosphere of bigotry, harassment and intolerance, and that it makes it difficult for them to learn.

The same students who insist that they be treated as adults when it comes to their sexuality, drinking and school work, beg to be treated like children when it comes to politics, speech and controversy. They whine to Big Father and Mother—the president or provost of the University—to "protect" them from offensive speech, instead of themselves trying to combat it in the marketplace of ideas.

Does this movement for political correctness—this intolerance of verbal and intellectual diversity—really affect college and university students today? Or is it, as some argue, merely a passing fad, exaggerated by the political right and the media?

It has certainly given the political right, not known for its great tolerance of different ideas—a hey day. Many hypocrites of the right, who would gladly impose their own speech codes if *they* had the power to enforce *their* way, are selectively wrapping themselves in the same First Amendment they willingly trash when it serves their political interest to do so.

But hypocrisy aside—since there is more than enough on both sides—the media is not exaggerating the problem of political correctness. It is a serious issue on college and university campuses. As a teacher, I can feel a palpable reluctance on the part of many students—particularly those with views in neither extreme and those who are anxious for peer acceptance—to experiment with unorthodox ideas, to make playful comments on serious subjects, to challenge politically correct views and to disagree with minority, feminist or gay perspectives.

I feel this problem quite personally, since I happen to agree—as a matter of substance—with most "politically correct" positions. But I am appalled at the intolerance of many who share my substantive views. And I worry about the impact of politically correct intolerance on the generation of leaders we are currently educating.

REVIEW AND DISCUSSION QUESTIONS

1. What does Dershowitz think is the real motive behind speech codes?
2. What is the distinction between ideas and epithets? Is it an important one, in thinking about free speech on campus?
3. What argument might be given on behalf of the view that speech codes should be enforced on university campuses? How, exactly, should such a code be written? Should it restrict only speech that refers to race, ethnicity, or gender?

4. What should a university's policy be toward students who believe homosexuality, for example, is wrong? What about speech that offends a religious minority? Could a professor be brought up on charges for raising questions about the existence of God?

5. Can the harmful effects of prejudice be successfully attacked while ignoring the private attitudes people have and focusing only on their behavior?

Pornography, Oppression, and Freedom: A Closer Look

Helen E. Longino

In this essay, Helen Longino first distinguishes pornography from both erotica and moral realism. Pornography involves the "degrading and demeaning portrayal of the role and status of the human female . . . as a mere sexual object to be exploited and manipulated sexually." Longino then describes the various ways in which pornography injures women, and concludes pornography should be banned because of these harms. Helen E. Longino is professor of philosophy at Rice University.

I. INTRODUCTION

The much-touted sexual revolution of the 1960's and 1970's not only freed various modes of sexual behavior from the constraints of social disapproval, but also made possible a flood of pornographic material. According to figures provided by WAVPM (Women Against Violence in Pornography and Media), the number of pornographic magazines available at newsstands has grown from zero in 1953 to forty in 1977, while sales of pornographic films in Los Angeles alone have grown from $15 million in 1969 to $85 million in 1976.[1]

Traditionally, pornography was condemned as immoral because it presented sexually explicit material in a manner designed to appeal to "prurient interests" or a "morbid" interest in nudity and sexuality, material which furthermore lacked any redeeming social value and which exceeded "customary limits of candor." While these phrases, taken from a definition of "obscenity" proposed in the 1954 American

Law Institute's *Model Penal Code*,[2] require some criteria of application to eliminate vagueness, it seems that what is objectionable is the explicit description or representation of bodily parts or sexual behavior for the purpose of inducing sexual stimulation or pleasure on the part of the reader or viewer. This kind of objection is part of a sexual ethic that subordinates sex to procreation and condemns all sexual interactions outside of legitimated marriage. It is this code which was the primary target of the sexual revolutionaries in the 1960's, and which has given way in many areas to more open standards of sexual behavior.

One of the beneficial results of the sexual revolution has been a growing acceptance of the distinction between questions of sexual mores and questions of morality. This distinction underlies the old slogan, "Make love, not war," and takes harm to others as the defining characteristic of immorality. What is immoral is behavior which causes injury to or violation of another person or people. Such injury may be physical or it may be psychological. To cause pain to another, to lie to another, to hinder another in the exercise of her or his rights, to exploit another, to degrade another, to misrepresent and slander another are instances of immoral behavior. Masturbation or engaging voluntarily in sexual intercourse with another consenting adult of the same or the other sex, as long as neither injury nor violation of either individual or another is involved, are not immoral. Some sexual behavior is morally objectionable, but not because of its sexual character. Thus, adultery is immoral not because it involves sexual intercourse with someone to whom one is not legally married, but because it involves breaking a promise (of sexual and emotional fidelity to one's spouse). Sadistic, abusive, or forced sex is immoral because it injures and violates another.

The detachment of sexual chastity from moral virtue implies that we cannot condemn forms of sexual behavior merely because they strike us as distasteful or subversive of the Protestant work ethic, or because they depart from standards of behavior we have individually adopted. It has thus seemed to imply that no matter how offensive we might find pornography, we must tolerate it in the name of freedom from illegitimate repression. I wish to argue that this is not so, that pornography is immoral because it is harmful to people.

II. WHAT IS PORNOGRAPHY?

I define pornography as *verbal or pictorial explicit representations of sexual behavior that,* in the words of the Commission on Obscenity and Pornography, *have as a distinguishing characteristic "the degrading and demeaning portrayal of the role and status of the human female . . . as a mere sexual object to be exploited and manipulated sexually."*[3] In pornographic books, magazines, and films, women are represented as passive and as slavishly dependent upon men. The role of female characters is limited to the provision of sexual services to men. To the extent that women's sexual pleasure is represented at all, it is subordinated to that of men and is never

an end in itself as is the sexual pleasure of men. What pleases women is the use of their bodies to satisfy male desires. While the sexual objectification of women is common to all pornography, women are the recipients of even worse treatment in violent pornography, in which women characters are killed, tortured, gang-raped, mutilated, bound, and otherwise abused, as a means of providing sexual stimulation or pleasure to the male characters. It is this development which has attracted the attention of feminists and been the stimulus to an analysis of pornography in general.[4]

Not all sexually explicit material is pornography, nor is all material which contains representations of sexual abuse and degradation pornography.

A representation of a sexual encounter between adult persons which is characterized by mutual respect is, once we have disentangled sexuality and morality, not morally objectionable. Such a representation would be one in which the desires and experiences of each participant were regarded by the other participants as having a validity and a subjective importance equal to those of the individual's own desire and experiences. In such an encounter, each participant acknowledges the other participant's basic human dignity and personhood. Similarly, a representation of a nude human body (in whole or in part) in such a manner that the person shown maintains self-respect—e.g., is not portrayed in a degrading position—would not be morally objectionable. The educational films of the National Sex Forum, as well as a certain amount of erotic literature and art, fall into this category. While some erotic materials are beyond the standards of modesty held by some individuals, they are not for this reason immoral.

A representation of a sexual encounter which is not characterized by mutual respect, in which at least one of the parties is treated in a manner beneath her or his dignity as a human being, is no longer simple erotica. That a representation is of degrading behavior does not in itself, however, make it pornographic. Whether or not it is pornographic is a function of contextual features. Books and films may contain descriptions or representations of a rape in order to explore the consequences of such an assault upon its victim. What is being shown is abusive or degrading behavior which attempts to deny the humanity and dignity of the person assaulted, yet the context surrounding the representation, through its exploration of the consequences of the act, acknowledges and reaffirms her dignity. Such books and films, far from being pornographic, are (or can be) highly moral, and fall into the category of moral realism.

What makes a work a work of pornography, then, is not simply its representation of degrading and abusive sexual encounters, but its implicit, if not explicit, approval and recommendation of sexual behavior that is immoral, i.e., that physically or psychologically violates the personhood of one of the participants. Pornography, then, is verbal or pictorial material which represents or describes sexual behavior that is degrading or abusive to one or more of the participants *in such a way as to endorse the degradation.* The participants so treated in virtually all heterosexual pornography are women or children, so heterosexual pornography is, as a matter of fact, material which endorses sexual behavior that is degrading and/or abusive to women and children. As I use the term "sexual behavior," this includes sexual encounters between persons, behavior which produces sexual stimulation or pleasure for one of the participants, and behavior which is preparatory to or invites sexual activity. Behavior that is degrading or abusive includes physical harm or abuse, and physical or psychological coercion. In addition, behavior which ignores or devalues the real interests, desires, and experiences of one or more participants in any way is degrading. Finally, that a person has chosen or consented to be harmed, abused, or subjected to coercion does not alter the degrading character of such behavior.

Pornography communicates its endorsement of the behavior it represents by various features of the pornographic context: the degradation of the female characters is represented as providing pleasure to the participant males and, even worse, to the participant females, and there is no suggestion that this sort of treatment of others is inappropriate to their status as human beings. These two features are together sufficient to constitute endorsement of the represented behavior. The contextual features which make material pornographic are intrinsic to the material. In addition to these, extrinsic features, such as the purpose for which the material is presented— i.e., the sexual arousal/pleasure/satisfaction of its (mostly) male consumers—or an accompanying text, may reinforce or make explicit the endorsement. Representations which in and of themselves do not show or endorse degrading behavior may be put into a pornographic context by juxtaposition with others that are degrading, or by a text which invites or recommends degrading behavior toward the subject represented. In such a case the whole complex—the series of representations or representations with text—is pornographic.

The distinction I have sketched is one that applies most clearly to sequential material—a verbal or pictorial (filmed) story—which represents an action and provides a temporal context for it. In showing the before and after, a narrator or film-maker has plenty of opportunity to acknowledge the dignity of the person violated or clearly to refuse to do so. It is somewhat more difficult to apply the distinction to single still representations. The contextual features cited above, however, are clearly present in still photographs or pictures that glamorize degradation and sexual violence. Phonograph album covers and advertisements offer some prime examples of such glamorization. Their representations of women in chains (the Ohio Players), or bound by ropes and black and blue (the Rolling Stones) are considered high-quality commercial "art" and glossily prettify the violence they represent. Since the standard function of prettification and glamorization is the communication of desirability, these albums and ads are communicating the desirability of violence against women. Representations of women bound or chained, particularly those of women bound in such a way as to make their breasts, or genital or anal areas vulnerable to any passerby, endorse the scene they represent by the absence of any indication that this treatment of women is in any way inappropriate.

To summarize: Pornography is not just the explicit representation or description of sexual behavior, nor even the explicit representation or description of sexual behavior which is degrading and/or abusive to women. Rather, it is material that explicitly represents or describes degrading and abusive sexual behavior so as to endorse and/or recommend the behavior as described. The contextual features, moreover, which communicate such endorsement are intrinsic to the material; that is, they are features whose removal or alteration would change the representation or description.

This account of pornography is underlined by the etymology and original meaning of the word "pornography." *The Oxford English Dictionary* defines pornography as "Description of the life, manners, etc. of prostitutes and their patrons . . . " hence the expression or suggestion of obscene or unchaste subjects in literature or art.[5]

Let us consider the first part of the definition for a moment. In the transactions between prostitutes and their clients, prostitutes are paid, directly or indirectly, for the use of their bodies by the client for sexual pleasure.[6] Traditionally males have obtained from female prostitutes what they could not or did not wish to get from their wives or women friends, who, because of the character of their relation to the male, must be accorded some measure of human respect. While there are limits to what treatment is seen as appropriate toward women as wives or women friends, the prostitute as prostitute exists to provide sexual pleasure to males. The female characters of contemporary pornography also exist to provide pleasure to males, but in the pornographic context no pretense is made to regard them as parties to a contractual arrangement. Rather, the anonymity of these characters makes each one. Every women, thus suggesting not only that all women are appropriate subjects for the enactment of the most bizarre and demeaning male sexual

fantasies, but also that this is their primary purpose. The recent escalation of violence in pornography—the presentation of scenes of bondage, rape, and torture of women for the sexual stimulation of the male characters or male viewers—while shocking in itself, is from this point of view merely a more vicious extension of a genre whose success depends on treating women in a manner beneath their dignity as human beings.

III. PORNOGRAPHY: LIES AND VIOLENCE AGAINST WOMEN

What is wrong with pornography, then, is its degrading and dehumanizing portrayal of women (and *not* its sexual content). Pornography, by its very nature, requires that women be subordinate to men and mere instruments for the fulfillment of male fantasies. To accomplish this, pornography must lie. Pornography lies when it says that our sexual life is or ought to be subordinate to the service of men, that our pleasure consists in pleasing men and not ourselves, that we are depraved, that we are fit subjects for rape, bondage, torture, and murder. Pornography lies explicitly about women's sexuality, and through such lies fosters more lies about our humanity, our dignity, and our personhood.

Moreover, since nothing is alleged to justify the treatment of the female characters of pornography save their womanhood, pornography depicts all women as fit objects of violence by virtue of their sex alone. Because it is simply being female that, in the pornographic vision, justifies being violated, the lies of pornography are lies about all women. Each work of pornography is on its own libelous and defamatory, yet gains power through being reinforced by every other pornographic work. The sheer number of pornographic productions expands the moral issue to include not only assessing the morality or immorality of individual works, but also the meaning and force of the mass production of pornography.

The pornographic view of women is thoroughly entrenched in a booming portion of the publishing, film, and recording industries, reaching and affecting not only all who look to such sources for sexual stimulation, but also those of us who are forced into an awareness of it as we peruse magazines at newsstands and record albums in record stores, as we check the entertainment sections of city newspapers, or even as we approach a counter to pay for groceries. It is not necessary to spend a great deal of time reading or viewing pornographic material to absorb its male-centered definition of women. No longer confined within plain brown wrappers, it jumps out from billboards that proclaim "Live X-rated Girls!" or "Angels in Pain" or "Hot and Wild," and from magazine covers displaying a woman's genital area being spread open to the viewer by her own fingers.[7] Thus, even men who do not frequent pornographic shops and movie houses are supported in the sexist objectification of women by their environment. Women, too, are crippled by internalizing as self-images those that are presented to us by pornographers. Isolated from one another and with no source of support for an alternative view of female sexuality, we may not always find the strength to resist a message that dominates the common cultural media.

The entrenchment of pornography in our culture also gives it a significance quite beyond its explicit sexual messages. To suggest, as pornography does, that the primary purpose of women is to provide sexual pleasure to men is to deny that women are independently human or have a status equal to that of men. It is, moreover, to deny our equality at one of the most intimate levels of human experience. This denial is especially powerful in a hierarchical, class society such as ours, in which individuals feel good about themselves by feeling superior to others. Men in our society have a vested interest in maintaining their belief in the inferiority of the female sex, so that no matter how oppressed and exploited by the society in which they live and work, they can feel that they are at least superior to someone or some category of individuals—a woman or women. Pornography, by presenting women as wanton, depraved, and made for

the sexual use of men, caters directly to that interest.[8] The very intimate nature of sexuality which makes pornography so corrosive also protects it from explicit public discussion. The consequent lack of any explicit social disavowal of the pornographic image of women enables this image to continue fostering sexist attitudes even as the society publicly proclaims its (as yet timid) commitment to sexual equality.

In addition to finding a connection between the pornographic view of women and the denial to us of our full human rights, women are beginning to connect the consumption of pornography with committing rape and other acts of sexual violence against women. Contrary to the findings of the Commission on Obscenity and Pornography a growing body of research is documenting (1) a correlation between exposure to representations of violence and the committing of violent acts generally, and (2) a correlation between exposure to pornographic materials and the committing of sexually abusive or violent acts against women.[9] While more study is needed to establish precisely what the causal relations are, clearly so-called hard-core pornography is not innocent.

From "snuff" films and miserable magazines in pornographic stores to *Hustler,* to phonography album covers and advertisements, to "Vogue," pornography has come to occupy its own niche in the communications and entertainment media and to acquire a quasi-institutional character (signaled by the use of diminutives such as "porn" or "porno" to refer to pornographic material, as though such familiar naming could take the hurt out). Its acceptance by the mass media, whatever the motivation, means a cultural endorsement of its message. As much as the materials themselves, the social tolerance of these degrading and distorted images of women in such quantities is harmful to us, since it indicates a general willingness to see women in ways incompatible with our fundamental human dignity and thus to justify treating us in those ways.[10] The tolerance of pornographic representations of the rape, bondage, and torture of women helps to create and maintain a climate more tolerant of the actual physical abuse of women.[11] The tendency on the part of the legal system to view the victim of a rape as responsible for the crime against her is but one manifestation of this.

In sum, pornography is injurious to women in at least three distinct ways:

1. Pornography, especially violent pornography, is implicated in the committing of crimes of violence against women.
2. Pornography is the vehicle for the dissemination of a deep and vicious lie about women. It is defamatory and libelous.
3. The diffusion of such a distorted view of women's nature in our society as it exists today supports sexist (i.e., male-centered) attitudes, and thus reinforces the oppression and exploitation of women.

Society's tolerance of pornography, especially pornography on the contemporary massive scale, reinforces each of these modes of injury: By not disavowing the lie, it supports the male-centered myth that women are inferior and subordinate creatures. Thus, it contributes to the maintenance of a climate tolerant of both psychological and physical violence against women. . . .

CONCLUSION

I have defined pornography in such a way as to distinguish it from erotica and from moral realism, and have argued that it is defamatory and libelous toward women, that it condones crimes against women, and that it invites tolerance of the social, economic, and cultural oppression of women. The production and distribution of pornographic material is thus a social and moral wrong. Contrasting both the current volume of pornographic production and its growing infiltration of the communications media with the status of women in this culture makes clear the necessity for its control. . . .

Appeals for action against pornography are sometimes brushed aside with the claim that such action is a diversion from the primary task of feminists—the elimination of sexism and of sexual inequality. This approach focuses on the enjoyment rather than the manufacture of pornography, and sees it as merely a product of sexism which will disappear when the latter has been overcome and the sexes are socially and economically equal. Pornography cannot be separated from sexism in this way: Sexism is not just a set of attitudes regarding the inferiority of women but the behaviors and social and economic rules that manifest such attitudes. Both the manufacture and distribution of pornography and the enjoyment of it are instances of sexist behavior. The enjoyment of pornography on the part of individuals will presumably decline as such individuals begin to accord women their status as fully human. A cultural climate which tolerates the degrading representation of women is not a climate which facilitates the development of respect for women. Furthermore, the demand for pornography is stimulated not just by the sexism of individuals but by the pornography industry itself. Thus, both as a social phenomenon and in its effect on individuals, pornography, far from being a mere product, nourishes sexism. The campaign against it is an essential component of women's struggle for legal, economic, and social equality, one which requires the support of all feminists.[12]

NOTES

1. *Women Against Violence in Pornography and Media Newspage,* Vol. II, No. 5, June 1978; and Judith Reisman in *Women Against Violence in Pornography and Media Proposal.*

2. American Law Institute *Model Penal Code,* sec. 251.4.
3. *Report of the Commission on Obscenity and Pornography* (New York: Bantam Books, 1970), p. 239. The Commission, of course, concluded that

the demeaning content of pornography did not adversely affect male attitudes toward women.

4. Among recent feminist discussions are Diana Russell, "Pornography: A Feminist Perspective" and Susan Griffin, "On Pornography," *Chrysalis,* Vol. I, No. 4, 1978; and Ann Garry, "Pornography and Respect for Women," *Social Theory and Practice,* Vol. 4, Spring 1978, pp. 395–421.

5. *The Oxford English Dictionary,* Compact Edition (London: Oxford University Press, 1971), p. 2242.

6. In talking of prostitution here, I refer to the concept of, rather than the reality of, prostitution. The same is true of my remarks about relationships between women and their husbands or men friends.

7. This was a full-color magazine cover seen in a rack at the check-out counter of a corner delicatessen.

8. Pornography thus becomes another tool of capitalism. One feature of some contemporary pornography—the use of Black and Asian women in both still photographs and films—exploits the racism as well as the sexism of its white consumers. For a discussion of the interplay between racism and sexism under capitalism as it relates to violent crimes against women, see Angela Y. Davis, "Rape, Racism, and the Capitalist Setting," *The Black Scholar,* Vol. 9, No. 7, April 1978.

9. Urie Bronfenbrenner, *Two Worlds of Childhoods* (New York: Russell Sage Foundation, 1970); H. J. Eysenck and D. K. B. Nias, *Sex, Violence and the Media* (New York: St. Martin's Press, 1978); and Michael Goldstein, Harold Kant, and John Hartman, *Pornography and Sexual Deviance* (Berkeley: University of California Press, 1973); and the papers by Diana Russell, Pauline Bart, and Irene Diamond

included in [Laura Lederer, ed., *Take Back the Night* (New York: William Morrow, 1980)].

10. This tolerance has a linguistic parallel in the growing acceptance and use of nonhuman nouns such as "chick," "bird," "filly," "fox," "doll," "babe," "skirt," etc., to refer to women, and of verbs of harm such as "fuck," "screw," "bang," to refer to sexual intercourse. See Robert Baker and Frederick Elliston, "'Pricks' and 'Chicks': A Plea for Persons." *Philosophy and Sex* (Buffalo, N.Y.: Prometheus Books, 1975).

11. This is supported by the fact that in Denmark the number of rapes committed has increased while the number of rapes reported to the authorities has decreased over the past twelve years. See *WAVPM Newspage,* Vol. II, No. 5, June, 1978, quoting M. Harry, "Denmark Today—The Causes and Effects of Sexual Liberty" (paper presented to The Responsible Society, London, England, 1976). See also Eysenck and Nias, *Sex, Violence and the Media* (New York: St. Martin's Press, 1978), pp. 120–124.

12. Many women helped me to develop and crystallize the ideas presented in this paper. I would especially like to thank Michele Farrell, Laura Lederer, Pamela Miller, and Dianne Romain for their comments in conversation and on the first written draft. Portions of this material were presented orally to members of the Society for Women in Philosophy and to participants in the workshops on "What Is Pornography?" at the Conference on Feminist Perspectives on Pornography, San Francisco, November 17, 18, and 19, 1978. Their discussion was invaluable in helping me to see problems and to clarify the ideas presented here.

REVIEW AND DISCUSSION QUESTIONS

1. Describe how Longino defines "pornography" and how her definition differs from the legal definition of "obscenity."

2. Explain why Longino thinks pornography involves "lies and violence" against women.

3. Discuss how one might use Longino's proposal to write a law. What political or philosophical problems might arise under such a law?

Feminism, Pornography, and Censorship

Mark R. Wicclair

In this essay, Mark Wicclair addresses Helen Longino's proposal that pornographic material be censored. He argues that it is unclear that the dangers of pornography are as grave as is suggested and that supporters of censorship also ignore or downgrade its potential risks. Mark R. Wicclair is professor of philosophy at West Virginia University.

It is sometimes claimed that pornography is objectionable because it violates conventional standards of sexual morality. Although feminists tend to agree that pornography is objectionable, they reject this particular argument against it.[1] This argument is unacceptable to feminists because it is associated with an oppressive Puritanical sexual ethic that inhibits the sexual fulfillment of all people, but especially women. In order to understand why feminists find pornography objectionable, one has to keep in mind that they do not equate the terms "pornographic" and "sexually explicit." Rather, sexually explicit material is said to be "pornographic" only if it depicts and condones the exploitation, dehumanization, subordination, abuse, or denigration of women. By definition, then, all pornography is sexist and misogynistic. Some pornographic material has the additional feature of depicting and condoning acts of *violence* against women (e.g., rape, brutality, torture, sadism). Thus there is a world of difference between harmless "erotica" and pornography. Whereas erotica depicts sexual activity in a manner which is designed to produce sexual arousal and is therefore likely to be objectionable only to those who subscribe to a Puritanical sexual ethic, pornography is "material that explicitly represents or describes degrading and abusive sexual behavior so as to endorse and/or recommend the behavior as described."[2]

Despite the general agreement among feminists that pornography, understood in the way just described, is objectionable, they are sharply divided over the question of its *censorship*. Whereas some feminists find pornography to be so objectionable that they call for its censorship, others oppose this proposal.[3] I will argue that anyone who supports the aims of feminism and who seeks the liberation of all people should reject the censorship of pornography.[4]

When discussing censorship, it is important to keep in mind that there are very strong reasons to be wary of its use. In our society, the importance of the principle of freedom of expression—an anticensorship principle—is widely recognized. The ability to speak one's mind and to express ideas and feelings without the threat of legal penalties or government control is rightly perceived as an essential feature of a truly free society. Moreover, an environment that tolerates the expression of differing views about politics, art, lifestyles, etc., encourages progress and aids in the search for truth and justice. In addition to the many important values associated with the principle of freedom of expression, it is also necessary to consider likely negative side effects of censorship. There is a serious risk that once any censorship is allowed, the power to censor will, over time, expand in unintended and undesirable directions (the "slippery slope"). This is not mere speculation, for such an expansion of the power to censor is to be expected in view of the fact that it is extremely difficult, if not impossible, to formulate unequivocal and unambiguous criteria of censorship. Then, too, the power to censor can all too easily be abused or misused. Even though it may arise in a genuine effort to promote the general welfare and to protect certain rights, officials and groups might use the power to censor as a means to advance their own interests and values and to suppress the rights, interests, and values of others. Thus, given the value of freedom of expression and the many dangers associated with censorship, there is a strong *prima facie* case against censorship. In other words, advocates of censorship have the burden of showing that there are sufficiently strong overriding reasons which would justify it in a specific area.

Like racist and antisemitic material, sexist and misogynistic films, books, and magazines surely deserve condemnation. But censorship is another matter. In view of the strength of the case against censorship in general, it is unwise to advocate it merely to prevent depicting morally objectionable practices in a favorable light. Fortunately, proponents of the censorship of pornography tend to recognize this, for they usually base their call for censorship on a claim about the *effects* of pornography. Pornography, it is held, is *injurious* or *harmful* to women because it fosters the objectionable practices that it depicts. Pornography generally is said to promote the exploitation, humiliation, denigration, subordination, etc., of women; and pornography that depicts acts of violence against women is said to cause murder, rape, assault, and other acts of violence. On the basis of the "harm principle"—a widely accepted principle that allows us to restrict someone's freedom in order to prevent harm to others—it would appear to be justified to override the principle of freedom of expression and to restrict the freedom of would-be producers, distributors, sellers, exhibitors, and consumers of pornography. In short it seems that censorship of pornography is a legitimate means of preventing harm to women.

However, there are a number of problems associated with this attempt to justify censorship. To begin with, it is essential to recognize the important difference between words and images, on the one hand, and actions, on the other hand. A would-be rapist poses a *direct* threat to his intended victim, and by stopping him, we prevent an act of violence. But if there is a connection between the depiction of a rape—even one which appears to condone it—and someone's committing an act of violence against a woman, the connection is relatively *indirect;* and stopping the production, distribution, sale, and exhibition of depictions of rape does not directly restrict the freedom of would-be rapists to commit acts of violence against women. In recognition of the important difference between restricting words and images and preventing harmful behavior, exceptions to the principle of freedom of expression are generally thought to be justified only if words or images present a "clear and present danger" of harm or injury. Thus, to cite a standard example, it is justified to

stop someone from falsely shouting "Fire!" in a crowded theater, for this exclamation is likely to cause a panic that would result in serious injury and even death.

It is doubtful that pornography satisfies the "clear and present danger" condition. For there does not seem to be conclusive evidence that establishes its *causal* significance. Most studies are limited to violent pornography. And even though some of these studies do suggest a *temporary* impact on *attitudes* (e.g., those who view violent pornography may be more likely to express the view that women seek and "enjoy" violence), this does not show that viewing violent pornography causes violent *behavior*. Moreover, there is some evidence suggesting that the effect on attitudes is only temporary and that it can be effectively counteracted by additional information.[5]

But even if there is no conclusive evidence that pornography causes harm, is it not reasonable to "play it safe," and does this not require censorship? Unfortunately, the situation is not as simple as this question appears to suggest. For one thing, it is sometimes claimed that exposure to pornography has a "cathartic" effect and that it therefore produces a net *reduction* in harm to women. This claim is based upon two assumptions, neither of which has been proven to be false: (1) Men who are not already violence-prone are more likely to be "turned off" than to be "turned on" by depictions of rape, brutality, dismemberment, etc. (2) For men in the latter category, exposure to pornography can function as a substitute for actually causing harm. It is also necessary to recall that there are significant values associated with the principle of freedom of expression, and that a failure to observe it involves a number of serious dangers. Since censorship has costs which are substantial and not merely speculative, the more speculative the connection between pornography and harm to women, the less basis there is for incurring the costs associated with censorship.

Just as it is easy to overlook the negative side of censorship, it is also common to overplay its positive effects. Surely it would be foolish to think that outlawing antisemitism in sexually explicit material would have halted the slaughter of Jews in Hitler's Germany or that prohibiting racism in sexually explicit material would reduce the suffering of Blacks in South Africa. Similarly, in view of the violent nature of American society generally and the degree to which sexism persists to this day, it is unlikely that censorship of pornography by itself would produce any significant improvement in the condition of women in the United States. Fortunately, there are other, more effective and direct means of eliminating sexism than by censoring pornography. Passage and strict enforcement of the Equal Rights Amendment, electing feminists to local, state, and national political office, achieving genuine economic justice for women, and securing their reproductive freedom will do considerably more to foster the genuine liberation of women in the United States than will the censorship of pornography. With respect to rape and other acts of violence, it has often been noted that American society is extremely violent, and, sadly, there are no magic solutions to the problems of rape and violence. But the magnitude of the problem suggests that censoring pornography only addresses a symptom and not the underlying disease. Although there is still much dispute about the causes of violence generally and rape in particular, it is unlikely that there will be a serious reduction in acts of violence against women until there are rather drastic changes in the socioeconomic environment and in the criminal justice system.

Those who remain concerned about the possible contribution of pornography to violence and sexism should keep in mind that it can be "neutralized" in ways that avoid the dangers of censorship. One important alternative to government censorship is to help people understand why pornography is objectionable and why it and its message should be rejected. This can be accomplished by means of educational campaigns, discussions of pornography on radio and television and at public forums, letter writing, and educational

picketing. In addition, attempts might be made to prevent or restrict the production, distribution, display, sale, and consumption of pornographic material by means of organized pickets, boycotts, and the like. Such direct measures by private citizens raise some troubling questions, but the dangers and risks which they pose are considerably less than those associated with government censorship.

There are several other reasons for questioning the view that the sexist and misogynistic nature of pornography justifies its censorship. Some of the more important of these include the following:

1. Although pornography depicts some practices that are both morally objectionable and illegal (e.g., rape, assault, torture), many of the practices depicted are morally repugnant *but do not break any law.* Thus, for example, our legal system does not explicitly prohibit men from treating women in a degrading or humiliating manner; and with some exceptions, it is not a crime to treat women exclusively as sex objects or to use them exclusively as means and not ends. But is it not odd to recommend making illegal the production, distribution, sale, and exhibition of materials that depict practices that are not themselves illegal?

2. It is essential that laws be clearly formulated and that vagueness be avoided. Vague laws can have a "chilling effect" on unobjectionable activities, and they tend to undermine the fair and effective enforcement of the law by giving police, prosecutors, and judges too much discretionary power. But those who call for the censorship of pornography on the grounds that it is sexist and misogynistic fail to recognize the difficulty of formulating laws which would have an acceptable degree of clarity and specificity. Proponents of censorship use terms like "degrading," "humiliating," "debasing," "exploitative," and "subordination of women." But these terms are far from unambiguous. In fact, they are highly subjective in the sense that different people have different criteria for deciding when something is degrading, humiliating, etc. For example, someone might think that the depiction of an unmarried female or a lesbian couple having and enjoying sex is "demeaning" or "debasing." Thus, in order to prevent censorship from being applied in unintended and undesirable ways, it is necessary to offer clear and unambiguous operational criteria for terms like "demeaning," "humiliating," etc. But the feasibility of articulating generally acceptable criteria of this sort remains highly doubtful.

3. Sexually explicit material that depicts violence against women or that depicts sexist practices is said to be subject to censorship only if it *condones* the objectionable practices. Thus, for example, news films, documentaries, and works which take a critical stance toward those practices are not to be censored. But it is exceedingly difficult in many cases to determine the "point of view" of films, books, photographs, etc.[6] If scholars who have advanced degrees in film, literature, and art can come to no general consensus about the "meaning" or "message" of certain works, is it plausible to think that prosecutors, judges, and juries are likely to fare any better?

4. Why call for the censorship of sexist and misogynistic books, magazines, films, and photographs only if they include an explicit depiction of *sexual activity?* There is no conclusive evidence showing that material that includes a depiction of sexual activity has a greater causal impact on attitudes and behavior.[7] Moreover, it will not do to claim that such material is not worthy of protection under the principle of freedom of expression. Surely, many works which include explicit depictions of sex are not totally devoid of significant and challenging ideas. Consequently, advocates of censorship are faced with a dilemma: Either they can call for the censorship of *all* material that contains objectionable images of women; or they can call for censorship only in the case of sexually explicit materials of that nature. If the first alternative is chosen, then given the pervasiveness of objectionable portrayals of women in art, literature, and the mass media, very little would

be immune from censorship. But in view of the strong *prima facie* case against censorship, this seems unacceptable. On the other hand, if the second alternative is chosen, this invites the suspicion that the restriction to sexual material is based upon the very same Puritanical sexual ethic which feminists rightly tend to reject. I am not suggesting that feminists who call for censorship wish to champion sexual oppression. But it is noteworthy that many conservatives who generally do not support the aims of feminism align themselves with feminists who advocate censoring pornography.

5. Why call for censorship of materials only if they depict violence or other objectionable practices in relation to *women?* Wouldn't consistency require censoring *all* violence and material that portrays *anyone* in a derogatory light? But this is clearly unacceptable. For so much of our culture is permeated with images of violence and morally distasteful treatment of people that it is hard to think of many films, television programs, books, or magazines which would be totally immune from censorship. Censorship would be the rule rather than an exception, and such pervasive censorship is incompatible with a truly free society. It also won't do to limit censorship to members of historically oppressed groups (e.g., women, Blacks, Jews). First, it is very unlikely that such "preferential censorship" would be accepted by the majority for too long. Sooner or later others would object and/or press for protection too. Second, in view of the significant costs of censorship, even if it were limited to the protection of historically oppressed groups, it would not be justified unless there were a demonstrable "clear and present danger"; and this remains doubtful. But what about the view that only pornography should be subject to censorship because *women need special protection?* This position is also unacceptable. For since men are victimized by acts of racism, antisemitism, and violence, and since there is no evidence to prove that depictions of objectionable practices have a greater effect on behavior in pornographic material than they do in nonpornographic material, this position seems to be based on the sexist assumption that women need greater protection than men because they are "naturally" more fragile and vulnerable.

I have tried to show that censorship of pornography is neither the most effective nor a legitimate means to achieve the aims of feminism. Much pornographic material is morally repugnant, but there are less costly ways to express one's moral outrage and to attempt to "neutralize" pornography than by censorship. Moreover, pornography is only a relatively minor manifestation of the sexist practices and institutions that still pervade our society. Hence, the genuine liberation of women—and men—is best served by directly attacking those oppressive practices and institutions. It may be easier to identify and attack pornography—and to win some battles—but the payoff would be slight, and the negative side effects would be substantial.

NOTES

1. Just as the civil rights movement in the United States in the 1950's and 1960's included many people who were not black, so one does not have to be a woman to be a feminist. As I am using the term, a feminist is any person who supports the fundamental goal of feminism: the liberation of women.
2. Helen E. Longino, "Pornography, Oppression, and Freedom: A Closer Look," in Laura Lederer, ed., *Take Back the Night* (New York: William Morrow and Company, Inc., 1980), p. 44. Longino also stipulates that the sexual activities depicted in pornography are degrading or abusive *to women.*
3. In response to the generally pro-censorship Women Against Violence in Pornography and Media, other feminists have organized the Feminist Anti-Censorship Task force.
4. Until recently, advocates of censorship have pressed for laws which prohibit or restrict the production, distribution, sale, and exhibition of pornographic material. However, pro-censorship feminists have hit upon a new strategy: Ordinances which stipulate that pornography is *sex discrimination,* enabling women to file sex discrimination lawsuits against producers, distributors, sellers, and exhibitors of pornography. Most of the criticisms of censorship which I discuss in this paper apply to both strategies.
5. For a discussion of research on the effects of pornography, see Edward Donnerstein and Neil Malamuth, eds., *Pornography and Sexual Aggression* (New York: Academic Press, 1984).
6. An informative illustration of how a film can resist unambiguous classification as either progressive or retrograde from a feminist perspective is provided in Lucy Fischer and Marcia Landy, "The Eyes of Laura Mars: A Binocular Critique," *Screen,* Vol. 23, Nos. 3–4 (September–October 1982).
7. In fact some researchers claim that the impact of depictions of violence is *greater* in material which is *not* pornographic See, for example, the contribution of Edward Donnerstein and Daniel Linz to a section on pornography, "Pornography: Love or Death?" in *Film Comment,* Vol. 20, No. 6 (December 1984), pp. 34–35.

REVIEW AND DISCUSSION QUESTIONS

1. Why does Wicclair think freedom of speech is so important?
2. Wicclair doubts that pornography causes harm. On what grounds does he make that claim?
3. Describe the five reasons he gives for thinking that despite its sexist nature pornography should be condemned but not censored.

Pornography

American Booksellers v. *Hudnut*

This case grew out of a challenge to an Indianapolis ordinance outlawing the production, sale, exhibition, and distribution of pornography, which it defined as any "graphic sexually explicit subordination of women" that also presented women as sexual objects "who enjoy rape, pain, or humiliation; enjoy being penetrated by objects or animals; in scenarios of degradation, injury, debasement, torture, shown as filthy or inferior; or presented as sexual objects for domination, conquest, violation, exploitation, possession, or use." The ordinance allowed women who can show they have been injured as a direct result of pornography to win private damages from the person who produced, sold, exhibited, or distributed it. Earlier Supreme Court decisions had held that "obscenity" is not protected by the First Amendment's guarantee of freedom of speech. In those cases the Court defined obscenity as work that (1) appeals to the "prurient" interest, (2) depicts sex in a "patently offensive way," and (3) lacks "serious literary, artistic, political, or scientific value" (*Miller* v. *California*). In *Hudnut,* however, the issue is pornography, not obscenity, and Judge Easterbrook of the Federal Appeals Court rejects the ordinance and affirms a lower court's decision that, unlike obscenity, pornography is constitutionally protected speech.

Judge Easterbrook: We do not try to balance the arguments for and against an ordinance such as this. The ordinance discriminates on the ground of the content of the speech. Speech treating women in the approved way—in sexual encounters "premised on equality"—is lawful no matter how sexually explicit. Speech treating women in the disapproved way—as submissive in matters sexual or as enjoying humiliation—is unlawful no matter how significant the literary, artistic, or political qualities of the work taken as a whole. The state may not ordain preferred viewpoints in this way. The Constitution forbids the state to declare one perspective right and silence opponents. . . .

"If there is any fixed star in our constitutional constellation, it is that no official, high or petty, can prescribe what shall be orthodox in politics, nationalism, religion, or other matters of opinion or force citizens to confess by word or act their faith therein." *West Virginia State Board of Education* v. *Barnette,* 319 U.S. 624, 642 (1943). Under the First Amendment the government must leave to the people the evaluation of ideas. Bald or subtle, an idea is as powerful as the audience allows it to be. . . . A belief may be pernicious—the beliefs of Nazis led to the death of millions, those of the Klan to the repression of millions. A pernicious belief may prevail. Totalitarian governments today rule much of the planet, practicing suppression of billions and spreading dogma that may enslave others. One of the things that separates our society from theirs is our absolute right to propagate opinions that the government finds wrong or even hateful. . . .

Under the ordinance graphic sexually explicit speech is "pornography" or not depending on the perspective the author adopts. Speech that "subordinates" women and also, for example, presents women as enjoying pain, humiliation, or rape, or even simply presents women in "positions of servility or submission or display" is forbidden, no matter how great the literary or political value of the work taken as a whole. Speech that portrays women in positions of equality is lawful, no matter how graphic

American Bookkeepers v. *Hudnut.* 771 F.2d 323 (1985).

the sexual content. This is thought control. It establishes an "approved" view of women, of how they may react to sexual encounters, of how the sexes may relate to each other. Those who espouse the approved view may use sexual images; those who do not, may not.

Indianapolis justifies the ordinance on the ground that pornography affects thoughts. Men who see women depicted as subordinate are more likely to treat them so. Pornography is an aspect of dominance. It does not persuade people so much as change them. It works by socializing, by establishing the expected and the permissible. In this view pornography is not an idea; pornography is the injury.

There is much to this perspective. Beliefs are also facts. People often act in accordance with the images and patterns they find around them. People raised in a religion tend to accept the tenets of that religion, often without independent examination. People taught from birth that black people are fit only for slavery rarely rebelled against that creed; beliefs coupled with the self-interest of the masters established a social structure that inflicted great harm while enduring for centuries. Words and images act at the level of the subconscious before they persuade at the level of the conscious. Even the truth has little chance unless a statement fits within the framework of beliefs that may never have been subjected to rational study.

Therefore we accept the premises for this legislation. Depictions of subordination tend to perpetuate subordination. The subordinate status of women in turn leads to affront and lower pay at work, insult and injury at home, battery and rape on the streets. . . .

Yet this simply demonstrates the power of pornography as speech. All of these unhappy effects depend on mental intermediation. Pornography affects how people see the world, their fellows, and social relations. If pornography is what pornography does, so is other speech. Hitler's orations affected how some Germans saw Jews. Communism is a world view, not simply a Manifesto by Marx and Engels or a set of speeches. Efforts to

suppress communist speech in the United States were based on the belief that the public acceptability of such ideas would increase the likelihood of totalitarian government. Religions affect socialization in the most pervasive way. The opinion in *Wisconsin* v. *Yoder* shows how a religion can dominate an entire approach to life, governing much more than the relation between the sexes. . . .

Racial bigotry, anti-semitism, violence on television, reporters' biases—these and many more influence the culture and shape our socialization. None is directly answerable by more speech, unless that speech too finds its place in the popular culture. Yet all is protected as speech, however insidious. Any other answer leaves the government in control of all of the institutions of culture, the great censor and director of which thoughts are good for us.

Sexual responses often are unthinking responses, and the association of sexual arousal with the subordination of women therefore may have a substantial effect. But almost all cultural stimuli provoke unconscious responses. Religious ceremonies condition their participants. Teachers convey messages by selecting what not to cover; the implicit message about what is off limits or unthinkable may be more powerful than the messages for which they present rational argument. Television scripts contain unarticulated assumptions. People may be conditioned in subtle ways. If the fact that speech plays a role in a process of conditioning were enough to permit governmental regulation, that would be the end of freedom of speech. . . .

Much of Indianapolis's argument rests on the belief that when speech is "unanswerable," and the metaphor that there is a "marketplace of ideas" does not apply, the First Amendment does not apply either. The metaphor is honored; Milton's *Areopagitica* and John Stuart Mill's *On Liberty* defend freedom of speech on the ground that the truth will prevail, and many of the most important cases under the First Amendment recite this position. The Framers undoubtedly believed it.

As a general matter it is true. But the Constitution does not make the dominance of truth a necessary condition of freedom of speech. To say that it does would be to confuse an outcome of free speech with a necessary condition for the application of the amendment.

A power to limit speech on the ground that truth has not yet prevailed and is not likely to prevail implies the power to declare truth. At some point the government must be able to say (as Indianapolis has said): "We know what the truth is, yet a free exchange of speech has not driven out falsity, so that we must now prohibit falsity." If the government may declare the truth, why wait for the failure of speech? Under the First Amendment, however, there is no such thing as a false idea. . . . The government may not restrict speech on the ground that in a free exchange truth is not yet dominant. . . .

We come, finally, to the argument that pornography is "low value" speech, that it is enough like obscenity that Indianapolis may prohibit it. Some cases hold that speech far removed from politics and other subjects at the core of the Framers' concerns may be subjected to special regulation. . . .

In *Pacifica* the FCC sought to keep vile language off the air during certain times. The Court held that it may; but the Court would not have sustained a regulation prohibiting scatological descriptions of Republicans but not scatological descriptions of Democrats, or any other form of selection among viewpoints. . . .

At all events, "pornography" is not low value speech within the meaning of these cases. . . . True, pornography and obscenity have sex in common. But Indianapolis left out of its definition any reference to literary, artistic, political, or scientific value. . . .

REVIEW AND DISCUSSION QUESTIONS

1. What did the law that is being challenged in this case do, exactly?
2. What is the difference between obscenity and pornography?
3. Describe the justification that Judge Easterbrook gives for overturning the statute. What precedents and principles does he rely on?
4. Explain why the Court might have thought obscenity is not protected speech, while pornography is protected. Do you think this position is reasonable? Explain.

Internet Censorship: A Debate

Jay A. Sekulow and Jerry Berman

Internet access has exploded, making information available on a scale that was unimaginable only a few years ago. For some, this holds out the promise of greater freedom as political organizations coordinate their activities via the Internet and as oppressed groups throughout the world gain access to information that their government is now no longer able to restrict. But what are the limits on Internet access? One issue that Congress has wrestled with is regulation of access by children to indecent and obscene material in libraries. The 1996 Telecommunications Act provides for discount "e-rate access" only to schools and libraries that put filters on their machines preventing access to certain Internet sites. Software thus serves as a censor, with the federal government encouraging it through economic incentives to localities. This raises many questions, including the responsibility (or at least right) of local governments to protect children against this material, the distinction between governmental censorship of material and its refusal to fund programs that do not limit access to material, and the use of filtering devices themselves. The following two selections are from testimony given by the authors before Congress, which was considering the Children's Internet Protection Act. Jay A. Sekulow is counsel to the American Center for Law and Justice. Jerry Berman is executive director of the Center for Democracy and Technology.

By Jay A. Sekulow

INTRODUCTION

Public libraries were created to lend books, provide research tools, and make available educational opportunities to its citizens. The Supreme Court has described a library as "a place dedicated to quiet, to knowledge, and to beauty." *Brown* v. *Louisiana,* 383 U.S. 131, 142 (1966). Libraries, therefore, have an affirmative duty to provide materials which will benefit the surrounding community and to restrict illegal and harmful materials.

Children's unrestricted access to the Internet fails to fulfill this duty. The Internet is obviously a very valuable educational resource, and many can benefit from access to that information resource free of charge at public libraries. The vast majority of the pornography which saturates the Web is neither educational, nor beneficial, and in many jurisdictions the exposure of minors to such materials is illegal. Therefore, to avoid liability, libraries will have to adopt some form of Internet filtering process for minors.

Additionally, libraries, like other employers, have an affirmative duty to provide a workplace which is free from pornography. Pornography creates a hostile work environment, as well as a hostile environment for patrons not wishing to be exposed to such material. Internet filtering prevents libraries from becoming peep show parlors. That is constitutionally sufficient for upholding the use of such software.

LIBRARIES HAVE AN AFFIRMATIVE RESPONSIBILITY TO PROTECT CHILDREN

Libraries have a duty to the public in their dealings with children. As the U.S. Supreme Court has stated: "It is evident beyond the need for elaboration that a State's interest in safeguarding the physical and psychological well-being of a minor is compelling... the legislative judgment, as well as the judgment found in relevant literature, is that the use of children as subjects of pornographic materials is harmful to the physiological, emotional, and mental health of the child. The judgment, we think, easily passes muster under the First Amendment." *New York* v. *Ferber, 458 U.S. 747, 756-758 (1982).*

Accordingly, the Supreme Court has long held that the government has a compelling interest in protecting the physical and psychological well-being of minors. . . . This compelling interest extends to the state acting in *loco parentis* for children. As the Supreme Court reiterated in *Bethel School Dist. No. 403* v. *Fraser,* 478 U.S. 675, 684 (1986):

This Court's First Amendment jurisprudence has acknowledged limitations on the otherwise absolute interest of the speaker in reaching an unlimited audience where the speech is sexually explicit and the audience may include children. In *Ginsberg* v. *New York,* 390 U.S. 629, 88 S.Ct. 1274, 20 L.Ed.2d 195 (1968), this Court upheld a New York statute banning the sale of sexually oriented material to minors, even though the material in question was entitled to First

From U.S. Senate. Committee on Commerce, Science, and Transportation. *Children's Internet Protection Act.* Hearing, March 4, 1999. Washington, DC: Government Printing Office, 1999. Some case citations omitted.

Amendment protection with respect to adults. And in addressing the question whether the First Amendment places any limit on the authority of public schools to remove books from a public school library, all Members of the Court, otherwise sharply divided, acknowledged that the school board has the authority to remove books that are vulgar. . . .

These cases recognize the obvious concern on the part of parents, and school authorities acting in *loco parentis,* to protect children especially in a captive audience from exposure to sexually explicit, indecent, or lewd speech.

Accordingly, the Court held that: "petitioner School District acted entirely within its permissible authority in imposing sanctions upon *Fraser* in response to his offensively lewd and indecent speech. Unlike the sanctions imposed on the students wearing arm bands in *Tinker* [v. *Des Moines Independent Sch. Dist.,* 393 U.S. 503, 506], the penalties imposed in this were unrelated to any political viewpoint. The First Amendment does not prevent the school officials from determining that to permit a vulgar and lewd speech such as respondent's would undermine the school's basic educational mission." *Id.* at 685.

There is absolutely no constitutional protection for child pornography, yet child pornography is on the Internet. As the Supreme Court held in *Osborne* v. *Ohio,* 495 U.S. 105, 111 (1989):

First, as *Ferber* recognized, the materials produced by child pornographers permanently records the victim's abuse. The pornography's continued existence causes the child victims continuing harm by haunting the children in years to come. The State's ban on possession and viewing encourages the possessors of these materials to destroy them. Second, encouraging the destruction of these materials is also desirable because evidence suggests that pedophiles use child pornography to seduce other children into sexual activity.

The use of children in pornography or predation of children on the Internet is not the only concern, however. It is the exposure of pornography to children which represents another real harm. The potential harm to children allows the imposition of regulations limiting Internet access. Filtering systems used for the purpose of protecting children is completely constitutional. As the Supreme Court ruled in this regard in *FCC* v. *Pacifica Foundation,* 438 U.S. 726, 749 (1978):

. . . broadcasting is uniquely accessible to children, even those too young to read. Although [comedian George] Carlin's written message might have been incomprehensible to a first grader, Pacifica's broadcast could have enlarged a child's vocabulary in an instant. Other forms of offensive expression may be withheld from the young without restricting the expression at its source. Bookstores and motion picture theaters, for example, may be prohibited from making indecent material available to children. We held in *Ginsberg* v. *New York,* 390 U.S. 629, 20 LEd2d 195, 88 S. Ct. 1274, 44 Ohio Ops 2d 339, that the government's interest in the "well-being of its youth" and in supporting "parents' claim to authority in their own household" justified the regulation of otherwise protected expression. *Id.,* at 640 and 639, 20 LEd2d 195, 88 S.Ct. 1274, 44 Ohio Ops 2d 339.

Similarly, the Internet (like broadcasting) "is uniquely accessible to children, even those too young to read." In the context of a library with unfiltered Internet access, it is more than possible that a child may be exposed to what an adult decides to view.

Unquestionably, the Internet contains material that is not suitable for children, and that could be harmful to them if allowed to view such material. The argument that children can make choices concerning pornography is not only counter-intuitive, it is in most states illegal. "[D]uring the formative years of childhood and adolescence, minors often lack experience, perspective, and judgment to recognize and avoid choices that could be detrimental to them." *Bellotti* v. *Baird,* 443 U.S. 622, 635 (1979). Therefore, to protect the welfare of children and to remove the possibility of any civil liability, libraries should take reasonable steps to ensure that children do not access indecent or pornographic material through the use of the Internet.

It is in the context of the protection of children, that libraries may constitutionally use filtering systems or segregate certain computer systems with filtering software for the use of children from "adult" computers. Otherwise, libraries open themselves up to liability for the inevitable harm caused to innocents viewing pornography for the first time. . . .

THE USE OF FILTERING SOFTWARE IS REASONABLE AND VIEWPOINT NEUTRAL

Content-based restrictions in such a forum must only be reasonable and viewpoint neutral. . . .

The Use of Filtering Software to Protect Children and Employees Is Reasonable

In *Arkansas Educ. Television Comm'n* v. *Forbes,* 118 S.Ct. 1633 (1998), the Court upheld the decision of a public broadcasting station denying a political candidate access to a televised public debate. The Court's reasoning was based on the broadcaster's duty "to schedule programming that serves the public interest, convenience, and necessity". *Id.* at 1639. In furtherance of this duty, "[p]ublic and private broadcasters alike are not only permitted, but indeed required, to exercise substantial editorial discretion in the selection and presentation of their programming." *Id.* The Court stated that forcing a broadcaster to include all candidates "would actually undermine the educational value and quality of the debates." *Id.* at 1643.

The television station put forth five reasons for excluding Forbes from the televised debate: "(1) the Arkansas voters did not consider him a serious candidate; (2) the news organizations also did not consider him a serious candidate; (3) the Associated Press and a national election result reporting service did not plan to run his name in results on election night;

(4) Forbes apparently had little, if any, financial support, failing to report campaign finances to the Secretary of State's office or to the Federal Election Commission; and (5) there was no 'Forbes for Congress' campaign headquarters other than his house." *Id.* at 1643–44. These reasons led the television station to conclude that Forbes had generated no appreciable public interest. The Court held that this was a reasonable basis for excluding Forbes from the debate. *Id.* at 1644.

Similarly, ensuring that pornographic material is not accessible at library computer terminals is a reasonable basis for utilizing Internet filtering software. Libraries are designed to serve the "public interest, convenience, and necessity." To further this purpose, libraries are required to "exercise substantial editorial discretion in the selection and presentation" of the material they make available to the public. If libraries were forced to make available every piece of information on the Internet, including obscene material, it would undermine the "educational value and quality" of the information provided by the library. Library officials, as opposed to the courts, are best equipped to make decisions as to the types of information that the library will make available to the public.

Libraries are designed to promote education in the surrounding communities. Intertwined with this purpose is the duty to promote community values and to protect children from harmful material. Due to the compelling interest in protecting children, placing Internet filtering software on library computers is a reasonable measure designed to protect children from accessing materials which could be harmful to them. Also, even though libraries are not compelled to use the least restrictive means, Internet filtering software is the least restrictive means to block harmful material on the Internet.

Opponents of Internet filtering software, such as the American Library Association (ALA) and the American Civil Liberties Union (ACLU), have proposed several alternatives which they argue would be less restrictive and just as effective. The following are the five alternatives proposed: (1) Acceptable Use Policies—provide carefully worded instructions for parents, teachers, students and libraries on use of the Internet; (2) Time Limits—establish content neutral time limits on use of the Internet, request that Internet access in schools be limited to school-related work; (3) "Driver's Ed" for Internet Users—condition Internet access for minors on completion of Internet seminar similar to a driver's education course; (4) Recommended Reading—publicize and provide link to websites recommended for children and teens; (5) Privacy Screens—install screens to protect users' privacy when viewing sensitive information and avoid unwanted viewing of websites by passers-by. . . .

First, the first four suffer from the same flaw in assuming that one can avoid offensive material simply by being educated about the Internet. One can hardly imagine a search on the Internet which will not yield at least a few pornographic sites. Many sites are designed to look innocent at first glance so that they can avoid being blocked by Internet filtering software. Second, establishing time limits would in no way limit children's access to pornography. It would only limit the amount of pornography that they could access. Third, these alternatives suffer from another faulty premise that, if educated, children will not access pornographic sites. In no other aspect of our society does the law trust minors to do what is in their best interest. Children are banned from accessing pornography in every other venue. Public libraries should not be the only place where children are allowed to access such material because we trust them to do what is in their best interest. Lastly, privacy screens will only foster minors' access of pornography by allowing them to do it in private without the fear or embarrassment of being caught. They will in no way decrease the minors' access of pornography. Therefore, none of the alternatives cited by the ALA and ACLU provide any reasonable proof that if placed in use they will be at all effective in curbing the problem of minors' access to pornography. . . .

In fact, not using Internet filtering software constitutes a significant change in the nature of libraries. Libraries have always been a safe haven for children; a place which parents could trust that would be beneficial to their children. Libraries are designed to enhance the educational process and to inculcate community values. However, pornographic material permeates the Internet and is readily accessible to the willing, and the unwilling, recipient. If Internet filtering software is not placed on library computers, it will drastically change the nature of public libraries, and parents can no longer be safe in assuming that their child's visit to the library will be beneficial to their upbringing.

The Use of Internet Filtering Software Is Viewpoint-Neutral

Viewpoint discrimination is an effort to suppress the speaker's activity due to disagreement with the speaker's view. *Rosenberger* v. *Rector & Visitors of Univ. of Virginia*, 515 U.S. 819, 829 (1995), A viewpoint is "a specific premise, a perspective, a standpoint from which a variety of subjects may be discussed and considered." *Id.* at 831. The Supreme Court has consistently recognized that the government may allocate funding according to criteria that would not be permissible in enacting a direct regulation.

This principle was reiterated in *Finley,* when the Court noted that, "the Government may allocate competitive funding according to criteria that would be impermissible were direct regulation of speech or a criminal penalty at stake." *Id.* at 2179. This principle is firmly ensconced in the Supreme Court's "It is preposterous to equate the denial of taxpayer subsidy with measures aimed at the suppression of dangerous ideas." *Regan* v. *Taxation with Representation*, 461 U.S. 540, 550 (1983). . . .

Just as the federal government may determine what types of art it chooses to fund, so also can public libraries choose the types of information they will make available to the public. A public library's decision to place Internet filtering software on computer terminals in no way restricts individuals' First Amendment rights. Libraries which do so have merely made a choice to, in the words of the NEA regulation, "tak[e] into consideration general standards of decency and respect for the diverse beliefs and values of the American public," *Finley* at 2172, when deciding which information to purchase.

This type of governmental decision stands in stark contrast to the broad provisions of the Communications Decency Act (CDA) which was struck down by the Court in *Reno* v. *American Civil Liberties* Union, 117 S. Cf. 2329 (1998). The major distinction between the CDA and this piece of legislation is that this is a control not over the Internet, but it is a control being exercised over the receipt of government funds. . . .

It simply limits a child's access to pornography on those computers to which children have access. Stated another way, as opposed to the CDA, this proposed legislation does not attempt to control the Internet at all. Instead, it controls the funding for the gateway through which children have access to the Internet. . . .

By Jerry Berman

MANDATORY USE OF FILTERING SOFTWARE RESTRICTS SPEECH UNCONSTITUTIONALLY

While the Supreme Court has upheld the government's right to restrict speech that it funds where the speech reflects government policy, the government may not restrict speech where the purpose of funding is to propagate a diverse range of private views. The mandatory filtering decision in Loudoun County found that libraries are a public forum for the purpose of analyzing access to information on the Internet. The reasoning the court used to reach that conclusion would be reinforced by the fact that Universal Service E-rate funding is explicitly designed to facilitate access to the Internet—a broad range of ideas and views— not to express a specific government policy.

Several studies of commercial available filters suggest that they curtail access to information on topics ranging from gay and lesbian issues, women's health, conservative politics, and many others. If libraries and schools are faced with a limited set of options, this approach may force them to censor more than they would choose and in effect discriminate against specific viewpoints.

This bill will alter adults' ability to access constitutionally protected material in ways that will constrain and in some instances violate their First Amendment rights. Currently adults and children are able to access information that falls into the "harmful to minors" category in the same way they access other information online. Instituting a supervisory override of the filtering tool would not be constitutionally sufficient.

Courts have ruled that the government may not require adults to affirmatively request controversial but protected material in order to receive it.

ALTERNATIVES TO LEGISLATION

While the Congress and courts around the country have been debating whether censorship laws can protect children online, companies and non-profit organizations have responded with wide-ranging efforts to create child-friendly content collections, teach children about appropriate online behavior, and develop voluntary, user-controlled, technology tools that offer parents the ability to protect their own children from inappropriate material. Unlike legislative approaches, these bottom-up solutions are voluntary. They protect children and assist parents and care-takers regardless of whether the material to be avoided is on a US or foreign Web site. They respond to local and family concerns. And they avoid government decisions about content. We would like to describe some of these initiatives to emphasize their diversity, their user-controlled nature, and their responsiveness to parental concerns.

Education, Green Spaces, and Other Initiatives

Many public-private initiatives are underway to help parents and children learn to navigate the Web safely, create kid-friendly content zones, and to work with law enforcement to ensure children's safety. They include:

- User-friendly, "One Click Away" content is currently being developed by libraries, parents, consumer and civil liberties groups and the Internet industry, to help Internet Service Providers comply with the "Dodd Amendment," which requires that such companies provide their customers with information about and access to User Empowerment tools including filtering software.
- Sites created by libraries and schools, to lists of useful sites compiled by libraries and educators, such as "Kids Connect Favorite Web Sites" selected by school librarians for K–12 students;
- Tools that guide kids while they explore the Internet, such as AOL NetFind Kids Only a search engine that links only to sites that are safe for kids; and
- Hotlines that connect concerned parents and adults to law enforcement resources, such as the National Center for Missing and Exploited Children's Cyber Tipline.

REVIEW AND DISCUSSION QUESTIONS

1. What special problems does allowing pornography into libraries raise, according to Sekulow?
2. Explain the idea of "viewpoint neutrality." Why has the Supreme Court thought that it is important to free speech?
3. On what basis does Sekulow distinguish this government regulation from ordinary cases of censorship in which the law forbids people from buying or selling certain material?
4. On what basis does Berman argue that filtering software restricts speech?
5. Describe the alternatives to filtering that Berman proposes.

Essay and Paper Topics for Section 12

1. Write an essay on hate speech by first defining it and then exploring the political, legal, and philosophical issues involved in censoring it.
2. Which position on the flag burning case do you think Alasdair MacIntyre would probably support, given his view about the virtue of patriotism?
3. Write an essay in which you assess the strengths and weaknesses of the arguments on behalf of censoring pornography. Be sure to explain just what you mean by the term, and how you would enforce the ban, legally.
4. Write an essay on censorship and the Internet. What impact has the Internet had on speech? Is it on balance good or bad that information is so readily available? In what ways do you think the Internet should be censored, if at all?
5. Universities are supposed to be places where free speech flourishes. Write an essay on the importance and limits of free speech on campus. Is "political correctness" on campus a form of censorship, or merely an attempt to be sure that everybody on campus feels welcome and is able to learn?

13

Equality and Difference

What do racial and gender equality require? Do women live in a world of male domination and oppression? Does evolutionary biology show that differences between the sexes are "natural" and therefore undermine (or strengthen) feminists' criticisms of society? And what would an ideal society think about racial and ethnic differences? Would it be blind to them, as we now are, more or less, to eye color? Or should government encourage citizens' sense of gender, racial, or ethnic identity? Essays in this section offer a variety of perspectives on these controversial and much discussed issues. The first reading in this section, by John Stuart Mill and Harriet Taylor, is perhaps the most important early work on women's rights and equality. Other readings explore the strengths and weaknesses of this early vision of sexual equality, including the alternative "dominance" approach advocated by some feminists and the relevance of evolutionary theory for sexual equality. The last two essays discuss racism and sexism—the extent to which they remain a problem and how an ideal society should treat such differences. Should identity politics be encouraged, or should law be color blind?

The Subjection of Women

John Stuart Mill and Harriet Taylor

As noted in the introduction to Mill's essay on utilitarianism, John Stuart Mill and Harriet Taylor enjoyed a lengthy and profoundly rewarding relationship. Her influence on Mill was extraordinary; indeed, there are many who believe it was she, as much or more than he, who was responsible for the following essay. In any event, this is a prescient essay on the subject of women's rights, and even today, more than a century later, it speaks to many issues still very much in the forefront of our discussions of sexual equality.

Mill and Taylor begin with an analysis of the situation faced by women, along with the possible causes of their plight. They then respond to those who would argue that the observed differences between the sexes are natural and those who believe women willingly accept their lot. They conclude with a discussion of the various reasons why women's equality should be advanced.

It is interesting to note that before Mill and Taylor were married, Mill signed an agreement renouncing all of the powers the law would normally bestow on him, asserting instead that his prospective wife was to retain the same rights to her property and personal freedom as if they had never married. When she died, Mill bought a house near the graveyard in France where Taylor was buried in order to spend his last years near his wife. The description of an ideal marriage appearing near the end of the essay mirrors Mill's own description of their relationship. (Because the essay was originally published under Mill's name alone, it is written using the first-person singular. Nonetheless, I have included Taylor as coauthor, as I believe Mill might have wished.)

Chapter 1. The object of this Essay is to explain as clearly as I am able, the grounds of an opinion which I have held from the very earliest period when I had formed any opinions at all on social or political matters, and which, instead of being weakened or modified, has been constantly growing stronger by the progress of reflection and the experience of life: That the principle which regulates the existing social relations between the two sexes—the legal subordination of one sex to the other—is wrong in itself, and now one of the chief hindrances to human improvement; and that it ought to be replaced by a principle of perfect equality, admitting no power or privilege on the one side, no disability on the other. . . .

The generality of a practice is in some cases a strong presumption that it is, or at all events once was, conducive to laudable ends. This is the case, when the practice was first adopted, or afterwards kept up, as a means to such ends, and was grounded on experience of the mode in which they could be most effectually attained. If the authority of men over women, when first established, had been the result of a conscientious comparison between different modes of constituting the government of society; if, after trying various other modes of social organization—the government of women over men, equality between the two, and such mixed and divided modes of government as might be invented—it had been decided, on the testimony of experience, that the mode in which women are wholly under the rule of men, having no share at all in public concerns, and each in private being under the legal obligation of obedience to the man with whom she has associated her destiny, was the arrangement most conducive to the happiness and well being of both; its general adoption might then be fairly thought to be some evidence that, at the time when it was adopted, it was the best: though even then the considerations which recommended it may, like so many other primeval social facts of the greatest importance, have subsequently, in the course of ages, ceased to exist. But the state of the case is in every respect the reverse of this. In the first place, the opinion in favour of the present system, which entirely subordinates the weaker sex to the stronger, rests upon theory only; for there never has been trial made of any other: so that experience, in the sense in which it is vulgarly opposed to theory, cannot be pretended to have pronounced any verdict. And in the second place, the adoption of this system of inequality never was the result of deliberation, or forethought, or any social ideas, or any notion whatever of what conduced to the benefit of humanity or the good order of society. It arose simply from the fact that from the very earliest twilight of human society, every woman (owing to the value attached to her by men, combined with her inferiority in muscular strength) was found in a state of bondage to some man. Laws and systems of polity always begin by recognising the relations they find already existing between individuals. They convert what was a mere physical fact into a legal right, give it the sanction of society, and principally aim at the substitution of public and organized means of asserting and protecting these rights, instead of the irregular and lawless conflict of physical strength. Those who had already been compelled to obedience became in this manner legally bound to it. . . . But this dependence, as it exists at present, is not an original institution,

From John Stuart Mill and Harriet Taylor, *The Subjection of Women* (1869).

taking a fresh start from considerations of justice and social expediency—it is the primitive state of slavery lasting on, through successive mitigations and modifications occasioned by the same causes which have softened the general manners, and brought all human relations more under the control of justice and the influence of humanity. It has not lost the taint of its brutal origin. No presumption in its favour, therefore, can be drawn from the fact of its existence. . . . The inequality of rights between men and women has no other source than the law of the strongest.

But, it will be said, the rule of men over women differs from all these others in not being a rule of force: it is accepted voluntarily; women make no complaint, and are consenting parties to it. In the first place, a great number of women do not accept it. Ever since there have been women able to make their sentiments known by their writings (the only mode of publicity which society permits to them), an increasing number of them have recorded protests against their present social condition. . . .

All causes, social and natural, combine to make it unlikely that women should be collectively rebellious to the power of men. They are so far in a position different from all other subject classes, that their masters require something more from them than actual service. Men do not want solely the obedience of women, they want their sentiments. All men, except the most brutish, desire to have, in the woman most nearly connected with them, not a forced slave but a willing one, not a slave merely, but a favourite. They have therefore put everything in practice to enslave their minds. The masters of all other slaves rely, for maintaining obedience, on fear; either fear of themselves, or religious fears. The masters of women wanted more than simple obedience, and they turned the whole force of education to effect their purpose. All women are brought up from the very earliest years in the belief that their ideal of character is the very opposite to that of men; not self-will, and government by self-control, but submission,

and yielding to the control of others. All the moralities tell them that it is the duty of women, and all the current sentimentalities that it is their nature, to live for others; to make complete abnegation of themselves, and to have no life but in their affections. And by their affections are meant the only ones they are allowed to have—those to the men with whom they are connected, or to the children who constitute an additional and indefeasible tie between them and a man. When we put together three things—first, the natural attraction between opposite sexes; secondly, the wife's entire dependence on the husband, every privilege or pleasure she has being either his gift, or depending entirely on his will; and lastly, that the principal object of human pursuit, consideration, and all objects of social ambition, can in general be sought or obtained by her only through him, it would be a miracle if the object of being attractive to men had not become the polar star of feminine education and formation of character. And, this great means of influence over the minds of women having been acquired, an instinct of selfishness made men avail themselves of it to the upmost as a means of holding women in subjection, by representing to them meekness, submissiveness, and resignation of all individual will into the hands of a man, as an essential part of sexual attractiveness. Can it be doubted that any of the other yokes which mankind have succeeded in breaking, would have subsisted till now if the same means had existed, and had been as sedulously used, to bow down their minds to it? . . .

Neither does it avail anything to say that the *nature* of the two sexes adapts them to their present functions and position, and renders these appropriate to them. Standing on the ground of common sense and the constitution of the human mind, I deny that any one knows, or can know, the nature of the two sexes, as long as they have only been seen in their present relation to one another. . . .

One thing we may be certain of—that what is contrary to women's nature to do, they never will be made to do by simply giving their nature free play. The anxiety of mankind to interfere in behalf of nature, for fear lest nature should not succeed in effecting its purpose, is an altogether unnecessary solicitude. . . .

Chapter 2. . . . Marriage being the destination appointed by society for women, the prospect they are brought up to, and the object which it is intended should be sought by all of them, except those who are too little attractive to be chosen by any man as his companion; one might have supposed that everything would have been done to make this condition as eligible to them as possible, that they might have no cause to regret being denied the option of any other. Society, however, both in this, and, at first, in all other cases, has preferred to attain its object by foul rather than fair means: but this is the only case in which it has substantially persisted in them even to the present day. Originally women were taken by force, or regularly sold by their father to the husband. . . .

[Today] the wife is the actual bondservant of her husband: no less so, as far as legal obligation goes, than slaves commonly so called. She vows a life-long obedience to him at the altar, and is held to it all through her life by law. Casuists may say that the obligation of obedience stops short of participation in crime, but it certainly extends to everything else. She can do no act whatever but by his permission, at least tacit. She can acquire no property but for him; the instant it becomes hers, even if by inheritance, it becomes *ipso facto* his. In this respect the wife's position under the common law of England is worse than that of slaves in the laws of many countries. . . . The two are called "one person in law," for the purpose of inferring that whatever is hers is his, but the parallel inference is never drawn that whatever is his is hers; the maxim is not applied against the man, except to make him responsible to third parties for her acts, as a master is for the acts of his slaves or of his cattle. I am far from pretending that wives are in general no better treated than slaves; but no slave is a slave to the same lengths, and in so full a sense of the word, as a wife is. Hardly any slave, except one immediately attached to the master's person, is a slave at all hours and all minutes; in general he has, like a soldier, his fixed task, and when it is done, or when he is off duty, he disposes, within certain limits, of his own time, and has a family life into which the master rarely intrudes. "Uncle Tom" under his first master had his own life in his "cabin," almost as much as any man whose work takes him away from home, is able to have in his own family. But it cannot be so with the wife. Above all, a female slave has (in Christian countries) an admitted right, and is considered under a moral obligation, to refuse to her master the last familiarity. Not so the wife: however brutal a tyrant she may unfortunately be chained to—though she may know that he hates her, though it may be his daily pleasure to torture her, and though she may feel it impossible not to loathe him—he can claim from her and enforce the lowest degradation of a human being, that of being made the instrument of an animal function contrary to her inclinations. While she is held in this worst description of slavery as to her own person, what is her position in regard to the children in whom she and her master have a joint interest? They are by law his children. He alone has any legal rights over them. Not one act can she do towards or in relation to them, except by delegation from him. Even after he is dead she is not their legal guardian, unless he by will has made her so. He could even send them away from her, and deprive her of the means of seeing or corresponding with them, until this power was in some degree restricted by Serjeant Talfourd's Act. This is her legal state. And from this state she has no means of withdrawing herself. If she leaves her husband, she can take nothing with her, neither her children nor anything which is rightfully her own. If he chooses, he can compel her to return, by law, or by physical force; or he may content himself with seizing for his own use anything which she may earn, or which may be given to her by her relations. . . .

When we consider how vast is the number of men, in any great country, who are little higher than brutes, and that this never prevents them from being able, through the law of marriage, to obtain a victim, the breadth and depth of human misery caused in this shape alone by the abuse of the institution swells to something appalling. . . . I grant that the wife, if she cannot effectually resist, can at least retaliate; she, too, can make the man's life extremely uncomfortable, and by that power is able to carry many points which she ought, and many which she ought not, to prevail in. But this instrument of self-protection —which may be called the power of the scold, or the shrewish sanction—has the fatal defect, that it avails most against the least tyrannical superiors, and in favour of the least deserving dependents. It is the weapon of irritable and self-willed women; of those who would make the worst use of power if they themselves had it, and who generally turn this power to a bad use. . . .

But how, it will be asked, can any society exist without government? In a family, as in a state, some one person must be the ultimate ruler. Who shall decide when married people differ in opinion? Both cannot have their way, yet a decision one way or the other must be come to.

It is not true that in all voluntary association between two people, one of them must be absolute master: still less that the law must determine which of them it shall be. . . .

It is quite true that things which have to be decided every day, and cannot adjust themselves gradually, or wait for a compromise, ought to depend on one will: one person must have their sole control. But it does not follow that this should always be the same person. The natural arrangement is a division of powers between the two; each being absolute in the executive branch of their own department, and any change of system and principle requiring the consent of both. . . .

The real practical decision of affairs, to whichever may be given the legal authority, will greatly depend, as it even now does, upon comparative qualifications. The mere fact that he is usually the eldest, will in most cases give the preponderance to the man; at least until they both attain a time of life at which the difference in their years is of no importance. There will naturally also be a more potential voice on the side, whichever it is, that brings the means of support. . . .

After what has been said respecting the obligation of obedience, it is almost superfluous to say anything concerning the more special point included in the general one—a woman's right to her own property; for I need not hope that this treatise can make any impression upon those who need anything to convince them that a woman's inheritance or gains ought to be as much her own after marriage as before. The rule is simple: whatever would be the husband's or wife's if they were not married, should be under their exclusive control during marriage. . . .

When the support of the family depends, not on property, but on earnings, the common arrangement, by which the man earns the income and the wife superintends the domestic expenditure, seems to me in general the most suitable division of labour between the two persons. If, in addition to the physical suffering of bearing children, and the whole responsibility of their care and education in early years, the wife undertakes the careful and economical application of the husband's earnings to the general comfort of the family; she takes not only her fair share, but usually the larger share, of the bodily and mental exertion required by their joint existence. If she undertakes any additional portion, it seldom relieves her from this, but only prevents her from performing it properly. The care which she is herself disabled from taking of the children and the household, nobody else takes; those of the children who do not die, grow up as they best can, and the management of the household is likely to be so bad, as even in point of economy to be a great drawback from the value of the wife's earnings. In an otherwise just state of things, it is not, therefore, I think, a desirable custom, that the wife should contribute by her labour to the income of the family. In an unjust state of things, her doing so may be useful to her, by making her of more value in the eyes of the man who is legally her master; but, on the other hand, it enables him still farther to abuse his power, by forcing her to work, and leaving the support of the family to her exertions, while he spends most of his time in drinking and idleness. The *power* of earning is essential to the dignity of a woman, if she has not independent property. But if marriage were an equal contract, not implying the obligation of obedience; if the connection were no longer enforced to the oppression of those to whom it is purely a mischief, but a separation, on just terms (I do not now speak of a divorce), could be obtained by any woman who was morally entitled to it; and if she would then find all honourable employments as freely open to her as to men; it would not be necessary for her protection, that during marriage she should make this particular use of her faculties. Like a man when he chooses a profession, so, when a woman marries, it may in general be understood that she makes choice of the management of a household, and the bringing up of a family, as the first call upon her exertions, during as many years of her life as may be required for the purpose; and that she renounces, not all other objects and occupations, but all which are not consistent with the requirements of this. The actual exercise, in a habitual or systematic manner, of outdoor occupations, or such as cannot be carried on at home, would by this principle be practically interdicted to the greater number of married women. But the utmost latitude ought to exist for the adaptation of general rules to individual suitabilities; and there ought to be nothing to prevent faculties exceptionally adapted to any other pursuit, from obeying their vocation notwithstanding marriage: due provision being made for supplying otherwise any falling-short which might become inevitable, in her full performance of the ordinary functions of mistress of a family. These things, if once opinion were rightly directed on the subject, might with perfect safety be left to be regulated by opinion, without any interference of law.

Chapter 3. On the other point which is involved in the just equality of women, their admissibility to all the functions and occupations hitherto retained as the monopoly of the stronger sex, I should anticipate no difficulty in convincing any one who has gone with me on the subject of the equality of women in the family. I believe that their disabilities elsewhere are only clung to in order to maintain their subordination in domestic life. . . . It is not sufficient to maintain that women on the average are less gifted than men on the average, with certain of the higher mental faculties, or that a smaller number of women than of men are fit for occupations and functions of the highest intellectual character. It is necessary to maintain that no women at all are fit for them, and that the most eminent women are inferior in mental faculties to the most mediocre of the men on whom those functions at present devolve. . . . Is there so great a superfluity of men fit for high duties, that society can afford to reject the service of any competent person? Are we so certain of always finding a man made to our hands for any duty or function of social importance which falls vacant, that we lose nothing by putting a ban upon one-half of mankind, and refusing beforehand to make their faculties available, however distinguished they may be? And even if we could do without them, would it be consistent with justice to refuse to them their fair share of honour and distinction, or to deny to them the equal moral right of all human beings to choose their occupation (short of injury to others) according to their own preferences, at their own risk? Nor is the injustice confined to them: it is shared by those who are in a position to benefit by their services. . . .

But (it is said) there is anatomical evidence of the superior mental capacity of men compared with women: they have a larger brain. I reply, that in the first place the fact itself is doubtful. It is by no means established that the brain of a woman is smaller than that of a man. . . . Next, I must observe that the precise relation which exists between the brain and the intellectual powers is not yet well understood, but is a subject of great dispute. . . . It would not be surprising—it is indeed an hypothesis which accords well with the differences actually observed between the mental operations of the two sexes—if men on the average should have the advantage in the size of the brain, and women in activity of cerebral circulation. The results which conjecture, founded on analogy, would lead us to expect from this difference of organization, would correspond to some of those which we most commonly see. In the first place, the mental operations of men might be expected to be slower. They would neither be so prompt as women in thinking, nor so quick to feel. Large bodies take more time to get into full action. On the other hand, when once got thoroughly into play, men's brains would bear more work. It would be more persistent in the line first taken; it would have more difficulty in changing from one mode of action to another, but, in the one thing it was doing, it could go on longer without loss of power or sense of fatigue. And do we not find that the things in which men most excel women are those which require most plodding and long hammering at a single thought, while women do best what must be done rapidly? A woman's brain is sooner fatigued, sooner exhausted; but given the degree of exhaustion, we should expect to find that it would recover itself sooner. I repeat that this speculation is entirely hypothetical. . . .

Let us take, then, the only marked case which observation affords, of apparent inferiority of women to men, if we except the merely physical one of bodily strength. No production in philosophy, science, or art, entitled to the first rank, has been the work of a woman. Is there any mode of accounting for this, without supposing that women are naturally incapable of producing them?

In the first place, we may fairly question whether experience has afforded sufficient grounds for an induction. It is scarcely three generations since women, saving very rare exceptions, have begun to try their capacity in philosophy, science, or art. It is only in the present generation that their attempts have been at all numerous; and they are even now

extremely few, everywhere but in England and France. It is a relevant question, whether a mind possessing the requisites of first-rate eminence in speculation or creative art could have been expected, on the mere calculation of chances, to turn up during that lapse of time, among the women whose tastes and personal position admitted of their devoting themselves to these pursuits. . . .

Chapter 4. There remains a question, not of less importance than those already discussed, and which will be asked the most importunately by those opponents whose conviction is somewhat shaken on the main point. What good are we to expect from the changes proposed in our customs and institutions? Would mankind be at all better off if women were free? If not, why disturb their minds, and attempt to make a social revolution in the name of an abstract right? . . .

To which let me first answer, [there is] the advantage of having the most universal and pervading of all human relations regulated by justice instead of injustice. The vast amount of this gain to human nature, it is hardly possible, by any explanation or illustration, to place in a stronger light than it is placed by the bare statement, to any one who attaches a moral meaning to words. All the selfish propensities, the self-worship, the unjust self-preference, which exist among mankind, have their source and root in, and derive their principal nourishment from, the present constitution of the relation between men and women. Think what it is to a boy, to grow up to manhood in the belief that without any merit or any exertion of his own, though he may be the most frivolous and empty or the most ignorant and stolid of mankind, by the mere fact of being born a male he is by right the superior of all and every one of an entire half of the human race. . . . What must be the effect on his character, of this lesson? And men of the cultivated classes are often not aware how deeply it sinks into the immense majority of male minds. For, among right-feeling and well-bred people, the inequality is kept as much as possible out of sight; above all, out of sight of the children. As much obedience is required from boys to their mother as to their father: they are not permitted to domineer over their sisters, nor are they accustomed to see these postponed to them, but the contrary; the compensations of the chivalrous feeling being made prominent, while the servitude which requires them is kept in the background. . . .

The second benefit to be expected from giving to women the free use of their faculties, by leaving them the free choice of their employments, and opening to them the same field of occupation and the same prizes and encouragements as to other human beings, would be that of doubling the mass of mental faculties available for the higher service of humanity. . . . This great accession to the intellectual power of the species, and to the amount of intellect available for the good management of its affairs, would be obtained, partly, through the better and more complete intellectual education of women. . . .

The opinion of women would then possess a more beneficial, rather than a greater, influence upon the general mass of human belief and sentiment. I say a more beneficial, rather than a greater influence; for the influence of women over the general tone of opinion has always, or at least from the earliest known period, been very considerable. . . .

The wife's influence tends, as far as it goes, to prevent the husband from falling below the common standard of approbation of the country. It tends quite as strongly to hinder him from rising above it. The wife is the auxiliary of the common public opinion. A man who is married to a woman his inferior in intelligence, finds her a perpetual dead weight, or, worse than a dead weight, a drag, upon every aspiration of his to be better than public opinion requires him to be. It is hardly possible for one who is in these bonds, to attain exalted virtue. . . .

Though it may stimulate the amatory propensities of men, it does not conduce to married happiness, to exaggerate by differences of education whatever may be the native differences of the sexes. If the married pair are well-bred and well-behaved people, they tolerate each other's tastes; but is mutual toleration what people look forward to, when they enter into marriage? . . .

What marriage may be in the case of two persons of cultivated faculties, identical in opinions and purposes, between whom there exists that best kind of equality, similarity of powers and capacities with reciprocal superiority in them—so that each can enjoy the luxury of looking up to the other, and can have alternately the pleasure of leading and of being led in the path of development—I will not attempt to describe. To those who can conceive it, there is no need; to those who cannot, it would appear the dream of an enthusiast. But I maintain, with the profoundest conviction, that this, and this only, is the ideal of marriage; and that all opinions, customs, and institutions which favour any other notion of it, or turn the conceptions and aspirations connected with it into any other direction, by whatever pretences they may be coloured, are relics of primitive barbarism. The moral regeneration of mankind will only really commence, when the most fundamental of the social relations is placed under the rule of equal justice, and when human beings learn to cultivate their strongest sympathy with an equal in rights and in cultivation.

REVIEW AND DISCUSSION QUESTIONS

1. Describe the situation of English women at the time Mill and Taylor were writing.
2. To what do the authors attribute the situation of women?
3. How do Mill and Taylor answer the claim that women are naturally inferior? That they willingly accept their status?
4. Describe the reasons the authors give for concluding that the current situation is intolerable.

5. What do Mill and Taylor see as the ideal marriage? Do you agree? Explain.

6. How does Mill's discussion of happiness and the good life, described in *Utilitarianism* and *On Liberty,* inform this essay on women and their plight?

7. Describe the connections you see between this essay and the limits on government that Mill defends in *On Liberty*. Are women who are raised in the environment he has described likely to be able to make truly "autonomous" choices?

Sexual Harassment

Ellison v. Brady

Legally, sexual harassment is a form of sex discrimination, which is prohibited under Title VII of the 1964 Civil Rights Act. That act makes it illegal for an employer to "discriminate" against any individual in "compensation, terms, conditions or privileges of employment" based on "race, color, religion, sex, or national origin." In *Meritor Savings Bank* v. *Vinson* (1986), the Supreme Court held that sexual harassment of a female employee constitutes "discrimination" based on "sex" within the meaning of that statute. The Court stated in *Meritor* that women could demand compensation for psychological as well as purely economic consequences of a "hostile workplace environment." Such harassment can include "unwelcome sexual advances, requests for sexual favors, and other verbal or physical conduct of a sexual nature." Having established in *Meritor* that sexual harassment is a form of sex discrimination, the courts then faced a variety of questions. What, precisely, are the bounds of sexual conduct in the workplace? From whose perspective should questions concerning the hostility of a work environment be judged: the average person, or the individual man or woman? *Ellison* v. *Brady* addresses these further questions about sexual harassment. (Though the actual defendant in the case was Brady, the person who allegedly harassed Ellison was named Gray. Often a named defendant will be a company, for instance, or a supervisor.)

Beezer, Circuit Judge: Kerry Ellison worked as a revenue agent for the Internal Revenue Service in San Mateo, California. During her initial training in 1984 she met Sterling Gray, another trainee, who was also assigned to the San Mateo office. The two co-workers never became friends, and they did not work closely together.

Gray's desk was twenty feet from Ellison's desk, two rows behind and one row over. Revenue agents in the San Mateo office often went to lunch in groups. In June of 1986 when no one else was in the office, Gray asked Ellison to lunch. She accepted. Gray had to pick up his son's forgotten lunch, so they stopped by Gray's house. He gave Ellison a tour of his house.

Ellison alleges that after the June lunch Gray started to pester her with unnecessary questions and hang around her desk. On October 9, 1986, Gray asked Ellison out for a drink after work. She declined, but she suggested that they have lunch the following week. She did not want to have lunch alone with him, and she tried to stay away from the office during lunch time. One day during the following week, Gray uncharacteristically dressed in a three-piece suit and asked Ellison out for lunch. Again, she did not accept.

Ellison v. *Brady*. 924 F.2d. 872 (1991).

On October 22, 1986 Gray handed Ellison a note he wrote on a telephone message slip which read:

> I cried over you last night and I'm totally drained today. I have never been in such constant term oil (sic). Thank you for talking with me. I could not stand to feel your hatred for another day.

When Ellison realized that Gray wrote the note, she became shocked and frightened and left the room. Gray followed her into the hallway and demanded that she talk to him, but she left the building.

Ellison later showed the note to Bonnie Miller, who supervised both Ellison and Gray. Miller said "this is sexual harassment." Ellison asked Miller not to do anything about it. She wanted to try to handle it herself. Ellison asked a male co-worker to talk to Gray, to tell him that she was not interested in him and to leave her alone. The next day, Thursday, Gray called in sick.

Ellison did not work on Friday, and on the following Monday, she started four weeks of training in St. Louis, Missouri. Gray mailed her a card and a typed, single-spaced, three-page letter. She describes this letter as "twenty times, a hundred times weirder" than the prior note. Gray wrote, in part:

> I know that you are worth knowing with or without sex. . . . Leaving aside the hassles and disasters of recent weeks. I have enjoyed you so much over these past few months. Watching you. Experiencing you from O so far away. Admiring your style and elan. . . . Don't you think it odd that two people who have never even talked together, alone, are striking off such intense sparks. . . . I will [write] another letter in the near future.[1]

Explaining her reaction, Ellison stated: "I just thought he was crazy. I thought he was nuts. I didn't know what he would do next. I was frightened."

She immediately telephoned Miller. Ellison told her supervisor that she was frightened and really upset. She requested that Miller transfer either her or Gray because she would not be comfortable working in the same office with him. . . .

Gray subsequently transferred to the San Francisco office. . . . After three weeks in San Francisco, Gray filed union grievances requesting a return to the San Mateo office. The IRS and the union settled the grievances in Gray's favor, agreeing to allow him to transfer back to the San Mateo office provided that he spend four more months in San Francisco and promise not to bother Ellison. On January 28, 1987, Ellison first learned of Gray's request in a letter from Miller. . . . After receiving the letter, Ellison was "frantic." She filed a formal complaint alleging sexual harassment on January 30, 1987 with the IRS. She also obtained permission to transfer to San Francisco temporarily when Gray returned.

Gray sought joint counseling. He wrote Ellison another letter which still sought to maintain the idea that he and Ellison had some type of relationship.

The IRS employee investigating the allegation agreed with Ellison's supervisor that Gray's conduct constituted sexual harassment. In its final decision, however, the Treasury Department rejected Ellison's complaint because it believed that the complaint did not describe a pattern or practice of sexual harassment covered by the EEOC regulations. After an appeal, the EEOC . . . concluded that the agency took adequate action to prevent the repetition of Gray's conduct.

Ellison filed a complaint in September of 1987 in federal district court. The court granted the government's motion for summary judgment on the ground that Ellison had failed to state a prima facie case of sexual harassment due to a hostile working environment. Ellison appeals. . . .

The government asks us to apply the reasoning of other courts which have declined to find Title VII violations on more egregious facts. In *Scott* v. *Sears, Roebuck & Co.* (7th Cir. 1986), the Seventh Circuit analyzed a female employee's working conditions for sexual harassment. It noted that she was repeatedly propositioned and winked at by her supervisor. When she asked for assistance, he asked "what will I get for it?" Co-workers slapped her buttocks and commented that she must moan and groan during sex. The court examined the evidence to see if "the demeaning conduct and sexual stereotyping cause[d] such anxiety and debilitation to the plaintiff that working conditions were 'poisoned' within the meaning of Title VII." The court did not consider the environment sufficiently hostile.

Similarly, in *Rabidue* v. *Osceola Refining Co.* (6th Cir. 1986), the Sixth Circuit refused to find a hostile environment where the workplace contained posters of naked and partially dressed women, and where a male employee customarily called women "whores," "cunt," "pussy," and "tits," referred to plaintiff as "fat ass," and specifically stated, "All that bitch needs is a good lay." Over a strong dissent, the majority held that the sexist remarks and the pin-up posters had only a de minimis effect and did not seriously affect the plaintiff's psychological well-being.

We do not agree with the standards set forth in *Scott* and *Rabidue,* and we choose not to follow those decisions. Neither *Scott*'s search for "anxiety and debilitation" sufficient to "poison" a working environment nor *Rabidue*'s requirement that a plaintiff's psychological well-being be "seriously affected" follows directly from language in *Meritor*. It is the harasser's conduct which must be pervasive or severe, not the alteration in the conditions of employment. Surely, employees need not endure sexual harassment until their psychological well-being is seriously affected to the extent that they suffer anxiety and debilitation. Although an isolated epithet by itself fails to support a cause of action for a hostile environment, Title VII's protection of employees from sex discrimination comes into play long before the point where victims of sexual harassment require psychiatric assistance.

We have closely examined *Meritor* and our previous cases, and we believe that Gray's

conduct was sufficiently severe and pervasive to alter the conditions of Ellison's employment and create an abusive working environment. We first note that the required showing of severity or seriousness of the harassing conduct varies inversely with the pervasiveness or frequency of the conduct. . . .

Next, we believe that in evaluating the severity and pervasiveness of sexual harassment, we should focus on the perspective of the victim. If we only examined whether a reasonable person would engage in allegedly harassing conduct, we would run the risk of reinforcing the prevailing level of discrimination. Harassers could continue to harass merely because a particular discriminatory practice was common, and victims of harassment would have no remedy.

We therefore prefer to analyze harassment from the victim's perspective. A complete understanding of the victim's view requires, among other things, an analysis of the different perspectives of men and women. Conduct that many men consider unobjectionable may offend many women.

We realize that there is a broad range of viewpoints among women as a group, but we believe that many women share common concerns which men do not necessarily share. For example, because women are disproportionately victims of rape and sexual assault, women have a stronger incentive to be concerned with sexual behavior. Women who are victims of mild forms of sexual harassment may understandably worry whether a harasser's conduct is merely a prelude to violent sexual assault. Men, who are rarely victims of sexual assault, may view sexual conduct in a vacuum without a full appreciation of the social setting or the underlying threat of violence that a woman may perceive.

In order to shield employers from having to accommodate the idiosyncratic concerns of the rare hyper-sensitive employee, we hold that a female plaintiff states a prima facie case of hostile environment sexual harassment when she alleges conduct which a reasonable woman[2] would consider sufficiently severe or pervasive to alter the conditions of employment and create an abusive working environment.[3]

We adopt the perspective of a reasonable woman primarily because we believe that a sex-blind reasonable person standard tends to be male-biased and tends to systematically ignore the experiences of women. The reasonable woman standard does not establish a higher level of protection for women than men. Instead, a gender-conscious examination of sexual harassment enables women to participate in the workplace on an equal footing with men. By acknowledging and not trivializing the effects of sexual harassment on reasonable women, courts can work towards ensuring that neither men nor women will have to "run a gauntlet of sexual abuse in return for the privilege of being allowed to work and make a living." *Henson* v. *Dundee* (11th Cir. 1982).

We note that the reasonable victim standard we adopt today classifies conduct as unlawful sexual harassment even when harassers do not realize that their conduct creates a hostile working environment. Well-intentioned compliments by co-workers or supervisors can form the basis of a sexual harassment cause of action if a reasonable victim of the same sex as the plaintiff would consider the comments sufficiently severe or pervasive to alter a condition of employment and create an abusive working environment.[4] That is because Title VII is not a fault-based tort scheme. . . .

The facts of this case illustrate the importance of considering the victim's perspective. Analyzing the facts from the alleged harasser's viewpoint, Gray could be portrayed as a modern-day Cyrano de Bergerac wishing no more than to woo Ellison with his words. There is no evidence that Gray harbored ill will toward Ellison. He even offered in his "love letter" to leave her alone if she wished. Examined in this light, it is not difficult to see why the district court characterized Gray's conduct as isolated and trivial.

Ellison, however, did not consider the acts to be trivial. Gray's first note shocked and frightened her. After receiving the three-page letter, she became really upset and frightened again. She immediately requested that she or Gray be transferred. Her supervisor's prompt response suggests that she too did not consider the conduct trivial. When Ellison learned that Gray arranged to return to San Mateo, she immediately asked to transfer, and she immediately filed an official complaint.

We cannot say as a matter of law that Ellison's reaction was idiosyncratic or hypersensitive. We believe that a reasonable woman could have had a similar reaction. After receiving the first bizarre note from Gray, a person she barely knew, Ellison asked a co-worker to tell Gray to leave her alone. Despite her request, Gray sent her a long, passionate, disturbing letter. He told her he had been "watching" and "experiencing" her; he made repeated references to sex; he said he would write again. Ellison had no way of knowing what Gray would do next. A reasonable woman could consider Gray's conduct, as alleged by Ellison, sufficiently severe and pervasive to alter a condition of employment and create an abusive working environment. . . .

We hope that over time both men and women will learn what conduct offends reasonable members of the other sex. When employers and employees internalize the standard of workplace conduct we establish today, the current gap in perception between the sexes will be bridged. . . .

Stephens, District Judge, Dissenting: . . . Nowhere in section 2000e of Title VII, the section under which the plaintiff in this case brought suit, is there any indication that Congress intended to provide for any other than equal treatment in the area of civil rights. The legislation is designed to achieve a balanced and generally gender neutral and harmonious workplace which would improve production and the quality of the employee's lives. In fact, the Supreme Court has shown a preference against systems that are not gender or race neutral, such as hiring quotas. . . . While women may be the most frequent targets of this type of conduct that is at issue in this case, they are not the only targets. I believe that it is incumbent upon the court in this case to use terminology that will meet the needs of all who seek recourse under this section of Title VII. Possible alternatives that are more in line with a gender neutral approach include "victim," "target," or "person."

The term "reasonable man" as it is used in the law of torts, traditionally refers to the average adult person, regardless of gender, and the conduct that can reasonably be expected of him or her. For the purposes of the legal issues that are being addressed, such a term assumes that it is applicable to all persons. . . . It is clear that the authors of the majority opinion intend a difference between the "reasonable woman" and the "reasonable man" in Title VII cases on the assumption that men do not have the same sensibilities as women. This is not necessarily true. A man's response to circumstances faced by women and their effect upon women can be and in given circumstances may be expected to be understood by men. . . .

The creation of the proposed "new standard" which applies only to women will not necessarily come to the aid of all potential victims of the type of misconduct that is at issue in this case. I believe that a gender neutral standard would greatly contribute to the clarity of this and future cases in the same area. . . .

NOTES

1. In the middle of the long letter, Gray did say "I am obligated to you so much that if you want me to leave you alone I will . . . If you want me to forget you entirely, I can not do that."
2. Of course, where male employees allege that co-workers engage in conduct which creates a hostile environment, the appropriate victim's perspective would be that of a reasonable man.
3. We realize that the reasonable woman standard will not address conduct which some women find offensive. Conduct considered harmless by many today may be considered discriminatory in the future. Fortunately, the reasonableness inquiry which we adopt today is not static. As the views of reasonable women change, so too does the Title VII standard of acceptable behavior.
4. If sexual comments or sexual advances are in fact welcomed by the recipient, they, of course, do not constitute sexual harassment. Title VII's prohibition of sex discrimination in employment does not require a totally desexualized work place.

REVIEW AND DISCUSSION QUESTIONS

1. Describe the events leading to Ms. Ellison's claim that she was sexually harassed. Was her work environment "hostile"?
2. On what basis does the Court reject the *Scott* and *Rabidue* decisions?
3. What is the "reasonable woman" standard? Why does the Court adopt it?
4. Explain the reason Judge Stephens dissents.
5. "This decision is unfair to men." Do you agree or disagree? Explain.
6. How do you think Mill and Taylor would respond to this case?

Sexual Equality and Discrimination: Difference vs. Dominance

Will Kymlicka

According to Will Kymlicka, sex discrimination is commonly interpreted as the arbitrary or irrational use of gender in the awarding of benefits or positions. That is, sex discrimination is unequal treatment that cannot be justified by reference to some sexual difference. This "difference approach" to discrimination perceives sexual equality in terms of the ability of women to compete under gender-neutral rules for various roles and positions. The problem, Kymlicka argues, is that these roles and positions may be defined in such a way as to make men more suited to them, even under gender-neutral competition. Will Kymlicka is professor of philosophy at Queen's University in Kingston, Ontario.

Until well into this century, most male theorists on all points of the political spectrum accepted the belief that there was a "foundation in nature" for the confinement of women to the family, and for the "legal and customary subjection of women to their husbands" within the family (Okin 1979: 200).[1] Restrictions on women's civil and political rights were said to be justified by the fact that women are, by nature, unsuited for political and economic activities outside the home. Contemporary theorists have progressively abandoned this assumption of women's natural inferiority. They have accepted that women, like men, should be viewed as "free and equal beings," capable of self-determination and a sense of justice, and hence free to enter the public realm. And liberal democracies have progressively adopted anti-discrimination statutes intended to ensure that women have equal access to education, employment, political office, etc.

But these anti-discrimination statutes have not brought about sexual equality. In the United States and Canada, the extent of job segregation in the lowest-paying occupations is increasing. Indeed, if present trends continue,

all of the people below the poverty line in America in the year 2000 will be women or children (Wietzman 1985: 350). Moreover, domestic violence and sexual assault are increasing, as are other forms of violence and degradation aimed at women. Catharine MacKinnon summarizes her survey of the effects of equal rights in the United States by saying that "sex equality law has been utterly ineffective at getting women what we need and are socially prevented from having on the basis of a condition of birth: a chance at productive lives of reasonable physical security, self-expression, individuation, and minimal respect and dignity" (MacKinnon 1987: 32).

Why is this? Sex discrimination, as commonly interpreted, involves the arbitrary or irrational use of gender in the awarding of benefits or positions. On this view, the most blatant forms of sex discrimination are those where, for example, someone refuses to hire a woman for a job even though gender has no rational relationship to the task being performed. MacKinnon calls this the "difference approach" to sexual discrimination, for it views as discriminatory unequal treatment that cannot be justified by reference to some sexual difference.

Sex discrimination law of this sort was modelled on race discrimination law. And just as race equality legislation aims at a "colour-blind" society, so sex equality law aims at a sex-blind society. A society would be non-discriminatory if race or gender never entered into the awarding of benefits. Of course, while it is conceivable that political and economic decisions could entirely disregard race, it is difficult to see how a society could be entirely sex-blind. A society which provides for pregnancy benefits, or for sexually segregated sports, takes sex into account, but this does not seem unjust. And while racially segregated washrooms are clearly discriminatory, most people do not feel that way about sex-segregated washrooms. So the "difference approach" accepts that there are legitimate instances of differential treatment of the sexes. These are not discriminatory, however, so long as there is a genuine sexual difference which explains and justifies the differential treatment. Opponents of equal rights for women often invoked the spectre of sexually integrated sports (or washrooms) as evidence that sex equality is misguided. But defenders of the difference approach respond that the cases of legitimate differentiation are sufficiently rare, and the cases of arbitrary differentiation so common, that the burden of proof rests on those who claim that sex is a relevant ground for assigning benefits or positions.

This difference approach, as the standard interpretation of sex equality law in most Western countries, has had some successes. Its "moral thrust" is to "grant women access to what men have access to," and it has indeed "gotten women some access to employment and education, the public pursuits, including academic, professional, and blue-collar work, the military, and more than nominal access to athletics" (MacKinnon 1987: 33, 35). The difference approach has helped create gender-neutral access to, or competition for, existing social benefits and positions.

But its successes are limited, for it ignores the gender inequalities which are built into the very definition of these positions. The difference approach sees sex equality in terms of the ability of women to compete under gender-neutral rules for the roles that men have defined. But equality cannot be achieved by allowing men to build social institutions according to their interests, and then ignoring the gender of the candidates when deciding who fills the roles in these institutions. The problem is that the roles may be defined in such a way as to make men more suited to them, even under gender-neutral competition.

Consider that fact that most jobs "require that the person, gender neutral, who is qualified for them will be someone who is not the primary caretaker of a preschool child" (MacKinnon 1987: 37). Given that women are still expected to take care of children in our society, men will tend to do better than women in competing for such jobs. This is not because women applicants are discriminated against. Employers may pay no attention to the gender of the applicants, or may in fact wish to hire more women. The problem is that many women lack a relevant qualification for the job—i.e. being free from child-care responsibilities. There is gender-neutrality, in that employers do not attend to the gender of applicants, but there is no sexual equality, for the job was defined under the assumption that it would be filled by men who had wives at home taking care of the children. The difference approach insists that gender should not be taken into account in deciding who should have a job, but it ignores the fact "that day one of taking gender into account was the day the job was structured with the expectation that its occupant would have no child care responsibilities" (MacKinnon 1987: 37).

Whether or not gender-neutrality yields sexual equality depends on whether and how gender was taken into account earlier. As Janet Radcliffe Richards says,

If a group is kept out of something for long enough, it is overwhelmingly likely that activities of that sort will develop in a way unsuited to the excluded group. We know for certain that women have been kept out of many kinds of work, and this means that the work is quite likely to be unsuited to them. The most obvious example of this is the incompatibility of most work with the bearing and raising of children; I am firmly convinced that if women had been fully involved in the running of society from the start they would have found a way of arranging work and children to fit each other. Men have had no such motivation, and we can see the results. (Radcliffe Richards 1980: 113–14)

This incompatibility that men have created between child-rearing and paid labour has profoundly unequal results for women. The result is not only that the most valued positions in society are filled by men, while women are disproportionately concentrated into lower-paying part-time work, but also that many women become economically dependent on men. Where most of the "household income" comes from the man's paid work, the woman who does the unpaid domestic work is rendered dependent on him for access to resources. The consequences of this dependence have become more apparent with the rising divorce rate. While married couples may share the same standard of living during marriage, regardless of who earns the income, the effects of divorce are catastrophically unequal. In California, men's average standard of living goes up 42 per cent after divorce, women's goes down 73 per cent, and similar results have been found in other states (Okin 1979: 161). However, none of these unequal consequences of the incompatibility of child care and paid work are discriminatory, according to the difference approach, for they do not involve arbitrary discrimination. The fact is that freedom from child-care responsibilities is relevant to most existing jobs, and employers are not being arbitrary in insisting on it. Because it is a relevant qualification, the difference approach says that it is not discriminatory to insist upon it, regardless of the disadvantages it creates for women. Indeed, the difference approach sees the concern with child-care responsibilities, rather than irrelevant criteria like gender, as evidence that sex discrimination has been eliminated. It cannot see that the relevance of child-care responsibilities is itself a profound source of

sexual inequality, one that has arisen from the way men have historically structured the economy to suit their interests.

So before we decide whether gender should be taken into account, we need to know how it has already been taken into account. And the fact is that almost all important roles and positions have been structured in gender-biased ways:

> Virtually every quality that distinguishes men from women is already affirmatively compensated in this society. Men's physiology defines most sports, their needs define auto and health insurance coverage, their socially-designed biographies define workplace expectations and successful career patterns, their perspectives and concerns define quality in scholarship, their experiences and obsessions define merit, their objectification of life defines art, their military service defines citizenship, their presence defines family, their inability to get along with each other—their wars and rulerships—defines history, their image defines god, and their genitals define sex. For each of their differences from women, what amounts to an affirmative action plan is in effect, otherwise known as the structure and values of American society. (MacKinnon 1987: 36)

All of this is "gender-neutral," in the sense that women are not arbitrarily excluded from pursuing the things society defines as valuable. But it is sexist, because the things being pursued in a gender-neutral way are based on men's interests and values. Women are disadvantaged, not because chauvinists arbitrarily favour men in the awarding of jobs, but because the entire society systematically favours men in the defining of jobs, merits, etc.

Indeed, the more society defines positions in a gendered way, the less the difference approach is able to detect an inequality. Consider a society which restricts access to contraception and abortion, which defines paying jobs in such a way as to make them incompatible with child-bearing and child-rearing, and which does not provide economic compensation for domestic labour. Every woman who faces an unplanned pregnancy, and who cannot both raise children and work for wages, is rendered economically dependent on someone who is a stable income-earner (i.e. a man). In order to ensure that she acquires this support, she must become sexually attractive to men. Knowing that this is their likely fate, many girls do not try as hard as boys to acquire employment skills which can only be exercised by those who avoid pregnancy. Where boys pursue personal security by increasing their employment skills, girls pursue security by increasing their attractiveness to men. This, in turn, results in a system of cultural identifications in which masculinity is associated with income-earning, and femininity is defined in terms of sexual and domestic service for men, and the nurturing of children. So men and women enter marriage with different income-earning potential, and this disparity widens during marriage, as the man acquires valuable job experience. Since the woman faces greater difficulty supporting herself outside of the marriage, she is more dependent on maintaining the marriage, which allows the man to exercise greater control within it.

In such a society, men as a group exercise control over women's general life-chances (through political decisions about abortion, and economic decisions concerning job requirements), and individual men exercise control over economically vulnerable women within marriages. Yet there need be no arbitrary discrimination. All of this is gender-neutral, in that one's gender does not necessarily affect how one is treated by those in charge of distributing contraception, jobs, or domestic pay. But whereas the difference approach takes the absence of arbitrary discrimination as evidence of the absence of sexual inequality, it may in fact be evidence of its pervasiveness. It is precisely because women are dominated in this society that there is no need for them to be discriminated against. Arbitrary discrimination in employment is not only unnecessary for the maintenance of male privilege, it is unlikely to occur, for most women will never be in a position to be arbitrarily discriminated against in employment.

Perhaps the occasional woman can overcome the social pressures supporting traditional sex-roles. But the greater the domination, the less the likelihood that any women will be in a position to compete for employment, and hence the less room for arbitrary discrimination. The more sexual inequality there is in society, the more that social institutions reflect male interests, the less arbitrary discrimination there will be.

None of the contemporary Western democracies correspond exactly to this model of a patriarchal society, but they all share some of its essential features. And if we are to confront these forms of injustice, we need to reconceptualize sexual inequality as a problem, not of arbitrary discrimination, but of domination. As MacKinnon puts it,

> to require that one be the same as those who set the standard—those which one is already socially defined as different from—simply means that sex equality is conceptually designed never to be achieved. Those who most need equal treatment will be the least similar, socially, to those whose situation sets the standard as against which one's entitlement to be equally treated is measured. Doctrinally speaking, the deepest problems of sex inequality will not find women 'similarly situated' to men. Far less will practices of sex inequality require that acts be intentionally discriminatory. (MacKinnon 1987: 44; cf. Taub and Schneider 1982: 134)

The subordination of women is not fundamentally a matter of irrational differentiation on the basis of sex, but of male supremacy, under which gender differences are made relevant to the distribution of benefits, to the systematic disadvantage of women (MacKinnon 1987: 42; Frye 1983: 38).

Since the problem is domination, the solution is not only the absence of discrimination, but the presence of power. Equality requires not only equal opportunity to pursue male-defined roles, but also equal power to create female-defined roles, or to create androgynous roles men and women have an equal interest in filling. The result of such empowerment could be very different from our society, or from the equal-opportunity-to-enter-male-institutions that is favoured by contemporary sex-discrimination theory. From a position of equal power, we would not have created a system of social roles that defines "male" jobs as superior to "female" jobs. For example, the roles of male and female health practitioners were redefined by men against the will of women in the field. With the professionalization of medicine, women were squeezed out of their traditional health care roles as midwives and healers, and relegated to the role of nurse—a position which is subservient to, and financially less rewarding than, the role of doctor. That redefinition would not have happened had women been in a position of equality, and will have to be rethought now if women are to achieve equality.

REFERENCES

Eisenstein, Z. (1981). *The Radical Future of Liberal Feminism.* Longman, New York.

Frye, M. (1983). *The Politics of Reality: Essays in Feminist Theory.* Crossing Press, Trumansburg.

Gross, E. (1986). "What Is Feminist Theory?," in C. Pateman and E. Gross (eds.), *Feminist Challenges, Social and Political Theory.* Northeastern University Press, Boston, MA.

MacKinnon, C. (1987). *Feminism Unmodified: Discourses on Life and Law.* Harvard University Press, Cambridge, MA.

Okin, S. (1979). *Women in Western Political Thought.* Princeton University Press, Princeton, NJ.

Radcliffe Richards, J. (1980). *The Skeptical Feminist: A Philosophical Enquiry.* Routledge and Kegan Paul, London.

Weitzman, L. (1985). *The Divorce Revolution.* The Free Press, New York.

NOTE

1. In accepting this prevailing view that there is "a Foundation in Nature" for the rule of the husband "as the abler and the stronger" (Locke, in Okin 1979: 200), classical liberals created a serious contradiction for themselves. For they also argued that all humans are by nature equal, that nature provides no grounds for an inequality of rights. This, we have seen, was the point of their state-of-nature theories. . . . Why should the supposed fact that men are "abler and stronger" justify unequal rights for women when, as Locke himself says, "differences in excellence of parts or ability" do not justify unequal rights? One cannot both maintain equality amongst men as a class, on the grounds that differences in ability do not justify different rights, and also exclude women as a class, on the grounds that they are less able. If women are excluded on the grounds that the average woman is less able than the average man, then all men who are less able than the average man must also be excluded. As Okin puts it, "If the basis of his individualism was to be firm, he needed to argue that individual women were equal with individual men, just as weaker men were with stronger ones" (Okin 1979: 199).

REVIEW AND DISCUSSION QUESTIONS

1. Why does Kymlicka think antidiscrimination laws have not achieved sex equality?
2. What is the "difference" approach to sex equality? Give an example of this approach.
3. What is the "dominance" approach to sex equality? How does it differ from the "difference" approach?
4. What specific proposals would be necessary to achieve genuine sex equality?
5. How would Mill and Taylor respond to this essay?

Feminists, Meet Mr. Darwin

Robert Wright

In this essay, Robert Wright argues that while feminists often ignore or mistrust Darwinian evolutionary theory, they have much to learn, and gain, from its results. Using recent discoveries of biologists about reproduction and other patterns of behavior, he argues that "difference," "radical," and "equity" feminists as well as anybody else interested in understanding male-female relationships can benefit from the deeper understanding of human nature that biology provides. Topics Wright discusses include sexual harassment, monogamy, rape, affirmative action, and the "ethics of care." Robert Wright is an editor and writer at *The New Republic* and the author of *The Moral Animal*.

History has not been kind to ideologies that rested on patently false beliefs about human nature. Communism, for example, isn't looking very robust these days. From the beginning communists held that human selfishness, the great crippler of communal utopias, was eradicable. They shaped scientific theory accordingly. Marx insisted that traits acquired through education—a more generous disposition, say—were biologically inherited by offspring. Up until 1964, long after Western geneticists had dismissed this idea, it was still an official doctrine of Soviet biology. Occasionally Soviet geneticists who failed to appreciate the doctrine were sent to prison. It would be melodramatic to say that today feminism is where communism was at midcentury. Still, it's tempting. Once again an ideology clings to a doctrine that, for better or worse, isn't true—in this case the idea that "gender" is essentially a "construct": that male and female nature are inherently more or less identical. Once again, the falseness of the doctrine is increasingly evident. And, once again, adherents of the ideology can admit this falseness only at some risk—not imprisonment, maybe, but an extremely chilly reception from fellow feminists.

Of course, there are the much-discussed "difference feminists." But even they don't believe—or, at least, don't admit to believing—that men and women are inherently different. They either stay silent on the question of where the differences come from or trace them to early social influences.

There has been much talk about the fragmentation of modern feminism. In addition to the difference feminists (e.g., psychologist Carol Gilligan, linguist Deborah Tannen), there are the "radical feminists" (e.g., Catharine MacKinnon, Andrea Dworkin), the liberal "equity feminists" (e.g., Supreme Court Justice Ruth Bader Ginsburg, writer Katha Pollitt) and assorted others. But as diverse as these thinkers seem, they are bound by a common thread: none is interested in the well-grounded study of human nature, of the male and female minds.

By "well-grounded study of human nature" I don't *just* mean, "grounded the way I think the study of human nature should be grounded" (although I do, of course, mean that). I mean grounded in comprehension of the process that designed human beings: natural selection. Specifically, the field of inquiry that I commend to feminists, and that they seem loath to explore, is a science called evolutionary psychology. Evolutionary psychology sees (among other things) some clear differences between the male and female minds. These differences aren't wholly immutable. The difference feminists are right to sense that culture matters; we are a pretty plastic species. Still, many of the differences between men and women are more stubborn than most feminists would like, and complicate the quest for—even the definition of—social equality between the sexes.

The feminist aversion to the Darwinian study of difference has as much to do with Darwinism as with difference. Traditionally, after all, Darwinism has been most potently wielded by the right wing. Feminists fear that it will again be used to justify oppression as "natural," as "in our genes," as beyond our control. That's certainly a danger, but it's not inevitable. And besides, it's not necessarily worse than the alternative danger: that feminism, like communism, will falter under the weight of its doctrinal absurdities; and that the laudable ideals it started with, rather than reaching a gritty compromise with reality, will begin to wither for lack of honest support.

It would be misleading to say that feminists casually disregard Darwinism. A fair amount of effort goes into the disregard. A few feminists have actually studied and then dismissed the Darwinian view of human nature. Unfortunately, they seem to have expended more energy on the dismissal than on the study.

A typical dismissal begins by mocking Darwin's observation that in species after species, "the differences between the sexes follow almost exactly the same rules; the males are almost always the wooers. . . . " The female, "with the rarest exception, is less eager than the male. . . . [S]he is coy. . . . The exertion of some choice on the part of the female seems almost as general a law as the eagerness of the male." This is a vital observation, for the evolutionary logic behind it (which wasn't grasped until a century after Darwin) underlies many psychological differences between men and women.

Darwin's observation has been ridiculed by Carol Tavris in her much-praised (by feminists) book *The Mismeasure of Woman.* Tavris calls it the "myth of the coy female." The pattern Darwin thought he saw, she asserts, isn't really there. We can no longer explain sex roles by "appealing to the universality of such behavior in other species" because "other species aren't cooperating."

Actually, they are. To be sure, there are many species whose females are less than devoutly monogamous. There are even species whose females are as sexually assertive as males, or more so. What Tavris doesn't seem to appreciate is how all this variety can specifically reinforce our belief that the general rule of *relative* female sexual reserve has a genetic basis.

To see this crucial point, you have to first see the modern Darwinian explanation for that reserve. A female can reproduce much less often than a male, because she is stuck with the time-sapping job of birthing and maybe even rearing the young. Thus it makes Darwinian sense for her to appraise carefully the quality of aspiring mates—both their genetic quality and, in species with "high male parental investment," like ours, their ability and willingness to help provide for the young after birth. This quality control helps keep the female from wasting one of her rare and arduous reproductive episodes creating offspring with poor survival prospects. (A woman needn't think about these things; rather, her genetically based impulses of attraction have been shaped by this logic over millions of years; genes encouraging selectivity have flourished, while genes allowing females to squander precious reproductive episodes have not.)

For a male, in contrast, reproduction can be a frequent and low-cost affair; the more sex partners, the more chances to get genes into the next generation. Hence the massively documented fact that males in our species, when sizing up sheerly *sexual* (not marital) opportunities, are on average less choosy than females. (Among the documentation are male and female tastes in pornography and prostitution, as well as the oft-noted fact that gay males are on average more promiscuous than gay females; both homosexual cultures are a de facto experiment in how one sex behaves when it doesn't have to compromise with the other.)

Now, as it happens, in a few eccentric "sex-reversed" species the *males* assume much of the burden of giving birth. Male sea horses have an incubation pouch in which the female deposits the eggs. Male phalaropes (sea snipes) sit in the nest and incubate the eggs, taking themselves out of commission and leaving their mates free to embark on another round of reproduction. And these are the species in which stereotypes of courtship behavior most reliably break down; female sea horses and phalaropes are quite sexually assertive. Thus these ostensible "exceptions" to Darwinian logic in fact comply with and bolster it. They are yet more evidence that the sex that can reproduce more often will typically be the randier sex. They are yet more reason to believe that *human* females, whose reproductive episodes are rare and arduous, are indeed genetically inclined to be more discriminating about sex partners than human males are.

The feminist Anne Fausto-Sterling, author of *Myths of Gender,* is thus missing the point by 180 degrees when she cites the phalaropes, with their reversed sex roles, and says sarcastically, "You name your animal species and make your political point." You name your animal species and it complies with evolutionary theory. Politics will have to adjust accordingly.

It turns out that females in our species are not, by nature, utterly coy or utterly monogamous. There is physiological evidence that they are "naturally" prone to promiscuity and infidelity under some circumstances. But they are not nearly so prone as males. More to the point: figuring out how naturally adventurous women are, and why, has depended on careful study of various species whose females, for various reasons, don't precisely fit the coy stereotype. (Some of the pioneering work was done by the anthropologist Sarah Blaffer Ilrdy, author of *The Woman That Never Evolved.*)

So, while Tavris is in one sense right to say the "myth of the coy female" is dead, she is exactly wrong to imply that this means women aren't by nature more sexually reserved than men, or that recent zoology has sapped confidence in the Darwinian comprehension of the human mind. For Tavris and

Fausto-Sterling to note that the crudest stereotypes about human sex roles aren't found throughout the animal kingdom, and then end the discussion there, is to get a C- in Evolutionary Biology 101. And these are the two most commonly cited feminist "experts" on Darwinism.

I cannot, in the space of this article, try to convince skeptics that men are "naturally" less discriminating about sex partners than women—or that men and women inherently differ in the various other ways I'll discuss. I would direct readers who seek deeper immersion in the arguments for modern Darwinism to various books, including Matt Ridley's *The Red Queen,* David Buss's *The Evolution of Desire* and (got a pencil handy?) my own recently published *The Moral Animal.* (Or, at a more academic level: Donald Symons's *The Evolution of Human Sexuality;* Martin Daly and Margo Wilson's *Sex, Evolution, and Behavior;* and *The Adapted Mind,* edited by Jerome Barkow, Leda Cosmides and John Tooby.)

In lieu of persuasion, I'll mostly confine my assertions about human nature to beliefs that are widely accepted within evolutionary psychology—doctrines subscribed to by, among others, many female (and male) Darwinians who would call themselves feminists. When discussing more speculative theories, I'll so label them. Of course, detached from the larger body of cross-cultural and cross-species evidence in which they're embedded, all these claims will strike any determined skeptic as "just-so stories." But do not excuse yourself from confronting them on grounds that they are just tired Darwinian doctrines, scrutinized by feminists and judiciously rejected. There is not a single well-known feminist who has learned enough about modern Darwinism to pass judgment on it.

Some of them would be well advised to. Though it is simplistic to say that evolutionary psychology vindicates one feminist school or another, some schools could use the field to support at least part of their platform. At the same time, every school can find something in the field that threatens cherished beliefs.

478   Robert Wright

Most feminists should have a love-hate relationship with modern Darwinism.

Oddly, given Darwinism's historical (and confused) association with right-wing politics, evolutionary psychology lends a kind of support to some of the most radical feminists, such as MacKinnon and Dworkin. Both have gotten lots of ink for saying genuinely nutty things (such as Dworkin's theatrical suggestion that all heterosexual sex is rape)—pronouncements that defy all attempts at justification. But both have other positions, of more measured extremity, that, if they can be justified at all, are best justified in Darwinian terms.

Consider sexual harassment. MacKinnon helped establish the "hostile environment" test for harassment, and she defines such environments broadly; by her reckoning, two-thirds of working women have been harassed. Whereas some feminists consider the Anita Hill affair a borderline harassment case (if a clear-cut indictment of Clarence Thomas's character), MacKinnon jumped vehemently to Hill's defense.

I can see why: a man who held power over Hill was alleged to have made persistent, if not explicit, sexual overtures. Naturally, Hill would feel great distress. But I can only take this view by thinking of Hill as a woman, with the kind of mind natural selection designed for women. A man might feel uncomfortable with a comparable undercurrent of sexual advance from a female boss, but it would be strange for him to feel deep distress.

Again, the logic goes back to the fact that for women reproductive opportunities are precious. Thus during evolution it was costly (genetically) for a woman to have sex with a man she didn't want to have sex with—often a man who (a) evidently had genes not conducive to viable and fertile offspring or (b) had no evident inclination to stick around and help provide for the offspring. The abhorrence women feel at the prospect of sex with a man they find unattractive is an expression of this logic.

For men, the logic is different. Being coerced into sex with a woman (a) wasn't an issue during evolution, since men can't have

sex unless physiologically aroused; and (b) would have had no large ill effects; the worst likely outcome for the man (in genetic terms) is that pregnancy would not ensue. And spending fifteen minutes failing to get a woman pregnant is hardly a major Darwinian disaster. There is no reason for evolution to have instilled in the male mind an aversion to coerced sex with women.

So, yes, I'd say Anita Hill was sexually harassed. She was under coercive, if subtle, pressure to have sex. But that judgment depends on her mind being a female mind, with female vulnerabilities.

Many feminists, even without any help from Darwin, have discerned the tension here: the more protection you want to provide women, the harder it is to argue that they don't by their nature need special protection; the more often you see them victimized, the stronger the implication that they are by nature victims, weaker than men. That is why some feminists resist MacKinnon's broader definitions of sexual harassment and of rape, and her view of pornography as an assault on women. That is why she is called a "victim" feminist—and not just by conservatives such as Christina Hoff Sommers, but by feminists further to the left, such as Naomi Wolf. Justice Ruth Bader Ginsburg, who as a liberal equity feminist professes to seek only equal treatment for women, remarked after hearing MacKinnon speak, "That woman has bad karma."

Yet the equity feminists have failed just as surely as MacKinnon to resolve the tension between protecting women and patronizing them. Consider the Supreme Court's unanimous ruling in the latest sexual harassment case. It concerned a woman at a forklift company and her creepy boss. He would joke about large breasts, ask female employees to fish through his pockets for coins and so on. The straw that broke the camel's back was his asking a subordinate if she had landed one of her accounts by meeting with the client at a Holiday Inn.

Ruling in support of the female worker, the Supreme Court tried to sustain a broad definition of "hostile environment." The victim, it said, needn't prove that she had been psychologically damaged—only that she might "reasonably" have found the comments hostile. But, in a bow to Ginsburg and the equity feminists, the Court cast its ruling in terms of a "reasonable person," not a "reasonable woman."

This simply won't wash. How does a "reasonable person" feel about the implication that he or she closed a deal by sleeping with a customer? Well, the average woman feels quite insulted, and the average man feels somewhere between mildly insulted and quite flattered. She is being called a whore. He is being called a stud.

It is tempting to dismiss these value-laden labels as file residue of centuries of patriarchy, or as echoes of the Victorian Madonna-whore dichotomy—ephemeral cultural pathologies that the Court needn't stoop to accommodate. But there is another explanation: these moral judgments may have a genetic basis.

To begin with, men tend to find a history of extreme promiscuity an exceedingly undesirable feature in a wife, and this makes perfect Darwinian sense. The more promiscuous the wife, the less likely that the children in which the man invests his time and energy are in fact carrying his genes. In other words, genes inclining men to abhor promiscuous long-term mates would do better at getting into ensuing generations than less discriminating genes. The logic isn't the same for women, since the children they give birth to always carry their genes (or, at least, did during evolution, before high technology—and that's what counts).

This isn't to say men don't find loose women sexy. From a Darwinian standpoint, loose women are in some ways great *sex* partners, because they're so easy to get—and for purposes of a man's genetic proliferation, remember, the more gettable women there are the better. (Contraception has now short-circuited this logic, too, but again, we're stuck with the minds the logic shaped.) A loose woman just isn't the genetically optimal woman to fall in *love* with; investing in her children is ill-advised.

Hence, it seems, the Madonna-whore distinction. Men appear to be designed by natural selection to feel merely lust for fast women but to feel love as well for (some) slower ones. They won't always insist on marrying a Madonna, of course, virgins being scarce, and, besides, the choice of a mate being a complex unconscious calculus full of tradeoffs. Still, men do often draw a morally colored distinction among their romantic prospects, viewing some kinds of women as full-fledged human beings, warranting extensive psychological exploration, and other kinds as something more like pieces of meat. And one of various features that can put a woman in the latter camp is a reputation for extreme promiscuity. Men seldom admit this to either kind of woman, and some men don't admit it to themselves. But if you listen carefully to men talking to one another, the attitude is there.

It is not surprising, then, that the average woman resists being publicly labeled "easy," regardless of her actual degree of promiscuity. During evolution, that label would have cut the chances of a man's investing in her offspring. (A general theme of evolutionary psychology is that we all naturally burnish our reputations in all kinds of ways, regardless of whether the gloss reflects our actual behavior.)

This idea of an inherent and morally charged male mental distinction between fast and slow women is just a theory. And, while it probably commands majority allegiance within evolutionary psychology (though only when given more nuance than space here permits), it is not as solidly established as, say, the idea of sex differences in promiscuity. Even more tentative is the idea that women have some natural aversion to accusations of extreme sexual looseness (though certainly women do, in general, resist them more than men). Still, the closer we look at the evidence, the better things look for the theory. Various culturally deterministic anthropologists, notably Margaret Mead, claimed to have found exotic cultures in which women were as prone to promiscuity as men and no one cared. These claims have collapsed upon reexamination. Mead's favorite example, Samoa, turns out to have featured a virtual male obsession with the virginity of mates. (In Samoan lore, as Derek Freeman noted in *Margaret Mead and Samoa,* a deflowered woman is called a "wanton woman, like an empty shell exposed by the ebbing tide." A song performed at defloration ceremonies went like this: "All others have failed to achieve entry. . . . Being first, he is foremost, O to be foremost.")

All of this explains what for almost everyone is the commonsense reaction to the forklift case, yet what few feminists will admit: the reason the remark about the Holiday Inn was offensive was because it was made to a woman. What evolutionary psychology suggests is that this relevance of gender to law is no fleeting creation of culture; jurists might as well reckon with it.

In the end, the problem with the Ginsburgian "reasonable person" formulation is not that it leads to a narrow definition of harassment, but that it leads to no definition at all. Asking what a "reasonable person" finds offensive is like asking what color a typical fruit is. The answer depends on whether you're talking apples or oranges.

The general truth suggested here is that we can either give women broad protection against sexual harassment that is grounded specifically in an understanding of the female mind, or we can ignore sex differences and give women much less protection. Or we can do what the Supreme Court did: carefully craft tortured legal doctrines that defy both common sense and our emerging comprehension of human nature—doctrines that are unlikely to withstand the test of time.

Evolutionary psychology's tendency to provide at least some support for radical feminism goes beyond sexual harassment. Dworkin's contention that "dehumanization is a basic part of the content of all pornography" is characteristically overstated, but in Darwinian light it looks far from crazy. Certainly most pornography rivets the "whore," not the "Madonna," part of the male mind. The women in *Hustler* aren't women a man would want to marry. They're women whose appeal has nothing to do with getting to know them.

Indeed, they're women who are exciting partly because they're portrayed as not demanding that he get to know them; they seem willing to be treated as meat, as optimally efficient sex objects.

To say that men objectify loose women isn't to say, alas, that men never see the lucky recipients of their lasting affection as objects. The male tendency to "possessively" guard mates against the advances of rivals may be more than mere metaphor. For men, "the same mental algorithms are apparently activated in the marital and mercantile spheres," write the evolutionary psychologists Martin Daly and Margo Wilson. Again, the reason seems to be the high genetic costs cuckoldry brings the male victim. As evolutionary psychologists have shown, the average woman isn't as threatened as the average man by the purely sexual infidelity of a mate, apparently because it doesn't so immediately threaten her genes.

Even the radical feminists' famously expansive definitions of rape have *some* Darwinian merit. One of MacKinnon's more moderate utterances on the subject is this: "Politically, I call it rape whenever a woman has sex and feels violated." Psychologically, too, you might call it that. When a woman has sex under a man's pretenses of enduring affection (Darwinian translation: pretenses of commitment to ensuing offspring) and then he never calls again, the evolutionary source of her anguish is the same as for the anguish following rape: she has had sex with a man she (unconsciously) deemed unworthy of her eggs, even though in this case the deeming was done after the fact, once evidence of his unworthiness surfaced.

Again, though, if you really want to claim such a broad realm of moral protection for women, you have to admit they're different from men and in some ways uniquely vulnerable. Men, after all, virtually never feel "violated" by sex with a woman. A man may feel crushed if a woman he loves leaves him, but it is an odd man indeed who regrets the sex.

Dworkin has distinguished between rape and seduction as follows: "In seduction, the rapist bothers to buy a bottle of wine." Another feminist has opined that rape is "on a continuum" with normal male sexual behavior. Some Darwinians would agree. They'd say rape is something men do when other forms of manipulation fail. It may be "natural" when men with a manifest inability to legitimately obtain a mate resort to sex with aggression. Hence the profile of the typical rapist: lacking the material and personal resources to attract women.

Dworkin has written, "A man wants what a woman has—sex. He can steal it (rape), persuade her to give it away (seduction), rent it (prostitution), lease it over the long term (marriage in the United States) or own it outright (marriage in most societies)." However depressing, this would strike some Darwinians as a fair thumbnail sketch of the situation. This doesn't mean men think of their pursuits this way (in general the radical feminists attribute too much conscious calculation to men); but it is a fairly apt functional analysis of the emotions men feel—from lust to love to the selective evaporation of affection upon conquest.

Plainly, the resonance between radical feminism and Darwinism isn't just that the former's implicit depiction of female vulnerabilities is explicit in the latter. Darwinism also depicts men as something like the animals that MacKinnon and Dworkin say they are. Human males are by nature oppressive, possessive, flesh-obsessed pigs. They're not beyond cultural improvement, thanks to the fact that love, compassion, guilt, remorse and the conscience are evolved parts of the mind, just like lust and jealous rage. Still, MacKinnon and Dworkin are probably right to suggest that the current cultural climate does a lackluster job of improving men.

I won't spend the next few weeks waiting for MacKinnon and Dworkin to call and thank me for empowering their worldview. For they don't want its power to run quite so deep. Dworkin denounces "Female" supremacists—some of the difference feminists—as being "biological determinists." (Remarkably, she does this one paragraph after asserting that "men as a class are moral cretins.") MacKinnon, hit by less radical feminists with the entirely apt label "victim feminist," tries to fob it off on the difference feminists. Her reaction to Gilligan's book *In a Different Voice*, which depicted women as more empathetic and less abstractly logical than men in their moral thinking, was to call this "different" voice "the voice of a victim."

This aversion to "biological determinism" (a misnomer) is one thing all major brands of feminism have in common. Even the difference feminists don't want to talk about *deep* differences. Tannen, in her bestseller *You Just Don't Understand* and her recent *Talking From 9 to 5*, says men are on average more concerned than women with status and hierarchy. This undeniable fact begs to be placed on its proper Darwinian foundation. During evolution, high male status seems to have expanded sexual access to females (as it does in many species, including our nearest relatives, chimpanzees). This Darwinian perk has been documented in "hunter-gatherer" societies, the closest living model of the social context of human evolution. Given this distinctively male link between social achievement and genetic proliferation, it is plausible, to say the least, that millions of years of evolution would endow males with a distinctive thirst for power.

Yet Tannen couches her explanation for this thirst in cultural terms. The tendency of boys to "jockey for center stage, challenge those who get it and deflect challenges" is "learned" by boys and not girls because boys' groups "tend to be more obviously hierarchical." Well, yes, lots of learning goes on, and every child has a range of flexibility whose bounds still aren't precisely known. Culture matters. But does that explain why the boys' groups are always more hierarchical in the first place? Tannen's overriding emphasis on culture would make more sense if she could point to a single one of the 1,200 societies on the anthropological record and show women, on average, pursuing social status and political power as fiercely and opportunistically as the average man. She can't.

Poor Tannen. Her evasion of Darwinism fails to keep her safe from the wrath of even the mild-mannered equity feminists. Katha Pollitt says Tannen and Gilligan "massage their findings to fit their theories," and that their prominence just proves that social science is "one part science and nine parts social. They say what people want to hear: women really are different, just the way we always thought." Maybe so. But did you ever wonder why it is that we've always thought that?

It's logical that liberal feminists would fear the idea of innate sex differences in ambition. For it imperils two liberal feminist legal principles. One is sex discrimination—in particular, the claim that a gross underrepresentation of women in high-paying jobs is by itself evidence of discrimination. This logic assumes not just that men and women are equally qualified, but that they pursue a given job or promotion with equal intensity. If men are on average more ambitious than women, this assumption falters.

The second legal doctrine imperiled by evolutionary psychology is affirmative action for women. It is sometimes (not always) justified on similar grounds: that, in the absence of discrimination, men and women would be equally represented at the higher levels of corporate and government life. But if men on average work harder at self-advancement, this rationale won't work.

As Ridley notes in *The Red Queen,* there are other possible rationales for affirmative action. Our emerging knowledge of male-female differences might lead us to favor quotas for women on grounds that they are less inclined than men to sacrifice the organization's welfare to personal advancement. In other words: if a meritocracy is a place where people are promoted according to their actual value to the employer, then affirmative action may be needed to make the workplace a meritocracy. (The business pages are full of tales of male primates who follow their impulses to no good corporate end. How much money did Barry Diller waste trying vainly to outbid his old rival, Sumner Redstone, in the battle over—as it were—Paramount? A lot, but

maybe not as much as Redstone wasted by "winning.")

Evolutionary psychology suggests that if affirmative action for women is to rest on coherent logic, the subject of sex differences will have to come into play. Once again: if women want broad protection, they can most cogently seek it as women, not as persons.

The deepest source of the feminist aversion to Darwinism is larger and vaguer than specific policy issues. Evolutionary psychology seems to paint a generally grim view of the "natural" order. Some of the ugliest things about the word—the very things that stirred modern feminist indignation to begin with—have biological roots. These include the male "patriarchy" that the radicals see everywhere they look, and men's attempts to control the sexuality of women. Even the classically reviled male hypocrisy over promiscuity—the "double standard"—appears to be a legacy of natural selection. Men not only are naturally inclined to cheat on their mates; men are also inclined to abhor, and thus fiercely condemn, the philandering of a mate. Women share both inclinations, but they aren't as strong as the male versions. Indeed, a woman may actually reinforce the double standard when she finds herself able to forgive a husband's sexual infidelity in order to head off what for her female ancestors was a much bigger threat—a male's desertion, his withdrawal of resources.

None of this is great news for feminism (or, really, for humankind). But it isn't *quite* as bad as it seems. By getting clear on what the word "natural" does and doesn't mean, we can isolate the parts of evolutionary psychology that should most worry feminists.

To infer that what's "natural" is morally "good" is an elementary logical error, famously labeled the "naturalistic fallacy" by the turn-of-the-century British ethicist G. E. Moore. Indeed, I would go further, Darwinism not only doesn't tell us that the double standard is morally right; it tells us that any intuitive sense men have of its rightness is untrustworthy. This sense is a mere vestige of natural selection, morally arbitrary so far as we know. A central lesson of evolutionary psychology by my lights is that we should cast a wary eye on our moral intuitions generally (including, for example, the sense that retribution is just); they are a voice not from God but from our genes, echoes of our amoral creator, natural selection. What's natural may or may not be good, but it's certainly not good *by virtue of the fact* that it's natural.

Another thing "natural" doesn't mean is unchangeable. There are cultures in which the "natural" male impulse to control female sexuality is expressed as ritual genital mutilation. There are cultures, like ours, in which men don't do such things. And there is no reason to think we've reached the biological limit of male malleability. Evolutionary psychologists aren't genetic determinists, and they aren't "biological determinists" except in a sense so broad as to encompass both genes and culture.

So much for the good news. The bad news is (a) The average beer-drinking, two-timing, wife-beating lout isn't going to change his moral views after being handed a copy of G. E. Moore's *Principia Ethica.* He is more likely to conveniently see modern Darwinism as a divine embrace of his loutishness, and (b) People, though malleable, aren't simply and infinitely malleable. They aren't malleable enough to make communism a productive economic system, and they aren't malleable enough to create a society of perfect behavioral symmetry between men and women. Some changes simply can't be made, and others will come only at some cost.

Here is where the word "natural" assumes a second import that is not so easily dismissed as the first, and that feminists may find uncomfortable. Here we can expect men to turn the tables and use evolutionary psychology to talk about *their* vulnerabilities, to make *their* appeals for special treatment on grounds of peculiar biological predicament. Thus, for example, a man could urge for the double standard by saying (a) that his own philandering is hard to control, and (b) that he is more "vulnerable" than his wife to the pain of a mate's sexual infidelity.

Obviously, this is a self-serving argument. And it can be combated in two ways: by

pointing to the social costs of male infidelity (which, I would argue, are extremely high in the current social environment); and by noting that "hard to control" doesn't mean "impossible to control." Still, this argument, though combatable, isn't laughable in the way the naturalistic fallacy is. It uses our understanding of "natural" impulses not to justify them as being *right,* strictly speaking, but to excuse them by stressing the psychic costs of defying them. Feminists are right to dread some of the rhetorical resistance Darwinism will abet.

Men seeking to stress their victim status can also lay claim to being "objectified" much as women are. Feminists complain about women's beauty and youth counting for so much in the eyes of men. (And this male obsession, according to evolutionary psychologists, isn't merely a product of Madison Avenue.) But men could just as easily complain about being viewed as walking wallets— about the fact that women place so much value on the social status and/or wealth of a mate. (This emphasis, too, appears to be a legacy of evolution, a deep aesthetic impulse that lives on after its evolutionary logic has been broken by a modern world in which women can earn their own wealth and status.) One reason you don't hear more about this male grievance is that low-status men have trouble getting their grievances heard. They aren't a very prominent group.

In the end, Darwinism's proper place in moral discourse is not to aid simplistic assertions about some natural order that is supposedly good or supposedly inevitable, but, rather to inform arguments about the social costs and benefits of alternative norms in light of human nature, with heightened awareness of which groups the costs and benefits fall on. The issue of what's "natural" will enter the debate, but by itself should confer no justification for anything.

Feminists' fear of the word "natural," and their attendant reluctance to confront sex differences, has left open a gaping intellectual niche. Perhaps it is poetic justice that the void is being semi-occupied by the scourge of name-brand feminism, the dreaded Camille Paglia. At least, Paglia professes to be a Darwinian; she talks about "instinctual drives" and says primal things like "sex crime means back to nature." Still, she has no evident grasp of evolutionary theory and prefers free-form literary explanation. For example, when men kill mates or ex-mates, it is usually out of jealousy, and many evolutionary psychologists would call this an extreme, pathological expression of a "natural" impulse to punish a woman for real or suspected infidelity. But Paglia has a different explanation: "Men who kill the women they love have reverted to pagan cult. She whom a man cannot live without has become a goddess, an avatar of his half-divinized, half-demonized mother, a magic fountain of cosmic creativity." Thanks for clearing that up.

For all her impressionistic excess, Paglia does tell a few simple, crude truths about sex differences, and this is one reason she's gotten where she is today (the other being the impressionistic excess). If name-brand feminists don't like the moral spin she puts on her comic-book Darwinism, there's one solution: to learn real Darwinism and put their own moral spin on it. It is certainly spinnable; like all theories of human behavior, evolutionary psychology has no inherent moral upshot. It merely limits the range of realistic moral and political discourse. Within the arena thus defined, interest groups will contest, each trying to shape the moral and legal codes to its ends. And the groups that aren't in the arena will lose.

In retrospect, much of the recent history of feminism might have been predicted with the help of evolutionary psychology. To begin with, the prime mover of modern feminism, the discontent of the 1950s suburban housewife, was entirely natural. To see this, you need only look at a hunter-gatherer society, which, being a rough approximation of the social context of human evolution, is a rough guide to the patterns of behavior "natural" to us, absent the influence of modern technological society. In hunter-gatherer societies, women have a career: gathering. This may

sound to an upper-middle-class feminist like menial labor; but it gets them out of the house. (And besides, menial compared to what—hunting?)

But women in such societies are also mothers, the primary caregivers. And reconciling their home and work lives is surprisingly practical. When they go out to gather food, child care is barely an issue; their children may go with them or, instead, stay with relatives. And when mothers, back from work, do care for children, the context is social, even communal. As the anthropologist Marjorie Shostak wrote after observing the !Kung San hunter-gatherers, "The isolated mother burdened with bored small children is not a scene that has parallels in !Kung daily life." Women weren't designed to be suburban housewives.

The generic suburban habitat of the '50s was more "natural," more congenial, for men. Like many hunter-gatherers, vintage suburban husbands spent a little time with children and a lot of time out bonding with males, in work, play or ritual. Thus the grievance that drove 1950s housewives toward feminism was solidly grounded: suburbia let men behave naturally while forcing mothers into artificial isolation—removed from their kin, often lacking close friends and devoid of purpose beyond child-rearing.

If this inequity is clear from a Darwinian vantage point, so is the reason that redressing it has been hard. It is no surprise that many working mothers feel not just harried by their dual identity but guilty about it—guilty about, say, spending forty hours a week away from a 1- or 2-year-old child while the child is in the hands of someone who is neither kin nor close friend. To judge by hunter-gatherer societies, this is quite an unnatural predicament. That doesn't mean women can't adapt to it. But anecdotal evidence suggests that they don't easily do so, and that some working mothers today aren't dramatically happier than the lonely suburban mothers of the 1950s.

This is one of the most pressing issues now facing women. Various partial solutions are possible, such as job-sharing and workplace-based child care. But if these are to be pursued vigorously *as feminist issues,* it would help to acknowledge that they are fundamentally the concerns of women; that, although men can certainly play a large role in childrearing, it's much easier for the average man than for the average woman to be away from young offspring—and that it always will be.

Many feminists will admit no such thing. The reason women have always been primary caregivers, Pollitt writes, has nothing in particular to do with their psychology. "Historically, women have taken care of children because high fertility and lack of other options left most of them no choice." Well, yes, that's been going on for a while—throughout human evolution, in fact. That's why any evolutionary psychologist finds it hard to believe that natural selection wouldn't have molded the female mind to this task. The task, after all, is pretty vital: protecting the vessel that carries the genes into the next generation.

Some consider the liberal equity feminists the most sober of the major schools of feminism, and Pollitt in particular has become known as the voice of calm reason. Yet she and the other mainstream liberals may have the most warped vision in all of feminism. Quite unlike the difference feminists, and more than the radical feminists, they are committed to ignoring basic features of reality. Imagine a social observer as acute as Pollitt not sensing how deeply—well, for lack of a better term—*maternal* women are compared with men. That must take a lot of perceptual restraint.

When Pollitt, under the pressure of overwhelming evidence, does concede some distinctive female feature, she seems disappointed, no matter how ostensibly laudable it is, and hastens to predict its demise. Thus she grants that "social scientists who look for it can find traces of empathy, caring and so on in some women who have risen in the world of work and power." But that's just because "we are in a transition period" and working women haven't yet learned the ropes. Thus, it seems, we can look forward to a day when working women will have been stripped of the last trace of empathy and caring. Then they'll be just like men. Congratulations.

The reductio ad absurdum of Pollitt's attitude has been performed by the feminist novelist Katherine Dunn. When she isn't celebrating the several women who have taken up boxing (equal opportunity brain damage!) Dunn spends her time trying to dispel some of the fuss about wife-beating. In both [*The New Republic*] and *Mother Jones,* she has touted some study that found that women strike their husbands about as often as men strike their wives. Well, maybe so (though probably not). But getting hit is not the essence of being an abused spouse. Chronic intimidation is. How many husbands live in fear of assault by their wives? How many husbands, while out with their wives, desperately avoid eye contact with the opposite sex lest they be beaten upon returning to their cage? That major liberal magazines are publishing articles whose predictable effect is to downplay the plight of battered wives is a sure sign that equity feminism's denial of harsh Darwinian truths is reaching pathological extremes.

To be sure, neither the difference feminists nor the radical feminists come close to getting the whole picture. The difference feminists often stress ways women are good, and the radical feminists always stress ways men are bad; both tend to ignore female badness and male goodness. Also, of course, both schools deny any important role for biology. Still, at least the larger project of the radical feminists and, especially, of the difference feminists, is quietly eroding that denial; the fit between Darwinian theory and the social reality they're documenting is too neat to go unnoticed. That these feminists are emphatically not Darwinians makes their database even more valuable as objective corroboration.

The radical feminists' penetrating perception of social reality, paired with delusion about its deepest roots, is reminiscent of Marxism. Though Marx fooled himself about human nature, his view of the way the upper classes exploit their power, manipulating ideology to the detriment of the less fortunate, is acute (and, actually, quite Darwinian), much like the radical feminists' keen attention to the levers of male sexual power. (Though the radical feminists tend to ignore the often subtler means by which women use their sexuality to control men.) And the parallels don't end there. Like the Marxists, the radical feminists are marginalizing themselves by the hyperbole of their indictment and by their dreams of a perfect post-revolution world. They depict an enemy of overwhelming force and envision its unconditional surrender.

With both Marxism and feminism, the struggle against the forces of oppression is worthy and, up to a point, practical. But in both cases, the struggle is best conducted with thorough comprehension of those forces and of their bases in human nature. If feminists— of all stripes—want to know their enemy, it is now available for inspection.

REVIEW AND DISCUSSION QUESTIONS

1. Why does Wright compare many contemporary feminists with communists?
2. How do biologists explain the relatively greater sexual reserve of females?
3. Why do men distinguish between "fast" and "slow" women, according to Wright?
4. Describe Wright's position on sexual harassment, and why he thinks the Supreme Court's approach is mistaken.
5. In what ways does Darwinian theory agree and disagree with the Dworkin-MacKinnon view of men?
6. Why does Wright think affirmative action for women is incompatible with biology?
7. Does Wright agree that what is "natural" is also "morally good"? Explain.
8. How can evolutionary theory explain the emergence of feminism out of the 1950s, according to Wright?
9. How might "dominance" feminists respond to this essay? Which view seems most reasonable to you? Explain.

On Racism and Sexism: Realities and Ideals

Richard A. Wasserstrom

Richard A. Wasserstrom discusses two important problems. One is the degree to which modern social realities continue to reflect racism and sexism. The second concerns the ideal: How would a decent society treat race and sex? Thus, Wasserstrom first describes important features of modern society having to do with racism and sexism, including its institutions, practices, and attitudes. Turning to questions about ideals, Wasserstrom distinguishes the assimilationist ideal from those of diversity and tolerance, and then defends the ideal of assimilation, that is, the view that race and sex should have no more institutional significance than eye color. Richard A. Wasserstrom is professor of philosophy at the University of California at Santa Cruz.

From Parts I and II of Richard A. Wasserstrom, "Racism, Sexism, and Preferential Treatment: An Approach to the Topics," *UCLA Law Review,* 24 (1977), 581–622. © 1977 by Richard A. Wasserstrom. Some footnotes have been deleted and the remaining ones renumbered. Reprinted by permission of the author.

INTRODUCTION

Racism and sexism are two central issues that engage the attention of many persons living within the United States today. But while there is relatively little disagreement about their importance as topics, there is substantial, vehement, and apparently intractable disagreement about what individuals, practices, ideas, and institutions are either racist or sexist—and for what reasons. In dispute are a number of related questions concerning how individuals ought to regard and respond to matters relating to race or sex. . . .

What I want to do in this essay is first propose a general way of looking at issues of racism and sexism, then look at several of the respects in which racism and sexism are alike and different, and then, finally, examine one somewhat neglected but fundamental issue; namely that of what a genuinely nonracist or nonsexist society might look like. . . .

1. SOCIAL REALITIES

A. The Position of Blacks and Women

Methodologically, the first thing it is important to note is that to talk about social realities is to talk about a particular social and cultural context. And in our particular social and cultural context race and sex are socially very important categories. They are so in virtue of the fact that we live in a culture which has, throughout its existence, made race and sex extremely important characteristics of and for all the people living in the culture.

It is surely possible to imagine a culture in which race would be an unimportant, insignificant characteristic of individuals. In such a culture race would be largely if not exclusively a matter of superficial physiology; a matter, we might say, simply of the way one looked. And if it were, then any analysis of race and racism would necessarily assume very different dimensions from what they do in our society. In such a culture, the meaning of the term "race" would itself have to change

substantially. This can be seen by the fact that in such a culture it would literally make no sense to say of a person that he or she was "passing."[1] This is something that can be said and understood in our own culture and it shows at least that to talk of race is to talk of more than the way one looks.[2]

Sometimes when people talk about what is wrong with affirmative action programs, or programs of preferential hiring, they say that what is wrong with such programs is that they take a thing as superficial as an individual's race and turn it into something important. They say that a person's race doesn't matter; other things do, such as qualifications. Whatever else may be said of statements such as these, as descriptions of the social realities they seem to be simply false. One complex but true empirical fact about our society is that the race of an individual is much more than a fact of superficial physiology. It is, instead, one of the dominant characteristics that affects both the way the individual looks at the world and the way the world looks at the individual. As I have said, that need not be the case. It may in fact be very important that we work toward a society in which that would not be the case, but it is the case now and it must be understood in any adequate and complete discussion of racism. That is why, too, it does not make much sense when people sometimes say, in talking about the fact that they are not racists, that they would not care if an individual were green and came from Mars, they would treat that individual the same way they treat people exactly like themselves. For part of our social and cultural history is to treat people of certain races in a certain way, and we do not have a social or cultural history of treating green people from Mars in any particular way. To put it simply, it is to misunderstand the social realities of race and racism to think of them simply as questions of how some people respond to other people whose skins are of different hues, irrespective of the social context.

I can put the point another way: Race does not function in our culture as does eye color. Eye color is an irrelevant category; nobody cares what color people's eyes are; it is not an important cultural fact; nothing turns on what eye color you have. It is important to see that race is not like that at all. And this truth affects what will and will not count as cases of racism. In our culture to be nonwhite—especially to be black—is to be treated and seen to be a member of a group that is different from and inferior to the group of standard, fully developed persons, the adult white males. To be black is to be a member of what was a despised minority and what is still a disliked and oppressed one. That is simply part of the awful truth of our cultural and social history, and a significant feature of the social reality of our culture today.

We can see fairly easily that the two sexual categories, like the racial ones, are themselves in important respects products of the society. Like one's race, one's sex is not merely or even primarily a matter of physiology. To see this we need only realize that we can understand the idea of a transsexual. A transsexual is someone who would describe himself or herself as a person who is essentially a female but through some accident of nature is trapped in a male body, or a person who is essentially a male but through some accident of nature is trapped in the body of a female. His (or her) description is some kind of a shorthand way of saying that he (or she) is more comfortable with the role allocated by the culture to people who are physiologically of the opposite sex. The fact that we regard this assertion of the transsexual as intelligible seems to me to show how deep the notion of sexual identity is in our culture and how little it has to do with physiological differences between males and females. Because people do pass in the context of race and because we can understand what passing means; because people are transsexuals and because we can understand what transsexuality means, we can see that the existing social categories of both race and sex are in this sense creations of the culture.

It is even clearer in the case of sex than in the case of race that one's sexual identity is a centrally important, crucially relevant category within our culture. I think, in fact, that it is more important and more fundamental than one's race. It is evident that there are substantially different role expectations and role assignments to persons in accordance with their sexual physiology, and that the positions of the two sexes in the culture are distinct. We do have a patriarchal society in which it matters enormously whether one is a male or a female. By almost all important measures it is more advantageous to be a male rather than a female. . . .

As is true for race, it is also a significant social fact that to be a female is to be an entity or creature viewed as different from the standard, fully developed person who is male as well as white. But to be female, as opposed to being black, is not to be conceived of as simply a creature of less worth. That is one important thing that differentiates sexism from racism: The ideology of sex, as opposed to the ideology of race, is a good deal more complex and confusing. Women are both put on a pedestal and deemed not fully developed persons. They are idealized; their approval and admiration is sought; and they are at the same time regarded as less competent than men and less able to live fully developed, fully human lives—for that is what men do. At best, they are viewed and treated as having properties and attributes that are valuable and admirable for humans of this type. For example, they may be viewed as especially empathetic, intuitive, loving, and nurturing. At best, these qualities are viewed as good properties for women to have, and, provided they are properly muted, are sometimes valued within the more well-rounded male. Because the sexual ideology is complex, confusing, and variable, it does not unambiguously proclaim the lesser value attached to being female rather than being male, nor does it unambiguously correspond to the existing social realities. For these, among other reasons, sexism could plausibly be regarded as a deeper phenomenon than racism. It is more deeply embedded in the culture, and thus less visible. . . .

Viewed from the perspective of social reality it should be clear, too, that racism and sexism should not be thought of as phenomena that consist simply in taking a person's race or sex into account, or even simply in taking a person's race or sex into account in an arbitrary way. Instead, racism and sexism consist in taking race and sex into account in a certain way, in the context of a specific set of institutional arrangements and a specific ideology which together create and maintain a specific system of institutions, role assignments, beliefs and attitudes. That system is one, and has been one, in which political, economic, and social power and advantage is concentrated in the hands of those who are white and male. . . .

Take, for instance, the most hideous of the practices, human slavery. The primary thing that was wrong with the institution was not that the particular individuals who were assigned the place of slaves were assigned there arbitrarily because the assignment was made in virtue of an irrelevant characteristic, i.e., their race. Rather, it seems to me clear that the primary thing that was and is wrong with slavery is the practice itself—the fact of some individuals being able to own other individuals and all that goes with that practice. It would not matter by what criterion individuals were assigned; human slavery would still be wrong. And the same can be said for many of the other discrete practices and institutions that comprised the system of racial discrimination even after human slavery was abolished. The practices were unjustifiable—they were oppressive—and they would have been so no matter how the assignment of victims had been made. What made it worse, still, was that the institutions and ideology all interlocked to create a system of human oppression whose effects on those living under it were as devastating as they were unjustifiable.

Some features of the system of sexual oppression are like this and others are different. For example, if it is true that women are socialized to play the role of servers of men and if they are in general assigned that position in the society, what is objectionable about that practice is the practice itself. It is not that

women are being arbitrarily or capriciously assigned the social role of server, but rather that such a role is at least *prima facie* unjustifiable as a role in a decent society. As a result, the assignment on any basis of individuals to such a role is objectionable.

The assignment of women to primary responsibility for child rearing and household maintenance may be different; it may be objectionable on grounds of unfairness of another sort. That is to say, if we assume that these are important but undesirable aspects of social existence—if we assume that they are, relatively speaking, unsatisfying and unfulfilling ways to spend one's time, then the objection is that women are unduly and unfairly allocated a disproportionate share of unpleasant, unrewarding work. Here the objection, if it is proper, is to the degree to which the necessary burden is placed to a greater degree than is fair on women, rather than shared equally by persons of both sexes. . . .

[T]he primary evil of the various schemes of racial segregation against blacks that the courts were being called upon to assess was not that such schemes were a capricious and irrational way of allocating public benefits and burdens. That might well be the primary wrong with racial segregation if we lived in a society very different from the one we have. The primary evil of these schemes was instead that they designedly and effectively marked off all black persons as degraded, dirty, less than fully developed persons who were unfit for full membership in the political, social, and moral community.

It is worth observing that the social reality of sexually segregated bathrooms appears to be different. The idea behind such sexual segregation seems to have more to do with the mutual undesirability of the use by both sexes of the same bathroom at the same time. There is no notion of the possibility of contamination; or even directly of inferiority and superiority. What seems to be involved—at least in part—is the importance of inculcating and preserving a sense of secrecy concerning the genitalia of the opposite sex. What seems to be at stake is the maintenance of that same sense of mystery or forbiddenness about the other sex's sexuality which is fostered by the general prohibition upon public nudity and the unashamed viewing of genitalia.

Sexually segregated bathrooms simply play a different role in our culture than did racially segregated ones. But that is not to say that the role they play is either benign or unobjectionable—only that it is different. Sexually segregated bathrooms may well be objectionable, but here too, the objection is not on the ground that they are *prima facie* capricious or arbitrary. Rather, the case against them now would rest on the ground that they are, perhaps, one small part of that scheme of sex-role differentiation which uses the mystery of sexual anatomy, among other things, to maintain the primacy of heterosexual sexual attraction central to that version of the patriarchal system of power relationships we have today.[3] Once again, whether sexually segregated bathrooms would be objectionable, because irrational, in the good society depends once again upon what the good society would look like in respect to sexual differentiation. . . .

B. Types of Racism or Sexism

Another recurring question that can profitably be examined within the perspective of social realities is whether the legal system is racist or sexist. Indeed, it seems to me essential that the social realities of the relationships and ideologies concerning race and sex be kept in mind whenever one is trying to assess claims that are made about the racism or sexism of important institutions such as the legal system. It is also of considerable importance in assessing such claims to understand that even within the perspective of social reality, racism or sexism can manifest itself, or be understood, in different ways. That these are both important points can be seen through a brief examination of the different, distinctive ways in which our own legal system might plausibly be understood to be racist. The mode of analysis I propose serves as well, I believe, for an analogous analysis of the sexism of the legal system,

although I do not undertake the latter analysis in this paper.

The first type of racism is the simplest and the least controversial. It is the case of overt racism, in which a law or a legal institution expressly takes into account the race of individuals in order to assign benefits and burdens in such a way as to bestow an unjustified benefit upon a member or members of the racially dominant group or an unjustified burden upon members of the racial groups that are oppressed. We no longer have many, if any, cases of overt racism in our legal system today, although we certainly had a number in the past. Indeed, the historical system of formal, racial segregation was both buttressed by, and constituted of, a number of overtly racist laws and practices. At different times in our history, racism included laws and practices which dealt with such things as the exclusion of nonwhites from the franchise, from decent primary and secondary schools and most professional schools, and the prohibition against interracial marriages.

The second type of racism is very similar to overt racism. It is covert, but intentional, racism, in which a law or a legal institution has as its purpose the allocation of benefits and burdens in order to support the power of the dominant race, but does not use race specifically as a basis for allocating these benefits and burdens. One particularly good historical example involves the use of grandfather clauses which were inserted in statutes governing voter registration in a number of states after passage of the fifteenth amendment.

Covert racism within the law is not entirely a thing of the past. Many instances of de facto school segregation in the North and West are cases of covert racism. At times certain school boards—virtually all of which are overwhelmingly white in composition—quite consciously try to maintain exclusively or predominantly white schools within a school district. . . .

I believe it is a mistake to think about the problem of racism in terms of overt or covert racial discrimination by state action, which is now banished, and racial prejudice, which still lingers, but only in the hearts of persons. For there is another, more subtle kind of racism—unintentional, perhaps, but effective—which is as much a part of the legal system as are overt and covert racist laws and practices. It is what some critics of the legal system probably mean when they talk about the "institutional racism" of the legal system.

There are at least two kinds of institutional racism. The first is the racism of sub-institutions within the legal system such as the jury, or the racism of practices built upon or countenanced by the law. These institutions and practices very often, if not always, reflect in important and serious ways a variety of dominant values in the operation of what is apparently a neutral legal mechanism. The result is the maintenance and reinforcement of a system in which whites dominate over non-whites. One relatively uninteresting (because familiar) example is the case of de facto school segregation. As observed above, some cases of de facto segregation are examples of covert racism. But even in school districts where there is no intention to divide pupils on grounds of race so as to maintain existing power relationships along racial lines, school attendance zones are utilized which are based on the geographical location of the pupil. Because it is a fact in our culture that there is racial discrimination against black people in respect to housing, it is also a fact that any geographical allocation of pupils—unless one pays a lot of attention to housing patterns—will have the effect of continuing to segregate minority pupils very largely on grounds of race. It is perfectly appropriate to regard this effect as a case of racism in public education. . . .

The second type of institutional racism is what I will call "conceptual" institutional racism. . . .

We use concepts. Quite often without realizing it, the concepts used take for granted certain objectionable aspects of racist ideology without our being aware of it. The second *Brown* case (*Brown II*) provides an example.[4] There was a second *Brown* case because, having decided that the existing system of racially segregated public education was

unconstitutional (*Brown I*),[5] the Supreme Court gave legitimacy to a second issue—the nature of the relief to be granted—by treating it as a distinct question to be considered and decided separately. That in itself was striking because in most cases, once the Supreme Court has found unconstitutionality, there has been no problem about relief (apart from questions of retroactivity): The unconstitutional practices and acts are to cease. As is well known, the Court in *Brown II* concluded that the desegregation of public education had to proceed "with all deliberate speed."[6] The Court said that there were "complexities arising from the transition to a system of public education freed from racial discrimination."[7] More specifically, time might be necessary to carry out the ruling because of

> problems related to administration, arising from the physical condition of the school plant, the school transportation system personnel, revision of school districts and attendance areas into compact units to achieve a system of determining admission to the public school on a nonracial basis, and revision of local laws and regulations which may be necessary in solving the foregoing problems.[8]

Now, I do not know whether the Court believed what it said in this passage, but it is a fantastic bit of nonsense that is, for my purposes, most instructive. Why? Because there was nothing complicated about most of the dual school systems of the southern states. . . . There was nothing difficult about deciding that—as of the day after the decision—half of the children in the county, say all those who lived in the southern part of the county, would go to "Robert E. Lee High School," and all those who lived in the northern half would go to "Booker T. Washington High School." *Brown I* could have been implemented the day after the Court reached its decision. But it was also true that the black schools throughout the South were utterly wretched when compared to the white schools. There never had been any system of separate but equal education. In almost every measurable respect, the black schools were inferior. One possibility is that, without being explicitly aware of it, the members of the Supreme Court made use of some assumptions that were a significant feature of the dominant racist ideology. If the assumptions had been made explicit, the reasoning would have gone something like this: Those black schools are wretched. We cannot order white children to go to those schools, especially when they have gone to better schools in the past. So while it is unfair to deprive blacks, to make them go to these awful, segregated schools, they will have to wait until the black schools either are eliminated or are sufficiently improved so that there are good schools for everybody to attend.

What seems to me to be most objectionable, and racist, about *Brown II* is the uncritical acceptance of the idea that during this process of change, black schoolchildren would have to suffer by continuing to attend inadequate schools. The Supreme Court's solution assumed that the correct way to deal with this problem was to continue to have the black children go to their schools until the black schools were brought up to par or eliminated. That is a kind of conceptual racism in which the legal system accepts the dominant racist ideology, which holds that the claims of black children are worth less than the claims of white children in those cases in which conflict is inevitable. It seems to me that any minimally fair solution would have required that during the interim process, if anybody had to go to an inadequate school, it would have been the white children, since they were the ones who had previously had the benefit of the good schools. But this is simply not the way racial matters are thought about within the dominant ideology.

A study of *Brown II* is instructive because it is a good illustration of conceptual racism within the legal system. It also reflects another kind of conceptual racism—conceptual racism about the system. . . . [T]he fact that we have, as well as inculcate, attitudes of effusive praise toward *Brown I* and *II* and its progeny reveals a kind of persistent conceptual racism in talk about the character of the legal system, and what constitutes the right way to have dealt with the social reality of American racial oppression of black people.

2. IDEALS

The second perspective . . . which is also important for an understanding and analysis of racism and sexism, is the perspective of the ideal. Just as we can and must ask what is involved today in our culture in being of one race or of one sex rather than the other, and how individuals are in fact viewed and treated, we can also ask different questions: namely, what would the good or just society make of race and sex, and to what degree, if at all, would racial and sexual distinctions ever be taken into account? Indeed, it could plausibly be argued that we could not have an adequate idea of whether a society was racist or sexist unless we had some conception of what a thoroughly nonracist or nonsexist society would look like. This perspective is an extremely instructive as well as an often neglected one. Comparatively little theoretical literature that deals with either racism or sexism has concerned itself in a systematic way with this perspective.

In order to ask more precisely what some of the possible ideals are of desirable racial or sexual differentiation, it is necessary to see that we must ask: "In respect to what?" And one way to do this is to distinguish in a crude way among three levels or areas of social and political arrangements and ctivities. . . . First, there is the area of basic political rights and obligations, including the rights to vote and to travel, and the obligation to pay income taxes. Second, there is the area of important, nongovernmental institutional benefits and burdens. Examples are access to and employment in the significant economic markets, the opportunity to acquire and enjoy housing in the setting of one's choice, the right of persons who want to marry each other to do so, and the duties (nonlegal as well as legal) that persons acquire in getting married. And third, there is the area of individual, social interaction, including such matters as whom one will have as friends, and what aesthetic preferences one will cultivate and enjoy.

As to each of these three areas we can ask, for example, whether in a nonracist society it would be thought appropriate ever to take the race of the individuals into account. Thus, one picture of a nonracist society is that which is captured by what I call the assimilationist ideal: a nonracist society would be one in which the race of an individual would be the functional equivalent of the eye color of individuals in our society today.[9] In our society no basic political rights and obligations are determined on the basis of eye color. No important institutional benefits and burdens are connected with eye color. Indeed, except for the mildest sort of aesthetic preferences, a person would be thought odd who even made private, social decisions by taking eye color into account. And for reasons that we could fairly readily state we could explain why it would be wrong to permit anything but the mildest, most trivial aesthetic preference to turn on eye color. The reasons would concern the irrelevance of eye color for any political or social institution, practice or arrangement. According to the assimilationist ideal, a nonracist society would be one in which an individual's race was of no more significance in any of these three areas than is eye color today.

The assimilationist ideal in respect to sex does not seem to be as readily plausible and obviously attractive here as it is in the case of race. In fact, many persons invoke the possible realization of the assimilationist ideal as a reason for rejecting the Equal Rights Amendment and indeed the idea of women's liberation itself. My own view is that the assimilationist ideal may be just as good and just as important an ideal in respect to sex as it is in respect to race. But many persons think there are good reasons why an assimilationist society in respect to sex would not be desirable.

To be sure, to make the assimilationist ideal a reality in respect to sex would involve more profound and fundamental revisions of our institutions and our attitudes than would be the case in respect to race. On the institutional level we would have to alter radically our practices concerning the family and marriage. If a nonsexist society is a society in which one's sex is no more significant than eye color in our society today, then laws that require the persons who are getting married to be of different sexes would clearly be sexist laws.

And on the attitudinal and conceptual level, the assimilationist ideal would require the eradication of all sex-role differentiation. It would never teach about the inevitable or essential attributes of masculinity or femininity; it would never encourage or discourage the ideas of sisterhood or brotherhood; and it would be unintelligible to talk about the virtues as well as disabilities of being a woman or a man. Were sex like eye color, these things would make no sense. Just as the normal, typical adult is virtually oblivious to the eye color of other persons for all major interpersonal relationships, so the normal, typical adult in this kind of nonsexist society would be indifferent to the sexual, physiological differences of other persons for all interpersonal relationships.

To acknowledge that things would be very different is, of course, hardly to concede that they would be undesirable. But still, perhaps the problem is with the assimilationist ideal. And the assimilationist ideal is certainly not the only possible, plausible ideal.

There are, for instance, two others that are closely related, but distinguishable. One I call the ideal of diversity; the other, the ideal of tolerance. Both can be understood by considering how religion, rather than eye color, tends to be thought about in our culture. According to the ideal of diversity, heterodoxy in respect to religious belief and practice is regarded as a positive good. On this view there would be a loss—it would be a worse society—were everyone to be a member of the same religion. According to the other view, the ideal of tolerance, heterodoxy in respect to religious belief and practice would be seen more as a necessary, lesser evil. On this view there is nothing intrinsically better about diversity in respect to religion, but the evils of achieving anything like homogeneity far outweigh the possible benefits.

Now, whatever differences there might be between the ideals of diversity and tolerance, the similarities are more striking. Under neither ideal would it be thought that the allocation of basic political rights and duties should take an individual's religion into account. And we would want equalitarianism even in respect to most important institutional benefits and burdens—for example, access to employment in the desirable vocations. Nonetheless, on both views it would be deemed appropriate to have some institutions (typically those that are connected in an intimate way with these religions) that do in a variety of ways take the religion of members of the society into account. For example, it might be thought permissible and appropriate for members of a religious group to join together in collective associations which have religious, educational and social dimensions. And on the individual, interpersonal level, it might be thought unobjectionable, or on the diversity view, even admirable, were persons to select their associates, friends, and mates on the basis of their religious orientation. So there are two possible and plausible ideals of what the good society would look like in respect to religion in which religious differences would be to some degree maintained because the diversity of religions was seen either as an admirable, valuable feature of the society, or as one to be tolerated. The picture is a more complex, less easily describable one than that of the assimilationist ideal.

It may be that in respect to sex (and conceivably, even in respect to race) something more like either of these ideals in respect to religion is the right one. But one problem then—and it is a very substantial one—is to specify with a good deal of precision and care what that ideal really comes to. Which legal, institutional and personal differentiations are permissible and which are not? Which attitudes and beliefs concerning sexual identification and difference are properly introduced and maintained and which are not? Part, but by no means all, of the attractiveness of the assimilationist ideal is its clarity and simplicity. In the good society of the assimilationist sort we would be able to tell easily and unequivocally whether any law, practice, or attitude was in any respect either racist or sexist. Part, but by no means all, of the unattractiveness of any pluralistic ideal is that it makes the question of what is racist or sexist a much more difficult and complicated one to answer. But although simplicity and lack of ambiguity may be virtues, they are not the only virtues to be taken into account in deciding among competing ideals. We quite appropriately take other considerations to be relevant to an assessment of the value and worth of alternative nonracist and nonsexist societies.

Nor do I even mean to suggest that all persons who reject the assimilationist ideal in respect to sex would necessarily embrace either something like the ideal of tolerance or the ideal of diversity. Some persons might think the right ideal was one in which substantially greater sexual differentiation and sex-role identification was retained than would be the case under either of these conceptions. Thus, someone might believe that the good society was, perhaps, essentially like the one they think we now have in respect to sex: equality of political rights, such as the right to vote, but all of the sexual differentiation in both legal and nonlegal institutions that is characteristic of the way in which our society has been and still is ordered. And someone might also believe that the usual ideological justifications for these arrangements are the correct and appropriate ones. . . .

The next question, of course, is that of how a choice is rationally to be made among these different, possible ideals. One place to begin is with the empirical world. For the question of whether something is a plausible and attractive ideal does turn in part on the nature of the empirical world. If it is true, for example, that any particular characteristic, such as sex, is not only a socially significant category in our culture but that it is largely a socially created one as well, then many ostensible objections to the assimilationist ideal appear immediately to disappear.

What I mean is this: It is obvious that we could formulate and use some sort of a crude, incredibly imprecise physiological concept of race. In this sense we could even say that race is a naturally occurring rather than a socially created feature of the world. There are diverse skin colors and related physiological characteristics distributed among human beings. But the fact is that except for skin hue and the related physiological characteristics, race is a socially created category. And skin hue, as I have shown, is neither a necessary nor a sufficient condition for being classified as black in our culture. Race as a naturally occurring characteristic is also a socially irrelevant category. There do not in fact appear to be any characteristics that are part of this natural concept of race and that are in any plausible way even relevant to the appropriate distribution of any political, institutional, or interpersonal concerns in the good society. Because in this sense race is like eye color, there is no plausible case to be made on this ground against the assimilationist ideal.[10]

There is, of course, the social reality of race. In creating and tolerating a society in which race matters, we must recognize that we have created a vastly more complex concept of race which includes what might be called the idea of ethnicity as well—a set of attitudes, traditions, beliefs, etc., which the society has made part of what it means to be of a race. It may be, therefore, that one could argue that a form of the pluralist ideal ought to be preserved in respect to race, in the socially created sense, for reasons similar to those that might be offered in support of the desirability of some version of the pluralist ideal in respect to religion. As I have indicated, I am skeptical, but for the purposes of this essay it can well be left an open question.

Despite appearances, the case of sex is more like that of race than is often thought.

What opponents of assimilationism seize upon is that sexual difference appears to be a naturally occurring category of obvious and inevitable social relevance in a way, or to a degree, which race is not. The problems with this way of thinking are twofold. To begin with, an analysis of the social realities reveals that it is the socially created sexual differences which tend in fact to matter the most. It is sex-role differentiation, not gender per se, that makes men and women as different as they are from each other, and it is sex-role differences which are invoked to justify most sexual differentiation at any of the levels of society.[11]

More importantly, even if naturally occurring sexual differences were of such a nature that they were of obvious *prima facie* social relevance, this would by no means settle the question of whether in the good society sex should or should not be as minimally significant as eye color. Even though there are biological differences between men and women in nature, this fact does not determine the question of what the good society can and should make of these differences. . . . For there appear to be very few, if any, respects in which the ineradicable, naturally occurring differences between males and females must be taken into account. The industrial revolution has certainly made any of the general differences in strength between the sexes capable of being ignored by the good society in virtually all activities. And it is sex-role acculturation, not biology, that mistakenly leads many persons to the view that women are both naturally and necessarily better suited than men to be assigned the primary responsibilities of child rearing. Indeed, the only fact that seems required to be taken into account is the fact that reproduction of the human species requires that the fetus develop *in utero* for a period of months. Sexual intercourse is not necessary, for artificial insemination is available. Neither marriage nor the family is required for conception or child rearing. Given the present state of medical knowledge and the natural realities of female pregnancy, it is difficult to see why any important institutional or interpersonal arrangements *must* take the existing gender difference of *in utero* pregnancy into account. . . .

There is, however, at least one more argument based upon nature, or at least the "natural," that is worth mentioning. Someone might argue that significant sex-role differentiation is natural not in the sense that it is biologically determined but only in the sense that it is a virtually universal phenomenon in human culture. By itself, this claim of virtual universality, even if accurate, does not directly establish anything about the desirability or undesirability of any particular ideal. But it can be made into an argument by the addition of the proposition that where there is a virtually universal social practice, there is probably some good or important purpose served by the practice. . . . The straightforward way to think about that . . . is to ask what would be good and what would be bad about a society in which sex functioned like eye color does in our society. We can imagine what such a society would look like and how it would work. It is hard to see how our thinking is substantially advanced by reference to what has typically or always been the case.

If it is true, as I think it is, that the sex-role differentiated societies we have had so far have tended to concentrate power in the hands of males, have developed institutions and ideologies that have perpetuated that concentration and have restricted and prevented women from living the kinds of lives that persons ought to be able to live for themselves, then this says far more about what may be wrong with any nonassimilationist ideal than does the conservative premise say what may be right about any nonassimilationist ideal.

Nor is this all that can be said in favor of the assimilationist ideal. For it seems to me that the strongest affirmative moral argument on its behalf is that it provides for a kind of individual autonomy that a nonassimilationist society cannot attain. Any nonassimilationist society will have sex roles. Any nonassimilationist society will have some institutions that distinguish between individuals by virtue of their gender, and any such society will necessarily teach the desirability of doing so. Any substantially nonassimilationist society will make one's sexual identity an important characteristic, so that there are substantial psychological, role, and status differences between persons who are males and those who are females. Even if these could be attained without systemic dominance of one sex over the other, they would, I think, be objectionable on the ground that they necessarily impaired an individual's ability to develop his or her own characteristics, talents and capacities to the fullest extent to which he or she might desire. Sex roles, and all that accompany them, necessarily impose limits—restrictions on what one can do, be or become. As such, they are, I think at least *prima facie* wrong.

To some degree, all role-differentiated living is restrictive in this sense. Perhaps, therefore, all role-differentiation in society is to some degree troublesome, and perhaps all strongly role-differentiated societies are objectionable. . . .

I do not believe that all I have said in this section shows in any conclusive fashion the desirability of the assimilationist ideal in respect to sex. I have tried to show why some typical arguments against the assimilationist ideal are not persuasive, and why some of the central ones in support of that ideal are persuasive. But I have not provided a complete account, or a complete analysis. At a minimum, what I have shown is how thinking about this topic ought to proceed, and what kinds of arguments need to be marshalled and considered before a serious and informed discussion of alternative conceptions of a non-sexist society can even take place. Once assembled, these arguments need to be individually and carefully assessed before any final, reflective choice among the competing ideals can be made. There does, however, seem to me to be a strong presumptive case for something very close to, if not identical with, the assimilationist ideal.

NOTES

1. Passing is the phenomenon in which a person who in some sense knows himself or herself to be black "passes" as white because he or she looks white. A version of this is described in Sinclair Lewis' novel *Kingsblood Royal* (1947), where the protagonist discovers when he is an adult that he, his father, and his father's mother are black (or, in the idiom of the late 1940's, Negro) in virtue of the fact that his great grandfather was black. His grandmother knew this and was consciously passing. When he learns about his ancestry, one decision he has to make is whether to continue to pass, or to acknowledge to the world that he is in fact "Negro."

2. That looking black is not in our culture a necessary condition for being black can be seen from the phenomenon of passing. That it is not a sufficient condition can be seen from the book *Black Like Me* (1960), by John Howard Griffin, where "looking black" is easily understood by the reader to be different from being black. I suspect that the concept of being black is, in our culture, one which combines both physiological and ancestral criteria in some moderately complex fashion.

3. This conjecture about the role of sexually segregated bathrooms may well be inaccurate or incomplete. The sexual segregation of bathrooms may have more to do with privacy than with patriarchy. However, if so, it is at least odd that what the institution makes relevant is sex rather than merely the ability to perform the eliminatory acts in private.

4. *Brown* v. *Board of Educ.*, 349 U.S. 294 (1955).

5. *Brown* v. *Board of Educ.*, 347 U.S. 483 (1954).

6. 349 U.S. at 301.

7. *Id.* at 299.

8. *Id.* at 300–01.

9. There is a danger in calling this ideal the "assimilationist" ideal. That term suggests the idea of incorporating oneself, one's values, and the like into the dominant group and its practices and values. I want to make it clear that no part of that idea is meant to be captured by my use of this term. Mine is a stipulative definition.

10. This is not to deny that certain people believe that race is linked with characteristics that *prima facie* are relevant. Such beliefs persist. They are, however, unjustified by the evidence. More to the point, even if it were true that such a linkage existed, none of the characteristics suggested would require that political or social institutions, or interpersonal relationships, would have to be structured in a certain way.

11. See, e.g., M. Mead, *Sex and Temperament in Three Primitive Societies* (1935): "These three situations [the cultures of the Anapesh, the Mundugumor, and the Tchambuli] suggest, then, a very definite conclusion. If those temperamental attitudes which we have traditionally regarded as feminine—such as passivity, responsiveness, and a willingness to cherish children—can so easily be set up as the masculine pattern in one tribe, and in another to be outlawed for the majority of women as well as for the majority of men, we no longer have any basis for regarding such aspects of behavior as sex-linked. . . . We are forced to conclude that human nature is almost unbelievably malleable, responding accurately and contrastingly to contrasting cultural conditions. . . . Standardized personality differences between the sexes are of this order, cultural creations to which each generation, male and female is trained to conform." *Id.* at 190–91. A somewhat different view is expressed in J. Sherman, *On the Psychology of Women* (1971). There, the author suggests that there are "natural" differences of a psychological sort between men and women, the chief ones being aggressiveness and strength of sex drive. See *Id.* at 238. However, even if she is correct as to these biologically based differences, this does little to establish what the good society should look like. Almost certainly the most complete discussion of this topic is E. Maccoby & C. Jacklin, *The Psychology of Sex Differences* (1974). The authors conclude that the sex differences which are, in their words, "fairly well established," are: (1) that girls have greater verbal ability than boys; (2) that boys excel in visual-spatial ability; (3) that boys excel in mathematical ability; and (4) that males are more aggressive. *Id.* at 351–52. They conclude, in respect to the etiology of these psychological sex differences, that there appears to be a biological component to the greater visual-spatial ability of males and to their greater aggressiveness. *Id.* at 360.

REVIEW AND DISCUSSION QUESTIONS

1. What point about race does Wasserstrom make in his discussion of "passing"?

2. How does Wasserstrom understand racism and sexism? What is their connection with social realities?

3. In what ways are racism and sexism similar? Different?

4. Describe the different types of racism and sexism Wasserstrom notes.

5. How do the Supreme Court's rulings in *Brown* v. *Board of Education* illustrate institutional racism, according to Wasserstrom?

6. Identify and explain briefly the three "ideals."

7. Why does Wasserstrom think the assimilationist ideal is preferable?

8. Assess the assimilationist ideal, indicating whether you agree that it is preferable to the other two. Is there another alternative that might be better? Explain.

9. In footnote 11 Wasserstrom discusses some of the evidence regarding biological differences between males and females. Compare his conclusions there with the position Robert Wright took in the previous reading.

10. Have events since 1977, when this essay was written, given us reason to question Wasserstrom's assessment of social realities? Explain.

Social Movements and the Politics of Difference

Iris Marion Young

In this essay, Iris Marion Young offers a wide-ranging and important discussion of the significance of group differences and personal identity to contemporary politics. Beginning with a critique of Wasserstrom's assimilationist ideal, she goes on to outline an alternative, "relational" ideal and defend the "politics of difference" as the best means to achieve genuine emancipation. Iris Marion Young is professor of political science at the University of Chicago.

In this chapter I criticize an ideal of justice that defines liberation as the transcendence of group difference, which I refer to as an ideal of assimilation. This ideal usually promotes equal treatment as a primary principle of justice. Recent social movements of oppressed groups challenge this ideal. *[Young earlier defined "oppression" as institutional processes that prevent people from developing "skills and capacities necessary for the good life" and "domination" as "constraints on self-determination."—Ed.]* Many in these movements argue that a positive self-definition of group difference is in fact more liberatory.

I endorse this politics of difference, and argue that at stake is the meaning of social difference itself. Traditional politics that excludes or devalues some persons on account of their group attributes assumes an essentialist meaning of difference; it defines groups as having different natures. An egalitarian politics of difference, on the other hand, defines difference more fluidly and relationally as the product of social processes.

An emancipatory politics that affirms group difference involves a reconception of the meaning of equality. The assimilationist ideal assumes that equal social status for all persons requires treating everyone according to the same principles, rules, and standards. A politics of difference argues, on the other hand, that equality as the participation and inclusion of all groups sometimes requires different treatment for oppressed or disadvantaged groups. To promote social justice, I argue, social policy should sometimes accord special treatment to groups. . . .

COMPETING PARADIGMS OF LIBERATION

In "On Racism and Sexism," Richard Wasserstrom develops a classic statement of the ideal of liberation from group-based oppression as involving the elimination of group-based difference itself. A truly nonracist, nonsexist society, he suggests, would be one in which the race or sex of an individual would be the functional equivalent of eye color in our society today. While physiological differences in skin color or genitals would remain, they would have no significance for a person's sense of identity or how others regard him or her. No political rights or obligations would be connected to race or sex, and no important institutional benefits would be associated with either. People would see no reason to consider race or gender in policy or everyday interactions. In such a society, social group differences would have ceased to exist.

Wasserstrom contrasts this ideal of assimilation with an ideal of diversity much like the one I will argue for, which he agrees is compelling. He offers three primary reasons, however, for choosing the assimilationist ideal of liberation over the ideal of diversity. First, the assimilationist ideal exposes the arbitrariness of group-based social distinctions which are thought natural and necessary. By imagining a society in which race and sex have no social significance, one sees more clearly how pervasively these group categories unnecessarily limit possibilities for some in existing society. Second, the assimilationist ideal presents a clear and unambiguous standard of equality and justice. According to such a standard, any group-related differentiation or discrimination is suspect. Whenever laws or rules, the division of labor, or other social practices allocate benefits differently according to group membership, this is a sign of injustice. The principle of justice is simple: treat everyone according to the same principles, rules, and standards. Third,

the assimilationist ideal maximizes choice. In a society where differences make no social difference people can develop themselves as individuals, unconstrained by group norms and expectations.

There is no question that the ideal of liberation as the elimination of group difference has been enormously important in the history of emancipatory politics. The ideal of universal humanity that denies natural differences has been a crucial historical development in the struggle against exclusion and status differentiation. It has made possible the assertion of the equal moral worth of all persons, and thus the right of all to participate and be included in all institutions and positions of power and privilege. The assimilationist ideal retains significant rhetorical power in the face of continued beliefs in the essentially different and inferior natures of women, Blacks, and other groups.

The power of this assimilationist ideal has inspired the struggle of oppressed groups and the supporters against the exclusion and denigration of these groups, and continues to inspire many. Periodically in American history, however, movements of the oppressed have questioned and rejected this "path to belonging." . . . Instead they have seen self-organization and the assertion of a positive group cultural identity as a better strategy for achieving power and participation in dominant institutions. Recent decades have witnessed a resurgence of this "politics of difference" not only among racial and ethnic groups, but also among women, gay men and lesbians, old people, and the disabled. . . .

None of the social movements asserting positive group specificity is in fact a unity. All have group differences within them. The Black movement, for example, includes middle-class Blacks and working-class Blacks, gays and straight people, men and women, and so it is with any other group. The implications of group differences within a social group have been most systematically discussed in the women's movement. Feminist conferences and publications have generated particularly fruitful, though often emotionally wrenching, discussions of the oppression of racial and ethnic blindness and importance of attending to group differences among women. . . . From such discussions emerged principled efforts to provide autonomously organized forums for Black women, Latinas, Jewish women, lesbians, differently abled women, old women, and any other women who see reason for claiming that they have as a group a distinctive voice that might be silenced in a general feminist discourse. Those discussions, along with the practices feminists instituted, structure discussion and interaction among differently identified groups of women and offer some beginning models for the development of a heterogeneous public. Each of the other social movements has also generated discussion of group differences that cut across their identities, leading to other possibilities of coalition and alliance.

EMANCIPATION THROUGH THE POLITICS OF DIFFERENCE

Implicit in emancipatory movements asserting a positive sense of group difference is a different ideal of liberation, which might be called democratic cultural pluralism. In this vision the good society does not eliminate or transcend group difference. Rather, there is equality among socially and culturally differentiated groups, who mutually respect one another and affirm one another in their differences. What are the reasons for rejecting the assimilationist ideal and promoting a politics of difference?

. . . Some deny the reality of social groups. For them, group difference is an invidious fiction produced and perpetuated in order to preserve the privilege of the few. Others, such as Wasserstrom, may agree that social groups do now exist and have real social consequences for the way people identify themselves and one another, but assert that such social group differences are undesirable. The assimilationist ideal involves denying either the reality or the desirability of social groups.

Those promoting a politics of difference doubt that a society without group differences is either possible or desirable. Contrary to the assumption of modernization theory, increased urbanization and the extension of equal formal rights to all groups has not led to a decline in particularist affiliations. If anything, the urban concentration and interactions among groups that modernizing social processes introduce tend to reinforce group solidarity and differentiation. Attachment to specific traditions, practices, languages, and other culturally specific forms is a crucial aspect of social existence. People do not usually give up their social group identifications, even when they are oppressed.

Whether eliminating social group difference is possible or desirable in the long run, however, is an academic issue. Today and for the foreseeable future societies are certainly structured by groups, and some are privileged while others are oppressed. New social movements of group specificity do not deny the official story's claim that the ideal of liberation as eliminating difference and treating everyone the same has brought significant improvement in the status of excluded groups. Its main quarrel is with the story's conclusion, namely, that since we have achieved formal equality, only vestiges and holdovers of differential privilege remain, which will die out with the continued persistent assertion of an ideal of social relations that make differences irrelevant to a person's life prospects. The achievement of formal equality does not eliminate social differences, and rhetorical commitment to the sameness of persons makes it impossible even to name how those differences presently structure privilege and oppression.

Though in many respects the law is now blind to group differences, some groups continue to be marked as deviant, as the Other. In everyday interactions, images, and decisions, assumptions about women, Blacks, Hispanics, gay men and lesbians, old people, and other marked groups continue to justify exclusion, avoidance, paternalism, and authoritarian treatment. Continued racist, sexist, homophobic, ageist, and ableist institutions and behavior create particular circumstances for these groups, usually disadvantaging them in their opportunity to develop their capacities. Finally, in part because they have been segregated from one another, and in part because they have particular histories and traditions, there are cultural differences among social groups —differences in language, style of living, body comportment and gestures, values, and perspectives on society.

Today in American society, as in many other societies, there is widespread agreement that no person should be excluded from political and economic activities because of ascribed characteristics. Group differences nevertheless continue to exist, and certain groups continue to be privileged. Under these circumstances, insisting that equality and liberation entail ignoring difference has oppressive consequences in three respects.

First, blindness to difference disadvantages groups whose experience, culture, and socialized capacities differ from those of privileged groups. The strategy of assimilation aims to bring formerly excluded groups into the mainstream. So assimilation always implies coming into the game after it is already begun, after the rules and standards have already been set, and having to prove oneself according to those rules and standards. In the assimilationist strategy, the privileged groups implicitly define the standards according to which all will be measured. Because their privilege involves not recognizing these standards as culturally and experientially specific, the ideal of a common humanity in which all can participate without regard to race, gender, religion, or sexuality poses as neutral and universal. The real differences between oppressed groups and the dominant norm, however, tend to put them at a disadvantage in measuring up to these standards, and for that reason assimilationist policies perpetuate their disadvantage. . . .

Second, the ideal of a universal humanity without social group differences allows privileged groups to ignore their own group specificity. Blindness to difference perpetuates cultural imperialism by allowing norms expressing the point of view and experience of privileged groups to appear neutral and universal.

The assimilationist ideal presumes that there is a humanity in general, an unsituated group-neutral human capacity for self-making that left to itself would make individuality flower, thus guaranteeing that each individual will be different. . . . Because there is no such unsituated group-neutral point of view, the situation and experience of dominant groups tend to define the norms of such a humanity in general. Against such a supposedly neutral humanist ideal, only the oppressed groups come to be marked with particularity; they, and not the privileged groups, are marked, objectified as the Others.

Thus, third, this denigration of groups that deviate from an allegedly neutral standard often produces an internalized devaluation by members of those groups themselves. When there is an ideal of general human standards according to which everyone should be evaluated equally, then Puerto Ricans or Chinese Americans are ashamed of their accents or their parents, Black children despise the female-dominated kith and kin networks of their neighborhoods, and feminists seek to root out their tendency to cry, or to feel compassion for a frustrated stranger. The aspiration to assimilate helps produce the self-loathing and double consciousness characteristic of oppression. The goal of assimilation holds up to people a demand that they "fit," be like the mainstream, in behavior, values, and goals. At the same time, as long as group differences exist, group members will be marked as different—as Black, Jewish, gay—and thus as unable simply to fit. When participation is taken to imply assimilation the oppressed person is caught in an irresolvable dilemma: to participate means to accept and adopt an identity one is not, and to try to participate means to be reminded by oneself and others of the identity one is.

A more subtle analysis of the assimilationist ideal might distinguish between a conformist and a transformational ideal of assimilation. In the conformist ideal, status quo institutions and norms are assumed as given, and disadvantaged groups who differ from those norms are expected to conform to

them. A transformational ideal of assimilation, on the other hand, recognizes that institutions as given express the interests and
perspective of the dominant groups.
Achieving assimilation therefore requires
altering many institutions and practices in
accordance with neutral rules that truly do
not disadvantage or stigmatize any person,
so that group membership really is irrelevant to
how persons are treated. Wasserstrom's ideal
fits a transformational assimilation, as does
the group-neutral ideal advocated by some
feminists (Taub and Williams, 1985). Unlike
the conformist assimilationist, the transformational assimilationist may allow that
group-specific policies, such as affirmative
action, are necessary and appropriate means
for transforming institutions to fit the assimilationist ideal. Whether conformist or transformational, however, the assimilationist
ideal still denies that group difference can be
positive and desirable; thus any form of the
ideal of assimilation constructs group difference as a liability or disadvantage.

Under these circumstances, a politics that
asserts the positivity of group difference is
liberating and empowering. In the act of
reclaiming the identity the dominant culture
has taught them to despise and affirming it
as an identity to celebrate, the oppressed
remove double consciousness. I am just what
they say I am—a Jewboy, a colored girl, a fag,
a dyke, or a hag—and proud of it. No longer
does one have the impossible project of trying
to become something one is not under circumstances where the very trying reminds
one of who one is. This politics asserts that
oppressed groups have distinct cultures, experiences, and perspectives on social life with
humanly positive meaning, some of which
may even be superior to the culture and perspectives of mainstream society. The rejection
and devaluation of one's culture and perspective should not be a condition of full participation in social life.

Asserting the value and specificity of the
culture and attributes of oppressed groups,
moreover, results in a relativizing of the dominant culture. When feminists assert the validity

of feminine sensitivity and the positive value of
nurturing behavior, when gays describe the
prejudice of heterosexuals as homophobic
and their own sexuality as positive and self-
developing, when Blacks affirm a distinct Afro-
American tradition, then the dominant culture
is forced to discover itself for the first time as
specific: as Anglo, European, Christian, masculine, straight. In a political struggle where
oppressed groups insist on the positive value
of their specific culture and experience, it
becomes increasingly difficult for dominant
groups to parade their norms as neutral and
universal, and to construct the values and
behavior of the oppressed as deviant, perverted, or inferior. By puncturing the univer-
salist claim to unity that expels some groups
and turns them into the Other, the assertion of
positive group specificity introduces the possibility of understanding the relation between
groups as merely difference, instead of exclusion, opposition, or dominance.

The politics of difference also promotes a
notion of group solidarity against the individualism of liberal humanism. Liberal humanism treats each person as an individual,
ignoring differences of race, sex, religion, and
ethnicity. Each person should be evaluated
only according to her or his individual efforts
and achievements. With the institutionaliza-
tion of formal equality some members of
formerly excluded groups have indeed succeeded, by mainstream standards. Structural
patterns of group privilege and oppression
nevertheless remain. When political leaders
of oppressed groups reject assimilation they
are often affirming group solidarity. Where
the dominant culture refuses to see anything
but the achievement of autonomous individuals, the oppressed assert that we shall not
separate from the people with whom we identify in order to "make it" in a white Anglo
male world. The politics of difference insists
on liberation of the whole group of Blacks,
women, American Indians, and that this can
be accomplished only through basic institutional changes. These changes must include
group representation in policymaking and an
elimination of the hierarchy of rewards that

forces everyone to compete for scarce positions at the top.

Thus the assertion of a positive sense of group difference provides a standpoint from which to criticize prevailing institutions and norms. Black Americans find in their traditional communities, which refer to their members as "brother" and "sister," a sense of solidarity absent from the calculating individualism of white professional capitalist society. Feminists find in the traditional female values of nurturing a challenge to a militarist worldview, and lesbians find in their relationships a confrontation with the assumption of complementary gender roles in sexual relationships. From their experience of a culture tied to the land American Indians formulate a critique of the instrumental rationality of European culture that results in pollution and ecological destruction. Having revealed the specificity of the dominant norms which claim universality and neutrality, social movements of the oppressed are in a position to inquire how the dominant institutions must be changed so that they will no longer reproduce the patterns of privilege and oppression.

From the assertion of positive difference the self-organization of oppressed groups follows. Both liberal humanist and leftist political organizations and movements have found it difficult to accept this principle of group autonomy. In a humanist emancipatory politics, if a group is subject to injustice, then all those interested in a just society should unite to combat the powers that perpetuate that injustice. If many groups are subject to injustice, moreover, then they should unite to work for a just society. The politics of difference is certainly not against coalition, nor does it hold that, for example, whites should not work against racial injustice or men against sexist injustice. This politics of group assertion, however, takes as a basic principle that members of oppressed groups need separate organizations that exclude others, especially those from more privileged groups. Separate organization is probably necessary in order for these groups to discover and reinforce the positivity of their specific experience, to collapse and eliminate double consciousness. In discussions within autonomous organizations, group members can determine their specific needs and interests. Separation and self-organization risk creating pressures toward homogenization of the groups themselves, creating new privileges and exclusions. . . . But contemporary emancipatory social movements have found group autonomy an important vehicle for empowerment and the development of a group-specific voice and perspective.

Integration into the full life of the society should not have to imply assimilation to dominant norms and abandonment of group affiliation and culture. If the only alternative to the oppressive exclusion of some groups defined as Other by dominant ideologies is the assertion that they are the same as everybody else, then they will continue to be excluded because they are not the same.

Some might object to the way I have drawn the distinction between an assimilationist ideal of liberation and a radical democratic pluralism. They might claim that I have not painted the ideal of a society that transcends group differences fairly, representing it as homogeneous and conformist. The free society envisaged by liberalism, they might say, is certainly pluralistic. In it persons can affiliate with whomever they choose; liberty encourages a proliferation of life styles, activities, and associations. While I have no quarrel with social diversity in this sense, this vision of liberal pluralism does not touch on the primary issues that give rise to the politics of difference. The vision of liberation as the transcendence of group difference seeks to abolish the public and political significance of group difference, while retaining and promoting both individual and group diversity in private, or nonpolitical, social contexts. . . . [But] this way of distinguishing public and private spheres, where the public represents universal citizenship and the private individual differences, tends to result in group exclusion from the public. Radical democratic pluralism acknowledges and affirms the public and political significance of social group differences as a means of ensuring the participation and inclusion of everyone in social and political institutions.

RECLAIMING THE MEANING OF DIFFERENCE

Many people inside and outside the movements I have discussed find the rejection of the liberal humanist ideal and the assertion of a positive sense of group difference both confusing and controversial. They fear that any admission by oppressed groups that they are different from the dominant groups risks justifying anew the subordination, special marking, and exclusion of those groups. Since calls for a return of women to the kitchen, Blacks to servant roles and separate schools, and disabled people to nursing homes are not absent from contemporary politics, the danger is real.

It may be true that the assimilationist ideal that treats everyone the same and applies the same standards to all perpetuates disadvantage because real group differences remain that make it unfair to compare the unequals. But this is far preferable to a reestablishment of separate and unequal spheres for different groups justified on the basis of group difference.

Since those asserting group specificity certainly wish to affirm the liberal humanist principle that all persons are of equal moral worth, they appear to be faced with a dilemma. Analyzing W.E.B. Du Bois's arguments for cultural pluralism, Bernard Boxill poses the dilemma this way: "On the one hand, we must overcome segregation because it denies the idea of human brotherhood; on the other hand, to overcome segregation we must self-segregate and therefore also deny the idea of human brotherhood" (Boxill, 1984, p. 174). . . .

These dilemmas are genuine, and exhibit the risks of collective life, where the consequences of one's claims, actions, and policies may not turn out as one intended because others have understood them differently or turned them to different ends. Since ignoring group differences in public policy does not mean that people ignore them in everyday life and interaction, however, oppression continues even when law and policy declare that all are equal. Thus I think for many groups and in many circumstances it is more empowering to affirm and acknowledge in political life the group differences that already exist in social life. One is more likely to avoid the dilemma of difference in doing this if the meaning of difference itself becomes a terrain of political struggle. Social movements asserting the positivity of group difference have established this terrain, offering an emancipatory meaning of difference to replace the old exclusionary meaning.

The oppressive meaning of group difference defines it as absolute otherness, mutual exclusion, categorical opposition. This essentialist meaning of difference submits to the logic of identity. One group occupies the position of a norm, against which all others are measured. The attempt to reduce all persons to the unity of a common measure constructs as deviant those whose attributes differ from the group-specific attributes implicitly presumed in the norm. The drive to unify the particularity and multiplicity of practices, cultural symbols, and ways of relating in clear and distinct categories turns difference into exclusion. . . .

The attempt to measure all against some universal standard generates a logic of difference as hierarchical dichotomy—masculine/feminine, civilized/savage, and so on. The second term is defined negatively as a lack of the truly human qualities; at the same time it is defined as the complement to the valued term, the object correlating with its subject, that which brings it to completion, wholeness, and identity. By loving and affirming him, a woman serves as a mirror to a man, holding up his virtues for him to see. By carrying the white man's burden to tame and educate the savage peoples, the civilized will realize universal humanity. The exotic orientals are there to know and master, to be the completion of reason's progress in history, which seeks the unity of the world. In every case the valued term achieves its value by its determinately negative relation to the Other.

In the objectifying ideologies of racism, sexism, anti-Semitism, and homophobia, only the oppressed and excluded groups are defined as different. Whereas the privileged groups are neutral and exhibit free and malleable subjectivity, the excluded groups are marked with an essence, imprisoned in a given set of possibilities. By virtue of the characteristics the group is alleged to have by nature, the ideologies allege that group members have specific dispositions that suit them for some activities and not others. Difference in these ideologies always means exclusionary opposition to a norm. There are rational men, and then there are women; there are civilized men, and then there are wild and savage peoples. The marking of difference always implies a good/bad opposition; it is always a devaluation, the naming of an inferiority in relation to a superior standard of humanity.

Difference here always means absolute otherness; the group marked as different has no common nature with the normal or neutral ones. The categorical opposition of groups essentializes them, repressing the differences within groups. In this way the definition of difference as exclusion and opposition actually denies difference. This essentializing categorization also denies difference in that its universalizing norms preclude recognizing and affirming a group's specificity in its own terms.

Essentializing difference expresses a fear of specificity, and a fear of making permeable the categorical border between oneself and the others. . . . The politics of difference confronts this fear, and aims for an understanding of group difference as indeed ambiguous, relational, shifting, without clear borders that keep people straight—as entailing neither amorphous unity nor pure individuality. By asserting a positive meaning for their own identity, oppressed groups seek to seize the power of naming difference itself, and explode the implicit definition of difference as deviance in relation to a norm, which freezes some groups into a self-enclosed nature. Difference now comes to mean not

otherness, exclusive opposition, but specificity, variation, heterogeneity. Difference names relations of similarity and dissimilarity that can be reduced to neither coextensive identity nor nonoverlapping otherness.

The alternative to an essentializing, stigmatizing meaning of difference as opposition is an understanding of difference as . . . relational rather than defined by substantive categories and attributes. A relational understanding of difference relativizes the previously universal position of privileged groups, which allows only the oppressed to be marked as different. When group difference appears as a function of comparison between groups, whites are just as specific as Blacks or Latinos, men just as specific as women, able-bodied people just as specific as disabled people. Difference thus emerges not as a description of the attributes of a group, but as a function of the relations between groups and the interaction of groups with institutions.

In this relational understanding, the meaning of difference also becomes contextualized. Group differences will be more or less salient depending on the groups compared, the purposes of the comparison, and the point of view of the comparers. Such contextualized understandings of difference undermine essentialist assumptions. For example, in the context of athletics, health care, social service support, and so on, wheelchair-bound people are different from others, but they are not different in many other respects. Traditional treatment of the disabled entailed exclusion and segregation because the differences between the disabled and the able-bodied were conceptualized as extending to all or most capacities.

In general, then, a relational understanding of group difference rejects exclusion. Difference no longer implies that groups lie outside one another. To say that there are differences among groups does not imply that there are not overlapping experiences, or that two groups have nothing in common. The assumption that real differences in affinity, culture, or privilege imply oppositional categorization must be challenged. Different groups are always similar in some respects, and always potentially share some attributes, experiences, and goals.

Such a relational understanding of difference entails revising the meaning of group identity as well. In asserting the positive difference of their experience, culture, and social perspective, social movements of groups that have experienced cultural imperialism deny that they have a common identity, a set of fixed attributes that clearly mark who belongs and who doesn't. Rather, what makes a group a group is a social process of interaction and differentiation in which some people come to have a particular *affinity* for others. My "affinity group" in a given social situation comprises those people with whom I feel the most comfortable, who are more familiar. Affinity names the manner of sharing assumptions, affective bonding, and networking that recognizably differentiates groups from one another, but not according to some common nature. The salience of a particular person's group affinities may shift according to the social situation or according to changes in her or his life. Membership in a social group is a function not of satisfying some objective criteria, but of a subjective affirmation of affinity with that group, the affirmation of that affinity by other members of the group, and the attribution of membership in that group by persons identifying with other groups. Group identity is constructed from a flowing process in which individuals identify themselves and others in terms of groups, and thus group identity itself flows and shifts with changes in social process.

Groups experiencing cultural imperialism have found themselves objectified and marked with a devalued essence from the outside, by a dominant culture they are excluded from making. The assertion of a positive sense of group difference by these groups is emancipatory because it reclaims the definition of the group by the group, as a creation and construction, rather than a given essence. To be sure, it is difficult to articulate positive elements of group affinity without essentializing them, and these movements do not always succeed in doing so. But they are developing

a language to describe their similar social situation and relations to one another, and their similar perceptions and perspectives on social life. These movements engage in the project of cultural revolution, . . . insofar as they take culture as in part a matter of collective choice. While their ideas of women's culture, Afro-American culture, and American Indian culture rely on past cultural expressions, to a significant degree these movements have self-consciously constructed the culture that they claim defines the distinctiveness of their groups.

Contextualizing both the meaning of difference and identity thus allows the acknowledgment of difference within affinity groups. In our complex, plural society, every social group has group differences cutting across it, which are potential sources of wisdom, excitement, conflict, and oppression. Gay men, for example, may be Black, rich, homeless, or old, and these differences produce different identifications and potential conflicts among gay men, as well as affinities with some straight men.

RESPECTING DIFFERENCE IN POLICY

A goal of social justice, I will assume, is social equality. Equality refers not primarily to the distribution of social goods, though distributions are certainly entailed by social equality. It refers primarily to the full participation and inclusion of everyone in a society's major institutions, and the socially supported substantive opportunity for all to develop and exercise their capacities and realize their choices. American society has enacted formal legal equality for members of all groups, with the important and shameful exception of gay men and lesbians. But for many groups social equality is barely on the horizon. Those seeking social equality disagree about whether group-neutral or group-conscious policies best suit that goal, and their disagreement often turns on whether they hold an assimilationist or culturally pluralist ideal. . . .

The issue of formally equal versus group-conscious policies arises primarily in the context of workplace relations and access to political power. I have already discussed one of the primary reasons for preferring group-conscious to neutral policies: policies that are universally formulated and thus blind to differences of race, culture, gender, age, or disability often perpetuate rather than undermine oppression. Universally formulated standards or norms, for example, according to which all competitors for social positions are evaluated, often presume as the norm capacities, values, and cognitive and behavioral styles typical of dominant groups, thus disadvantaging others. Racist, sexist, homophobic, ageist, and ableist aversions and stereotypes, moreover, continue to devalue or render invisible some people, often disadvantaging them in economic and political interactions. Policies that take notice of the specific situation of oppressed groups can offset these disadvantages.

It might be objected that when facially neutral standards or policies disadvantage a group, the standards or policies should simply be restructured so as to be genuinely neutral, rather than replaced by group-conscious policies. For some situations this may be appropriate, but in many the group-related differences allow no neutral formulation. Language policy might be cited as paradigmatic here, but as I will discuss shortly, some gender issues may be as well.

More important, however, some of the disadvantages that oppressed groups suffer can be remedied in policy only by an affirmative acknowledgment of the group's specificity. For example, removing oppressive stereotypes of Blacks, Latinos, Indians, Arabs and Asians and portraying them in the same roles as whites will not eliminate racism from television programming. Positive and interesting portrayals of people of color in situations and ways of life that derive from their own self-perceptions are also necessary, as well as a great deal more positive presence of all these groups than currently exists. These considerations produce a second reason for justice of group-conscious policies, in addition to their function in countering oppression and disadvantage. Group-conscious policies are sometimes necessary in order to affirm the solidarity of groups, to allow them to affirm their group affinities without suffering disadvantage in the wider society.

Some group-conscious policies are consistent with an assimilationist ideal in which group difference has no social significance, as long as such policies are understood as means to that end, and thus as temporary divergences from group-neutral norms. Many people look upon affirmative action policies this way and people typically understand bilingual education in this way. A culturally pluralist democratic ideal, however, supports group-conscious policies not only as means to the end of equality, but also as intrinsic to the ideal of social equality itself. Groups cannot be socially equal unless their specific experience, culture, and social contributions are publicly affirmed and recognized.

The dilemma of difference exposes the risks involved both in attending to and in ignoring differences. The danger in affirming difference is that the implementation of group-conscious policies will reinstate stigma and exclusion. In the past, group-conscious policies were used to separate those defined as different and exclude them from access to the rights and privileges enjoyed by dominant groups. A crucial principle of democratic cultural pluralism, then, is that group-specific rights and policies should stand together with general civic and political rights of participation and inclusion. Group-conscious policies cannot be used to justify exclusion of or discrimination against members of a group in the exercise of general political and civil rights. A democratic cultural pluralism thus requires a dual system of rights: a general system of rights which are the same for all, and a more specific system of group-conscious policies and rights. . . .

[Young goes on to claim that "group differences of gender, age, and sexuality should not be ignored, but publicly acknowledged and accepted. Even more so should group

differences of nation or ethnicity be accepted. In the twentieth century the ideal state is composed of a plurality of nations or cultural groups, with a degree of self-determination and autonomy compatible with federated equal rights and obligations of citizenship." She then argues in other sections of the book on behalf of racial and ethnic preferences, policies that *make child-raising and childbirth "costless" to women, comparable worth laws mandating equal pay to women and men who perform similar work, equal funding for men's and women's athletics, and for a "bilingual-bicultural" education that aims to promote the students' native language, culture, and sense of identity as well as teach them English.—Ed.]*

BIBLIOGRAPHY

Bastian, Ann, et al., *Choosing Equality: The Case for Democratic Schooling* (Philadelphia: Temple University Press, 1986).

Boxill, Bernard, *Blacks and Social Justice* (Totowa, NJ: Rowman and Allenheld, 1984).

Canter, Norma V., "Testimony from Mexican American Legal Defense and Education Fund," *Congressional Digest* (March 1987).

Karst, Kenneth, "Paths to Belonging: The Constitution and Cultural Identity," *North Carolina Law Review* 64 (1986), 303–77.

Littleton, Christine, "Reconstructing Sexual Equality," *California Law Review* 75 (July 1987), 1279–1377.

Sears, David O., and Leonia Huddy, "Bilingual Education: Symbolic Meaning and Support Among Non-Hispanics." Paper presented at the annual meeting of the American Political Science Association, Chicago, September 1987.

Taub, Nadine, and Wendy Williams, "Will Equality Require More than Assimilation, Accommodation or Separation from the Existing Social Structure?" *Rutgers Law Review* 31 (1985) 825–44.

Wasserstrom, Richard, "On Racism and Sexism," in *Philosophy and Social Issues* (Notre Dame, IN: Notre Dame University Press, 1980).

REVIEW AND DISCUSSION QUESTIONS

1. How does Young characterize Wasserstrom's ideal of "assimilation"? Is it an accurate description of his position? Explain.
2. What objections does Young raise against the ideal of assimilation?
3. What is the difference between the "conformist" and the "transformational" versions of assimilation?
4. How does Young distinguish those who "essentialize difference" from the "relational" understanding of difference?
5. Why does Young think that equality for women and others is best achieved by group-conscious policies instead of neutral ones that rely on "formal" equality?
6. Compare Young's idea of dominance with John Stuart Mill's discussion of autonomy and rights.

Essay and Paper Topics for Section 13

1. Compare the positions of Kymlicka and Mill and Taylor on gender equality.
2. How would Held (section 2) and/or Kymlicka respond to Wright's essay and to Wasserstrom's comments in footnote 11 about biological differences between women and men? Are some theorists wrong in ignoring evolutionary theory when thinking about gender equality? Explain.

3. Randall Kennedy, an African American law professor at Harvard, has written recently that identity politics is "mere superstition and prejudice." "I eschew racial pride," says Kennedy, "because of my conception of what should properly be the object of pride for an individual: something that he or she has accomplished. I can feel pride in a good deed I have done or a good effort I have made. I cannot feel pride in some state of affairs that is independent of my contribution to it. I did not achieve my racial designation" (*Atlantic Monthly,* May 1997, p. 56). Do you agree? Explain, indicating how you think other authors you have read in this section might respond.

4. Using the authors in this section, write an essay on how you understand the "self" and its relation to privacy, history, ethnicity, and race.

5. Using the authors you have read in this section, write an essay in which you discuss the nature of equality: what it is, and what it demands of social relations and political institutions.

14

Affirmative Action and Reparations

Readings in this section address some of the most controversial subjects in American politics: affirmative action policies that give preference to members of certain racial or ethnic minorities (and also sometimes women) who are applying for admission to universities or seeking government contracts or employment as well as reparations for past racial oppression. The essays explore a wide range of positions on the subject, from the wisdom of affirmative action policies (are they worth the price?) to questions of their fairness and justice. Is it unjust to white males who are passed over on the basis of race? Are they being treated unequally by such policies, for example, or does it deny their right not to be refused admission based on race? Others contend, however, that justice *requires* that preferences be given to minorities, either due to past injustices or to compensate for current inequities. Behind these debates lies the question of what causes the gaps in achievement among different racial and ethnic groups and whether racism or other social ills cause it. The section concludes with a discussion of the idea that society owes "reparations" to the living descendants of slaves and other victims of racial oppression.

Affirmative Action in Universities

Regents of the University of California v. Bakke

The term *affirmative action* was first used by President John Kennedy in 1961. His Executive Order 10295 required that contractors working for the federal government take "affirmative action to ensure that applicants are employed without regard to their race, creed, color, or national origin." Over the next decade, however, this requirement moved slowly away from racial neutrality and toward preferences and quotas as the government tried to expand opportunities for minorities. In 1965, President Lyndon Johnson's secretary of labor issued guidelines for federal contractors that included "goals and timetables" to increase minority employment; and, today, preferences based on race, ethnicity, and gender are commonplace. The focus of discussion is often admission policies at universities, although the implications of the debate extend far beyond that.

Affirmative action programs are often defended as efforts to help rectify the racial, sexual, and socioeconomic inequalities in our society. Yet critics of affirmative action contend that it violates the principle of equality by showing preference to members of certain groups.

The controversy over affirmative action came to a head in the famous Supreme Court case, *Regents of the University of California* v. *Bakke.*

Allan Bakke applied for admission to the medical school at the University of California at Davis. Only a tiny percentage of doctors are not white, and in order to help remedy this situation, the University of California at Davis had an affirmative action program that set aside 16 out of its 100 entrance places for minority students. If qualified minority students could not be found, those places were not to be filled. In addition to the special admission process, minority students were free to compete through the regular admission process for one of the unrestricted 84 positions. Bakke was refused admission, but he sued the University of California, contending that he had been discriminated against in violation of both the 1964 Civil Rights Act and the equal protection clause of the Constitution. He argued that he would have won admission if those 16 places had not been withdrawn from open competition and reserved for minority students. The University of California did not deny this but contended that its program was legally permissible and socially necessary. (The Court reported that Bakke scored in the 97th percentile on the MCAT, whereas the average of the minority students admitted under the quota system was the 30th; Bakke's GPA was 3.44, whereas the GPA for the minority students who were admitted was 2.42.)

A badly divided Supreme Court reached a compromise. Although striking down rigid quotas for minority applicants, it also held that universities need not be color-blind in their admissions policies but may instead consider racial diversity as a goal in selecting students. Justice Powell delivered the opinion of the Court, while Justice Brennan dissented in part.

Mr. Justice Powell: Although many of the Framers of the Fourteenth Amendment conceived of its primary function as bridging the vast distance between members of the Negro race and the white "majority," the Amendment itself was framed in universal terms, without reference to color, ethnic origin, or condition of prior [servitude.] . . .

Over the past 30 years, this Court has embarked upon the crucial mission of interpreting the Equal Protection Clause with the view of assuring to all persons "the protection of equal laws" in a Nation confronting a legacy of slavery and racial discrimination. . . .

Petitioner [U.C. Davis] urges us to adopt for the first time a more restrictive view [and] hold that discrimination against members of the white "majority" cannot be suspect if its purpose can be characterized as "benign." [But it] is far too late to argue that the guarantee of equal protection to all persons permits the recognition of special wards entitled to a degree of protection greater than that accorded others. . . .

The concepts of "majority" and "minority" necessarily reflect temporary arrangements and political judgments. The white "majority" itself is composed of various minority groups, most of which can lay claim to a history of prior discrimination at the hands of the state and private individuals. Not all of these groups can receive preferential treatment and corresponding judicial tolerance of distinctions drawn in terms of race and nationality, for then the only "majority" left would be a new minority of White Anglo-Saxon Protestants. There is no principled basis for deciding which groups would merit "heightened judicial solicitude" and which would not. . . .

Moreover, there are serious problems of justice connected with the idea of preference itself. . . . Preferential programs may only reinforce common stereotypes holding that certain groups are unable to achieve success without special protection based on a factor having no relationship to individual worth. . . . There is [also] a measure of inequity in forcing innocent persons in respondent's position to bear

Regents of the University of California v. *Bakke.* 438 U.S. 265 (1978).

the burdens of redressing grievances not of their making.

In this case, [there] has been no determination by the legislature or a responsible administrative agency that the University engaged in a discriminatory practice requiring remedial efforts. . . . [When] a classification denies an individual opportunities or benefits enjoyed by others solely because of his race or ethnic background, it must be regarded as suspect.

[The] special admissions program purports to serve the purposes of: (i) "reducing the historic deficit of traditionally disfavored minorities in medical schools and the medical profession"; (ii) countering the effects of societal discrimination; (iii) increasing the number of physicians who will practice in communities currently underserved; and (iv) obtaining the educational benefits that flow from an ethnically diverse student body. It is necessary to decide which, if any, of these purposes is substantial enough to support the use of a suspect classification.

A. If petitioner's purpose is to assure within its student body some specified percentage of a particular group merely because of its race or ethnic origin, such preferential purpose must be rejected not as insubstantial but as facially invalid. Preferring members of any one group for no reason other than race or ethnic origin is discrimination for its own sake. This the Constitution forbids.

B. The State certainly has a legitimate and substantial interest in ameliorating, or eliminating where feasible, the disabling effects of identified discrimination. . . . We have never approved a classification that aids persons perceived as members of relatively victimized groups at the expense of other innocent individuals in the absence of judicial, legislative, or administrative findings of constitutional or statutory violations. . . . Petitioner does not purport to have made, and is in no position to make, such findings. . . .

Hence, the purpose of helping certain groups whom the faculty of the Davis Medical School perceived as victims of "societal discrimination" does not justify a classification that imposes disadvantages upon persons like respondent, who bear no responsibility for whatever harm the beneficiaries of the special admissions program are thought to have suffered. . . .

C. Petitioner identifies, as another purpose of its program, improving the delivery of health care services to communities currently underserved. . . . It may be correct to assume that some of them will carry out this intention, and that it is more likely they will practice in minority communities than the average white doctor. . . . An applicant of whatever race who has demonstrated his concern for disadvantaged minorities in the past and who declares that practice in such a community is his primary professional goal would be more likely to contribute to alleviation of the medical shortage than one who is chosen entirely on the basis of race and disadvantage. . . .

D. The fourth goal asserted by petitioner is the attainment of a diverse student body. . . . Physicians serve a heterogeneous population. An otherwise qualified medical student with a particular background—whether it be ethnic, geographic, culturally advantaged or disadvantaged—may bring to a professional school of medicine experiences, outlooks and ideas that enrich the training of its student body and better equip its graduates to render with understanding their vital service to humanity.

Ethnic diversity, however, is only one element in a range of factors a university properly may consider in attaining the goal of a heterogeneous student body. . . . [The] diversity that furthers a compelling state interest encompasses a far broader array of qualifications and characteristics of which racial or ethnic origin is but a single though important element. Petitioner's special admissions program, focused *solely* on ethnic diversity, would hinder rather than further attainment of genuine diversity. . . .

The experience of other university admissions programs, which take race into account in achieving the educational diversity valued by the First Amendment, demonstrates that the assignment of a fixed number of places to a minority group is not a necessary means toward that end. An illuminating example is found in the Harvard College program.

In such an admissions program, race or ethnic background may be deemed a "plus" in a particular applicant's file, yet it does not insulate the individual from comparison with all [others]. . . . This kind of program treats each applicant as an individual in the admissions process. The applicant who loses out [to] another candidate receiving a "plus" on the basis of ethnic background will not have been foreclosed from all consideration [simply] because he was not the right color or had the wrong surname. . . .

It has been suggested that an admissions program which considers race only as one factor is simply a subtle and more sophisticated—but no less effective—means of according racial preference than the Davis program. A facial intent to discriminate, however, is evident [in] this case. No such facial infirmity exists in an admissions program where race or ethnic background is simply one element—to be weighed fairly against other elements—in the selection process. . . .

[W]hen a State's distribution of benefits or imposition of burden hinges on the color of a person's skin or ancestry, that individual is entitled to a demonstration that the challenged classification is necessary to promote a substantial state interest. Petitioner has failed to carry this burden. . . .

In enjoining petitioner from ever considering the race of any applicant, however, the courts below failed to recognize that the State has a substantial interest that legitimately may be served by a properly devised admissions program involving the competitive consideration of race and ethnic origin. For this reason, so much of the California court's judgment as enjoins petitioner from any consideration of the race of any applicant must be reversed.

Mr. Justice Brennan, Concurring in the Judgment and Dissenting in Part: Since we conclude that the [program] is constitutional, we would reverse the judgment below in all respects. Mr. Justice Powell agrees that some uses of race in university admissions are permissible and, therefore, he joins with us to make five votes reversing the judgment below insofar as it prohibits the University from establishing race-conscious programs in the future. . . .

[E]ven today officially sanctioned discrimination is not a thing of the past. Against this background, claims that law must be "color-blind" or that the datum of race is no longer relevant to public policy must be seen as aspiration rather than as description of reality. This is not to denigrate aspiration; for reality rebukes us that race has too often been used by those who would stigmatize and oppress minorities. Yet we cannot [let] color blindness become myopia which masks the reality that many "created equal" have been treated within our lifetimes as inferior both by the law and by their fellow citizens. . . .

[A] government practice or statute which restricts "fundamental rights" or which contains "suspect classifications" is to be subjected to "strict scrutiny." But no fundamental right is involved here. . . . Nor do whites as a class have any of the "traditional indicia of suspectedness: the class is not saddled with such disabilities, or subjected to such a history of purposeful unequal treatment, or relegated to such a position of political powerlessness as to command extraordinary protection from the majoritarian political process." . . .

Moreover, [this] is not a case where racial classifications are "irrelevant and therefore prohibited." Nor has anyone suggested that the University's purposes contravene the cardinal principle that racial classifications that stigmatize—because they are drawn on the presumption that one race is inferior to another or because they put the weight of government behind racial hatred and separatism—are invalid without more. . . .

Davis had a sound basis for believing that the problem of underrepresentation of minorities was substantial and chronic and that the problem was attributable to handicaps imposed on minority applicants by past and present racial discrimination. Until at least 1973, the practice of medicine in this country [was] largely the prerogative of whites. . . .

Davis clearly could conclude that the serious and persistent underrepresentation [is] the result of handicaps under which minority applicants labor as a consequence of a background of deliberate, purposeful discrimination against minorities in education and in society generally, as well as in the medical profession. . . .

The habit of discrimination and the cultural tradition of race prejudice [were] not immediately dissipated [*by Brown I*]. Rather, massive official and private resistance prevented, and to a lesser extent still prevents, attainment of equal opportunity in education at all levels and in the professions. The generation of minority students applying to Davis Medical School since it opened in 1968—most of whom were born before or about the time *Brown I* was decided—clearly have been victims of this discrimination. Judicial decrees recognizing discrimination in public education in California testify to the fact of widespread discrimination suffered by California-born minority applicants; many minority group members living in California, moreover, were born and reared in school districts in southern States segregated by law. [T]he conclusion is inescapable that applicants to medical school must be few indeed who endured the effects of de jure segregation, the resistance to *Brown I,* or the equally debilitating pervasive private discrimination fostered by our long history of official discrimination, and yet come to the starting line with an education equal to whites.

It is not even claimed that Davis' program in any way operates to stigmatize or single out any discrete and insular, or even any identifiable, nonminority group. Nor will harm comparable to that imposed upon racial minorities by exclusion or separation on grounds of race be the likely result of the program. It does not, for example, establish an exclusive preserve for minority [students]. Rather, its purpose is to overcome the effects of segregation by bringing the races together. True, whites are excluded from participation in the special admissions program, but this fact only operates to reduce the number of whites to be admitted in the regular admissions program in order to permit admission of a reasonable percentage—less than their proportion of the California population—of otherwise underrepresented qualified minority applicants.

Nor was Bakke in any sense stamped as inferior by [rejection].

Unlike discrimination against racial minorities, the use of racial preferences for remedial purposes does not inflict a pervasive injury upon individual whites in the sense that wherever they go or whatever they do there is a significant likelihood that they will be treated as second-class citizens because of their color. This distinction does not mean that the exclusion of a white resulting from the preferential use of race is not sufficiently serious to require justification; but it does mean that the injury inflicted by such a policy is not distinguishable from disadvantages caused by a wide range of government actions, none of which has ever been thought impermissible for that reason alone.

In addition, there is simply no evidence that the Davis program discriminates intentionally or unintentionally against any minority group which it purports to benefit. The program does not establish a quota in the invidious sense of a ceiling on the number of minority applicants to be admitted. Nor can the program reasonably be regarded as stigmatizing the program's beneficiaries or their race as inferior. The Davis program does not simply advance less qualified applicants; rather, it compensates applicants, whom it is uncontested are fully qualified to study medicine, for educational disadvantage which it was reasonable to conclude was a product of state-fostered discrimination. Once admitted, these students must satisfy the same degree [requirements]; they are taught by the same faculty in the same classes; and their performance is evaluated by the same standards by which regularly admitted students are judged. . . . We disagree with the lower courts' conclusion that the Davis program's use of race was unreasonable in light of its objectives. First, as petitioner argues, there are no practical means by which it could achieve its ends in the foreseeable future without the use of race-conscious measures. . . .

Second, [the] program does not simply equate minority status with disadvantage. Rather, Davis considers [each] applicant's personal history to determine whether he or she has likely been disadvantaged by racial discrimination. The record makes clear that only minority applicants likely to have been isolated from the mainstream of American life are considered in the special [program].

Finally, Davis' special admissions program cannot be said to violate the Constitution simply because it has set aside a predetermined number of places for qualified minority applicants rather than using minority status as a positive factor to be considered in evaluating the applications of disadvantaged minority applicants. For purposes of constitutional adjudication, there is no difference between the two approaches.

REVIEW AND DISCUSSION QUESTIONS

1. This was an unusual case. Four of the justices wanted to hold the California program constitutional along the lines described by Justice Brennan. Four others thought that the California program violated the 1964 Civil Rights Act's promise that no person shall be "discriminated against" on the basis of race and, following usual practice, did not address the constitutional question of whether it also denied Bakke equal protection of the law under the Fourteenth Amendment. The ninth judge, Justice Powell, said that the policy did, in fact, trigger "strict scrutiny" because a fundamental constitutional right was at stake. What is that right? Why does Justice Brennan disagree?

2. Which of the university's reasons for having the program does Justice Powell reject, and why?

3. What reason(s) for the program does Justice Powell accept?

4. Summarize the reasoning behind Justice Brennan's dissent.

5. How might it be argued that affirmative action programs are owed, as a matter of right, to minorities?

The Rights of Allan Bakke

Ronald Dworkin

Do quotas requiring that a certain number of minority applicants get into medical school violate the moral or constitutional rights of white males who would have gotten in had race not been taken into account? That question was raised by Allan Bakke, who, having been refused admission to medical school, filed suit claiming that his rights under the 1964 Civil Rights Act and the Equal Protection Clause of the Fourteenth Amendment (which applies to all governmental agencies) had been violated. Soon after this article was published, the Supreme Court ruled five to four that the quota system at Davis was unconstitutional. (See the previous reading for more information about the case and the Court's opinion.) The Court also held, however, that preferential admissions are not per se unconstitutional as long as quotas are avoided. The "fatal flaw" in the Davis program, according to Justice Powell, is that it tells applicants "who are not Negro, Asian, or Chicano that they are totally excluded from a specific percentage of seats in an entering class." Interestingly, four of the justices argued that the Davis policy was a violation of the 1964 Civil Rights Act, while four others contended that it violated neither that act nor the Constitution. The outcome was therefore a compromise that only one of the Justices supported in total. In the following article, Ronald Dworkin argues that Bakke's rights were not violated by the Davis policy. Ronald Dworkin teaches philosophy and law at New York University and London University. (See the introduction to the Bakke decision, reprinted above, for further background of the decision.)

On October 1, 1977 the Supreme Court heard oral argument in the case of *The Regents of the University of California* v. *Allan Bakke.* No lawsuit has ever been more widely watched or more thoroughly debated in the national and international press before the Court's decision. Still, some of the most pertinent facts set before the Court have not been clearly summarized.

The medical school of the University of California at Davis has an affirmative action program (called the "task force program") designed to admit more black and other minority students. It sets sixteen places aside for which only members of "educationally and economically disadvantaged minorities" compete. Allan Bakke, white, applied for one of the remaining eighty-four places; he was rejected but, since his test scores were relatively high, the medical school has conceded that it could not prove that he would have been rejected if the sixteen places reserved had been open to him. Bakke sued, arguing that the task force program deprived him of his constitutional rights. The California Supreme Court agreed, and ordered the medical school to admit him. The university appealed to the Supreme Court.

The Davis program for minorities is in certain respects more forthright (some would say cruder) than similar plans now in force in many other American universities and professional schools. Such programs aim to increase the enrollment of black and other minority students by allowing the fact of their race to count affirmatively as part of the case for admitting them. Some schools set a "target" of a particular number of minority places instead of setting aside a flat number of places.

But Davis would not fill the number of places set aside unless there were sixteen minority candidates it considered clearly qualified for medical education. The difference is therefore one of administrative strategy and not of principle.

So the constitutional question raised by Bakke is of capital importance for higher education in America, and a large number of universities and schools have entered briefs amicus curiae urging the Court to reverse the California decision. They believe that if the decision is affirmed then they will no longer be free to use explicit racial criteria in any part of their admissions programs, and that they will therefore be unable to fulfill what they take to be their responsibilities to the nation.

It is often said that affirmative action programs aim to achieve a racially conscious society divided into racial and ethnic groups, each entitled, as a group, to some proportionable share of resources, careers, or opportunities. That is a perverse description. American society is currently a racially conscious society; that is the inevitable and evident consequence of a history of slavery, repression, and prejudice. Black men and women, boys and girls, are not free to choose for themselves in what roles—or as members of which social groups—others will characterize them. They are black, and no other feature of personality or allegiance or ambition will so thoroughly influence how they will be perceived and treated by others, and the range and character of the lives that will be open to them.

The tiny number of black doctors and professionals is both a consequence and a continuing cause of American racial consciousness, one link in a long and self-fueling chain

---

This article originally appeared as "Why Bakke Has No Case," in *The New York Review of Books,* November 10, 1977. Reprinted with the permission from *The New York Review of Books.* © 1977 Nyrev, Inc.

reaction. Affirmative action programs use racially explicit criteria because their immediate goal is to increase the number of members of certain races in these professions. But their long-term goal is to reduce the degree to which American society is overall a racially conscious society.

The programs rest on two judgments. The first is a judgment of social theory: that America will continue to be pervaded by racial divisions as long as the most lucrative, satisfying, and important careers remain mainly the prerogative of members of the white race, while others feel themselves systematically excluded from a professional and social elite. The second is a calculation of strategy: that increasing the number of blacks who are at work in the professions will, in the long run, reduce the sense of frustration and injustice and racial self-consciousness in the black community to the point at which blacks may begin to think of themselves as individuals who can succeed like others through talent and initiative. At that future point the consequences of nonracial admissions programs, whatever these consequences might be, could be accepted with no sense of racial barriers or injustice.

It is therefore the worst possible misunderstanding to suppose that affirmative action programs are designed to produce a balkanized America, divided into racial and ethnic subnations. They use strong measures because weaker ones will fail; but their ultimate goal is to lessen not to increase the importance of race in American social and professional life.

According to the 1970 census, only 2.1 percent of US doctors were black. Affirmative action programs aim to provide more black doctors to serve black patients. This is not because it is desirable that blacks treat blacks and whites treat whites, but because blacks, for no fault of their own, are now unlikely to be well served by whites, and because a failure to provide the doctors they trust will exacerbate rather than reduce the resentment that now leads them to trust only their own. Affirmative action tries to provide more blacks as classmates for white doctors, not

because it is desirable that a medical school class reflect the racial makeup of the community as a whole, but because professional association between blacks and whites will decrease the degree to which whites think of blacks as a race rather than as people, and thus the degree to which blacks think of themselves that way. It tries to provide "role models" for future black doctors, not because it is desirable for a black boy or girl to find adult models only among blacks, but because our history has made them so conscious of their race that the success of whites, for now, is likely to mean little or nothing for them.

The history of the campaign against racial injustice since 1954, when the Supreme Court decided *Brown* v. *Board of Education,* is a history in large part of failure. We have not succeeded in reforming the racial consciousness of our society by racially neutral means. We are therefore obliged to look upon the arguments for affirmative action with sympathy and an open mind. Of course, if Bakke is right that such programs, no matter how effective they may be, violate his constitutional rights then they cannot be permitted to continue. But we must not forbid them in the name of some mindless maxim, like the maxim that it cannot be right to fight fire with fire, or that the end cannot justify the means. If the strategic claims for affirmative action are cogent, they cannot be dismissed simply on the ground that racially explicit tests are distasteful. If such tests are distasteful it can only be for reasons that make the underlying social realities the programs attack more distasteful still.

The New Republic, in a recent editorial opposing affirmative action, missed that point. "It is critical to the success of a liberal pluralism," it said, "that group membership itself is not among the permissible criteria of inclusion and exclusion." But group membership is in fact, as a matter of social reality rather than formal admission standards, part of what determines inclusion or exclusion for us now. If we must choose between a society that is in fact liberal and an illiberal society that scrupulously avoids formal racial criteria, we can hardly appeal to the ideals of liberal pluralism to prefer the latter.

Professor Archibald Cox of Harvard Law School, speaking for the University of California in oral argument, told the Supreme Court that this is the choice the United States must make. As things stand, he said, affirmative action programs are the only effective means of increasing the absurdly small number of black doctors. The California Supreme Court, in approving Bakke's claim, had urged the university to pursue that goal by methods that do not explicitly take race into account. But that is unrealistic. We must distinguish, as Cox said, between two interpretations of what the California court's recommendation means. It might mean that the university should aim at the same immediate goal, of increasing the proportion of black and other minority students in the medical school, by an admissions procedure that on the surface is not racially conscious.

That is a recommendation of hypocrisy. If those who administer the admissions standards, however these are phrased, understand that their immediate goal is to increase the number of blacks in the school, then they will use race as a criterion in making the various subjective judgments the explicit criteria will require, because that will be, given the goal, the only right way to make those judgments. The recommendation might mean, on the other hand, that the school should adopt some nonracially conscious goal, like increasing the number of disadvantaged students of all races, and then hope that that goal will produce an increase in the number of blacks as a by-product. But even if that strategy is less hypocritical (which is far from plain), it will almost certainly fail because no different goal, scrupulously administered in a nonracially conscious way, will in fact significantly increase the number of black medical students.

Cox offered powerful evidence for that conclusion, and it is supported by the recent and comprehensive report of the Carnegie Council on Policy Studies in Higher Education. Suppose, for example, that the medical school sets aside separate places for applicants "disadvantaged" on some racially neutral test,

like poverty, allowing only those disadvantaged in that way to compete for these places. If the school selected these from that group who scored best on standard medical school aptitude tests, then it will take almost no blacks, because blacks score relatively low even among the economically disadvantaged. But if the school chooses among the disadvantaged on some basis other than test scores, just so that more blacks will succeed, then it will not be administering the special procedure in a nonracially conscious way.

So Cox was able to put his case in the form of two simple propositions. A racially conscious test for admission, even one that sets aside certain places for qualified minority applicants exclusively, serves goals that are in themselves unobjectionable and even urgent. Such programs are, moreover, the only means that offer any significant promise of achieving these goals. If these programs are halted, then no more than a trickle of black students will enter medical or other professional schools for another generation at least.

If these propositions are sound, then on what ground can it be thought that such programs are either wrong or unconstitutional? We must notice an important distinction between two different sorts of objections that might be made. These programs are intended, as I said, to decrease the importance of race in the United States in the long run. It may be objected, first, that the programs will in fact harm that goal more than they will advance it. There is no way now to prove that that is so. Cox conceded, in his argument, that there are costs and risks in these programs.

Affirmative action programs seem to encourage, for example, a popular misunderstanding, which is that they assume that racial or ethnic groups are entitled to proportionate shares of opportunities, so that Italian or Polish ethnic minorities are, in theory, as entitled to their proportionate shares as blacks or Chicanos or American Indians are entitled to the shares the present programs give them. That is a plain mistake: the programs are not based on the idea that those who are aided are entitled to aid, but only on the strategic hypothesis that helping them is now an effective way of attacking a national problem. Some medical schools may well make that judgment, under certain circumstances, about a white ethnic minority. Indeed it seems likely that some medical schools are even now attempting to help white Appalachian applicants, for example, under programs of regional distribution.

So the popular understanding is wrong, but so long as it persists it is a cost of the program because the attitudes it encourages tend to a degree to make people more rather than less conscious of race. There are other possible costs. It is said, for example, that some blacks find affirmative action degrading; they find that it makes them more rather than less conscious of prejudice against their race as such. This attitude is also based on a misperception, I think, but for a small minority of blacks at least it is a genuine cost.

In the view of the many important universities who have such programs, however, the gains will very probably exceed the losses in reducing racial consciousness overall. This view is hardly so implausible that it is wrong for these universities to seek to acquire the experience that will allow us to judge whether they are right. It would be particularly silly to forbid these experiments if we know that the failure to try will mean, as the evidence shows, that the status quo will almost certainly continue. In any case, this first objection could provide no argument that would justify a decision by the Supreme Court holding the programs unconstitutional. The Court has no business substituting its speculative judgment about the probable consequences of educational policies for the judgment of professional educators.

So the acknowledged uncertainties about the long-term results of such programs could not justify a Supreme Court decision making them illegal. But there is a second and very different form of objection. It may be argued that even if the programs *are* effective in making our society less a society dominated by race, they are nevertheless unconstitutional because they violate the individual constitutional rights of those, like

Allan Bakke, who lose places in consequence. In the oral argument Reynold H. Colvin of San Francisco, who is Bakke's lawyer, made plain that his objection takes this second form. Mr. Justice White asked him whether he accepted that the goals affirmative action programs seek are important goals. Mr. Colvin acknowledged that they were. Suppose, Justice White continued, that affirmative action programs are, as Cox had argued, the only effective means of seeking such goals. Would Mr. Colvin nevertheless maintain that the programs are unconstitutional? Yes, he insisted, they would be, because his client has a constitutional right that the programs be abandoned, no matter what the consequences.

Mr. Colvin was wise to put his objections on this second ground; he was wise to claim that his client has rights that do not depend on any judgment about the likely consequences of affirmative action for society as a whole, because if he makes out that claim then the Court must give him the relief he seeks.

But can he be right? If Allan Bakke has a constitutional right so important that the urgent goals of affirmative action must yield, then this must be because affirmative action violates some fundamental principle of political morality. This is not a case in which what might be called formal or technical law requires a decision one way or the other. There is no language in the Constitution whose plain meaning forbids affirmative action. Only the most naive theories of statutory construction could argue that such a result is required by the language of any earlier Supreme Court decision or of the Civil Rights Act of 1964 or of any other congressional enactment. If Mr. Colvin is right it must be because Allan Bakke has not simply some technical legal right but an important moral right as well.

What could that right be? The popular argument frequently made on editorial pages is that Bakke has a right to be judged on his merit. Or that he has a right to be judged as an individual rather than as a member of a social group. Or that he has a right, as much as any black man, not to be sacrificed or excluded from any opportunity because of his race alone. But these catch phrases are deceptive here, because, as reflection demonstrates, the only genuine principle they describe is the principle that no one should suffer from the prejudice or contempt of others. And that principle is not at stake in this case at all. In spite of popular opinion, the idea that the Bakke case presents a conflict between a desirable social goal and important individual rights is a piece of intellectual confusion.

Consider, for example, the claim that individuals applying for places in medical school should be judged on merit, and merit alone. If that slogan means that admissions committees should take nothing into account but scores on some particular intelligence test, then it is arbitrary and, in any case, contradicted by the long-standing practice of every medical school. If it means, on the other hand, that a medical school should choose candidates that it supposes will make the most useful doctors, then everything turns on the judgment of what factors make different doctors useful. The Davis medical school assigned to each regular applicant, as well as to each minority applicant, what it called a "benchmark score." This reflected not only the results of aptitude tests and college grade averages, but a subjective evaluation of the applicant's chances of functioning as an effective doctor, in view of society's present needs for medical service. Presumably the qualities deemed important were different from the qualities that a law school or engineering school or business school would seek, just as the intelligence tests a medical school might use would be different from the tests these other schools would find appropriate.

There is no combination of abilities and skills and traits that constitutes "merit" in the abstract; if quick hands count as "merit" in the case of a prospective surgeon, this is because quick hands will enable him to serve the public better and for no other reason. If a black skin will, as a matter of regrettable fact, enable another doctor to do a different medical job better, then that black skin is by the same token "merit" as well. That argument may strike some as dangerous; but only because they confuse its conclusion—that

black skin may be a socially useful trait in particular circumstances—with the very different and despicable idea that one race may be inherently more worthy than another.

Consider the second of the catch phrases I have mentioned. It is said that Bakke has a right to be judged as an "individual," in deciding whether he is to be admitted to medical school and thus to the medical profession, and not as a member of some group that is being judged as a whole. What can that mean? Any admissions procedure must rely on generalizations about groups that are justified only statistically. The regular admissions process at Davis, for example, set a cutoff figure for college grade-point averages. Applicants whose averages fell below that figure were not invited to any interview, and therefore rejected out of hand.

An applicant whose average fell one point below the cutoff might well have had personal qualities of dedication or sympathy that would have been revealed at an interview, and that would have made him or her a better doctor than some applicant whose average rose one point above the line. But the former is excluded from the process on the basis of a decision taken for administrative convenience and grounded in the generalization, unlikely to hold true for every individual, that those with grade averages below the cutoff will not have other qualities sufficiently persuasive. Indeed, even the use of standard Medical College Aptitude tests (MCAT) as part of the admissions procedure requires judging people as part of groups because it assumes that test scores are a guide to medical intelligence which is in turn a guide to medical ability. Though this judgment is no doubt true statistically, it hardly holds true for every individual.

Allan Bakke was himself refused admission to two other medical schools, not because of his race but because of his age: these schools thought that a student entering medical school at the age of thirty-three was likely to make less of a contribution to medical care over his career than someone entering at the standard age of twenty-one. Suppose these schools relied, not on any detailed investigation of whether Bakke himself had abilities that would contradict the generalization in his specific case, but on a rule of thumb that allowed only the most cursory look at applicants over (say) the age of thirty. Did these two medical schools violate his right to be judged as an individual rather than as a member of a group?

The Davis Medical School permitted whites to apply for the sixteen places reserved for members of "educationally or economically disadvantaged minorities," a phrase whose meaning might well include white ethnic minorities. In fact several whites have applied, though none has been accepted, and the California Court found that the special committee charged with administering the program had decided, in advance, against admitting any. Suppose that decision had been based on the following administrative theory: it is so unlikely that any white doctor can do as much to counteract racial imbalance in the medical professions as a well-qualified and trained black doctor can do that the committee should for reasons of convenience proceed on the presumption no white doctor could. That presumption is, as a matter of fact, more plausible than the corresponding presumption about medical students over the age of thirty, or even the presumption about applicants whose grade-point averages fall below the cutoff line. If the latter presumptions do not deny the alleged right of individuals to be judged as individuals in an admissions procedure, then neither can the former.

Mr. Colvin, in oral argument, argued the third of the catch phrases I mentioned. He said that his client had a right not to be excluded from medical school because of his race alone, and this as a statement of constitutional right sounds more plausible than claims about the right to be judged on merit or as an individual. It sounds plausible, however, because it suggests the following more complex principle. Every citizen has a constitutional right that he not suffer disadvantage, at least in the competition for any public benefit, because the race or religion or sect or region or other natural or artificial group to which he belongs is the object of prejudice or contempt.

That is a fundamentally important constitutional right, and it is that right that was systematically violated for many years by racist exclusions and anti-Semitic quotas. Color bars and Jewish quotas were not unfair just because they made race or religion relevant or because they fixed on qualities beyond individual control. It is true that blacks or Jews do not choose to be blacks or Jews. But it is also true that those who score low in aptitude or admissions tests do not choose their levels of intelligence. Nor do those denied admission because they are too old, or because they do not come from a part of the country underrepresented in the school, or because they cannot play basketball well, choose not to have the qualities that made the difference.

Race seems different because exclusions based on race have historically been motivated not by some instrumental calculation, as in the case of intelligence or age or regional distribution or athletic ability, but because of contempt for the excluded race or religion as such. Exclusion by race was in itself an insult, because it was generated by and signaled contempt.

Bakke's claim, therefore, must be made more specific than it is. He says he was kept out of medical school because of his race. Does he mean that he was kept out because his race is the object of prejudice or contempt? That suggestion is absurd. A very high proportion of those who were accepted (and, presumably, of those who run the admissions program) were members of the same race. He therefore means simply that if he had been black he would have been accepted, with no suggestion that this would have been so because blacks are thought more worthy or honorable than whites.

That is true: no doubt he would have been accepted if he were black. But it is also true, and in exactly the same sense, that he would have been accepted if he had been more intelligent, or made a better impression in his interview, or, in the case of other schools, if he had been younger when he decided to become a doctor. Race is not, in his case, a different matter from these other factors equally beyond his control. It is not a different matter because in his case race is not distinguished by the special character of public insult. On the contrary, the program presupposes that his race is still widely if wrongly thought to be superior to others.

In the past, it made sense to say that an excluded black or Jewish student was being sacrificed because of his race or religion; that meant that his or her exclusion was treated as desirable in itself, not because it contributed to any goal in which he as well as the rest of society might take pride. Allan Bakke is being "sacrificed" because of his race only in a very artificial sense of the word. He is being "sacrificed" in the same artificial sense because of his level of intelligence, since he would have been accepted if he were more clever than he is. In both cases he is being excluded not by prejudice but because of a rational calculation about the socially most beneficial use of limited resources for medical education.

It may now be said that this distinction is too subtle, and that if racial classifications have been and may still be used for malign purposes, then everyone has a flat right that racial classifications not be used at all. This is the familiar appeal to the lazy virtue of simplicity. It supposes that if a line is difficult to draw, or might be difficult to administer if drawn, then there is wisdom in not making the attempt to draw it. There may be cases in which that is wise, but those would be cases in which nothing of great value would as a consequence be lost. If racially conscious admissions policies now offer the only substantial hope for bringing more qualified black and other minority doctors into the profession, then a great loss is suffered if medical schools are not allowed voluntarily to pursue such programs. We should then be trading away a chance to attack certain and present injustice in order to gain protection we may not need against speculative abuses we have other means to prevent. And such abuses cannot, in any case, be worse than the injustice to which we would then surrender.

We have now considered three familiar slogans, each widely thought to name a constitutional right that enables Allan Bakke to stop programs of affirmative action no matter how effective or necessary these might be. When we inspect these slogans, we find that they can stand for no genuine principle except one. This is the important principle that no one in our society should suffer because he is a member of a group thought less worthy of respect, as a group, than other groups. We have different aspects of that principle in mind when we say that individuals should be judged on merit, that they should be judged as individuals, and that they should not suffer disadvantages because of their race. The spirit of that fundamental principle is the spirit of the goal that affirmative action is intended to serve. The principle furnishes no support for those who find, as Bakke does, that their own interests conflict with that goal.

It is of course regrettable when any citizen's expectations are defeated by new programs serving some more general concern. It is regrettable, for example, when established small businesses fail because new and superior roads are built; in that case people have invested more than Bakke has. And they have more reason to believe their businesses will continue than Bakke had to suppose he could have entered the Davis medical school at thirty-three even without a task force program.

There is, of course, no suggestion in that program that Bakke shares in any collective or individual guilt for racial injustice in America; or that he is any less entitled to concern or respect than any black student accepted in the program. He has been disappointed, and he must have the sympathy due that disappointment, just as any other disappointed applicant—even one with much worse test scores who would not have been accepted in any event—must have sympathy. Each is disappointed because places in medical schools are scarce resources and must be used to provide what the more general society most needs. It is hardly Bakke's fault that racial justice is now a special need—but he has no right to prevent the most effective measures of securing that justice from being used.

REVIEW AND DISCUSSION QUESTIONS

1. Dworkin says that affirmative action programs rest on two premises. Explain them.
2. How does Dworkin answer critics of those two premises?
3. How does Dworkin respond to the claim that Bakke's right to be judged on the basis of merit was infringed?
4. How does he respond to the claim that Bakke was not "judged as an individual"?
5. In fact, Bakke's lawyer claimed he had a right not to be excluded from medical school because of race. How does Dworkin answer that charge?
6. Setting aside questions of justice or rights, describe the potential social and economic advantages and disadvantages of affirmative action policies.
7. How might it be argued that some people have a right to affirmative action programs? Are those the same people that benefit from such a program? Explain.
8. The *Journal of the American Medical Association* reported that in 1988, medical school graduates passed the National Board of Medical Examiners certifying test at the following rates: white males, 89 percent; while females, 84 percent; black males, 54 percent; black females, 44 percent. It also reported that the large majority of those who first fail will eventually pass the exam. Are those figures significant for this debate? Explain.

Affirmative Racism

Charles Murray

Even the most well-intentioned social policies sometimes have unforeseen results. In this essay, Charles Murray offers a broad-based attack on affirmative action, arguing, among other things, that preferential treatment for blacks has actually worked against their interests by encouraging a new form of racism. He develops his argument by inventing a narrative involving three students applying to college with very different educational and ethnic backgrounds. Charles Murray is a fellow at the American Enterprise Institute.

A few years ago, I got into an argument with a lawyer friend who is a partner in a New York firm. I was being the conservative, arguing that preferential treatment of blacks was immoral; he was being the liberal, urging that it was the only way to bring blacks to full equality. In the middle of all this he abruptly said, "But you know, let's face it. We must have hired at least ten blacks in the last few years, and none of them has really worked out." He then returned to his case for still stronger affirmative action, while I wondered what it had been like for those ten blacks. And if he could make a remark like that so casually, what remarks would he be able to make some years down the road, if by that time it had been fifty blacks who hadn't "really worked out"?

My friend's comment was an outcropping of a new racism that is emerging to take its place alongside the old. It grows out of preferential treatment for blacks, and it is not just the much-publicized reactions, for example, of the white policemen or firemen who are passed

Charles Murray, "Affirmative Racism," *The New Republic,* December 31, 1984. Reprinted by permission of *The New Republic.* © 1984, The New Republic, Inc.

over for promotion because of an affirmative action court order. The new racism that is potentially most damaging is located among the white elites—educated, affluent, and occupying the positions in education, business, and government from which this country is run. It currently focuses on blacks; whether it will eventually extend to include Hispanics and other minorities remains to be seen.

The new racists do not think blacks are inferior. They are typically longtime supporters of civil rights. But they exhibit the classic behavioral symptom of racism: they treat blacks differently from whites, because of their race. The results can be as concretely bad and unjust as any that the old racism produces. Sometimes the effect is that blacks are refused an education they otherwise could have gotten. Sometimes blacks are shunted into dead-end jobs. Always, blacks are denied the right to compete as equals.

The new racists also exhibit another characteristic of racism: they *think* about blacks differently from the way they think about whites. Their global view of blacks and civil rights is impeccable. Blacks must be enabled to achieve full equality. They are still unequal, through no fault of their own (it is the fault of racism, it is the fault of inadequate opportunity, it is the legacy of history). But the new racists' local view is that the blacks they run across professionally are not, on the average, up to the white standard. Among the new racists, lawyers have gotten used to the idea that the brief a black colleague turns in will be a little less well-rehearsed and argued than the one they would have done. Businessmen expect that a black colleague will not read a balance sheet as subtly as they do. Teachers expect black students to wind up toward the bottom of the class.

The new racists also tend to think of blacks as a commodity. The office must have a sufficient supply of blacks, who must be treated with special delicacy. The personnel problems this creates are more difficult than most because whites barely admit to themselves what's going on.

What follows is a foray into very poorly mapped territory. I will present a few numbers that explain much about how the process gets started. But the ways that the numbers get translated into behavior are even more important. The cases I present are composites constructed from my own observations and taken from firsthand accounts. All are based on real events and real people, stripped of their particularities. But the individual cases are not intended as evidence, because I cannot tell you how often they happen. They have not been the kind of thing that social scientists or journalists have wanted to count. I am writing this because so many people, both white and black, to whom I tell such stories know immediately what I am talking about. It is apparent that a problem exists. How significant is it? What follows is as much an attempt to elicit evidence as to present it.

As in so many of the crusades of the 1960s, the nation began with a good idea. It was called "affirmative action," initiated by Lyndon Johnson through Executive Order 11246 in September 1965. It was an attractive label and a natural corrective to past racism: actively seek out black candidates for jobs, college, or promotions, without treating them differently in the actual decision to hire, admit, or promote. The term originally evoked both the letter and the spirit of the order.

Then, gradually, affirmative action came to mean something quite different. In 1970 a federal court established the legitimacy of quotas as a means of implementing Johnson's executive order. In 1971 the Supreme Court ruled that an employer could not use minimum credentials as a prerequisite for hiring if the credential acted as a "built-in headwind" for minority groups—even when there was no discriminatory intent and even when the hiring procedures were "fair in form." In 1972 the Equal Employment Opportunity Commission acquired broad, independent enforcement powers.

Thus by the early 1970s it had become generally recognized that a good-faith effort to recruit qualified blacks was not enough—especially if one's school depended on federal grants or one's business depended on federal contracts. Even for businesses and schools not directly dependent on the government, the simplest way to withstand an accusation of violating Title VII of the Civil Rights Act of 1964 was to make sure not that they had not just interviewed enough minority candidates, but that they had actually hired or admitted enough of them. Employers and admissions committees arrived at a rule of thumb: if the blacks who are available happen to be the best candidates, fine; if not, the best available black candidate will be given some sort of edge in the selection process. Sometimes the edge will be small; sometimes it will be predetermined that a black candidate is essential, and the edge will be very large.

Perhaps the first crucial place where the edge applies is in admission to college. Consider the cases of the following three students: John, William, and Carol, 17 years old and applying to college, are all equal on paper. Each has a score of 520 in the mathematics section of the Scholastic Aptitude Test, which puts them in the top third—at the 67th percentile—of all students who took the test. (Figures are based on 1983 data.)

John is white. A score of 520 gets him into the state university. Against the advice of his high school counselor, he applies to a prestigious school, Ivy U., where his application is rejected in the first cut—its average white applicant has math scores in the high 600s.

William is black, from a middle-class family who sent him to good schools. His score of 520 puts him at the 95th percentile of all blacks who took the test. William's high school counselor points out that he could probably get into Ivy U. William applies and is admitted—Ivy U. uses separate standards for admission of whites and blacks, and William is among the top blacks who applied.

Carol is black, educated at an inner-city school, and her score of 520 represents an extraordinary achievement in the face of terrible schooling. An alumnus of Ivy U. who regularly looks for promising inner-city candidates finds her, recruits her, and sends her off with a full scholarship to Ivy U.

When American universities embarked on policies of preferential admissions by race,

they had the Carols in mind. They had good reason to be optimistic that preferential treatment would work—for many years, the best universities had been weighting the test scores of applicants from small-town public schools when they were compared against those of applicants from the top private schools, and had been giving special breaks to students from distant states to ensure geographic distribution. The differences in preparation tended to even out after the first year or so. Blacks were being brought into a long-standing and successful tradition of preferential treatment.

In the case of blacks, however, preferential treatment ran up against a large black-white gap in academic performance combined with ambitious goals for proportional representation. This gap has been the hardest for whites to confront. But though it is not necessary or even plausible to believe that such differences are innate, it is necessary to recognize openly that the differences exist. By pretending they don't, we begin the process whereby both the real differences and the racial factor are exaggerated.

The black-white gap that applies most directly to this discussion is the one that separates blacks and whites who go to college. In 1983, for example, the mean Scholastic Aptitude Test score for all blacks who took the examination was more than 100 points below the white score on both the verbal and the math sections. Statistically, it is an extremely wide gap. To convert the gap into more concrete terms, think of it this way: in 1983, the same Scholastic Aptitude Test math score that put a black at the 50th percentile of all blacks who took the test put him at the 16th percentile of all whites who took the test.

These results clearly mean we ought to be making an all-out effort to improve elementary and secondary education for blacks. But that doesn't help much now, when an academic discrepancy of this magnitude is fed into a preferential admissions process. As universities scramble to make sure they are admitting enough blacks, the results feed the new racism. Here's how it works:

In 1983, only 66 black students nationwide scored above 700 in the verbal section of the Scholastic Aptitude Test, and only 205 scored above 700 in the mathematics section. This handful of students cannot begin to meet the demand for blacks with such scores. For example, Harvard, Yale, and Princeton have in recent years been bringing an aggregate of about 270 blacks into each entering class. If the black students entering these schools had the same distribution of scores as that of the freshman class as a whole, then every black student in the nation with a verbal score in the 700s, and roughly 70 percent of the ones with a math score in the 700s, would be in their freshman classes.

The main problem is not that a few schools monopolize the very top black applicants, but that these same schools have much larger implicit quotas than they can fill with those applicants. They fill out the rest with the next students in line—students who would not have gotten into these schools if they were not black, who otherwise would have been showing up in the classrooms of the nation's less glamorous colleges and universities. But the size of the black pool does not expand appreciably at the next levels. The number of blacks scoring in the 600s on the math section in 1983, for example, was 1,531. Meanwhile, 31,704 nonblack students in 1983 scored in the 700s on the math section and 121,640 scored in the 600s. The prestige schools cannot begin to absorb these numbers of other highly qualified freshmen, and they are perforce spread widely throughout the system.

At schools that draw most broadly from the student population, such as the large state universities, the effects of this skimming produce a situation that confirms the old racists in everything they want most to believe. There are plenty of outstanding students in such student bodies (at the University of Colorado, for example, 6 percent of the freshmen in 1981 had math scores in the 700s and 28 percent had scores in the 600s), but the skimming process combined with the very small raw numbers means that almost none of them are black. What students and instruc-tors see in their day-to-day experience in the classroom is a disproportionate number of blacks who are below the white average, relatively few blacks who are at the white average, and virtually none who are in the first rank. The image that the white student carries away is that blacks are less able than whites.

I am not exalting the SAT as an infallible measure of academic ability, or pointing to test scores to try to convince anyone that blacks are performing below the level of whites. I am simply using them to explain what instructors and students already notice, and talk about, among themselves.

They do not talk openly about such matters. One characteristic of the new racism is that whites deny in public but acknowledge in private that there are significant differences in black and white academic performance. Another is that they dismiss the importance of tests when black scores are at issue, blaming cultural bias and saying that test scores are not good predictors of college performance. At the same time, they watch anxiously over their own children's test scores.

The differences in academic performance do not disappear by the end of college. Far from narrowing, the gap separating black and white academic achievement appears to get larger. Various studies, most recently at Harvard, have found that during the 1970s blacks did worse in college (as measured by grade point average) than their test scores would have predicted. Moreover, the black-white gap in the Graduate Record Examination is larger than the gap in the Scholastic Aptitude Test. The gap between black and white freshmen is a bit less than one standard deviation (the technical measure for comparing scores). Black and white seniors who take the Graduate Record Examination reveal a gap of about one and a quarter standard deviations.

Why should the gap grow wider? Perhaps it is an illusion—for example, perhaps a disproportionate number of the best black students never take the examination. But there are also reasons for suspecting that in fact blacks get a worse education in college than whites do. Here are a few of the hypotheses that deserve full exploration.

Take the situation of William—a slightly above-average student who, because he is black, gets into a highly competitive school. William studies very hard during the first year. He nonetheless gets mediocre grades. He has a choice. He can continue to study hard and continue to get mediocre grades, and be seen by his classmates as a black who cannot do very well. Or he can explicitly refuse to engage in the academic game. He decides to opt out, and his performance gets worse as time goes on. He emerges from college with a poor education and is further behind the whites than he was as a freshman.

If large numbers of other black students at the institution are in the same situation as William, the result can be group pressure not to compete academically. (At Harvard, it is said, the current term among black students for a black who studies like a white is "incognegro.") The response is not hard to understand. If one subpopulation of students is conspicuously behind another population and is visibly identifiable, then the population that is behind must come up with a good excuse for doing poorly. "Not wanting to do better" is as good as any.

But there is another crucial reason why blacks might not close the gap with whites during college: they are not taught as well as whites are. Racist teachers impeding the progress of students? Perhaps, but most college faculty members I know tend to bend over backward to be "fair" to black students—and that may be the problem. I suggest that inferior instruction is more likely to be a manifestation of the new racism than the old.

Consider the case of Carol, with outstanding abilities but deprived of decent prior schooling: she struggles the first year, but she gets by. Her academic skills still show the aftereffects of her inferior preparation. Her instructors diplomatically point out the more flagrant mistakes, but they ignore minor lapses, and never push her in the aggressive way they push white students who have her intellectual capacity. Some of them are being patronizing (she is doing quite well, considering). Others are being prudent: teachers who criticize black students can find themselves being called racists in the classroom, in the campus newspaper, or in complaints to the administration.

The same process continues in graduate school. Indeed, because there are even fewer blacks in graduate schools than in undergraduate schools, the pressure to get black students through to the degree, no matter what, can be still greater. But apart from differences in preparation and ability that have accumulated by the end of schooling, the process whereby we foster the appearance of black inferiority continues. Let's assume that William did not give up during college. He goes to business school, where he gets his Masters degree. He signs up for interviews with the corporate recruiters. There are 100 persons in his class, and William is ranked near the middle. But of the 5 blacks in his class, he ranks first (remember that he was at the 95th percentile of blacks taking the Scholastic Aptitude Test). He is hired on his first interview by his first-choice company, which also attracted the very best of the white students. He is hired alongside 5 of the top-ranking white members of the class.

William's situation as one of 5 blacks in a class of 100 illustrates the proportions that prevail in business schools, and business schools are by no means one of the more extreme examples. The pool of black candidates for any given profession is a small fraction of the white pool. This works out to a 20-to-1 edge in business; it is even greater in most of the other professions. The result, when many hiring institutions are competing, is that a major gap between the abilities of new black and white employees in any given workplace is highly likely. Everyone needs to hire a few blacks, and the edge that "being black" confers in the hiring decision warps the sequence of hiring in such a way that a scarce resource (the blacks with a given set of qualifications) is exhausted at an artificially high rate, producing a widening gap in comparison with the remaining whites from which an employer can choose.

The more aggressively affirmative action is enforced, the greater the imbalance. In general, the first companies to hire can pursue strategies that minimize or even eliminate the difference in ability between the new black and white employees. IBM and Park Avenue law firms can do very well, just as Harvard does quite well in attracting the top black students. But the more effectively they pursue these strategies, the more quickly they strip the population of the best black candidates.

To this point I have been discussing problems that are more or less driven by realities we have very little hope of manipulating in the short term except by discarding the laws regarding preferential treatment. People do differ in acquiring abilities. Currently, acquired abilities in the white and black populations are distributed differently. Schools and firms do form a rough hierarchy when they draw from these distributions. The results follow ineluctably. The dangers they represent are not a matter of statistical probabilities, but of day-to-day human reactions we see around us.

The damage caused by these mechanistic forces should be much less in the world of work than in the schools, however. Schools deal in a relatively narrow domain of skills, and "talent" tends to be assigned specific meanings and specific measures. Workplaces deal in highly complex sets of skills, and "talent" consists of all sorts of combinations of qualities. A successful career depends in large part upon finding jobs that elicit and develop one's strengths.

At this point the young black professional must sidestep a new series of traps laid by whites who need to be ostentatiously non-racist. Let's say that William goes to work for the XYZ Corporation, where he is assigned with another management trainee (white) to a department where much of the time is spent preparing proposals for government contracts. The white trainee is assigned a variety of scud work—proofreading drafts, calculating the costs of minor items in the bid, making photocopies, taking notes at conferences. William gets more dignified work. He is assigned portions of the draft to write (which are later rewritten by more experienced staff), sits in on planning sessions, and even goes to Washington as a highly visible part of the team to present the bid. As time goes on, the white trainee learns a great deal about how the company operates, and is seen as a go-getting young member of the team. William is perceived to be a bright enough fellow, but not much of a detail man and not really much of a self-starter.

Even if a black is hired under terms that put him on a par with his white peers, the subtler forms of differential treatment work against him. Particularly for any corporation that does business with the government, the new employee has a specific, immediate value purely because he is black. There are a variety of requirements to be met and rituals to be observed for which a black face is helpful. These have very little to do with the long-term career interests of the new employee; on the contrary, they often lead to a dead end as head of the minority-relations section of the personnel department.

Added to this is another problem that has nothing to do with the government. When the old racism was at fault (as it often still is), the newly hired black employee was excluded from the socialization process because the whites did not want him to become part of the group. When the new racism is at fault, it is because many whites are embarrassed to treat black employees as badly as they are willing to treat whites. Hence another reason that whites get on-the-job training that blacks do not: much of the early training of an employee is intertwined with menial assignments and mild hazing. Blacks who are put through these routines often see themselves as racially abused (and when a black is involved, old-racist responses may well have crept in). But even if the black is not unhappy about the process, the whites are afraid that he is, and so protect him from it. There are many variations, all having the same effect: the black is denied an apprenticeship that the white has no way of escaping. Without serving the apprenticeship, there is no way of becoming part of the team.

Carol suffers a slightly different fate. She and a white woman are hired as reporters by a major newspaper. They both work hard, but after a few months there is no denying it: neither one of them can write. The white woman is let go. Carol is kept on, because the paper cannot afford to have any fewer blacks than it already has. She is kept busy with reportorial work, even though they have to work around the writing problem. She is told not to worry—there's lots more to being a journalist than writing.

It is the mascot syndrome. A white performing at a comparable level would be fired. The black is kept on, perhaps to avoid complications with the Equal Employment Opportunity Commission (it can be very expensive to fire a black), perhaps out of a more diffuse wish not to appear discriminatory. Everybody pretends that nothing is wrong—but the black's career is at a dead end. The irony, of course, is that the white who gets fired and has to try something else has been forced into accepting a chance of making a success in some other line of work whereas the black is seduced into *not* taking the same chance.

Sometimes differential treatment takes an even more pernicious form: the conspiracy to promote a problem out of existence. As part of keeping Carol busy, the newspaper gives her some administrative responsibilities. They do not amount to much. But she has an impressive title on a prominent newspaper and she is black—a potent combination. She gets an offer from a lesser paper in another part of the country to take a senior editorial post. Her current employer is happy to be rid of an awkward situation and sends along glowing references. She gets a job that she is unequipped to handle—only this time, she is in a highly visible position, and within a few weeks the deficiencies that were covered up at the old job have become the subject of jokes all over the office. Most of the jokes are openly racist.

It is important to pause and remember who Carol is: an extremely bright young woman, not (in other circumstances) a likely object of condescension. But being bright is no protection. Whites can usually count on the market to help us recognize egregious career mistakes and to prevent us from being promoted too far from a career line that fits our strengths, and too far above our level of readiness. One of the most prevalent characteristics of white differential treatment of blacks has been to exempt blacks from these market considerations, substituting for them a market premium attached to race.

The most obvious consequence of preferential treatment is that every black professional, no matter how able, is tainted. Every black who is hired by a white-run organization that hires blacks preferentially has to put up with the knowledge that many of his coworkers believe he was hired because of his race; and he has to put up with the suspicion in his own mind that they might be right.

Whites are curiously reluctant to consider this a real problem—it is an abstraction, I am told, much less important than the problem that blacks face in getting a job in the first place. But black professionals talk about it, and they tell stories of mental breakdowns; of people who had to leave the job altogether; of long-term professional paralysis. What white would want to be put in such a situation? Of course it would be a constant humiliation to be resented by some of your coworkers and condescended to by others. Of course it would affect your perceptions of yourself and your self-confidence. No system that produces such side effects—as preferential treatment must do—can be defended unless it is producing some extremely important benefits.

And that brings us to the decisive question. If the alternative were no job at all, as it was for so many blacks for so long, the resentment and condescension are part of the price of getting blacks into the positions they deserve. But is that the alternative today? If the institutions of this country were left to their own devices now, to what extent would they refuse to admit, hire, and promote people because they were black? To what extent are American institutions kept from being racist by the government's intervention?

It is another one of those questions that are seldom investigated aggressively, and I have no evidence. Let me suggest a hypothesis that bears looking into: that the signal event in the struggle for black equality during the last thirty years, the one with real impact, was not the Civil Rights Act of 1964 or Executive Order 11246 or any other governmental act. It was the civil rights movement itself. It raised to a pitch of acute and lasting discomfort the racial consciousness of the generations of white Americans who are now running the country. I will not argue that the old racism is dead at any level of society. I will argue, however, that in the typical corporation or in the typical admissions office, there is an abiding desire to be not-racist. This need not be construed as brotherly love. Guilt will do as well. But the civil rights movement did its job. I suggest that the laws and the court decisions and the continuing intellectual respectability behind preferential treatment are not holding many doors open to qualified blacks that would otherwise be closed.

Suppose for a moment that I am right. Suppose that, for practical purposes, racism would not get in the way of blacks if preferential treatment were abandoned. How, in my most optimistic view, would the world look different?

There would be fewer blacks at Harvard and Yale; but they would all be fully competitive with the whites who were there. White students at the state university would encounter a cross-section of blacks who span the full range of ability, including the top levels, just as whites do. College remedial courses would no longer be disproportionately black. Whites rejected by the school they wanted would quit assuming they were kept out because a less-qualified black was admitted in their place. Blacks in big corporations would no longer be shunted off to personnel-relations positions, but would be left on the mainline tracks toward becoming comptrollers and sales managers and chief executive officers. Whites would quit assuming that black colleagues had been hired because they were black. Blacks would quit

worrying that they had been hired because they were black.

Would blacks still lag behind? As a population, yes, for a time, and the nation should be mounting a far more effective program to improve elementary and secondary education for blacks than it has mounted in the last few decades. But in years past virtually every ethnic group in America has at one time or another lagged behind as a population, and has eventually caught up. In the process of catching up, the ones who breached the barriers were evidence of the success of that group. Now blacks who breach the barriers tend to be seen as evidence of the inferiority of that group.

And that is the evil of preferential treatment. It perpetuates an impression of inferiority. The system segments whites and blacks who come in contact with each other so as to maximize the likelihood that whites have the advantage in experience and ability. The system then encourages both whites and blacks to behave in ways that create self-fulfilling prophecies even when no real differences exist.

It is here that the new racism links up with the old. The old racism has always openly held that blacks are permanently less competent than whites. The new racism tacitly accepts that, in the course of overcoming the legacy of the old racism, blacks are temporarily less competent than whites. It is an extremely fine distinction. As time goes on, fine distinctions tend to be lost. Preferential treatment is providing persuasive evidence for the old racists, and we can already hear it *sotto voce:* "We gave you your chance, we let you educate them and push them into jobs they couldn't have gotten on their own and coddle them every way you could. And see: they still aren't as good as whites, and you are beginning to admit it yourselves." Sooner or later this message is going to be heard by a white elite that needs to excuse its failure to achieve black equality.

The only happy aspect of the new racism is that the corrective—to get rid of the policies encouraging preferential treatment—is so natural. Deliberate preferential treatment by race has sat as uneasily with America's equal-opportunity ideal during the post-1965 period as it did during the days of legalized segregation. We had to construct tortuous rationalizations when we permitted blacks to be kept on the back of the bus—and the rationalizations to justify sending blacks to the head of the line have been just as tortuous.

Both kinds of rationalization say that sometimes it is all right to treat people of different races in different ways. For years, we have instinctively sensed this was wrong in principle but intellectualized our support for it as an expedient. I submit that our instincts were right. There is no such thing as good racial discrimination.

REVIEW AND DISCUSSION QUESTIONS

1. Using the three stories, describe why Murray thinks reverse discrimination encourages racism.
2. What is the "mascot syndrome"?
3. Are the dangers Murray emphasizes outweighed by the longer term advantages of preferential admission and hiring? What are those advantages?
4. California recently abolished preferences in admissions to its universities. The result, so far, has been a decline in black, Hispanic, and Native American enrollment at California's most competitive universities and an increase in white and Asian enrollment. Is that relevant to Murray's description of the world without preferential treatment? Are there features of the situation he overlooks?
5. Are the responses of those whites whom Murray describes as racist reasonable, given their circumstances? Should their feelings be given significant weight in assessing affirmative action? Explain.

Reverse Discrimination

James Rachels

In this essay, James Rachels considers affirmative action from two perspectives. First, he asks whether it is a wise policy. Is society better off giving preferences to minorities than it would be if it didn't? Rachels then considers the claim that under certain circumstances, affirmative action is required by considerations of justice. This is the third section of a longer essay Rachels wrote titled "What People Deserve," reprinted in section 9. James Rachels teaches philosophy at the University of Alabama at Birmingham.

Is it right to give preferential treatment to blacks, women, or members of other groups who have been discriminated against in the past? I will approach this issue by considering the deserts of the individuals involved.

[*Rachels earlier argued in this essay that past actions, especially effort, are important factors in distributing punishment, rewards, and other goods. By respecting past effort, he contends, we show respect for the autonomous choices of*

From James Rachels, "What People Deserve," originally printed in John Arthur and William H. Shaw, Eds., *Justice and Economic Distribution* (Prentice Hall, 1978). Reprinted by permission.

those who both win and lose. See "What People Deserve" section 9—Ed.] "Reverse Discrimination" is not a particularly good label for the practices in question because the word "discrimination" has come to have such unsavory connotations. Given the way that word is now used, to ask whether reverse *discrimination* is justified already prejudices the question in favor of a negative answer. But in other ways the term is apt: the most distinctive thing about reverse discrimination is that it *reverses* past patterns, so that those who have been discriminated against are now given preferential treatment. At any rate, the label is now part of our common vocabulary, so I will stay with it.

The following example incorporates the essential elements of reverse discrimination. The admissions committee of a certain law school assesses the qualifications of applicants by assigning numerical values to their college grades, letters of recommendation, and test scores, according to some acceptable formula. (The better the grades, etc., the higher the numerical values assigned.) From past experience the committee judges that a combined score of 600 is necessary for a student to have a reasonable chance of succeeding in the school's program. Thus in order to be minimally qualified for admission an applicant must score at least 600. However, because there are more qualified applicants than places available, many who score over 600 are nevertheless rejected.

Against this background two students, one black and one white, apply for admission. The black student's credentials are rated at 700, and the white student's credentials are rated at 720. So although both exceed the minimum requirement by a comfortable margin, the white student's qualifications are somewhat better. But the white applicant is rejected and the black applicant is accepted. The officials of the school explain that this decision is part of a policy designed to bring more blacks into the legal profession. The scores of the white applicants are generally higher than those of the blacks; so, some blacks with lower scores must be admitted in order to have a fair number of black students in the entering class. . . .

Now a number of arguments can be given in support of the law school's policy, and other policies like it. Black people have been, and still are, the victims of racist discrimination. One result is that they are poorly represented in the professions. In order to remedy this it is not enough that we simply stop discriminating against them. For, so long as there are not enough "role models" available—i.e., black people visibly successful in the professions, whom young blacks can recognize as models to emulate—young blacks cannot be expected to aspire to the professions and prepare for careers in the way that young whites do. It is a vicious cycle: while there are relatively few black lawyers, relatively few young blacks will take seriously the possibility of becoming lawyers, and so they will not be prepared for law school. But if relatively few young blacks are well-prepared for law school, and admissions committees hold them to the same high standards as the white applicants, there will be relatively few black lawyers. Law school admissions committees may try to help set things right, and break this cycle, by temporarily giving preferential treatment to black applicants.

Moreover, although many people now recognize that racist discrimination is wrong, prejudice against blacks is still widespread. One aspect of the problem is that a disproportionate number of blacks are still poor and hold only menial jobs, while the most prestigious jobs are occupied mostly by whites. So long as this is so, it will be easy for the white majority to continue with their old stereotyped ideas about black people. But if there were more black people holding prestigious jobs, it would be much more difficult to sustain the old prejudices. So in the long run law school admissions policies favoring black applicants will help reduce racism throughout the society.

I believe these arguments, and others like them, show that policies of reverse discrimination can be socially useful, although this is certainly a debatable point. For one thing, the resentment of those who disapprove of such policies will diminish their net utility. For another, less qualified persons will not perform as well in the positions they attain. However, I will not discuss these issues any further. I will concentrate instead on the more fundamental question of whether policies of reverse discrimination are unjust. After all, the rejected white student may concede the utility of such policies and nevertheless still complain that he has been treated unjustly. He may point out that he has been turned down simply because of his race. If he had been black, and had had exactly the same qualifications, he would have been accepted. This, he may argue, is equally as unjust as discriminating against black people on account of their race. Moreover, he can argue that, even if black people have been mistreated, he was not responsible for it, and so it is unfair to penalize him for it now. These are impressive arguments and, if they cannot be answered, the rightness of reverse discrimination will remain in doubt regardless of its utility.

I will argue that whether the white applicant has been treated unjustly depends on why he has better credentials than the black, that is, it depends on what accounts for the 20-point difference in their qualifications.

Suppose, for example, that his higher qualifications are due entirely to the fact that he has worked harder. Suppose the two applicants are equally intelligent, and have had the same opportunities. But the black student has spent a lot of time enjoying himself, going to the movies, and so forth, while the white student has passed by such pleasures to devote himself to his studies. If *this* is what accounts for the difference in their qualifications, then it seems that the white applicant really has been treated unjustly. For he has earned his superior qualifications; he deserves to be admitted ahead of the black student because he has worked harder for it.

But now suppose a different explanation is given as to why the white student has ended up with a 20-point advantage in qualifications.

Suppose the applicants are equally intelligent and they have worked equally hard. However, the black student has had to contend with obstacles which his white competitor has not had to face. For example, his early education was at the hands of ill-trained teachers in crowded, inadequate schools, so that by the time he reached college he was far behind the other students and despite his best efforts he never quite caught up. If *this* is what accounts for the difference in qualifications, things look very different. For now the white student has not earned his superior qualifications. He has done nothing to deserve them. His record is, of course, the result of things he's done, just as the black student's record is the result of things the black student has done. But the fact that he has a *better* record than the black student is not due to anything he has done. That difference is due only to his good luck in having been born into a more advantaged social position. Surely he cannot deserve to be admitted into law school ahead of the black simply because of *that*.

Now in fact black people in the United States have been, and are, systematically discriminated against, and it is reasonable to believe that this mistreatment does make a difference to black people's ability to compete with whites for such goods as law school admission. Therefore, at least some actual cases probably do correspond to the description of my example. Some white students have better qualifications for law school only because they have not had to contend with the obstacles faced by their black competitors. If so, their better qualifications do not automatically entitle them to prior admission.

Thus it is not the fact that the applicant is black that matters. What is important is that, as a result of past discriminatory practices, he has been unfairly handicapped in trying to achieve the sort of academic standing required for admission. If he has a claim to "preferential" treatment now, it is for *that* reason.

It follows that, even though a system of reverse discrimination might involve injustice for some whites, in many cases no injustice will be done. In fact, the reverse is true: If no such system is employed—if, for example, law school admissions are granted purely on the basis of "qualifications"—*that* may involve injustice for the disadvantaged who have been unfairly handicapped in the competition for qualifications.

It also follows that the most common arguments against reverse discrimination are not valid. The white student in our example cannot complain that he is being rejected simply because he is white. The effect of the policy is only to *neutralize an advantage* that he has had because he is white, and that is very different.[1] Nor will it do any good for the white to complain that, while blacks may have suffered unjust hardships, *he* is not responsible for it and so should not be penalized for it. The white applicant is not being penalized, or being made to pay reparations, for the wrongs that have been done to blacks. He is simply not being allowed to *profit* from the fact that those wrongs were done, by now besting the black in a competition that is "fair" only if we ignore the obstacles which one competitor, but not the other, has had to face.

NOTE

1. See George Sher, "Justifying Reverse Discrimination in Employment," *Philosophy and Public Affairs*, 4, no. 2 (Winter 1975), 159–170. Sher also argues that "reverse discrimination is justified insofar as it neutralizes competitive disadvantages caused by past privations" (p. 165). I have learned a lot from Sher's paper.

REVIEW AND DISCUSSION QUESTIONS

1. What are the potential advantages of affirmative action that Rachels identifies?
2. What are the potential costs to society of affirmative action, according to Rachels?
3. Describe the factors that could mean that preference in hiring or admission is deserved, as a matter of justice.
4. "Reverse discrimination only serves to prevent some people from cashing in on an unfair system; it's rather like awarding a prize to a horse that came in second but would have won had the race been fair." Would Rachels agree or disagree with this statement? Explain.
5. "Since many minorities enjoy education and economic advantages while many whites are poor and suffer educational and other disadvantages, Rachels has not shown that preference based on race or gender is justified." Do you agree? Explain.

Racism and Reparations

John Arthur

What does society owe to people it has wronged in the past? Increasingly, the answer that is proposed is reparations, at least for the most eggregious forms of injustice, such as slavery and the racial oppression of Jim Crow. In this article John Arthur discusses the argument that

© 2001 by John Arthur. Thanks to various people who read and commented on this paper, including Rebecca Haimowitz, Katie Janssen, Mel Leffler, Phyllis Leffler, Steve Scalet, and Amy Shapiro. Needless to say, their providing me with helpful and sometimes critical comments does not imply their agreement.

reparations are owed to the African American descendants of slaves and victims of other forms of injustice. After a brief consideration of the goal of reparations, which he terms *restitution,* Arthur goes on to weigh several misguided objections. Nonetheless, he argues, reparations are not owed for either recent or long-past racial injustices. Along the way he discusses current racial attitudes of whites; the causes of contemporary economic inequality and poverty among blacks; and the role of family breakdown, crime, poor educational achievement, and I.Q. The last section addresses the related questions of what in fact *should* be done to help the black underclass, why pressing for reparations is not a good political strategy, and finally whether an apology rather than reparations should be offered. John Arthur is professor of philosophy and director of the Program in Philosophy, Politics and Law at Binghamton University.

Reparations is a hot topic. A fury erupted recently over whether college newspapers should accept an advertisement entitled "Ten Reasons Why Reparations for Blacks Is a Bad Idea." But paying reparations for slavery and discrimination is also gathering political and legal support. To date, about a dozen major U.S. cities have passed resolutions asking the federal government to study the reparations issue. For many years, representative John Conyers (D-Michigan) has introduced a bill in Congress calling for a similar study, though the proposal has never gotten out of committee. Human Rights Watch has also called for a study. A recent issue of the *Harvard Law Bulletin* [1] includes an article describing plans by law professor Charles Ogletree and author Randall Robinson to bring lawsuits demanding reparations for the enslavement of and discrimination against the ancestors of African Americans. Roy L. Brooks of the University of San Diego Law School recently proposed on ABC news that monetary reparations should be paid based on the average income gap between African Americans and whites.

In what follows I assume that reparations, like restitution in law, are compensation to people who have been wrongfully harmed. Defenders of reparations for African Americans rest their case on premises that I want first to acknowledge as both true and important: (1) slaves and their descendants suffered gross injustices and (2) like all victims of injustice, those individuals who suffered under slavery and Jim Crow laws should have been compensated. The issue I address,

however, is whether the *living* descendants of those who suffered under slavery and Jim Crow are entitled to reparations, who should compensate, who should receive compensation, and what form the reparations should take.

Randall Robinson defends reparations by first pointing out that slavery is "a human rights crime without parallel in the modern world. For it produces its victims, *ad infinitum*, long after the active stage of the crime has ended."[2] The goal of reparations, he points out, is "repairing the victim" or making the victim "whole."[3] I agree that refusing to pay reparations can be a serious injustice. In tort law, acts of negligence often require compensation in the form of payment for medical expenses, lost wages, and "pain and suffering" of the victim, though damages can also include loss of ability to use part of one's body, loss of a spouse's companionship, and much more. Sometimes compensation is demanded under tort law when the harm was intentional rather than negligent. If Jones assaults Smith, Smith is entitled to compensation, just as he would be if Jones negligently injured Smith.

Just what full reparation would require in practice is controversial, although in theory full compensation is not achieved until harm done to the victim of the wrongdoing has been fully repaired.[4] Restitution for African Americans thus raises many questions. The first is whether there is a debt owed to today's African Americans—a topic that will require looking closely at the lingering effects of past injustices and causes of contemporary economic inequalities among groups of Americans. In later sections, I ask who might be made to pay restitution, and what form the payment should take. In the last sections, I discuss the politics of reparations, including the potential dangers of pressing for reparations, equality of opportunity, and apologies. First, however, I turn to some common but mistaken reasons for rejecting reparations.

FOUR MISTAKEN OBJECTIONS TO REPARATIONS

Reparations are often dismissed out of hand, for a variety of familiar but mistaken reasons. It is sometimes claimed, for example, that since the injustices were done to long-dead slaves and other victims of discrimination, nothing could be owed to their descendants. But that is a mistake: nothing in the theory behind reparations rules out the possibility that negligence and intentional injustices create debts extending well beyond immediate victims and their contemporaries. Art stolen long ago and passed down from generation to generation should still be returned to the descendants of its rightful owner, just as negligence against a parent that also harms her children should be compensated.[5]

Another oft-heard objection appeals to the fact that nobody living today was responsible or blameworthy for slavery; but again this misses the mark. Reparations are not necessarily about *blaming* the perpetrators of past injustices. A corporation may be required to compensate for harm it caused despite the fact that no individual in the corporation was morally or legally responsible for the negligence. The law treats the corporation *as if* it were a single, responsible person and asks whether what it did, *if* done by a person, was negligent. If the answer is yes, then the corporation may be liable even if no single individual in the corporation was culpable. Strict liability laws work similarly, holding a person responsible despite the absence of moral culpability.

A third objection to reparations focuses on the question of who owes them. Reparations

seem to many to suggest not just that an injustice occurred, but also that some individual or group benefited from the injustice and therefore owes compensation to the victims. Thus, when Mari Matsuda argues for reparations, she describes the "defendant" as the "perpetrator descendants and *current beneficiaries of past injustice*."[6] But this way of thinking about reparations is open to an obvious objection, often made by critics: how are we to decide who has benefited unjustly and therefore should be forced to compensate? Is it only the direct descendants of the slave owners and racists who inherited wealth produced by slaves or who benefited from Jim Crow laws who should pay? Defenders of reparations could deny this, of course, claiming that society as a whole (including some living African Americans?) benefited from the general economic prosperity flowing from slavery and discrimination. But this is controversial, since it can also be argued that slavery and discrimination were *not* economically efficient, that the general economic situation in the South would have been better without slavery, and indeed that rather than benefiting, the entire country actually suffered economically from discrimination and segregation. Furthermore, if we say that *everybody* benefited from slavery rather than the few descendants of slave owners, reparations would then be owed by living African Americans to themselves—a distinctly paradoxical result. And finally, critics ask, what about all those who have come to the United States since the end of slavery and Jim Crow? Must they pay reparations? In what sense do poor Vietnamese immigrants and unemployed white Appalachian miners owe reparations to wealthy African Americans?

These critics of reparations assume, following Matsuda, that reparations are owed by those persons who benefited from the injustice to those who suffered the injustice. But why suppose that somebody must benefit before reparations are owed? When a corporation compensates for its negligence, there is no requirement that its employees or owners have benefited from its negligence. Similarly when the government of Germany paid reparations to Jews who suffered in the Holocaust and the U.S. government compensated Japanese Americans who had been forced into camps during World War II, there was again no suggestion that any person had benefited from those injustices. In these cases, reparations were owed simply because an institution, whether a corporation or government, had done an injustice.

A fourth objection to reparations appeals to the fact that at that time slavery and discrimination were widespread and often accepted practices. It is wrong, according to this argument, to hold past generations and governments to contemporary standards. In tort law, just as in our private moral relationships with one another, we would not hold a person liable unless we were convinced a "reasonable person" would have behaved differently at the time. We do not demand perfection of one another, only what we can reasonably expect of another human being. But again this objection misses the point, which is that there is a difference between what individuals owe and what governments owe. We now know that what the government did was unjust, and governments owe not just a reasonable *attempt* at justice to their citizens, but justice itself. When a government fails to live up to that in an especially egregious fashion, it has a duty to repair the damage.

The fact that there are plausible responses to these familiar objections is important. It means reparations could still be owed by the United States to descendants of slaves despite the fact that no living individual was blameworthy or benefited from the injustice. It also suggests that the question is more complex than many have supposed. But having thus set aside, for the sake of argument, these easy objections, the key question still remains: are reparations owed for slavery and past discrimination, and if so why and to whom?

ECONOMIC INEQUALITY AND RACISM

Defenders of reparations often point to what they see as the lingering effects of slavery and discrimination, which were either legally sanctioned or at least tolerated by the government. Robinson and Ogletree explain that the justification of their lawsuit is the fact that "256 years of slavery, 100 years of Jim Crow laws, and continuing discrimination have taken their toll on the African-American community," a toll that includes "pervasive disparities between African Americans and other Americans in areas including health care, education and employment."[7] Matsuda makes a similar claim in her defense of reparations: "Reparations claims are based on continuing stigma and economic harm. The wounds are fresh and the action timely given ongoing discrimination."[8] Derrick Bell paints a particularly bleak picture of the failure of American law to remedy past injustices visited on African Americans:

> In spite of dramatic civil rights movements and periodic victories in the legislatures, black Americans by no means are equal to whites. . . . The reality is that blacks still suffer disproportionately higher rates of poverty, joblessness, and insufficient health care than other ethnic populations in the U.S. . . . The racial realism we must seek is simply a hard-eyed view of racism as it is and our subordinate role in it."[9]

Poverty, joblessness, and poor health are serious problems for many African Americans. But the reparations argument must link these with past injustices for which compensation is due. So the key question is how best to explain the disparities in wealth and other disadvantages suffered by the black underclass. Are they the result of slavery and racial oppression?

Sometimes it is thought sufficient simply to point to the fact that economic inequalities and poverty fall disproportionately on African Americans to show racism's lingering effects. Kimberle Crenshaw, for instance, *assumes* that all we need to know is that African Americans do less well. The "expansive" view of equality, which she favors, "stresses equality as a result, and it looks to real consequences for African-Americans. It [seeks] the eradication of the substantive conditions of black subordination . . . and the effects of racial oppression." [10] The question, of course, is whether inequality *is* the result of slavery and racism.

Standing alone, however, differences in wealth and poverty between contemporary African Americans and others in society prove nothing about the effects of slavery and discrimination. Major economic disparities exist between many groups, not just between blacks and whites or between oppressed and oppressor. Indeed, those other disparities are often *greater* than the black/white one. The figures are striking. Overall, the average family income of native-born U.S. whites is $35,975 and that of African Americans is $20,209. To Crenshaw and Matsuda, that must be the result of racism, but look at the figures more closely. Americans of Japanese and Chinese descent earn an average of $52,728 and $56,762, far above the average for whites. Those of Cuban descent also earn more than whites ($37,452). There is also wide variation among white ethnic groups: Greek Americans, for instance, do much better than Polish Americans.

These economic disparities are relevant to the reparations dispute for two reasons. First, we know that many cultural and other factors contribute to economic differences among groups, so that slavery and racism need not *necessarily* be behind such differences. Second, these figures raise doubts about the importance of slavery and racism because other groups, also victims of discrimination (and in the case of Jews, slavery), have not suffered economically.[11] So to make the case for reparations, it would have to be shown that the cultural or other factors at work explaining inequality among other groups do not explain the economic differences between African American and whites. We need to know much more before we can join Crenshaw and Matsuda in attributing the lower income and high poverty rates of blacks to racism.

Defenders of reparations often do not distinguish between the lingering effects of slavery and Jim Crow laws on one hand, and the supposed effects of *contemporary* racism on the other. Matsuda, in the essay quoted earlier, speaks of "ongoing discrimination" as well as slavery as the reasons reparations are justified, and Bernard Boxill defends reparations exclusively on the ground that blacks today suffer from discrimination.[12] So before returning to the argument based on slavery and racism against past generations, I want first to look at the assumption that widespread racism persists in the United States and that poverty among African Americans is its result.

CONTEMPORARY ECONOMIC REALITIES AND RACIAL ATTITUDES

It is important to remember first that almost half of all African Americans now describe themselves as middle class, so whatever impediments racism poses have not prevented vast numbers of blacks from succeeding and in many cases accumulating great wealth. Other indicators also suggest that life has improved substantially for African Americans since the mid-1960s. The proportion of blacks who have attended college rose from about 15 percent in 1965 to nearly half in 1995, and the percentage graduating from college has risen from less than 7 percent to *more* than 15 percent.[13] Perhaps most interesting, of those who complete college, black women with a college degree now actually earn 7 percent *more* than what comparably educated white women earn.[14] Overall, the economic position of blacks improved markedly in the mid-1900s. The percentage of black families below the poverty line decreased from 87 percent in 1940 to about 30 percent in 1970. But it has remained pretty constant ever since, declining to about 26 percent today.[15] That 26 percent, then, is the crux of the debate.

The reason that poverty has not continued to decline is not that the American people suddenly became more racist in the last quarter of the twentieth century. In fact, the reverse is true: racial attitudes have consistently improved, just as legal protections against discrimination were secured by civil rights laws of the 1960s and 1970s and affirmative action policies were put in place giving preferences to African Americans in education and employment. From 1944 to 1963, for example, the percentage of white Americans saying that blacks should "have as good a chance as white people to get any kind of job" rose from 42 percent to 83 percent.[16] By 1972, that figure had increased to 97 percent. Similarly, by 1972, 84 percent of whites favored integrated schools and 85 percent expressed no reservation about having a black neighbor. Changes since then have continued this trend.[17] Americans are also far more tolerant of inter-racial marriages, which are becoming commonplace. Nor of course do publicized random acts of violence by whites against blacks show society is more racist. More than half of the victims of violent crimes by blacks are white, and 89 percent of inter-racial crime is committed by black perpetrators against white victims.[18]

But what about the fact that whites often generalize about criminal behavior of young African American males? Does that indicate racism? I think not. In a survey done in 1991 by the University of California, *more blacks than whites* said blacks are "aggressive or violent" while many more blacks than whites also reported being afraid to walk out alone at night.[19]

What figures do show is that beginning in the 1960s the U.S. experienced a huge increase in crime—what two sociologists describe as the "worst crime wave in its history"—and that young black males were responsible for a disproportionate share of reported offenses. While large numbers of young blacks have been arrested for drug offenses, they are also arrested and convicted in much larger proportions for other crimes. In 1995, for example, more than half of those arrested for murder and robbery were black (54 percent and 59 percent respectively) despite the fact that they represent about 12 percent of the population as a whole.[20] "Fear of blacks," wrote Norman Podhoretz in 1993, "has become the dirty little secret of our political culture."[21]

The lesson then is not that people have stopped stereotyping based on race, for plainly they have not. But generalizing based on evidence is not a racist act. People cannot force themselves to believe what they know to be false and should not be criticized for failing to do so. A black woman who is fearful of an approaching skinhead is only behaving reasonably given the chances that he is a racist and she should therefore not be thought prejudiced against prematurely bald men and chemotherapy patients.

Finally it is sometimes assumed that opposition to affirmative action and welfare are themselves proof or racism[22], but again the evidence does not support that claim.[23] Much of the opposition to these policies is based on principles such as equality before the law and the work ethic, and "most of those who oppose more government spending on behalf of blacks are not bigots."[24] Opposition takes on a racial character because African Americans are disproportionately represented among welfare recipients and affirmative action beneficiaries, and both welfare and affirmative action programs are controversial. None of this means genuine racism has disappeared, of course. But the assertion that inequalities in income and poverty among African Americans can be attributed to modern-day racism does not withstand scrutiny.

THE REAL CAUSES OF POVERTY

We return then to the heart of the matter: is poverty among African Americans the result of the racist history of the United States? I argue that while there is no simple answer to the causes of persistent African American poverty, the claim that slavery and discrimination against past generations of African Americans caused it flies in the face of the facts. The reason is that we have other, better explanations—ones that have little or nothing to do with racism.

The first, very important factor that explains poverty is a surge in black children being born to single women. *Regardless of race*, children growing up in households headed by a single parent tend overwhelmingly to be poor, which means that because disproportionately large numbers of black children are in single-parent families, they are disproportionately poor. In 1995, 70 percent of all black births were out of wedlock[25] while 85 percent of black children who were poor lived in families without a father present.[26] Indeed, the majority (62 percent) of black children living with only their mother are poor, while only 13 percent of black children living with both parents are poor. The income for female-headed black families was just over a third of the income of black married couples.[27]

Besides the economic disadvantages of being raised by a single-earner parent who may herself be poor, statistics show that being raised in a single-parent family is an educational handicap as well. Educational achievement is lower for children of single parents than for children raised by two adults, even when income levels are the same.[28] Family breakdown is thus a doubly important factor: not only is it directly correlated with poverty but it is also an indirect disadvantage because of its negative effect on educational achievement.

Increased crime is a second factor contributing to poverty. While it is often assumed that unemployment and poverty cause crime, the reverse is also the case. Crime is often the cause of poverty as well its effect. This complexity in the relationship between poverty and crime is confirmed by the fact that crime exploded *not* during the 1930s and early 1940s when black poverty was rampant but instead beginning in the 1960s, during a period of sustained economic progress among blacks. The crime rise continued into the 1990s, which was again a time of economic progress for most blacks and even slight increases for the poorest.

Specifically, crime contributes to poverty at least four ways. High rates of crime (1) encourage the perception that young black males are not responsible employees and so reduces their ability to get good jobs; (2) increase the cost and risk of doing business in high crime areas, often African American neighborhoods, causing businesses to move away; (3) mean that people engaged in criminal activities or in prison are not earning income for themselves or their families (or at least not income that is counted when figures are compiled); and (4) reduce the value of home ownership, which for many families of all races is their major source of wealth and has been a standard stepping-stone to the middle class.

Added to growth in single-parent families and increased crime is another important predictor of economic success: educational performance. First, there are large gaps in the college graduation rates of black and other students. Although blacks graduate from high school in about the same proportion as whites, less than 13 percent of African Americans complete college, while almost 25 percent of whites have a college degree.[29] While, as Orlando Patterson put it, a sixfold increase since 1940 in college completion that leaves African Americans "among the most educated persons in the world, with median years of schooling and college completion rates higher than those of most West Europeans is nothing to sniff at," the disparity with other groups remains a serious matter.[30]

Equally troubling is the gap in achievement scores. Black seventeen-year-olds, for instance, range from three to almost six grades behind whites in educational achievement.[31] That matters in understanding poverty because not only is graduation a major factor in predicting economic success, with college-educated people earning more than those not finishing college, but those with high skills do better than those who lack them. Unlike females, college-educated black males earn only 77 percent of comparably educated white males.[32] This difference is attributable in part to the fact that fewer black male college graduates go into high-paying professions such as medicine, law, and accounting. (This also explains some of the income differences noted earlier among other groups of Americans. Different groups tend to pursue different career paths.) But that is only part of the story. Studies also show significant disparities between comparably educated black and white males on basic tests involving arithmetical reasoning, reading comprehension, and vocabulary, which themselves influence career choices and ultimate success.[33] Large disparities also exist on SAT Achievement tests across the board: the most recent evidence suggests that blacks average 524 on both History and English SAT II, while the national average is 736.[34]

My goal here is not to explore precisely *how much* economic inequality can be explained by such factors as family breakdown, crime, and educational achievement. The point is that plausible reasons that explain poverty raise doubts about whether slavery and racism play a significant role. Perhaps, however, it could be argued that these cultural and social factors that do explain economic inequalities are *themselves* the lingering, indirect effects of slavery and discrimination against African Americans many generations ago. If this is true, then reparations might still be owed as compensation for the fact that slavery and racism cause the family breakdown, crime, and poor educational achievement that in turn cause the poverty. Rather than undermining the case for reparations, then, these social problems would support it.

IS SLAVERY THE *INDIRECT* CAUSE OF INEQUALITY?

But is this true? Are the factors that explain poverty *themselves* the lingering effects of slavery and discrimination for which reparations might be owed? In this section, I indicate briefly how difficult it would be to sustain such an argument, and indeed how unlikely a race-based explanation is.

First, as I noted earlier, great differences exist in the economic levels of many different groups that cannot plausibly be attributed to racism. While that fact does undermine the *assumption* that inequality must be caused by racial oppression, it still might be argued that because of the uniqueness of American slavery, its effects were worse than other forms of discrimination that apparently had no lasting economic impact on Chinese, Japanese, and Jewish Americans. Just *how* slavery and Jim Crow laws might have had such a long-term effect is subject to much conjecture, with many simply assuming it *must* be true. It is sometimes suggested, for example, that the destruction of the family was in some way the result of slavery's denigration of the importance of marriage, or that laws forbidding slaves to learn to read have a lingering effect on educational achievement. In his book *The Debt,* Randall Robinson claims that the destruction of African cultural identity as a result of slavery continues to harm African Americans and warrants reparations.[35]

It should be noted first, however, that all such claims face the important objection that the increases in single-parent families and crime began in the 1960s and 1970s, and not immediately after slavery and Jim Crow. It seems unlikely that slavery's effects would remain dormant for generations, only to emerge in the 1960s and later.

Equally important is the fact that we already have on hand better explanations for poverty than slavery and Jim Crow. To appreciate the true complexity of the situation, we need first to note the important economic changes that took place in the last part of the Twentieth Century. Harvard economist William Julius Wilson, for example, claims that unemployment, crime, and poverty are rooted in recent changes in industrial production and labor markets, as blue-collar jobs disappeared and were replaced on one hand by jobs requiring more education and other skills and on the other by relatively low-paying service jobs. The effects of this economic shift were felt disproportionately by African Americans.[36]

Though important, however, that does not yet explain *why* these economic dislocations were felt disproportionately by African Americans, and why a large proportion of African Americans were unable to take advantage of educational and other opportunities in response to the economic conditions by moving to better paying jobs requiring higher skill and education levels. The most obvious reason for this, which I believe needs to be taken very seriously, is that public education has failed. While nobody is legally barred from getting re-training, it does seem likely that the often disastrously poor quality of many inner-city schools affects people's economic prospects, including their ability to adapt to economic changes.

I believe this is an argument that should be taken seriously, because I also believe that one of the fundamental requirements of justice is that government provide fair equality of opportunity for all citizens.[37] If government fails in this important duty, it would at least justify a serious and possibly expensive effort to improve educational opportunities and perhaps even compensation to all those who, of whatever race, were harmed by that injustice.[38]

That said, however, two further points should be made. First, this argument is not grounded on racism and discrimination but instead on class. Many poor whites suffer from unequal educational opportunities, and so would also be entitled to whatever poor blacks should get. The argument is therefore very different from the claim I am considering here, which is that slavery and racism require reparations. Second, this claim is complicated by the fact that inadequate funding is only part of the cause of poor educational opportunity; other problems include familiar ones of family breakdown and crime as well as administrative inefficiencies. Washington D.C., for example, is among the nation's highest cities in per-pupil expenditures and yet among the lowest in educational achievement. So the topic is complex. While government is required to do all it can to provide equality of opportunity, it cannot be expected to replace the family or perhaps even to convert recalcitrant teachers' unions.

We seem left, then, with a complex web of factors explaining economic inequalities between blacks and other groups. The causes include major structural changes in the economy, single-parent families, crime, poor educational achievement, and failure of society to secure equal educational opportunity for the country's poor—many of whom are black. If there is injustice at work, however, it is not race based or grounded in slavery but instead involves failure to provide fair equality of opportunity.

All that being granted (if it is) one further issue needs airing. It has sometimes been argued that while social factors such as crime, single-parent families, general economic changes, and educational disadvantages play their roles, another more basic cause of lower incomes is differences in scores on I.Q. tests. (I do not assume I.Q. tests measure anything worth having. They are important for these purposes only based on what they are able to explain.) And indeed I.Q. tests do predict many of the factors that themselves predict poverty, and they do so for all groups, including African Americans. Single white women with I.Q. scores in the bottom 20 percent have a 70 percent chance of being poor, for example, while women with high I.Q.s have only about a 10 percent possibility. Differences in educational achievement also reflect variations in I.Q. scores. Not only does I.Q. predict which children succeed in high school, but I.Q. is an even *more important* predictor of high school graduation than the parents' socio economic status. In addition to poverty and educational achievement, I.Q. also predicts welfare dependency for all groups. White women with an I.Q. in the bottom 20 percent constitute 55 percent of those who go on welfare within a year of the birth of their first child, while those in the top 20 percent of I.Q. account for only 1 percent. Even after marital status and poverty are taken into account, I.Q. remains an important factor in determining whether white women become welfare dependent over a long period.[39]

These economic consequences of I.Q. scores are relevant for understanding economic inequality because African Americans score approximately 15 points or one standard deviation below whites on I.Q. tests. In other words, the average white scores higher than 84 percent of blacks, while the average African American scores higher than 16 percent of whites.[40] (Jews score substantially above the average for all whites, while East Asians probably score higher on mathematical tests but not verbal, though the data on that are less clear.)[41] Nor are these differences in I.Q. among groups the result of variations in wealth and income: the I.Q. scores of both blacks and whites go up with income, but the difference in scores between blacks and whites does not diminish substantially. Wealthy blacks not only score lower than wealthy whites, but they also do not score as high as poor whites, while African Americans from families with incomes over $50,000 do less well on I.Q. tests than East Asians from families earning $6,000 or less.[42]

Not surprisingly, the impact of these group-based differences in I.Q. on the income differentials between African Americans and whites is profound. Controlling for I.Q., the differences in wages between blacks and whites (as will as Latinos) actually shrink from thousands to just over five hundred dollars per worker per year. In other words, African Americans and whites with similar I.Q. scores receive virtually identical incomes. Similar patterns emerge with regard to I.Q. and educational achievement. Blacks with the same I.Q. as whites are even slightly *more* likely to graduate from college. The same is true for post-graduate degrees: the proportion of blacks who earn a Ph.D. almost perfectly matches the proportion of blacks who have an I.Q. above 130, which is the average for all people who get a Ph.D.[43] (In that sense, there is no "under representation" of African Americans among college professors.)

As would be expected, in addition to predicting income and education levels for both whites and blacks, I.Q. scores are also correlated with welfare dependency, out-of-wedlock childbirth, and crime.[44] What all this suggests, then, is that instead of slavery and

discrimination, I.Q. may be the ultimate explanation of both economic inequalities and their underlying social problems. In other words, if we really want to understand differences in income levels and poverty, we should look not *just* to single-parent families, poor educational achievement, and crime but also to I.Q. It predicts income success generally and also accounts for these other factors that, I have argued, are themselves predictors of poverty. But that then opens up still another question: is it not possible that differences in I.Q. scores are *themselves* somehow the result of racism and slavery?

It is widely agreed that both environment and inheritance (i.e., nurture and nature) play a role. And while there is little doubt that biological inheritance substantially influences I.Q. scores *among individuals*, there is deep controversy about the relative importance of environmental factors and inherited ones in explaining group I.Q. differences. One study of identical twins raised in different environments found that their I.Q. scores were consistently similar and concluded that between .75 and .80 of intelligence is inheritable while .25 or less of the variance in I.Q. scores is attributable to environmental factors.[45] Siblings who are not identical twins but were also raised apart show a less significant correlation in I.Q., approximately .4, while half-siblings, who share even less genetic material, show still less correlation. Additional evidence showing that I.Q. differences are not determined by environmental factors comes from studies of transracial adoptions. The Minnesota Transracial Adoption Study, for instance, compared the I.Q. scores of black and white children raised by white middle-class families. For African American high school age children, the mean I.Q. was 89, while white children raised in the same families had a mean I.Q. of 105.[46]

So there is little room for doubt that individuals' I.Q. scores are influenced by genetic as well as by environmental factors. These studies do not prove conclusively, however, that I.Q. differences between *groups* are biologically based, since it is at least theoretically possible that something unknown to us today about the environment of a group of people accounts for group I.Q. differences, even though much of the variation between individuals within each group is inherited.[47] But that said, it does seem unlikely that slavery and racial oppression generations ago could have had such an effect on I.Q., for a variety of reasons. First, it is far from clear intuitively how the culture-neutral parts of I.Q. tests, such as the ability to repeat a series of numbers backwards, could be affected by past discrimination and slavery. Second, the effects of slavery on blacks would have to be vast if it is to explain the substantial variation in I.Q., since only 16 percent of blacks achieve above the average of whites. Third, the lingering effects of slavery must be at least as effective at explaining the low I.Q. scores of wealthy blacks as poor blacks. Finally, slavery's effects would have to take hold in early childhood, when I.Q. is largely settled.[48] Given all those facts, the claim that low I.Q. scores result from slavery and racial oppression seems not just unproved but also quite doubtful.[49]

Finally, it should also be emphasized that even the environmental factors affecting I.Q.s of different groups are not necessarily evidence of past discrimination. Some cultural groups emphasize literacy and numeracy more than others, which may do much to explain variations in I.Q. It is a further, controversial question whether such cultural variations are attributable to historical discrimination or to a wealth of other possible factors.[50] Even the proportion of I.Q. that is not genetically determined may have little to do with racial discrimination.

So in sum, we know that a substantial narrowing of the economic gap between African Americans and other groups has taken place, though a black underclass remains that is marked by poverty, crime, single-parent families, and poor educational performance. The causes of the persistence of the black underclass are complex and often controversial, but it is difficult to attribute economic inequalities and poverty either directly to contemporary racism or indirectly, to the legacy of slavery and legal discrimination. Structural shifts in

the economy and variations in I.Q. scores have been offered as explanations, and each likely plays a part along with cultural differences among groups. But whatever the causes, I have argued, the claim that economic inequalities and poverty result from slavery and Jim Crow is at best unsubstantiated if not completely disproved.

WHO OWES WHAT TO WHOM?

In this section and the next, I set the objections I have just raised aside and offer other reasons why reparations should still be rejected. These reasons vary, from the importance of subsequent actions of later generations of African Americans themselves to the impossibility of determining how much is owed and to whom it should be given.

The first objection focuses on events after slavery and Jim Crow and depends on a principle known in law as the doctrine of the "last clear chance." Normally, if a person who was wronged had the opportunity to avoid the damages she suffered, but she then failed to do so, her claim to reparations is undermined. Intervening actions and failures to act can break the linkage of responsibility that would otherwise go back to the one who originally caused the harm. So, for example, if your negligence causes somebody else to break a leg, but then the injured person refuses medical help to repair the leg, you are not responsible for damages that your victim could have avoided by a trip to the doctor. Your responsibility is limited to what your victim could not reasonably have avoided; the rest is his own responsibility. I will assume that this principle applies in morality and politics as well as law.

The principle is relevant to the reparations debate because *even if we assume* there are lingering effects of Jim Crow and slavery, they would not render the contemporary descendants of slaves incapable of obeying the law, working hard in school, avoiding drugs, or forming a family and taking a serious interest in their children's welfare. If a father is harmed by a negligent driver, and cannot support his children, then the children may claim damages. But if after the accident the father chooses to abandon his children the harm the abandonment causes is not the driver's responsibility. Sometimes it *is* proper to "blame the victim," or at least to deny a victim reparations when he is at fault.

That is not to say, of course, that every poor African American is in a position to do more to help himself or herself; many plainly are not. Children are not responsible for their parent's misdeeds. But neither is the government always responsible for all the failings and choices people make, even those making us or our children worse off. This is relevant for our purposes because there is some evidence that part of the reason young black males do not succeed in school and employment has to do with their own behavior and attitudes. In their book *Crime and Human Nature,* Richard Hernstein and James Q. Wilson write that in a study of ghetto boys, "Every boy interviewed had been employed at one time, but the turnover was very high. When asked why they left the job, they typically answered that they found it monotonous or low paying. . . . Being able to 'make it' while avoiding the 'work game' is a strong, pervasive and consistent goal."[51] Other researchers have found similar behavior and attitudes.[52] This raises deep issues since, as I suggested earlier, government does have an obligation to provide fair equality of opportunity. My only point, however, is that it is a two-way street: people must also do their part in making the best of their opportunities, and insofar as poverty results from uncoerced choices people make rather than past injustices, their claim to reparations is undermined.

Another, even more fundamental objection to reparations questions whether it is possible ever to determine the nature of the compensation that is owed to African Americans. The assumption behind the reparations claim is that past injustices harmed, in some way, the current descendants of slavery and segregation. But this raises a host of problems. First, we immediately confront the role of other

Africans. It is widely acknowledged by historians that Africans were active participants in the slave trade in capturing and selling slaves to the European slave traders. In that way, slavery was very much a mutual undertaking between Europeans and Africans: just as illegal drugs require both a supplier and a purchaser, and both are partly responsible, so too with slavery. The suggestion, then, is that if reparations are owed to African Americans, they are the responsibility of not just Americans and Europeans but also Africans themselves.

But that is only the beginning of the problems. In order to determine whether a past unjust or negligent action caused harm, we must be able compare the victim's current situation with some other one, a baseline, in which the injustice did not occur. Sometimes the right baseline seems obvious: if a watch is stolen, the baseline measure of harm compares the current situation to one in which the thief did not steal the watch. In the case of negligent drivers, we may also feel confident that our baseline is the one in which the accident victim would still be working, without the medical bills and the pain endured.

Determining harm, therefore, actually involves three steps: first *choosing* the appropriate baseline of comparison, then *describing* what would actually have happened to current victims under that imagined baseline, and finally *evaluating* the harm done by comparing what actually happened with how history would have progressed under that baseline. So the first task is to choose the baseline that is the relevant initial point of comparison.[53] But the choice of the right baseline in the case of slavery and past discrimination is far more difficult than in cases such as the ones I mentioned, for a variety of reasons.

Setting aside the role of other Africans in slavery, there are at least four possible baselines. One would be to compare the current situation of African Americans with where they would be had their ancestors been captured and brought to this country not as slaves but as free and equal citizens. Or we could imagine a baseline in which (like other immigrants) the ancestors were merely allowed to come if they could find their own way, rather than being forced. A third possibility would be to ask how contemporary blacks would have fared had somebody helped their ancestors to come as free citizens by providing free transportation to the ports and on to America. Finally, we could assume that there had never been any migration or slavery and compare the lives of current African Americans with a baseline in which their ancestors stayed in Africa.

The question is: which baseline is the "right" one? Why *not* imagine that they remained in Africa, as some have suggested, either to live as natives or perhaps even to be sold as slaves to Arabs, other Africans, or someone else? The other three baselines, where they were either forced, allowed, or helped to immigrate to the United States, have the best prospect of justifying reparations, though we must also assume that Africans brought here would have flourished rather than starved or been killed by Native Americans. The problem, then, is that while this choice is critical, it also seems arbitrary. What reason do we have for choosing one baseline rather than the others?

One answer might be to choose the baseline that is the most likely actually to have occurred. It is difficult to know, of course, but it does seems unlikely there would have been massive voluntary immigration from Africa to the European colonies of North America. Still, who knows? If on the other hand, the choice is made based on whether the person choosing likes the idea of reparations, as I suspect is likely, then we are begging the question by assuming to know the answer to the problem we are trying to resolve with the choice of a baseline.

The second problem in determining a baseline is how to describe the historical implications of whatever baseline we do choose. Even if we could agree for good reasons on a particular baseline, we need to be able to say with some confidence and detail how history would have proceeded. But can we do that? How could we know what would have happened

had Africans been allowed or enabled to come to America? Would they have chosen to come? What would have happened to them after they arrived? So unlike normal legal cases in which we are confident that but for the negligence the injuries to the victim would not have occurred, reparations raises questions without answers. (It is worth remembering that reparations paid to Jewish victims of the Holocaust went to actual victims who lost property and suffered under the Nazis, not to their descendants.)

Third, even if we could identify the right baseline and also describe its course through history with some assurance, we would still need to compare the harm (and benefits) of slavery against the advantages and disadvantages of that baseline. Given that average per capita income in Africa is something like $300 a year, the baseline in which there was no slavery and Africans remained in Africa might justify no reparations at all, on the ground that the injustice of slavery did not harm the descendants given what their position would have been had they stayed in Africa. Wanting to defend reparations, Randall Robinson suggests that we focus on harm caused by the loss of African language and culture.[54] But that again raises a host of thorny questions, including the relative advantages and disadvantages of replacing an African language with English and an African tribe's way of life with a Western one. If loss of one's language and cultural identity is *ipso facto* damaging, do the assimilated descendants of Greek or Mexican immigrants have reason to demand reparations from *their* great grandparents? On what basis could we answer such a question? Many suppose such comparisons are not just difficult but impossible: the values of one culture cannot be compared to those of another. If it *is* possible to make comparisons, however, is it relevant that so many Africans wish to emigrate to the United States while so few Americans emigrate to Africa?

Finally, and most speculatively, because we are thinking about the effects of slavery on *currently living* African Americans, it is also clear that had there been no slavery, none of those African Americans now claiming compensation would even have been conceived. Their parents would likely never have met, let alone conceived that child when they did. Without slavery, different generations would have been born. The question then arises: does the fact that their very *existence depends on slavery* undermine their claim that they were *harmed by slavery*? Can we just say that if a past injustice resulted in a person's being conceived, the person cannot then also claim damages from the injustice?

Besides these many problems and objections, involving the principle of the last clear chance and the impossibility of identifying a baseline, describing its implications and then evaluating the amount of harm, there is also a question whether the descendants of slavery have not already received compensation. In his advertisement attacking reparations, David Horowitz suggested that welfare payments and affirmative action policies giving preference to African Americans are all the reparation that could be owed. It has also been claimed that restitution was paid by the blood of Union soldiers in the Civil War. My point again is not to defend either claim but to highlight the earlier problem. Besides having no way to know what baseline to choose, let alone how to describe and evaluate the situation of contemporary African Americans had history gone according to another scenario instead of slavery, we also have no way to know whether compensation has already been paid. The upshot of all this is that even if slavery and past discrimination were the source of the black underclass (which I argued they were not), we have no way to know if the compensation is owed or, if it is, has already been paid.

One final question involves the form that compensation should take if it were owed and had not already been paid. Robinson recommends cash payments to make up for lost wages, which he thinks would total perhaps "a trillion and a half" as well as several trillion more for wage discrimination.[55] Yet it is not at all clear that a cash payment would ultimately be of much help. Those most deserving of

reparations would presumably be those who are in the worst position today; certainly that seems to be the thinking of people who contemplate bringing a lawsuit for reparations. Yet those are the same people who have shown themselves least able and willing to take advantage of opportunities they have already been given. Another suggestion, which perhaps makes more sense than a cash payment, would be to provide compensation in the form of better schools and fuller opportunities. This has obvious advantages, but I want to suggest in the last section why that is a goal better justified without appealing to reparations for slavery.

I should emphasize, finally, that I am not arguing against all discrimination-based reparations. I support compensation to Holocaust victims, to interred Japanese Americans and to women abused by the Japanese Army in World War II. Perhaps there are some African Americans still alive who do continue to suffer the effects of racial discrimination during their childhood.[56] Merely remembering segregated schools and bathrooms is not enough, however, any more than Jews who today recall quotas at universities warrant reparations. So if my argument against reparations for slavery is right, the defense of reparations will always be complicated. But reparations for living victims of racial and other injustices, for those who can trace the harm directly to more recent injustices, is not my subject.

THE POLITICS OF REPARATIONS

Paying reparations to African Americans for slavery and Jim Crow laws is not only unjustified, as I have been arguing, but also both unfair and politically unwise. Paying reparations is unfair because it ignores all the injustices that other groups have endured, from Native Americans and Hispanics to Asians, the Irish, and the Jews. Though slavery is undoubtedly a worse injustice than many other forms of discrimination, if reparations are justified, they are justified to all who are in a worse position today as a result of past injustices. Why select only African Americans?

Reparations are also politically misguided. They encourage the mistaken thought that descendants of slaves and Jim Crow are not responsible for their own conduct: poor performance in school, crime, and family breakup are assumed to be the outgrowth of historical processes over which nobody has control or responsibility. Paying reparations would therefore reinforce the self-destructive attitudes that work cannot pay off and that the system offers little opportunity for poor African Americans. As William James emphasized in another context, what we believe we can do and what we expect of others shapes how things ultimately go in our own lives.

There is also a larger political issue, grounded in a tension between reparations and the background conditions of civil society that make achieving social justice possible. Social justice assumes a shared commitment among fellow citizens, especially by the more powerful, that all in society will be shown a special concern. In a democratic society, justice depends on the sense of a shared relationship among citizens that is not found among strangers or with citizens of other nations. Reparations are controversial and divisive, as Horowitz's suggestion that welfare payments are all the reparations that are owed shows. The worry, then, is based on the fact that demands for reparations appeal to group-based entitlements. They are a demand that compensation be paid for past injustices to all members of a particular group. This differs from the ordinary requirements of social justice, which are owed to all citizens individually and equally: to respect basic rights, secure fair equality of opportunity, and meet basic economic needs for those unable to provide for themselves. Demanding reparations, therefore, runs the risk of encouraging the attitude that group membership trumps shared citizenship, undercutting more powerful, justice-based efforts to improve the conditions of the African American underclass based on fair equality of opportunity. But providing fair equality of opportunity is not divisive in that way. Unlike group-based reparations, equal opportunity is owed to all and at the same time is widely accepted as an important responsibility of government. It does not have the air of special pleading or seeking an undeserved, group-based advantage.

Finally, instead of encouraging feelings of dependence on government largesse, as reparations could do, demanding equality of opportunity calls attention to the responsibilities of not only government to provide sound education and training but also of citizens to take advantage of those opportunities. So besides being more compatible with the social concern that motivates social justice and less socially divisive, equality of opportunity also encourages attitudes among citizens that are likely to prove helpful rather than self-destructive.

AN APOLOGY FOR SLAVERY?

As I have said, I believe that the real, serious injustices done to today's poor children, of whatever group, have nothing to do with slavery and reparations—and little to do with race. Rather, it is this systematic failure of government, and society, to secure fair equality of opportunity for all. No child should be deprived of an equal chance to a decent life, which includes a good education. Pleas for reparations risk undermining the social ground on which that important claim rests. Apologies, on the other hand, are a different story. Suppose the parent of an adult child did something long ago that the parent now knows was wrong or unjust. Perhaps the parent showed favoritism to another child or abused or neglected one child. The parent now feels ashamed and deeply regrets what he did. But the parent also realizes that the long-term effects of that wrong on the child, done long ago, are completely unknowable. For those reasons, restitution in the sense of returning the child to where she would have been without that injustice is impossible.

Should that parent nonetheless now acknowledge the wrong and apologize to the child? No compensation is possible, I assume, and we might even add that the child is now indifferent to getting the apology. Perhaps the two have lost touch. It still seems to me that despite all these facts, the parent should express sorrow and ask forgiveness of the child. But the reason has little to do with the child, who may not be made to feel more kindly toward the parent or even feel satisfied by the

apology. The beneficiary of the apology is in a sense the parent. Though the wrong cannot be made right, and the child may not even care, it is still a better world if the wrong is acknowledged and an apology offered. I can see no reason why a government that is also guilty of a gross injustice owes its citizens anything less. But neither, I have argued, does it owe more—specifically not reparations for slavery and Jim Crow.

NOTES

1. Emily Newburger, "Breaking the Chain," *Harvard Law Bulletin* Vol. 52, No. 3, Summer 2001.
2. *Ibid.*, p. 19.
3. *Ibid.*, p. 21.
4. One way to think about this more concretely is to require that the victim be compensated until she is indifferent to either of two scenarios: the one in which she was never harmed, and the actual one in which the victim was wronged but then compensated.
5. For obvious reasons law does not attempt to compensate *all* those who have been harmed, however remote. But our concern here is with political morality. Whether it is practical, or wise, as a policy matter to pay reparations for slavery is a question I touch on in the last section.
6. Mari J. Matsuda, "Looking to the Bottom: Critical Legal Studies and Reparations" in *Critical Race Theory*, ed. Kimberle Crenshaw, Neil Gotanda, Gary Peller, and Kendall Thomas (New York: The New Press, 1995), p. 70.
7. Newburger, "Breaking the Chain," p. 19.
8. Matsuda, "Looking to the Bottom," p. 72.
9. Derrick Bell, "Racial Realism" in Crenshaw et al. *Critical Race Theory*, pp. 302 and 308.
10. Kimberle Crenshaw, "Race, Reform, and Retrenchment," in Crenshaw et al. *Critical Race Theory*, p. 105.
11. Although as Steve Scalet pointed out to me, it might be that what needs explaining is how these other groups managed to be so successful and overcome the effects of slavery and discrimination. But if other groups did overcome the effects, why not blacks too? We still need an explanation of *that*.
12. Bernard Boxill, *Blacks and Social Justice* (New York: Roman and Littlefield, 1992), pp. 147–172.
13. From U.S. Department of Education, *Youth Indicators 1996: Trends in the Well-Being of American Youth* (Washington DC: U.S. Government Printing Office, 1996) p. 70. Quoted in Stephan Thernstrom

and Abigail Thernstrom, *America in Black and White* (New York: Simon & Shuster, 1997), p. 391.
14. U.S. Bureau of Census, *Current Population Reports: March 1995* (Washington D.C.: Government Printing Office, 1996), table 9. Quoted in Thernstrom and Thernstrom, *America in Black and White*, p. 445.
15. Thernstrom and Thernstrom, *America in Black and White*, p. 233. (Taken from census figures.)
16. *Ibid.*, p. 141. (Figures from various sources.)
17. *Ibid.*, p. 500. (Figures from various sources.)
18. U.S. Department of Justice, Bureau of Justice Statistics, *Criminal Victimization in the United States, 1993* (Washington D.C.: U.S. Department of Justice, 1996), p. 45 and 49. Quoted in Thernstrom and Thernstrom, *America in Black and White*, p. 272.
19. Thernstrom and Thernstrom, *America in Black and White*, p. 141.
20. U.S. Department of Justice, *Crime in the United States–1995* (Washington, D.C.: U.S. Government Printing Office, 1996), p. 226. Quoted in Thernstrom and Thernstrom, *America in Black and White*, pp, 262–264.
21. Norman Podhoretz, "Postscript (1993)" in *Blacks and Jews: Alliances and Arguments*, ed. Paul Berman (New York: Bantam Doubleday Dell, 1994), p. 94.
22. See for example Charles R. Lawrence III, "The Id, the Ego, and Equal Protection: Reckoning With Unconscious Racism" in Crenshaw et al., *Critical Race Theory*.
23. Paul M. Sniderman and Thomas Piazza, *The Scar of Race* (Cambridge: Harvard University Press, 1993), pp. 35–65.
24. *Ibid.,* p.105.
25. *Ibid.*, p. 237. (Figures from various sources.)
26. Thernstrom and Thernstrom, *America in Black and White* pp. 236–237. (Figures from various sources.)
27. *Ibid.,* p. 241. (Figures from various sources.)
28. *Ibid.*, p. 358.

29. Orlando Patterson, "The Paradox of Integration," *The New Republic*, November 6, 1995. Reprinted in John Arthur and Amy Shapiro, *Color, Class Identity: The New Politics of Race* (Boulder: Westview Press, 1996), p. 27.

30. *Ibid.*, p. 67.

31. Thernstrom and Thernstrom, *America in Black and White*, p. 355. (Figures from various sources.)

32. U.S. Bureau of Census, *Current Population Reports: March 1995* (Washington D.C.: Government Printing Office, 1996), table 9. Quoted in Thernstrom and Thernstrom, *America in Black and White*, p. 445.

33. Thernstrom and Thernstrom, *America in Black and White*, p. 446.

34. "Bilingual Students Use Language Tests to Get a Leg Up on College Admissions," *Wall Street Journal*, June 26, 2001, p. 1.

35. Randall Robinson, *The Debt: What America Owes Blacks* (New York: E.P. Dutton, 2000).

36. William Julius Wilson, *The Truly Disadvantaged* (Chicago: The University of Chicago Press, 1987).

37. Fair equality of opportunity means that any two equally talented and motivated children have the same prospects for economic success, regardless of socioeconomic class. See "Fair Equality of Opportunity and Pure Procedural Justice" in John Rawls, *A Theory of Justice* (Cambridge: Harvard University Press, 1971).

38. It might therefore be argued that some form of reparations is due because of failure to provide fair equality of opportunity.

39. Figures in this paragraph from various sources, quoted in Richard J. Herrnstein and Charles Murray, *The Bell Curve: Intelligence and Class Structure in American Life* (New York: The Free Press, 1994) pp. 138, 149, 194, 198.

40. *Ibid.,* p. 269.

41. *Ibid.*, pp. 272–275.

42. Leonard Ramist and Solomon Arbeiter, *Profiles, College-Bound Seniors*, 1985 (New York: College Entrance Examination Board, 1986), pp. 27, 37, 47, 57.

43. Michael Levin, "Race, Biology and Justice," *Public Affairs Quarterly* Vol. 8, No. 3 (1994), p. 274.

44. Figures in this paragraph are mainly from the *National Longitudinal Study of Youth*, quoted in Herrnstein and Murray, *The Bell Curve*, pp. 320–324, 374–378.

45. J. J. Boucharad, D. T. Lykken, M. McGue, N. L. Segal, and A. Tellegen, "Sources of Human Psychological Differences: The Minnesota Study of Twins Reared Apart." *Science* Vol. 250, (1990), 223–228.

46. R. Weinberg, S. Searr, and I. Waldman, "The Minnesota Transracial Adoption Study: A Follow-up of IQ Test Performance at Adolescence," *Intelligence* Vol. 16 (1992), 1192.

47. Those who argue that group differences in test scores are environmentally rather than genetically based sometimes point to a study showing that after World War II, no significant difference was found between the I.Q.s of children fathered by black and white American soldiers in Germany. [See John Loehlin, Gardner Lindzey, and J. N. Spuhler, *Race Differences in Intelligence* (San Francisco: W.H. Freeman Co., 1975), p. 183.] But while such historical variations in I.Q. do seem to suggest that environment is a major factor in shaping test scores, these figures would also imply that the decline in test scores among blacks has taken place only in recent decades—a fact that is impossible to square with the claim that the test differences are due to slavery and Jim Crow.

48. While tests given to very young children are unreliable predictors of future scores, I.Q. differences are largely set by the age of 10, with very little variance after that. [B. S. Bloom, *Stability and Change in Human Characteristics* (New York, Wiley: 1960).]

49. There is also some additional evidence, albeit controversial, suggesting that differences in group I.Q.s are genetic and not primarily the result of environmental factors of any sort, let alone slavery. First, native Africans score lower on I.Q. tests than do African Americans, including on those tests that are the least susceptible to cultural bias. [R. Lynn, "Race Differences in Intelligence: A Global Perspective," *Mankind Quarterly* Vol. 31 (1991), pp. 254–269; see also K. Owen, "The Suitability of Raven's Standard Progressive Matrices for Various Groups in South Africa," *Personality and Individual Differences*, Vol. 13 (1992), pp. 149–159.] Similarly, South African students of "mixed" white and black African ancestry show I.Q.'s similar to African Americans. [D. Owen, *None of the Above: Behind the Myth of Scholastic Aptitude,* (Boston: Houghton Mifflin, 1985).]

50. As a non-Jew, I have often been struck in attending a Bar Mitzvah or Bat Mitzvah by the strong emphasis placed on language, history, and interpretation. Presumably that has something to do with the fact that there are so many Jewish lawyers.

51. Richard Hernstein and James Q. Wilson, *Crime and Human Nature* (New York: Simon & Schuster, 1985), pp. 304, 335.

52. See for example Edward Banfield, *The Unheavenly City Revisited* (Boston: Little, Brown, 1974). In the 1991 *National Survey on Race*, more blacks than whites said they agree with the statement "blacks are lazy" and nearly twice the percentage of blacks than whites agreed that "blacks are irresponsible." [Sniderman and Piazza, *The Scar of Race*, p. 45.]

53. For a discussion of the problem of baselines in the context of original acquisition of unowned property, see John Arthur, "Property Acquisition and Harm," *Canadian Journal of Philosophy* Vol. 17, No. 2, (June 1987).

54. Robinson, *The Gift.*

55. Quoted in Newburger, "Breaking the Chain," p. 21.

56. Thanks to Phyllis Leffler for pressing the importance of this on me.

REVIEW AND DISCUSSION QUESTIONS

1. Some have argued that reparations are not justified because no currently living individuals were responsible for slavery or benefited from it. How does Arthur answer those objections?

2. How does Arthur respond to those who argue that current racial attitudes and racist practices justify reparations? What is the importance of group-based differences in income among various groups, according to Arthur?

3. What does Arthur think are the underlying social problems that do explain the black underclass, if not slavery, racial oppression, and Jim Crow?

4. Explain the role of I.Q. in predicting economic success. Why does Arthur think I.Q. differences cannot be explained by slavery and racial oppression?

5. Explain the significance of this essay for arguments about race-based preferences and affirmative action.

6. Why does Arthur favor pressing for equality of opportunity and an apology rather than reparations?

Essay and Paper Topics for Section 14

1. Compare the justification Rachels gives for affirmative action with that offered by the Supreme Court in the Bakke case. Which seems to have the stronger position?

2. Affirmative action is sometimes defended as an attempt to compensate for society's failure to provide equality of opportunity. Is that a sound argument for such policies? Explain.

3. Affirmative action is now commonly defended on the ground suggested by Justice Powell in the Bakke case: that it promotes "diversity." Write an essay in which you first analyze what, precisely, would be good or valuable about having a diverse student body or faculty and, second, whether or not you think preferences based on race, skin color, or ethnicity achieve the goal of diversity.

4. Using one of the moral theories from Part I, write an essay in which you either defend or criticize affirmative action from within that theoretical perspective.

5. After California eliminated affirmative action preferences in admissions to its universities, the proportion of black and Hispanic students at the most competitive universities decreased while the proportions at less competitive ones increased. Other states have replaced racial preferences with guarantees that the top students at any high school will be admitted to universities. Do you agree that this is better than affirmative action?

6. Compare Arthur's position on racism with those of Wasserstrom and Young in Section 13.

PART IV

Personal Relationships

15

Sex, Love, and Friendship

Sexual relationships, sexual morality, and friendship are oft-discussed, intensely personal, emotional, and profoundly important to most people. Should sex be limited to marriage? Or at least to friends? What is sex, ideally? Merely a pleasant experience? An expression of friendship or love? Essays in this section begin with Kant's famous discussion of sexual duty, followed by a series of different perspectives on the nature of sex, homosexuality, and date rape. The last essay is on friendship, a topic in the background of other discussions in this section. In it, the author considers the impact of modern communications and information technology on our relationships with other people and on our own sense of self.

Duties Toward the Body
in Respect to Sexual Impulse

Immanuel Kant

In this reading, Immanuel Kant discusses the nature of the "sexual impulse" and people's needs to control it, as well as his views on marriage. Kant sees sexual desire as threatening people's higher, rational nature, and in particular the requirement that we respect ourselves and others by acting only on principles we can will to become universal laws. Specifically, he thinks some sexual practices violate the fundamental ethical principle that we must never treat another person merely as a means, but always as an end. Prostitution, concubinage, and extramarital sex are all, Kant argues, inconsistent with this most fundamental of moral requirements. He then goes on to describe the moral basis of marriage and the morality of homosexuality. Kant's biography can be found in section 1.

Amongst our inclinations there is one which is directed towards other human beings. They themselves, and not their work and services, are its Objects of enjoyment. It is true that man has no inclination to enjoy the flesh of another—except, perhaps, in the vengeance of war, and then it is hardly a desire—but none the less there does exist an inclination which we may call an appetite for enjoying another human being. We refer to sexual impulse. Man can, of course, use another human being as an instrument for his service; he can use his hands, his feet, and even all his powers; he can use him for his own purposes with the other's consent. But there is no way in which a human being can be made an Object of indulgence for another except through sexual impulse. This is in the nature of a sense, which we can call the sixth sense; it is an appetite for another human being. We say that a man loves someone when he has an inclination towards another person. If by this love we mean true human love, then it admits of no distinction between types of persons, or between young and old. But a love that springs merely from sexual impulse cannot be love at all, but only appetite. Human love is goodwill, affection, promoting the happiness of others and finding joy in their happiness. But

it is clear that, when a person loves another purely from sexual desire, none of these factors enter into the love. Far from there being any concern for the happiness of the loved one, the lover, in order to satisfy his desire and still his appetite, may even plunge the loved one into the depths of misery. Sexual love makes of the loved person an Object of appetite; as soon as that appetite has been stilled, the person is cast aside as one casts away a lemon which has been sucked dry. Sexual love can, of course, be combined with human love and so carry with it the characteristics of the latter, but taken by itself and for itself, it is nothing more than appetite. Taken by itself it is a degradation of human nature; for as soon as a person becomes an Object of appetite for another, all motives of moral relationship cease to function, because as an Object of appetite for another a person becomes a thing and can be treated and used as such by every one. This is the only case in which a human being is designed by nature as the Object of another's enjoyment. Sexual desire is at the root of it; and that is why we are ashamed of it, and why all strict moralists, and those who had pretensions to be regarded as saints, sought to suppress, and extirpate it. It is true that without it a man

From Immanuel Kant, *Lectures in Ethics,* translated by Louis Infield (London: Methuen & Co., 1963). Reprinted by permission.

would be incomplete; he would rightly believe that he lacked the necessary organs, and this would make him imperfect as a human being; none the less men made pretence on this question and sought to suppress these inclinations because they degraded mankind.

Because sexuality is not an inclination which one human being has for another as such, but is an inclination for the sex of another, it is a principle of the degradation of human nature, in that it gives rise to the preference of one sex to the other, and to the dishonouring of that sex through the satisfaction of desire. The desire which a man has for a woman is not directed towards her because she is a human being, but because she is a woman; that she is a human being is of no concern to the man; only her sex is the object of his desire. Human nature is thus subordinated. Hence it comes that all men and women do their best to make not their human nature but their sex more alluring and direct their activities and lusts entirely towards sex. Human nature is thereby sacrificed to sex. If then a man wishes to satisfy his desire, and a woman hers, they stimulate each other's desire; their inclinations meet, but their object is not human nature but sex, and each of them dishonours the human nature of the other. They make of humanity an instrument for the satisfaction of their lusts and inclinations, and dishonour it by placing it on a level with animal nature. Sexuality, therefore, exposes mankind to the danger of equality with the beasts. But as man has this desire from nature, the question arises how far he can properly make use of it without injury to his manhood. How far may persons allow one of the opposite sex to satisfy his or her desire upon them? Can they sell themselves, or let themselves out on hire, or by some other contract allow use to be made of their sexual faculties? Philosophers generally point out the harm done by this inclination and the ruin it brings to the body or to the commonwealth, and they believe that, except for the harm it does, there would be nothing contemptible in such conduct in itself. But if this were so, and if giving vent to this desire was not in itself abominable and did not involve immorality,

then any one who could avoid being harmed by them could make whatever use he wanted of his sexual propensities. For the prohibitions of prudence are never unconditional; and the conduct would in itself be unobjectionable, and would only be harmful under certain conditions. But in point of fact, there is in the conduct itself something which is contemptible and contrary to the dictates of morality. It follows, therefore, that there must be certain conditions under which alone the use of the *facultates sexuales* would be in keeping with morality. There must be a basis for restraining our freedom in the use we make of our inclinations so that they conform to the principles of morality. We shall endeavour to discover these conditions and this basis. Man cannot dispose over himself because he is not a thing; he is not his own property; to say that he is would be self-contradictory; for in so far as he is a person he is a Subject in whom the ownership of things can be vested, and if he were his own property, he would be a thing over which he could have ownership. But a person cannot be a property and so cannot be a thing which can be owned, for it is impossible to be a person and a thing, the proprietor and the property.

Accordingly, a man is not at his own disposal. He is not entitled to sell a limb, not even one of his teeth. But to allow one's person for profit to be used by another for the satisfaction of sexual desire, to make of oneself an Object of demand, is to dispose over oneself as over a thing and to make of oneself a thing on which another satisfies his appetite, just as he satisfies his hunger upon a steak. But since the inclination is directed towards one's sex and not towards one's humanity, it is clear that one thus partially sacrifices one's humanity and thereby runs a moral risk. Human beings are, therefore, not entitled to offer themselves, for profit, as things for the use of others in the satisfaction of their sexual propensities. In so doing they would run the risk of having their person used by all and sundry as an instrument for the satisfaction of inclination. This way of satisfying sexuality is *vaga libido* [prostitution], in which one satisfies the inclinations of others for gain. It is possible for either sex. To let one's person out on hire and to surrender it to another for the satisfaction of his sexual desire in return for money is the depth of infamy. The underlying moral principle is that man is not his own property and cannot do with his body what he will. The body is part of the self; in its togetherness with the self it constitutes the person; a man cannot make of his person a thing, and this is exactly what happens in *vaga libido*. This manner of satisfying sexual desire is, therefore, not permitted by the rules of morality. But what of the second method, namely *concubinatus* [sex outside marriage]? Is this also inadmissible? In this case both persons satisfy their desire mutually and there is no idea of gain, but they serve each other only for the satisfaction of sexuality. There appears to be nothing unsuitable in this arrangement, but there is nevertheless one consideration which rules it out. Concubinage consists in one person surrendering to another only for the satisfaction of their sexual desire whilst retaining freedom and rights in other personal respects affecting welfare and happiness. But the person who so surrenders is used as a thing; the desire is still directed only towards sex and not towards the person as a human being. But it is obvious that to surrender part of oneself is to surrender the whole, because a human being is a unity. It is not possible to have the disposal of a part only of a person without having at the same time a right of disposal over the whole person, for each part of a person is integrally bound up with the whole. But concubinage does not give me a right of disposal over the whole person but only over a part, namely the *organa sexualia*. It presupposes a contract. This contract deals only with the enjoyment of a part of the person and not with the entire circumstances of the person. Concubinage is certainly a contract, but it is one-sided; the rights of the two parties are not equal. But if in concubinage I enjoy a party of a person, I thereby enjoy the whole person; yet by the terms of the arrangement I have not the rights over the whole person, but only over a part;

I, therefore, make the person into a thing. For that reason this method of satisfying sexual desire is also not permitted by the rules of morality. The sole condition on which we are free to make use of our sexual desire depends upon the right to dispose over the person as a whole—over the welfare and happiness and generally over all the circumstances of that person. If I have the right over the whole person, I have also the right over the part and so I have the right to use the person's *organa sexualia* for the satisfaction of sexual desire. But how am I to obtain these rights over the whole person? Only by giving that person the same rights over the whole of myself. This happens only in marriage. Matrimony is an agreement between two persons by which they grant each other reciprocal rights, each of them undertaking to surrender the whole of their person to the other with a complete right to disposal over it. We can now apprehend by reason how a *commercium sexuale* [sexual relationship] is possible without degrading humanity and breaking the moral laws. Matrimony is the only condition in which use can be made of one's sexuality. If one devotes one's person to another, one devotes not only sex but the whole person; the two cannot be separated. If, then, one yields one's person, body and soul, for good and ill and in every respect, so that the other has complete rights over it, and if the other does not similarly yield himself in return and does not extend in return the same rights and privileges, the arrangement is one-sided. But if I yield myself completely to another and obtain the person of the other in return, I win myself back; I have given myself up as the property of another, but in turn I take that other as my property, and so win myself back again in winning the person whose property I have become. In this way the two persons become a unity of will. Whatever good or ill, joy or sorrow befall either of them, the other will share in it. Thus sexuality leads to a union of human beings, and in that union alone its exercise is possible. This condition of the use of sexuality, which is only fulfilled in marriage, is a moral condition. But let us pursue this aspect further and examine the case of a man who takes two wives. In such a case each wife would have but half a man, although she would be giving herself wholly and ought in consequence to be entitled to the whole man. To sum up: *vaga libido* is ruled out on moral grounds; the same applies to concubinage; there only remains matrimony, and in matrimony polygamy is ruled out also for moral reasons; we, therefore, reach the conclusion that the only feasible arrangement is that of monogamous marriage. Only under that condition can I indulge my *facultas sexualis.* We cannot here pursue the subject further. . . .

Crimina carnis [crimes of the flesh] are contrary to self-regarding duty because they are against the ends of humanity. They consist in abuse of one's sexuality. Every form of sexual indulgence, except in marriage, is a misuse of sexuality, and so a *crimen carnis.* . . . Adultery cannot take place except in marriage; it signifies a breach of marriage. Just as the engagement to marry is the most serious and most inviolable engagement between two persons and binds them for life, so also is adultery the greatest breach of faith that there can be, because it is disloyalty to an engagement than which there can be none more important. For this reason adultery is cause for divorce. Another cause is incompatibility and inability to be at one, whereby unity and concord of will between the two persons is impossible. . . .

Uses of sexuality which are contrary to natural instinct and to animal nature are *crimina carnis contra naturam.* First amongst them we have onanism [masturbation]. This is abuse of the sexual faculty without any object, the exercise of the faculty in the complete absence of any object of sexuality. The practice is contrary to the ends of humanity and even opposed to animal nature. By it man sets aside his person and degrades himself below the level of animals. A second *crimen carnis contra naturam* is intercourse between *sexus homogenii* [same sex], in which the object of sexual impulse is a human being but there is homogeneity instead of heterogeneity of sex, as when a woman satisfies her desire on a woman, or a man on a man. This practice too is contrary to the ends of humanity; for the end of humanity in respect of sexuality is to preserve the species without debasing the person; but in this instance the species is not being preserved (as it can be by a *crimen carnis secundum naturam*), but the person is set aside, the self is degraded below the level of the animals, and humanity is dishonoured. The third *crimen carnis contra naturam* occurs when the object of the desire is in fact of the opposite sex but is not human. Such is sodomy, or intercourse with animals. This, too, is contrary to the ends of humanity and against our natural instinct. It degrades mankind below the level of animals, for no animal turns in this way from its own species. All *crimina carnis contra naturam* degrade human nature to a level below that of animal nature and make man unworthy of his humanity. He no longer deserves to be a person. From the point of view of duties towards himself such conduct is the most disgraceful and the most degrading of which man is capable. Suicide is the most dreadful, but it is not as dishonourable and base as the *crimina carnis contra naturam.* . . . These vices make us ashamed that we are human beings and, therefore, capable of them.

REVIEW AND DISCUSSION QUESTIONS

1. What is the difference between love and sexual desire, according to Kant?
2. Kant says that sex can subordinate another human being by treating her (or him) not as a human being but as a sexual creature. Explain what you think he might mean.
3. Explain how Kant seems to understand the nature of persons: are we minds, bodies, or both? What does he mean when he says we are "not at our own disposal"?

4. In what way does sex outside marriage or concubinage presuppose a "contract" that deals "only with a part of the person"? How can people gain "rights over the whole person," according to Kant? What does he mean by that phrase?

5. Explain Kant's objection to homosexuality. How might it be argued that homosexual relations are compatible with, rather than contrary to, Kant's view of the legitimate use of our sexual faculties?

6. Kant writes elsewhere that polygamy is ruled out because the contract is unequal: one person gives up more than the other. In marriage, however, the relationship is reciprocal and therefore acceptable. Explain why Kant would think that, given his general moral view.

What's Wrong with Homosexuality?

John Finnis

Many, these days, regard those who oppose homosexual conduct as "homophobic," which means not that they fear homosexuals, but that they are prejudiced against them. John Finnis argues, however, that certain sorts of sexual activities, whether performed by people of the same or opposite sex, are wrong. Finnis's reasoning is based on the idea of a "common good" that is realized only in certain forms of sexual activity. Other forms of sexual activity involve a use of one's body in ways that fail to live up to that ideal and are in other ways damaging to society as well as to the participants. This selection is from Finnis's testimony in a Colorado court. The case arose because citizens of Colorado had amended their constitution to bar localities from passing ordinances protecting gays and lesbians against discrimination. The amendment was challenged in the courts and eventually held by the U.S. Supreme Court to be unconstitutional on the ground that it singled out a particular group, homosexuals, and denied them the equal protection of the law. John Finnis is professor of moral and legal philosophy at Oxford University.

The underlying thought is on the following lines. In masturbating, as in being masturbated or sodomized, one's body is treated as instrumental for the securing of the experiential satisfaction of the conscious self. Thus one disintegrates oneself in two ways, (1) by treating one's body as a mere instrument of the consciously operating self, and (2) by making one's choosing self the quasi-slave of the experiencing self which is demanding gratification. The worthlessness of the gratification, and the disintegration of oneself, are both the result of the fact that, in these sorts of behavior, one's conduct is not the actualizing and experiencing of a real common good. Marriage, with its double blessing—procreation and friendship—is a real common good. Moreover, it is a common good that can be both actualized and experienced in the orgasmic union of the reproductive organs of a man and a woman united in commitment to that good. Conjugal sexual activity, and—as Plato and Aristotle and Plutarch and Kant all argue,—*only* conjugal activity is free from the shamefulness of instrumentalization that is found in masturbating and in being masturbated or sodomized.

At the very heart of the reflections of Plato, Xenophon, Aristotle, Musonius Rufus, and Plutarch on the homoerotic culture around them is the very deliberate and careful

Excerpts from legal depositions from the 1993 trial over the constitutionality of Colorado Amendment 2.

judgment that homosexual *conduct* (and indeed all extramarital sexual gratification) is radically incapable of participating in, or actualizing, the common good of friendship. Friends who engage in such conduct are following a natural impulse and doubtless often wish their genital conduct to be an intimate expression of their mutual affection. But they are deceiving themselves. The attempt to express affection by orgasmic nonmarital sex is the pursuit of an illusion. The orgasmic union of the reproductive organs of husband and wife really unites them biologically (and their biological reality is part of, not merely an instrument of, their *personal* reality); that orgasmic union therefore can actualize and allow them to experience their real common good—their marriage with the two goods, children and friendship, which are the parts of its wholeness as an intelligible common good. But the common good of friends who are not and cannot be married (man and man, man and boy, woman and woman) has nothing to do with their having children by each other, and their reproductive organs cannot make them a biological (and therefore a personal) unit. So their genital acts together cannot do what they may hope and imagine.

In giving their considered judgment that homosexual conduct cannot actualize the good of friendship, Plato and the many philosophers who followed him intimate an answer to the questions why it should be considered shameful to use, or allow another to use, one's body to give pleasure, and why this use of one's body differs from one's bodily participation in countless other activities (e.g., games) in which one takes and/or gets pleasure. Their response is that pleasure is indeed a good, when it is the experienced aspect of one's participation in some intelligible good, such as a task going well, or a game or a dance or a meal or a reunion. Of course, the activation of sexual organs with a view to the pleasures of orgasm is sometimes spoken of as if it were a game. But it differs from real games in that its point is not the exercise of skill; rather, this activation of reproductive organs is focused upon the body precisely as a source of

pleasure for one's consciousness. So this is a "use of the body" in a strongly different sense of "use." The body now is functioning not in the way one, as a bodily person, acts to instantiate some other intelligible good, but precisely as providing a service to one's consciousness, to satisfy one's desire for satisfaction.

This disintegrity is much more obvious when masturbation is solitary. Friends are tempted to think that pleasuring each other by some forms of mutual masturbation could be an instantiation or actualization or promotion of their friendship. But that line of thought overlooks the fact that if their friendship is not marital . . . activation of their reproductive organs cannot be, in reality, an instantiation or actualization of their friendship's common good. In reality, whatever the generous hopes and dreams with which the loving partners surround their use of their genitals, *that use* cannot express more than is expressed if two strangers engage in genital activity to give each other orgasm, or a prostitute pleasures a client, or a man pleasures himself. Hence, Plato's judgment, at the decisive moment of the *Gorgias,* that there is no important distinction in essential moral worthlessness between solitary masturbation, being sodomized as a prostitute and being sodomized for the pleasure of it. . . .

Societies such as classical Athens and contemporary England (and virtually every other) draw a distinction between behavior found merely (perhaps extremely) offensive (such as eating excrement) and behavior to be repudiated as destructive of human character and relationships. Copulation of humans with animals is repudiated because it treats human sexual activity and satisfaction as something appropriately sought in a manner that, like the coupling of animals, is divorced from the expressing of an intelligible common good—and so treats human bodily life, in one of its most intense activities, as merely animal. The deliberate genital coupling of persons of the same sex is repudiated for a very similar reason. It is not simply that it is sterile and disposes the participants to an abdication of responsibility for the future of humankind. Nor is it simply that it cannot *really* actualize the mutual devotion that some homosexual persons hope to manifest and experience by it; nor merely that it harms the personalities of its participants by its disintegrative manipulation of different parts of their one personal reality. It is also that it treats human sexual capacities in a way that is deeply hostile to the self-understanding of those members of the community who are willing to commit themselves to real marriage [even one that happens to be sterile] in the understanding that its sexual joys are not mere instruments or accompaniments to, or mere compensation for, the accomplishments of marriage's responsibilities, but rather are the *actualizing and experiencing* of the intelligent commitment to share in those responsibilities. . . .

This pattern of judgment, both widespread and sound, concludes as follows. Homosexual orientation—the deliberate willingness to promote and engage in homosexual acts— is a standing denial of the intrinsic aptness of sexual intercourse to actualize and give expression to the exclusiveness and open-ended commitment of marriage as something good in itself. All who accept that homosexual acts can be a humanly appropriate use of sexual capacities must, if consistent, regard sexual capacities, organs, and acts as instruments to be put to whatever suits the purposes of the individual "self" who has them. Such an acceptance is commonly (and in my opinion rightly) judged to be an active threat to the stability of existing and future marriages; it makes nonsense, for example, of the view that adultery is per se (and not merely because it may involve deception), and in an important way, inconsistent with conjugal love. A political community that judges that the stability and educative generosity of family life is of fundamental importance to the community's present and future can rightly judge that it has a compelling interest in denying that homosexual conduct is a valid, humanly acceptable choice and form of life, and in doing whatever it properly can, as a community with uniquely wide but still subsidiary functions, to discourage such conduct.

REVIEW AND DISCUSSION QUESTIONS

1. What, exactly, is the "common good" that Finnis thinks cannot be realized by certain forms of sexual conduct? Why can't it be realized through masturbation or sodomy?
2. How would Finnis respond to a person who said: "I agree that sodomy and masturbation are not perfect. But they are better than nothing"?
3. Is Finnis right in supposing that sex with animals is on a par with sodomy and masturbation, assuming that the animal doesn't mind?
4. Besides failing to realize people's common good, what other concerns does Finnis express about homosexual conduct?
5. Would allowing homosexual marriage address some of the problems Finnis raises?

Plain Sex

Alan H. Goldman

Critical of Kant and other defenders of the "means-end" conception of sex, Goldman offers an alternative "plain fact" understanding of human sexuality. Rather than serving another goal, such as reproduction or the expression of love, sex on Goldman's view is something far simpler: the desire for physical contact. Goldman concludes with discussions of the nature of love, and of sexual perversion. Alan H. Goldman is professor of philosophy at the University of Miami.

1. SEX AS THE DESIRE FOR PHYSICAL CONTACT

. . . I shall suggest here that sex continues to be misrepresented in recent writings, at least in philosophical writings, and I shall criticize the predominant form of analysis which I term "means-end analysis." Such conceptions attribute a necessary external goal or purpose to sexual activity, whether it be reproduction, the expression of love, simple communication, or interpersonal awareness. They analyze sexual activity as a means to one of these ends, implying that sexual desire is a desire to reproduce, to love or be loved, or to communicate with others. All definitions of this type suggest false views of the relation of sex to perversion and morality by implying that sex which does not fit one of these models or fulfill one of these functions is in some way deviant or incomplete.

The alternative, simpler analysis with which I will begin is that sexual desire is desire for contact with another person's body and for the pleasure which such contact produces; sexual activity is activity which tends to fulfill such desire of the agent. . . . This definition in terms of the general goal of sexual desire appears preferable to an attempt to more explicitly list or define specific sexual activities, for many activities such as kissing, embracing, massaging, or holding hands may or may not be sexual, depending upon the context and more specifically upon the purposes, needs, or desires into which such activities fit. The generality of the definition also represents a refusal (common in recent psychological texts) to overemphasize orgasm as the goal of sexual desire or genital sex as the only norm of sexual activity (this will be hedged slightly in the discussion of perversion below).

Central to the definition is the fact that the goal of sexual desire and activity is the physical contact itself, rather than something else which this contact might express. By contrast, what I term "means-end analyses" posit ends which I take to be extraneous to plain sex, and they view sex as a means to these ends. . . .

This initial [plain sex] analysis may seem to some either over- or underinclusive. It might seem too broad in leading us to interpret physical contact as sexual desire in activities such as football and other contact sports. In these cases, however, the desire is not for contact with another body per se, it is not directed toward a particular person for that purpose, and it is not the goal of the activity—the goal is winning or exercising or knocking someone down or displaying one's prowess. If the desire is purely for contact with another specific person's body, then to interpret it as sexual does not seem an exaggeration. A slightly more difficult case is that of a baby's desire to be cuddled and our natural response in wanting to cuddle it. In the case of the baby, the desire may be simply for the physical contact, for the pleasure of the caresses. If so, we may characterize this desire, especially in keeping with Freudian theory, as sexual or protosexual. It will differ nevertheless from full-fledged sexual desire in being more amorphous, not directed outward toward another specific person's body. It may also be that what the infant unconsciously desires is not physical contact per se but signs of affection, tenderness, or security, in which case we have further reason for hesitating to characterize its wants as clearly sexual. The intent of our response to the baby is often the showing of affection, not the pure physical contact, so that our definition in terms of action which fulfills sexual desire *on the part of the agent* does not capture such actions, whatever we say of the baby. (If it is intuitive to character our response as sexual as well, there is clearly no problem here for my analysis.) The same can be said of signs of affection (or in some cultures polite greeting) among men or women: these certainly need not be homosexual when the intent is only to show friendship, something extrinsic to plain sex although valuable when added to it.

Our definition of sex in terms of the desire for physical contact may appear too narrow in that a person's personality, not merely her or his body, may be sexually attractive to another, and in that looking or conversing in a certain way can be sexual in a given context without bodily contact. Nevertheless, it is not the contents of one's thoughts per se that are sexually appealing, but one's personality as embodied in certain manners of behavior. Furthermore, if a person is sexually attracted by another's personality, he or she will desire not just further conversation, but actual sexual contact. While looking at or conversing with someone can be interpreted as sexual in given contexts it is so when intended as preliminary to, and hence parasitic upon, elemental sexual interest. Voyeurism or viewing a pornographic movie qualifies as a sexual activity, but only as an imaginative substitute for the real thing

(otherwise a deviation from the norm as expressed in our definition). The same is true of masturbation as a sexual activity without a partner. . . ,

This characterization of sex as an intensely pleasurable physical activity and acute physical desire may seem to some to capture only its barest level. But it is worth distinguishing and focusing upon this least common denominator in order to avoid the false views of sexual morality and perversion which emerge from thinking that sex is essentially something else.

2. THE REPRODUCTIVE MODEL

We may turn then to what sex is not, to the arguments regarding supposed conceptual connections between sex and other activities which it is necessary to conceptually distinguish. The most comprehensible attempt to build an extraneous purpose into the sex act identifies that purpose as reproduction, its primary biological function. While this may be "nature's" purpose, it certainly need not be ours (the analogy with eating, while sometimes overworked, is pertinent here). While this identification may once have had a rational basis which also grounded the identification of the value and morality of sex with that applicable to reproduction and childrearing, the development of contraception rendered the connection weak. Methods of contraception are by now so familiar and so widely used that it is not necessary to dwell upon the changes wrought by these developments in the concept of sex itself and in a rational sexual ethic dependent upon that concept. In the past, the ever present possibility of children rendered the concepts of sex and sexual morality different from those required at present. There may be good reasons, if the presence and care of both mother and father are beneficial to children, for restricting reproduction to marriage. Insofar as society has a legitimate role in protecting children's interests, it may be justified in giving marriage a legal status, although this question is complicated by the fact (among others) that children born to single mothers deserve no penalties. In any case, the point here is simply that these questions are irrelevant at the present time to those regarding the morality of sex and its potential social regulation. (Further connections with marriage will be discussed below.) . . .

3. THE SEX-LOVE MODEL

Before discussing further relations of means-end analyses to false or inconsistent sexual ethics and concepts of perversion, I turn to [another example of means-end analysis]. One common position views sex as essentially an expression of love or affection between the partners. It is generally recognized that there are other types of love besides sexual, but sex itself is taken as an expression of one type, sometimes termed "romantic" love. Various factors again ought to weaken this identification. First, there are other types of love besides that which it is appropriate to express sexually, and "romantic" love itself can be expressed in many other ways. I am not denying that sex can take on heightened value and meaning when it becomes a vehicle for the expression of feelings of love or tenderness, but so can many other usually mundane activities such as getting up early to make breakfast on Sunday, cleaning the house, and so on. Second, sex itself can be used to communicate many other emotions besides love, and, as I will argue below, can communicate nothing in particular and still be good sex.

On a deeper level, an internal tension is bound to result from an identification of sex, which I have described as a physical-psychological desire, with love as a long-term, deep emotional relationship between two individuals. As this type of relationship, love is permanent, at least in intent, and more or less exclusive. A normal person cannot deeply love more than a few individuals even in a lifetime. We may be suspicious that those who attempt or claim to love many love them weakly if at all. Yet, fleeting sexual desire can

arise in relation to a variety of other individuals one finds sexually attractive. It may even be, as some have claimed, that sexual desire in humans naturally seeks variety, while this is obviously false of love. For this reason, monogamous sex, even if justified, almost always represents a sacrifice or the exercise of self-control on the part of the spouses, while monogamous love generally does not. There is no such thing as casual love in the sense in which I intend the term "love." It may occasionally happen that a spouse falls deeply in love with someone else (especially when sex is conceived in terms of love), but this is relatively rare in comparison to passing sexual desires for others; and while the former often indicates a weakness or fault in the marriage relation, the latter does not.

If love is indeed more exclusive in its objects than is sexual desire, this explains why those who view sex as essentially an expression of love would again tend to hold a repressive or restrictive sexual ethic. As in the case of reproduction, there may be good reasons for reserving the total commitment of deep love to the context of marriage and family—the normal personality may not withstand additional divisions of ultimate commitment and allegiance. There is no question that marriage itself is best sustained by a deep relation of love and affection; and even if love is not naturally monogamous, the benefits of family units to children provide additional reason to avoid serious commitments elsewhere which weaken family ties. It can be argued similarly that monogamous sex strengthens families by restricting and at the same time guaranteeing an outlet for sexual desire in marriage. But there is more force to the argument that recognition of a clear distinction between sex and love in society would help avoid disastrous marriages which result from adolescent confusion of the two when sexual desire is mistaken for permanent love, and would weaken damaging jealousies which arise in marriages in relation to passing sexual desires. The love and affection of a sound marriage certainly differs from the adolescent romantic variety, which is often a mere substitute for sex in the context of a repressive sexual ethic.

In fact, the restrictive sexual ethic tied to the means-end analysis in terms of love again has failed to be consistent. At least, it has not been applied consistently, but forms part of the double standard which has curtailed the freedom of women. It is predictable in light of this history that some women would now advocate using sex as another kind of means, as a political weapon or as a way to increase unjustly denied power and freedom. The inconsistency in the sexual ethic typically attached to the sex-love analysis, according to which it has generally been taken with a grain of salt when applied to men, is simply another example of the impossibility of tailoring a plausible moral theory in this area to a conception of sex which builds in conceptually extraneous factors.

I am not suggesting here that sex ought never to be connected with love or that it is not a more significant and valuable activity when it is. Nor am I denying that individuals need love as much as sex and perhaps emotionally need at least one complete relationship which encompasses both. Just as sex can express love and take on heightened significance when it does, so love is often naturally accompanied by an intermittent desire for sex. But again love is accompanied appropriately by desires for other shared activities as well. What makes the desire for sex seem more intimately connected with love is the intimacy which is seen to be a natural feature of mutual sex acts. Like love, sex is held to lay one bare psychologically as well as physically. Sex is unquestionably intimate, but beyond that the psychological toll often attached may be a function of the restrictive sexual ethic itself, rather than a legitimate apology for it. The intimacy involved in love is psychologically consuming in a generally healthy way, while the psychological tolls of sexual relations, often including embarrassment as a correlate of intimacy, are too often the result of artificial sexual ethics and taboos. The intimacy involved in both love and sex is insufficient in any case in light of previous points to render a means-end analysis in these terms appropriate. . . .

4. PLATONIC MORALITY

I have now criticized various types of analysis sharing or suggesting a common means-end form. . . . The reproductive model brands oral-genital sex a deviation, but cannot account for kissing or holding hands; . . . the sex-love model makes most sexual desire seem degrading or base. [Its defenders] . . . condemn extramarital sex on the sound but irrelevant grounds that reproduction and deep commitment are best confined to family contexts. The romanticization of sex and the confusion of sexual desire with love operate in both directions: sex outside the context of romantic love is repressed; once it is repressed, partners become more difficult to find and sex becomes romanticized further, out of proportion to its real value for the individual.

What . . . these analyses share in addition to a common form is accordance with and perhaps derivation from the Platonic-Christian moral tradition, according to which the animal or purely physical element of humans is the source of immorality, and plain sex in the sense I defined it is an expression of this element, hence in itself to be condemned. All the analyses examined seem to seek a distance from sexual desire itself in attempting to extend it conceptually beyond the physical. The love . . . [analysis seeks] refinement or intellectualization of the desire; plain physical sex becomes vulgar, and too straightforward sexual encounters without an aura of respectable cerebral communicative content are to be avoided. [Robert] Solomon explicitly argues that sex cannot be a "mere" appetite, his argument being that if it were subway exhibitionism and other vulgar forms would be pleasing.[1] This fails to recognize that sexual desire can be focused or selective at the same time as being physical. Lower animals are not attracted by every other member of their species, either. Rancid food forced down one's throat is not pleasing, but that certainly fails to show that hunger is not a physical appetite. Sexual desire lets us know that we are physical beings and, indeed, animals; this is why traditional Platonic morality is so thorough in its condemnation. Means-end analyses continue to reflect this tradition, sometimes unwittingly. They show that in conceptualizing sex it is still difficult, despite years of so-called revolution in this area, to free ourselves from the lingering suspicion that plain sex as physical desire is an expression of our "lower selves," that yielding to our animal natures is subhuman or vulgar.

5. SEX AND MORALITY

Having criticized these analyses for the sexual ethics and concepts of perversion they imply, it remains to contrast my account along these lines. To the question of what morality might be implied by my analysis, the answer is that there are no moral implications whatever. Any analysis of sex which imputes a moral character to sex acts in themselves is wrong for that reason. There is no morality intrinsic to sex, although general moral rules apply to the treatment of others in sex acts as they apply to all human relations. We can speak of a sexual ethic as we can speak of a business ethic, without implying that business in itself is either moral or immoral or that special rules are required to judge business practices which are not derived from rules that apply elsewhere as well. Sex is not in itself a moral category, although like business it invariably places us into relations with others in which moral rules apply. It gives us opportunity to do what is otherwise recognized as wrong, to harm others, deceive them or manipulate them against their wills. Just as the fact that an act is sexual in itself never renders it wrong or adds to its wrongness if it is wrong on other grounds (sexual acts toward minors are wrong on other grounds, as will be argued below), so no wrong act is to be excused because done from a sexual motive. If a "crime of passion" is to be excused, it would have to be on grounds of temporary insanity rather than sexual context (whether insanity does constitute a legitimate excuse for certain actions is

too big a topic to argue here). Sexual motives are among others which may become deranged, and the fact that they are sexual has no bearing in itself on the moral character, whether negative or exculpatory, of the actions deriving from them. Whatever might be true of war, it is certainly not the case that all's fair in love or sex.

Our first conclusion regarding morality and sex is therefore that no conduct otherwise immoral should be excused because it is sexual conduct, and nothing in sex is immoral unless condemned by rules which apply elsewhere as well. The last clause requires further clarification. Sexual conduct can be governed by particular rules relating only to sex itself. But these precepts must be implied by general moral rules when these are applied to specific sexual relations or types of conduct. The same is true of rules of fair business, ethical medicine, or courtesy in driving a car. In the latter case, particular acts on the road may be reprehensible, such as tailgating or passing on the right, which seem to bear no resemblance as actions to any outside the context of highway safety. Nevertheless their immorality derives from the fact that they place others in danger, a circumstance which, when avoidable, is to be condemned in any context. This structure of general and specifically applicable rules describes a reasonable sexual ethic as well. To take an extreme case, rape is always a sexual act and it is always immoral. A rule against rape can therefore be considered an obvious part of sexual morality which has no bearing on nonsexual conduct. But the immorality of rape derives from its being an extreme violation of a person's body, of the right not to be humiliated, and of the general moral prohibition against using other persons against their wills, not from the fact that it is a sexual act.

The application elsewhere of general moral rules to sexual conduct is further complicated by the fact that it will be relative to the particular desires and preferences of one's partner (these may be influenced by and hence in some sense include misguided beliefs about sexual morality itself). This means that there will be fewer specific rules in the area of sexual ethics than in other areas of conduct, such as driving cars, where the relativity of preference is irrelevant to the prohibition of objectively dangerous conduct. More reliance will have to be placed upon the general moral rule, which in this area holds simply that the preferences, desires, and interests of one's partner or potential partner ought to be taken into account. This rule is certainly not specifically formulated to govern sexual relations; it is a form of the central principle of morality itself. But when applied to sex, it prohibits certain actions, such as molestation of children, which cannot be categorized as violations of the rule without at the same time being classified as sexual. I believe this last case is the closest we can come to an action which is wrong *because* it is sexual, but even here its wrongness is better characterized as deriving from the detrimental effects such behavior can have on the future emotional and sexual life of the naive victims, and from the fact that such behavior therefore involves manipulation of innocent persons without regard for their interests. Hence, this case also involves violation of a general moral rule which applies elsewhere as well.

Aside from faulty conceptual analyses of sex and the influence of the Platonic moral tradition, there are two more plausible reasons for thinking that there are moral dimensions intrinsic to sex acts per se. The first is that such acts are normally intensely pleasurable. According to a hedonistic, utilitarian moral theory they therefore should be at least prima facie morally right, rather than morally neutral in themselves. To me this seems incorrect and reflects unfavorably on the ethical theory in question. The pleasure intrinsic to sex acts is a good, but not, it seems to me, a good with much positive moral significance. Certainly I can have no duty to pursue such pleasure myself, and while it may be nice to give pleasure of any form to others, there is no ethical requirement to do so, given my right over my own body. The exception relates to the context of sex acts themselves, when one partner derives pleasure from the

other and ought to return the favor. This duty to reciprocate takes us out of the domain of hedonistic utilitarianism, however, and into a Kantian moral framework, the central principles of which call for just such reciprocity in human relations. Since independent moral judgments regarding sexual activities constitute one area in which ethical theories are to be tested, these observations indicate here, as I believe others indicate elsewhere, the fertility of the Kantian, as opposed to the utilitarian, principle in reconstructuring reasoned moral consciousness.

It may appear from this alternative Kantian viewpoint that sexual acts must be at least prima facie wrong in themselves. This is because they invariably involve at different stages the manipulation of one's partner for one's own pleasure, which might appear to be prohibited on the formulation of Kant's principle which holds that one ought not to treat another as a means to such private ends. A more realistic rendering of this formulation, however, one which recognizes its intended equivalence to the first universalizability principle [the principle requiring we act only on a maxim whereby we can at the same time will that it should become a universal law], admits no such absolute prohibition. Many human relations, most economic transactions for example, involve using other individuals for personal benefit. These relations are immoral only when they are one-sided, when the benefits are not mutual, or when the transactions are not freely and rationally endorsed by all parties. The same holds true of sexual acts. The central principle governing them is the Kantian demand for reciprocity in sexual relations. In order to comply with the second formulation of the categorical imperative, one must recognize the subjectivity of one's partner. . . . Even in an act which by its nature "objectifies" the other, one recognizes a partner as a subject with demands and desires by yielding to those desires, by allowing oneself to be a sexual object as well, by giving pleasure or ensuring that the pleasures of the acts are mutual. It is this kind of reciprocity which forms the basis for morality in sex, which distinguishes right acts from wrong in this area as in others. (Of course, prior to sex acts one must gauge their effects upon potential partners and take these longer range interests into account.)

6. LOVE

I suggested earlier that in addition to generating confusion regarding the rightness or wrongness of sex acts, false conceptual analyses of the means-end form cause confusion about the value of sex to the individual. My account recognizes the satisfaction of desire and the pleasure this brings as the central psychological function of the sex act for the individual. Sex affords us a paradigm of pleasure, but not a cornerstone of value. For most of us it is not only a needed outlet for desire but also the most enjoyable form of reaction we know. Its value is nevertheless easily mistaken by being confused with that of love, when it is taken as essentially an expression of that emotion. Although intense, the pleasures of sex are brief and repetitive rather than cumulative. They give values to the specific acts which generate them, but not the lasting kind of value which enhances one's whole life. The briefness of these pleasures contributes to their intensity (or perhaps their intensity makes them necessarily brief), but it also relegates them to the periphery of most rational plans for the good life.

By contrast, love typically develops over a long term relation; while its pleasures may be less intense and physical, they are of more cumulative value. The importance of love to the individual may well be central in a rational system of value. And it has perhaps an even deeper moral significance relating to the identification with the interests of another person, which broadens one's possible relationships with others as well. Marriage is again important in preserving this relation between adults and children, which seems as important to the adults as it is to the children in broadening concerns which have a tendency to become selfish. Sexual desire, by contrast, is desire for another which is nevertheless essentially self-regarding. Sexual pleasure is certainly a good for the individual, and for many it may be necessary in order for them to function in a reasonably cheerful way. But it bears little relation to those other values just discussed, to which some analyses falsely suggest a conceptual connection.

7. PERVERTED SEX

While my initial analysis lacks moral implications in itself, as it should, it does suggest by contrast a concept of sexual perversion. Since the concept of perversion is itself a sexual concept, it will always be defined relative to some definition of normal sex; and any conception of the norm will imply a contrary notion of perverse forms. The concept suggested by my account again differs sharply from those implied by the means-end analyses examined above. Perversion does not represent a deviation from the reproductive function (or kissing would be perverted), from a loving relationship (or most sexual desire and many heterosexual acts would be perverted), or from efficiency in communicating (or unsuccessful seduction attempts would be perverted). It is a deviation from a norm, but the norm in question is merely statistical. Of course, not all sexual acts that are statistically unusual are perverted—a three-hour continuous sexual act would be unusual but not necessarily abnormal in the requisite sense. The abnormality in question must relate to the *form of the desire* itself in order to constitute sexual perversion; for example, desire, not for contact with another, but for merely looking, for harming or being harmed, for contact with items of clothing. This concept of sexual abnormality is that suggested by my definition of normal sex in terms of its typical desire. However not all unusual desires qualify either, only those with the typical physical sexual effects upon the individual who satisfies them. These effects, such as erection in males, were not built into the original definition of sex in terms of sexual desire, for they do not always occur in activities that are properly characterized as sexual, say, kissing for the pleasure of it. But they do seem to bear a close relation to the definition of activities as perverted. (For those who consider only genital sex sexual, we could build such symptoms into a narrower definition, then speak of sex in a broad sense as well as "proper" sex.)

Solomon . . . [disagrees] with this statistical notion of perversion. For [him] the concept is evaluative rather than statistical. I do not deny that the term "perverted" is often used evaluatively (and purely emotively for that matter), or that it has a negative connotation for the average speaker. I do deny that we can find a norm, other than that of statistically usual desire, against which all and only activities that properly count as sexual perversions can be contrasted. Perverted sex is simply abnormal sex, and if the norm is not to be an idealized or romanticized extraneous end or purpose, it must express the way human sexual desires usually manifest themselves. Of course not all norms in other areas of discourse need be statistical in this way. Physical health is an example of a relatively clear norm which does not seem to depend upon the numbers of healthy people. But the concept in this case achieves its clarity through the connection of physical health with other clearly desirable physical functions and characteristics, for example, living longer. In the case of sex, that which is statistically abnormal is not necessarily incapacitating in other ways, and yet these abnormal desires with sexual effects upon their subject do count as perverted to the degree to which their objects deviate from usual ones. The connotations of the concept of perversion beyond those connected with abnormality or statistical deviation derive more from the attitudes of those likely to call certain acts perverted than from specifiable features of the acts themselves. These connotations add to the concept of abnormality, that of *sub*normality, but there is no norm against which the latter can be measured intelligibly in accord with all and only acts intuitively called perverted.

The only proper evaluative norms relating to sex involve degrees of pleasure in the acts and moral norms, but neither of these scales coincides with statistical degrees of abnormality, according to which perversion is to be measured. The three parameters operate independently (this was implied for the first two when it was held above that the pleasure of sex is a good, but not necessarily a moral good). Perverted sex may be more or less enjoyable to particular individuals than normal sex, and more or less moral, depending upon the particular relations involved. Raping a sheep may be more perverted than raping a woman, but certainly not more condemnable morally.[2] It is nevertheless true that the evaluative connotations attaching to the term "perverted" derive partly from the fact that most people consider perverted sex highly immoral. Many such acts are forbidden by long-standing taboos, and it is sometimes difficult to distinguish what is forbidden from what is immoral. Others, such as sadistic acts, are genuinely immoral, but again not at all because of their connection with sex or abnormality. The principles which condemn these acts would condemn them equally if they were common and nonsexual. It is not true that we properly could continue to consider acts perverted which were found to be very common practice across societies. Such acts, if harmful, might continue to be condemned properly as immoral, but it was just shown that the immorality of an act does not vary with its degree of perversion. If not harmful, common acts previously considered abnormal might continue to be called perverted for a time by the moralistic minority; but the term when applied to such cases would retain only its emotive negative connotation without consistent logical criteria for application. It would represent merely prejudiced moral judgments.

To adequately explain why there is a tendency to so deeply condemn perverted acts would require a treatise in psychology beyond the scope of this paper. Part of the reason undoubtedly relates to the tradition of repressive sexual ethics and false conceptions of sex;

another part to the fact that all abnormality seems to disturb and fascinate us at the same time. The former explains why sexual perversion is more abhorrent to many than other forms of abnormality; the latter indicates why we tend to have an emotive and evaluative reaction to perversion in the first place. It may be, as has been suggested according to a Freudian line,[3] that our uneasiness derives from latent desires we are loathe to admit, but this thesis takes us into psychological issues I am not competent to judge. Whatever the psychological explanation, it suffices to point out here that the conceptual connection between perversion and genuine or consistent moral evaluation is spurious and again suggested by misleading means-end idealizations of the concept of sex.

The position I have taken in this paper against those concepts is not totally new.

Something similar to it is found in Freud's view of sex, which of course was genuinely revolutionary, and in the body of writings deriving from Freud to the present time. But in his revolt against romanticized and repressive conceptions, Freud went too far—from a refusal to view sex as merely a means to a view of it as the end of all human behavior, although sometimes an elaborately disguised end. This pansexualism led to the thesis (among others) that repression was indeed an inevitable and necessary part of social regulation of any form, a strange consequence of a position that began by opposing the repressive aspects of the means-end view. Perhaps the time finally has arrived when we can achieve a reasonable middle ground in this area, at least in philosophy if not in society.

NOTES

1. Robert Solomon, "Sex and Perversion," *Philosophy and Sex,* R. Baker and F. Elliston, eds. (Buffalo: Prometheus, 1975).
2. The example is like one from Sara Ruddick, "Better Sex," *Philosophy and Sex,* p. 96.
3. See Michael Slote, "Inapplicable Concepts and Sexual Perversion," *Philosophy and Sex.*

REVIEW AND DISCUSSION QUESTIONS

1. What is the "plain sex" view that Goldman defends? How does he contrast it with "means-end" views?
2. Why does Goldman reject the reproductive and the sex-love models?
3. On what grounds does Goldman reject Kant's account of sexual morality?
4. Discuss Goldman's understanding of "perversion" and its connection with morality. Why does he think people tend to condemn perversion?
5. Compare Goldman's understanding of love with that of Kant. Which one seems most reasonable to you? Why do you think that?

Gay Basics: Some Questions, Facts, and Values

Richard D. Mohr

In this essay, Richard D. Mohr surveys the wide array of issues surrounding homosexuality. He begins with a discussion of some of the important facts about homosexuals and homosexuality, including a discussion of the most prominent stereotypes, which, he points out, are in fact contradictory. He then reviews different forms of discrimination experienced by gays, considers arguments that homosexuality is wrong, and concludes with a discussion of social policies that affect gays. Richard D. Mohr is professor of philosophy at the University of Illinois.

WHO ARE GAYS ANYWAY?

A recent Gallup poll found that only one in five Americans reports having a gay or lesbian acquaintance.[1] This finding is extraordinary given the number of practicing homosexuals in America. Alfred Kinsey's 1948 study of the sex lives of 5,000 white males shocked the nation: 37 percent had at least one homosexual experience to orgasm in their adult lives; an additional 13 percent had homosexual fantasies to orgasm; 4 percent were exclusively homosexual in their practices; another 5 percent had virtually no heterosexual experience; and nearly one-fifth had at least as many homosexual as heterosexual experiences.[2]

Two out of five men one passes on the street have had orgasmic sex with men. Every second family in the country has a member who is essentially homosexual, and many more people regularly have homosexual experiences. Who are homosexuals? They are your friends, your minister, your teacher, your bank teller, your doctor, your mail carrier, your secretary, your congressional representative, your sibling, parent, and spouse. They are everywhere, virtually all ordinary, virtually all unknown.

Several important consequences follow. First, the country is profoundly ignorant of the actual experience of gay people. Second, social attitudes and practices that are harmful to gays have a much greater overall harmful impact on society than is usually realized. Third, most gay people live in hiding—in the closet—making the "coming out" experience the central fixture of gay consciousness and invisibility the chief characteristic of the gay community.

IGNORANCE, STEREOTYPE, AND MORALITY

Ignorance about gays, however, has not stopped people from having strong opinions about them. The void which ignorance leaves has been filled with stereotypes. Society holds chiefly two groups of antigay stereotypes; the two are an oddly contradictory lot. One set of stereotypes revolves around alleged mistakes in an individual's gender identity: Lesbians are women that want to be, or at least look and act like, men—bulldykes, diesel dykes; while gay men are those who want to be, or at least look and act like, women—queens, fairies, limp-wrists, nellies. These stereotypes of mismatched genders provide the materials through which gays and lesbians become the butts of ethnic-like jokes. These stereotypes and jokes, though derisive, basically view gays and lesbians as ridiculous.

Another set of stereotypes revolves around gays as a pervasive sinister conspiratorial threat. The core stereotype here is the gay person as child molester and, more generally, as sex-crazed maniac. These stereotypes carry with them fears of the very destruction of family and civilization itself. Now, that which is essentially ridiculous can hardly have such a staggering effect. Something must be afoot in this incoherent amalgam.

Sense can be made of this incoherence if the nature of stereotypes is clarified. Stereotypes are not *simply* false generalizations from a skewed sample of cases examined. Admittedly, false generalizing plays some part in the stereotypes a society holds. If, for instance, one takes as one's sample homosexuals who are in psychiatric hospitals or prisons, as was done in nearly all early investigations, not surprisingly one will probably find homosexuals to be of a crazed and criminal cast. Such false generalizations, though, simply confirm beliefs already held on independent grounds, ones that likely led the investigator to the prison and psychiatric ward to begin with. Evelyn Hooker, who in the late '50s carried out the first rigorous studies to use nonclinical gays, found that psychiatrists, when presented with case files including all the standard diagnostic psychological profiles—but omitting indications of sexual orientation—were unable to distinguish gay files from straight ones, even though they believed gays to be crazy and supposed themselves to be experts in detecting craziness.[3] These studies proved a profound embarrassment to the psychiatric establishment, the financial well-being of which has been substantially enhanced by "curing" allegedly insane gays. The studies led the way to the American Psychiatric Association finally dropping homosexuality from its registry of mental illnesses in 1973.[4] Nevertheless, the stereotype of gays as sick continues apace in the mind of America.

False generalizations *help maintain* stereotypes, they do not *form* them. As the history of Hooker's discoveries shows, stereotypes have a life beyond facts; their origin lies in a culture's ideology—the general system of beliefs by which it lives—and they are sustained across generations by diverse cultural transmissions, hardly any of which, including slang and jokes, even purport to have a scientific basis. Stereotypes, then, are not the products of bad science but are social constructions that perform central functions in maintaining society's conception of itself.

On this understanding, it is easy to see that the antigay stereotypes surrounding gender identification are chiefly means of reinforcing still powerful gender roles in society. If, as this stereotype presumes and condemns, one is free to choose one's social roles independently of gender, many guiding social divisions, both domestic and commercial, might be threatened. The socially gender-linked distinctions between breadwinner and homemaker, boss and secretary, doctor and nurse, protector and protected would blur. The accusations "fag" and "dyke" exist in significant part to keep women in their place and to prevent men from breaking ranks and ceding away theirs.

The stereotypes of gays as child molesters, sex-crazed maniacs, and civilization destroyers function to displace (socially irresolvable) problems from their actual source to a foreign (and so, it is thought, manageable) one. Thus, the stereotype of child molester functions to give the family unit a false sheen of absolute innocence. It keeps the unit from being examined too closely for incest, child abuse, wife battering, and the terrorism of constant threats. The stereotype teaches that the problems of the family are not internal to it, but external.[5]

One can see these cultural forces at work in society's and the media's treatment of current reports of violence, especially domestic violence. When a mother kills her child or a father rapes his daughter—regular Section B fare even in major urban papers—this is never taken by reporters, columnists, or pundits as evidence that there is something wrong with heterosexuality or with traditional families. These issues are not even raised. But when a homosexual child molestation is reported, it is taken as confirming evidence of the way homosexuals are. One never hears of heterosexual murders, but one regularly hears of "homosexual" ones. Compare the social treatment of Richard Speck's sexually motivated mass murder of Chicago nurses with that of John Wayne Gacy's murders of Chicago youths. Gacy was in the culture's mind taken as symbolic of gay men in general. To prevent the possibility that "The Family" was viewed as anything but an innocent victim in this affair, the mainstream press knowingly failed to mention that most of Gacy's adolescent victims were homeless hustlers. That knowledge would be too much for the six o'clock news and for cherished beliefs.

Because "the facts" largely don't matter when it comes to the generation and maintenance of stereotypes, the effects of scientific and academic research and of enlightenment generally will be, at best, slight and gradual in the changing fortunes of lesbians and gay men. If this account of stereotypes holds, society has been profoundly immoral. For its treatment of gays is a grand scale rationalization, a moral sleight-of-hand. The problem is not that society's usual standards of evidence and procedure in coming to judgments of social policy have been misapplied to gays; rather, when it comes to gays, the standards themselves have simply been ruled out of court and disregarded in favor of mechanisms that encourage unexamined fear and hatred.

ARE GAYS DISCRIMINATED AGAINST? DOES IT MATTER?

Partly because lots of people suppose they don't know any gay people and partly through willful ignorance of its own workings, society at large is unaware of the many ways in which gays are subject to discrimination in consequence of widespread fear and hatred. Contributing to this social ignorance of discrimination is the difficulty for gay people, as an invisible minority, even to complain of discrimination. For if one is gay, to register a complaint would suddenly target one as a stigmatized person, and so in the absence of any protections against discrimination, would simply invite additional discrimination. Further,

many people, especially those who are persistently downtrodden and so lack a firm sense of self to begin with, tend either to blame themselves for their troubles or to view injustice as a matter of bad luck rather than as indicating something wrong with society. The latter recognition would require doing something to rectify wrong, and most people, especially the already beleaguered, simply aren't up to that. So for a number of reasons discrimination against gays, like rape, goes seriously under-reported.

First, gays are subject to violence and harassment based simply on their perceived status rather than because of any actions they have performed. A recent extensive study by the National Gay Task Force found that over 90 percent of gays and lesbians had been victimized in some form on the basis of their sexual orientation.[6] Greater than one in five gay men and nearly one in ten lesbians had been punched, hit, or kicked, a quarter of all gays had had objects thrown at them, a third had been chased, a third had been sexually harassed, and 14 percent had been spit on— all just for being perceived as gay.

The most extreme form of antigay violence is queerbashing—where groups of young men target a person who they suppose is a gay man and beat and kick him unconscious and sometimes to death amid a torrent of taunts and slurs. Such seemingly random but in reality socially encouraged violence has the same social origin and function as lynchings of blacks —to keep a whole stigmatized group in line. As with lynchings of the recent past, the police and courts have routinely averted their eyes, giving their implicit approval to the practice.

Few such cases with gay victims reach the courts. Those that do are marked by inequitable procedures and results. Frequently judges will describe queerbashers as "just all-American boys." Recently a District of Columbia judge handed suspended sentences to queerbashers whose victim had been stalked, beaten, stripped at knife-point, slashed, kicked, threatened with castration, and pissed on, because the judge thought the bashers were good boys at heart—after all, they went to a religious prep school.[7]

Police and juries will simply discount testimony from gays; they typically construe assaults on and murders of gays as "justified" self-defense—the killer need only claim his act was a panicked response to a sexual overture. Alternatively, when guilt seems patent, juries will accept highly implausible "diminished capacity" defenses, as in the case of Dan White's 1978 assassination of openly gay San Francisco city [supervisor] Harvey Milk—Hostess Twinkies made him do it.[8]

These inequitable procedures and results collectively show that the life and liberty of gays, like those of blacks, simply count for less than the life and liberty of members of the dominant culture.

The equitable rule of law is the heart of an orderly society. The collapse of the rule of law for gays shows that society is willing to perpetrate the worst possible injustices against them. Conceptually there is only a difference in degree between the collapse of the rule of law and systematic extermination of members of a population simply for having some group status independently of any act an individual has performed. In the Nazi concentration camps, gays were forced to wear pink triangles as identifying badges, just as Jews were forced to wear yellow stars. In remembrance of that collapse of the rule of law, the pink triangle has become the chief symbol of the gay rights movement.[9]

Gays are subject to widespread discrimination in employment—the very means by which one puts bread on one's table and one of the chief means by which individuals identify themselves to themselves and achieve personal dignity. Governments are leading offenders here. They do a lot of discriminating themselves, require that others do it ([such as] government contractors), and set precedents favoring discrimination in the private sector. The federal government explicitly discriminates against gays in the armed forces, the CIA, FBI, National Security Agency, and the State Department. The federal government refuses to give security clearances to gays and so forces the country's considerable private- sector military and aerospace contractors to fire known gay employees. State and local governments regularly fire gay teachers, policemen, firemen, social workers, and anyone who has contact with the public. Further, states through licensing laws officially bar gays from a vast array of occupations and professions—everything from doctors, lawyers, accountants, and nurses to hairdressers, morticians, and used car dealers. The American Civil Liberties Union's handbook *The Rights of Gay People* lists 307 such prohibited occupations.[10]

Gays are subject to discrimination in a wide variety of other ways, including private-sector employment, public accommodations, housing, immigration and naturalization, insurance of all types, custody and adoption, and zoning regulations that bar "singles" or "nonrelated" couples. All of these discriminations affect central components of a meaningful life; some even reach to the means by which life itself is sustained. In half the states, where gay sex is illegal, the central role of sex to meaningful life is officially denied to gays.

All these sorts of discriminations also affect the ability of people to have significant intimate relations. It is difficult for people to live together as couples without having their sexual orientation perceived in the public realm and so becoming targets for discrimination. Illegality, discrimination, and the absorption by gays of society's hatred of them all interact to impede or block altogether the ability of gays and lesbians to create and maintain significant personal relations with loved ones. So every facet of life is affected by discrimination. Only the most compelling reasons could justify it.

BUT AREN'T THEY IMMORAL?

Many people think society's treatment of gays is justified because they think gays are extremely immoral. To evaluate this claim, a different sense of *moral* must be distinguished. Sometimes by *morality* is meant the

overall beliefs affecting behavior in a society—its mores, norms, and customs. On this
understanding, gays certainly are not moral:
Lots of people hate them and social customs
are designed to register widespread disapproval of gays. The problem here is that this
sense of morality is merely a *descriptive* one.
On this understanding *every* society has a
morality—even Nazi society, which had
racism and mob rule as central features of its
"morality" understood in this sense. What is
needed in order to use the notion of morality
to praise or condemn behavior is a sense of
morality that is *prescriptive* or *normative*—a
sense of morality whereby, for instance, the
descriptive morality of the Nazis is found
wanting.

As the Nazi example makes clear, that
something is descriptively moral is nowhere
near enough to make it normatively moral.
[The fact that] a lot of people in a society say
something is good, even over eons, does not
make it so. Our rejection of the long history of
socially approved and state-enforced slavery
is another good example of this principle at
work. Slavery would be wrong even if nearly
everyone liked it. So consistency and fairness
require that we abandon the belief that gays
are immoral simply because most people dislike or disapprove of gays or gay acts, or even
because gay sex acts are illegal.

Furthermore, recent historical and anthropological research has shown that opinion
about gays has been by no means universally
negative. Historically, it has varied widely
even within the larger part of the Christian era and even within the church itself.[11]
There are even societies—current ones—
where homosexuality is not only tolerated
but a universal compulsory part of social
maturation.[12] Within the last thirty years,
American society has undergone a grand
turnabout from deeply ingrained, near total
condemnation to near total acceptance on
two emotionally charged "moral" or "family"
issues: contraception and divorce. Society
holds its current descriptive morality of gays
not because it has to, but because it chooses to.

If popular opinion and custom are not
enough to ground moral condemnation of
homosexuality, perhaps religion can. Such
argument[s] proceed along two lines. One
claims that the condemnation is a direct revelation of God, usually through the Bible; the
other claims to be able to detect condemnation in God's plan as manifested in nature.

One of the more remarkable discoveries
of recent gay research is that the Bible
may not be as univocal in its condemnation of homosexuality as has been usually
believed.[13] Christ never mention[ed] homosexuality. Recent interpreters of the Old
Testament have pointed out that the story of
Lot at Sodom is probably intended to condemn inhospitality rather than homosexuality.
Further, some of the Old Testament condemnations of homosexuality seem simply to be
ways of tarring those of the Israelites' opponents who happen to accept homosexual practices when the Israelites themselves did not. If
so, the condemnation is merely a quirk of history and rhetoric rather than a moral precept.

What does seem clear is that those who
regularly cite the Bible to condemn an activity like homosexuality do so by reading it
selectively. Do ministers who cite what they
take to be condemnations of homosexuality in
Leviticus maintain in their lives all the
hygienic and dietary laws of Leviticus? If they
cite the story of Lot at Sodom to condemn
homosexuality, do they also cite the story of
Lot in the cave to praise incestuous rape? It
seems then not that the Bible is being used to
ground condemnations of homosexuality as
much as society's dislike of homosexuality is
being used to interpret the Bible.[14]

Even if a consistent portrait of condemnation could be gleaned from the Bible, what
social significance should it be given? One of
the guiding principles of society, enshrined in
the [U.S.] Constitution as a check against the
government, is that decisions affecting social
policy are not made on religious grounds. If
the real ground of the alleged immorality
invoked by governments to discriminate
against gays is religious (as it has explicitly

been even in some recent court cases involving teachers and guardians), then one of the major commitments of our nation is violated.

BUT AREN'T THEY UNNATURAL?

The most noteworthy feature of the accusation of something being unnatural (where a moral rather than an advertising point is being made) is that the plaint is so infrequently made. One used to hear the charge leveled against abortion, but that has pretty much faded as antiabortionists have come to lay all their chips on the hope that people will come to view abortion as murder. Incest used to be considered unnatural but discourse now usually assimilates it to the moral machinery of rape and violated trust. The charge comes up now in ordinary discourse only against homosexuality. This suggests that the charge is highly idiosyncratic and has little, if any, explanatory force. It fails to put homosexuality in a class with anything else so that one can learn by comparison with clear cases of the class just exactly what it is that is allegedly wrong with it.

Though the accusation of unnaturalness looks whimsical, in actual ordinary discourse when applied to homosexuality, it is usually delivered with venom of forethought. It carries a high emotional charge, usually expressing disgust and evincing queasiness. Probably it is nothing but an emotional charge. For people get equally disgusted and queasy at all sorts of things that are perfectly natural—to be expected in nature apart from artifice—and that could hardly be fit subjects for moral condemnation. Two typical examples in current American culture are some people's responses to mothers' suckling in public and to women who do not shave body hair. When people have strong emotional reactions, as they do in these cases, without being able to give good reasons for them, we think of them not as operating morally, but rather as being obsessed and manic. So the feelings of disgust that some people have to gays will hardly

ground a charge of immorality. People fling the term *unnatural* against gays in the same breath and with the same force as when they call gays "sick" and "gross." When they do this, they give every appearance of being neurotically fearful and incapable of reasoned discourse.

When *nature* is taken in *technical* rather than ordinary usage, it looks like the notion also will not ground a charge of homosexual immorality. When *unnatural* means "by artifice" or "made by humans," it need only be pointed out that virtually everything that is good about life is unnatural in this sense, that the chief feature that distinguishes people from other animals is their very ability to make over the world to meet their needs and desires, and that their well-being depends upon these departures from nature. On this understanding of human nature and the natural, homosexuality is perfectly unobjectionable.

Another technical sense of *natural* is that something is natural, and so, good, if it fulfills some function in nature. Homosexuality on this view is unnatural because it allegedly violates the function of genitals, which is to produce babies. One problem with this view is that lots of bodily parts have lots of functions and just because some one activity can be fulfilled by only one organ (say, the mouth for eating) this activity does not condemn other functions of the organ to immorality (say, the mouth for talking, licking stamps, blowing bubbles, or having sex). So the possible use of the genitals to produce children does not, without more, condemn the use of the genitals for other purposes, say, achieving ecstasy and intimacy.

The functional view of nature will only provide a morally condemnatory sense to the unnatural if a thing which might have many uses has but one proper function to the exclusion of other possible functions. But whether this is so cannot be established simply by looking at the thing. For what is seen is all its possible functions. The notion of function seemed like it might ground moral authority, but instead it turns out that moral authority is needed to define proper function. Some people try to fill in this moral authority by appeal to the "design" or "order" of an organ, saying, for instance, that the genitals are designed for the purpose of procreation. But these people cheat intellectually if they do not make explicit *who* the designer and orderer is. If it is God, we are back to square one—holding others accountable for religious beliefs.

Further, ordinary moral attitudes about child-rearing will not provide the needed supplement, which, in conjunction with the natural function view of bodily parts, would produce a positive obligation to use the genitals for procreation. Society's attitude toward a childless couple is that of pity not censure—even if the couple could have children. The pity may be an unsympathetic one, that is, not registering a course one would choose *for oneself,* but this does not make it a course one would *require* of others. The couple who discovers it cannot have children is viewed not as having thereby had a debt canceled, but rather as having to forgo some of the richness of life, just as a quadriplegic is not viewed as absolved from some moral obligation to hop, skip, and jump, but is viewed as missing some of the richness of life. Consistency requires then that, at most, gays who do not or cannot have children are to be pitied rather than condemned. What is immoral is the willful preventing of people from achieving the richness of life. Immorality in this regard lies with those social customs, regulations, and statutes that prevent lesbians and gay men from establishing blood or adoptive families, not with gays themselves.

Sometimes people attempt to establish authority for a moral obligation to use bodily parts in a certain fashion simply by claiming that moral laws are natural laws and vice versa. On this account, inanimate objects and plants are good in that they follow natural laws by necessity, animals by instinct, and persons by a rational will. People are special in that they must first discover the laws that govern them. Now, even if one believes the view—dubious in the post-Newtonian, post-Darwinian world—that natural laws in the

usual sense (e = mc^2, for instance) have some moral content, it is not at all clear how one is to discover the laws in nature that apply to people.

If, on the one hand, one looks to people themselves for a model—and looks hard enough—one finds amazing variety, including homosexuality as a social ideal (upper-class 5th-century Athenians) and even as socially mandatory (Melanesia today). When one looks to people, one is simply unable to strip away the layers of social custom, history, and taboo in order to see what's really there to any degree more specific than that people are the creatures that make over their world and are capable of abstract thought. That this is so should raise doubts that neutral principles are to be found in human nature that will condemn homosexuality.

On the other hand, if one looks to nature apart from people for models, the possibilities are staggering. There are fish that change gender over their lifetimes: Should we "follow nature" and be operative transsexuals? Orangutans, genetically our next of kin, live completely solitary lives without social organization of any kind: Ought we to "follow nature" and be hermits? There are many species where only two members per generation reproduce: Shall we be bees? The search in nature for people's purpose—far from finding sure models for action—is likely to leave one morally rudderless.

BUT AREN'T GAYS WILLFULLY THE WAY THEY ARE?

It is generally conceded that if sexual orientation is something over which an individual—for whatever reason—has virtually no control, then discrimination against gays is especially deplorable, as it is against racial and ethnic classes, because it holds people accountable without regard for anything they themselves have done. And to hold a person accountable for that over which the person has no control is a central form of prejudice.

Attempts to answer the question whether or not sexual orientation is something that is reasonably thought to be within one's own control usually appeal simply to various claims of the biological or "mental" sciences. But the ensuing debate over genes, hormones, twins, early childhood development, and the like is as unnecessary as it is currently inconclusive.[15] All that is needed to answer the question is to look at the actual experience of gays in current society, and it becomes fairly clear that sexual orientation is not likely a matter of choice. For coming to have a homosexual identity simply does not have the same sort of structure that decision-making has.

On the one hand, the "choice" of the gender of a sexual partner does not seem to express a trivial desire which might be as easily well fulfilled by a simple substitution of the desired object. Picking the gender of a sex partner is decidedly dissimilar, that is, to such activities as picking a flavor of ice cream. If an ice-cream parlor is out of one's flavor, one simply picks another. And if people were persecuted, threatened with jail terms, shattered careers, loss of family and housing and the like for eating, say, Rocky Road ice cream, no one would ever eat it; everyone would pick another easily available flavor. That gay people abide in being gay even in the face of persecution shows that being gay is not a matter of easy choice.

On the other hand, even if establishing a sexual orientation is not like making a relatively trivial choice, perhaps it is nevertheless relevantly like making the central and serious life choices by which individuals try to establish themselves as being of some type. Again, if one examines gay experience, this seems not to be the case. For one never sees anyone setting out to become a homosexual, in the way one does see people setting out to become doctors, lawyers, and bricklayers. One does not find gays-to-be picking some end—"At some point in the future, I want to become a homosexual"—and then setting about planning and acquiring the ways and means to that end, in the way one does see people deciding that they want to become

lawyers, and then sees them planning what courses to take and what sort of temperaments, habits, and skills to develop in order to become lawyers. Typically gays-to-be simply find themselves having homosexual encounters and yet at least initially resisting quite strongly the identification of being homosexual. Such a person even very likely resists having such encounters but ends up having them anyway. Only with time, luck, and great personal effort, but sometimes never, does the person gradually come to accept her or his orientation, to view it as a given material condition of life, coming as materials do with certain capacities and limitations. The person begins to act in accordance with his or her orientation and its capacities, seeing its actualization as a requisite for an integrated personality and as a central component of personal well-being. As a result, the experience of coming out to oneself has for gays the basic structure of a discovery, not the structure of a choice. And far from signaling immorality, coming out to others affords one of the few remaining opportunities in ever more bureaucratic, mechanistic, and socialistic societies to manifest courage.

HOW WOULD SOCIETY AT LARGE BE CHANGED IF GAYS WERE SOCIALLY ACCEPTED?

Suggestions to change social policy with regard to gays are invariably met with claims that to do so would invite the destruction of civilization itself: After all, isn't that what did Rome in? Actually Rome's decay paralleled not the flourishing of homosexuality, but its repression under the later Christianized emperors.[16] Predictions of American civilization's imminent demise have been as premature as they have been frequent. Civilization has shown itself rather resilient here, in large part because of the country's traditional commitments to a respect for privacy, to individual liberties, and especially to people minding their own business. These all give society an open texture and the flexibility to try out things to see what works. And because of this one now need not speculate about what changes reforms in gay social policy might bring to society at large. For many reforms have already been tried.

Half the states have decriminalized homosexual acts. Can you guess which of the following states still have sodomy laws? Wisconsin, Minnesota; New Mexico, Arizona; Vermont, New Hampshire; Nebraska, Kansas. One from each pair does and one does not have sodomy laws. And yet one would be hard pressed to point out any substantial difference between the members of each pair. (If you're interested: It is the second of each pair with them.) Empirical studies have shown that there is no increase in other crimes in states that have decriminalized [homosexual acts].[17] Further, sodomy laws are virtually never enforced. They remain on the books not to "protect society" but to insult gays and, for that reason, need to be removed.

Neither has the passage of legislation barring discrimination against gays ushered in the end of civilization. Some 50 counties and municipalities, including some of the country's largest cities (like Los Angeles and Boston) have passed such statutes and among the states and [counties] Wisconsin and the District of Columbia have model protective codes. Again, no more brimstone has fallen in these places than elsewhere. Staunchly antigay cities, like Miami and Houston, have not been spared the AIDS crisis.

Berkeley, California, has even passed domestic partner legislation giving gay couples the same rights to city benefits as married couples, and yet Berkeley has not become more weird than it already was.

Seemingly hysterical predictions that the American family would collapse if such reforms would pass proved false, just as the same dire predictions that the availability of divorce would lessen the ideal and desirability of marriage proved completely unfounded. Indeed, if current discriminations, which drive gays into hiding and into anonymous relations, were lifted, far from seeing gays raze American families, one would see gays forming them.

Virtually all gays express a desire to have a permanent lover. Many would like to raise or foster children—perhaps [from among the] alarming number of gay kids who have been beaten up and thrown out of their "families" for being gay. But currently society makes gay coupling very difficult. A life of hiding is a pressure-cooker existence not easily shared with another. Members of non-gay couples are here asked to imagine what it would take to erase every trace of their own sexual orientation for even just a week

Even against oppressive odds, gays have shown an amazing tendency to nest. And those gay couples who have survived the odds show that the structure of more usual couplings is not a matter of destiny but of personal responsibility. The so-called basic unit of society turns out not to be a unique immutable atom but can adopt different parts, be adapted to different needs, and even be improved. Gays might even have a thing or two to teach others about divisions of labor, the relation of sensuality and intimacy, and stages of development in such relations.

If discrimination ceased, gay men and lesbians would enter the mainstream of the human community openly and with self-respect. The energies that the typical gay person wastes in the anxiety of leading a day-to-day existence of systematic disguise would be released for use in personal flourishing. From this release would be generated the many spin-off benefits that accrue to a society when its individual members thrive.

Society would be richer for acknowledging another aspect of human richness and diversity. Families with gay members would develop relations based on truth and trust rather than lies and fear. And the heterosexual majority would be better off for knowing that they are no longer trampling their gay friends and neighbors.

Finally and perhaps paradoxically, in extending to gays the rights and benefits it has reserved for its dominant culture, America would confirm its deeply held vision of itself as a morally progressing nation, a nation itself advancing and serving as a beacon for others—especially with regard to human rights. The words with which our national pledge ends—"with liberty and justice for all"—are not a description of the present but a call for the future. Ours is a nation given to a prophetic political rhetoric which acknowledges that morality is not arbitrary and that justice is not merely the expression of the current collective will. It is this vision that led the black civil rights movement to its successes. Those

congressmen who opposed that movement and its centerpiece, the 1964 Civil Rights Act, on obscurantist grounds, but who lived long enough and were noble enough came in time to express their heartfelt regret and shame at what they had done. It is to be hoped and someday to be expected that those who now grasp at anything to oppose the extension of that which is best about America to gays will one day feel the same.

NOTES

1. "Public Fears—and Sympathies," *Newsweek,* August 12, 1985, p. 23.
2. Alfred C. Kinsey, *Sexual Behavior in the Human Male* (Philadelphia: Saunders, 1948), pp. 650–51. On the somewhat lower incidences of lesbianism, see Alfred C. Kinsey, *Sexual Behavior in the Human Female* (Philadelphia: Saunders, 1953), pp. 472–75.
3. Evelyn Hooker, "The Adjustment of the Male Overt Homosexual," *Journal of Projective Techniques* 21 (1957), pp. 18–31, reprinted in Hendrik M. Ruitenbeek, ed., *The Problem of Homosexuality* (New York: Dutton, 1963), pp. 141–61.
4. See Ronald Bayer, *Homosexuality and American Psychiatry* (New York: Basic Books, 1981).
5. For studies showing that gay men are no more likely—indeed, are less likely—than heterosexuals to be child molesters and that the largest classes and most persistent sexual abusers of children are the children's fathers, stepfathers, or mother's boyfriends, see Vincent De Francis, *Protecting the Child Victim of Sex Crimes Committed by Adults* (Denver: The American Humane Association, 1969), pp. vii,

38, 69–70; A. Nicholas Groth, "Adult Sexual Orientation and Attraction to Underage Persons," *Archives of Sexual Behavior* 7 (1978), pp. 175–81; Mary J. Spencer, "Sexual Abuse of Boys," *Pediatrics* 78:1 (July 1986), pp. 133–38.
6. See National Gay Task Force, *Antigay/Lesbian Victimization* (New York: NGTF, 1984).
7. "2 St. John's Students Given Probation in Assault on Gay," *The Washington Post,* May 15, 1984, p. 1.
8. See Randy Shilts, *The Mayor of Castro Street: The Life and Times of Harvey Milk* (New York: St. Martin's, 1982), pp. 308–25.
9. See Richard Plant, *The Pink Triangle: The Nazi War Against Homosexuals* (New York: Holt, 1986).
10. E. Carrington Boggan, *The Rights of Gay People: The Basic ACLU Guide to a Gay Person's Rights* (New York: Avon, 1975), pp. 211–35.
11. John Boswell, *Christianity, Social Tolerance, and Homosexuality: Gay People in Western Europe from the Beginning of the Christian Era to the Fourteenth Century* (Chicago: The University of Chicago Press, 1980).

REVIEW AND DISCUSSION QUESTIONS

1. Who, according to Mohr, are gays? What are the consequences of the fact that homosexuality is commonplace, according to Mohr?
2. Describe the stereotypes Mohr finds about gays, along with the false generalizations he says lie behind them.
3. In what ways does he argue gays experience discrimination? Is it important, in this connection, that according to Mohr sexual orientation is not chosen?
4. How does Mohr respond to the argument that homosexuality is unnatural?
5. What policy changes does Mohr recommend, and why?

Date Rape: A Feminist Analysis

Lois Pineau

In this article, Lois Pineau discusses a range of issues associated with date rape, including myths about consent and sexuality that make conviction difficult. She defends what she terms a "communicative" mode of sexuality, which, she argues, better describes the mutuality of sexual relationships and provides a better test for consent than the contractualist model she believes is currently used in law. Lois Pineau is professor philosophy at Kansas State University.

Date rape is nonaggravated sexual assault, nonconsensual sex that does not involve physical injury, or the explicit threat of physical injury. But because it does not involve physical injury, and because physical injury is often the only criterion that is accepted as evidence that the *actus reus* [*wrongful act—Ed.*] is nonconsensual, what is really sexual assault is often mistaken for seduction. . . .

[If] a man is to be convicted, it does not suffice to establish that the *actus reas* was nonconsensual. In order to be guilty of sexual assault a man must have the requisite *mens rea*, i.e., he must either have believed that his victim did not consent or that she was probably not consenting. . . .

The criteria for *mens rea*, for the reasonableness of belief, and for consent are closely related. For although a man's sincere belief in the consent of his victim may be sufficient to defeat *mens rea*, the court is less likely to believe his belief is sincere if his belief is unreasonable. If his belief is reasonable, they are more likely to believe in the sincerity of his belief. But evidence of the reasonableness of his belief is also evidence that consent really did take place. For the very things that make it reasonable for him to believe that the defendant consented are often the very things that incline the court to believe that she consented. What is often missing is the voice of the woman herself, an account of what it would be reasonable for *her* to agree to, that is to say, an account of what is reasonable from *her* standpoint. . . .

The following statements by self-confessed date rapists reveal how our lack of a solution for dealing with date rape protects rapists by failing to provide their victims with legal recourse:

All of my rapes have been involved in a dating situation where I've been out with a woman I know. . . . I wouldn't take no for an answer. I think it had something to do with my acceptance of rejection. I had low self-esteem and not much self-confidence and when I was rejected for something which I considered to be rightly mine, I became angry and I went ahead anyway. And this was the same in any situation, whether it was rape or it was something else.[1]

. . . There is, at this time, nothing to protect women from this kind of unscrupulous victimization. A woman on a casual date with a virtual stranger has almost no chance of bringing a complaint of sexual assault before the courts. One reason for this is the prevailing criterion for consent. According to this criterion, consent is implied unless some emphatic episodic sign of resistance occurred, and its occurrence can be established. But if no episodic act occurred, or if it did occur, and the defendant claims that it didn't, or if the defendant threatened the plaintiff but won't admit it in court, it is almost impossible to find any evidence that would support the plaintiff's word against the defendant. This difficulty is exacerbated by suspicion on the part of the courts, police, and legal educators that even where an act of resistance occurs, this act should not be interpreted as a withholding of consent, and this suspicion is especially upheld where the accused is a man who is known to the female plaintiff.

In Glanville Williams's classic textbook on criminal law we are warned that where a man is unknown to a woman, she does not consent if she expresses her rejection in the form of an episodic and vigorous act at the "vital moment." But if the man is known to the woman she must, according to Williams, make use of "all means available to her to repel the man."[2] Williams warns that women often welcome a "mastery advance" and present a token resistance. He quotes Byron's couplet,

A little still she strove, and much repented
And whispering "I will ne'er consent"—
consented

by way of alerting law students to the difficulty of distinguishing real protest from pretence.[3] Thus, while in principle, a firm unambiguous stand, or a healthy show of temper ought to be sufficient, if established, to show nonconsent, in practice the forceful overriding of such a stance is apt to be taken as an indication that the resistance was not seriously intended, and that the seduction had succeeded. The consequence of this is that it is almost impossible to establish the defendant's guilt beyond a reasonable doubt.

Thus, on the one hand, we have a situation in which women are vulnerable to the most exploitive tactics at the hands of men who are known to them. On the other hand, almost nothing will count as evidence of their being assaulted, including their having taken an emphatic stance in withholding their consent. The new laws have done almost nothing to change this situation. Yet clearly, some solutions must be sought. Moreover, the road to that solution presents itself clearly enough as

a need for a reformulation of the criterion of consent. It is patent that a criterion that collapses whenever the crime itself succeeds will not suffice. . . .

THE PROBLEM OF THE CRITERION

The reasoning that underlies the present criterion of consent is entangled in a number of mutually supportive mythologies which see sexual assault as masterful seduction, and silent submission as sexual enjoyment. Because the prevailing ideology has so much informed our conceptualization of sexual interaction, it is extraordinarily difficult for us to distinguish between assault and seduction, submission and enjoyment, or so we imagine. At the same time, this failure to distinguish has given rise to a network of rationalizations that support the conflation of assault with seduction, submission with enjoyment. I therefore want to begin my argument by providing an example which shows both why it is so difficult to make this distinction, and that it exists. Later, I will identify and attempt to unravel the lines of reasoning that reinforce this difficulty.

The woman I have in mind agrees to see someone because she feels an intimate attraction to him and believes that he feels the same way about her. She goes out with him in the hope that there will be mutual enjoyment and in the course of the day or evening an increase of mutual interest. Unfortunately, these hopes of mutual and reciprocal interest are not realized. We do not know how much interest she has in him by the end of their time together, but whatever her feelings she comes under pressure to have sex with him, and she does not want to have the kind of sex he wants. She may desire to hold hands and kiss, to engage in more intense caresses or in some form of foreplay, or she may not want to be touched. She may have reasons unrelated to desire for not wanting to engage in the kind of sex he is demanding. She may have religious reservations, concerns about pregnancy or disease, a disinclination to be just another conquest. She may be engaged in a seduction program of her own which sees abstaining from sexual activity as a means of building an important emotional bond. She feels she is desirable to him, and she knows, and he knows that he will have sex with her if he can. And while she feels she doesn't owe him anything, and that it is her prerogative to refuse him, this feeling is partly a defensive reaction against a deeply held belief that if he is in need, she should provide. If she buys into the myth of insistent male sexuality she may feel he is suffering from sexual frustration and that she is largely to blame.

We do not know how much he desires her, but we do know that his desire for erotic satisfaction can hardly be separated from his desire for conquest. He feels no dating obligation, but has a strong commitment to scoring. He uses the myth of "so hard to control" male desire as a rhetorical tactic, telling her how frustrated she will leave him. He becomes overbearing. She resists, voicing her disinclination. He alternates between telling her how desirable she is and taking a hostile stance, charging her with misleading him, accusing her of wanting him, and being coy, in short of being deceitful, all the time engaging in rather aggressive body contact. It is late at night, she is tired and a bit queasy from too many drinks, and he is reaffirming her suspicion that perhaps she has misled him. She is having trouble disengaging his body from hers, and wishes he would just go away. She does not adopt a strident angry stance, partly because she thinks he is acting normally and does not deserve it, partly because she feels she is partly to blame, and partly because there is always the danger that her anger will make him angry, possibly violent. It seems that the only thing to do, given his aggression, and her queasy fatigue, is to go along with him and get it over with, but this decision is so entangled with the events in process it is hard to know if it is not simply a recognition of what is actually happening. She finds the whole encounter a thoroughly disagreeable experience, but he does not take any notice, and wouldn't have changed course if he had. He congratulates himself on his sexual prowess and is confirmed in his opinion that aggressive tactics pay off. Later she feels that she has been raped, but paradoxically tells herself that she let herself be raped.

The paradoxical feelings of the woman in our example indicate her awareness that what she feels about the incident stands in contradiction to the prevailing cultural assessment of it. She knows that she did not want to have sex with her date. She is not so sure, however, about how much her own desires count, and she is uncertain that she has made her desires clear. Her uncertainty is reinforced by the cultural reading of this incident as an ordinary seduction.

As for us, we assume that the woman did not want to have sex, but just like her, we are unsure whether her mere reluctance, in the presence of high-pressure tactics, constitutes non-consent. We suspect that submission to an overbearing and insensitive lout is no way to go about attaining sexual enjoyment, and we further suspect that he felt no compunction about providing it, so that on the face of it, from the outside looking in, it looks like a pretty unreasonable proposition for her.

Let us look at this reasoning more closely. Assume that she was not attracted to the kind of sex offered by the sort of person offering it. Then it would be *prima facie* unreasonable for her to agree to have sex, unreasonable, that is, unless she were offered some pay-off of her stoic endurance, money perhaps, or tickets to the opera. The reason is that in sexual matters, agreement is closely connected to attraction. Thus, where the presumption is that she was not attracted, we should at the same time presume that she did not consent. Hence, the burden of proof should be on her alleged assailant to show that she had good reasons for consenting to an unattractive proposition.

This is not, however, the way such situations are interpreted. In the unlikely event that the example I have described should come before the courts, there is little doubt that the law would interpret the woman's eventual acquiescence or "going along with" the sexual encounter as consent. But along with this interpretation would go the implicit understanding that she had consented because when all was said and done, when the "token" resistances to the "masterful advances" had been made, she had wanted to after all. Once the courts have constructed this interpretation, they are then forced to conjure up some horror story of feminine revenge in order to explain why she should bring charges against her "seducer."

In the even more unlikely event that the courts agreed that the woman had not consented to the above encounter, there is little chance that her assailant would be convicted of sexual assault.[4] The belief that the man's aggressive tactics are a normal part of seduction means that *mens rea* cannot be established. Her eventual "going along" with his advances constitutes reasonable grounds for his believing in her consent. These "reasonable" grounds attest to the sincerity of his belief in her consent. This reasonableness means that *mens rea* would be defeated even in jurisdictions which make *mens rea* a function of objective standards of reasonableness. Moreover, the sympathy of the court is more likely to lie with the rapist than with his victim, since, if the court is typical, it will be strongly inclined to believe that the victim had in some way "asked for it."

The position of the courts is supported by the widespread belief that male aggression and female reluctance are normal parts of seduction. Given their appearance in this model, the logic of their response must be respected. For if sexual aggression is a part of ordinary seduction, then it cannot be inconsistent with the legitimate consent of the person allegedly seduced by this means. And if it is normal for a woman to be reluctant, then this reluctance must be consistent with her consent as well. The position of the courts is not inconsistent just so long as they allow that some sort of protest on the part of a woman counts as a refusal. As we have seen, however, it frequently happens that no sort of a protest would count as a refusal. Moreover, if no sort of protest, or at least if precious few count, then the failure to register these protests will amount to "asking for it," it will amount, in other words, to agreeing. . . .

RAPE MYTHS

The belief that the natural aggression of men and the natural reluctance of women somehow makes date rape understandable underlies a number of prevalent myths about rape and human sexuality. . . . These myths are not just popular, however, but often emerge in the arguments of judges who acquit date rapists, and policemen who refuse to lay charges.

The claim that the victim provoked a sexual incident, that "she asked for it," is by far the most common defense given by men who are accused of sexual assault. . . .

Attempts to explain that women have a right to behave in sexually provocative ways without suffering dire consequences still meet with surprisingly tough resistance. Even people who find nothing wrong or sinful with sex itself, in any of its forms, tend to suppose that women must not behave sexually unless they are prepared to carry through on some fuller course of sexual interaction. The logic of this response seems to be that at some point a woman's behavior commits her to following through on the full course of a sexual encounter as it is defined by her assailant. At some point she has made an agreement, or formed a contract, and once that is done, her contractor is entitled to demand that she satisfy the terms of that contract. Thus, this view about sexual responsibility and desert is supported by other assumptions about contracts and agreement. But we do not normally suppose that casual nonverbal behavior generates agreements. Nor do we normally grant private persons the right to enforce contracts. What rationale would support our conclusion in this case?

The rationale, I believe, comes in the form of a belief in the especially insistent nature of male sexuality, an insistence which lies at the root of natural male aggression, and which is extremely difficult, perhaps impossible, to contain. At a certain point in the arousal process, it is thought, a man's rational will gives way to the IOU of nature. His sexual need can and does reach a point where it is uncontrollable, and his natural masculine aggression kicks in to assure that this need is met. Women, however, are naturally more contained, and so it is their responsibility not to provoke the irrational in the male. If they do go so far as that, they have both failed in their responsibilities, and subjected themselves to the inevitable. One does not go into the lion's cage and expect not to be eaten. Natural feminine reluctance, it is thought, is no protection against a sexually aroused male.

The belief about the normal aggressiveness of male sexuality is complemented by common knowledge about female gender development. Once, women were taught to deny their sexuality and to aspire to ideals of chastity. Things have not changed so much. Women still tend to eschew conquest mentalities in favor of a combination of sex and affection. Insofar as this is thought to be merely a cultural requirement, however, there is an expectation that women will be coy about their sexual desire. The assumption that women both want to indulge sexually, and are inclined to sacrifice this desire for higher ends, gives rise to the myth that they want to be raped. After all, doesn't rape give them the sexual enjoyment they *really* want, at the same time that it relieves them of the responsibility for admitting to and acting upon what they want? And how then can we blame men, who have been socialized to be aggressively seductive precisely for the purpose of overriding female reserve? If we find fault at all, we are inclined to cast our suspicions on the motives of the woman. For it is on her that the contradictory roles of sexual desirer and sexual denier have been placed. Our awareness of the contradiction expected of her makes us suspect her honesty. In the past, she was expected to deny her complicity because of the shame and guilt she felt at having submitted. This expectation persists in many quarters today, and is carried over into a general suspicion about her character, and the fear that she might make a false accusation out of revenge, or some other low motive. . . .

DISPELLING THE MYTHS

. . . The belief that a woman generates some sort of contractual obligation whenever her behavior is interpreted as seductive is the most indefensible part of the mythology of rape. In law, contracts are not legitimate just because a promise has been made. In particular, the use of pressure tactics to extract agreement is frowned upon. . . .

Even if we assume that a woman has initially agreed to an encounter, her agreement does not automatically make all subsequent sexual activity to which she submits legitimate. If during coitus a woman should experience pain, be suddenly overcome with guilt or fear of pregnancy, or simply lose her initial desire, those are good reasons for her to change her mind. Having changed her mind, neither her partner nor the state has any right to force her to continue. But then if she is forced to continue she is assaulted. Thus, establishing that consent occurred at a particular point during a sexual encounter should not conclusively establish the legitimacy of the encounter. What is needed is a reading of whether she agreed throughout the encounter.

If the "she asked for it" contractual view of sexual interchange has any validity, it is because there is a point at which there is no stopping a sexual encounter, a point at which that encounter becomes the inexorable outcome of the unfolding of natural events. If a sexual encounter is like a slide on which I cannot stop halfway down, it will be relevant whether I enter the slide of my own free will, or am pushed.

But there is no evidence that the entire sexual act is like a slide. While there may be a few seconds in the "plateau" period just prior to orgasm in which people are "swept" away by sexual feelings to the point where we could justifiably understand their lack of heed for the comfort of their partner, the greater part of a sexual encounter comes well within the bounds of morally responsible control of our own actions. Indeed, the available evidence shows that most of the activity involved in sex has to do with building the requisite level of desire, a task that involves the proper use of foreplay, the possibility of which implies control over the form that foreplay will take.

Modern sexual therapy assumes that such control is universally accessible, and so far there has been no reason to question that assumption. All are unanimous, moreover, in holding that mutual sexual enjoyment requires an atmosphere of comfort and communication, a minimum of pressure, and an ongoing check-up on one's partner's state. They maintain that different people have different predilections, and that what is pleasurable for one person is very often anathema to another. These findings show that the way to achieve sexual pleasure, at any time at all, let alone with a casual acquaintance, decidedly does not involve overriding the other person's express reservations and providing them with just any kind of sexual stimulus. . . . In this case science seems to concur with women's perception that aggressive incommunicative sex is not what they want. But if science and the voice of women concur, if aggressive seduction does not lead to good sex, if women do not like it or want it, then it is not rational to think that they would agree to it. Where such sex takes place, it is therefore rational to presume that the sex was not consensual. . . .

In conclusion, there are no grounds for the "she asked for it" defence. Sexually provocative behaviour does not generate sexual contracts. Even where there are sexual agreements, they cannot be legitimately enforced either by the State, or by private right, or by natural prerogative. Secondly, all the evidence suggests that neither women nor men find sexual enjoyment in rape or in any form of noncommunicative sexuality. Thirdly, male sexual desire is containable, and can be subjected to moral and rational control. Fourthly, since there is no reason why women should not be sexually provocative, they do not "deserve" any sex they do not want. This last is a welcome discovery. The taboo on sexual provocativeness in women is a taboo both on sensuality and on teasing. But sensuality is a source of delight, and teasing is playful and inspires wit. What a relief to learn that it is not sexual provocativeness, but its enemies, that constitutes a danger to the world.

COMMUNICATIVE SEXUALITY: REINTERPRETING THE KANTIAN IMPERATIVE

The present criterion of consent sets up sexual encounters as contractual events in which sexual aggression is presumed to be consented to unless there is some vigorous act of refusal. As long as we view sexual interaction on a contractual model, the only possibility for finding fault is to point to the presence of such an act. But it is clear that whether or not we can determine such a presence, there is something strongly disagreeable about the sexual aggression described above.

In thinking about sex we must keep in mind its sensual ends, and the facts show that aggressive high-pressure sex contradicts those ends. Consensual sex in dating situations is presumed to aim at mutual enjoyment. It may not always do this, and when it does, it might not always succeed. There is no logical incompatibility between wanting to continue a sexual encounter, and failing to derive sexual pleasure from it.

But it seems to me that there is a presumption in favour of the connection between sex and sexual enjoyment, and that if a man wants to be sure that he is not forcing himself on a woman, he has an obligation either to ensure that the encounter really is mutually enjoyable, or to know the reasons why she would want to continue the encounter in spite of her lack of enjoyment. A closer investigation of the nature of this obligation will enable us to construct a more rational and a more plausible norm of sexual conduct.

Onara O'Neill has argued that in intimate situations we have an obligation to take the ends of others as our own, and to promote those ends in a non-manipulative and non-paternalistic manner. Now it seems that in honest sexual encounters just this is required . . . But the obligation to promote the sexual ends of one's partner implies the obligation to know what those ends are, and also the obligation to know how those ends are attained. Thus, the problem comes down to a problem of epistemic responsibility, the responsibility to know. The solution, in my view, lies in the practice of a communicative sexuality, one which combines the appropriate knowledge of the other with respect for the dialectics of desire.

So let us, for a moment, conceive of sexual interaction on a communicative rather than a contractual model. Let us look at it the way I think it should be looked at, as if it were a proper conversation rather than an offer from the Mafia. . . .

The communicative interaction involved in conversation is concerned with a good deal more than didactic content and argument. Good conversationalists are intuitive, sympathetic, and charitable. Intuition and charity aid the conversationalist in her effort to interpret the words of the other correctly and sympathy enables her to enter into the other's point of view. Her sensitivity alerts her to the tone of the exchange. Has her point been taken good-humouredly or resentfully? Aggressively delivered responses are taken as a sign that *ad hominems* are at work, and that the respondent's self-worth has been called into question. Good conversationalists will know to suspend further discussion until this sense of self-worth has been reestablished. Angry responses, resentful responses, bored responses, even over-enthusiastic responses require that the emotional ground be cleared before the discussion be continued. Often it is better to change the topic, or to come back to it on another day under different circumstances. Good conversationalists do not overwhelm their respondents with a barrage of their own opinions. While they may be persuasive, the forcefulness of their persuasion does not lie in their being overbearing, but rather in their capacity to see the other's point of view, to understand what it depends on, and so to address the essential point, but with tact and clarity.

Just as communicative conversationalists are concerned with more than didactic content, persons engaged in communicative sexuality will be concerned with more than achieving coitus. They will be sensitive to the responses of their partners. They will, like good conversationalists, be intuitive, sympathetic, and charitable. Intuition will help them to interpret their partner's responses; sympathy will enable them to share what their partner is feeling; charity will enable them to care. Communicative sexual partners will not overwhelm each other with the barrage of their own desires. They will treat negative, bored, or angry responses as a sign that the erotic ground needs to be either cleared or abandoned. Their concern with fostering the desire of the other must involve an ongoing state of alertness in interpreting her responses.

Just as a conversationalist's prime concern is for the mutuality of the discussion, a person engaged in communicative sexuality will be most concerned with the mutuality of desire. As such, both will put into practice a regard for their respondent that is guaranteed no place in the contractual language of rights, duties, and consent. The *dialectics* of both activities reflect the dialectics of desire insofar as each person's interest in continuing is contingent upon the other person wishing to do so too, and each person's interest is as much fueled by the other's interest as it is by her own. . . .

CULTURAL PRESUMPTIONS

. . . Traditionally, the decision to date indicates that two people have an initial attraction to each other, that they are disposed to like each other, and look forward to enjoying each other's company. Dating derives its implicit meaning from this tradition. It retains this meaning unless other aims are explicitly stated, and even then it may not be possible to alienate this meaning. It is a rare woman who will not spurn a man who states explicitly, right at the onset, that he wants to go out with her solely on the condition that he have sexual intercourse with her at the end of the evening, and that he has no interest in her company apart from gaining that end, and no concern for mutual satisfaction.

Explicit protest to the contrary aside, the conventions of dating confer on it its social meaning, and this social meaning implies a relationship which is more like friendship than the cutthroat competition of opposing teams. As such, it requires that we do more than stand on our rights with regard to each other. As long as we are operating under the auspices of a dating relationship, it requires that we behave in the mode of friendship and trust. But if a date is more like friendship than a business contract, then clearly respect for the dialectics of desire is incompatible with the sort of sexual pressure that is inclined to end in date rape. And clearly, also, a conquest mentality which exploits a situation of trust and respect for purely selfish ends is morally pernicious. Failure to respect the dialectics of desire when operating under the auspices of friendship and trust is to act in flagrant disregard of the moral requirement to avoid manipulative, coercive, and explotive behaviour. Respect for the dialectics of desire is *prima facie* inconsistent with the satisfaction of one person at the expense of the other. The proper end of friendship relations is mutual satisfaction. But the requirement of mutuality means that we must take a communicative approach to discovering the ends of the other, and this entails that we respect the dialectics of desire.

But now that we know what communicative sexuality is, and that it is morally required, and that it is the only feasible means to mutual sexual enjoyment, why not take this model as the norm of what is reasonable in sexual interaction? The evidence strongly indicates that women whose partners are aggressively uncommunicative have little chance of experiencing sexual pleasure. But it is not reasonable for women to consent to what they have little chance of enjoying. Hence it is not reasonable for women to consent to aggressive noncommunicative sex. Nor can we reasonably suppose that women have consented to sexual encounters which we know and they know they do not find enjoyable. With the communicative model as the norm, the aggressive contractual model should strike us as a model of deviant sexuality, and sexual encounters patterned on that model should

strike us as encounters to which *prima facie* no one would reasonably agree. But if acquiescence to an encounter counts as consent only if the acquiescence is reasonable, something to which a reasonable person, in full posession of knowledge relevant to the encounter, would agree, then acquiescence to aggressive noncommunicative sex is not reasonable. Hence, acquiescence under such conditions should not count as consent.

Thus, where communicative sexuality does not occur, we lack the main ground for believing that the sex involved was consensual. Moreover, where a man does not engage in communicative sexuality, he acts either out of reckless disregard, or out of willful ignorance. For he cannot know, except through the practice of communicative sexuality, whether his partner has any sexual reason for continuing the encounter. And where she does not, he runs the risk of imposing on her what she is not willing to have. All that is needed then, in order to provide women with legal protection from "date rape," is to make both reckless indifference and willful ignorance a sufficient condition of *mens rea* and to make communicative sexuality the accepted norm of sex to which a reasonable woman would agree. Thus, the appeal to communicative sexuality as a norm for sexual encounters accomplishes two things. It brings the aggressive sex involved in "date rape" well within the realm of sexual assault, and it locates the guilt of date rapists in the failure to approach sexual relations on a communicative basis.

. . . Where communicative sexuality is taken as the norm, and aggressive sexual tactics as a presumption against [legal] consent, . . . the communicative model of normal sexuality gives us a handle on a solution to the problem of [legally establishing] date rape. If [we were to say, as I think we should, that] noncommunicative sexuality establishes a resumption of nonconsent, then where there are no overriding reasons for thinking that consent occurred, we have a criterion for a category of sexual assault that does not require evidence of physical violence or threat. If we are serious about date rape, then the next step is to take this criterion as objective grounds for establishing that date rape has occurred. The proper legislation is the shortest route to establishing this criterion.

NOTES

1. Sylvia Levine and Joseph Loenig, eds., *Why Men Rape* (Toronto: Macmillan, 1980), p. 83.
2. Williams, *Textbook of Criminal Law* (1983), p. 238.
3. Ibid.
4. See Jeanne C. Marsh, Allison Geist, and Nathan Caplan, *Rape and the Limits of Law Reform* (Boston: Auburn House, 1982), p. 32. According to Marsh's study on the impact on the Michigan reform of rape laws, convictions were increased for traditional conceptions of rape, i.e., aggravated assault. However, date rape, which has a much higher incidence than aggravated assault, has a very low rate of arrest and an even lower one of conviction.

REVIEW AND DISCUSSION QUESTIONS

1. What is Pineau's definition of date rape?
2. Describe the problems that prosecutors face in proving date rape.
3. In the example she discusses, why is it unlikely that the man would be convicted of rape?
4. Describe the myths that Pineau points to about sex and rape, indicating why she thinks they should be dispelled.
5. What is the "communicative" model of sexuality? How is it different from the alternative view?
6. How does Pineau link communicative sexuality with consent?
7. Do you think the hypothetical case she describes is date rape? Explain.
8. How does Pineau think the communicative model can help solve the problem of establishing in a court whether date rape occurred?

An Interview About Date Rape

Camille Paglia

In this two-part interview with Celia Farber for *SPIN* magazine, Camille Paglia defends a different view about sex and male-female relations than does Pineau, one that leads her to criticize the behavior of some who see themselves as victims of date rape. Rather than communication, Paglia sees in sex an inherent aggressiveness of males. Women, she thinks, must both acknowledge the true nature of sex and take responsibility for themselves and the risks they take. Camille Paglia is professor of humanities at the University of the Arts in Philadelphia.

Paglia: I'm noticing that many people coming into the media now are people whose minds have been poisoned by their training at Yale and other Ivy League places. For example, I see where this whole date-rape thing is coming from. I recognize the language of these smart girls who are entering the media; they are coming from these schools. They have this stupid, pathetic, completely-removed-from-reality view of things that they've gotten from these academics who are totally off the wall, totally removed. Whereas my views on sex are coming from the fact that I am a football fan and I am a rock fan. Rock and football are revealing something true and permanent and eternal about male energy and sexuality. They are revealing the fact that women, in fact, *like* the idea of flaunting, strutting, wild masculine energy. . . . This date-rape propaganda has been primarily coming out of the elite schools, where the guys are all these cooperative, literate, introspective, sit-on-their-ass guys, whereas you're not getting it that much down in the football schools where people accept the fact of the beauty and strength of masculinity. You see jocks on the campus all the time—they understand what manhood is down there. It's only up here where there is this idea that they can get men on a leash. It's these guys in the Ivy League schools who get used to obeying women. They're sedentary guys. It's ironic that you're getting the biggest bitching about men from the schools where the men are just eunuchs and bookworms.

SPIN: That point about primordial male sexuality is also at odds with much contemporary pop psychology. I'm referring to the twelve-step, women-who-love-too-much school of thought, which insists that a woman's attraction to an "untamed" man, as it were, is necessarily a sign of sickness—a sign of a warped emotional life that invariably traces back to childhood, and the attention span of the father. It never considers such an attraction to be a naturally occurring phenomenon—a force of nature. I think the approach to remedying the problem is simplistic, even dangerously so at times.

Paglia: I agree. I'm a Freudian. I like Freud very much, even though I adapt him and add things to him. But his system of analysis is extremely accurate. It's a conflict-based system that allows for paradox. It's also very self-critical and self-analytical. I've watched therapy getting more and more mushy in the

past fifteen years in America. . . . It's become what I call coercive compassion. It's disgusting, it's condescending, it's insulting, it's coddling, it keeps everyone in an infantile condition rather than in the adult condition that was postulated as the ultimate goal of Freudian analysis. You were meant to be totally self-aware as a Freudian. Now, it's everyone who will help you, the group will help you. It's awful. It's a return to the Fifties conformist model of things. It's this victim-centered view of the world, which is very pernicious. We cannot have a world where everyone is a victim. "I'm this way because my father made me this way. I'm this way because my husband made me this way." Yes, we are indeed formed by traumas that happened to us. But then you must take charge, you must take over, you are responsible. Personal responsibility is at the heart of my system. But today's system is this whining thing, "Why won't you help me, Mommy and Daddy?" It's like this whole thing with date rape.

SPIN: One point that hasn't been made in the whole rape debate is women's role over men, sexually. In the case of a rape, a man has to use brute force to obtain something that a woman has—her very sex. So naturally she's weaker physically, and will always be oppressed by him physically. But in that moment when he decides that the only way he can get what he wants from her emotionally, or sexually, or whatever, is to rape her, he is confessing to a weakness that is all-encompassing. She is abused, but he is utterly tragic and pathetic. One is temporary and the other is permanent. I was raped once and it helped me to think of it like that. Not at all to apologize for him, but to focus on my power instead of my helplessness. It was a horrible experience, but it certainly didn't destroy my whole life or my psyche, as much as contemporary wisdom insisted it must have.

Paglia: Right, we *have* what they want. I think woman is the dominant sex. Men have to

From Celia Farber, "An Interview with Camille Paglia," *SPIN*, September–October 1991. Reprinted by permission.

do all sorts of stuff to prove that they are worthy of a woman's attention. It's very interesting what you said about the rape, because one of the German magazine reporters who came to talk to me—she's been living in New York for ten years—she came to talk to me about two weeks ago and she told me a very interesting story, very similar to yours. She lives in Brooklyn, and she let this guy in whom she shouldn't have, and she got raped. She said that, because she's a feminist, of course she had to go for counseling. She said it was awful, that the minute she arrived there, the rape counselors were saying, "You will never recover from this, what's happened to you is so terrible." She said, what the hell, it was a terrible experience, but she was going to pick herself up, and it wasn't that big a deal. The whole system now is designed to make you feel that you are maimed and mutilated forever if something like that happens. She said it made her feel worse. It's absolutely American—it is not European—and the whole system is filled with these clichés about sex. I think there is a fundamental prudery about sex in all this. Rape is one of the risk factors in getting involved with men. It's a risk factor. It's like driving a car. My attitude is, it's like gambling. If you go to Atlantic City—these girls are going to Atlantic City, and when they lose, it's like "Oh, Mommy and Daddy, I lost." My answer is stay home and do your nails, if that's the kind of person you are. My Sixties attitude is, yes, go for it, take the risk, take the challenge—if you get raped, if you get beat up in a dark alley in a street, it's okay. That was part of the risk of freedom, that's part of what we've demanded as women. Go with it. Pick yourself up, dust yourself off, and go on. We cannot regulate male sexuality. The uncontrollable aspect of male sexuality is part of what makes sex interesting. And yes, it can lead to rape in some situations. What feminists are asking for is for men to be castrated, to make eunuchs out of them. The powerful, uncontrollable force of male sexuality has been censored out of white middle-class homes. But it's still there in black culture, and in Spanish culture.

SPIN: In the first part of our interview, the section about rape upset every single woman who read it—in the offices at *SPIN* and even at the typesetters. They all seemed to feel that you were defending the rapist.

Paglia: No, that's not it at all. The point is, these white, upper-middle-class feminists believe that a pain-free world is achievable. I'm saying that a pain-free world will be achievable only under totalitarianism. There is no such thing as risk-free anything. In fact, all valuable human things come to us from risk and loss. Therefore we value beauty and youth because they are transient. Part of the sizzle of sex is the danger, the risk of loss of identity in love. That's part of the drama of love. My generation demanded no more overprotection of women. We wanted women to be able to freely choose sex, to freely have all the adventures that men could have. So women began to hike on mountain paths and do all sorts of dangerous things. That's the risk of freedom. If women break their legs on mountain bikes, that's the risk factor. I'm not defending the rapist—I'm defending the freedom to risk rape. I don't want sexual experience to be protected by society. A part of it is that since women are physically weaker than men, in our sexual freedom, women are going to get raped. We should be angry about it, but it's a woman's personal responsibility now, in this age of sexual liberation, to make herself physically fit, so that she can fight off as best she can man's advances. She needs to be alert in her own mind to any potential danger. It's up to the woman to give clear signals of what her wishes are. If she does not want to be out of control of the situation, she should not get drunk, she should not be in a private space with a man whom she does not know. Rape does not destroy you forever. It's like getting beaten up. Men get beat up all the time.

SPIN: But don't you think that people see a man getting beat up and a woman getting raped as completely different? Do you think rape should be considered as serious a crime as murder?

Paglia: That's absurd. I dislike anything that treats women as if they are special, frail little creatures. We don't need special protection. Rape is an assault. If it is a totally devastating psychological experience for a woman, then she doesn't have a proper attitude toward sex. It's this whole stupid feminist thing about how we are basically nurturing, benevolent people, and sex is a wonderful thing between two equals. With that kind of attitude, then of course rape is going to be a total violation of your entire life, because you have had a stupid, naive, Mary Poppins view of life to begin with. Sex is a turbulent power that we are not in control of; it's a dark force. The sexes are at war with each other. That's part of the excitement and interest of sex. It's the dark realm of the night. When you enter the realm of the night, horrible things can happen there. You can be attacked on a dark street. Does that mean we should never go into dark streets? Part of my excitement as a college student in the Sixties was coming out of the very protective Fifties. I was wandering those dark streets understanding that not only could I be raped, I could be killed. It's like the gay men going down to the docks and having sex in alleyways and trucks; it's the danger. Feminists have no idea that some women like to flirt with danger because there is a sizzle in it. You know what gets me sick and tired? The battered-woman motif. It's so misinterpreted, the way we have to constantly look at it in terms of male oppression and tyranny, and female victimization. When, in fact, everyone knows throughout the world that many of these working-class relationships where women get beat up have hot sex. They ask why she won't leave him? Maybe she won't leave him because the sex is very hot. I say we should start looking at the battered-wife motif in terms of sex. If gay men go down to bars and like to get tied up, beaten up, and have their asses whipped, how come we can't allow that a lot of wives like the kind of sex they are getting in these battered-wife relationships? We can't consider that women might have kinky tastes, can we? No, because women are naturally benevolent and nurturing, aren't they? Everything is so damn Mary Poppins and sanitized.

SPIN: What do you think is the main quality that women have within them that they aren't using?

Paglia: What women have to realize is their dominance as a sex. That women's sexual powers are enormous. All cultures have seen it. Men know it. Women know it. The only people who don't know it are feminists. Desensualized, desexualized, neurotic women. I wouldn't have said this twenty years ago because I was militant feminist myself. But as the years have gone on, I begin to see more and more that the perverse, neurotic psychodrama projected by these women is coming from their own problems with sex.

REVIEW AND DISCUSSION QUESTIONS

1. Explain what Paglia means when she speaks of some women's "victim-centered" view. Who has that view? What is it?

2. What is the "fifties" view of sex that Paglia rejects, as contrasted with her own?

3. In answering a question during another interview about whether a woman has a right to wear "sexually provocative" clothes in public, Paglia answered: "We have the *right* to leave our purse on a park bench in Central Park and go play twenty-five feet away and hope the purse is going to be there when we return, okay? Now, this is just simply stupid behavior. If someone steals the purse, we pursue the thief, we put him in jail. We also say to you, 'That was really *stupid!*' Now, the same thing here. You may have the *right* to leave your purse there, you may have the *right* to dress in that way, but you are running a *risk!*" Do you agree with Paglia? Explain.

4. Discuss the claim that Paglia has a much higher opinion of women than of men.

The Saturated Self: Persons and Relationships in the Information Age

Kenneth Gergen

We often focus on the advantages of new technologies. We want the newest computers, the fastest Internet access, the greatest number of cable TV channels, and the cheapest cell phones; all of these have obvious benefits. Advances in applied science have made these technologies available at prices that many can afford, so their use is widespread. We tend to be less aware of the costs that accompany the cultural transformations resulting from such technologies. Kenneth Gergen develops an impressionistic account of the effects of communications technologies on social relations and personal identity. When personal relations are mediated electronically, we are able to experience many more individuals and to maintain more friendships. At the same time, our knowledge of others becomes more fragmented, and our relationships become thinner. He suggests that while TV, e-mail, and other communication technologies enhance our knowledge about relationships, they also expand our desires and our obligations. Increasingly, we are drawn in different directions and experience what he calls "multiphrenia," a new pattern of divided self-consciousness. Gergen takes an equivocal stance toward these changes. The reader is left to form a summative evaluation of the costs and benefits of the Information Age that he identifies. Kenneth Gergen is professor of psychology at Swarthmore College.

A century ago, social relationships were largely confined to the distance of an easy walk. Most were conducted in person, within small communities: family, neighbors, townspeople. Yes, the horse and carriage made longer trips possible, but even a trip of thirty miles could take all day. The railroad could speed one away, but cost and availability limited such travel. If one moved from the community, relationships were likely to end. From birth to death one could depend on relatively even-textured social surroundings. Words, faces, gestures, and possibilities were relatively consistent, coherent, and slow to change.

For much of the world's population, especially the industrialized West, the small, face-to-face community is vanishing into the pages of history. We go to country inns for weekend outings, we decorate condominium interiors with clapboards and brass beds, and we dream of old age in a rural cottage. But as a result of the technological developments just described, contemporary life is a swirling sea of social relations. Words thunder in by radio, television, newspaper, mail, telephone, fax, wire service, electronic mail, billboards, Federal Express, and more. Waves of new faces are everywhere—in town for a day, visiting for the weekend, at the Rotary lunch, at the church social—and incessantly and incandescently on television. Long weeks in a single community are unusual; a full day within a single neighborhood is becoming rare. We travel casually across town, into the countryside, to neighboring towns, cities, states; one might go thirty miles for coffee and conversation.

Through the technologies of the century, the number and variety of relationships in which we are engaged, potential frequency of contact, expressed intensity of relationship, and endurance through time all are steadily increasing. As this increase becomes extreme we reach a state of social saturation. Let us consider this state in greater detail.

In the face-to-face community the cast of others remained relatively stable.[1] There were changes by virtue of births and deaths, but moving from one town—much less state or country—to another was difficult. The number of relationships commonly maintained in today's world stands in stark contrast. Counting one's family, the morning television news, the car radio, colleagues on the train, and the local newspaper, the typical commuter may confront as many different persons (in terms of views or images) in the first two hours of a day as the community-based predecessor did in a month. The morning calls in a business office may connect one to a dozen different locales in a given city, often across the continent, and very possibly across national boundaries. A single hour of prime-time melodrama immerses one in the lives of a score of individuals. In an evening of television, hundreds of engaging faces insinuate themselves into our lives. It is not only the immediate community that occupies our thoughts and feelings, but a constantly changing cast of characters spread across the globe.

Two aspects of this expansion are particularly noteworthy. First there is what may be termed the *perseverance of the past.* Formerly, increases in time and distance between persons typically meant loss. When someone moved away, the relationship would languish. Long-distance visits were arduous, and the mails slow. Thus, as one grew older, many active participants would fade from one's life. Today, time and distance are no longer such serious threats to a relationship. One may sustain an intimacy over thousands of miles by frequent telephone raptures punctuated by occasional visits. One may similarly retain relationships with high-school chums, college roommates, old military cronies, or friends from a Caribbean vacation five years earlier. Birthday books have become a standard household item; one's memory is inadequate to record the festivities for which one is responsible. In effect, as we move through life, the cast of relevant characters is ever expanding. For some this means an ever-increasing sense of stress: "How can we make friends with them?

We don't even have time for the friends we already have!" For others there is a sense of comfort, for the social caravan in which we travel through life remains always full.

Yet at the same time that the past is preserved, continuously poised to insert itself into the present, there is an *acceleration of the future.* The pace of relationships is hurried, and processes of unfolding that once required months or years may be accomplished in days or weeks. A century ago, for example, courtships were often carried out on foot or horseback, or through occasional letters. Hours of interchange might be punctuated by long periods of silence, making the path from acquaintanceship to intimacy lengthy. With today's technologies, however, it is possible for a couple to maintain almost continuous connection. Not only do transportation technologies chip away at the barrier of geographic distance, but through telephone (both stable and cordless), overnight mail, cassette recordings, home videos, photographs, and electronic mail, the other may be "present" at almost any moment. Courtships may thus move from excitement to exhaustion within a short time. The single person may experience not a handful of courtship relationships in a lifetime but dozens. In the same way, the process of friendship is often accelerated. Through the existing technologies, a sense of affinity may blossom into a lively sense of interdependence within a brief space of time. As the future opens, the number of friendships expands as never before. . . .

New patterns of relationship also take shape. In the face-to-face community one participated in a limited set of relationships—with family, friends, storekeepers, clerics, and the like. Now the next telephone call can thrust us suddenly into a new relationship—with a Wall Street broker, a charity solicitor, an alumni campaigner from the old school, a childhood friend at a nearby convention, a relative from across the country, a child of a friend, or even a sex pervert. One may live in a suburb with well-clipped neighbors, but commute to a city for frequent confrontation with street people, scam merchants, panhandlers, prostitutes, and threatening bands of juveniles. One may reside in Houston, but establish bonds—through business or leisure travel—with a Norwegian banker, a wine merchant from the Rhine Pfalz, or an architect from Rome.

Of course, it is television that most dramatically increases the variety of relationships in which one participates—even if vicariously. One can identify with heroes from a thousand tales, carry on imaginary conversations with talk-show guests from all walks of life, or empathize with athletes from around the globe. One of the most interesting results of this electronic expansion of relationships occurs in the domain of parent-child relationships. As Joshua Meyrowitz proposes in *No Sense of Place,* children of the preceding century were largely insulated from information about the private lives of adults.[2] Parents, teachers, and police could shield children from their adult proceedings by simply conducting them in private places. Further, books dealing with the misgivings, failings, deceits, and conflicts of the adult world were generally unavailable to children. Children remained children. Television has changed all that. Programming systematically reveals the full panoply of "backstage" trials and tribulations to the child. As a result the child no longer interacts with one-dimensional, idealized adults, but with persons possessing complex private lives, doubt-filled and vulnerable. In turn, parents no longer confront the comfortably naive child of yesteryear, but one whose awe is diminished and whose insights may be acute.

The technology of the age both expands the variety of human relationships and modifies the form of older ones. When relationships move from the face-to-face to the electronic mode, they are often altered. Relationships that were confined to specific situations—to offices, living rooms, bedrooms—become "unglued." They are no longer geographically confined, but can take place anywhere. Unlike face-to-face relationships, electronic relationships also conceal visual information (eye

movement, expressive movements of the mouth), so a telephone speaker cannot read the facial cues of the listener for signs of approval or disapproval. As a result, there is a greater tendency to create an imaginary other with whom to relate. One can fantasize that the other is feeling warm and enthusiastic or cold and angry, and act accordingly. An acquaintance told me that he believed his first marriage to be a product of the heavy phoning necessary for a long-distance courtship. By phone she seemed the most desirable woman in the world; it was only months after the wedding that he realized that he had married a mirage.

Many organizations are now installing electronic-mail systems, which enable employees to carry out their business with each other by computer terminals rather than by traditional, face-to-face means. Researchers find that employee relations have subtly changed as a result. Status differences begin to crumble as lower-ranking employees feel freer to express their feelings and question their superiors electronically than in person. Harvard Business School's Shoshana Zuboff suggests that the introduction of "smart machines" into businesses is blurring the distinctions between managers and workers. Managers are no longer the "thinkers" while the workers are consigned to the "doing."[3] Rather, out of necessity the workers now become managers of information, and as a result, they considerably augment their power . . .

Consider the moments:

- Over lunch with friends you discuss Northern Ireland. Although you have never spoken a word on the subject, you find yourself heatedly defending British policies.
- You work as an executive in the investments department of a bank. In the evenings you smoke marijuana and listen to the Grateful Dead.
- You sit in a café and wonder what it would be like to have an intimate relationship with various strangers walking past.
- You are a lawyer in a prestigious midtown firm. On the weekends you work on a novel about romance with a terrorist.

- You go to a Moroccan restaurant and afterward take in the latest show at a country-and-western bar.

In each case individuals harbor a sense of coherent identity or self-sameness, only to find themselves suddenly propelled by alternative impulses. They seem securely to be one sort of person, but yet another comes bursting to the surface—in a suddenly voiced opinion, a fantasy, a turn of interests, or a private activity. Such experiences with variation and self-contradiction may be viewed as preliminary effects of social saturation. They may signal a *populating of the self,* the acquisition of multiple and disparate potentials for being. It is this process of self-population that begins to undermine the traditional commitments to both romanticist and modernist forms of being. It is of pivotal importance, in setting the stage for the postmodern turn. Let us explore.

The technologies of social saturation expose us to an enormous range of persons, new forms of relationship, unique circumstances and opportunities, and special intensities of feeling. One can scarcely remain unaffected by such exposure. As child-development specialists now agree, the process of socialization is life-long. We continue to incorporate information from the environment throughout our lives. When exposed to other persons, we change in two major ways. We increase our capacities for *knowing that* and for *knowing how.* In the first case, through exposure to others we learn myriad details about their words, actions, dress, mannerisms, and so on. We ingest enormous amounts of information about patterns of interchange. Thus, for example, from an hour on a city street, we are informed of the clothing styles of blacks, whites, upper class, lower class, and more. We may learn the ways of Japanese businessmen, bag ladies, Sikhs, Hare Krishnas, or flute players from Chile. We see how relationships are carried out between mothers and daughters, business executives, teenage friends, and construction workers. An hour in a business office may expose us to the political views of a Texas oilman, a Chicago lawyer, and a gay activist from San Francisco. Radio commentators espouse views on boxing, pollution, and child abuse; pop music may advocate machoism, racial bigotry, and suicide. Paperback books cause hearts to race over the unjustly treated, those who strive against impossible odds, those who are brave or brilliant. And this is to say nothing of television input. Via television, myriad figures are allowed into the home who would never otherwise trespass. Millions watch as talk-show guests—murderers, rapists, women prisoners, child abusers, members of the KKK, mental patients, and others often discredited—attempt to make their lives intelligible. There are few six-year-olds who cannot furnish at least a rudimentary account of life in an African village, the concerns of divorcing parents, or drug-pushing in the ghetto. Hourly our storehouse of social knowledge expands in range and sophistication.

This massive increase in knowledge of the social world lays the groundwork for a second kind of learning, a *knowing how.* We learn how to place such knowledge into action, to shape it for social consumption, to act so that social life can proceed effectively. And the possibilities for placing this supply of information into effective action are constantly expanding. The Japanese businessman glimpsed on the street today, and on the television tomorrow, may be well confronted in one's office the following week. On these occasions the rudiments of appropriate behavior are already in place. If a mate announces that he or she is thinking about divorce, the other's reaction is not likely to be dumb dismay. The drama has so often been played out on television and movie screens that one is already prepared with multiple options. If one wins a wonderful prize, suffers a humiliating loss, faces temptation to cheat, or learns of a sudden death in the family, the reactions are hardly random. One more or less knows how it goes, is more or less ready for action. Having seen it all before, one approaches a state of ennui.

In an important sense, as social saturation proceeds we become pastiches, imitative assemblages of each other. In memory we carry others' patterns of being with us. If the conditions are favorable, we can place these patterns into action. Each of us becomes the other, a representative, or a replacement. To put it more broadly, as the century has progressed selves have become increasingly populated with the character of others.[4] We are not one, or a few, but like Walt Whitman, we "contain multitudes." We appear to each other as single identities, unified, of whole cloth. However, with social saturation, each of us comes to harbor a vast population of hidden potentials—to be a blues singer, a gypsy, an aristocrat, a criminal. All the selves lie latent, and under the right conditions may spring to life.

The populating of the self not only opens relationships to new ranges of possibility, but one's subjective life also becomes more fully laminated. Each of the selves we acquire from others can contribute to inner dialogues, private discussions we have with ourselves about all manner of persons, events, and issues. These internal voices, these vestiges of relationships both real and imagined, have been given different names: *invisible guests* by Mary Watkins, *social imagery* by Eric Klinger, and *social ghosts* by Mary Gergen, who found in her research that virtually all the young people she sampled could discuss many such experiences with ease.[5] Most of these ghosts were close friends, often from earlier periods of their lives. Family members were also frequent, with the father's voice predominating, but grandparents, uncles, aunts, and other relatives figured prominently. Relevant to the earlier discussion of relations with media figures, almost a quarter of the ghosts mentioned were individuals with whom the young people had never had any direct interchange. Most were entertainers: rock stars, actors and actresses, singers, and the like. Others were religious figures such as Jesus and Mary, fictitious characters such as James Bond and Sherlock Holmes, and celebrities such as Chris Evert, Joe Montana, Barbara Walters, and the president.

The respondents also spoke of the many ways the social ghosts functioned in their lives. It was not simply that they were there for conversation or contemplation; they also served as models for action. They set standards for behavior; they were admired and were emulated. As one wrote, "Connie Chung was constantly being used as a role model for me and I found myself responding to a question about what I planned to do after graduation by saying that I wanted to go into journalism just because I had been thinking of her." Or, as another wrote of her grandmother, "She showed me how to be tolerant of all people and to show respect to everyone regardless of their state in life." Ghosts also voiced opinions on various matters. Most frequently they were used to bolster one's beliefs. At times such opinions were extremely important. As one wrote of the memory of an early friend, "She is the last link I have to Christianity at this point in my life when I am trying to determine my religious inclinations." Still other respondents spoke of the way their ghosts supported their self-esteem: "I think my father and I know that he would be proud of what I have accomplished." Many mentioned the sense of emotional support furnished by their ghosts: "My grandmother seems to be watching me and showing that she loves me even if I am not doing so well."

In closely related work, the psychologists Hazel Markus and Paula Nurius speak of *possible selves,* the multiple conceptions people harbor of what they might become, would like to become, or are afraid to become.[6] In each case, these possible selves function as private surrogates for others to whom one has been exposed—either directly or via the media. The family relations specialists Paul Rosenblatt and Sara Wright speak similarly of the *shadow realities* that exist in close relationships.[7] In addition to the reality that a couple shares together, each will harbor alternative interpretations of their lives together—interpretations that might appear unacceptable and threatening if revealed to the partner. These shadow realities are typically generated and supported by persons outside the relationship—possibly members of the extended family, but also figures from the media. Finally, the British psychologist Michael Billig and his colleagues have studied the values, goals, and ideals to which people are committed in their everyday lives.[8] They found the typical condition of the individual to be internal conflict: for each belief there exists a strong countertendency. People feel their prejudices are justified, yet it is wrong to be intolerant; that there should be equality but hierarchies are also good; and that we are all basically the same, but we must hold on to our individuality. For every value, goal, or ideal, one holds to the converse as well. Billig proposes that the capacity for contradiction is essential to the practical demands of life in contemporary society.

This virtual cacophony of potentials is of no small consequence for either romanticist or modernist visions of the self. For as new and disparate voices are added to one's being, committed identity becomes an increasingly arduous achievement. How difficult for the romantic to keep a firm grasp on the helm of an idealistic undertaking when a chorus of internal voices sing the praises of realism, skepticism, hedonism, and nihilism. And can the committed realist, who believes in the powers of rationality and observation, remain arrogant in the face of inner urges toward emotional indulgence, moral sentiment, spiritual sensitivity, or aesthetic fulfillment? Thus, as social saturation adds incrementally to the population of self, each impulse toward well-formed identity is cast into increasing doubt; each is found absurd, shallow, limited, or flawed by the onlooking audience of the interior. . . .

It is sunny Saturday morning and he finishes breakfast in high spirits. It is a rare day in which he is free to do as he pleases. With relish he contemplates his options. The back door needs fixing, which calls for a trip to the hardware store. This would allow a much-needed haircut; and while in town he could get a birthday card for his brother, leave off his shoes for repair, and pick up shirts at the cleaners. But, he ponders, he really should get some exercise; is there time for jogging in the

afternoon? That reminds him of a championship game he wanted to see at the same time. To be taken more seriously was his ex-wife's repeated request for a luncheon talk. And shouldn't he also settle his vacation plans before all the best locations are taken? Slowly his optimism gives way to a sense of defeat. The free day has become a chaos of competing opportunities and necessities.

If such a scene is vaguely familiar, it attests only further to the pervasive effects of social saturation and the populating of the self. More important, one detects amid the hurly-burly of contemporary life a new constellation of feelings or sensibilities, a new pattern of self-consciousness. This syndrome may be termed *multiphrenia,* generally referring to the splitting of the individual into a multiplicity of self-investments. This condition is partly an outcome of self-population, but partly a result of the populated self's efforts to exploit the potentials of the technologies of relationship. In this sense, there is a cyclical spiraling toward a state of multiphrenia. As one's potentials are expanded by the technologies, so one increasingly employs the technologies for self-expression; yet, as the technologies are further utilized, so do they add to the repertoire of potentials. It would be a mistake to view this multiphrenic condition as a form of illness, for it is often suffused with a sense of expansiveness and adventure. Someday there may indeed be nothing to distinguish multiphrenia from simply "normal living."

However, before we pass into this oceanic state, let us pause to consider some prominent features of the condition.[9] Three of these are especially noteworthy.

With the technology of social saturation, two of the major factors traditionally impeding relationships—namely time and space—are both removed. The past can be continuously renewed—via voice, video, and visits, for example—and distance poses no substantial barriers to ongoing interchange. Yet this same freedom ironically leads to a form of enslavement. For each person, passion, or potential incorporated into oneself exacts a penalty

—a penalty both of *being* and of *being with*. In the former case, as others are incorporated into the self, their tastes, goals, and values also insinuate themselves into one's being. Through continued interchange, one acquires, for example, a yen for Thai cooking, the desire for retirement security, or an investment in wildlife preservation. Through others one comes to value whole-grain breads, novels from Chile, or community politics. Yet as Buddhists have long been aware, to desire is simultaneously to become a slave of the desirable. To "want" reduces one's choice to "want not." Thus, as others are incorporated into the self, and their desires become one's own, there is an expansion of goals—of "musts," wants, and needs. Attention is necessitated, effort is exerted, frustrations are encountered. Each new desire places its demands and reduces one's liberties.

There is also the penalty of being with. As relationships develop, their participants acquire local definitions—friend, lover, teacher, supporter, and so on. To sustain the relationship requires an honoring of the definitions—both of self and other. If two persons become close friends, for example, each acquires certain rights, duties, and privileges. Most relationships of any significance carry with them a range of obligations—for communication, joint activities, preparing for the other's pleasure, rendering appropriate congratulations, and so on. Thus, as relations accumulate and expand over time, there is a steadily increasing range of phone calls to make and answer, greeting cards to address, visits or activities to arrange, meals to prepare, preparations to be made, clothes to buy, makeup to apply. . . . And with each new opportunity—for skiing together in the Alps, touring Australia, camping in the Adirondacks, or snorkling in the Bahamas—there are "opportunity costs." One must unearth information, buy equipment, reserve hotels, arrange travel, work long hours to clear one's desk, locate babysitters, dogsitters, homesitters. . . . Liberation becomes a swirling vertigo of demands.

In the professional world this expansion of "musts" is strikingly evident. In the university of the 1950s, for example, one's departmental colleagues were often vital to one's work. One could walk but a short distance for advice, information, support, and so on. Departments were often close-knit and highly interdependent; travels to other departments or professional meetings were notable events. Today, however, the energetic academic will be linked by post, long-distance phone, fax, and electronic mail to like-minded scholars around the globe. The number of interactions possible in a day is limited only by the constraints of time. The technologies have also stimulated the development of hundreds of new organizations, international conferences, and professional meetings. A colleague recently informed me that if funds were available he could spend his entire sabbatical traveling from one professional gathering to another. A similar condition pervades the business world. One's scope of business opportunities is no longer so limited by geography; the technologies of the age enable projects to be pursued around the world. (Colgate Tartar Control toothpaste is now sold in over forty countries.) In effect, the potential for new connection and new opportunities is practically unlimited. Daily life has become a sea of drowning demands, and there is no shore in sight. . . .

It is not simply the expansion of self through relationships that hounds one with the continued sense of "ought." There is also the seeping of self-doubt into everyday consciousness, a subtle feeling of inadequacy that smothers one's activities with an uneasy sense of impending emptiness. In important respects this sense of inadequacy is a by-product of the populating of self and the presence of social ghosts. For as we incorporate others into ourselves, so does the range of proprieties expand—that is, the range of what we feel a "good," "proper," or "exemplary" person should be. Many of us carry with us the "ghost of a father," reminding us of the values of honesty and hard work, or a mother challenging us to be nurturing and understanding. We may also absorb from a friend the values of maintaining a healthy body, from a lover the goal of self-sacrifice, from a teacher the ideal of worldly knowledge, and so on. Normal development leaves most people with a rich range of "goals for a good life," and with sufficient resources to achieve a sense of personal well-being by fulfilling these goals.

But now consider the effects of social saturation. The range of one's friends and associates expands exponentially; one's past life continues to be vivid; and the mass media expose one to an enormous array of new criteria for self-evaluation. A friend from California reminds one to relax and enjoy life; in Ohio an associate is getting ahead by working eleven hours a day. A relative from Boston stresses the importance of cultural sophistication, while a Washington colleague belittles one's lack of political savvy. A relative's return from Paris reminds one to pay more attention to personal appearance, while a ruddy companion from Colorado suggests that one grows soft.

Meanwhile newspapers, magazines, and television provide a barrage of new criteria of self-evaluation. Is one sufficiently adventurous, clean, well traveled, well read, low in cholesterol, slim, skilled in cooking, friendly, odor-free, coiffed, frugal, burglarproof, family-oriented? The list is unending. More than once I have heard the lament of a subscriber to the Sunday *New York Times*. Each page of this weighty tome will be read by millions. Thus each page remaining undevoured by day's end will leave one precariously disadvantaged—a potential idiot in a thousand unpredictable circumstances.

Yet the threat of inadequacy is hardly limited to the immediate confrontation with mates and media. Because many of these criteria for self-evaluation are incorporated into the self—existing within the cadre of social ghosts—they are free to speak at any moment. The problem with values is that they are sufficient unto themselves. To value justice, for example, is to say nothing of the value of love; investing in duty will blind one to the value of spontaneity. No one value in itself recognizes the importance of any alternative value. And so it is with the chorus of

social ghosts. Each voice of value stands to discredit all that does not meet its standard. All the voices at odds with one's current conduct thus stand as internal critics, scolding, ridiculing, and robbing action of its potential for fulfillment. One settles in front of the television for enjoyment, and the chorus begins: "twelve-year-old," "couch potato," "lazy," "irresponsible." . . . One sits down with a good book, and again, "sedentary," "antisocial," "inefficient," "fantasist." . . . Join friends for a game of tennis and "skin cancer," "shirker of household duties," "underexercised," "overly competitive" come up. Work late and it is "workaholic," "heart attack–prone," "overly ambitious," "irresponsible family member." Each moment is enveloped in the guilt born of all that was possible but now foreclosed. . . .

A third dimension of multiphrenia is closely related to the others. The focus here is on the rationality of everyday decision making—instances in which one tries to be a "reasonable person." Why, one asks, is it important for one's children to attend college? The rational reply is that a college education increases one's job opportunities, earnings, and likely sense of personal fulfillment. Why should I stop smoking? one asks, and the answer is clear that smoking causes cancer, so to smoke is simply to invite a short life. Yet these "obvious" lines of reasoning are obvious only so long as one's identity remains fixed within a particular group.

The rationality of these replies depends altogether on the sharing of opinions—of each incorporating the views of others. To achieve identity in other cultural enclaves turns these "good reasons" into "rationalizations," "false consciousness," or "ignorance." Within some subcultures a college education is a one-way ticket to bourgeois conventionality—a white-collar job, picket fence in the suburbs, and chronic boredom. For many, smoking is an integral part of a risky lifestyle; it furnishes a sense of intensity, offbeatness, rugged individualism. In the same way, saving money for old age is "sensible" in one family, and "oblivious to the erosions of inflation" in another. For most Westerners, marrying for love is the only reasonable (if not conceivable) thing to do. But many Japanese will point to statistics demonstrating greater longevity and happiness in arranged marriages. Rationality is a vital by-product of social participation.

Yet as the range of our relationships is expanded, the validity of each localized rationality is threatened. What is rational in one relationship is questionable or absurd from the standpoint of another. The "obvious choice" while talking with a colleague lapses into absurdity when speaking with a spouse, and into irrelevance when an old friend calls that evening. Further, because each relationship increases one's capacities for discernment, one carries with oneself a multiplicity of competing expectations, values, and beliefs about "the obvious solution." Thus, if the options are carefully evaluated, every decision becomes a leap into gray vapors. Hamlet's bifurcated decision becomes all too simple, for it is no longer being or nonbeing that is in question, but to which of multifarious beings one can be committed. T. S. Eliot began to sense the problem when Prufrock found "time yet for a hundred indecisions / And for a hundred visions and revision, / Before taking of a toast and tea."[10]

The otherwise simple task of casting a presidential vote provides a useful illustration. As one relates (either directly or vicariously) to various men and women, in various walks of life, and various sectors of the nation or abroad, one's capacities for discernment are multiplied. Where one might have once employed a handful of rational standards, or seen the issues in only limited ways, one can now employ a variety of criteria and see many sides of many issues. One may thus favor candidate A because he strives for cuts in the defense budget, but also worry about the loss of military capability in an unsteady world climate. Candidate B's plans for stimulating the growth of private enterprise may be rational from one standpoint, but the resulting tax changes seem unduly to penalize the middle-class family. At the same time,

there is good reason to believe that A's cuts in defense spending will favor B's aims for a stimulated economy, and that B's shifts in the tax structure will make A's reductions in the military budget unnecessary. To use one criterion, candidate A is desirable because of his seeming intelligence, but from another, his complex ideas seem both cumbersome and remote from reality. Candidate B has a pleasing personality, useful for him to garner popular support for his programs, but in another sense his pleasant ways suggest he cannot take a firm stand. And so on.

Increasing the criteria of rationality does not, then, move one to a clear and univocal judgment of the candidates. Rather, the degree of complexity is increased until a rationally coherent stand is impossible. In effect, as social saturation steadily expands the population of the self, a choice of candidates approaches the arbitrary. A toss of a coin becomes equivalent to the diligently sought solution. We approach a condition in which the very idea of "rational choice" becomes meaningless.

So we find a profound sea change taking place in the character of social life during the twentieth century. Through an array of newly emerging technologies the world of relationships becomes increasingly saturated. We engage in greater numbers of relationships, in a greater variety of forms, and with greater intensities than ever before. With the multiplication of relationships also comes a transformation in the social capacities of the individual—both in knowing how and knowing that. The relatively coherent and unified sense of self inherent in a traditional culture gives way to manifold and competing potentials. A multiphrenic condition emerges in which one swims in ever-shifting, concatenating, and contentious currents of being. One bears the burden of an increasing array of oughts, of self-doubts and irrationalities. The possibility for committed romanticism or strong and single-minded modernism recedes, and the way is opened for the postmodern being.

NOTES

1. A useful description of communication in the traditional or "monocultural" community is furnished by W. Barnett Pearce in *Communication and the Human Condition* (Carbondale: University of Northern Illinois Press, 1989).
2. Joshua Meyrowitz, *No Sense of Place* (New York: Oxford University Press, 1985). A similar thesis is developed by Neil Postman in *The Disappearance of Childhood* (New York: Delacorte, 1982).
3. Shoshana Zuboff, *In the Age of the Smart Machine* (New York: Basic Books, 1988).
4. Bruce Wilshire describes the process by which humans come to imitate each other as *mimetic engulfment*. See his "Mimetic Engulfment and Self-Deception," in Amelie Rorty, ed., *Self-Deception* (Berkeley: University of California Press, 1988). Many social scientists believe that such tendencies are innate, appearing as early as the first two weeks of life.
5. Mary Watkins, *Invisible Guests: The Development of Imaginal Dialogues* (Hillsdale, N.J.: Analytic Press, 1986); Eric Klinger, "The Central Place of Imagery in Human Functioning," in Eric Klinger, ed., *Imagery, Volume 2: Concepts, Results, and Applications* (New York: Plenum, 1981); Mary Gergen, "Social

Ghosts, Our Imaginal Dialogues with Others" (paper presented at American Psychological Association Meetings, New York, August 1987). See also Mark W. Baldwin and John G. Holmes, "Private Audiences and Awareness of the Self," *Journal of Personality and Social Psychology* 52 (1987): 1087–198.
6. Hazel Markus and Paula Nurius, "Possible Selves," *American Psychologist* 41 (1986): 954–69. Closely related is Barbara Konig's fascinating novel, *Personen-Person* (Frankfurt: Carl Hanser Verlag, 1981). The narrator realizes that she may be soon meeting an attractive man. The entire volume is then composed of a dialogue among her many inner voices—the residuals of all her past relations.
7. Paul C. Rosenblatt and Sara E. Wright, "Shadow Realities in Close Relationships," *American Journal of Family Therapy* 12 (1984): 45–54.
8. Michael Billig et al., *Ideological Dilemmas* (London: Sage, 1988).
9. See Peter Berger, Brigitte Berger, and Hansfried Kellner, *The Homeless Mind* (New York: Random House, 1973), for a precursor to the present discussion.
10. T. S. Eliot, "The Love Song of J. Alfred Prufrock," in *The Waste Land and Other Poems* (New York: Harvest, 1930).

REVIEW AND DISCUSSION QUESTIONS

1. According to Gergen, how have our social relationships been transformed by recent technological advances?
2. How does Gergen think social saturation affects our lives? On balance do you think the effects are beneficial?
3. What features of "multiphrenia" does Gergen highlight?
4. Why does he think that modern communications technologies increase our sense of obligation and threaten our capacity for rationality?
5. Do you think that the benefits of the Information Age outweigh its costs? If not, can we avoid these costs or prevent the transformation of our culture?

Essay and Paper Topics for Section 15

1. Compare and critically assess the different views on sex and sexuality defended in this section.
2. Paglia has also written, "Aggression and eroticism are deeply intertwined. Hunt, pursuit, and capture are biologically programmed into male sexuality." Compare her view of sexuality and violence with the positions of others you have read in this book.
3. Using readings from this section, write an essay describing what is wrong with rape, and who is responsible for it.

4. Hume and others have argued that morality is, at root, about the responses of people and their attitudes toward certain actions and institutions. Is disgust at homosexual conduct an example of a moral response? If not, how might disgust be distinguished from a moral attitude?

5. Discuss the nature of and the relationships among sex, love, and friendship.

Marriage and the Family

Contemporary society has undergone, and continues to undergo, remarkable changes in its attitudes toward marriage and the family. These changes take many forms and raise many issues. They include the nature of marriage and the duty of fidelity, the impact of modern technology and of economics on our understanding of parenting, the implications for families of feminism and the emergence of women into public life, and the responsibilities of grown children for their aging parents. Readings in this section discuss all of these topics, and more.

Is Adultery Immoral?

Richard A. Wasserstrom

Richard Wasserstrom considers various reasons that might be given for supposing adultery is wrong, including claims that it involves promise breaking and deception. He concludes with a discussion of the importance of fidelity as a support for the institution of marriage and whether adultery may be wrong just because it constitutes an attack on marriage. Richard A. Wasserstrom is professor of philosophy at the University of California, Santa Cruz.

I propose in this paper to think about the topic of sexual morality, and to do so in the following fashion. I shall consider just one kind of behavior that is often taken to be a case of sexual immorality—adultery. I am interested in pursuing at least two questions. First, I want to explore the question of in what respects adulterous behavior falls within the domain of morality at all: For this surely is one of the puzzles one encounters when considering the topic of sexual morality. It is often hard to see on what grounds much of the behavior is deemed to be either moral or immoral, for example, private homosexual behavior between consenting adults. I have purposely selected adultery because it seems a more plausible candidate for moral assessment than many other kinds of sexual behavior.

The second question I want to examine is that of what is to be said about adultery, without being especially concerned to stay within the area of morality. I shall endeavor, in other words, to identify and to assess a number of the major arguments that might be advanced against adultery. I believe that they are the chief arguments that would be given in support of the view that adultery is immoral, but I think they are worth considering even if some of them turn out to be nonmoral arguments and considerations.

A number of the issues involved seem to me to be complicated and difficult. In a number of places I have at best indicated where further philosophical exploration is required without having successfully conducted the exploration myself. The paper may very well be more useful as an illustration of how one might begin to think about the subject of sexual morality than as an elucidation of important truths about the topic.

Before I turn to the arguments themselves there are two preliminary points that require some clarification. Throughout the paper I shall refer to the immorality of such things as breaking a promise, deceiving someone, etc. In a very rough way, I mean by this that there is something morally wrong that is done in doing the action in question. I mean that the action is, in a strong sense of *"prima facie"* *prima facie* wrong or unjustified. I do not mean that it may never be right or justifiable to do the action; just that the fact that it is an action of this description always does count against the rightness of the action. I leave entirely open the question of what it is that makes actions of this kind immoral in this sense of "immoral."

The second preliminary point concerns what is meant or implied by the concept of adultery. I mean by "adultery" any case of extramarital sex, and I want to explore the arguments for and against extramarital sex, undertaken a variety of morally relevant situations. Someone might claim that the concept of adultery is conceptually connected with the concept of immorality, and that to characterize behavior as adulterous is already to characterize it as immoral or unjustified in the sense described above. There may be something to this. Hence the importance of making it clear that I want to talk about extramarital sexual relations. If they are always immoral, this is something that must be shown by argument. If the concept of adultery does in some sense entail or imply immorality, I want to ask whether that connection is a rationally based one. If not all cases of extramarital sex are immoral (again, in the sense described above), then the concept of adultery should either be

weakened accordingly or restricted to those classes of extramarital sex for which the predication of immorality is warranted.

One argument for the immorality of adultery might go something like this: what makes adultery immoral is that it involves the breaking of a promise, and what makes adultery seriously wrong is that it involves the breaking of an important promise. For, so the argument might continue, one of the things the two parties promise each other when they get married is that they will abstain from sexual relationships with third persons. Because of this promise both spouses quite reasonably entertain the expectation that the other will behave in conformity with it. Hence, when one of the parties has sexual intercourse with a third person he or she breaks that promise about sexual relationships which was made when the marriage was entered into, and defeats the reasonable expectations of exclusivity entertained by the spouse.

In many cases the immorality involved in breaching the promise relating to extramarital sex may be a good deal more serious than that involved in the breach of other promises. This is so because adherence to this promise may be of much greater importance to the parties than is adherence to many of the other promises given or received by them in their lifetime. The breaking of this promise may be much more hurtful and painful than is typically the case.

Why is this so? To begin with, it may have been difficult for the nonadulterous spouse to have kept the promise. Hence that spouse may feel the unfairness of having restrained himself or herself in the absence of reciprocal restraint having been exercised by the adulterous spouse. In addition, the spouse may perceive the breaking of the promise as an indication of a kind of indifference on the part of the adulterous spouse. If you really cared about me and my feelings—the spouse might say—you would not have done this to me. And third, and related to the above, the spouse may see the act of sexual intercourse with another as a sign of affection for the other person and as an additional rejection of the nonadulterous spouse as the one who is loved by the adulterous spouse. It is not just that the adulterous spouse does not take the feelings of the spouse sufficiently into account, the adulterous spouse also indicates through the act of adultery affection for someone other than the spouse. I will return to these points later. For the present, it is sufficient to note that a set of arguments can be developed in support of the proposition that certain kinds of adultery are wrong just because they involve the breach of a serious promise which, among other things, leads to the intentional infliction of substantial pain by one spouse upon the other.

Another argument for the immorality of adultery focuses not on the existence of a promise of sexual exclusivity but on the connection between adultery and deception. According to this argument, adultery involves deception. And because deception is wrong, so is adultery.

Although it is certainly not obviously so, I shall simply assume in this paper that deception is always immoral. Thus the crucial issue for my purposes is the asserted connection between extramarital sex and deception. Is it plausible to maintain, as this argument does, that adultery always does involve deception and is on that basis to be condemned?

The most obvious person on whom deceptions might be practiced is the nonparticipating spouse, and the most obvious thing about which the nonparticipating spouse can be deceived is the existence of the adulterous act. One clear case of deception is that of lying. Instead of saying that the afternoon was spent in bed with A, the adulterous spouse asserts that it was spent in the library with B, or on the golf course with C.

There can also be deception even when no lies are told. Suppose, for instance, that a person has sexual intercourse with someone other than his or her spouse and just does not tell the spouse about it. Is that deception? It may not be a case of lying if, for example, the spouse is never asked by the other about the situation. Still, we might say, it is surely deceptive because of the promises that were exchanged

at marriage. As we saw earlier, these promises provide a foundation for the reasonable belief that neither spouse will engage in sexual relationships with any other persons. Hence the failure to bring the fact of extramarital sex to the attention of the other spouse deceives that spouse about the present state of the marital relationship.

Adultery, in other words, can involve both active and passive deception. An adulterous spouse, may just keep silent or, as is often the fact, the spouse may engage in an increasingly complex way of life devoted to the concealment of the facts from the nonparticipating spouse. Lies, half-truths, clandestine meetings, and the like may become a central feature of the adulterous spouse's existence. These are things that can and do happen, and when they do they make the case against adultery an easy one. Still, neither active nor passive deception is inevitably a feature of an extramarital relationship.

It is possible, though, that a more subtle but pervasive kind of deceptiveness is a feature of adultery. It comes about because of the connection in our culture between sexual intimacy and certain feelings of love and affection. The point can be made indirectly at first by seeing that one way in which we can, in our culture, mark off our close friends from our mere acquaintances is through the kinds of intimacies that we are prepared to share with them. I may, for instance, be willing to reveal my very private thoughts and emotions to my closest friends or to my wife, but to no one else. My sharing of these intimate facts about myself is from one perspective a way of making a gift to those who mean the most to me. Revealing these things and sharing them with those who mean the most to me is one means by which I create, maintain, and confirm those interpersonal relationships that are of most importance to me.

Now in our culture, it might be claimed, sexual intimacy is one of the chief currencies through which gifts of this sort are exchanged. One way to tell someone—particularly someone of the opposite sex—that you have feelings of affection and love for them is by sharing with them sexual behaviors that one doesn't share with the rest of the world. This way of measuring affection was certainly very much a part of the culture in which I matured. It worked something like this. If you were a girl, you showed how much you liked someone by the degree of sexual intimacy you would allow. If you liked a boy only a little, you never did more than kiss—and even the kiss was not very passionate. If you liked the boy a lot and if your feeling was reciprocated, necking, and possibly petting, was permissible. If the attachment was still stronger and you thought it might even become a permanent relationship, the sexual activity was correspondingly more intense and more intimate, although whether it would ever lead to sexual intercourse depended on whether the parties (and particularly the girl) accepted fully the prohibition on nonmarital sex. The situation of the boy was related, but not exactly the same. The assumption was that males did not naturally link sex with affection in the way in which females did. However, since women did, males had to take this into account. That is to say, because a woman would permit sexual intimacies only if she had feelings of affection for the male and only if those feelings were reciprocated, the male had to have and express those feelings, too, before sexual intimacies of any sort would occur.

The result was that the importance of a correlation between sexual intimacy and feelings of love and affection was taught by the culture and assimilated by those growing up in the culture. The scale of possible positive feelings toward persons of the opposite sex ran from casual liking at the one end to the love that was deemed essential to and characteristic of marriage at the other. The scale of possible sexual behavior ran from brief, passionless kissing or hand-holding at the one end to sexual intercourse at the other. And the correlation between the two scales was quite precise. As a result, any act of sexual intimacy carried substantial meaning with it, and no act of sexual intimacy was simply a pleasurable set of bodily sensations. Many such acts were, of course, more pleasurable to

the participants because they were a way of saying what the participants' feelings were. And sometimes they were less pleasurable for the same reason. The point is, however, that in any event sexual activity was much more than mere bodily enjoyment. It was not like eating a good meal, listening to good music, lying in the sun, or getting a pleasant back rub. It was behavior that meant a great deal concerning one's feelings for persons of the opposite sex in whom one was most interested and with whom one was most involved. It was among the most authoritative ways in which one could communicate to another the nature and degree of one's affection.

If this sketch is even roughly right, then several things become somewhat clearer. To begin with, a possible rationale for many of the rules of conventional sexual morality can be developed. If, for example, sexual intercourse is associated with the kind of affection and commitment to another that is regarded as characteristic of the marriage relationship, then it is natural that sexual intercourse should be thought properly to take place between persons who are married to each other. And if it is thought that this kind of affection and commitment is only to be found within the marriage relationship, then it is not surprising that sexual intercourse should only be thought to be proper within marriage.

Related to what has just been said is the idea that sexual intercourse ought to be restricted to those who are married to each other as a means by which to confirm the very special feelings that the spouses have for each other. Because the culture teaches that sexual intercourse means that the strongest of all feelings for each other are shared by the lovers, it is natural that persons who are married to each other should be able to say this is to each other in this way. Revealing and confirming verbally that these feelings are present is one thing that helps to sustain the relationship; engaging in sexual intercourse is another.

In addition, this account would help to provide a framework within which to make sense of the notion that some sex is better than other sex. As I indicated earlier, the fact that sexual intimacy can be meaningful in the sense described tends to make it also the case that sexual intercourse can sometimes be more enjoyable than at other times. On this view, sexual intercourse will typically be more enjoyable where the strong feelings of affection are present than it will be where it is merely "mechanical." This is so in part because people enjoy being loved, especially by those whom they love. Just as we like to hear words of affection, so we like to receive affectionate behavior. And the meaning enhances the independently pleasurable behavior.

More to the point, moreover, an additional rationale for the prohibition on extramarital sex can now be developed. For given this way of viewing the sexual world, extramarital sex will almost always involve deception of a deeper sort. If the adulterous spouse does not in fact have the appropriate feelings of affection for the extramarital partner, then the adulterous spouse is deceiving that person about the presence of such feelings. If, on the other hand, the adulterous spouse does have the corresponding feelings for the extramarital partner but not toward the nonparticipating spouse, the adulterous spouse is very probably deceiving the nonparticipating spouse about the presence of such feelings toward that spouse. Indeed, it might be argued, whenever there is no longer love between the two persons who are married to each other, there is deception just because being married implies both to the participants and to the world that such a bond exists. Deception is inevitable, the argument might conclude, because the feelings of affection that ought to accompany any act of sexual intercourse can only be held toward one other person at any given time in one's life. And if this is so, then the adulterous spouse always deceives either the partner in adultery or the nonparticipating spouse about the existence of such feelings. Thus extramarital sex involves deception of this sort and is for this reason immoral even if no deception vis-à-vis the occurrence of the act of adultery takes place.

What might be said in response to the foregoing arguments? The first thing that might be said is that the account of the connection between sexual intimacy and feelings of affection is inaccurate. Not inaccurate in the sense that no one thinks of things that way, but in the sense that there is substantially more divergence of opinion than that account suggests. For example, the view I have delineated may describe reasonably accurately the concepts of the sexual world in which I grew up, but it does not capture the sexual *Weltanschauung* of today's youth at all. Thus, whether or not adultery implies deception in respect to feelings depends very much on the persons who are involved and the way they look at the "meaning" of sexual intimacy.

Second, the argument leaves to be answered the question of whether it is desirable for sexual intimacy to carry the sorts of messages described above. For those persons for whom sex does have these implications, there are special feelings and sensibilities that must be taken into account. But it is another question entirely whether any valuable end—moral or otherwise—is served by investing sexual behavior with such significance. That is something that must be shown and not just assumed. It might, for instance, be the case that substantially more good than harm would come from a kind of demystification of sexual behavior: one that would encourage the enjoyment of sex more for its own sake and one that would reject the centrality both of the association of sex with love and of love with only one other person.

I regard these as two of the more difficult, unresolved issues that our culture faces today in respect to thinking sensibly about the attitudes toward sex and love that we should try to develop in ourselves and in our children. Much of the contemporary literature that advocates sexual liberation of one sort or another embraces one or the other of two different views about the relationship between sex and love.

One view holds that sex should be separated from love and affection. To be sure sex is probably better when the partners genuinely like and enjoy each other. But sex is basically an intensive, exciting sensuous activity that can be enjoyed in a variety of suitable settings with a variety of suitable partners. The situation in respect to sexual pleasure is no different from that of the person who knows and appreciates fine food and who can have a very satisfying meal in any number of good restaurants with any number of congenial companions. One question that must be settled here is whether sex can he so demystified; another, more important question is whether it would be desirable to do so. What would we gain and what might we lose if we all lived in a world in which an act of sexual intercourse was no more or less significant or enjoyable than having a delicious meal in a nice setting with a good friend? The answer to this question lies beyond the scope of this paper.

The second view seeks to drive the wedge in a different place. It is not the link between sex and love that needs to be broken; rather, on this view, it is the connection between love and exclusivity that ought to be severed. For a number of the reasons already given, it is desirable, so this argument goes, that sexual intimacy continue to be reserved to and shared with only those for whom one has very great affection. The mistake lies in thinking that any "normal" adult will only have those feelings toward one other adult during his or her lifetime—or even at any time in his or her life. It is the concept of adult love, not ideas about sex, that, on this view, needs demystification. What are thought to be both unrealistic and unfortunate are the notions of exclusivity and possessiveness that attach to the dominant conception of love between adults in our and other cultures. Parents of four, five, six, or even ten children can certainly claim and sometimes claim correctly that they love all of their children, that they love them all equally, and that it is simply untrue to their feelings to insist that the numbers involved diminish either the quantity or the quality of their love. If this is an idea that is readily understandable in the case of parents and children, there is no necessary reason why it is an impossible or undesirable ideal in the case

of adults. To be sure, there is probably a limit to the number of intimate, "primary" relationships that any person can maintain at any given time without the quality of the relationship being affected. But one adult ought surely to be able to love two, three, or even six other adults at any one time without that love being different in kind or degree from that of the traditional, monogamous, lifetime marriage. And as between the individuals in these relationships, whether within a marriage or without, sexual intimacy is fitting and good.

The issues raised by a position such as this one are also surely worth exploring in detail and with care. Is there something to be called "sexual love" which is different from parental love or the nonsexual love of close friends? Is there something about love in general that links it naturally and appropriately with feelings of exclusivity and possession? Or is there something about sexual love, whatever that may be, that makes these feelings especially fitting here? Once again the issues are conceptual, empirical, and normative all at once: What is love? How could it be different? Would it be a good thing or a bad thing if it were different?

Suppose, though, that having delineated these problems we were now to pass them by. Suppose, moreover, we were to be persuaded of the possibility and the desirability of weakening substantially either the links between sex and love or the links between sexual love and exclusivity. Would it not then be the case that adultery could be free from all of the morally objectionable features described so far? To be more specific, let us imagine that a husband and wife have what is today sometimes characterized as an "open marriage." Suppose, that is, that they have agreed in advance that extramarital sex is—under certain circumstances—acceptable behavior for each to engage in. Suppose, that as a result there is no impulse to deceive each other about the occurrence or nature of any such relationships, and that no deception in fact occurs. Suppose, too, that there is no deception in respect to the feelings involved between the adulterous spouse and the extramarital partner. And suppose, finally, that one or the other or both of the spouses then has sexual intercourse in circumstances consistent with these understandings. Under this description, so the argument might conclude, adultery is simply not immoral. At a minimum, adultery cannot very plausibly be condemned either on the ground that it involves deception or on the ground that it requires the breaking of a promise. . . .

The remaining argument seeks to justify the prohibition by virtue of the role that it plays in the development and maintenance of nuclear families. The argument, or set of arguments, might, I believe, go something like this.

Consider first a farfetched nonsexual example. Suppose a society were organized so that after some suitable age—say, 18, 19, or 20—persons were forbidden to eat anything but bread and water with anyone but their spouse. Persons might still choose in such a society not to get married. Good food just might not be very important to them because they have underdeveloped taste buds. Or good food might be bad for them because there is something wrong with their digestive system. Or good food might be important to them, but they might decide that the enjoyment of good food would get in the way of the attainment of other things that were more important. But most persons would, I think, be led to favor marriage in part because they preferred a richer, more varied, diet to one of bread and water. And they might remain married because the family was the only legitimate setting within which good food was obtainable. If it is important to have society organized so that persons will both get married and stay married, such an arrangement would be well suited to the preservation of the family, and the prohibitions relating to food consumption could be understood as fulfilling that function.

It is obvious that one of the more powerful human desires is the desire for sexual gratification. The desire is a natural one, like hunger and thirst, in the sense that it need not be learned in order to be present within us and operative upon us. But there is in addition much that we do learn about what the act of

sexual intercourse is like. Once we experience sexual intercourse ourselves—and in particular once we experience orgasm—we discover that it is among the most intensive, short-term pleasures of the body.

Because this is so, it is easy to see how the prohibition upon extramarital sex helps to hold marriage together. At least during that period of life when the enjoyment of sexual intercourse is one of the desirable bodily pleasures, persons will wish to enjoy those pleasures. If one consequence of being married is that one is prohibited from having sexual intercourse with anyone but one's spouse, then the spouses in a marriage are in a position to provide an important source of pleasure for each other that is unavailable to them elsewhere in the society.

The point emerges still more clearly if this rule of sexual morality is seen as of a piece with the other rules of sexual morality. When this prohibition is coupled, for example, with the prohibition on nonmarital sexual intercourse, we are presented with the inducement both to get married and to stay married. For if sexual intercourse is only legitimate within marriage, then persons seeking that gratification which is a feature of sexual intercourse are furnished explicit social directions for its attainment: namely marriage.

Nor, to continue the argument, is it necessary to focus exclusively on the bodily enjoyment that is involved. Orgasm may be a significant part of what there is to sexual intercourse, but it is not the whole of it. We need only recall the earlier discussion of the meaning that sexual intimacy has in our own culture to begin to see some of the more intricate ways in which sexual exclusivity may be connected with the establishment and maintenance of marriage as the primary heterosexual, love relationship. Adultery is wrong, in other words, because a prohibition on extramarital sex is a way to help maintain the institutions of marriage and the nuclear family.

Now I am frankly not sure what we are to say about an argument such as this one. What I am convinced of is that, like the arguments discussed earlier, this one also reveals something of the difficulty and complexity of the issues that are involved. So, what I want now to do—in the brief and final portion of this paper—is to try to delineate with reasonable precision what I take several of the fundamental, unresolved issues to be.

The first is whether this last argument is an argument for the *immorality* of extramarital sexual intercourse. What does seem clear is that there are differences between this argument and the ones considered earlier. The earlier arguments condemned adulterous behavior because it was behavior that involved breaking of a promise, taking unfair advantage, or deceiving another. To the degree to which the prohibition on extramarital sex can be supported by arguments which invoke considerations such as these, there is little question but that violations of the prohibition are properly regarded as immoral. And such a claim could be defended on one or both of two distinct grounds. The first is that things like promise-breaking, and deception are just wrong. The second is that adultery involving promise-breaking or deception is wrong because it involves the straightforward infliction of harm on another human being—typically the non-adulterous spouse—who has a strong claim not to have that harm so inflicted.

The argument that connects the prohibition on extramarital sex with the maintenance and preservation of the institution of marriage is an argument for the instrumental value of the prohibition. To some degree this counts, I think, against regarding all violations of the prohibition as obvious cases of immorality. This is so partly because hypothetical imperatives are less clearly within the domain of morality than are categorical ones, and even more because instrumental prohibitions are within the domain of morality only if the end they serve or the way they serve It is itself within the domain of morality.

What this should help us see, I think, is the fact that the argument that connects the prohibition on adultery with the preservation of marriage is at best seriously incomplete. Before we ought to be convinced by it, we ought to have reasons for believing that marriage is a morally desirable and just social institution. And this is not quite as easy or obvious a task as it may seem to be. For the concept of marriage is both a loosely structured and a complicated one. There may be all sorts of intimate, interpersonal relationships which will resemble but not be identical, with the typical marriage relationship presupposed by the traditional sexual morality. There may be a number of distinguishable sexual and loving arrangements which can all legitimately claim to be called *marriages*. The prohibitions of the traditional sexual morality may be effective ways to maintain some marriages and ineffective ways to promote and preserve others. The prohibitions of the traditional sexual morality may make good psychological sense if certain psychological theories are true, and they may be purveyors of immense psychological mischief if other psychological theories are true. The prohibitions of the traditional sexual morality may seem obviously correct if sexual intimacy carries the meaning that the dominant culture has often ascribed to it, and they may seem equally bizarre when sex is viewed through the perspective of the counterculture. Irrespective of whether instrumental arguments of this sort are properly deemed moral arguments, they ought not to fully convince anyone until questions like these are answered.

REVIEW AND DISCUSSION QUESTIONS

1. Describe the various ways that adultery may involve deception.
2. How might one argue that adultery is wrong based on the importance of marriage? Does Wasserstrom accept this argument?
3. Suppose adultery does weaken the marriage institution. Does that mean It is wrong? Are people obligated never to weaken a useful institution?

4. Is "passive" deception always wrong? Explain, using examples, and then indicate if you think this is a problem for Wasserstrom's position.

5. Is Wasserstrom's argument relevant to the discussions of the nature of sex in section 15? Explain.

Polygamy Is Good Feminism

Elizabeth Joseph

In this essay, Elizabeth Joseph, one of the nine wives of Alex Joseph, defends the practice of polygamy. She does so on the ground that polygamy is in fact better from the perspective of the wives as well, she suggests, as the husband. Elizabeth Joseph is a lawyer.

I married a married man. In fact, he had six wives when I married him 17 years ago. Today, he has nine. In March, the Utah Supreme Court struck down a trial court's ruling that a polygamist couple could not adopt a child because of their marital style. Last month, the national board of the American Civil Liberties Union, in response to a request from its Utah chapter, adopted a new policy calling for the legalization of polygamy.

Polygamy, or plural marriage, as practiced by my family is a paradox. At first blush, it sounds like the ideal situation for the man and an oppressive one for the women. For me, the opposite is true. While polygamists believe that the Old Testament mandates the practice of plural marriage, compelling social reasons make the life style attractive to the modern career woman. Pick up any women's magazine and you will find article after article about the problems of successfully juggling career, motherhood and marriage. It is a complex act that many women struggle to manage daily; their frustrations fill up the pages of those magazines and consume the hours of afternoon talk shows. In a monogamous context, the only solutions are compromises. The kids need to learn to fix their own breakfast, your husband needs to get used to occasional microwave dinners, you need to divert more of your income to insure that your pre-schooler is in a good day care environment.

I am sure that in the challenge of working through these compromises, satisfaction and success can be realized. But why must women only embrace a marital arrangement that requires so many trade-offs? When I leave for the 60-mile commute to court at 7 A.M., my 2-year-old daughter, London, is happily asleep in the bed of my husband's wife, Diane. London adores Diane. When London awakes, about the time I'm arriving at the courthouse, she is surrounded by family members who are as familiar to her as the toys in her nursery.

My husband, Alex, who writes at night, gets up much later. While most of his wives are already at work, pursuing their careers, he can almost always find one who's willing to chat over coffee. I share a home with Delinda, another wife, who works in town government. Most nights, we agree we'll just have a simple dinner with our three kids. We'd rather relax and commiserate over the pressures of our work day than chew up our energy cooking and doing a ton of dishes. Mondays, however, are different. That's the night Alex eats with us. The kids, excited that their father is coming to dinner, are on their best behavior. We often invite another wife or one of his children. It's a special event because it only happens once a week. Tuesday night, it's back to simplicity for us. But for Alex and the household he's dining with that night, it's their special time.

The same system with some variation governs our private time with him. While spontaneity is by no means ruled out, we basically use an appointment system. If I want to spend Friday evening at his house, I make an appointment. If he's already "booked," I either request another night or if my schedule is inflexible, I talk to the other wife and we work out an arrangement. One thing we've all learned is that there's always another night. Most evenings, with the demands of career

and the literal chasing after the needs of a toddler, all I want to do is collapse into bed and sleep. But there is also the longing for intimacy and comfort that only he can provide, and when those feelings surface, I ask to be with him.

Plural marriage is not for everyone. But it is the life style for me. It offers men the chance to escape from the traditional, confining roles that often isolate them from the surrounding world. More important, it enables women, who live in a society full of obstacles, to fully meet their career, mothering and marriage obligations. Polygamy provides a whole solution. I believe American women would have invented it if it didn't already exist.

REVIEW AND DISCUSSION QUESTIONS

1. Explain the advantages of polygamy for women that Joseph describes.
2. Are there disadvantages to the relationship that she does not mention? If so, indicate which aspects of polygamy you think might be serious problems, and why.
3. Is it of any significance that very few nonhuman primates are naturally monogamous?

Same-Sex Marriage: A Debate

William Bennett and Andrew Sullivan

Marriage is changing, and encouraged by the media, people are now having children outside marriage far more frequently than in the past. But while some are questioning the institution's value, others who would like to participate in it—homosexuals—are denied the opportunity. This exchange began with an article by Andrew Sullivan in which he claimed, as a conservative, that conservatives should support same-sex marriage. In his book *Virtually Normal* he wrote that such a proposal "seeks merely to promote monogamy, fidelity and the disciplines of family life among people who have long been cast to the margins of society. And what could be a more conservative project than that?" This provoked a response, which we begin with here, by William Bennett (who besides having a career in a politics is also a philosopher). In his essay, Bennett doubts that this proposal would benefit the institution of marriage, and also wonders whether it is compatible with the nature of marriage itself. Andrew Sullivan then responds to Bennett's claim that his position is based on "sexual relativism" and would require him to condone polygamy or marriage between a parent and child. He also denies the claim that this change would alter his, and Bennett's, conception of monogamous marriage. William

Bennett was Secretary of Education under Ronald Reagan. Andrew Sullivan writes for *The New Republic,* and is also an author and political commentator.

By William Bennett

There are at least two key issues that divide proponents and opponents of same-sex marriage. The first is whether legally recognizing same-sex unions would strengthen or weaken the institution. The second has to do with the basic understanding of marriage itself.

The advocates of same-sex marriage say that they seek to strengthen and celebrate marriage. That may be what some intend. But I am certain that it will not be the reality. Consider: the legal union of same-sex couples would shatter the conventional definition of marriage, change the rules which govern behavior, endorse practices which are completely antithetical to the tenets of all of the world's major religions, send conflicting signals about marriage and sexuality, particularly to the young, and obscure marriage's enormously consequential function—procreation and child-rearing.

Broadening the definition of marriage to include same-sex unions would stretch it almost beyond recognition—and new attempts to expand the definition still further would surely follow. On what *principled* ground can Andrew Sullivan exclude others who most desperately want what he wants, legal recognition and social acceptance? Why on earth would Sullivan exclude from marriage a bisexual who wants to marry two other people? After all, exclusion would be a denial of that person's sexuality. The same holds true of a father and daughter who want to marry. Or two sisters. Or men who want (consensual) polygamous arrangements. Sullivan may think some of these arrangements are unwise. But having employed sexual relativism in his own defense, he has effectively lost the capacity to draw any lines and make moral distinctions.

Forsaking all others is an essential component of marriage. Obviously it is not always honored in practice. But it is the ideal to which we rightly aspire, and in most marriages the ideal is in fact the norm. Many advocates of same-sex marriage simply do not share this ideal; promiscuity among homosexual males is well known. Sullivan himself has written that gay male relationships are served by the "openness of the contract" and that homosexuals should resist allowing their "varied and complicated lives" to be flattened into a "single, moralistic model." But that "single, moralistic model" has served society exceedingly well. The burden of proof ought to be on those who propose untested arrangements for our most important institution.

A second key difference I have with Sullivan goes to the very heart of marriage itself. I believe that marriage is not an arbitrary construct which can be redefined simply by those who lay claim to it. It is an honorable estate, instituted of God and built on moral, religious, sexual and human realities. Marriage is based on a natural teleology, on the different, complementary nature of men and women—and how they refine, support, encourage and complete one another. It is the institution through which we propagate, nurture, educate and sustain our species.

That we have to engage in this debate at all is an indication of how steep our moral slide has been. Worse, those who defend, the traditional understanding of marriage are routinely referred to (though not to my knowledge by Sullivan) as "homophobes," "gay-bashers," "intolerant" and "bigoted." Can one defend an honorable, 4,000-year-old tradition and not be called these names?

This is a large, tolerant, diverse country. In America people are free to do as they wish, within broad parameters. It is also a country in sore need of shoring up some of its most crucial institutions: marriage and the family, schools, neighborhoods, communities. But marriage and family are the greatest of these. That is why they are elevated and revered. We should keep them so.

By Andrew Sullivan

It wasn't that we hadn't prepped. Testifying on the Hill was a first for me, and those of us opposing the "Defense of Marriage Act" had been chatting for days about possible questions. But we hadn't quite expected this one. If a person had an "insatiable desire" to marry more than one wife, Congressman Bob Inglis of South Carolina wanted to know, what argument did gay activists have to deny him a legal, polygamous marriage? It wasn't a stray question. Republican after Republican returned gleefully to a Democratic witness who, it turned out, was (kind of) in favor of polygamy. I hastily amended my testimony to deal with the question. Before long, we were busy debating on what terms Utah should have been allowed into the Union and whether bisexuals could have legal harems.

Riveting stuff, compared to the Subcommittee on the Constitution's usual fare. But also revealing. In succeeding days, polygamy dominated the same-sex marriage debate. . . . Bill Bennett . . . used the polygamy argument as a first line of defense against same-sex marriage. . . . Bennett in particular accused the same-sex marriage brigade of engaging in a "sexual relativism" with no obvious stopping place and no "principled ground" to oppose the recognition of multiple spouses.

Well, here's an attempt at a principled ground. The polygamy argument rests, I think, on a couple of assumptions. The first is that polygamous impulses are morally and psychologically equivalent to homosexual impulses, since both are diversions from the healthy heterosexual norm, and that the government has a role to prevent such activities. But I wonder whether Bennett really agrees with this. Almost everyone seems to accept, even if they find homosexuality morally troublesome, that it occupies a deeper level of human consciousness than a polygamous impulse. Even the Catholic Church, which believes that homosexuality is an "objective disorder," concedes that it is a profound element of human identity. It speaks of "homosexual persons," for example, in a way it

would never speak of "polygamous persons." And almost all of us tacitly assume this, even in the very use of the term "homosexuals." We accept also that multiple partners can be desired by gays and straights alike; that polygamy is an *activity*, whereas both homosexuality and heterosexuality are *states*.

So where is the logical connection between accepting same-sex marriage and sanctioning polygamy? Rationally, it's a completely separate question whether the government should extend the definition of marriage (same-sex or different-sex) to include more than one spouse or whether, in the existing institution between two unrelated adults, the government should continue to discriminate between its citizens. Politically speaking, the connection is even more tenuous. To the best of my knowledge, there is no polygamists' rights organization poised to exploit same-sex marriage to return the republic to polygamous abandon. Indeed, few in the same-sex marriage camp have anything but disdain for such an idea. And, as a matter of social policy, same-sex marriage is, of course, the opposite of Bennett's relativism. Far from opening up the possibilities of multiple partners for homosexuals, it actually closes them down.

Bennett might argue, I suppose, that any change in marriage opens up the possibility of any *conceivable* change in marriage. But this is not an argument, it's a panic. If we're worried about polygamy, why not the threat of legally sanctioned necrophilia? Or bestiality? The same panic occurred when interracial marriage became constitutional—a mere thirty years ago—and when women no longer had to be the legal property of their husbands. The truth is, marriage has changed many, many times over the centuries. Each change should be judged on its own terms, not as part of some seamless process of alleged disintegration.

So Bennett must move to his next point, which is that homosexuals understand the institution of marriage so differently than heterosexuals do that to admit them into it would be to alter the institution entirely. To argue this, he has to say that gay men are so naturally promiscuous that they are constitutively unable to sustain the monogamous requirements of marriage and so fail to meet the requirements of membership. He has even repeatedly—and misleadingly—quoted my book, *Virtually Normal,* to buttress this point.

Bennett claims that I believe male-male marriage would and should be adulterous—and cites a couple of sentences from the epilogue to that effect. In context, however, it's clear that the sentences he cites refer to some cultural differences between gay and straight relationships, as they exist today *before same-sex marriage has been made legal.* He ignores the two central chapters of my book—and several articles—in which I unequivocally argue for monogamy as central to all marriage, same-sex or opposite-sex.

That some contemporary gay male relationships are "open" doesn't undermine my point; it supports it. What I do concede, however, is that, in all probability, gay male marriage is not likely to be identical to lesbian marriage, which isn't likely to be identical to heterosexual marriage. The differences between the genders, the gap between gay and straight culture, the unique life experiences that divide as well as unite heterosexuals and homosexuals, will probably create an institution not easily squeezed into a completely uniform model. And a small minority of male-male marriages may perhaps fail to uphold monogamy as

successfully as many opposite-sex marriages. But what implications does that assertion have for the same-sex marriage debate as a whole?

Bennett argues that non-monogamous homosexual marriages will fatally undermine an already enfeebled institution. He makes this argument for one basic reason: men are naturally more promiscuous and male-male marriages will legitimize such promiscuity. But this argument has some problems. If you believe that men are naturally more promiscuous than women, then it follows that lesbian marriages will actually be more monogamous than heterosexual ones. So the alleged damage male-male marriages might do to heterosexual marriage would be countered by the good example that lesbian marriages would provide. It's a wash. And if you take the other conservative argument—that marriage exists not to reward monogamy but to encourage it—then Bennett is also in trouble. There is surely no group in society, by this logic, more in need of marriage rights than gay men. They are the group that most needs incentives for responsible behavior, monogamy, fidelity, and the like.

I'm not trying to be facetious here. The truth is, I think, marriage acts both as an incentive for virtuous behavior—and as a social blessing for the effort. In the past, we have wisely not made nitpicking assessments as to who deserves the right to marry and who does not. We have provided it to anyone prepared to embrace it and hoped for the best.

REVIEW AND DISCUSSION QUESTIONS

1. On what basis does Bennett claim same-sex marriage will undermine the institution?
2. Why does Bennett think same-sex marriage is incompatible with the nature of the institution?
3. How does Sullivan respond to Bennett's two claims?
4. Is part of the issue dividing these two about the morality of homosexual conduct itself?

Surrogate Motherhood as Prenatal Adoption

Bonnie Steinbock

Bonnie Steinbock begins with a discussion of the famous Baby M case, in which Mary Beth Whitehead originally agreed to serve as a surrogate mother but later changed her mind. Steinbock then considers different arguments in support of surrogacy and concludes with a discussion of the objections to surrogacy: that it involves exploitation, that it is incompatible with human dignity, that it violates the right to privacy of the birth mother, and that it harms the offspring resulting from the contract. Bonnie Steinbock is professor of philosophy at the State University of New York at Albany.

The recent case of "Baby M" has brought surrogate motherhood to the forefront of American attention. Ultimately, whether we permit or prohibit surrogacy depends on what we take to be good reasons for preventing people from acting as they wish. A growing number of people want to be, or hire, surrogates; are there legitimate reasons to prevent them? Apart from its intrinsic interest, the issue of surrogate motherhood provides us with an opportunity to examine different justifications for limiting individual freedom.

In the first section, I examine the Baby M case, and the lessons it offers. In the second section, I examine claims that surrogacy is ethically unacceptable because exploitive, inconsistent with human dignity, or harmful to the children born of such arrangements. I conclude that these reasons justify restrictions on surrogate contracts, rather than an outright ban.

I. BABY M

Mary Beth Whitehead, a married mother of two, agreed to be inseminated with the sperm of William Stern, and to give up the child to him for a fee of $10,000. The baby (whom Mrs. Whitehead named Sara, and the Sterns named Melissa) was born on March 27, 1986. Three days later, Mrs. Whitehead took her home from the hospital, and turned her over to the Sterns.

Then Mrs. Whitehead changed her mind. She went to the Sterns' home, distraught, and pleaded to have the baby temporarily. Afraid that she would kill herself, the Sterns agreed. The next week, Mrs. Whitehead informed the Sterns that she had decided to keep the child, and threatened to leave the country if court action was taken.

At that point, the situation deteriorated into a cross between the Keystone Kops and Nazi stormtroopers. Accompanied by five policemen, the Sterns went to the Whitehead residence armed with a court order giving them temporary custody of the child. Mrs. Whitehead managed to slip the baby out of a window to her husband, and the following morning the Whiteheads fled with the child to Florida, where Mrs. Whitehead's parents lived. During the next three months, the Whiteheads lived in roughly twenty different hotels, motels, and homes to avoid apprehension. From time to time, Mrs. Whitehead telephoned Mr. Stern to discuss the matter: He taped these conversations on advice of counsel. Mrs. Whitehead threatened to kill herself, to kill the child, and falsely to accuse Mr. Stern of sexually molesting her older daughter.

At the end of July 1986, while Mrs. Whitehead was hospitalized with a kidney infection, Florida police raided her mother's

From Bonnie Steinbock, "Surrogate Motherhood as Prenatal Adoption," *Law, Medicine and Health Care,* 16, no. 1 (Spring/Summer 1988), 44–50. Reprinted with permission of the author.

home, knocking her down, and seized the child. Baby M was placed in the custody of Mr. Stern, and the Whiteheads returned to New Jersey, where they attempted to regain custody. After a long and emotional court battle, Judge Harvey R. Sorkow ruled on March 31, 1987, that the surrogacy contract was valid, and that specific performance was justified in the best interests of the child. Immediately after reading his decision, he called the Sterns into his chambers so that Mr. Stern's wife, Dr. Elizabeth Stern, could legally adopt the child.

This outcome was unexpected and unprecedented. Most commentators had thought that a court would be unlikely to order a reluctant surrogate to give up an infant merely on the basis of a contract. Indeed, if Mrs. Whitehead had never surrendered the child to the Sterns, but had simply taken her home and kept her there, the outcome undoubtedly would have been different. It is also likely that Mrs. Whitehead's failure to obey the initial custody order angered Judge Sorkow, and affected his decision.

The decision was appealed to the New Jersey Supreme Court, which issued its decision on February 3, 1988. Writing for a unanimous court, Chief Justice Wilentz reversed the lower court's ruling that the surrogacy contract was valid. The court held that a surrogacy contract which provides money for the surrogate mother, and which includes her irrevocable agreement to surrender her child at birth, is invalid and unenforceable. Since the contract was invalid, Mrs. Whitehead did not relinquish, nor were there any other grounds for terminating, her parental rights. Therefore, the adoption of Baby M by Mrs. Stern was improperly granted, and Mrs. Whitehead remains the child's legal mother.

The Court further held that the issue of custody is determined solely by the child's best interests, and it agreed with the lower court that it was in Melissa's best interests to remain with the Sterns. However, Mrs. Whitehead, as Baby M's legal as well as natural mother, is entitled to have her own interest in visitation considered. The determination of

what kind of visitation rights should be granted to her, and under what conditions, was remanded to the trial court.

The distressing details of this case have led many people to reject surrogacy altogether. Do we really want police officers wrenching infants from their mothers' arms, and prolonged custody battles when surrogates find they are unable to surrender their children, as agreed? Advocates of surrogacy say that to reject the practice wholesale, because of one unfortunate instance, is an example of a "hard case" making bad policy. Opponents reply that it is entirely reasonable to focus on the worst potential outcomes when deciding public policy. Everyone can agree on at least one thing: This particular case seems to have been mismanaged from start to finish, and could serve as a manual of how not to arrange a surrogate birth.

First, it is now clear that Mary Beth Whitehead was not a suitable candidate for surrogate motherhood. Her ambivalence about giving up the child was recognized early on, although this information was not passed on to the Sterns.[1] Second, she had contact with the baby after birth, which is usually avoided in "successful" cases. Typically, the adoptive mother is actively involved in the pregnancy, often serving as the pregnant woman's coach in labor. At birth, the baby is given to the adoptive, not the biological, mother. The joy of the adoptive parents in holding their child serves both to promote their bonding, and to lessen the pain of separation of the biological mother.

At Mrs. Whitehead's request, no one at the hospital was aware of the surrogacy arrangement. She and her husband appeared as the proud parents of "Sara Elizabeth Whitehead," the name on her birth certificate. Mrs. Whitehead held her baby, nursed her, and took her home from the hospital—just as she would have done in a normal pregnancy and birth. Not surprisingly, she thought of Sara as her child, and she fought with every weapon at her disposal, honorable and dishonorable, to prevent her being taken away. She can hardly be blamed for doing so.[2]

Why did Dr. Stern, who supposedly had a very good relation with Mrs. Whitehead before the birth, not act as her labor coach? One possibility is that Mrs. Whitehead, ambivalent about giving up her baby, did not want Dr. Stern involved. At her request, the Sterns' visits to the hospital to see the newborn baby were unobtrusive. It is also possible that Dr. Stern was ambivalent about having a child. The original idea of hiring a surrogate was not hers, but her husband's. It was Mr. Stern who felt a "compelling" need to have a child related to him by blood, having lost all his relatives to the Nazis.

Furthermore, Dr. Stern was not infertile, as was stated in the surrogacy agreement. Rather, in 1979 she was diagnosed by two eye specialists as suffering from optic neuritis, which meant that she "probably" had multiple sclerosis. (This was confirmed by all four experts who testified.) Normal conception was ruled out by the Sterns in late 1982, when a medical colleague told Dr. Stern that his wife, a victim of multiple sclerosis, had suffered a temporary paralysis during pregnancy. "We decided the risk wasn't worth it," Mr. Stern said.[3]

Mrs. Whitehead's lawyer, Harold J. Cassidy, dismissed the suggestion that Dr. Stern's "mildest case" of multiple sclerosis determined their decision to seek a surrogate. He noted that she was not even treated for multiple sclerosis until after the Baby M dispute had started. "It's almost as though it's an afterthought," he said.[4]

Judge Sorkow deemed the decision to avoid conception "medically reasonable and understandable." The Supreme Court did not go so far, noting that "her anxiety appears to have exceeded the actual risk, which current medical authorities assess as minimal."[5] Nonetheless the Court acknowledged that her anxiety, including fears that pregnancy might precipitate blindness and paraplegia, was "quite real." Certainly, even a woman who wants a child very much, may reasonably wish to avoid becoming blind and paralyzed as a result of pregnancy. Yet is it believable that a woman who really wanted a child would

decide against pregnancy solely on the basis of someone else's medical experience? Would she not consult at least one specialist on her own medical condition before deciding it wasn't worth the risk? The conclusion that she was at best ambivalent about bearing a child seems irresistible.

This possibility conjures up many people's worst fears about surrogacy: That prosperous women, who do not want to interrupt their careers, will use poor and educationally disadvantaged women to bear their children. I will return shortly to the question of whether this is exploitive. The issue here is psychological: What kind of mother is Dr. Stern likely to be? If she is unwilling to undergo pregnancy, with its discomforts, inconveniences, and risks, will she be willing to make the considerable sacrifices which good parenting requires? Mrs. Whitehead's ability to be a good mother was repeatedly questioned during the trial. She was portrayed as immature, untruthful, hysterical, overly identified with her children, and prone to smothering their independence. Even if all this is true—and I think that Mrs. Whitehead's inadequacies were exaggerated—Dr. Stern may not be such a prize either. The choice for Baby M may have been between a highly strung, emotional, over-involved mother, and a remote, detached, even cold one.

The assessment of Mrs. Whitehead's ability to be a good mother was biased by the middle-class prejudices of the judge and mental health officials who testified. Mrs. Whitehead left school at 15, and is not conversant with the latest theories on child rearing: She made the egregious error of giving Sara teddy bears to play with, instead of the more "age-appropriate," expert-approved pans and spoons. She proved to be a total failure at patty-cake. If this is evidence of parental inadequacy, we're all in danger of losing our children.

The Supreme Court felt that Mrs. Whitehead was "rather harshly judged" and acknowledged the possibility that the trial court was wrong in its initial award of custody. Nevertheless, it affirmed Judge Sorkow's decision to allow the Sterns to retain custody, as being in Melissa's best interests. George Annas disagrees with the "best interests" approach. He points out that Judge Sorkow awarded temporary custody of Baby M to the Sterns in May 1986 without giving the Whiteheads notice or an opportunity to obtain legal representation. That was a serious wrong and injustice to the Whiteheads. To allow the Sterns to keep the child compounds the original unfairness: " . . . justice requires that reasonable consideration be given to returning Baby M to the permanent custody of the Whiteheads."[6]

But a child is not a possession, to be returned to the rightful owner. It is not fairness to all parties that should determine a child's fate, but what is best for her. As Chief Justice Wilentz rightly stated, "The child's interests come first: We will not punish it for judicial errors, assuming any were made."[7]

Subsequent events have substantiated the claim that giving custody to the Sterns was in Melissa's best interests. After losing custody, Mrs. Whitehead, whose husband had undergone a vasectomy, became pregnant by another man. She divorced her husband and married Dean R. Gould last November. These developments indicate that the Whiteheads were not able to offer a stable home, although the argument can be made that their marriage might have survived, but for the strains introduced by the court battle, and the loss of Baby M. But even if Judge Sorkow had no reason to prefer the Sterns to the Whiteheads back in May 1986, he was still right to give the Sterns custody in March 1987. To take her away then, at nearly eighteen months of age, from the only parents she had ever known, would have been disruptive, cruel, and unfair to her.

Annas's preference for a just solution is premised partly on his belief that there is no "best interest" solution to this "tragic custody case." I take it that he means that however custody is resolved, Baby M is the loser. Either way, she will be deprived of one parent. However, a best interests solution is not a perfect solution. It is simply the solution which is on balance best for the child, given the realities of the situation. Applying this standard, Judge Sorkow was right to give the Sterns custody, and the Supreme Court was right to uphold the decision.

The best interests argument is based on the assumption that Mr. Stern has at least a *prima facie* claim to Baby M. We certainly would not consider allowing a stranger who kidnapped a baby, and managed to elude the police for a year, to retain custody on the grounds that he was providing a good home to a child who had known no other parent. However, the Baby M case is not analogous. First, Mr. Stern is Baby M's biological father and, as such, has at least some claim to raise her, which no non-parental kidnapper has. Second, Mary Beth Whitehead *agreed* to give him their baby. Unlike the miller's daughter in *Rumpelstiltskin,* the fairy tale to which the Baby M case is sometimes compared, she was not forced into the agreement. Because both Mary Beth Whitehead and Mr. Stern have *prima facie* claims to Baby M, the decision as to who should raise her should be based on her present best interests. Therefore we must, regretfully, tolerate the injustice to Mrs. Whitehead, and try to avoid such problems in the future.

It is unfortunate that the Court did not decide the issue of visitation on the same basis as custody. By declaring Mrs. Whitehead Gould the legal mother, and maintaining that she is entitled to visitation, the Court has prolonged the fight over Baby M. It is hard to see how this can be in her best interests. This is no ordinary divorce case, where the child has a relation with both parents which it is desirable to maintain. As Mr. Stern said at the start of the court hearing to determine visitation, "Melissa has a right to grow and be happy and not be torn between two parents."[8]

The court's decision was well-meaning but internally inconsistent. Out of concern for the best interests of the child, it granted the Sterns custody. At the same time, by holding Mrs. Whitehead Gould to be the legal mother, with visitation rights, it precluded precisely what is most in Melissa's interest, a resolution of the situation. Further, the decision leaves open the distressing possibility that a Baby M situation could happen again. Legislative efforts should be directed toward ensuring that this worst-case scenario never occurs.

II. SHOULD SURROGACY BE PROHIBITED?

On June 27, 1988, Michigan became the first state to outlaw commercial contracts for women to bear children for others. Yet making a practice illegal does not necessarily make it go away: Witness black market adoption. The legitimate concerns which support a ban on surrogacy might be better served by careful regulation. However, some practices, such as slavery, are ethically unacceptable, regardless of how carefully regulated they are. Let us consider the arguments that surrogacy is intrinsically unacceptable.

A. Paternalistic Arguments

These arguments against surrogacy take the form of protecting a potential surrogate from a choice she may later regret. As an argument for banning surrogacy, as opposed to providing safeguards to ensure that contracts are freely and knowledgeably undertaken, this is a form of paternalism.

At one time, the characterization of a prohibition as paternalistic was a sufficient reason to reject it. The pendulum has swung back, and many people are willing to accept at least some paternalistic restrictions on freedom. Gerald Dworkin points out that even Mill made one exception to his otherwise absolute rejection of paternalism: He thought that no one should be allowed to sell himself into slavery, because to do so would be to destroy his future autonomy.

This provides a narrow principle to justify some paternalistic interventions. To preserve freedom in the long run, we give up the freedom to make certain choices, those which have results which are "far-reaching, potentially dangerous and irreversible."[9] An example would be a ban on the sale of crack.

Virtually everyone who uses crack becomes addicted and, once addicted, a slave to its use. We reasonably and willingly give up our freedom to buy the drug, to protect our ability to make free decisions in the future.

Can a Dworkinian argument be made to rule out surrogacy agreements? Admittedly, the decision to give up a child is permanent, and may have disastrous effects on the surrogate mother. However, many decisions may have long-term, disastrous effects (e.g., postponing childbirth for a career, having an abortion, giving a child up for adoption). Clearly we do not want the state to make decisions for us in all these matters. Dworkin's argument is rightly restricted to paternalistic interferences which protect the individual's autonomy or ability to make decisions in the future. Surrogacy does not involve giving up one's autonomy, which distinguishes it from both the crack and selling-oneself-into-slavery examples. Respect for individual freedom requires us to permit people to make choices which they may later regret.

B. Moral Objections

Four main moral objections to surrogacy were outlined in the Warnock Report.[10]

1. It is inconsistent with human dignity that a woman should use her uterus for financial profit.
2. To deliberately become pregnant with the intention of giving up the child distorts the relationship between mother and child.
3. Surrogacy is degrading because it amounts to child-selling.
4. Since there are some risks attached to pregnancy, no woman ought to be asked to undertake pregnancy for another in order to earn money.

We must all agree that a practice which exploits people or violates human dignity is immoral. However, it is not clear that surrogacy is guilty on either count.

1. Exploitation. The mere fact that pregnancy is risky does not make surrogate agreements exploitive, and therefore morally wrong. People often do risky things for money; why should the line be drawn at undergoing pregnancy? The usual response is to compare surrogacy and kidney-selling. The selling of organs is prohibited because of the potential for coercion and exploitation. But why should kidney-selling be viewed as intrinsically coercive? A possible explanation is that no one would do it, unless driven by poverty. The choice is both forced and dangerous, and hence coercive.

The situation is quite different in the case of the race car driver or stuntman. We do not think that they are *forced* to perform risky activities for money: They freely choose to do so. Unlike selling one's kidneys, these are activities which we can understand (intellectually, anyway) someone choosing to do. Movie stuntmen, for example, often enjoy their work, and derive satisfaction from doing it well. Of course they "do it for the money," in the sense that they would not do it without compensation; few people are willing to work "for free." The element of coercion is missing, however, because they enjoy the job, despite the risks, and could do something else if they chose.

The same is apparently true of most surrogates. "They choose the surrogate role primarily because the fee provides a better economic opportunity than alternative occupations, but also because they enjoy being pregnant and the respect and attention that it draws."[11] Some may derive a feeling of self-worth from an act they regard as highly altruistic: Providing a couple with a child they could not otherwise have. If these motives are present, it is far from clear that the surrogate is being exploited. Indeed, it seems objectionably paternalistic to insist that she is.

2. Human Dignity. It may be argued that even if womb-leasing is not necessarily exploitive, it should still be rejected as inconsistent with human dignity. But why? As John Harris points out, hair, blood and other tissue is often donated or sold; what is so special about the uterus?[12]

Human dignity is more plausibly invoked in the strongest argument against surrogacy, namely, that it is the sale of a child. Children are not property, nor can they be bought or sold. It could be argued that surrogacy is wrong because it is analogous to slavery, and so is inconsistent with human dignity.

However, there are important differences between slavery and a surrogate agreement. The child born of a surrogate is not treated cruelly or deprived of freedom or resold; none of the things which make slavery so awful are part of surrogacy. Still, it may be thought that simply putting a market value on a child is wrong. Human life has intrinsic value; it is literally priceless. Arrangements which ignore this violate our deepest notions of the value of human life. It is profoundly disturbing to hear the boyfriend of a surrogate say, quite candidly in a television documentary on surrogacy, "We're in it for the money."

Judge Sorkow accepted the premise that producing a child for money denigrates human dignity, but he denied that this happens in a surrogate agreement. Mrs. Whitehead was not paid for the surrender of the child to the father: She was paid for her willingness to be impregnated and carry Mr. Stern's child to term. The child, once born, is his biological child. "He cannot purchase what is already his."

This is misleading, and not merely because Baby M is as much Mrs. Whitehead's child as Mr. Stern's. It is misleading because it glosses over the fact that the surrender of the child was part—indeed, the whole point—of the agreement. If the surrogate were paid merely for being willing to be impregnated and carrying the child to term, then she would fulfill the contract upon giving birth. She could take the money *and* the child. Mr. Stern did not agree to pay Mrs. Whitehead merely to *have* his child, but to provide him with a child. The New Jersey Supreme Court held that this violated New Jersey's laws prohibiting the payment or acceptance of money in connection with adoption.

One way to remove the taint of baby-selling would be to limit payment to medical expenses associated with the birth or incurred by the surrogate during pregnancy (as is allowed in many jurisdictions, including New Jersey, in ordinary adoptions). Surrogacy could be seen, not as baby-selling, but as a form of adoption. Nowhere did the Supreme Court find any legal prohibition against surrogacy when there is no payment, and when the surrogate has the right to change her mind and keep the child. However, this solution effectively prohibits surrogacy, since few women would become surrogates solely for self-fulfillment or reasons of altruism.

The question, then, is whether we can reconcile paying the surrogate, beyond her medical expenses, with the idea of surrogacy as prenatal adoption. We can do this by separating the terms of the agreement, which include surrendering the infant at birth to the biological father, from the justification for payment. The payment should be seen as compensation for the risks, sacrifice, and discomfort the surrogate undergoes during pregnancy. This means that if, through no fault on the part of the surrogate, the baby is stillborn, she should still be paid in full, since she has kept her part of the bargain. (By contrast, in the Stern-Whitehead agreement, Mrs. Whitehead was to receive only $1,000 for a stillbirth.) If, on the other hand, the surrogate changes her mind and decides to keep the child, she would break the agreement, and would not be entitled to any fee, or compensation for expenses incurred during pregnancy.

C. The Right of Privacy

Most commentators who invoke the right of privacy do so in support of surrogacy. However, George Annas makes the novel argument that the right to rear a child you have borne is also a privacy right, which cannot be prospectively waived. He says:

[Judge Sorkow] grudgingly concedes that [Mrs. Whitehead] could not prospectively give up her right to have an abortion during pregnancy. . . . This would be an intolerable restriction on her liberty and under *Roe* v.

Wade, the state has no constitutional authority to enforce a contract that prohibits her from terminating her pregnancy. But why isn't the same logic applicable to the right to rear a child you have given birth to? Her constitutional rights to rear the child she has given birth to are even stronger since they involve even more intimately, and over a lifetime, her privacy rights to reproduce and rear a child in a family setting.[13]

Absent a compelling state interest (such as protecting a child from unfit parents), it certainly would be an intolerable invasion of privacy for the state to take children from their parents. But Baby M has two parents, both of whom now want her. It is not clear why only people who can give birth (i.e., women) should enjoy the right to rear their children.

Moreover, we do allow women to give their children up for adoption after birth. The state enforces those agreements, even if the natural mother, after the prescribed waiting period, changes her mind. Why should the right to rear a child be unwaivable before, but not after, birth? Why should the state have the constitutional authority to uphold postnatal, but not prenatal, adoption agreements? It is not clear why birth should affect the waivability of this right, or have the constitutional significance which Annas attributes to it.

Nevertheless, there are sound moral and policy, if not constitutional, reasons to provide a postnatal waiting period in surrogate agreements. As the Baby M case makes painfully clear, the surrogate may underestimate the bond created by gestation, and the emotional trauma caused by relinquishing the baby. Compassion requires that we acknowledge these feelings, and not deprive a woman of the baby she has carried because, before conception, she underestimated the strength of her feelings for it. Providing a waiting period, as in ordinary postnatal adoptions, will help protect women from making irrevocable mistakes, without banning the practice.

Some may object that this gives too little protection to the prospective adoptive parents. They cannot be sure that the baby is theirs until the waiting period is over. While this is hard on them, a similar burden is placed on other adoptive parents. If the absence of a guarantee serves to discourage people from entering surrogacy agreements, that is not necessarily a bad thing, given all the risks inherent in such contracts. In addition, this requirement would make stricter screening and counselling of surrogates essential, a desirable side effect.

D. Harm to Others

Paternalistic and moral objections to surrogacy do not seem to justify an outright ban. What about the effect on the offspring of such contracts? We do not yet have solid data on the effects of being a "surrogate child." Any claim that surrogacy creates psychological problems in the children is purely speculative. But what if we did discover that such children have deep feelings of worthlessness from learning that their natural mothers deliberately created them with the intention of giving them away? Might we ban surrogacy as posing an unacceptable risk of psychological harm to the resulting children?

Feelings of worthlessness are harmful. They can prevent people from living happy, fulfilling lives. However, a surrogate child, even one whose life is miserable because of these feelings, cannot claim to have been harmed by the surrogate agreement. Without the agreement, the child would never have existed. Unless she is willing to say that her life is not worth living because of these feelings, that she would be better off never having been born, she cannot claim to have been harmed by being born of a surrogate mother.

Children can be *wronged* by being brought into existence, even if they are not, strictly speaking, *harmed*. They are wronged if they are deprived of the minimally decent existence to which all citizens are entitled. We owe it to our children to see that they are not born with such serious impairments that their most basic interests will be doomed in advance. If being born to a surrogate is a handicap of this magnitude, comparable to being born blind or deaf or severely mentally retarded, then surrogacy can be seen as

wronging the offspring. This would be a strong reason against permitting such contracts. However, it does not seem likely. Probably the problems arising from surrogacy will be like those faced by adopted children and children whose parents divorce. Such problems are not trivial, but neither are they so serious that the child's very existence can be seen as wrongful.

If surrogate children are neither harmed nor wronged by surrogacy, it may seem that the argument for banning surrogacy on grounds of its harmfulness to the offspring evaporates. After all, if the children themselves have no cause for complaint, how can anyone else claim to reject it on their behalf? Yet it seems extremely counterintuitive to suggest that the risk of emotional damage to the children born of such arrangements is not even relevant to our deliberations. It seems quite reasonable and proper—even morally obligatory—for policymakers to think about the possible detrimental effects of new reproductive technologies, and to reject those likely to create physically or emotionally damaged people. The explanation for this must involve the idea that it is wrong to bring people into the world in a harmful condition, even if they are not, strictly speaking, harmed by having been brought into existence. Should evidence emerge that surrogacy produces children with serious psychological problems, that would be a strong reason for banning the practice.

There is some evidence on the effect of surrogacy on the other children of the surrogate mother. One woman reported that her daughter, now 17, who was 11 at the time of the surrogate birth, ". . . is still having problems with what I did, and as a result she is still angry with me." She explains, "Nobody told me that a child could bond with a baby while you're still pregnant. I didn't realize then that all the times she listened to his heartbeat and felt his legs kick that she was becoming attached to him."[14]

A less sentimental explanation is possible. It seems likely that her daughter, seeing one child given away, was fearful that the same might be done to her. We can expect anxiety and resentment on the part of children whose mothers give away a brother or sister. The psychological harm to these children is clearly relevant to a determination of whether surrogacy is contrary to public policy. At the same time, it should be remembered that many things, including divorce, remarriage, and even moving to a new neighborhood, create anxiety and resentment in children. We should not use the effect on children as an excuse for banning a practice we find bizarre or offensive.

CONCLUSION

There are many reasons to be extremely cautious of surrogacy. I cannot imagine becoming a surrogate, nor would I advise anyone else to enter into a contract so fraught with peril. But the fact that a practice is risky, foolish, or even morally distasteful is not sufficient reason to outlaw it. It would be better for the state to regulate the practice, and minimize the potential for harm, without infringing on the liberty of citizens.

NOTES

1. Had the Sterns been informed of the psychologist's concerns as to Mrs. Whitehead's suitability to be a surrogate, they might have ended the arrangement, costing the Infertility Center its fee. As Chief Justice Wilentz said, "It is apparent that the profit motive got the better of the Infertility Center." In the matter of Baby M, Supreme Court of New Jersey, A-39, at 45.
2. "[W]e think it is expecting something well beyond normal human capabilities to suggest that this mother should have parted with her newly born infant without a struggle. . . . We . . . cannot conceive of any other case where a perfectly fit mother was expected to surrender her newly born infant, perhaps forever, and was then told she was a bad mother because she did not." *Id.* at 79.
3. "Father Recalls Surrogate Was 'Perfect,'" *New York Times,* January 6, 1987, p. B2.
4. *Id.*
5. In the matter of Baby M, *supra* note 1, at 8.
6. G. J. Annas, "Baby M: Babies (and Justice) for Sale," *Hastings Center Report* 17 (3): 15, 1987.
7. In the matter of Baby M, *supra* note 1, at 75.
8. "Anger and Anguish at Baby M Visitation Hearing," *New York Times,* March 29, 1988, p. 17.
9. G. Dworkin, "Paternalism," in ed. R. A. Wasserstrom, *Morality and the Law* (Belmont, CA: Wadsworth, 1971) reprinted in J. Feinberg and H. Gross, eds., *Philosophy of Law,* 3rd ed. (Belmont, CA: Wadsworth, 1986), p. 265.
10. M. Warnock, chair, *Report of the Committee of Inquiry into Human Fertilization and Embryology* (London, Her Majesty's Stationery Office, 1984).
11. J. A. Robertson, "Surrogate Mothers: Not So Novel after All," *Hastings Center Report* 13 (5): 29, 1983. Citing P. Parker, "Surrogate Mother's Motivations: Initial Findings," *American Journal of Psychiatry* (140): 1, 1983.
12. J. Harris, *The Value of Life* (London: Routledge & Kegan Paul, 1985) p. 144.
13. Annas, *supra* note 6.
14. "Baby M Case Stirs Feelings of Surrogate Mothers," *New York Times,* March 2, 1987, p. B1.

REVIEW AND DISCUSSION QUESTIONS

1. Describe the factual and legal situation surrounding the Baby M case.
2. How might it be argued that laws banning surrogacy are paternalistic? Are they? Explain.
3. What is exploitation, and how might it be argued that surrogacy is an instance of it?
4. In what sense(s) might surrogacy involve the right to privacy?
5. Does surrogacy harm anybody? Explain.
6. What sorts of regulations does Steinbock suggest are appropriate? Do you agree with her that surrogacy should only be regulated, not banned? Explain.

Selling Babies

Richard A. Posner

Judge Richard A. Posner criticizes current adoption practices that outlaw baby selling. A freer market (though one that is still regulated in important respects) would have many advantages, he claims, including lower prices and higher quality. Nor, he argues, should we be persuaded by "symbolic" claims that baby selling might lead to abuses or slavery. Indeed, we already have in place something like a market in babies, although it is highly regulated and often hidden from view. Richard A. Posner is a judge of the U.S. Court of Appeals for the Seventh Circuit and a senior lecturer at the University of Chicago Law School.

1. CHARACTERISTICS OF AND DESIRABLE CONSTRAINTS ON THE BABY MARKET

A. The Question of Price

For heuristic purposes (only!) it is useful to analogize the sale of babies to the sale of an ordinary good, such as an automobile or a television set. We observe, for example, that although the supply of automobiles and of television sets is rationed by price, not all the automobiles and television sets are owned by wealthy people. On the contrary, the free market in these goods has lowered prices, through competition and innovation, to the point where the goods are available to a lot more people than in highly controlled economies such as that of the Soviet Union. There is even less reason for thinking that if babies could be sold to adoptive parents the wealthy would come to monopolize babies. Wealthy people (other than those few who owe their wealth to savings or inheritance rather than to a high income) have high costs of time.

It therefore costs them more to raise a child—child rearing still being a time-intensive activity—than it costs the nonwealthy. As a result, wealthy couples tend to have few rather than many children. This pattern would not change if babies could be bought. Moreover, since most people have a strong preference for natural, as distinct from adopted, children, wealthy couples able to have natural children are unlikely (to say the least) to substitute adopted ones.

It is also unlikely that allowing people to bid for babies with dollars would drive up the price of babies, thereby allocating the supply to wealthy demanders. Today we observe a high black-market price conjoined with an artificially low price for babies obtained from adoption agencies and through lawful independent adoptions. The "blended" or average price is hard to calculate; but probably it is very high. The low price in the lawful market is deceptive. It ignores the considerable queuing costs—most people would pay a considerable premium to get their adopted baby now, not five or ten years from now. And for people unable to maneuver successfully in the complex market created by the laws against baby selling, the price is infinite. Quality-adjusted prices in free markets normally are lower than black market prices, and there is no reason to doubt that this would be true in a free market for adoptions. Thus, . . . the words "black market" ought to be italicized. It is not the free market, but unwarranted restrictions on the operation of that market, that has raised the black market price of babies beyond the reach of ordinary people.

Thus far I have implicitly been speaking only of the market for healthy white infants.

From Richard A. Posner, "The Regulation of the Market in Adoption," *Boston University Law Review*, January 1987. Reprinted by permission. © Richard A. Posner.

There is no shortage of nonwhite and of handicapped infants, and of any children who are no longer infants, available for adoption. Such children are substitutes for healthy white infants, and the higher price of the latter, the greater will be the demand for the former. The network of regulations that has driven up the full price (including such nonmonetary components of price as delay) of adopting a healthy, white infant may have increased the willingness of childless couples to consider adopting a child of a type not in short supply, though how much (if at all) no one knows. The present system is, in any event, a grossly inefficient, as well as covert, method of encouraging the adoption of the hard-to-place child. If society wants to subsidize these unfortunate children, the burden of the subsidies should be borne, if not by the natural parents of these children, then by the taxpaying population at large—rather than by just the nation's childless white couples, who under the present unsystematic system bear the lion's share of the burden by being denied the benefits of an efficient method of allocating healthy white infants for adoption in the hope that this will induce them to adopt nonwhite, handicapped, or older children.

B. The Question of Quality

As soon as one mentions quality, people's hackles rise and they remind you that one is talking about a traffic in human beings, not in inanimate objects. The observation is pertinent, and at least five limitations might have to be placed on the operation of the market in babies for adoption. The first, already mentioned and already in place, is that the buyers can have no right to abuse the thing bought, as they would if the thing were a piece of steel or electronics. This really should go without saying. The laws against child abuse have never distinguished among different methods of acquiring custody of the child. Natural parents are not permitted to abuse a child because they are natural rather than adoptive parents; and people who acquire their children illegally through the black market are no more exempt from the child-abuse laws than people with illegal income are exempt from paying income tax on it. If I were arrested for torturing my cat and charged with violation of the laws forbidding cruelty to animals, it would be no defense that I had bought the cat for forty dollars.

If the laws against child abuse were perfectly efficacious, nothing more would have to be said on the subject. But they are not. The abuse occurs in secret, and the victim may be too young and too dependent to bring it to the attention of the authorities—or indeed to know what is going on. In addition, many child abusers may be so mentally or psychologically abnormal that they cannot be deterred even by very harsh penalties. In such a setting, preventive as well as punitive measures may be justified. Today, all adoptive parents are, in theory anyway, screened for fitness. Adoption agencies are charged with this responsibility, and if we moved toward a freer market in babies the agencies could be given the additional function of investigating and certifying prospective purchasers, who would pay the price of the service.

But let us not make too much of screening. The idea that a significant number of people are lurking about who if given the chance would buy babies for criminal purposes is a bogeyman. Most child abuse occurs as a result either of stresses arising from the experience of parenthood or from the sexual maturing of the child; it is not planned in advance when a baby is conceived or when steps are initiated to adopt a baby. As I will note in a moment, a market in babies for adoption should only be allowed to operate with regard to infants; a couple should not be allowed to sell its thirteen-year-old daughter for immoral (or any other) purposes.

Moreover, since we do not screen natural parents, and any proposal to do so would be met with justifiable protests against governmental intrusion into private matters, the case for screening adoptive parents can hardly be considered self-evident. Maybe, since people like their own children more than strangers' children, the child molester is less likely to molest his own children than other people's children. But people who adopt children do so not out of a mild affection toward children in general, which might easily be overborne by a tendency to abuse children, but in the hope of creating the same close bonds of affection with the adopted child as natural parents have with their children. Allowing price to play a bigger role in adoptions is not likely to change this. But whether screening adoptive parents is a good or a bad idea is not the issue in this article. Whatever screening is deemed necessary for persons who adopt through an agency or by independent adoption would also be necessary for persons who adopted children in a free(r) market. Freeing the adoption market from price regulation would leave the case for or against screening largely, perhaps entirely, unaffected.

The third limitation on a baby market concerns remedies for breach of contract. In an ordinary market a buyer can both reject defective goods and, if the seller refuses to deliver and damages would be an inadequate remedy for the refusal, get specific performance of the contract. Natural parents are not permitted to reject their baby, either when it is born or afterward, because it turns out to be handicapped or otherwise not in conformity with their expectations; no more should adoptive parents who buy their babies. Nor should the adoptive parents be able to force the natural mother to surrender the baby to them if she changes her mind, unless some competent authority determines that the baby would be better off adopted. For the welfare of the baby must be considered along with that of the contracting parties. Refusing to grant specific performance in circumstances in which it appears that forcing the sale to go through would harm the baby is consistent with the basic equity principle that the third-party effects of equitable remedies must be considered in deciding whether to grant such a remedy or confine the plaintiff to damage remedies. The child is an interested third party whose welfare would be disserved by a mechanical application of the remedies available to buyers in the market for inanimate goods.

For the same reason (the child's welfare) neither natural nor adopting parents should be allowed to sell their children after infancy, that is, after the child has established a bond with its parents. Nor should the natural mother be allowed to take back the baby after adoption, any more than a seller of a conventional good or service can (except in extraordinary circumstances) rescind the sale after delivery and payment in accordance with his contract with the buyer, unless, once again, a competent authority decides that the baby's welfare would be increased. I shall not try to resolve the question whether, in any of these remedial settings, the welfare of the child should be paramount or should be balanced with that of the adult parties.

The last limitation on the baby market that I shall discuss relates to eugenic breeding. Although prospects still seem remote, one can imagine an entrepreneur in the baby market trying to breed a race of *Übermenschen* who would command premium prices. The external effects of such an endeavor could be very harmful, and would provide an appropriate basis for governmental regulation.

I am not so sanguine about the operation of a baby market, even with the limitations I have discussed, that I am prepared to advocate the complete and immediate repeal of the laws forbidding the sale of babies for adoption. That such a market might give somewhat greater scope for child abusers and might encourage weird and potentially quite harmful experiments in eugenic breeding should be enough to give anyone pause. But to concentrate entirely on the downside would be a mistake. One million abortions a year is a serious social problem regardless of where one stands on the underlying ethical issues; so is a flourishing black market in babies combined with a severe shortage in the lawful market. The severity of the shortage is, admittedly, a matter of fair debate. In our 1978 article Dr. Landes and I estimated that about 130,000 married couples who at present are childless might adopt a child under free-market conditions. More recent research suggests this estimate is reasonable. A study conducted by the National Center for Health Statistics found that 46% of the estimated 274,000 currently married women who are between 30 and 44 years of age and sterile have adopted a child. If all those who have not adopted would like to, and would be willing to pay a free-market price, then the 148,000 married couples in the relevant population who have not yet adopted a child are unsatisfied demanders. But some unknown fraction of this number either do not want to have children at all or do not want to have adopted children. Dr. Landes and I noted that 96% of couples marrying in 1975 in which the wife was between 18 and 24 years old expected to have a child. Since most people who marry young do not know whether they have a fertility problem, it seems a fair guess that almost all of the 274,000 married couples who are sterile planned when they got married to have children, and hence that most of the 148,000 who have not yet adopted a child would like, or at some time in the past would have liked, to adopt a child. Of course, wanting something and being willing to pay for it are two different things, and it might seem that many childless couples would be unwilling or unable to pay for a baby if they had to pay free market prices. But this seems unlikely. The purchase price on the free market would probably be lower than under the present system (for reasons discussed earlier), and in any event only a small fraction of the total cost (even discounted to present value) of raising a child. Bear in mind, too, that adoptive parents save the medical and opportunity costs of pregnancy. Marrying couples who expected to have a child, notwithstanding the cost, are unlikely to be deterred by the small, probably zero or even negative, incremental cost of adopting a child in a free market.

True, some couples decide after marriage that they don't want to have a child. This is particularly likely if the couple anticipates a high probability of divorce. About half of American marriages end in divorce, and

some of these divorces are anticipated before children enter the picture. Another consideration is that some couples do not consider an adopted child a good substitute for the natural child they cannot have, and they may therefore decide to remain childless even if the price of an adopted child is low and the quality high.[1] Although these factors suggest a downward adjustment in my estimates, there are three offsetting factors to consider. First, some unknown fraction of adoptions is of babies bought in the black market, and the part of the demand for a good that is satisfied in a black market reflects the shortage in the lawful market. Second, the 148,000 figure excludes married couples who become sterile after having one or more children and who would like to adopt. In fact, 20% of married couples who become sterile after having one child go on to adopt a child, and 42% of married couples with one child say that they would adopt a second child if they became sterile. Finally, and bearing particularly on the experiment that Dr. Landes and I proposed, ten times as many premarital pregnancies end in "pregnancy loss" (miscarriage, stillbirth, and no doubt the biggest category, abortion) as in putting the baby up for adoption.

One reason people fear the operation of a free market in babies for adoption is that they extrapolate from experience with the illegal market. Critics who suggest that baby selling offers the promise of huge profits to middlemen—the dreaded "baby brokers"—fail to distinguish between an illegal market, in which sellers demand a heavy premium (an apparent, though not real, profit) in order to defray the expected costs of punishment, and a legal market, in which the premium is eliminated. Seemingly exorbitant profits, low quality, poor information, involvement of criminal elements—these widely asserted characteristics of the black market in babies are no more indicative of the behavior of a lawful market than the tactics of the bootleggers and rum-runners during Prohibition were indicative of the behavior of the liquor industry after Prohibition was repealed. . . .

II. THE OBJECTION FROM SYMBOLISM AND THE ISSUE OF SEMANTICS

Even if partial deregulation of the baby market might make practical utilitarian sense along the lines just suggested, some will resist on symbolic grounds. If we acknowledge that babies can be sold, the argument goes, we open the door to all sorts of monstrous institutions—including slavery. We regularly resist this type of argument in analogous contexts, and I have difficulty understanding why it stubbornly persists in this one. Some people argue that military conscription is wrong because it legitimates government coercion of the civilian labor force, or because it is a form of slavery; others that the sale of blood should be forbidden because it treats human life as a commodity; others that medicine should be socialized so that the wealthy can't use their wealth to increase their chances of a long and healthy life, relative to the poor; others that parents should not be allowed to spank their children because that is treating the children like slaves; others that capital punishment should be outlawed because it implicates the state in murder. The common thread in these arguments is the reprobating of social practices not because of any demonstrable or even probable bad effects, but because the practices have a symbolic affinity with practices that do have horrible effects. Allowing parents to sell their children into slavery would be a monstrous idea. Allowing the prospective mother of an illegitimate child to receive money in exchange for giving up the child for adoption, when described in shorthand as "baby selling," seems to many people uncomfortably close to the type of real baby selling that is found in slave societies—that was found in the slave societies of the South before the Civil War. No doubt it requires more thought than most people are willing to give to the problem to hold these quite different concepts separate in their minds. But if they are not held separate we may find ourselves condemned to perpetuate the painful spectacle of mass abortion and illegitimacy in a society in which, to a significant extent, children are not available for adoption by persons unwilling to violate the law.

One should always be suspicious of arguments against the market when they are made by people who have no desire to participate in it themselves, people who want to restrict the availability of goods to other people. Most people who invoke vague symbols in opposition to "baby selling" have no interest in or expectation of either adopting a child or conceiving one out of wedlock. They have little empathy with the needs of people who find themselves involuntarily childless or involuntarily pregnant.

The opponents of "baby selling" are unwilling to acknowledge that what we have today, even apart from the black market, is closer to a free market in babies than a free market in babies would be to slavery or torture (always bearing in mind that a free market in an economic sense is one in which due consideration is given the welfare of affected third parties, here the babies themselves). As I said at the outset, adoption agencies do lawfully "sell" babies, and many charge thousands of dollars. Moreover, in independent adoptions, the mother herself may "sell" her baby, for it is not considered unlawful to use a part of the fee paid by the adoptive parents to defray the medical and other maintenance costs of the mother during pregnancy. It seems that to obtain lawfully a healthy, white infant (rarely available through adoption agencies), a couple must be prepared to lay out at least $5,000. Black-market prices of $25,000, even $50,000, have been rumored, but the equilibrium baby price in a free market (by which I do not mean an entirely unregulated market, for I suggested that the market should be regulated in various ways) might not exceed $5,000. As a matter of fact, though baby selling is everywhere unlawful, almost half the states have no specific restrictions on fees payable for adoption, and in many other states the restrictions are porous. No doubt many lawful and semi-lawful "baby sales" are taking place today at approximately free-market prices.

Two other important examples of legal baby selling should be mentioned. One is the "family compact" doctrine, which allows a woman to enter into an enforceable contract to give up her baby for adoption by a close relative. The other is surrogate motherhood, by which (at least in some states) a married couple in which the wife is infertile can make an enforceable contract with another woman whereby the latter agrees to be artificially inseminated with the husband's sperm and to carry the baby to term and give it up to the couple. In the first case the close family relative "buys" the baby, in the second the father (and his wife) "buys out" the natural mother's "share" in their joint product.

So we have legal baby selling today; the question of public policy is not whether baby selling should be forbidden or allowed but how extensively it should be regulated. I simply think it should be regulated less stringently than is done today.

NOTE

1. The potential importance of this point is brought out by a 1977 study that found that, of then-married women who had no children and wanted to have one or more, only 62% said they would adopt a child. See Bonham, "Who Adopts: The Relationship of Adoption and Social-Demographic Characteristics of Women," *Journal of Marriage and Family* 39, 295, 300 tab. 3 (1977). If 46% of sterile couples have adopted a child, and 62% would like to, it might seem that the fraction of unsatisfied demanders (to be multiplied by 274,000 to yield an estimate of their number) would be 16% rather than 54%. But apart from other factors mentioned in the text, a statement of nonintention to adopt a child may simply reflect awareness of the obstacles to adoption under the present system. As we shall see, the nonintending 38% (100%–62%) is almost twice the percentage of couples who become sterile after having one child and then adopt—suggesting a very large unsatisfied demand among this group.

REVIEW AND DISCUSSION QUESTIONS

1. Why would a market in babies improve the (current) price structure, according to Posner?
2. What impact does Posner think a freer market would have on "quality"? Explain why.
3. Explain the limitations Posner would place on the baby market.
4. Describe the "objection from symbolism," along with Posner's response to it.
5. What is your overall assessment of Posner's proposal? What are its major strengths? Major weaknesses?

No-Fault Family Law and the Unencumbered Self

Michael J. Sandel

Earlier in his book, Michael Sandel argued that contemporary liberalism, which is the dominant public philosophy, has emphasized personal freedom and insisted that government remain neutral among different conceptions of personal and family relationships. Behind this, he claimed, lies a commitment to respecting the free, autonomous choices of individuals; the political ideal of a neutral, procedural government; and a conception of the person or self as "unencumbered." This liberal, unencumbered self acknowledges only obligations that are voluntarily made, like promises, or else are universally applicable to all persons, such as the duty to help others we meet who are in need. This unencumbered self and its narrow view of duty contrasts with the earlier, situated conception of the self that understands persons as located in a web of family, religious, fraternal, and other institutions and practices, all of which make demands on us whatever we may choose or want. History and biology rather than free choices and universal duties form the foundation of the situated self and its responsibilities. Besides influencing constitutional law, according to Sandel, this liberal picture of governmental neutrality and the unencumbered self has also found its way into our understanding of marriage, divorce, and child-rearing, where it has produced neither genuine freedom for the individual nor stable, successful families. Michael Sandel is professor of government at Harvard University.

NO-FAULT FAMILY LAW

Recent decades have brought "a diminution of the law's discourse in moral terms about the relations between family members, and the transfer of many moral decisions from the law to the people the law once regulated."[1] At the same time, the law increasingly treats persons as individual selves independent of their family roles. These changes have affected the law's treatment of divorce, alimony, marital property, child custody, and family support requirements in virtually every state in the country.[2]

The law of divorce offers the most telling example. For over a century, divorce law reflected and enforced a particular ideal of marriage and "of the proper moral relations between husband and wife."[3] This ideal included duties of lifelong mutual responsibility and fidelity, tied to traditional gender-based roles. The husband had the duty of economic support; the wife, the duty of domestic service. The mutual responsibilities of marriage constituted "a unity that transcended the parties' individual interests." Only a serious breach of moral duties, such as adultery, cruelty, or desertion, provided grounds for divorce. And the obligations of marriage could persist long after divorce, in the form of alimony payments by the husband to his former wife.[4]

In 1970 the state of California enacted the first "no-fault" divorce law in the country. Its effect was to bracket the moral considerations that had traditionally governed the law of divorce. The new law removed all reference to guilt and innocence and provided for divorce upon either party's claim that "irreconcilable differences" had caused the marriage to break down. Moral grounds were no longer required, neither spouse had to prove fault or guilt, nor did the spouses have to agree to end their marriage. Either could decide unilaterally to get a divorce, without the consent of the other. Whereas the old law implied "'a right' to remain married if one adhered to one's marriage contract, the new law elevates one's 'right' to divorce by permitting divorce at either party's request."[5]

Like the divorce itself, financial awards were also detached from moral considerations of guilt and innocence, punishment and reward. Alimony payments and property settlements are now based on financial need, not marital behavior. "Under the old law the adulterous husband or wife typically had to pay for his or her infidelity with a disadvantageous property or alimony award. Today, in contrast, there are no penalties for adultery and no rewards for fidelity."[6] Instead of concerning themselves with guilt or innocence, the courts now employ such "nonjudgmental" criteria as the economic needs and resources of the parties.

The new law brackets marital roles as well as fault. The gender-based responsibilities of the old law give way to gender neutrality in the new. Husbands are no longer held responsible for the financial support of their former wives, and women are expected to become

Reprinted by permission of the publisher from *Democracy's Discontents:* by Michael J. Sandel, 108–115. Cambridge MA: Harvard University Press. ©1996 by Michael J. Sandel.

self-sufficient after divorce. The law now views alimony as a temporary, not a lifelong, obligation, whose purpose is to ease the wife's transition from economic dependence to self-sufficiency. In the wake of the reform, permanent alimony dropped from 62 to 32 percent of alimony awarded. By 1972 "two-thirds of the spousal support awards were transitional awards for a limited and specified duration," about two years on average. By 1978 only 17 percent of divorced women were awarded any alimony at all.[7]

The California law also rejects traditional role-based responsibilities in child custody and support. It replaces the old preference for maternal custody with a gender-neutral standard, although in practice most children continue to live with their mothers. It also makes both parents responsible for child support.[8]

California's revolution in family law quickly spread across the country. By 1985 every state in the nation had adopted some version of no-fault divorce. Some, like California, rejected moral grounds for divorce altogether, while others added "no-fault" as an option, alongside traditional versions. A few even provided for divorce by mail.[9]

Most states have also banned fault as a factor in alimony awards. Even the language of spousal support has changed in ways that reflect the rejection of desert-based considerations. For example, a Colorado court recently distinguished between "alimony," which presupposes fault, and "maintenance," which seeks simply to ensure that "the basic (economic) needs of a disadvantaged spouse are met." Such maintenance is sometimes called "rehabilitative alimony," as if to suggest that the role of homemaker and mother is a kind of infirmity from which entry into the labor market constitutes recovery. An Indiana law goes further and restricts alimony to "physically or mentally handicapped spouses.[10]

Child support obligations continue in law but often go unenforced in practice. In 1975 only one-fourth of divorced, separated, or single women with children received any child support payments.[11] Court-ordered child support and alimony combined rarely amount to even one-third of the husband's income, and fewer than half of child support awards are ever, actually paid.[12] A Wisconsin law sought to enforce payment by preventing fathers in arrears on child support from getting a marriage license, but the U.S. Supreme Court struck it down for infringing the right to marry.[13]

The law also reflects the decline of obligations beyond the conjugal family. "Filial responsibility" statutes requiring adults to support indigent parents or grandparents are gradually disappearing, and those that remain are rarely enforced. Meanwhile, interest groups have formed to press for the recognition of "grandparents' visiting rights."[14]

The new family law has proven at best a mixed success. The removal of fault as grounds for divorce has spared couples the pain and humiliation of airing their disputes in public, and spared the courts the sordid task of assessing guilt in broken marriages. The advent of gender neutrality does away with outmoded assumptions about the roles of husbands and wives and gives legal recognition to the ideal of sexual equality.

On the other hand, reform has brought economic hardship for women and children that its proponents did not foresee. Treating men and women equally in the division of marital property and in expectations of self-sufficiency overlooks the inequality of earning capacity, especially for women who devoted their lives to child rearing while their husbands pursued careers. And since women continue to retain custody of children in most cases, they must meet greater responsibilities with fewer economic resources. Few mothers are awarded alimony (only 13 percent of mothers with preschool children), and child support payments average only $2,200 per year, often for the support of two or more children. For men, divorce brings a 42 percent increase in standard of living, while divorced women and their children suffer a 73 percent decline.[15] As a result, "divorce now constitutes a major cause of poverty among women and their children."[16]

Further reforms giving greater attention to the economic conditions of women and children after divorce might alleviate the hardships while preserving some of the gains of the new family law. In the 1990s, efforts in this direction included national legislation to strengthen enforcement of child support obligations.[17] While some such efforts can be defended in terms consistent with procedural liberalism, the new family law that unfolded in the 1970s and 1980s nonetheless offered a striking expression of assumptions drawn from the liberal conception of the person and displayed some of the difficulties to which it gives rise.

MARRIAGE, DIVORCE, AND THE UNENCUMBERED SELF

First, the rejection of fault as grounds for divorce and property settlements reflects the liberal resolve to bracket moral judgments, to make law neutral among competing conceptions of the good. As in liberal theories of distributive justice, so now in divorce settlements, distributive shares are not intended to reward virtue but simply to meet the economic needs of the parties. Under the new law, unlike the old, the principles that determine the distribution of marital assets upon divorce "do not mention moral desert, and there is no tendency for distributive shares to correspond to it."[18]

Second, the provision for divorce as a unilateral decision without mutual consent, the rejection of marital roles tied to lifelong obligations, and the emphasis on self-sufficiency after divorce all reflect the liberal conception of persons as unencumbered selves independent of their roles and unbound by moral ties they choose to reject. The old law treated persons as situated selves, whose identity as legal persons was tied to their roles as husbands, wives, and parents. The new law loosens the relation between the self and its roles; it makes family roles easier to shed and relaxes the obligations that attach to them.

More than a reflection of law alone, the image of the unencumbered self is consistent with actual developments in American family life in recent decades. Divorce rates more than doubled from the 1960s to the late 1970s, to

the point where half of all marriages are expected to end in divorce.[19] With the rise in divorce came a growing tendency to cast off the obligations of parenthood. A leading demographer observes that "since 1960 the conjugal family has begun to divest itself of care for children in much the same way that it did earlier for the elderly," and that this phenomenon is due mainly to "a disappearing act by fathers." The percentage of births out of wedlock rose from 5.3 percent in 1960 to 18.4 percent in 1980, reaching 30.1 percent by 1992. Of children born in wedlock, as many as half are expected to experience the breakup of their parents' marriage before they reach age seventeen, up from 22 percent in the mid-1960s. Most children of divorced parents live with their mothers, and over half of these children have not seen their fathers in the past year. Only about 40 percent receive any child support payments from their father. Not surprisingly, 56 percent of children in single female-headed households live in poverty.[20]

Quite apart from the social pathology of broken families and missing fathers, national surveys conducted in the 1950s and 1970s found a growing tendency among Americans to conceive their identities as independent of familial or parental roles.[21] One indication of this shift was a growing view of children as encumbrances, as obstacles to parents' freedom. Asked in 1976 how having children changes one's life, 45 percent of adults mentioned only the restrictions parenthood imposes, such as the added responsibility, the need to think of someone else, the lost freedom. In 1957 only 30 percent responded by citing restrictions alone.[22]

The same survey found that married persons in the 1950s tended to describe their family life in terms of their duties as husbands, wives, and parents. By the 1970s people described family life less as an arrangement of roles and more as a relationship of persons behind the roles. In the 1950s, for example, parents were concerned largely with such role-based responsibilities as the physical care and financial support of their children. In the 1970s parents were more concerned with their personal relationships with their children—how much time they spent together, how well they got along. "While earlier generations stressed role aspects of parenthood," concluded the authors of the survey, "later generations adopted [a] more psychological, interpersonal orientation." Especially among men, the 1970s brought "a very large shift toward seeing parental inadequacies in terms of affiliative relationships with children."[23]

As these attitudes suggest, the liberal self-image has had beneficial consequences as well as destructive ones. For better and for worse, however, the new views of family life support the conclusion that Americans increasingly conceive of themselves as bearers of selves independent of their roles. As a popular inspirational book called *Personhood* proclaims, "We have a right to choose our own selves, even if that self is different from the selves of others."[24] In family life as in family law, "role and status designations have become objects of suspicion, as though they were different from—and even contradictory to—the core self, the essential person."[25] In the procedural republic the unencumbered self not only governs public life but penetrates the precincts of family life as well.

The new law of divorce illustrates two difficulties with the liberal assumptions it embodies. One concerns the notion of respect for persons; the other, the claim to be neutral among conceptions of the good.

First, by treating all persons as bearers of a self independent of its roles, the new law fails to respect mothers and homemakers of traditional marriages whose identity is constituted by their roles, who have lived their married lives as situated selves. By insisting on self-sufficiency after divorce, it penalizes women whose economic reliance on their husbands expressed the mutual dependence of traditional marital roles. Her care for children and home enabled him to pursue a career. But when the marriage dissolves, he has the career, with its income and status, while she has the children and a sudden requirement to enter a labor market that rewards the skills she has forgone while making his career possible.

Since the law now brackets the roles that defined her identity and made sense of her dependence, she is typically left with half the marital property (less than $10,000 on average), no alimony, minimal child support that may never be paid, and responsibility for the care of children. Although courts supposedly consider the earning capacity of the parties, in the majority of cases even women married fifteen years or longer receive no alimony.[26]

For the woman whose identity is tied to family rather than to career, the injury goes beyond the risk of economic hardship should her marriage end in divorce. By failing to reward women's unpaid contributions to child rearing, homemaking, and husband's career, the new law of divorce devalues those contributions and erodes the significance of the roles they reflect. It strengthens the assumption that the work that counts is work for pay outside the home. Even those whose marriages remain intact suffer the loss of social status that goes with this assumption. Among professional classes, for example, the woman's reply to the proverbial question "What do you do?" sadly reflects the loss of esteem accorded those whose work is in the home: "I'm just a mother."

Second, the new divorce law calls into question the liberal assumption that treating persons as independent selves expands rather than constrains their choice of lives, and so is neutral among conceptions of the good. For as we have seen, the ideals of independence and self-sufficiency embodied in the new law do not simply enlarge the range of possible lives; they also make some ways of life more difficult, especially those like traditional marriage that involve a high degree of mutual dependence and obligation.

Although couples are free in principle to divide the roles of breadwinner and homemaker and to tie their identities to family roles and obligations, the new law poses a powerful obstacle to such arrangements. It gives married persons, and especially women, a harsh incentive not to devote themselves too completely to the care of children and family, but to pursue a career as a hedge against the day when they may have to fend for themselves. As sociologist Lenore Weitzman has observed, the clear message of current divorce settlements is that "women had better not forgo any of their own education, training, and career development to devote themselves fully or even partially to their families. The law assures that they will not be rewarded for their devotion, either in court or in the job market, and they will suffer greatly if their marriage dissolves.[27]

Liberals often argue that the good of community can be fully accounted for "by a conception of justice that in its theoretical basis is individualistic."[28] Given a neutral framework of individual rights, people are free to join in voluntary association on whatever terms they choose, whether to pursue their private ends or to enjoy the communal sentiments that such cooperation often inspires. "[W]ithin this framework communitarian aims may be pursued, and quite possibly by the vast majority of persons.[29]

But the new law of divorce offers a counterexample to this claim. By making dependence a dangerous thing, it burdens the practice of marriage as a community in the constitutive sense. By bracketing moral judgments, celebrating self-sufficiency, and loosening the relation between the self and its roles, the law is not neutral among competing visions of married life, but recasts the institution of marriage in the image of the unencumbered self.

Some see in this conception a long-term threat to family life as such. As growing numbers of women understand that they cannot count on the economic stability of marriage, they seek to assure their economic security by committing themselves to a career.. As men and women find that greater benefits derive from holding a job, family life will diminish in relative importance to the world of work, and people will invest less in the family than in their individual lives and careers.[30] That careers have come to matter more and families less in modern life may explain why the law now makes it easier to divorce a spouse than to fire an employee. While much of the labor force can only be fired for "good cause," no-fault divorce makes marriage a relationship that can be "terminated at will.[31]

Whether or not these worries are well-founded, whatever the merits or drawbacks of the new arrangements, it is clear in any case that the new family law, for all its liberating promise, does not simply free people to arrange their marital roles as they choose. It is not neutral among conceptions of the good, but favorable to certain visions of family life, inhospitable to others.

NOTES

1. Carl E. Schneider, "Moral Discourse in Family Law," *Michigan Law Review, 83* (1985), 1807–08.
2. Illuminating accounts of these developments include ibid.; Mary Ann Glendon, *The New Family and the New Property* (Toronto: Butterworths, 1981); Lenore J. Weitzman, *The Divorce Revolution* (New York: Free Press, 1985); and Herbert Jacob, *Silent Revolution* (Chicago: University of Chicago Press, 1988).
3. Schneider, "Moral Discourse in Family Law," p. 1808.
4. Weitzman, *The Divorce Revolution, pp.* 4–7.
5. Ibid., p. 27 and, generally, pp. 15–41.
6. Ibid., p. 24.
7. Ibid., pp. 32–33. Figures are for Los Angeles County.
8. Ibid., pp. 36–37.
9. Schneider, "Moral Discourse in Family Law," p. 1809; Weitzman, *The Divorce Revolution, pp.* 41–43.
10. Weitzman, *The Divorce Revolution, pp.* 43–46, 167, Glendon, *The New Family,* pp. 52–57; Schneider, "Moral Discourse in Family Law," p. 1810. The Uniform Marriage and Divorce Act provides that maintenance awards shall be determined "without regard to marital misconduct"; sec. 308(b), 9A U.L.A. 160 (1979).
11. U.S. Bureau of the Census, "Divorce, Child Custody, and Child Support," in *Current Population Reports,* Series P-23, no. 84 (Washington, D.C., 1979), cited in Glendon, *The New Family, p.* 69.
12. Weitzman, *The Divorce Revolution,* pp. 267 (figures for Los Angeles County, 1978) and 262, citing U.S. Bureau of the Census, "Child Support and Alimony: 1981," *Current Population Reports,* Series P-23, no. 124 (Washington, D.C., 1983).
13. *Zablocki v. Redhail,* 434 U.S. 374 (1978).

14. The number of states with filial responsibility statutes declined from thirty-eight in 1956 to twenty-seven in 1980. See Schneider, "Moral Discourse in Family. Law," p. 1813; and Glendon, *The New Family,* pp. 49–5 1. On grandparents' visiting rights, see S. Con. Res. 40, 98th Cong., 1st sess. (1983), cited in Schneider, p. 1858, n. 212.

15. Weitzman, *The Divorce Revolution, pp.* 186, 265, 338–339, 362. Alimony and standard-of-living figures are for Los Angeles County, 1977 and 1978. Child-support figure is for the United States, 1981, reported in U.S. Bureau of the Census, "Child Support and Alimony: 1981."

16. Arland Thornton and Deborah Freedman, "The Changing American Family," *Population Bulletin,* 38, no. 4 (October 1983), p. 10.

17. See "Elements of Child-Support Bill Pass," *Congressional Quarterly Almanac,* 50 (1994), 375.

18. John Rawls, *A Theory of Justice* (Cambridge, Mass.: Harvard University Press, 1971), p. 311.

19. Thornton and Freedman, "The Changing American Family," pp. 3, 7.

20. Samuel Preston, "Children and the Elderly: Divergent Paths for America's Dependents," *Demography,* 21 (November 1984), 435, 443–444. The figure for 1992 is from National Center for Health Statistics, "Advance Report of Final Natality Statistics, 1992," *Monthly Vital Statistics Report,* 43, no. 5, supp. (1994).

21. Joseph Veroff, Elizabeth Douvan, and Richard A. Kulka, *The Inner American: A Self-Portrait from 1957 to 1976* (New York: Basic Books, 1981),

pp. 147, 201. Figures are based on national surveys conducted in 1957 and 1976.

22. Ibid., p. 200.

23. Ibid., pp. 209, 215, 239–240, 531. Women, however, showed an increased concern for providing children material support, possibly as a reflection of the increase in female-headed households.

24. Leo F. Buscaglia, *Personhood: The Art of Being Fully Human* (New York: Fawcett Columbine, 1978), p. 100.

25. Veroff, Douvan, and Kulka, *The Inner American, p.* 141.

26. Weitzman, *The Divorce Revolution, pp.* 169, 177. Alimony is more frequent for housewives of long marriages who have never held a job, but even in this category, over a third of women are awarded no alimony. Figures are for Los Angeles County, 1977.

27. Weitzman, *The Divorce Revolution, p.* 372.

28. Rawls, *A Theory of Justice,* pp. 264–265.

29. John Rawls, "Fairness to Goodness," *Philosophical Review,* 84 (October 1975), 550.

30. This argument is made in William J. Goode, "Individual Investments in Family Relationship over the Coming Decades," *Tocqueville Review,* 6, no. 1 (1984), 51–83. For an opposing view, see Theodore Caplow et al., *Middletown Families* (Minneapolis: University of Minnesota Press, 1982), pp. 322-334.

31. This contrast is a major theme of Glendon, *The New Family,* esp. pp. 1–8, 151–170, 198.

REVIEW AND DISCUSSION QUESTIONS

1. What does Sandel mean by the "unencumbered" self? How is that different from the "situated" self?

2. Explain what Sandel means by "no-fault" family law.

3. What are the advantages of the no-fault system?

4. What effects does Sandel think no-fault family law has had on children? How has the growth of the idea of an "unencumbered" self influenced these changes?

5. Why does Sandel think that the new liberalism has not, in fact, merely increased the options open to women?

6. How would Sandel respond to those who, like Richard Posner, propose allowing people to sell children?

Licensing Parents

Hugh LaFollette

Undertaking to raise a child is an act with vast consequences, for good or ill—far greater than those that result from driving a car, for example. Yet society requires a license to make certain that people are at least minimally capable of driving safely, let alone practice medicine and law or give psychological counseling. Why, then, shouldn't parenting be an activity that also requires some sort of assurances of minimal competence? Hugh LaFollette argues that it should, and that neither the theoretical nor the practical objections that might be brought against licensing parents are sufficiently strong to justify allowing people to have children when they are incapable of raising them competently. Hugh LaFollette is professor of philosophy at East Tennessee State University.

In this essay I shall argue that the state should require all parents to be licensed. My main goal is to demonstrate that the licensing of parents is theoretically desirable, though I shall also argue that a workable and just licensing program actually could be established.

My strategy is simple. After developing the basic rationale for the licensing of parents, I shall consider several objections to the proposal and argue that these objections fail to undermine it. I shall then isolate some striking similarities between this licensing program and our present policies on the adoption of children. If we retain these adoption policies—as we surely should—then, I argue, a general licensing program should also be established. Finally, I shall briefly suggest that the reason many people object to licensing is that they think parents, particularly biological parents, own or have natural sovereignty over their children.

REGULATING POTENTIALLY HARMFUL ACTIVITIES

Our society normally regulates a certain range of activities; it is illegal to perform these activities unless one has received prior permission to do so. We require automobile operators to have licenses. We forbid people from practicing medicine, law, pharmacy, or psychiatry unless they have satisfied certain licensing requirements.

Society's decision to regulate just these activities is not ad hoc. The decision to restrict admission to certain vocations and to forbid some people from driving is based on an eminently plausible, though not often explicitly formulated, rationale. We require drivers to be licensed because driving an auto is an activity which is potentially harmful to others, safe performance of the activity requires a certain competence, and we have a moderately reliable procedure for determining that competence. The potential harm is obvious: incompetent drivers can and do maim and kill people. The best way we have of limiting this harm without sacrificing the benefits of automobile travel is to require that all drivers demonstrate at least minimal competence. We likewise license doctors, lawyers, and psychologists because they perform activities which can harm others. Obviously they must be proficient if they are to perform these activities properly, and we have moderately reliable procedures for determining proficiency. Imagine a world in which everyone could legally drive a car, in which everyone could legally perform surgery,

From Hugh LaFollette, "Licensing Parents," *Philosophy & Public Affairs*, 9, no. 2, (1980):182–197. © 1980 by Princeton University Press. Reprinted by permission of Princeton University Press. Some footnotes omitted.

prescribe medications, dispense drugs, or offer legal advice. Such a world would hardly be desirable.

Consequently, any activity that is potentially harmful to others and requires certain demonstrated competence for its safe performance, is subject to regulation—that is, it is theoretically desirable that we regulate it. If we also have a reliable procedure for determining whether someone has the requisite competence, then the action is not only subject to regulation but ought, all things considered, to be regulated.

It is particularly significant that we license these hazardous activities, even though denying a license to someone can severely inconvenience and even harm that person. Furthermore, available competency tests are not 100 percent accurate. Denying someone a driver's license in our society, for example, would inconvenience that person acutely. In effect that person would be prohibited from working, shopping, or visiting in places reachable only by car. Similarly, people denied vocational licenses are inconvenienced, even devastated. We have all heard of individuals who had the "life-long dream" of becoming physicians or lawyers, yet were denied that dream. However, the realization that some people are disappointed or inconvenienced does not diminish our conviction that we must regulate occupations or activities that are potentially dangerous to others. Innocent people must be protected even if it means that others cannot pursue activities they deem highly desirable.

Furthermore, we maintain licensing procedures even though our competency tests are sometimes inaccurate. Some people competent to perform the licensed activity (for example, driving a car) will be unable to demonstrate competence (they freeze up on the driver's test). Others may be incompetent, yet pass the test (they are lucky or certain aspects of competence—for example, the sense of responsibility—are not tested). We recognize clearly—or should recognize clearly— that no test will pick out all and only competent drivers, physicians, lawyers, and so

on. Mistakes are inevitable. This does not mean we should forget that innocent people may be harmed by faulty regulatory procedures. In fact, if the procedures are sufficiently faulty, we should cease regulating that activity entirely until more reliable tests are available. I only want to emphasize here that tests need not be perfect. Where moderately reliable tests are available, licensing procedures should be used to protect innocent people from incompetents.

These general criteria for regulatory licensing can certainly be applied to parents. First, parenting is an activity potentially very harmful to children. The potential for harm is apparent: each year more than half a million children are physically abused or neglected by their parents.[1] Many millions more are psychologically abused or neglected—not given love, respect, or a sense of self-worth. The results of this maltreatment are obvious. Abused children bear the physical and psychological scars of maltreatment throughout their lives. Far too often they turn to crime.[2] They are far more likely than others to abuse their own children.[3] Even if these maltreated children never harm anyone, they will probably never be well-adjusted, happy adults. Therefore, parenting clearly satisfies the first criterion of activities subject to regulation.

The second criterion is also incontestably satisfied. A parent must be competent if he is to avoid harming his children; even greater competence is required if he is to do the "job" well. But not everyone has this minimal competence. Many people lack the knowledge needed to rear children adequately. Many others lack the requisite energy, temperament, or stability. Therefore, child-rearing manifestly satisfies both criteria of activities subject to regulation. In fact, I dare say that parenting is a paradigm of such activities since the potential for harm is so great (both in the extent of harm any one person can suffer and in the number of people potentially harmed) and the need for competence is so evident. Consequently, there is good reason to believe that all parents should be licensed. The only ways to avoid this conclusion are to deny the need for licensing any potentially harmful activity; to deny that I have identified the standard criteria of activities which should be regulated; to deny that parenting satisfies the standard criteria; to show that even though parenting satisfies the standard criteria there are special reasons why licensing parents is not theoretically desirable; or to show that there is no reliable and just procedure for implementing this program.

While developing my argument for licensing I have already identified the standard criteria for activities that should be regulated, and I have shown that they can properly be applied to parenting. One could deny the legitimacy of regulation by licensing, but in doing so one would condemn not only the regulation of parenting, but also the regulation of drivers, physicians, druggists, and doctors. Furthermore, regulation of hazardous activities appears to be a fundamental task of any stable society.

Thus only two objections remain. In the next section I shall see if there are any special reasons why licensing parents is not theoretically desirable. Then, in the following section, I shall examine several practical objections designed to demonstrate that even if licensing were theoretically desirable, it could not be justly implemented.

THEORETICAL OBJECTIONS TO LICENSING

Licensing is unacceptable, someone might say, since people have a right to have children, just as they have rights to free speech and free religious expression. They do not need a license to speak freely or to worship as they wish. Why? Because they have a right to engage in these activities. Similarly, since people have a right to have children, any attempt to license parents would be unjust.

This is an important objection since many people find it plausible, if not self-evident. However, it is not as convincing as it appears. The specific rights appealed to in this analogy are not without limitations. Both slander and human sacrifice are prohibited by law; both could result from the unrestricted exercise of freedom of speech and freedom of religion. Thus, even if people have these rights, they may sometimes be limited in order to protect innocent people. Consequently, even if people had a right to have children, that right might also be limited in order to protect innocent people, in this case children. Secondly, the phrase "right to have children" is ambiguous; hence, it is important to isolate its most plausible meaning in this context. Two possible interpretations are not credible and can be dismissed summarily. It is implausible to claim either that infertile people have rights to be *given* children or that people have rights to intentionally create children biologically without incurring any subsequent responsibility to them.

A third interpretation, however, is more plausible, particularly when coupled with observations about the degree of intrusion into one's life that the licensing scheme represents. On this interpretation people have a right to rear children if they make good-faith efforts to rear procreated children the best way they see fit. One might defend this claim on the ground that licensing would require too much intrusion into the lives of sincere applicants.

Undoubtedly one should be wary of unnecessary governmental intervention into individuals' lives. In this case, though, the intrusion would not often be substantial, and when it is, it would be warranted. Those granted licenses would face merely minor intervention; only those denied licenses would encounter marked intrusion. This encroachment, however, is a necessary side-effect of licensing parents—just as it is for automobile and vocational licensing. In addition, as I shall argue in more detail later, the degree of intrusion arising from a general licensing program would be no more than, and probably less than, the present (and presumably justifiable) encroachment into the lives of people who apply to adopt children. Furthermore, since some people hold unacceptable views about what is best for children (they think children should be abused regularly), people do not automatically have rights to rear children just because they will rear them in a way they deem appropriate.

Consequently, we come to a somewhat weaker interpretation of this right claim: a person has a right to rear children if he meets certain minimal standards of child rearing. Parents must not abuse or neglect their children and must also provide for the basic needs of the children. This claim of right is certainly more credible than the previously canvassed alternatives, though some people might still reject this claim in situations where exercise of the right would lead to negative consequences, for example, to over-population. More to the point, though, this conditional right is compatible with licensing. On this interpretation one has a right to have children only if one is not going to abuse or neglect them. Of course the very purpose of licensing is just to determine whether people *are* going to abuse or neglect their children. If the determination is made that someone will maltreat children, then that person is subject to the limitations of the right to have children and can legitimately be denied a parenting license.

In fact, this conditional way of formulating the right to have children provides a model for formulating all alleged rights to engage in hazardous activities. Consider, for example, the right to drive a car. People do not have an unconditional right to drive, although they do have a right to drive if they are competent. Similarly, people do not have an unconditional right to practice medicine; they have a right only if they are demonstrably competent. Hence, denying a driver's or physician's license to someone who has not demonstrated the requisite competence does not deny that person's rights. Likewise, on this model, denying a parenting license to someone who is not competent does not violate that person's rights.

Of course someone might object that the right is conditional on actually being a person who will abuse or neglect children, whereas my proposal only picks out those we can reasonably predict will abuse children. Hence,

this conditional right would be incompatible with licensing.

There are two ways to interpret this objection and it is important to distinguish these divergent formulations. First, the objection could be a way of questioning our ability to predict reasonably and accurately whether people would maltreat their own children. This is an important practical objection, but I will defer discussion of it until the next section. Second, this objection could be a way of expressing doubt about the moral propriety of the prior restraint licensing requires. A parental licensing program would deny licenses to applicants judged to be incompetent even though they had never maltreated any children. This practice would be in tension with our normal skepticism about the propriety of prior restraint.

Despite this healthy skepticism, we do sometimes use prior restraint. In extreme circumstances we may hospitalize or imprison people judged insane, even though they are not legally guilty of any crime, simply because we predict they are likely to harm others. More typically, though, prior restraint is used only if the restriction is not terribly onerous and the restricted activity is one which could lead easily to serious harm. Most types of licensing (for example, those for doctors, drivers, and druggists) fall into this latter category. They require prior restraint to prevent serious harm, and generally the restraint is minor—though it is important to remember that some individuals will find it oppressive. The same is true of parental licensing. The purpose of licensing is to prevent serious harm to children. Moreover, the prior restraint required by licensing would not be terribly onerous for many people. Certainly the restraint would be far less extensive than the presumably justifiable prior restraint of, say, insane criminals. Criminals preventively detained and mentally ill people forcibly hospitalized are denied most basic liberties, while those denied parental licenses would be denied only that one specific opportunity. They could still vote, work for political candidates, speak on controversial topics, and so on. Doubtless some individuals would find the restraint onerous. But when compared to other types of restraint currently practiced, and when judged in light of the severity of harm maltreated children suffer, the restraint appears *relatively* minor.

Furthermore, we could make certain, as we do with most licensing programs, that individuals denied licenses are given the opportunity to reapply easily and repeatedly for a license. Thus, many people correctly denied licenses (because they are incompetent) would choose (perhaps it would be provided) to take counseling or therapy to improve their chances of passing the next test. On the other hand, most of those mistakenly denied licenses would probably be able to demonstrate in a later test that they would be competent parents.

Consequently, even though one needs to be wary of prior restraint, if the potential for harm is great and the restraint is minor relative to the harm we are trying to prevent—as it would be with parental licensing—then such restraint is justified. This objection, like all the theoretical objections reviewed, has failed.

PRACTICAL OBJECTIONS TO LICENSING

I shall now consider five practical objections to licensing. Each objection focuses on the problems or difficulties of implementing this proposal. According to these objections, licensing is (or may be) theoretically desirable; nevertheless, it cannot be efficiently and justly implemented.

The first objection is that there may not be, or we may not be able to discover, adequate criteria of "a good parent." We simply do not have the knowledge, and it is unlikely that we could ever obtain the knowledge, that would enable us to distinguish adequate from inadequate parents.

Clearly there is some force to this objection. It is highly improbable that we can formulate criteria that would distinguish precisely between good and less than good parents. There is too much we do not know about child development

and adult psychology. My proposal, however, does not demand that we make these fine distinctions. It does not demand that we license only the best parents; rather it is designed to exclude only the very bad ones. This is not just a semantic difference, but a substantive one. Although we do not have infallible criteria for picking out good parents, we undoubtedly can identify bad ones—those who will abuse or neglect their children. Even though we could have a lively debate about the range of freedom a child should be given or the appropriateness of corporal punishment, we do not wonder if a parent who severely beats or neglects a child is adequate. We know that person isn't. Consequently, we do have reliable and useable criteria for determining who is a bad parent; we have the criteria necessary to make a licensing program work.

The second practical objection to licensing is that there is no reliable way to predict who will maltreat their children. Without an accurate predictive test, licensing would be not only unjust, but also a waste of time. Now I recognize that as a philosopher (and not a psychologist, sociologist, or social worker), I am on shaky ground if I make sweeping claims about the present or future abilities of professionals to produce such predictive tests. Nevertheless, there are some relevant observations I can offer.

Initially, we need to be certain that the demands on predictive tests are not unreasonable. For example, it would be improper to require that tests be 100 percent accurate. Procedures for licensing drivers, physicians, lawyers, druggists, etc., plainly are not 100 percent (or anywhere near 100 percent) accurate. Presumably we recognize these deficiencies yet embrace the procedures anyway. Consequently, it would be imprudent to demand considerably more exacting standards for the tests used in licensing parents.

In addition, from what I can piece together, the practical possibilities for constructing a reliable predictive test are not all that gloomy. Since my proposal does not require that we make fine-line distinctions between good and less than good parents, but rather that we weed out those who are potentially very bad, we can use existing tests that claim to isolate relevant predictive characteristics—whether a person is violence-prone, easily frustrated, or unduly self-centered. In fact researchers at Nashville General Hospital have developed a brief interview questionnaire which seems to have significant predictive value. Based on their data, the researchers identified 20 percent of the interviewees as a "risk group"—those having great potential for serious problems. After one year they found "the incidence of major breakdown in parent-child interaction in the risk group was approximately four to five times as great as in the low risk group."[4] We also know that parents who maltreat children often have certain identifiable experiences; for example, most of them were themselves maltreated as children. Consequently, if we combined our information about these parents with certain psychological test results, we would probably be able to predict with reasonable accuracy which people will maltreat their children.

However, my point is not to argue about the precise reliability of present tests. I cannot say emphatically that we now have accurate predictive tests. Nevertheless, even if such tests are not available, we could undoubtedly develop them. For example, we could begin a longitudinal study in which all potential parents would be required to take a specified battery of tests. Then these parents could be "followed" to discover which ones abused or neglected their children. By correlating the test scores with information on maltreatment, a usable, accurate test could be fashioned. Therefore, I do not think that the present unavailability of such tests (if they are unavailable) would count against the legitimacy of licensing parents.

The third practical objection is that even if a reliable test for ascertaining who would be an acceptable parent were available, administrators would unintentionally misuse that test. These unintentional mistakes would clearly harm innocent individuals. Therefore, so the argument goes, this proposal ought to be scrapped. This objection can be dispensed with fairly easily unless one assumes there is some special reason to believe that more mistakes will be made in administering parenting licenses than in other regulatory activities. No matter how reliable our proceedings are, there will always be mistakes. We may license a physician who, through incompetence, would cause the death of a patient; or we may mistakenly deny a physician's license to someone who would be competent. But the fact that mistakes are made does not and should not lead us to abandon attempts to determine competence. The harm done in these cases could be far worse than the harm of mistakenly denying a person a parenting license. As far as I can tell, there is no reason to believe that more mistakes will be made here than elsewhere.

The fourth proposed practical objection claims that any testing procedure will be intentionally abused. People administering the process will disqualify people they dislike, or people who espouse views they dislike, from rearing children.

The response to this objection is parallel to the response to the previous objection, namely, that there is no reason to believe that the licensing of parents is more likely to be abused than driver's license tests or other regulatory procedures. In addition, individuals can be protected from prejudicial treatment by pursuing appeals available to them. Since the licensing test can be taken on numerous occasions, the likelihood of the applicant's working with different administrative personnel increases and therefore the likelihood decreases that intentional abuse could ultimately stop a qualified person from rearing children. Consequently, since the probability of such abuse is not more than, and may even be less than, the intentional abuse of judicial and other regulatory authority, this objection does not give us any reason to reject the licensing of parents.

The fifth objection is that we could never adequately, reasonably, and fairly enforce such a program. That is, even if we could establish a reasonable and fair way of determining which people would be inadequate parents, it would be difficult, if not impossible, to enforce the program. How would one deal with violators and what could we do with babies so conceived? There are difficult problems here, no doubt, but they are not insurmountable. We might not punish parents at all—we might just remove the children and put them up for adoption. However, even if we are presently uncertain about the precise way to establish a just and effective form of enforcement, I do not see why this should undermine my licensing proposal. If it is important enough to protect children from being maltreated by parents, then surely a reasonable enforcement procedure can be secured. At least we should assume one can be unless someone shows that it cannot.

AN ANALOGY WITH ADOPTION

So far I have argued that parents should be licensed. Undoubtedly many readers find this claim extremely radical. It is revealing to notice, however, that this program is not as radical as it seems. Our moral and legal systems already recognize that not everyone is capable of rearing children well. In fact, well-entrenched laws require adoptive parents to be investigated—in much the same ways and for much the same reasons as in the general licensing program advocated here. For example, we do not allow just anyone to adopt a child; nor do we let someone adopt without first estimating the likelihood of the person's being a good parent. In fact, the adoptive process is far more rigorous than the general licensing procedures I envision. Prior to adoption the candidates must first formally apply to adopt a child. The applicants are then subjected to an exacting home study to determine whether they really want to have children and whether they are capable of caring for and rearing them adequately. No one is allowed to adopt a child until the administrators can reasonably predict that the person will be an adequate parent. The results of these procedures are impressive. Despite the trauma children often face before they are finally adopted, they are five times less likely to be abused than children reared by their biological parents.[5]

Nevertheless we recognize, or should recognize, that these demanding procedures exclude some people who would be adequate parents. The selection criteria may be inadequate; the testing procedures may be somewhat unreliable. We may make mistakes. Probably there is some intentional abuse of the system. Adoption procedures intrude directly in the applicants' lives. Yet we continue the present adoption policies because we think it better to mistakenly deny some people the opportunity to adopt than to let just anyone adopt.

Once these features of our adoption policies are clearly identified, it becomes quite apparent that there are striking parallels between the general licensing program I have advocated and our present adoption system. Both programs have the same aim—protecting children. Both have the same drawbacks and are subject to the same abuses. The only obvious dissimilarity is that the adoption requirements are *more* rigorous than those proposed for the general licensing program. Consequently, if we think it is so important to protect adopted children, even though people who want to adopt are less likely than biological parents to maltreat their children, then we should likewise afford the same protection to children reared by their biological parents.

I suspect, though, that many people will think the cases are not analogous. The cases are relevantly different, someone might retort, because biological parents have a natural affection for their children and the strength of this affection makes it unlikely that parents would maltreat their biologically produced children.

Even if it were generally true that parents have special natural affections for their biological offspring, that does not mean that all parents have enough affection to keep them from maltreating their children. This should be apparent given the number of children abused each year by their biological parents. Therefore, even if there is generally such a bond, that does not explain why we should not have licensing procedures to protect children of parents who do not have a sufficiently strong bond. Consequently, if we continue our practice of regulating the adoption of children, and certainly we should, we are rationally compelled to establish a licensing program for all parents.

However, I am not wedded to a strict form of licensing. It may well be that there are alternative ways of regulating parents which would achieve the desired results—the protection of children—without strictly prohibiting nonlicensed people from rearing children. For example, a system of tax incentives for licensed parents, and protective services scrutiny of nonlicensed parents, might adequately protect children. If it would, I would endorse the less drastic measure. My principal concern is to protect children from maltreatment by parents. I begin by advocating the more strict form of licensing since that is the standard method of regulating hazardous activities.

I have argued that all parents should be licensed by the state. This licensing program is attractive, not because state intrusion is inherently judicious and efficacious, but simply because it seems to be the best way to prevent children from being reared by incompetent parents. Nonetheless, even after considering the previous arguments, many people will find the proposal a useful academic exercise, probably silly, and possibly even morally perverse. But why? Why do most of us find this proposal unpalatable, particularly when the arguments supporting it are good and the objections to it are philosophically flimsy?

I suspect the answer is found in a long-held, deeply ingrained attitude toward children, repeatedly reaffirmed in recent court decisions, and present, at least to some degree, in almost all of us. The belief is that parents own, or at least have natural sovereignty over, their children. It does not matter precisely how this belief is described, since on both views parents legitimately exercise extensive and virtually unlimited control over their children. Others can properly interfere with or criticize parental decisions only in unusual and tightly prescribed circumstances—for example, when parents severely and repeatedly abuse their children. In all other cases, the parents reign supreme.

This belief is abhorrent and needs to be supplanted with a more child-centered view. Why? Briefly put, this attitude has adverse effects on children and on the adults these children will become. Parents who hold this view may well maltreat the children. If these parents happen to treat their children well, it is only because they want to, not because they think their children deserve or have a right to good treatment. Moreover, this belief is manifestly at odds with the conviction that parents should prepare children for life as adults. Children subject to parents who perceive children in this way are unlikely to be adequately prepared for adulthood. Hence, to prepare children for life as adults and to protect them from maltreatment, this attitude toward children must be dislodged. As I have argued, licensing is a viable way to protect children. Furthermore, it would increase the likelihood that more children will be adequately prepared for life as adults than is now the case.

NOTES

1. The statistics on the incidence of child abuse vary. Probably the most recent detailed study (Saad Nagi, *Child Maltreatment in the United States* [Columbia University Press, 1977]) suggests that between 400,000 and 1 million children are abused or neglected each year. Other experts claim the incidence is considerably higher.

2. According to the National Committee for the Prevention of Child Abuse, more than 80 percent of incarcerated criminals were, as children, abused by their parents. In addition, a study in the *Journal of the American Medical Association* 168, no. 3: 1755–1758, reported that first-degree murderers from middle-class homes and who have "no history

of addiction to drugs, alcoholism, organic disease of the brain, or epilepsy" were frequently found to have been subject to "remorseless physical brutality at the hands of the parents."

3. "A review of the literature points out that abusive parents were raised in the same style that they have recreated in the pattern of rearing children. . . . An individual who was raised by parents who used physical force to train their children and who grew up in a violent household has had as a role model the use of force and violence as a means of family problem solving." R. J. Gelles, "Child Abuse as Psychopathology—A Sociological Critique and Reformulation," *American Journal of Orthopsychiatry* 43, no. 4 (1973): 618–19.

4. The research gathered by Altemeir was reported by Ray Helfer in "Review of the Concepts and a Sampling of the Research Relating to Screening for the Potential to Abuse and/or Neglect One's Child."

Helfer's paper was presented at a workshop sponsored by the National Committee for the Prevention of Child Abuse, 3–6 December 1978.

5. According to a study published by the Child Welfare League of America, at least 51 percent of the adopted children had suffered, prior to adoption, more than minimal emotional deprivation. See Elizabeth A. Lawder et al., *A Follow-up Study of Adoptions: Post-Placement Functioning of Adoption Families* (New York, 1969).

According to a study by David Gil (*Violence Against Children* [Cambridge: Harvard University Press, 1970]) only .4 percent of abused children were abused by adoptive parents. Since at least 2 percent of the children in the United States are adopted (*Encyclopedia of Social Work*, National Association of Social Workers, New York, 1977), that means the rate of abuse by biological parents is five times that of adoptive parents.

REVIEW AND DISCUSSION QUESTIONS

1. What provides the motivation behind LaFollette's proposal? Is his concern warranted?
2. Describe LaFollette's response to the claim that parents have a right to raise children.
3. Describe the practical objections LaFollette discusses, along with his response to each.
4. On balance, do you think LaFollette's arguments are sufficiently sound to overcome the objections he considers? Explain.

Who Controls a Child's Education?

Wisconsin v. Yoder

This well-known case arose in response to a Wisconsin law requiring all children to be sent to school until the age of sixteen. The Amish parents of two children, ages fourteen and fifteen, refused to comply, arguing that compulsory school attendance beyond eighth grade violated their constitutional right of "free exercise" of religion protected by the First Amendment to the U.S. Constitution. The case went all the way to the Supreme Court, and the Court overturned the law, upholding the right of the Amish parents to guide the religious future and education of their children. In his dissenting opinion, Justice Douglas discusses problems associated with allowing parents to impose their religious notions on children as well as the possible effects of the Court's ruling on the children's educational development.

Mr. Chief Justice Burger: On complaint of the school district administrator for the public schools, respondents [Mr. and Mrs. Yoder] were charged, tried, and convicted of violating the compulsory-attendance law in Green County Court and were fined the sum of $5 each. Respondents defended on the ground that the application of the compulsory-attendance

Wisconsin v. Yoder. 406 U.S. 205 (1972).

law violated their rights under the First and Fourteenth Amendments. The trial testimony showed that respondents believed, in accordance with the tenets of Old Order Amish communities generally, that their children's attendance at high school, public or private, was contrary to the Amish religion and way of life. . . . The State stipulated that respondents' religious beliefs were sincere.

In support of their position, respondents presented as expert witnesses scholars on religion and education whose testimony is uncontradicted. They expressed their opinions on the relationship of the Amish belief concerning school attendance to the more general tenets of their religion, and described the impact that compulsory high school attendance could have on the continued survival of Amish communities as they exist in the United States today. . . .

Amish beliefs require members of the community to make their living by farming or closely related activities. Broadly speaking, the Old Order Amish religion pervades and determines the entire mode of life of its adherents. . . .

Amish objection to formal education beyond the eighth grade is firmly grounded in these central religious concepts. They object to the high school, and higher education generally, because the values they teach are in marked variance with Amish values and the Amish way of life; they view secondary school education as an impermissible exposure of their children to a "worldly" influence in conflict with their beliefs. The high school tends to emphasize intellectual and scientific accomplishments, self-distinction, competitiveness, worldly success, and social life with other students. Amish society emphasizes informal learning-through-doing; a life of "goodness," rather than a life of intellect; wisdom, rather than technical knowledge; community welfare, rather than competition; and separation from, rather than integration with, contemporary worldly society.

Formal high school education takes [Amish children] away from their community, physically and emotionally, during the crucial and formative adolescent period of life. During this period, the children must acquire Amish attitudes favoring manual work and self-reliance and the specific skills needed to perform the adult role of an Amish farmer or housewife. They must learn to enjoy physical labor. . . . And, at this time in life, the Amish child must also grow in his faith and his relationship to the Amish community if he is to be prepared to accept the heavy obligations imposed by adult baptism. . . .

The Amish do not object to elementary education through the first eight grades as a general proposition because they agree that their children must have basic skills in the "three Rs" in order to read the Bible, to be good farmers and citizens, and to be able to deal with non-Amish people when necessary in the course of daily affairs. They view such a basic education as acceptable because it does not significantly expose their children to worldly values or interfere with their development in the Amish community during the crucial adolescent period. . . .

On the basis of such considerations, [an expert] testified that compulsory high school attendance could not only result in great psychological harm to Amish children, because of the conflicts it would produce, but would also, in his opinion, ultimately result in the destruction of the Old Order Amish church community as it exists in the United States today. . . .

In order for Wisconsin to compel school attendance beyond the eighth grade against a claim that such attendance interferes with the practice of a legitimate religious belief, it must appear either that the State does not deny the free exercise of religious belief by its requirement, or that there is a state interest of sufficient magnitude to override the interest claiming protection under the Free Exercise Clause. . . .

A way of life, however virtuous and admirable, may not be interposed as a barrier to reasonable state regulation of education if it is based on purely secular considerations; to have the protection of the Religion Clauses, the claims must be rooted in religious belief.

Although a determination of what is a "religious" belief or practice entitled to constitutional protection may present a most delicate question, the very concept of ordered liberty precludes allowing every person to make his own standards on matters of conduct in which society as a whole has important interests. Thus, if the Amish asserted their claims because of their subjective evaluation and rejection of the contemporary secular values accepted by the majority, much as Thoreau rejected the social values of his time and isolated himself at Walden Pond, their claims would not rest on a religious basis. Thoreau's choice was philosophical and personal rather than religious, and such belief does not rise to the demands of the Religion Clauses.

Giving no weight to such secular considerations, however, we see that the record in this case abundantly supports the claim that the traditional way of life of the Amish is not merely a matter of personal preference, but one of deep religious conviction, shared by an organized group, and intimately related to daily living. That the Old Order Amish daily life and religious practice stem from their faith is shown by the fact that it is in response to their literal interpretation of the Biblical injunction from the Epistle of Paul to the Romans, "be not conformed to this world. . . . "

Their way of life in a church-oriented community, separated from the outside world and "worldly" influences, their attachment to nature and the soil, is a way inherently simple and uncomplicated, albeit difficult to preserve against the pressure to conform. Their rejection of telephones, automobiles, radios, and television, their mode of dress, of speech, their habits of manual work do indeed set them apart from much of contemporary society; these customs are both symbolic and practical. . . .

The State advances two primary arguments in support of its system of compulsory education. It notes, as Thomas Jefferson pointed out early in our history, that some degree of education is necessary to prepare citizens to participate effectively and intelligently in our open political system if we are to preserve freedom and independence. Further, education prepares individuals to be self-reliant and self-sufficient participants in society. We accept these propositions.

However, the evidence adduced by the Amish in this case is persuasively to the effect that an additional one or two years of formal high school for Amish children in place of their long-established program of informal vocational education would do little to serve those interests. . . .

It is one thing to say that compulsory education for a year or two beyond the eighth grade may be necessary when its goal is the preparation of the child for life in modern society as the majority live, but it is quite another if the goal of education be viewed as the preparation of the child for life in the separated agrarian community that is the keystone of the Amish faith. . . .

Whatever their idiosyncrasies as seen by the majority, the Amish community has been a highly successful social unit within our society, even if apart from the conventional "mainstream."

Its members are productive and very law-abiding members of society; they reject public welfare in any of its usual modern forms. . . .

This case involves the fundamental interest of parents, as contrasted with that of the State, to guide the religious future and education of their children. The history and culture of Western civilization reflect a strong tradition of parental concern for the nurture and upbringing of their children. This primary role of the parents in the upbringing of their children is now established beyond debate as an enduring American tradition. . . .

To be sure, the power of the parent, even when linked to a free exercise claim, may be subject to limitation if it appears that parental decisions will jeopardize the health or safety of the child, or have a potential for significant social burdens. But in this case, the Amish have introduced persuasive evidence undermining the arguments the State has advanced to support its claims in terms of the welfare of the child and society as a whole.

Mr. Justice Douglas, Dissenting in Part: The Court's analysis assumes that the only interests at stake in the case are those of the Amish parents on the one hand, and those of the State on the other. The difficulty with this approach is that, despite the Court's claim, the parents are seeking to vindicate not only their own free exercise claims, but also those of their high-school-age children. . . .

No analysis of religious-liberty claims can take place in a vacuum. If the parents in this case are allowed a religious exemption, the inevitable effect is to impose the parents' notions of religious duty upon their children. Where the child is mature enough to express potentially conflicting desires, it would be an invasion of the child's rights to permit such an imposition without canvassing his views. . . . As the child has no other effective forum, it is in this litigation that his rights should be considered. And, if an Amish child desires to attend high school, and is mature enough to have that desire respected, the State may well be able to override the parents' religiously motivated objections.

This issue has never been squarely presented before today. Our opinions are full of talk about the power of the parents over the child's education. . . . And we have in the past analyzed similar conflicts between parent and State with little regard for the views of the child. . . .

Recent cases, however, have clearly held that the children themselves have constitutionally protectible interests.

These children are "persons" within the meaning of the Bill of Rights. . . . While the parents, absent dissent, normally speak for the entire family, the education of the child is a matter on which the child will often have decided views. He may want to be a pianist or an astronaut or an oceanographer. To do so he will have to break from the Amish tradition. . . .

If a parent keeps his child out of school beyond the grade school, then the child will be forever barred from entry into the new and amazing world of diversity that we have today. . . .

[In the cases in which the Court held antipolygamy laws constitutional,] action which the Court deemed to be antisocial could be punished even though it was grounded on deeply held and sincere religious convictions. What we do today, at least in this respect, opens the way to give organized religion a broader base than it has ever enjoyed.

In another way, however, the Court retreats when in reference to Henry Thoreau it says his "choice was philosophical and personal rather than religious, and such belief does not rise to the demands of the Religion Clauses." That is contrary to what we held in *United States* v. *Seeger,* where we were concerned with the meaning of the words "religious training and belief" in the Selective Service Act, which were the basis of many conscientious objector claims. We said: "Within that phrase would come all sincere religious beliefs which are based upon a power or being, or upon a faith, to which all else is subordinate or upon which all else is ultimately dependent. The test might be stated in these words: A sincere and meaningful belief which occupies in the life of its possessor a place parallel to that filled by the God of those admittedly qualifying for the exemption comes within the statutory definition. This construction avoids imputing to Congress an intent to classify different religious beliefs, exempting some and excluding others, and is in accord with the well-established congressional policy of equal treatment for those whose opposition to service is grounded in their religious tenets."

REVIEW AND DISCUSSION QUESTIONS

1. Describe the legal issue in this case.
2. Does Justice Burger seem to rely more on religious freedom or the rights of parents over children? Explain.

3. On what basis does Justice Douglas dissent?

4. Does Justice Burger think the Constitution should be "neutral" among different religions? Explain.

5. Children will eventually have the right to make decisions for themselves in many areas, independent of what government or others may think. Can parents sometimes damage their children's future right to self-determination? Explain, giving examples.

What Do Grown Children Owe Their Parents?

Jane English

One way to view the responsibilities of grown children to their parents is to suppose that children owe their parents love, respect, and financial or other help on the basis of past sacrifices parents have made. Jane English rejects this form of argument, claiming instead that friendship is a better model than debts owed for understanding the parent-child relationship. Jane English taught philosophy at the University of North Carolina.

What do grown children owe their parents? I will contend that the answer is "nothing." Although I agree that there are many things that children ought to do for their parents, I will argue that it is inappropriate and misleading to describe them as things "owed." I will maintain that parents' voluntary sacrifices, rather than creating "debts" to be "repaid," tend to create love or "friendship." The duties of grown children are those of friends and result from love between them and their parents, rather than being things owed in repayment for the parents' earlier sacrifices. Thus, I will oppose those philosophers who use the word "owe" whenever a duty or obligation exists. Although the "debt" metaphor is appropriate in some moral circumstances, my argument is that a love relationship is not such a case.

Misunderstandings about the proper relationship between parents and their grown children have resulted from reliance on the "owing" terminology. For instance, we hear parents complain, "You owe it to us to write

home (keep up your piano playing, not adopt a hippie lifestyle), because of all we sacrificed for you (paying for piano lessons, sending you to college)." The child is sometimes even heard to reply, "I didn't ask to be born (to be given piano lessons, to be sent to college)." This inappropriate idiom of ordinary language tends to obscure, or even to undermine, the love that is the correct ground of filial obligation.

1. FAVORS CREATE DEBTS

There are some cases, other than literal debts, in which talk of "owing," though metaphorical, is apt. New to the neighborhood, Max barely knows his neighbor, Nina, but he asks her if she will take in his mail while he is gone for a month's vacation. She agrees. If, subsequently, Nina asks Max to do the same for her, it seems that Max has a moral obligation to agree (greater than the one he would have had if Nina had not done the same for him),

From Jane English, "What Do Grown Children Owe Their Parents?" in *Having Children,* Onora O'Neill and William Ruddick, eds. (New York: Oxford University Press, 1979). Reprinted by permission.

unless for some reason it would be a burden far out of proportion to the one Nina bore for him. I will call this a *favor:* when A, at B's request, bears some burden for B, then B incurs an obligation to reciprocate. Here the metaphor of Max's "owing" Nina is appropriate. It is not literally a debt, of course, nor can Nina pass this IOU on to heirs, demand payment in the form of Max's taking out her garbage, or sue Max. Nonetheless, since Max ought to perform one act of similar nature and amount of sacrifice in return, the term is suggestive. Once he reciprocates, the debt is "discharged"—that is, their obligations revert to the condition they were in before Max's initial request.

Contrast a situation in which Max simply goes on vacation and, to his surprise, finds upon his return that his neighbor has mowed his grass twice weekly in his absence. This is a voluntary sacrifice rather than a favor, and Max has no duty to reciprocate. It would be nice for him to volunteer to do so, but this would be supererogatory on his part. Rather than a favor, Nina's action is a friendly gesture. As a result, she might expect Max to chat over the back fence, help her catch her straying dog, or something similar—she might expect the development of a friendship. But Max would be chatting (or whatever) out of friendship, rather than in repayment for mown grass. If he did not return her gesture, she might feel rebuffed or miffed, but not unjustly treated or indignant, since Max has not failed to perform a duty. Talk of "owing" would be out of place in this case.

It is sometimes difficult to distinguish between favors and non-favors, because friends tend to do favors for each other, and those who exchange favors tend to become friends. But one test is to ask how Max is motivated. Is it "to be nice to Nina" or "because she did x for me"? Favors are frequently performed by total strangers without any friendship developing. Nevertheless, a temporary obligation is created, even if the chance for repayment never arises. For instance, suppose that Oscar and Matilda, total strangers, are waiting in a long checkout line at the supermarket. Oscar, having forgotten the oregano, asks Matilda to watch his cart for a second. She does. If Matilda now asks Oscar to return the favor while she picks up some tomato sauce, he is obliged to agree. Even if she had not watched his cart, it would be inconsiderate of him to refuse, claiming he was too busy reading the magazines. He may have a duty to help others, but he would not "owe" it to her. But if she had done the same for him, he incurs an additional obligation to help, and talk of "owing" is apt. It suggests an agreement to perform equal, reciprocal, canceling sacrifices.

2. THE DUTIES OF FRIENDSHIP VERSUS DEBTS

The terms "owe" and "repay" are helpful in the case of favors, because the sameness of the amount of sacrifice on the two sides is important; the monetary metaphor suggests equal quantities of sacrifice. But friendship ought to be characterized by *mutuality* rather than reciprocity: friends offer what they can give and accept what they need, without regard for the total amounts of benefits exchanged. And friends are motivated by love rather than by the prospect of repayment. Hence, talk of "owing" is singularly out of place in friendship.

For example, suppose Alfred takes Beatrice out for an expensive dinner and a movie. Beatrice incurs no obligation to "repay" him with a goodnight kiss or a return engagement. If Alfred complains that she "owes" him something, he is operating under the assumption that she should repay a favor, but on the contrary his was a generous gesture done in the hopes of developing a friendship. We hope that he would not want her repayment in the form of sex or attention if this was done to discharge a debt rather than from friendship. Since, if Alfred is prone to reasoning in this way, Beatrice may well decline the invitation or request to pay for her own dinner, his attitude of expecting a "return" on his "investment" could hinder the development of a friendship.

Beatrice should return the gesture only if she is motivated by friendship.

Another common misuse of the "owing" idiom occurs when the Smiths have dined at the Joneses' four times, but the Joneses at the Smiths' only once. People often say, "We owe them three dinners." This line of thinking may be appropriate between business acquaintances, but not between friends. After all, the Joneses invited the Smiths not in order to feed them or to be fed in turn, but because of the friendly contact presumably enjoyed by all on such occasions. If the Smiths do not feel friendship toward the Joneses, they can decline future invitations and not invite the Joneses; they owe them nothing. Of course, between friends of equal resources and needs, roughly equal sacrifices (though not necessarily roughly equal dinners) will typically occur. If the sacrifices are highly out of proportion to the resources, the relationship is closer to servility than to friendship.

Another difference between favors and friendship is that after a friendship ends, the duties of friendship end. The party that has sacrificed less owes the other nothing. For instance, suppose Elmer donated a pint of blood that his wife Doris needed during an operation. Years after their divorce, Elmer is in an accident and needs one pint of blood. His new wife, Cora, is also of the same blood type. It seems that Doris not only does not "owe" Elmer blood, but that she should actually refrain from coming forward if Cora has volunteered to donate. To insist on donating not only interferes with the newlyweds' friendship, but it belittles Doris and Elmer's former relationship by suggesting that Elmer gave blood in hopes of favors returned instead of simply out of love for Doris. It is one of the heart-rending features of divorce that it attends to quantity in a relationship previously characterized by mutuality. If Cora could not donate, Doris's obligation is the same as that for any former spouse in need of blood; it is not increased by the fact that Elmer similarly aided her. It is affected by the degree to which they are still friends, which in turn may (or may not) have been influenced by Elmer's donation.

In short, unlike the debts created by favors, the duties of friendship do not require equal quantities of sacrifice. Performing equal sacrifices does not cancel the duties of friendship, as it does the debts of favors. Unrequested sacrifices do not themselves create debts, but friends have duties regardless of whether they requested or initiated the friendship. Those who perform favors may be motivated by mutual gain, whereas friends should be motivated by affection. These characteristics of the friendship relation are distorted by talk of "owing."

3. PARENTS AND CHILDREN

The relationship between children and their parents should be one of friendship characterized by mutuality rather than one of reciprocal favors. The quantity of parental sacrifice is not relevant in determining what duties the grown child has. The medical assistance grown children ought to offer their ill mothers in old age depends upon the mothers' need, not upon whether they endured a difficult pregnancy, for example. Nor do one's duties to one's parents cease once an equal quantity of sacrifice has been performed, as the phrase "discharging a debt" may lead us to think.

Rather, what children ought to do for their parents (and parents for children) depends upon (1) their respective needs, abilities, and resources and (2) the extent to which there is an ongoing friendship between them. Thus, regardless of the quantity of childhood sacrifices, an able, wealthy child has an obligation to help his needy parents more than does a needy child. To illustrate, suppose sisters Cecile and Dana are equally loved by their parents, even though Cecile was an easy child to care for, seldom ill, while Dana was often sick and caused some trouble as a juvenile delinquent. As adults, Dana is a struggling artist living far away, while Cecile is a wealthy lawyer living nearby. When the parents need visits and financial aid, Cecile has an obligation to bear a higher proportion of these burdens than her sister. This results from her abilities, rather than from the quantities of sacrifice made by the parents earlier.

Sacrifices have an important causal role in creating an ongoing friendship, which may lead us to assume incorrectly that it is the sacrifices that are the source of the obligation. That the source is the friendship instead can be seen by examining cases in which the sacrifices occurred but the friendship, for some reason, did not develop or persist. For example, if a woman gives up her newborn child for adoption, and if no feelings of love ever develop on either side, it seems that the grown child does not have an obligation to "repay" her for her sacrifices in pregnancy. For that matter, if the adopted child has an unimpaired love relationship with the adoptive parents, he or she has the same obligations to help them as a natural child would have.

The filial obligations of grown children are a result of friendship, rather than owed for services rendered. Suppose that Vance married Lola despite his parents' strong wish that he marry within their religion, and that as a result, the parents refuse to speak to him again. As the years pass, the parents are unaware of Vance's problems, his accomplishments, the birth of his children. The love that once existed between them, let us suppose, has been completely destroyed by this event and thirty years of desuetude. At this point, it seems, Vance is under no obligation to pay his parents' medical bills in their old age, beyond his general duty to help those in need. An additional, filial obligation would only arise from whatever love he may still feel for them. It would be irrelevant for his parents to argue, "But look how much we sacrificed for you when you were young," for that sacrifice was not a favor but occurred as part of a friendship which existed at that time but is now, we have supposed, defunct. A more appropriate message would be, "We still love you, and we would like to renew our friendship."

I hope this helps to set the question of what children ought to do for their parents in a new light. The parental argument, "You ought to do x because we did y for you," should be replaced by, "We love you and you will be happier if you do x," or "We believe you love us, and anyone who loved us would do x." If the parents' sacrifice had been a favor, the child's reply, "I never asked you to do y for me," would have been relevant; to the revised parental remarks, this reply is clearly irrelevant. The child can either do x or dispute one of the parents' claims: by showing that a love relationship does not exist, or that love for someone does not motivate doing x, or that he or she will not be happier doing x.

Seen in this light, parental requests for children to write home, visit, and offer them a reasonable amount of emotional and financial support in life's crises are well founded, so long as a friendship still exists. Love for others does call for caring about and caring for them. Some other parental requests, such as for more sweeping changes in the child's lifestyle or life goals, can be seen to be insupportable, once we shift the justification from debts owed to love. The terminology of favors suggests the reasoning, "Since we paid for your college education, you owe it to us to make a career of engineering, rather than becoming a rock musician." This tends to alienate affection even further, since the tuition payments are depicted as investments for a return rather than done from love, as though the child's life goals could be "bought." Basing the argument on love leads to different reasoning patterns. The suppressed premise, "If A loves B, then A follows B's wishes as to A's lifelong career" is simply false. Love does not even dictate that the child adopt the parents' values as to the desirability of alternative life goals. So the parents' strongest available argument here is, "We love you, we are deeply concerned about your happiness, and in the long run you will be happier as an engineer." This makes it clear that an empirical claim is really the subject of the debate.

The function of these examples is to draw out our considered judgments as to the proper relation between parents and their grown children, and to show how poorly they fit the model of favors. What is relevant is the ongoing friendship that exists between parents and children. Although that relationship developed partly as a result of parental sacrifices for the child, the duties that grown children have to their parents result from the friendship rather than from the sacrifices. The idiom of owing favors to one's parents can actually be destructive if it undermines the role of mutuality and leads us to think in terms of quantitative reciprocal favors.

REVIEW AND DISCUSSION QUESTIONS

1. What differences does English find between duties to friends and the obligation to repay debts?
2. Why does English advocate the model of friendship rather than of reciprocal favors in describing the parent-child relationship?
3. Does the friendship model exhaust the duties of children? Is the mere fact of a biological connection between parent and child morally irrelevant? Explain.
4. Suppose a parent has not been a "friend" to the child, but instead has been strict, remote, and uncompromising but also self-sacrificing. Does the adult child then owe the parent nothing?

Essay and Paper Topics for Section 16

1. Using the general moral theory you found most reasonable from Part I, write an essay in which you evaluate the position of two philosophers you have read on the subject of selling babies and licensing parents.
2. How would LaFollette respond to *Wisconsin* v. *Yoder?* Do you agree with that position?
3. Compare English's position with the view of parent-child relationships described by Judith Jarvis Thomson in her article on abortion.
4. Using the essays by Godwin ("Comparing Human Lives"), Sandel ("No Fault Divorce and the Unencumbered Self,") and English ("What Do Grown Children Owe Their Parents?") (reprinted earlier) discuss the importance of impartiality and how it is relevant to the family.

Postscript to Instructors

This book has been used as the basic text for courses in ethics, applied ethics, and social and political philosophy. Many instructors organize the class around specific moral or political controversies, choosing among the range of possibilities the book provides. But I and others who have used the book in the past have sometimes chosen an alternative approach, one that puts more emphasis on ethical or political theory. I have therefore put together two alternative syllabi that indicate how such classes might be organized. In each case selections representing a particular theory are coupled with articles illustrating how that theoretical perspective has been applied to specific topics. Though I have put the theory sections first, followed by practical applications, the two can be done in either order.

Alternative Ethics Syllabus

I. **Utilitarianism**
   A. **Theory**
      1. Mill, *Utilitarianism*
      2. Singer, *All Animals Are Equal*
   B. **Practice**
      1. Brandt, *Defective Newborns and the Morality of Termination*
      2. Godwin, *Comparing Human Lives: The Archbishop and the Chamber Maid*
      3. Baxter, *People or Penguins*
      4. Singer, *Rich and Poor*

II. **Natural Rights**
   A. **Theory**
      1. Hobbes, *Leviathan*
      2. Locke, *The Second Treatise of Government*
      3. Ross, *Intuitionism*
   B. **Practice**
      1. Nozick, *The Entitlement Theory*
      2. Thomson, *A Defense of Abortion*
      3. Dworkin, *Taking Rights Seriously*

III. **Kantianism**
   A. **Theory**
      1. Kant, *The Fundamental Principles of the Metaphysic of Morals*
      2. O'Neill, *Kant and Utilitarianism Contrasted*
      3. Nagel, *Ethics*
      4. Rawls, *A Theory of Justice*
   B. **Practice**
      1. Kant, *Duties Toward the Body in Respect to Sexual Impulse*
      2. Pinau, *Date Rape: A Feminist Analysis*

3. Perlmutter, *Desert and Capital Punishment*
4. Steinbock, *Speciesism and the Idea of Equality*
5. Goodin, *The Ethics of Smoking*

IV. **Virtue Ethics**
   A. **Theory**
      1. Aristotle, *Nichomachean Ethics*
      2. MacIntyre, Is *Patriotism a Virtue?*
   B. **Practice**
      1. Marquis, *An Argument that Abortion Is Wrong*
      2. Dyck, *An Alternative to the Ethic of Euthanasia*
      3. Calicott, *The Land Ethic*
      4. Plato, *Crito*
      5. Rachels, *What People Deserve*
      6. Walzer, *Markets and Hard Work*

V. **Feminist Ethics**
   A. **Theory**
      1. Mill, *The Subjection of Women*
      2. Held, *Feminist Transformations of Moral Theory*
      3. Kymlicka, *Sex Equality and Discrimination*
      4. Radcliffe Richards, *Freedom, Contitioning and the Real Woman*
      5. Wright, *Feminists, Meet Mr. Darwin*
   B. **Practice**
      1. Sexual Harassment: *Ellison v. Brady*
      2. Longino, *Pornography, Oppression and Freedom: A Closer Look*
      3. Joseph, *Polygamy is Good Feminism*
      4. Sandel, *No-Fault Family Law*

Alternative Social and Political Philosophy Syllabus

I. **Libertarianism**
   A. **Theory**
      1. Hobbes, *Leviathan*
      2. Locke, *The Second Treatise of Government*
      3. Nozick, *The Entitlement Theory*
   B. **Practice**
      1. Thomson, *A Defense of Abortion*
      2. *Requiring Medical Treatment: JFK Hospital v. Heston*
      3. Szasz, *The Ethics of Addiction: An Argument in Favor of Letting Americans Take Any Drug They Want*
      4. Shapiro, *Addiction and Drug Policy*

II. **Utilitarianism**
   A. **Theory**
      1. Hume, *Of Justice*
      2. Mill, *Utilitarianism*
      3. Mill, *On Liberty*
   B. **Practice**
      1 Singer, *Rich and Poor*
      2. Mill, *Of the Liberty of Thought and Discussion*
      3. *Flag Burning as Constitutionally Protected: Texas v. Johnson; Nazi Marches: Village of Skokie v. National Socialism Party;* Lawrence and Gunther, *Prohibiting Racist Speech on Campus: A Debate*
      4. Singer, *All Animals are Equal*
      5. Posner, *Selling Babies*

III. **Liberal Egalitarianism**
   A. **Theory**
      1. Dworkin, *Taking Rights Seriously*
      2. Kant, *The Fundamental Principles of the Metaphysic of Morals*
      3. Rawls, *A Theory of Justice*
   B. **Practice**
      1. Cohen, *The Arc of the Moral Universe*

      2. Plato, *Crito*
      3. Rawls, Civil *Disobedience and the Social Contract*

IV. **Marxism and Communitarianism**
   A. **Theory**
      1. Marx and Engels, *The Communist Manifesto*
      2. Walzer, *Markets and Hard Work*
      3. Rachels, *What People Deserve*
      4. MacIntyre, *Is Patriotism a Virtue?*
   B. **Practice**
      1. Wasserstrom, *On the Morality of War*
      2. Sandel, *No-Fault Family Law*
      3. *Who Controls a Child's Education? Wisconsin v. Yoder*

V. **Equality and Discrimination**
   A. **Racism, Affirmative Action and Reparations**
      1. Wasserstrom, *On Racism and Sexism: Realities and Ideals*
      2. Young, *Social Movements and the Politics of Difference*
      3. Dworkin, *The Rights of Allan Bakke*
      4. Rachels, *Reverse Discrimination*
      5. Murray, *Affirmative Racism*
      6. Arthur, *Racism and Reparations*
   B. **Sex Equality, Pornography and Feminism**
      1. Mill, *The Subjection of Women*
      2. Held, *Feminist Transformations of Moral Theory*
      3. Longino, *Pornography, Oppression and Freedom: A Closer Look*
      4. Radcliffe Richards, *Freedom, Conditioning and the Real Woman*
      5. Kymlicka, *Sex Equality and Discrimination: Difference v. Dominance*
      6. Wright, *Feminists, Meet Mr. Darwin*